APA Handbook of

Sexuality and Psychology

APA Handbooks in Psychology

APA Handbook of Sexuality and Psychology

VOLUME 1

Person-Based Approaches

Deborah L. Tolman and Lisa M. Diamond, *Editors-in-Chief*

José A. Bauermeister, William H. George, James G. Pfaus, and L. Monique Ward, *Associate Editors*

American Psychological Association • Washington, DC

Published by
American Psychological Association
750 First Street, NE
Washington, DC 20002-4242
www.apa.org

To order
APA Order Department
P.O. Box 92984
Washington, DC 20090-2984
Tel: (800) 374-2721; Direct: (202) 336-5510
Fax: (202) 336-5502; TDD/TTY: (202) 336-6123
Online: www.apa.org/pubs/books/
E-mail: order@apa.org

In the U.K., Europe, Africa, and the Middle East, copies may be ordered from
American Psychological Association
3 Henrietta Street
Covent Garden, London
WC2E 8LU England

AMERICAN PSYCHOLOGICAL ASSOCIATION STAFF
Gary R. VandenBos, PhD, *Publisher*
Julia Frank-McNeil, *Senior Director, APA Books*
Theodore J. Baroody, *Director, Reference, APA Books*
Katherine R. Lenz, *Project Editor, APA Books*

Typeset in Berkeley by Cenveo Publisher Services, Columbia, MD

Printer: Edwards Brothers, Inc., Lillington, NC
Cover Designer: Naylor Design, Washington, DC

Library of Congress Cataloging-in-Publication Data

APA handbook of sexuality and psychology / Deborah L. Tolman and
Lisa M. Diamond, editors-in-Chief ; José A. Bauermeister, William H.
George, James G. Pfaus, and L. Monique Ward, Associate Editors.
volumes ; cm. — (APA handbooks in psychology)
Includes bibliographical references and index.
ISBN-13: 978-1-4338-1369-6
ISBN-10: 1-4338-1369-6
1. Sex (Psychology) I. Tolman, Deborah L.
BF692.A63 2013
155.3—dc23
2013012916

British Library Cataloguing-in-Publication Data
A CIP record is available from the British Library.

Printed in the United States of America
First Edition

http://dx.doi.org/10.1037/14193-000

Contents

Volume 1: Person-Based Approaches

Editorial Board

About the Editors-in-Chief

Deborah L. Tolman, EdD, is professor of social welfare and psychology at The Silberman School of Social Work at Hunter College and The Graduate Center of The City University of New York, where she trains doctoral students studying women's lives and sexuality-related topics. Dr. Tolman is an applied developmental psychologist whose research has focused on adolescent sexuality, gender development, gender equity, and research methods. Her groundbreaking book on adolescent girls' sexuality, *Dilemmas of Desire: Teenage Girls Talk About Sexuality*, published in 2002, was awarded the 2003 Distinguished Book Award from the Association for Women in Psychology. Her research has covered the impact of television on adolescent sexuality, the roles of beliefs about masculinity and femininity in adolescent girls' and boys' experiences of sexual and romantic relationships and mental health, and adolescent girls' experiences with fellatio. She is currently revisiting how adolescent girls are negotiating their own sexuality in the current complex social landscape of sexualization and choice and other contradictory messages about female and adolescent sexuality. Her work has been supported by the National Institute of Child Health and Development, the Spencer Foundation, the Ford Foundation, the Atlantic Philanthropies, and the NoVo Foundation. She has published more than 75 peer-reviewed articles and book chapters and several books on adolescent sexuality, research methods, and feminist theory. Dr. Tolman is a Fellow of the American Psychological Association (APA), the Society for the Psychology of Women (APA Division 35) and the Society for the Psychological Study of Social Issues (SPSSI, APA Division 9) and has received wide recognition for her contributions to female adolescent development. She was a member of APA's Task Force on the Sexualization of Girls and an author of its report, the most frequently downloaded document on APA's website, which was the impetus for her cofounding SPARK, an intergenerational girl-fueled social movement to challenge the sexualization of girls (http://www.sparkmovement.org). Through this work, she is building a bridge between academia and activism to create enabling conditions in which girls can develop healthy sexuality and well-being. Among the awards she has received are APA's Committee on Women's Leadership Award and SPSSI's Louise Kidder Early Career Award. She earned her doctorate in human development and psychology at the Harvard Graduate School of Education in 1992. She was senior research scientist and associate director at the Center for Research on Women at Wellesley College, and professor of sexuality studies and founding director of the Center for Research on Gender and Sexuality at San Francisco State University.

Lisa M. Diamond, PhD, is professor of psychology and gender studies at the University of Utah. Her research focuses on close relationships and sexuality over the life span, with a particular emphasis on their biobehavioral underpinnings and health implications. The three primary areas of her research are the development of sexual desire, identity, and orientation over the life span; influences of close relationships on mental and physical health; and the role of biologically based capacities for emotion regulation in shaping the development and experience of intimate relationships. Dr. Diamond is best known for her unprecedented longitudinal study of 100 lesbian, bisexual, heterosexual, and "unlabeled" women, whom she has been interviewing approximately every two years since 1995, tracking changes in their sexual identities, attractions, and behaviors over time. Her 2008 book, *Sexual Fluidity*, describes the changes and transformations that her respondents underwent from late adolescence to adulthood, and profiles some of the most intriguing women in detail. *Sexual Fluidity* has been awarded the Distinguished Book Award from the American Psychological Association (APA) Society for the Study of Lesbian/Gay/Bisexual/Transgendered Issues. Dr. Diamond has received numerous awards for her work from the APA Committee on Lesbian, Gay, Bisexual, and Transgender Concerns; the American Association of University Women; the Society for the Scientific Study of Sexuality; and the Society for the Psychological Study of Social Issues. In 2011 she was granted Fellow status in APA's Society for the Psychological Study of Lesbian, Gay, Bisexual and Transgender Issues (Division 44). Dr. Diamond has been awarded grants in support of her research from the National Institute for Mental Health, the W. T. Grant Foundation, the American Psychological Foundation, the American Institute for Bisexuality, and the Templeton Foundation. Her current work focuses on understanding associations between day-to-day changes in gonadal hormone levels and day-to-day changes in same-sex and other-sex desires, investigating the psychological and biological mechanisms through which sexual activity relates to mental and physical health, and understanding the origins of individual differences in sexual fluidity.

Contributors

V. Bede Agocha, PhD, Department of Psychology, University of Connecticut, Storrs

Marysol Asencio, DrPH, Department of Human Development and Family Studies, University of Connecticut, Storrs

José A. Bauermeister, PhD, MPH, Department of Health Behavior and Health Education, University of Michigan, Ann Arbor

Heather Blunt, PhD, MPH, Department of Community and Family Health, University of South Florida, Tampa

Walter O. Bockting, PhD, LGBT Health Initiative, Division of Gender, Sexuality, and Health, New York State Psychiatric Institute/Columbia Psychiatry, and Columbia University School of Nursing, New York, NY

Jennifer A. Bossio, MSc, Department of Psychology, Queen's University, Kingston, Ontario, Canada

Christin P. Bowman, MS, Department of Psychology, The City University of New York, New York

Elizabeth A. Boylan, MA, Department of Sexuality Studies, San Francisco State University, San Francisco, CA

Lori A. Brotto, PhD, Department of Obstetrics and Gynaecology, University of British Columbia, Vancouver, British Columbia, Canada

Eric R. Buhi, PhD, MPH, Department of Community and Family Health, University of South Florida, Tampa

Sheana S. Bull, PhD, MPH, Department of Community and Behavioral Health, University of Colorado–Denver, Anschutz Medical Campus, Aurora

E. Sandra Byers, PhD, Department of Psychology, University of New Brunswick, Fredericton, New Brunswick, Canada

Sarah K. Calabrese, PhD, Center for Interdisciplinary Research on AIDS, Yale University, New Haven, CT

Meredith L. Chivers, PhD, Department of Sexuality Studies, Queen's University, Kingston, Ontario, Canada

Jennifer B. Clark, MA, Department of Sexuality Studies, San Francisco State University, San Francisco, CA

Sonia Corrêa, Associação Brasileira Interdisciplinar de AIDS (The Brazilian Interdisciplinary AIDS Association) and Sexuality Policy Watch, Rio de Janeiro, Brazil

Brian R. Davis, MA, Department of Psychology, The City University of New York, New York
Kelly Cue Davis, PhD, School of Social Work, University of Washington, Seattle
Carlos Ulises Decena, PhD, Department of Women's and Gender Studies, Rutgers University, New Brunswick, NJ
Lisa M. Diamond, PhD, Departments of Psychology and Gender Studies, University of Utah, Salt Lake City
Sarah Diefendorf, BA, Department of Sociology, University of Washington, Seattle
Katherine S. Elkington, PhD, HIV Center of Clinical and Behavioral Studies, New York State Psychiatric Institute and Columbia University, New York
Breanne Fahs, PhD, Department of Women and Gender Studies, Arizona State University, Phoenix
J. Dennis Fortenberry, MD, MS, Department of Pediatrics, Indiana University School of Medicine, Indianapolis
Monica Foust, MA, Department of Psychology, University of Michigan, Ann Arbor
David M. Frost, PhD, Heilbrunn Department of Population and Family Health, Columbia University, New York, NY
Jonathan Garcia, PhD, Department of Sociomedical Sciences, Columbia University, New York, NY
Nicola Gavey, PhD, School of Psychology, The University of Auckland, Auckland, New Zealand
William H. George, PhD, Department of Psychology, University of Washington, Seattle
Janniko R. Georgiadis, PhD, Department of Neuroscience, University Medical Center Groningen, Groningen, the Netherlands
Shira M. Goldenberg, PhD, Department of Medicine, University of California–San Diego, La Jolla
Louis F. Graham, DrPH, Department of Health Behavior and Health Education, University of Michigan, Ann Arbor
George J. Greene, PhD, Department of Medical Social Sciences, Northwestern University, Chicago, IL
Gert Martin Hald, PhD, Department of Public Health, University of Copenhagen, Copenhagen, Denmark
Carolyn T. Halpern, PhD, Department of Maternal and Child Health, The University of North Carolina at Chapel Hill
Peter Hegarty, PhD, School of Psychology, University of Surrey, Guildford, England
Devon J. Hensel, PhD, Department of Pediatrics, Indiana University School of Medicine, Indianapolis
Debby Herbenick, PhD, MPH, Department of Applied Health Science, Indiana University, Bloomington
Krystal M. Hernandez, PhD, Department of Counseling and Psychological Services, Ohio University, Athens
David Huebner, PhD, MPH, Department of Psychology, University of Utah, Salt Lake City
Janet S. Hyde, PhD, Department of Psychology, University of Wisconsin–Madison
Emily A. Impett, PhD, Department of Psychology, University of Toronto Mississauga, Mississauga, Ontario, Canada
Christine E. Kaestle, PhD, Department of Human Development, Virginia Polytechnic Institute and State University, Blacksburg

Sabra L. Katz-Wise, PhD, Division of Adolescent and Young Adult Medicine, Boston Children's Hospital, Boston, MA; and Department of Pediatrics, Harvard Medical School, Boston, MA

Nancy Kendall, PhD, Department of Educational Policy Studies, University of Wisconsin–Madison

Peggy J. Kleinplatz, PhD, School of Psychology, University of Ottawa, Ottawa, Ontario, Canada

Laura Kuper, MA, Department of Psychology, University of Illinois at Chicago

Sharon Lamb, EdD, Department of Counseling and School Psychology, University of Massachusetts–Boston

Daniel Linz, PhD, Department of Communication, University of California–Santa Barbara

Julia E. Mackaronis, MS, Department of Psychology, University of Utah, Salt Lake City

Annette Mahoney, PhD, Department of Psychology, Bowling Green State University, Bowling Green, OH

Lesley Marson, PhD, Department of Surgery, The University of North Carolina at Chapel Hill

N. Tatiana Masters, MSW, PhD, School of Social Work, University of Washington, Seattle

Sara I. McClelland, PhD, Departments of Psychology and Women's Studies, University of Michigan, Ann Arbor

Anne McGlynn-Wright, BA, Department of Sociology, University of Washington, Seattle

Amy Muise, PhD, Department of Psychology, University of Toronto Mississauga, Mississauga, Ontario, Canada

Miguel Muñoz-Laboy, DrPH, Department of Sociomedical Sciences, Columbia University, New York, NY

Brian Mustanski, PhD, Department of Medical Social Sciences, Northwestern University, Chicago, IL

Hong V. Nguyen, MS, Department of Psychology, University of Washington, Seattle

Jeanette Norris, PhD, Alcohol and Drug Abuse Institute, University of Washington, Seattle

Lucia F. O'Sullivan, PhD, Department of Psychology, University of New Brunswick, Fredericton, New Brunswick, Canada

Mark Padilla, PhD, MPH, Department of Global and Sociocultural Studies, Florida International University, Miami

Kenneth I. Pargament, PhD, Department of Psychology, Bowling Green State University, Bowling Green, OH; and Institute for Spirituality and Health at the Texas Medical Center, Houston

Richard Parker, PhD, Departments of Sociomedical Sciences and Anthropology, Columbia University, New York, NY

Diana Peragine, BSc, Department of Psychology, University of Toronto Mississauga, Mississauga, Ontario, Canada

Michael A. Perelman, PhD, Departments of Psychiatry, Reproductive Medicine, and Urology, Weill Medical College of Cornell University, New York, NY

Michael Pettit, PhD, Department of Psychology, York University, Toronto, Ontario, Canada

James G. Pfaus, PhD, Center for Studies in Behavioral Neurobiology, Department of Psychology, Concordia University, Montreal, Quebec, Canada

Aleksandra Plocha, MS, Department of Counseling and School Psychology, University of Massachusetts–Boston

Ronna Popkin, MS, Department of Sociomedical Sciences, Columbia University, New York, NY

Lauren Reed, MA, Department of Psychology, University of Michigan, Ann Arbor

Uzma S. Rehman, PhD, Department of Psychology, University of Waterloo, Waterloo, Ontario, Canada

Margaret Rosario, PhD, Department of Psychology, The City College of the City University of New York, New York

John Santelli, MD, MPH, Heilbrunn Department of Population and Family Health, Columbia University, New York

Lisa A. Scepkowski, MA, Department of Psychology, Boston University, Boston, MA

Vanessa Schick, PhD, Division of Management, Policy, and Community Health, The University of Texas School of Public Health, Houston

Eric W. Schrimshaw, PhD, Department of Sociomedical Sciences, Columbia University, New York, NY

Pepper Schwartz, PhD, Department of Sociology, University of Washington, Seattle

Christopher Seaman, MA, Department of Communication, University of California–Santa Barbara

Charlene Y. Senn, PhD, Department of Psychology, University of Windsor, Windsor, Ontario, Canada

Kate Shannon, PhD, Department of Medicine, University of British Columbia, Vancouver, British Columbia, Canada

Kelly B. Smith, PhD, Department of Obstetrics and Gynaecology, University of British Columbia, Vancouver, British Columbia, Canada

Donald S. Strassberg, PhD, Department of Psychology, University of Utah, Salt Lake City

Steffanie A. Strathdee, PhD, Department of Medicine, University of California–San Diego, La Jolla

Kelly D. Suschinsky, PhD, Department of Psychology, Queen's University, Kingston, Ontario, Canada

Ashley E. Thompson, BS, Department of Psychology, University of New Brunswick, Fredericton, New Brunswick, Canada

Amanda D. Timmers, BAH, Department of Psychology, Queen's University, Kingston, Ontario, Canada

Deborah L. Tolman, EdD, Silberman School of Social Work, Hunter College and The Graduate Center, The City University of New York, New York

Sarah L. Trinh, MA, Department of Psychology, University of Michigan, Ann Arbor

Lianne A. Urada, PhD, MSW, LCSW, Department of Medicine, University of California–San Diego, La Jolla

L. Monique Ward, PhD, Department of Psychology, University of Michigan, Ann Arbor

Christopher Wheldon, MSPH, Department of Community and Family Health, University of South Florida, Tampa

Series Preface

The *APA Handbook of Sexuality and Psychology* is the 11th publication to be released in the American Psychological Association's *APA Handbooks in Psychology*™ series, instituted in 2010. The series primarily comprises multiple two- and three-volume sets focused on core subfields. Additionally, some single-volume handbooks on highly focused content areas within core subfields will be released in coming years.

The ten previously released sets are as follows:

- *APA Handbook of Industrial and Organizational Psychology*—three volumes; Sheldon Zedeck, Editor-in-Chief
- *APA Handbook of Ethics in Psychology*—two volumes; Samuel J. Knapp, Editor-in-Chief
- *APA Educational Psychology Handbook*—three volumes; Karen R. Harris, Steve Graham, and Tim Urdan, Editors-in-Chief
- *APA Handbook of Research Methods in Psychology*—three volumes; Harris Cooper, Editor-in-Chief
- *APA Addiction Syndrome Handbook*—two volumes; Howard J. Shaffer, Editor-in-Chief
- *APA Handbook of Counseling Psychology*—two volumes; Nadya A. Fouad, Editor-in-Chief
- *APA Handbook of Behavior Analysis*—two volumes; Gregory J. Madden, Editor-in-Chief
- *APA Handbook of Psychology, Religion, and Spirituality*—two volumes; Kenneth I. Pargament, Editor-in-Chief
- *APA Handbook of Testing and Assessment in Psychology*—three volumes; Kurt F. Geisinger, Editor-in-Chief
- *APA Handbook of Multicultural Psychology*—two volumes; Frederick T. L. Leong, Editor-in-Chief

Each set is primarily formulated to address the reference interests and needs of researchers, clinicians, and practitioners in psychology and allied behavioral fields. Each also targets graduate students in psychology who require well-organized, detailed supplementary texts, not only for "filling in" their own specialty areas but also for gaining sound familiarity with other established specialties and emerging trends across the breadth of psychology. Moreover, many of the sets will bear strong interest for professionals in pertinent complementary fields (i.e., depending on content area), be they corporate executives and human resources personnel; doctors, psychiatrists, and other health personnel; teachers and school administrators; cultural diversity and pastoral counselors; legal professionals; and so forth.

Under the direction of small and select editorial boards consisting of top scholars in the field, with chapters authored by both senior and rising researchers and practitioners, each reference set is committed to a steady focus on best science and best practice. Coverage converges on what is currently known in the particular subject area (including basic historical reviews) and the identification of the most pertinent sources of information in both core and evolving literature. Volumes and chapters alike pinpoint practical issues; probe unresolved and controversial topics; and present future theoretical, research, and practice trends. The editors provide clear guidance to the "dialogue" among chapters, with internal cross-referencing that demonstrates a robust integration of topics to lead the user to a clearer understanding of the complex interrelationships within each field.

With the imprimatur of the largest scientific and professional organization representing psychology in the United States and the largest association of psychologists in the world, and with content edited and authored by some of its most respected members, the *APA Handbooks in Psychology* series will be the indispensable and authoritative reference resource to turn to for researchers, instructors, practitioners, and field leaders alike.

Gary R. VandenBos
APA Publisher

Foreword

To see two new volumes emerge on the topic of human sexuality, and an APA-designed handbook, is of substantial interest to all of those whose work relies on developing or disseminating sexual knowledge. We can thus welcome the considerable effort made to bring this material forward.

The perspective taken across the chapters is broadly psychological, meaning the reference point is a person's experience, not their biology, and the social context in which they live. That is the unapologetic focus and allows the emphasis on methods that maximizes the findings on the personal. This is important and legitimate. Measuring subjective experience continues to be a core challenge. The authors discuss, and many have used, multiple-level qualitative and quantitative measures to pursue both the surface and depth of understanding different sexual feelings, thoughts, and ideas and, importantly, to challenge researchers in their own assumptions. To take subjective measurement seriously and critically is a service to sexual science.

Furthermore, the last two sections of the book, nearly 20% of the chapters, go further by addressing sexual rights, social institutions, and social change. These topics push the envelope of how we scientifically study sexuality beyond typical methods and frameworks. While the authors will make their own cases, I would offer that this addition has become a type of imperative given the realities of HIV research, sexual minority visibility, health disparity research, and the need for broader access to sexual information and health.

These chapters are written primarily from and by those working in the United States and Canada. The current status of conducting sex research in the United States is contextualized by direct or indirect political interference and the pressure for science, even social science, to produce results conforming to social values. Nevertheless or perhaps in part spurred on by these factors, many who seek answers to understanding sexuality soldier on, pursue what seems important, and conduct research despite often challenging conditions. A number of those individuals are authors of the chapters in this volume.

For the future, what this work brings to mind is the following thought: Sexuality research needs a strong base in personal/subjective experience and the individual's interaction with social and cultural systems. Meanwhile biological research is moving quickly with a dramatic recasting of biology as a variable, malleable component of human existence, also shaped by environmental factors. There are genomics and proteomics but there are also epigenetics and exposomics. Just as biological research in general becomes more microbiological, it suffers from fragmentation and isolation from psychosocial measurement; until translation research is really needed, this separation is likely to continue. The same holds true for sexuality research. Psychologists, including cognitive and neuropsychologists, and social, developmental, and clinically oriented, have an excellent opportunity and position to make links across this great, and artificial, divide. Are we all up to this challenge? These volumes suggest it is necessary, and we are ready.

Julia R. Heiman, PhD
Director, Kinsey Institute for Research in Sex, Gender, and Reproduction
Professor, Psychological and Brain Sciences
Professor, Clinical Psychiatry
Indiana University, Bloomington

Introduction

The simple question "What is sexuality?" has perennially defied any easy answer. Sexuality is the proverbial nested dimension of human experience—individuals within relationships within communities within cultures. Sexuality cannot be distilled down to one essential element but is composed of many; sexuality can also be understood as fundamentally relational, not a "something" at all, produced in the interplay within or among individuals, interpersonal interactions, or institutions. Sexuality can be understood as a laundry list of individual and social experiences and attributes, including desires, behaviors, identities, fantasies, preferences, orientations, and identities at the individual level and incorporating both mind and body, as well as sexual mores, laws, standards, communities, institutions, and cultures, at the social level. These intersecting dimensions coalesce and disaggregate to form a dynamic and changing system. Even basic distinctions such as "individual" and "social" become blurred as soon as one names them; what seems at first to be an individual quality of sexuality—desire, emotion, decision making, identity—is quickly revealed to be intricately intertwined with a variety of social and cultural processes, ranging from family beliefs and relationships to social norms, discourses, and transactions of power and privilege that foster some expressions of sexuality while punishing or obscuring others. Distinct and even contradictory conceptions about the human condition run through how people think about, understand, experience, and conceive of sexuality: Are people biologically wired to perceive and treat potential sexual partners in highly specific ways, on the basis of the evolutionary objective to propagate the species? Or are humans fundamentally distinct from their mammalian brethren because of their capacity to move beyond such wiring, using their enormous brains and cognitive capacities to imagine and realize sexual ideas, desires, communities, beliefs, and practices that supersede and even undermine the basic evolutionary goal of reproduction? Clearly, sexuality is a domain in which people cannot help but perceive and project notions of their humanity and morality. Accordingly, it is subject in profound ways to social regulation and control and has provided the impetus for resistance and revolution. It is as unruly as it is codified and institutionalized.

When embarking on this handbook, the question we posed to ourselves was "What is sexuality for psychology?" Many authors of these chapters responded with some version of "everything and everywhere." That sex and sexuality have become almost perversely definitional of who humans are at this historical moment is cause for both celebration and complaint. Query it, queer it, or quell it, sexuality is an element of the human condition that demands attention and analysis. Psychology is certainly not the only discipline charged with this task, but we would argue that it is among the most important.

Historically, the discipline of psychology has had a fraught relationship with the complex range of human experiences encompassed by sexuality. On one hand, psychologists have contributed extensively to research, clinical practice, health care, and education about sexuality (from the elementary school level to graduate education). On the other hand, psychology has tended to legitimize a relatively narrow set of questions or concerns about sexuality as important psychology scholarship. The American Psychological Association is the voice of the discipline in the United States, and historically it has said relatively little about sexuality. This handbook therefore represents a watershed moment not only for the field of sexuality scholarship but also for the discipline of psychology. It represents the discipline's first comprehensive effort to define, explain, and understand human sexuality in all of its complexity, at multiple analytical levels, and to place a marker specifying what we know at this particular historical moment and, perhaps more important, what we have yet to learn.

We originally conceived this handbook as one volume, but it quickly became apparent that one volume would be woefully inadequate in scope and depth. From the beginning, we have been committed to producing a handbook that is a state-of-the-art review of current empirical research on sexuality and a synthesis of the dominant theoretical perspectives that have guided both research and clinical practice. We have also been committed to representing sexuality at both a person level and a context level. Our target audience primarily includes established psychology researchers and practitioners, but the handbook is intended to be a resource for allied social and behavioral scientists, as well as professionals in complementary fields such as education, social work, public health, and public policy. Professors and graduate students in general will find the chapters in the handbook extremely valuable as supplementary text, not only for filling in their own specialty areas but also for gaining a sound familiarity with this particular field of study.

Every chapter integrates an understanding of the social and cultural contexts and institutions that fundamentally organize the basic human phenomenon of sexuality. Key although not exclusive among these are race, gender, ethnicity, sexual orientation, and social class. We have called on all authors to represent these organizing forces and social locations rather than segregating these discussions to single chapters (i.e., there is no chapter on Latino sexuality or Asian American sexuality). Instead, each chapter addresses the variability associated with and shaped by various contexts and standpoints and also notes gaps in the literature stemming from the historical inattention to these factors. In each chapter, the authors also consider and convey how clinicians might use sexual knowledge in their practice, mindful of the fact that sexuality is a dimension of every single presenting patient or client, even if it is not a presenting problem. Issues of cultural location are also primary: Although the American Psychological Association's mandate concerns the United States, it is impossible to meaningfully discuss sexuality without remaining mindful of cultural variation in its development and expression and the way it has been profoundly infused by globalization. Several chapters address global concerns specifically, and most chapters include research from different parts of the world.

ROAD MAP

Our answer to the question "What is sexuality?" can be found in 38 chapters organized into seven sections across two volumes. The first volume is titled *Person-Based Approaches*. In

Part I, we sketch out the lay of the land, consisting of the interplay of sexuality research with theory, history, and notions of gender, three foundational dimensions that have played a fundamental role in organizing knowledge about sexuality. In our chapter on sexuality theory and research, we begin with a focus on theory and a review of the essentialist–constructionist debates that come to subsume the primary theoretical battles in the field. Yet contrary to much previous work (including our own) arguing for greater integration of essentialist and social constructionist (and, relatedly, between logical–positivist and postmodern) perspectives on sexuality, we instead argue that the continuing tension between these perspectives is fundamentally generative and productive. We highlight how sexuality research has been made up of profoundly different types of inquiries, using diverse conceptual assumptions and methods, and has yielded a startlingly diverse constellation of sexual knowledge. Our call is for the recognition of these productive differences and a stronger dose of respect for the questions that are asked by researchers occupying different epistemological positions. At the same time, we recognize that knowledge about sexuality is "hot," with profound implications for social justice, social hierarchies, and the material and psychological conditions of people's life experiences. Under this rubric, we review some theoretical innovations in sexuality research located in these very different epistemologies, arguing that researchers have a responsibility to make their theoretical grounding explicit in order to enable all of us to understand the conceptual underpinnings of different types of sexual knowledge.

Katz-Wise and Hyde, in their analysis of gender and sexuality (Chapter 2), help to complete the larger project of illuminating the explicit connection between psychology and sexuality. Gender has always been conceived of as fundamentally important to the experience and analysis of sexuality, and the relationship between sexuality and gender has been both ambiguous and contested over the years. We view the study of gender as fundamental to the study of sexuality, even as recent work increasingly pulls at the threads of the familiar categories of male and female. Katz-Wise and Hyde review the basic dimensions of gender as an organizing principle of sexuality research, address the epistemological questions and challenges posed by gender, examine major theories and methods in the field, and discuss salient controversies, including the nature of gender differences in sexuality (such as women's "naturally low" sex drives). They conclude by considering new theoretical developments and research questions in the field, among them the orgasm gap, implications of new technologies for biological measurement, and the sexual excitation–inhibition model. Pettit and Hegarty (Chapter 3) situate contemporary sexuality research in what they call historical time, distinguished from the evolutionary time of the species as well as the developmental time of an individual, inviting readers to recognize the interplay between historically specific conceptual events and the history of psychology. To do so, they examine four events that have unfolded in historical time that have profoundly influenced the nexus of psychology and sexuality: changes in sexual experiences, norms, epistemologies, and selves. They invite researchers to be alert to their own historical time as sexuality researchers—the questions, contexts, assumptions, and methods that are at this moment at the heart of the production of sexual knowledge.

In some ways, sexuality research is idiosyncratic as a set of social science practices. Hence, we turn next to research methodologies, and Part II of the first volume offers insights into the tools of research used to produce sexual knowledge, explicating how the topic of sexuality demands a range of strategies and considering how sexuality researchers deploy them. Because sexuality itself is so multidimensional, so too are the tools and techniques that enable the field to engage in such an enormous enterprise of inquiry. Three of the most significant methodological families are presented by some of the leading practitioners of those methods in the field: survey methods (Schick, Calabrese, and Herbenick; Chapter 4); experimental, neuroimaging, and psychophysiological methods (Chivers, Suschinsky, Timmers, and Bossio; Chapter 5); and phenomenological methods (Frost, McClelland, Clark, and Boylan; Chapter 6).

Part III covers five principal dimensions of sexuality that have generated a rich and controversial body of research. In Chapter 7, Pfaus, Scepkowski, Marson, and Georgiadis synthesize the enormous body of research on the biology of sexuality and sexual response, with a critical emphasis on what they describe as the most important sexual organ in the body: the brain. Situating this body of research at the intersection of context and biology, with an awareness of the fundamental processes through which biologically based behaviors are modified by experience, they review the literature addressing central questions about how the body and the brain mutually regulate sexual responding, how people cognitively and affectively interpret sexual stimuli, and why orgasms feel so good. Providing a meticulous integration of both animal and human studies, Pfaus and colleagues illuminate the neural and hormonal organization of sexual behavior; physiological mechanisms of sexual desire and arousal; and mechanisms of sexual stimulation, reward, and inhibition. They explicate how biological substrates are enormously adaptive and flexible; how the brain provides a meeting place for the interplay of bodies and their multidimensional social and physical contexts; and the complex, fundamental, and yet flexible relationship between sexual practices and reproduction. In Chapter 8, Brotto and Smith then take up the thorny issues of sexual desire and pleasure, deeply excavating what is currently known and directly addressing persistent unanswered questions. They delve into critical controversies that have erupted around conceptions, characteristics, and real-life implications of what they define as "subjective awareness of desire for sexual satisfaction, irrespective of sexual activity" (p. 205). Working from the perspective that sexual desire is simultaneously experienced as physiological, cognitive, emotional, and interpersonal, they review the multiple models of sexual desire and pleasure that currently circulate in both research and clinical contexts and have informed recent revisions to the *Diagnostic and Statistical Manual of Mental Disorders* (*DSM*); consider what asexuality can tell researchers about sexual desire and pleasure; articulate what is known about developmental processes and psychological, physiological, and neurological mechanisms; and demonstrate how a multiplicity of social contexts inform experiences of desire and pleasure.

Kleinplatz and Diamond (Chapter 9) address questions of diversity in sexual practice, dispensing with the notion that there is a stable set of normative and natural sexual interests, arousal patterns, behaviors, and relationships and elucidating the wide range of practices and circumstances through which people express their sexuality. In their review, they provide an overview of the current state of psychological knowledge regarding alternative—colloquially known as "kinky"—sexual interests and practices. They address theoretical and ideological debates and assumptions regarding these practices, most notably regarding recent revisions to the *DSM*, and they review the literature on some of the more common forms of alternative sexual interest and behavior, including bondage, domination, sadism, and masochism; fetishes; and polyamory. Impett, Muise, and Peragine then take up the question of interpersonal relationships in Chapter 10. Given that interpersonal relationships remain the primary context in which sexuality is conventionally understood—and in which sexual expression usually occurs—a review of this extensive literature (which has its own established tradition within the discipline of psychology) is critical but daunting. The (often surprising) caveat that the psychological research on sexuality and psychological research on intimate relationships have grown up largely independent of one another, and that only recently have the primary theories and insights of these two traditions begun to substantively influence one another, makes this review an important synthesis. Impett, Muise, and Peragine provide a comprehensive framework for understanding how sexuality informs the formation and development of romantic relationships (and vice versa), from initial experiences of sexual attraction to the longer term role of sexuality in the maintenance of established romantic relationships. They review how attachment, sexual desire, and sexual satisfaction twine together within the rich context of sexually and emotionally intimate ties, and they devote much needed attention to a number of highly specific (and historically understudied) contexts, such as same-sex relationships and relationships at specific stages of life, in particular adolescence and later adulthood. They also consider what they call "the dark side" of sexuality in romantic relationships, covering sexual aggression, sexual jealousy, and sexual infidelity. They encourage the consideration of the changing social landscape as research on sexuality and relationships continues to coalesce, and they note the increasing role of the Internet and social media in diversifying the contemporary landscape of sexual and romantic intimacy beyond conventional heterosexual monogamous marriage.

The next two chapters cover what might be considered two ends of a single spectrum. Byers and Rehman address sexual well-being in Chapter 11, situating this topic within theories and research on broader psychological well-being. They anchor sexual well-being in sexual satisfaction, a global emotional response that arises from cognitive appraisals and affective responses to various aspects of an individual's sexual life. For many people, sexual well-being is linked to partners and their experiences. In this chapter, the authors review research on individual and demographic factors; personality, affective and cognitive factors (sexual motives, sexual cognitions, body image); and the role of relationships, with particular attention to the interpersonal exchange model of sexual satisfaction. On the opposite end of this continuum of well-being, in Chapter 12 Gavey and Senn interrogate and explicate the topic of sexual violence, challenging the traditional portrayal of sexual violence as a phenomenon perpetrated uniformly by men against women. They use a feminist sociocultural analysis to understand the ways in which most sexual violence is not, in fact, about sex at all and to excavate the complex interconnections between sexuality and violence at the level of motivation and behavior. Their review of the prevalence and history of social and legal understandings and responses to sexual violence addresses fundamental assumptions that have pervaded this domain, such as the common attribution of sexual violence to miscommunication, misperceptions about women's sexual interest, and the complex issue of token resistance. Their review addresses what is and is not known about the gray areas of unwanted, nonconsensual, and yet "compliant" sex, showing how normative standards governing heterosexual sex facilitate this phenomenon. They show how relational and gendered norms regarding sexuality and sexual desire (particularly among women) constitute a primer for sexual violence, and they conclude with a review of how interventions that empower women sexually may enable women to navigate these complex contours.

Part IV of Volume 1 addresses the life course as a critical context for the study of sexuality. Historically, developmental perspectives on sexuality have primarily been limited to sexual development at the physical level, focusing on normative development of the sexual body and reproductive capacities. The chapters in Part IV provide an important corrective to this limited approach, beginning in Chapter 13 with Hensel and Fortenberry's offer of an important new developmental model of sexuality based in a sexual health perspective and incorporating notions of multidimensionality, agelessness, continuity, and connectedness. They conceive of sexuality as a lifelong process in which a variety of experiences and behaviors provide important contexts for individual learning around sexuality at each life stage, with experiences in each stage feeding forward to critically shape later stages. Addressing what they call "two meaningful threads" of sexuality, partnering and sexual behaviors, they review the socially significant and contiguous life stages of adolescence, adulthood, and later life. They posit a lifelong process by which sexuality remains a primary aspect of identity and a core part of health and well-being during every life stage. They present the developmental literature in a framework of ongoing continuity and change across multiple sexual dimensions, with both new and past experiences informing current and future experiences. The other chapters in this section build on this framework by providing comprehensive and in-depth reviews of distinct moments of the sexual life cycle. They address key differences in how sexuality is understood and expressed at different life stages, how people negotiate what has been framed as normal or problematic at certain developmental junctures, and how sexuality serves as both a conduit and an expression of the developing and changing self, shaped and bounded by social expectations, norms, and possibilities that take different forms and have different implications depending on one's life stage. In childhood, for example, the very possibility of sexuality remains a controversial notion that Lamb and Plocha (Chapter 14) address directly in reviewing a surprisingly robust scope of knowledge about childhood sexuality. O'Sullivan and Thompson (Chapter 15) address the enormous body of literature on sexuality in adolescence, reflecting the manner in which societal anxieties about adolescent risk have produced a voluminous body of research on this topic, and note the tension between people's grasp of the normative reality of adolescent sexuality and their cultural ambivalence about its potential repercussions. In Chapter 16, Halpern and Kaestle provide the first comprehensive review of the newest developmental moment in the psychological literature—emerging adulthood—a stage between adolescence and adulthood during which young people are substantively negotiating their adult sexuality in an ever-growing variety of contexts, caught between a shifting terrain of their own and others' expectations and norms. Finally, in Chapter 17 Schwartz, Diefendorf, and McGlynn-Wright address the growing body of research on sexuality in later life, a topic that has garnered increased attention as society has gradually shown greater comfort with the reality that individuals continue to seek and enjoy sexual experience as they age.

Part V of the first volume incorporates three chapters that distill and integrate what is known about same-sex sexuality, one of sexuality research's growth areas in recent years. These chapters review different bodies of research that have grown exponentially in three domains and that remain fundamental and also contested: Rosario and Scrimshaw provide an extensive review of the variety of theoretical foundations and various perspectives on the etiology of same-sex sexuality (Chapter 18), and Mustanski, Kuper, and Greene articulate the multiple perspectives on how same-sex sexuality—disaggregating orientation and identity—develops (Chapter 19). In Chapter 20, Diamond addresses the critical question of gender, unpacking and integrating the large body of research suggesting fundamental gender differences in the experience and expression of same-sex sexuality, and considers the causes and implications of these differences.

The final section of Volume 1, Part VI, addresses questions of sexual bodies and sexual embodiment. Although sexuality is of course always about the body (be it individual bodies, bodies in relationship, or bodies as they interact and interplay with institutions), in this section the body takes center stage as a site of fundamental experience and expression of sexuality. Covering the intersection of health and sexuality, George, Norris, Nguyen, Masters, and Davis (Chapter 21) review the deleterious and beneficial associations between sexuality and both physical and mental health, including both psychological and social domains, understood as being inextricably interwoven with experiences of biological sexual processes and functions. In their conception of sexual health, they include sexual wellness and highlight how experiences of sexual coercion, abuse, exploitation, violence, and oppression undermine positive sexual health. Their conception of health incorporates physical health syndromes, mental health syndromes, and sexually transmitted infections and diseases, and they substantively address the ways in which substance use influences and is influenced by sexual health. Finally, they review the health benefits of sex, providing an important corrective to the long-standing assumption that links between sexuality and health are fundamentally about risk and danger rather than benefit and well-being.

HIV is the pandemic of our time and has been both a lightning rod for sexuality research and a powerful reminder of the importance of critically understanding the complexity of sexuality. Bauermeister, Elkington, and Huebner's Chapter 22 provides an historical synthesis of HIV/AIDS prevention efforts, which have had sexual behavior at their center. After a brief overview of the HIV/AIDS epidemic, they address the full array of HIV/AIDS prevention approaches that have focused on individual, interpersonal, ecologic, and biomedical strategies. In conclusion, they argue for integrated, multilevel HIV/AIDS research to inform and shape comparable intervention approaches. Unpacking and reconnecting sexuality and reproductive health, Popkin and Santelli demonstrate in Chapter 23 how the context of public health has provided the landscape in which the concept of sexual health has been developed and operationalized in research, programs, and policies. They synthesize the relatively small body of research in which these two generally distinct lines of inquiry meet. In the following chapter (Chapter 24), Bockting addresses the growing body of research on transgender sexuality, a domain in which the sexual body itself has been fundamentally challenged as predictable, bounded, and coherent, with respect to the conventional gender binary that has dominated researchers' conceptions of sexuality and sexual bodies. In his review, Bockting reminds readers first that there have virtually always been people whose identities and bodies have challenged the entrenched conception of gender as necessarily situated within the male–female binary, and he shows how differently gendered individuals have adopted a variety of strategies to name and locate themselves in new spaces and continua that provide alternative understandings of gender, from no gender to third genders, pan genders, and, increasingly, transgender or genderqueer. His chapter reviews the extant literature on the identity development and health of transgender people and demonstrates how these identity issues remain distinct from, albeit related to, issues of sexual orientation, attraction, and behavior. Finally, in Chapter 25 Tolman, Bowman, and Fahs address the new and provocative body of research on sexual embodiment, a theoretical framework that enables new ways of understanding how conceptions and experiences regarding the corporeal body inform sexual phenomenology. They provide the first comprehensive review of sexuality research on this topic, showing how sexuality is an intrinsic dimension of an embodied self and summarizing the diverse range of conceptions and theories of embodiment that have emerged in recent years, focusing particularly on those that align with psychological theory on sexuality. They present a critical review of a wide range of empirical research on sexuality that has used a lens of embodiment, including research on gendered sexual bodies, the sexual body and its parts, the sexual body in action, the sexual body across the life span, sexual minority sexual bodies, and what they call the "disobedient" sexual body.

The second volume of the handbook can be broadly construed as shifting the figure–ground constellation of person-based approaches to focus on the contexts that shape and define people's sexuality, that is, contextual approaches. In Part I, the first three chapters elaborate on forms of commodification that organize sexuality. At a moment in history that has seen a startling increase in the widespread local, global, and technological commodification of sex, these chapters provide a critical baseline for tracking key arenas that are likely to continue growing and changing in the coming decades. In Chapter 1, Hald, Seaman, and Linz provide a newly updated accounting of what is known about pornography and sexuality, from its psychological and social impact to the ways in which it has shifted from taboo to mainstream in the cultural landscape and the everyday lives of individuals. Although sex work has in a sense always been a venue for commodified sexuality, Urada, Goldenberg, Shannon, and Strathdee explicate in Chapter 2 what sex work means in the 21st century, who sex workers are, and the effects—on individuals and social conditions—of cultural changes that have rendered sex work and sex workers both marginalized and pervasive. New technologies represent another domain of rapid change for sexual experience and expression. In Chapter 3, Buhi, Blunt, Wheldon, and Bull review the growing body of knowledge about how new technologies are created and how existing technologies are repurposed—for sexual expression and communication, for seeking and engaging in a wide variety of sexual behaviors, and for accessing information about sexuality. In their chapter, they focus on digital technology used for sexual exploration and expression, considering both the potential benefits, such as support, and the potential problems, such as exposure to inadvertently sexually explicit materials or to new forms of social risk or consequences. They review the literature on how sexuality has been affected as new technologies have emerged, theoretical considerations in technology-related research on sexuality, and how new technologies are contributing to positive sexuality and sexual health.

Two chapters make up Part II of Volume 2 on clinical treatment of sexuality, both addressing how the concept of treatment emerged in relation to sexuality and how it is implemented in the current climate and casting a critical eye toward the social contexts in which sexuality and treatment become joined at the hip. Strassberg and Mackaronis (Chapter 4) provide a comprehensive accounting of how psychologists are working with the range of issues that arise in sex therapy, from specific diagnoses to the threads of sexuality that weave through a plethora of psychotherapeutic contexts. In Chapter 5, Perelman provides the first thorough accounting of what is relatively recent history: the development of sexual medicine as a field of practice and a community of practitioners.

In Part III of this volume, we turn mindfully to the emergent discourses, practices, and implications of positioning sexuality in terms of rights and as a potent force and reason for social change. Sexual rights are institutionalized protections and freedoms that make it possible for individuals, groups, and communities to engage in diverse sexual self-expression and to develop healthy sexualities. To highlight the ways in which culture shapes, informs, and affects sexuality, Agocha, Asencio, and Decena set the stage with a very broad, remarkably thoughtful and highly comprehensive chapter on sexuality and culture, focusing attention on what can only be described as one of the most fundamental dimensions of sexuality and one that permeates all chapters of the handbook. Parker, Garcia, and Muñoz-Laboy (Chapter 7) review the formation of communities on the basis of sexual identities and subsequent sexual social movements, in particular what they call the "high-impact global movements"—gay and lesbian movements, feminist movements, and HIV- and AIDS-related movements—tracing the emergent movements by transgender communities, how the Internet and social media are shaping sexual movements, and the globalization of these sexual social movements. It is in this section that a global lens is most evident in the handbook, in part an effect of how social justice conceptions of sexuality have burned especially brightly beyond U.S. borders, although these conceptions are increasingly salient and evident within the United States. In Chapter 8, Graham and Padilla review the literature on sexual rights for marginalized populations. Their assessment illuminates how heteronormativity and unequal gender hierarchies are forms of oppression shaping public policies affecting sexual rights, demonstrating the deleterious effects that such policies have had on the development of sexuality and on sexual health. Corrêa, Davis, and Parker (Chapter 9) invite an interdisciplinary consideration of the complex intersections among genders, sexualities, and globalization. They recount the development of sexual rights as human rights and the development of this organizing framework in both transnational and localized contexts. Among the many effects of globalization for genders and sexualities, they observe constitutive linkages between expanding inequalities in the North and South and problematic and unexamined outward migration of Western sexual concepts and categories. These exported concepts and categories often conflict with local systems of living and meaning, in particular regarding sexual identities and practices, and carry with them insidious colonial and racial biases.

The final part of Volume 2 is on sexuality and public institutions and contains four chapters covering the major institutions that anchor sexuality and within which individual and social experiences are critically embedded and from which they emerge. Each of these chapters is anchored in an understanding of how sexuality is regulated explicitly and through discourse and practice, as well as how it is enabled and constrained through both formal and informal norms, rules, and codes. In Chapter 10, McClelland and Frost provide an understanding of the slippery concept of policy as driving networks of formal and informal rules about sexuality that govern people, groups, and communities through a combination of means, including laws, regulatory measures, courses of action, and funding priorities. They name five qualities of sexuality—sexual knowledge, sexual behavior, reproduction and family formation, the sexual body, and institutional infrastructures designed to address sexuality issues—enabling an assessment of the processes, impact, and target of sexual policies. For each of these "entry points," they provide analysis of specific policies and their intended and unintended effects from a psychological perspective, illuminating both the policies themselves and this overall guiding approach to policy analysis. They conclude by encouraging a departure from the inclusion–support framework of policy analysis and responsive action to a critical and creative engagement with how policies about sexuality can have both positive and negative effects. In Chapter 11, Kendall takes readers through the complexities that sexuality education has wrought in the past 2 decades, braiding together the vicissitudes of school-based sexuality education with how policies, practices, anxieties, and assumptions outside of the school walls inform what happens in the corridors, as well as considering what does and could constitute sexuality education within and beyond schools. Ward, Reed, Trinh, and Foust (Chapter 12) take on the mighty task of reviewing the exploding literature on sexuality and the media in the past decade, where both representations of sexuality and forms of media have proliferated, from predictors and outcomes of interaction with media associated with sexuality to media as endemic to sexual socialization to how individuals and communities are engaging with the multiplicity of media inputs and outputs to inform and form sexuality. Hernandez, Mahoney, and Pargament (Chapter 13) provide the often overlooked and absolutely vital perspective on how sexuality intersects with religion as a highly diversified institution in the United States, noting how religious ideologies and institutions both collide and collaborate with sexual practices and identities.

We are hopeful that this exemplary roster of authors representing a diverse, multidisciplinary approach to sexuality will deepen and enrich psychological understanding of this critical facet of human experience. The authors' comprehensive synthesis of each topic area testifies to their collective commitment to enhancing the representation of sexuality within the field of psychology as a whole, at the level of both research and clinical practice. We, along with the editorial board for this handbook—José Bauermeister, Bill George, Jim Pfaus, and L. Monique Ward—feel it has met its single overriding goal: to convey the remarkably diverse and rich body of contemporary research at the intersection of sexuality and psychology and to lay the groundwork for the future, charting a multidisciplinary pathway that represents the diversity and complexity of sexuality itself.

Deborah L. Tolman and Lisa M. Diamond
Editors-in-Chief

Part I

INTRODUCTION AND OVERVIEW

CHAPTER 1

SEXUALITY THEORY: A REVIEW, A REVISION, AND A RECOMMENDATION

Deborah L. Tolman and Lisa M. Diamond

Practically all social scientists would agree that science entails an ongoing dialectic between the development, testing, and refinement of theory. Yet they would certainly disagree about the defining characteristics of theory, what qualifies as a test, and the very definition of science itself. These disagreements are particularly acute within the domain of sexuality research, in which vociferous debates about what is normal, natural, biological, social, and political about sexuality have played a central role in driving the field. In this chapter, we review some of the major theoretical perspectives underlying research on sexuality, but we also wrestle with the very meaning and function of theory itself, especially in the context of the essentialist–social constructionist debates that have historically dominated sexuality research. In particular, we want to push back against our own earlier argument that the notion that sexuality research would be enhanced by a more cohesive and internally consistent theoretical framework, one that attempts to specify and integrate biological and sociocultural influences at every possible level. Rather, we want to argue for the value and significance of theoretical diversity, even theoretical promiscuity, in the service of broadening, challenging, questioning, and ultimately enhancing what is known about sexuality and how it is known.

There is unlikely to be any such thing as a unified field theory in sexuality, and instead of attempting to resolve theoretical debates about, for example, the relative role of genes versus environment in the development of sexual desires, we believe it might be more fruitful for social scientists to continue stoking rather than resolving debates and to oscillate between creating and disrupting established bodies of knowledge regarding sexuality. The reason we believe this to be so important is that sexuality (along with race and gender) is one of those domains in which the status of scientific facts is particularly suspicious and important. The stakes are arguably much higher than for other fields of inquiry, which places a special burden on sexuality researchers to question their own theoretical and ideological assumptions, not only about the sexual phenomena under study, but also about the basic practices, techniques, perspectives, and methodologies used to study it. Sexual facts have profoundly important consequences in a culture (such as that of the United States) that grants special status to scientific knowledge as the basis for ethics, ideology, and social policy and rigorously regulates sexuality. Hence, responsible scientific practice, in our opinion, requires an open and honest reckoning and wrestling with one's own theoretical perspective, whether implicit or explicit; its implications for research practice; and its implications for the interpretation and dissemination of research findings. Accordingly, we begin with some reflections about the role of theory more generally in sexuality research and particularly the long-standing and, we believe, fundamentally productive, tension between essentialism and social constructionism.

INTEGRATIONISM: NOT ALL IT'S CRACKED UP TO BE

More than a decade ago, the two of us wrote an article arguing for greater integration of biological and

http://dx.doi.org/10.1037/14193-001
APA Handbook of Sexuality and Psychology: Vol. 1. Person-Based Approaches, D. L. Tolman and L. M. Diamond (Editors-in-Chief)

cultural perspectives on sexuality (and particularly sexual desire) and critiquing the long-standing battle between essentialist and social constructionist understandings of sexual phenomena (Tolman & Diamond, 2001). In short form, the debate is grounded in fundamentally different epistemologies. Essentialists perceive sexuality as governed by basic, biologically programmed drives and behaviors. Although people's basic sexual essence may have been repressed, celebrated, sublimated, and stigmatized to different degrees in different cultures and historical periods, its basic operation was presumed until recently to be a fundamentally biological rather than sociocultural phenomenon. In contrast, social constructionist perspectives maintain that sexual identities, experiences, and expressions are constituted through meaning making rather than natural biological processes. Social constructionism also necessitates the assumption of the political context of constitutive scripts and discourses by highlighting the systematic social forces that collectively define and reproduce specific conceptualizations of sexuality in different cultures and historical periods. Unadulterated social constructionist accounts of sexuality that altogether ignore the contribution of bodies and biology cannot elucidate the mechanisms and parameters constraining and potentiating the relationship between social scripts and subjective sexual experiences. Similarly, inflexible essentialism basically boils down to "anatomy is destiny," a conclusion that is not only contradicted by voluminous data on variation within and across cultures and history in subjective sexual experiences but by psychological research on the processes by which individuals internalize culturally and historically specific sexual scripts (Gagnon & Simon, 1973). More detailed treatments of the core tenets of each view can be found elsewhere (DeLamater & Hyde, 1998; Hammack, 2005; Kitzinger, 1995).

In 2001 we argued that both of these theoretical positions, at least in their extreme or pure forms, provided only a partial understanding of human experience and that only by integrating the core constructs, methods, and perspectives of each standpoint could social scientific research on sexuality make meaningful strides forward. As we readily acknowledged, similar arguments for interactionist, conjoint, biosocial, and biocultural approaches have been made by many other scholars over the years (DeLamater & Hyde, 1998; Ehrhardt, 2000; McClintock & Herdt, 1996; Udry, Talbert, & Morris, 1986), and these calls have continued apace since the publication of our article (e.g., Hammack, 2005). In short, not much has changed. As noted by Plummer (2007), social constructionist views of sexuality, specifically with regard to challenging historically and culturally specific understandings of what is sexually "normal" or "natural" and spotlighting the political context of sex and sex research, have come to dominate certain areas of sexuality research (such as those grounded in the humanities, sociology, anthropology, and critical feminist thought) but have had little impact on others (such as medicine, clinical sexology, and numerous specialties within conventional psychology, especially as practiced within the United States). Despite oft-repeated calls for greater interaction, integration, and "cross-talk" between the social–cultural and biological camps of sexuality research, it has rarely happened in a substantive way. Furthermore, as aptly noted by DeLamater and Hyde (1998), even researchers who claim to conduct interactionist research often fail to do so, instead producing additive models of social and biological forces (in which both make unique and independent contributions to sexual experience and development) rather than truly integrated models that focus on processes through which social–cultural or biological factors truly transform the influence of the other. Although at some level multiple or mixed methods have created some useful linkages between the biological and the social (i.e., Brotto, Heiman, & Tolman, 2009; McClelland, 2011), these efforts, though productive, do end up skirting, glossing over, or simply sidestepping the debate rather than integrating or resolving its terms, practicing pragmatism rather than transforming paradigms.

Hence, one possible approach to this chapter on theory in sexuality research would be to bemoan—yet again—the continued dominance of the essentialist–constructionist debate, such that researchers on each side of the divide produce, publish, and disseminate work that has limited relevance or intelligibility to those on the other.

This critique would be relatively easy to make; after all, we and, as we have noted, plenty of others have already made it. However, we have come to have reservations about the validity and value of this recommendation for resolution. After revisiting our 2001 article and carefully considering some of the most exciting, challenging, and generative work that has been published over the past decade, we suggest that continued calls for integration between essentialist and constructionist perspectives on sexuality may be not only idealistic but perhaps even misguided. We argued previously (Tolman & Diamond, 2001) that the segregation of sexuality research into different camps inevitably weakened its impact and quality. Yet we are now finding ourselves of a different mind. Some of the best contemporary research in sexuality is located squarely in one camp or another, with those distinct epistemologies still linked to mindfully circumscribed methods and conceptual assumptions and anchors. Ten years ago, we would have looked at this situation and begun wringing our hands ever harder, stepping back to review all of the new evidence for continued, debilitating stalemate.

Instead, we want to suggest that these limitations do not necessarily hinder the capacity of this work to make important contributions to the understanding of sexual phenomena. If this were the case, social scientific research on sexuality would be dwindling and dying, becoming increasingly marginalized with every passing year, and in fact just the opposite is happening. The number of social scientific articles on sexuality submitted and published has been increasing steadily over the past several decades and shows no signs of abating. Studies of sexuality are being published in increasingly high-profile, high-impact journals (e.g., the *Journal of Personality and Social Psychology, JAMA, Developmental Psychology, Journal of Research on Adolescence, Journal of Adolescent Health,* and *Journal of Consulting and Clinical Psychology*). This record suggests that the field of sexuality research is thriving, broadening its reach and furthermore gaining credibility as a core intellectual endeavor with critically important scientific and social implications. Additionally, the proliferation and ever-increasing circulation and impact of journals dedicated specifically to sexuality research (*Journal of Sex Research; Archives of Sexual Behavior; Culture, Health and Sexuality*) is yet another measure of this trend, as is the increasing visibility and status of journals that were once considered "rogue" or alternative outlets (*Feminism and Psychology, Sexualities*). Hence, sexuality research is now garnering far wider audiences than ever before, aided by the democratization of knowledge dissemination brought about by electronic access. As a result, a wide variety of perspectives on sexuality, from quantitative analyses of large-scale representative surveys to intensive analyses of culturally specific discourses about sexuality, are commingling in the marketplace of ideas and pushing the field forward on multiple fronts. University presses and respected publishers also publish sexuality research at increasingly high rates, indicating the value they perceive in these topics and their marketability to a wide audience, even in highly complex, specialized treatments. The number of federally funded studies of sexuality is actually on the rise, and federal calls for research have encouraged a plethora of questions and methods, often insisting on interdisciplinary, translational, multimethod research with clear real-world implications and impact.

If the field as a whole is flourishing, then why do so many sexuality researchers, ourselves included, continue to ruminate over the meaning and implications of the essentialist–constructionist divide? We suspect that it is because this debate has less to do with boots-on-the-ground research and much more to do with larger, metaquestions about the status of sexuality research in society at large as well as within academic communities. We would argue that the essentialist–constructionist debate, which appears by all accounts to have outlived its scholarly usefulness, is in fact standing in for a larger and more important set of epistemological issues having less to do with specific research questions such as "What causes homosexuality?" and more to do with the terms of such questions themselves. The real debate, we would argue, is not about which side is "right" (i.e., is homosexuality an essential biological property of humans or a culturally constructed phenomenon?) but about the status of such a question as meaningful and answerable. From where we sit now, relatively few sexuality researchers are duking it out in a debate about which side produces a more accurate, valid, rigorous understanding of human sexuality and are instead engaged in an increasingly dynamic and productive dialogue about the very meaning of validity, accuracy, and rigor; about the criteria used to judge intellectual inquiries as empirical, scientific, verifiable, objective, and important; and about the criteria by which certain ideas are treated as facts, opinions, hypotheses, models, and theories. The scope of the chapters that constitute this handbook bears witness to this claim. Hence, the real question at hand in this particular example is not really "What causes homosexuality?" but "What do we mean by *cause*?" "What do we mean by *homosexuality*?"

One useful analogy, we think, is that of a multiple-course meal. The appetizer course and the dessert course are utterly different, using fundamentally different ingredients, cooking techniques, and standards for presentation, and they have fundamentally different goals (stimulating further appetite vs. finishing the meal). Each course makes a valid, distinct, and important contribution to the experience of the meal, but none is sufficient to stand on its own. Each is inherently partial but still independently important. One does not achieve a better or more complete meal by integrating them into a single unpalatable plate. That process would retain none of their unique strengths and contributions and would produce something that might be interesting as a novel experiment but would lack integrity, intelligibility, and unique flavors. It is their separate existence within the larger project of the meal itself that makes their contributions meaningful and important. By extension, pastry chefs need not master grilling techniques to produce better pastries. Rather, we would hope that all chefs have a working familiarity and respect for the divergent techniques, goals, and rules of different courses to understand and enhance their own work, and the work of others, in context.

Despite the hurdles that sexuality researchers clearly face in wrestling with the continued standoff between essentialist and constructionist approaches to sexuality, it is important to note that theory, as a larger project across or despite this divide, has been instrumental in the progress of sexuality research over the past decade and continues to provide the promise of enabling researchers to document, discover, unearth, and understand more about this key anchor of the human experience. We view theory as critically important to sexuality research in two key ways. The first concerns its role in shaping and organizing knowledge about sexuality itself. The second concerns its role in shaping and organizing knowledge about such knowledge and about the social forces shaping the process of perceiving, making meaning of, and representing facts and truths about sexuality more broadly. Our goal in this chapter is to highlight both types of theoretical contributions and thus illuminate the productive tensions between them. We review some of the leading theories in both conceptual domains and the kinds of sexual knowledge that each theoretical framework, and perspective on the use of theory, generates. To conclude, we argue that in sexuality research in particular, theory in fact goes beyond specific epistemologies, questions, and methods into the politics of dissemination, both within and beyond the academy; the subsequent impact that these politics have for the production and use of various forms that sexual knowledge takes; and the obligations of being epistemologically explicit and taking responsibility, an ethics of sexuality research that we believe is incumbent on the field.

SEXUAL STRATEGIES THEORY

Sexual strategies theory (Buss & Schmitt, 1993) is perhaps the best-known example of an essentialist, evolutionary model of the factors that drive men and women to seek different types of sexual and romantic liaisons in going about the basic human business of mating and reproduction. More important, it does not make claims about the immediate, proximal mechanisms that shape men's and women's behavior (such as specific cognitions or emotions), but about the distal influences that shape men's and women's bodies and brains during the environment of evolutionary adaptedness. Sexual strategies theory argues that the legacy of these influences, preserved in women's and men's genetic makeup, can still be observed today in the many differences between men's and women's attitudes and behaviors regarding sexuality and close relationships.

Sexual strategies theory is essentially an extension of the parental investment theory proposed by Trivers (1972). Trivers basically argued that sex differences in mating behavior arise as a function of sex differences in what it costs men versus women to successfully get their genes into the next generation for sexual mating. As Trivers noted, women face a more uphill battle on this front than do men. Men are capable of inseminating many different women very quickly, and they can be reasonably sure that any offspring resulting from these encounters will be cared for and nurtured by the mothers, regardless of whether they choose to invest any effort or resources in the child's welfare. Hence, the costs to men in terms of parental investment are minimal. A woman, however, must invest 9 months of pregnancy and then several years of intensive childcare to ensure the survival of a single child (and her own genetic legacy). Hence, her costs in terms of parental investment strategies are enormous. According to sexual strategies theory, this fundamental asymmetry gives rise to hard-wired sex differences in general approaches to mating and reproduction. Specifically, men should be genetically predisposed to seek sexual contact with a wide variety of young, attractive women and to avoid investing too many resources on any particular mate. In contrast, women should be sexually reticent (lest they squander several years of intensive childcare on the offspring of a mate with low genetic fitness) and should prefer men who indicate a willingness to invest precious resources in their child.

Support for sexual strategies theory comes from research demonstrating that around the world, men report a greater preference for physical attractiveness in mates than do women, and women report a greater preference for mates with status and resources than do men. For example, Buss (1989) found this to be the case in a study conducted in 37 different cultures, including more than 10,000 respondents in all. Support for sexual strategies theory also comes from the fact that men are more likely than are women to cheat on a present partner and to express preferences for cheating (Shackelford & Buss, 1997). Finally, sexual strategies theory has been invoked to explain gender differences in the types of infidelity that provoke distress and jealousy. According to the theory, men should be primarily distressed by the prospect of sexual infidelity, because their reproductive success is directly threatened if their female mate engages in sexual contact with another man (particularly because they have no way to confirm who is the father of any resulting offspring). Women, in contrast, should be primarily distressed by the prospect of emotional infidelity, because their reproductive success is maximized by obtaining a high level of parental investment from their mate. This investment would be directly threatened if their male partner became emotionally motivated to make these investments in another woman. Harris (2000, 2003) has referred to this prediction as the "jealousy as a specific innate module" (JSIM) effect because it purports an evolved, genetically based psychological module for the detection of threats to one's reproductive success.

Numerous social psychological studies have been conducted to test the existence, magnitude, and context of these predicted gender differences in sexual versus emotional jealously. In early studies that simply asked men and women which type of infidelity they found most troubling, the results confirmed Buss's predictions (Buss, Larsen, Westen, & Semmelroth, 1992; Buss et al., 1999; Buunk, Angleitner, Oubaid, & Buss, 1996). Studies using different methodologies and samples, however (particularly samples not made up of undergraduate students), sometimes failed to replicate the effect (reviewed in DeSteno, Bartlett, Braverman, & Salovey, 2002; Harris, 2000; Sabini & Green, 2004) One well-known critique of Buss's interpretation of the JSIM effect is the double-shot hypothesis (DeSteno & Salovey, 1996; Harris & Christenfeld, 1996), which maintains that women are more distressed by emotional infidelity because they presume that a man's emotional infidelity is usually accompanied by sexual infidelity (thereby providing a double shot of infidelity), whereas men are more distressed by sexual infidelity because they presume that a woman's sexual infidelity is usually accompanied by emotional infidelity (also thereby providing a double shot).

Additionally, recent work by Sabini and Green (2004) failed to confirm a key tenet of the JSIM hypothesis, namely that women have a greater fear of resource withdrawal from men who are emotionally involved with another woman than from men who are sexually involved with another woman. Sabini and Green therefore concluded that the JSIM effect is "replicable but not robust" (p. 1385). Variation in findings across samples has been interpreted to suggest that in some cases, the JSIM may reflect local norms, and also life course—specific perspectives on mating and parenting, rather than an innate evolved and universal jealousy module. Additionally, researchers have argued that jealousy itself is not a discrete, evolved, sexually dimorphic psychological module but consists of multiple other affective statuses that are collectively "recruited" in a context-specific manner to serve the ultimate goal of mate guarding (DeSteno et al., 2002; Sabini & Green, 2004).

Sexual strategies theory has been criticized for placing inordinate emphasis on gender differences in mating and ignoring the evolved similarities between men and women regarding basic processes of pair-bonding (Bem, 1993; Hazan & Diamond, 2000). Other evolutionary theorists have challenged the assumption of a uniformly lower sex drive in women, calling attention to the extensive evidence that human and nonhuman primate females show voracious sexual appetites under certain circumstances, sometimes mating with every single male in the vicinity, especially during ovulation, contrary to the notion that females should be especially sexually reticent when the probability of conception is high (reviewed in Small, 1993; Wallen, 1995; Wrangham, 1993). Sexual promiscuity around the time of ovulation would be foolhardy from a sexual strategies perspective, but it makes sense if one takes into account the phenomenon of sperm competition, in which the sperm of different males compete within the female's reproductive tract to reach her egg (Shackelford & Goetz, 2006; Shackelford, Goetz, McKibbin, & Starratt, 2007; Shackelford, Pound, & Goetz, 2005). Sperm competition has garnered increasing attention from evolutionary biologists and theorists in recent years, partly because it poses such an interesting challenge to conventional views of female sexual reticence. If one takes sperm competition into account, then a woman should not hold back and carefully evaluate a potential mate's fitness before engaging in sex. Rather, she should have sex with as many different males as possible during ovulation and let the fittest sperm win. The emerging inquiry into sperm competition demonstrates that evolutionary models of sexuality come in different forms, making strikingly different predictions about male and female sexual natures. Whereas sexual strategies theory would appear to reify conventional cultural assumptions about gender differences in sexuality (i.e., sexually voracious males and sexually reticent females), research on sperm competition challenges these assumptions. What these perspectives share, however, is the view that sexual motivation and behavior is governed—at least in part—by evolved psychological mechanisms that remain a basic part of humans' genetic makeup. Whether one views women as naturally lusty or naturally reticent, an essentialist perspective suggests that such a trait is biologically and not culturally driven.

ATTACHMENT AND STEROID–PEPTIDE THEORY

A long-standing critique of many theories of sexuality, especially those grounded in evolutionary perspectives, is their often myopic focus on sexual desire and behavior at the expense of a comprehensive integration with current theoretical and empirical knowledge regarding the (similarly evolutionarily relevant) processes of pair-bonding and emotional attachment (Diamond, 2003; Hazan & Diamond, 2000). Attachment theory views sexuality as part of an evolved pair-bonding system that integrates sexual desire and behavior with the processes of seeking protection and security from and providing it to a pair-bonded reproductive partner (Shaver, Hazan, & Bradshaw, 1988). Attachment theory was originally developed to explain emotional bonding between infants and caregivers. Specifically, Bowlby (1958, 1982) conceptualized attachment as an evolved behavioral system designed to regulate infants' proximity to caregivers and thereby maximize chances for survival. When an infant experiences distress, he or she immediately seeks contact with the attachment figure. In normative cases, this proximity reassures and soothes the infant, who subsequently comes to associate the presence of the attachment figure with emotional security and alleviation of distress. The attachment system remains active over the life course but undergoes important developmental changes. As argued by Hazan and Shaver (1987), adults do not typically continue to use parents as their primary bases of emotional security but instead turn to romantic or sexual partners for that function. Hence, adult love relationships are thought to be functionally analogous to infant–caregiver attachments and based in the same neurobiologically mediated social–behavioral system. The fundamental correspondence between infant–caregiver attachment and adult romantic ties is supported by extensive research documenting that these phenomena share the same core emotional and behavioral dynamics: heightened proximity maintenance, resistance to separation, and use of the partner as a preferred target for comfort and security seeking (reviewed in Hazan & Zeifman, 1999). Even more powerful evidence is provided by the voluminous animal research documenting that two types of affectional bonding are mediated by the same opioid- and oxytocin-based neural circuitry (Carter, 1998).

Sexual behavior and functioning play very different roles within attachment-based models of mating than within models that are based on sexual strategies theory (Hazan & Diamond, 2000). For example, whereas sexual strategies theory views sexual desire and activity as exclusively geared toward reproduction, attachment theory also emphasizes the role of sexual desire and behavior—and the close physical contact that it affords and motivates—in helping to cement an emotional bond between partners, as a result of oxytocin- and dopamine-mediated conditioning processes that are sensitive to intimate physical contact (Hazan & Zeifman, 1994). Recently, van Anders, Goldey, and Kuo (2011) developed a model of sexual motivation that more fully accounts for the pair-bonding context of sexual activity and that considers the distinct hormonal underpinnings of different types of sexual relationships. Their steroid–peptide theory of social bonding is notable not only for its conjoint focus on both mating and pair-bonding but for its specific focus on neuroendocrine factors as proximal mechanisms through which the evolutionary goals of mating and pair-bonding are accomplished in different contexts. They began the explication of their model by noting an important unexplained problem in contemporary research on the evolution of pair-bonds: Specifically, van Anders et al. reviewed research indicating that the basic neurobiological system that structures nurturance and attachment between adult reproductive partners (the oxytocin- and vasopressin-mediated attachment) is the same basic system that structures nurturance and attachment between parents and offspring. Yet, obviously, these types of bonds are critically different with respect to the role of sexuality. As van Anders et al. queried, "How could the same physiological system promote nurturance within pair and parent offspring bonds, but also facilitate sexual contact exclusively within pairs?" (p. 1267).

The solution posited by van Anders et al. (2011) involves the partitioning of intimacy into two types, with different hormonal profiles: *sexual intimacy* (defined as sexual contact oriented around pleasure, reproduction, or power) and *nurturant intimacy* (defined as warm loving contact that enhances social bonds). They posited that both sexual and nurturant intimacy are associated with higher levels of oxytocin and vasopressin (which enhance social bonding) but that only sexual intimacy is associated with higher levels of testosterone (which inhibits social bonding). They similarly partitioned aggression into two types, with different hormonal profiles: *antagonistic aggression* (oriented around gaining territory, status, mates, or dominance) and *protective aggression* (oriented around protecting and safeguarding close social partners, most notably family members). They posited that both antagonistic and protective aggression are associated with higher levels of testosterone (which facilitates aggression but inhibits social bonding), but that only protective aggression is also associated with vasopressin, which enhances social bonds. Hence, the elegance of the steroid–peptide theory is its attempt to develop an integrative, empirically grounded neuroendocrine perspective on human sociosexual behavior that takes into account—and attempts to unpack physiologically—the multiple functions served by complex human behaviors such as aggression and sexuality. Not only does the theory resolve long-standing paradoxes in the field of social neuroendocrinology (such as the fact that sexuality is known to enhance social bonding and yet testosterone is positively associated with sexual motivation and negatively associated with social bonding), but it generates more sophisticated predictions about human social and sexual behavior—and their hormonal underpinnings—as a function of different social and interpersonal contexts (see Chapter 10, this volume). In other words, their model suggests that global predictions about male and female sexuality are simply untenable: The goals, motives, and interpersonal contexts of sexual intimacy must be fully understood to understand its neurobiological architecture. As van Anders et al. argued, the same evolutionarily relevant behavior may serve notably different evolutionary goals according to context (e.g., whether physically affectionate cuddling is pursued between two sexually active pair-bonded partners vs. between parents and infants), and psychobiological models of these behaviors must take this context specificity into account.

REWARD AND CONDITIONING THEORIES

Interestingly, a core tenet of social constructionist theories of sexuality—that sexual desires are acquired in specific contexts and not rigidly biologically programmed—has received new empirical and theoretical support from biologically oriented psychologists using animal models of sexual functioning (thereby demonstrating that biological models of sexuality are not, in fact, intrinsically determinist in nature). Specifically, Pfaus et al. (2012) recently reviewed extensive evidence indicating a thoroughgoing role for reward and conditioning processes in sexuality. They began their argument with a provocative challenge to determinist evolutionary models of sexual desire:

> If the ultimate desire for reproductive success causes us to select potential sex partners with epigamic characteristics that denote good genetic material . . . why would we ever have a difference of opinion? Why would we have a "billion wicked thoughts" (Ogdas & Gaddam, 2011) instead of a few that denote reproductive success? Why would we ever need to learn anything about, or from, sex? (p. 32)

Their answer is that the neural systems that govern sexual response are intrinsically plastic, designed to respond flexibly to the different options and opportunities afforded by different environments and to learn—through basic processes of reward-based conditioning—what people desire (see Chapter 7, this volume). One's desires do not unfold fully formed; they develop on the basis of direct, contextually embedded experience (see Chapter 8, this volume). As stated by Pfaus et al., innate predispositions are forged into stable patterns of desire and behavior through the individual's ongoing experience with sexual reward and with the process of linking reward with specific sets of cues over time. Notably, Pfaus et al. highlighted the fact that this notion of adult sexual desire and behavior as the developmental outcome of dynamic interactions between predispositions and direct experiences is fully consistent with Tinbergen's (1963) influential model of "the complementary nature of ultimate and proximate causality" (p. 33) as well as newer work on epigenetic processes, through which experience alters the manner in which genetic predispositions are expressed and passed on (i.e., Bale, 2011). They emphasized the fact that such plasticity, even in behaviors as evolutionarily crucial as reproduction, makes good adaptive sense when one considers the changing environments that humans have had to contend with over the course of their evolutionary history. Across different environments, different reproductive strategies (which are initiated and sustained by different cues for sexual motivation) have had different cost–benefit ratios, and those cost–benefit ratios are subject to substantial, rapid, and unpredictable change (as when the population density, sex ratio, or availability of food undergoes sudden change). As summarized by Pfaus et al., "Those who learn to respond in the wake of sudden changes to a niche . . . will likely out-reproduce those who do not learn" (p. 33). They posited reward-based conditioning mechanisms as sitting in the middle between ultimate and proximate causes of behavior, exemplifying Ainsworth and Baumeister's (2012) call for mid-level theories of sexuality capable of identifying the specific psychological and biological processes underlying sexual experience and functioning.

The theoretical perspective outlined by Pfaus et al. (2012) is one in which the critical features of sexuality that are refined through interactions between predispositions and experience are the who, what, where, and when of sexuality. In other words, they provided evidence (on the basis of rodent experimental models of sexual functioning) that learning processes are critical to the identification of appropriate targets for sexual activity (of the "correct" gender and reproductive status), the specific sequence of motor behaviors necessary for successful sexual functioning, and the preferred places and times for sexuality. The juvenile animal does not enter into these learning experiences as a blank slate: Pfaus et al. argued that there are species-typical underpinnings to sexual functioning as well as genetically based individual differences (most notably, differences in sexual orientation) that bias the course of future development. More important, however, none of these biases are viewed as deterministic. Instead, innate predispositions—whether for uniform, species-typical features of sexuality or for individual differences—are always in interaction with context-specific, reward-based learning processes (reviewed in Hoffmann, Janssen, & Turner, 2004; Pfaus, Kippin, & Centeno, 2001). Hence, the capacity for context-sensitive plasticity in the development of sexual tastes, patterns, and profiles is an evolved, hard-wired feature of the human brain (providing a useful corrective to the long-standing popular assumption that neurobiological substrates of sexuality foster rigidity and uniformity rather than plasticity and environmentally based change). Of course, given that the extensive research reviewed by Pfaus et al. (and their own collaborative work in this area) focused on rodent sexual behavior, critics might argue that such findings, and their associated conceptual speculations, cannot meaningfully inform the understanding of human sexuality. Yet Pfaus, Kippin, and Coria-Avila (2003) have argued convincingly otherwise, developing a cogent, theoretically grounded, and empirically based framework for using the results of experimental studies of animals to generate and test hypotheses about the basic processes and neuroendocrine mechanisms underlying mammalian and human sexuality more generally (see Chapter 5, this volume).

Another key component of the model put forth by Pfaus et al. (2012) is the notion of critical periods for the development of sexual profiles. Specifically, they argued that at certain critical ages and during certain critical events (i.e., first experiences of sexual desire, masturbation, sexual release, first partnered sexual activity), the sensory, cognitive, affective, and motoric aspects of sexuality become fundamentally integrated, organized by direct experiences of reward and pleasure. Through learning and conditioning processes, these integrated experiences crystallize into stable preferences for certain sexual acts and certain partner characteristics, even if these acts and characteristics are maladaptive in the evolutionary sense or deviant with respect to cultural norms.

More important, Pfaus et al. (2012) are not arguing that sexual orientation, as commonly conceived, represents one such learned preference. To the contrary, they interpret the extant evidence for genetic contributions to sexual orientation as suggesting that innate orientations might in fact represent prepotent constraints on the overall reward-based sexual learning processes, given that some sexual targets will—from an early age—provide stronger sexual rewards than do others (see Chapters 18 and 19, this volume). Yet here, too, they emphasize the importance of learning processes in further enhancing and strengthening gender-based orientations, especially during critical periods in adolescent social and emotional development. In their model, same-sex attractions are likely to be naturally and intrinsically rewarded through the adolescent's direct experience with attractions and emotional attachments to peers, followed in many cases by rewarding sexual experiences or fantasies that directly pair experiences of sexual pleasure and gratification with gender-based cues. Hence, even prepotent orientations require a range of learning experiences, experienced during successive, critical periods of sociosexual development, to develop into comprehensive sexual gestalts (Pfaus et al., 2012, p. 33). This model helps to make sense of the enormous range of variation in the developmental trajectories of sexual minorities, some of whom begin identifying and acting on their same-sex attractions at a very early age and others of whom do not even recall a conscious awareness of same-sex attractions until late adulthood (reviewed in Diamond, 2008). This model also helps to explain the experiences of individuals who, despite manifesting nearly exclusive same-sex or other-sex attractions and behavior during adulthood, report that as adolescents they had pleasurable and rewarding sexual interactions and relationships with individuals of the "wrong" gender for their orientation. Such experiences are perplexing from the standpoint of determinist models of sexual orientation, which presume that sexual experiences with the wrong gender are intrinsically distasteful. Yet such experiences are fully intelligible from the perspective of Pfaus et al.'s model, in which prepotent biases do not obviate the possibility of periodic, atypical experiences of sexual pleasure and reward from the "wrong" type of partner, they simply make it less likely that such rewarding experiences will provide enough rewarding feedback to redirect the individual's sexual development away from its prepotent disposition.

SOCIAL EXCHANGE THEORY

Social exchange theory represents interpersonal behavior as a function of each partner's motives to maximize their rewards and minimize their costs as well as to achieve relative equity in their respective inputs and outcomes (Walster, Berscheid, & Walster, 1973). Applied to the domain of sexuality, Lawrance and Byers (1992; Byers & Wang, 2004) have argued that an individual's sexual satisfaction in a relationship is determined by (a) the overall balance of one's sexual rewards and costs, (b) how these rewards and costs compare with one's expectations, (c) perceptions of equity between one's own rewards and costs and those of one's partner, and (d) the quality of the nonsexual dimensions of the relationship. The rewards associated with sexuality might include such factors as physical pleasure, release of tension, emotional expression, and feelings of closeness with one's partner; the costs associated with sexuality might include dislike of certain practices, embarrassment, or sexual dysfunction (Lawrance & Byers, 1992). The key contribution of the exchange perspective is that these rewards and costs are not conceived as independent and isolated predictors of sexual satisfaction—rather, their relevance derives from how individuals appraise the overall ratio of sexual rewards to costs. Hence, a woman who has highly pleasurable orgasms during sex might actually have low levels of sexual satisfaction if this reward comes with numerous pernicious costs that, for her, outweigh the rewarding nature of the orgasms (e.g., feelings of shame, stigmatization from others, partners' complaints about how long it takes her to reach orgasm). A man with untreatable erectile dysfunction might have extremely high sexual satisfaction if the costs associated with his sexual dysfunction are balanced out by important rewards that he experiences sexually (e.g., the excitement of experimenting with alternative sexual practices with his partner, the climate of warmth and acceptance from his partner).

Numerous studies have confirmed that individuals' perceptions of a high ratio of sexual rewards to sexual costs (regardless of the specific nature of each reward and cost) reliably predict their sexual satisfaction (Byers & Demmons, 1999; Lawrance & Byers, 1995). The social exchange perspective is also particularly useful for understanding discrepancies between partners' sexual satisfaction, because partners may assign different values to certain aspects of their sexual relationship. Such discrepancies are particularly notable in heterosexual relationships because they tend to align with traditional gender differences regarding the valuation of physical versus emotional intimacy. For example, relationship dynamics such as emotional closeness, security, and open communication play a larger role in women's sexual arousal and sexual satisfaction than is the case for men (Basson, 2001; Byers, 2002; Lawrance & Byers, 1992).

The importance of perceived equity to individuals' sexual satisfaction in a relationship has also received extensive support (Hatfield, Greenberger, Traupmann, & Lambert, 1982; Traupmann, Hatfield, & Wexler, 1983), although this association appears to be mediated by the association between perceived equity and overall relationship satisfaction.

Specifically, when individuals feel "underbenefited" in their relationship (i.e., their ratio of positive inputs to positive outcomes in the relationship is lower than that of their partner), they report more relationship distress and lower sexual satisfaction. Yet, it is not clear whether the causal arrow runs from equity to satisfaction or vice versa, and in fact both pathways are likely to operate (Byers & Wang, 2004). Finally, expectations and comparison levels make important contributions to sexual satisfaction, and some studies have found that they make more significant contributions than either rewards or costs and perceived equity (Byers & Demmons, 1999; Lawrance & Byers, 1995; Michaels, Edwards, & Acock, 1984). Lawrance and Byers (1992) found that the majority of individuals, when evaluating their own sexual satisfaction, compare their experiences with generalized expectations regarding how positive and negative sexual relationships should be. Individuals who perceive large discrepancies between what they have and what they expect (regardless of whether their expectations are reasonable) report less satisfaction (Byers & Demmons, 1999; Lawrance & Byers, 1995; Michaels et al., 1984). Hence, although some might critique social exchange perspectives for appearing to provide an overly mechanistic and utilitarian approach to sexual intimacy (reviewed in Byers & Wang, 2004), these models offer a powerful and comprehensive framework within which to understand how two individuals with potentially divergent sexual histories, interests, and expectations come together to negotiate the delicate, dyadic terrain of satisfying sexual intimacy (see Chapter 10, this volume).

Baumeister and Vohs (2004) have proposed revisions to the classic social exchange perspective on sexuality to better accommodate gender differences in what they called the resource value of sexuality. Specifically, they argued for greater attention to the fact that because men have greater sex drives than do women (an obviously controversial claim for which they reviewed the evidence in Baumeister, Catanese, & Vohs, 2001), men are chronically in a position of lower relative power than women when it comes to seeking sexual activity. As they reviewed, the principle of least interest (Waller & Hill, 1938/1951) predicts that in the course of an exchange, the party who is least invested in the outcome of the exchange (and who is therefore more willing to abandon the exchange if it does not meet his or her needs and demands) has more relative power to drive the terms of the exchange. Applied to sexuality, Baumeister and Vohs predicted that because the average woman is less invested in obtaining sex from her male partner than vice versa, she has more relative power. Hence, her sexuality (or, more accurately, access to her sexuality) is a valuable resource that she can exchange for other resources (money, economic security, children, etc.). Furthermore, this perspective predicts certain sexual dynamics between women and men. Specifically, given that principles of economic exchange predict that perceived scarcity increases the value of resources, Baumeister and Vohs maintained that women have an interest in restricting men's sexual access to them to increase the value of sexual activity and hence its exchange value. At the same time (and also following the principles of economic theory), if they restrict access significantly more than competing "sellers," they risk forfeiting the exchange value of their resource altogether (i.e., a man to whom they denied sexual access might simply seek sexual access from another woman). Hence, this theoretical model yields testable predictions about how the average heterosexual man and woman might behave in sexual interactions, according to a clear-cut set of rules and principles.

Although this particular theory of gender differences in sexuality is obviously subject to criticism for its adherence to what some would call reductionistic and outdated assumptions about gender differences in sex drive, Baumeister and Vohs (2004) would likely have argued that the more important foundation of their theory of sexual economics is the widespread and long-standing cultural assumption that men should want sex more than women do, along with the fact that the costs associated with "loose" sexual behavior are greater for women than for men. Hence, even if a woman does, in fact, want sex from a male partner just as much as he wants it from her, social and cultural norms will make it more costly for her to reveal a strong desire for sex, and in fact she will confront profound cultural motives (over her entire life span) to disattend to, suppress, and deny her own sexual desires (see Chapters 2, 8, and 11, this volume). Accordingly, even if one does not share Baumeister and Vohs' (2004) assumption that women are intrinsically less interested in the physical gratification of sex than are men, one can still grant that in the economic marketplace of sex, women have generally been relegated to the cultural role of sexual refusers and men have generally been relegated to the cultural role of sexual seekers, and according to these roles, women have greater ability than men to trade sexual access for other desirable resources. One important testable prediction arising from the theory of sexual economics is that in sexual marketplaces that operate under different cultural rules (e.g., social environments in which women are encouraged—and given cultural permission—to seek just as much sexual gratification as are men), the relative value of sexual access for women and men should be different, and this should change the nature of gender differences in sexual and interpersonal behavior.

Now that we have provided an overview of some of the most important and influential logical–positivist theories that have informed research on sexuality over the past several decades, we take a shift in perspective toward influential theories that represent a social-constructionist approach that fundamentally critiques not necessarily the conclusions of the theories we have outlined but their fundamental epistemological assumptions. To summarize, whereas these theories seek to articulate and test competing truths about human sexuality using an arsenal of empirical methods that meet the standards of the contemporary scientific community, the social constructionist approaches reviewed next are deeply suspicious of the very project of identifying and testing such truths and of the methods and tools legitimated by the scientific community in the service of this project.

POSTMODERN AND CRITICAL THEORY

Critical theory is predicated on a postmodern analysis of sexuality, originating in Foucault's (1969, 1978, 1980) reconceptualization of sexuality not as a distinct thing that individuals have but as a condition of the time and place in which individuals, social institutions, and individuals' material bodies are always situated, unfixed rather than static. Foucault (1969, 1980) demonstrated that sexuality is a dynamic relationship between sexual bodies, sexual practices, institutional power, and knowledge. Rather than being predetermined and ahistorical biological mandates, instinctual impulses, or essential categories that structure human experience, sexuality is a production. In other words, sexual individuals—or subjects—are constantly coming into being, and becoming recognizable to themselves and others, through discourses, or constitutive systems of meaning and language that create, control, enable, regulate, and surveil sexual experience and expression. These discourses exist simultaneously nowhere and everywhere, difficult to pinpoint but reliably effective in shaping and regulating the very experiences that people come to perceive as natural. Thus, people's entire experience of sexuality can be viewed as a context- and culture-specific story that they come to live, most often without conscious awareness that they are doing so (Cohler & Hammack, 2006; Plummer, 1995). For example, people perceive their desires as fundamentally natural and context independent because the sociocultural forces that shape their subjective experiences of sexuality are largely invisible to them.

Discourses are a central driver in Foucault's (1969) notion of power: Power is not a thing but a relation; power is not simply repressive but productive. By *discourse,* Foucault meant not simply a way of speaking but an integrated way of being and knowing that includes the body, the mind, and relationships. Hegemonic or dominant discourses exert intangible but forceful pressure to comply with a set of interlocking norms or ideologies, communicated through language and produced, reproduced, and sanctioned through practices that both reflect and enact these discourses (Foucault, 1969). He demonstrated how hegemonic—that is, dominant—and condoned discourses about sexuality emerged and continue to both enable and constrain how sexuality might be known, understood, experienced, and lived in relation to the management of all aspects of sexuality (not only identities, behaviors, and relationships but also the larger discourses establishing which of these are normal and natural versus marginalized, pathological, or both). In his concept of biopower, Foucault articulated how discourses deployed by the state serve as mechanisms of control to regulate the subjugation of bodies and control of populations. Explication of discourse and its organizing effects on human experience has birthed a now large body of sexuality research (see Volume 2, Chapters 7, 8, and 9, this handbook).

Sexuality and sexuality research have always been entangled with the terms, realities, and justifications of oppression. Kinsey's research (Kinsey, Pomeroy, & Martin, 1948; Kinsey, Pomeroy, Martin, & Gebhard, 1953) was predicated on a rejection of norms rendering anathema so much of the variability in sexuality that was based on a demonstration of the range of sexual expression, yet even as Kinsey used (or, as postmodern theory would dictate, deployed) science to make his case, his research demonstrated how discourse simultaneously normalizes and marginalizes in his use of heterosexual marital status as the primary organizing category of his objective project of nonjudgmental catalogue. Much recent sexuality research has excavated and explicated various forms, experiences, and effects of multiple vectors of oppression, often occurring simultaneously in or for a single body. A marker of research on social dimensions of sexuality in the past decade is the spiraling suspicion of the usefulness of generalization and an impulse, instead, toward deep documentation and thick description (Geertz, 1973/2003) of specific lives of marginalized individuals and collectives of people (see Chapter 6, this volume). In addition, this approach seeks to understand how it is that certain practices become differentially condoned, pathologized, and marginalized, whereas others are tolerated, celebrated, or downright valorized and the specific meanings, histories, positionalities, and geographies that collectively produce these effects and give rise to particular sexual lives (see Chapters 3 and 9, this volume; see also Volume 2, Chapters 2, 7, and 13, this handbook).

FEMINIST AND QUEER THEORIES

Although feminist theory has been critical to both debates and developments in sexuality research since the late 1970s (Padgug, 1979; Ross & Rapp, 1981), at the dawn of the 21st century, the use of feminist theories is well accepted and, in a sense, a mainstreamed vector in postmodern and critical queries about sexuality. Classic feminist sexuality theories, including Rich's (1980) theory of compulsory heterosexuality and Rubin's (1984) theory of sex and gender, continue to be widely used in sexuality research in the United States and globally, as more and more girls' and women's sexual lives are filled with both old and new dangers and pleasures, emerging in migration (González-López, 2005), commodification (Gill, 2009), and technology (S. Jackson & Vares, 2011; see Chapters 12 and 25, this volume; Volume 2, Chapters 1, 3, and 9, this handbook). For instance, in 2004, a conference on the 20th anniversary of Vance's theory of pleasure and danger (Epstein & Renold, 2005) yielded a set of articles on topics ranging from how popular culture is now shot through with representations of women's sexual pleasure as fashionable, nonthreatening, feminine, and aesthetically pleasing (Attwood, 2005) to how female genital cosmetic surgery is positioned as enhancing female pleasure both in magazines and in interviews with surgeons (Braun, 2005) to bisexual women's accounts of how assumptions of promiscuity and nonmonogamous sexual and relational practices impact them (Klesse, 2005). Inquiry into women's experiences and navigation of sexuality as fundamentally relational and gendered dimensions and meanings of sexual desire, sexual identities, sexual behavior, and sexual relationships has extended into almost every corner of sexuality research, from traditional domains of predicting sexual risk and sexual behaviors to the complex and contradictory realms of sexual empowerment and sexual practices. Numerous feminists have built on Foucault's (1980) analysis by highlighting the extent to which conventional understandings of sexuality both spring from and reproduce hierarchies of gender that privilege (White, middle-class) men and oppress women (Bartky, 1990; Duggan, 1990; Ramazanoğlu & Holland, 1993; Rich, 1980; Tiefer, 1999), by restricting not only their freedom to act on sexual desires but their very experiences of sexual desire. For example, Fine (1988) noted that school-based discourses about adolescent sexuality within sex education made frequent references to male but not female sexual desire. In her analysis, this missing discourse of desire effectively robs adolescent girls of a strong sense of sexual subjectivity and sexual agency. Along similar lines, Hollway (1984, 1989) identified several related cultural discourses organizing the contours, contents, and limits of "typical" heterosexuality, including have–hold discourse, male sexual drive discourse, permissive discourse; more recently, Braun, Gavey, and McPhillips (2003) articulated a discourse of reciprocity. By sending powerful messages that women do not have the same types of desires as men, culture (translated through institutions, media, and everyday talk) creates a kind of self-fulfilling prophecy. Women may not recognize their own bodily experiences of sexual desire, in part because available discourses do not offer this interpretation of embodied feelings (Burns, Futch, & Tolman, 2011; Holland & Thomson, 2010; Tolman, 2002). From this perspective, experiences of sexual desire are inextricably linked to the historically and culturally specific belief systems in which people are embedded, and therefore rendering suspect the notion of a culture- or context-free, biologically determined experience of sexual desire.

The other major theoretical advance is the extensive use of queer theory in sexuality research in the social sciences. Although the specific origin and history of queer theory remain contested, queer theory—broadly construed—illuminates how social organizations (rather than natural biological urges) produce and reproduce heterosexuality by both assuming and insisting on it. Queer theory seeks to challenge entrenched and familiar binaries, not only heterosexual–homosexual and male–female but also natural–unnatural, normal–deviant, and so forth, and to elucidate how these binaries gain legitimacy and regulatory force to produce and maintain systems of bodily, social, and political privilege as well as marginalization. A plethora of questions and research programs have demonstrated both how these twin processes of privileging–legitimation and marginalization–punishment are produced and how they can be resisted, to reveal that these binaries organize experience while at the same time demonstrating the ways in which they are social fictions (Sedgwick, 1990; Warner, 1999). Queer theory enables research illuminating how homosexuality has been positioned as "abjected" or marginalized and how it is constituted through the positioning of heterosexuality as normal and central. Queer theory also elucidates how multiple institutions serve the larger purpose of organizing the status and sustenance of heterosexuality and how the effects of this social organization pervade individuals' relationships, communities, behaviors, and subjective experiences. Research informed by queer theory illuminates how individuals construct and live identities that are not heterosexual, enact sets of sexual practices associated with (though by no means engaged in only by) individuals who are not heterosexual, and negotiate relationships and membership in excluded communities (see Chapter 25, this volume; see also Volume 2, Chapters 7 and 9, this handbook). This line of research traces how regulatory discourses operate successfully and also are subverted. For instance, discourses of masculinity offer important insights into gay men's sexuality. In a study of online engagement on barebacking Internet sites as sites of productive sexual culture, Dowsett, Williams, Ventuneac, and Carballo-Diéguez (2008) traced how notions of "taking it like a man" reposition receptive anal sex—receiving semen—not as feminine but as a mechanism for establishing and performing a new kind of masculinity, subverting conventional meanings. They observed the contradiction of how these sites challenge public health concerns of safe sex even as they enable a technologically mediated space for managing HIV/AIDS risk.

Predicated on Foucault's (1980) explication of sexual subjects and practices as situated in culture and produced through discourse and regulatory relations of power, queer theory can be understood as a direct descendent of and intersecting partner with feminist theory. Butler (1990) put forth the notion of gender performativity, that gender is a constant set of performances of appropriate bodily, emotional, interpersonal, and identity practices that makes gender appear to be a stable characteristic but at the same time, when performances are interrupted, resisted, or slipped up, reveal its unstable surface. It is the potential (and perhaps inevitable) slip-up that reveals the regulatory power and control that gender norms, and conceptions of gender as natural, obfuscate. Building on Rich's (1980) explication of heterosexuality as an institution and as fundamentally compulsory, Butler (1990) also introduced the concept of the heterosexual matrix, which is now a commonplace theoretical framework in postmodern and social constructionist sexuality research. This concept refers to

> that grid of cultural intelligibility through which bodies, genders, and desires are naturalized. . . . a hegemonic discursive/epistemological mode of gender intelligibility that assumes that for bodies to cohere and make sense there must be a stable sex expressed through a stable gender (masculine expresses male, feminine expresses female) that is oppositionally and hierarchically defined through the compulsory practice of heterosexuality. (Butler, 1990, p. 151)

Renold (2005, 2007) has argued that heterosexuality itself, even as it is compulsory, is not fixed but is packaged in a hegemonic form, and she has identified shifting and multiple versions of heterosexuality that are subject to regulation among children and in schools.

Queer theory has anchored not only a large number of studies of lesbian, gay, and bisexual sexuality, as lived by individuals and communities and in relation to social norms and policies, but has also been elaborated in theorizing on and researching heterosexual sexuality. For instance, Hill (2006) articulated a model of feminine heterosexual men—that is, those who have fewer macho pretensions or are averse to appearing aggressive or dominant, are overtly concerned with style or "prettiness," and value and present nurturance, kindness, or emotionality—suggesting that such men may find attracting a female partner more challenging but, once they do, may be more likely to have satisfying and strong relationships. Theory specific to transgender bodies and experiences has served both destabilizing and generative purposes in sexuality research (i.e., Valentine, 2007). Stryker (2004) characterized transgender theory as queer theory's "evil twin" that "willfully disrupts the privileged family narratives that favor sexual identity labels (like gay, lesbian, bisexual, and heterosexual) over the gender categories (like man and woman) that enable desire to take shape and find its aim" (p. 212). Overall, then, queer theory—and related developments in transgender theory—are likely to be increasingly influential in social constructionist understandings of sexuality that seek to question the naturalness and inevitability of gender–sex categories, the ways in which such categories have been studied and reproduced through scientific discourse (as critiqued by Jordan-Young, 2010), and their social and political implications.

INTERSECTIONALITY THEORIES

The foregoing discussion of feminist and queer theory may give the mistaken impression of a monolithic critical understanding of patriarchy and a corresponding consensus about "woman" and "man" as meaningful social entities. Yet this is not the case. The advent of intersectionality theories has highlighted the degree to which these discourses can and must recognize how structural differences organize people's experiences. Hence, intersectionality theory demands a systematic accounting of the complexities and specificities of individuals' and groups' standpoints or perspectives (Cole, 2009; Crenshaw, 1991; Nielsen, 1990). Using these perspectives or standpoints in framing and interpreting research is requisite for making diversity meaningful and for meaningfully incorporating social hierarchies into both participants' making sense of those experiences and researchers' interpretations. In particular, intersectionality theory articulates that individuals occupy multiple structural positions that locate their experience, knowledge, choices, and practices in particular histories and in specific relationship to dominant culture's understanding of what is real, normal, acceptable, and even possible. Social markers such as race, ethnicity, and socioeconomic status position each person in relation to beliefs and assumptions grounded in the dominant culture and can be used to marginalize or to highlight points of view that may otherwise not be recognized. For instance, an African American lesbian woman's experience is in some ways distinctive because of how present and past discourses about these different structural dimensions of who she is position her own subjectivity, how she understands her experience, and how others and society itself make sense of her. These aspects of who she is cannot, according to intersectionality, be put into a hierarchy of importance or even controlled for because they are mutually constitutive of her and thus cannot meaningfully be separated out or prioritized. Recent transnational feminist theories are a newer instantiation of intersectionality theory and are increasingly being parlayed in an ever more globalized body of sexuality research (Blackwood, 2005). Anthias and Yuval-Davis (1992), for example, articulated how women are connected to politics of nation-states, including as reproducers of members of ethnic collectivities, of boundaries between ethnic or national groups, and as transmitters of national and ethnically specific cultures that have been demonized, marginalized, or virtually eradicated under colonialism. These theories take as fundamental the critical role played in women's and men's lives by histories of colonization and realities of postcolonial nation-states, and they highlight the embattled nature of cultural, nationalistic, ethnic, and racial discourses on gender and sex. For example, in a study of desire and sexuality among middle-class heterosexual women in postcolonial India, Puri (1999) heard women narrate their internalization of being compelled to protect their vulnerable bodies from male aggression, so that maintaining a respectable female sexual body, and the security and protection that comes with that respectability, was both their responsibility as women and also as members of "respectable" society, charged with enacting and reproducing its norms and hierarchies. Yet women's narratives showed that their passionate sexual desire for, and sexual experiences with, their husbands were the source of considerable social anxieties for these women. Although such desires and behaviors were acceptable within this cultural context, they nonetheless transgressed cultural norms—within their own community and also at a broader, transnational level—regarding women's inherent sexual containment. These examples demonstrate how intersectionality theories are critical in shaping understanding of the construction of gendered and sexual selves across diverse contexts.

Embodiment Theory

One compelling theoretical development that speaks directly to, and in some sense alleviates or subverts the old terms of, the essentialist–social constructionist debates is the increasing use of embodiment theory in sexuality research. The elaboration of embodiment, especially within feminist, queer, and critical theories, has been an exciting development for social constructionist sexuality research, providing the theoretical capacity to recuperate bodies and bodily experience—so central to sexuality—beyond the binaries of mind–body, male–female, and normal–pathological. Embodiment theory has both forced and enabled greater attention by these sexuality researchers to the physical sexual body and also to the subjectivities attached to such bodies through analysis of how institutional and social power are produced and lived by individuals in context. It has increasingly been used to investigate people's lived experiences and to understand how and where the body itself is social at the individual, interpersonal, and cultural levels (see Chapter 25, this volume).

Embodiment refers to the experience of living in, perceiving, and experiencing the world from one's body, one's corporeality. The concept of embodiment is twofold and can mean both *being embodied* (the awareness of bodily sensations, perceptions, and feelings) and *embodying the social* (social inscription or inscribed embodiment, or how social and historical contexts become part of and entangled with one's body). These two components can be at work independently, in tandem, or interactively. By living day to day in a society that makes certain demands on their bodies and psyches, people come to internalize these norms or discourses and embody them (e.g., Bartky, 1990; Foucault, 1980).

Embodiment theory seeks to investigate how culture infuses the body with meaning but also respects the materiality and situatedness of people's bodies as they intersect with other structural contexts. For instance, in a study of adolescent girls, Maxwell and Aggleton (2012) found that some girls who positioned themselves as powerful narrated how sensation experienced on or within the body motivated agentic sexual practices, with both physical and verbal practices being used. These researchers suggested an alternative to framing practices as accommodating or resisting norms, presenting as an alternative four strategies discernible in these girls' narratives—assertive, refusing, proactive, and interrogative—that enable such agency. An intersectional perspective emphasizes how every corporeal body is situated within, and constructed and experienced through, interlocking and inseparable standpoints constituted by specific structural realities and meanings. Feminist theorists have made the case for how female bodies (or those "marked" as female) are under pressure, internally and externally, to become socially inscribed as female–male or feminine–masculine (Bartky, 1990; Bordo, 1993; Young, 1990). Embodiment theory also shows how "transgressive bodies"—not heterosexual, not properly gendered, not recognizable as potentially sexual—are actually necessary in constituting and consolidating heterosexual bodies and sexual practices as natural and normal. Embodiment theory explicates how such transgressive bodies and sexualities raise questions about and transform social norms that underpin "appropriate" sexuality and acceptable embodiments (Berlant & Warner, 1998; Butler, 1993).

CRITICAL THEORIES AT WORK: SEXUAL SUBJECTIVITIES

The study of the sexual self has a long tradition in sexuality research (see, e.g., the influential work on sexual self-schemas by Andersen & Cyranowski, 1994). Sexual subjectivity can in fact have somewhat shifting meanings. One is Foucault's (1980) notion of the sexual subject, whereby subjectivity must be constituted by the subject in the course of social relations; he or she "takes up" subject positions in discourse or can be understood to perform subject positions or to be made up of (potentially changing, multiple, and contradictory) subjectivities. Research stemming from this construct is predicated on the insidious nature of discourses as a form of power, deriving from their invisibility. These discourses ensure that the very self that abides by the state's regulations and interests inevitably reproduces these regulations and entrenches their power at the individual and the social levels. "Secondary virginity" (Carpenter, 2011) serves as a potent example, whereby an available subject position as virginal can be taken up by a young person who has already had sexual intercourse, thus not simply engaging in postcoital ongoing abstinence but as a recuperated identity enabling access to and reinforcing a place-specific form of privilege organized by religion, gender, and sexuality. Another is the growing body of work on how discourses of masculinity operate to organize boys' and men's understanding, experiences, and navigation of sexuality. In an excellent example of Foucault's concept of biopower, Loe (2004) followed how notions of a broken machine flowed through men's narratives about Viagra and erectile dysfunction, ranging from men finding relief for their masculinity experienced as running amok in the face of erection loss to men critical of the press to understand their bodies as troubled, instead delineating the techno-fix as contributing to or even creating a social problem. The regulatory function of masculinity emerges strongly in high school, as Pascoe (2011) found in boys' narrations of their strategies for dealing with "fag discourse," deployed to establish and maintain acceptable heterosexual masculinity. Boys who failed to shed all traces of a feminine voice, who failed to beat other boys into submission, or who failed to gain sexual access to girls were sure to face retaliation, both emotional and physical, by being deemed a "fag" and thus justifiably subjected to bullying, violence, and shunning. Pascoe found that White boys were subject to fag discourses more than African American boys, and she argued that this derived from the fact that such sociosexual regulation of masculine heterosexuality was less necessary in light of the pervasive stereotype of African American boys as possessing an out-of-control hypersexuality. Mooney-Somers and Ussher (2010) inquired how heterosexual men navigated the masculine imperative to commodify sex in constructing sexual subjectivities. They found that men discursively reproduced the value of sex as quantity rather than quality, as an experience of male bodily pleasure using women as a prop to achieve it, and as having a sexual drive in need of control. Yet they also described sexual competence, by which men sought to recognize themselves as figuring out women's desires and needs to manage their gatekeeping function and also attached notions of maturity to attempts to pursue sex as part of a deeper emotional attachment in a relationship (rather than an end in itself).

Yet sexual subjectivity incorporates the capacity for agency; sexual subjects are not doomed to discursive regulation but can recognize, circumvent, resist, or refuse dominant discourses, transgressing social agreements about acceptability and normality (i.e., S. M. Jackson & Cram, 2003; Maxwell & Aggleton, 2012; Renold & Ringrose, 2011; Tolman & McClelland, 2011). Another line of research on sexual subjectivities is predicated on phenomenological and narrative theories of human experience, in particular in the construction of identities and a felt sense of the self (Hammack, 2008; Josselson & Lieblich, 1997; Riessman, 2008). A phenomenological approach or method of research holds that experience is people's complex, nuanced, and often contradictory perceptions and understanding of their thoughts, feelings, behavior, relationships, and social worlds rather than a set of extant principles or characteristics that cannot encompass or account for the complexity of experience. Narrative theories of identity explicate how people internalize and evolve a dynamic sense of self—or multiple selves—through story or narrative, often using William James's concept of the subjective self or the self-as-I (as cited in McAdams, 2001). These perspectives understand identity not as a final accomplishment but as ongoing identity work; life stories develop and change over time and across different dimensions of one's life, including sexuality (Cohler, 1983). For example, in a study of how sexual minority youths construct or configure their sexual identities, Hammack, Thompson, and Pilecki (2009) identified master narratives about heterosexual and homosexual desire that took different forms for individuals with different configurations of gender and ethnicity. One young man narrated an integrated gay identity, grounded in an untroubled sense of difference that "just happened" in a school culture that supported all forms of diversity and a family who accepted his sexuality, and another struggled with assuming a gay identity, describing a felt sense of self as weird, confused, and ambivalent, managing a fractured identity in the traumatic wake of his mother's rejection.

In a somewhat different direction, the development of "sexual citizenship" is another proliferating line of research about sexual selves in which sexuality is a vector for social justice for both individuals and groups (Seidman, 2005). Linking concepts of citizenship to sexuality makes visible the interplay between sexual norms and subsequent sexual hierarchies and access to rights, resources, and full social participation and protections (Evans, 1993; see Volume 2, Chapters 10, 11, and 13, this handbook). This body of research deconstructs and reconstructs how heteronormativity organizes who is labeled or has access to the status of good sexual citizen in venues as diverse as schools, workplaces, and families. An example is Fields and Hirschman's (2007) analysis of how abstinence-only sex education denies lesbian, gay, and bisexual youths (as well as children from "nonlegitimate" families) the right to a safe and productive educational climate.

Critical sexuality theories have been usefully combined with psychological and other social theories that are not about sexuality per se to generate what Tolman (1999) has called a web of theory for sexuality research. For instance, Fasula, Carry, and Miller (2012) argued for a multidimensional theory of the sexual double standard for young women. They integrated sexual scripting theory (Simon & Gagnon, 1986), recognizing the interplay among broader cultural scripts, scripts that organize interpersonal interactions, and intrapersonal scripts, with feminist analysis of gender as a dynamic system of power and control (Connell, 1987) and recognition of the shifting meanings of the sexual double standard and its effects by race in historical context (Collins, 2000). Thus, for African American young women, the sexual double standard is infused with past and current implications of racial inequality as well as the specific forms that gendered power, binaries, and ideologies take under these conditions. In a study of stigma as a form of minority stress (i.e., stress associated with social marginalization, combining coping theory [Folkman, Moskowitz, Ozer, & Park, 1997] with queer theory), Meyer, Ouellette, Haile, and McFarlane (2011) found in the narratives of sexual minority men and women that stigma deprived them of access to critical possibilities and opportunities, especially with regard to safety and acceptance, yet it also yielded adoption of a positive and collective outlook on those very stigmatized identities. McClelland (2011) developed a theory of intimate justice that integrates sociopolitical experiences of inequity into how individuals think about and evaluate the quality of their sexual and relational experiences, demonstrating how social conditions have an impact on what individuals feel, and feel entitled to, in their sexual lives. In an effort to systematically describe the limitations of current research on sexual satisfaction, she conducted a study of individuals' use of sexual satisfaction scales and interviewed them to determine how they understood scale items. She found that women and sexual minority men often reported on their partners' satisfaction rather than their own.

CONCLUSIONS: TAKING RESPONSIBILITY FOR THEORY AND ITS POLITICAL IMPLICATIONS

Be it essentialist or social constructionist, logical–positivist or postmodern, theory is instrumental in revealing new questions that have yet to be asked, in addition to helping to reorganize understanding of questions that have seemingly been answered. Theory provides a lens to make visible or provide insight into observations, narratives, and models in unexpected and generative ways. Theory can provide explanations for existing phenomena and can guide researchers to identify and help them make sense of phenomena they do not yet recognize. Theory can account for universal processes of the human condition and can reveal dimensions of experience that are historically and culturally specific. Theory is also, we argue, critically important for revealing and analyzing the political dimensions of sexuality and its study.

As is the case across the social sciences, in sexuality research theory is inextricably linked to methodology and epistemology and hence speaks to researchers' understanding of just what they are doing when they embark on projects of "sexual science." This ethos is, to be sure, a point of some controversy among researchers studying sexuality who have different, often incompatible, intellectual commitments. Those from social constructionist and postmodern traditions take for granted that their work is inherently political and that the study of sexuality is fundamentally shaped by the sociocultural frame and lens of the researcher and his or her particular positioning within the social institutions that house academic research. Yet researchers from logical–positivist traditions have been trained to strive for total objectivity and to cast out any hint of historical, cultural, or political specificity in their mode of observation or analyses. Even those who admit that pure and total objectivity and neutrality are probably impossible typically agree that it is the scientist's goal to strive for it.

Hence, we suggest that the true wrangling may be more about the nature of science and the role of researchers in accounting for the translation of their work into real-life, socially and politically embedded contexts. On this front, we think it is important to note that in the contemporary cultural context, certain forms of scientific practice have more social legitimacy and hence sociopolitical currency than others: Studies that approach sexuality from a logical–positivist frame, and that emphasize the quantification of sexual phenomena, are the ones that have the most cultural intelligibility as real science and are hence the ones that tend to infiltrate public discourse and count as evidence to be trusted and accommodated. In contrast, phenomenological and narrative studies and studies using other methods anchored in critical theories, such as participatory action research, that focus on highly particularized experiences, or analyses critiquing broader, invisible social and explicitly political dynamics, are often not apprehended as real research and can often be treated as human interest versions of science within as well as beyond the academy. This hierarchy of what counts as science means that in the marketplace of ideas and social currency, essentialist perspectives on sexuality and logical–positivist approaches to studying it often hold greater sway and have tended to set the terms of public debate. Although change in this condition is gradual at best, we argue that researchers studying sexuality, and people, colleagues and otherwise, consuming this research, should be mindful of the hierarchy of knowledge and knowledge production that grants some scientific stories more status, greater dissemination, and more power than others.

Going back to our multiple-course meal metaphor in arguing for theoretical promiscuity and a vigorous and active dialectic between incompatible theoretical perspectives, we want to advocate for the necessity and desirability of all courses to make up a complete and satisfying meal. In other words, psychobiologists who have never read Foucault and critical psychologists who have no interest in oxytocin need one another. They need not get along or like the same dishes (though a diet of only, say, meatloaf, can be seen as unhealthy, unadventurous, or simply limited), but the larger project of sexuality research requires that their respective bodies of work continue to vigorously question, challenge, disturb, and distress one another, ideally in a larger dialogue characterized by respect and in which each of their voices has an equal chance of being heard and disseminated. Because our intellectual commitments are so often a part of our proverbial DNA, we recognize that our argument not simply for tolerance but for engagement may be a difficult one to embrace. We know from personal experience the challenge of reaching across this divide, yet we also know how productive this reach can be.

We hope that by making explicit some of the fundamental theoretical assumptions and practices inherent in these perspectives rather than striving for a potentially problematic and elusive golden key of integration, scholars studying sexuality should instead strive for explicitness and responsibility in the conduct of theoretically driven research. By *explicitness,* we mean that all researchers should begin from the premise that their work has a distinct theoretical perspective, even those who stridently maintain that they are simply producing objective, neutral observations, and that these theoretical perspectives must be made explicit. This is already a common practice for some sexuality researchers. For example, those guided by evolutionary models of sexuality usually make this clear from the outset and clarify the major tenets and assumptions of this standpoint, and poststructuralists typically lay out their premise of the instability of knowledge production, the articulation of the standpoint from which they and their participants engage in inquiry, and the practice of producing knowledge about aspects of sexuality that continue to be marginalized and hidden. However, by no means do all sexuality researchers situate their research clearly in specific epistemologies. We are asserting that a basic requirement of conducting and disseminating one's work requires an explicit wrestling and discussion of its theoretical bases, in the same way that basic discussions of methodology, study design, and analyses are pro forma.

Responsibility is a broader and somewhat more elastic construct, but we mean this term to refer to the manner in which researchers consider and participate in the dissemination of their work within a larger social context in which questions about natural causes and normal forms in the domain of sexuality have real and important social and political implications. We think that sexuality researchers have a greater responsibility to wrestle with these implications than other social science researchers because of the unique status of sexuality as a site of intense resistance, control, stigma, and straightforward political battling beyond the halls of the academy. In short, the stakes of this panoply of theoretical perspectives and hierarchies are higher in the field of sexuality than they are in other domains, and we argue that ethical scholarly practice therefore requires taking responsibility for ensuring that the strengths and limitations of one's perspective are adequately described.

Outing such an ethics of sexuality research has consequences for the production and consumption of our work. We stand firm that the walls of the academy are porous for sexuality research, whether researchers are interested in extending their reach beyond them or not. In tandem with psychology, we conclude that is incumbent on sexuality researchers to use theory with wisdom, grace, and an urgent sense of the impact that their contributions to sexual knowledge have for people's lives.

References

Ainsworth, S. E., & Baumeister, R. F. (2012). Changes in sexuality: How sexuality changes across time, across relationships, and across sociocultural contexts. *Clinical Neuropsychiatry: Journal of Treatment Evaluation, 9,* 32–38.

Andersen, B. L., & Cyranowski, J. M. (1994). Women's sexual self-schema. *Journal of Personality and Social Psychology, 67,* 1079–1100. doi:10.1037/0022-3514.67.6.1079

Anthias, F., & Yuval-Davis, N. (1992). *Racialized boundaries: Race, nation, gender, color and class and the anti-racist struggle.* New York, NY: Routledge.

Attwood, F. (2005). Fashion and passion: Marketing sex to women. *Sexualities, 8*, 392–406. doi:10.1177/1363460705056617

Bale, T. L. (2011). Sex differences in prenatal epigenetic programing of stress pathways. *Stress, 14*, 348–356.

Bartky, S. L. (1990). *Femininity and domination: Studies in the phenomenology of oppression*. New York, NY: Routledge.

Basson, R. (2001). Using a different model for female sexual response to address women's problematic low sexual desire. *Journal of Sex and Marital Therapy, 27*, 395–403. doi:10.1080/713846827

Baumeister, R. F., Catanese, K. R., & Vohs, K. D. (2001). Is there a gender difference in strength of sex drive? Theoretical views, conceptual distinctions, and a review of relevant evidence. *Personality and Social Psychology Review, 5*, 242–273. doi:10.1207/S15327957PSPR0503_5

Baumeister, R. F., & Vohs, K. D. (2004). Sexual economics: Sex as female resource for social exchange in heterosexual interactions. *Personality and Social Psychology Review, 8*, 339–363. doi:10.1207/s15327957pspr0804_2

Bem, S. L. (1993). *The lenses of gender: Transforming the debate on sexual inequality*. New Haven, CT: Yale University Press.

Berlant, L., & Warner, M. (1998). Sex in public. *Critical Inquiry, 24*, 547–566. doi:10.1086/448884

Blackwood, E. (2005). Transnational sexualities in one place: Indonesian readings. *Gender and Society, 19*, 221–242. doi:10.1177/0891243204272862

Bordo, S. (1993). *Unbearable weight: Feminism, Western culture, and the body*. Berkeley: University of California Press.

Bowlby, J. (1958). The nature of the child's tie to his mother. *International Journal of Psycho-Analysis, 39*, 350–373.

Bowlby, J. (1982). *Attachment and loss: Vol. 1. Attachment* (2nd ed.). New York, NY: Basic Books.

Braun, V. (2005). In search of (better) sexual pleasure: Female genital "cosmetic" surgery. *Sexualities, 8*, 407–424. doi:10.1177/1363460705056625

Braun, V., Gavey, N., & McPhillips, K. (2003). The "fair deal"? Unpacking accounts of reciprocity in heterosex. *Sexualities, 6*, 237–261. doi:10.1177/1363460703006002005

Brotto, L. A., Heiman, J. R., & Tolman, D. L. (2009). Narratives of desire in mid-aged women with and without arousal difficulties. *Journal of Sex Research, 46*, 387–398. doi:10.1080/00224490902792624

Burns, A., Futch, V. A., & Tolman, D. L. (2011). "It's like doing homework": Academic achievement discourse in adolescent girls' fellatio narratives. *Sexuality Research and Social Policy, 8*, 239–251. doi:10.1007/s13178-011-0062-1

Buss, D. M. (1989). Sex differences in human mate preferences: Evolutionary hypotheses tested in 37 cultures. *Behavioral and Brain Sciences, 12*, 1–49. doi:10.1017/S0140525X00023992

Buss, D. M., Larsen, R. J., Westen, D., & Semmelroth, J. (1992). Sex differences in jealousy: Evolution, physiology, and psychology. *Psychological Science, 3*, 251–255. doi:10.1111/j.1467-9280.1992.tb00038.x

Buss, D. M., & Schmitt, D. P. (1993). Sexual strategies theory: A contextual evolutionary analysis of human mating. *Psychological Review, 100*, 204–232. doi:10.1037/0033-295X.100.2.204

Buss, D. M., Shackelford, T. K., Kirkpatrick, L. A., Choe, J. C., Lim, H. K., Hasegawa, M., . . . Bennett, K. (1999). Jealousy and beliefs about infidelity: Tests of competing hypotheses in the United States, Korea, and Japan. *Personal Relationships, 6*, 125–150. doi:10.1111/j.1475-6811.1999.tb00215.x

Butler, J. P. (1990). *Gender trouble: Feminism and the subversion of identity*. London, England: Routledge.

Butler, J. P. (1993). *Bodies that matter: On the discursive limits of sex*. New York, NY: Routledge.

Buunk, B. P., Angleitner, A., Oubaid, V., & Buss, D. M. (1996). Sex differences in jealousy in evolutionary and cultural perspective: Tests from the Netherlands, Germany, and the United States. *Psychological Science, 7*, 359–363. doi:10.1111/j.1467-9280.1996.tb00389.x

Byers, E. S. (2002). Evidence for the importance of relationship satisfaction for women's sexual functioning. *Women and Therapy, 24*, 23–26. doi:10.1300/J015v24n01_04

Byers, E. S., & Demmons, S. (1999). Sexual satisfaction and sexual self-disclosure within dating relationships. *Journal of Sex Research, 36*, 180–189. doi:10.1080/00224499909551983

Byers, E. S., & Wang, A. (2004). Understanding sexuality in close relationships from a social exchange perspective. In J. H. Harvey, A. Wenzel, & S. Sprecher (Eds.), *The handbook of sexuality in close relationships* (pp. 203–234). Mahwah, NJ: Erlbaum.

Carpenter, L. M. (2011). Like a virgin . . . again? Secondary virginity as an ongoing gendered social construction. *Sexuality and Culture, 15*, 115–140. doi:10.1007/s12119-010-9085-7

Carter, C. S. (1998). Neuroendocrine perspectives on social attachment and love. *Psychoneuroendocrinology, 23*, 779–818. doi:10.1016/S0306-4530(98)00055-9

Cohler, B. J. (1983). Personal narrative and life course. In P. B. Baltes (Ed.), *Life span development and behavior* (Vol. 4, pp. 205–241). Mahwah, NJ: Erlbaum.

Cohler, B. J., & Hammack, P. L. (2006). Making a gay identity: Life story and the construction of a coherent self. In D. P. McAdams, R. Josselson, & A. Lieblich (Eds.), *Identity and story: Creating self in narrative* (pp. 151–172). Washington, DC: American Psychological Association. doi:10.1037/11414-007

Cole, E. R. (2009). Intersectionality and research in psychology. *American Psychologist, 64*, 170–180. doi:10.1037/a0014564

Collins, P. H. (2000). *Black feminist thought: Knowledge, consciousness, and the politics of empowerment.* New York, NY: Routledge.

Connell, R. W. (1987). *Gender and power: Society, the person and sexual politics.* Stanford, CA: Stanford University Press.

Crenshaw, K. (1991). Mapping the margins: Intersectionality, identity politics, and violence against women of color. *Stanford Law Review, 43*, 1241–1299. doi:10.2307/1229039

DeLamater, J. D., & Hyde, J. S. (1998). Essentialism vs. social constructionism in the study of human sexuality. *Journal of Sex Research, 35*, 10–18. doi:10.1080/00224499809551913

DeSteno, D., Bartlett, M. Y., Braverman, J., & Salovey, P. (2002). Sex differences in jealousy: Evolutionary mechanism or artifact of measurement? *Journal of Personality and Social Psychology, 83*, 1103–1116. doi:10.1037/0022-3514.83.5.1103

DeSteno, D., & Salovey, P. (1996). Evolutionary origins of sex differences in jealousy? Questioning the "fitness" of the model. *Psychological Science, 7*, 367–372. doi:10.1111/j.1467-9280.1996.tb00391.x

Diamond, L. M. (2003). What does sexual orientation orient? A biobehavioral model distinguishing romantic love and sexual desire. *Psychological Review, 110*, 173–192. doi:10.1037/0033-295X.110.1.173

Diamond, L. M. (2008). *Sexual fluidity: Understanding women's love and desire.* Cambridge, MA: Harvard University Press.

Dowsett, G. W., Williams, H., Ventuneac, A., & Carballo-Diéguez, A. (2008). "Taking it like a man": Masculinity and barebacking online. *Sexualities, 11*, 121–141. doi:10.1177/1363460707085467

Duggan, L. (1990). From instincts to politics: Writing the history of sexuality in the U.S. *Journal of Sex Research, 27*, 95–109. doi:10.1080/00224499009551544

Ehrhardt, A. A. (2000). Gender, sexuality, and human development. In J. H. Bancroft (Ed.), *The role of theory in sex research* (pp. 3–16). Bloomington: Indiana University Press.

Epstein, D., & Renold, E. (2005). Introduction. *Sexualities, 8*, 387–391. doi:10.1177/1363460705056615

Evans, G. (1993). *Sexual citizenship.* New York, NY: Routledge.

Fasula, A. M., Carry, M., & Miller, K. S. (2012). A multidimensional framework for the meanings of the sexual double standard and its application for the sexual health of young Black women in the US. *Journal of Sex Research.* Advance online publication. doi:10.1080/00224499.2012.716874

Fields, J., & Hirschman, C. (2007). Citizenship lessons in abstinence-only sexuality education. *American Journal of Sexuality Education, 2*, 3–25. doi:10.1300/J455v02n02_02

Fine, M. (1988). Sexuality, schooling, and adolescent females: The missing discourse of desire. *Harvard Educational Review, 58*, 29–53.

Folkman, S., Moskowitz, J. T., Ozer, E. M., & Park, C. L. (1997). Positive meaningful events and coping in the context of HIV/AIDS. In B. H. Gottlieb (Ed.), *Coping with chronic stress* (pp. 293–314). New York, NY: Plenum Press.

Foucault, M. (1969). *The archaeology of knowledge.* New York, NY: Routledge.

Foucault, M. (1978). *Discipline and punish: The birth of the prison.* New York, NY: Pantheon Books.

Foucault, M. (1980). *The history of sexuality* (Vol. 1). New York, NY: Vintage.

Gagnon, J. H., & Simon, W. (1973). *Sexual conduct: The social sources of human sexuality.* Chicago, IL: Aldine.

Geertz, C. (2003). Thick description: Toward an interpretive theory of culture. In C. Jenks (Ed.), *Culture: Critical concepts in sociology* (Vol. 1, pp. 173–196). New York, NY: Psychology Press. (Original work published 1973)

Gill, R. (2009). Supersexualize me! Advertising and the midriffs. In F. Attwood (Ed.), *Mainstreaming sex: The sexualization of Western culture* (pp. 93–110). London, England: I. B. Taurus.

González-López, G. (2005). *Erotic journeys: Mexican immigrants and their sex lives.* Berkeley: University of California Press.

Hammack, P. L. (2005). The life course development of human sexual orientation: An integrative paradigm. *Human Development, 48*, 267–290. doi:10.1159/000086872

Hammack, P. L. (2008). Narrative and the cultural psychology of identity. *Personality and Social Psychology Review, 12*, 222–247. doi:10.1177/1088868308316892

Hammack, P. L., Thompson, E. M., & Pilecki, A. (2009). Configurations of identity among sexual minority youth: Context, desire, and narrative. *Journal of Youth and Adolescence, 38*, 867–883. doi:10.1007/s10964-008-9342-3

Harris, C. R. (2000). Psychophysiological responses to imagined infidelity: The specific innate modular view of jealousy reconsidered. *Journal of Personality and Social Psychology, 78*, 1082–1091. doi:10.1037/0022-3514.78.6.1082

Harris, C. R. (2003). A review of sex differences in sexual jealousy, including self-report data, psychophysiological responses, interpersonal violence, and morbid jealousy. *Personality and Social Psychology Review, 7*, 102–128. doi:10.1207/S15327957PSPR0702_102-128

Harris, C. R., & Christenfeld, N. (1996). Gender, jealousy, and reason. *Psychological Science, 7*, 364–366. doi:10.1111/j.1467-9280.1996.tb00390.x

Hatfield, E., Greenberger, D., Traupmann, J., & Lambert, P. (1982). Equity and sexual satisfaction in recently married couples. *Journal of Sex Research, 18*, 18–32. doi:10.1080/00224498209551131

Hazan, C., & Diamond, L. M. (2000). The place of attachment in human mating. *Review of General Psychology, 4*, 186–204. doi:10.1037/1089-2680.4.2.186

Hazan, C., & Shaver, P. R. (1987). Romantic love conceptualized as an attachment process. *Journal of Personality and Social Psychology, 52*, 511–524. doi:10.1037/0022-3514.52.3.511

Hazan, C., & Zeifman, D. (1994). Sex and the psychological tether. In D. Perlman & K. Bartholomew (Eds.), *Advances in personal relationships: Vol. 5. A research annual* (pp. 151–177). London, England: Jessica Kingsley.

Hazan, C., & Zeifman, D. (1999). Pair-bonds as attachments: Evaluating the evidence. In J. Cassidy & P. R. Shaver (Eds.), *Handbook of attachment theory and research* (pp. 336–354). New York, NY: Guilford Press.

Hill, D. B. (2006). "Feminine" heterosexual men: Subverting heteropatriarchal sexual scripts? *Journal of Men's Studies, 14*, 145–159. doi:10.3149/jms.1402.145

Hoffmann, H., Janssen, E., & Turner, S. L. (2004). Classical conditioning of sexual arousal in women and men: Effects of varying awareness and biological relevance of the conditioned stimulus. *Archives of Sexual Behavior, 33*, 43–53. doi:10.1023/B:ASEB.0000007461.59019.d3

Holland, J., & Thomson, R. (2010). Revisiting youthful sexuality: Continuities and changes over two decades. *Sexual and Relationship Therapy, 25*, 342–350. doi:10.1080/14681991003767370

Hollway, W. (1984). Gender difference and the production of subjectivity. In J. Henriques (Ed.), *Changing the subject: Psychology, social regulation and subjectivity* (pp. 227–263). London, England: Methuen.

Hollway, W. (1989). *Subjectivity and method in psychology*. Thousand Oaks, CA: Sage.

Jackson, S., & Vares, T. (2011). Media "sluts": "Tween" girls' negotiation of postfeminist sexual subjectivities in popular culture. In R. Gill & C. Scharff (Eds.), *New femininities: Postfeminism, neoliberalism and subjectivity* (pp. 134–146). Basingstoke, England: Palgrave-Macmillan.

Jackson, S. M., & Cram, F. (2003). Disrupting the sexual double standard: Young women's talk about heterosexuality. *British Journal of Social Psychology, 42*, 113–127. doi:10.1348/014466603763276153

Jordan-Young, R. M. (2010). *Brain storm: The flaws in the science of sex differences*. Cambridge, MA: Harvard University Press.

Josselson, R., & Lieblich, A. (1997). *The narrative study of lives*. Newbury Park, CA: Sage.

Kinsey, A. C., Pomeroy, W. B., & Martin, C. E. (1948). *Sexual behavior in the human male*. Philadelphia, PA: W. B. Saunders.

Kinsey, A. C., Pomeroy, W. B., Martin, C. E., & Gebhard, P. H. (1953). *Sexual behavior in the human female*. Philadelphia, PA: W. B. Saunders.

Kitzinger, C. (1995). Social constructionism: Implications for lesbian and gay psychology. In A. R. D'Augelli & C. Patterson (Eds.), *Lesbian, gay, and bisexual identities over the lifespan* (pp. 136–162). New York, NY: Oxford University Press. doi:10.1093/acprof:oso/9780195082319.003.0006

Klesse, C. (2005). Bisexual women, non-monogamy and differentialist anti-promiscuity discourses. *Sexualities, 8*, 445–464. doi:10.1177/1363460705056620

Lawrance, K.-A., & Byers, E. S. (1992). Development of the interpersonal exchange model of sexual satisfaction in long term relationships. *Canadian Journal of Human Sexuality, 1*, 123–128.

Lawrance, K.-A., & Byers, E. S. (1995). Sexual satisfaction in long-term heterosexual relationships: The interpersonal exchange model of sexual satisfaction. *Personal Relationships, 2*, 267–285. doi:10.1111/j.1475-6811.1995.tb00092.x

Loe, M. (2004). *The rise of Viagra: How the little blue pill changed sex in America*. New York, NY: New York University Press.

Maxwell, C., & Aggleton, P. (2012). Bodies and agentic practice in young women's sexual and intimate relationships. *Sociology, 46*, 306–321. doi:10.1177/0038038511419192

McAdams, D. P. (2001). The psychology of life stories. *Review of General Psychology, 5*, 100–122. doi:10.1037/1089-2680.5.2.100

McClelland, S. I. (2011). Who is the "self" in self reports of sexual satisfaction? Research and policy implications. *Sexuality Research and Social Policy, 8*, 304–320. doi:10.1007/s13178-011-0067-9

McClintock, M. K., & Herdt, G. (1996). Rethinking puberty: The development of sexual attraction.

Current Directions in Psychological Science, 5, 178–183. doi:10.1111/1467-8721.ep11512422

Meyer, I. H., Ouellette, S. C., Haile, R., & McFarlane, T. A. (2011). "We'd be free": Narratives of life without homophobia, racism, or sexism. *Sexuality Research and Social Policy, 8*, 204–214. doi:10.1007/s13178-011-0063-0

Michaels, J. W., Edwards, J. N., & Acock, A. C. (1984). Satisfaction in intimate relationships as a function of inequality, inequity, and outcomes. *Social Psychology Quarterly, 47*, 347–357. doi:10.2307/3033637

Mooney-Somers, J., & Ussher, J. M. (2010). Sex as commodity: Single and partnered men's subjectification as heterosexual men. *Men and Masculinities, 12*, 353–373. doi:10.1177/1097184X08322620

Nielsen, J. M. (1990). *Feminist research methods: Exemplary readings in the social sciences.* Boulder, CO: Westview Press.

Padgug, R. A. (1979). Sexual matters: On conceptualizing sexuality in history. *Radical History Review, 20*, 3–23. doi:10.1215/01636545-1979-20-3

Pascoe, C. J. (2011). *Dude, you're a fag: Masculinity and sexuality in high school.* Berkeley: University of California Press.

Pfaus, J. G., Kippin, T. E., & Centeno, S. (2001). Conditioning and sexual behavior: A review. *Hormones and Behavior, 40*, 291–321. doi:10.1006/hbeh.2001.1686

Pfaus, J. G., Kippin, T. E., & Coria-Avila, G. (2003). What can animal models tell us about human sexual response? *Annual Review of Sex Research, 14*, 1–63.

Pfaus, J. G., Kippin, T. E., Coria-Avila, G. A., Gelez, H., Afonso, V. M., Ismail, N., & Parada, M. (2012). Who, what, where, when (and maybe even why)? How the experience of sexual reward connects sexual desire, preference, and performance. *Archives of Sexual Behavior, 41*, 31–62. doi:10.1007/s10508-012-9935-5

Plummer, K. (1995). *Telling sexual stories.* New York, NY: Routledge. doi:10.4324/9780203425268

Plummer, K. (2007). Queers, bodies, and postmodern sexualities: A note on revisiting the "sexual" in symbolic interactionism. In M. Kimmel (Ed.), *The sexual self: The construction of sexual scripts* (pp. 16–30). Nashville, TN: Vanderbilt University Press.

Puri, J. (1999). *Woman, body, desire in post-colonial India: Narratives of gender and sexuality.* New York, NY: Routledge.

Ramazanoğlu, C., & Holland, J. (1993). Women's sexuality and men's appropriation of desire. In C. Ramazanoğlu (Ed.), *Up against Foucault* (pp. 239–264). New York, NY: Routledge.

Renold, E. (2005). *Girls, boys and junior sexualities.* New York, NY: Routledge.

Renold, E. (2007). Primary school "studs": (De)constructing young boys' heterosexual masculinities. *Men and Masculinities, 9*, 275–297. doi:10.1177/1097184X05277711

Renold, E., & Ringrose, J. (2011). Schizoid subjectivities? Retheorizing teen girls' sexual cultures in an era of sexualization. *Journal of Sociology, 47*, 389–409. doi:10.1177/1440783311420792

Rich, A. (1980). Compulsory heterosexuality and lesbian existence. *Signs: Journal of Women in Culture and Society, 5*, 631–660. doi:10.1086/493756

Riessman, C. K. (2008). *Narrative methods for the social sciences.* Newbury Park, CA: Sage.

Ross, E., & Rapp, R. (1981). Sex and society: A research note from social history and anthropology. *Comparative Studies in Society and History, 23*, 51–72. doi:10.1017/S0010417500009683

Rubin, G. (1984). Thinking sex: Notes for a radical theory of the politics of sexuality. In C. S. Vance (Ed.), *Pleasure and danger: Exploring female sexuality* (pp. 267–319) Boston, MA: Routledge & Kegan Paul.

Sabini, J., & Green, M. C. (2004). Emotional responses to sexual and emotional infidelity: Constants and differences across genders, samples, and methods. *Personality and Social Psychology Bulletin, 30*, 1375–1388. doi:10.1177/0146167204264012

Sedgwick, E. K. (1990). *Epistemology of the closet.* Berkeley: University of California Press.

Seidman, S. (2005). Regulating sex: The politics of intimacy and identity. In E. Bernstein & L. Schaffner (Eds.), *Regulating sex: The politics of intimacy and identity* (pp. 225–245). New York, NY: Routledge.

Shackelford, T. K., & Buss, D. M. (1997). Anticipation of marital dissolution as a consequence of spousal infidelity. *Journal of Social and Personal Relationships, 14*, 793–808. doi:10.1177/0265407597146005

Shackelford, T. K., & Goetz, A. T. (2006). Comparative evolutionary psychology of sperm competition. *Journal of Comparative Psychology, 120*, 139–146. doi:10.1037/0735-7036.120.2.139

Shackelford, T. K., Goetz, A. T., McKibbin, W. F., & Starratt, V. G. (2007). Absence makes the adaptations grow fonder: Proportion of time apart from partner, male sexual psychology, and sperm competition in humans (*Homo sapiens*). *Journal of Comparative Psychology, 121*, 214–220. doi:10.1037/0735-7036.121.2.214

Shackelford, T. K., Pound, N., & Goetz, A. T. (2005). Psychological and physiological adaptations to sperm competition in humans. *Review of General Psychology, 9*, 228–248. doi:10.1037/1089-2680.9.3.228

Shaver, P. R., Hazan, C., & Bradshaw, D. (1988). Love as attachment: The integration of three behavioral systems. In J. Sternberg & M. L. Barnes (Eds.), *The psychology of love* (pp. 193–219). New Haven, CT: Yale University Press.

Simon, W., & Gagnon, J. H. (1986). Sexual scripts: Permanence and change. *Archives of Sexual Behavior, 15*, 97–120. doi:10.1007/BF01542219

Small, M. F. (1993). *Female choices: Sexual behavior of human primates*. Ithaca, NY: Cornell University Press.

Stryker, S. (2004). Transgender studies: Queer theory's evil twin. *GLQ: A Journal of Gay and Lesbian Studies, 10*, 212–215.

Tiefer, L. (1999). Challenging sexual naturalism, the shibboleth of sex research and popular sexology. In D. Bernstein (Ed.), *Gender and motivation* (pp. 143–172). Lincoln: University of Nebraska Press.

Tinbergen, N. (1963). On aims and methods of ethology. *Zeitschrift für Tierpsychologie, 20*, 410–433.

Tolman, D. L. (1999). Femininity as a barrier to positive sexual health for adolescent girls. *Journal of the American Medical Women's Association, 54*, 133–138.

Tolman, D. L. (2002). *Dilemma of desire: Teenage girls and sexuality*. Cambridge, MA: Harvard University Press.

Tolman, D. L., & Diamond, L. M. (2001). Desegregating sexuality research: Combining cultural and biological perspectives on gender and desire. *Annual Review of Sex Research, 12*, 33–74.

Tolman, D. L., & McClelland, S. I. (2011). Normative sexuality development in adolescence: A decade in review, 2000–2009. *Journal of Research on Adolescence, 21*, 242–255. doi:10.1111/j.1532-7795.2010.00726.x

Traupmann, J., Hatfield, E., & Wexler, P. (1983). Equity and sexual satisfaction in dating couples. *British Journal of Social Psychology, 22*, 33–40. doi:10.1111/j.2044-8309.1983.tb00563.x

Trivers, R. L. (1972). Parental investment and sexual selection. In B. Campbell (Ed.), *Sexual selection and the descent of man* (pp. 1136–1179). Chicago, IL: Aldine.

Udry, J. R., Talbert, L. M., & Morris, N. M. (1986). Biosocial foundations for adolescent female sexuality. *Demography, 23*, 217–230. doi:10.2307/2061617

Valentine, D. (2007). *Imagining transgender: An ethnography of a category*. Durham, NC: Duke University Press.

van Anders, S. M., Goldey, K. L., & Kuo, P. X. (2011). The steroid/peptide theory of social bonds: Integrating testosterone and peptide responses for classifying social behavioral contexts. *Psychoneuroendocrinology, 36*, 1265–1275. doi:10.1016/j.psyneuen.2011.06.001

Wallen, K. (1995). The evolution of female sexual desire. In P. R. Abramson & S. D. Pinkerton (Eds.), *Sexual nature/sexual culture* (pp. 57–79). Chicago, IL: University of Chicago Press.

Waller, W., & Hill, R. (1951). *The family: A dynamic interpretation*. New York, NY: Dryden. (Original work published 1938)

Walster, E., Berscheid, E., & Walster, G. W. (1973). New directions in equity research. *Journal of Personality and Social Psychology, 25*, 151–176. doi:10.1037/h0033967

Warner, M. (1999). *The trouble with normal: Sex, politics, and the ethics of queer life*. New York, NY: Free Press.

Wrangham, R. W. (1993). The evolution of sexuality in chimpanzees and bonobos. *Human Nature, 4*, 47–79. doi:10.1007/BF02734089

Young, I. M. (Ed.). (1990). *Throwing like a girl and other essays in feminist philosophy and social theory*. Bloomington: University of Indiana Press.

CHAPTER 2

SEXUALITY AND GENDER: THE INTERPLAY

Sabra L. Katz-Wise and Janet S. Hyde

Sexuality and gender are central to a person's identity and well-being. *Sexuality* is a broad term encompassing many aspects of the human experience. The Sexuality Information and Education Council of the United States (SIECUS; 2012a) has defined *sexuality* as "the sexual knowledge, beliefs, attitudes, values, and behaviors of individuals," involving "the anatomy, physiology, and biochemistry of the sexual response system; identity, orientation, roles, and personality; and thoughts, feelings, and relationships" (SIECUS, 2012a, Human Sexuality section, para. 1). Furthermore, SIECUS proposed that sexuality is influenced by "ethical, spiritual, cultural, and moral concerns." *Gender* is defined as "the attitudes, feelings, and behaviors that a given culture associates with a person's biological sex" (American Psychological Association [APA], 2012, p. 11). Rather than treating them as separate variables in psychological research and theory, it is important to understand the interplay between these two aspects of the self.

In this chapter, we first address basic issues related to psychological research on gender and sexuality, including epistemology, major theories in the field, methodological issues, development of sexuality, and gender differences and similarities in sexuality. Then we discuss salient controversies in the field, such as cultural versus biological influences, erotic plasticity of women's sexuality, women's "naturally low" sex drives. Finally, we explore key research questions and theoretical developments in the field, including the sexualization of girls and boys, dilemmas of desire for adolescent girls, the orgasm gap, the new view of women's sexual problems, sexual fluidity, implications of new technologies for biological measurement, the sexual excitation–inhibition model, and advances in measurement of environmental factors. Finally, we offer a number of directions for future research. It is our hope that this chapter will provide an overview of the current state of research on sexuality and gender in the field of psychology as well as draw new connections and encourage readers to stretch their thinking about the interplay of sexuality and gender.

BASIC ISSUES

Epistemology

Sexuality and gender researchers operate under a variety of assumptions about epistemology, and we begin there. *Epistemology* refers to the origin and methods of human knowledge. Whether people are laypersons or scientists, how do they know or produce knowledge? The two dominant epistemologies for sexuality and gender researchers are positivism and social constructionism. Our goal here is not to advocate for one epistemology over another but to point out the strengths and usefulness of each. Both positivism and social constructionism have been the grounds for important knowledge production through research on gender and sexuality (see Chapter 1, this volume).

Positivism, or *logical positivism*, is an epistemology asserting that knowledge is objective and value free; science obtains this objective, value-free knowledge through proper application of the scientific method (Breen & Darlaston-Jones, 2010). The

http://dx.doi.org/10.1037/14193-002
APA Handbook of Sexuality and Psychology: Vol. 1. Person-Based Approaches, D. L. Tolman and L. M. Diamond (Editors-in-Chief)

idea is that scientists can know reality accurately and directly if they use appropriate methods. The results of these scientific inquiries are considered facts that constitute truth. Positivism was originally theorized by the French philosopher August Comte in the mid-1800s and had an enormous impact throughout the sciences. It was a basic guiding principle for psychology from the time of its founding in the late 1800s. The influence of positivism on psychology was particularly potent in that scientific psychologists worked within the paradigm that psychology was a science, just like physics or biology. This approach dominated the field until the 1960s, when social constructionism became influential (e.g., Berger & Luckmann, 1966).

Social constructionism challenges the tenets of positivism that science is or can be objective and value free and that reality can be observed or known directly. It asserts instead that reality is socially constructed (Berger & Luckmann, 1966; DeLamater & Hyde, 1998). Social constructionism holds that humans (including scientists) do not—and even cannot—discover or observe reality directly; no objective reality exists to be discovered. Instead, reality is constituted by individuals and groups through meanings and interpretations of events in the environment, on the basis of perspectives, perceptions, experiences, knowledge, and beliefs (Gergen, 1985; Hare-Mustin & Marecek, 1988; Marecek, Crawford, & Popp, 2004). Although social constructionism has not been embraced in many areas of psychology, it is dominant in feminist psychology, which has contributed most significantly to theorizing and studying gender, and in some approaches to sexuality research. The foundations for a social constructionist approach to sexuality were laid by Foucault (1978), who argued that sexuality is not a biological drive but a constellation of discourses that constitute meaning through language and social institutions.

Intersectionality is an analytic approach found primarily in feminist psychology and critical race theory, which asserts that one cannot understand the meaning of gender or the meaning of sexuality in isolation from other structural dimensions of individuals' lives or social contexts (Cole, 2009). Strictly speaking, intersectionality is not an epistemology, but it has profound implications for epistemology, so we address it here. Sexuality and gender are each conditioned by other categories, especially race/ethnicity, social class, and religion. Gender, sexual orientation, race/ethnicity, social class, and religion all intersect for the individual and are often the basis of both personal and social identities. Moreover, they describe categories not only of identity but also of difference and disadvantage. In the context of this chapter, a lens of intersectionality demands that, for instance, to conceptualize female sexuality, one must also consider the standpoints of sexual orientation, race/ethnicity, social class, and religion. More recent versions of intersectionality also include disability. Intersectionality argues that one should not consider a social category in isolation but must instead always consider how multiple social categories jointly shape individuals' experiences and outcomes.

Major Theories

Two broad theoretical approaches have been influential in understanding sexuality and gender: biological theories (including evolutionary theories) and sociocultural theories. Biological theorists seek to explain phenomena using biological processes, such as genes, hormones, or structural differences in the brain. LeVay's (2011) book reviewing scientific evidence for causes of homosexuality takes this approach in proposing that sexual orientation stems from an interaction among genes, sex hormones, and cells in a person's developing body and brain. In contrast, sociocultural theories take a different approach in seeking to explain phenomena using social and cultural contexts. We discuss evolutionary and sociocultural theories next.

Evolutionary theories. Sociobiology (Wilson, 1975) and evolutionary psychology (Buss, 1995; Buss & Schmitt, 1993; Geary, 1998; Tooby & Cosmides, 1992) are two theoretical frameworks that apply evolutionary theory to understanding behavior, including gender and sexuality. Essential to the evolutionary theories is the principle of natural selection, originally formulated by Charles Darwin (1871). Natural selection relied on Darwin's observation that there is differential survival within a species, with some individuals surviving to pass their genes on to the next generation and others not surviving and not reproducing. In evolutionary theory, *fitness* refers to the number of its genes that an animal contributes to the next generation. Over generations, characteristics that promote fitness are selected for and become more frequent in the population, whereas characteristics that reduce fitness should become less frequent. Current human behaviors must be a product of evolution through natural selection, and these behaviors must be adaptive because they promoted the fitness of our evolutionary ancestors. The evolutionary theories understand human behavior, especially sexuality, in tandem with reproduction, as driven by the biological factors that have survived as functional for both biological and social dimensions.

In particular, the evolutionary theorists believe that human gender characteristics and differences are biological in origin and are a result of natural selection. In explaining gender differences, evolutionary theorists rely on two additional concepts: parental investment and sexual selection. *Parental investment* refers to behaviors or other investments of the parent with respect to the offspring that increase the offspring's chance of survival but that also cost the parent something (Trivers, 1972). Given a heavier investment (e.g., 9 months of pregnancy, birth, nursing), mothers will be more dedicated to child care than are fathers to see a return on their large investment. Mothers will also be choosy about a mate, wanting to maximize the fitness of this single offspring, whereas it is to males' evolutionary advantage to inseminate many females, producing many offspring and relying on the females to raise them successfully to maturity.

Sexual selection, originally proposed by Darwin, is a form of selection that acts in concert with natural selection. It consists of two processes: (a) Members of one gender (usually males) compete among themselves to gain mating privileges with members of the other gender (usually females) and (b) members of the other gender (usually females) have preferences for certain members of the first gender (usually males) and decide with which of them they are willing to mate. Sexual selection is important to evolutionary theorists because they believe that it is the evolutionary mechanism that creates gender differences, for example, the greater size, strength, and aggressiveness of males who must compete with each other to mate with females.

Evolutionary psychologist David Buss has added sexual strategies theory to evolutionary theorizing about sexuality and gender (Buss & Schmitt, 1993). This theory distinguishes between short-term mating strategies (e.g., a one-night stand) and long-term mating strategies (e.g., married with children) and proposes that women and men have different problems to solve in both short-term and long-term mating. Men put more time and energy into short-term mating, gaining evolutionary advantage by inseminating many women. Women put more of their energy into long-term mating because they have the greater parental investment and want to maximize the chance of their offspring's survival, which in humans would be enhanced by the presence of the father, who provides resources.

Evolutionary theories have had profound implications for the understanding of gender and sexuality but remain contentious as convincing explanations and accounts. One argument is that evolutionary psychology is based on an outdated and oversimplified version of evolutionary theory that modern biologists would consider naïve (Buller, 2005; Gould, 1987). Yet others have suggested that more sophisticated evolutionary analyses are not linear but acknowledge plasticity in behavior and brain function (Kenrick, Li, & Butner, 2003; Lickliter & Honeycutt, 2003; Lloyd & Feldman, 2002; see also Chapter 7, this volume). This flexibility yields a multitude of selection pressures, some of them related to individual survival and others to survival of the species, thus producing gendered sexual and other salient social behaviors (Chaine & Lyon, 2008; Widemo & Saether, 1999).

Sociocultural theory. *Sociocultural theory,* or *social–structural theory,* has been articulated particularly by Eagly and Wood (1999) as an alternative to the biological determinism found in the evolutionary theories. According to this theory, the division of labor by gender drives psychological gender differences. Once the gendered division of labor is established and men have more power, both women and men adapt to these roles in their psychological attributes and behaviors, creating gender roles. For example, women cultivate the quality of nurturance for their work caring for children, and men acquire skills in aggression so that they perform well in warfare. However, gender roles are not limited to the division of labor; rather, they extend to gender differences in sexuality. In particular, psychological attributes and behaviors that may be adaptive for women's and men's roles in a gender-differentiated workplace may have negative consequences for women's sexuality. For instance, the patriarchal hierarchy accompanying the gendered division of labor and male aggression might play into violence against women, especially sexualized violence, in which the perpetrator is typically male (Watts & Zimmerman, 2002).

However, wide variations exist across cultures in the extent of gender inequality, the empowerment of women, and the roles taken on by men and women (see Volume 2, Chapter 6, this handbook). Whereas evolutionary theorists emphasize cross-cultural universals in patterns of gender differences, sociocultural theorists emphasize variations across cultures in gender differences. For example, on the basis of his 37 cultures study, Buss (1989) emphasized the finding of a large gender difference in the extent to which a potential mate's earning capacity was important in mate selection, with women rating it as substantially more important than did men, consistently across cultures. Eagly and Wood (1999), however, found a large negative correlation across the cultures between the magnitude of this gender difference and a measure of women's empowerment in the cultures created by the United Nations. That is, to the extent that women are more empowered in a culture—including having more access to education and good jobs—the smaller the gender difference is in finding earning capacity important in mate selection. These and similar analyses provide evidence that these mate preferences are not universal across cultures, but are shaped by the relative power of women and men in the cultures.

Sociocultural theory proposes that sex-differentiated behavior originates in the concentration of women and men in differing roles that yield structural inequalities for women and men (Eagly & Wood, 1999). Rather than directly contradicting evolutionary theory, this articulation of sociocultural theory proposes that sex-differentiated roles are determined in part by the biological endowment of women and men, which has necessarily evolved over time. For instance, greater upper body strength in men has resulted in a greater concentration of men in occupations that require such strength. At the same time, the amount of time that women spend childbearing and breastfeeding has resulted in women having priority in roles related to child care and has caused conflict with roles that require extended absences from home. However, with these physical differences becoming less important with industrialization and the technological revolution, there has been a lessening of some gender role differences—especially from an intersectional perspective (Cole, 2009)—suggesting the growing salience of social contexts infusing meaning into gender role norms, expectations, and possibilities.

More recent iterations of sociocultural theory have provided a clear contrast to evolutionary theory, particularly in understanding how the relationship between gender and sexuality changes over time. Biological evolution happens much more slowly than cultural evolution, which is not captured in evolutionary theory. For instance, Petersen and Hyde's (2010) meta-analysis of gender differences in sexuality found that between 1993 and 2007, some gender differences increased, and others decreased, suggesting that changes regarding these aspects of gender and sexuality are more likely related to cultural factors than biological factors. Therefore, in contrast to evolutionary theory, sociocultural theory emphasizes the importance of social and cultural contexts in shaping gender and sexuality.

Methodology

The methods used to study sexuality and gender include a wide variety of quantitative and qualitative methods, and their use typically depends on the epistemological approach of the researchers and their research questions. Those approaching the study of sexuality from a positivist stance might use more quantitative methods, such as experimental design and biological and physiological measures (see Chapter 5, this volume). For example, in a study of gender differences in sexual arousal, participants of different sexual orientations watched audiovisual sexual stimuli consisting of different gender pairings: male–male, female–female, and male–female (Chivers, Rieger, Latty, & Bailey, 2004). Genital arousal was measured during the film viewing, using measures of penile erection and the amount of blood flow to the vagina, and subjective sexual arousal was measured using a self-report measure. Researchers found sexual arousal to be more category specific in men than in women; for example, heterosexual men were more aroused by female than male sexual stimuli, whereas homosexual men showed the opposite response. The strengths of using quantitative methods are numerous, including generalizability; determination of biological and physiological bases for specific aspects of sexuality, such as behavior; and the ability to ascribe a causal explanation through use of experimental design. Quantitative approaches also enable identification of attitudes, demographics, and characteristics to predict or explain sexual behaviors, for instance, through survey research and the use of standardized scales (see Chapter 4, this volume). Quantitative approaches may be used to examine interactions among predictors or the mediating role of a specific construct in accounting for the relationship between two variables. For instance, a meta-analysis of sexual orientation–based victimization revealed an interaction between gender and sexual orientation yielding differences in rates of reported victimization; lesbian, gay, and bisexual (LGB) individuals experienced more physical and sexual assault than heterosexual individuals, but the difference was larger among males than among females (Katz-Wise & Hyde, 2012).

Despite the numerous strengths of using a quantitative approach, we should mention a number of weaknesses. First, the use of forced-choice questions in surveys may gloss over the complexities of certain processes because it is impossible to anticipate every possible response to an open-ended question. Related to this issue, formulated response options limit the ability to draw more nuanced conclusions that might not be captured in the available responses. Finally, researchers can never be sure whether all participants understand a particular question in the same way.

Those approaching the study of sexuality from a social constructionist epistemology might favor survey research or qualitative approaches such as interviews and participant observation, although social constructionist researchers may also use quantitative methods. This epistemology is often served by producing in-depth pictures of particular phenomena or understanding a participant's lived experience through his or her own words (see Chapter 6, this volume). Qualitative methods are particularly useful for research on new or understudied topics because they often use an exploratory approach that allows for theory generation from the data itself, rather than beginning the research with a base of knowledge and theory about the topic. For instance, Gagné, Tewksbury, and McGaughey (1997) conducted interviews with male-to-female transgender individuals to explore themes of transgender identity formation. They used a qualitative approach to understand and begin to document the process of transgender identity formation, which had not been much studied at the time the study was conducted. Interviews also allow participants to explain their answers in greater detail, which can be useful if a population is understudied or if the purpose of the research is to gain detailed knowledge about the participants' experiences and processes. Qualitative approaches have many strengths but also a number of weaknesses. In particular, qualitative studies often have a small sample size that does not permit generalizability, nor do they allow for conclusions of a causal nature. We should note that many quantitative studies cannot draw causal conclusions either, because they are correlational or seek to explain variation in outcomes. However, some quantitative methods, such as experimental studies or some longitudinal population-based studies, are able to draw causal conclusions, whereas no qualitative methods are able to do so. Having an impact on public policy can be a challenge in societies that understand only quantification as appropriate knowledge (see Tolman, Hirschman, & Impett, 2005, for an argument of how qualitative sexuality research can be leveraged in public policy; see also Volume 2, Chapter 10, this handbook).

In summary, both quantitative and qualitative methods are used for studying sexuality and gender, and both approaches have strengths and weaknesses.

A mixed-methods approach may provide the best overview of a particular phenomenon, because it allows for statistical testing and generalizability of findings, in addition to an in-depth exploration of the topic of interest (Lund, 2012). For all of the methods we have mentioned, we discuss a number of issues that should be taken into consideration.

Definition and measurement. The first methodological issue concerns definition and measurement. What exactly is sexuality? *Sexuality* is broadly defined in research and has often in recent years been conflated with the more specific term *sexual orientation*. As we previously articulated, *sexuality* is a broad term encompassing many aspects of the human experience, including attitudes, feelings, and behaviors as well as identity, orientation, and relationships (SIECUS, 2012a). Sexual orientation falls within the broader concept of sexuality and is a multidimensional construct including specific components of identity, attractions, behaviors, and fantasies (Savin-Williams, 2005; Striepe & Tolman, 2003). Thus, it is important to clearly define and operationalize the construct of interest. For instance, if a study is measuring risky sexual behavior in youths, it is important to define *sexual behavior*. Are the researchers only interested in heterosexual penile–vaginal sexual intercourse? Is anal sex included? What about oral sex or manual stimulation? Does it matter if the respondent is giving versus receiving oral sex? Does the gender of the partner matter? Of course, defining what constitutes sexual behavior depends on the research question being addressed. If the researchers are interested in measuring sexual behaviors that place the individual at greater risk for sexually transmitted infections (STIs), then it would be important to define *sexual behavior* as those behaviors that are riskier for STI transmission. As Price and Hyde (2009) discussed in their article on predictors of early sexual behavior in adolescents, oral sex and intercourse both place an individual at risk for STI transmission (unless protection is used); therefore, they included both oral sex and penile–vaginal intercourse as measures of risky sexual behaviors in adolescents (see Chapter 15, this volume).

As another example of the importance of defining sexual behavior in relation to the research question of interest, researchers have recently begun to study the cultural phenomenon of hooking up (e.g., Bogle, 2008; Owen & Fincham, 2011). The term *hooking up* may be defined differently by the researcher than it is by the participants and differently by men than by women. Furthermore, age, geography, or social location are often key factors. The definition of hooking up provided by Owen and Fincham (2011) is "a sexual encounter ranging from kissing to intercourse that occurs on one occasion and where the partners do not necessarily expect future physical encounters or a committed relationship" (p. 321). As their definition states, hooking up may or may not involve sexual intercourse. Because this particular study addressed emotional reactions to hooking up among college students, as well as associations with behaviors such as alcohol consumption and condom use, it is important to distinguish in which sexual behaviors participants are actually engaging. Indeed, Owen and Fincham found that the degree of physical intimacy influenced their participants' emotional reactions; specifically, women who engaged in both coital (oral sex, intercourse, or both) and noncoital (kissing, petting, or both) hook-ups had more negative emotional reactions than men who engaged in coital hook-ups. This study serves as an example of the importance of specificity of definition and measurement, particularly regarding sexual behavior.

Measurement of sexual orientation varies widely and is based on multiple definitions: romantic attraction, sexual attraction, sexual behavior, sexual identity, and sexual fantasies (see also Chapter 18, this volume). Researchers should think carefully about which aspect of sexual orientation they are most interested in, given the research questions. A recent meta-analysis examining the prevalence of sexual orientation–based victimization found that 66% of the studies reviewed used self-identification as lesbian, gay, or bisexual to classify sexual orientation, 11% used same-sex behavior, 3% used same-sex attraction, 2% used the Kinsey scale (which is a continuous measure and focuses on behavior), and 17% used combined features (Katz-Wise & Hyde, 2012). In explaining why sexual minorities might be victimized more than heterosexual people—which this meta-analysis found—it is important to consider how sexual orientation is defined. Are sexual minorities more likely to be victimized because they identify as lesbian, gay, or bisexual; because they have same-gender sexual partners; because they are attracted to members of the same gender; or because of their gender presentation?

Age and development. The second methodological issue to consider in conducting research on sexuality concerns age and development (see Chapters 13 through 17, this volume). Sexuality develops over time, particularly in relation to gender, and specific aspects of sexuality are likely to differ for different age groups. Regardless of what the specific research questions are, it is important to clearly identify the age of the sample. For instance, if a study is conducted on the onset of sexual behavior in adolescents, it is important to clearly define the range of ages that are included in the category of adolescents. Should the sample consist of early adolescents, middle adolescents, late adolescents, emerging adults, young adults, or some combination of these? Price and Hyde (2009) identified a limitation of previous research on early sexual behavior in adolescents, such that researchers have measured puberty only in terms of menarche (first menstruation in girls). Use of this measure fails to measure pubertal maturation in boys and may also lead to inaccuracies in the data when used as a measure of early maturation, because it is one of the final stages of pubertal development for girls. Cognitive, social, contextual, and other differences over the course of adolescence and early adulthood are important to consider, especially longitudinally from these earlier ages to later adulthood.

As another example, Katz-Wise and Hyde (2012) identified age as a salient methodological issue in research on victimization of LGB people. It is unlikely that LGB adolescents, adults, and older adults would experience the same rates of victimization—in part because the degree of "outness" as a sexual minority might differ among these age groups. It is important—especially for policy reasons—to identify the prevalence of victimization in different age groups of LGB people as well as the specific types of victimization that occur in each age group. In the studies included in Katz-Wise and Hyde's meta-analysis, reporting of descriptive statistics for the age of the sample (e.g., mean, standard deviation, range) was inconsistent. As a result, a developmental analysis of the results was impossible. If multiple age groups are used in research on sexuality and gender, it is important to conduct analyses to examine each age group separately if it is hypothesized that the aspect of sexuality being measured might differ across age groups. Furthermore, there is a need for greater understanding of how processes related to gender and sexuality might develop or change over time. Finally, clear reporting of descriptive statistics for the sample and analyses is crucial to defining the population being studied and conveying the results to other researchers.

Ethnicity. A third methodological issue related to research on sexuality is ethnicity. From a social constructionist perspective, sexuality is largely influenced by culture and society (see Volume 2, Chapter 6, this handbook). Different cultures and ethnic groups hold different gender norms and expectations regarding sexuality. Blackwood (2000) explored how cultural systems of gender create different sexual practices for women and men. For example, she described the practice of intimate friendships between schoolgirls in South Africa, termed *mummy–baby relationships* (Gay, 1986) and the practice of ingesting semen as a ritual of masculinity among Sambian adolescent boys in Papua New Guinea (Herdt, 1981). Both of these cultures construct gender and sexuality differently than Western cultures such as the United States, where gender roles for adolescents are defined in a different manner.

Some ethnic and cultural groups in the United States may also define gender and sexuality differently. For example, an ethnographic study of racial, class, and gender dynamics of an abstinence-only program for low-income Black girls indicated that Black adults found the girls to be sexually vulnerable because of racism and class inequality (Froyum, 2010). This study also provided an example of how the framework of intersectionality is productive in studying sexuality as contextualized by social differences, such as race and class (see also P. Collins, 2004). It is important not only to study how sexuality might be different among different cultural and ethnic groups but also to recruit ethnic minorities to address the common problem in U.S.-based research of largely White, college-age samples, especially for studies of normative sexuality development.

Self-report. Two specific methods are particularly relevant for the study of sexuality and gender today: self-reports and Internet- or web-based research. Self-report is commonly used in sexuality and gender research (e.g., self-reported sexual arousal measured by Chivers et al., 2004). Given the sensitive nature of sexuality, it is important to consider the conditions under which participants are most likely to provide accurate reports of their sexuality. In a study specifically addressing this issue, in terms of whether gender differences in sexuality may be an artifact of cultural stereotypes that are influential in respondents' answers, researchers measured self-reported sexual behavior using questionnaires in three conditions (Alexander & Fisher, 2003). In the first condition, exposure threat, participants believed that their responses would be seen by a peer; in the second condition, participants believed their answers would remain anonymous; and in the third condition a bogus pipeline procedure was used, in which participants were hooked up to a fake polygraph machine and were led to believe that dishonest answers to the survey would be detected by the machine (Jones & Sigall, 1971). Alexander and Fisher (2003) found that gender differences in reported sexual behavior were greatest in the exposure threat condition (viewed by a peer) and least in the bogus pipeline condition (measured by polygraph), suggesting that participants provided the most accurate reports of their sexuality under the condition that they believed provided additional information about the veracity of their responses.

Internet- or web-based research. The other method that is relevant for and growing rapidly in the study of sexuality and gender today is Internet- or web-based research (see Volume 2, Chapter 3, this handbook). The majority of the Western population either owns a personal computer or has ready access to one. To take advantage of this trend, much of the research conducted today—especially survey research—uses the Internet. A number of considerations should be made when using the Internet to conduct research on sexuality and gender. Mustanski (2001) reviewed the risks and rewards of using the Internet for such research. As he discussed, positive aspects of conducting research using this method are the low cost, ease of data collection, and recruitment of large sample sizes, and because the Internet affords a degree of anonymity, participants might be more likely to share truthful information about their sexuality with the researchers. However, the ease of data collection comes at the cost of experimental control because the researcher cannot control the conditions under which the survey is completed. For example, experimental control might be compromised if one participant completes the survey while alone in a quiet room, and another completes the survey while having a conversation at a noisy coffee shop. Furthermore, rather than increasing personal disclosure, the anonymity of the Internet might also cause people to lie or create a self that is untrue (Mustanski, 2001). Therefore, it is important to pay attention to issues of internal validity and experimental control when conducting Internet research on sexuality.

Development of Sexuality

The development of sexuality is not limited to a particular age group. Sexuality begins before birth and changes throughout the lifetime (see Chapter 13, this volume). Therefore, we take a life-span approach to the development of sexuality similar to the gendered-sexuality-over-the-life-course model (L. Carpenter & DeLamater, 2012). This model assumes that sexuality plays a significant role in people's lives at all ages and frequently interacts with gender to produce both differences and similarities, as we discuss. This model also assumes that gender and sexuality are jointly constructed within specific sociostructural contexts. In other words, "transitions in an individual's sexuality trajectory will affect his or her gender trajectory, even as the gender-related transitions he or she experiences help construct his or her sexuality trajectory" (L. Carpenter, 2010, p. 161). For example, exposure to gendered norms of sexual conduct can affect adolescents' sexual behavior in terms of choosing whether or not to use protection against STIs or pregnancy. Adolescent girls who received the message that "good girls wait to have sex" are more likely to engage in risky sex and thus experience an unplanned pregnancy, which may then influence future sexual relationships (Thompson, 1995). Another important point to note is that patterns of gender differences in sexuality may change at different times in the life span (see Chapters 14 through 17, this volume).

Sexuality in infancy and childhood. Research has indicated that physiological sexual response is present from birth, and possibly prenatally as well. Masters, Johnson, and Kolodny (1982) reported data from ultrasound studies that showed reflex erections in male fetuses and vaginal lubrication in female infants 24 hours after birth. Prenatally and during infancy, when these genital responses are a response to blood flow rather than directed toward or an effect of sexual arousal or pleasure, these physiological responses indicate an innate capacity for human sexual response rather than a sexual response per se. That is, although infants and young children may experience pleasurable feelings, it is not appropriate to equate them with an adult understanding of sexual feelings (Pfaus et al., 2012; see also Chapter 14, this volume).

Masturbation is a common form of sexuality in children. In a large U.S. sample, mothers reported that 60% of boys and 44% of girls ages 2 to 5 years touched their genitals (Friedrich, Fisher, Broughton, Houston, & Shafran, 1998), although this is probably not the intentional masturbation that appears later in childhood. Another study of 7- to 12-year-old Black children and White children found that genital touching and masturbatory behaviors were more common among boys than among girls (Thigpen, 2012). The gender difference found in these studies is in line with other research suggesting that boys begin masturbating at a younger age than girls. In a study of high school seniors in Sweden, 42% of boys and 20% of girls reported masturbating to orgasm by age 12 (Larsson & Svedin, 2002). Childhood sexuality is also social, and many young children begin exploring their sexuality during this developmental time period through play. For example, "playing doctor" is common among children ages 4 to 5 (Gundersen, Melas, & Skar, 1981). Same-gender sexual play is also common during late childhood and preadolescence (8–12 years) and may in fact be more common than other-gender sexual play (Martinson, 1994).

The development of sexuality in childhood (and adolescence) is related to multiple sociocultural influences, including peers, parents, the school system, culture, and the media. Peer influences begin with the aforementioned sexual play but extend to knowledge about sex. Because many parents might restrict conversations about sex, children engage in sexual play and use their peers as sources of information about sex (Martinson, 1994). Boys typically learn about masturbation from their male peers through being told or watching them, whereas girls typically learn about masturbation through self-discovery (Langfeldt, 1981). Children may also learn about sex from their parents. A survey of youths ages 14 to 16 found that information about sex and sexual intercourse came primarily from friends (75%), teachers (62%), mothers (61%), and media (57%; Bleakley, Hennessy, Fishbein, & Jordan, 2009). Many parents may be embarrassed to talk to their children about sex or afraid that teaching their children about sex will lead them to engage in sexual behaviors earlier than they would otherwise. This reluctance on the part of parents means that the responsibility for sexual education lies with the school system and the media. Indeed, most schools today have some sort of sexuality education, although debates continue as to what the appropriate focus of these programs should be (i.e., abstinence-only vs. comprehensive sex education; see also Volume 2, Chapter 11, this handbook). As Bleakley and colleagues (2009) found, however, youths also learn about sex and sexuality from the media (see also Volume 2, Chapter 12, this handbook). In the Sexualization of Girls and Boys section, we discuss some potential negative consequences for children and teens of learning about sex from this cultural source.

Sexuality in adolescence. Sexuality in adolescence (ages 13–19 years) is largely related to pubertal development, including bodily changes and awareness of these changes, rising levels of sex hormones, increased peer and cultural emphasis on sexuality, and being seen or interacted with as a sexual adult. For example, in a study of sociological and biological factors associated with adolescent sexuality, results demonstrated that testosterone levels were strongly related to sexual activity for adolescent boys and also, to a lesser degree, for girls (Udry,

1988). Many adolescents also begin to engage in heterosexual intercourse during this developmental period. In Udry's (1988) study of youths ages 13 to 16, 35% of boys and 14% of girls had engaged in heterosexual intercourse. Similar to the gender difference in first masturbation, boys are more likely to experience first heterosexual intercourse at a younger age than girls, although the age difference is not large (Wells & Twenge, 2005). However, more recent data from the National Survey of Family Growth, collected in 2006 to 2010, found that the average age of first intercourse was 17.1 for both women and men (National Center for Health Statistics, 2012), suggesting that the gender difference may have disappeared. Some adolescents also engage in same-gender sexual behavior. Data from the National Survey of Family Growth collected between 2006 and 2008 found that 11% of adolescent girls and 2.5% of adolescent boys ages 15 to 19 had engaged in sexual activity with same-sex partners in their lifetime (Chandra, Mosher, & Copen, 2011; see also Chapter 19, this volume). However, a methodological point should be made that girls were asked a much broader question about sexual behavior than boys, which could account for the gender difference (see Chapter 15, this volume).

Much of the research on the development of sexuality in adolescents has been conducted within the framework of risk, in which sexual behaviors are inherently risky for this age group, leading to STI and teen pregnancy. Indeed, these outcomes are a reality, with approximately 19 million new STIs each year, almost half of which are among youths and young adults ages 15 to 24 (Centers for Disease Control and Prevention, 2011). Furthermore, in the United States, approximately 9% of all teenage girls younger than age 20 become pregnant each year (Guttmacher Institute, 2006). The statistics on teen pregnancy focus concerns much more on girls' early sexual initiation than on boys'.

Although STI and teen pregnancy rates are certainly causes for concern about the well-being of adolescents, much of sexual behavior during this developmental period is normative and a result of curiosity and exploration (Russell, 2005). Some researchers of adolescent sexuality have begun to conceptualize it as positive sexuality development or healthy sexuality development (e.g., Diamond, 2006; Russell, 2005) rather than solely within a risk framework. Russell, van Campen, and Muraco (2012) referred to an alternative approach to adolescent sexuality in some European countries, such as Germany and the Netherlands, in which adolescent sexuality is viewed more positively. As a result, adolescents in these countries have better sexuality-related health outcomes than those in the United States, such as lower rates of teen pregnancy and abortion (Russell et al., 2012). In a review of the research on adolescent sexuality over the past decade, Tolman and McClelland (2011) concluded that the development of sexual subjectivity, a sense of the self as having the capacity to enact sexuality, has been established in a substantive body of research and is related to and predictive of sexual behavioral and psychological outcomes. Tolman and McClelland proposed a framework integrating positive and risky dimensions of sexuality development in adolescence and considered both dimensions to be normative.

This tension in the framing of adolescent sexuality as risky versus healthy also informs the (largely political) sex education debate: comprehensive sexuality education (including information about the benefits of abstinence) versus abstinence-only sex education (Fine & McClelland, 2006). Advocates for comprehensive sexuality education argue that youths need information and tools to make informed decisions about engaging in sexual behavior, whereas advocates for abstinence-only sex education argue that youths need to hear a single clear message that premarital sex is wrong and harmful to their physical and emotional health (Solomon-Fears, 2011). Research from a multiyear experimental study comparing outcomes of abstinence-only programs with control programs that did not use this approach found that youths in the abstinence-only group were no more likely than youths in the control group to have abstained from sex, and those who reported having had sex had similar numbers of sexual partners and had initiated sex at the same mean age (Trenholm et al., 2007). It appears that providing adolescents with more knowledge about their sexuality does not lead to their having more sex or initiating sex at a younger age.

Abstinence-only education may also be problematic in promoting stereotypes about gender and sexuality. Research examining gender stereotypes in current, abstinence-only until marriage sex education curricula has found that modern ideals of choice and equality were represented more often than older stereotypes of boys as sexual pursuers and girls as passive recipients (Lamb, Graling, & Lustig, 2011). However, the language of choice and equality promoted problematic stereotypes about female sexuality, such as girls being "manipulative temptresses" who trick boys into having sex with them or "girls gone wild" who are sexual aggressors (Lamb et al., 2011, pp. 373–374). In addition, regarding objectification of women, these curricula propose that women deserve respect because they are "special" and not because they are equals. Lamb et al. classified this message as a form of benevolent sexism, which is "subjectively positive but patronizing in tone and reflects the desire to protect and idealize women" (p. 375; Glick & Fiske, 1996). All forms of sexuality education should work to present accurate information to youths without further promoting gendered stereotypes of sexuality.

Sexuality in adulthood. Sexuality in adulthood largely, though not exclusively, revolves around the initiation and dissolution of relationships. The majority of heterosexual adults in the United States get married at some point in their lives. In 2002, approximately 46% of women and 42% of men ages 15 to 44 were currently married (Goodwin, Mosher, & Chandra, 2010). Many adults who do not marry instead choose to cohabit long-term with a partner. In 2002, 9% of U.S. women and men ages 15 to 44 were currently cohabiting (Goodwin et al., 2010). Although people in same-gender relationships face the additional issue of the illegality of same-gender marriage in many states, many still cohabit in long-term relationships, and same-gender marriage is increasingly becoming legalized. Data from the 2000 Census indicated that of the 5.5 million couples in the United States who were living together but not married, one in nine was a same-gender couple (Simons & O'Connell, 2003). The pattern of long-term relationships remains the norm for most adults, regardless of sexual orientation (see Chapters 10 and 16, this volume).

Despite the popularity of long-term relationships, the divorce rate in the United States has risen in recent decades, with the current rate being one third of first marriages ending in divorce or separation before reaching the 10th anniversary (Goodwin et al., 2010). Research has also suggested that lesbian and gay couples are more likely to dissolve their relationships than heterosexual couples (Blumstein & Schwartz, 1983; Kurdek, 2004). The difference in rate of relationship dissolution between the two types of couples has been explained in part by the lack of institutional social, religious, and legal barriers for lesbian and gay (and cohabiting couples) in comparison with heterosexual married couples (Kurdek, 2005). Although limited data exist regarding rates of divorce among same-gender couples because the lack of access to same-gender marriage in most U.S. states, some research has investigated couples who obtained civil unions in Vermont, which was the first state to legalize same-gender relationships in 2000. Balsam, Beauchaine, Rothblum, and Solomon (2008) conducted a 3-year follow-up study of female and male same-gender couples who obtained civil unions in Vermont in the 1st year in which same-gender relationships were legalized in the state. They compared same-gender couples in civil unions, same-gender couples not in civil unions, and heterosexual married couples on numerous outcome variables and reported that same-gender couples not in civil unions were more likely to have ended their relationship than the other two groups; however, they found no difference in rates of divorce between same-gender couples in civil unions and married heterosexual couples.

Although people seek divorce for many different reasons, a primary factor is extramarital affairs. Among both women and men, dissatisfaction with marriage and specifically with marital sex is linked to likelihood of infidelity (Buss & Shackelford, 1997). Thus far, the patterns related to relationships in adults have largely reflected gender similarities, but extramarital affairs are an area in which women and men differ. Data from the National Health and

Social Life Survey indicated that 15% of married women and 25% of married men reported having engaged in extramarital sex at least once (Laumann, Gagnon, Michael, & Michaels, 1994).

Relationship satisfaction, whether or not it leads to dissolution, may also be linked to a decline in partner sexual activity over time within the context of long-term relationships. Call, Sprecher, and Schwartz (1995) found a sharp decline in frequency of sex after the 1st year of marriage and a slow and steady decline afterward. Although sex is an important factor in relationship satisfaction, it is one of many factors affecting each partner's satisfaction with their relationship. For both same-gender and other-gender couples, relationship satisfaction is linked to many factors other than frequency of partner sex, such as characteristics that each partner brings to the relationship, how each partner views the relationship, how partners behave toward each other, and perceived level of support for the relationship (Kurdek, 2005).

Although there is certainly variability among married heterosexual couples, the frequency of sexual intercourse typically drops from once per week at ages 50 to 59 to 0.3 times per week after age 70 (Smith, 2003). Less is known about other types of sexual behavior, such as oral sex and mutual masturbation in married heterosexual couples, which would be a fruitful area of future research. The two explanations most commonly proposed for the decline in marital sex are biological aging and habituation to sex with one's partner (Call et al., 1995; see also Chapter 8, this volume). Physiological factors that might account for the decline are decreased vaginal lubrication in women and general poor health in older adults. The theory about habituation proposes that a person becomes less sexually desirable over time because he or she becomes more familiar. This theory is supported by the pattern of findings described earlier in which frequency of sex declines after the 1st year of marriage (Call et al., 1995). Dishabituation can occur when couples engage in sexual activity in new or different locations, such as on vacation, or engage in new types of sexual activities, such as role-playing or use of sex toys. However, the rise in sexual activity prompted by dishabituation may return to the previous level of decline before the dishabituation when couples return to the same location or same behaviors to which they previously became habituated. This pattern of behavior can be understood within the conceptual framework of the dual control model, which proposes that sexual excitation and sexual inhibition are the two basic processes that underlie human sexual response (Bancroft, Graham, Janssen, & Sanders, 2009). Pfaus (2009) described a similar pattern in terms of interactive neural systems of excitation and inhibition that are related to sexual desire. We explore the dual control model further in the Sexual Excitation–Inhibition Model section.

Sexuality in older adults. Despite commonly held assumptions about older adults, sexuality continues to evolve and change during this developmental period. Bretschneider and McCoy (1988) studied a sample of healthy older adults ages 80 to 102 and found that 30% of women and 62% of men reported still engaging in sexual intercourse. Despite these findings, sexual behavior and interest do decline somewhat with age. The decline in sexual frequency from mid to later life may show a different pattern regarding contextual factors for women versus men. Karraker, DeLamater, and Schwartz (2011) found that the decline in frequency of sexual activity—defined as any mutually voluntary activity with another person that involves sexual contact, whether or not intercourse or orgasm occurred—is more related to a change in marital status (typically becoming widowed) for women, whereas it is more related to declines in physical health for men. Karraker and colleagues suggested that marital status might be more relevant for women's sexual behavior than for men's. Women who become widowed have fewer choices in new partners because men tend to die earlier than women. Additionally, older women are in a cohort in which they may have been socialized to view sexual intimacy as taking place only in the context of marriage. The decline in sexual frequency being related to declining physical health only for men suggests that men's physical health is more important for heterosexual partnered sex than women's physical health (see Chapters 17 and 21, this volume).

Sexual orientation development. Development of sexual orientation can also be considered in relation to age and gender. Traditional views of sexual orientation development have until recently assumed that it is completed by adolescence (Bell, Weinberg, & Hammersmith, 1981; Money, 1988). Stage models of sexual minority identity formation (e.g., Cass, 1979; Meyer & Schwitzer, 1999) follow the same assumption as well as assuming that all nonheterosexual individuals progress through these developmental stages in a linear fashion. Diamond (2008b) termed this view of sexual orientation the *master narrative,* including developmental milestones such as feeling different, gender-atypical behaviors, fascination with the same gender, gradual realization of romantic and sexual feelings toward the same gender, and consciously questioning sexual identity. However, these models tend to be most applicable to the experiences of gay men and not as applicable to lesbians or bisexual men and women (see Chapter 19, this volume).

Following the traditional stage model framework, Weinberg, Williams, and Pryor (1994) developed a model of bisexual identity development. The main difference between homosexual and bisexual identity development models lies in the final stage. In the bisexual model, Weinberg and colleagues suggested that rather than attaining a secure sense of self as a sexual minority, bisexual identity development is characterized by ongoing uncertainty about one's sexuality. This uncertainty was later reinterpreted as a resistance to the label "bisexual" and the struggle to find a suitable alternative (Gurevich, Bower, Mathieson, & Dhayanandhan, 2007) rather than uncertainty about one's sexual orientation. Although the bisexual identity development model represents an attempt to be inclusive of sexual identities beyond gay and lesbian, this theory still relies on a traditional conceptualization of sexual orientation as developing early and remaining stable over time that is being challenged by recent research on sexuality that raises questions about stable identity categories.

Diamond (2008a) has proposed that sexual identity formation is a process rather than a developmental endpoint, and her research has demonstrated nonheterosexual identities among women to be fluctuating rather than linear. Furthermore, sexual minorities have demonstrated a range of developmental histories regarding when and how each of the master narrative developmental milestones is reached (e.g., Charbonneau & Lander, 1991; Diamond, 1998; Diamond & Savin-Williams, 2000; Kitzinger & Wilkinson, 1995). In response to these findings, researchers have suggested use of a differential developmental trajectories perspective in studying the development of sexual minority youths (and adults) that acknowledges the possibility of multiple developmental pathways to sexual identity development (Savin-Williams, 2001; Savin-Williams & Diamond, 1999). This perspective highlights the importance of attending to within-group differences in sexuality (e.g., lesbians vs. gay men) in addition to between-groups differences (e.g., heterosexual vs. nonheterosexual) and similarities.

Gender Differences and Similarities in Sexuality

Although the media and many researchers have emphasized gender differences in sexuality, many similarities exist as well. Hyde (2005) proposed the *gender similarities hypothesis,* which states that males and females are similar on most, but not all, psychological variables. Evidence for the hypothesis comes from Hyde's synthesis of 46 meta-analyses of research on psychological gender differences, yielding 124 effect sizes from meta-analysis. The results indicated that 30% of the effect sizes, d, fell between 0 and 0.10, which is a trivial difference. An additional 48% fell in the small range, 0.11 to 0.35. Overall, then, 78% of the effect sizes were small or very close to nonexistent. The meta-analyses that were synthesized covered a wide range of behaviors and attributes, including mathematical performance, attributions for success and failure, interruptions in conversations, smiling, aggressive behavior, sexuality, and leadership.

Hyde (2005) noted exceptions to the overall pattern of psychological gender similarities. Some of those were in the area of sexuality. To give a clear picture of these gender differences and similarities, we turn to a recent meta-analysis. Petersen and Hyde (2010) conducted a meta-analysis of relevant research on sexuality appearing between 1993 and 2007. The meta-analysis covered 30 behaviors and attitudes and included 834 samples as well as data from seven large national datasets. Gender similarities were evident in many areas, with $d < .10$ for same-gender sexual behavior and oral sex and for attitudes toward sex when a couple is engaged, attitudes about condom use, the double standard, and attitudes toward lesbians. Petersen and Hyde found more substantial gender differences for masturbation ($d = 0.53$), use of pornography ($d = 0.63$), and attitudes about casual sex ($d = 0.45$), with males scoring higher in all cases. However, none of these differences were large. A helpful comparison is the magnitude of the gender difference in height for humans, which is $d = 2.0$ (Niewenweg, Smit, Walenkamp, & Wit, 2003).

Earlier, we discussed sociocultural theory (Eagly & Wood, 1999), which asserts that psychological gender differences are the result of the division of labor by gender and imbalances of power between men and women. In the Petersen and Hyde (2010) meta-analysis, a measure of gender empowerment was significantly negatively correlated, across nations, with the magnitude of the gender difference in masturbation. That is, the more gender equality in a nation, the smaller the gender difference in masturbation. Similarly, the gender empowerment measure was significantly negatively correlated with the gender difference in attitudes about gay marriage. That is, the gender gap in attitudes was smaller in more egalitarian nations and larger in nations with more gender inequality. These findings are consistent with the predictions of sociocultural theory.

SALIENT CONTROVERSIES

Sexuality is a field of research in which approaches to research and the findings themselves are often controversial in nature. Part of this stems from the connection between sexuality and morality, particularly in Western cultures such as the United States. We discuss four controversies in the field of sexuality research especially salient to gender: cultural versus biological influences, erotic plasticity, and women's "naturally low" sex drives.

Cultural Versus Biological Influences

One salient controversy in the field of sexuality research is whether the focus should be on cultural or biological influences (also framed as nature vs. nurture). Although most researchers have agreed that the best approach is some combination of these two types of influence, some still argue for an emphasis on one or the other. This alliance is often related to the researcher's epistemological standpoint. Those who subscribe to a more positivist approach may be more likely to emphasize biological influences or to include social variables but study them using the classic scientific method, whereas those who come from a social constructionist standpoint may be more likely to attend to cultural influences. In most cases, it is nearly impossible to tease apart cultural versus biological influences, but many researchers attempt to do just this (see Chapter 1, this volume).

One of the most infamous cases of nature versus nurture related to gender is that of David Reimer, documented by Colapinto (2000). Reimer was a patient of Dr. John Money, a prolific sex researcher at Johns Hopkins University, who was well known for his research on sex reassignment surgery and a strong proponent of the view that gender is largely malleable and influenced by the environment. Reimer was born an identical twin, with both biological males having XY chromosomes and normal male genitalia. When Reimer was 7 months old, he had a botched circumcision. Under Money's advice, Reimer underwent a vaginoplasty procedure to turn his penis into a vagina and was raised by his parents as a girl named Brenda. In Money's writings, this case was presented as a successful example of the environmental malleability of gender (e.g., Money, 1975), although he was later criticized by the Intersex Society of North America (1993–2008) for misrepresenting what actually happened. Rather than successfully forming a female gender identity, Reimer later claimed a male identity and transitioned back to being male, including having a phalloplasty to reconstruct his penis. The negative psychological consequences of his attempted gender reassignment were long term; he later committed suicide. This case provides evidence for the biological underpinnings of gender, in contrast to Money's view that gender is subject to change exclusively on the basis of environmental influences.

Cultural influences on gender and sexuality have been demonstrated in research with individuals who identify as male-to-female transsexual. These individuals (also referred to as *transwomen*) are born with a male body but come to identify themselves as female, and many transition some or all aspects of their physical bodies—especially those aspects associated with gender and sexuality—and their social and personal identities with the use of hormones and gender reassignment surgery to present themselves to others as female. Many transwomen adopt stereotypical cultural expressions associated with the female gender, such as wearing makeup and skirts, speaking softly, or becoming more emotionally expressive. A study of male-to-female transsexual, female-to-male transsexual, cisgender (non-transgender) male, and cisgender female individuals' levels of femininity and masculinity found that male-to-female transsexual individuals had the highest level of femininity compared with the other groups (Herman-Jeglínska, Grabowska, & Dulko, 2002). That is, the transwomen were more feminine than the cisgender women. Rather than being inherent to an individual, these aspects of female gender expression are culturally and socially constructed. Transwomen may not be socialized to have these qualities because they are born with male bodies, but they later adopt or express these qualities as they transition to becoming women, highlighting the role of cultural influence on gendered expressions and behavior (see also Chapter 24, this volume).

Despite the division of biological and cultural influences on sexuality and gender in the field of psychology, many researchers now view these influences as combined and jointly constructing gender and sexuality (Tolman & Diamond, 2001). Furthermore, it is difficult to parse factors influencing sexuality and gender as biological or cultural. In Diamond's (2008b) discussion of the usefulness of the dynamical systems approach to understanding women's sexuality, she stated, "Trying to identify the specific percentage of genetic versus environmental determinants of any complex phenomenon—such as same-sex sexuality—is as futile as trying to pull apart a chocolate cake into the flour, sugar, eggs, and butter that went into it" (p. 240). In the end, researchers can only attempt to identify biological and cultural influences while recognizing that both are at work, likely in tandem, in producing sexuality and gender.

Erotic Plasticity

Another salient controversy in the field of sexuality and gender research concerns the concept of *erotic plasticity*, which is defined as "the degree to which a person's sex drive can be shaped and altered by cultural and social factors" (Baumeister, 2000, p. 348). Baumeister (2000) argued for gender differences in erotic plasticity; that is, that compared with males, females' sex drive is more malleable in response to sociocultural and situation factors. This malleability is evidenced by individual women displaying more flexibility across time in their sexuality, by female sexuality being shaped more strongly by sociocultural forces than is male sexuality, and by greater consistency between attitudes and behavior for men than for women. Baumeister cited evidence from multiple sources and phenomena. For example, he argued that compared with male sexuality, female sexuality varies more across societies. Similarly, within a culture, female sexuality varies more by educational level than does male sexuality. Baumeister concluded that the gender difference in erotic plasticity results from men's sexuality being determined mainly by physical factors and less by cultural factors, whereas women's sexuality is more determined by sociocultural factors. Baumeister also concluded that these different patterns were the result of evolutionary selection rather than other factors such as the double standard.

Other researchers challenged Baumeister's (2000) assertions. Hyde and Durik (2000) argued that the gender differences catalogued by Baumeister were better explained by gender differences in power, with men having greater power than women (to varying degrees in various societies) at many levels from the institutional to the interpersonal. Andersen, Cyranowski, and Aarestad (2000) noted that Baumeister focused exclusively on gender differences in sexuality, despite much evidence of gender similarities in sexuality.

Women's Naturally Low Sex Drives

In Western cultures, women are believed to have naturally low sex drives. *Sex drive* refers to sexual motivation, including frequency and intensity of sexual desires, and may be measured in numerous ways, such as sexual thoughts, fantasies, desired frequency of intercourse, number of partners, and masturbation (Baumeister, Catanese, & Vohs, 2001, p. 242). This cultural assumption is thought to have originated in Victorian times, which can be characterized as particularly repressive for women in terms of sexuality. The assumption that all women have a low sex drive has changed somewhat over time—as evidenced by the title of Baumeister and colleagues' (2001) review "Is There a Gender Difference in Strength of Sex Drive?"—allowing for more within-gender differences. However, the cultural expectation still remains that women have a lower sex drive than men, which has been substantiated in some studies. For example, Baumeister and colleagues found evidence in their review of the research that on average, men report having a higher sex drive than women. Another study using a large sample found that heterosexual men self-reported a higher sex drive than heterosexual women; women's sex drive was also found to be more variable than men's (Lippa, 2009). Although this research provides information about gender differences in sex drive, it does not address how the assumption that women have a lower sex drive originated in Western culture.

The "natural" aspect of women's low sex drive is based on an epistemological framework that emphasizes traits as biologically innate rather than socially constructed or shaped. This view ignores the cultural construction of women's sexuality, which is evident in the change over time in expectations for women's level of sexual desire. The evolution of cultural expectations for women's sexuality also indicates a shift from the expectation that men should always initiate sexual activity to a context in which it is more acceptable for women to initiate sex with men; however, men still report initiating sex more than women (Peplau, 2003). Likewise, women and men have more similar numbers of sexual partners today, compared with previous time periods in which men had more sexual partners than women (Petersen & Hyde, 2010). These examples of change over time in women's sexuality raise questions about women's low sex drive and whether variability in women's sex drive is social, physical, or an interplay between the two (see also Chapters 7 and 8, this volume).

The assumption that women have a naturally low sex drive has numerous negative implications for women's sexuality, primarily in terms of limiting women's ability to have agency in sexual encounters, which places them at increased risk for being victimized in the context of dating and intimate partner violence (Tolman & Higgins, 1996; see also Chapters 11 and 12, this volume). Women might feel that because they are not expected to have sexual desires, they are not able to voice their desires in situations in which sex is wanted or in situations in which sex is unwanted. This assumption also relates to the dilemma of desire for adolescent girls, wherein women are sexualized in the media and in popular culture but are unable to act on their desires because they are expected to remain passive in sexual encounters and act like "good girls" (Tolman & Higgins, 1996). If women are assumed to have naturally low sex drives, this assumption may create a situation in which women with higher than expected sex drives are viewed negatively as promiscuous or as behaving inappropriately by initiating sexual activity, according to gendered cultural scripts of sexuality.

The assumption that women have a naturally low sex drive may also lead to a lack of education for women about their own sexuality. It is already the case that sex education focuses on reproduction rather than sexual pleasure, leaving women (and men) lacking knowledge about women's bodies in relation to sexuality (Pastor, 2009; see also Chapter 23, this volume; Volume 2, Chapter 11, this handbook). If women are also assumed not to want sex in the first place, then it might seem less important to educate women about their bodies. This lack of education leads to other negative outcomes, such as initiating sex at an early age when girls may not be mature enough to make responsible decisions about using protection against pregnancy and STIs. In a study of sex education and sexual behaviors and outcomes in teens and young adults using data from the longitudinal National Survey of Family Growth, results indicated that sex education of any type is linked to delay of first sex by both women and men (Lindberg & Maddow-Zimet, 2012). In addition, youths who received more comprehensive sex education were more likely to use contraception or a condom at first sexual intercourse. It is clear that educating adolescent girls about sex is linked to positive sexual health outcomes. Educating both girls and boys about cultural assumptions regarding gender and sex drive is another necessary step toward promoting positive sexuality in all adolescents. SIECUS (2012b) proposed that culture and society are a key part of sexuality and suggested addressing society and culture, including gender roles, in comprehensive sexuality education. This content should include attention to gendered conceptions of sexuality, such as sex drive.

Another negative consequence of women's ostensibly low sex drive can be seen in the context of women's same-gender relationships. The concept of *lesbian bed death* refers to the pattern that women in long-term romantic relationships with other women have less sex over time, leading to a shift in their relationship from sexual intimacy to emotional intimacy only (Nichols, 2004). In evidence, a major finding of Blumstein and Schwartz's (1983) study comparing lesbian, gay, heterosexual married, and heterosexual unmarried couples was that lesbian couples experienced less frequent sexual activity than other types of couples. Although this pattern is common over time in long-term relationships of any gender configuration (Call et al., 1995), it has been particularly noted in women's same-gender romantic relationships (Blumstein & Schwartz, 1983), although more recent research did not find a difference in rates of sexual frequency between heterosexual and lesbian women (Matthews, Tartaro, & Hughes, 2002). The pattern of lesbian bed death has been proposed to be linked to cultural expectations about women's sexuality; women are less likely to be sexual together over time because they have a lower libido, lower rates of general sexual activity, and less assertiveness around sexuality (Peplau, 2003). Therefore, if women are expected to have low sex drives and be uninterested in sex, this gendered conception of female sexuality may play out in a same-gender female relationship in terms of decreasing frequency of partner sex over time (see also Chapter 20, this volume). More research is needed to clarify whether female couples actually have less frequent sexual activity than heterosexual couples and whether factors other than societal expectations of women's sexuality are related to this difference in rates of sexual activity.

KEY RESEARCH QUESTIONS AND NEW DEVELOPMENTS

Sexuality is a burgeoning field of research in which new theoretical and methodological approaches are frequently developed. In addition, topics related to gender and sexuality that were not originally considered when the field began have become of interest and represent key directions for future research. We review the following key research areas and new developments: sexualization of girls and boys, dilemmas of desire for adolescent girls, the orgasm gap, the new view of women's sexual problems, sexual fluidity, implications of new biological measurements for sexuality research, the sexual excitation–inhibition model, and advances in measurement of environmental factors related to sexuality.

Sexualization of Girls and Boys

A key research topic in recent decades has been the sexualization of children, particularly in the United States. According to the APA Task Force on the Sexualization of Girls (2007), sexualization occurs when a person's value comes only from sexual appeal or sexual behavior, when a person is held to a standard that defines physical attractiveness as being sexy, when a person is sexually objectified, or when sexuality is inappropriately imposed on a person. This report by the APA task force suggested that sexualization of children occurs on both a larger cultural level and an interpersonal level. Culturally, girls are sexualized through media representations, such as on television, the Internet, or in print magazines. Sexualization of girls is also seen in products such as toys, clothing, books, and dolls (e.g., Barbie, Bratz). A recent study of self-sexualization among girls ages 6 to 9 found that girls chose a sexualized doll over a nonsexualized doll for their ideal self (Starr & Ferguson, 2012), suggesting that they might be internalizing cultural messages that girls should be sexy. Sexualization of boys occurs on a cultural level through messages that boys and men should be muscular and sexually dominant, including dominating women for sexual pleasure (D. Levin, 2009). For example, music videos shown on television stations such as MTV often contain sexually explicit images (Brown & Steele, 1996) and combine these images with aggression (Sommers-Flanagan, Sommers-Flanagan, & Davis, 1993).

Sexualization of children has numerous negative implications for the development of sexuality and mental and physical health. Sexualization may lead to low self-esteem, appearance anxiety in social interactions, body image dissatisfaction, impaired cognitive functioning and physical performance, and reduced educational and occupational goals (APA Task Force on the Sexualization of Girls, 2007). Sexualization may also contribute to the problem of violence against women, particularly sexualized violence. For girls who are sexualized, sexual objectification may lead to initiation of sexual behavior at an early age or engaging in risky sexual behaviors (e.g., not using protection during sexual intercourse). Longitudinal studies of adolescents have found that those who view more sexual content in the media are more likely to progress to more advanced sexual activities and initiate sexual contact earlier (Ashby, Arcari, & Edmonson, 2006; Brown et al., 2006; R. Collins et al., 2004). Girls may also be more likely to become involved in unwanted sexual activity and relationships if they are sexualized. For example, child abuse sexual victimization, an extreme form of sexualization, has been linked to risky sexual behavior in adolescence and adulthood (Quina, Morokoff, Harlow, & Zurbriggen, 2004). Additionally, the messages received through the media that sexual domination of women is desirable may lead both genders to accept violence against women (e.g., Milburn, Mather, & Conrad, 2000; Ward, Hansbrough, & Walker, 2005; see also Chapter 12, this volume; Volume 2, Chapter 12, this handbook).

The APA task force report suggested a number of ways in which sexualization of children can be addressed (APA Task Force on the Sexualization of Girls, 2007). One way is to address media consumption and education by providing media literacy programs and comprehensive sexuality education in schools. The task force also suggested increased involvement of parents, particularly in exhibiting control over media that their children are exposed to, such as limiting television or Internet time. Additionally, parents can view media with their children and comment on appropriate and inappropriate content as a way of providing tools for media literacy. A final way to address the problem of sexualizing children is to engage in activism, such as boycotting companies that use sexualized images to sell products or magazines that display such advertisements (see SPARK [http://www.sparksummit.com], a response to the *Report of the APA Task Force on the Sexualization of Girls*, for more on activism related to sexualization of girls and women).

Dilemmas of Desire for Adolescent Girls

Adolescent girls develop their sexuality within a specific set of cultural expectations of how women and men should think and behave with regard to sexuality; typically, men are expected to be the sexual initiators and aggressors, and women are expected to be sexually passive. The portrayal of men's sexuality as a natural, uncontrollable urge has been termed the *discourse of male sexual drive* (Hollway, 1984). Tolman (2002) described how adolescent girls are expected to hold the responsibility for making appropriate choices about sexual behavior, because teenage boys are assumed to be the age group of males least in control of their sexuality. However, girls are expected to act passively rather than with agency. Tolman proposed that these expectations set up a situation in which adolescent girls are both responsible for their sexual decision making and penalized for acting on their sexual desires. Furthermore, Tolman identified how adolescent girls are subject to specific messages about their sexuality: Girls who are sexual are either bad girls who have desire and sexual agency or good girls who are passively victimized by boys and male hormones. At the same time, adolescent girls are subjected to sexualized images of women that encourage sexual behavior and dressing sexually. This, then, is the dilemma of desire: Adolescent girls are sexualized and encouraged through media and cultural representations to be sexual, but at the same time they are punished if they are sexual because they are defying cultural expectations for women's sexuality.

The dilemma of desire has implications for adolescent girls' safety in the context of sexual violence. Tolman (2002) proposed that both U.S. culture and law assign women the responsibility for regulating heterosexual sex by resisting male aggression. At the same time, girls receive cultural messages that good girls are not sexual and should not act with sexual agency. Tolman suggested that by discouraging women's sexual agency (and men's sexual responsibility), these cultural messages increase girls' vulnerability to sexual coercion and psychological distress.

The dilemma of desire for adolescent girls is a key area of research for sexuality and gender because it highlights the cultural difference in expectations around sexuality for girls compared with boys. It is important to recognize how contradictory expectations for girls' sexuality can have a negative impact on their sexual experiences and development of sexuality (see Chapter 13, this volume). In this situation, the interplay of sexuality and gender produces differences in socially constructed experiences of sexuality for women and men. Recent debates about the appearance of young women's growing sexual empowerment have raised questions about the ways in which girls are negotiating desire in the context of highly commodified and ever more sexualized social worlds, the possibilities for sexual agency under demands for performance of assertive sexuality, and how the perpetuation of gender inequalities informs observations of girls gone wild (Gavey, 2012; Gill, 2008; Lamb & Peterson, 2012; Tolman, 2012). Evidence of the persistence of the double standard underscores the need to understand what sexual empowerment might mean in relation to sexual desire, embodiment, and sexual agency (see Chapter 25, this volume). Lamb (2010) critiqued the desire model, suggesting that placing desire, pleasure, and sexuality at the center of an ideal healthy sexuality is problematic and that sexuality education should address ideologies of sexuality and gender as a way of helping adolescent girls construct a healthy sexuality. It is clear that more research and theoretical work needs to be done in this area before researchers can draw conclusions about healthy sexualities for female adolescents.

The Orgasm Gap

Another key research area in sexuality and gender is the *orgasm gap,* which refers to the finding that men are more likely than women to report having orgasm as a result of heterosexual partner sex (typically intercourse; Douglass & Douglass, 1997). Specifically, 75% of men report orgasm in heterosexual partner sex on a regular basis compared with 29% of women (Laumann et al., 1994). Laumann and colleagues (1994) also found that women report having orgasms more reliably from same-gender sexual contact (83% of the time) and from masturbation (67%–84% of the time) than from heterosexual partner sex (type of sex not reported for this statistic). However, this notion of the orgasm gap is complicated by varied definitions of orgasm, for example, whether each ejaculation in men is considered to be an orgasm or how women know whether they have had an orgasm. For our purposes, the orgasm gap refers to rates of reported orgasms, regardless of how participants define orgasm for themselves. At the same time, it is important to recognize that an unresolved debate remains about how to conceptualize, define, and operationalize orgasm in sexuality research (R. Levin, 2004). For example, King, Belskey, Mah, and Binik (2011) identified four different types of female orgasms that are associated with evolutionarily salient sexual partner characteristics (King & Belsky, 2012). These different types would not be captured in a study of female sexual response that does not carefully operationalize orgasm. In addition, many questions remain regarding orgasm in men, including a lack of research on phenomenological experiences of orgasm in men and research beyond ejaculation as a marker of orgasm. These debates raise new and significant questions about the orgasm gap and also suggest an important new area for research (see Chapter 8, this volume).

Douglass and Douglass (1997) identified four myths that have implications for sexual culture in the United States that relate directly to the orgasm gap. The first is that women are associated with sex, or rather that the symbol for sex is the body of a young, beautiful, scantily clad woman. This myth is also associated with the sexualization of girls and sexual objectification, described in the preceding section. Douglass and Douglass proposed that because women are expected to look attractive and sexual for others, a woman might never come to understand her own sexual desires, because her sexuality develops on the basis of how others see her and thus how she sees and evaluates herself (Bartky, 1990).

The second myth that Douglass and Douglass (1997) identified is that sex is defined exclusively as penile–vaginal intercourse. Indeed, penile penetration of the vagina is the defining act of sex for most heterosexual people; this expectation has been termed the *coital imperative* (McPhillips, Braun, &

Gavey, 2001). In heterosexual partnered sex, other sexual activities such as oral sex or manual stimulation typically preclude or imitate intercourse. A large survey of Australian adults found that the women who were least likely to have orgasms were those in situations in which intercourse was the only sexual activity with their partner (Richters, Visser, Rissel, & Smith, 2003).

The third myth is that women and men are sexually different and unequal. This myth is based on the beliefs that women have a lesser sex drive than men, that women do not need orgasm as much as men do, and that women have "lesser" genitals than men. The first belief, that women have a naturally low sex drive in comparison to men, was discussed in the Salient Controversies section. The fourth myth is that women want intimacy, and men want sex. This myth extends the third myth of gender differences to suggest that women and men engage in sex for different reasons. This myth does not hold up in research findings; as evidence, both women and men prefer sex within the context of a relationship to recreational sex (Laumann et al., 1994). Other research has suggested that adolescents ages 17 to 19 describe their sexualities using both dominant and resistant discourses of female and male sexuality (Allen, 2003). However, the case is that despite popular representations to the contrary, recreational or casual sex remains more acceptable for men than for women (Petersen & Hyde, 2010).

Other theories attempting to explain the orgasm gap propose that it stems from a combination of education and socialization related to gender and sexuality (Pastor, 2009). Pastor (2009) described how sex education for children is largely focused on heterosexual intercourse for the purpose of reproduction rather than pleasure. The focus on reproduction in sex education necessitates teaching children about male external genitalia and female internal genitalia, but not about female external genitalia. Bem (1989) found that before puberty, girls had more knowledge of boys' genitals than of their own. Pastor proposed that as a result of this lack of education, women (and men) have less knowledge about female sexual response and are therefore less likely to know how best to engage in heterosexual partner activity to reach female orgasm. Additionally, because sex education focuses on reproduction rather than pleasure, youths are not taught about female sexual response because female orgasm is not necessary to reproduction as is male orgasm. Therefore, men—and women themselves—are less aware of how to produce an orgasm in women, leading to a lower rate of female orgasm during heterosexual partner sex.

The orgasm gap can also be explained by socialization related to gender and sexuality. As we discussed previously regarding the dilemma of desire for adolescent girls and women's naturally low sex drives, cultural expectations for women's sexuality can produce a context in which sexual pleasure is not central for women. For example, men report initiating sex in the context of relationships more often than do women (Peplau, 2003), and men tend to have more sexual partners than women (Petersen & Hyde, 2010). This context may lead to the gender difference in orgasm frequency because women often have less agency in terms of initiating partner sex or in telling their partner how to maximize their pleasure during partner sex.

How can the orgasm gap be addressed? One solution lies in the reform of sex education toward a comprehensive model rather than an abstinence-only model to enable less gender-differentiated sexual socialization. Although the trend of sex education has moved in this direction in the United States, abstinence is still a focus in sex education programs (Guttmacher Institute, 2012). Teaching about both sexual response and reproduction in sex education is important to provide women—and men—with information about pleasure and sexuality for women so that the gender difference in orgasm frequency during heterosexual partner sex can be diminished. It is important to note that a focus on orgasm has itself possibly undermined a full understanding of women's (and men's) sexual pleasure, which may be less focused on orgasm. Pleasure beyond orgasm is another missing piece in public discourse, including in sex education. In particular, women's sexual pleasure is underrepresented by the inattention to female orgasm, whereas men's sexual pleasure is underrepresented by focusing on orgasm as the only means to obtaining sexual pleasure (see also Chapter 8, this volume).

New View of Women's Sexual Problems

Leonore Tiefer's (2001) work on reframing women's sexual problems represents another key area of discussion about research on sexuality and gender. Her work is based on a critique of what she calls the "medicalization of male sexuality," which refers to "the process of promoting a medical classification system, market, and scientific literature for men's sexual problems" (Tiefer, 2001, p. 89) and is evidenced by the popularity of Viagra to treat erectile dysfunction since its approval in 1998 (see also Volume 2, Chapter 5, this handbook). The medicalization of male sexuality prompted a similar view of women's sexuality within a medical framework, emphasizing physical causes, physical aspects of sexual experience, and physiological assessments and treatment of women's sexual problems (Tiefer, 2002). As a response to the medicalization of women's sexuality, the new view of women's sexual problems proposed a meaning-centered, political, and humanistic approach to sexuality research, theory, practice, and education (Connell & Dowsett, 1992; Evans, 1993; Weeks, 1995).

To fully understand how the new view of women's sexual problems represented an important departure from the medical model, we must first describe the context of medicalization and the purpose behind this approach. Modern medicalization of sexuality is based on the work of Masters and Johnson (1966, 1970), which focused on the physiology of sexual response. The American Psychiatric Association's (2000) fourth text revision of the *Diagnostic and Statistical Manual of Mental Disorders* further contributed to the medicalization of sexuality by providing diagnostic criteria for sexual problems. According to critics, the medical model includes a focus on the individual person as well as a separation of mind and body, producing an understanding of sexuality that emphasizes genital function and the physiology underlying sexual behavior and response (Boyle, 1994; Tiefer, 1999). Underlying this medicalized approach is a specific norm of sexuality that largely focuses on correct genital performance (Tiefer, 2001). Furthermore, Tiefer (2001) proposed that this norm of sexuality dictates that a successful sexual experience must include sexual desire, genital arousal, orgasm, and enjoyment of vaginal penetration. These components leave little room for other aspects of sexuality, such as desire for intimacy, and types of sex other than penile–vaginal intercourse.

Tiefer (2001) suggested that one of the primary problems with the medicalization of sexuality is the omission of the relational aspects of sexual experiences as a potential primary source of problems. Tiefer also critiqued medicalized treatments of women's sexual problems for addressing physiology first rather than incorporating physiology into a larger understanding of women's sexual problems. Drugs such as Viagra focus on the physiological functioning of the genitals while ignoring the larger context of when, where, how, and with whom a sexual experience will occur. The medicalization of sexuality also overlooks cultural variability in sexuality, treating cultural and religious factors as less important than biology (Tiefer, 2001). Instead, the medical model proposes a universal approach to physiology. This approach is problematic because meaning and motivation for sexual activity are largely derived from cultural sexual scripts (Tiefer, 2001); for example, one of the cultural scripts for sexuality in the United States holds gendered expectations such as sexual aggressiveness for men and passivity for women. Therefore, female sexual problems for a couple within this cultural context could be related to a reluctance on the part of the woman to express that she is not being sexually satisfied by the acts performed by her partner. Finally, Tiefer (2001) proposed that another limitation of the medical approach to sexual problems is the neglect and denial of issues of power. Men's and women's sexual problems are assumed to be equally represented within the medical model of sexuality; instead, the focus is on the functioning (or lack of functioning) of the penis, whereas women's lack of sexual satisfaction (vs. functioning, i.e., sufficient lubrication for penile–vaginal intercourse) is largely ignored. This focus is representative of the larger political and economic subordination of women that has been well documented by feminist researchers (e.g., Kramarae & Spender, 1992).

The response of the new view campaign to the medicalization of women's sexuality has been to combine feminist scholarship and activism that focuses on the experiences of women themselves with a social constructionist view of sexual experiences that assumes that many aspects of sexuality are not universal (Tiefer, 2001). Within the new view campaign, women's sexual problems are defined as "discontent or dissatisfaction with any emotional, physical, or relational aspect of sexual experience" (Tiefer, 2001, p. 91) and are perceived as typically based on larger social and cultural factors, such as gender stereotyping or issues of social inequality. The model recognizes that bases for women's sexual problems can be physiological but suggests that this conclusion be the last resort rather than the first in evaluating a woman's report of sexual difficulties. Within this framework, the experience of a woman who is dissatisfied with her sexual experiences might be linked to causal factors such as fatigue or lack of time because of family and work obligations rather than her own inability to enjoy sexual intercourse; that is, experiences that are labeled *sexual dysfunctions* may well be effects of social conditions rather than a "broken" body.

Perhaps the most noteworthy aspect of the categorization of women's sexual problems within the new view is that the category of problems caused by sociocultural, political, or economic factors is the largest, whereas the category of medical and physical problems is the smallest. In stark contrast to medical models of women's sexuality, which exist across various scholarships, the new view emphasizes social and cultural factors. This is a promising new direction for investigating women's experiences of sexuality—not just for disorders, but also for optimal functioning. The new view approach, simultaneously social constructionist and feminist, puts women's lives in context at the center of evaluation of sexual troubles rather than as a deviation from the male norm. At the same time, this model is largely theoretical and has yet to be evaluated empirically, even as therapists recognize the complexity that many women are experiencing in relation to their sexuality. In addition, other biopsychological research exists that examines women's sexual response (e.g., Pfaus, 2006; see also Chapters 7 and 8, this volume). This research can serve either to provide evidence of a biological basis for women's sexual problems or to rule out these factors, allowing for a sociocultural explanation. The current environment is characterized by a polarization around women's sexual problems, with medical options growing out of a desire to find a "female Viagra" (Hartley, 2006) and the new view holding a virtually opposing position in diminishing a focus on sexual dysfunction that may have organic roots.

Operating in parallel to Tiefer (2001), Basson (2002) and Basson and colleagues (2004) have also proposed revised views of women's sexuality. These alternative views deemphasize genital congestion and instead emphasize intimacy-based sexual motivation and responsive desire, the notion that,for women, desire often follows from sexual stimulation rather than preceding it, particularly in long-term relationships. The reality that many women do report dissatisfaction, unhappiness, or dysfunction regarding their sexuality emphasizes the need for more research that accounts for social, cultural, gendered, and physiological factors in research on women's sexual distress.

Sexual Fluidity

Sexual fluidity—sometimes referred to as *erotic plasticity*—has been defined as situation-dependent flexibility in sexual responsiveness, which may manifest in changes in sexual identity over time (Baumeister, 2000; Diamond, 2008b). Therefore, sexual fluidity can involve changes in attractions or identity. This concept has been studied mainly in women, with Diamond's (2008b) longitudinal study as the most well-known example. In this study, Diamond followed young adult sexual minority women across 10 years and found that two thirds of the women had changed their sexual identity label since the beginning of the study, and one third had changed their label two or more times. In another study of sexual minority women, using retrospective self-report, 75% of the bisexual women reported that they had previously identified as lesbian, whereas 40% of lesbians had previously identified as bisexual (Rust, 1993).

Traditionally, sexual minority men's sexual orientation has been assumed to develop early and remain stable over time. However, a number of studies have begun to explore changes in men's sexual identity (e.g., Baumeister, 2000; Rosario, Schrimshaw, Hunter, & Braun, 2006). Weinberg and colleagues

(1994) found changes in men's sexual identity over time, and a study of young adults in New Zealand found that movement away from heterosexual attraction was more common for both women and men, although more change was seen in women (Dickson, Paul, & Herbison, 2003). Although much of the existing research on sexual fluidity in men suggests that it is not as common as sexual fluidity in women (Baumeister, 2000; Dickson et al., 2003), some studies have indicated a different pattern. Rosario and colleagues (2006) examined changes in sexual identity among female and male LGB youths ages 14 to 21 and found that females were less likely to change identities than males. In a recent study investigating sexual identity development and sexual fluidity in young adult sexual minority women and men ages 18 to 26, no significant difference was found between the gender groups in likelihood of sexual fluidity (Katz-Wise, 2012). More research is needed in this area to fully understand men's experiences of changes in attractions and identity. In particular, future research would benefit from attention to shifting cultural norms regarding male homosexuality that may open possibilities for sexual fluidity in men to occur (see also Chapters 19 and 20, this volume).

Although sexual fluidity has primarily been examined in sexual minority women (and to some degree in sexual minority men), some researchers have proposed that some fluidity is a general property of sexuality (Blumstein & Schwartz, 1990; Weinberg et al., 1994). Indeed, some studies have demonstrated sexual fluidity in heterosexual people as well. Diamond (2008b) interviewed a number of heterosexually identified women and found some evidence for sexual fluidity, although the process was different from the sexual minority women in her original study—in part because most heterosexual women never think about or question their sexual identity. Diamond found that both sexual minority and heterosexual women described current or past emotionally intense bonds to female friends; however, for sexual minority women, the distinction between sexual and romantic (or emotional) attraction was not always clear, whereas heterosexual women expressed that "if their attractions to women are exclusively emotional, then they are probably not gay" (Diamond, 2008b, p. 79). Weinberg and colleagues (1994) also found some change in the sexuality of heterosexual people in their sample of people living in San Francisco in the 1980s, although more change was seen among LGB people.

The gender difference commonly found in sexual fluidity research, with women experiencing greater fluidity than men (e.g., Dickson et al., 2003), has been explained in a number of ways. One line of reasoning has pointed to gender differences in the specificity of sexual arousability. In a study of physiological experiences of sexual arousal that was discussed earlier, researchers found that men were more specific in the set of stimuli that they found arousing than were women (Chivers et al., 2004). Specifically, gay men were aroused only to videos with men, and heterosexual men were aroused only to videos with women, whereas lesbian and heterosexual women were generally aroused to any video depicting sexual behavior, regardless of the gender of the actors. This finding suggests that women might have more flexibility around their sexual arousal, which could lead to greater sexual fluidity.

Another line of reasoning to explain the gender difference in sexual fluidity relates to sociocultural factors. Gender socialization related to expressions of sexuality provides more restrictive expectations for men in terms of displaying affection toward members of the same gender in the context of male–male friendships. Society prohibits open displays of affection between heterosexual men but permits them between women (Nardi, 1992). Additionally, intimate and affectionate same-gender relationships are seen to indicate homosexuality more often when occurring between men than when occurring between women (Derlega, Lewis, Harrison, Winstead, & Constanza, 1989). Derlega, Catanzaro, and Lewis (2001) conducted a more recent study of perceptions of tactile intimacy in same-gender compared with other-gender pairs and found that heterosexual men and women rated high tactile intimacy as less appropriate in male–male pairs than in male–female or female–female pairs. The researchers also found that in the high tactile intimacy group, heterosexual men and women attributed more sexual involvement to male–male pairs and to male–female pairs than to female–female pairs. This cultural context might create more situations in which women's same-gender friendships cross over into romantic relationships, whereas the same may not be true as often for men.

More recent research has indicated that rather than demonstrating gender differences in sexual fluidity, women and men were equally likely to experience changes in attractions and sexual identity (Katz-Wise, 2012). Katz-Wise's study used mixed methods to examine sexual identity development and sexual fluidity in young adult sexual minority women and men. Responses to an online questionnaire indicated that 64% of women and 52% of men had experienced changes in attractions to others over time, with no significant gender difference. Although women and men had a similar likelihood of experiencing sexual fluidity in attractions, they differed in their interpretations of those changes both in an open-ended question on the online questionnaire and during qualitative interviews. For instance, in response to the open-ended question on the online questionnaire, women were more likely to mention specific romantic or sexual experiences as being related to changes in attractions and sexual identity, whereas men were more likely to mention heteronormativity, the societal context within which heterosexuality is considered the norm. In particular, some men explained their sexual fluidity in terms of growing up and living in a heteronormative society in which they did not initially have the option to be attracted to other men or to act on those attractions. They described how the process of overcoming heteronormativity contributed to initial development of a sexual minority identity in addition to later changes in their attractions and sexual identity.

Sexual fluidity is a key area of theory and future research in particular because it demonstrates the importance of considering sexuality and gender as interacting rather than as separate constructs. Although recent research has demonstrated a gender similarity in prevalence of sexual fluidity, this same research has suggested that sexual fluidity may operate differently in men than in women. Specifically, some of the explanations for sexual fluidity in women (e.g., many women experience person-based attractions rather than gender-based attractions; Diamond, 2008b) may not apply to men. Therefore, it is important to consider how gender intersects with sexuality rather than assume that sexual fluidity does not occur in men.

Implications of New Technologies for Biological Measurement

Over the past 2 decades, two major technological developments have substantially advanced researchers' capabilities for biological measurement. One is imaging techniques—primarily functional MRI—that allow researchers to measure brain activity in alive, awake, behaving humans. The other, emerging with the Human Genome Project, is the capacity to genotype human participants at relatively low cost. Both have enormous potential to advance research on sexuality and gender, although it is very early in the research process in applications of both technologies. That said, we have examples of some exciting advances.

In the realm of genetics, we may be able to look forward to research that identifies specific genes that contribute, for example, to tendencies toward sexual excitation or sexual inhibition. Evolutionary theorists have been long on theory and short on specifying exact genetic mechanisms that underlie the behaviors that are said to be the product of evolution. The evolutionary theorists therefore have the opportunity to fill in the missing links. In one genomewide association study, Mustanski and colleagues (2005) identified several regions on chromosomes that were linked to sexual orientation in men. There are many exciting possibilities.

Use of these new biological measures need not result in a biologically deterministic approach to gender and sexuality. Indeed, it is important to consider how these measures can contribute to—but not completely explain—phenomena related to gender and sexuality (Salk & Hyde, 2012). Biological measures can be combined with measures of sociocultural factors to allow for a more complete examination of a particular issue. For example, Brotto, Heiman, and Tolman (2009) investigated sexual desire in middle-aged women with and without arousal disorders, using narrative descriptions to contribute a qualitative understanding of women's sexual problems. In addition, modern neuroscience has emphasized neural plasticity and the responsiveness of the brain to the environment (Eliot, 2009; Jordan-Young, 2010).

Neuroscientists do not use the term *hard wired.* The brain is anything but. The implication is that if, for example, a researcher discovers that different brain regions are activated during orgasm for males compared with females, the difference might be due to factors such as organizing influences during prenatal development, but it might also be due to different experiences that males and females have had in relation to sexuality. Moreover, recent evidence with nonhumans has indicated that sexual behavior can create neural changes in the brain (Gheusi, Ortega-Perez, Murray, & Lledo, 2009; Holmes, Seney, Goldman, & Forger, 2011; see also Chapter 7, this volume).

The Sexual Excitation–Inhibition Model

One major theoretical development is the dual control model, or the sexual excitation–inhibition model, developed by researchers at the Kinsey Institute at Indiana University (Bancroft et al., 2009). The model proposes that two basic processes underlie human sexual response: sexual excitation (responding with arousal to potentially sexual stimuli) and sexual inhibition (inhibiting sexual arousal to a potential sexual stimulus). The Kinsey researchers argued that most sex research has focused on the excitation component but that the inhibition component is equally important. They observed that inhibition of sexual response is adaptive across species; sexual arousal can be a powerful distraction that could become disadvantageous or even dangerous in certain situations.

According to the sexual excitation–inhibition model, tendencies toward sexual excitation and toward sexual inhibition vary widely from one person to the next. Most people fall in the moderate range on both and function well. Some sexual problems result, however, for people who fall at the extremes. For example, people who are very high on inhibition and low on excitation are more vulnerable to sexual disorders such as desire and arousal disorders. People who are very high on excitation and low on inhibition can be sex offenders or may engage in risky sexual behavior, such as sex addiction.

The Kinsey team has developed self-report scales that measure sexual excitation and inhibition, with parallel scales for men and women (Graham, Sanders, & Milhausen, 2006; Janssen, Vorst, Finn, & Bancroft, 2002). Men on average score higher than women on sexual excitation, and women score higher on inhibition than do men. In a sample of college students, the effect size (d) for gender differences was .67 for excitation, −.57 on one inhibition scale (threat of performance failure), and −.92 on the second inhibition scale (threat of performance consequences; D. Carpenter, Janssen, Graham, Vorst, & Wicherts, 2008). These differences are relatively large. Bisexual women score higher on excitation, on average, than do straight and lesbian women. Gay men, on average, score higher on excitation than straight men (Bancroft et al., 2009).

The dual control model is important because it gets at very basic processes that are involved with sexuality. The model recognizes biological contributions to both excitation and inhibition but also recognizes the forces that shape excitation and inhibition. As such, its implications are wide ranging. For example, clinical assessment of sexual arousal problems can use the framework of the dual control model to consider when inhibition of sexual response may be adaptive and when it may reflect vulnerability, leading to problems related to sexual functioning and satisfaction (Bancroft et al., 2009). In another use of this approach, a recent study assessed similarities in sexual excitation and inhibition in newlywed couples and found that similarities between members of the couple predicted sexual problems and satisfaction (Lykins, Janssen, Newhouse, Heiman, & Rafaeli, 2012). This model promises to be useful in advancing researchers' understanding of gender and sexuality, particularly in areas such as sexual disorders and sexual coercion (see Chapter 7, this volume; Volume 2, Chapter 5, this handbook).

Advances in Measurement of the Environment

Discussion of the major advances in biological measurement raises the question of whether equivalent advances have occurred in measurement of the environment, that is, variables, scales, and other assessments of dimensions of sociocultural, community, family, and interpersonal contexts. Measurement of both biological and environmental factors is necessary to enable examination of the complex ways in which sexuality and gender interact. At the level of culture, the measures of gender equality developed by the United Nations and by the Organisation for Economic Co-operation and Development represent great advances, as reflected in some of the research reported earlier in the chapter (Else-Quest & Grabe, 2012).

In particular, measurements of the environment are needed that are not strictly self-report. A behavioral, reaction-time measure of the individual's internalization of cultural stereotypes, such as gender stereotypes, is now available. The Implicit Attitudes Test (e.g., Nosek et al., 2009) is a viable alternative to a self-report measure that diminishes the weaknesses of the more common self-report measure. We foresee many applications that will illuminate the interplay between gender and sexuality. For example, research on the sexual double standard that is based on self-reports has produced mixed results; now, however, a sexual double standard Implicit Attitudes Test is available, and it is not vulnerable to factors such as socially desirable responding (Sakaluk & Milhausen, 2012).

The field of cultural psychology has taken off (e.g., Heine, 2008; Matsumoto & Juan, 2013). Many readers are familiar with measures of individualism and collectivism that appeared at the beginning of the field (Triandis, 1989). Today, much more research is available that reflects a dimensional approach to studying culture. This type of approach operationalizes differences between cultures as they are manifested in dominant value systems, such as individualism or collectivism (Hofstede, 2001; Hofstede & McCrae, 2004). Dimensions of culture are conceptualized as similar to factors or dimensions in models of personality, such as the Five-Factor Model of Personality (Digman, 1990). Another dimensional approach to studying culture involves the tightness versus looseness of a society, reflecting the strength of social norms and the strength of punishments for violations of such norms (Pelto, 1968). For example, Indian society is relatively tight, whereas Greek society is relatively loose (Gelfand et al., 2011). This dimension has much potential in the study of sexuality and gender across cultures.

In addition to studying phenomena cross-culturally, other researchers have examined differences in sexual outcomes between ethnic groups in a culture such as the United States or Canada. In one study, for example, Chinese Canadian women reported more sex guilt and less sexual desire than did European Canadians (Woo, Brotto, & Gorzalka, 2012). Moreover, more Westernized Chinese women reported less sex guilt and more desire than their less acculturated peers. Studies such as this one speak to the powerful role of culture in shaping sexuality. A review of all the advances in cultural psychology is beyond the scope of this chapter; interested readers can consult some of the excellent reviews that are available (Heine, 2008; Matsumoto & Juan, 2013; see also Volume 2, Chapters 6 and 9, this handbook). We believe that the approaches of cultural psychology can and should be applied to the study of the interplay between sexuality and gender.

CONCLUSION

Having provided an overview of the ways in which sexuality and gender interact within psychological research and theory, it is important to consider where to go from here. Many areas of psychology on sexuality and gender have yet to be explored and represent opportunities for exciting advancements in the field. For example, in the Development of Sexuality section, we discussed the decline in sexual activity over time in long-term relationships as well as across the life span. The majority of the work in this area has focused on penile–vaginal intercourse in heterosexual married couples. It is important to expand this research not only to couples of other gender configurations but also to other types of sexual activity.

We must also consider how much of previous psychological research and theory on sexuality and gender has originated from a Western standpoint. Assumptions that are central to this culture limit the overall understanding of gender and sexuality in failing to consider how other cultures and societies might view and experience the same phenomena differently. As such, we hope to see more transnational research on sexuality and gender as well as more cross-cultural research collaborations.

To advance the field, sexuality and gender researchers must capitalize on new advances in biology (e.g., Salk & Hyde, 2012) while at the same time incorporating advances in measurement of the environment, especially structural and sociocultural factors. Researchers will need to develop measures of specific environments that are relevant to sexuality, such as family environments that are pro-sex, anti-sex, or double standard. More emphasis on behavioral measures, rather than self-report measures, is badly needed. The Implicit Attitudes Test measures described earlier are noteworthy examples. Additionally, more sophisticated ways to collect and analyze qualitative data are needed, so that all forms of data can be integrated into larger, more complex and nuanced pictures.

In conclusion, sexuality and gender research has a long history in psychology, and much has changed over time. The field is moving in exciting new directions as it continues to evolve. As theories and methodologies change, however, it is important that researchers approach sexuality and gender as interacting constructs, variables, and discourses. We hope we have made it evident that exploring the interplay between sexuality and gender is crucial to moving research on these topics forward in the field of psychology.

References

Alexander, M. G., & Fisher, T. D. (2003). Truth and consequences: Using the bogus pipeline to examine sex differences in self-reported sexuality. *Journal of Sex Research, 40*, 27–35. doi:10.1080/00224490309552164

Allen, L. (2003). Girls want sex, boys want love: Resisting dominant discourses of (hetero)sexuality. *Sexualities, 6*, 215–236. doi:10.1177/1363460703006002004

American Psychiatric Association. (2000). *Diagnostic and statistical manual of mental disorders* (4th ed., text rev.). Washington, DC: Author.

American Psychological Association. (2012). Guidelines for psychological practice with lesbian, gay, and bisexual clients. *American Psychologist, 67*, 10–42. doi:10.1037/a0024659

American Psychological Association, Task Force on the Sexualization of Girls. (2007). *Report of the APA Task Force on the Sexualization of Girls*. Washington, DC: American Psychological Association. Retrieved from http://www.apa.org/pi/wpo/sexualization.html

Andersen, B. L., Cyranowski, J. M., & Aarestad, S. (2000). Beyond artificial, sex-linked distinctions to conceptualize female sexuality: Comment on Baumeister (2000). *Psychological Bulletin, 126*, 380–384. doi:10.1037/0033-2909.126.3.380

Ashby, S. L., Arcari, C. M., & Edmonson, M. B. (2006). Television viewing and risk of sexual initiation by young adolescents. *Archives of Pediatrics and Adolescent Medicine, 160*, 375–380. doi:10.1001/archpedi.160.4.375

Balsam, K. F., Beauchaine, T. P., Rothblum, E. D., & Solomon, S. E. (2008). Three-year follow-up of same-sex couples who had civil unions in Vermont, same-sex couples not in civil unions, and heterosexual married couples. *Developmental Psychology, 44*, 102–116. doi:10.1037/0012-1649.44.1.102

Bancroft, J., Graham, C. A., Janssen, E., & Sanders, S. A. (2009). The dual control model: Current status and future directions. *Journal of Sex Research, 46*, 121–142. doi:10.1080/00224490902747222

Bartky, S. L. (1990). *Femininity and domination: Studies in the phenomenology of oppression*. New York, NY: Routledge.

Basson, R. (2002). Women's sexual desire: Disordered or misunderstood? *Journal of Sex and Marital Therapy, 28*, 17–28. doi:10.1080/00926230252851168

Basson, R., Leiblum, S., Brotto, L., Derogatis, L., Fourcroy, J., Fugl-Meyer, K., . . . Schultz, W. W. (2004). Revised definitions of women's sexual dysfunctions. *Journal of Sexual Medicine, 1*, 40–48. doi:10.1111/j.1743-6109.2004.10107.x

Baumeister, R. F. (2000). Gender differences in erotic plasticity: The female sex drive as socially flexible and responsive. *Psychological Bulletin, 126*, 347–374. doi:10.1037/0033-2909.126.3.347

Baumeister, R. F., Catanese, K., & Vohs, K. (2001). Is there a gender difference in strength of sex drive? Theoretical views, conceptual distinctions, and a review of relevant evidence. *Personality and Social Psychology Review, 5*, 242–273. doi:10.1207/S15327957PSPR0503_5

Bell, A. P., Weinberg, M. S., & Hammersmith, S. K. (1981). *Sexual preference*. Bloomington: Indiana University Press.

Bem, S. L. (1989). Genital knowledge and gender constancy in preschool children. *Child Development, 60*, 649–662. doi:10.2307/1130730

Berger, P., & Luckmann, T. (1966). *The social construction of reality: A treatise in the sociology of knowledge*. Garden City, NY: Doubleday.

Blackwood, E. (2000). Culture and women's sexualities. *Journal of Social Issues, 56*, 223–238. doi:10.1111/0022-4537.00162

Bleakley, A., Hennessy, M., Fishbein, M., & Jordan, A. (2009). How sources of sexual information relate to adolescents' beliefs about sex. *American Journal of Health Behavior, 33*, 37–37-48. doi:10.5993/AJHB.33.1.4

Blumstein, P., & Schwartz, P. (1990). Intimate relationships and the creation of sexuality. In D. P. McWhirter, S. A. Sanders, & J. M. Reinisch (Eds.), *Homosexuality/heterosexuality: Concepts of sexual orientation* (pp. 307–320). New York, NY: Oxford University Press.

Blumstein, P. W., & Schwartz, P. (1983). *American couples*. New York, NY: Morrow.

Bogle, K. (2008). *Hooking up: Sex, dating, and relationships on campus*. New York, NY: New York University Press.

Boyle, M. (1994). Gender, science, and sexual dysfunction. In T. R. Sarbin & J. I. Kitsuse (Eds.), *Constructing the social* (pp. 101–118). London, England: Sage.

Breen, L. J., & Darlaston-Jones, D. (2010). Moving beyond the enduring dominance of positivism in psychological research: Implications for psychology in Australia. *Australian Psychologist, 45*, 67–76. doi:10.1080/00050060903127481

Bretschneider, J. G., & McCoy, N. L. (1988). Sexual interest and behavior in healthy 80- and 102-year-olds. *Archives of Sexual Behavior, 17*, 109–129. doi:10.1007/BF01542662

Brotto, L. A., Heiman, J. R., & Tolman, D. L. (2009). Narratives of desire in mid-age women with and without arousal difficulties. *Journal of Sex Research, 46*, 387–398. doi:10.1080/00224490902792624

Brown, J., & Steele, J. R. (1996). Sexuality and the mass media: An overview. *SIECUS Report, 24*, 3–9.

Brown, J. D., L'Engle, K. L., Pardun, C. J., Guo, G., Kenneavy, K., & Jackson, C. (2006). Sexy media matter: Exposure to sexual content in music, movies, television, and magazines predicts Black and White adolescents' sexual behavior. *Pediatrics, 117*, 1018–1027. doi:10.1542/peds.2005-1406

Buller, D. J. (2005). *Adapting minds: Evolutionary psychology and the persistent quest for human nature*. Cambridge, MA: MIT Press.

Buss, D., & Shackelford, T. (1997). Susceptibility to infidelity in the first year of marriage. *Journal of Research in Personality, 31*, 193–221. doi:10.1006/jrpe.1997.2175

Buss, D. M. (1989). Sex differences in human mate preferences: Evolutionary hypotheses tested in 37 cultures. *Behavioral and Brain Sciences, 12*, 1–14. doi:10.1017/S0140525X00023992

Buss, D. M. (1995). Evolutionary psychology: A new paradigm for psychological science. *Psychological Inquiry, 6*, 1–30. doi:10.1207/s15327965pli0601_1

Buss, D. M., & Schmitt, D. P. (1993). Sexual strategies theory: An evolutionary perspective on human mating. *Psychological Review, 100*, 204–232. doi:10.1037/0033-295X.100.2.204

Call, V., Sprecher, S., & Schwartz, P. (1995). The incidence and frequency of marital sex in a national sample. *Journal of Marriage and the Family, 57*, 639–652. doi:10.2307/353919

Carpenter, D., Janssen, E., Graham, C., Vorst, H., & Wicherts, J. (2008). Women's scores on the Sexual Inhibition/Sexual Excitation Scales (SIS/SES): Gender similarities and differences. *Journal of Sex Research, 45*, 36–48. doi:10.1080/00224490701808076

Carpenter, L. M. (2010). Gendered sexuality over the life course: A conceptual framework. *Sociological Perspectives, 53*, 155–178. doi:10.1525/sop.2010.53.2.155

Carpenter, L. M., & DeLamater, J. (2012). Studying gendered sexualities over the life course: A conceptual framework. In L. M. Carpenter & J. DeLamater (Eds.), *Sex for life: From virginity to Viagra, how sexuality changes throughout our lives* (pp. 23–41). New York, NY: New York University Press.

Cass, V. C. (1979). Homosexual identity formation: A theoretical model. *Journal of Homosexuality, 4*, 219–235. doi:10.1300/J082v04n03_01

Centers for Disease Control and Prevention. (2011). *STD trends in the United States: 2010 national data for gonorrhea, chlamydia, and syphilis*. Retrieved from http://www.cdc.gov/std/stats10/trends2010.pdf

Chaine, A. S., & Lyon, B. E. (2008). Adaptive plasticity in female mate choice dampens sexual selection on male ornaments in the lark bunting. *Science, 319*, 459–462. doi:10.1126/science.1149167

Chandra, A., Mosher, W. D., & Copen, C. (2011). Sexual behavior, sexual attraction, and sexual identity in the United States: Data from the 2006–208 National Survey of Family Growth. *National Health Statistics Reports, 36*, 1–36.

Charbonneau, C., & Lander, P. S. (1991). Redefining sexuality: Women becoming lesbian in midlife. In B. Sang, J. Warshow, & A. J. Smith (Eds.), *Lesbians at midlife: The creative transition* (pp. 35–43). San Francisco, CA: Spinsters.

Chivers, M. L., Rieger, G., Latty, E., & Bailey, J. M. (2004). A sex difference in the specificity of sexual arousal. *Psychological Science, 15*, 736–744. doi:10.1111/j.0956-7976.2004.00750.x

Colapinto, J. (2000). *As nature made him*. New York, NY: HarperCollins.

Cole, E. R. (2009). Intersectionality and research in psychology. *American Psychologist, 64*, 170–180. doi:10.1037/a0014564

Collins, P. H. (2004). *Black sexual politics: African Americans, gender, and the new racism*. New York, NY: Routledge. doi:10.4324/9780203309506

Collins, R. L., Elliott, M. N., Berry, S. H., Kanouse, D. E., Kunkel, D., Hunter, S. B., & Miu, A. (2004). Watching sex on television predicts adolescent initiation of sexual behavior. *Pediatrics, 114*, e280–e289. doi:10.1542/peds.2003-1065-L

Connell, R. W., & Dowsett, G. W. (1992). "The unclean motion of the generative parts": Frameworks in Western thought on sexuality. In R. W. Connell & G. W. Dowsett (Eds.), *Rethinking sex: Social theory and sexuality research* (pp. 49–75). Melbourne, Australia: Melbourne University Press.

Darwin, C. (1871). *The descent of man and selection in relation to sex*. London, England: Murray.

DeLamater, J. D., & Hyde, J. S. (1998). Essentialism vs. social constructionism in the study of human sexuality. *Journal of Sex Research, 35*, 10–18. doi:10.1080/00224499809551913

Derlega, V. J., Catanzaro, D., & Lewis, R. J. (2001). Perceptions about tactile intimacy in same-sex and opposite-sex pairs based on research participants' sexual orientation. *Psychology of Men and Masculinity, 2*, 124–132. doi:10.1037/1524-9220.2.2.124

Derlega, V. J., Lewis, R. J., Harrison, S., Winstead, B., & Constanza, R. (1989). Gender differences in the initiation and attribution of tactile intimacy. *Journal of Nonverbal Behavior, 13*, 83–96. doi:10.1007/BF00990792

Diamond, L. M. (1998). Development of sexual orientation among adolescent and adult young women. *Developmental Psychology, 34*, 1085–1095. doi:10.1037/0012-1649.34.5.1085

Diamond, L. M. (2006). Introduction: In search of good sexual-developmental pathways for adolescent girls. *New Directions for Child and Adolescent Development, 2006*, 1–7. doi:10.1002/cd.158

Diamond, L. M. (2008a). Female bisexuality from adolescence to adulthood: Results from a 10-year longitudinal study. *Developmental Psychology, 44*, 5–14. doi:10.1037/0012-1649.44.1.5

Diamond, L. M. (2008b). *Sexual fluidity: Understanding women's love and desire*. Cambridge, MA: Harvard University Press.

Diamond, L. M., & Savin-Williams, R. C. (2000). Explaining diversity in the development of same-sex sexuality among young women. *Journal of Social Issues, 56*, 297–313. doi:10.1111/0022-4537.00167

Dickson, N., Paul, C., & Herbison, P. (2003). Same-sex attraction in a birth cohort: Prevalence and persistence in early adulthood. *Social Science and Medicine, 56*, 1607–1615. doi:10.1016/S0277-9536(02)00161-2

Digman, J. M. (1990). Personality structure: Emergence of the Five-Factor Model. *Annual Review of Psychology, 41*, 417–440. doi:10.1146/annurev.ps.41.020190.002221

Douglass, M., & Douglass, L. (1997). *The sex you want: A lovers' guide to women's sexual pleasure*. Chicago, IL: Browne & Miller Literary Associates.

Eagly, A. H., & Wood, W. (1999). The origins of sex differences in human behavior: Evolved dispositions versus social roles. *American Psychologist, 54*, 408–423. doi:10.1037/0003-066X.54.6.408

Eliot, L. (2009). *Pink brain, blue brain: How small differences grow into troublesome gaps—And what we can do about it*. Boston, MA: Houghton Mifflin.

Else-Quest, N. M., & Grabe, S. (2012). The political is personal: Measurement and application of nation-level indicators of gender equity in psychological research. *Psychology of Women Quarterly, 36*, 131–144. doi:10.1177/0361684312441592

Evans, D. T. (1993). *Sexual citizenship: The material construction of sexualities*. New York, NY: Routledge. doi:10.4324/9780203412398

Fine, M., & McClelland, S. I. (2006). Sexuality education and desire: Still missing after all these years. *Harvard Educational Review, 76*, 297–338.

Foucault, M. (1978). *The history of sexuality: Vol. 1. An introduction*. New York, NY: Pantheon.

Friedrich, W. N., Fisher, J., Broughton, D., Houston, M., & Shafran, C. R. (1998). Normative sexual behavior in children: A contemporary sample. *Pediatrics, 101*, e9. doi:10.1542/peds.101.4.e9

Froyum, C. M. (2010). Making "good girls": Sexual agency in the sexuality education of low-income black girls. *Culture, Health, and Sexuality, 12*, 59–72. doi:10.1080/13691050903272583

Gagné, P., Tewksbury, R., & McGaughey, D. (1997). Coming out and crossing over: Identity formation and proclamation in a transgender community. *Gender and Society, 11*, 478–508. doi:10.1177/089124397011004006

Gavey, N. (2012). Beyond "empowerment"? Sexuality in a sexist world. *Sex Roles, 66*, 718–724. doi:10.1007/s11199-011-0069-3

Gay, J. (1986). "Mummies and babies" and friends and lovers in Lesotho. In E. Blackwood (Ed.), *The many faces of homosexuality: Anthropological approaches to homosexual behavior* (pp. 97–116). New York, NY: Harrington Park Press.

Geary, D. C. (1998). *Male, female: The evolution of human sex differences*. Washington, DC: American Psychological Association. doi:10.1037/10370-000

Gelfand, M. J., Raver, J. L., Nishii, L., Leslie, L. M., Lun, J., Lim, B. C., . . . Yamaguchi, S. (2011). Differences between tight and loose cultures: A 33-nation study. *Science, 332*, 1100–1104. doi:10.1126/science.1197754

Gergen, K. J. (1985). The social constructionist movement in modern psychology. *American Psychologist, 40*, 266–275. doi:10.1037/0003-066X.40.3.266

Gheusi, G., Ortega-Perez, I., Murray, K., & Lledo, P. (2009). A niche for adult neurogenesis in social behavior. *Behavioural Brain Research, 200*, 315–322. doi:10.1016/j.bbr.2009.02.006

Gill, R. (2008). Empowerment/sexism: Figuring female sexual agency in contemporary advertising. *Feminism and Psychology, 18*, 35–60. doi:10.1177/0959353507084950

Glick, P., & Fiske, S. T. (1996). The ambivalent sexism inventory: Differentiating hostile and benevolent sexism. *Journal of Personality and Social Psychology, 70*, 491–512. doi:10.1037/0022-3514.70.3.491

Goodwin, P. Y., Mosher, W. D., & Chandra, A. (2010). Marriage and cohabitation in the United States: A statistical portrait based on Cycle 6 (2002) of the National Survey of Family Growth. *Vital and Health Statistics, 23*(28).

Gould, S. J. (1987). *An urchin in the storm: Essays about books and ideas.* New York, NY: Norton.

Graham, C. A., Sanders, S. A., & Milhausen, R. R. (2006). The Sexual Excitation and Sexual Inhibition Inventory for Women: Psychometric properties. *Archives of Sexual Behavior, 35*, 397–409. doi:10.1007/s10508-006-9041-7

Gundersen, B., Melas, P. S., & Skar, J. E. (1981). Sexual behavior of preschool children. In L. L. Constantine & F. M. Martinson (Eds.), *Children and sex* (pp. 45–62). Boston, MA: Little, Brown.

Gurevich, M., Bower, J., Mathieson, C. M., & Dhayanandhan, B. (2007). "What do they look like and are they among us?": Bisexuality, (dis)closure, and (un)viability. In V. Clarke & E. Peel (Eds.), *Out in psychology: Lesbian, gay, bisexual, trans, and queer perspectives* (pp. 217–41). Chichester, England: Wiley.

Guttmacher Institute. (2006). *Facts on American teens' sexual and reproductive health.* New York, NY: Author.

Guttmacher Institute. (2012). *State policies in brief: Sex and HIV education.* New York, NY: Author. Retrieved from http://www.guttmacher.org/statecenter/spibs/spib_SE.pdf

Hare-Mustin, R. T., & Marecek, J. (1988). The meaning of difference: Gender theory, postmodernism, and psychology. *American Psychologist, 43*, 455–464. doi:10.1037/0003-066X.43.6.455

Hartley, H. (2006). The "pinking" of Viagra culture: Drug industry efforts to create and repackage sex drugs for women. *Sexualities, 9*, 363–378. doi:10.1177/1363460706065058

Heine, S. J. (2008). *Cultural psychology.* New York, NY: Norton.

Herdt, G. (1981). *Guardians of the flute.* New York, NY: McGraw-Hill.

Herman-Jeglínska, A., Grabowksa, A., & Dulko, S. (2002). Masculinity, femininity, and transsexualism. *Archives of Sexual Behavior, 31*, 527–534. doi:10.1023/A:1020611416035

Hofstede, G. (2001). *Culture's consequences: Comparing values, behaviors, institutions and organizations across nations* (2nd ed.). Thousand Oaks, CA: Sage.

Hofstede, G., & McCrae, R. R. (2004). Personality and culture revisited: Linking traits and dimensions of culture. *Cross-Cultural Research, 38*, 52–88. doi:10.1177/1069397103259443

Hollway, W. (1984). Women's power in heterosexual sex. *Women's Studies International Forum, 7*, 63–68. doi:10.1016/0277-5395(84)90085-2

Holmes, M. M., Seney, M. L., Goldman, B. D., & Forger, N. G. (2011). Social and hormonal triggers of neural plasticity in naked mole-rats. *Behavioural Brain Research, 218*, 234–239. doi:10.1016/j.bbr.2010.11.056

Hyde, J. S. (2005). The gender similarities hypothesis. *American Psychologist, 60*, 581–592. doi:10.1037/0003-066X.60.6.581

Hyde, J. S., & Durik, A. M. (2000). Gender differences in erotic plasticity—Evolutionary or sociocultural forces? Comment on Baumeister (2000). *Psychological Bulletin, 126*, 375–379. doi:10.1037/0033-2909.126.3.375

Intersex Society of North America. (1993–2008). *Who was David Reimer (also, sadly, known as "John/Joan")?* Retrieved from http://www.isna.org/faq/reimer

Janssen, E., Vorst, H., Finn, P., & Bancroft, J. (2002). The Sexual Inhibition (SIS) and Sexual Excitation (SES) Scales: I. Measuring sexual inhibition and excitation proneness in men. *Journal of Sex Research, 39*, 114–126. doi:10.1080/00224490209552130

Jones, E. E., & Sigall, H. (1971). The bogus pipeline: A new paradigm for measuring affect and attitude. *Psychological Bulletin, 76*, 349–364. doi:10.1037/h0031617

Jordan-Young, R. M. (2010). *Brain storm: The flaws in the science of sex differences.* Cambridge, MA: Harvard University Press.

Karraker, A., DeLamater, J., & Schwartz, C. R. (2011). Sexual frequency decline from midlife to later life. *Journals of Gerontology, Series B: Psychological Sciences and Social Sciences, 66*, 502–512. doi:10.1093/geronb/gbr058

Katz-Wise, S. L. (2012). *Beyond labels: Sexual fluidity and sexual identity development in sexual minority young adults.* Unpublished doctoral dissertation, University of Wisconsin–Madison.

Katz-Wise, S. L., & Hyde, J. S. (2012). Victimization experiences of lesbian, gay, and bisexual individuals: A meta-analysis. *Journal of Sex Research, 49*, 142–167. doi:10.1080/00224499.2011.637247

Kenrick, D. T., Li, N. P., & Butner, J. (2003). Dynamical evolutionary psychology: Individual decision rules and emergent social norms. *Psychological Review, 110*, 3–28. doi:10.1037/0033-295X.110.1.3

King, R., & Belsky, J. (2012). A typological approach to testing the evolutionary functions of human female orgasm. *Archives of Sexual Behavior, 41*, 1145–1160. doi:10.1007/s10508-012-0001-0

King, R., Belsky, J., Mah, K., & Binik, Y. (2011). Are there different types of female orgasm? *Archives of Sexual Behavior, 40*, 865–875. doi:10.1007/s10508-010-9639-7

Kitzinger, C., & Wilkinson, S. (1995). Transitions from heterosexuality to lesbianism: The discursive production of lesbian identities. *Developmental Psychology, 31*, 95–104. doi:10.1037/0012-1649.31.1.95

Kramarae, C., & Spender, D. (Eds.). (1992). *The knowledge explosion: Generations of feminist scholarship.* New York, NY: Columbia University Teachers College Press.

Kurdek, L. A. (2004). Are gay and lesbian cohabiting couples *really* different from heterosexual married couples? *Journal of Marriage and the Family, 66*, 880–900. doi:10.1111/j.0022-2445.2004.00060.x

Kurdek, L. A. (2005). What do we know about gay and lesbian couples? *Current Directions in Psychological Science, 14*, 251–254. doi:10.1111/j.0963-7214.2005.00375.x

Lamb, S. (2010). Feminist ideals for a healthy female adolescent sexuality: A critique. *Sex Roles, 62*, 294–306. doi:10.1007/s11199-009-9698-1

Lamb, S., Graling, K., & Lustig, K. (2011). Stereotypes in four current AOUM sexuality education curricula: Good girls, good boys, and the new gender equality. *American Journal of Sexuality Education, 6*, 360–380. doi:10.1080/15546128.2011.624477

Lamb, S., & Peterson, Z. D. (2012). Adolescent girls' sexual empowerment: Two feminists explore the concept. *Sex Roles, 66*, 703–712. doi:10.1007/s11199-011-9995-3

Langfeldt, T. (1981). Childhood masturbation. In L. L. Constantine & F. M. Martinson (Eds.), *Children and sex* (pp. 63–74). Boston, MA: Little, Brown.

Larsson, I., & Svedin, C. G. (2002). Sexual experiences in childhood: Young adults' recollections. *Archives of Sexual Behavior, 31*, 263–273. doi:10.1023/A:1015252903931

Laumann, E. O., Gagnon, J. H., Michael, R. T., & Michaels, S. (1994). *The social organization of sexuality: Sexual practices in the United States.* New York, NY: Columbia University Press.

LeVay, S. (2011). *Gay, straight, and the reason why: The science of sexual orientation.* New York, NY: Oxford University Press. doi:10.1007/s11199-011-9997-1

Levin, D. (2009). So sexy, so soon: The sexualization of childhood. In S. Olfman (Ed.), *The sexualization of childhood* (pp. 75–88). Westport, CT: Praeger.

Levin, R. J. (2004). An orgasm is . . . who defines what an orgasm is? *Sexual and Relationship Therapy, 19*, 101–107. doi:10.1080/14681990410001641663

Lickliter, R., & Honeycutt, H. (2003). Developmental dynamics: Toward a biologically plausible evolutionary psychology. *Psychological Bulletin, 129*, 819–835. doi:10.1037/0033-2909.129.6.819

Lindberg, L. D., & Maddow-Zimet, I. (2012). Consequences of sex education on teen and young adult sexual behaviors and outcomes. *Journal of Adolescent Health, 51*, 332–338. doi:10.1016/j.jadohealth.2011.12.028

Lippa, R. A. (2009). Sex differences in sex drive, sociosexuality, and height across 53 nations: Testing evolutionary and social structural theories. *Archives of Sexual Behavior, 38*, 631–651. doi:10.1007/s10508-007-9242-8

Lloyd, E. A., & Feldman, M. W. (2002). Evolutionary psychology: A view from evolutionary biology. *Psychological Inquiry, 13*, 150–156. doi:10.1207/S15327965PLI1302_04

Lund, T. (2012). Combining qualitative and quantitative approaches: Some arguments for mixed methods research. *Scandinavian Journal of Educational Research, 56*, 155–165. doi:10.1080/00313831.2011.568674

Lykins, A. D., Janssen, E., Newhouse, S., Heiman, J. R., & Rafaeli, E. (2012). The effects of similarity in sexual excitation, inhibition, and mood on sexual arousal problems and sexual satisfaction in newlywed couples. *Journal of Sexual Medicine, 9*, 1360–1366. doi:10.1111/j.1743-6109.2012.02698.x

Marecek, J., Crawford, M., & Popp, D. (2004). On the construction of gender, sex, and sexualities. In A. H. Eagly, A. E. Beall, & R. J. Sternberg (Eds.), *The psychology of gender* (pp. 192–216). New York, NY: Guilford Press.

Martinson, F. M. (1994). *The sexual life of children.* Westport, CT: Bergin & Garvey.

Masters, W. H., & Johnson, V. E. (1966). *Human sexual response.* Boston, MA: Little, Brown.

Masters, W. H., & Johnson, V. E. (1970). *Human sexual inadequacy.* Boston, MA: Little, Brown.

Masters, W. H., Johnson, V. E., & Kolodny, R. C. (1982). *Human sexuality.* Boston, MA: Little, Brown.

Matsumoto, D., & Juan, L. (2013). *Culture and psychology* (5th ed.). Belmont, CA: Cengage.

Matthews, A. K., Tartaro, J., & Hughes, T. L. (2002). A comparative study of lesbian and heterosexual women in committed relationships. *Journal of Lesbian Studies, 7*, 101–114. doi:10.1300/J155v07n01_07

McPhillips, K., Braun, V., & Gavey, N. (2001). Defining (hetero)sex: How imperative is the "coital imperative"? *Women's Studies International Forum, 24*, 229–240. doi:10.1016/S0277-5395(01)00160-1

Meyer, S., & Schwitzer, A. M. (1999). Stages of identity development among college students with minority sexual orientations. *Journal of College Student Psychotherapy, 13*, 41–65. doi:10.1300/J035v13n04_05

Milburn, M., Mather, R., & Conrad, S. (2000). The effects of viewing R-rated movie scenes that objectify women on perceptions of date rape. *Sex Roles, 43*, 645–664. doi:10.1023/A:1007152507914

Money, J. (1975). Ablatio penis: Normal male infant sex-reassigned as a girl. *Archives of Sexual Behavior, 4*, 65–71. doi:10.1007/BF01541887

Money, J. (1988). *Gay, straight, and in-between: The sexology of erotic orientation.* New York, NY: Oxford University Press.

Mustanski, B. S. (2001). Getting wired: Exploiting the Internet for the collection of valid sexuality data. *Journal of Sex Research, 38*, 292–301. doi:10.1080/00224490109552100

Mustanski, B. S., DuPree, M. G., Nievergelt, C. M., Bocklandt, S., Schork, N. J., & Hamer, D. H. (2005). A genomewide scan of male sexual orientation. *Human Genetics, 116*, 272–278. doi:10.1007/s00439-004-1241-4

Nardi, P. M. (1992). "Seamless souls": An introduction to men's friendships. In P. Nardi (Ed.), *Men's friendships* (pp. 1–14). Newbury Park, CA: Sage.

National Center for Health Statistics. (2012). *Sexual activity between males and females.* Retrieved from http://www.cdc.gov/nchs/nsfg/abc_list_s.htm#vaginalsexual

Nichols, M. (2004). Lesbian sexuality/female sexuality: Rethinking "lesbian bed death." *Sexual and Relationship Therapy, 19*, 363–371. doi:10.1080/14681990412331298036

Niewenweg, R., Smit, M. L., Walenkamp, M. J. E., & Wit, J. M. (2003). Adult height corrected for shrinking and secular trend. *Annals of Human Biology, 30*, 563–569. doi:10.1080/0301446032000112661

Nosek, B. A., Smyth, G. L., Sriram, N., Lindner, N. M., Devos, T., Ayala, A., . . . Greenwald, A. G. (2009). National differences in gender-science stereotypes predict national sex differences in science and math achievement. *Proceedings of the National Academy of Sciences, United States of America, 106*, 10593–10597. doi:10.1073/pnas.0809921106

Owen, J., & Fincham, F. D. (2011). Young adults' emotional reactions after hooking up encounters. *Archives of Sexual Behavior, 40*, 321–330. doi:10.1007/s10508-010-9652-x

Pastor, S. K. (2009). Education for sexual intimacy and agency. In N. Worcester & M. H. Whatley (Eds.), *Women's health: Readings on social, economic, and political issues* (5th ed., pp. 440–447). Dubuque, IA: Kendall/Hunt.

Pelto, P. J. (1968). The differences between "tight" and "loose" societies. *Trans-Action, 5*, 37–40. doi:10.1007/BF03180447

Peplau, L. A. (2003). Human sexuality: How do men and women differ? *Current Directions in Psychological Science, 12*, 37–40. doi:10.1111/1467-8721.01221

Petersen, J. L., & Hyde, J. S. (2010). A meta-analytic review of research on gender differences in sexuality, 1993–2007. *Psychological Bulletin, 136*, 21–38. doi:10.1037/a0017504

Pfaus, J. G. (2006). Of rats and women: Preclinical insights into the nature of female sexual desire. *Sexual and Relationship Therapy, 21*, 463–476. doi:10.1080/14681990600967011

Pfaus, J. G. (2009). Pathways of sexual desire. *Journal of Sexual Medicine, 6*, 1506–1533. doi:10.1111/j.1743-6109.2009.01309.x

Pfaus, J. G., Kippin, T. E., Coria-Avila, G. A., Gelez, H., Afonso, V. M., Ismail, N., & Parada, M. (2012). Who, what, where, when (and maybe even why)? How the experience of sexual reward connects sexual desire, preference, and performance. *Archives of Sexual Behavior, 41*, 31–62. doi:10.1007/s10508-012-9935-5

Price, M. N., & Hyde, J. S. (2009). When two isn't better than one: Predictors of early sexual activity in adolescence using a cumulative risk model. *Journal of Youth and Adolescence, 38*, 1059–1071. doi:10.1007/s10964-008-9351-2

Quina, K., Morokoff, P. J., Harlow, L. L., & Zurbriggen, E. L. (2004). Cognitive and attitudinal paths from childhood trauma to adult HIV risk. In L. J. Koenig, A. O'Leary, L. S. Doll, & W. Pequegnat (Eds.), *From child sexual abuse to adult sexual risk: Trauma, revictimization, and intervention* (pp. 117–134). Washington, DC: American Psychological Association. doi:10.1037/10785-006

Richters, J., Visser, R., Rissel, C., & Smith, A. (2003). Sex in Australia: Sexual difficulties in a representative sample of adults. *Australian and New Zealand Journal of Public Health, 27*, 164–170. doi:10.1111/j.1467-842X.2003.tb00804.x

Rosario, M., Schrimshaw, E. W., Hunter, J., & Braun, L. (2006). Sexual identity development among lesbian, gay, and bisexual youths: Consistency and change over time. *Journal of Sex Research, 43*, 46–58. doi:10.1080/00224490609552298

Russell, S. T. (2005). Conceptualizing positive adolescent sexuality development. *Sexuality Research and Social Policy, 2*, 4–12. doi:10.1525/srsp.2005.2.3.4

Russell, S. T., van Campen, K. S., & Muraco, J. A. (2012). Sexuality development in adolescence. In L. M. Carpenter & J. DeLamater (Eds.), *Sex for life: From virginity to Viagra, how sexuality changes throughout our lives* (pp. 70–87). New York, NY: New York University Press.

Rust, P. C. (1993). "Coming out" in the age of social constructionism: Sexual identity formation among lesbian and bisexual women. *Gender and Society, 7*, 50–77. doi:10.1177/089124393007001004

Sakaluk, J. K., & Milhausen, R. R. (2012). Factors influencing university students' explicit and implicit sexual double standards. *Journal of Sex Research, 49*, 464–476. doi:10.1080/00224499.2011.569976

Salk, R., & Hyde, J. S. (2012). Contemporary genetics for gender researchers: Not your grandma's genetics anymore. *Psychology of Women Quarterly, 36*, 395–410. doi:10.1177/0361684312461774

Savin-Williams, R., & Diamond, L. (1999). Sexual orientation. In W. Silverman & T. Ollendick (Eds.), *Developmental issues in the clinical treatment of children* (pp. 241–258). Needham Heights, MA: Allyn & Bacon.

Savin-Williams, R. C. (2001). A critique of research on sexual-minority youths. *Journal of Adolescence, 24*, 5–13. doi:10.1006/jado.2000.0369

Savin-Williams, R. C. (2005). *The new gay teenager*. Cambridge, MA: Harvard University Press.

Sexuality Information and Education Council of the United States. (2012a). *Culture and society* [Position statement]. Retrieved from http://www.siecus.org/index.cfm?fuseaction=Page.viewPage&pageId=494&parentID=472#culture%20and%20society

Sexuality Information and Education Council of the United States. (2012b). *Human sexuality* [Position statement]. Retrieved from http://www.siecus.org/index.cfm?fuseaction=Page.viewPage&pageId=494&parentID=472#human%20sexuality

Simons, T., & O'Connell, M. (2003). *Married-couple and unmarried-partner households: 2000*. Washington, DC: U.S. Census Bureau. Retrieved from http://www.census.gov/prod/2003pubs/censr-5.pdf

Smith, T. (2003). *American sexual behavior: Trends, socio-demographic differences, and risk behavior* (GSS Topical Report No. 25). Chicago, IL: University of Chicago, National Opinion Research Center.

Solomon-Fears, C. (2011). *Teenage pregnancy prevention: Statistics and programs*. Washington, DC: Congressional Research Service.

Sommers-Flanagan, R., Sommers-Flanagan, J., & Davis, B. (1993). What's happening on music television? A gender role content analysis. *Sex Roles, 28*, 745–753. doi:10.1007/BF00289991

Starr, C. R., & Ferguson, G. M. (2012). Sexy dolls, sexy grade-schoolers? Media and maternal influences on young girls' self-sexualization. *Sex Roles, 67*, 463–476. doi:10.1007/s11199-012-0183-x

Striepe, M. I., & Tolman, D. L. (2003). Mom, Dad, I'm straight: The coming out of gender ideologies in adolescent sexual-identity development. *Journal of Clinical Child and Adolescent Psychology, 32*, 523–530. doi:10.1207/S15374424JCCP3204_4

Thigpen, J. W. (2012). Childhood sexuality: Exploring culture as context. In L. M. Carpenter & J. DeLamater (Eds.), *Sex for life: From virginity to Viagra, how sexuality changes throughout our lives* (pp. 45–69). New York, NY: New York University Press.

Thompson, S. (1995). *Going all the way*. New York, NY: Hill & Wang.

Tiefer, L. (1999). Challenging sexual naturalism, the Shibboleth of sex research and popular sexology. In D. Bernstein (Ed.), *Current theory and research in motivation* (pp. 143–172). Lincoln: University of Nebraska Press.

Tiefer, L. (2001). A new view of women's sexual problems: Why new? Why now? *Journal of Sex Research, 38*, 89–96. doi:10.1080/00224490109552075

Tiefer, L. (2002). Arriving at a "new view" of women's sexual problems: Background, theory and activism. *Women and Therapy, 24*, 63–98. doi:10.1300/J015v24n01_12

Tolman, D. L. (2002). *Dilemmas of desire: Teenage girls talk about sexuality*. Cambridge, MA: Harvard University Press.

Tolman, D. L. (2012). Female adolescents, sexual empowerment and desire: A missing discourse of gender inequity. *Sex Roles, 66*, 746–757. doi:10.1007/s11199-012-0122-x

Tolman, D. L., & Diamond, L. M. (2001). Desegregating sexuality research: Cultural and biological perspectives on gender and desire. *Annual Review of Sex Research, 12*, 33–74.

Tolman, D. L., & Higgins, T. E. (1996). How being a good girl can be bad for girls. In N. B. Maglin & D. Perry (Eds.), *Bad girls/good girls: Women, sex, and power in the nineties* (pp. 205–225). Piscataway, NJ: Rutgers University Press.

Tolman, D. L., Hirschman, C., & Impett, E. A. (2005). There is more to the story: The place of qualitative research on female adolescent sexuality in policy making. *Sexuality Research and Social Policy, 2*, 4–17. doi:10.1525/srsp.2005.2.4.4

Tolman, D. L., & McClelland, S. I. (2011). Normative sexuality development in adolescence: A decade in review, 2000–2009. *Journal of Research on Adolescence, 21*, 242–255. doi:10.1111/j.1532-7795.2010.00726.x

Tooby, J., & Cosmides, L. (1992). The psychological foundations of culture. In J. Barkow, L. Cosmides, & J. Tooby (Eds.), *The adapted mind: Evolutionary psychology and the generation of culture* (pp. 19–136). New York, NY: Oxford University Press.

Trenholm, C., Devaney, B., Fortson, K., Quay, L., Wheeler, J., & Clark, M. (2007). *Impacts of four Title V, Section 510 abstinence education programs: Final report.* Princeton, NJ: Mathematica Policy Research.

Triandis, H. C. (1989). The self and social behavior in differing cultural contexts. *Psychological Review, 96*, 506–520. doi:10.1037/0033-295X.96.3.506

Trivers, R. L. (1972). Parental investment and sexual selection. In B. Campbell (Ed.), *Sexual selection and the descent of man* (pp. 136–179). Chicago, IL: Aldine.

Udry, J. R. (1988). Biological predispositions and social control in adolescent sexual behavior. *American Sociological Review, 53*, 709–722. doi:10.2307/2095817

Ward, L. M., Hansbrough, E., & Walker, E. (2005). Contributions of music video exposure to Black adolescents' gender and sexual schemas. *Journal of Adolescent Research, 20*, 143–166. doi:10.1177/0743558404271135

Watts, C., & Zimmerman, C. (2002). Violence against women: Global scope and magnitude. *Lancet, 359*, 1232–1237. doi:10.1016/S0140-6736(02)08221-1

Weeks, J. (1995). *Invented moralities: Sexual values in an age of uncertainty*. New York, NY: Columbia University Press.

Weinberg, M. S., Williams, C. J., & Pryor, D. W. (1994). *Dual attraction: Understanding bisexuality*. New York, NY: Oxford University Press.

Wells, B., & Twenge, J. (2005). Changes in young people's sexual behavior and attitudes, 1943–1999: A cross-temporal meta-analysis. *Review of General Psychology, 9*, 249–261. doi:10.1037/1089-2680.9.3.249

Widemo, F., & Saether, S. A. (1999). Beauty is in the eye of the beholder: Causes and consequences of variation in mating preferences. *Trends in Ecology and Evolution, 14*, 26–31. doi:10.1016/S0169-5347(98)01531-6

Wilson, E. O. (1975). *Sociobiology: The new synthesis.* Cambridge, MA: Harvard University Press.

Woo, J. S. T., Brotto, L. A., & Gorzalka, B. B. (2012). The relationship between sex guilt and sexual desire in a community sample of Chinese and Euro-Canadian women. *Journal of Sex Research, 49*, 290–298. doi:10.1080/00224499.2010.551792

CHAPTER 3

PSYCHOLOGY AND SEXUALITY IN HISTORICAL TIME

Michael Pettit and Peter Hegarty

Sex and sexuality are inconceivable outside of time. Like all living things, humans are fundamentally entities that unfold over time in a unidirectional fashion. They think, feel, and behave in time. To explain human conduct, psychologists have looked to at least four different kinds of temporality: (a) the very slow *evolutionary* time that has shaped the species, (b) the considerably less slow *historical* time within which cultural change happens, (c) the *developmental* time within which individual lives are lived, and (d) the immediate *situational* time that can be captured by experiments and studies of interventions, lasting anywhere from milliseconds to a few weeks. These kinds of time are not mutually exclusive because time is continuous. These temporalities are nested within each other. Historically, when it comes to sexuality, psychology's methods and theories have tended to privilege lines of debates between evolutionary time versus developmental time, or nature versus nurture. Such dichotomies (and even discussions of their interaction) particularly neglect the relationship between psychology and events that unfold in historical time courses that vary in length between the span of human history to a single generation. In this chapter, we explain why psychologists ought not to let historical time slip from their view.

Several features of U.S. psychology have contributed to the dismissal of a historical perspective on sexuality. First, psychology has long been shaped by dilemmas between its status as a science and its status as a field of application. In particular, the rise of clinical psychology and mental health expertise in the latter half of the 20th century has led to tensions between rationales for the application of psychology and standards of disinterested scientific description and explanation. Many psychologists spend much of their lives engaged in urgent work helping people with unbearable distress. For such psychologists, it can appear that there is little pragmatic benefit in developing an understanding of the historical events that constrain and shape both them and their clients.

Second, since at least the 1940s almost every psychologist has espoused some form of interactionism in which individual conduct is the product of the intersecting, or sometimes competing, influences of nature and nurture or biology and environment (see Chapter 1, this volume). When human sexuality is understood as the interaction of evolution and development, it becomes impossible to tease apart the effects of consistency within or between people that are the result of evolutionary or historical time. Indeed, in our current moment, psychology is still wrestling with a history of making universal claims on the basis of samples of people drawn from highly particular societies, such as U.S. campuses (Arnett, 2008; Henrich, Heine, & Norenzayan, 2010). One could argue that the recent turn to culture is another way of assessing the effects of historical time. Our concern is that without recognizing the events of historical time, cultural psychology risks overemphasizing gross and static contrasts between Western individualistic and Eastern collectivist societies

This research was supported by a Social Sciences and Humanities Research Council standard research grant to Michael Pettit.

http://dx.doi.org/10.1037/14193-003
APA Handbook of Sexuality and Psychology: Vol. 1. Person-Based Approaches, D. L. Tolman and L. M. Diamond (Editors-in-Chief)

(Adams & Markus, 2004). In other words, we advocate an "eventful" (Sewell, 2005) psychology that recognizes change over historical time within a culture and is attentive to the past circumstances that went into making current conditions. An eventful psychology adopts a dynamic ontology of cultures as interactive rather than bounded and as entities characterized by internal fragmentation rather than homogeneity (see Volume 2, Chapter 6, this handbook).

A focus on historical events has much to contribute to the psychology of sexuality. The psychology of sexuality lends itself particularly well to an eventful psychology because historians have documented notable shifts in how humans have performed, sanctioned, understood, and embodied sexuality. In this chapter, we first survey developments in the history of psychology and the history of sexuality, two intellectual traditions that have only begun to engage explicitly in recent years. Next, we examine four kinds of events that unfold in historical time and that profoundly influence the psychology of sexuality: changes in sexual experiences, norms, epistemologies, and selves. By so doing, we aim to flesh out the general point that we have made that psychologists' core concerns manifest themselves in historical time.

PSYCHOLOGY AND ITS HISTORY

As historian John O'Donnell (1979) pointed out, psychologists have engaged in the writing of their discipline's history since the beginning of modern science in the late 19th century. History served a pedagogical function, socializing students into the discipline by foregrounding some achievements and diminishing others, by identifying certain areas and methods as legitimate while excluding others. The 1970s saw the emergence of histories more critical of psychology's narratives of progressive development. This new history had several distinguishing features, namely a return to the primary—and especially unpublished archival—sources to detail the discipline's history (Samelson, 1974) and a debunking of the myths conveyed by textbooks surrounding famous experiments or scientists (Harris, 1979). The uncovering of such "invented traditions" (Hobsbawm & Ranger, 1983) in psychology textbooks raised questions about objectivity: Who is selecting which stories from the past and with what effect on the future? Feminist and antiracist histories of psychology attempted to recover the history of previously ignored and excluded psychologists (Guthrie, 1976; Scarborough & Furumoto, 1987). Historical inquiry showed psychology frequently intervened in organizations with ostensibly value-neutral scientific motives that nonetheless tipped struggles between workers and management in favor of the latter (Finison, 1976). Intense debates about race and IQ preoccupied the social sciences in the 1970s and prompted new histories about both "race"[1] and IQ testing in U.S. psychology (e.g., Richards, 1997). Psychologists on all sides of this debate made strategic use of this history. In contrast, important feminist work on the history of psychology (e.g., Cherry, 1995; Morawski, 1985; Scarborough & Furumoto, 1987; Shields, 1975) remained marginal among both historians and psychologists for a longer period of time (Bayer, 2004).

The new history issued yet another challenge to psychology: It questioned the very objects of "the individual," "the mind," and "behavior" that psychologists have often presumed to be natural kinds (Danziger, 1997). By the early 1990s, cultural psychologists successfully forced the recognition within the United States that the assumption that humans were all individualist was a false universalism and might well have been an expression of ethnocentrism in U.S. psychology (Markus & Kitayama, 1991). Qualitative researchers, largely outside the United States, developed nonindividualistic methods for studying discourses that have been taken up less in the United States than in any other country (e.g., Potter & Wetherell, 1987). Along with these developments, historians engaged with more substantive questions about what the range of psychology might be when individualist assumptions are suspended (Smith, 1988), used historical methods to explain how U.S. psychology came to take individual subjects as its objects of study (Danziger, 1990), and

[1]We have put the term *race* in quotation marks following Richards's (1997, pp. x–xi) own usage to distance the term from the idea that social categories named as "race" have a biological basis.

articulated how such methods were at odds with feminist theories of science (Morawski, 1994). In short, the new and revised history was less concerned with chronicling the achievements of the past and aimed instead to contextualize and offer a critical space to ask such questions as "Where in the world is psychology?" and "How can psychology be put in its place?" (Richards, 2009).

TOWARD A HISTORICAL UNDERSTANDING OF SEXUALITY

Even within such revisionist histories of psychology, remarkably little sustained attention has been paid to sexuality as a core topic of analysis. With the notable exception of Freud's theory of psychosexual development, sex is rarely mentioned in textbooks on the history of psychology. And yet, even the sex lives of psychologists themselves have had determinative effects on their lives, from the affair between John Watson and Rosalie Rayner leading to his dismissal from the academy (Buckley, 1994) to the arrest of Alan Turing on charges of gross indecency for having sex with another man in private (Hodges, 1983). Classic experiments have been read for their sexual politics, such as Nicholson's (2011) reading of reactions to Milgram's obedience studies as being shaped by Cold War anxieties about American manhood. Feminist histories of psychology have unearthed numerous ways that assumptions about the relationship between reproductive potential and intellectual capacity have shaped the opportunities for women and men to participate in science (Shields, 1975). In spite of these turning points in history, historians of psychology—as have other students of psychology—have been tutored to ignore sex or to confine it to the margins and footnotes, such as the almost total neglect of lesbian, gay, and bisexual lives in the psychology textbooks of all areas (Barker, 2007).

Contrast this situation with the outpouring of work on the history of sexuality in recent decades in which psychology, psychiatry, pedagogy, and psychoanalysis have featured prominently (Lunbeck, 1994; Meyerowitz, 2004; Nye, 1993). Psychology and sex research have figured particularly in historical narratives about a shift away from religious authority to determine norms for sexual conduct toward secular medical and legal authority (D'Emilio & Freedman, 1998). For example, histories of shifting norms about masturbation make frequent reference to psychologist G. Stanley Hall's 1904 book *Adolescence* (Laqueur, 2003). Histories of homosexuality (Terry, 1999), eugenics (Kline, 2001; Stern, 2005), and sex survey research methods (Ericksen & Steffen, 2001) have all made new sense out of IQ pioneer Lewis Terman's research on individual differences in sexuality and gender. Donna Haraway's (1989) ground-breaking feminist histories of biology engage substantively with such key comparative psychologists as Robert Yerkes and Harry Harlow. The actions of psychologists and psychiatrists in detecting straight men, who they assumed were pretending to be gay, are pivotal to understanding the history of the exclusion of gay and lesbian people from serving in the U.S. armed forces (Bérubé, 2010). Although psychologists' ways for accounting for the history of sexuality in historical terms are often limited to biographical references to events in the lives of individuals, historians who are interested in power, social movements, and broader shifts in the history of science and medicine have found themselves telling stories about psychologists and their social influence. Only in recent years has the study of the history of sexuality begun to affect the small research community in the history of psychology with particular force.

Around the same time as North American historians of psychology were engaging with more critical histories of the discipline, the French philosopher–historian Michel Foucault (1978) published his *The History of Sexuality: An Introduction*. As were evolutionary psychologists (Cassidy, 2007), Foucault was frustrated by the limited explanatory potential of both Freudian and Marxist schemes, and he particularly targeted theorists who argued that societies varied primarily in the extent to which sexuality was repressed or liberated within them (e.g., Marcuse, 1955). Foucault recast the Victorian era not as a period of sexual repression but as one in which the policing and management of sexuality led to the production of discourses around sex. Rather than being rarefied and confined, talk about sex intensified, multiplied, and became diffuse. For Foucault, a *discourse* was a system of ideas, especially problems, that structured perception and action. Defining certain behaviors as problematic led to the creation of specific sexual identities. In other words, Foucault presented an eventful history of Western cultures in which events influenced the form that individual sexualities would take, quite independent of the nature of the species or the individual or group differences within it. His approach to discourses made him skeptical of all claims about species or individual nature, because they were inseparable from the discourses that produced them. Foucault argued that these discourses proliferated through medical and legal practices that bore a close resemblance to the Catholic practice of confession. Indeed, Foucault characterized early 20th-century psychoanalysis as exemplary of this confessional model of truth about the self. Some of these identities are still with us, such as the homosexual or the sexual criminal. Other identities that used to cohere as medical types now exist largely as slang, including masturbators or hysterics. Masturbation was once considered a serious illness (Laqueur, 2003). Today, people are unlikely to think that there is a medical diagnosis that corresponds to the insult that someone is a jerk-off (in North America) or a wanker (in the United Kingdom).

Foucault's (1978) work stands out for its use of sexuality to forward a general account of the history of power. Rather than seeing power as concentrated in particular institutions (as Marxists might assume) or as organized by familial dynamics (as Freudians might assume), Foucault argued that power was produced through historical events and operated in a reciprocal fashion in all human relationships. Foucault's *The History of Sexuality* deserves to be considered a landmark event in the intellectual history of sexuality. In the history of the history of sexuality, its publication was an event in historical time that constituted a radical break from conceptualizing the link between sex, power, and nature in terms of repression and toward an understanding of this history in terms of the productive power of proliferating discourses (Hegarty, 2007).

This is not to say that Foucault's (1978) schema is the last or the most authoritative word on the history of sexuality. Gay and lesbian historians have taken very different approaches to the hypothesis that homosexuality as an identity came into being in the late 19th century (Boswell, 1980; Halperin, 1990). Foucault's pessimism about the possibility of individual agency seemed to offer little room for the emancipation from power relations promised by contemporary claims about sexual liberation, gay liberation, or women's liberation (Fraser, 1989). Even historians sympathetic to Foucault's approach criticized the stark contrast he made between Asian erotic arts centered on pleasure and European *scientia sexualis* organized around knowledge and power (Chiang, 2010; Stoler, 1995). In some Western sites in which discourses of sexuality have proliferated, such as prisons, sexual behavior has not followed the narrative of constructing types on the basis of behavior (Kunzel, 2008). Nor can Foucault's behavior-to-species narrative account for opposition to it, such as that affected by Kinsey's insistence that sexuality was continuous and that one cannot separate "the sheep from the goats" (Hegarty, 2013, Chapter 4). Rather than comb Foucault's words for eternal truths, we urge psychologists to look at these works and at such peer-reviewed journals as *Sexualities, GLQ,* and *Journal of the History of Sexuality,* all of which have published articles about the production of discourses of sexuality in historical time.

All three of these journals, which began publishing in the 1990s, are but one sign of how the history of sexuality became a recognized specialty during that decade. Simultaneously, the center of gravity for professional history was moving from a social history, which consisted of studying the behavioral patterns of the lives of politically marginalized people, toward a cultural history, which focused on identities and symbolic representations of meaning (Scott, 1986). Rather than assume that the categories of race, class, and gender referred to fixed and static things, the goal was to trace their changing contours and meaning in order to demonstrate their contingency and fluidity. For example, there was a shift away from histories of the African American experience toward an understanding of the meaning of Blackness in the United States. Many social historians in the 1970s devoted considerable attention to examining marriage patterns under slavery and after emancipation. In contrast, cultural historians in the

1990s focused more on the imagery of African American sexuality in mass culture—such as the myth of the Black rapist—to better understand perceptions of racial difference. The history of sexuality as a whole expanded to include not only the recovery of famous homosexual individuals and accounts of liberation movements, but an analysis of the historically shifting meanings ascribed to sex in different times and places (see Volume 2, Chapter 9, this handbook).

This historical literature offers tremendous intellectual resources for psychologists engaged in diverse scientific and therapeutic work. Focusing almost exclusively on examples from English-speaking countries from the past 2 centuries—the sites that are overrepresented in the current limited understandings of psychology's international history (Brock, 2006)—we use the rest of the space in this chapter to outline the work done by historians to map the significant changes in four key areas of sexuality: (a) bodies, behaviors, and pleasures; (b) sexual norms; (c) sexual epistemologies and concepts; and (d) sexual selves. We then conclude with some general points about how psychologists might use this work.

Bodies, Behaviors, and Pleasures

People have not had the same kinds of bodies or enjoyed the same kinds of sexual practices with the same kinds of frequency in all places in all cultures in all times. Obtaining reliable evidence of sexual conduct, which is often scripted as private and frequently restricted by religious, moral, and legal codes, is difficult. Historians have used vital statistics, oral histories, police records, and readings of the proscriptive literature "against the grain" to get some indication of stability and change in sexual practices in historical time.

Consider, for example, Cook's (2004) sophisticated historical account of sexual behavior that used both fertility statistics and sex manuals to suggest that a long sexual revolution characterized Britain in the period between 1820 and 1975. Birth rates declined across Western Europe in the late 19th century, whereas marriage rates did not. Without reliable contraception, this demographic change suggests that married women sought to control their reproduction by avoiding coitus. More speculatively, Cook argued that for women who were trained to dislike their genitals through particularly harsh toilet training regimes, the rejection of sexual desire in favor of strict sexual self-control (including the avoidance of masturbation) represented an important form of female agency and resistance to existing gendered expectations. Beginning in the 1920s, sex reform literature provided men and women with positive information about sexuality and promised effective means of birth control. These new norms eroded the ideal of female emotional and sexual self-control that had previously led to low frequencies of intercourse. In England, both marital fertility rates and the number of illegitimate children began to rise in 1933. The provisions provided by the postwar welfare state further diminished the risks for women associated with childbearing. The introduction of the contraceptive pill in 1960 offered women a novel means of controlling their fertility while engaging in intercourse, and the National Health Service's coverage of the contraceptive pill for unmarried women beginning in the 1970s completed this historical transformation. Rather than reducing these behavioral and demographic changes simply to technology or the inevitable imperatives of modernization, Cook focused on how culturally and historically specific attitudes about sex shaped behavior while also focusing on the agency of women in managing their sexuality (see also Chapter 25, this volume).

Such detailed histories help to reframe overly generalized theories about cultural change. According to the demographic transition theory of modernization, all populations experience the following sequence: (a) a traditional equilibrium resulting from both high fertility and infant mortality rates; (b) an explosion as urbanization and industrialization lower mortality without affecting fertility; and (c) a new equilibrium as people embrace the advantages of limiting their fertility (Ramsden, 2002). Demographic transition became one of the primary ways in which U.S. economists and social planners intervened in the developing world, seeking to alter existing reproductive patterns to initiate the first stage of modernization (Connelly, 2008; Murphy, 2013). Long-term research on more than a thousand provinces in different European countries by Princeton University's European Fertility Project failed to identify a single universal transition pattern (Greenhalgh, 1995). Although general theories of modernization continue to be cited as causal determinants of attitudes toward sexuality and gender, histories that focus on events in particular locales show the limits of assuming that modernization is the same thing everywhere. Briggs's (2002) account of the politics of population in 20th-century Puerto Rico is a particularly salient reminder to attend to conditions on the ground. She documented the surprising alignment of local women's groups and U.S. population experts that were often in tension with the views of Puerto Rican Catholic nationalists and mainland feminist organizations (see also Volume 2, Chapters 8 and 9, this handbook). This global history of attempts at managing reproduction shows that not only homosexuality but also heterosexuality has a history (see also Katz, 1995).

Norms and the Regulation of Sexuality

Social norms that encourage and forbid sexual conduct are a persistent concern for psychologists, who often aim their science at understanding the effects of such norms and their therapeutic interventions at undoing the harm they can cause. We have already mentioned the profound shifts in norms about masturbation over the 20th century, and psychologists' historical entanglement with the pathologization of homosexuality is another clear case in point. In this domain, norms have clearly changed throughout recent historical time, and psychologists have been involved as historical actors in these events in multiple ways. Since the 1970s, homosexuality has largely been understood through a stigma paradigm, and psychologists have been widely concerned with the effects of constricted sexual norms that fail to recognize same-sex expression on the well-being of lesbian, gay, and bisexual people (Meyer, 2003). In an era of diagnosis, psychologists were not concerned with studying same-sex relationships because they were interpreted as expressions of gay and lesbian individuals' pathology (Morin, 1977). Now, psychological research on same-sex relationships promises to be historically important in legal battles over marriage equality (e.g., Peplau & Fingerhut, 2007). Norms shift dramatically over historical time.

The history of sexuality helps psychologists to understand how some contemporary arguments against marriage equality involve invented traditions that do not match with the best scholarly literature on the past. The conviction that the purpose of marriage is traditionally that of securing the happiness and satisfaction of a necessarily heterosexual couple has a surprisingly recent historical vintage. Not until the 1920s did U.S. social scientists and sex reformers began to use the term *companionate marriage* to designate a novel vision of family life among the middle class (Davis, 2008). Marriage was defined as an equal partnership focused on mutual emotional and sexual satisfaction rather than governed by patriarchal control (Lindsey & Evans, 1927). Marital advice for the middle classes assured readers that marital happiness could be ensured through the use of contraception, premarital sex, and easy divorce (Neuhaus, 2000). Even eugenicists endorsed these norms, as they seemed to ensure stable families for the rearing of "fit" children (Kline, 2001). More an anticipatory imagining of what marriage could become than an empirical description of middle-class sexual relations, the new ideal of companionate marriage reflected historical changes in divorce, legal rights for women, and the use of contraception (Davis, 2008). Although contraception became legally available in the 1930s, psychologists turned away from the idea that good sex made for healthy marriages, focusing instead on the now-familiar hypothesis that happy partners had similar personalities (Terman, 1938). We describe the companionate marriage movement not to suggest that "affective individualism" or feelings among spouses and children did not exist before this period (Stone, 1977). Rather, a new social ideal emerged at this time, one that emphasized how a marriage should first and foremost be about emotional compatibility and sexual satisfaction, with economic, religious, or communal commitments and demands becoming secondary.

Historical changes in sexual behavior and affect are often deeply entangled with changes in norms, and such norms are most obviously expressed through the legal regulation of sex (see Volume 2, Chapter 10, this handbook). Over the 20th century, citizenship in the United States has become more intertwined with sexuality rather than less. Opponents of marriage equality often refer to "traditional marriage" and "family values" to support their arguments that it is un-American, or simply unsafe, to allow people of the same sex to marry each other. Since the colonial period, various legislatures have passed laws and ordinances prohibiting certain sexual acts between humans, and between humans and animals. In the 20th century, antisodomy laws increasingly focused on homosexuals as a class of people, consistent with Foucault's hypothesis about the shift from the regulation of behavior to the regulation of groups of people (Chauncey, 2004).

The shifts between the experience of homosexuality as conduct and as identity trouble the contemporary understanding that gay people are either in or out of the closet. Chauncey (1994) argued that the closet is the wrong spatial metaphor for understanding gay identity, because homosexuality was a highly visible element in the sexualized public spaces of New York City's Prohibition Era nightlife, which prominently featured drag balls and beauty parades. His history challenges the image of homosexual men living primarily closeted lives in isolation from one another before the Stonewall riots in 1969. This modern gay sociality began in the working-class Bowery district of the 1890s, where a multitude of sexualities flourished. In this social world, "normal" masculinity hinged on exclusively performing the insertive role during intercourse rather than the sex of one's partner. Policemen and sailors engaged in the trade without identifying as homosexual. In contrast to the more circumspect and privacy-seeking middle-class "queers" who visited the district, working-class "fairies" exaggerated their feminine qualities through dress and bodily gesture. The power of Chauncey's account is the detail with which he documented the geographical diffusion of this culture to different New York neighborhoods, where it took on new meanings, and the importance of racial, class, and gendered imperatives in fragmenting sexual identities. This culture reached its apex during the 1920s because many elite New Yorkers flaunted the law and social conventions to partake in the world of speakeasies and Harlem club life. The increased policing of liquor establishments after the repeal of Prohibition erased much of "Gay New York." Elites had less inclination to venture pseudoanonymously into less reputable neighborhoods to find pleasure. The legalization of alcohol meant that the public sociality associated with now licensed bars and clubs met with greater surveillance. This led to a solidified heterosexual–homosexual binary and the invention of the closet at midcentury (Chauncey, 1994; Katz, 1995).

The immediate postwar period witnessed a host of new federal restrictions on sexuality. A 1945 ruling denied the welfare state benefits extending from the G.I. Bill to those dishonorably discharged from the military because of homosexual acts or tendencies (Canaday, 2009). In 1950, the Senate struck an inquiry to investigate the extent of the government's employment of homosexuals and other sex perverts. Three years later, Dwight D. Eisenhower issued Executive Order 10450, which defined loyalty among government employees in terms of conduct and character and excluded individuals with a history of same-sex behavior on the grounds that their sexual perversion compromised national security (Johnson, 2004). In 1952, Congress formally prohibited the immigration of gay people as "sex psychopaths" and allowed for the deportation of people who hid their sexual inclinations on entry. In *Boutlier v. INS* (1967), the same Supreme Court upheld that statute (Stein, 2010). Between the 1930s and 1960s, legislatures rewrote these statutes to specifically regulate the lives of homosexual people of all genders rather than the sex acts. Between the 1987 *Bowers v. Hardwick* and 2003 *Lawrence v. Texas* judgments, U.S. law was compromised by the error of assuming that the legal category of sodomy defined a class of people as homosexual (Chauncey, 2004).

During the late 1960s, a number of landmark Supreme Court decisions supported companionate marriage. *Griswold v. Connecticut* (1965) interpreted the Constitution as guaranteeing a right to privacy when it protected married couples in their pursuit of contraception. The court extended this right to unmarried individuals with *Eisenstadt v. Baird* (1972). *Loving v. Virginia* (1967) struck down Virginia's 1924 antimiscegenation law, declaring that the states could not prohibit individuals from marrying on the basis of their race. Most famously, *Roe v. Wade* (1973) granted legal protection to abortion not on the grounds of a woman's right to choose but by extending the right to privacy principle from *Griswold v. Connecticut*. The normalization of companionate marriage by the 1960s led many social scientists to problematize the structure of the African American family. The prevalence of single-mother households was seen as a marker of social pathology: a damaged Black psyche resulting from the long-term effects of slavery as a system that did not acknowledge the sanctity of marriage and permitted the breakup of families for economic gain (Cohen, 1997). Others countered that the standard of the nuclear family was misplaced and that rather than exhibiting the antisocial effects of slavery, the matrilineal and multigeneration kinship networks reflected the survival of African cultural norms (Feldstein, 2000). In sum, the midcentury sexual revolution had uneven impacts and legacies on different U.S. groups and communities.

Shifting Epistemologies

The debate over the "pathology" of the African American family indicates how scientific research on sexuality was closely bound to changing political realties. As suggested by Foucault (1978), the second half of the 19th century saw the proliferation of scientific attempts to ascertain the truth about sex. Historians of science are very interested in the different methods deployed by psychologists and sexologists and the different—often incompatible—forms of knowledge that they generate. Psychologists have written case histories, conducted surveys, and experimented on humans and other species. The case history probably represents the earliest form of scientific knowledge about sexuality. Emerging from the clinical encounter between doctor and patient, psychoanalysis exemplifies this style of reasoning. Other important contributors to this genre include psychiatrist Richard von Krafft-Ebing's *Psychopathia Sexualis* (1886) and sexologist Havelock Ellis's *Sexual Inversion* (Ellis & Symonds, 1897). The Committee for Research in Problems of Sex (CRPS; 1921–1961) was initiated by the Rockefeller Foundation in response to concerns about prostitution, and it became the major funder of sex research in the United States for several decades, encouraging both experimental and survey studies. The CRPS was born out of eugenic concerns to solve social problems such as prostitution and the spread of sexually transmitted diseases. Zoologist Frank Lillie managed to lobby the committee to focus on basic research, and the CRPS became the major U.S. patron of the endocrinology gold rush during the 1920s (Clarke, 1998). Despite this focus, psychologists such as Robert Yerkes dominated the leadership of the CRPS (Pickren, 1997). In 1931, it refocused its attention on the psychobiology of sex, starting to fund Kinsey's major surveys a decade later.

Although psychological scientists might examine differences between methods to triangulate, or to tease out new empirical questions, and applied psychologists might examine them to close the gap between theory and practice, historians narrate how different methods produce different truths at different points in historical time. Considerable historical debate has occurred over the role that sexology has played in pathologizing sexual deviance. Some historians have emphasized the eugenic concerns of scientists who studied sexual variance in the hopes of eliminating it and who erased complicated sexual subjectivities in their scientific writing (Haraway, 1989; Rosario, 1997; Serlin, 2012; Terry, 1999). Other historians have suggested a more collaborative relationship between physicians and gay rights advocates. From Weimar Germany to the Cold War United States, members of the homophile movement hoped that spreading knowledge about sexual variation would aid in its decriminalization. Psychiatrists backed decriminalization less out of pro-homosexual sentiments and more to wrest control over this issue from the legal system and to bolster their own authority (Crozier, 2000; Minton, 2002; Sengoopta, 1998). Recently, we have narrated events that unfolded in time when CRPS funds were channeled into projects leading to unanticipated political and epistemological complications emerging from interactions between researchers, their assistants, and their human and animal participants (Hegarty, 2012; Pettit, 2012).

This divergence in interpretation of the historical effects of sex research is partially a consequence of the ways in which the moral authority of nature (Daston & Vidal, 2004) has played different roles in social scientific discussions of sexuality compared with other forms of identity. When it came to race and gender, the consensus among late 20th-century scientists was that these were fictions from a biological standpoint and largely the product of social convention. In contrast, many liberal social scientists embraced "born that way" arguments grounded in genetics, prenatal hormones, and animal models to combat assertions that homosexual behavior constituted a form of unnatural deviance. This has especially been the case since the 1970s, as conservative activists sought to overturn modest civil rights legislation for lesbian, gay, bisexual, and transgender people (Pettit, 2011). Nevertheless, much is missed in this search for the somatic homosexual body. For example, suggestive evidence exists that cultural norms mediate the influence of hormones over human behavior (Kim et al., 2010). As historians of psychology, we would emphasize not only how culture affects hormones in the bodies of research subjects but also the sense that scientists make of such patterns of data (see Chapter 19, this volume). Over the 20th century, the same sexual behavior in rats has been ignored, seen as homosexual, interpreted as suggestive of innate bisexuality, and dismissed as merely representing the artifice of caged conditions (Pettit, 2012).

One of the most salient effects of these new scientific epistemologies was an explosion in the vocabulary to discuss sex: *heterosexuality, gender, sexual orientation, sexual identity,* and *asexuality* (see Chapter 18, this volume). The story of *sex* and *gender,* two basic keywords for understanding sexuality, is illustrative. The psychologist John Money did much to popularize the idea that *sex* refers to one's biology and *gender* refers to one's social role (Money & Ehrhardt, 1972). Money's concepts emerged from his clinical work with intersex infants at his Gender Identity Clinic at Johns Hopkins University starting in 1950s. He held that early childhood was when one's sense of one's own gender was fluid, but that ambiguous gender roles in adulthood were pathological. As a result, he recommended fixing a gender (identity) to children with ambiguous genitals soon after their birth and performing the required surgeries, so that their conduct could be steered toward the appropriate gender role. In the 1970s, the sex–gender distinction became the benchmark of second-wave feminist interventions in the social sciences, and many feminists cited Money's work with enthusiasm (e.g., Weisstein, 1971). Separating gender from sex suggested that it was possible to intervene with and ameliorate the social conditioning that led to unequal gender roles (see Chapter 2, this volume). In the past 2 decades, intersex activists and later feminist scholars have drawn attention to the harms done to intersex people that occurred in the era of historical time affected by Money's work (e.g., Chase, 1998; Fausto-Sterling, 2000; Kessler, 1998). It is an open question as to whether new medical consensus statements that acknowledge these harms and emphasize the psychosocial needs of people who are intersexed has brought about a substantively different period of historical time in which 21st-century intersex lives will be lived (Hughes, Houk, Ahmed, & Lee, 2006).

Large shifts in the epistemologies deployed by psychology to make sense of sexuality have occurred in the past. When it comes to addressing public policy, psychology has moved from viewing homosexuality as a sign of sickness to understanding homosexuality as a species to understanding homosexuality as a kind of subjectivity (Hammack & Windell, 2011). During the 1950s, the experimental psychologist Evelyn Hooker conducted experiments demonstrating the inability of expert clinicians to distinguish the Rorschach responses of heterosexual and homosexual men as they had previously claimed to be able to do (Hegarty, 2003). She quickly became the most prominently homophilic scientist in the country, chairing the National Institute of Mental Health Task Force on Homosexuality from 1967 to 1969. Although Nixon's election delayed the final report's publication, it signaled a shift in how liberal scientists perceived the question of sexual minorities (Minton, 2002). Over the course of the 1970s, the institutions of psychology and mental health officially abandoned earlier views that equated differences in sexuality with forms of deficiency and pathology (Herek, 2010). In 1972, the psychotherapist George Weinberg popularized the term *homophobia* to designate an irrational fear of individuals attracted to the same sex. Whereas many physicians had previously viewed homosexual desire as a form of sickness, Weinberg and his allies in the gay liberation movement now suggested that prejudice toward such people represented both an illiberal attitude and an unhealthy mentality.

One of the legacies of the gay rights advocates' interaction with psychiatry during the 1970s was the conviction that the movement could and should engage biomedicine by challenging scientific procedures and rules. During the AIDS epidemic, many sufferers and their allies acquired considerable knowledge about immunology and virology to challenge the diagnosis and treatment of patients. In part, this was because the epidemiology of the disease targeted a recently organized and politicized community, which often included young and educated members who did not feel symptoms immediately after diagnosis. In particular, gay male sufferers resisted the model of risk built into randomized clinical trials for new treatments, demanding immediate access to new drugs such as AZT (Epstein, 1996). These challenges represented a revolution in common sense for bioethics, one that continues to shape research design in psychology. There was a shift from an ideal of protecting vulnerable populations (e.g., women of childbearing years) to a new awareness about the risk of withholding potentially life-saving drugs from those most in need and a desire to tailor treatments to specific populations (Epstein, 2007). The National Institutes of Health Revitalization Act of 1993 canonized this transformation, demanding that the clinical trials it funded demonstrate the validity of the analysis for women and ethnic minorities. Ironically, this feminist intervention helped reinforce the categories of sex and race as fixed, natural kinds in public health discourse (Epstein, 2007).

Selves: Making People Up?

The changes in behavior, norms, epistemologies, and concepts we have outlined resulted in different kinds of lives being lived in different times. As such, it is possible to speak of history "making" new kinds of people. New concepts such as the homosexual and the masturbator reflect widespread recognition of new sexual experiences while providing novel means through which people can understand their own sexuality. Indeed, much of the dispute between constructionists and essentialists revolves around how seriously one should take this linguistic evidence as impinging on the embodied experience of sex. This proliferation of these discourses had much to do with the emergence of a science of sex and the pursuit of precision therein. Even the terms *essentialist* and *constructionist* as supposed sides in this debate emerged at a specific historical moment and under particular conditions. Yet these concepts acquired a life of their own as they became important to social and intellectual movements organized around sexuality.

Much recent research on the history of the human sciences has embraced Ian Hacking's (2002) framework of historical ontology. He adapted this term from Foucault to circumvent the realist–antirealist debate within the philosophy of science. Scientific objects have biographies insofar as they come into being (and sometimes pass away) under specific historical conditions. As can the biographer, the historian can document the events, circumstances, and institutions that shape the life of a scientific object. Understanding these historical changes tells one much about the nature of the scientific object at hand but says little about whether it is real. Hacking suggested whatever enables action should count as real. He did distinguish most of the natural sciences that dealt with indifferent kinds (e.g., atoms, quarks) from the human sciences that traffic in interactive kinds. Humans have dynamic relationships with the categories ascribed to them. They respond to how they are classified, and these classifications provide a repertoire for describing their own actions to themselves. As new descriptions emerge, so too do new possibilities for action. These new actions lead to revisions in descriptions and classification (Hacking, 1999). Such an approach eschews the once-fashionable mantra of social construction, because society does not exist as a separate and autonomous thing acting on individuals.

Hacking (1995) developed many of these ideas in relationship to his long-term engagement with survivors of child abuse. He wrote about child abuse not to debunk the concept or to diminish the gravitas of the harm caused by it. Hacking asserted that child abuse is evil and that heightened awareness of its existence was the result of one of the most valuable social movements in his lifetime. Yet child abuse is also fundamentally historical. He highlighted crucial ruptures between Victorian campaigns against child cruelty and talk about child abuse since 1960. There was a 50-year gap in which the problem seemingly disappeared from public discussions, and juvenile delinquency seemed to be a more pressing issue. Class and religious differences defined Victorian anticruelty, with Protestant reformers seeking to remove children from impoverished Catholic homes. In contrast, modern child abuse is seen as a classless issue potentially lurking in every household. Hacking suggested that this broadening of concern about harm to children had much to do with the way that sex, and especially incest, became foundational to what it meant to be abused in the contemporary era. Child abuse began in a medical context with its methodologies and authority when pediatrician Walter Kempe and colleagues first spoke about battered child syndrome (Kempe, Silverman, Steele, Droegemueller, & Silver, 1962). At the outset, there was no clear definition of child abuse that led to identifying instances of it. Rather, sensitivity to the possibility of abuse led to new acts being classified under this rubric. The topic fused in complicated ways with the emergent second-wave feminist movement and consciousness raising as a way of knowing. Even the experience of what suffering abuse entails seems to shift historically. In the late 1980s, it seemed to almost inexorably lead to multiple personality disorder, but under other circumstances this equation was met with deep skepticism (Hacking, 1995).

Similarly, the contours of the category of sex offender, originally the sexual psychopath, have undergone dramatic permutations in historical time. Historians have documented the disjuncture between rates of sexual assault and the attention given to these acts by law enforcement, psychiatrists, and the media. The origins of the category of the sex offender lay in the Progressive Era impulse not to punish as harshly those people deemed not fully responsible for their crimes. This shift involved attending to the social conditions that led to crime, but courts soon turned to psychiatric expertise. A widely publicized and particularly brutal assault on a child in 1937 led to a moral panic around sex crimes and the passing of the first sexual psychopath statute. Although incidents of sexual assault did not dissipate during the Second World War, talk about sexual psychopaths disappeared from the national discussion only to reappear between 1947 and 1955 (Freedman, 1987). The diagnosis of sexual psychopathy was intended to demarcate people who did not meet the standard for criminal insanity but who were deemed not wholly responsible because of mental illness. The goal was to treat and hopefully rehabilitate such individuals in specialized psychiatric hospitals rather than punish them in prisons. From the outset, many psychiatrists expressed skepticism about sexual psychopathy as a distinct clinical entity. Crafted to prevent violent rapes and murders, for much of its history the category encompassed petty sex offenses, including homosexual acts, peeping, and exhibitionism. The management of such individuals shifted from confinement in low-security facilities to surgical and chemical castration to more recent community notification campaigns. Each of these judicial interventions leads to different lives as a sex offender (Cole, 2000).

It is not simply unusual kinds of people, such as abused children and sex offenders, who get materialized in relation to the human sciences. By analyzing hundreds of letters sent to Kinsey, Igo (2007) found considerable evidence to suggest that reading about his surveys encouraged Americans to create a new and more forgiving standard by which to judge and classify their own conduct. Numerous Americans were eager to volunteer as participants and cast their sexual past into Kinsey's categories. Igo did not suggest that Kinsey unleashed an unheralded promiscuity; rather, her argument and evidence pertained to the novel conceptual schema people applied to already existing behavior, allowing them to craft new identities. The circulation of numbers about the population, especially in the form of opinion polls, transformed how people related to their communities, which led to a new definition of the public and the social as statistical aggregates with variation. The 20th century saw the birth of a new kind of person: the citizen as social scientific subject whose opinions and attitudes are measured and who demands that her or his individuality is represented in such measures.

ON NOT LEARNING THE LESSONS OF HISTORY

In the introduction, we noted that many psychologists are interactionists who tend to conceptualize individual conduct as the interplay of nature and nurture. From such a perspective, we could be accused of overemphasizing cultural factors, having missed the reality or essence of sexuality. Alternatively, we could be accused of being historical determinists who underplay the scope of individuals to determine their own destinies. Our aim has been to explicate nondichotomous thinking about the temporality of the factors that affect human conduct in the domain of sexuality by discussing historical events that are neither easily understood as natural or as effects of environment that can be studied as individual differences in a cohort or an experiment. For example, intersex people living today are not only affected by the ways that their bodies are naturally formed and by the environmental influences on their conduct but also by a history of mistreatment, of neglect of the contingent ways that their embodiment and their cultural position can affect their well-being, and of the challenges of a history of medicine—played out in historical time—that has left medicine ill equipped to understand or respond to that contingency (e.g., Jordan-Young, 2012; Ogilvie et al., 2006; Stout, Litvak, Robbins, & Sandberg, 2010).

Some psychologists might be concerned that describing sexual practices as influenced by history rather than nature might make those practices seem less credible and more likely to be stigmatized. In particular, many psychologists believe that it is necessary to strategically engage in biological determinism to assert the value of particular sexual practices or groups. This belief is most obvious in the case of arguments that homosexuality is genetic. By pursuing this strategy, such psychologists are seeking to work as historical actors to change society (albeit for the better). There is a mismatch between their implicit belief in their own capacity to use science as a tool of historical agency and the equally implicit rejection of the importance of historical time in their science. One of the remarkable things about the Supreme Court's decision in *Lawrence v. Texas* (2003) was that the majority adopted a historicist argument to secure rights for homosexual people (see Volume 2, Chapter 8, this handbook). Embracing a historicist perspective on the expression of sexuality actually places psychologists at the forefront of legal and activist thinking about how best to secure rights. Indeed, examination of social science data collected over historical time has suggested that there is little grounds for the argument that people in the United States became more gay friendly because they came to endorse the theory that homosexuality was biological (Lewis, 2009).

Against this reliance on nature, history has also shown that accounts of nature vary widely. For example, Victorian images of sexual nature as a dangerous flaw in the human condition are different from midcentury American visions of sexual nature as a positive force that most characterizes vigorous, healthy people. Neither account is similar to the account of nature that focuses on ostensibly natural differences among people, as in contemporary theories about the biological basis of sexual orientation. Rather than take comfort in the moral authority of nature, many psychological approaches work on nature and deliberately remake it (e.g., AZT, intersex bodies, demographic transition, Viagra, categories of the *Diagnostic and Statistical Manual of Mental Disorders,* interventions for pedophiles). Researchers need critical distance from their technophobia and technophilia. These things are real, existent, and historical.

Perhaps the publication of this handbook will be a historic moment in psychology: an event that will bring about new ways of theorizing, examining, and therapeutically intervening around sex and sexuality by psychologists in their interactions with people both in the United States and elsewhere. It may interrupt disciplinary silences about sex. As historians of psychology, we share a concern for the lack of multidisciplinary attention to sex in psychology. In this chapter, we conveyed how a historical sensibility makes distinct contributions to this endeavor. The history of sexuality is not a narrative of greater enlightenment and universal emancipation, but an uneven and event-filled terrain featuring surprising reversals. Furthermore, the object of the psychology of sexuality is not historically stable because sexual subjects interact in complicated ways with the knowledge produced about them. To better understand sexuality, psychologists need to grapple with their history.

References

Adams, G., & Markus, H. (2004). Toward a conception of culture suitable for a psychology of culture. In M. Schaller & C. Crandall (Eds.), *The psychological foundations of culture* (pp. 335–360). Mahwah, NJ: Erlbaum.

Arnett, J. J. (2008). The neglected 95%: Why American psychology needs to become less American. *American Psychologist, 63*, 602–614. doi:10.1037/0003-066X.63.7.602

Barker, M. (2007). Heteronormativity and the exclusion of bisexuality in psychology. In V. Clarke & E. Peel (Eds.), *Out in psychology* (pp. 95–117). Chichester, England: Wiley. doi:10.1002/9780470713099.ch6

Bayer, B. (2004). On cultural history as transformation—or, what's the matter with psychology anyway? In A. Brock, J. Louw, & W. Hoorn (Eds.), *Rediscovering the history of psychology* (pp. 119–140). New York, NY: Springer.

Bérubé, A. (2010). *Coming out under fire: The history of gay men and women in World War II* (2nd ed.). Chapel Hill: University of North Carolina Press.

Boswell, J. (1980). *Christianity, social tolerance, and homosexuality: Gay people in Western Europe from the beginning of the Christian era to the 14th century.* Chicago, IL: University of Chicago Press.

Boutlier v. INS, 387 U.S. 118 (1967).

Bowers v. Hardwick, 478 U.S. 186 (1987).

Briggs, L. (2002). *Reproducing empire: Race, sex, science, and U.S. imperialism in Puerto Rico.* Berkeley: University of California Press.

Brock, A. C. (Ed.). (2006). *Internationalizing the history of psychology.* New York, NY: New York University Press.

Buckley, K. W. (1994). Misbehaviorism: The case of John B. Watson's dismissal from Johns Hopkins University. In J. T. Todd & E. K. Morris (Eds.), *Modern perspectives on John B. Watson and classical behaviorism* (pp. 19–36). Westport, CT: Greenwood Press.

Canaday, M. (2009). *The straight state: Sexuality and citizenship in 20th-century America.* Princeton, NJ: Princeton University Press.

Cassidy, A. (2007). The (sexual) politics of evolution: Popular controversy in the late 20th-century United Kingdom. *History of Psychology, 10*, 199–226. doi:10.1037/1093-4510.10.2.199

Chase, C. (1998). Hermaphrodites with attitude: Mapping the emergence of intersex political activism. *GLQ: A Journal of Lesbian and Gay Studies, 4*, 189–211.

Chauncey, G. (1994). *Gay New York: Gender, urban culture, and the making of the gay male world, 1890–1940.* New York, NY: Basic Books.

Chauncey, G. (2004). "What gay studies taught the court": The historians' amicus brief in Lawrence v. Texas. *GLQ: A Journal of Lesbian and Gay Studies, 10*, 509–538. doi:10.1215/10642684-10-3-509

Cherry, F. (1995). *The "stubborn particulars" of social psychology: Essays on the research process.* London, England: Routledge.

Chiang, H. H. (2010). Liberating sex, knowing desire: Scientia sexualis and epistemic turning points in the history of sexuality. *History of the Human Sciences, 23*, 42–69. doi:10.1177/0952695110378947

Clarke, A. E. (1998). *Disciplining reproduction: Modernity, American life science, and "the problem of sex."* Berkeley: University of California Press.

Cohen, C. (1997). Punks, bulldaggers, and welfare queens: The radical potential of queer politics? *GLQ: A Journal of Lesbian and Gay Studies, 4*, 437–465. doi:10.1215/10642684-3-4-437

Cole, S. A. (2000). From the sexual psychopath statute to "Megan's Law": Psychiatric knowledge in the diagnosis, treatment, and adjudication of sex criminals in New Jersey, 1949–1999. *Journal of the History of Medicine and Allied Sciences, 55*, 292–314. doi:10.1093/jhmas/55.3.292

Connelly, M. J. (2008). *Fatal misconception: The struggle to control world population.* Cambridge: Harvard University Press.

Cook, H. (2004). *The long sexual revolution: English women, sex, and contraception, 1800–1975.* Oxford, England: Oxford University Press.

Crozier, I. (2000). Havelock Ellis, Eonism and the patient's discourse; or, writing a book about sex. *History of Psychiatry, 11*, 125–154. doi:10.1177/0957154X0001104201

Danziger, K. (1990). *Constructing the subject: Historical origins for psychological research.* Cambridge, England: Cambridge University Press. doi:10.1017/CBO9780511524059

Danziger, K. (1997). *Naming the mind: How psychology found its language.* Beverly Hills, CA: Sage.

Daston, L., & Vidal, F. (Eds.). (2004). *The moral authority of nature.* Chicago, IL: University of Chicago Press.

Davis, R. L. (2008). "Not marriage at all, but simple harlotry": The companionate marriage controversy. *Journal of American History, 94*, 1137–1163. doi:10.2307/25095323

D'Emilio, J., & Freedman, E. B. (1998). *Intimate matters: A history of sexuality in America.* Chicago, IL: University of Chicago Press.

Eisenstadt v. Baird, 405 U.S. 438 (1972).

Ellis, H., & Symonds, J. A. (1897). *Sexual inversion.* London, England: Wilson & Macmillan.

Epstein, S. (1996). *Impure science: AIDS, activism, and the politics of knowledge.* Berkeley: University of California Press.

Epstein, S. (2007). *Inclusion: The politics of difference in medical research.* Chicago, IL: University of Chicago Press.

Ericksen, J. A., & Steffen, S. A. (2001). *Kiss and tell: Surveying sex in the 20th century.* Cambridge, England: Harvard University Press.

Fausto-Sterling, A. (2000). *Sexing the body: Gender politics and the construction of sexuality.* New York, NY: Basic Books.

Feldstein, R. (2000). *Motherhood in Black and White: Race and sex in American liberalism, 1930–1965.* Ithaca, NY: Cornell University Press.

Finison, L. J. (1976). Unemployment, politics, and the history of organized psychology. *American Psychologist, 31,* 747–755. doi:10.1037/0003-066X.31.11.747

Foucault, M. (1978). *The history of sexuality.* New York, NY: Pantheon.

Fraser, N. (1989). *Unruly practices: Power, discourse, and gender in contemporary social theory.* Minneapolis: University of Minnesota Press.

Freedman, E. B. (1987). "Uncontrolled desires": The response to the sexual psychopath, 1920–1960. *Journal of American History, 74,* 83–106. doi:10.2307/1908506

Greenhalgh, S. (Ed.). (1995). *Situating fertility: Anthropology and demographic inquiry.* Cambridge, England: Cambridge University Press. doi:10.1017/CBO9780511621611

Griswold v. Connecticut, 381 U.S. 479 (1965).

Guthrie, R. V. (1976). *Even the rat was white: A historical view of psychology.* New York, NY: Harper & Row.

Hacking, I. (1995). *Rewriting the soul: Multiple personality and the sciences of memory.* Princeton, NJ: Princeton University Press.

Hacking, I. (1999). *The social construction of what?* Cambridge, MA: Harvard University Press.

Hacking, I. (2002). *Historical ontology.* Cambridge, England: Harvard University Press.

Halperin, D. M. (1990). *One hundred years of homosexuality: and other essays on Greek love.* New York, NY: Routledge.

Hammack, P. L., & Windell, E. P. (2011). Psychology and the politics of same-sex desire in the United States: An analysis of three cases. *History of Psychology, 14,* 220–248. doi:10.1037/a0024541

Haraway, D. (1989). *Primate visions: Gender, race, and nature in the world of modern science.* New York, NY: Routledge.

Harris, B. (1979). Whatever happened to little Albert? *American Psychologist, 34,* 151–160. doi:10.1037/0003-066X.34.2.151

Hegarty, P. (2003). Homosexual signs and heterosexual silences: Rorschach research on male homosexuality from 1921 to 1969. *Journal of the History of Sexuality, 12,* 400–423. doi:10.1353/sex.2004.0009

Hegarty, P. (2007). Getting dirty: Psychology's history of power. *History of Psychology, 10,* 75–91. doi:10.1037/1093-4510.10.2.75

Hegarty, P. (2012). Getting miles away from Terman: Did the CRPS fund Catharine Cox Miles's unsilenced psychology of sex? *History of Psychology, 15,* 201–208. doi:10.1037/a0025725

Hegarty, P. (2013). *Gentlemen's disagreement: Alfred Kinsey, Lewis Terman and the sexual politics of smart men.* Chicago, IL: University of Chicago Press.

Henrich, J., Heine, S. J., & Norenzayan, A. (2010). The weirdest people in the world? *Behavioral and Brain Sciences, 33,* 61–83. doi:10.1017/S0140525X0999152X

Herek, G. M. (2010). Sexual orientation differences as deficits: Science and stigma in the history of American psychology. *Perspectives on Psychological Science, 5,* 693–699. doi:10.1177/1745691610388770

Hobsbawm, E. J., & Ranger, T. O. (1983). *The invention of tradition.* Cambridge, England: Cambridge University Press.

Hodges, A. (1983). *Alan Turing: The enigma.* New York, NY: Simon & Schuster.

Hughes, I. A., Houk, C., Ahmed, S. F., & Lee, P. A. (2006). Consensus statement on management of intersex disorders. *Archives of Disease in Childhood, 91,* 554–563. doi:10.1136/adc.2006.098319

Igo, S. E. (2007). *The averaged American: Surveys, citizens, and the making of a mass public.* Cambridge, MA: Harvard University Press.

Johnson, D. K. (2004). *The lavender scare: The Cold War persecution of gays and lesbians in the federal government.* Chicago, IL: University of Chicago Press.

Jordan-Young, R. M. (2012). Hormones, context, and "brain gender": A review of evidence from congenital adrenal hyperplasia. *Social Science and Medicine, 74,* 1738–1744. doi:10.1016/j.socscimed.2011.08.026

Katz, J. N. (1995). *The invention of heterosexuality.* Chicago, IL: University of Chicago Press.

Kempe, C. H., Silverman, F. N., Steele, B. F., Droegemueller, W., & Silver, H. K. (1962). The battered-child syndrome. *JAMA, 181*, 17–24. doi:10.1001/jama.1962.03050270019004

Kessler, S. (1998). *Lessons from the intersexed.* New Brunswick, NJ: Rutgers University Press.

Kim, H. S., Sherman, D. K., Sasaki, J. Y., Xu, J., Chu, T. Q., Ryu, C., . . . Taylor, S. E. (2010). Culture, distress, and oxytocin receptor polymorphism (OXTR) interact to influence emotional support seeking. *Proceedings of the National Academy of Sciences of the United States of America, 107*, 15717–15721. doi:10.1073/pnas.1010830107

Kline, W. (2001). *Building a better race: Gender, sexuality, and eugenics from the turn of the century to the Baby Boom.* Berkeley: University of California Press.

Kunzel, R. G. (2008). *Criminal intimacy: Prison and the uneven history of modern American sexuality.* Chicago, IL: University of Chicago Press.

Laqueur, T. W. (2003). *Solitary sex: A cultural history of masturbation.* New York, NY: Zone Books.

Lawrence v. Texas, 539 U.S. 558 (2003).

Lewis, G. B. (2009). Does believing homosexuality is innate increase support for gay rights? *Policy Studies Journal, 37*, 669–693. doi:10.1111/j.1541-0072.2009.00330.x

Lindsey, B. B., & Evans, W. (1927). *Companionate marriage.* New York, NY: Boni & Liveright.

Loving v. Virginia, 388 U.S. 1 (1967).

Lunbeck, E. (1994). *The psychiatric persuasion: Knowledge, gender, and power in modern America.* Princeton, NJ: Princeton University Press.

Marcuse, H. (1955). *Eros and civilization: A philosophical inquiry into Freud.* Boston, MA: Beacon Press.

Markus, H. R., & Kitayama, S. (1991). Culture and the self: Implications for cognition, emotion, and motivation. *Psychological Review, 98*, 224–253. doi:10.1037/0033-295X.98.2.224

Meyer, I. H. (2003). Prejudice, social stress, and mental health in lesbian, gay, and bisexual populations: Conceptual issues and research evidence. *Psychological Bulletin, 129*, 674–697. doi:10.1037/0033-2909.129.5.674

Meyerowitz, J. (2004). *How sex changed: A history of transsexuality in the United States.* Cambridge, England: Harvard University Press.

Minton, H. L. (2002). *Departing from deviance: A history of homosexual rights and emancipatory science in America.* Chicago, IL: University of Chicago Press.

Money, J., & Ehrhardt, A. A. (1972). *Man and woman, boy and girl: The differentiation and dimorphism of gender identity from conception to maturity.* Baltimore, MD: Johns Hopkins University Press.

Morawski, J. G. (1985). The measurement of masculinity and femininity: Engendering categorical realities. *Journal of Personality, 53*, 196–223. doi:10.1111/j.1467-6494.1985.tb00364.x

Morawski, J. G. (1994). *Practicing feminisms, reconstructing psychology: Notes on a liminal science.* Ann Arbor: University of Michigan Press.

Morin, S. F. (1977). Heterosexual bias in psychological research on lesbianism and male homosexuality. *American Psychologist, 32*, 629–637. doi:10.1037/0003-066X.32.8.629

Murphy, M. (2013). Economization of life: Calculative infrastructures of population and economy. In P. Rawes (Ed.), *Relational ecologies: Subjectivity, sex, nature, and architecture.* London, England: Routledge.

National Institutes of Health Revitalization Act of 1993, Pub. L. 103–43, 107 Stat. 122.

Neuhaus, J. (2000). The importance of being orgasmic: Sexuality, gender, and marital sex manuals in the United States, 1920–1963. *Journal of the History of Sexuality, 9*, 447–473.

Nicholson, I. (2011). "Shocking" masculinity: Stanley Milgram, "Obedience to Authority," and the "crisis of manhood" in Cold War America. *Isis, 102*, 238–268. doi:10.1086/660129

Nye, R. A. (1993). *Masculinity and male codes of honor in modern France.* New York, NY: Oxford University Press.

O'Donnell, J. M. (1979). The crisis of experimentalism in the 1920s: E. G. Boring and his uses of history. *American Psychologist, 34*, 289–295. doi:10.1037/0003-066X.34.4.289

Ogilvie, C. M., Crouch, N. S., Rumsby, G., Creighton, S. M., Liao, L.-M., & Conway, G. S. (2006). Congenital adrenal hyperplasia in adults: A review of medical, surgical, and psychological issues. *Clinical Endocrinology, 64*, 2–11.

Peplau, L. A., & Fingerhut, A. W. (2007). The close relationships of lesbians and gay men. *Annual Review of Psychology, 58*, 405–424. doi:10.1146/annurev.psych.58.110405.085701

Pettit, M. (2011). The SPSSI Task Force on Sexual Orientation, the nature of sex, and the contours of activist science. *Journal of Social Issues, 67*, 92–105. doi:10.1111/j.1540-4560.2010.01685.x

Pettit, M. (2012). The queer life of a lab rat. *History of Psychology, 15*, 217–227. doi:10.1037/a0027269

Pickren, W. (1997). Robert Yerkes, Calvin Stone, and the beginning of programmatic sex research by psychologists, 1921–1930. *American Journal of Psychology, 110*, 603–619. doi:10.2307/1423412

Potter, J., & Wetherell, M. (1987). *Discourse and social psychology: Beyond attitudes and behavior.* London, England: Sage.

Ramsden, E. (2002). Carving up population science: Eugenics, demography, and the controversy over the "biological law" of population growth. *Social Studies of Science, 32,* 857–899. doi:10.1177/03063127020 3200509

Richards, G. (1997). *"Race," racism and psychology: Towards a reflexive history*. Hove, England: Routledge.

Richards, G. (2009). *Putting psychology in its place: Critical historical perspectives* (3rd ed.). Hove, England: Routledge.

Roe v. Wade, 410 U.S. 113 (1973).

Rosario, V. A. (1997). *Science and homosexualities.* New York, NY: Routledge.

Samelson, F. (1974). History, origin myth and ideology: Discovery of social psychology. *Journal for the Theory of Social Behaviour, 4,* 217–232. doi:10.1111/j.1468-5914.1974.tb00338.x

Scarborough, E., & Furumoto, L. (1987). *Untold lives: The first generation of American women psychologists.* New York, NY: Columbia University Press.

Scott, J. W. (1986). Gender: A useful category of historical analysis. *American Historical Review, 91,* 1053. doi:10.2307/1864376

Sengoopta, C. (1998). Glandular politics: Experimental biology, clinical medicine, and homosexual emancipation in fin-de-siècle central Europe. *Isis, 89,* 445–473. doi:10.1086/384073

Serlin, D. (2012). Carney Landis and the psychosexual landscape of touch in mid-20th-century America. *History of Psychology, 15,* 209–216. doi:10.1037/a0027142

Sewell, W. H. (2005). *Logics of history: Social theory and social transformation.* Chicago, IL: University of Chicago Press.

Shields, S. (1975). Functionalism, Darwinism, and the psychology of women. *American Psychologist, 30,* 739–754. doi:10.1037/h0076948

Smith, R. (1988). Does the history of psychology have a subject? *History of the Human Sciences, 1,* 147–177. doi:10.1177/095269518800100201

Stein, M. (2010). *Sexual injustice: Supreme Court decisions from Griswold to Roe.* Chapel Hill: University of North Carolina Press.

Stern, A. M. (2005). *Eugenic nation: Faults and frontiers of better breeding in modern America.* Berkeley: University of California Press.

Stoler, A. L. (1995). *Race and the education of desire: Foucault's History of Sexuality and the colonial order of things.* Durham, NC: Duke University Press.

Stone, L. (1977). *The family, sex, and marriage in England, 1500–1800.* New York, NY: Harper & Row.

Stout, S. A., Litvak, M., Robbins, N. M., & Sandberg, D. E. (2010). Congenital adrenal hyperplasia: Classification of studies employing psychological endpoints. *International Journal of Pediatric Endocrinology, 2010,* Article ID 191520.

Terman, L. M. (1938). *Psychological factors in marital happiness.* New York, NY: McGraw-Hill.

Terry, J. (1999). *An American obsession: Science, medicine, and homosexuality in modern society.* Chicago, IL: University of Chicago Press.

von Krafft-Ebing, R. (1886). *Psychopathia Sexualis: eine Klinisch–Forensische Studie* [Sexual psychopathy: A clinical–forensic study]. Stuttgart, Germany: Enke.

Weisstein, N. (1971). Psychology constructs the female; or The fantasy life of the male psychologist (with some of the fantasies of his friends, the male biologist and the male anthropologist). *Social Education, 35,* 362–373.

Part II

METHODOLOGIES OF SEXUALITY RESEARCH

CHAPTER 4

SURVEY METHODS IN SEXUALITY RESEARCH

Vanessa Schick, Sarah K. Calabrese, and Debby Herbenick

Because of the privacy in which sexual behaviors are often enacted, the scientific methods available to study these phenomena are limited relative to other topics. In the United States, most people report engaging in sexual behavior in private locations such as their home or the home of a sexual partner (Herbenick et al., 2010), eliminating opportunities for naturalistic observation and complicating laboratory studies of sexual behavior. The range of sexual behaviors that can be captured or manipulated in a laboratory setting is limited, in part because most ethical guidelines pertaining to human subjects research prohibit the coercion of sexual behavior from an individual or between individuals. Moreover, the artificial context, observer effects, and self-selection bias inherent in studies involving what some may consider taboo behavior limit the generalizability of laboratory findings. Surveys provide an alternative and, in many cases, superior method of gathering information about sexual behavior and other dimensions of human sexuality (e.g., identity, intentions, knowledge).

We begin this chapter by presenting three landmark studies in sex survey research and reviewing their methods and limitations. We then discuss survey design (e.g., item construction, response formatting), modalities of administration (e.g., written self-report, computerized self-interviewing), and psychometric considerations in the context of sex research. Throughout the chapter, we provide examples and highlight considerations specific to research in the domain of sexuality.

THE EVOLUTION OF SEX SURVEYS: HISTORICAL EXAMPLES

In this section, we highlight the methods and limitations of three historical studies to set the stage for subsequent review of and commentary on sex survey research.

1948–1953: Alfred Kinsey and Colleagues' *Sexual Behavior in the Human Male* and *Sexual Behavior in the Human Female*

Art, literature, and poetry demonstrate that human beings have long pondered sexual behavior and expression. However, Alfred Kinsey's work (e.g., Kinsey, Pomeroy, & Martin, 1948; Kinsey, Pomeroy, Martin, & Gebhard, 1953), which included interviews with more than 18,000 people in the United States, marked the first systematic and large-scale scientific study of sexual behavior. Kinsey and his research team at Indiana University's Institute for Sex Research demonstrated that it was possible to use objective methods to collect highly sensitive information about sexual attitudes, fantasies, and behavior from women and men, even in a culture in which many aspects of sexual expression remained taboo, if not illegal, at the time. Through the use of one-on-one face-to-face interviews, Kinsey and his team were able to uncover much about Americans' sexual experiences at the time. Major findings include the prevalence of premarital intercourse, which was reported by approximately half of women and two thirds of men, as well as the commonness of same-sex attraction and activity, one or both of

http://dx.doi.org/10.1037/14193-004
APA Handbook of Sexuality and Psychology: Vol. 1. Person-Based Approaches, D. L. Tolman and L. M. Diamond (Editors-in-Chief)

which was experienced at some point in the lives of most men and women. In addition, 93% of men and 62% of women acknowledged engaging in masturbation, and about half of both sexes reported participating in oral–genital sexual contact (Kinsey et al., 1948, 1953).

Although this work was a major milestone in the field of sex research, the research methods used by Kinsey and his team (1948, 1953) were not without their limitations. The relative oversampling of residents of the Midwestern United States, prisoners, prostitutes, and homosexual men, as well as the relative undersampling of older adults, raised questions about the representativeness of the Kinsey group's sample and the applicability of their findings with respect to the U.S. population. Additionally, the face-to-face nature of the interviews and primarily White male research staff who conducted them led to speculation about participants' biasing their responses in accordance with perceived social expectation (e.g., underreporting of female masturbation), despite efforts of the research staff to emphasize confidentiality and provide a nonjudgmental atmosphere. Also, proportionally few older Americans were interviewed, a fact acknowledged by the researchers in their male (Kinsey et al., 1948) and female (Kinsey et al., 1953) volumes, and thus findings were mainly applicable to individuals between the ages of 18 and 50. Nevertheless, through the use of interview-based survey methods, Kinsey's work transformed Americans' understanding of human sexuality (see Chapter 3, this volume) and advanced—and many would say helped create—an interdisciplinary field of study related to human sexuality.

1992: Edward O. Laumann and Colleagues' National Health and Social Life Survey

Although the Kinsey team's (1948, 1953) research raised more questions about sexual behavior than it answered, it was decades before another large-scale scientific study of sex in the United States occurred. The first nationally representative, survey-based study of sexual behavior in the United State, the National Health and Social Life Survey (NHSLS), was conducted in 1992 by Edward O. Laumann and colleagues (Laumann, 1996). More than 3,000 women and men were interviewed in a face-to-face format, yielding new insights into Americans' psychological and physical experiences of their sexuality. The NHSLS represented a significant advancement in sampling methodologies in that the researchers were able to survey women and men who represented Americans ages 18 to 59. In doing so, they were able to overcome the criticisms of Kinsey's work related to the generalizability of study findings. Notable findings from the NHSLS included that married couples had more frequent sex than single or cohabitating couples, that more individuals experienced same-sex behavior than identified as gay or lesbian, and that noncoital behaviors such as oral sex were common (Michael, Gagnon, Laumann, & Kolata, 1994).

Given the timing of the study relative to the beginnings of the HIV/AIDS epidemic in the United States in the 1980s, findings were of particular interest to public health officials, health care providers, and the general public not simply for the sake of understanding or fulfilling curiosity but also for health maintenance and disease prevention purposes (see Chapter 22, this volume).

Despite methodological improvements over Kinsey's early work (e.g., a demographic profile matching the U.S. population), the NHSLS still encountered its share of criticism, including the actual representativeness of the "nationally representative" sample; the sample excluded adolescents younger than 18 and adults older than 59, oversampled certain ethnic groups (e.g., Black, Hispanic), was language limited (English only), and excluded institutionalized adults. Whereas Kinsey's interviews were mostly conducted by White men, these interviews were largely conducted by middle-aged White women. Additionally, the in-home interview setting, which facilitated access to participants, also meant that other household members were sometimes at home in a proximal room and potentially within earshot. This perceived threat to privacy could have influenced participants' reports of particularly sensitive aspects of their sexual behavior; the low rates of infidelity (16%) reported in this study relative to others (less than 25%) lend credence to this argument (Blow & Hartnett, 2005).

That said, the NHSLS was important for several reasons. First, the research served as a reminder that the study of human sexual experiences has scientific merit and that a society that does not understand the sexual behavior of its people may be ill prepared to understand or manage some of the more challenging outcomes of such behavior (e.g., unintended pregnancy, HIV/AIDS). Second, the research provided a snapshot of sexual behavior through which Americans could examine, understand, and ask questions of themselves about their own sexual behavior. The NHSLS also provided a wealth of data that could be made available to clinicians, parents, teachers, and health educators who, in turn, could provide information to others. In short, the NHSLS was a significant milestone in the study of human sexual behavior and experiences in the United States.

2009: Indiana University Center for Sexual Health Promotion's National Survey of Sexual Health and Behavior

Since the NHSLS (Michael et al., 1994), numerous large-scale national and international studies have assessed sexual health issues (e.g., the National Social Life, Health, and Aging Project; Global Study of Sexual Attitudes and Behavior; Australian Study of Health and Relationships; Laumann et al., 2005; Lindau et al., 2007; Smith, Rissel, Richters, Grulich, & de Visser, 2003). One of the more recent is the National Survey of Sexual Health and Behavior (NSSHB) conducted by researchers at the Center for Sexual Health Promotion at Indiana University in 2009 (Vanessa Schick and Debby Herbenick were among the researchers who conducted the NSSHB). This comprehensive study of nearly 6,000 people ages 14 to 94 living in the United States circumvented many of the pitfalls that befell earlier studies. The sampling itself was conducted by Knowledge Networks, which used address-based sampling and random-digit dialing in combination to identify a nationally representative sample, including age groups previously excluded by many studies, such as adolescents and older adults. Beyond improved sampling strategies, a major strength of this study was its Internet-based survey method, which included the provision of hardware and Internet access to participants as needed (see Volume 2, Chapter 3, this handbook). This approach was intended to foster an enhanced sense of privacy and anonymity relative to face-to-face interviewing, maximizing the potential for honest responding. The primary drawbacks of this survey study were the lack of data it yielded regarding sexual and gender minorities, which could only have been obtained via deliberate oversampling, as well as the exclusion of institutionalized adults and the shortage of qualitative insights that were gathered given the quantitative nature of most survey items (Herbenick et al., 2010; Reece et al., 2010). Also, because the NSSHB was conducted online, the team was also unable to clarify any confusing terms or questions, as Kinsey et al. (1948, 1953) and the NHSLS would have been able to do in their in-person interviews.

Indiana University's NSSHB was conducted nearly two decades after the NHSLS. In addition, the NSSHB was the first nationally representative study of sexual behavior and experiences conducted in the United States after the introduction of the Internet, which many have speculated has changed sexual experiences, particularly because it provides increased access to sexually explicit images (see Volume 2, Chapter 1, this handbook). In addition to assessing sexual behaviors, the NSSHB also assessed how people experience their sexual lives. Major findings of the NSSHB included the following: (a) The prevalence of anal sex reported by women and men was substantially higher than in the NHSLS data; (b) adolescents ages 14 to 17 who were sexually active with a partner were among the most consistent users of condoms; (c) approximately 30% of women reported pain during their most recent sexual experience, compared with about 5% of men; (d) far fewer women than men reported experiencing orgasm during their most recent sexual experience; and (e) sexual variety (i.e., diverse sexual behaviors) was common and associated with greater sexual pleasure and reports of orgasm (see also Chapter 11, this volume). Of course, the NSSHB represents only the most recent chapter—and certainly not the final one—in a relatively young history of using survey methods for understanding and assessing human sexual experiences.

SURVEY DESIGN

For any survey—whether it is conducted as an in-person interview or using a paper-based questionnaire—one of the earliest steps is to identify and develop the measures, or item sets, that will make up the survey. In this section, we discuss the use and adaptation of preexisting measures and the development of new measures in the context of sexuality research.

Utilization and Adaptation of Preexisting Measures

When approaching measurement of a particular construct, a commonly used strategy is to select a measure of that construct that is already in existence. Using a measure that has been published in the peer-reviewed literature and has already been validated in at least one other sample is advantageous, because it provides assurance that new data gathered via that measure will reflect the construct of interest. This increases the confidence of researchers and their critics in any findings derived from such data. Furthermore, using a preexisting measure allows the researcher and his or her readership to make more direct comparisons with other studies that have also used that measure. In the field of sexuality, many prevalidated measures of sex-related constructs are not only found in peer-reviewed journal articles, but have also been compiled into reference books (e.g., *Handbook of Sexuality Related Measures;* Fisher, 2011) along with descriptions, psychometric properties, and scoring guidelines.

If a researcher opts to use a preexisting measure, he or she may often deem one or more modifications to be necessary. For example, the researcher may judge that the instructions need elaboration, the language needs simplification, or items need clarification for the measure to be appropriate for use with a particular sample in a given study. In sexuality research, this is commonly the case when using pre-established measures with sexual minority samples, because measures are often designed for use with heterosexual individuals or those having sex with other-sex partners. For instance, the original instructions for the Female Sexual Function Index, a popular measure used to assess women's experiences of their sexuality (e.g., orgasm, desire, satisfaction, lubrication, pain) over a 4-week period, define *sexual intercourse* as vaginal penetration (Rosen et al., 2000). Although this definition encompasses the extent of intercourse practiced by many people, it fails to capture forms of vaginal penetration practiced by individuals who insert fingers, sex toys, or other items into their vaginas in addition to, or in lieu of, penile penetration. Therefore, researchers who use this measure with participants who may be engaging in forms of vaginal penetration other than penile–vaginal intercourse (e.g., women who have sex exclusively with women) sometimes choose to modify the definition of sexual intercourse to be more inclusive of women's diverse sexual experiences (e.g., Schick, Rosenberger, Herbenick, & Reece, 2012). Another way that measures are sometimes modified is by adopting their framework to assess a different yet related construct when other measures specific to that construct are unavailable. For instance, a measure designed to assess general body satisfaction may be modified to assess a specific component of women's bodies (e.g., their genitals; Schick, Calabrese, Rima, & Zucker, 2010).

At times, a researcher may choose to omit items from a scale or measure altogether. For instance, if a researcher was interested in measuring sexual self-efficacy among a sample of middle-aged mothers using Rosenthal, Moore, and Flynn's (1991) Sexual Self-Efficacy Scale, a measure that was originally developed for use with college students, asking the participants to rate their certainty that they could be honest with their friends about not having had sex would not be developmentally appropriate or yield the desired information; thus, the researcher would likely opt to exclude this item. In some cases, a researcher chooses to omit many items, using only a subset of items from an existing measure instead of the scale in its entirety, for conceptual or practical reasons. For example, if the researcher has specific interest in only one aspect of a multidimensional scale, a limit on the number of items that could be included in the survey, concerns about participants' fatigue, or time constraints, he or she may opt to exclude entire subscales or administer prevalidated short forms (reduced item versions) of the original measure if available in the published literature (e.g., the International Index of Erectile Function; Rosen, Cappelleri, Smith, Lipsky, & Pena, 1999).

Whether rephrasing, shortening, expanding, or otherwise adapting a preexisting measure, it is important to recognize that any deviation from the original form on which previously established psychometric properties were based has the potential to influence those properties, for example, reducing construct validity. This word of caution excludes subscales and short forms of a measure, which are generally validated independently of the parent measure, thus preserving psychometric soundness if used in isolation.

Development of New Measures

Scientific, survey-based research on sexuality has been conducted for more than 60 years in the United States, yet much remains unknown about people's mental and physical experience of their sexuality. As new phenomena are discovered and documented, a corresponding need for methods of measuring those phenomena develops. Moreover, at times, new methods of measuring "old" phenomena are also desired because of identified flaws in existing approaches. Whatever the motivation, researchers commonly choose to create new measures to capture phenomena of interest.

Consultation in the process of survey development. Developing a measure from scratch can be a daunting task for any researcher. Even if a researcher considers himself or herself to be an ingroup member of the community under study, a scientific expert on the particular topic of interest, or both, the researcher needs to be cognizant of the limitations to his or her knowledge, carefully differentiating evidence-based facts from subjective experiences and assumptions. Most research is conducted to investigate the unknown, and in sexuality research, the often private context of this unknown only furthers a researcher's understanding of the topic. Thus, measure development should be regarded as a multistep process in which consultation on the topic of interest with members of the population of interest is essential.

In the preliminary stages of survey development, the researcher should consult the scientific literature to generate research ideas and familiarize himself or herself with the available evidence surrounding the topic of interest. Subsequently, open-ended questions and discussion about the general topic of interest with members of the targeted population can help the researcher to define the specific construct he or she wants to measure and generate a more nuanced understanding of that construct as it relates to the population of interest.

The data gathered via consultation can be used in conjunction with the information gleaned from the scientific literature as a knowledge base to draw from when creating survey items and responses. If the researcher's intent is to develop a quantitative scale made up of multiple items that will measure a construct, it is initially useful to cast a wide net in drafting items in terms of quantity and variety to ensure that the construct is captured. Either way, it is helpful to present drafted items to an expert panel exclusive of the research team for review. Ideally, the panel would be composed of research scientists with both topical and survey expertise, who can identify methodological problems with the measure, and members of the community of interest with experience pertinent to the construct, who can provide feedback about the measure's cultural relevance, comprehensiveness, clarity, and sensitivity. Cognitive interviewing, a one-on-one style of interviewing during which a participant vocalizes his or her thoughts and reactions while proceeding through a measure (McColl, 2006), may be a particularly valuable approach with regard to the latter. Input from both sources can be integrated and used to refine the drafted measure (see, e.g., Mavhu, Langhaug, Manyonga, Power, & Cowan, 2008). The next step is to pilot test the refined measure with a sample drawn from the target population. Statistical analysis (e.g., factor analysis) of quantitative pilot data can be used to pare down quantitative measures, retaining only subsets of items that tap into shared constructs for use as subscales. Pilot data yielded from quantitative and qualitative items can also illuminate a need for item addition or adaptation to capture the construct of interest (see, e.g., Herbenick & Reece, 2010). Once the measure has been finalized, a remaining step is to validate it. Description of this process is beyond the scope of this chapter; we encourage researchers to refer to DeVellis (2003) for detailed guidelines.

Item wording and ordering. When asking questions about sex and sexuality related topics, it is important to be sensitive to several issues, including the language and order of items. The way that an item is worded and the order in which it appears may increase comfort and clarity for the participants. The sections that follow offer several suggestions.

Asking about sexual behavior and other sensitive topics: Threat minimization. Many aspects of sexuality (e.g., behavior, fantasy, anatomy) continue to be taboo topics in U.S. society. Accordingly, participants can easily perceive inquiries about such sensitive subject matter as invasive and a threat to privacy. A researcher can use multiple techniques when designing a survey that will help to minimize perceived threat. The following suggestions are derived from a guide to survey development written by Bradburn, Sudman, and Wansink (2004).

One tactic researchers can use is to gradually lead into sensitive material by placing relatively benign questions ahead of uncomfortable or provocative questions (Bradburn et al., 2004). For instance, researchers may want to consider asking about routine health care (e.g., dental care) before asking about screening for sexually transmitted infections (STIs). Similarly, when asking questions about behavior that the participant might judge to be socially undesirable, asking about past participation is generally perceived as less threatening than asking about current behavior and should therefore lead if both types of questions are to be asked (Bradburn et al., 2004).

Another useful approach is normalizing a given behavior, perception, or cognition before asking about it (Bradburn et al., 2004). This approach is especially relevant to sexuality research because the physical and psychological sexual experiences of others are often not readily accessible to an individual for comparative purposes, making it difficult for that individual to gauge the normalcy of his or her own experiences. Thus, providing reassurance that survey respondents' experiences are likely common—or at least experienced by others—before inquiring about them may minimize respondents' motivation to misrepresent their experiences. For example, if inquiring about women's experiences with heterosexual anal sex (i.e., penile–anal intercourse), it may be helpful to preface the question by stating, "Anal sex with a male partner is a common practice among women" or, to normalize both engagement in and abstinence from anal sex, "There is considerable variation in women's anal sex practices with male partners; some women engage in anal sex regularly, whereas others do so rarely or never."

In a similar vein, asking questions about others might be a useful lead into asking questions about the self (Bradburn et al., 2004). For example, inquiries about masturbation practices may be less jarring if they are framed as follows: "1. Do you know of other women who masturbate? 2. How about yourself?" In sum, researchers would be well advised to be thoughtful about the questions they ask and to consider framing their questions in ways that enhance honest and valid reporting. This can be particularly important when asking questions about socially taboo topics such as human sexuality.

Defining sex-related terminology: Ensuring common understanding. Many *sex*-related terms communicate different meanings to different people. In fact, the meaning of the term *sex* itself is highly variable, with some participants defining *sex* as only penile–vaginal intercourse and others including oral and anal sexual activities in their definition of *sex* (Bogart, Cecil, Wagstaff, Pinkerton, & Abramson, 2000; Carpenter, 2001; Pitts & Rahman, 2001; Sanders & Reinisch, 1999). In the absence of an explicit definition, heteronormative assumptions about sex being synonymous with penile–vaginal intercourse can lead to misinterpretation of the self-reported sexual behavior of men who have sex with men and women who have sex with women. Even with regard to heterosexual activity, consensus about the meaning of the term *sex* is sometimes lacking. For example, some adolescents who engage in penile–anal penetration consider themselves virgins because of their lifetime abstinence from penile–vaginal penetration (Carpenter, 2001) and could potentially endorse the "no" response option if asked about lifetime incidence of sex. Others who have never engaged in either penile–anal or penile–vaginal penetration might endorse the "yes" option on the basis of their past performance of oral sex or participation in activity that culminated in orgasm (Mehta, Sunner, Head, Crosby, & Shrier, 2011). Thus, a researcher's failure to clearly define sexual behavior terminology has the potential to introduce variability in item interpretation across participants and foster researcher misunderstanding of collected survey data. In spite of this imperative, a recent review of sexual behavior survey research published in sexual health journals over the past 6 years revealed that only 32% of articles explicitly defined sexual behavior terminology (Malacad & Hess, 2011).

The ambiguity surrounding sexual behavior terminology extends to other aspects of sexuality as well. For example, researchers commonly ask participants to identify their sexual orientation via single-item measures with limited response options (e.g., "homosexual/gay/lesbian," "bisexual," "heterosexual/straight," or "other"). However, as highlighted by Klein's Sexual Orientation Grid (Klein, Sepekoff, & Wolf, 1985), *sexual orientation* can refer to same-sex versus other-sex preference in terms of multiple dimensions (e.g., attraction, fantasy, behavior) and has the potential to vary across these dimensions within a single individual (see also Chapters 18 and 19, this volume). Further complicating measurement is the potential variation according to time frame (present, past, ideal) given the fluidity of sexual preference across the life span (Klein et al., 1985). Thus, ensuring shared meaning across participants as well as between the research team and participants can present a formidable challenge to any researcher.

A few simple strategies for addressing the ambiguity surrounding many sex-related terms are (a) to include simple definitions of potentially confusing terms in items or measures containing such terms (e.g., "By *anal sex,* we mean putting your penis in another man's ass/anus or another man putting his penis in your ass/anus"), (b) to replace vague terms with more specific descriptors to represent the construct of interest (e.g., substituting "men who have sex with men (MSM)" for "gay men" when seeking to isolate men with a behavioral same-sex preference, irrespective of how they define their sexual identity), and (c) to consult with members of the targeted population, soliciting direct feedback about their interpretation of a term or item.

Particular care in defining sex-related terminology must be taken when working with sexual and gender minority communities because heteronormative assumptions can lead a researcher to pose questions that are potentially confusing to respondents and fail to solicit the desired information. For example, when operationalizing sexual risk as condom use during penile–anal intercourse among men who have sex with men in a study of sexual safety, simply asking whether a condom was worn without contextualizing condom wearing according to partner (self vs. other) and sexual position (insertive or receptive) potentially groups men who engaged in behaviors of vastly different levels of risk into a single category. For instance, men who were the insertive partner only and wore a condom the entire time could be grouped with men who occupied both positions, wearing a condom in the insertive position but being penetrated by their partner without a condom in the receptive position. When working with transgender individuals, inferring the type of genitalia a participant possesses on the basis of his or her gender identity (e.g., assuming a self-identified man has a penis) can cause researchers to develop items that are insensitive, irrelevant, and difficult to answer.

Additional language considerations. Careful wording of survey items is imperative to the quality of the data produced. Item phrasing ought to be as clear, simple, and direct as possible. In this section, we discuss several common wording errors in the context of sex-related survey research. Additional examples are provided in Table 4.1.

Double-barreled items. Double-barreled items refers to items that assess more than one construct per question, such that respondents must respond to two inquiries with one response (Bradburn et al., 2004; DeVellis, 2003). Consider the following item hypothetically posed in a true–false format: "Vibrators make orgasms easier to achieve and make sex more pleasurable." If a participant agreed with the first part of that statement but not the second, the appropriate response option is not immediately obvious. Furthermore, if a researcher were to find that the majority of participants endorsed the "false" response for that statement, then concluding that participants disagreed with one part independent of the other, such as stating that the majority of participants disagreed that vibrators make orgasms easier, would be an inappropriate claim because the "false" responses could have been driven by their opinions on vibrators making sex more pleasurable.

Negative and double-negative items. Negatively worded items should be used with caution given

TABLE 4.1

Common Measurement Errors to Avoid When Developing Survey Items

Name	Description	Error example	Potential solution
Double-barreled items	Items that assess more than one construct per question	Women should not feel ashamed if they masturbate because almost all women masturbate.	Women should not feel ashamed if they masturbate.
Strongly worded items	Items that include bold or extreme language	I find the idea of using lubricants appalling.	I find the idea of using lubricants unappealing.
Double-negative items	Items that include two negative statements	I do not clean my vibrator when I do not use a condom on my vibrator.	I clean my vibrator when I do not use a condom on my vibrator.
Verbally complex items	Items that include vocabulary requiring advanced education or training to comprehend	Have you ever had any symptoms of vulvodynia?	Have you ever had any unexplained pain in your genital region?

the added layer of cognitive complexity they contribute and the confusion they may foster among respondents. On such items, participants possessing a positive view about a construct sometimes need to endorse a negative response option, which may feel confusing to them. For example, expressing pro–birth control views using a response scale ranging from *disagree* to *agree* is arguably more challenging if the item is phrased "I do not approve of my partner using birth control," requiring participants to disagree with not approving, versus "I approve of my partner using birth control," which allows them to agree with approving. Even more complicated than single-negative items are double-negative items, or items that include two negatives (e.g., "I do not approve of my partner not using birth control"). Such items typically have even greater potential to confuse participants while adding little benefit and are therefore discouraged in nearly all circumstances.

Despite the risk of added confusion inherent in negatively worded items, researchers sometimes have an incentive to include negatively worded items that correspond to parallel, positively worded items within a survey to ensure that participants are consistent in the views they are expressing across both versions (e.g., agreeing with using birth control and disagreeing with not using birth control). Thus, researchers need to weigh the risk of participant confusion against the gain of establishing internal consistency when deciding whether to include such items.

An additional consideration is that phrasing items only in a positive way (e.g., "Do you approve of your partner using birth control?") may implicitly suggest that there is a "right" answer, which could bias participants toward agreement (Dillman, Smyth, & Christian, 2009). One proposed solution is to include both the positively and the negatively worded options within a single item (e.g., "Do you or do you not approve of your partner using birth control?"), conveying permission to endorse either, and to provide parallel response options (e.g., "(1) do approve; (2) do not approve"; Dillman et al., 2009).

Verbally complex items. Regardless of the sociodemographic composition of the target sample, a survey should be designed for a broad audience, and participants should not need advanced education or training to understand and respond to it. Researchers should be cautious about using vocabulary that exceeds a sixth-grade reading level and avoid using scientific jargon unless accompanied by a colloquial definition. For instance, rather than asking a male participant, "Did you engage in receptive penile–anal penetration with a male partner?" it may be more appropriate to ask, "Did a man put his penis in your anus ("fuck you in the ass")?" Consultation with the members of the population of interest can help the researcher identify appropriate colloquial language and ensure that the wording he or she considers to be simple is perceived that way by participants (see Herbenick et al., 2010, for examples of how sexual behavior items were pilot tested among adolescents). In addition to wording items as simply as possible, diagrams and illustrations may be helpful aids. For instance, when asking participants about specific parts of their genitals, a labeled anatomical diagram would enable participants to respond even if they were unfamiliar with both the medical and the slang terms for these parts (e.g., Gartrell & Mosbacher, 1984).

Strongly worded items. Many researchers believe that strongly worded items (e.g., "I hate it when my partner performs cunnilingus on me") should be avoided because they could increase the likelihood of unanimous endorsement of a particular response option among participants (Bradburn et al., 2004) as opposed to the variability across participants in response selection that is typically desired in research. Softer language (e.g., "I feel uncomfortable when my partner performs cunnilingus on me") may generate the preferred distribution across response categories. However, depending on the construct being examined, the opposite may be true; a loaded item could produce greater variability than a softly worded version of the item if the item is assessing a construct that most people tend to share an opinion about. For instance, most people who have been exposed to public health messages regarding sexual health and safety would probably agree with the statement "Condoms are usually an effective way to reduce the likelihood of STI/HIV transmission," whereas a more strongly worded version of that item, for example, "Condoms are always an effective way to reduce the likelihood of STI/HIV transmission," may be more divisive. In sum, the use of strongly worded items ought to depend on the nature of the construct of interest.

Response formatting. When constructing survey items, the response options may provide as much meaning as the questions themselves. Therefore, it is important to take great care when deciding on the response options that will be provided to the participant. The sections that follow present several possible options.

Open-ended versus close-ended questions. When considering the response options to be provided to participants, researchers must first reflect on their research question and the nature of the data that they want to collect. Open-ended questions permit qualitative data to be collected. Thus, participants are encouraged to use their own words to express their opinions or describe their lived experiences in response to a given question; they are not constrained or influenced by preestablished categories (see also Chapter 6, this volume). This form of data collection generates rich, detailed information about a given topic (Dillman et al., 2009) and is particularly useful when exploring a new area of inquiry (Bradburn et al., 2004). Qualitative questions have produced insights into the reasons why men who have sex with men engage in unsafe sex (Adam, Husbands, Murray, & Maxwell, 2005; Carballo-Diéguez et al., 2011), women's experiences of sex during menstruation (Fahs, 2011), and women's introduction of or negotiation techniques regarding female condom use (Choi, Wojcicki, & Valencia-Garcia, 2004). Open-ended questions are also invaluable in the process of developing a measure because they can be used to solicit feedback that can further refine the measure, for example, identifying the need to reword questions to clarify context, simplify complex language, and define vague terms using culturally relevant terminology. However, qualitative surveys require significant expenditures on the part of both researchers and participants. In the absence of preexisting response categories, researchers must devote considerable amounts of time and energy to coding written responses and deciphering meaningful themes. Likewise, greater patience, time, and thought are demanded of participants in responding to open-ended versus close-ended questions (Bradburn et al., 2004), rendering this form of questioning more vulnerable to participant fatigue and incompletion. To motivate participants to provide thoughtful and complete responses, it is useful to limit the number of open-ended questions asked and to preface open-ended questions with a statement emphasizing the importance and value of their response (Dillman et al., 2009). For example, prefacing "Please describe the barriers you have experienced to accessing condoms on campus" with the statement "Your input on this topic is extremely important to helping us improve our university's condom distribution program" could enhance the quantity and quality of responses received.

Close-ended questions refer to items attached to preestablished and limited sets of response options. This type of questioning can take multiple formats, including traditional multiple choice, for which participants are invited to select one of several listed choices or to rank those choices. This form of questioning is advantageous when the researcher is confident that he or she can capture the full range of possible answers in the response set provided (e.g., "What is your HIV status? A. Positive, B. Negative, C. Unknown") and is more conducive to quantitative data analysis with large samples.

A third form of question is a hybrid of the other two. The partially closed question format offers a set of response options that includes an "other" option and space for participants to specify this otherness (Dillman et al., 2009). This type of question may be ideal for inquiries about such topics as sexual identity because numerous, commonly known identity labels exist (e.g., *gay, bisexual, straight*), yet the researcher may be uncertain about the existence of others and does not want to force a participant to choose a label that he or she would not ordinarily self-apply.

Response options for close-ended questions. Once the survey items are written, the response options also need to be carefully considered because the types of response options provided will influence the type of data collected. As with item writing, a few common pitfalls should be avoided to increase the clarity of the responses. Examples of each are provided in Table 4.2.

Overlapping response options. In items requiring respondents to endorse a single response option, mutual exclusivity of the response options provided is an important but easily overlooked principle. Failure to follow this principle can taint data and frustrate a participant and ought to be actively monitored.

Unequal distribution of response options. When using a bipolar response scale, according to which two different dimensions are considered endpoints of a continuum (e.g., *strongly disagree* and *strongly agree*), response options should be evenly balanced on either side of the center point. If there are an uneven number of response options on one side relative to the other, participant endorsement on the side possessing more response options may be

TABLE 4.2

Common Measurement Errors to Avoid When Creating Survey Response Options

Name	Description	Error example	Potential solution
Overlapping response options	Response options that are not distinct from one another	1–3 times per day 3–6 times per day 6 or more times per day	1–3 times per day 4–6 times per day 7 or more times per day
Unequal distribution of response options	Response options on a bipolar scale that are unevenly distributed between poles	Strongly disagree Moderately disagree Somewhat disagree Agree	Strongly disagree Somewhat disagree Somewhat agree Strongly agree
Vague quantifiers	Response options that are open to participant interpretation	Never Sometimes Frequently Always	0 of the last 10 times 1–4 of the last 10 times 5–9 of the last 10 times 10 of the last 10 times
Calculations	Response options that require the participant to perform a calculation	Body mass index = [(weight in pounds) / (height in inches)^2]* 703 = ___	Height = ___ feet and ___ inches Weight = ___ pounds
Overly specific response options	Response options that require information that is too detailed for participants to provide	How many ounces of lubricant did you use during your last sexual event?	How many times did you apply lubricant during your last sexual event?
Overly general response options	Response options that are too broad to establish variation across participants	How many bottles of lubricant did you use during your last sexual event?	How many times did you apply lubricant during your last sexual event?

artificially inflated as a result of the extra option (Dillman et al., 2009).

Vague quantifiers. Use of vague quantifiers, or quantitative terminology lacking objective criteria (e.g., *rarely* or *frequently*) may lead to variable interpretation by respondents and erroneous conclusions by researchers. When possible, concrete percentage or frequency values (e.g., "50% of the time" or "one out of every two times") should be specified to ensure common meaning. That said, vague quantifiers are occasionally appropriate or even preferable to concrete values, such as in research assessing participants' perception of their behavior.

Calculations. To eliminate potential mathematical errors, researchers should avoid asking participants to perform calculations and instead request only the raw data needed for such calculations.

Overly specific and overly general response options. When formulating research questions, a researcher must be conscientious about the degree of specificity being asked of participants relative to the level of detail participants are realistically capable of providing. As shown in Table 4.2, if responses are quantitative in nature, then the unit of measurement (e.g., ounces, drops) must be familiar to participants and assessable with regard to the construct to be quantified (e.g., lubricant). At the same time, response categories or units of measurement that are overly general (e.g., bottles) may fail to generate variability across response categories. Thus, the researcher should aim to offer response options that will differentiate participants but require only a level of detail that participants can provide with accuracy.

SURVEY MODALITIES

With the technological advances that have occurred over the past several decades, numerous modes of survey administration have emerged as supplements or alternatives to traditional methods. In this section, we provide a brief review of the options available to modern-day sex researchers.

Face-to-Face Interviewing

Before the 1960s, face-to-face interviewing was the predominant and most widely accepted method of survey research in the United States. Interviewers were sent to people's homes or places of work to conduct one-on-one interviews, an approach that yielded high rates of cooperation at the time (e.g., 70%–90%). Social courtesy, the perceived sincerity of the interviewer, and the individualized attention received by participants have been suggested factors contributing to this success (Dillman et al., 2009). Indeed, Alfred Kinsey's groundbreaking studies of sexual behavior used a face-to-face interviewing method (Kinsey et al., 1948, 1953), and many present-day sexuality researchers continue to do so today. As discussed earlier, a major advantage of face-to-face interviewing is that the researcher can clarify confusing terms of questions, thus enhancing the validity of participant responses. However, a disadvantage—particularly with socially taboo topics—is that some participants may not feel comfortable disclosing certain of their sexual behaviors or experiences in person to a researcher. Indeed, some individuals may be more comfortable reporting about sensitive topics in settings that feel more private or anonymous, such as via the Internet.

Beyond the traditional one-on-one format, face-to-face interviewing can also occur in a group format; focus groups generate data from multiple interviewees simultaneously, with the interaction between participants providing an additional layer of information (Basch, 1987; Montell, 1999). Whether conducted in a one-on-one or a group format, interviews can vary by degree of structure, ranging from an interviewer-administered questionnaire, in which a specified order and wording of questions and response options are strictly followed, to an open-ended format, in which the interviewer prepares only a few general questions to guide the discussion. Although face-to-face interviewing has received broad criticism as a mode of data collection that is particularly vulnerable to social desirability bias, which is of particular concern in sexuality research given the sensitivity of the topic, several recent reviews of sexual behavior research comparing face-to-face interviewing with other survey modes have suggested that this heightened vulnerability might exist for some aspects of sexuality (e.g., forced sex) but not for others (e.g., virginity status, number of sexual partners) and may vary by sociodemographic characteristics (e.g., geographic location, education) and other factors (Hamilton & Morris, 2010; McCallum & Peterson, 2012; Phillips, Gomez, Boily, & Garnett, 2010).

Telephone Interviewing

Although telephone surveying was commonly considered an inferior method of data collection relative to face-to-face interviews before the 1960s, it became more favorable in the 1970s and 1980s with the development of area codes to enable direct-dial calls, decreased long-distance charges, improved telephone line quality, and increased prevalence of telephone service among U.S. households. In its original form, this method of data collection maintained human interaction, albeit remote, and in so doing conveyed a sense of legitimacy to respondents. Later, such interaction was sometimes replaced by automated processes, including touch-tone data entry and interactive voice response. Telephone interviewing has been challenged by people's decreased willingness to accept unsolicited calls, the addition of multiple phone lines per household, and the widespread use of cellular telephones (Dillman et al., 2009). In addition, in an age in which text messages and other forms of electronic communication have become common substitutions for telephone calls, some people simply do not have the experience with or the desire for prolonged telephone conversations or survey taking. Also, considering that people take their phones with them, they may not be in a private setting when a phone call is received and may thus decline participation in a survey or, if they accept, may provide answers that are not accurate. For these reasons, telephone interviews have become less common and may not provide valid responding for studying many aspects of sexuality. However, some researchers are now exploring the utility of text messaging and Internet-based reporting via smartphones.

Written Questionnaires

Paper-and-pencil self-administered questionnaires present an alternative method of survey research that has existed for decades and continues to be used today. Similar to telephone interviewing, it was once considered inferior to face-to-face interviewing but became more popular with technological advances (e.g., copy machines; Dillman et al., 2009). Written questionnaires are commonly used in classroom settings, for example, and in communities in which access to telephones, computers, or other digital devices for data collection are sparse or only in the hands of those with significant financial resources. If study participants are spaced apart so as to enhance their sense of privacy, written questionnaires can be used to collect valid data about participants' sexual experiences. However, if study participants are closely seated so as to compromise their sense of privacy or confidentiality, the validity of survey responses may be severely compromised.

Computer-Assisted Interviewing and Other Electronic Technology

Several forms of computer-assisted interviewing are available, including computer-assisted telephone interviewing, in which a telephone interviewer administers a scripted questionnaire and enters the participant's responses directly into the computer; computer-assisted personal interviewing, in which a face-to-face interviewer administers a scripted questionnaire and enters the participant's responses directly into the computer; and computer-assisted self-administered interviewing, in which a participant self-administers a computerized questionnaire (Dillman et al., 2009). Computer-assisted interviewing, particularly of the latter form, has become increasingly popular for multiple reasons, including

- the elimination of clerical errors caused by human interviewers;
- removal of interviewer bias;
- programmability of complex skip patterns;
- capacity for easy integration of images, sounds, and video (including dictated instructions, questions, and response options for participants with low literacy);
- potential for randomization of question order, answer choices, or both;
- ability to automatically customize items later in the survey with information entered during earlier items;
- capability to restrict response options; and
- automatic timing and data entry (Bradburn et al., 2004).

As mentioned earlier, in addition to computers, other mobile technologies, including personal digital assistants and smartphones, have emerged as methods of data collection in sex research, offering convenient data entry, assurance of accurate delivery of complicated instructions, programmability of skip patterns, and sampling via random-digit dialing (McCallum & Peterson, 2012). These methods represent a significant advance in the field because they minimize the time lag in reporting of sexual behavior. As technology evolves at an ever-quickening pace, researchers will need to weigh the pros and cons of each new technology, as well as consider their likely limited financial resources and the types of technologies their population of interest has access to and comfort with, when making decisions about data collection methodologies.

Internet-Based Surveys

Since the mid-1990s, the Internet has emerged as a popular mechanism for survey administration given its ability to generate large sample sizes and eliminate costs associated with other methods (e.g., travel and office space for face-to-face interviews, long distance charges for telephone interviews, computer-assisted self-interviewing software for computerized self-interviewing, postage and printing for written surveys). Given the abundance of websites, social networks, and chat rooms available online that are tailored to particular groups of people, the Internet also facilitates access to populations that are difficult to reach via traditional methods, such as sexual minorities. An additional advantage is the enhanced perception of anonymity afforded by this method given that no direct human interaction is required for participation, which could potentially enhance participation among stigmatized group members. At the same time, the lack of a researcher's presence during survey administration makes it difficult if not impossible to clarify survey instructions or items, connect participants reporting mental or physical health problems with appropriate resources, or intervene in an emergency situation (e.g., self-reported suicidal ideation). See, for example, Couper, Traugott, and Lamias (2001).

The advent of Internet-based surveying technology has facilitated event-specific data collection in sexual behavior research using diaries. As a data collection method, *diaries* generally refer to self-reported behavioral logs, with entries repeated over a period of days, weeks, months, or longer. These longitudinal self-reports enable event-level analysis of sexual behavior, including the examination of situational and relational dimensions of a given sexual event. With the exception of data gathered at baseline, diary items typically inquire about participants' sexual cognitions or behaviors in real time or since the prior diary entry, reducing the likelihood of recall bias. Reminder text messages or emails containing hyperlinks to the online survey can be programmed for daily delivery to participants, maximizing the ease and convenience of participation. One caveat is that such a method requires that participants have daily access to the Internet, whether via computer or another electronic device. Although this method does demand daily (or almost daily) participation, previous success using this form of data collection for sexuality research has been reported, with generally low attrition rates, even over extended periods of time (e.g., several months; Fortenberry, Orr, Katz, Brizendine, & Blythe, 1997; McAuliffe, DiFranceisco, & Reed, 2007).

PSYCHOMETRIC CONSIDERATIONS

Ensuring that a measure is a reliable and valid assessment of the construct is an important part of the survey development process. The sections that follow review several of these considerations.

Sampling and Validity

External validity refers to the extent to which a study's findings can be generalized or extended to other individuals. As with many forms of research, sex survey researchers often face the challenge of accessing hard-to-reach populations and collecting data that are representative of such populations. Information provided by the U.S. Census Bureau is key in defining the sociodemographic profile of certain subpopulations and is a common reference point for researchers attempting to collect nationally representative data via matched sampling. However, the annual census does not inquire about sexual orientation when surveying the U.S. population and thus does not provide a sociodemographic profile of sexual minorities that can be used for matching purposes. Moreover, many people who experience same-sex attraction or behavior do not identify as gay; for example, some men who engage in penile–anal or penile–oral intercourse with other men identify as heterosexual (Rietmeijer, Wolitski, Fishbein, Corby, & Cohn, 1998); thus, even if the census did inquire about sexual orientation and all respondents answered truthfully, resulting statistics would not fully represent the subset of people in the United States who experience same-sex attraction or engage in same-sex behavior. Given the uncertainty about the sociodemographic composition of the subset of the U.S. population who engage in same-sex behavior or experience same-sex attraction, often identified as a hard-to-reach population, generating a nationally representative sample of various sexual minority groups is difficult. Recruitment of participants from these groups may be further challenged by the continued stigmatization of same-sex attraction and behavior, which may be particularly salient within certain minority communities (e.g., Rothblum, 1994). Therefore, researchers commonly rely on targeted sampling strategies as opposed to using a standard approach to reach such communities, compromising the external validity of their findings. For additional information on issues to consider when sampling hard-to-reach populations, see Crosby, Salazar, DiClemente, and Lang (2010).

Validity and Reliability Checks

Despite the deeply rooted history of survey methodology in sex research, many present-day critics continue to question whether data attained through a survey instrument, and researchers' translation of that data, are a valid reflection of people's actual lived experiences. This is a reasonable concern given that participants may not accurately report their experiences for a number of reasons, both intentional (e.g., concerns about confidentiality, impression management) and unintentional (e.g., self-deception, recall error, misinterpretation of the survey item; Bertrand & Mullainathan, 2001; McCallum & Peterson, 2012; Warner, 1965; Willis, Royston, & Bercini, 1991), and researchers may not accurately interpret participants' responses. However, multiple methods can be used to combat this threat.

Social desirability scales. One way that some researchers attempt to identify participants who intentionally misrepresent their thoughts, feelings, or behaviors in an effort to cast themselves in a more positive light is to embed a direct measure of social desirability among the other survey measures (Nederhof, 1985). Such measures are designed to be sensitive to high self-monitoring in a manner consistent with social norms and sanctions. Failure to acknowledge common flaws such as occasional resentment of others or reluctance to admit a mistake suggests increased self-monitoring (i.e., decreased honest responding), alerting the researcher to the possibility that response validity on the other self-report measures in the survey may be compromised. Unfortunately, it does not provide a clear indication of the extent of such compromise or a method of compensating for it.

Biomarkers. Examining biomarkers is another method of supporting the validity of some forms of self-reported survey data, and it is a method that is becoming increasingly popular in sexuality research (Hewett et al., 2008; Orr, Fortenberry, & Blythe, 1997). Within this field, *biomarkers* typically refer to biological outcomes detected via laboratory testing of samples of blood, urine, semen, or vaginal secretions that are used to corroborate self-reported sexual behavior or symptoms. For example, previous studies comparing self-reported sexually transmitted infection (STI) status with STI testing results have found that most participants who test negative for STIs self-report that status accurately (Harrington et al., 2001; Kahn, Goodman, Kaplowitz, Slap, & Emans, 2000), whereas a smaller proportion of those who test positive disclose their diagnosis (Clark, Brasseux, Richmond, Getson, & D'Angelo, 1997; Harrington et al., 2001; Hewett et al., 2008), though this varies by type of STI (Harrington et al., 2001; Hornberger, Rosenthal, Biro, & Stanberry, 1995). In addition to STI diagnoses, researchers may use a variety of biomarkers (e.g., hormones, sperm) to validate self-reported behavior (Minnis et al., 2009; Udry & Morris, 1967). Although biomarkers often provide important information, financial barriers, ethical barriers, or both may limit a researcher's access to biomarkers. Moreover, use of biomarkers has been criticized for the high rates of false positive results they generate (Hamilton & Morris, 2010) and their inapplicability to other dimensions of sexuality (McCallum & Peterson, 2012).

Partner reports. Because sexual behavior (excluding masturbation) generally occurs in the presence of at least one other person, an individual's account of the sexual activities that occurred during a given encounter should be verifiable via comparison with the account of another individual who witnessed or partook in the encounter. Overall, reports between sexual partners tend to be consistent for questions that assess participation in behavior as a simple dichotomous variable. For instance, one study found agreement within all couples with regard to penile–vaginal intercourse when variables were dichotomized as yes or no (Padian, Aral, Vranizan, & Bolan, 1995). However, more inconsistency between partners (4%–13%) has been reported when calculations or frequency estimates are required, such as condom use more than 75% of the time (Padian et al., 1995), sexual events over the past 30 days (Ellish, Weisman, Celentano, & Zenilman, 1996), or frequency of sexual contact in the past month (Van Duynhoven, Nagelkerke, & Van De Laar, 1999). This inconsistency between partner reports on items requiring frequency estimates might cue a researcher to reevaluate the objectivity of the question and interpret his or her results cautiously.

Member checks. Data can often be interpreted in a number of ways, and it is the researchers' responsibility to ensure that their interpretation authentically represents the intended meanings of their participants. For example, in a sample of African American women ages 26 to 76, 75% of women disagreed with the statement "A woman like me should use her sexuality to get what she wants." A researcher could easily jump to the conclusion that disagreement with this response represented a moral objection to using sex for personal gain. However, one-on-one, open-ended interviews revealed a diversity of reasons for saying "no" to the item: Whereas, some regarded the behavior as "belittling," others objected because they consider it a way to "do something the easy way," or a strategy with "no guarantee" (Calabrese et al., 2012). Thus, verification of data interpretation with participants in a process termed *member checks* enhances researchers' confidence in the validity of their findings and provides an opportunity to reevaluate initial interpretations of the data (Creswell, 1998). If such consultation is not possible, then researchers need to clearly distinguish conclusions that are mere speculation from data-driven findings.

Repeating survey administration. Another method of verifying the accuracy of data is to collect data for the same construct at two (or more) different time points and determine whether participants responded consistently between those time points. This is sometimes referred to as *test–retest reliability* or *temporal stability* of an item or a scale and is only applicable to constructs for which change in one or both directions would not be anticipated. For instance, among one group of adolescents, the number of self-reported sexual experiences, which should remain stable or increase over time, decreased for approximately 15% of participants between eighth and ninth grades, and age of first sexual experience, which should remain the same, was inconsistently reported across the two time points by more than half of participants (Alexander, Somerfield, Ensminger, Johnson, & Kim, 1993). This unreliable reporting raises questions about the validity of the data. Notably, in a nationally representative sample of adolescents (Brener et al., 2002), the reliability of self-reported sexual behavior was substantially higher than the reliability of many other types of activity (e.g., violence, physical activity, dietary behaviors), suggesting other types of behaviors may be similarily or more affected by self-report bias in this population.

CONCLUDING REMARKS

Survey methods remain one of the only ways to assess participants' mental and physical sexual experiences. The creation of survey items and decisions about which survey modality or modalities to use for a given study are processes requiring careful contemplation of the research question, population of interest, and resources available. In addition to considering common methodological concerns, researchers should be aware of specific challenges to sex research and be cognizant of their own heteronormative biases, which could interfere with developing strong measures and generating meaningful data. Finally, researchers should continue to explore ways in which they can design surveys to reach and capture the experiences of populations with diverse sexual experiences. As new technologies emerge and evolve, researchers will have a broad range of tools available for administering surveys—which can be invigorating as well as daunting. Although studying human sexual behaviors and experiences has significant challenges, it remains an exciting field of study, particularly because of the many unanswered questions in such a young field and the value of sexuality to so many people's lives, families, and relationships.

References

Adam, B. D., Husbands, W., Murray, J., & Maxwell, J. (2005). AIDS optimism, condom fatigue, or self-esteem? Explaining unsafe sex among gay and bisexual men. *Journal of Sex Research, 42*, 238–248. doi:10.1080/00224490509552278

Alexander, C. S., Somerfield, M. R., Ensminger, M. E., Johnson, K. E., & Kim, Y. J. (1993). Consistency of adolescents' self-report of sexual behavior in a longitudinal study. *Journal of Youth and Adolescence, 22*, 455–471. doi:10.1007/BF01537710

Basch, C. E. (1987). Focus group interview: An underutilized research technique for improving theory and practice in health education. *Health Education and Behavior, 14*, 411–448. doi:10.1177/109019818701400404

Bertrand, M., & Mullainathan, S. (2001). Do people mean what they say? Implications for subjective survey data. *American Economic Review, 91*, 67–72. doi:10.1257/aer.91.2.67

Blow, A. J., & Hartnett, K. (2005). Infidelity in committed relationships II: A substantive review. *Journal of Marital and Family Therapy, 31*, 217–233. doi:10.1111/j.1752-0606.2005.tb01556.x

Bogart, L. M., Cecil, H., Wagstaff, D. A., Pinkerton, S. D., & Abramson, P. R. (2000). Is it "sex"? College students' interpretations of sexual behavior terminology. *Journal of Sex Research, 37*, 108–116. doi:10.1080/00224490009552027

Bradburn, N., Sudman, S., & Wansink, B. (2004). *Asking questions: The definitive guide to questionnaire design—for market research, political polls, and social and health questionnaires* (Rev. ed.). San Francisco, CA: Wiley.

Brener, N. D., Kann, L., McManus, T., Kinchen, S. A., Sundberg, E. C., & Ross, J. G. (2002). Reliability of the 1999 Youth Risk Behavior Survey Questionnaire. *Journal of Adolescent Health, 31*, 336–342. doi:10.1016/S1054-139X(02)00339-7

Calabrese, S. K., Zea, M. C., Poppen, P. J., Bowleg, L., Young, M., & Plankey, M. W. (2012, November). *Psychosexual implications of sex as a commodity for HIV+ and high-risk, HIV– African American women*. Paper presented at the Annual Meeting of the Society for the Scientific Study of Sexuality, Tampa, FL.

Carballo-Diéguez, A., Ventuneac, A., Dowsett, G., Balan, I., Bauermeister, J., Remien, R., . . . Mabragaña, M. (2011). Sexual pleasure and intimacy among men who engage in "bareback sex." *AIDS and Behavior, 15*(1, Suppl.), 57–65. doi:10.1007/s10461-011-9900-7

Carpenter, L. M. (2001). The ambiguity of "having sex": The subjective experience of virginity loss in the United States. *Journal of Sex Research, 38*, 127–139. doi:10.1080/00224490109552080

Choi, K.-H., Wojcicki, J., & Valencia-Garcia, D. (2004). Introducing and negotiating the use of female condoms in sexual relationships: Qualitative interviews with women attending a family planning clinic. *AIDS and Behavior, 8*, 251–261. doi:10.1023/B:AIBE.0000044073.74932.6f

Clark, L. R., Brasseux, C., Richmond, D., Getson, P., & D'Angelo, L. J. (1997). Are adolescents accurate in self-report of frequencies of sexually transmitted diseases and pregnancies? *Journal of Adolescent Health, 21*, 91–96. doi:10.1016/S1054-139X(97)00042-6

Couper, M. P., Traugott, M. W., & Lamias, M. J. (2001). Web survey design and administration. *Public Opinion Quarterly, 65*, 230–253. doi:10.1086/322199

Creswell, J. W. (1998). *Qualitative inquiry and research design: Choosing among five traditions*. Thousand Oaks, CA: Sage.

Crosby, R. A., Salazar, L. F., DiClemente, R. J., & Lang, D. L. (2010). Balancing rigor against the inherent limitations of investigating hard-to-reach populations. *Health Education Research, 25*, 1–5. doi:10.1093/her/cyp062

DeVellis, R. F. (2003). *Scale development: Theory and applications* (2nd ed.). Thousand Oaks, CA: Sage.

Dillman, D. A., Smyth, J. D., & Christian, L. M. (2009). *Internet, mail, and mixed-mode surveys: The tailored design method* (3rd ed.). Hoboken, NJ: Wiley.

Ellish, N. J., Weisman, C. S., Celentano, D., & Zenilman, J. M. (1996). Reliability of partner reports of sexual history in a heterosexual population at a sexually transmitted diseases clinic. *Sexually Transmitted Diseases, 23*, 446–452. doi:10.1097/00007435-199611000-00002

Fahs, B. (2011). Sex during menstruation: Race, sexual identity, and women's accounts of pleasure and disgust. *Feminism and Psychology, 21*, 155–178. doi:10.1177/0959353510396674

Fisher, T. D. (2011). *Handbook of sexuality-related measures* (3rd ed.). New York, NY: Routledge.

Fortenberry, J. D., Orr, D. P., Katz, B. P., Brizendine, E. J., & Blythe, M. J. (1997). Sex under the influence: A diary self-report study of substance use and sexual behavior among adolescent women. *Sexually Transmitted Diseases, 24*, 313–319. doi:10.1097/00007435-199707000-00001

Gartrell, N., & Mosbacher, D. (1984). Sex differences in the naming of children's genitalia. *Sex Roles, 10*, 869–876. doi:10.1007/BF00288510

Hamilton, D. T., & Morris, M. (2010). Consistency of self-reported sexual behavior in surveys. *Archives of Sexual Behavior, 39*, 842–860. doi:10.1007/s10508-009-9505-7

Harrington, K. F., DiClemente, R. J., Wingood, G. M., Crosby, R. A., Person, S., Oh, M. K., & Hook, E. W. (2001). Validity of self-reported sexually transmitted diseases among African American female adolescents participating in an HIV/STD prevention intervention trial. *Sexually Transmitted Diseases, 28*, 468–471. doi:10.1097/00007435-200108000-00009

Herbenick, D., & Reece, M. (2010). Development and validation of the female genital self image scale. *Journal of Sexual Medicine, 7*, 1822–1830. doi:10.1111/j.1743-6109.2010.01728.x

Herbenick, D., Reece, M., Schick, V., Sanders, S. A., Dodge, B., & Fortenberry, J. D. (2010). An event-level analysis of the sexual characteristics and composition among adults ages 18 to 59: Results from a national probability sample in the United States. *Journal of Sexual Medicine, 7*(Suppl. 5), 346–361. doi:10.1111/j.1743-6109.2010.02020.x

Hewett, P. C., Mensch, B. S., Ribeiro, M. C. S. A., Jones, H. E., Lippman, S. A., Montgomery, M. R., & Wijgert, J. H. H. M. D. (2008). Using sexually transmitted infection biomarkers to validate reporting of sexual behavior within a randomized, experimental evaluation of interviewing methods. *American Journal of Epidemiology, 168*, 202–211. doi:10.1093/aje/kwn113

Hornberger, L. L., Rosenthal, S. L., Biro, F. M., & Stanberry, L. R. (1995). Sexual histories of adolescent girls: Comparison between interview and chart. *Journal of Adolescent Health, 16*(3), 235–239.

Kahn, J. A., Goodman, E., Kaplowitz, R. A., Slap, G. B., & Emans, S. J. (2000). Validity of adolescent and young adult self-report of Papanicolaou smear results. *Obstetrics and Gynecology, 96*, 625–631. doi:10.1016/S0029-7844(00)00987-X

Kinsey, A. C., Pomeroy, W. B., & Martin, C. E. (1948). *Sexual behavior in the human male*. Philadelphia, PA: Saunders.

Kinsey, A. C., Pomeroy, W. B., Martin, C. E., & Gebhard, P. H. (1953). *Sexual behavior in the human female*. Philadelphia, PA: Saunders.

Klein, F., Sepekoff, B., & Wolf, T. J. (1985). Sexual orientation. *Journal of Homosexuality, 11*, 35–49. doi:10.1300/J082v11n01_04

Laumann, E. O. (1996). *National Health and Social Life Survey, 1992*. Ann Arbor, MI: Interuniversity Consortium for Political and Social Research.

Laumann, E. O., Nicolosi, A., Glasser, D. B., Paik, A., Gingell, C., Moreira, E., & Wang, T. (2005). Sexual problems among women and men aged 40–80 years: Prevalence and correlates identified in the Global Study of Sexual Attitudes and Behaviors. *International Journal of Impotence Research, 17*, 39–57. doi:10.1038/sj.ijir.3901250

Lindau, S. T., Schumm, L. P., Laumann, E. O., Levinson, W., O'Muircheartaigh, C. A., & Waite, L. J. (2007). A study of sexuality and health among older adults in the United States. *New England Journal of Medicine, 357*, 762–774. doi:10.1056/NEJMoa067423

Malacad, B. L., & Hess, G. C. (2011). Sexual behaviour research using the survey method: A critique of the literature over the last six years. *European Journal of Contraception and Reproductive Health Care, 16*, 328–335. doi:10.3109/13625187.2011.600479

Mavhu, W., Langhaug, L., Manyonga, B., Power, R., & Cowan, F. (2008). What is "sex" exactly? Using cognitive interviewing to improve the validity of sexual behaviour reporting among young people in rural Zimbabwe. *Culture, Health, and Sexuality, 10*, 563–572. doi:10.1080/13691050801948102

McAuliffe, T. L., DiFranceisco, W., & Reed, B. R. (2007). Effects of question format and collection mode on the accuracy of retrospective surveys of health risk behavior: A comparison with daily sexual activity diaries. *Health Psychology, 26*, 60–67. doi:10.1037/0278-6133.26.1.60

McCallum, E. B., & Peterson, Z. D. (2012). Investigating the impact of inquiry mode on self-reported sexual behavior: Theoretical considerations and review of the literature. *Journal of Sex Research, 49*, 212–226. doi:10.1080/00224499.2012.658923

McColl, E. (2006). Cognitive interviewing. A tool for improving questionnaire design. *Quality of Life Research, 15*, 571–573. doi:10.1007/s11136-005-5263-8

Mehta, C. M., Sunner, L. E., Head, S., Crosby, R., & Shrier, L. A. (2011). "Sex isn't something you do with someone you don't care about": Young women's definitions of sex. *Journal of Pediatric and Adolescent Gynecology, 24*, 266–271. doi:10.1016/j.jpag.2011.03.003

Michael, R. T., Gagnon, J. H., Laumann, E. O., & Kolata, G. (1994). *Sex in America: A definitive survey*. New York, NY: Warner.

Minnis, A. M., Steiner, M. J., Gallo, M. F., Warner, L., Hobbs, M. M., van der Straten, A., . . . Padian, N. S. (2009). Biomarker validation of reports of recent sexual activity: Results of a randomized controlled study in Zimbabwe. *American Journal of Epidemiology, 170,* 918–924. doi:10.1093/aje/kwp219

Montell, F. (1999). Focus group interviews: A new feminist method. *NWSA Journal, 11,* 44–71. doi:10.2979/NWS.1999.11.1.44

Nederhof, A. J. (1985). Methods of coping with social desirability bias: A review. *European Journal of Social Psychology, 15,* 263–280. doi:10.1002/ejsp.2420150303

Orr, D. P., Fortenberry, D. J., & Blythe, M. J. (1997). Validity of self-reported sexual behaviors in adolescent women using biomarker outcomes. *Sexually Transmitted Diseases, 24,* 261–266. doi:10.1097/00007435-199705000-00005

Padian, N. S., Aral, S., Vranizan, K., & Bolan, G. (1995). Reliability of sexual histories in heterosexual couples. *Sexually Transmitted Diseases, 22,* 169–172. doi:10.1097/00007435-199505000-00008

Phillips, A. E., Gomez, G. B., Boily, M.-C., & Garnett, G. P. (2010). A systematic review and meta-analysis of quantitative interviewing tools to investigate self-reported HIV and STI associated behaviours in low- and middle-income countries. *International Journal of Epidemiology, 39,* 1541–1555. doi:10.1093/ije/dyq114

Pitts, M., & Rahman, Q. (2001). Which behaviors constitute "having sex" among university students in the UK? *Archives of Sexual Behavior, 30,* 169–176. doi:10.1023/A:1002777201416

Reece, M., Herbenick, D., Schick, V., Sanders, S. A., Dodge, B., & Fortenberry, J. D. (2010). Condom use rates in a national probability sample of males and females ages 14 to 94 in the United States. *Journal of Sexual Medicine, 7,* 266–276. doi:10.1111/j.1743-6109.2010.02017.x

Rietmeijer, C. A., Wolitski, R. J., Fishbein, M., Corby, N. H., & Cohn, D. L. (1998). Sex hustling, injection drug use, and non-gay identification by men who have sex with men: Associations with high-risk sexual behaviors and condom use. *Sexually Transmitted Diseases, 25,* 353–360. doi:10.1097/00007435-199808000-00006

Rosen, R., Brown, C., Heiman, J., Leiblum, S., Meston, C., Shabsigh, R., . . . D'Agostino, R. (2000). The Female Sexual Function Index (FSFI): A multidimensional self-report instrument for the assessment of female sexual function. *Journal of Sex and Marital Therapy, 26,* 191–208. doi:10.1080/009262300278597

Rosen, R. C., Cappelleri, J. C., Smith, M. D., Lipsky, J., & Pena, B. M. (1999). Development and evaluation of an abridged, 5-item version of the International Index of Erectile Function (IIEF-5) as a diagnostic tool for erectile dysfunction. *International Journal of Impotence Research, 11,* 319–326. doi:10.1038/sj.ijir.3900472

Rosenthal, D., Moore, S., & Flynn, I. (1991). Adolescent self-efficacy, self-esteem, and sexual risk-taking. *Journal of Community and Applied Social Psychology, 1,* 77–88. doi:10.1002/casp.2450010203

Rothblum, E. D. (1994). "I only read about myself on bathroom walls": The need for research on the mental health of lesbians and gay men. *Journal of Consulting and Clinical Psychology, 62,* 213–220. doi:10.1037/0022-006X.62.2.213

Sanders, S. A., & Reinisch, J. M. (1999). Would you say you "had sex" if . . .? *JAMA, 281,* 275–277. doi:10.1001/jama.281.3.275

Schick, V., Rosenberger, J., Herbenick, D., & Reece, M. (2012). Sexual behaviour and risk reduction strategies among a multinational sample of women who have sex with women. *Sexually Transmitted Infections, 88,* 407–412. doi:10.1136/sextrans-2011-050404

Schick, V. R., Calabrese, S. K., Rima, B. N., & Zucker, A. N. (2010). Genital appearance dissatisfaction: Implications for women's genital image self-consciousness, sexual esteem, sexual satisfaction, and sexual risk. *Psychology of Women Quarterly, 34,* 394–404. doi:10.1111/j.1471-6402.2010.01584.x

Smith, A. M. A., Rissel, C. E., Richters, J., Grulich, A. E., & de Visser, R. O. (2003). Sex in Australia: The rationale and methods of the Australian Study of Health and Relationships. *Australian and New Zealand Journal of Public Health, 27,* 106–117. doi:10.1111/j.1467-842X.2003.tb00797.x

Udry, J. R., & Morris, N. M. (1967). A method for validation of reported sexual data. *Journal of Marriage and the Family, 29,* 442–446. doi:10.2307/349579

Van Duynhoven, Y. T. H. P., Nagelkerke, N. J. D., & Van De Laar, M. J. W. (1999). Reliability of self-reported sexual histories: Test–retest and interpartner comparison in a sexually transmitted diseases clinic. *Sexually Transmitted Diseases, 26,* 33–42. doi:10.1097/00007435-199901000-00006

Warner, S. L. (1965). Randomized response: A survey technique for eliminating evasive answer bias. *Journal of the American Statistical Association, 60,* 63–69. doi:10.1080/01621459.1965.10480775

Willis, G. B., Royston, P., & Bercini, D. (1991). The use of verbal report methods in the development and testing of survey questionnaires. *Applied Cognitive Psychology, 5,* 251–267. doi:10.1002/acp.2350050307

CHAPTER 5

EXPERIMENTAL, NEUROIMAGING, AND PSYCHOPHYSIOLOGICAL METHODS IN SEXUALITY RESEARCH

Meredith L. Chivers, Kelly D. Suschinsky, Amanda D. Timmers, and Jennifer A. Bossio

> Hence, even in the domain of natural science, the aid of the experimental method becomes indispensable whenever the problem set is the analysis of transient and impermanent phenomena, and not merely the observation of persistent and relatively constant objects.
>
> —W. Wundt (1904)

In this chapter, we provide an introductory overview of experimental and observational methodologies used in sex research, including sexual psychophysiology, cognitive measures of sexual attitudes and interests, hormone sampling, and neuroimaging. Along with a brief discussion of notable findings to inform participant selection and research design, we provide reliability and validity data when possible, make recommendations, and direct the reader to more comprehensive reviews for further reading.

SEXUAL PSYCHOPHYSIOLOGY

Sexual psychophysiological methods involve assessing the physiological aspect of sexual response in combination with cognitive, behavioral, and emotional processes and experiences (Rosen & Beck, 1988). Although sexual response has several components, including desire, arousal, and orgasm (Basson, 2000), most sexual psychophysiological methods assess one of the initial phases of sexual response, typically sexual arousal or sexual desire. The development of these methods has facilitated a variety of basic and applied questions, including investigating how sexual arousal interacts with other emotions (e.g., Peterson & Janssen, 2007), hormonal or other somatic factors that may influence sexual response (e.g., Laan, Van Lunsen, & Everaerd, 2001), sexual preferences (e.g., Freund, 1963), the effectiveness of various treatments for sexual dysfunctions (e.g., Brotto, Basson, & Luria, 2008), and how sexual responses may be learned or conditioned (e.g., Hoffmann, 2010; see also Chapter 8, this volume).

Measuring Sexual Arousal

In the sections that follow we briefly review some of the commonly used measures of sexual arousal; for more information about the applications of sexual psychophysiological methods, see Janssen (2007).

Self-report. The most straightforward way to assess whether someone feels sexually aroused is to simply ask; yet how, what, and who one asks are important matters to consider. There are two primary methods of assessing self-reported arousal. In *discrete response methods,* participants report their subjective level of arousal once or repeatedly at different intervals, usually after the presentation of a sexual stimulus (Henson, Rubin, Henson, & Williams, 1977). Alternatively, with *continuous response methods,* participants rate their arousal (either overall feelings of sexual arousal or perception of genital sensations) throughout an entire stimulus by moving a lever or computer mouse (Rellini, McCall, Randall, & Meston, 2005) or by raising and lowering a visual representation of a bar (e.g., Chivers, Seto, & Blanchard, 2007). Laan (1994) reported good internal consistency ($\alpha = .82$) for a discrete measure of women's self-reported

http://dx.doi.org/10.1037/14193-005
APA Handbook of Sexuality and Psychology: Vol. 1. Person-Based Approaches, D. L. Tolman and L. M. Diamond (Editors-in-Chief)

sexual arousal that included items assessing overall sexual arousal, strongest sexual arousal, and genital sensations, rated using unipolar visual analog scales. Although men's self-reported sexual arousal is often assessed, similar reports on consistency have not been published. To date, no research on other measures of subjective response reliability (e.g., test–retest reliability) has been reported.

What one asks depends on what aspect of the experience of sexual arousal one wants to assess. Participants may be asked to report their overall experience or feelings of sexual arousal (e.g., "How sexually aroused do you feel?") or their perception of genital or extragenital physiological changes associated with sexual arousal (e.g., "Do you feel any genital throbbing or pulsing?"; Heiman & Rowland, 1983). It is unclear to what degree one's experience or feelings of sexual arousal are influenced by one's perception of genital responding, or vice versa, but these aspects of self-reported sexual arousal are highly positively correlated in both women (Slob, Bax, Hop, Rowland, & van der Werff ten Bosch, 1996) and men (Rowland & Heiman, 1991), indicating that they may be inextricably linked.

Who one asks may also be an important factor to consider; however, most research has shown little difference when comparing self-reported sexual arousal across groups. Women may report slightly less sexual arousal to sexual stimuli than men, but usually in response to pornography relative to erotica and when tested alone or in small groups (Murnen & Stockton, 1997). More recent research, however, has indicated that heterosexual women and men report similar degrees of sexual arousal in response to heterosexual sexual stimuli (Suschinsky, Lalumière, & Chivers, 2009). Likewise, self-reported sexual arousal tends to be similar across participants of different sexual orientations (e.g., Brotto & Yule, 2011; Chivers et al., 2007), even among those participants who report no sexual attraction toward others (Brotto & Yule, 2011). Participants with sexual dysfunction may report less sexual arousal than participants without sexual difficulties (e.g., Heiman & Rowland, 1983), though this is not always the case (e.g., Brotto, Klein, & Gorzalka, 2009). To date, limited research has been conducted to examine ethnic differences in self-reported sexual arousal (e.g., Yule, Woo, & Brotto, 2010). Sex offenders' self-reported arousal may not differ from non–sex offenders' self-reported sexual arousal (e.g., Quinsey, Steinman, Bergersen, & Holmes, 1975). These results must be interpreted with caution; because self-reports are prone to response biases, forensic researchers and clinicians often include measures of genital arousal to obtain an objective measure of the sexual response, at least in men.

Genital. Sexual arousal involves a range of physiological changes reflecting activation in the sympathetic nervous system (e.g., pupil dilation, cardiovascular responses, and respiratory responses); the most reliable and valid change is genital vasocongestion, resulting in vulvar, clitoral, and vaginal epithelium vasoengorgement and vaginal lubrication in women (Levin, 2003) and penile erection in men. The most commonly used measure of genital vasocongestion in women is the vaginal photoplethysmograph (Palti & Bercovici, 1967), a clear, tampon-shaped plastic probe containing a light source (most commonly an infrared LED) and a light detector (photoresistor). The light source illuminates the capillary bed of the vaginal wall and the blood circulating within it, and the amount of back-scattered light serves as an indirect measurement of vasocongestion because the amount of reflected light varies in relation to the amount of blood in the vaginal tissue. Women insert the gauge themselves, therefore minimizing experimenter contact. The vaginal photoplethysmograph produces two signals: *vaginal blood volume,* the direct-current-coupled component of the signal, provides an index of slow changes in the pooling of blood, and *vaginal pulse amplitude* (VPA), the alternating-current-coupled signal component, reflects the dynamic changes in vasocongestion with each heartbeat, with higher amplitudes indicating higher levels of arousal (Prause & Janssen, 2005). Increases in VPA are specific to sexual stimuli (e.g., Suschinsky et al., 2009), whereas vaginal blood volume tends to increase in response to sexual and nonsexual anxiety-inducing stimuli (Laan, Everaerd, & Evers, 1995).

In addition to being a valid measure of genital response, VPA demonstrates good reliability (Prause, Janssen, Cohen, & Finn, 2002). There is also evidence of its predictive and discriminant validity. Increases in postlaboratory sexual behavior are associated with increased vaginal responses to sexual stimuli (Both, Spiering, Everaerd, & Laan, 2004). Variation in the VPA signal can distinguish premenopausal women from postmenopausal women (Laan et al., 2001), heterosexual from same-gender-attracted women when using stimuli depicting solitary men and women (Chivers et al., 2007), and women with and without sexual arousal disorders (Basson & Brotto, 2003). However, the majority of studies have found no differences in genital response between sexually functional and dysfunctional groups (see Laan, Van Driel, & Van Lunsen, 2008, for a review).

Thermography, the second most commonly used measure of genital vasocongestion, involves measuring changes in genital temperature resulting from increased blood flow using either thermistors (i.e., small temperature gauges) that attach to the labia or penis (e.g., Henson et al., 1977; Webster & Hammer, 1983) or thermal imaging cameras that detect and record changes in the skin's electrochemical energy during sexual response (Kukkonen, Binik, Amsel, & Carrier, 2010). Because the dependent measure, temperature change, is identical for women and men, thermography may facilitate cross-sex comparisons; however, the range of responding differs between women and men and may also differ between individuals (Kukkonen et al., 2010). Both thermistors and thermal imaging cameras reliably detect increases in genital temperature with exposure to sexual, but not neutral or humorous, stimuli (Henson et al., 1977; Kukkonen et al., 2010). VPA, vaginal blood volume, and labial temperature tend to be positively correlated with each other during sexual stimuli, but less so during nonerotic stimuli (Henson, Rubin, & Henson, 1979). Labial temperature may be more stable across testing sessions than genital blood flow responses (Henson et al., 1979); the reliability of genital responses assessed with thermal imaging has yet to be reported. Despite the advantages and the validity of temperature measurements, these devices are less frequently used because of slower onset of temperature change during sexual response, lengthy return-to-baseline intervals, and, for thermal imaging, equipment and operational costs (Kukkonen et al., 2010; Webster & Hammer, 1983).

Other measures of women's genital sexual response have been validated but are less commonly used. These measures include the labial photoplethysmograph, a small clip containing a pulse plethysmograph that attaches to the labia minora (Prause, Cerny, & Janssen, 2005); laser Doppler imaging, which measures cutaneous blood flow to the vulvar skin through laser imaging (Waxman & Pukall, 2009); and the clitoral photoplethysmograph for measuring clitoral blood volume changes during sexual response (Gerritsen et al., 2009).

Penile plethysmography (the measurement of erectile response to various stimulus conditions) is the most commonly used measure of genital vasocongestion in men. Volumetric plethysmography measures changes in penile volume via air displacement from a cylinder placed over the penis, detected by a pressure transducer (Freund, 1963). This method is very sensitive to small changes in genital vasocongestion (Kuban, Barbaree, & Blanchard, 1999), but it is technologically demanding and is only used in clinical forensic settings to assess atypical and problematic sexual interests, such as pedophilia (e.g., Freund & Watson, 1991). Circumferential plethysmography, which is much more commonly used in both clinical and research laboratories, measures changes in the circumference of the penis using a strain gauge—either a thin rubber band (C. Fisher, Gross, & Zuch, 1965) or a metal cuff (e.g., Barlow gauge; Barlow, Becker, Leitenberg, & Agras, 1970)—that the man places on the midshaft of his penis himself. Penile vasocongestion is strongly related to men's sexual interests and attractions, and patterns of penile responses to sexual stimuli can be reliably used to assess partner gender preferences (e.g., Freund, 1963) and age preferences (e.g., Freund & Watson, 1991). Penile responses to preferred and nonpreferred sexual stimuli differentiate rapists and nonrapists (e.g., Lalumière, Quinsey, Harris, Rice, & Trautrimas, 2003) and sexually sadistic and nonsadistic men (e.g., Seto, Lalumière, Harris, & Chivers, 2012). Men with sexual dysfunctions also have different penile responses relative to men without sexual dysfunctions (e.g., Rowland, Van Diest, Incrocci, & Slob, 2005). In addition to its discriminative validity, penile plethysmography also exhibits predictive validity: Penile responses to stimuli depicting children or sexual violence are an important predictor of sexual reoffending among sex offenders (Hanson & Morton-Bourgon, 2005), and penile responses to sexual stimuli in the laboratory are associated with increases in sexual behavior on the day after the laboratory session in non–sexual offenders (Both et al., 2004). Because penile plethysmography can differentiate men on the basis of their sexual preferences, it has become the leading measure in assessing problematic sexual interests, though several limits to its use have been reported, including the ability of both sexual offenders and nonoffenders to fake sexual response patterns to some degree (Marshall & Fernandez, 2000).

Additional anatomically equivalent measures that facilitate cross-sex comparisons do exist (other than thermography) but have received less attention. For example, changes in anal blood volume and muscle tension have been measured in men and women (e.g., Bohlen & Held, 1979). The anal probe consists of an LED–transistor photoplethysmograph and a pressure transducer encased within a small structure of silicone rubber tubing, with electrical signals from the probe being sent directly to a recording device. Imaging techniques, including functional MRI (fMRI), have also been used to assess anatomical structures in men and women during sexual activity (e.g., Weijmar-Schultz, van Andel, Sabelis, & Mooyaart, 1999). Electrical activity generated by skeletal muscles in the genital region has also been assessed with electromyography separately in men (e.g., Jiang, Speel, Wagner, Meuleman, & Wijkstra, 2003) and women (Both & Laan, 2007), but to our knowledge, genital responses in men and women have yet to be directly compared with electromyography.

Agreement between self-report and genital measures. Traditional psychometric theory uses agreement between multiple measures of a construct as an index of a measurement's construct validity (Campbell & Fiske, 1959). In sexual psychophysiology, a consistent gender difference in agreement between genital and self-reported sexual arousal, termed *sexual concordance,* has raised concerns regarding the construct validity of genital vasocongestion as a measurement of sexual arousal in women and debate regarding the validity of a model of sexual response whereby genital and affective responses are expected to be strongly related (cf. Basson, 2000). In a recent meta-analysis of 132 sexual psychophysiological studies, Chivers, Seto, Lalumière, Laan, and Grimbos (2010) noted that although women's sexual concordance tends to be positive (average Pearson $r = .26$ across studies), suggesting moderate construct validity, it is significantly lower than men's sexual concordance (average $r = .66$), suggestive of a systematic gender difference in the relationship between physiological and psychological processes relating to sexual arousal.

Currently, why women exhibit lower sexual concordance than men is not known. Chivers et al.'s (2010) meta-analysis indicated that the gender difference in sexual concordance is not the result of several methodological factors, including stimulus characteristics (e.g., stimulus length, modality of presentation, male- versus female-centered content, number of trials), sample characteristics (e.g., age and hormonal contraceptive use in women), statistical factors (e.g., type of correlation computed), and type of vaginal photoplethysmography component used (i.e., vaginal blood volume or VPA). Likewise, the gender difference does not seem to be an extension of women's lower accuracy in reporting nonsexual physiological responses in laboratory settings (e.g., Suschinsky & Lalumière, 2012, 2013). The gender difference is robust across testing sessions (Suschinsky & Lalumière, 2011b) and across different methods of calculating sexual concordance (Suschinsky, Chivers, & Lalumière, 2013). Although women's sexual concordance may be higher when using thermographic measures of arousal (Kukkonen et al., 2010), a significant degree of variability in women's sexual concordance scores remains, with more women than men exhibiting negative or zero correlations between their genital and self-reported sexual arousal. Further research is required to better understand whether low sexual concordance reflects a partial independence between women's physiology and psychology and whether this disconnect has a significant impact on their sexuality.

A related gender difference concerns the relationship between self-reported sexual attractions and patterns of sexual response. Men's genital and self-reported sexual arousal are *category-specific*, meaning their patterns of response correspond to their preferred categories of sexual stimuli including gender, age, and preferred sexual activities (cf. Chivers, 2005). Women's self-reported arousal, much like men's, tends to be somewhat category-specific and corresponds with their stated sexual preferences or interests (cf. Chivers, 2010). Women's genital arousal, however, tends to be more complex and *category-nonspecific*. Heterosexual women's genital sexual arousal is not restricted to stimuli that correspond with their stated sexual preferences or interests, with respect to the sex of the actors depicted (reviewed in Chivers, 2010) or the activities depicted (Suschinsky & Lalumière, 2011a). Depictions of less intense sexual stimuli (e.g., nude individuals exercising or masturbating rather than a couple engaging in sexual intercourse) do elicit category-specific genital responses in same-gender-attracted women, but stimuli depicting partnered sexual interactions elicit nonspecific genital responses in these same women (Chivers et al., 2007). Women even show significant genital arousal to nonhuman sexual stimuli (Chivers & Bailey, 2005; Chivers et al., 2007).

One possible explanation for the gender differences in sexual arousal patterns is that different endpoints of vasocongestion are measured for women and men when patterns of arousal using vaginal photoplethysmography and penile plethysmography are compared. Often, researchers compare vaginal vasoengorgement in women, a precursor to vaginal lubrication, with men's penile erection. Although penile responses are well understood, the relationship between vaginal vasocongestion and lubrication is not (Levin, 2003). Some researchers have tried to measure lubrication more directly: Measures of lubrication in laboratory settings have involved inserting weighted absorbent materials (e.g., tampons) into the vagina during stimulus presentation and then reweighing the material on removal to determine the amount of fluid produced. Similar to thermography, however, these procedures do not allow for assessment of rapid changes in genital vasocongestion or multiple measurements (Levin, 2003). Given that nonspecific responses to sexual stimuli have been reported using nongenital methods of assessing sexual interests, such as viewing time (cf. Chivers, 2010), it is unlikely that measurement differences account for the gender difference in the specificity of sexual response.

Using self-reported measures of sexual arousal assumes that participants are aware of their arousal and comfortable with reporting this information to others. It is unclear whether participants are aware of their sexual arousal at all times (see the earlier discussion of women's lower sexual concordance), but evidence has indicated that some participants are less comfortable with reporting their arousal relative to others in certain testing conditions. For example, women's discrete reports, but not their continuous reports, of their sexual arousal are significantly negatively correlated with their desire to present themselves in a socially favorable manner (Huberman, Suschinsky, Lalumière, & Chivers, in press). Thus, continuous measures of self-reported sexual arousal, which appear to be less affected by socially desirable responding, are recommended whenever possible to assess sexual arousal.

Genital responses are considered to be a more objective measure of sexual arousal because they are more difficult for participants to consciously or unconsciously alter relative to self-reported sexual arousal. They may be used to assess sexual preferences (in men) and sexual dysfunctions, but some limitations are still associated with their use. For example, people may consider genital measures of sexual arousal to be more invasive than self-reports of arousal, which may introduce ascertainment biases (e.g., Strassberg & Lowe, 1995). Even among those individuals who are comfortable with participating in studies that measure genital arousal, a small subset of "nonresponders," or people who do not exhibit a genital response, is often found. Although reasons for nonresponse have not been systematically explored, they may include discomfort with the assessment process that may induce an arousal-quashing performance demand, disliking the sexual stimuli, or possible sexual dysfunction. Because of the limitations associated with measuring self-reported and genital responses, indirect means of assessing sexual interests are a natural complement to the use of sexual psychophysiology.

Cognitive Measures of Sexual Interests and Attitudes

A perennial issue in sex research is concern about the biases inherent in self-report (see Chapter 4, this volume). For example, people with atypical sexual interests, such as pedophilia, may, for a variety of reasons, be unwilling to disclose those interests. Indirect cognitive measures may help circumvent these concerns; by examining participants' responses to a cognitive task, researchers can infer sexual preferences or attitudes participants may not be aware of endorsing or are unwilling to disclose. In this way, the construct being measured, such as sexual attraction to children, is not assessed directly but is inferred through measurement of other behaviors (see Snowden, Craig, & Gray, 2011, for a full review).

The information processing model of sexual arousal (Janssen, Everaerd, Spiering, & Janssen, 2000) suggests that both conscious and deliberate and automatic and unconscious cognitive processes are engaged during sexual arousal. In Janssen et al.'s (2000) model, sexual arousal is the product of an unconscious/automatic appraisal stage and a response generation stage. In the appraisal stage, a stimulus is given emotional meaning through a process of stimulus encoding and matching to stimuli from memory. The response generation stage is described as an integrative stage in which the meaning of the stimulus is integrated with response generation or motor plans (e.g., a sexual stimulus elicits physiological sexual arousal). Attentional processes and other higher order mechanisms may affect or be triggered by the appraisal and response-generation stages. Cognitive tasks, as such, may be among the best methods for assessing the stimuli associated with the initiation of sexual behavior, assessing how sexual information is processed and responded to, indirect assessment of sexual interests and attractions, and the measurement of sexual attitudes.

Implicit Association Test. The Implicit Association Test (IAT) was developed by Greenwald, McGhee, and Schwartz (1998) to assess implicit attitudes that stem from underlying, automatically activated, and largely unconscious evaluations. The IAT achieves this goal through a series of cognitive tasks that begin with an initial discrimination task, in which the participant must distinguish examples as belonging to one of two categories (e.g., pictures of men vs. pictures of women). In the most typical IAT design, participants will respond using their left hand to identify the example as belonging to the first class (e.g., pictures of men) and their right hand to classify the example as belonging to the second class (e.g., pictures of women). The next step in the test involves identifying the attribute dimension of examples provided. Typically, the participant must categorize examples (e.g., target words) given on two (usually evaluative) dimensions, such as *sexually attractive* (e.g., the words *arousing* and *sexy*) and *sexually unattractive* (e.g., the words *ugly* and *repulsive*). Finally, the discrimination and attribute dimensions are presented together, pairing first one set (e.g., women and sexually attractive, men and sexually unattractive) and then the second set (e.g., women and sexually unattractive, men and sexually attractive) of discrimination dimensions. If the participant has an automatic association between one particular category and attribute (e.g., pictures of women are sexually attractive), then the first pairing should be considerably easier for the participant to categorize than the second pairing (in which the pictures-of-women dimension is paired with the sexually unattractive dimension), resulting in a faster response time.

The previous example is drawn from a study by Snowden and Gray (2012) that found that heterosexual men and lesbian women had greater facility in categorizing pictures and words when their preferred gender was paired with the sexually attractive dimension, whereas heterosexual women did not show any preference on the basis of gender, replicating previous findings of specificity of sexual response examining sexual arousal (mentioned previously). This facility may be operationalized through reaction time/response latency in each of the pairing tasks. Left–right response assignments may be changed throughout the testing to ensure that responses are not a product of handedness or general left–right bias.

Although widely used in studies examining stereotypes and racial discrimination (e.g., Greenwald,

Pickrell, & Farnham, 2002; Rudman & Ashmore, 2007), the IAT has not yet found much purchase in the field of sexuality research. In those studies that have used the IAT, however, it has shown promising results: In one study, the IAT showed very high accuracy in identifying participants' sexual orientation, through the pairing of male or female faces with the word *sexy* (area under the curve = .97; Snowden, Wichter, & Gray, 2008). The IAT has also been used to distinguish accurately between child sex offenders and sex offender controls (the Child–Sex IAT; Gray, Brown, MacCulloch, Smith, & Snowden, 2005), to examine gender differences in sexual attitudes (Geer & Robertson, 2005) and sexual double standards (Sakaluk & Milhausen, 2012), to examine homophobic response biases (e.g., Meier, Robinson, Gaither, & Heinert, 2006), and to investigate the cognitive processes in women with a history of childhood sexual abuse (Rellini, Ing, & Meston, 2011). The IAT's test–retest reliability (r = .50) and internal validity (α = .79) have been found to be fairly good (Hofmann, Gawronski, Gschwendner, Le, & Schmitt, 2005; Lane, Banaji, Nosek, & Greenwald, 2007), making the IAT an ideal choice for examining sexual interests and preferences indirectly. Although the IAT may identify cognitive associations, the researcher may not always be able to infer why these associations exist; for example, a participant may associate sex more strongly with children than with adults because of a pedophilic interest, decreased interest in sex with adults in general, or childhood sexual abuse or other sexual experiences the participant had early in life (Snowden et al., 2011). As such, results should be interpreted cautiously.

Implicit Relational Assessment Procedure. A similar measure to the IAT, the Implicit Relational Assessment Procedure (Barnes-Holmes et al., 2006), assesses participants' implicit attitudes by asking them to assess the veracity of statements such as "child—sexual" using a true–false response choice (Dawson, Barnes-Holmes, Gresswell, & Gore, 2009). Participants are asked to evaluate these statements in a fashion consistent with social norms and, later, in a fashion inconsistent with social norms. Response contingencies consistent with social norms (e.g., "child—nonsexual") should be cognitively easier and faster to process than response contingencies that are inconsistent with social norms (e.g., "child—sexual"); therefore, the response latency for "inconsistent" trials should be greater than the response latency for "consistent" trials. The Implicit Relational Assessment Procedure has most notably found support among researchers studying sexual offenders, showing nonsignificantly less discriminant validity than the IAT for identifying child sex offenders (Gray et al., 2005; see Snowden, Craig, & Gray, 2011, for a full review). Split-half reliability for the Implicit Relational Assessment Procedure has also been found to be reasonable (r = .72; Barnes-Holmes, Murtagh, & Barnes-Holmes, 2010). Similar to the IAT, however, interpretation of these response latencies may be limited.

Sexual content–induced delay. More attention is paid (particularly by women) to stimuli that are sexual in nature than to stimuli that are nonsexual, which results in attenuated responding to a button press to indicate whether a stimulus is sexual, termed the *sexual content–induced delay* (Geer & Bellard, 1996). The sexual content–induced delay describes situations in which saliently presented sexual cues or stimuli interfere with the completion of some task or result in a delay in responding (Geer & Bellard, 1996). For example, Spiering, Everaerd, and Laan (2004) found that participants were slower at categorizing targets as sexual or nonsexual when they were preceded by sexual versus neutral supraliminal primes. The sexual content–induced delay is posited to be the result of a response and appraisal bias toward sexual cues (Geer & Bellard, 1996). Indeed, this appears to be the case for women with sexual dysfunction, who tend to show an attentional bias to sexual words (Beard & Amir, 2010).

Choice reaction time. In a choice reaction-time paradigm, participants must identify the location of a dot that is superimposed over an image that varies according to stimulus condition (e.g., sexual or nonsexual image). In accordance with literature on the sexual content–induced delay, the participant is expected to display the longest response times to conditions in which the participant finds the image sexually interesting or exciting. In this way, the choice reaction-time task has become a popular method in assessing paraphilic sexual interests (e.g., Giotakos, 2006; Poeppl et al., 2011). To date, internal reliability of choice reaction-time tests have been found to be strong ($\alpha > .90$; Wright & Adams, 1994), though further research is required to fully understand the advantages and limitations of this cognitive technique.

Stroop interference. In the traditional Stroop paradigm, participants identify the text color for each word presented to them. Because reading is such an automatic response, participants must actively suppress the meaning of the words they are reading to focus on the color of the word, a cognitively challenging task termed *Stroop interference*. Interestingly, women have been found to perform better on traditional (nonsexual) Stroop tasks during the menstrual phase than during the mid-luteal phase (Hatta & Nagaya, 2009). A modified version of the Stroop task, known as the "E-Stroop" task, has been used in sexual offending populations to discriminate between sex offenders and controls. In the modified task, participants must identify the color in which neutral or emotionally salient (e.g., sexual) words or images are presented. Sex offenders have been shown to demonstrate the greatest cognitive interference (operationalized as response latency) to sex-related words compared with controls (e.g., Smith & Waterman, 2004). Although test–retest reliability for the traditional Stroop task has been found to be high, findings of the E-Stroop should be interpreted cautiously because test–retest reliability has been found to be poor on the E-Stroop when difference scores are used, as opposed to measuring response latency alone (see Strauss, Allen, Jorgensen, & Cramer, 2005). Interpretation of the E-Stroop may also be difficult because response latencies may be affected by constructs other than deviant sexual interests, such as childhood sexual abuse (Snowden et al., 2011). Because of these difficulties, Snowden et al. (2011) recommended the use of other validated methods, such as the IAT.

Rapid serial visual presentation. In the rapid serial visual presentation task, participants are shown two stimuli (T1 and T2) within 500 milliseconds of each other. With this time sequencing, participants' perceptual report of the second stimulus (T2) is typically reduced because their attention has been captured by the preceding stimulus (T1). This phenomenon is known as the *attentional blink* (Raymond, Shapiro, & Arnell, 1992), indicative of people's limited capacity for working memory and attentional resources (Johnston, Linden, & Shapiro, 2012). The more interested the participant is in the first stimulus, the more attention is captured, and the longer and stronger the attentional blink should be.

The few studies that have used rapid serial visual presentation to examine sexual interests have found mixed results. In one study, child sex offenders were found to have a sustained attentional blink after the presentation of a child (Beech et al., 2008); however, an elevated interest in children may be shared by parents, teachers, and grandparents and may not be indicative of a sexual interest in children per se. In another study, no differences in the attentional blink were detected between adolescent sexual offenders and non–sexual offenders, possibly owing to low-potency sexual stimuli (Crooks, Rostill-Brookes, Beech, & Bickley, 2009). Test–retest reliability estimates of rapid serial visual presentation in measuring the attentional blink are good ($r = .70$; Saint-Aubin & Klein, 2004). Because of these mixed results, however, we recommend caution when using rapid serial visual presentation to assess sexual interests.

Lexical decision priming task. The lexical decision priming task (Meyer & Schvaneveldt, 1971) typically involves the presentation of a prime, which may or may not be semantically related to a word (presented as a series of letters) that follows it. For example, in a study by Rudman and Borgida (1995), participants were randomly assigned to one of two priming conditions: a neutral prime condition and a "women-as-sexual-objects" priming condition. After the participants had been primed, they were shown a series of letter strings, which formed either sexist words (e.g., *playboy, bimbo, babe*) or nonsexist words pertaining to women (e.g., *sister, mother*). Participants in the women-as-sexual-objects priming condition were much faster at recognizing the sexist words pertaining to women and slower at recognizing the nonsexist words than those in the neutral priming condition. In this way, the lexical decision priming task can be an indirect means of assessing cognitive associations held by participants. The lexical decision priming task has been used to assess cognitive associations in sexual offenders (see Snowden et al., 2011, for a full review). Caution is advised when interpreting results of the lexical decision priming task, however, because reliability has been found to be moderate ($r = .38$; Stolz, Besner, & Carr, 2005).

Sexual arousal affects cognition. Although many researchers are interested in how cognition can affect sexual interests and arousal, we should also note that sexual attraction and arousal could, in turn, affect cognitions, raising concerns about the validity of cognitive measures. In one study, men were found to exhibit significantly more future-discounting behavior (preferring smaller rewards after a short delay vs. a larger reward after a longer delay) after having viewed an attractive woman's face (Wilson & Daly, 2004). Likewise, men exposed to the scent of a woman during the periovulatory (most fertile) phase of her menstrual cycle had increased accessibility to sexual concepts and, after face-to-face interactions with fertile women, were more likely to make risky decisions (Miller & Maner, 2011). Men have also been found to be interested in a wider array of sexual activities, to be more willing to engage in morally questionable behavior for sexual gratification (e.g., using drugs to incapacitate a sexual partner), and to be more likely to engage in unsafe sexual behaviors while sexually aroused (Ariely & Loewenstein, 2006). Fewer research studies have examined cognitions of sexually aroused women, though one study did report that women who were sexually aroused made significantly more risky choices on a risky-choice task (Kennedy, 2011).

Eye-Tracking

Eye-tracking technology is a reliable and valid measure of visual attention (Rayner, 1995) that provides precise measures of eye movements during scene viewing (Rayner, 1998). Studies of visual attention use fixations—periods of time in which the visual point of interest is unchanged—as the dependent measure (Henderson & Hollingworth, 1998). Eye movements are not contingent on explicit processes (Richardson & Spivey, 2000) that may otherwise influence responding in sexuality research, such as social desirability. For example, in a society that discriminates against same-sex-attracted individuals, participants may not have an incentive to report attraction to members of the same sex. However, when presented with pictures of a heterosexual couple engaging in sexual activity, naturally cycling heterosexual women have been shown to spend as much time as heterosexual men looking at the female body in the picture (Rupp & Wallen, 2007).

Within sexuality research, eye-tracking has been used to examine attention to erotic stimuli (Lykins, Meana, & Strauss, 2008), viewing patterns for same- and opposite-sex faces (G. M. Alexander & Charles, 2009), and attention to erotic and nonerotic images (Lykins, Meana, & Kambe, 2006). This methodology has been validated across a wide range of populations, including healthy opposite-sex-attracted (Rupp & Wallen, 2007) and same-sex-attracted (Samson & Janssen, 2012) men and women and individuals with sexual dysfunction (Lykins, Meana, & Minimi, 2010). Eye-tracking has also been used as a diagnostic tool for assessing pedophilic sexual interests in men (Renaud et al., 2009). Eye-tracking studies have revealed a gender difference in gaze patterns such that women using hormonal contraceptives spend more time looking at contextual cues—specifically, clothing and background as opposed to genitals, naked bodies, or the actor's faces—than naturally cycling women or men (Rupp & Wallen, 2007). One of the major shortcomings of eye-tracking is that inferences regarding the cognitive processes underlying gaze patterns are limited. For example, without real-time comparisons of sexual arousal and eye-gaze patterns, one cannot assume that visual attention to sexual stimuli is associated with physiological sexual arousal (Rupp & Wallen, 2008).

Hormones

With the recent increase in relatively inexpensive and accessible means of collecting and analyzing hormones, sex steroid analyses are more frequently included in sexuality research. Progesterone, estrogen, and testosterone are the most commonly studied hormones, with the latter two being those most studied in relation to sexual functioning in both women and men. To collect valid and reliable hormone data, a range of methodological factors and target sample characteristics must be considered, including (a) sample acquisition, handling, and storage; (b) biological rhythms including diurnal and seasonal variation, menstrual cycles, and age-related changes; (c) body composition, medication, and substance use; (d) relationship status and orientation; and (e) interactions with sexual behaviors. In this section, we provide a brief overview of the factors relevant to sexuality research. For a more detailed discussion of methodological considerations, please see van Anders, Goldey, and Bell (2013).

Sample acquisition, handling, and storage. Biomarkers present in blood, urine, and saliva are typically used to measure sex steroid concentrations. Blood or serum testing provides the most direct and accurate assessment of circulating hormones and is used as the gold standard against which salivary and urinary assays are compared (Vitzthum, 2009). Circulating androgens and estrogens consist of protein-bound portions (e.g., sex hormone–binding globulin) and free—or unbound—portions, which are bioavailable, or free to act on target cells. This distinction is an important one because bioavailable portions may be more relevant to behavior outcomes; in the case of testosterone, for example, unbound levels are positively associated with sex drive and sexual functioning in men (Gades et al., 2008). Serum measures give estimates of total hormone concentration and unbound hormone concentrations; the latter is estimated by relative assessment of total concentration and measures of sex hormone–binding globulin to determine bound portions (Wierman et al., 2010). Although considered the gold standard in terms of reliability, serum assessment of hormone levels requires trained personnel for their collection and specific equipment for preparation and storage. Furthermore, venipuncture may be a deterrent for some participants. Similarly, urine sampling, though superior in terms of robustness to diurnal fluctuations, is methodologically cumbersome because total urine output over a 24-hour period is typically required to obtain reliable estimates (Talalay, 1960). Immediate freezing of samples is recommended.

Salivary hormone testing is now commonly used in psychological research, providing a simple, noninvasive, easily repeatable measure that circumvents the stress associated with venipuncture and its unintended elevation of cortisol levels that may distort readings. Collection of salivary samples is relatively straightforward and can be done by the participant both in and outside the laboratory; however, the use of substances to increase saliva production (termed *sialogogues*), such as chewing gum, is not recommended because their use may distort assay results (van Anders, 2010). Similarly, participants should refrain from eating, drinking, or smoking before providing a saliva sample. Unlike serum testing, saliva samples can be reliably stored in a noncycling freezer, and shipping to an assay laboratory is relatively straightforward. Salivary measures are reliable and accurate (Dabbs, 1990; Granger, Shirtcliff, Booth, Kivlighan, & Schwartz, 2004) and yield an estimate of bioavailable hormone that is typically highly correlated with total hormone blood concentrations, though some conflicting findings raise the possibility that salivary estimates of testosterone underestimate hormone–behavior relationships in women (van Anders, 2013).

Biological rhythms and life-cycle fluctuations. Hormone levels are not static but show daily (e.g., testosterone), monthly (e.g., estrogen, progesterone), seasonal (e.g., testosterone), and life-cycle fluctuations. Testosterone and estrogen levels are highest in the morning, just before waking (Axelsson, Ingre, Akerstedt, & Holmback, 2005). Estrogen, progesterone, and testosterone (along with luteinizing hormone and follicular-stimulating hormone) fluctuate within women's menstrual cycle, with ovulation-linked peaks in estrogen and testosterone and mid-luteal peaks in progesterone. Testosterone shows seasonal variation, with the highest values recorded in the fall for women and men, possibly related to seasonal variation in nutrition, caloric intake, and energy expenditure (van Anders, 2013). Hormones vary across the life cycle, with onset of higher sex steroid levels at puberty (testosterone for boys, testosterone and estrogen for girls), age-related decline in testosterone in men, and menopausal drops in estrogen in women. Researchers assessing hormone levels must keep these variations in mind when designing a research protocol, such as testing at the same time of day, controlling for menstrual cycle effects, and being mindful of age cohort effects.

Changes in women's sexuality associated with the menstrual cycle are particularly worth noting from a methodological standpoint. Menstrual cycle–related fluctuations in women's sexuality include changes in mate preference, interest in sex, and likelihood of erotic fantasies (for a review, see Gangestad, Thornhill, & Garver-Apgar, 2005). Exogenous sex hormone use, such as hormonal contraceptives, also has known effects on women's sexuality, including shifts in sexual desire and mate preferences (e.g., Little, Jones, & Burriss, 2007). Because of these effects, researchers are encouraged to, at the very least, identify day of the menstrual cycle (see van Anders, 2013, for a discussion of methods), assess hormonal contraceptive status, and examine cycle and hormone status as potential covariates in research examining sexual response and mating preferences.

The reproductive life cycle also involves hormonal fluctuations for women and men (see Chapter 23, this volume). Pregnancy and lactation are associated with dramatic hormonal changes, including lactation amenorrhea, a period of infertility during breastfeeding as a result of hormones that stimulate milk production (including prolactin and oxytocin) and suppression of gonadal steroids (such as testosterone). This period also results in a reduction in sexual interest and enjoyment, ostensibly because of decreased androgens (Alder & Bancroft, 1988) and reduced vaginal lubrication associated with estrogen suppression from elevated prolactin (LaMarre, Paterson, & Gorzalka, 2003). Researchers studying sexuality in the perinatal period should assess breastfeeding status to control for these effects. Parenthood is also associated with systematic differences in hormone profiles; parents have lower testosterone than nonparents, and the drop in testosterone is associated with the birth of a child (van Anders, 2013).

Body composition, medication, and substance use. Sex steroids are synthesized from hormone precursors in body fat; therefore, gonadal hormone levels are associated with fatty tissue levels in the body, producing a range of effects that differ for women and men. In men, testosterone levels are negatively correlated with body weight and fat, with this relationship thought to reflect the fact that increased body fat causes aromatization of testosterone to estradiol in peripheral tissues (van Anders, 2013). In women, there is a positive relationship between testosterone and body weight and fat, whereas a curvilinear relationship has been found between estrogen and body fat, with the leanest and heaviest women showing the lowest levels (Ziomkiewicz, Ellison, Lipson, Thune, & Jasienska, 2008). Subsequently, researchers are strongly encouraged to assess body mass index and use this individual difference as a covariate in their analyses.

Any exogenous source of sex steroids will influence endogenous hormone levels; therefore, researchers are encouraged to obtain detailed personal medication histories from participants. Hormonal contraceptives vary in their dosages of estrogen and progesterone, and their use may reduce levels of these naturally occurring hormones along with androgens (Bancroft, Sherwin, Alexander, Davidson, & Walker, 1991). Factors such as undergoing sex reassignment and the presence of polycystic ovarian disease are associated with hormonal differences, the latter because of amplified endogenous androgen production, and both because exogenous hormones are likely to be prescribed. Psychological factors such as stress and related mental health concerns (e.g., anxiety, depression) can affect hormone levels through cortisol elevations. Nicotine is also known to reduce testosterone levels (Xue et al., 2010), and it is also suggested that researchers control for nicotine use.

Relationship status and orientation. Despite the growing body of research investigating the relationship–hormone association, the direction of this effect is still unclear because most of the studies investigating this topic have been cross-sectional as opposed to longitudinal (van Anders & Watson, 2006). Relationship status (being single or partnered) and relationship orientation (likelihood of entering into one or multiple relationships, whether they be monogamous or polyamorous) are associated with different hormonal statuses. For example, lower testosterone has been reported in partnered men compared with single men (Mazur & Michalek, 1998), and higher testosterone has been reported in polyamorous men with multiple partners than in monogamous men with a single partner (van Anders, Hamilton, & Watson, 2007). Women in polyamorous relationships had higher testosterone than single women, monogamously partnered women, or women with a polyamorous lifestyle, also showing an interaction between relationship status and orientation. Partnered heterosexual men and nonheterosexual women had lower testosterone than their unpartnered counterparts, but this effect was not found for nonheterosexual men or heterosexual women, suggesting that the relationship between testosterone and partnering status may only manifest in individuals sexually and romantically attracted to women (van Anders & Watson, 2006).

Relationship status and partner proximity differentially affect hormone status in women and men; single men consistently have higher testosterone than partnered men, but single women and women in long distance relationships have lower testosterone levels than women in same-city relationships (van Anders & Watson, 2007). Testosterone levels before and after entering into a relationship also show strong associations with relationship status and likelihood of entering into a relationship in men and women. For example, testosterone is higher in single or divorced men than in married men (Mazur & Michalek, 1998). Stage of relationship (early stages vs. comfortable long-term commitment) and testosterone levels also appear to have a strong relationship that differs by gender; testosterone increases in partnered men as they enter into the comfortable long-term stages of a relationship, whereas the opposite is true for women (Marazziti & Canale, 2004). The growing body of research suggesting that hormones, such as testosterone, are tied to relationship status and orientation illustrates the importance of taking relationship factors into consideration when studying human sexuality (see Chapter 10, this volume). In addition to relationship status and orientation, researchers should consider additional moderating factors between hormone levels and relationship status including sexual attraction, frequency of partnered sex, frequency and desire of partnered versus solitary orgasms, familiarity of partners (Hirschenhauser, Frigerio, Grammer, & Magnusson, 2002), and self-reported interest in additional new partners (van Anders et al., 2007).

Sexual behavior. Hormone concentrations are not static but are responsive to sexual behavior. Sexual intercourse increases testosterone levels over physically intimate contact (e.g., cuddling; van Anders et al., 2007), and more frequent sexual activity is associated with higher testosterone (van Anders & Goldey, 2010). Testosterone is associated with increased orgasm frequency, is higher after sexual activity, and is associated with sexual desire or orgasmic experience (van Anders et al., 2007). Testosterone and estrogen are positively correlated with orgasm experience and assertiveness in men and women (van Anders & Dunn, 2009), and motivation for sexual behaviors is associated with hormone status in heterosexual (van Anders et al., 2007) and nonheterosexual samples (Diamond & Wallen, 2011). Hormone levels also fluctuate with sexual response to sexual stimuli. For example, exposure to films depicting sexually explicit content compared with neutral content has been shown to increase testosterone in men (Stoléru, Ennaji, Cournot, & Spira, 1993), but possibly not in women (Heiman, Rowland, Hatch, & Gladue, 1991). However, sexual thoughts raise testosterone levels in men and women who are instructed to engage in sexual fantasy (Goldey & van Anders, 2011). Rupp and Wallen (2007) found that testosterone is associated with interest in sexual stimuli. Estrogen administration to premenopausal women (van Anders, Brotto, Farrell, & Yule, 2009) and postmenopausal women (Archer, Love-Geffen, Herbst-Dam, Swinney, & Chang, 2006) increases neural responses to sexual stimuli. These data are instructive for research design, suggesting that investigators may want to limit participants' sexual behaviors before hormone sampling in the laboratory or control for sexual behaviors in their analysis.

Research investigating the influence of hormones on sexuality has spanned various populations and contexts, offering important insights into sexuality research methodology. Hormones experience micro- as well as macro-level fluctuations; thus, factors such as time of day, age, and even season should be considered when measuring physiological or subjective arousal. Information on research participants should be gathered to account for individual variables such as body composition, medical issues, and medication use, which may all have an effect on hormone levels. Hormone concentrations are also contingent on contextual factors, such as relationship status, sexual orientation, or partner proximity. Finally, careful attention should be paid to the dynamic link between hormone levels and sexual behavior, because this relationship may influence experimental results on the basis of the type of sexual stimuli used, how sexual interest or arousal is measured, or recency of participants' last sexual encounter.

Neuroimaging

Since the mid-1990s, a variety of neuroimaging techniques have been used to study brain structure and function in relation to human sexuality. Most of these efforts have focused on three main lines of research: (a) brain structure correlates of individual differences in sexuality, such as variations in sexual interests; (b) functional brain changes associated with events related to sexual response, including sexual arousal, sexual desire, and orgasm, and comparisons between individuals with and without problematic sexual response (see Stoléru, Fonteille, Cornelis, Joyal, & Moulier, 2012, for an extensive quantitative review of sexual response in women and men); and (c) electroencephalogram (EEG) assessments of sexual stimulus processing (Ortigue, Patel, & Bianchi-Demicheli, 2009).

Structural imaging is performed using computerized axial tomography (CAT) or magnetic resonance imaging (MRI). CAT scans produce three-dimensional images through the compilation of a series of two-dimensional X-ray images. MRI produces images of brain (or other body) tissues by measuring magnetic field fluctuations induced by the magnet in the scanner and reconstructing this information to produce a three-dimensional image of the structures being measured. Research questions investigating relationships between sexual interests and brain structure, such as examining white matter deficiencies in pedophilic men (Cantor et al., 2008), can be addressed using these methods.

Functional imaging is performed using positron emission tomography (PET) or fMRI. Both of these methods involve measurement of physiological changes associated with increases in cellular metabolism in specific brain regions, including local blood flow and oxygenation, termed *brain perfusion*. PET scanning involves measurement of positrons emitted from an intravenously injected, radioisotope-tagged biological compounds (usually water or glucose) because these compounds are metabolized during brain function. fMRI involves measurement of changes in blood oxygenation as metabolic demands increase in imaged brain regions. Multiple forms of fMRI exist, with blood oxygenation level–dependent fMRI being the most common. Others, however, such as arterial spin labeling fMRI, are more amenable to longer testing times associated with slower brain changes during sexual response, such as those induced by means of sexual stimulation by a partner in men (Georgiadis et al., 2010).

EEG involves recording the electrical activity on the scalp associated with neuronal activity (e.g., during processing of sexual stimuli or sexual activity). Event-related potentials (ERP) make up the averaged EEG activity during stimulus processing and consist of a series of positive and negative voltage deflections. Multiple components of ERPs have been identified as corresponding to cognitive processes associated with stimulus recognition, attention, memory, and so forth. For example, the contingent negative variation is thought to reflect expectancy that is enhanced under conditions promoting interest and attention, such as in preferred stimuli. In a classic study, Costell, Lunde, Kopell, and Wittner (1972) demonstrated that heterosexual women's and men's contingent negative variation responses were significantly greater to preferred than nonpreferred sexual stimuli (nude pictures of women and men), though women also showed significant contingent negative variation response to pictures of nude women, a response pattern reminiscent of nonspecific sexual responding among heterosexual women demonstrated using sexual psychophysiological techniques (Chivers, 2010). More recently, methodological advances have facilitated more sophisticated examination of the temporal dynamics of brain activity and the estimation of brain sources of EEG signals (see Ortigue et al., 2009, for a review of sexuality-relevant methodologies).

In general, the research designs in neuroimaging studies examine brain responses to sexual stimuli contrasted with responses to nonsexual control stimuli to identify stimulus-specific patterns of brain activity. To date, most paradigms involve passive processing of sexual stimuli by simply viewing or listening to sexual stimuli; however, newer research studies have used active paradigms involving decision making regarding sexual stimuli (Rupp et al., 2009) or measurement of brain response during active sexual behaviors (Georgiadis et al., 2010). Stoléru et al. (2012) have also proposed including subliminal stimulus presentation paradigms as a means of circumventing inhibition of brain responses associated with sexual arousal.

Spatial and temporal resolution, that is, the degree of acuity of the resulting image and the time taken for each measurement to be acquired, respectively, is a major methodological issue that warrants careful consideration when neuroimaging sexuality-related phenomena. Structural methods such as MRI provide good spatial resolution (MRI is superior to CAT), particularly with higher power magnets; however, because the image is static, there is no temporal component. Functional neuroimaging methods differ in the temporal resolution, typically 2 to 3 seconds for fMRI and about 1 minute for PET (Stoléru et al., 2012). Spatial resolution for functional imaging varies with the technical characteristics of the scanner but is about 1 to 3 millimeters. EEG has the highest temporal resolution, measuring brain activity occurring within milliseconds. The choice of methodology will therefore rest on the nature of the behavior being measured and the research question.

METHODOLOGICAL CONSIDERATIONS AND CONCLUSIONS

Although the majority of the methods and devices discussed in this chapter are valid and reliable, researchers must be cognizant of the biases in sexuality research. For example, there is a well-replicated ascertainment bias in sexuality research; individuals who volunteer to participate in research (particularly sexual arousal research) tend to be more sexually experienced (both in terms of partnered sexual activity and use of erotic materials), report lower degrees of sex guilt, and have more positive attitudes toward sexuality (e.g., Strassberg & Lowe, 1995). Given this bias, one may question the generalizability of the results obtained from sexuality research. Strassberg and Lowe's (1995) study illustrates the problem of sampling biases; only one third of their initial sample (of 1,063 undergraduate students) completed a subsequent anonymous sexuality questionnaire. Our experience has been that participation rates in sexual psychophysiology are similar, with about 30% of individuals who indicate interest in participation (an already selected group) actually completing the study.

Researchers must also consider the influence of the social context within which sexuality research is situated, particularly with respect to gender norms, or cultural expectations about appropriate sexual behavior for women and men (M. G. Alexander & Fisher, 2003; see also Chapter 2, this volume; Volume 2, Chapter 6, this handbook). Experimental manipulations, such as the bogus pipeline, can encourage less biased responding; however, implementing this methodology is somewhat cumbersome. Researchers may, instead, be able to promote honest responding by creating environments that promote anonymity (M. G. Alexander & Fisher, 2003) and use same-gender experimenters, particularly for male participants (T. D. Fisher, 2007). Care must be taken regarding the information that is directly and indirectly communicated to participants; for example, women's and men's reports of infidelity in previous relationships are higher when they are under the impression that confederate research assistants endorse sexual promiscuity (T. D. Fisher, 2009). Considering the local norms and possibly providing participants with gender- and age-specific information, when possible, may encourage participants to provide less biased responses.

Alternatively, researchers may want to engage the contextual and sociocultural factors that can influence responses in experimental paradigms (rather than control them) and critically examine tacit assumptions that experimental methodologies yield more valid representations of human sexuality. The biases themselves, such as those observed by M. G. Alexander and Fisher (2003), may indeed, for some, be the most fascinating and informative aspects of the research findings. The belief that objective measures produce truer representations of psychological constructs is a common epistemological divide in psychology research, and the study of human sexuality is no exception (see Chapter 1, this volume). For example, cognitive measures, however effective at measuring biases and interests, do not necessarily correspond to sexual behaviors outside of the lab. Although a heterosexual woman may show substantial visual attention to same-sex stimuli, this may not translate into a nonheterosexual sexual orientation or the propensity to engage in sexual acts with a same-sex partner (Chivers, 2010). Researchers are increasingly using mixed-methods research designs, in which multiple qualitative and quantitative methods are used (e.g., Brotto, Knudson, Inskip, Rhodes, & Erskine, 2010; Tolman & Szalacha, 1999). Similarly, multimethod approaches in experimental research are also emerging (e.g., Banse, Schmidt, & Clabour, 2010). The integration of experimental methods with qualitative approaches is both a challenge and an opportunity for researchers to better characterize sexual phenomena, both inside and outside of the sexuality research laboratory.

References

Alder, E., & Bancroft, J. (1988). The relationship between breastfeeding persistence, sexuality and mood in postpartum women. *Psychological Medicine, 18*, 389–396. doi:10.1017/S0033291700007935

Alexander, G. M., & Charles, N. (2009). Sex differences in adults' relative visual interest in female and male faces, toys, and play styles. *Archives of Sexual Behavior, 38*, 434–441. doi:10.1007/s10508-008-9429-7

Alexander, M. G., & Fisher, T. D. (2003). Truth and consequences: Using the bogus pipeline to examine sex differences in self-reported sexuality. *Journal of Sex Research, 40*, 27–35. doi:10.1080/00224490309552164

Archer, J. S., Love-Geffen, T. E., Herbst-Dam, K. L., Swinney, D. A., & Chang, J. R. (2006). Effect of estradiol versus estradiol and testosterone brain-activation patterns in postmenopausal women. *Menopause, 13*, 528–537. doi:10.1097/01.gme.0000188737.46746.cd

Ariely, D., & Loewenstein, G. (2006). The heat of the moment: The effect of sexual arousal on sexual decision making. *Journal of Behavioral Decision Making, 19*, 87–98. doi:10.1002/bdm.501

Axelsson, J., Ingre, M., Akerstedt, T., & Holmback, U. (2005). Effects of acutely displaced sleep on testosterone. *Journal of Clinical Endocrinology and Metabolism, 90*, 4530–4535. doi:10.1210/jc.2005-0520

Bancroft, J., Sherwin, B. B., Alexander, G. M., Davidson, D. W., & Walker, A. (1991). Oral contraceptives, androgens, and the sexuality of young women: II. The role of androgens. *Archives of Sexual Behavior, 20*, 121–135. doi:10.1007/BF01541939

Banse, R., Schmidt, A. F., & Clabour, J. (2010). Indirect measures of sexual interest in child sex offenders: A multi-method approach. *Criminal Justice and Behavior, 37*, 319–335. doi:10.1177/0093854809357598

Barlow, D. H., Becker, R., Leitenberg, H., & Agras, W. S. (1970). A mechanical strain gauge for recording penile circumference change. *Journal of Applied Behavior Analysis, 3*, 73–76. doi:10.1901/jaba.1970.3-73

Barnes-Holmes, D., Barnes-Holmes, Y., Power, P., Hayden, E., Milne, R., & Stewart, I. (2006). Do you know what you believe? Developing the Implicit Relational Assessment Procedure as a direct measure of implicit beliefs. *Irish Psychologist, 32*, 169–177.

Barnes-Holmes, D., Murtagh, L., & Barnes-Holmes, Y. (2010). Using the Implicit Association Test and the Implicit Relational Assessment Procedure to measure attitudes toward meat and vegetables in vegetarians and meat-eaters. *Psychological Record, 60*, 287–306.

Basson, R. (2000). The female sexual response: A different model. *Journal of Sex and Marital Therapy, 26*, 51–65. doi:10.1080/009262300278641

Basson, R., & Brotto, L. A. (2003). Sexual psychophysiology and effects of sildenafil citrate in estrogenized women with acquired genital arousal disorder and impaired orgasm. *British Journal of Obstetrics and Gynaecology, 110*, 1014–1024. doi:10.1111/j.1471-0528.2003.02438.x

Beard, C., & Amir, N. (2010). Attention bias for sexual words in female sexual dysfunction. *Journal of Sex and Marital Therapy, 36*, 216–226. doi:10.1080/00926231003719616

Beech, A. R., Kalmus, E., Tipper, S. P., Baudouin, J. Y., Flak, V., & Humphreys, G. W. (2008). Children induce an enhanced attentional blink in child molesters. *Psychological Assessment, 20*, 397–402. doi:10.1037/a0013587

Bohlen, J. G., & Held, J. P. (1979). An anal probe for monitoring vascular and muscular events during sexual response. *Psychophysiology, 16*, 318–323. doi:10.1111/j.1469-8986.1979.tb02998.x

Both, S., & Laan, E. (2007). Simultaneous measurement of pelvic floor muscle activity and vaginal blood flow: A pilot study. *Journal of Sexual Medicine, 4*, 690–701. doi:10.1111/j.1743-6109.2007.00457.x

Both, S., Spiering, M., Everaerd, W., & Laan, E. (2004). Sexual behavior and responsiveness to sexual stimuli following laboratory-induced sexual arousal. *Journal of Sex Research, 41*, 242–258. doi:10.1080/00224490409552232

Brotto, L. A., Basson, R., & Luria, M. (2008). A mindfulness-based group psychoeducational intervention targeting sexual arousal disorder in women. *Journal of Sexual Medicine, 5*, 1646–1659. doi:10.1111/j.1743-6109.2008.00850.x

Brotto, L. A., Klein, C., & Gorzalka, B. B. (2009). Laboratory-induced hyperventilation differentiates female sexual arousal subtypes. *Archives of Sexual Behavior, 38*, 463–475. doi:10.1007/s10508-007-9288-7

Brotto, L. A., Knudson, G., Inskip, J., Rhodes, K., & Erskine, Y. (2010). Asexuality: A mixed-methods approach. *Archives of Sexual Behavior, 39*, 599–618. doi:10.1007/s10508-008-9434-x

Brotto, L. A., & Yule, M. (2011). Psychological and subjective sexual arousal in asexual women: A pilot study of sexual orientation groups. *Archives of Sexual Behavior, 40*, 699–712. doi:10.1007/s10508-010-9671-7

Campbell, D. T., & Fiske, D. W. (1959). Convergent and discriminant validation by the multitrait–multimethod matrix. *Psychological Bulletin, 56*, 81–105. doi:10.1037/h0046016

Cantor, J. M., Kabani, N., Christensen, B. K., Zipursky, R. B., Barbaree, H. E., Dickey, R., . . . Blanchard, R. (2008). Cerebral white matter deficiencies in pedophilic men. *Journal of Psychiatric Research, 42*, 167–183. doi:10.1016/j.jpsychires.2007.10.013

Chivers, M. L. (2005). A brief review and discussion of sex differences in the specificity of sexual arousal. *Sexual and Relationship Therapy, 20*, 377–390. doi:10.1080/14681990500238802

Chivers, M. L. (2010). A brief update on the specificity of sexual arousal. *Sexual and Relationship Therapy, 25*, 407–414. doi:10.1080/14681994.2010.495979

Chivers, M. L., & Bailey, J. M. (2005). A sex difference in features that elicit genital response. *Biological Psychology, 70*, 115–120. doi:10.1016/j.biopsycho.2004.12.002

Chivers, M. L., Seto, M. C., & Blanchard, R. (2007). Gender and sexual orientation differences in sexual response to the sexual activities versus the gender of actors in sexual films. *Journal of Personality and Social Psychology, 93*, 1108–1121. doi:10.1037/0022-3514.93.6.1108

Chivers, M. L., Seto, M. C., Lalumière, M. L., Laan, E., & Grimbos, T. (2010). Agreement of self-reported and genital measures of sexual arousal among men and women: A meta-analysis. *Archives of Sexual Behavior, 39*, 5–56. doi:10.1007/s10508-009-9556-9

Costell, R. M., Lunde, D. T., Kopell, B. S., & Wittner, W. K. (1972). Contingent negative variation as an indicator of sexual object preference. *Science, 177*, 718–720. doi:10.1126/science.177.4050.718

Crooks, V. L., Rostill-Brookes, H., Beech, A. R., & Bickley, J. A. (2009). Applying rapid serial visual presentation to adolescent sexual offenders: Attentional bias as a measure of deviant sexual interest? *Sexual Abuse: A Journal of Research and Treatment, 21*, 135–148. doi:10.1177/1079063208328677

Dabbs, J. M., Jr. (1990). Salivary testosterone measurements: Reliability across hours, days, and weeks. *Physiology and Behavior, 48*, 83–86. doi:10.1016/0031-9384(90)90265-6

Dawson, D. L., Barnes-Holmes, D., Gresswell, D. M., Hart, A. J., & Gore, N. J. (2009). Assessing the implicit beliefs of sexual offenders using the implicit relational assessment procedure: A first study. *Sexual Abuse: A Journal of Research and Treatment, 21*, 57–75. doi:10.1177/1079063208326928

Diamond, L. M., & Wallen, K. (2011). Sexual minority women's sexual motivation around the time of ovulation. *Archives of Sexual Behavior, 40*, 237–246. doi:10.1007/s10508-010-9631-2

Fisher, C., Gross, J., & Zuch, J. (1965). Cycle of penile erection synchronous with dreaming (REM) sleep. *Archives of General Psychiatry, 12*, 29–45. doi:10.1001/archpsyc.1965.01720310031005

Fisher, T. D. (2007). Sex of experimenter and social norm effects on reports of sexual behavior in young men and women. *Archives of Sexual Behavior, 36*, 89–100. doi:10.1007/s10508-006-9094-7

Fisher, T. D. (2009). The impact of socially conveyed norms on the reporting of sexual behavior and attitudes by men and women. *Journal of Experimental Social Psychology, 45*, 567–572. doi:10.1016/j.jesp.2009.02.007

Freund, K. (1963). A laboratory method for diagnosing predominance of homo- or hetero-erotic interest in the male. *Behaviour Research and Therapy, 1*, 85–93. doi:10.1016/0005-7967(63)90012-3

Freund, K., & Watson, R. J. (1991). Assessment of the sensitivity and specificity of a phallometric test: An update of phallometric diagnosis of pedophilia. *Psychological Assessment, 3*, 254–260. doi:10.1037/1040-3590.3.2.254

Gades, N. M., Jacobson, D. J., McGree, M. E., St. Sauver, J. L., Lieber, M. M., Nehra, A., . . . Jacobsen, S. J. (2008). The associations between serum sex hormones, erectile function, and sex drive: The Olmsted County study of urinary symptoms and health status among men. *Journal of Sexual Medicine, 5*, 2209–2220.

Gangestad, S. W., Thornhill, R., & Garver-Apgar, C. E. (2005). Adaptations to ovulation: Implications for sexual selection and social behaviour. *Current Directions in Psychological Science, 14*, 312–316. doi:10.1111/j.0963-7214.2005.00388.x

Geer, J. H., & Bellard, H. S. (1996). Sexual content induced delays in unprimed lexical decisions: Gender and context effects. *Archives of Sexual Behavior, 25*, 379–395. doi:10.1007/BF02437581

Geer, J. H., & Robertson, G. G. (2005). Implicit attitudes and sexuality: Gender differences. *Archives of Sexual Behavior, 34*, 671–677. doi:10.1007/s10508-005-7923-8

Georgiadis, J. R., Farrell, M. J., Boessen, R., Denton, D. A., Gavrilescu, M., Kortekass, R., . . . Egan, G. F. (2010). Dynamic subcortical blood flow during male sexual activity with ecological validity: A perfusion fMRI study. *NeuroImage, 50*, 208–216. doi:10.1016/j.neuroimage.2009.12.034

Gerritsen, J., van der Made, F., Bloemers, J., van Ham, D., Kleiverda, G., Everaerd, W., . . . Tuiten, A. (2009). The clitoral photoplethysmography: A new way of assessing genital arousal in women. *Journal of Sexual Medicine, 6*, 1678–1687. doi:10.1111/j.1743-6109.2009.01228.x

Giotakos, O. (2006). A combination of viewing reaction time and incidental learning task in child molesters, rapists, and control males and females. *Annals of General Psychiatry, 5*, S114. doi:10.1186/1744-859X-5-S1-S114

Goldey, K. L., & van Anders, S. M. (2011). Sexy thoughts: Effects of sexual cognitions on testosterone, cortisol, and arousal in women. *Hormones and Behavior, 59*, 754–764. doi:10.1016/j.yhbeh.2010.12.005

Granger, D. A., Shirtcliff, E. A., Booth, A., Kivlighan, K. T., & Schwartz, E. B. (2004). The "trouble" with testosterone. *Psychoneuroendocrinology, 29*, 1229–1240. doi:10.1016/j.psyneuen.2004.02.005

Gray, N. S., Brown, A. S., MacCulloch, M. J., Smith, J., & Snowden, R. J. (2005). An implicit test of the associations between children and sex in pedophiles. *Journal of Abnormal Psychology, 114*, 304–308. doi:10.1037/0021-843X.114.2.304

Greenwald, A. G., McGhee, D. E., & Schwartz, J. L. K. (1998). Measuring individual differences in implicit cognition: The Implicit Association Test. *Journal of Personality and Social Psychology, 74*, 1464–1480. doi:10.1037/0022-3514.74.6.1464

Greenwald, A. G., Pickrell, J. E., & Farnham, S. D. (2002). Implicit partisanship: Taking sides for no reason. *Journal of Personality and Social Psychology, 83*, 367–379. doi:10.1037/0022-3514.83.2.367

Hanson, R. K., & Morton-Bourgon, K. (2005). The characteristics of persistent sexual offenders: A meta-analysis of recidivism studies. *Journal of Consulting and Clinical Psychology, 73*, 1154–1163. doi:10.1037/0022-006X.73.6.1154

Hatta, T., & Nagaya, K. (2009). Menstrual cycle phase effects on memory and Stroop task performance. *Archives of Sexual Behavior, 38*, 821–827. doi:10.1007/s10508-008-9445-7

Heiman, J. R., & Rowland, D. L. (1983). Affective and physiological sexual response patterns: The effects of instructions on sexually functional and dysfunctional men. *Journal of Psychosomatic Research, 27*, 105–116. doi:10.1016/0022-3999(83)90086-7

Heiman, J. R., Rowland, D. L., Hatch, J. P., & Gladue, B. A. (1991). Psychophysiological and endocrine responses to sexual arousal in women. *Archives of Sexual Behavior, 20*, 171–186. doi:10.1007/BF01541942

Henderson, J. M., & Hollingworth, A. (1998). Eye movements during scene viewing: An overview. In G. Underwood (Ed.), *Eye guidance in reading and scene perception* (pp. 269–293). Oxford, England: Elsevier Science. doi:10.1016/B978-008043361-5/50013-4

Henson, C., Rubin, H. B., & Henson, D. E. (1979). Women's sexual arousal concurrently assessed by three genital measures. *Archives of Sexual Behavior, 8*, 459–469. doi:10.1007/BF01541413

Henson, D. E., Rubin, H. B., Henson, C., & Williams, J. R. (1977). Temperature change of the labia minora as an objective measure of female eroticism. *Journal of Behavior Therapy and Experimental Psychiatry, 8*, 401–410. doi:10.1016/0005-7916(77)90011-8

Hirschenhauser, K., Frigerio, D., Grammer, K., & Magnusson, M. S. (2002). Monthly patterns of testosterone and behavior in prospective fathers. *Hormones and Behavior, 42*, 172–181. doi:10.1006/hbeh.2002.1815

Hoffmann, H. (2010). Hot and bothered: Classical conditioning of sexual incentives in humans. In T. R. Schachtman & S. Reilly (Eds.), *Associative learning and conditioning theory: Human and non-human applications* (pp. 532–550). New York, NY: Oxford University Press.

Hofmann, W., Gawronski, B., Gschwendner, T., Le, H., & Schmitt, M. (2005). A meta-analysis on the correlation between the Implicit Association Test and explicit self-report measures. *Personality and Social Psychology Bulletin, 31*, 1369–1385. doi:10.1177/0146167205275613

Huberman, J. S., Suschinsky, K. D., Lalumière, M. L., & Chivers, M. L. (in press). The relationship between impression management and three measures of women's self-reported sexual arousal. *Canadian Journal of Behavioural Science.*

Janssen, E. (2007). *The psychophysiology of sex.* Bloomington: Indiana University Press.

Janssen, E., Everaerd, W., Spiering, M., & Janssen, J. (2000). Automatic processes and the appraisal of sexual stimuli: Toward an information processing model of sexual arousal. *Journal of Sex Research, 37*, 8–23. doi:10.1080/00224490009552016

Jiang, X. G., Speel, T. G. W., Wagner, G., Meuleman, E. J. H., & Wijkstra, H. (2003). The value of corpus cavernosum electromyography in erectile dysfunction: Current status and future prospect. *European Urology, 43*, 211–218. doi:10.1016/S0302-2838(03)00011-3

Johnston, S. J., Linden, D. E., & Shapiro, K. L. (2012). Functional imaging reveals working memory and attention interact to produce the attentional blink. *Journal of Cognitive Neuroscience, 24*, 28–38. doi:10.1162/jocn_a_00054

Kennedy, G. (2011). *The effects of sexual arousal on risky decision-making* (unpublished master's thesis). University of Lethbridge, Lethbridge, Alberta, Canada.

Kuban, M., Barbaree, H. E., & Blanchard, R. (1999). A comparison of volume and circumference phallometry: Response magnitude and method agreement. *Archives of Sexual Behavior, 28*, 345–359. doi:10.1023/A:1018700813140

Kukkonen, T. M., Binik, Y. M., Amsel, R., & Carrier, S. (2010). An evaluation of the validity of thermography as a physiological measure of sexual arousal in a non-university adult sample. *Archives of Sexual Behavior, 39*, 861–873. doi:10.1007/s10508-009-9496-4

Laan, E. (1994). *Determinants of sexual arousal in women.* Unpublished doctoral dissertation, University of Amsterdam, Amsterdam, the Netherlands.

Laan, E., Everaerd, W., & Evers, A. (1995). Assessment of female sexual arousal: Response specificity and construct validity. *Psychophysiology, 32*, 476–485. doi:10.1111/j.1469-8986.1995.tb02099.x

Laan, E., Van Driel, E. M., & Van Lunsen, R. H. W. (2008). Genital responsiveness in healthy women with and without sexual arousal disorder. *Journal of Sexual Medicine, 5*, 1424–1435. doi:10.1111/j.1743-6109.2008.00827.x

Laan, E., Van Lunsen, R. T., & Everaerd, W. (2001). The effects of tibolone on vaginal blood flow, sexual desire, and arousability in postmenopausal women. *Climacteric, 4*, 28–41.

Lalumière, M. L., Quinsey, V. L., Harris, G. T., Rice, M. E., & Trautrimas, C. (2003). Are rapists differentially aroused by coercive sex in phallometric assessments? *Annals of the New York Academy of Sciences, 989*, 211–224. doi:10.1111/j.1749-6632.2003.tb07307.x

LaMarre, A. K., Paterson, L. Q., & Gorzalka, B. B. (2003). Breastfeeding and postpartum maternal sexual functioning: A review. *Canadian Journal of Human Sexuality, 12*, 151–168.

Lane, K. A., Banaji, M. R., Nosek, B. A., & Greenwald, A. G. (2007). Understanding and using the Implicit Association Test IV: What we know (so far) about the method. In B. Wittenbrink & N. Schwarz (Eds.), *Implicit measures of attitudes* (pp. 59–102). New York, NY: Guilford Press.

Levin, R. J. (2003). The ins and outs of vaginal lubrication. *Sexual and Relationship Therapy, 18*, 509–513. doi:10.1080/14681990310001609859

Little, A. C., Jones, B. C., & Burriss, R. P. (2007). Preferences for masculinity in male bodies change across the menstrual cycle. *Hormones and Behavior, 51*, 633–639. doi:10.1016/j.yhbeh.2007.03.006

Lykins, A. D., Meana, M., & Kambe, G. (2006). Detection of differential viewing patterns to erotic and non-erotic stimuli using eye-tracking methodology. *Archives of Sexual Behavior, 35*, 569–575. doi:10.1007/s10508-006-9065-z

Lykins, A. D., Meana, M., & Minimi, J. (2010). Visual attention to erotic images in women reporting pain with intercourse. *Journal of Sex Research, 48*, 43–52. doi:10.1080/00224490903556374

Lykins, A. D., Meana, M., & Strauss, G. P. (2008). Sex differences in visual attention to erotic and non-erotic stimuli. *Archives of Sexual Behavior, 37*, 219–228. doi:10.1007/s10508-007-9208-x

Marazziti, D., & Canale, D. (2004). Hormonal changes when falling in love. *Psychoneuroendocrinology, 29*, 931–936. doi:10.1016/j.psyneuen.2003.08.006

Marshall, W. L., & Fernandez, Y. M. (2000). Phallometric testing with sexual offenders: Limits to its value. *Clinical Psychology Review, 20*, 807–822. doi:10.1016/S0272-7358(99)00013-6

Mazur, A., & Michalek, J. (1998). Marriage, divorce, and male testosterone. *Social Forces, 77*, 315–330.

Meier, B. P., Robinson, M. D., Gaither, G. A., & Heinert, N. J. (2006). A secret attraction or defensive loathing? Homophobia, defense, and implicit cognition. *Journal of Research in Personality, 40*, 377–394. doi:10.1016/j.jrp.2005.01.007

Meyer, D. E., & Schvaneveldt, R. W. (1971). Facilitation in recognizing pairs of words: Evidence of a dependence between retrieval operations. *Journal of Experimental Psychology, 90*, 227–234. doi:10.1037/h0031564

Miller, S. L., & Maner, J. K. (2011). Ovulation as a male mating prime: Subtle signs of women's fertility influence men's mating cognition and behavior. *Journal of Personality and Social Psychology, 100*, 295–308. doi:10.1037/a0020930

Murnen, S. K., & Stockton, M. (1997). Gender and self-reported sexual arousal to sexual stimuli: A meta-analytic review. *Sex Roles, 37*, 135–153. doi:10.1023/A:1025639609402

Ortigue, S., Patel, N., & Bianchi-Demicheli, F. (2009). New EEG neuroimaging methods of analyzing brain activity applicable to the study of human sexual response. *Journal of Sexual Medicine, 6*, 1830–1845. doi:10.1111/j.1743-6109.2009.01271.x

Palti, Y., & Bercovici, B. (1967). Photoplethysmographic study of the vaginal blood pulse. *American Journal of Obstetrics and Gynecology, 97*, 143–153.

Peterson, Z. D., & Janssen, E. (2007). Ambivalent affect and sexual response: The impact of co-occurring positive and negative emotions on subjective and physiological responses to erotic stimuli. *Archives of Sexual Behavior, 36*, 793–807. doi:10.1007/s10508-006-9145-0

Poeppl, T. B., Nitschke, J., Dombert, B., Santilla, P., Greenlee, M. W., Osterheider, M., & Mokros, A. (2011). Functional cortical and subcortical abnormalities in pedophilia: A combined study using a choice reaction time task and fMRI. *Journal of Sexual Medicine, 8*, 1660–1674. doi:10.1111/j.1743-6109.2011.02248.x

Prause, N., Cerny, J., & Janssen, E. (2005). The labial photoplethysmograph: A new instrument for assessing genital hemodynamic changes in women. *Journal of Sexual Medicine, 2*, 58–65. doi:10.1111/j.1743-6109.2005.20106.x

Prause, N., & Janssen, E. (2005). Blood flow: Vaginal photoplethysmography. In I. Goldstein, C. M. Meston, S. Davis, & A. Traish (Eds.), *Textbook of female sexual dysfunction* (pp. 361–369) London, England: Taylor & Francis Medical.

Prause, N., Janssen, E., Cohen, J., & Finn, P. (2002, June). *Effects of acute ethanol consumption on sexual arousal and sexual risk taking*. Poster presented at the meeting of the International Academy of Sex Research, Hamburg, Germany.

Quinsey, V. L., Steinman, C. M., Bergersen, S. G., & Holmes, T. F. (1975). Penile circumference, skin conductance, and ranking responses of child molesters and "normals" to sexual and non-sexual visual stimuli. *Behavior Therapy, 6*, 213–219. doi:10.1016/S0005-7894(75)80143-2

Raymond, J. E., Shapiro, K. L., & Arnell, K. M. (1992). Temporary suppression of visual processing in an RSVP task: An attentional blink? *Journal of Experimental Psychology: Human Perception and Performance, 18*, 849–860. doi:10.1037/0096-1523.18.3.849

Rayner, K. (1995). Eye movements and cognitive processes in reading, visual search, and scene perception. In J. M. Findlay, R. Walker, & R. W. Kentridge (Eds.), *Eye movement research: Mechanisms, processes and applications* (pp. 3–22). Amsterdam, the Netherlands: North Holland. doi:10.1016/S0926-907X(05)80003-0

Rayner, K. (1998). Eye-movements in reading and information processing: 20 years of research. *Psychological Bulletin, 124*, 372–422. doi:10.1037/0033-2909.124.3.372

Rellini, A. H., Ing, A. D., & Meston, C. M. (2011). Implicit and explicit sexual processes in survivors of childhood sexual abuse. *Journal of Sexual Medicine, 8*, 3098–3107. doi:10.1111/j.1743-6109.2011.02356.x

Rellini, A. H., McCall, K. M., Randall, P. K., & Meston, C. M. (2005). The relationship between women's subjective and physiological sexual arousal. *Psychophysiology, 42*, 116–124. doi:10.1111/j.1469-8986.2005.00259.x

Renaud, P., Chartier, S., Roulear, J., Proulx, J., Decarie, J., Trottier, D., . . . Bouchard, S. (2009). Gaze behavior nonlinear dynamics assessed in virtual immersion as a diagnostic index of sexual deviancy: Preliminary results. *Journal of Virtual Reality and Broadcasting, 6*(3).

Richardson, D. C., & Spivey, M. J. (2000). Representation, space, and Hollywood squares: Looking at things that aren't there anymore. *Cognition, 76*, 269–295. doi:10.1016/S0010-0277(00)00084-6

Rosen, R., & Beck, J. G. (1988). *Patterns of sexual arousal: Psychophysiological process and clinical applications.* New York, NY: Guilford Press.

Rowland, D., Van Diest, S., Incrocci, L., & Slob, A. K. (2005). Psychosexual factors that differentiate men with inhibited ejaculation from men with no dysfunction or another sexual dysfunction. *Journal of Sexual Medicine, 2*, 383–389. doi:10.1111/j.1743-6109.2005.20352.x

Rowland, D. L., & Heiman, J. R. (1991). Self-reported and genital arousal changes in sexually dysfunctional men following a sex therapy program. *Journal of Psychosomatic Research, 35*, 609–619. doi:10.1016/0022-3999(91)90055-S

Rudman, L. A., & Ashmore, R. D. (2007). Discrimination and the Implicit Association Test. *Group Processes and Intergroup Relations, 10*, 359–372. doi:10.1177/1368430207078696

Rudman, L. A., & Borgida, E. (1995). The afterglow of construct accessibility: The behavioural consequences of priming men to view women as sexual objects. *Journal of Experimental Social Psychology, 31*, 493–517. doi:10.1006/jesp.1995.1022

Rupp, H. A., James, T. W., Ketterson, E. D., Sengelaub, D. R., Janssen, R., & Heiman, J. R. (2009). The role of the anterior cingulate cortex in women's sexual decision making. *Neuroscience Letters, 449*, 42–47. doi:10.1016/j.neulet.2008.10.083

Rupp, H. A., & Wallen, K. (2007). Relationship between testosterone and interest in sexual stimuli: The effect of experience. *Hormones and Behavior, 52*, 581–589. doi:10.1016/j.yhbeh.2007.07.015

Rupp, H. A., & Wallen, K. (2008). Sex differences in response to visual sexual stimuli: A review. *Archives of Sexual Behavior, 37*, 206–218. doi:10.1007/s10508-007-9217-9

Saint-Aubin, J., & Klein, R. M. (2004). One missing-letter effect: Two methods of assessment. *Canadian Journal of Experimental Psychology, 58*, 61–66. doi:10.1037/h0087440

Sakaluk, J. K., & Milhausen, R. R. (2012). Factors influencing university students' explicit and implicit sexual double standards. *Journal of Sex Research, 49*, 464–476. doi:10.1080/00224499.2011.569976

Samson, L., & Janssen, E. (2012). *Sexual and affective responses to same- and opposite-sex stimuli in heterosexual and homosexual men: The impact of visual attention.* Retrieved from http://www.kinseyinstitute.org/newsletter/sp2012/Samson_Janssen2012.pdf

Seto, M. C., Lalumière, M. L., Harris, G. T., & Chivers, M. L. (2012). The sexual responses of sexual sadists. *Journal of Abnormal Psychology, 121*, 739–753. doi:10.1037/a0028714

Slob, A. K., Bax, C. M., Hop, W. C. J., Rowland, D., & van der Werff ten Bosch, J. J. (1996). Sexual arousability and the menstrual cycle. *Psychoneuroendocrinology, 21*, 545–558. doi:10.1016/0306-4530(95)00058-5

Smith, P., & Waterman, M. (2004). Processing bias for sexual material: The Emotional Stroop and sexual offenders. *Sexual Abuse: A Journal of Research and Treatment, 16*, 163–171. doi:10.1177/107906320401600206

Snowden, R. J., Craig, R. L., & Gray, N. S. (2011). Indirect behavioral measures of cognition among sexual offenders. *Journal of Sex Research, 48*, 192–217. doi:10.1080/00224499.2011.557750

Snowden, R. J., & Gray, N. S. (2012). Implicit sexual associations in heterosexual and homosexual women and men. *Archives of Sexual Behavior.* Advance online publication. doi:10.1007/s10508-012-9920-z

Snowden, R. J., Wichter, J., & Gray, N. S. (2008). Implicit and explicit measurements of sexual preference in gay and heterosexual men: A comparison of priming techniques and the Implicit Association Task. *Archives of Sexual Behavior, 37*, 558–565. doi:10.1007/s10508-006-9138-z

Spiering, M., Everaerd, W., & Laan, E. (2004). Conscious processing of sexual information: Mechanisms of appraisal. *Archives of Sexual Behavior, 33*, 369–380. doi:10.1023/B:ASEB.0000028890.08687.94

Stoléru, S. G., Ennaji, A., Cournot, A., & Spira, A. (1993). LH pulsatile secretion and testosterone blood levels are influenced by sexual arousal in human males. *Psychoneuroendocrinology, 18*, 205–218. doi:10.1016/0306-4530(93)90005-6

Stoléru, S. G., Fonteille, V., Cornelis, C., Joyal, C., & Moulier, V. (2012). Functional neuroimaging studies of sexual arousal and orgasm in healthy men and women: A review and meta-analysis. *Neuroscience and Biobehavioral Reviews, 36*, 1481–1509. doi:10.1016/j.neubiorev.2012.03.006

Stolz, J. A., Besner, D., & Carr, T. H. (2005). Implications of measures of reliability for theories of priming: Activity in semantic memory is inherently noisy and uncoordinated. *Visual Cognition, 12*, 284–336. doi:10.1080/13506280444000030

Strassberg, D. S., & Lowe, K. (1995). Volunteer bias in sexuality research. *Archives of Sexual Behavior, 24*, 369–382. doi:10.1007/BF01541853

Strauss, G. P., Allen, D. N., Jorgensen, M. L., & Cramer, S. L. (2005). Test-retest reliability of standard and emotional Stroop tasks: An investigation of color-word and picture-word versions. *Assessment, 12*, 330–337. doi:10.1177/1073191105276375

Suschinsky, K. D., Chivers, M. L., & Lalumière, M. L. (2013). *A test of an information-processing model of sexual arousal and sexual concordance.* Manuscript in preparation.

Suschinsky, K. D., & Lalumière, M. L. (2011a). Prepared for anything? An investigation of female genital arousal to rape cues. *Psychological Science, 22*, 159–165. doi:10.1177/0956797610394660

Suschinsky, K. D., & Lalumière, M. L. (2011b). Sexual arousal category-specificity and sexual concordance: The stability of sex differences in sexual arousal patterns. *Canadian Journal of Human Sexuality, 20*, 93–108.

Suschinsky, K. D., & Lalumière, M. L. (2012). Is sexual concordance related to awareness of internal states? *Archives of Sexual Behavior, 41*, 199–208. doi:10.1007/s10508-012-9931-9

Suschinsky, K. D., & Lalumière, M. L. (2013). *The relationship between sexual concordance and interoception in anxious and nonanxious women.* Manuscript submitted for publication.

Suschinsky, K. D., Lalumière, M. L., & Chivers, M. L. (2009). Sex difference in patterns of genital sexual arousal: Measurement artifacts or true phenomena? *Archives of Sexual Behavior, 38*, 559–573. doi:10.1007/s10508-008-9339-8

Talalay, P. (1960). Enzymatic analysis of steroid hormones. In D. Glick (Ed.), *Methods of biochemical analysis* (Vol. 8, pp. 119–143). Hoboken, NJ: Wiley.

Tolman, D. L., & Szalacha, L. A. (1999). Dimensions of desire: Bridging qualitative and quantitative methods in a study of female adolescent sexuality. *Psychology of Women Quarterly, 23*, 7–39. doi:10.1111/j.1471-6402.1999.tb00338.x

van Anders, S. M. (2010). Chewing gum has large effects on salivary testosterone, estradiol, and secretory immunoglobulin A assays in women and men. *Psychoneuroendocrinology, 35*, 305–309. doi:10.1016/j.psyneuen.2009.06.009

van Anders, S. M. (2013). *Testosterone and androgens in human behavioral neuroendocrine research: Methodological considerations*. Manuscript submitted for publication.

van Anders, S. M., Brotto, L., Farrell, J., & Yule, M. (2009). Associations among physiological and subjective sexual response, sexual desire, and salivary steroid hormones in healthy premenopausal women. *Journal of Sexual Medicine, 6*, 739–751. doi:10.1111/j.1743-6109.2008.01123.x

van Anders, S. M., & Dunn, E. J. (2009). Are gonadal steroids linked with orgasm perceptions and sexual assertiveness in women and men? *Hormones and Behavior, 56*, 206–213. doi:10.1016/j.yhbeh.2009.04.007

van Anders, S. M., & Goldey, K. L. (2010). Testosterone and partnering are linked via relationship status for women and "relationship orientation" for men. *Hormones and Behavior, 58*, 820–826. doi:10.1016/j.yhbeh.2010.08.005

van Anders, S. M., Goldey, K. L., & Bell, S. N. (2013). *Testosterone and androgens in human sexuality research: Methodological considerations*. Manuscript submitted for publication.

van Anders, S. M., Hamilton, L. D., & Watson, N. V. (2007). Multiple partners are associated with higher testosterone in North American men and women. *Hormones and Behavior, 51*, 454–459. doi:10.1016/j.yhbeh.2007.01.002

van Anders, S. M., & Watson, N. V. (2006). Relationship status and testosterone in North American men and women of diverse orientations: Cross-sectional and longitudinal findings. *Psychoneuroendocrinology, 31*, 715–723. doi:10.1016/j.psyneuen.2006.01.008

van Anders, S. M., & Watson, N. V. (2007). Testosterone levels in women and men who are single, in long-distance relationships, or same-city relationships. *Hormones and Behavior, 51*, 286–291. doi:10.1016/j.yhbeh.2006.11.005

Vitzthum, V. J. (2009). The ecology and evolutionary endocrinology of reproduction in the human female. *American Journal of Physical Anthropology, 140*(Suppl. 49), 95–136. doi:10.1002/ajpa.21195

Waxman, S. E., & Pukall, C. F. (2009). Laser Doppler imaging of genital blood flow: A direct measure of female sexual arousal. *Journal of Sexual Medicine, 6*, 2278–2285. doi:10.1111/j.1743-6109.2009.01326.x

Webster, J. S., & Hammer, D. (1983). Thermistor measurement of male sexual arousal. *Psychophysiology, 20*, 111–115. doi:10.1111/j.1469-8986.1983.tb00911.x

Weijmar-Schultz, W., van Andel, P., Sabelis, I., & Mooyaart, E. (1999). Magnetic resonance imaging of male and female genitals during coitus and female sexual arousal. *British Medical Journal, 319*, 1596–1600. doi:10.1136/bmj.319.7225.1596

Wierman, M. E., Nappi, R. E., Avis, N., Davis, S. R., Labrie, F., Rosner, W., & Shifren, J. (2010). Endocrine aspects of women's sexual function. *Journal of Sexual Medicine, 7*, 561–585. doi:10.1111/j.1743-6109.2009.01629.x

Wilson, M., & Daly, M. (2004). Do pretty women inspire men to discount the future? *Proceedings of the Royal Society of London B: Biological Sciences, 271*(Suppl. 4), S177–S179.

Wright, L. W., & Adams, H. E. (1994). Assessment of sexual preference using a choice reaction time task. *Journal of Psychopathology and Behavioral Assessment, 16*, 221–231. doi:10.1007/BF02229209

Wundt, W. (1904). *Principles of physiological psychology* (5th German edition, Vol. 1; E. B. Titchener, Trans.). New York, NY: Macmillan.

Xue, Y., Morris, M., Ni, L., Guthrie, S., Zubieta, J.-K., Gonzalez, K., . . . Domino, E. (2010). Venous plasma nicotine correlates of hormonal effects of tobacco smoking. *Pharmacology Biochemistry and Behavior, 95*, 209–215. doi:10.1016/j.pbb.2010.01.007

Yule, M., Woo, J. S., & Brotto, L. A. (2010). Sexual arousal in East Asian and Euro-Canadian women: A psychophysiological study. *Journal of Sexual Medicine, 7*, 3066–3079. doi:10.1111/j.1743-6109.2010.01916.x

Ziomkiewicz, A., Ellison, P. T., Lipson, S. F., Thune, I., & Jasienska, G. (2008). Body fat, energy balance and estradiol levels: A study based on hormonal profiles from complete menstrual cycles. *Human Reproduction, 23*, 2555–2563. doi:10.1093/humrep/den213

CHAPTER 6

PHENOMENOLOGICAL RESEARCH METHODS IN THE PSYCHOLOGICAL STUDY OF SEXUALITY

David M. Frost, Sara I. McClelland, Jennifer B. Clark, and Elizabeth A. Boylan

In this chapter, we review issues central to the use of phenomenological research methods in the psychological study of sexuality. Phenomenological methods are characterized by close attention to the details of participants' lived experience as well as an emphasis on participants' interpretation of their experience. This group of methods is essential in psychological research on sexuality because it helps researchers to understand the phenomenon of sexuality as it is experienced in everyday life and under constant change. Beginning with a summary of the epistemological foundations of phenomenological research methods in psychology, we present an overview of several popular approaches to data collection and analysis that facilitate phenomenological investigations of sexuality. Classical foundations, future directions, limitations, advantages, and clinical and policy relevance are discussed via key exemplar studies of sexuality-related phenomena using phenomenological research methods.

SEXUALITY AS COMPLEX AND VARIED PHENOMENA

Human sexuality is complex, given that it is inclusive of a number of related, but distinct, phenomena. These phenomena include, but are not limited to, sexual behavior, desire, pleasure, orientation, and identity. Psychologists and other social scientists often operationalize these aspects of sexuality categorically at the level of groups and populations to facilitate comparative study (e.g., heterosexual vs. sexual minority; penetrative vs. nonpenetrative sex). However, within these groups and categories, psychological experiences of sexuality-related phenomena are enormously varied. For example, people vary greatly in the content and object of their sexual desires, hold complex and multiple sexual identity structures, imbue their own and others' sexual behaviors with subjective meanings, and become energized to engage in sexual behavior by diverse motivations (see Chapters 10, 19, 20, and 25, this volume). In addition to this high degree of interpersonal or within-group variability, there is also a great deal of intrapersonal variability in the psychological experience of sexuality. As people develop over time and move between social contexts, their psychological experiences of sexuality often follow suit. Thus, for any given person, sexual desires, identities, behaviors, and motives may change from one moment to the next. With all of these variations in mind, researchers are tasked with developing and using methods that are able to adequately capture the diversity of individuals' psychological experiences of sexuality, including the multitude of dimensions within the experience of sexuality.

In addition, pressing clinical concerns in the area of sexuality require both a nuanced understanding of people's subjective meanings of their experience of sexuality and an identification of possible ways to intervene (see Volume 2, Chapter 4, this handbook). For example, researchers have addressed a number of issues, including the following with which we have engaged in our own research: how same-sex couples negotiate experiences of stigma and intimacy within long-term romantic relationships (Frost, 2011b), what motivations gay men have for seeking

http://dx.doi.org/10.1037/14193-006
APA Handbook of Sexuality and Psychology: Vol. 1. Person-Based Approaches, D. L. Tolman and L. M. Diamond (Editors-in-Chief)

partners of the same HIV status (Frost, Stirratt, & Ouellette, 2008), how women's experiences of their sexuality align with contemporary survey measures of sexual function (McClelland, 2012), and how young adults experience and define their own sexual satisfaction (McClelland, 2011). In the domain of sexuality, it is increasingly important to consider the clinical applications of psychological research, given that findings from studies are often quickly applied to questions of diagnosis and treatment. For example, understanding diverse experiences within diagnostic categories (Tiefer, 2002) and attending to the subjective evaluation of sexual experiences are concerns for those working close to the interface between sexuality, health, and well-being (see Chapters 11 and 13, this volume). These and similar research and therapeutic questions begin with the proposition that variability and complexity in the subjective experience of sexuality are not simply unexplainable error variance but matters worthy of investigation and explanation in their own right.

Thus, faced with the sometimes daunting complexity inherent in the psychological experience of sexuality, researchers and clinicians need to engage with methodological approaches that are specifically designed to investigate individuals' experiences and interpretations of their sexuality. These methods stand in contrast to other methods that might, for example, address the frequency or type of sexual behaviors but not examine someone's rationale for engaging in behaviors, record an individual's current sexual identity but not explore the development of that identity, or collect individuals' articulations of sexual desire but without a focus on the social and historical limitations imposed on some individuals speaking about their desire. In this chapter, we discuss these approaches—broadly categorized as *phenomenological approaches*—to the psychological study of sexuality. Before delving further into an overview of phenomenological epistemologies and methods in psychology, we provide a brief overview of why understanding the complexities and subjective lived experiences of sexuality-related phenomena is important. These insights are, we argue, essential not only for improved basic social scientific knowledge of human sexuality but for understanding and improving people's health and well-being and informing sexuality-related social policies (see Chapter 22, this volume; Volume 2, Chapter 8, this handbook).

STAKES OF PSYCHOLOGICAL RESEARCH ON SEXUALITY-RELATED PHENOMENA

Sexuality is an area that has historically been of interest to local and federal policymakers (Foucault, 1976/1998) and is often one in which politics and social norms play an important role in people's lives. Sexuality-related social policies are at times designed to exert social control over sexual bodies and behaviors and are often intended to extend the sexual morals of some individuals and groups with legislative authority to all individuals (for an in-depth review of psychological concerns related to social policy and sexuality, see Volume 2, Chapter 10, this handbook). Alternatively, sexuality-related social policies are also extended in order to distribute social resources, such as education, protections against harms, and equal rights.

State and federal policies directed at sexual behaviors, relationships, education, and health have enormous ramifications in people's lives. Policymakers often rely on research to help guide decisions, interventions, and laws that aim to protect groups and equitably distribute resources. Psychological research in the field of sexuality has often been influential in shaping and changing social policies related to sexual health, sexual rights, and sexual behaviors (see Volume 2, Chapters 8 and 10, this handbook). Researchers have consistently provided data concerning individuals' sexual development, experiences, relationships, and health—data that are important in the formation of policies surrounding topics such as the legal recognition of same-sex relationships (Peplau & Fingerhut, 2007), sex education in schools (Fine & McClelland, 2006, 2007; see Volume 2, Chapter 11, this handbook), and abortion rights (Major et al., 2000). Sexual relationships, in particular, have historically been an area of state regulation and prohibition, as witnessed in three specific examples of laws and policies enacted over the past half-century: (a) laws prohibiting interracial marriage (antimiscegenation laws, e.g., *Loving v. Virginia,* 1967), (b) same-sex marriage (the Defense of Marriage Act, 1996), and (c) the U.S. military's "Don't Ask, Don't Tell" policy (Policy Concerning Homosexuality in the Armed Forces, 2006) that prohibited people who "demonstrate a propensity or intent to engage in homosexual acts" from serving in the armed forces of the United States. Although enforced through different policy mechanisms, each of these laws has aimed to control who can have sex with whom, the contexts in which sex is valued or devalued, and the consequences of engaging in sex that is deemed immoral (see Volume 2, Chapter 10, this handbook).

The enactment of policies pertaining to sexuality brings about a need to understand how people's lives are affected when their sexual identity, intimate relationships, or sexual behaviors are defined as problematic and subsequently stigmatized. Phenomenological research—via its focus on subjective interpretations of lived experience—has the potential to illustrate complex variability in the negative consequences of limiting and discriminatory policy or to demonstrate the need for new policies that support the well-being of individuals left out of existing policies (Frost & Ouellette, 2011). For example, the Defense of Marriage Act has prevented many same-sex couples from obtaining legal recognition for their relationships, thereby reinforcing a marginalized social status for their relationships and excluding them from full participation in society (Frost, 2011a; Herdt & Kertzner, 2006). In spite of these numerous and severe forms of social devaluation and discrimination, many same-sex couples are able to have personally meaningful relationships that are both healthy and rewarding. By focusing on the experiences of same-sex couples through phenomenological investigation, psychologists are able to better understand how policies are perceived (e.g., threats vs. challenges to their relationships), the moments in their lives when policies exert the most (and least) influence, and the nuanced social creativity individuals exercise to circumvent delimiting social structures that seek to control their sexualities (e.g., community commitment ceremonies in lieu of formal legal recognition; Frost, 2011b, 2011c; Frost & Ouellette, 2011).

These examples provide a brief insight into several important characteristics of sexuality research and methods. In sum, phenomenological methods are able to contribute three elements to the study of sexuality: (a) the acknowledgment of the enormous variability in individuals' intimate and sexual experiences and their interpretations of these experiences; (b) the recognition of consistently high stakes in sexuality research, including applications in clinical, medical, and policy settings; and (c) attention to the diversity of sexual experiences as well as the patterns and meanings that exist within and between people. It is at the crossroads of these three elements that phenomenological methods sit.

OVERVIEW OF PHENOMENOLOGICAL PSYCHOLOGY AND ITS EPISTEMOLOGICAL FOUNDATIONS

In its broadest sense, phenomenological psychology is concerned with the study of the subjective meanings of lived experience (e.g., Giorgi, 1997; Smith, 2004; Wertz, 2005). Its roots lie primarily in the philosophies of Edmund Husserl's phenomenology (e.g., Husserl, 1977), Merleau-Ponty's (1962) phenomenology of perception, and the existential phenomenological philosophies of Martin Heidegger (1927/1962) and Jean-Paul Sartre (1943), and they have given rise to clinical and empirically oriented approaches in psychology. For extensive historical and epistemological reviews, see Langdridge (2007) and Giorgi (2010a, 2010b).

In its traditional formulations, one major focus of phenomenology and its use in psychology has been the description of consciousness and the mechanisms underlying consciousness (Giorgi, 1997, 2006). Phenomenology assumes that consciousness is not entirely biological but is produced through subjective perception and mutually constituted intersubjectivities—with a specific focus on the intersubjective experience between one who perceives and one being perceived (Giorgi, 1997, 2006). Researchers and clinicians are thus able to gain insight into the meanings of a singular experience by describing the subjective nature of that experience as relayed through patients' or participants' reflective talk or textual data. Through reflection, therefore, a description of any given phenomenon can be produced.

Phenomenological approaches in psychology have grown to incorporate hermeneutic traditions from other related branches of psychology, such as humanistic psychology (Klein & Westcott, 1994). The inclusion of hermeneutics (i.e., ways of interpretation; see Dilthey, 1977; Gadamer, 1975) expanded the boundaries of phenomenological psychology by moving the focus of research beyond description toward the meanings that individuals make out of lived experiences. In other words, with the addition of hermeneutic approaches, phenomenological psychology has grown to include both description and analysis of participants' accounts of their experiences.

This linking of descriptive elements provided by participants with analytic elements is what sets phenomenological methods apart from the larger category of qualitative methods. Although qualitative and phenomenological methods share a commitment to description as a powerful way of understanding a phenomenon, qualitative methods are a more inclusive and broader category. For example, qualitative methods, on one hand, may generate descriptive data from various sources other than a participant (e.g., ethnographic descriptions provided by a researcher or interviews with friends and family of a participant), may produce limited responses from participants that are light on description (e.g., an open-ended survey question), and may contain only descriptive elements that do not include analytic elements (e.g., describing elements of a participant's daily routine). Phenomenological methods, on the other hand, prioritize the viewpoint of the subject or participant, often use qualitative data collection methods to better understand this viewpoint, and additionally use analysis strategies (described later) to examine the social, cultural, historical, and political contexts in which the data emerged.

The combination of analytical and descriptive aims has been of particular importance in the psychological study of sexuality. Possibilities were opened to not solely describe sexual phenomena, such as sexual identity, sexual satisfaction, and intimacy, but also to compare experiences of phenomena across individuals and from one point in time to the next and, perhaps most important, describe how changes across time were experienced by individuals. In addition, as participants' interpretations of their own experience were increasingly treated as meaningful data, researchers' interpretations were increasingly considered meaningful. This inclusion of multiple perspectives on participant-generated descriptions and analysis has resulted in an area of rich psychological theory and empirical work, particularly for feminist psychologists (see Josselson, 2004; Kitzinger & Wilkinson, 1997; McClelland & Fine, 2008b; Morawski, 1997; Tolman, 2002).

For example, McClelland (2011) demonstrated how individuals who experienced greater marginalization in the sexual domain were also more likely to describe their sexual experiences from the perspective of their partner rather than themselves. This study linked several layers of data: (a) participants' descriptions of the criteria they used to decide whether they were sexually satisfied; (b) participants' analysis of their criteria and how these criteria had changed over time; and (c) an analysis strategy that assessed which groups consistently imagined themselves as the primary beneficiaries of sexual encounters and which did not. Linking participants' descriptions of their subjective experiences (in this case, of sexual satisfaction) with analysis of the social and historical contexts in which individuals were asked to appraise the quality of their lives (in this case, their sexual lives) is a hallmark of phenomenological research.

Last, it is important to note that the boundaries defining the subfield of phenomenological psychology are unclear at best. Debate over how broadly or narrowly to conceive the subfield has been extensive (e.g., Giorgi, 2006; Klein & Westcott, 1994). The present overview of phenomenological psychology construes the subfield in its broadest possible sense to provide readers with a useful array of methodological approaches to the psychological study of sexuality-related phenomena. In doing so, we follow Langdridge's (2007) four key characteristics of phenomenological psychology: focus on human experience, concern with how meaning arises for individuals, focus on description and relationships, and recognition of the researcher's role in the coconstruction of the topic under investigation.

PHENOMENOLOGICAL METHODS IN THE STUDY OF SEXUALITY

Before presenting specific phenomenological methods that are commonly used in the psychological study of sexuality, it is important to note which aspects of research design are influenced by phenomenological concerns. In short, we suggest that all aspects of the design process should be attentive to principles of phenomenological psychology for the study to successfully achieve its goals of describing and interpreting complex meanings of sexuality-related phenomena. This includes the initial formulation of research questions and hypotheses, the selection of participants, the mode of data collection, the method of data analysis, and the presentation and discussion of the findings. Although the remainder of this chapter focuses primarily on methods of data collection and analysis, these design elements are nested within a larger research process. The research process typically begins with the generation of a research question or set of research questions. Example research questions concerned with the study of the subjective meanings of the lived experience of sexuality were presented earlier. Sampling, data collection, analysis, and presentation of findings stem directly from and inform the study's research questions (Ouellette, 2003). The blanket term *methods* is often used to refer to sampling, data collection, and analysis strategies. However, there are important distinctions and interrelationships between these study components, several of which we highlight here.

Approaches to Data Collection in Phenomenological Research

One of the most frequently used methods of data collection in phenomenological studies of sexuality-related phenomena is the qualitative interview. There are many different types of interviewing methods, ranging from the structured interview method, which asks a consistent set of questions in a systematic order and with the same exact wording; to the semistructured interview, which relaxes these constraints of wording and sequence; to the clinical interview, which more often takes its cues from the participant concerning the appropriate order and emphases within the interview setting (e.g., Diamond, 2008; Frost et al., 2008; Kvale, 1994; Tolman, 2002). In the clinical interview, the aim is (sometimes) to arrive at a clinical diagnosis or some other form of assessment. Also common in phenomenological studies in psychology is the life history interview, a specific subtype of qualitative interview focused on revealing the developmental trajectory of a person's life, often articulated through the narration of significant past events. Life history interviews can be both undirected (e.g., the participant tells the story of his or her life in whatever sequence and structure he or she sees fit in discourse with the interviewer; e.g., Mishler, 1986) or semistructured (e.g., a participant is directed by the interview protocol to talk about specific periods of his or her life—childhood, adolescence—or define the chapters of his or her life story; McAdams, 1995).

Although these methods of interviewing are often used to categorize distinct approaches to conducting interviews, it is important to recognize that they represent different approaches to collecting data and can sometimes be used within a single interview. For example, a psychologist who is interested in gaining insight into motivations for engaging in sexual risk behaviors might begin an interview with a series of structured questions to determine exactly which behaviors are relevant to a participant, followed by a less structured set of questions in which she asks a participant to tell her about the last time the participant engaged in a particular sexual behavior, thereby allowing motivational determinants to emerge naturally from the participant's descriptions. Alternatively, a psychologist interested in developmental questions might be interested in understanding the meanings and experiences of being a gay man across a participant's life course. He might begin his interview by asking a participant, "What memories do you have about your childhood and first sexual thoughts?" Once a participant expands on his experience in this regard, the interviewer might ask specific follow-up questions that are relevant only in relation to what the participant had already talked about and develop the interview in relationship to these early experiences and how they relate to later experiences of sexual identity.

Throughout the process of creating and conducting an interview, researchers must take steps to be conscious of how aspects of their own social location contribute to the decisions they make in study design, interview question selection, and reactions to participants' responses. This process, often referred to as *reflexivity* (e.g., Morawski, 1994, 2005), is necessary for the interviewer or researcher to take into consideration how aspects of one's positionality (e.g., race, gender, sexual orientation, socioeconomic status, education) profoundly shape the interaction between researcher and participant (Harding, 1993; see McCorkel & Myers, 2003, for an example). In her study of sexual desire among adolescent girls, Tolman (1994) likened the process of reflexivity to that of countertransference in the clinical or therapeutic setting. The interviewer's approach and reactions to the interviewee shape how the interviewee responds to the interviewer and, thus, what is ultimately said in the interview. Reflexivity is necessary to understand the contextual influence of the research setting on data collection and analysis (described next).

Not all data need to be collected using in-person interviews to be useful in a phenomenological investigation. Many elements of interview-based data collection strategies underlie the collection of other forms of data, including written data. For example, some researchers interested in collecting life story data have used structured writing prompts (e.g., guided autobiography; McAdams, 1995) to elicit participants' written narrative accounts of important events in their lives. Additionally, phenomenological researchers have increasingly used diary-based data collection strategies whereby participants are asked to keep diaries or journals with guided prompts that elicit written accounts surrounding a specific experience as it unfolds temporally over time. For example, in a study of the experience of pregnancy and how it shapes women's sense of self as mothers, Smith (1999) asked participants to keep weekly diaries in which they wrote down their thoughts and feelings related to being pregnant and becoming a mother. Such diary methods, sometimes referred to as *experience sampling methods* (Mehl & Conner, 2011), can also involve daily reporting of behaviors, emotions, and motivations in response to quantitative scales. Data collected via these methods can provide important insight into the subjective reality of phenomena as they vary within people over the course of a day or week, for example, thus allowing for a dynamic understanding of intrapersonal variability in the phenomena under investigation.

Defining Units of Analysis

Closely tied to data collection methods are decisions regarding the unit of analysis in an investigation. The unit of analysis is typically established by the researcher in the planning stage; thinking ahead to the analysis process, researchers should anticipate whether the data collected will be useful in answering their research questions. For example, if an investigator is examining why people engage in a behavior, data on how often someone engages in a behavior will not be sufficient; the investigator will need to consider a unit of analysis that provides information on meanings and motivations for the behavior of interest, not simply its frequency. When considering interview data, a unit of analysis can be defined in numerous ways. Some research questions will be best served by considering larger units (e.g., participants' life stories), and therefore the entire interview may be considered the unit of analysis. Other research questions may not require the entire interview but rather a subset of questions, themes, or images that emerge from the data. In short, researchers may identify specific aspects of the collected data as relevant units of analysis for a given research question.

As an illustrative example, the following text is drawn from a series of written relationship stories collected from individuals in long-term same-sex and heterosexual relationships (Frost, 2011c, 2012). The text was provided by a 55-year-old lesbian woman in a 10-year relationship in response to a prompt that asked her to "tell a story about an important decision you made in your relationship." Her response begins by describing when she and her partner decided to buy a house together:

> In 2000, [my partner and I] bought a house together. This was a major decision, especially because it meant that [I] would have to sell the house that [I] had owned for 15 years, a house to which [I] was very attached emotionally. But that house had several drawbacks, one of which was that it wasn't ["our"] house. The new house was more expensive than [we] felt they could afford, but [we] both loved it, so [we] took a chance and

> bought it. *[We] trusted that [we] would either make it work, and [we] agreed that, if at some future time [we] could no longer manage the mortgage payments, [we] would sell it and find a smaller house. This was an important decision because both [of us] have had to rely on each other to keep up with the mortgage payments as well as the housework.* Also, in another time and place, lesbian neighbors might not be accepted, but in this particular neighborhood, nobody seems to care who lives next door as long as they keep their lawn mowed. (Participant names have been removed; emphasis added during coding procedure.)

In an investigation of how participants' experiences of relationship stories shaped their relational well-being, Frost (2012) identified how individuals described moments of intimacy within significant relationship events. Frost's unit of analysis in this study focused on sentences within the relationship stories (e.g., the two italicized sentences in the preceding text illustrating themes of trust, commitment, and communicative intimacy). As a comparison, in another study using the same data, Frost (2011c) investigated how individuals in same-sex relationships negotiated experiences of stigma. In this study, he used the story as a whole as his unit of analysis, noting how the story evolved over the course of the narrative. This analysis demonstrated how participants narrated social stigma as "not as bad as it used to be" (as in the preceding example) or more simply as a heavy weight on their relationship (see Frost, 2011c). These depictions of the meanings of stigma are the result of an analysis of the whole story rather than of isolating specific parts. Because the same text can be analyzed in multiple ways for different purposes, it is essential that researchers clearly identify their units of analysis and ensure that their units of analysis are appropriate for the aims of their studies.

Phenomenological Approaches to Data Analysis

Once units of analysis have been defined and data have been collected, researchers proceed with the process of data analysis. Multiple approaches to the analysis of qualitative data are relevant within phenomenological projects (for a review, see Madill & Gough, 2008). We highlight two analytic approaches from phenomenological investigations into the psychological experience of sexuality to provide readers with an introduction to some analytical approaches commonly used in the field. These approaches are thematic analysis (Braun & Clarke, 2006) and narrative analysis (Riessman, 2008). We refer to thematic and narrative analysis as *approaches* because they provide means to guide and organize data analysis. These approaches provide the basis for more specific operational analysis strategies and procedures, such as interpretive phenomenological analysis (Smith, 2004) and the Listening Guide (Gilligan, Spencer, Weinberg, & Bertsch, 2003; Tolman, 1994), which are discussed later.

Thematic analysis is one of the most commonly used approaches to the analysis of qualitative data (Braun & Clarke, 2006). According to Braun and Clarke (2006) in their now classic overview of thematic approaches to analysis in psychology, "Thematic analysis is a method for identifying, analysing and reporting patterns (themes) within data. It minimally organizes and describes your data set in (rich) detail" (p. 79). A theme, therefore, "captures something important about the data in relation to the research question, and represents some level of patterned response or meaning within the data set" (Braun & Clarke, 2006, p. 82).

Thematic approaches within phenomenological investigations focus on identifying themes that capture, represent, and explicate the meanings and complexities of a given experience. Accordingly, researchers using thematic analytical approaches follow a step-by-step iterative process of thematic code development. First, each unit of analysis is subjected to initial readings by the researcher or group of researchers, who take initial notes on their overarching impressions of central themes. Next, transcripts are reread, and this time researchers attempt to code each transcript for these themes. Third, researchers adjust the initial definitions of the themes as the data warrant, thereby creating a codebook for final application. This codebook outlines the themes coded in a given study as well as the conceptual and operational definitions of each theme (Weston et al., 2001). Transcripts are then read again, and the finalized codes are applied to the data. In instances in which the aims of the study require an indication for the reliability of the thematic coding scheme, multiple individuals code data for the presence or absence of themes. A significant amount of controversy exists in the field regarding the applicability of reliability and validity in the analysis of qualitative data; however, many have argued for the retention of these concepts and apply them in ways consistent with the aims of qualitative inquiry as opposed to statistical research (cf. Fine, 2006; Morse, Barrett, Mayan, Olsen, & Spiers, 2002). Once codes have been applied, researchers are able to look across the dataset to observe the central themes in relation to the research questions.

For example, Frost et al. (2008) interviewed 32 HIV-positive and HIV-negative gay men about their approaches to finding sexual and relationship partners of the same HIV status. They followed a three-step iterative process of thematic code development: first, reading each interview transcript independently and developing an initial list of salient themes; second, attempting to code each transcript for these themes; and third, adjusting the themes as the data warranted. In defining intimacy for initial coding, they started with a theory-derived definition of intimacy motivation: the desire or need to feel sexually, physically, emotionally, or communicatively close to another (following Prager, 1995). As themes elicited from the narratives required this definition to change, their iterative approach to thematic analysis allowed for necessary flexibility. The final operational definition of intimacy used in this study included the theory-derived definition but was supplemented with notions of how participants described a sense of having a shared future with a partner as well as experiences and expectations of care provision for themselves, their partner, or both. Illuminating the ways in which themes of intimacy emerged in men's interviews in relation to themes of HIV risk reduction allowed Frost et al. to highlight how a desire for intimacy with a partner can both facilitate and undermine sexual health decision making (e.g., decisions to use or not use condoms in newly forming relationships).

Narrative analysis is another common approach to the analysis of qualitative data in psychology. Although not limited to phenomenological studies, narrative analysis is focused on uncovering the ways in which individuals' stories reveal how people make meaning of their everyday lived experience and aspects of their social contexts (e.g., Frost & Ouellette, 2011; Riessman, 2008). Narrative analytical approaches are grounded in the fundamental notion that people use narratives (or stories) to make sense of the world and construct a sense of self (e.g., Bruner, 1991). Unlike thematic analysis, narrative analysis is focused on understanding the storied nature of lived experience and therefore requires that data have a narrative structure. Narrative structure involves a temporally organized sequence of events—though not necessarily a linear one—that involves actors and actions. The elements of a participant's story are then subjected to analytical readings designed to understand the plot and purpose of the story and its subjective importance to the teller.

What actually happened in the event is not typically prioritized in a narrative analysis. Rather, the way a participant tells the story is considered to be revealing of the subjective meanings of the elements of the event (behaviors, emotions, relationships with people involved, cultural factors). Narrative analysis thus borrows from literary analysis, in that it often seeks to document the coherence of a narrative (how the parts fit together), the affective tone of a participant's telling (positive, negative), perspective (distancing, inclusive), linguistic referent (*I/my, we/ours*), and type of narrative arc (redemptive plots, contamination plots; McAdams, 2006). For example, in the narrative study of members of same-sex couples' relationship stories described earlier, Frost (2011c) did not seek to understand whether stigma affected intimacy in same-sex couples; he instead sought to understand how participants made both positive and negative meanings of experiences of intimacy in events involving stigmatization.

In short, in narrative analytical approaches, the participant's story is the unit of analysis, and the way in which it is built from its component parts is analyzed to reveal the subjective meanings of the experience under investigation. However, as is often the case with longer interviews (e.g., clinical interviews, life story interviews), one interview transcript may contain multiple narratives. For instance, a life history interview may contain specific event narratives (e.g., parents' divorce, birth of first child), but there is often an overarching narrative structure to the life story as a whole (e.g., early struggles led to later success; McAdams, 2006). Recognizing which narratives enter into the process of analysis is part of the task of selecting relevant units of analysis. Including all of the narratives that emerge in a given interview can be useful in identifying the metanarratives, or overarching story structures, that shape what (and how) smaller narratives are told in a given interview.

Approaches to thematic analysis and narrative analysis typically involve inductive foundations. Inductive foundations—of which grounded theory is one (Charmaz, 2006; Glaser & Strauss, 1967)—involve only minimal theoretical knowledge and assumptions before analysis. Unlike with many psychological research methods, approaching thematic or narrative analysis from an inductive foundation does not seek to test theory or prove a causal relationship between constructs. Instead, it seeks to build or expand theoretical understandings of lived experience within an underexplored area of investigation (e.g., McClelland, 2011). Starting from the assumption that theories are often inadequate to describe the populations or processes to which they are applied, inductive approaches such as thematic and narrative analysis seek to expand existing theories to more adequately attend to the diversity of experiences. This is especially important in studies of sexuality, in which contemporary ideologies, norms, and laws often guide the development of sexuality theories both implicitly and explicitly (see Chapters 1 and 3, this volume). An essential task of research is to encourage the formation of new ideas and to note when old ideologies fall away, for example, the increasing treatment of adolescent sexuality as a normative aspect of development rather than as merely a sign of pathology or deviance (Tolman & McClelland, 2011). Phenomenological methods, overall, share an interest in developing theoretical and empirical research that expands ideological assumptions about human diversity.

PUTTING IT ALL TOGETHER: EXAMPLES OF PHENOMENOLOGICAL APPROACHES TO THE PSYCHOLOGICAL STUDY OF SEXUALITY

Thus far, we have discussed approaches to data collection and analysis separately. This distinction—although helpful in highlighting the important decisions needed for each step—creates an artificial impression that data collection and analysis are not dependent on one another. Data collection and analysis are, in fact, related processes and need to be planned for as such in the design of any phenomenological investigation into the psychological experience of sexuality. Three studies are presented in this section as a way to illustrate several forms of phenomenological research methods as they are put into practice to examine topics central to the psychological experience of sexuality.

Example 1: The Narrative Study of Lives

Summary of aims. Hammack, Thompson, and Pilecki (2009) is an excellent example of the use of the narrative study of lives to understand the phenomenon of how young people come to develop a sexual identity amid shifting sexual norms and social contexts that influence when, how, and with whom one can have sex, can desire, and build community (see Chapters 13 and 20, this volume). Noting recent significant shifts in the cultural contexts in which sexual minority youths develop, Hammack et al. (2009) aimed to understand how same-sex-attracted emerging adults develop sexual identities. More specifically, these researchers sought to understand the relationships between sociopolitical contexts, desire, and sexual identity. They aimed to shift the discourse on sexual minority youth development, which has largely focused on discourses of struggles with coming out and assumptions about committing to a singular identity (i.e., gay, lesbian, or bisexual) toward a direction more closely reflecting the complicated experiences of young people's sexual development.

Hammack et al. (2009) used a theoretical and methodological approach to the study of sexual identity development grounded in the narrative study of lives (Cohler, 2007; Gregg, 2007; McAdams, 2006), which allowed them to examine how the common but limited discourses of sexual identity affected individual identity construction as well as strategies that incorporated, synthesized, and restructured these discourses. The study was primarily focused on understanding how sexual identities were experienced and made meaningful in lived experiences of same-sex-attracted emerging adults through the process of narrative engagement. The concept of narrative engagement was operationalized as the ways in which same-sex-attracted emerging adults told their life stories, which evidenced how they constructed their own identities in relation to prevailing societal discourses. This conceptualization of identity as a dynamic and evolving life story (Hammack, 2008; McAdams & Pals, 2006) sits in contrast to more common notions of sexual identity as singular and categorical (e.g., gay, lesbian, or bisexual; see Chapter 18, this volume).

Data collection strategies. Focusing primarily on description and interpretation of individual participant experiences rather than on aggregation of data across cases, Hammack et al. (2009) collected life story data from four youths, two self-identified men and two self-identified women, in semistructured interviews that lasted from 2 to 4 hours. The interview was divided into three parts: (a) an exercise allowing participants to draw a "lifeline" representing their life trajectory thus far, explaining the ups and downs as they corresponded to life events; (b) McAdams's (1995) Life Story Interview, composed of questions regarding life experiences (e.g., name chapters in your life; identify and describe a high point in your life, a low point); and (c) questions relating to sexual identity, desire, behavior and experience. The first two portions of the interview protocol contained no explicit reference to sexuality and allowed researchers to evaluate the emergence and integration of same-sex desire in personal identity configuration. As a result, Hammack et al. (2009) could examine how participants constructed sexuality in their narratives before interviewer prompting, and the protocol allowed participants to narrate sexual identities that would potentially not fit within categorical measures.

Data analysis strategies. In their analysis, Hammack et al. (2009) focused on how participants' discussions of desire and behavior were narrated as integrated with one another or in conflict as evidence of their roles in shaping identity. In this regard, the ways in which desire and behavior were (or were not) interrelated within participants' interviews was treated as evidence of the process of narrative engagement in their construction of identity as a life story. Thus, each participant's overarching life story narrative constituted the unit of analysis, rather than specific event descriptions or individual sentences. The research team paid close attention to moments in the narrative when participants referenced the relevance of or their interactions with social discourses (e.g., historical, familial, religious, and cultural attitudes and expectations surrounding sexuality). This revealed the role of social factors in emerging adults' lived experiences of sexual desire and behavior.

Summary of study conclusions. Hammack et al.'s (2009) phenomenological narrative approach produced findings that (a) descriptively revealed the individualized aspects of behavior, desire, and identity and (b) analytically linked these individual experiences to the larger contexts of available opportunities, social support systems, and accessible narratives. For example, although one participant, Francine, assumed her same-sex desire required embracing a categorical lesbian identity, she still felt attracted to men and referred to herself behaviorally as bisexual. The other-sex desire she continued to experience conflicted with the social, historical, and cultural expectations for the lesbian identity Francine committed to at an early age. In their analysis, Hammack et al. found her to be grappling with bisexual feelings in a biphobic social context (i.e., she felt prejudice against bisexuals), which prevented her from integrating her desire and behavior within an integrative life story narrative. In other words, simply claiming a bisexual identity was not an authentic option for Francine, given that she perceived negative societal and historical connotations associated with identifying as bisexual. Thus, she remained committed to a lesbian identity even though this identity category may not have sufficiently reflected and integrated her sexual behavior and desire.

In highlighting "the idiographic complexity of individual lives" (Hammack et al., 2009, p. 879), this study revealed the importance of context at both a sociocultural and an individual level. Hammack et al. (2009) concluded that their phenomenological approach to studying narrative engagement bridged the individual with the social, conceiving of neither as producing the other and instead revealing the ways in which social discourses and lived experience are inextricably interrelated. The researchers found that the categories of sexual identity with which participants narratively engaged in their construction of life stories lacked stability; because individuals sometimes drew on multiple categories (e.g., lesbian, bisexual) and social discourses, they continually renegotiated boundaries and definitions of what sexual identity meant to them. Sexual identity was not the unchanging, singular experience that previous psychological research and commonly held societal assumptions portrayed. Instead, Hammack et al.'s findings demonstrated that sexual identity is negotiated and restructured to construct a life story and identity, which can at times be coherent but is inclusive of seemingly contradictory desires and behaviors.

Utility of phenomenological methods. This analysis of emerging adult narratives, grounded in the narrative-study-of-lives approach, highlighted both personal context and cultural factors that shape identity within the process of narrative engagement. Although the study did not offer a singular generalizable process guiding sexual minority identity development, it highlights the importance of the interaction between lived experience and particular social contexts (e.g., biphobia and the limitations of singular identity categories) in the process of meaning-making and individual development and endorses further study of sexual identity using the narrative study of lives.

Example 2: Phenomenological Uses of Clinical Interviewing and Thematic Analysis

Summary of aims. Tolman's (1994) study of female sexuality is an excellent example of a study that pairs a common approach to qualitative data collection (i.e., clinical interviewing) with an analysis of narrative data with a phenomenological aim: to understand the complexities of adolescent girls' lived experience of sexual desire. Tolman's research integrated findings from previous research on adolescent girls' relational selves (Brown & Gilligan, 1992; Gilligan, 1989) with research concerning girls' sexual stories and how these stories include, or more often lack, recognition of sexual desire (Fine, 1988; Thompson, 1984, 1990). Specifically, Tolman aimed to describe what adolescent girls' experiences of sexual desire looked like within their own lived experience as well as to understand and explain how adolescent girls described their experiences of (and responses to) their own sexual desire. Tolman was, furthermore, interested in understanding how sociocultural factors defined the boundaries of female sexual freedom.

Data collection strategies. To accomplish these aims, Tolman (1994) used a clinical interview protocol that favored the elicitation of narratives as opposed to direct answers to specific prompts. The resulting narratives provided data that privileged the girls' own voices in their retelling of their experiences and responses to their own sexual desire. Tolman collected 30 semistructured, one-on-one clinical interviews from adolescent girls of various racial and ethnic backgrounds, religions, sexual experiences, and school environments (e.g., urban and suburban). Given Tolman's interests in the sociocultural factors that shaped girls' sexuality, sampling for diversity along these social dimensions ensured that she would be able to examine variability across the girls' lived experiences as well as analyze the data for whether that variability was related to differences in social context.

Data analysis strategies. Tolman (1994) used a specific narrative analytic approach—the Listening Guide—to conduct a discursive narrative analysis (Brown, Debold, Gilligan, & Tappan, 1991; Brown & Gilligan, 1992; Brown, Tappan, Gilligan, Miller, & Argyris, 1989). The Listening Guide highlights the multiple voices that are often present in the telling of a narrative and was developed as a way to discern the polyphonic nature of girls' narratives. The Listening Guide approach requires multiple readings of each interview, with each reading focusing on a particular voice. Tolman identified four voices, defined as "a way of speaking that has an identifiable set of coherent features" (Tolman & Szalacha, 1999, p. 14): the self, erotic voice, voice of the body, and voice of response to one's desire. The Listening Guide's discursive features allow the researcher to focus on the roles and interplay of these multiple voices in constructing narratives of lived experience as well as on how such voices are often in implicit conversation with cultural discourses (e.g., media portrayals, historical constructions, and normative expectations of sexual desire).

Through recognition of both the listener and the participant as subjective coconstructors of the text, the analysis included notation of the interviewer's thoughts and reactions to the participant's narratives. Tolman paid specific attention in the processes of interviewing and analysis to how she, as the researcher, shaped the context in which the data arose, thus illuminating how the researcher exists as an audience for whom stories are told. For example, asking questions about participants' bodily experience of sexuality gave participants opportunities to talk about embodied experiences of their desire that were new to some, highlighting both the silencing of physical pleasure in girls' lives outside of the interview context, but also giving them an opportunity to voice such experiences within the interview (see Chapter 25, this volume).

Summary of study conclusions. Tolman's (1994) analysis revealed that although two thirds of participants spoke about their own bodily experiences of sexual feelings, three participants perceived their bodies as silent, and the remainder related confusion about their experience of sexual desire. All who spoke of feeling sexual desire described a conflict between these feelings and cultural expectations or socially constructed problems as connected to female sexual desire (see Volume 2, Chapter 6, this handbook).

Participants' narratives revealed intrapersonal discrepancies in the form of intense conflict between their sexual feelings and their awareness of the social and relational consequences of desire. For example, one participant, Megan, who identified as bisexual, voiced confusion as she described feeling responsible for subduing her male partner's sexual desire despite her own strong desires; she worried that her failure to do so would categorize her as a slut. Megan also related confusion as she described silencing her bodily feelings for girls and her perception that society deemed her same-sex attraction unnatural. These intrapersonal conflicts in Megan's narratives of her sexual desire evidenced how social context (e.g., societal expectations of sexual restraint and heteronormativity) played important and distinct roles in her subjective experiences of sexual desire for both other-sex and same-sex partners.

This study design also granted Tolman (1994) access to girls' solutions to what she termed *sexual desire dilemmas,* or feelings of conflict between wanting to experience sexual desire and pleasure while also responding to social demands to silence their desire and pleasure. For example, a heterosexual participant from an urban school, Rochelle, described feelings of sexual desire but fearfully equated acting on them with increasing her vulnerability to the stigma of a bad reputation, the possibility of sexually transmitted infections, and the reality of male violence. Although sometimes able to experience her desire privately when alone and safe from her feared social consequences, Rochelle's narratives illustrated how some girls might be able to solve the problem of struggling with their sexual feelings in an unsafe social context. The ways in which dilemmas of desire were negotiated privately by girls was deemed problematic in that it potentially diminished girls' own experiences and did not challenge the limiting social contexts that continued to silence and problematize female sexuality.

Utility of phenomenological methods. This study's clinical interviewing and narrative analysis allowed for the discovery of layered complexity in girls' experiences of their own sexual desire and revealed the wide range of meanings participants attached to their bodily feelings. The narrative collection and analysis of data, centered on the Listening Guide approach, enabled Tolman (1994) to look beyond the presence or absence of girls' sexual desire and revealed the ways in which adolescent female sexuality was understood and expressed in relationship to the particular limitations and freedoms afforded by social environments (see Chapter 15, this volume).

Rooted in feminist psychological foundations, evidence of the social forces that oppress and silence female sexuality offered potential insights into intervention opportunities. Specifically, Tolman's (1994) findings suggested that on an individual level, educating girls about sexual desire, as well as talking to them about their own sexual feelings, could ease their psychological dilemmas and reduce their experiences of internalized oppression. However, additional intervention is needed on a social level to challenge the societal oppression and silencing of women's sexual selves by creating opportunity structures for women to be able to express and act on their sexual desire.

Example 3: Interpretive Phenomenological Analysis

Summary of aims. Touroni and Coyle's (2002) study of lesbian couples and parenthood is an excellent example of a phenomenological approach to thematic data analysis as a means to better understand qualities in reproduction and family formation in lesbian families. Although many previous studies had focused on children's development in lesbian-parented families, Touroni and Coyle (2002) sought to investigate internal and external factors affecting decisions to have children, including paternal involvement or anonymity and parenting roles. Given that the decision to have a child is just the first in a string of decisions and negotiations lesbian parents must make, this investigation aimed to understand the complexities of the lived experiences of lesbian parenting and provide further information for professionals who assist lesbian couples desiring to become parents (see Chapter 23, this volume; Volume 2, Chapter 7, this handbook).

Data collection strategies. Touroni and Coyle (2002) recruited lesbian couples who were expecting or who already had at least one child in the context of their current relationship. These individuals were recruited for the study because they were presumed to have engaged in the negotiating or decision-making process of planning to have a child and were well positioned to provide retrospective accounts of their experiences of becoming parents. Nine couples were interviewed together in their homes for between 1 hour and 1.75 hours. Notably, the interviewer posed questions to the couple, rather than to each individual, to "obtain a negotiated account from each couple in which partners could contribute their individual recollections to the construction of an agreed version of events" (Touroni & Coyle, 2002, p. 196). Interviewers began by asking background questions and collecting basic demographic data and then asking questions concerning the couple's motivations to become parents, decision making throughout this process, and negotiations of biological and nonbiological parent roles. This interviewing method was designed to recognize and model the collaborative nature of the decision-making process to become parents, given that the participants were essentially required to collaborate in their joint responses to the interviewers' questions. Their interactions with each other in the interview context provided the researchers with further insight into the interpersonal dynamic of each couple.

Data analysis strategies. Touroni and Coyle's (2002) study used a specific type of thematic analysis—interpretative phenomenological analysis (IPA; Smith, 2004)—to focus on the subjective experience of decision making in the context of planned lesbian parenting. Unlike forms of thematic analysis that simply focus on the presence or absence of themes in a given set of interviews, IPA emphasizes both the description and the interpretation (i.e., analysis) of participants' experiences through a focus on the construction of the meaning of a given phenomenon within the research context. Emerging themes are thus illustrative of components of the overarching meaning of an experience. IPA requires an iterative process of thematic code development requiring multiple readings of the data. Specifically, Touroni and Coyle's use of IPA required readings of the interview transcripts and the production of summary notes on key phrases and concepts emerging within each individual transcript regarding motivations, concerns, and negotiations during the pregnancy planning process. The researchers solidified initial themes in the data by reviewing these notes. Analysis then shifted toward reading across all of the transcripts, comparing interview notes, and identifying common or superordinate themes across all interviews. This process resulted in a hierarchical structure to the findings, which represented the relationships between the themes as lived by the participants. For example, concerns about paternal involvement and conception fell under the overarching theme of decision making about using known or anonymous sperm donors and were distributed across two subordinate themes of opting for a known donor and opting for an anonymous donor. It is important to note that the analytical focus was on how couples negotiated these aspects of becoming same-sex parents, as identified by the emergent themes.

Touroni and Coyle (2002) were especially interested in the interactions between researcher and participant rather than providing an objective account of participant experience, as determined by the researchers. Interviewing itself was conceptualized as a reflexive and dynamic process; participants' accounts were considered to be shaped by both interviewer and participant. For example, the researchers discussed and assessed the possible contributions of their roles as a lesbian counseling psychologist and a gay male social psychologist to the interview and analysis process. Their shared identities as sexual minorities may have provided them with unique insight into some of their participants' experiences. However, not being parents may have allowed them to hear more from participants regarding experiences of parental decision making that may not have been shared with other same-sex parents because participants may have assumed some aspects of the experience to be taken for granted by similar others.

Summary of study conclusions. The use of IPA identified four overarching themes emerging from conversations about planning parenthood with lesbian couples, including (a) internal factors motivating couples to have children, (b) external factors contextualizing their experience, (c) decisions regarding paternal anonymity or involvement, and (d) parental roles for the biological and nonbiological parent. Internal factors primarily involved a desire to have children and a feeling that it was the right time in one's life and relationship. When considering external factors, participants identified the relatively recent positive shift in public discourses conceptualizing the possibility of parenthood for lesbian couples. Still, some participants noted a distinct lack of role models for lesbian parenting, and discrimination concerns remained present in their minds. Decisions to opt for a known sperm donor were motivated by a desire to have control of the conception process and for a child to know his or her biological father. However, negotiating paternal involvement could then become a complex issue. Some couples opted for an anonymous donor on the basis of a desire to avoid conflict with the biological father and the potential strain he might create. Finally, parent–child relationships were frequently discussed as they related to the bonds of biological parent and nonbiological parent. Whereas the biological parent, or mother, seemed to have a stable identity, more work went into developing, defining, and negotiating the role of the nonbiological parent.

Utility of phenomenological methods. IPA is a particularly useful form of thematic data analysis in that it allows for both an understanding of what elements of an experience matter to participants (through a description of emergent themes) and the meaning of the experience (through interpretive analysis; Smith & Osborn, 2003). In their application of IPA, Touroni and Coyle (2002) revealed unique factors relevant to lesbian parenting that influence women's decisions to parent and the decisions that often follow from wanting to become a parent. By collecting accounts from couples rather than interviewing individuals, Touroni and Coyle examined the decision-making processes surrounding each of the concerns of lesbian parents identified in their analysis. As a result, their study provides an in-depth account of the factors and struggles (e.g., lack of role models, discrimination) that lesbian parents confront. These findings offer important insight for practitioners working with lesbian couples who seek to provide support and guidance throughout the process of becoming parents.

ADDITIONAL CONSIDERATIONS

The three exemplar studies discussed in the preceding section demonstrate how phenomenological data collection and analysis methods provide important perspectives on the study of sexuality. These perspectives include increased attention to intrapersonal and interpersonal variability, the roles of time and sociohistorical changes in people's lives, and analysis of the ways in which the meanings of lived experience are inexorably linked to social context. However, just as with any method, phenomenological methods come with limitations. Two of these limitations are the role of generalizability to larger populations and a focus on participants' access to language and voice as the route to self-knowledge. We discuss both in detail next.

Question of Generalizability

Phenomenological methods focus on participants' descriptions and analysis of their lived experience. Data are typically collected from a small number of participants because of the in-depth and time-consuming nature of the data collection. Although some investigators use phenomenological methods to make interpretive claims by examining patterns across participants to speak to a larger shared experience in a population, phenomenological methods do not test causal or explanatory hypotheses. In short, traditional notions of statistical generalizability cannot be applied when gauging the value of findings from phenomenological research. What phenomenological methods do provide, however, are insights into the ways in which social, political, and historical contexts interact with individual development (e.g., how same-sex couples experience and subvert discriminatory social policy).

For example, the narrative study of lives does not seek to estimate the average experience of or parameters within a population. The power of the narrative study of lives lies in its ability to provide detailed analysis of the interactive processes shaping human development, as evidenced in the discussion of narrative engagement with sexual identity (Hammack et al., 2009). Although this method does not give one a complete account of the frequency of any given experience, phenomenological methods paint a detailed and nuanced picture of a small set of subjective accounts to offer a sense of the processes that occur at the level of everyday lived experience (e.g., Frost & Ouellette, 2011). This kind of detail is especially useful when researchers are interested in understanding the meanings and experiences of sexuality-related phenomena that are not well understood or are insufficiently theorized (see Chapter 1, this volume).

Role of Language and Voice

The strengths of phenomenological methods of data collection, such as clinical interviewing, are that they often ask participants to describe their sexuality-related experiences. Although relying on participants' voice and self-generated description enables greater insight into how participants are making meaning of their experiences, these methods are limited to aspects of sexuality that participants are able and willing to communicate. It is possible that in an interview, participants are limited by broader constraints that maintain the invisibility of important aspects of their experiences, including limited self-understanding, image management, social stigmas, and (perhaps most important) experiences that have been lived but not yet languaged (i.e., turned from inchoate experiences to communicable utterances; see McClelland & Fine, 2008a). The language available to individuals for making sense of their sexualities may differ on the basis of their social location and access to privilege in many forms, including but not limited to educational attainment, sex education, and being native speakers of the language of investigation.

McClelland and Fine (2008b) described the methodological dilemma inherent in research with young women on topics concerning sexual desire: Researchers want to rely on participants' subjective descriptions and interpretations but are often faced with participants who have been systematically marginalized and may lack adequate language to describe their experiences. Building from Fine's (1988) seminal writing on the missing discourse of desire, McClelland and Fine (2008b) offered a series of methodological release points that aim to help researchers navigate this dilemma, including research practices such as asking participants to reflect on previously published findings about adolescent sexual behavior as a way to collect young people's insights into these data or using focus groups to inquire about topics that might be read as shaming by research participants struggling to adhere to sexual norms. Last, McClelland and Fine (2008a) theorized an emerging version of sexual desire in the form of want. McClelland and Fine (2008a) argued that want may offer a quieter form of expression and may provide an additional lens by which to inquire about and assess young women's experiences of developing sexualities.

McClelland and Fine (2008a, 2008b, in press), along with other psychological researchers, have worked to shine a light on how and what participants talk about when they describe their sexuality while still drawing attention to the difficult balance between telling it like it is (Midgley, 2006) and critically analyzing the ideologies and discourses that participants speak with and through. The image of being wrapped in cellophane provides a metaphor for the limitations that both researcher and participant face when trying to communicate about topics related to sexuality, topics that are often weighted with sexual stigmas (McClelland & Fine, 2008b). When reflecting on the role of voice in phenomenological research, it is essential "to recognize that when someone speaks . . . we must assume that there are other relevant words both unspoken and not-yet-spoken" (McClelland & Fine, 2008b, p. 240). It is in these spaces between participant and researcher, and between the spoken and the yet-to-be-spoken, that researchers must work to listen, document, and critically assess the lives of individuals, groups, and psychological phenomena.

Reflections on Phenomenological Methods

Given the wide range of research methods and analysis strategies available to the psychologically oriented researcher studying sexuality, what do phenomenological methods offer that other methods do not? Sex and sexuality are in some sense mundane in that they represent everyday phenomena. Both have also been defined as extraordinary, taboo, and areas of intense speculation, regulation, and curiosity. This tension between sexuality's mundaneness and its extraordinariness creates a unique space for study: Individuals must negotiate this space within themselves and often with partners and families as they develop and change throughout their lifetime (see Chapter 13, this volume). This quality highlights that there may be something unique about sexuality (and the research questions it produces) that demands research methods that are capable of examining these dimensions, attending to temporal shifts, and understanding the role of social norms in individuals' lives.

There are many different ways to understand the phenomena of sex and sexuality. Understanding the physiological responses within individuals related to their sexuality (e.g., brain response during orgasm or hormone levels during arousal) offers one type of insight (see Chapter 5, this volume); assessing the frequency of sexual behaviors or the number of individuals who identify as lesbian, gay, bisexual, or transgender offers yet another type of insight into the phenomenon of sexuality (see Chapter 4, this volume). Yet the need remains to examine other aspects of sexuality, many of which researchers remain unaware or only vaguely aware. In this regard, phenomenological methods provide an important alternative or complement to other, more widely used research methods in the psychological study of sexuality.

Phenomenological methods uniquely allow psychologists to understand the wide range of variability in the psychological experience and meanings of sexuality in particular and how these experiences shape and are shaped by social and historical contexts. Thus, by uncovering new social scientific knowledge stemming from the documentation of subjective experiences, other nomothetically oriented projects in psychology can build better assessment techniques and more accurately define sexual well-being outcomes (e.g., Edwards & Coleman, 2004; McClelland, 2011, 2012; Peterson & Muehlenhard, 2007; Sanders et al., 2010) as well as better document the need for sexuality-related social and clinical policy change (for reviews, see Frost & de Vries, 2011, and Volume 2, Chapter 10, this handbook). This is the important role that phenomenological research plays within the broader psychological study of sexuality.

FUTURE DIRECTIONS

In this chapter, we presented several of the foundational components of phenomenological inquiry into the psychological experience of sexuality and highlighted specific approaches to conducting this kind of research. Along the way, we have pointed out the benefits of and limitations to phenomenological approaches with regard to their abilities to contribute to the growing body of research on psychology and human sexuality. This discussion is designed to aid researchers interested in gaining the tools necessary to begin their own psychological investigations into sexuality-related phenomena as well as to interest them in these new avenues of inquiry. In further service of this interest, we close with a discussion of potential new directions and advancements in phenomenological investigations into the psychological experience of sexuality.

Thus far, given their roots in pursuit of idiographic and individual experience, phenomenological methods have been well applied to the understanding of individuals' meanings and experiences of sexuality (e.g., identity, desire, behavior). However, sexuality is also, at times, a relational phenomenon, and thus methods limited to capturing the experience of one individual are inherently limited in their ability to explicate relational meanings and the coconstruction of the experience of sexuality. For example, Frost (2011b, 2011c, 2012; Frost & Ouellette, 2004, 2011) has used narrative research methods in efforts to understand the meanings of intimacy that individuals have within their romantic relationships. Given that romantic relationships involve more than one individual, this research is limited, and necessary next steps in this line of inquiry require an understanding how meanings of experience are coconstructed within couples, as shown by Touroni and Coyle (2002; see also Chapter 10, this volume). This will require advancing phenomenological research methods to incorporate dyadic data collection and analysis strategies. Phenomenological psychologists have voiced concerns over such methodological expansions (e.g., focus groups; see Smith, 2004), given the concomitant shift in focus away from the meaning of individual experiences. These concerns must be addressed in advancing a relational phenomenology of the psychological experience of sexuality.

Moreover, given that phenomenological data collection methods traditionally involve intensive face-to-face interviews, phenomenological investigations into the psychological experience of sexuality have been geographically bound to only those locations accessible to the researchers. Location restrictions bias all forms of research into experiences and qualities of individuals that may be geographically unique. As Internet-based research methods in psychology continue to develop, they may offer tools to phenomenological researchers that can help address this limitation. For example, narrative researchers have used the Internet to recruit geographically diverse samples of individuals to provide written narrative accounts of events (e.g., Frost, 2011b; van Eeden-Moorefield, Proulx, & Pasley, 2008). Given that psychological experiences of sexuality-related phenomena are grounded in cultural and structural contexts that are often geographically specific, expanding the boundaries of phenomenological methods in the psychological study of sexuality is a necessary next step if psychologists are interested in understanding how location, place, and psychology are related (Ittelson, Proshansky, Rivlin, & Winkel, 1974; Proshansky, 1987).

An additional limitation is the retrospective bias of cross-sectional interview methods in attempting to study development and change over time. Phenomenological approaches must expand to include longitudinal designs to improve their claims regarding the lived change in sexuality-related phenomena over time. Most notable in this regard is Diamond's (2008) research on sexual fluidity. With repeated interviewing of a cohort of young women over 10 years who initially identified as nonheterosexual, Diamond's study yielded knowledge about intraperson stability and change in sexual desire, identity, and behavior and how these processes influenced and were influenced by women's social and relational contexts (i.e., changing norms about family, trans identities, and legal restrictions on same-sex relationships). Additional research on change in other aspects of sexuality can benefit from longitudinal methods that have grown increasingly popular in nomothetic investigations, such as experience sampling and daily diary methods (e.g., Impett, Strachman, Finkel, & Gable, 2008; Impett et al., 2010).

Future research on the meanings and experiences of sexuality-related phenomena must also explore the direct and indirect utility of forms of data other than qualitative, first-person accounts.

Research by Tolman and Szalacha (1999) has highlighted potential expanded insights into the psychological experience of sexuality that can be gained from bringing both qualitative and quantitative data to bear on a single research question in a mixed-methods approach. Such approaches are distinct from multimethod approaches that use separate methods (e.g., interview and survey) to produce separate data sets to answer separate research questions. Mixed-methods designs relevant to phenomenological approaches in psychology begin with units of analysis that provide idiographic insights. Researchers (and participants) can apply quantitative coding schemes to those original data that allow for additional insight into observable patterns and the ability to make nomothetic conclusions about subjective phenomenological experience (e.g., Frost, 2012; McClelland, 2011; Tolman & Szalacha, 1999).

CONCLUSIONS

As evidenced by the work highlighted in this chapter, phenomenological methods offer the psychological study of sexuality a means to understand the high degree of intrapersonal and interpersonal variability in lived experiences of sexuality. In other words, understanding the complex meanings of sexuality with which we began this chapter is a task well suited to psychologists who use phenomenological methods in their research. As the need for knowledge surrounding the nuances of the subjective experience of sexuality grows increasingly scientifically and socially salient, future work on the psychology of sexuality will greatly benefit from the implementation and integration of phenomenological methods.

References

Braun, V., & Clarke, V. (2006). Using thematic analysis in psychology. *Qualitative Research in Psychology, 3*, 77–101. doi:10.1191/1478088706qp063oa

Brown, L., Debold, E., Gilligan, C., & Tappan, M. (1991). Reading narratives of conflict for self and moral voice: A relational method. In W. Kurtines & J. Gewirtz (Eds.), *Handbook of moral behavior and development: Theory, research and application* (pp. 25–61). Hillsdale, NJ: Erlbaum.

Brown, L., & Gilligan, C. (1992). *Meeting at the crossroads*. Cambridge, MA: Harvard University Press.

Brown, L., Tappan, M., Gilligan, C., Miller, B., & Argyris, P. (1989). Reading for self and moral voice: A method for interpreting narratives of real-life, moral conflict and choice. In M. Packer & R. Addison (Eds.), *Entering the circle: Hermeneutic investigation in psychology* (pp. 141–164). Albany: State University of New York Press.

Bruner, J. (1991). The narrative construction of reality. *Critical Inquiry, 18*, 1–21. doi:10.1086/448619

Charmaz, K. (2006). *Constructing grounded theory: A practical guide through qualitative analysis*. Thousand Oaks, CA: Sage.

Cohler, B. J. (2007). *Writing desire: Sixty years of gay autobiography*. Madison: University of Wisconsin Press.

Defense of Marriage Act, Pub. L. 104-199, 110 Stat. 2419 (1996).

Diamond, L. M. (2008). *Sexual fluidity: Understanding women's love and desire*. Cambridge, MA: Harvard University Press.

Dilthey, W. (1977). *Descriptive psychology and historical understanding* (R. Zaner & K. Heiges, Trans.). The Hague, the Netherlands: Martinus Nijhoff. (Original work published 1910)

Edwards, W. M., & Coleman, E. (2004). Defining sexual health: A descriptive overview. *Archives of Sexual Behavior, 33*, 189–195. doi:10.1023/B:ASEB.0000026619.95734.d5

Fine, M. (1988). Sexuality, schooling, and adolescent females: The missing discourse of desire. *Harvard Educational Review, 58*, 29–53.

Fine, M. (2006). Bearing witness: Methods for researching oppression and resistance—A textbook for critical research. *Social Justice Research, 19*, 83–108.

Fine, M., & McClelland, S. I. (2006). Sexuality education and desire: Still missing after all these years. *Harvard Educational Review, 76*, 297–338.

Fine, M., & McClelland, S. I. (2007). The politics of teen women's sexuality: Public policy and the adolescent female body. *Emory Law Journal, 56*, 993–1038.

Foucault, M. (1998). *The history of sexuality: Vol. 1. The will to knowledge*. London, England: Penguin. (Original work published 1976)

Frost, D. M. (2011a). Similarities and differences in the pursuit of intimacy among sexual minority and heterosexual individuals: A personal projects analysis. *Journal of Social Issues, 67*, 282–301. doi:10.1111/j.1540-4560.2011.01698.x

Frost, D. M. (2011b). Social stigma and its consequences for the socially stigmatized. *Social and Personality Psychology Compass, 5*, 824–839. doi:10.1111/j.1751-9004.2011.00394.x

Frost, D. M. (2011c). Stigma and intimacy in same-sex relationships: A narrative approach. *Journal of Family Psychology, 25*, 1–10. doi:10.1037/a0022374

Frost, D. M. (2012). The narrative construction of intimacy and affect in relationship stories: Implications for relationship quality, stability, and mental health. *Journal of Social and Personal Relationships*. Advance online publication. doi: 10.1177/0265407512454463

Frost, D. M., & de Vries, B. (2011). Narrative research, sexuality, and social policy. *Sexuality Research and Social Policy, 8*, 147–150. doi:10.1007/s13178-011-0064-z

Frost, D. M., & Ouellette, S. C. (2004). Meaningful voices: How psychologists, speaking as psychologists, can inform social policy. *Analyses of Social Issues and Public Policy, 4*, 219–226. doi:10.1111/j.1530-2415.2004.00044.x

Frost, D. M., & Ouellette, S. C. (2011). A search for meaning: Recognizing the potential of narrative research in social policy-making efforts. *Sexuality Research and Social Policy, 8*, 151–161. doi:10.1007/s13178-011-0061-2

Frost, D. M., Stirratt, M. J., & Ouellette, S. C. (2008). Understanding why gay men seek HIV seroconcordant partners: Intimacy and risk reduction motivations. *Culture, Health, and Sexuality, 10*, 513–527. doi:10.1080/13691050801905631

Gadamer, H.-G. (1975). *Truth and method* (W. Glen-Doepel, Trans.). London, England: Sheed & Ward.

Gilligan, C. (1989). Teaching Shakespeare's sister. In C. Gilligan, N. Lyons, and T. Hamner (Eds.), *Making connections: The relational world of adolescent girls at Emma Willard School* (pp. 6–29). Cambridge, MA: Harvard University Press.

Gilligan, C., Spencer, R., Weinberg, K. M., & Bertsch, T. C. (2003). On the *Listening Guide*: A voice-centered relational model. In P. M. Carnic, J. E. Rhodes, & L. Yardley (Eds.), *Qualitative research in psychology: Expanding perspectives in methodology and design* (pp. 157–172). Washington, DC: American Psychological Association. doi:10.1037/10595-009

Giorgi, A. (1997). The theory, practice, and evaluation of the phenomenological method as a qualitative research procedure. *Journal of Phenomenological Psychology, 28*, 235–260. doi:10.1163/15691629 7X00103

Giorgi, A. (2006). Concerning variations in the application of the phenomenological method. *Humanistic Psychologist, 34*, 305–319. doi:10.1207/s15473333thp3404_2

Giorgi, A. (2010a). Phenomenological psychology: A brief history and its challenges. *Journal of Phenomenological Psychology, 41*, 145–179. doi:10.1163/156916210X532108

Giorgi, A. (2010b). Phenomenology and the practice of science. *Existential Analysis, 21*(1), 3–22.

Glaser, B. G., & Strauss, A. L. (1967). *The discovery of grounded theory: Strategies for qualitative research*. New York, NY: Aldine de Gruyter.

Gregg, G. S. (2007). *Culture and identity in a Muslim society*. New York, NY: Oxford University Press.

Hammack, P. L. (2008). Narrative and the cultural psychology of identity. *Personality and Social Psychology Review, 12*, 222–247. doi:10.1177/1088868308316892

Hammack, P. L., Thompson, E. M., & Pilecki, A. (2009). Configurations of identity among sexual minority youth: Context, desire, and narrative. *Journal of Youth and Adolescence, 38*, 867–883. doi:10.1007/s10964-008-9342-3

Harding, S. (1993). Rethinking standpoint epistemology: "What is strong objectivity?" In L. Alcoff & E. Potter (Eds.), *Feminist epistemologies* (pp. 49–82). New York, NY: Routledge.

Heidegger, M. (1962). *Being and time* (J. Macquarrie & E. Robinson, Trans.). London, England: SCM Press. (Original work published 1927)

Herdt, G., & Kertzner, R. (2006). I do, but I can't: The impact of marriage denial on the mental health and sexual citizenship of lesbians and gay men in the United States. *Sexuality Research and Social Policy, 3*, 33–49. doi:10.1525/srsp.2006.3.1.33

Husserl, E. (1977). *Phenomenological psychology* (J. Scanlon, Trans.). The Hague, the Netherlands: Martinus Nijhoff. doi:10.1007/978-94-010-1083-2

Impett, E. A., Gordon, A. M., Kogan, A., Oveis, C., Gable, S. L., & Keltner, D. (2010). Moving toward more perfect unions: Daily and long-term consequences of approach and avoidance goals in romantic relationships. *Journal of Personality and Social Psychology, 99*, 948–963. doi:10.1037/a0020271

Impett, E. A., Strachman, A., Finkel, E. J., & Gable, S. L. (2008). Maintaining sexual desire in intimate relationships: The importance of approach goals. *Journal of Personality and Social Psychology, 94*, 808–823. doi:10.1037/0022-3514.94.5.808

Ittelson, W. H., Proshansky, H., Rivlin, L., & Winkel, G. (1974). *An introduction to environmental psychology*. New York, NY: Holt, Rinehart & Winston.

Josselson, R. (2004). The hermeneutics of faith and the hermeneutics of suspicion. *Narrative Inquiry, 14*, 1–28. doi:10.1075/ni.14.1.01jos

Kitzinger, C., & Wilkinson, S. (1997). Validating women's experience? Dilemmas in feminist research. *Feminism and Psychology, 7*, 566–574. doi:10.1177/0959353597074012

Klein, P., & Westcott, M. R. (1994). The changing character of phenomenological psychology. *Canadian Psychology/Psychologie Canadienne, 35*, 133–158.

Kvale, S. (1994). *InterViews: An introduction to qualitative research interviewing.* Thousand Oaks, CA: Sage.

Langdridge, D. (2007). *Phenomenological psychology: Theory, research and method.* London, England: Prentice Hall.

Loving v. Virginia, 388 U.S. 1 (1967).

Madill, A., & Gough, B. (2008). Qualitative research and its place in psychological science. *Psychological Methods, 13,* 254–271. doi:10.1037/a0013220

Major, B., Cozzarelli, C., Cooper, M. L., Zubeck, Z., Richards, C., Wilhite, M., & Gramzow, M. H. (2000). Psychological responses of women after first trimester abortion. *Archives of General Psychiatry, 57,* 777–784. doi:10.1001/archpsyc.57.8.777

McAdams, D. P. (1995). *The life story interview.* Evanston, IL: Northwestern University Press.

McAdams, D. P. (2006). *The redemptive self: Stories Americans live by.* New York, NY: Oxford University Press. doi:10.1093/acprof:oso/9780195176933.001.0001

McAdams, D. P., & Pals, J. L. (2006). A new Big Five: Fundamental principles for an integrative science of personality. *American Psychologist, 61,* 204–217. doi:10.1037/0003-066X.61.3.204

McClelland, S. I. (2011). Who is the "self" in self-reports of sexual satisfaction? Research and policy implications. *Sexuality Research and Social Policy, 8,* 304–320. doi:10.1007/s13178-011-0067-9

McClelland, S. I. (2012). Measuring sexual quality of life: Ten recommendations for health psychologists. In A. Baum, T. A. Revenson, & J. Singer (Eds.), *Handbook of health psychology* (2nd ed., pp. 247–269). New York, NY: Taylor & Francis.

McClelland, S. I., & Fine, M. (2008a). Rescuing a theory of adolescent sexual excess: Young women and wanting. In A. Harris (Ed.), *Next wave cultures: Feminism, subcultures, activism* (pp. 83–102). London, England: Routledge.

McClelland, S. I., & Fine, M. (2008b). Writing *on* cellophane: Studying teen women's sexual desires, inventing methodological release points. In K. Gallagher (Ed.), *The methodological dilemma: Creative, critical, and collaborative approaches to qualitative research* (pp. 232–260). London, England: Routledge.

McClelland, S. I., & Fine, M. (in press). Over-sexed and under surveillance: Adolescent sexualities, cultural anxieties and thick desire. In M. L. Rasmussen, K. Quinlivan, & L. Allen (Eds.), *Interrogating the politics of pleasure in sexuality education: Pleasure bound.* New York, NY: Routledge.

McCorkel, J. A., & Myers, K. (2003). What difference does difference make? Position and privilege in the field. *Qualitative Sociology, 26,* 199–231. doi:10.1023/A:1022967012774

Mehl, M. R., & Conner, T. S. (Eds.). (2011). *Handbook of research methods for studying daily life.* New York, NY: Guilford Press.

Merleau-Ponty, M. (1962). *Phenomenology of perception* (C. Smith, Trans.). New York, NY: Routledge & Kegan Paul.

Midgley, N. (2006). Psychoanalysis and qualitative psychology: Complementary or contradictory paradigms? *Qualitative Research in Psychology, 3,* 213–231. doi:10.1191/1478088706qrp065oa

Mishler, E. G. (1986). *Research interviewing: Context and narrative.* Cambridge, MA: Harvard University Press.

Morawski, J. G. (1994). *Practicing feminisms, reconstructing psychology: Notes on a liminal science.* Ann Arbor: University of Michigan Press.

Morawski, J. G. (1997). The science behind feminist research methods. *Journal of Social Issues, 53,* 667–681. doi:10.1111/j.1540-4560.1997.tb02455.x

Morawski, J. G. (2005). Reflexivity and the psychologist. *History of the Human Sciences, 18,* 77–105. doi:10.1177/0952695105058472

Morse, J. M., Barrett, M., Mayan, M., Olsen, K., & Spiers, J. (2002). Verification strategies for establishing reliability and validity in qualitative research. *International Journal of Qualitative Methods, 1*(2), 13–22.

Ouellette, S. C. (2003). Painting lessons. In R. Josselson, A. Lieblich, & D. P. McAdams (Eds.), *Up close and personal: The teaching and learning of narrative research* (pp. 13–28). Washington, DC: American Psychological Association. doi:10.1037/10486-001

Peplau, L. A., & Fingerhut, A. W. (2007). The close relationships of lesbians and gay men. *Annual Review of Psychology, 58,* 405–424. doi:10.1146/annurev.psych.58.110405.085701

Peterson, Z. D., & Muehlenhard, C. L. (2007). Conceptualizing the "wantedness" of women's consensual and nonconsensual sexual experiences: Implications for how women label their experiences with rape. *Journal of Sex Research, 44,* 72–88.

Policy concerning homosexuality in the armed forces, 10 U.S.C. 37 § 654 (2006).

Prager, K. J. (1995). *The psychology of intimacy.* New York, NY: Guilford Press.

Proshansky, H. M. (1987). The field of environmental psychology: Securing its future. In D. Stokols & I. Altman (Eds.), *Handbook of environmental psychology* (pp. 1467–1488). New York, NY: Wiley.

Riessman, C. (2008). *Narrative methods for the human sciences.* Thousand Oaks, CA: Sage.

Sanders, S. A., Hill, B. J., Yarber, W. L., Graham, C. A., Crosby, R. A., & Milhausen, R. R. (2010). Misclassification bias: Diversity in conceptualisations about having "had sex." *Sexual Health, 7,* 31–34. doi:10.1071/SH09068

Sartre, J. (1958). *Being and nothingness* (H. E. Barnes, Trans.). London, England: Routledge. (Original work published 1943)

Smith, J. A. (1999). Towards a relational self: Social engagement during pregnancy and psychological preparation for motherhood. *British Journal of Social Psychology, 38*, 409–426. doi:10.1348/014466699164248

Smith, J. A. (2004). Reflecting on the development of interpretative phenomenological analysis and its contribution to qualitative research in psychology. *Qualitative Research in Psychology, 1*(1), 39–54.

Smith, J. A., & Osborn, M. (2003). Interpretative phenomenological analysis. In J. A. Smith (Ed.), *Qualitative methods: A practical guide to research methods* (pp. 51–80). London, England: Sage.

Thompson, S. (1984). Search for tomorrow: On feminism and the reconstruction of teen romance. In C. Vance (Ed.), *Pleasure and danger: Exploring female sexuality* (pp. 350–384). Boston, MA: Routledge & Kegan Paul.

Thompson, S. (1990). Putting a big thing in a little hole: Teenage girls' accounts of sexual initiation. *Journal of Sex Research, 27*, 341–361. doi:10.1080/00224499009551564

Tiefer, L. (2002). Arriving at a "new view" of women's sexual problems: Background, theory, and activism. *Women and Therapy, 24*, 63–98. doi:10.1300/J015v24n01_12

Tolman, D., & Szalacha, L. (1999). Dimensions of desire: Bridging qualitative and quantitative methods in a study of female adolescent sexuality. *Psychology of Women Quarterly, 23*, 7–39. doi:10.1111/j.1471-6402.1999.tb00338.x

Tolman, D. L. (1994). Doing desire: Adolescent girls' struggles for/with sexuality. *Gender and Society, 8*, 324–342. doi:10.1177/089124394008003003

Tolman, D. L. (2002). *Dilemmas of desire: Teenage girls talk about sexuality*. Cambridge, MA: Harvard University Press.

Tolman, D. L., & McClelland, S. I. (2011). Normative sexuality development in adolescence: A decade in review 2000–2009. *Journal of Research on Adolescence, 21*, 242–255. doi:10.1111/j.1532-7795.2010.00726.x

Touroni, E., & Coyle, A. (2002). Decision-making in planned lesbian parenting: An interpretative phenomenological analysis. *Journal of Community and Applied Social Psychology, 12*, 194–209. doi:10.1002/casp.672

van Eeden-Moorefield, B., Proulx, C. M., & Pasley, K. (2008). A comparison of Internet and face-to-face (FTF) qualitative methods in studying the relationships of gay men. *Journal of GLBT Family Studies, 4*, 181–204. doi:10.1080/15504280802096856

Wertz, F. J. (2005). Phenomenological research methods for counseling psychology. *Journal of Counseling Psychology, 52*, 167–177. doi:10.1037/0022-0167.52.2.167

Weston, C., Gandell, T., Beauchamp, J., McAlpine, L., Wiseman, C., & Beauchamp, C. (2001). Analyzing interview data: The development and evolution of a coding system. *Qualitative Sociology, 24*, 381–400. doi:10.1023/A:1010690908200

Part III

DIMENSIONS OF SEXUALITY

CHAPTER 7

BIOLOGY OF THE SEXUAL RESPONSE

James G. Pfaus, Lisa A. Scepkowski, Lesley Marson, and Janniko R. Georgiadis

Sex lies at the root of life, and we can never learn how to reverence life until we know how to understand sex.

—Havelock Ellis (1859–1939)

Sex is a part of nature. I go along with nature.

—Marilyn Monroe (1926–1962)

Sex is everywhere. It imbues our lives with meaning at so many levels, from sexual identity to the proficiency with which we work within (and around) culturally imposed rules regarding sexual conduct. Sex gives us pleasure and pain, self-worth and self-doubt. It can be solitary or enjoyed with others. It can lead us toward or away from love depending on our experiences and expectations. It can elude us, trick us, and turn us into liars or arouse us to poetry, prose, music, and art. It is the best and the worst of us. And, of course, until recently, it has been necessary for human reproduction, entangling us in the subsequent joys and sorrows of nurturing our offspring. Because no one ever dies from lack of sex, it is easy to make believe that sex occupies a less important place on the motivational totem pole than, say, eating. However, the amount of time we spend thinking about it and learning what to do to have it belies its importance in our lives.

Yet even as sex pervades our lives, fundamental questions about it persist. How do the body and brain regulate sexual responding? How do we interpret sexual stimuli? Is there a difference between sexual arousal and desire? Why do orgasms feel so good? How is sexual pleasure related to desire and preference? Do women and men differ in their sexual responses? What is the nature of sexuality and sexual responding? Context and biology interact at the level of the brain for behavior to be modified by experience, allowing even animals to learn about sex. Humans and animals incorporate their experiences with sexual reward and inhibition into a set of Pavlovian predictions about, and operant responses to, their sexual world. In turn, experiences with the world exert a reciprocal influence on neurobiological processes (e.g., Li, 2003). Similarities in the brain's response during different kinds of social and sexual circumstances in all animals, and indeed between males and females, encourage researchers to consider the interactions between sociocultural and biological levels of analysis (e.g., Tolman & Diamond, 2001; see also Chapter 1, this volume). This research has led to more sophisticated experimental designs in the animal literature and has made the behavioral and social contexts in which brain mechanisms of sexual response are studied of vital importance. The human literature has begun to reflect an understanding of context not only as a cultural and political entity (i.e., Tiefer, 2004) but as a biological occasion setter that primes the brain toward (or away from) sexual arousal and desire. The biological mechanisms we discuss here stem from a view of sexuality that blends social, behavioral, biological, and molecular analyses of different sexual responses. In this chapter, we consider research on females and males within and among different species to illuminate a biological core in the brain and periphery that mediates how sexual stimuli are perceived and acted on.

http://dx.doi.org/10.1037/14193-007
APA Handbook of Sexuality and Psychology: Vol. 1. Person-Based Approaches, D. L. Tolman and L. M. Diamond (Editors-in-Chief)

For all animals, this biological core is organized into excitatory and inhibitory systems in the brain and periphery that respond to sexual stimulation and generate arousal in terms of physical activation of the body (and in particular the genitals), desire in terms of responding to preferred stimuli that predict sexual reward (often referred to as *incentive* responding; Toates, 1992), sexual pleasure and reward from different types of sexual stimulation, and inhibition during refractoriness or stress (Pfaus, 2009). Accordingly, we discuss the mechanisms of each of these divisions of sexual response from the standpoint of behavioral, pharmacological, and neuroanatomical research done with animals and psychophysiological and brain imaging research done with humans to synthesize core biological variables that direct different sexual responses.

Key to researchers' understanding of those variables, however, is the fact that sexual responses in all animals, including humans, derive their expression from two sources. One is a set of primarily innate and species-specific motor patterns and physiological responses that are subserved by known pathways in the brain and peripheral nervous system, activated by relevant unconditioned sexual stimuli, and potentiated by gonadal hormones, such as estrogen and testosterone. The other is a set of neural systems in the brain that link arousal and desire to the experience of pleasure and reward. These systems are driven less by hormones and more by mechanisms operating in the brain during sexual experiences. Experience with sexual pleasure and reward comes to sensitize attention, arousal, and bonding to sexual stimuli that predict reward, even if those stimuli have no place in the evolutionary history of the animal (e.g., fetishes involving inanimate objects). Responses to such stimuli depend critically on an animal's first sexual experiences (Pfaus et al., 2012). Of course, laboratory settings allow researchers to control the experiences animals have to test hypotheses efficiently. Although the external control of sexuality in humans is also pervasive, it is derived haphazardly from a morass of cultural and subcultural norms and the imposition of systems of morality and legality, which makes the external control of human sexual behavior amenable to study largely after the fact. It is a testament to the power of reward, however, that despite many sources of internal and external inhibitory control, most animals and many humans find their way toward sexual pleasure with preferred partners and preferred modes of expression. Sex is in no insignificant part driven by pleasure systems in the brain (Georgiadis, Kringelbach, & Pfaus, 2012). Where sex and pleasure intersect, reproduction may well be a secondary benefit (or cost).

COMPARING ANIMAL AND HUMAN SEXUAL BEHAVIORS

Because a substantial portion of knowledge concerning the neurobiology of sexual behavior has been derived from research with laboratory animals such as rats, hamsters, and gerbils, and to a lesser extent with primates such as rhesus macaques (and lesser still with humans), it is important to understand how their behavior, as with that of all animals that engage in sexual behavior, is similar to that of humans. This is not to say that there are no differences that might give rise to limitations in the use of animal sexual behaviors as models of human sexual behavior. Indeed, animal sexual behavior looks different in many respects. Compared with the variety and diversity of human sexual behavior, that of animals appears more fixed, more driven by gonadal hormone effects in the brain and periphery, and more sex stereotyped. Researchers cannot know an animal's subjective experience except in the most rudimentary way as it might be expressed through behavior and expectancy. Although animals live naturally in diverse social systems, as far as researchers can tell they do not have from a self-defining morality that imposes different expectations on individuals by virtue of their genetic and anatomical sex (vs. the gender they believe they are), race, or socioeconomic status. An extreme example is the fact that females of virtually all species initiate and control the rate of sexual responding during their behavioral estrus (the period when they are sexually receptive). When they are not sexually receptive, sex simply does not occur. Males that try are severely attacked by the females, resulting in a very steep inhibitory learning curve in which males learn not to attempt copulation with sexually nonreceptive females

(Pfaus & Pinel, 1989). No culture of low self-esteem or low socioeconomic status drives nonhuman females to accept copulation that they do not want or to copulate for secondary rewards such as money.

Yet for all animals, sex serves a core of common end points related to reward and reproduction. Sex is pleasurable and rewarding when it is desired and when there is sufficient arousal for it. Animals can indeed learn to perform many tricks to get it, navigating around impediments and learning to master the imposition of complex sequences of behavior to gain access to a receptive sex partner. They also easily learn to associate neutral cues (e.g., neutral odors such as almond or lemon) with both sexual arousal and reward, such that those cues end up priming neurochemical systems that excite sexual arousal, desire, and copulatory behavior, along with bonding mechanisms that lead to mate preferences for partners bearing the cue. Sexual behavior occurs in a sequence or "cascade" of behavioral events. Beach (1956) recognized the heuristic value of separating sexual behavior into respective appetitive and consummatory phases. Essentially, this scheme followed from the work of early ethologists such as Craig (1918) and experimental psychologists such as Woodworth (1918), who defined *appetitive* (or *preparatory*) behaviors as those that bring an animal from distal to proximal and into contact with goal objects or incentives. In contrast, *consummatory* behaviors are performed once an animal is in direct contact with the incentive (i.e., to "consummate" the goal). Consummatory behaviors tend to be species specific, sexually differentiated, and stereotyped, whereas appetitive behaviors are more flexible. Indeed, survival often depends on an animal's ability to learn a variety of strategies to obtain goals in different circumstances. Thus, despite differences in the way sexual behaviors appear between species, they share a common set of principles and end points that define them, along with neural mechanisms that make them successful. Animals must be able to respond to hormonal and neurochemical changes that signal sexual desire and arousal. This ability underlies moment-to-moment levels of sexual arousability (Whalen, 1966) and defines the internal state that is commonly referred to as *sex drive*. Sexual responding also requires learning and feedback that allow competent anticipation of, and interaction with, external sexual incentives. Animals must be able to identify external stimuli that predict where potential sex partners can be found; to seek out, solicit, court, or otherwise work to obtain sex partners; to distinguish external cues and behavioral patterns of potential sex partners from those of partners that are not sexually receptive; and to pursue sex partners once sexual contact has been made. Thus, by using a rich combination of unconditioned appetitive responses and conditioned copulatory behaviors, a rational understanding of the neurobiology of sexual behavior can be constructed using preclinical animal models that possess predictive validity for humans (e.g., Pfaus, Giuliano, & Gelez, 2007).

MODELS OF SEXUAL RESPONSE

To grasp the big picture of how biological functions underlie sexual response, it has been useful to place findings from both animal and human literatures into overarching models that attempt to distill the behavioral components down to core variables that can be applied across different species, different situations, or both, given homologous or analogous behaviors (e.g., Figure 7.1). The important implication here is that the brain contains separate systems for those variables and a neuroanatomical organization that allows them to interact. For example, although sexual arousal and desire are often experienced together, they can be perturbed separately, as in the case of a sexual arousal difficulty without a concomitant loss of desire, or vice versa. Thus, models of sexual response are heuristics that guide the understanding of behavioral organization at different levels of analysis. Another important implication is that although some models are derived exclusively from human observations (e.g., Bancroft, 1989; Barlow, 1986; Basson, 2005; Masters & Johnson, 1966), they can apply to animals as well. Likewise, some models of behavior and integrated neural organization derived from animal studies (e.g., Beach, 1956; Pfaff, 1980; Whalen, 1966) can also apply to humans. These two implications are critical when taking a unified approach to understanding the biology of sexual response.

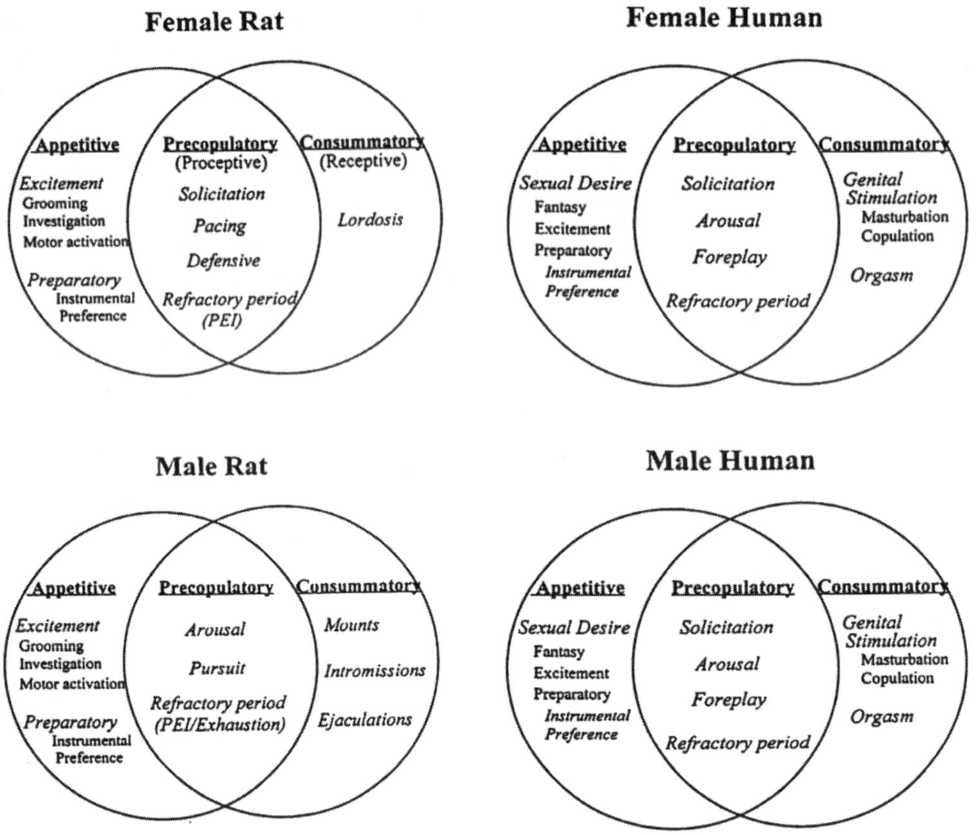

FIGURE 7.1. Incentive sequences for female and male sexual behavior in humans and rats. The behavioral stream moves from left to right, through appetitive, precopulatory, and consummatory phases of behavior, which conforms to the movement of animals from distal to proximal to interactive with respect to the sexual incentive. Three types of appetitive responding reflect relative degrees of learning and necessity. Preparatory behaviors are learned responses that animals must make to acquire the incentive (e.g., operant behaviors, pursuit). Anticipatory behaviors are learned responses that occur in anticipation of an incentive but that are not necessary to obtain it (e.g., conditioned psychomotor stimulation that characterizes behavioral excitement). Unlearned appetitive responses also exist that are instinctual (e.g., arousal induced by touching, kissing, anogenital investigation). These aspects of behavior also occur once copulatory contact has been made, especially if copulation occurs in bouts (as it does in rats). From "Revisiting the Concept of Sexual Motivation," by J. G. Pfaus, 1999, *Annual Review of Sex Research, 10*, p. 141. Copyright 1999 by Taylor & Francis. Adapted with permission.

Most early sexological models described relatively straightforward complementary forces, such as Moll's (1897) notion of the interactive impulses of detumescence, the drive to reduce sexual tension, and contrectation, the drive to approach, touch, and otherwise interact with a sexual incentive (which resembles the later drive-reduction theory of C. Hull [1943] that was based largely on animal studies). *Detumescence* referred to the physical processes taking place in the genital organs specifically, and *contrectation* referred to parts of the sexual impulse taking the form of the higher "psychical" processes "tending towards bodily and mental approximation to another individual" (Moll, 1908/1912, p. 29). In this later work, Moll (1908/1912) characterized these components as distinct, even suggesting that the detumescence impulse could manifest alone, but he noted that these processes are usually so intimately associated that only artificial analysis can separate them.

Ellis (1900), building on Moll's (1897) early description of these processes, argued for viewing the sexual impulse as consisting of tumescence and detumescence. In his view, Moll had left out the most significant part of the sexual process because detumescence could not occur before tension was built up in the first place. During tumescence, desires and images form in the mind while the organism is energized and the genitals become congested with blood. During detumescence, accumulated tension discharges via the genitals amid high sexual excitement, resulting in relief. Ellis described these phenomena as distinct, consecutive stages of the same process. Thus, these types of models characterize the sexual impulse as consisting of complementary drives for approach, for arousal, and for tension reduction that follow a roughly linear pattern. Similarly, the ethological notion of appetitive and consummatory behaviors described earlier are complementary and flow in time as animals move from distal to proximal to interactive with a sexual incentive or partner (e.g., Beach, 1956; Pfaus, 1999).

Perhaps the most well-known linear model of sexual response is Masters and Johnson's (1966) "EPOR" model, also referred to as the *sexual response cycle*. This model emphasized a cascade of sexual responses that formed around the build-up and release of sexual excitement, starting with a steep increase in sexual excitement (E) during sexual desire and arousal, a less-steep plateau (P) during actual sexual stimulation, the abrupt release of sexual excitement or tension during orgasm (O), followed by a prolonged period of relaxation known as resolution (R). This model applied to the sexual responses of both men and women, although individual differences existed in the actual response patterns, especially concerning the ability of women to experience multiple orgasms. The sexual behavior of all animals can be described using this model. Although it is not known whether other animals have orgasms as humans understand them, it has been established that reward ensues from paced copulatory stimulation in female rats and from ejaculation in male rats (Paredes & Vazquez, 1999; Pfaus et al., 2012). Kaplan (1974) proposed a similar but triphasic model suggesting a sequence of desire, excitement, and orgasm, which explicitly added the element of sexual interest that was viewed by many as missing from the Masters and Johnson model (see Chapters 8 and 11, this volume; Volume 2, Chapters 4 and 5, this handbook).

Linear models that are focused on sexual physiology tend to be descriptive and situational, leaving out anything that occurs between the end of an episode of sexual activity and the start of a next one. However, they provide common understanding of a typical physiological and behavioral progression on which models proposing more complex interactions of sexual events in time have been built. More intricate models tend to address one or more additional important features of sexual response, such as dynamic relationships between physiological, psychological, and sociocultural variables; the presence of excitatory and inhibitory processes; and the mechanisms by which disruptions in sexual response can occur.

Bancroft (1989) proposed a "psychosomatic circle of sex" to describe the interplay of psychological and somatic processes involved in a sexual experience. Individual feedback loops were specified and linked together into five dimensions that relay information processing throughout the central and autonomic nervous systems. The first two dimensions involve the brain: cognitive processes in the cortex that influence emotional processes in limbic and hypothalamic systems. In this case, *cognitions* span a range of conditioned responses, including cultural beliefs and attitudes, attentional mechanisms, learned sexual incentives, and learned inhibition over sexual responding. The affective dimension came from the interaction of cortical structures with limbic–hypothalamic structures. Together, these systems influence the spinal cord and autonomic processes related to the mechanics of sexual response: sexual reflex centers in the spinal cord, parasympathetic genital responses such as erection, and other sympathetic autonomic responses consistent with sexual arousal (e.g., increased heart rate).

The autonomic nervous system also played a central role in Barlow's (1986) cognitive–affective model, which outlined the process by which sexual arousal was attained in functional individuals alongside the process by which a pattern of sexual dysfunction could develop in others. The key mechanism in this model is the relationship between selective attention and autonomic arousal in the context of sexual situations. In individuals with sexual dysfunction, erotic cues and expectations regarding sexual performance induce negative affect and increase focus on task-irrelevant, nonsexual stimuli (e.g., performance concerns). Autonomic arousal serves to further narrow attention onto those stimuli, leading to sexual inhibition via facilitated distraction from relevant cues. In contrast, in individuals without sexual difficulties, selective attention and autonomic arousal work reciprocally to enhance processing of sexual stimuli. Positive and negative feedback loops in the model demonstrate how expectancies related to previous functional and dysfunctional experiences influence future sexual responding. Feedback was also critical in the information processing models of Everaerd and colleagues (Everaerd, 1995; Laan, Everaerd, van der Velde, & Geer, 1995), in which the positive or negative outcome of a sexually motivated state was dependent on interpretation from cognitive feedback. These models were similar to that proposed by Pfaff (1980, 1999) to account for quantum neural control of lordosis in female rats by different brain "modules" that compile and interpret different types of sensory and hormonal stimulation.

In Basson's (2005) model of women's sexual response, in the absence of inhibitory processes psychological and biological processing of sexual stimuli lead to physical arousal and sexual responding mediated by subjective arousal. Within this model, sexual interest either arises spontaneously, for example, through hormone actions in the brain and periphery, or reactively in response to external sexual incentives. Basson expanded the array of incentives feeding sexual motivation in this model to include a wide range of nonsexual rewards and reasons (e.g., emotional intimacy, guilt about sexual infrequency; see Chapter 8, this volume). The net behavioral output in this system depends on the interaction of arousal and desire as modified by expectations and previous outcomes. Similarly, Pfaus and Scepkowski (2005; see Figure 7.2) proposed a dynamic model applicable to humans and animals describing the mechanisms by which physiological variables and sexual experiences and expectations interact with arousability and processing of internal and external stimuli to produce a sexual response. Excitatory and inhibitory feedback occurring at any point in the model serve to either enhance or diminish sexual responding.

Despite very little agreement about which kind of model of sexual behavior fits the data best (e.g.,

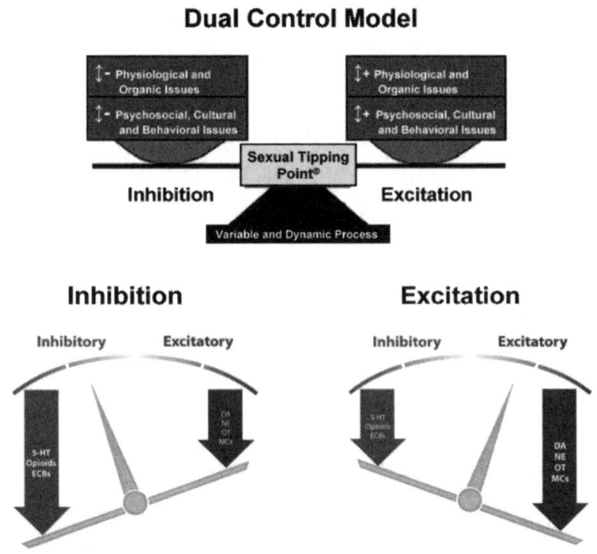

FIGURE 7.2. Dual-control model, after Perelman (2006), and mechanisms of sexual excitation and inhibition, after Pfaus (2009). Top: The interplay between mechanisms of excitation and inhibition generate a Sexual Tipping Point® that results in an individual's level of sexual responsiveness at any given time. Bottom: Sexual excitation (right) involves the activation of neurotransmitters such as noradrenaline (NE) and oxytocin (OT), which stimulate sexual arousal, and dopamine (DA) and melanocortins (MCs), which stimulate attention and desire, within regions of the hypothalamus and limbic system, in response to sexual cues and stimulation. Sexual inhibition (left) involves the activation of transmitters such as opioids, which are released in the cortex, limbic system, hypothalamus, and midbrain during orgasm or sexual reward; serotonin (5-HT), which is released in those regions to induce refractoriness and sexual satiety; and endocannabinoids (ECBs) that mediate sedation. From "A New Combination Treatment for Premature Ejaculation: A Sex Therapist's Perspective," by M. A. Perelman, 2006, *Journal of Sexual Medicine, 3,* p. 1007, and "Pathways of Sexual Desire," by J. G. Pfaus, 2009, *Journal of Sexual Medicine, 6,* pp. 1510, 1516. Copyright 2006 and 2009 by Wiley-Blackwell. Adapted with permission.

Sand & Fisher, 2007), models serve as heuristics that help to guide the understanding of how the components might fit together. To be most useful, a sexual model must be able to address the mechanisms by which its factors of interest interact and influence the psychological and physiological processes driving sexual response and activity. As noted earlier, in most normative examples in both animals and humans many components co-occur, for example, physiological and subjective sexual arousal.

Desire may precede this arousal if spontaneous or follow it if reactive. During an individual's initial sexual experiences, the brain pieces together the components into wholes and assigns them both cognitive and emotional meaning, along with behavioral interpretation, memory, and expectancy. As behavior becomes automated or habitual, a sense of one's "pattern" emerges as a relatively stable factor (e.g., Larsson, 1956; Pfaus et al., 2012), although one that can be altered with subsequent experience in either a positive direction with each new experience of enhanced sexual pleasure or in a negative direction with unexpected difficulties obtaining sexual arousal, desire, or pleasure. The multivariate models discussed earlier for the most part account for increases and decreases in sexual responding by allowing for excitatory and inhibitory feedback loops during and between sexual encounters. Recent models have capitalized on this common theme of opposing forces, for example, brain mechanisms that subserve sexual excitation and inhibition (Bancroft & Janssen, 2000; Perelman, 2006; Pfaus, 2009). These models typically posit a balance of two forces that leads to competent and flexible sexual responding, with a fixation or overactivation of one or the other force that leads to disordered sexual responding (either hyper or hypo, as depicted in Figure 7.3). From this perspective, it is easy to see how many of these models overlap and can be merged. For example, both excitatory and inhibitory neurochemical systems mediate the individual components of the EPOR model and could easily be imagined to enhance or diminish individual phases of the Basson (2005) model. In fact, such an interplay among systems reflects current thinking about how the brain is organized for sexual behavior (reviewed in Pfaus, 2009).

NEURAL AND HORMONAL ORGANIZATION OF SEXUAL BEHAVIOR

In applying a modular neural concept to the control of sexual behavior, it is necessary to understand how the peripheral and autonomic nervous systems send sensory information about genital and erogenous sexual arousal and stimulation to the spinal cord and brain and how the brain derives a feeling of desire and pleasure from such stimulation that feeds forward to copulation, culminating in a threshold amount of sympathetic arousal for orgasm (or homologous responses in animals) and immediate sexual pleasure that activates inhibitory mechanisms related to euphoria (e.g., orgasm–reward), satiety, and refractoriness.

Autonomic Processing

The autonomic nervous system (Gabella, 1995; Iverson, Iverson, & Saper, 2000) consists of three divisions, sympathetic, parasympathetic, and enteric (the latter of which controls the gut and is not discussed further). The role of the sympathetic system is to up- or down-regulate homeostatic and cardiovascular mechanisms to prepare the body for action (sometimes referred to as the *stress response* or the *fight-or-flight response*). Such action can be defined in terms of good stress (eustress) or bad stress (distress) depending on the nature of the event (Selye, 1974). In either case, the sympathetic system initiates immediate pupil dilation (allowing for greater processing of the visual field), increased heart rate and blood pressure, dilation of the bronchioles of the lungs (to increase oxygenation of the blood), constriction of blood vessels, and inhibited digestion. It is also responsible for ejaculation and orgasm once sexual stimulation is underway. The sympathetic system activates the adrenal gland (located just above the kidney) to induce a massive release of adrenaline from the adrenal medulla (which activates and potentiates sympathetic outflow in most organs all at once, except the gonads) and glucocorticoids such as corticosterone or cortisol from the adrenal cortex (which increases glucose concentrations in the blood, inhibits inflammation that might occur in response to injury, and potentiates arousal in the central nervous system and phenomena such as place learning in the hippocampus of the brain's limbic system). The sympathetic nervous system extends from the spinal cord between the thoracic and lumbar divisions and consists of short preganglionic nerves that contain the transmitter acetylcholine, which excites postganglionic neurons, and long postganglionic nerves that contain noradrenaline (which inhibits prolonged muscle contractions). The ganglia collect incoming

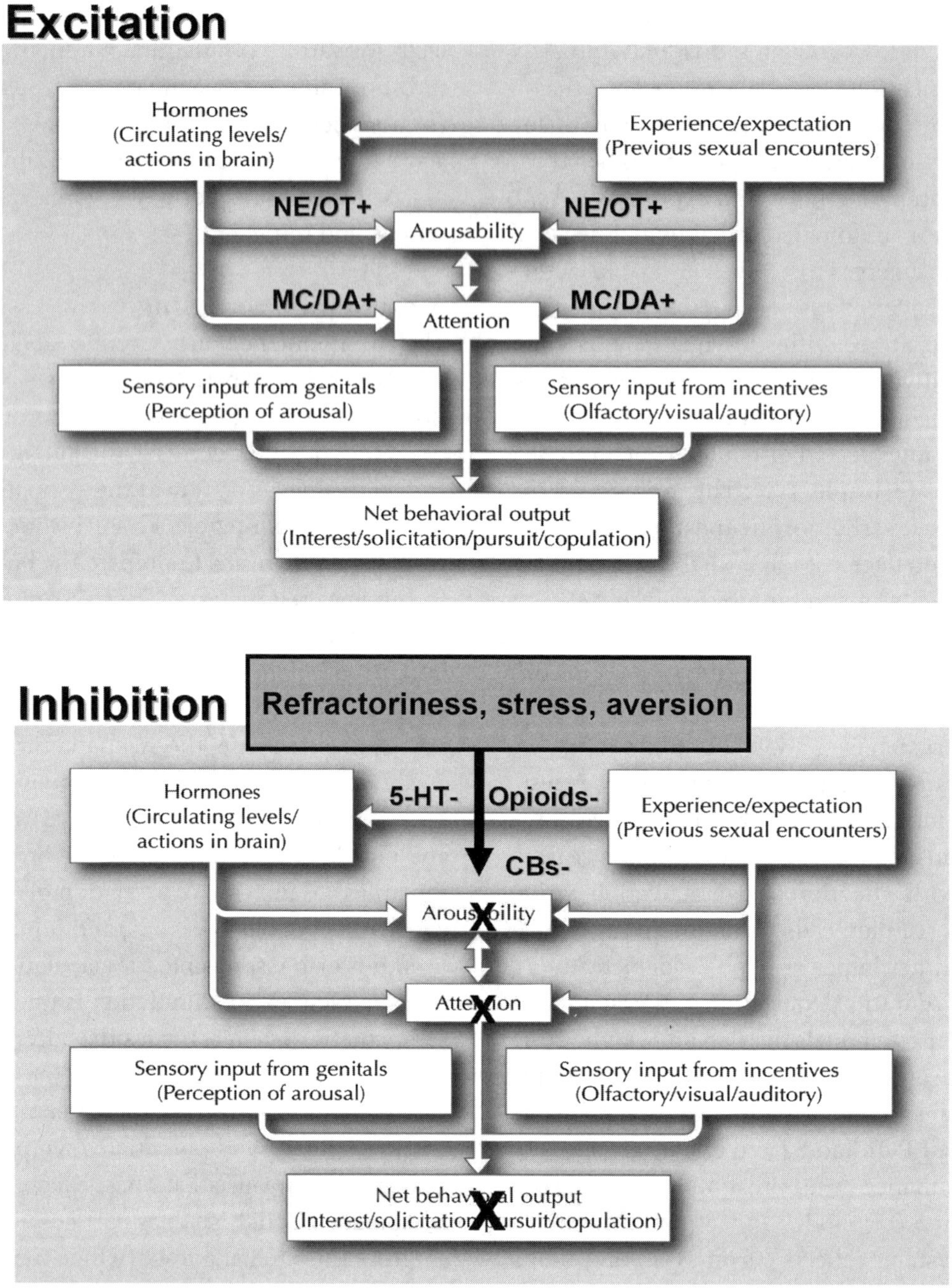

FIGURE 7.3. Interactive model by Pfaus and Scepkowski (2005) depicting how neurochemical mechanisms of sexual excitation and inhibition control the hormonal and associative learning (experiential) systems that subserve sexual arousal, desire, and behavior. Top: Excitation produced by hormone action, experientially derived activation of arousability (via activation of norepinephrine [NE] and oxytocin [OT]), or both and attention (via the activation of melanocortin [MC] and dopamine [DA]) that mixes with peripheral arousal and sexual stimuli to drive net behavioral output. Bottom: Inhibition from refractory states, stress, or aversion. Inhibitory systems activate serotonin (5-HT), opioids, and endocannabinoids (CBs) to induce satiety, pleasure, and sedation, respectively, although such systems are activated in stressful or aversive circumstances. From "The Biological Basis for Libido," by J. G. Pfaus and L. A. Scepkowski, 2005, *Current Sexual Health Reports, 2*, p. 96. Copyright 2005 by Springer Science + Business Medica B.V. Reprinted with permission.

preganglionic fibers and distribute the postganglionic fibers to the organs in the abdominal and pelvic regions.

In contrast, the parasympathetic nervous system opposes the actions of the sympathetic system at each organ within each division. Its role is to calm the system down after stress, though it can be activated within each division on its own (e.g., as bright sunlight induces constriction of the pupil). The parasympathetic division is literally around ("para") the sympathetic division and extends long fibers of the cranial nerves III, VII, IX, and X (occulomotor, facial, glossopharyngeal, and vagus) to innervate ganglia close to the organs. The postganglionic fibers going to the orgasm are short. Both pre- and postganglionic fibers contain acetylcholine, which excites neurons and contracts smooth muscle. The pre–post relationship is more specific (e.g., 1:3) than the sympathetic division (which is greater than 1:10). Because the parasympathetic division causes dilation of blood vessels, it is critical for the stimulation of erection in clitoris, vagina, and penis, along with other erogenous erectile tissues (e.g., nipples) and for draining the blood out of erectile tissues after ejaculation or orgasm.

Peripheral autonomic blood flow is felt far more readily than internal flow (unless the particular organ is sensitive to pressure, as in the case of the heart and kidneys, which have baroreceptors that allow heart rate to be detected by the brain and allow the kidneys to detect a hypovolemic state). When cold, regulatory systems in the hypothalamus activate the sympathetic nervous system to keep blood in the center of the body, thus keeping the core organs warm. However, this necessarily causes constriction of blood vessels in the fingers, making them feel painfully cold, which in turn sensitizes the limbic, motor, and cortical systems to find warmth and shelter. Likewise, blood flow to the penis is sensed far more readily than blood flow to smaller external organs such as the clitoris or labia, and indeed both are more readily sensed than internal blood flow to the vagina or prostate. The reliance on vaginal arousal as a measure of sexual arousal may well account for the relative lack of concordance between physiological and subjective measures of sexual arousal in women relative to that observed between physiological and subjective measures of sexual arousal in men (Chivers & Rosen, 2010).

Central Processing

The brain organizes all stimulation that is sexual in nature into modules (e.g., Pfaff, 1980) that reflect different levels of processing and interpretation. Although sexual responding is typically thought of as highly emotional and base in terms of horny people or animals abandoning rationality for immediate gratification, sexual responding has a huge cognitive component that involves cortical activation. This activation controls the coding of information into gestalts (e.g., sets of physical or interpersonal characteristics that individuals find conditionally attractive or unattractive; contexts that are suitable or unsuitable for sexual activity, following from Pavlov, 1927) and involves the activation of prefrontal cortex and the descending inhibition of motor acts as part of executive function.

Information is also encoded into attentional and emotional components that involve the activation of the limbic system, notably the nucleus accumbens (NAc), septum, and amygdala, which provide pleasure and attention that can focus itself on pleasure-related stimuli in the environment; the hippocampus, which provides spatial maps of the external world and episodic memory for important sexual encounters; and the paleocortex (e.g., anterior cingulate gyrus), which regulates autonomic function along with anticipation of reward, decision making, and empathy (Bush et al., 2002; Carter et al., 1998).

Although sexual responses can be thoughts and fantasies (at least in humans), they are reflected in all animals as behavior. Coordinated purposeful behavior comes from both fine and gross motor acts that are derived from the coordinated activation of motor cortex and the basal ganglia, along with other motor structures in the midbrain and the cerebellum. In addition to coordinating body movements in space and time, these structures crystallize motor memory, a function that is critical for motor habit formation (the phenomenon whereby motor acts at the beginning of behavioral learning are choppy and uncoordinated but become virtually automated with practice). As with all other motor function, practice makes perfect. Indeed, the formation of motor habits protects sexual behavior against treatments or situations that might disrupt it, including novel environments, stress, castration, genital anesthesia, and brain lesions (reviewed in Pfaus et al., 2012).

Finally, regulatory components in the hypothalamus sum gonadal steroid actions into a primitive drive state (Pfaff, 1980, 1999). This state then feeds forward to inhibit other hypothalamic regulatory states (e.g., feeding) and interacts with the limbic system to direct appropriate attention and bias. The limbic system interacts with the basal ganglia to generate appropriate and competent movements in response to sexual cues, and the cortex (along with related subcortical structures) provides interpretation, learning, memory, and expectation. Inhibition can be exerted in both a bottom-up and a top-down fashion, and inhibitory loops exist in all modules. Inhibition can occur as part of the general behavioral inhibition stimulated by the medial prefrontal cortex in its control of executive function or as part of a hypothalamic system that turns on feeding or parental behavior at the expense of sexual responding.

Hormones Set the Stage

The brain does not interpret sexual stimuli in a vacuum. It relies on the generation of an internal drive state based on steroid hormone action and the anticipation of sexual reward based on the interpretation of both unconditional sexual stimuli (e.g., odors, certain phenotypical body features) and conditional sexual stimuli that are associated with sexual pleasure and drive incentive attentional mechanisms in the limbic system (notably dopamine [DA] release in the NAc) that come to predict sexual reward. Steroid hormone secretion by the ovaries and testes acts in the periphery to maintain the integrity of both internal and external genital tissues and in the brain to increase the sensitivity of an individual to sexual incentives. However, the pattern of circulating steroid hormone levels differs between the sexes. It occurs in two phases in mammals: (a) an organizational phase in which the male phenotype differentiates from the female "default" through the combined action of androgens and estrogens during a critical perinatal period that "sculpt" a male brain and (b) during a subsequent activational phase in which gonadal steroid secretion acts on those differentiated brain regions to activate the neuroendocrine systems necessary for reproduction and the behaviors that will bring it about (Bonthuis et al., 2010; Lenz & McCarthy, 2010; Nelson, 2005). Thus, the brains of male mammals are differentiated from the female default by early hormone actions, which leads to different patterns of sexual responding in adulthood driven by two distinct steroid hormone secretion patterns, one continuous (male) and one cyclic (female).

The cyclic actions of estradiol, testosterone, and progesterone in females leads to changes in sexual responding and increases in sexual arousal and desire around the time of ovulation in all vertebrate species, including humans (Slob, Ernste, & van der Werff ten Bosch, 1991; Stanislaw & Rice, 1988), although a smaller increase has been reported around the time of menstruation (Singer & Singer, 1972). Of the three steroids released from the ovaries of mammalian females, testosterone is at its highest during ovulation, whereas estradiol rises a few days earlier, peaking just before ovulation. Progesterone levels begin to rise during and after ovulation. This hormonal milieu during the periovulatory follicular phase alters the way in which visual sexual stimuli are processed in women (Gizewski et al., 2006; Krug, Plihal, Fehm, & Born, 2000; Mass, Hölldorfer, Moll, Bauer, & Wolf, 2009; Rupp et al., 2009), which presumably leads to a shift in the incentive value of the stimuli. Analogous findings have been reported in other primates, for example, in approaches and solicitations made around the time of the mid-cycle estradiol peak in rhesus macaques (Wallen, Winston, Gaventa, Davis-DaSilva, & Collins, 1984) and in the appetitive and consummatory sexual behaviors that characterize the periovulatory period of female rats (e.g., Beach, 1976; Erskine, 1989; McClintock, 1984; Pfaff, 1980, 1999; Pfaus, Kippin, & Coria-Avila, 2003). This cycle in females contrasts with the relatively stable and continuous testicular androgen secretion in mammalian males (and its aromatization to neural estradiol in different regions of the brain) that maintains sexual arousability and responsiveness in a relatively continuous manner (E. M. Hull & Dominguez, 2007).

MECHANISMS OF SEXUAL AROUSAL

Physiological sexual arousal in humans and other animals can be defined as increased autonomic activation that prepares the body for sexual activity. It includes activation of the parasympathetic system that keeps blood in genital and erectile tissues, in particular the clitoris, labia, vaginal epithelium, and penis, and sympathetic blood flow from the heart to striated and smooth muscle that participate in sexual responses, as depicted in Figure 7.4. Sexual arousal also includes a central component that increases neural tone, or preparedness to respond to sexual incentives, and forms around an intricate interaction of hormone priming and noradrenergic activity in different regions of the brain. Both peripheral and central arousal may be detected as part of the perception of subjective sexual arousal, and both clearly lead to changes in responsiveness

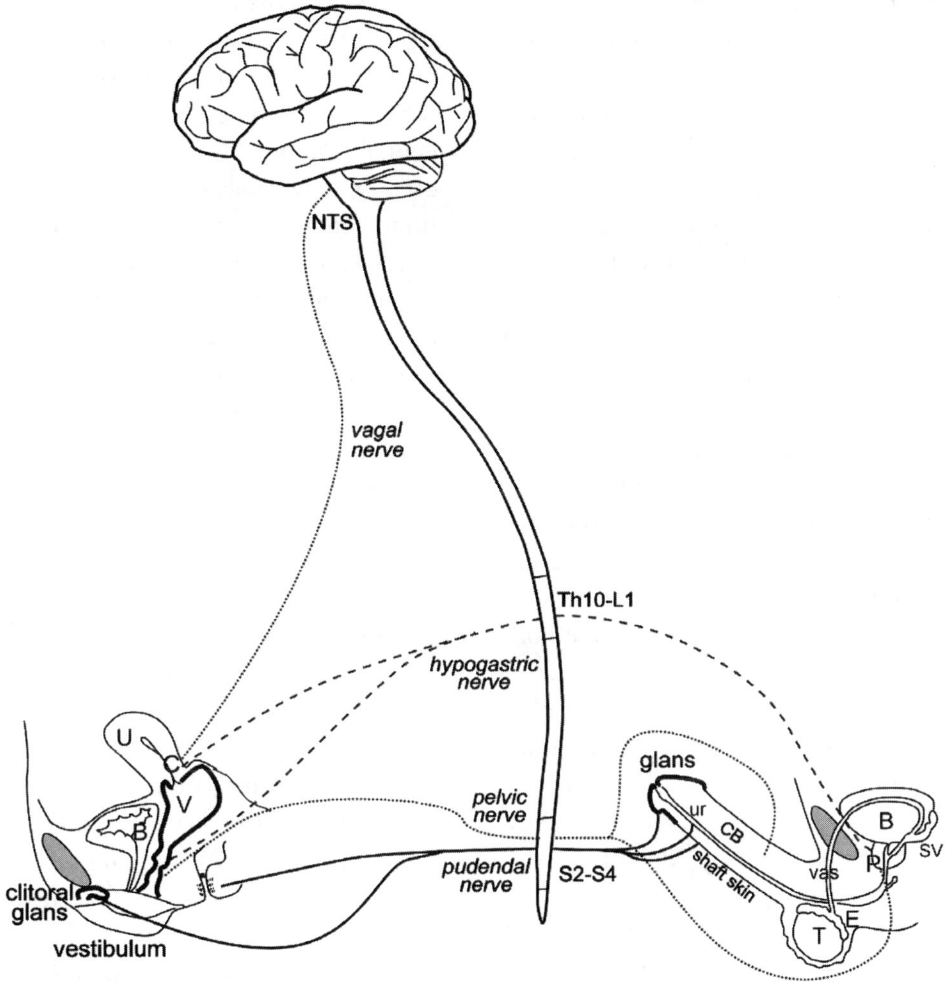

FIGURE 7.4. Mechanisms of peripheral genitosensory stimulation in women and men. Stimulation of the clitoris and glans penis is transduced by the pudendal nerve, whereas stimulation of the vagina and cervix and the lower penile shaft activates the pelvic nerve. Both enter the spinal cord in the sacral region. The hypogastric nerve innervates the vagina and cervix and the prostate and enters the spinal cord in the lower thoracic and upper lumbar region. Finally, the vagus nerve innervates the uterus, although its role in males is more controversial. As a cranial nerve, it enters the brain directly at the level of the nucleus of the solitary tract (NTS). B = bladder; C = cervix; CB = cannabinoid; E = epididymus; P = prostate; SV = seminal vesicle; T = testes; U = uterus; ur = urethra; V = vagina; vas = vas deferens. From "Sex for Fun: Bringing Together Human and Animal Neurobiology," by J. R. Georgiadis, M. L. Kringelbach, and J. G. Pfaus, 2012, *Nature Reviews Urology, 9*, p. 491. Copyright 2012 by Nature Publishing Group. Reprinted with permission.

in genital tissues and control certain copulatory responses, such as the latency to orgasm or ejaculation (with shorter latencies indicating an increase in arousal).

Male Sexual Arousal

A considerable degree of similarity exists between male rats and men in terms of the neuroanatomical, neuroendocrine, and neurochemical regulation of penile erection and ejaculation (see Andersson, 2011; McKenna, 1999; and Meisel & Sachs, 1994, for comprehensive reviews). Penile erections in men can be either physiological or psychogenic in response to parasympathetic arousal. As previously mentioned, they can be studied using mercury-in-rubber strain gauges either during the night (to gain an unbiased measure of physiological erectile capability) or in response to different types of erotic or somatosensory stimuli (to measure psychogenic arousal). Latency to erection, percentage of full erection, and duration of erection can be studied after the administration of drugs that either enhance or delay parasympathetic arousal. Such studies are important diagnostically in distinguishing psychological from physiological erectile dysfunction or in determining spared erectile capability in men with spinal cord injury (see Chapter 21, this volume). Relative to erection, fewer studies have addressed ejaculation in men. One method has been to allow participants to masturbate in the presence of different types of erotic stimulation after an experimental treatment. Ejaculation latencies are recorded along with physiological measurements of ejaculate volume, sperm motility, or subjective measurements of orgasm intensity (e.g., Mah & Binik, 2002; Rowland, Strassberg, de Gouveia Brazao, & Slob, 2000). Ejaculation has also been studied in heterosexual men using the stopwatch method (Waldinger, Zwinderman, Olivier, & Schweitzer, 2005), in which men's partners start a stopwatch on vaginal entry and record the amount of time taken to achieve ejaculation (referred to as the *intravaginal ejaculation latency*). Subjective sexual arousal, or the ability of people to describe or monitor their own sexual arousal, is impossible to determine in animals.

In men, erections in the presence of distal sexual cues such as erotic pictures, audio, or videos are used to study both subjective and physiological sexual arousal. The advantage here is that central mechanisms can be studied directly with the use of brain imaging techniques, and correlations made between the activation of certain brain regions and the stimulation of penile erection by different types of distal erotica (reviewed in Georgiadis et al., 2012; Georgiadis & Kringelbach, 2012).

Although sexual arousal is likely to happen during prolonged exposure to video-type visual sexual stimulation (VSS), it is, on the one hand, not always explicitly evaluated by subjective reports or objective measurements. On the other hand, all studies in which genital responses were measured have shown that the video-type VSS was effective in eliciting genital responses. Relative to the brief "sexual interest" photo-VSS designs, the video-type VSS, penile tumescence, or both induce a shift in brain activity (Georgiadis & Kringelbach, 2012). First, much stronger activity is found on the cortical convexity, especially in the occipitotemporal cortex, in the intraparietal cortex and secondary somatosensory cortex, and in the ventral part of the premotor cortex. Contrary to photo VSS, video-type VSS usually depicts moving images of sexual interaction between two or more individuals. This stronger activity can be explained by the longer exposure time of the video-type VSS, allowing subjects more time to process the images (Bühler, Vollstädt-Klein, Klemen, & Smolka, 2008; Georgiadis & Kringelbach, 2012), and also by the higher complexity of the video-type VSS (Ferretti et al., 2005). However, increased presentation time and complexity may also induce a different way of processing the VSS; occipitotemporal, intraparietal, and ventral premotor cortices have consistently been implicated in mental action imitation (Caspers, Zilles, Laird, & Eickhoff, 2010) and in understanding the emotional states of others (Keysers & Gazzola, 2009). Participants watching video-type VSS are thus not only more likely to develop sexual arousal, including genital responses, their brain activity changes are indicative of more intense and empathic processing of the VSS. Recruitment of occipitotemporal, intraparietal cortex, and ventral premotor cortex may not only track the switch to sexual arousal, it may actually be predictive of it. In an interesting study, activity in these areas was shown to precede the penile response

(Mouras et al., 2008). Female sexual arousal is underexplored but is also likely to draw on similar central mechanisms (Arnow et al., 2009).

In rats, penile erections can be studied in isolation to obtain measures of physiological arousal (summarized in Meisel & Sachs, 1994) or in response to different types of sexually arousing stimuli (e.g., noncontact erections in response to estrous odors) to obtain measures of psychogenic arousal (Sachs, Akasofu, Citron, Daniels, & Natoli, 1994). Latency to erection and the frequency of specific genital reflexes are counted after an experimental treatment (e.g., systemic or central drug administration, brain lesions, or lesions of different nerves that innervate the pelvic ganglia). Many treatments that enhance penile erection in men (e.g., phosphodiesterase type 5 inhibitors such as sildenafil; DA agonists such as apomorphine, prostaglandin E_1, and oxytocin; α_2-adrenergic receptor antagonists such as yohimbine, idazoxan, and imiloxan; and vasodilators that act through nitric oxide substrates, such as nitroglycerine, sodium nitroprusside, and linsidomine) also enhance penile erection in rats (reviewed in Andersson, 2011; McKenna, 1999; Meisel & Sachs, 1994). Erectile responses to these drugs have also been studied by monitoring intracavernosal pressure with electrodes (e.g., Andersson et al., 1999; Bernabé, Rampin, Sachs, & Giuliano, 1999). Conversely, drugs that reduce sexual arousal in men, for example, DA antagonists such as haloperidol (Crenshaw & Goldberg, 1996), also reduce penile reflexes in rats (Pehek, Thompson, Eaton, Bazzett, & Hull, 1988). Infusions of oxytocin to the paraventricular nucleus of the hypothalamus, ventral subiculum of the hippocampus, or ventral tegmental area (VTA) induce erections in male rats (Melis & Argiolas, 2011; Melis et al., 2007), an effect that appears to involve a necessary interaction with DA in both the medial preoptic area (mPOA) and the NAc, along with oxytocin actions in the spinal cord. Likewise, the melanocortin agonist bremelanotide induces penile erection after systemic administration (Hallam, Spana, Earle, Shadiack, & Sharma, 2007). Identical doses of bremelanotide induce DA release in the mPOA (Pfaus et al., 2007), further supporting a DA substrate in the hypothalamic control of penile erection.

Psychogenic erections in rats occur in response to estrous odors or inaccessible females behind an opaque or mesh screen (Sachs et al., 1994). As with men viewing VSS, these erections do not require direct somatosensory stimulation of the penis for their induction. The neurochemical and hormonal mechanisms that control their expression have been studied in detail (e.g., nitric oxide release in the paraventricular hypothalamus [Melis, Succu, Spano, & Argiolas, 2000], DA in the mPOA [Adachi et al., 2003], peripheral and central actions of androgens [Manzo, Cruz, Hernandez, Pacheco, & Sachs, 1999]).

Ejaculations in rats can be studied in much the same way they are studied in humans, with the latency from first mount or intromission to ejaculation being the key variables (e.g., Pattij, Olivier, & Waldinger, 2005). Male rats typically ejaculate after several penile intromissions and can ejaculate several times before becoming sexually exhausted, in which the male no longer responds to estrous odors or female solicitations (Beach & Jordan, 1956). During successive ejaculatory series, the refractory period or postejaculatory interval between each ejaculation and the subsequent resumption of copulation increases progressively (Larsson, 1956). Penile intromission requires erection, and ejaculation typically requires sensory feedback from the penis that accumulates with multiple intromissions. The number of intromissions before ejaculation, the number of ejaculations achieved in a timed test, and the length of the postejaculatory interval are all dependent on autonomic arousal and can be enhanced or disrupted by drugs that have similar effects on copulatory performance in men (see Bitran & Hull, 1987; Dornan & Malsbury, 1989; Meisel & Sachs, 1994; and Pfaus & Gorzalka, 1987, for selective reviews). Yohimbine increased the rate of mounting in male rats (Clark, Smith, & Davidson, 1985), except at high doses, when it inhibited mounting altogether. Conversely, lesions of noradrenergic cells in the locus ceruleus increase the postejaculatory refractory period of male rats, and administration of noradrenaline synthesis inhibitors increases the mount and intromission latencies, suggesting a decrement in sexual desire (McIntosh & Barfield, 1984). Such a decrement could be explained by sluggish arousal induced by diminished noradrenaline transmission and subsequent decreases in sexual desire owing to insufficient general arousal, particularly among hypoarousable individuals. Conversely, drugs that delay or abolish orgasm in men (e.g., the selective serotonin reuptake inhibitor [SSRI] fluoxetine) increase the ejaculation latencies and reduce the total number of ejaculations in rats (Wieseler Frank, Hendricks, & Olson, 2000; Yells, Prendergast, Hendricks, & Nakamura, 1994). As in men, the reduced ability to ejaculate is more pronounced in rats following long-term administration (Cantor, Binik, & Pfaus, 1999). Acute alcohol intoxication also delays ejaculation in men (Malatesta, Pollack, Wilbanks, & Adams, 1979) and in rats (Pfaus & Pinel, 1989).

Short ejaculation latencies in rats, ejaculation with fewer than normal preejaculatory intromissions, or an increased number of ejaculations in a timed test or before sexual exhaustion sets in suggests an enhancement of sympathetic arousal. Although at first glance, faster ejaculation or ejaculation with fewer intromissions suggests that the male may be a more proficient copulator, such behavior in the wild would be less likely to get a female rat pregnant (e.g., Adler, 1969) and should be considered a disruption of normal copulatory responding. Such behavior is more reminiscent of premature ejaculation in humans and can be induced by drugs that stimulate sympathetic arousal (e.g., cocaine; reviewed in Pfaus, Wilkins et al., 2010) or by experiential conditions that increase sympathetic arousal in sexual circumstances. For example, male rats ejaculate faster, and with fewer intromissions, if the stimulus female is removed from the test chamber for periods of as much as 1 minute between successive intromissions (an effect referred to as the *enforced interval effect;* Larsson, 1956). Although this effect could constitute a rat analogue model of premature ejaculation (PE), it remains to be seen whether drugs that can counteract PE in men, such as alcohol or fluoxetine, can increase the latency of male rats to ejaculate in this condition.

Female Sexual Arousal

A long-standing assumption was that genital blood flow in women followed the same physiological and psychological rules as in men (e.g., Barlow, 1986). Certainly, drugs or highly stressful circumstances that block erections in men also block vaginal and clitoral blood volume in women. However, general autonomic activation by drugs, mild to moderate stressors, or exciting environmental circumstances may be translated into sexual arousal in women, especially in the presence of an appropriate sexual incentive, which is reminiscent of the idea put forth by the ancient Roman poet Ovid (1930) in *Ars Amatoria* that under the right circumstances and occasion setting, general arousal induced by stress can be manipulated into sexual arousal in women but not in men. Such an effect is also consistent with the notion by Meston and colleagues (Meston, 2000; Meston & Gorzalka, 1996) that sympathetic arousal provides a necessary background for the perception of sexual arousal in women. Real differences may exist between men and women in patterns of sexual arousal and in the types of psychogenic stimuli that elicit genital blood flow (e.g., Palace & Gorzalka, 1990; Rosen & Beck, 1988). However, the original clinical results with sildenafil in women with sexual arousal disorders were inconclusive (Basson, McInnes, Smith, Hodgson, & Koppiker, 2002; Berman et al., 2001; Rosen, 2000), likely as a result of differences in propensity for genital blood flow and its perception across the ovulatory cycle. In addition, women appear to manifest discordance between subjective and physiological measures of sexual arousal (Bailey, 2009; Chivers & Bailey, 2005; Chivers & Rosen, 2010; Chivers, Seto, Lalumière, Laan, & Grimbos, 2010; Laan, Everaerd, & Evers, 1995; Laan, Everaerd, van der Velde, & Geer, 1995; see Chapters 2 and 8, this volume). Men do not manifest this discordance, which may stem from the fact that vaginal blood flow is internal and less perceptible than the external blood flow that characterizes penile erection. However, it was recently reported (Chivers, Roy, Grimbos, Cantor, & Seto, in press) that women who practice bondage, discipline, dominance, submission, sadism, and masochism show concordance between subjective and physiological measures of sexual arousal when viewing erotic videos that depict sadistic and masochistic themes relative to heteronormative erotic themes (see Chapter 9, this volume). Thus, context may play the most important role of all in women's perception of sexual arousal, denoting both culturally imposed and experientially bound perceptions of arousal.

Women also experience cyclic fluctuations in attention and arousability, with peak incidents of female-initiated sexual activity coinciding with ovulation (Wallen, 1995). Indeed, event-related potentials that correspond to attention and stimulus processing for working memory (e.g., the P3 amplitude) increase after the presentation of sexually arousing pictures, but not pictures of babies or body care products, to women during the ovulatory phase (Krug et al., 2000). The same pictures do not activate those event-related potential components during other phases of the menstrual cycle or in women taking oral contraceptives (Krug, Pietrowsky, Fehm, & Born, 1994). Another study used functional MRI (fMRI) to compare brain activation of premenopausal women in mid-luteal or menstrual phases of the cycle in response to erotic video clips relative to neutral video clips (Gizewski et al., 2006). Increased activation in response to the erotic clips was observed in the anterior cingulate cortex, left insula, and orbitofrontal cortices during the mid-luteal phase relative to the menstrual phase. The ability of erotic visual stimuli to activate limbic and cortical structures is reduced after menopause but can be restored to premenopausal levels after combined estradiol and testosterone treatment (Sherwin, Gelfand, & Brender, 1985), as can sexual desire and subsequent sexual activity in postmenopausal women who experience its loss (Archer, Love-Geffen, Herbst-Damm, Swinney, & Chang, 2006; Kingsberg, Simon, & Goldstein, 2008; Segraves, 2008). Timing, context, and hormonal milieus may thus be extremely important when studying sexual arousal in women relative to men. Such a relationship has been established for rats and other species. Female rats display sexual heat only during the periovulatory period of their estrous cycle, a state that can be induced in ovariectomized (OVX) rats by means of sequential administration of estrogen and progesterone (Bolling & Blandau, 1939) or estradiol and testosterone (Jones, Ismail, King, & Pfaus, 2012).

Animal models of female genital arousal have been developed using rabbits and rats (e.g., Min et al., 2003; Munarriz, Kim, Kim, Traish, & Goldstein, 2003; Traish, Kim, Munarriz, Moreland, & Goldstein, 2002). In these models, electrical stimulation of the pelvic nerve is applied to mimic the type of stimulation normally received by females during vaginal intromission and results in increased vaginal blood flow, vaginal wall pressure, vaginal length, clitoral intracavernosal pressure and blood flow, and decreased vaginal luminal pressure. Similar effects have been reported after pelvic nerve stimulation in female rats (Giuliano, Rampin, & Allard, 2002; Vachon, Simmerman, Zahran, & Carrier, 2000). In addition to vaginal and clitoral blood flow responses, vaginal smooth muscle preparations have been developed to examine the ability of different neurotransmitters to induce muscle contraction and relaxation. These studies have shown that ovariectomy diminishes vaginal blood flow, lubrication, and epithelial cell morphology and that treatment with estradiol restores these measures of vaginal response. Moreover, the nitric oxide–cyclic guanosine monophosphate (GMP) pathway appears to be critical for vaginal blood flow, as it is for penile blood flow. Treatment with androgens facilitates vaginal nitric oxide synthase activity, along with vaginal smooth muscle relaxation. Although how these vaginal responses might be integrated with behavioral responses in female rats is not yet known, Whalen and Lauber (1986) hypothesized that cyclic GMP was a common target for drugs that substitute for progesterone in the facilitation of lordosis in rats. Inhibition of the ability of nitric oxide to stimulate cyclic GMP in the rat brain results in a profound disruption of lordosis (Chu & Etgen, 1997), suggesting that the brain is an important target for activation of lordosis stimulated by nitric oxide–GMP. However, it remains an intriguing possibility that increased vaginal blood flow could be perceived by females and help stimulate behavioral measures of sexual arousal. This increase may occur naturally during ovulation. To that end, it is intriguing indeed that despite the relative failure of phosphodiesterase type 5 inhibitors such as sildenafil to increase subjective sexual arousal in women while increasing vaginal blood volume (Berman et al., 2001; Meston & Frolich, 2001), a phosphodiesterase type 5 inhibitor combined with testosterone can increase sexual satisfaction in women with arousal and desire disorders (Poels et al., 2012) and increase solicitations in female rats primed with low levels of estradiol (Bijlsma et al., 2012).

What About Sympathetic Activation?

Before the measurement of sexual arousal with genital blood flow measures, indexes of sympathetic autonomic activation were routinely measured in human psychophysiological research. Sexual response, considered by many as one of the primary emotions alongside fear, rage, and so forth (e.g., Watson, 1919), was a target of psychophysiological study in the early 20th century. Landis and Gullette (1925) observed increases in systolic blood pressure while subjects viewed pornographic pictures, although they suggested that "complexes and inhibitions," as opposed to a sex emotion, might have determined their response to "such bold vulgarity" (p. 236). Responses to nude art and the reading of sex case histories in the same study produced highly variable blood pressure responses. Scott (1930) observed increases in systolic blood pressure in men watching films depicting a love scene and suggestive dance, but inconsistent reactions to fear and anger stimuli. Wenger, Averill, and Smith (1968) found that blood pressure and electrodermal activity increased while young men viewed erotic reading material on slides; changes in observed peripheral vasomotor activity suggested that overall the observed responses reflected a complex pattern of both sympathetic and parasympathetic activity. They theorized that in the absence of overt muscle activity, initial stages of sexual excitement were characterized by parasympathetic dominance followed by increasing sympathetic activation until orgasm was reached.

As genital measures of parasympathetic arousal were developed by the mid-1970s, sympathetic arousal continued to be measured concurrently in laboratories, but these measures were noted as being unable to discriminate between emotional stimulus types (e.g., Heiman, 1977; Hoon, Wincze, & Hoon, 1976; Lake Polan et al., 2003), and they generally went unused until recently when emotion researchers began incorporating erotic images into their stimulus sets. For example, Ritz, Thöns, Fahrenkrug, and Dahme (2005) observed strong increases in respiratory sinus arrhythmia in men and women viewing erotic images compared with other image categories, suggesting an increase in cardiac vagal tone during exposure to sexual stimuli. That result supports the notion that the initial stage of sexual excitation is due to parasympathetic dominance, as suggested previously by Wenger et al. (1968). Other recent studies have demonstrated significant increases in skin conductance in response to erotic images compared with neutral or negatively valenced stimuli in both men and women (Codispoti, Ferrari, & Bradley, 2006; Sarlo, Palomba, Buodo, Minghetti, & Stegagno, 2005), with more explicit images inducing the greatest increases (Costa & Esteves, 2008). Sarlo et al. (2005) noted that significant increases in blood pressure were observed only in men while viewing erotic images, suggesting a greater reactivity of that measure moderated by gender and specific to sexual stimuli. Laeng and Falkenberg (2007) found that women's pupil dilation responses to pictures of their sexual partners were highest during the ovulatory phase of the menstrual cycle, an effect that was absent in women who used oral contraceptive pills.

Meston and colleagues (Meston, 2000; Meston & Gorzalka, 1996), reported that acute exercise can elevate vaginal pulse amplitude in response to erotic VSS in unmedicated women and women taking SSRIs (Ahrold & Meston, 2009). In contrast, the α2-noradrenergic receptor agonist clonidine (which reduces sympathetic tone) diminished precopulatory appetitive behaviors and lordosis in female rats (Meston, Moe, & Gorzalka, 1996) and reduced the ability of exercise to elevate both subjective and physiological arousal in response to VSS (Meston, Gorzalka, & Wright, 1997). There appears to be an inverted U-shaped optimality function in which an optimal degree of sympathetic tone facilitates sexual arousal in women, harking back to Ovid's (second-century) prediction about the role of acute stressors and stimulation of women's sexual arousal and possibly desire. The optimality hypothesis for sympathetic tone and sexual responding was also discussed recently by Rowland (2010), who found that men with PE evidenced higher average heart rate increases during VSS and vibrotactile stimulation than men without PE, lending evidence to the notion that early or excessive increases in sympathetic arousal could contribute to the etiology of PE. A similar phenomenon may underlie the more rapid ejaculation in male rats exposed to Larsson's (1956) enforced interval effect, discussed earlier, and in male rats that develop baseline rates of more rapid ejaculation with fewer intromissions when learning to copulate in conditions in which they have to wait longer to copulate with females (Ismail, Zhao, & Pfaus, 2008). It would appear that sympathetic activity is critical to the stimulation of sexual arousal, as it is for the stimulation of orgasm (see next section).

Conditioned Sexual Arousal

Responsive sexual arousal is, by definition, conditional on the sexual stimuli being adequate to activate the necessary sympathetic (e.g., increased heart rate) and parasympathetic (e.g., genital blood flow) divisions of the autonomic nervous system, including the context in which the arousal takes place, acting as an occasion setter. Sexual arousal is constrained further by experience. In addition to habituation that occurs when the same actions are done repeatedly and inhibition that occurs during a refractory period, reward-related occasion setting may well underlie the ability of external cues (and in their most obvious human manifestation, fetish objects) to control sexual arousal and thereby control when to have sex. Inanimate objects, such as articles of clothing, particular forms and textures, and, in fact, any antecedent tactile, olfactory, auditory, or visual stimulation, can, during an animal's initial experiences with sexual reward, come to control both arousal and desire. Thus, the development of paraphilias may well follow the rules of associative (Pavlov, 1927) and operant (Skinner, 1938) learning (e.g., as described in case reports by von Krafft-Ebing, 1886/1929).

It is possible that anything that predicts sexual reward becomes an occasion setter for sexual arousal (and maybe desire too). Although sexual reward may be studied objectively in animals, in humans the notion is muddled in peculiar definitions, along with particular phases of the human sexual response (Pfaus, 1999). It is also the case that human subjects in laboratory settings show relatively weaker effects than are typically observed in animals, which may be because the typical human subject has already acquired sexual experience before the study, an effect that reduces the possibility of robust conditioning. Thus, the unconditioned stimuli (UCSs) used in studies of conditioned sexual arousal in humans may not create a strong enough sexual reward state for a neutral stimulus to become a potent enough conditioned stimulus (CS), given that their pairing occurs long after the early critical period of sexual behavior development (reviewed in Pfaus et al., 2012).

Several notable attempts have been made to condition sexual arousal in humans (see Hoffmann, 2012). Rachman (1966) and Rachman and Hodgson (1968) found that after pairing with erotic visual slides, a pair of women's boots was able to elicit erections in men. Similarly, McConaghy (1970, 1974) demonstrated conditioned erection elicited by colored circles or squares previously paired with erotic videos or still pictures in heterosexual and homosexual men. A particularly informative study by Kantorowitz (1978) examined the nature of association between the UCS and conditioned arousal induced by still pictures and found that stimuli paired with the plateau phase produced an increase in penile erection, whereas stimuli paired with the refractory phase produced a decrease in erection. Remarkably, those responses were still present after 3 months. Lalumière and Quinsey (1998) reported significant conditioned genital arousal in heterosexual men to a picture of a moderately attractive, partially nude woman that was paired with a video depicting highly arousing sexual interaction. A control group that received access to the picture alone (without the video) showed habituation.

Although Letourneau and O'Donohue (1997) failed to find significant effects of conditioning on sexual arousal in women, they noted that the UCSs (erotic films) produced only moderate levels of arousal; thus, this failure to demonstrate conditioned arousal in women may have been due to an ineffective UCS. Indeed, Both, Laan, et al. (2008) found that neutral pictures of male headshots paired with 2 seconds of intensely pleasurable vibrotactile clitoral stimulation produced greater vaginal pulse amplitude during extinction in the paired versus unpaired groups (see also Both, Brauer, & Laan,

2011). In another study, stimuli were presented briefly (30 milliseconds), followed by a masking stimulus (Both, Spiering, et al., 2008). Although only the paired group showed increased vaginal pulse amplitude to the CS during the first extinction trial, there was no increase in the conscious affective value of the stimulus. Finally, Hoffmann, Janssen, and Turner (2004) varied the duration and relevance of a CS (abdominal area vs. a gun) that was paired with short erotic film clips in both men and women. Interestingly, when the stimuli were presented subliminally for brief durations, the relevant abdominal stimulus increased arousal in both men and women. However, when the stimuli were presented for longer periods before the erotic film clips, a sex difference emerged in which the relevant CS alone (abdominal area) induced genital arousal in men, but the presumably irrelevant stimulus alone (gun) induced genital arousal in women. This latter effect may indicate that women require CSs that increase autonomic arousal to a higher extent than men, a potential corollary of the discordance experienced by women, but not men, between genital and subjective sexual arousal (Chivers & Rosen, 2010). It may also be the case that anything that activates the sympathetic nervous system sufficiently in women may generate a genital blood flow response, regardless of whether the stimulus is sexual in nature. This suggestion is similar to Ovid's, regarding general arousal.

Animals also show sexual arousal in response to cues associated with sexual reward. Rats live in a largely olfactory world, making odors and scents potential CSs for conditioning studies. For example, J. M. Graham and Desjardins (1980) placed sexually naïve male rats in a chamber scented with a methyl salicylate (wintergreen oil) CS for 7 minutes before transferring them to an adjacent chamber with an unscented receptive female for 15 minutes of copulation (UCS). Control males received the CS alone, UCS alone, or handling. Training occurred once a day for 14 days. On the 15th day, males were placed in either the CS or the UCS chamber, and blood was analyzed for luteinizing hormone and testosterone. Exposure to females increased concentrations of both hormones in plasma, whereas the CS was effective only in males in the paired group. Sachs and Garinello (1978) reported that placing male rats into a chamber in which copulation had previously occurred dramatically reduced the latency for males to display penile erections. Male rats trained to associate an almond odor with copulation to ejaculation (see Sexual Preference, Conditioned Attraction, and Mate Choice section) initiated copulation faster with an almond-scented receptive female than with an unscented receptive female (Kippin & Pfaus, 2001b). Similarly, male marmosets trained to copulate to ejaculation with lemon-scented receptive females displayed erections and increased place preference in response to the odor alone relative to unpaired males (Snowdon, Tannenbaum, Schultz-Darken, Ziegler, & Ferris, 2011).

Placement of male rats into a holding cage has been used as a conditioned contextual stimulus to signal exposure of males to an inaccessible receptive female behind a wire-mesh screen (Zamble, Hadad, Mitchell, & Cutmore, 1985; Zamble, Mitchell, & Findlay, 1986). Placing males into the holding cage before a final test of unrestricted copulation resulted in significantly shorter latencies to intromit and ejaculate relative to males placed directly from their home cages into the copulatory condition. Subsequent studies found that second-order CSs (e.g., a plastic toy fish found in the holding cage) were effective in enhancing the same measures of arousal (Zamble et al., 1985), and such conditioning in sexually naive or sluggish males could increase the proportion of males that copulated on a subsequent test (Cutmore & Zamble, 1988). Hollis, Cadieux, and Colbert (1989) demonstrated that repeatedly pairing a light with noncontact exposure to a receptive female resulted in conditioning of sexual behavior in male gouramie fish. Males that received the conditioning treatment displayed significantly lower latencies to initiate copulation and lower levels of aggression toward females when the CS was presented before access to a female. Similar results have been demonstrated in Japanese quail. Male quail that received repeated exposure to females after the presentation of a CS light displayed significantly shorter latencies to initiate copulation when the stimulus was present than when it was absent (e.g., Domjan, O'Vary, & Greene, 1988).

Finally, if male rats are given their first copulatory trials wearing a Velcro tethering jacket, the jacket will become a CS for sexual arousal (Pfaus et al., 2012). Sexually naïve males in the paired group were given nine multiejaculatory trials at 4-day intervals with the jacket on, whereas males in the unpaired group received the same number of trials without the jacket. On the 10th trial, males in both groups were assigned randomly to two subgroups, one with the jacket on and one with the jacket off, and given a final 30-minute test of copulation. Males that had been trained without the jacket displayed normal baseline rates of copulatory behavior with or without the jacket, as did males trained with the jacket and that had the jacket on during the final test. In contrast, males trained with the jacket but that had the jacket off during the final test displayed a severe copulatory deficit, including significantly increased mount, intromission, and ejaculation latencies, a decreased number of conditioned level changes, and a reduction in the proportion of males that achieved ejaculation during the test. The pattern suggests significantly diminished sexual arousal and desire and a failure to engage sympathetic tone for ejaculation (Pfaus, 2009). Thus, the jacket had become a CS for sexual arousal only in the paired group that had their early formative sexual experiences with it. This result is reminiscent of von Krafft-Ebing's (1886/1929) description of boys' early peripubertal experience with fetish objects that predicted sexual arousal being reinforced by fantasy and masturbation. To date, no studies have attempted to examine conditioned sexual arousal in female animals, in contrast to a rather large literature on conditioned sexual desire (see the next section).

MECHANISMS OF SEXUAL DESIRE

When an individual expresses sexual desire, it follows that attention and behavior focus on obtaining some form of positive sexual reinforcement. This reinforcement can occur alone in fantasies or together with others in goal-directed social and sexual behaviors. Thus, in addition to a conscious awareness of feeling horny (with or without corresponding arousal), desire encompasses the work people will perform to obtain sexual rewards, the excitement displayed in anticipation of such rewards, and the strength of the incentive value ascribed to a particular sexual stimulus. As mentioned earlier, much of the research about biological systems in sexual desire has been derived from animal studies and more recently from human brain imaging during the presentation of VSS. As with people, animals manifest excitement in anticipation of sexual reward. They will increase their motor output in anticipation of copulation (e.g., moving between levels of a bilevel chamber) and work for the opportunity to copulate or to obtain rewards associated with copulation; such behavior can be viewed as analogous to desire (Pfaus et al., 2003). Sexual rewards may come in the form of primary reinforcers (e.g., orgasm in humans; ejaculation in male rats or pacing in female rats) or secondary reinforcers, such as stimuli associated with sexual gratification (e.g., certain facial features, clothes, or smells in humans; certain odors or place cues in rats). In male rats, precopulatory behaviors have included performance in obstruction boxes, straight-alley running, maze learning, crossing of electrified grids, nose-pokes, and other attempts to get to a potential sex partner behind a wire-mesh screen; digging through sand; and bar-pressing for a sex partner or for cue lights associated with the arrival of a sex partner. Indeed, to gain access to receptive females, male guinea pigs will learn to run an alley, male pigeons will learn to peck keys, and male stickleback fish will learn to swim through rings (see Pfaus, Kippin, & Centano, 2001; Pfaus et al., 2003, for reviews of these behaviors). Animals with more desire will display more robust behavior than animals with less desire.

Male rats in bilevel chambers display an increase in level changing in anticipation of the arrival of a sexually receptive female (Pfaus, Mendelson, & Phillips, 1990; Van Furth & Van Ree, 1996). Typically, when males are placed into the testing chamber for an adaptation period before the placement of a receptive female, anticipatory behaviors develop naturally over a few trials. Systemic administration of DA receptor antagonists decrease the number of anticipatory level changes displayed by male rats in bilevel chambers at doses that do not alter copulatory responses once receptive females are placed into the chamber (Pfaus & Phillips, 1991). Interestingly, a loss of desire and interest in sex is a common complaint among patients taking DA antagonists as major tranquilizers (Crenshaw & Goldberg, 1996). Long-term use of the stimulant drug cocaine has also been reported to decrease sexual desire in men (Siegel, 1982), and long-term administration of cocaine to sexually active male rats decreases conditioned level changes progressively over time (Pfaus, Wilkins et al., 2010). Conversely, systemic administration of the melanocortin agonist bremelanotide increases anticipatory-level changes in male rats (Pfaus, 2009), an effect that presumably reflects increased DA release in the mPOA.

Some appetitive instrumental sexual responses are also expressed without much prior experience (e.g., nose-pokes, digging, obstruction box performance, crossing electrified grids), whereas others require some degree of training (e.g., maze learning, bar pressing). These behaviors can be reduced after castration, indicating that gonadal steroid actions in the brain are necessary for their development or maintenance (Everitt, Fray, Kostarczyk, Taylor, & Stacey, 1987; Nissen 1929). They can also be reduced after a devaluation of the reward offered by the incentive the male is working for (e.g., switching from receptive female to no female, an extinction procedure) or after infusions of DA antagonists to the NAc (Everitt, 1990; Mendelson & Pfaus, 1989) or mPOA (Warner et al., 1991). Systemic administration of DA antagonists to male rats reduces running speed in a runway that leads to a goal box containing a sexually receptive female (López & Ettenberg, 2001). Different DA terminal regions likely play a role in different types of unconditioned and conditioned sexual activity. Although many of these paradigms have been in the literature for more than 50 years, they have not been mined extensively by sex researchers to study the effects of drugs that activate or inhibit other neurotransmitter systems.

Fewer studies have examined operant conditioning in females, but the basic phenomenon is the same. Female rats learn to run mazes (Drewett, 1973) and bar press to gain access to gonadally intact, sexually active males (Bermant, 1961; Bermant & Westbrook, 1966; French, Fitzpatrick, & Law, 1972) and will nose-poke a lever to gain access to penile intromissions by a male (Matthews et al., 1997). Becker and colleagues (Becker, Rudick, & Jenkins, 2001; Jenkins & Becker, 2003; Mermelstein & Becker, 1995) found increased DA release in the striatum and NAc of females that had to press a lever to gain access to a male, or run back and forth from behind an opaque barrier, relative to females that did not. Indeed, lesions of the striatum reduced the efficiency of females to pace the copulatory interactions (a behavior female rats find rewarding), whereas lesions of the NAc resulted in females that avoided sexual contact (Jenkins & Becker, 2003).

Sexual Preference, Conditioned Attraction, and Mate Choice

Sexual desire can be inferred from the strength of preference for particular features of a person or conspecific or for a place in which potential sex partners have been found in the past. As with other instrumental responses, preferences are typically displayed before sexual interaction so that animals and people can focus their forward trajectories toward sexual incentives (Pfaus et al., 2012). In humans, preferences exist for gender, and within gender for certain individually defined physical features (e.g., shape of face, smile, eye or hair color, body type) and personality characteristics (e.g., introvert vs. extravert; naughty vs. nice) that people find attractive. Recent evidence has indicated that animals show preferences for specific features, many of which are learned during experience with sexual reward rather than driven instinctually to maximize reproductive fitness. This latter dimension represents an exciting new foray into a level of animal behavior that approximates that of humans.

Some preferences seem instinctual and hard wired by hormonal influences on the brain. For example, numerous studies have shown that male rats spend more time near sexually receptive than nonreceptive females (reviewed in Pfaus et al., 2003). Likewise, sexually receptive females spend more time near gonadally intact, sexually active males versus castrated, sexually inactive males (Gilman & Westbrook, 1978). Male rats also show unconditioned preferences for the odors of sexually receptive versus nonreceptive females (Bakker, van Ophemert, & Slob, 1996; Carr, Wylie, & Loeb, 1970). These studies have been conducted in

Y-mazes, T-mazes, radial-arm mazes, or open fields that contain goal boxes baited with tethered receptive versus nonreceptive conspecifics (e.g., Gilman & Westbrook, 1978), different conspecifics behind wire-mesh screens (e.g., Ågmo, 2003a, 2003b; Bakker et al., 1996), or different anesthetized stimulus animals contained at opposite ends (e.g., Landauer, Wiese, & Carr, 1977). Castration of male rats abolishes their preference to remain near a sexually receptive female, whereas replacement with testosterone restores the preference (Ågmo, 2003a). Moreover, gonadally intact, sexually experienced males display significant preferences for sexually receptive versus nonreceptive females and for sexually receptive females versus males, but not for sexually nonreceptive females versus males. Those data suggest that amount of time spent near the receptive female is based on the intensity of her olfactory cues. Indeed, Ågmo (1999) reported that the intensity of preference for a live receptive female could be generated by bedding that contained estrous odors, suggesting that olfactory cues are important sensory determinants of incentive value in the rat. Estrous odors are known to induce DA release unconditionally in the NAc of intact, sexually inexperienced male rats (Mitchell & Gratton, 1991, 1992; Wenkstern, Pfaus, & Fibiger, 1993), and such odors increase neural activation in several key brain regions known from lesion studies to be critical for male sexual behavior, including the mPOA, bed nucleus of the stria terminalis, medial amygdala, NAc, and VTA (reviewed in Pfaus & Heeb, 1997; Veening & Coolen, 1998).

The studies of Mitchell and Gratton (1991, 1992) are of particular interest because they suggest that endogenous opioid release in the VTA occurs in response to estrous odor cues, and this release in turn disinhibits ascending mesolimbic DA neurons. However, systemic treatment with a DA agonist or antagonist (amphetamine, cis-flupenthixol) or opioid agonist or antagonist (morphine, naloxone) did not alter the amount of time sexually experienced males spent near a sexually receptive versus nonreceptive female in an open field, except at higher doses that induced motor deficits (Ågmo, 2003a). Although Ågmo's (2003a) data suggest that DA and opioid systems are not necessary for the processing of unconditioned incentive cues, infusions of the DA antagonist flupenthixol to the VTA of male rats decreases the percentage of time spent near a sexually receptive female in an X-maze (Warner et al., 1991) and, as mentioned earlier, infusions of the DA antagonist haloperidol to the NAc or mPOA deceases conditioned level changing in bilevel chambers (Pfaus & Phillips, 1991). Sexually experienced males are also known to be relatively resistant to many treatments that disrupt sexual behavior in inexperienced males, including castration, penile anesthesia, novelty of a testing chamber, olfactory deprivation, and age (reviewed in Pfaus et al., 2012). It is not clear whether experience may have buffered Ågmo's males from the effects of DA or opioid drugs.

Some preferences are not instinctual, in the sense of being hard wired, but rather reflect a process of Pavlovian conditioning in which neutral stimuli associated with sexual reward become conditioned sexual incentives. Such conditioned preferences can be assessed along with copulation in sequence. For example, male Japanese quail respond differentially to females on the basis of the presence of stimuli (e.g., plumage colors and adornments) previously paired with copulation (Domjan et al., 1988; Nash & Domjan, 1991). Domjan and Hall (1986) also demonstrated that males would stay in the vicinity of a window in their home cage through which they could see a sexually receptive female during a precopulatory period, but only if the males had the opportunity to copulate with the female after the precopulatory period. Balthazart, Reid, Absil, Foidart, and Ball (1995) demonstrated that castrated males do not develop this kind of conditioned proximity behavior, nor do males that do not copulate. Indeed, as in male rats, DA levels in male Japanese quail increase during appetitive phases of sexual behavior and further increase during copulation (Kleitz-Nelson, Dominguez, & Ball, 2010). Moreover, males that failed to copulate did not show a precopulatory increase in DA. Thus, brain DA systems in birds and mammals have analogous—if not identical—functions in the control of appetitive and consummatory sexual behaviors.

The role of associative learning has also been examined for sexual partner preferences in male and female rats during sexual interaction. Kippin, Talianakis, Schattmann, Bartholomew, and Pfaus (1998) trained male rats to associate an almond odor smeared on the back of the neck and anogenital area of females that were either sexually receptive or nonreceptive. Males trained consistently with the almond odor paired with receptive females and no odor paired with nonreceptive females ejaculated preferentially with the scented females, while displaying no significant preference of female to receive mounts and intromissions. Subsequent studies established that the conditioned ejaculatory preference developed only if males were in the vicinity of the females during their postejaculatory refractory period (Kippin & Pfaus, 2001a) and was more robust if males had more ejaculations (Kippin, Samaha, Sotiropoulos, & Pfaus, 2001). Conditioned ejaculatory preference did not develop if males were allowed only to intromit or if the female was removed immediately after ejaculation. An analysis of the conditioned response showed that males became choosy during the last three mounts before ejaculation and directed those mounts at the female bearing the familiar cue (Kippin & Pfaus, 2001b) because this is a period in which males are sensitive to their impending ejaculation and emit a 50-kilohertz call that attracts females immediately before ejaculation (McGinnis & Vakulenko, 2003).

Association with reward can also reduce the impact of aversive stimuli. For example, although rats initially reject a bitter morphine solution that replaces their drinking water, they learn to like the bitter taste as the morphine reward state sensitizes over time (Zellner, Berridge, Grill, & Ternes, 1985). The sexual reward state in males is not only powerful enough to condition a preference for a neutral odor, but it is also powerful enough to blunt the impact of an unconditionally aversive odor such as cadaverine, a polyamine that is produced in decaying flesh (Pfaus et al., 2001). Male rats who had been given their first sexual experiences with cadaverine-scented females pursued, copulated, and ejaculated with both scented and unscented females, indicating that the aversive properties of cadaverine had been diminished after pairing with sexual reward.

Female rats also show olfactory-conditioned partner preference for males associated with a pacing-induced reward state (Coria-Avila, Ouimet, Pacheco, Manzo, & Pfaus, 2005). This preference was accomplished easily by placing the rats in unilevel pacing chambers in which the paced condition involved the placement of either a one-hole or a four-hole Plexiglas divider through which the female could regulate the initiation and rate of copulation. The nonpaced condition involved copulation in the same chamber but without the divider. Females in the paired group were given paced copulation with males that had the almond odor smeared on their necks and anogenital area or nonpaced copulation with males that had distilled water smeared on the same areas. After four paced versus nonpaced trials, females were placed into a large open field with two tethered males, one scented and the other unscented, and the choice of male to solicit, copulate with, and receive ejaculations from was recorded. Females for which the odor was paired with the paced condition selectively solicited, copulated with, and received ejaculations from the scented male. Females that had the odor explicitly unpaired or paired randomly with pacing did not display a preference.

Sexually naïve female rats given manual clitoral stimulation in the presence of a cotton gauze pad soaked in almond extract chose to copulate selectively with almond-scented males over unscented males during their first sexual experience in a large open field with both males (Parada, Abdul-Ahad, Censi, Sparks, & Pfaus, 2011). Interestingly, they did not show a preference to receive the scented male's ejaculations, suggesting that the vaginocervical stimulation (VCS) received from males during paced copulation induced a further reproductive or mate choice. Whether this finding stems from specific stimulation of the cervix (and pelvic nerve) or from full stimulation of internal and external aspects of the clitoris is not yet known. Experience with paced, relative to nonpaced, copulation in unilevel chambers induces significant neurogenesis in the granular layer of the accessory olfactory bulbs (Corona, Larriva-Sahd, & Paredes, 2011), a region known to contain intrinsic memory systems related to pheromonal stimulation and recognition of conspecifics (Brennan & Keverne, 1997). Thus, as Darwin (1859) suggested, females are indeed more choosy than males in terms of choosing a male with which to copulate and mate. However, as with males, they base this choice on the external (epigamic) characteristics of the male associated with their own experience of a copulatory reward state.

Desire in Copulatory Measures

Sexual desire can also be inferred from certain unconditioned copulatory measures. The speed with which male rats mount sexually receptive females is typically interpreted as a measure of sexual motivation and the desire for copulation. Males with lesions of the mPOA will not mount females, and as a result the rest of the copulatory sequence is abolished (e.g., Heimer & Larsson, 1967). E. M. Hull et al. (1989, 1999) have argued that the D1–D2 receptor ratio in the mPOA of male rats is critical for the stimulation of penile erection and mounting (D1) and ejaculation (D2) through integrated control of behavior and autonomic processes. This ratio makes the coordinated activation of mPOA and NAc critical in the stimulation of sexual arousal and copulation (Pfaus, 1999). Interestingly, ejaculation decreases DA release precipitously in the mPOA and NAc, but not the striatum, of male rats (Blackburn, Pfaus, & Phillips, 1992). This decline lasts through the absolute refractory period and is followed by a progressive increase during the relative refractory period, when arousing stimuli can activate copulation in male rats (Meisel & Sachs, 1994). Interestingly, in males that copulate to sexual exhaustion, DA in the NAc reduces to precopulatory baseline levels (Fiorino, Coury, & Phillips, 1997). Removal and reintroduction of the familiar female does not increase DA release, but placement of a new receptive female in with the male results in a small increase. However, this increase is not of sufficient magnitude to induce a full copulatory response.

The rate at which female rats will solicit and pace their copulatory contact with males, and the willingness of males to chase females, can be considered analogues of desire (and possibly arousal). These measures can be recorded unambiguously in bilevel chambers (Pfaus, Smith, & Coopersmith, 1999), pacing chambers (Erskine, 1989; Paredes & Alonso, 1997; Paredes & Vazquez, 1999), mazes, or choice boxes (e.g., Ågmo, 1999). Solicitations by the female usually result in mounts and intromissions by the male. After intromission, the female runs away to control or pace the rate of copulation. To the extent that solicitations and pacing inversely reflect a general desire for sexual contact, then experimental treatments that increase solicitations or keep pacing durations low may increase desire in women. For example, OVX female rats primed with estrogen and progesterone, or estrogen alone, and administered the melanocortin agonist bremelanotide display a dramatic and selective increase in solicitations (Pfaus et al., 2007; Pfaus, Shadiack, Van Soest, Tse, & Molinoff, 2004). In clinical trials, this drug was shown to increase subjective and vaginal arousal along with ratings of desire in women viewing a female-centric erotic film (Diamond et al., 2006), making solicitations in female rats a predictive homologue of sexual desire in women. As with penile erections and mounting behavior in males, solicitations in female rats depend critically on the mPOA. Lesions of the mPOA abolish solicitations (Hoshina, Takeo, Nakano, Sato, & Sakuma, 1994). Infusions of DA agonists to the mPOA facilitate solicitations in OVX females primed with a low dose of estradiol (M. D. Graham & Pfaus, 2010), whereas infusions of D1 receptor antagonists decrease solicitations in OVX females primed fully with estradiol and progesterone (M. D. Graham & Pfaus, 2012). Finally, the stimulation of solicitations by systemic administration of bremelanotide can be reversed by infusions of a D1 receptor antagonist to the mPOA, indicating that the melanocortin stimulation of solicitations works through the subsequent activation of DA release in the mPOA.

Another female copulatory behavior that is taken as a measure of the willingness to have sex is lordosis (Beach, 1976). More is known about the hormonal, neurochemical, and neuroanatomical control of lordosis than any other mammalian sexual behavior (Pfaff, 1980; Pfaff, Schwartz-Giblin, McCarthy, & Kow, 1994). This reflex is dependent on estrogen, although treating OVX females with estrogen alone produces only a moderate activation of the reflex in response to flank stimulation by the male. Full receptivity depends on additional activation by progesterone. Indeed, so does the full expression of proceptive behaviors, such as solicitation, and the normally low expression of pacing (Beach, 1976; Pfaus et al., 1999). Drugs that bind to D1 DA receptors, α_1-adrenergic receptors, oxytocin receptors, delta opioid receptors, or gamma-aminobutyric acid receptors in certain regions of the hypothalamus can increase lordosis in OVX rats primed with estrogen alone (see Kow, Mobbs, & Pfaff, 1994, and Pfaff, 1999, for reviews). These substances may work on neurochemical substrates normally activated by progesterone or could work via cell-signaling cascades that activate progesterone receptors (e.g., as has been described by Mani, Allen, Clark, Blaustein, & O'Malley, 1994, for DA in the ventromedial hypothalamus). If these drugs also enhance solicitations and delay the increase in pacing normally observed at the beginning of estrus termination, they might stand as suitable candidates for the treatment of hypoactive sexual desire disorder.

In males, the willingness to mount, intromit, and pursue females can be used as analogues of male desire. Several drugs are known to decrease mount and intromission latencies in sexually naive or sluggish male rats, including the opioid receptor antagonist naloxone (Pfaus & Gorzalka, 1987). Although chasing behavior displayed by male rats in open fields or bilevel chambers has not been studied in detail, DA antagonists have been noted to reduce this behavior in bilevel chambers at doses that did not alter the initiation of copulation (Pfaus & Phillips, 1991).

Neural Correlates of Desire in Animals

One of the strengths of the olfactory conditioned partner preference paradigm is that the odor can be presented alone in the animal's bedding or on a cotton gauze pad and neuroanatomical and neurochemical activation in response to the odor can be examined. This procedure takes the mess of copulation (and interpretation on the basis of different types or amounts of sensory stimulation) out of the analysis and makes the study far more cognitive in terms of examining responses made to a second-order conditioned cue. In fact, it is now possible using this paradigm to relate areas of the rat brain activated by the conditioned odor with areas of the human brain activated by visual erotic cues.

Activation of the immediate-early gene product Fos occurs in neurons that have been stimulated sufficiently by sensory inputs. Significant activation was found after presentation of the odor alone in paired versus unpaired groups in a number of brain regions that constitute a sexual circuit similar to that found activated in fMRI studies of sexual arousal and desire in men and women (reviewed in Georgiadis et al., 2012; Georgiadis & Kringelbach, 2012). These regions include cortical structures such as the medial prefrontal cortex, piriform cortex, insula, and anterior cingulate gyrus; limbic–motor regions such as the olfactory tubercle, NAc, dorsal striatum, lateral septum, and basolateral and medial amygdala; hypothalamic regions such as the mPOA, bed nuclei of the stria terminalis, anterior and lateral hypothalamus, and the midbrain anterior ventral tegmentum (a region that gives rise to the mesolimbic DA system) of males (Kippin, Cain, & Pfaus, 2003) and females (Coria-Avila & Pfaus, 2007) after presentation of the paired odor alone relative to the odor unpaired or random. Previous studies showed these regions to be activated by unconditioned olfactory or genitosensory stimulation during copulation (reviewed in Pfaus & Heeb, 1997); thus, their conditional activation by the odor suggests that they are activating a representation of the UCS, as Pavlov (1927) originally suggested for all positive CSs. Notably, a nearly identical set of regions is activated by stimuli that predict cocaine or heroin reward (Childress et al., 2008; Garavan et al., 2000), suggesting that these regions function together as a general system for appetitive arousal and desire related to reward.

The conditioned odor also stimulated DA release in the NAc of paired–trained male rats in response to the almond odor but not in that of unpaired–trained males. Conditioned activation of Fos was also found within parvocellular oxytocin neurons of the paraventricular nucleus that likely project to other forebrain regions. Fos was also found to be activated by the conditioned odor in magnocellular vasopressin neurons of the supraoptic nucleus that likely project into the posterior pituitary. Finally, systemic injections of oxytocin, but not vasopressin, to sexually naïve male rats during their first exposure to almond-scented receptive females resulted in one-trial conditioned ejaculatory preference (Pfaus et al., 2012). These data suggest that mechanisms of bonding are coactivated by sexual reward as part of the stimulation of desire, which allows animals to direct their desire toward preferred partners. The conditioned cue acts as a priming stimulus to activate cortical, limbic, and hypothalamic circuits involved in the facilitation of sexual arousal and desire, in the suppression of inhibitory systems, or both (Figure 7.5). Some of those circuits involve selective processing of the sexual stimulation that generates the reward state (UCS), the olfactory stimulus (CS), and a system that integrates the CS and UCS so that animals can focus their attention and engage in appropriate forward-directed locomotion toward the CS when it is present (Robinson & Berridge, 1993). What is immediately obvious from Figure 7.5 is that systems for sexual reward and incentive responding overlap with systems proposed for sexual (and maternal) bonding (e.g., Young & Wang, 2004). These systems involve the interaction of at least three neurochemical systems, including

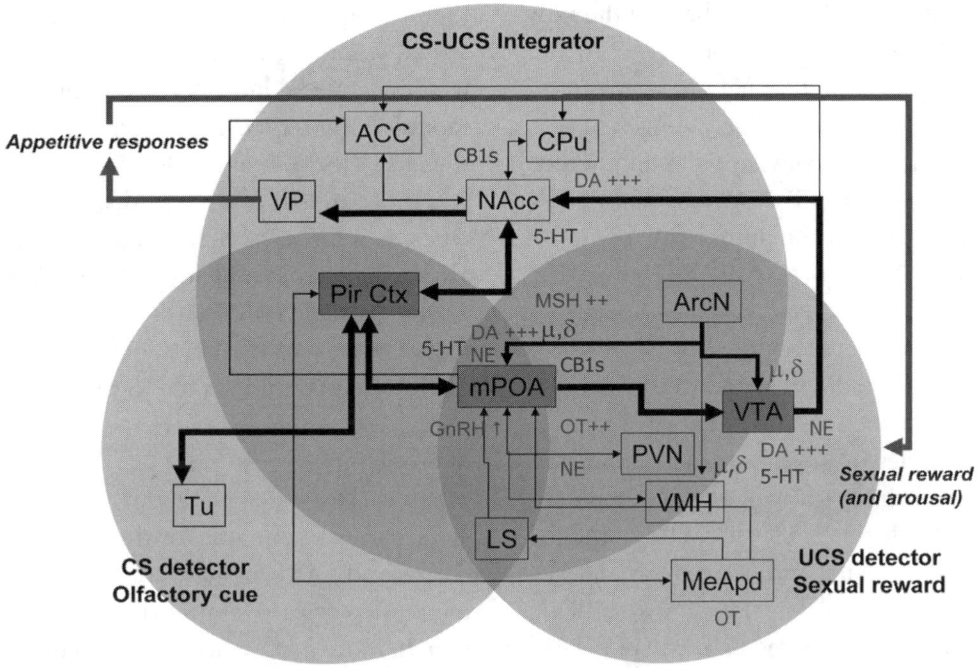

FIGURE 7.5. Neural systems that are critical for the display of conditioned olfactory preferences in the rat. Appetitive behaviors made toward conditioned stimuli lead to sexual reward that is processed by three interactive systems. Two systems process olfactory stimuli and sexual reward relatively independently, whereas a third, mesolimbic DA system acts to integrate both the conditioned olfactory cue and its rewarding sexual outcome. Three common regions, the piriform cortex, mPOA, and VTA, are activated in male and female rats by conditioned olfactory stimuli. Opioid actions in the VTA potentiate mesolimbic DA activation, whereas opioid actions in the mPOA inhibit sexual arousal and desire. Note that opioids can be excitatory in the VTA, inhibitory in the mPOA, or either in the VMH (depending on the receptor type). ACC = anterior cingulate cortex; ArcN = arcuate nucleus of the hypothalamus; CB1 = cannabinoid Type 1 receptor; CPu = caudate–putamen (striatum); CS = conditioned stimulus; DA = dopamine; δ = delta opioid receptors; GnRH = gonadotropin-releasing hormone; LS = lateral septum; MeApd = posterior–dorsal nucleus of the medial amygdala; mPOA = medial preoptic area; MSH = melanocyte-stimulating hormone; μ = mu opioid receptors; NAcc = nucleus accumbens; NE = noradrenaline; OT = oxytocin; Pir Ctx = piriform cortex; PVN = paraventricular nucleus of the hypothalamus; Tu = olfactory tubercle; UCS = unconditioned stimulus; VMH = ventromedial nucleus of the hypothalamus; VP = ventral pallidum; VTA = ventral tegmental area; 5-HT = serotonin. From "Sexual Motivation," by J. G. Pfaus, N. Ismail, and G. A. Coria-Avila, in *Encyclopedia of Behavioral Neuroscience* (Vol. 3, p. 206), edited by G. Koob, D. Thompson, and M. Le Moal, 2010, New York, NY: Elsevier. Copyright 2010 by Elsevier. Adapted with permission.

mesolimbic DA, hypothalamic oxytocin, and opioids that inhibit hypothalamic structures such as the mPOA but sensitize mesolimbic DA systems through a process of disinhibition (Kalivas & Stewart, 1991). This pattern is strikingly similar to the proposal by Fisher, Aron, Mashek, Li, and Brown (2002) of three primary emotional systems for mating, reproduction, and parenting.

Neural Correlates of Desire in Humans

Human subjects with genetically predisposed high synaptic DA are more likely to have been with many sexual partners (Guo, Tong, Xie, & Lange, 2007) and to have a low age of first sexual intercourse (Guo & Tong, 2006), which strongly suggests that mesolimbic DA drives sexual wanting. Subliminally induced ventral striatum (VS)–NAc responses are sensitive to pharmacological manipulation of DA (Oei, Rombouts, Soeter, van Gerven, & Both, 2012), suggesting that DA sensitizes or prepares sexual desire. Moreover, inside the realm of conscious processing, the VS–NAc readily respond to briefly presented photo VSS (which primarily depict single nudes; for an overview of studies, see Georgiadis et al., 2012; Georgiadis & Kringelbach, 2012; Stoléru, Fonteille, Cornélis, Joyal, & Moulier, 2012). Indeed, VS–NAc activity correlated with the perceived sexual attractiveness of bodily depictions (Walter et al., 2008), which may be considered an index of perceived sexual wanting. However, long excerpts of video-type VSS that induce genital responses (mainly penile erection) very rarely yield measurable activity in the VS–NAc (Georgiadis & Kringelbach, 2012). Mesolimbic DA transmission may thus be especially critical for the onset of sexual desire but may be less so for ensuing sexual arousal. In women, VS–NAc activity induced by anticipation of a monetary reward varies over the course of the menstrual cycle (Ossewaarde et al., 2011) and can be manipulated by exogenous testosterone (Hermans et al., 2010), suggesting that gonadal hormones and mesolimbic DA interact to fine tune the reward system.

The ventral prefrontal cortex (orbitofrontal cortex [OFC] and ventromedial prefrontal cortex [vmPFC]) and pregenual anterior cingulate cortex (pACC) seem to play an important role in evaluation of sexual attractiveness. Faces considered to be attractive activate the vmPFC more than unattractive faces (Ishai, 2007; Kranz & Ishai, 2006), and seeing a waist-to-hip ratio of 0.7 (generally considered most attractive by Western men) activated the OFC more strongly than other ratios (Platek & Singh, 2010). Nonparaphilic heterosexual men activate the OFC more strongly when presented with images of adult women versus images of underaged girls (Schiffer et al., 2008). Interestingly, this effect is not seen (but also not reversed) in heterosexual pedophiles (Schiffer et al., 2008; Walter et al., 2007). In heterosexual women, OFC activity to male faces is modulated by gonadal hormone levels, and this modulation predicts the perceived attractiveness of the faces (Rupp et al., 2009). In the pACC, activity was independent of perceived sexual arousal levels, whereas it did correlate with the perceived sexual attractiveness of bodily depictions (Walter et al., 2008). As with the OFC, the pACC responded to naked women more than to naked underaged girls only in nonparaphilic men (Schiffer et al., 2008). pACC activity also predicted reported self-relevance of erotic pictures but not of nonerotic emotional pictures (Heinzel et al., 2006). This evidence suggests a possible role for the ventral prefrontal cortex and pACC in evaluating the reward value of external reward stimuli (Kringelbach, 2005), which, in turn, may instate sexual desire. These areas have widespread anatomical and functional connections between them and with many other parts of the brain (Mesulam & Mufson, 1982; Taylor, Seminowicz, & Davis, 2009; Vogt & Pandya, 1987), which puts them in a good position to take into account other information, for example, related to context, prior experiences, and one's moral reference.

Whether a stimulus comes to elicit sexual desire is often the result of learning. For instance, Klucken et al. (2009) paired two different geometric shapes (CS) with either VSS (UCS) or nonrewarding (neutral) stimuli (non-UCS). The positive CS activated the OFC, pACC, anterior insula, VS–NAc, and midbrain, whereas the negative CS did not. Of note, strong awareness of the CS–UCS contingency corresponded with stronger activity in this network and with greater sexual desire. The involvement of the

VS–NAc in this sexual reward-based learning paradigm thus fits nicely with the results shown in animals, described previously.

Only one fMRI study has investigated sexual expectancy (Sescousse, Redouté, & Dreher, 2010). The paradigm was designed such that expectancies ranged from a low chance of getting a minor sexual reward to a high chance of obtaining a reasonable sexual reward. The positive subjective value assigned to the stimuli correlated with activity in a number of brain regions, most notably the OFC, pACC, anterior insula, VS–NAc, and midbrain. More important, the same set of brain regions were involved in processing the reward prediction error, that is, the degree of incongruence between the reward expected and obtained.

MECHANISMS OF SEXUAL STIMULATION AND REWARD

Sexual stimulation typically means genital stimulation (external and internal clitoris and cervix in women; penis and maybe prostate in men) but often includes stimulation of other erectile tissues, such as nipples, or erogenous areas of the body (e.g., lips, tongue, neck). Copulation often leads to orgasm, followed by a period of sexual satisfaction and satiety. Although all sexual activity is imbued with rewarding properties, the pleasures derived from copulation and those following orgasm are qualitatively (if not also quantitatively) different.

Sexual reward shares many features with sexual desire. In fact, in an incentive motivational analysis, desire typically reflects an expectancy of reward. Despite this, it is exceedingly difficult to define what is and is not rewarding about sexual interaction for any person or even within a culture (see Volume 2, Chapter 6, this handbook). Is it genital stimulation? Is it orgasm? Is it the chase or just the anticipation of sexual interaction? Moreover, sexual behavior can occur for reasons that have nothing to do with sexual gratification per se. Sexual reward as a general concept, however, has a more pervasive problem: its association in psychology with positive reinforcement. Positive reinforcers are traditionally considered events or stimuli that increase the probability of subsequent behavior (e.g., Ferster & Skinner, 1957). Playing with one's hair or sideways glances during a bout of flirting would also be considered positive reinforcers if they increase the degree of responding between the flirting pair (Perper, 1985). Consider satiety, however. All behaviors have a beginning, middle, and end, and satiety mechanisms place negative feedback on behavior by activating inhibitory neural pathways. Satiety mechanisms are absolutely critical for any regulatory behavior (e.g., Toates, 1992). In any motivational system, reward must be considered a dynamic function with an inverted U–shaped optimality relationship to ongoing behavior: Low rewards might sustain a small amount of behavior, moderate rewards might sustain more behavior, and high rewards might induce the inhibitory feedback that characterizes satiety. With regard to sexual behavior, rewards that sustain sexual arousal and desire might be considered low to moderate, whereas high rewards such as orgasm might be those that induce a period of sexual refractoriness. The reward value of satiety may also depend on the time frame. Although sexual satiety decreases sexual responding in the short term, the reward associated with it in male and female rats is necessary for the conditioning of sexual preferences in the long term. Satiety, however, is also defined along a continuum to aversion. For example, in the study of feeding, continued food ingestion after one is full leads to emesis. Likewise, continued genital stimulation after orgasm can be experienced as aversive in both men and women (Masters, Johnson, & Kolodny, 1983). So what is rewarding about sex, and how could one ever really know?

Wanting or craving sexual interaction goes hand in hand with a state of intense arousability (Whalen, 1966) in the presence of sexual stimuli. In an incentive motivational analysis (e.g., Pfaus, 1999; Toates, 1992), sexually motivated individuals will work hard to obtain a sex partner and some known or predicted degree of sexual gratification. The coactivation of brain DA and noradrenergic systems combines attention and arousal, bringing potential sex partners into sharp focus and galvanizing behavioral output toward a successful sexual interaction. What defines success? Although the early phases of sexual interaction can be powerful, exciting, and magic (e.g., first touch, first kiss), an important, positively reinforcing set of end points includes genital stimulation and orgasm.

Pathways for Genital Stimulation and Orgasm in Humans

As we have mentioned, sexual encounters generally engage very high sympathetic arousal, which, combined with parasympathetic activation and maintenance of blood in erectile tissues along with genital sensory feelings, may lead to the subjective experience of sexual arousal. In humans, this arousal is exemplified by markedly elevated cardiovascular arousal (Exton et al., 1999; Krüger et al., 1998) and elevated norepinephrine levels measured in cerebrospinal fluid during masturbation-induced sexual arousal and ejaculation (Krüger et al., 2006). Insufficient general arousal during sex jeopardizes sexual function (Weil, Zhang, Hornung, Blizard, & Pfaff, 2010), whereas, generally speaking, sympathetic arousal is strongly coupled with mood and pleasure (Pfaff, Kieffer, & Swanson, 2008). Sympathetic activity can evoke chills whose occurrence coincides with the perceived pleasantness of a musical piece (Salimpoor, Benovoy, Cooperstock, & Zatorre, 2009) or sexual pleasure (Georgiadis & Kringelbach, 2012) during erogenous stimulation.

Genital sensory input. Both psychogenic and physical stimulation induce sexual arousal and desire that can lead to sexual behavior. Under normal conditions, peripheral genital stimulation enhances excitability within sensory afferents that innervate spinal cord neural circuits. These spinal pathways contain the neural components for reflexive vasodilation and orgasm and receive and send information to brain regions that perceive and modulate the signals that drive or inhibit sexual behavior. Although the brain and spinal pathways have important differences that mediate sexual function in males and females, largely related to sexual differentiation resulting from gonadal steroid hormone actions during fetal development, there is also substantial similarity between the central nervous system mechanisms mediating sexual desire, arousal, and orgasm in males and females. These mechanisms include those involved in genital and psychological arousal; vasodilation in the penis, clitoris, and vagina; smooth and skeletal muscle contractions; and rewarding sensations including orgasm.

The pudendal nerve (which branches into the dorsal penile nerve and dorsal clitoral nerve) provides the major sensory input from the vagina, clitoris, penis, and skin and provides the efferent (motor) innervations of the striated muscles of the pelvic floor and perineum (Marson 2009; Marson & McKenna 1996; McKenna, 1999; see Figure 7.4). Stimulation of the sensory branch of the pudendal nerve elicits vasodilation of the penis, clitoris, and vagina and ejaculation (Adler, Davis, & Komisaruk, 1977; Cai, Alexander, & Marson, 2008; McKenna, 1999; Munarriz et al., 2003; Wiedey, Alexander, & Marson, 2008). The increase in vaginal blood flow in response to sensory pudendal nerve stimulation was reduced by bilateral pelvic nerve cuts, suggesting that somatic afferents activate automatic spinal pathways to mediate the changes in vaginal blood flow that lead to vasocongestion (Cai et al., 2008).

The pelvic and hypogastric nerves (Figure 7.4) convey sensory and noxious information from the internal reproductive organs, vagina, and skin (Marson 2011). The cavernous nerve regulates penile and clitoral erections. Stimulation of pelvic nerve afferents can evoke an increase in vaginal blood flow, modeling genital arousal (Munarriz et al., 2003). Vagal afferents from the uterus and cervix provide direct connections to the brain stem and may sense orgasmic responses after spinal cord injury (Komisaruk et al., 2004), although the role of the vagus nerve in males has not been verified. The distribution of the sensory afferents in the pelvis allows them to transmit considerable information relevant to mating, such as initiation and strength of sexual arousal, the location and movement of the penis, and climax. The glans penis contains specialized nerve endings that become very sensitive during erection that might enhance sensation during intercourse (Halata & Munger 1986; Johnson & Halata 1991).

Spinal pathways. The sympathetic, parasympathetic, and somatic branches of the nervous system are highly coordinated and highly interconnected through important spinal pathways. This coordination allows the physiological and psychological (orgasmic sensation) sensory inputs to produce the appropriate sexual response—vasodilation of erectile tissue, lubrication, increased sensitivity of erogenous zones, and muscle contractions during orgasm. In females, the sympathetic spinal regions in the lower thoracic–lumbar segments play a role in psychogenic arousal (Paick & Lee, 1994; Sipski, Alexander, Gomez-Marin, & Spalding, 2007). Genital responses occur only if the lumbosacral spinal cord that contains the pelvic and pudendal afferents and efferents is intact. The brain stem nuclei (nucleus paragigantocellularis) exert a tonic inhibition over the spinal pathways, and different regions of the brain (cortex, limbic system, mPOA) can be activated (directly or via visual sexual stimulation) to initiate genital responses (reviewed in Marson, 2011).

The pudendal nerve and pelvic nerve afferents course primarily along the medial and lateral dorsal horn, respectively, of the fifth segment of the lumbar spine (L5) through the first vertebra of the sacrum (S1) of the rat, with some afferent fibers penetrating into the dorsal gray commissure and toward the parasympathetic preganglionic nucleus. In contrast, the hypogastric nerve afferents of the rat are relatively sparse and terminate in the superficial dorsal horn and medial gray of the 13th segment of the thoracic spine through the third segment of the lumbar spine (Marson & McKenna, 1996).

Mating, VCS, urethral stimulation, and pudendal or pelvic nerve stimulation all activate Fos in neurons in similar spinal segments and subregions (Lee & Erskine, 1996; Wiedey et al., 2008) Activated spinal neurons were located in the superficial dorsal horn, the dorsal gray commissure of L5–S1 segments, overlapping with pelvic and pudendal sensory nerve innervations. Additional spinal neurons were activated in the intermediate gray and lateral gray dorsal to the parasympathetic preganglionic neurons. The distribution of activated spinal interneurons was similar in males and females. In parallel, electrophysiological studies identified similar spinal interneurons in the medial lumbosacral spinal gray matter after stimulation of the pudendal nerve and pelvic viscera (Fedirchuk, Song, Downie, & Shefchyk, 1992; Honda, 1985).

Neuroanatomical tracing studies using neurotrophic viruses that are transported transneuronally through several synapses (e.g., pseudorabies virus) have also been used to map spinal and brain neurons that innervate the penis, perineal muscles, clitoris, vagina, or uterus (Marson, 1995; Marson & Carson, 1999; Marson & Foley, 2004; Marson & McKenna, 1996; Papka, Williams, Miller, Copelin, & Puri, 1998). The majority of labeled neurons in the spinal cord were located in the dorsal gray commissure and in the vicinity of the sympathetic and parasympathetic preganglionic neurons, in the same regions as the Fos-activated neurons.

Within the medial gray is a subpopulation of neurons, termed the *lumbar spinothalamic neurons,* that has been shown to be critical for ejaculation in rats (Allard, Truitt, McKenna, & Coolen, 2005; Truitt & Coolen, 2002). The lumbar spinothalamic cells are thought to be part of the spinal pattern generator for ejaculation. These cells are not activated in females during copulation or the urethrogenital reflex, suggesting that activation of these neurons may be specific to ejaculation in males (Marson, Cai, & Makhanova, 2003; Truitt, Shipley, Veening, & Coolen, 2003). Further elucidation of the spinal generator mediating female genital responses is required.

These neuroanatomical and electrophysiological studies have revealed that genital afferents synapse on multiple interneurons in the spinal cord, which then relay through a spinal pattern generator the preganglionic and postganglionic neurons and motor neurons to mediate, enhance, trigger, and maintain genital sexual responses. This complex spinal system allows coordination of sexual reflexes and modulation of these responses by the brain.

Brain activation. Sensory information is relayed to the brain via the spinothalamic and spinoreticular pathways. These pathways terminate primarily in the posterolateral nucleus and medial thalamus. Spinoreticular fibers terminate in the brain stem reticular formation. These nuclei, in turn, project to specific areas of the cortex. Activation of many brain sites can evoke sexual responses, and these areas receive genital sensory information indicating that the central nervous system pathways mediating sexual responses are influenced by peripheral stimuli. For example, the nucleus paragigantocellularis, paraventricular nucleus and ventromedial nuclei of the hypothalamus, periaqueductal gray, mPOA, and medial amygdala have all been shown to contain neurons that are activated with pelvic sensory input (Coolen, Peters, & Veening, 1998; Marson, 2009, 2011; Marson & McKenna, 1996). DA release in NAc, striatum, and mPOA are activated in male and female rats in a continuous manner during copulation, although in males, DA release in the mPOA and NAc declines abruptly with ejaculation and stays low during the absolute refractory phase (reviewed in Blackburn et al., 1992).

During partnered sexual stimulation of the penis, a number of brain regions track the changing subjective sexual arousal and penile circumference (Georgiadis et al., 2010). Some of these regions are particularly interesting in the context of arousal regulation. Middle cingulate cortex activity is known to increase with enhanced sympathetic arousal (Critchley, Corfield, Chandler, Mathisa, & Dolan, 2000; Critchley, Nagai, Gray, & Mathias, 2011), and middle cingulate cortex activity is logically seen in diverse emotional and arousing situations (Blood & Zatorre, 2001; Breiter et al., 1997; Mobbs et al., 2009; Vogt, 2005). This shared neuronal substrate might give clues about how people can transfer from a nonsexual high-arousal state (e.g., anger) to sexual arousal, or vice versa if the arousal is not correctly identified as sexual (Pfaus, 2009). Conversely, the subgenual part of the cingulate cortex was most active during the steepest decline in penile tumescence after stimulation had ceased (Georgiadis et al., 2010), which is in line with exaggerated activity in this area in people with major depression (Hamani et al., 2011; Mayberg, 1997). A similar dichotomy is seen in the hypothalamus. Activity in the lateral hypothalamus correlated with penile tumescence, whereas the anteroventral hypothalamus was active only during penile detumescence after stimulation ceased, which is remarkably similar to hypothalamic arousal systems identified in animal models (Saper, Scammell, & Lu, 2005).

The ventral pallidum showed a specific association with penis stimulation onset and termination, which resembles its role in food intake and food liking (Berridge, 2009). Other areas showing a strong positive association with genitally induced high sexual arousal were the occipitotemporal cortex, inferior parietal lobule, and ventral premotor cortex (Georgiadis et al., 2010), which were also found to be associated with visually induced sexual arousal and psychogenic penile erection (reviewed in Georgiadis & Kringelbach, 2012; Stoléru et al., 2012). Other areas tracking sexual arousal were sensorimotor areas, such as the genital primary somatosensory cortex, intraparietal cortex and secondary somatosensory cortex, posterior insula, supplementary motor areas, and pelvic floor motor cortex (Georgiadis et al., 2010). Putative sensorimotor areas may thus actively take part in sexual activity and arousal, which has been confirmed by a recent study on affective touch showing that primary somatosensory cortex processing depends on whether the toucher is a man or a woman (Gazzola et al., 2012).

Activity in some brain regions decreases as sexual pleasure increases. This is true for the amygdala even when the amygdala readily responds to distant visual erotica (reviewed in Georgiadis & Kringelbach, 2012). However, prolonged amygdala activity corresponds to heightened vigilance, which promotes avoidant responses and precludes physical interaction (Rauch et al., 2000). Conversely, people are less sensitive to a sudden burst of white noise during sexual arousal (Koukounas & McCabe, 2001). Down-regulated neural activity associated with sexual liking is seen not only in the amygdala but also in parts of the medial temporal lobe and ventromedial prefrontal cortex (reviewed in Georgiadis & Kringelbach, 2012). These areas have been well documented to play a critical role in moral affiliations, self–other relations, self-awareness, and interpersonal judgments (Forbes & Grafman, 2010; Lou, Gross, Biermann-Ruben, Kjaer, & Schnitzler, 2010). One way to conceptualize deactivation of these areas in relation to high sexual arousal is that it helps to dissolve normal body boundaries, thereby facilitating sexual interactions, which in turn might contribute significantly to the experience of sexual arousal.

Orgasm. Orgasm is an autonomic and somatic reflex. It is controlled in part by the mPOA, which regulates parasympathetic and sympathetic outflow (E. M. Hull et al., 1999) in response to sexual stimulation, and potentially by the release of oxytocin and vasopressin from the posterior pituitary immediately before orgasm. During copulation, the parasympathetic division of the autonomic nervous system keeps blood in engorged erectile tissues (clitoris, penis, vaginal walls, nipples). As shown in Figure 7.6, orgasm engages sympathetic outflow to increase blood flow, systolic blood pressure, heart rate, breathing rate, and core temperature (Courtois et al., 2011; Komisaruk, Beyer-Flores, & Whipple, 2006). In turn, the climax during orgasm is experienced in conjunction with endogenous opioid release

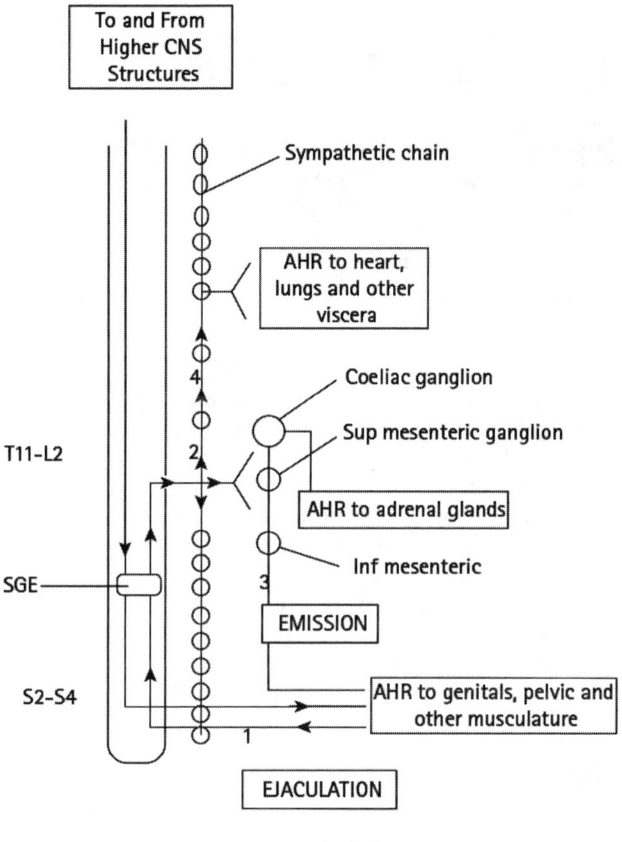

FIGURE 7.6. Spinal and autonomic systems that underlie ejaculation and autonomic hyperreflexia. Inputs from the genitals are conveyed to the sacral segments (S2–S4) of the spinal cord until the threshold for ejaculation is reached (1). Then the splanchnic (2)–hypogastric (3) and splanchnic–sympathetic chain (4) connections are activated to trigger emission and climax at the same time. AHR = autonomic hyperreflexia; CNS = central nervous system; L = lumbar; SGE = spinal generator of ejaculation; T = thoracic. From "Assessing and Conceptualizing Orgasm After Spinal Cord Injury," by F. Courtois, K. Charvier, J. G. Vézina, N. M. Journel, S. Carrier, G. Jacquemin, and I. Côté, 2011, *BJU International, 108*, p. 1631. Copyright 2011 by Wiley and Sons. Reprinted with permission.

in limbic regions that creates a rush of pleasurable ecstasy, along with the release of serotonin and endocannabinoids that create longer lasting feelings of satiety and sedation (Pfaus, 2009). Orgasm also increases pain thresholds and action consistent with the release of opioids (Whipple & Komisaruk, 1985).

Male orgasm is assumed to be synonymous with ejaculation and therefore biologically necessary for reproduction. Women's orgasms, however, have been difficult to understand (e.g., Lloyd, 2005; see Chapter 8, this volume), despite the fact that orgasm induces a reflexive tenting of the vagina and dipping of the cervix (that could come into contact with a semen pool), along with gentle peristalsis of the uterus that likely aids in sperm transport (Levin, 2005; Shafik, Shafik, El Sibai, & Shafik, 2006). However, both men and women differentiate the quality of orgasms from masturbation and copulation, and women in particular differentiate the deep orgasms from vaginal stimulation (involving both external and internal clitoral stimulation and cervical stimulation) from the focused orgasms induced by external clitoral stimulation alone (Ladas, Whipple, & Perry, 1982). Orgasm-induced sexual reward might well lay a sufficient foundation for activation of bonding mechanisms that ensure some degree of sociosexual and parental monogamy in pairs and social cohesion in groups (e.g., as in bonobos; Parish & De Waal, 2000).

A few studies have examined human brain activation during orgasm using fMRI and positron emission tomography (reviewed in Georgiadis & Kringelbach; Georgiadis et al., 2006; Stoléru et al., 2012). In general, these studies have suggested an activation of reward-related regions of the limbic system (e.g., VS–NAc, septum, hippocampus, insula, cingulate cortex) and activation of the cerebellum, but a deactivation of a number of regions that are associated with ongoing inhibition and vigilance (e.g., vmPFC, OFC, and amygdala) with a reactivation of amygdala, vmPFC, and OFC as refractoriness ensues (Figure 7.7). Human orgasms are exceptionally difficult to study, primarily because of their unpredictable and uncontrolled nature. Currently, the most insightful orgasm data come from a partnered clitoral stimulation positron emission tomography imaging study in women (Georgiadis et al.,

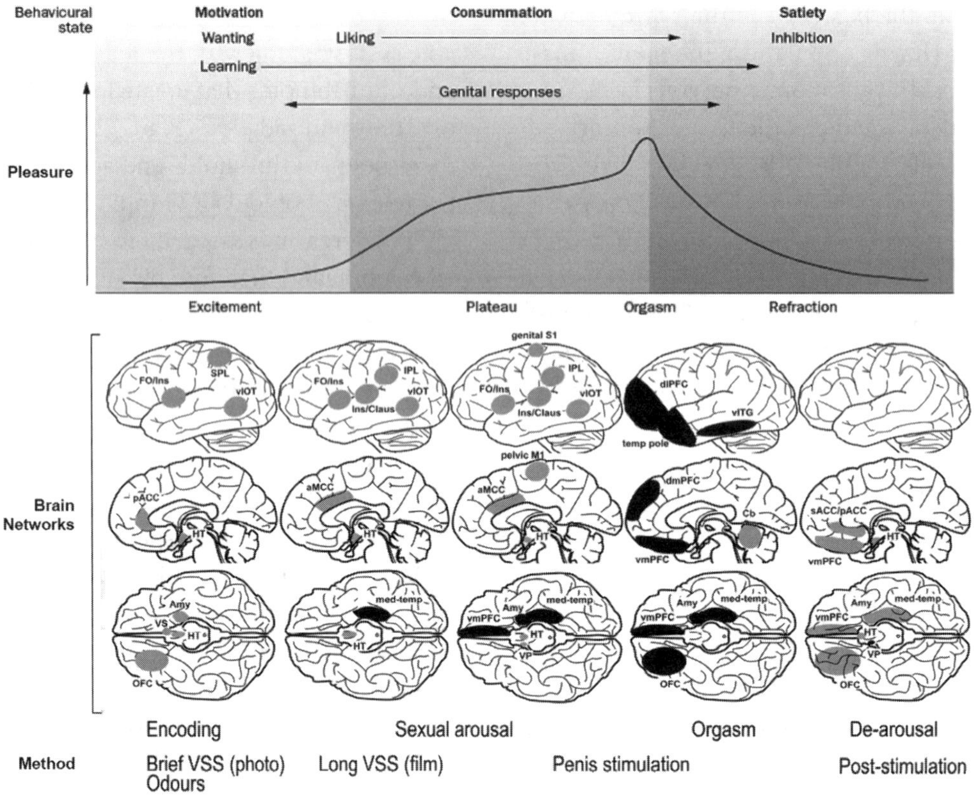

FIGURE 7.7. Human brain activation during the sexual pleasure–response cycle. The sexual response cycle involves phases related to excitement, plateau, orgasm, and refraction, which can also be expressed in terms of wanting, liking, and inhibition. Sexual liking typically peaks at orgasm but is by no means restricted to it. Orgasm (especially in men) tends to signal transition to the satiety phase, which can temporally prevent the individual from entering the cycle again. The sexual response cycle typically occurs over a relatively short time span (from minutes to hours) and may or may not include all of the phases and elements described. Neuroimaging studies have elucidated the key nodes and hubs that are responsible for sustaining and switching between the different phases of the pleasure cycle and can lead to changes in behavior. VSS paradigms are likely to elicit sexual motivation and wanting. Genital stimulation is usually required to enter the consummatory plateau. The brain regions involved in mediating changes in the sexual response cycle are shown on only one side of the brain, but most regions are involved bilaterally. Some regions have multiple roles at different points in the sexual response cycle; for example, activity in the amygdala is involved in encoding sexual salience, sexual arousal, orgasm, and poststimulation. Gray zones denote activation, and black zones denote inhibition during the various phases of the sexual response cycle. aMCC = middle cingulate cortex (anterior part); Amy = amygdala; Cb = cerebellum; dlPFC = dorsolateral prefrontal cortex; dmPFC = dorsomedial prefrontal cortex; FO/Ins = frontal operculum–anterior insula; genital S1 = primary somatosensory cortex of external genitalia; HT = hypothalamus; Ins/Claus = posterior insula–claustrum; IPL = intraparietal lobule; Med-temp = medial temporal lobe; OFC = orbitofrontal cortex; pACC = pregenual anterior cingulate cortex; pelvic M1 = primary motor cortex of pelvic floor; sACC = subgenual anterior cingulate cortex; SPL = superior parietal lobule; Temp pole = temporal pole; vITG = ventral aspect of inferior temporal gyrus; vlOT = ventrolateral occipitotemporal cortex; vmPFC = ventromedial prefrontal cortex; VP = ventral pallidum; VS = ventral striatum–nucleus accumbens; VSS = visual sexual stimulation. From "The Human Sexual Response Cycle: Brain Imaging Evidence Linking Sex to Other Pleasures," by J. R. Georgiadis, M. L. Kringelbach, & J. G. Pfaus, 2012, *Progress in Neurobiology, 98,* p. 488. Copyright 2012 by Elsevier. Reprinted with permission.

2006). Orgasm in women was verified by measuring fast rectal pressure fluctuations that reflect involuntary pelvic muscular activity (Bohlen, Held, Sanderson, & Ahlgren, 1982; van Netten, Georgiadis, Nieuwenburg, & Kortekaas, 2008). Activity in prefrontal, but not so much temporal, areas correlated with the frequency of rectal pressure fluctuations, so that fast fluctuations were associated with low prefrontal cortex activity. This association indicates a relative loss of voluntary behavioral control (Bechara, 2005), which is supported by the lack of pelvic floor motor cortex activity during orgasm (Georgiadis et al., 2006). The brain effect most specific to orgasm was observed in the mid-anterior and medial subregion of the OFC because activity in this area was most representative of the difference between sexual clitoral stimulation (a high sexual arousal control) and orgasm. Thus, OFC activity is unlikely to reflect general or sexual arousal but could reflect satiation or the loss of behavioral control. This activity was different in ventromedial temporal and ventromedial prefrontal cortices, which showed activity clearly related to perceived sexual arousal (Georgiadis et al., 2006). Caution must be taken when interpreting these data. Given that the temporal resolution of positron emission tomography is approximately 1 minute, the results described here might also be related to postorgasmic satiety or preorgasmic sexual arousal. For the same reason, it is possible that areas active specifically during orgasm might no longer be identified when data are pooled over a 1-minute period.

Sexual Reward in Animals

The sensory inputs from the clitoris, cervix, penis, and prostate in other female and male mammals are virtually identical to those in humans (Giraldi et al., 2004; Giuliano et al., 2010). Much of the data reviewed earlier on sexual desire and partner preference in rats double as a reflection of the reward state used to induce it. As we have noted, in males this reward state occurs in the aftermath of ejaculation (Ågmo & Berenfeld, 1990; Everitt, 1990; Kippin & Pfaus, 2001a). In females, it occurs as a function of being able to pace the copulatory contact (clitoral and cervical stimulation) at their preferred rate (Erskine, 1989; Paredes & Alonso. 1997; Paredes & Vazquez, 1999). These reward states can be assessed relatively unambiguously using the conditioned place preference (CPP) paradigm, in which animals experience a putative reward state in one of two perceptually distinctive sides of the apparatus and a control state in the other side. On a final test, animals are placed into a start compartment and allowed to roam freely between the two sides. If a reward state existed during conditioning, animals spend significantly more time in the side associated with reward relative to the side associated with the control condition.

Contextual factors, such as settings, are important components of positive sexual experiences for both men and women (e.g., Hoon, 1984; Kinsey, Pomeroy, & Martin, 1948; Kinsey, Pomeroy, Martin, & Gebhard, 1953). In male rats, sexual CPPs have been established using both copulatory and postejaculatory CPP procedures that produce effects of similar magnitude in male rats; however, differences are found in the underlying neurobiology. The opioid receptor antagonist naloxone disrupts both copulatory and postejaculatory CPPs, but in different ways. Ågmo and Berenfeld (1990) found that the development of postejaculatory CPP was blocked by injections of naloxone before each training session. Conversely, the development of a copulatory CPP was unaffected by naloxone before each training session (Mehrara & Baum, 1990). However, once a copulatory CPP had developed, its expression was blocked by naloxone injections before the final test (Hughes, Everitt, & Herbert, 1990; Mehrara & Baum, 1990). The site of action of naloxone is different for these effects. Ågmo and Gómez (1993) found that naloxone's disruption of the development of postejaculatory CPP occurred after infusions into the mPOA, whereas infusions of naloxone into this brain region did not disrupt the expression of a copulatory CPP (Hughes et al., 1990). In females, pacing-related CPP was blocked by systemic injections of naloxone (Paredes & Martinez, 2001) or after infusions of naloxone to the mPOA, ventromedial nucleus of the hypothalamus (VMH), or medial amygdala, but not to the NAc (García-Horsman, Ågmo, & Paredes, 2008). The data suggest that common opioid systems in the brains of male and female rats are activated by sex-related cues (Paredes & Martinez, 2001) and constitute a primary reward signal.

CPPs have also been demonstrated in female rats and hamsters. Oldenburger, Everitt, and de Jonge (1992) found that when copulation occurred within one of the distinctive compartments of a CPP apparatus, female rats showed a weak CPP. Subsequently, Paredes and Alonso (1997) and Paredes and Vazquez (1999) demonstrated a robust CPP in female rats that depended on whether the females were able to pace the rate of copulation without having to use defensive behaviors.

What about paced copulation leads to CPP in females? Meerts and Clark (2009) reported that artificial VCS distributed at 30-second intervals for a total of 15 stimulations induced a reliable CPP in OVX females primed with estradiol and progesterone. Given that VCS stimulates both the internal clitoris and the cervix, could clitoral stimulation alone could induce CPP? In two studies (Cibrian-Llanderal et al., 2012; Parada, Chamas, Censi, Coria-Avila, & Pfaus, 2010), clitoral stimulation was administered either with a lubricated paintbrush or a small cotton-tipped vibrator at preferred intervals for 10 to 15 minutes over five to six reinforced sessions. Both types of stimulation induced robust CPP. More important, clitoral reward can be induced in OVX females without hormone priming (Parada, Vargas, Kyres, Burnside, & Pfaus, 2012), indicating that sexual reward is independent of steroid priming, although such priming would normally be required for females to show lordosis, which allows them to experience clitoral stimulation from mounts with pelvic thrusting (Pfaff, Montgomery, & Lewis, 1977).

In summary, sexual reward in the form of ejaculation in male rats or paced copulation in female rats involves the activation of brain opioid systems that feed forward to sensitize mesolimbic DA in the presence of positively rewarding sexual cues. A similar system underlies copulatory reward in male and female Japanese quail, suggesting that it has been conserved as a pleasure–desire system across significant evolutionary time. Interestingly, heroin addicts often state that the drug effect reminds them of the pleasure experienced at orgasm (reviewed in Pfaus & Gorzalka, 1987), an effect referred to explicitly as a *pharmacogenic orgasm* by Chessick (1960). As with the reward state induced by heroin or cocaine, both male and female rats spend more time in contexts associated with a state induced by sexual reward. Moreover, conditioned contextual stimuli associated with those reward states activate pituitary and gonadal hormone release in male rats, suggesting a priming or occasion-setting response that gets males and females ready to copulate.

MECHANISMS OF SEXUAL INHIBITION

Sexual inhibition generally occurs during a sexual refractory period but also occurs in response to threat or stress. As an adaptive response, sexual inhibition serves both reproductive and social end points, for example, to keep individuals out of trouble or to allow a sufficient amount of sexual reward to induce a restorative state of sexual satiety during a refractory phase. Kinsey et al. (1948) hypothesized that sexual refractoriness in males occurs after ejaculation to allow time to generate more sperm for a subsequent ejaculation. Bancroft and Janssen (2000) argued that a normal amount of sexual inhibition keeps individuals from engaging in risky or inappropriate sexual behaviors, which a lack of inhibition would promote (as occurs in individuals with Kluver-Bucy syndrome or dementia or when individuals have sustained fronto-temporal cortical and amygdala damage after head trauma; Góscínski, Kwiatkowski, Polak, & Orlowiejska, 1997; Green, Clemente, & de Groot, 1957). Conversely, too much central inhibition was viewed as increasing the risk of sexual dysfunction, including inhibited arousal, desire, and diminished capacity to achieve sexual gratification. Excessive inhibition may thus lead to a numbing of intimacy and disruption of bonding between partners to the point that sexual activity, if it is engaged in at all, becomes a routine of going through the motions rather than an enriching and rewarding experience.

The concept of inhibition is further related to the cognitive principle of executive function, in which individuals have to choose among several possibilities and create hierarchies on the basis of expectancies, planned actions, and calculations. Cognitive psychologists view executive functions as the role of the prefrontal cortex (Robbins, 2007), which must inhibit a complex and ongoing interplay of motor tendencies to arrive at planned and sustained actions. People or rats with disrupted prefrontal function have great difficulty focusing attention on tasks, are unable to inhibit competing responses, and experience retroactive and proactive interference (Robbins, 2007; Tamm, Menon, & Reiss, 2002; Van der Linden, 2001; Winn, 1998). With regard to sexual behavior, it is assumed that cultures superimpose a moral value of "right" and "wrong" on the hierarchies so that some behaviors that feel good are right and can be experienced without guilt, whereas others are wrong and carry the weight of guilt or rule of law against them. This type of inhibition represents an approach–avoidance conflict in which the expectation of reward drives the desire, but the inhibition imposed by the real or perceived aversive consequences of engaging in sexual activity blunts the initiation of behavior. Finally, sexual inhibition can also be induced by sexual nonreward. This type of inhibition suppresses components of desire directly (Perelman, 2006; Pfaus, 2009). Accordingly, the "prosexual" nature of drugs such as alcohol or cocaine may be a function of their ability to disinhibit such suppressed sexual responding (see Chapter 21, this volume). For example, sexually active male rats have to learn to inhibit their sexual advances toward sexually nonreceptive females (Pfaus & Pinel, 1989). Once learned, this inhibition can be disinhibited by low doses of alcohol (see the Inhibition Related to Aversion or Nonreward section).

Stress and Inhibition

Stress activates the autonomic nervous system. Typically, threatening stimuli activate the sympathetic arm, increasing blood flow and oxygen uptake to muscles and organs that need it. A small degree of stress or threat (i.e., something naughty or even painful) can be arousing, especially for individuals with low levels of arousability. Translated to a sexual situation, such arousal could be directed into sexual activity, perhaps to the point in some individuals that it becomes a necessary antecedent. The stimuli that evoke excitation and inhibition may be different for different individuals, and what inhibits one person may actually excite another.

Although shock can suppress a variety of appetitive and consummatory behaviors in rats (Mackintosh, 1994), such punishment has never been reported to induce sexual inhibition in males (Beach & Fowler, 1959; Hayward, 1957; Zimbardo, 1958). In fact, shock or short-term pain (e.g., tail-pinch), or neutral stimuli paired with them, actually stimulate mounting in sexually sluggish or inactive male rats, an effect referred to as the *dud-to-stud phenomenon* (Barfield & Sachs, 1968; Caggiula, 1972; Crowley, Popolaw, & Ward, 1973). Foot-shock also reduces the number of intromissions required for ejaculation in sexually active males (Beach & Fowler, 1959; Sachs & Barfield, 1976). As mentioned earlier, both male and female rats will readily cross electrified grids to gain access to sexually receptive partners (Moss, 1924). Thus, low-level shock or pain does not induce an inhibitory state. Indeed, arousal is a necessary antecedent to sexual activity in both male and female rats. Drugs that decrease the activity of the sympathetic nervous system (e.g., α_2-adrenergic receptor agonists such as clonidine) decrease sexual responding in both male and female rats (Clark et al., 1985; Meston et al., 1996).

Inhibition Related to Aversion or Nonreward

More effective situational inhibition has been induced in rats using more ecologically valid procedures. Rodents live in a predominantly olfactory world, and pairing estrous odors with gastrointestinal distress (induced by contingent injections of lithium chloride that make animals sick) induces a conditioned odor aversion in male rats and hamsters that translates to avoidance of female vaginal secretions (Zahorik & Johnston, 1976), increased mount and intromission latencies (Johnston, Zahorik, Immler, & Zakon, 1978), decreased proportion of males that ejaculate (Peters, 1983), or avoidance of copulation altogether (Peters, 1983; however, see Lawrence & Keifer, 1987). This effect occurred if conditioning took place when the males were juveniles (Koch & Peters, 1987), and conditioned males uttered distress vocalizations in the presence of vaginal secretions (Peters, Koch, Blythe, & Sufka, 1988). Using a choice paradigm, Ågmo (2002) showed that males allowed to copulate to one ejaculation with females scented with capelin oil, after which they were injected with lithium chloride, avoided copulation with capelin-scented females, although they continued to copulate normally with unscented females. Finally, Frohmader, Bateman, Lehman, and Coolen (2010) found that methamphetamine administered before or after the sexual behavior–lithium chloride pairings disrupted the acquisition of conditioned sex aversion. This finding suggests that amplification of brain DA, norepinephrine levels, or both during conditioning delays the activation of inhibition.

Adult male rats in the wild are rarely observed to attempt copulation with sexually nonreceptive females (Barnett, 1963; Calhoun, 1962), which is in marked contrast to most laboratory settings in which males will attempt to copulate with nonreceptive females placed into chambers in which the males have previously copulated with sexually receptive females. Training sexually active male rats to differentiate between sexually receptive and nonreceptive females on alternating test trials leads quickly to a substantial reduction in the proportion of males that attempt to copulate with nonreceptive females (Pfaus & Pinel, 1989). By virtue of the females being nonreceptive, these behaviors are paired with a lack of estrous odors. Males learn quickly to differentiate the presence of estrous odors with appetitive precopulatory and receptive behaviors and the lack of estrous odors with thwarted sexual advances and female aggression. In the wild, such conditioning may occur normally during adolescence.

The inhibition induced by pairing male rats with sexually nonreceptive females can be reversed by low to moderate doses of alcohol (Pfaus & Pinel, 1989) such that a dose-dependent increase in sex behavior is seen with alcohol treatment. However, if the alcohol dose was high enough to induce motor disruption, the males did not attempt any copulation with the nonreceptive females. These findings are of interest because alcohol intoxication figures in high-risk sexual activity (Castilla, Barrio, Belza, & de la Fuente, 1999) and is one of the strongest antecedent predictors of men actually carrying out a rape (Rada, 1975; Ranieri-Collins, 1995)

A sexual nonreward state can also be conditioned to a neutral odor. One of the control conditions used in studies of conditioned ejaculatory preference reviewed earlier was an explicitly unpaired group that received copulatory trials with unscented sexually receptive females and inhibitory trials with scented nonreceptive females (e.g., Kippin et al., 1998; Kippin & Pfaus, 2001a). When placed with two sexually receptive females in an open field, one scented and the other unscented, males in the unpaired group copulated and ejaculated significantly more frequently with unscented females. In female rats, a similar sequential pairing of scent on males in a nonpacing condition and no scent on males in a pacing condition led them to solicit and receive ejaculations more frequently from unscented males (Coria-Avila et al., 2005). Indeed, Parada et al. (2011) reported that sexually naïve females that received clitoral stimulation in the presence of a scented male behind a wire-mesh screen attempted to solicit the male (who cannot respond). Subsequently, on their first copulatory trial in an open field with two sexually vigorous males, one scented and the other unscented, the females solicited and received ejaculations selectively from the unscented male.

Finally, sexual nonreward can be induced by administration of the opioid receptor antagonist naloxone during conditioning trials. Naloxone treatment during training blocks both sexual CPP and sexually conditioned partner preference in male and female rats (Coria-Avila et al., 2008; Ismail, Girard-Bériault, Nakanishi, & Pfaus, 2009). This blocking occurs as a function of expectancy and not as an effect of naloxone per se. In another study (Pfaus et al., 2012), naloxone or saline was administered to females on their 1st six multiejaculatory pairings with sexually vigorous males. On the seventh trial, all females received saline. The females trained with saline had high numbers of full solicitations, hops, and darts and showed full lordosis, and the males mounted and ejaculated at a normal rate. In contrast, females trained with naloxone had dramatically lower levels of solicitations and hops and darts and lower magnitude lordoses and received fewer intromissions and ejaculations from the males. In fact, this group of females displayed far more defensive behaviors toward the males, despite being fully primed with estradiol and progesterone. This example is one of the first in the rat of expectancy of sexual nonreward overshadowing the sexual excitement induced by ovarian steroid hormone treatment.

Inhibition Induced by Sexual Satiety

Sexual satiety is said to occur when animals no longer engage in sexual behavior after copulation, as occurs during a period of sexual refractoriness after orgasm. Males of a variety of species show behavioral quiescence after ejaculation and are not responsive to female solicitations. In rats, this period is marked by an abrupt decrease in DA release in the NAc and mPOA during the "absolute" refractory period (Blackburn et al., 1992), but it reinstates over time. If male rats are allowed to copulate to sexual exhaustion, they display reduced or completely inhibited responsiveness to female solicitations, and many will not copulate to ejaculation for 24 to 48 hours (Beach & Jordan, 1956; Larsson, 1956; Tiefer, 1969). This inhibition is due to neurochemical events that underlie sexual satiety and can be partly or fully reversed by treatments that elevate noradrenaline or block serotonin release or opioid receptors (Fernández-Guasti & Rodríguez-Manzo, 2003; Rodríguez-Manzo, 1999; Rodríguez-Manzo & Fernández-Guasti, 1994; 1995a, 1995b). This reversal suggests that increased release of serotonin and endogenous opioids, and decreased release of noradrenaline, underlies the neurochemical state of sexual satiety. Interestingly, the generation of sexual satiety can be delayed by changing the stimulus female for every ejaculatory series (i.e., by inducing a "Coolidge effect"; Rodríguez-Manzo, 1999). Sexual satiety also leads to a complete suppression of DA release in the NAc (Fiorino et al., 1997).

Sexual satiety in females is more difficult to assess. In the wild, females of a variety of species approach and solicit males around the time of ovulation, but those behaviors diminish after a period of copulation (e.g., McClintock, 1984; Wallen, 1995). Female rats show a marked decline in solicitations and an increase in rejection responses after receiving four series of mounts, intromissions, and ejaculations per male (Pfaus, Smith, Byrne, & Stephens, 2000). The progressive decline in sexual approach, solicitation, and receptivity, with concomitant increases in rejection responses, characterizes the phenomenon of estrus termination (Erskine & Baum, 1982; Lodder & Zeilmaker, 1976; Pfaus et al., 2000). Estrus termination is facilitated by manually applied VCS using a lubricated glass rod at intervals similar to those of paced intromissions (Pfaus et al., 2000). This type of stimulation activates the ventrolateral region of the VMH and other brain areas in a manner indistinguishable from male intromissions over the same time period (Pfaus, Kleopoulos, Mobbs, Gibbs, & Pfaff, 1993; Pfaus, Marcangione, Smith, Manitt, & Abillamaa, 1996). Transection of the pelvic nerve eliminates the effect of VCS on both estrus termination (Lodder & Zeilmaker, 1976) and activation of ventrolateral VMH (Pfaus, Manitt, & Coopersmith, 2006), suggesting that VCS activates an inhibitory system that abbreviates the duration of estrus. Treatment of OVX rats with estradiol benzoate and progesterone reduces the cellular response to VCS in the VMH and decreases Fos activation in glutamate neurons, which can be reversed by blockade of the α-amino-3-hydroxy-5-methyl-4-isoxazolepropionic acid–kainite receptor by the glutamate antagonist 6,7-dinitroquinoxaline-2, 3-dione (Georgescu, Cyr, & Pfaus, 2012; Georgescu, Sabongui, Del Corpo, Marsan, & Pfaus, 2009). Thus, the actions of ovarian steroids in the VMH inhibit the ability of VCS to activate the glutamate-driven system that brings about estrus termination, thereby allowing females to receive the requisite amount of sexual stimulation so neuroendocrine changes necessary for sexual reward and pregnancy can occur.

Neurochemical Mechanisms of Inhibition

What is striking in the animal data is the similar pattern of inhibition that emerges from states of aversion, nonreward (induced either by frustration or by pharmacological blockade of opioid transmission), and satiety: a suppression of sexual interest, desire, or arousal; an increase in rejection responses in females; and a progressive decline in copulatory behavior. To the extent that sexual refractoriness blunts attention to sexual incentives and inhibits sexual responses as a natural end point of sexual behavior, one can speculate that inhibitory systems exist in the brain that are activated by mechanisms of sexual reward and satiety. These systems inhibit the activation of excitatory mechanisms reviewed earlier and possibly shift attention and behavior to nonsexual stimuli or situations. At least three neurochemical systems may do this simultaneously in the brain (depicted in Figure 7.2): serotonin, which induces satiety; opioids, which mediate sexual reward states; and endocannabinoids, which induce sedation (reviewed in Pfaus, 2009). The combined action of those systems may well underlie the suppression and subsequent reinstatement of forebrain activity that characterizes orgasm and its immediate aftermath (Hajós, Gartside, Varga, & Sharp, 2003).

Serotonin. Serotonin plays a crucial role in the mediation of satiety and behavioral inhibition that characterizes executive function via activation of the medial prefrontal cortex. Ascending serotonin fibers innervate the prefrontal cortex (Goldman-Rakic, 1987) and modulate descending outputs to a variety of limbic, thalamic, hypothalamic, and midbrain regions, including the mPOA, NAc, and DA neurons in the VTA (Room, Russchen, Groenewegen, & Lohman, 1985; Sesack & Pickel, 1992). Serotonin neurons that descend down the spinal cord from the Raphé and the nucleus paragigantocellularis also play a role in maintaining control over ejaculation (and possibly orgasm in general) via descending inhibition. This inhibition is itself disinhibited by several neurochemicals, including oxytocin released from the posterior pituitary. In fact, drugs that activate serotonin transmission, including certain SSRIs such as fluoxetine, delay or abolish orgasm in both men and women and in many cases blunt sexual arousal and desire (Pfaus, 2009; Rowland et al., 2000; Waldinger et al., 2005). This effect can be reproduced acutely when serotonin is reverse-dialyzed into the mPOA (Dominguez & Hull, 2010). Chronic fluoxetine treatment also disrupts patterns of appetitive and consummatory sexual behavior in female hamsters (Frye & Rhodes, 2010). Given their ability to delay ejaculation, some well-tolerated SSRIs are being used to treat premature ejaculation (e.g., Hoy & Scott, 2010).

Endogenous opioids. Opiates such as heroin produce a rush of euphoria followed by a long-lasting period of relaxation (Pfaus & Gorzalka, 1987). This pattern is extremely similar to that observed during and after orgasm and is typically referred to by heroin addicts in sexual terms. Drug reward states induced by virtually all drugs with abuse potential activate endogenous opioid systems, which in turn modulate the sensitization of mesolimbic DA neurons (Aston-Jones & Harris, 2004; Tzschentke, 2001) and thus increased attention and goal-directed motor output in the presence of drug-related cues. Essentially, drugs usurp the reward mechanisms that exist for natural reinforcers such as sex (e.g., Childress et al., 2008).

Infusions of mu opioid receptor agonists to the mPOA inhibit sexual behavior in male rats (Band & Hull, 1990; Hughes, Everitt, & Herbert, 1987; Matuszewich, Ormsby, Moses, Lorrain, & Hull, 1995), and infusions to the mPOA or VMH inhibit sexual behavior in female rats (Acosta-Martinez & Etgen, 2002b). Conversely, mu opioid receptors are activated in the mPOA after copulation in male rats (Coolen, Fitzgerald, Yu, & Lehman, 2004), and infusions of a mu antagonist to the mPOA, but not the NAc, block sexually conditioned place preference (Ågmo & Gómez, 1993). Enkephalin levels are also elevated in the frontal cortex, hypothalamus, and midbrain of sexually exhausted or inactive male rats (Rodríguez-Manzo, Asai, & Fernández-Guasti, 2002). These data suggest that opioid release in the hypothalamus, and in particular the mPOA, produces a reward state and is a major factor in the immediate induction of sexual refractoriness.

In contrast to the induction of sexual refractoriness in the mPOA, opioids in the VTA stimulate sexual activity in sexually sluggish male rats, presumably by disinhibition of DA neurons. For example, infusions of morphine or dynorphin 1-13 to the VTA stimulated female-directed behavior and mounting in male rats, and repeated administration of morphine to this region sensitized DA release in the NAc (Mitchell & Stewart, 1990). More interesting, repeated exposure of male rats to sexually receptive females sensitizes DA release in the NAc, an effect that is attenuated by pretreatment with naloxone (Mitchell & Gratton, 1992).

Finally, infusion of delta receptor agonists to the lateral ventricles or VMH facilitates sexual behavior in female rats (Acosta-Martinez & Etgen, 2002a; Pfaus & Pfaff, 1992), whereas infusion to the mPOA inhibits female sexual behavior (Sinchak, Mills, Eckersell, & Micevych, 2004). A similar effect has been reported for gamma-aminobutyric acid–A agonists in the VMH and mPOA of female rats (McCarthy,

Malik, & Feder, 1990). Local effects of opioids in different hypothalamic regions may modulate the overall electrophysiological responsiveness of neurons to change the way that sexual stimuli are processed or responded to (Devidze et al., 2008), and estrogens may set this up by stimulating the synthesis of enkephalin in the VMH (Lauber, Romano, Mobbs, Howells, & Pfaff, 1990). An interesting finding is that in the mPOA, estrogen causes the internalization of mu opioid receptors (a signature of activation), but progesterone decreases this internalization, suggesting a mechanism by which the pattern of estrogen and progesterone actions could time sexual behavior to coincide with ovulation in the rat (Sinchak & Micevych, 2001).

Endocannabinoids. Engaging in sexual activity to ejaculation or orgasm induces a state of sedation leading to reduced responses to anxiety-provoking or stressful stimuli (Rodríguez-Manzo, López-Rubalcava, & Fernández-Guasti, 1999). The sedative effects of cannabinoids have been known for centuries (Pazos, Núñez, Benito, Tolón, & Romero, 2005). The discovery of the cannabinoid Type 1 receptor (CB1) in motor, limbic, and hypothalamic regions of the mammalian brain and endogenous ligands for those receptors in diffuse populations of neurons and glial cells generated a flurry of research into their endogenous function (Pars & Howes, 1977). It has become clear that a variety of emotional and regulatory functions, such as pain, anxiety, feeding, and sexual desire, are mediated by endocannabinoids. In addition, endocannabinoids appear to "cross-talk" with hormone receptor–induced changes in second-messenger actions in the hypothalamus to generate changes in behavior (Mani, Mitchell, & O'Malley, 2001). Several cannabinoid agonists and antagonists have been suggested for clinical use in the treatment of pain, inflammation, feeding, and sexual desire disorders (Baker, Pryce, Giovannoni, & Thompson, 2003).

Sexually, cannabinoid agonists have effects similar to alcohol, with disinhibited sexual desire in putatively inhibited individuals but also a blunting of somatosensory awareness that leads to an increase in erection and ejaculation latencies (Crenshaw & Goldberg, 1996; Gorzalka, Hill, & Chang, 2010; Gorzalka, Morish, & Hill, 2008; López, 2010). Similar effects have been reported in male rats with both tetrahydrocannabinol and the endogenous cannabinoid agonist anadamide (Martínez-González et al., 2004; Navarro et al., 1993). Antagonists of the CB1 receptor facilitate erection and ejaculation (Gorzalka et al., 2008; Melis, Succu, Mascia, & Argiolas, 2004; Succu et al., 2006). Approach of males toward a sexually receptive female was impaired by tetrahydrocannabinol treatment (Navarro et al., 1993). Although tetrahydrocannabinol facilitates lordosis in female rats (Gorzalka et al., 2010; Mani et al., 2001; Turley & Floody, 1981), CB1 agonists can inhibit both lordosis and precopulatory hops and darts (Ferrari, Ottani, & Giuliani, 2000). Conversely, treatment of estrogen-primed female rats with a CB1 antagonist increases both lordosis and solicitation behaviors (López, Webb, & Nash, 2009). As in male rats, appetitive sexual motivation can be enhanced by CB1 antagonists, suggesting that a state of endocannabinoid activation may carry with it a concomitant inhibition of sexual desire (López et al., 2009).

Patterns of Brain Activation and Inhibition

As shown in Figure 7.7, orgasm creates a sudden and dramatic shift in brain activation patterns, with some brain regions being activated selectively at orgasm and afterward, whereas others activated during sexual stimulation become quiescent (Georgiadis et al., 2012). One fMRI study scanned men during the period 3 to 30 minutes postejaculation (Mallick, Tandon, Janannathan, Gulia, & Kumar, 2007) and found that the septal area–anterior hypothalamus, temporal lobe, and amygdala were involved. Another study found these areas with the addition of vmPFC, subgenual anterior cingulate cortex, and pACC to be related to poststimulatory dearousal (Georgiadis et al. 2010). Studies with hypogonadal individuals have indicated that sexual inhibition correlates with prefrontal hyperactivity (Arnow et al., 2009; Redouté et al., 2000) and that this hyperactivity can be down-regulated by treatments that enhance testosterone (Redouté et al., 2000) or central DA levels (Montorsi et al., 2003). Studies of psychogenic hyposexual patients have suggested that increased activity in the ventral prefrontal (Arnow et al., 2009; Cera et al., 2012) and dorsal parietal areas and decreased activity in the middle cingulate cortex (Bianchi-Demicheli et al., 2011; Cera et al., 2012) are indicative of psychogenic sexual difficulties. Interestingly, male hyposexual patients showed sustained superior parietal activity during an erotic video (and a failure to achieve erection), whereas control patients demonstrated a drop in superior parietal activity and a rise in middle and posterior insula activity in association with penile erection (Cera et al., 2012). Indeed, volitional inhibition of sexual arousal in healthy men elevated neural activity in the superior parietal and ventrolateral prefrontal cortex (Beauregard, Lévesque, & Bourgouin, 2001). These observations suggest that sexual inhibition is related to exaggerated activity in areas that are implicated generally in saliency detection and alertness, which likely prevents the focus on sexual arousal and desire specifically. Hyposexual patients might still be able to identify sexual incentives, but these incentives fail to produce a switch to a different processing mode.

CONCLUSIONS

Sexual behavior epitomizes the whole-body relationship between autonomic activation and central nervous system function. Yet part of that biological substrate is an enormous adaptive flexibility in the brain that allows individual and idiosyncratic Pavlovian and operant associations to be made between external stimuli, behavioral responses, and sexual reward. Excitatory and inhibitory neuroanatomical and neurochemical systems exist in the brain for sexual responding, some of which are general and related to incentive motivation (e.g., mesolimbic DA) and executive function (e.g., serotonin and medial prefrontal cortex activity), whereas others are specifically related to sexual arousal, desire, and reward processing (e.g., DA and opioid actions in the mPOA and NAc) and the activation of bonding (oxytocin). In all sexually responding organisms, these systems are activated by competent sexual stimuli, the competence of which is determined by the interaction of temperamental variables, such as the endogenous capacity for arousability and expression of inhibition (including where individuals are at any particular time in their own sexual response cycle), steroid hormone levels, learned associations between external cues and sexual pleasure, and the responses made to achieve such pleasure. Indeed, a high degree of homology exists in the excitatory and inhibitory neural systems controlling sexual responding that appears to have been conserved for at least 450 million years. This homology makes it possible to predict how a drug that disrupts ejaculation in rats might disrupt it in humans or how alcohol-induced sexual disinhibition in humans might be expressed in rats. The convergence of animal and human data on the biological bases of sexual responding illuminates how a behavioral science can become translational and predictive (Beach, 1978; Pfaus et al., 2007).

As the technology of human brain imaging increases in sensitivity, it will become possible to view activation patterns with greater resolution in response to more sophisticated behavioral or sensory paradigms. Sexual motivation or desire may exist before genital responses can be measured, and it would be important to get a better handle on such behavioral responses, even inside the scanner. A potentially powerful method could be to use a combination of fMRI and transcranial magnetic stimulation to manipulate activity of certain areas and subsequently the impact of this manipulation on behavior (Volman, Roelofs, Koch, Verhagen, & Toni, 2011). The use of partnered protocols, and hence the possibility for sexual partners to interact, significantly enhances the ecological validity of neuroimaging designs, but this use could be expanded. Possibilities include the manipulation of expectancy and the element of choice and allowing the subject to touch the partner.

Animal studies have also increased in behavioral sophistication and, combined with advances in molecular and neurochemical techniques, it will be possible to view gene activation and epigenetic modifications (e.g., DNA methylation or chromatin alterations) in response to sexual learning. Such experience-induced changes may well mirror those that are found to differentiate monogamous from polygamous species (e.g., vasopressin and DA receptor differences between prairie and meadow voles; Aragona et al., 2006; Young & Wang, 2004). Such plasticity may allow for abrupt changes in mating strategies when dramatic environmental shifts occur or when population dynamics change. Differences in susceptibility to reward and bonding or to inhibition, for example, may be more or less responsive to early sexual experiences in different individuals. The genetics that create that difference may also play a vitally important role in the way individuals respond to drugs of abuse, or indeed to any other reward.

Obvious limitations exist in the extent to which the study of animal sexual behavior can guide the understanding of human sexual behavior. Despite new knowledge of a common biological core of brain and autonomic activation that underlies sexual behavior in all animals, whether rats or other animals have self-aware and socially constructed definitions of their own sexuality is not known. As we have noted, they do not speak in languages readily understood, nor do they seem to be poked by a culture that requires them to conform to sexual expression on the basis of gender or sexual orientation. Animals probably do not have a sense of gender or orientation as people understand it. Although male rats can be conditioned to prefer to spend time near another male versus a sexually receptive female (Cibrian-Llanderal et al., 2012), this preference may be social and not necessarily sexual. Even when same-sex partner and copulatory preferences clearly exist and are driven by sexual reward (as in female Japanese macaques; Vasey & Duckworth, 2006; Vasey & Jiskoot, 2010), they clearly do not possess a history of political, cultural, or scientific debate about their orientation. Although myriad sex differences are found in sexual and other behaviors in animals (Nelson, 2005), these differences are not based on socially constructed concepts of gender or gender-appropriate versus gender-inappropriate behaviors (see Chapter 2, this volume).

Although rats and other animals experience sexual pleasure and reward, we have no idea whether they experience orgasm as we understand it. And therein lies another set of questions that require common effort from essentialists and constructionists (see Chapter 1, this volume): What is an orgasm? What and who defines it? Is it a unidimensional phenomenon in the spinal cord but interpreted in a multidimensional way in the brain (e.g., Mah & Binik, 2002)? Is it synonymous with ejaculation in men? Does it differ qualitatively between sex with a romantic partner relative to a one-night stand? Does it differ qualitatively given the amount of time it takes to achieve it? Is it elusive in some women regardless of expectation and sexual position but expressed easily in others just by fantasy alone? Regarding women, clearly clitoral orgasms differ qualitatively from vaginal orgasms (King, Belsky, Mah, & Binik, 2011; Meston, Levin, Sipski, Hull, & Heiman, 2004), but what causes this? Could the difference reflect solitary masturbation versus sexual intercourse with a live partner (who may or may not provide competent stimulation)? Could it reflect a difference between external clitoral stimulation and stimulation of the rest of the two thirds of the clitoris that is internal (Foldes & Buisson, 2009)? Could it reflect the addition of cervical stimulation? Could it be expressed differently in different women as a normal function of individual differences in genitosensory inputs? Can nipples or earlobes be involved with the right stimulation? Stimulation parameters will become important for human brain activation studies and could reveal differences in neural activation patterns with different types of orgasms. To that end, use of subjective orgasm rating scales (e.g., King et al., 2011; Mah & Binik, 2002) would be one important way to correlate the subjective experience with the physiological activation patterns.

For all the questions still needing answers, we may be nearing the time at which we can begin to offer some answers as to why we have sex. For all its primitive reproductive benefits, animal, and especially human, sexuality comes in an astounding variety of behaviors and preferences. In addition to the conditioning data reviewed in this chapter, male goats and sheep cross-fostered to the other mother subsequently display partner preferences for females of the mother's species (Kendrick, Hinton, Atkins, Haupt, & Skinner, 1998). Female bonobos will copulate to resolve intermale conflicts (Parish & De Waal, 2000). Of course, many human sexual practices offer little, if anything, in the way of reproductive success. This can be true even when people satisfactorily go through a full sexual response cycle with oral or anal sexual stimulation, same-sex practices, solitary practices, or fetish activities. Conversely, even when sexual behavior is completely functional in a reproductive sense, it does not necessarily comply with social or cultural norms (e.g., rape or sexual abuse), nor is it necessarily perceived as pleasurable or satisfactory. Some preferences raise tremendous controversy but also vary across cultures or epochs of time within a culture (e.g., rates of anal sex between the original Kinsey et al. [1948, 1953] samples and those of the more recent National Survey of Sexual Health and Behavior [Herbenick et al., 2010a, 2010b]). These and other intricacies of human sexuality strongly suggest that biological predispositions, including primitive sexual reflexes and pleasurable genital feelings, interact with context, learning, and self-referential and normative thinking to determine the meaning of any sexual act or thought. That this integration occurs in the brain makes it the ultimate sex organ.

References

Acosta-Martinez, M., & Etgen, A. M. (2002a). Activation of mu-opioid receptors inhibits lordosis behavior in estrogen and progesterone-primed female rats. *Hormones and Behavior, 41*, 88–100. doi:10.1006/hbeh.2001.1741

Acosta-Martinez, M., & Etgen, A. M. (2002b). The role of delta-opioid receptors in estrogen facilitation of lordosis behavior. *Behavioural Brain Research, 136*, 93–102. doi:10.1016/S0166-4328(02)00103-1

Adachi, H., Sato, Y., Kato, R., Hisasue, S., Suzuki, K., Masumori, N., . . . Tsukamoto, T. (2003). Direct evidence of facilitative actions of dopamine in the medial preoptic area on reflexive and noncontact erections in male rats. *Journal of Urology, 169*, 386–389. doi:10.1016/S0022-5347(05)64133-X

Adler, N. T. (1969). The effect of the male's copulatory behavior on successful pregnancy of the female rat. *Journal of Comparative and Physiological Psychology, 69*, 613–622. doi:10.1037/h0028244

Adler, N. T., Davis, P. G., & Komisaruk, B. R. (1977). Variation in the size and sensitivity of a genital sensory field in relation to the estrous cycle in rats. *Hormones and Behavior, 9*, 334–344. doi:10.1016/0018-506X(77)90068-X

Ågmo, A. (1999). Sexual motivation—An inquiry into events determining the occurrence of sexual behavior. *Behavioural Brain Research, 105*, 129–150. doi:10.1016/S0166-4328(99)00088-1

Ågmo, A. (2002). Copulation-contingent aversive conditioning and sexual incentive motivation in male rats: Evidence for a two-stage process of sexual behavior. *Physiology and Behavior, 77*, 425–435. doi:10.1016/S0031-9384(02)00874-0

Ågmo, A. (2003a). Lack of opioid or dopaminergic effects on unconditioned sexual incentive motivation in male rats. *Behavioral Neuroscience, 117*, 55–68. doi:10.1037/0735-7044.117.1.55

Ågmo, A. (2003b). Unconditioned sexual incentive motivation in the male Norway rat (*Rattus norvegicus*). *Journal of Comparative Psychology, 117*, 3–14. doi:10.1037/0735-7036.117.1.3

Ågmo, A., & Berenfeld, R. (1990). Reinforcing properties of ejaculation in the male rat: The role of opioids and dopamine. *Behavioral Neuroscience, 104*, 177–182. doi:10.1037/0735-7044.104.1.177

Ågmo, A., & Gómez, M. (1993). Sexual reinforcement is blocked by infusion of naloxone into the medial preoptic area. *Behavioral Neuroscience, 107*, 812–818. doi:10.1037/0735-7044.107.5.812

Ahrold, T. K., & Meston, C. M. (2009). Effects of SNS activation on SSRI-induced sexual side effects differ by SSRI. *Journal of Sex and Marital Therapy, 35*, 311–319. doi:10.1080/00926230902851322

Allard, J., Truitt, W. A., McKenna, K. E., & Coolen, L. M. (2005). Spinal cord control of ejaculation. *World Journal of Urology, 23*, 119–126. doi:10.1007/s00345-004-0494-9

Andersson, K.-E. (2011). Mechanisms of penile erection and basis for pharmacological treatment of erectile dysfunction. *Pharmacological Reviews, 63*, 811–859. doi:10.1124/pr.111.004515

Andersson, K.-E., Gemalmaz, H., Waldeck, K., Chapman, T. N., Tuttle, J. B., & Steers, W. D. (1999). The effect of sildenafil on apomorphine-evoked increases in intracavernous pressure in the awake rat. *Journal of Urology, 161*, 1707–1712. doi:10.1016/S0022-5347(05)69009-X

Aragona, B. J., Liu, Y., Yu, Y. J., Curtis, J. T., Detwiler, J. M., Insel, T. R., & Wang, Z. (2006). Nucleus accumbens dopamine differentially mediates the formation and maintenance of monogamous pair bonds. *Nature Neuroscience, 9*, 133–139. doi:10.1038/nn1613

Archer, J. S., Love-Geffen, T. E., Herbst-Damm, K. L., Swinney, D. A., & Chang, J. R. (2006). Effect of estradiol versus estradiol and testosterone on brain-activation patterns in postmenopausal women. *Menopause, 13*, 528–537. doi:10.1097/01.gme.0000188737.46746.cd

Arnow, B. A., Millheiser, L., Garrett, A., Lake, P. M., Glover, G. H., Hill, K. R., & Desmond, J. E. (2009). Women with hypoactive sexual desire disorder compared to normal females: A functional magnetic resonance imaging study. *Neuroscience, 158*, 484–502. doi:10.1016/j.neuroscience.2008.09.044

Aston-Jones, G., & Harris, G. C. (2004). Brain substrates for increased drug seeking during protracted withdrawal. *Neuropharmacology, 47*(Suppl. 1), 167–179. doi:10.1016/j.neuropharm.2004.06.020

Bailey, J. M. (2009). What is sexual orientation and do women have one? *Nebraska Symposium on Motivation Nebraska Symposium on Motivation, 54*, 43–63. doi:10.1007/978-0-387-09556-1_3

Baker, D., Pryce, G., Giovannoni, G., & Thompson, A. J. (2003). The therapeutic potential of cannabis. *Lancet Neurology, 2*, 291–298. doi:10.1016/S1474-4422(03)00381-8

Bakker, J., van Ophemert, J., & Slob, A. K. (1996). Sexual differentiation of odor and partner preference in the rat. *Physiology and Behavior, 60*, 489–494. doi:10.1016/S0031-9384(96)80023-0

Balthazart, J., Reid, J., Absil, P., Foidart, A., & Ball, G. F. (1995). Appetitive as well as consummatory aspects of male sexual behavior in quail are activated by androgens and estrogens. *Behavioral Neuroscience, 109*, 485–501. doi:10.1037/0735-7044.109.3.485

Bancroft, J., & Janssen, E. (2000). The dual control model of male sexual response: A theoretical approach to centrally mediated erectile dysfunction. *Neuroscience and Biobehavioral Reviews, 24*, 571–579. doi:10.1016/S0149-7634(00)00024-5

Bancroft, J. H. (1989). *Human sexuality and its problems.* Edinburgh, Scotland: Churchill Livingstone.

Band, L. C., & Hull, E. M. (1990). Morphine and dynorphin(1–13) microinjected into the medial preoptic area and nucleus accumbens: Effects on sexual behavior in male rats. *Brain Research, 524*, 77–84. doi:10.1016/0006-8993(90)90494-V

Barfield, R. J., & Sachs, B. (1968). Sexual behavior: Stimulation by painful electrical shock to the skin in male rats. *Science, 161*, 392–395. doi:10.1126/science.161.3839.392

Barlow, D. H. (1986). Causes of sexual dysfunction. *Journal of Consulting and Clinical Psychology, 54*, 140–148. doi:10.1037/0022-006X.54.2.140

Barnett, S. A. (1963). *The rat: A study in behavior.* Chicago, IL: Aldine.

Basson, R. (2005). Women's sexual dysfunction: Revised and expanded definitions. *Canadian Medical Association Journal, 172*, 1327–1333. doi:10.1503/cmaj.1020174

Basson, R., McInnes, R., Smith, M. D., Hodgson, G., & Koppiker, N. (2002). Efficacy and safety of sildenafil citrate in women with sexual dysfunction associated with female sexual arousal disorder. *Journal of Women's Health and Gender-Based Medicine, 11*, 367–377. doi:10.1089/152460902317586001

Beach, F. A. (1956). Characteristics of masculine "sex drive." In M. R. Jones (Ed.), *Nebraska Symposium on Motivation Nebraska Symposium on Motivation* (pp. 1–32). Lincoln: University of Nebraska.

Beach, F. A. (1976). Sexual attractivity, proceptivity, and receptivity in female mammals. *Hormones and Behavior, 7*, 105–138. doi:10.1016/0018-506X(76)90008-8

Beach, F. A. (1978). Animal models for human sexuality. *Ciba Foundation Symposium, 16*, 113–143.

Beach, F. A., & Fowler, H. (1959). Effects of situational anxiety on sexual behavior in male rats. *Journal of Comparative and Physiological Psychology, 52*, 245–248. doi:10.1037/h0040726

Beach, F. A., & Jordan, L. (1956). Sexual exhaustion and recovery in the male rat. *Quarterly Journal of Experimental Psychology, 8*, 121–133. doi:10.1080/17470215608416811

Beauregard, M., Lévesque, J., & Bourgouin, P. (2001). Neural correlates of conscious self-regulation of emotion. *Journal of Neuroscience, 21*, RC165.

Bechara, A. (2005). Decision making, impulse control and loss of willpower to resist drugs: A neurocognitive perspective. *Nature Neuroscience, 8*, 1458–1463. doi:10.1038/nn1584

Becker, J. B., Rudick, C. N., & Jenkins, W. J. (2001). The role of dopamine in the nucleus accumbens and striatum during sexual behavior in the female rat. *Journal of Neuroscience, 21*, 3236–3241.

Berman, J. R., Berman, L. A., Lin, H., Flaherty, E., Lahey, N., Goldstein, I., & Kantey-Kiser, J. (2001). Effect of sildenafil on subjective and physiologic parameters of the female sexual response in women with sexual arousal disorder. *Journal of Sex and Marital Therapy, 27*, 411–420. doi:10.1080/713846815

Bermant, G. (1961). Response latencies of female rats during sexual intercourse. *Science, 133*, 1771–1773. doi:10.1126/science.133.3466.1771

Bermant, G., & Westbrook, W. H. (1966). Peripheral factors in the regulation of sexual contact by female rats. *Journal of Comparative and Physiological Psychology, 61*, 244–250. doi:10.1037/h0023152

Bernabé, J., Rampin, O., Sachs, B. D., & Giuliano, F. (1999). Intracavernous pressure during erection in rats: An integrative approach based on telemetric recording. *American Journal of Physiology, 276*(2, Pt. 2), R441–R449.

Berridge, K. C. (2009). "Liking" and "wanting" food rewards: Brain substrates and roles in eating disorders. *Physiology and Behavior, 97*, 537–550. doi:10.1016/j.physbeh.2009.02.044

Bianchi-Demicheli, F., Cojan, Y., Waber, L., Recordon, N., Vuilleumier, P., & Ortigue, S. (2011). Neural bases of hypoactive sexual desire disorder in women: An event-related FMRI study. *Journal of Sexual Medicine, 8*, 2546–2559. doi:10.1111/j.1743-6109.2011.02376.x

Bijlsma, E. Y., Jonker, M., Bloemers, J., Tuiten, A., Olivier, B., & Oosting, R. S. (2012). The facilitating effects of testosterone–sildenafil cotreatment on sexual behavior in sub-primed female rats depends on the delayed effects of testosterone. In *Abstracts of the 2012 Annual Meeting of the Society for Neuroscience* (2012 Neuroscience Meeting Planner). Retrieved from http://www.abstractsonline.com/plan/start.aspx?mkey=%7B70007181-01C9-4DE9-A0A2-EEBFA14CD9F1%7D

Bitran, D., & Hull, E. M. (1987). Pharmacological analysis of male rat sexual behavior. *Neuroscience and Biobehavioral Reviews, 11*, 365–389. doi:10.1016/S0149-7634(87)80008-8

Blackburn, J. R., Pfaus, J. G., & Phillips, A. G. (1992). Dopamine function in appetitive and defensive behaviors. *Progress in Neurobiology, 39*, 247–279. doi:10.1016/0301-0082(92)90018-A

Blood, A. J., & Zatorre, R. J. (2001). Intensely pleasurable responses to music correlate with activity in brain regions implicated in reward and emotion. *Proceedings of the National Academy of Sciences of the United States of America, 98*, 11818–11823. doi:10.1073/pnas.191355898

Bohlen, J. G., Held, J. P., Sanderson, M. O., & Ahlgren, A. (1982). The female orgasm: Pelvic contractions. *Archives of Sexual Behavior, 11*, 367–386. doi:10.1007/BF01541570

Boling, J. L., & Blandau, R. J. (1939). The estrogen-progesterone induction of mating responses in the spayed female rat. *Endocrinology, 25*, 359–364. doi:10.1210/endo-25-3-359

Bonthuis, P. J., Cox, K. H., Searcy, B. T., Kumar, P., Tobet, S., & Rissman, E. F. (2010). Of mice and rats: Key species variations in the sexual differentiation of brain and behavior. *Frontiers in Neuroendocrinology, 31*, 341–358. doi:10.1016/j.yfrne.2010.05.001

Both, S., Brauer, M., & Laan, E. (2011). Classical conditioning of sexual response in women: A replication. *Journal of Sexual Medicine, 8*, 3116–3131. doi:10.1111/j.1743-6109.2011.02453.x

Both, S., Laan, E., Spiering, M., Nilsson, T., Oomens, S., & Everaerd, W. (2008). Appetitive and aversive classical conditioning of female sexual response. *Journal of Sexual Medicine, 5*, 1386–1401. doi:10.1111/j.1743-6109.2008.00815.x

Both, S., Spiering, M., Laan, E., Belcome, S., van den Heuvel, B., & Everaerd, W. (2008). Unconscious classical conditioning of sexual arousal: Evidence for the conditioning of female genital arousal to subliminally presented sexual stimuli. *Journal of Sexual Medicine, 5*, 100–109.

Breiter, H. C., Gollub, R. L., Weisskoff, R. M., Kennedy, D. N., Makris, N., Berke, J. D., & Hyman, S. E. (1997). Acute effects of cocaine on human brain activity and emotion. *Neuron, 19*, 591–611. doi:10.1016/S0896-6273(00)80374-8

Brennan, P. A., & Keverne, E. B. (1997). Neural mechanisms of mammalian olfactory learning. *Progress in Neurobiology, 51*, 457–481. doi:10.1016/S0301-0082(96)00069-X

Bühler, M., Vollstädt-Klein, S., Klemen, J., & Smolka, M. N. (2008). Does erotic stimulus presentation design affect brain activation patterns? Event-related vs. blocked fMRI designs. *Behavioral and Brain Functions, 4*, 30. doi:10.1186/1744-9081-4-30

Bush, G., Vogt, B. A., Holmes, J., Dale, A. M., Greve, D., Jenike, M. A., & Rosen, B. R. (2002). Dorsal anterior cingulated cortex: A role in reward-based decision making. *Proceedings of the National Academy of Sciences of the United States of America, 99*, 523–528. doi:10.1073/pnas.012470999

Caggiula, A. R. (1972). Shock-elicited copulation and aggression in male rats. *Journal of Comparative and Physiological Psychology, 80*, 393–397. doi:10.1037/h0032987

Cai, R. S., Alexander, M. S., & Marson, L. (2008). Activation of somatosensory afferents elicit changes in vaginal blood flow and the urethrogenital reflex via autonomic efferents. *Journal of Urology, 180*, 1167–1172. doi:10.1016/j.juro.2008.04.139

Calhoun, J. B. (1962). *The ecology and sociology of the Norway rat* (U.S. Public Health Service Publication No. 1008). Washington, DC: U.S. Government Printing Office.

Cantor, J. M., Binik, Y. M., & Pfaus, J. G. (1999). Chronic fluoxetine inhibits sexual behavior in the male rat: Reversal with oxytocin. *Psychopharmacology, 144*, 355–362. doi:10.1007/s002130051018

Carr, W. J., Wylie, N. R., & Loeb, L. S. (1970). Responses of adult and immature rats to sex odors. *Journal of Comparative and Physiological Psychology, 72*, 51–59. doi:10.1037/h0029326

Carter, C. S., Braver, T. S., Barch, D. M., Botvinick, M. M., Noll, D., & Cohen, J. D. (1998). Anterior cingulate cortex, error detection, and the online monitoring of performance. *Science, 280*, 747–749. doi:10.1126/science.280.5364.747

Caspers, S., Zilles, K., Laird, A. R., & Eickhoff, S. B. (2010). ALE meta-analysis of action observation and imitation in the human brain. *NeuroImage, 50*, 1148–1167. doi:10.1016/j.neuroimage.2009.12.112

Castilla, J., Barrio, G., Belza, M., & de la Fuente, L. (1999). Drug and alcohol consumption and sexual risk behavior among young adults: Results from a national survey. *Drug and Alcohol Dependence, 56*, 47–53. doi:10.1016/S0376-8716(99)00008-3

Cera, N., Di Pierro, E. D., Sepede, G., Gambi, F., Perrucci, M. G., Merla, A., & Ferretti, A. (2012). The role of left superior parietal lobe in male sexual behavior: Dynamics of distinct components revealed by fMRI. *Journal of Sexual Medicine, 6*, 1602–1612. doi:10.1111/j.1743-6109.2012.02719.x

Chessick, R. D. (1960). The "pharmacogenic orgasm" in the drug addict. *Archives of General Psychiatry, 3*, 545–556. doi:10.1001/archpsyc.1960.01710050095010

Childress, A. R., Ehrman, R. N., Wang, Z., Li, Y., Sciortino, N., Hakun, J., . . . O'Brien, C. P. (2008). Prelude to passion: Limbic activation by "unseen" drug and sexual cues. *PLoS One, 3*, e1506.

Chivers, M. L., & Bailey, J. M. (2005). A sex difference in features that elicit genital response. *Biological Psychology, 70*, 115–120. doi:10.1016/j.biopsycho.2004.12.002

Chivers, M. L., & Rosen, R. C. (2010). Phosphodiesterase type 5 inhibitors and female sexual response: Faulty protocols or paradigms? *Journal of Sexual Medicine, 7*, 858–872. doi:10.1111/j.1743-6109.2009.01599.x

Chivers, M. L., Roy, C., Grimbos, T., Cantor, J. M., & Seto, M. C. (in press). Specificity of sexual arousal for preferred sexual activities in men and women with conventional and masochistic sexual interests. *Archives of Sexual Behavior.*

Chivers, M. L., Seto, M. C., Lalumière, M. L., Laan, E., & Grimbos, T. (2010). Agreement of self-reported and genital measures of sexual arousal in men and women: A meta-analysis. *Archives of Sexual Behavior, 39*, 5–56. doi:10.1007/s10508-009-9556-9

Chu, H. P., & Etgen, A. M. (1997). A potential role of cyclic GMP in the regulation of lordosis behavior of female rats. *Hormones and Behavior, 32*, 125–132. doi:10.1006/hbeh.1997.1413

Cibrian-Llanderal, T., Rosas-Aguilar, V., Triana-Del Rio, R., Perez, C. A., Manzo, J., Garcia, L. I., & Coria-Avila, G. A. (2012). Enhanced D2-type receptor activity facilitates the development of conditioned same-sex partner preference in male rats. *Pharmacology, Biochemistry and Behavior, 102*, 177–183. doi:10.1016/j.pbb.2012.04.007

Clark, J. T., Smith, E. R., & Davidson, J. M. (1985). Evidence for the modulation of sexual behavior by alpha-adrenoceptors in male rats. *Neuroendocrinology, 41*, 36–43. doi:10.1159/000124151

Codispoti, M., Ferrari, V., & Bradley, M. M. (2006). Repetitive picture processing: Autonomic and cortical correlates. *Brain Research, 1068*, 213–220. doi:10.1016/j.brainres.2005.11.009

Coolen, L. M., Fitzgerald, M. E., Yu, L., & Lehman, M. N. (2004). Activation of mu opioid receptors in the medial preoptic area following copulation in male rats. *Neuroscience, 124*, 11–21. doi:10.1016/j.neuroscience.2003.10.045

Coolen, L. M., Peters, H. J., & Veening, J. G. (1998). Anatomical interrelationships of the medial preoptic area and other brain regions activated following male sexual behavior: A combined fos and tract-tracing study. *Journal of Comparative Neurology, 397*, 421–435. doi:10.1002/(SICI)1096-9861(19980803)397:3<421::AID-CNE8>3.0.CO;2-4

Coria-Avila, G. A., Ouimet, A. J., Pacheco, P., Manzo, J., & Pfaus, J. G. (2005). Olfactory conditioned partner preference in the female rat. *Behavioral Neuroscience, 119*, 716–725. doi:10.1037/0735-7044.119.3.716

Coria-Avila, G. A., & Pfaus, J. G. (2007). Neuronal activation by stimuli that predict sexual reward in female rats. *Neuroscience, 148*, 623–632. doi:10.1016/j.neuroscience.2007.05.052

Coria-Avila, G. A., Solomon, C. E., Barbosa Vargas, E., Lemme, I., Ryan, R., Ménard, S., . . . Pfaus, J. G. (2008). Neurochemical basis of conditioned partner preference in the female rat: I. Disruption by naloxone. *Behavioral Neuroscience, 122*, 385–395. doi:10.1037/0735-7044.122.2.385

Corona, R., Larriva-Sahd, J., & Paredes, R. G. (2011). Paced mating increases the number of adult new born cells in the internal cellular (granular) layer of the accessory olfactory bulb. *PLoS ONE, 6*, e19380. doi:10.1371/journal.pone.0019380

Costa, R. M., & Esteves, F. (2008). Skin conductance responses to visual sexual stimuli. *International Journal of Psychophysiology, 67*, 64–69. doi:10.1016/j.ijpsycho.2007.10.005

Courtois, F., Charvier, K., Vézina, J. G., Journel, N. M., Carrier, S., Jacquemin, G., & Côté, I. (2011). Assessing and conceptualizing orgasm after spinal cord injury. *BJU International, 108*, 1624–1633. doi:10.1111/j.1464-410X.2011.10168.x

Craig, W. (1918). Appetites and aversions as constituents of instincts. *Biological Bulletin, 34*, 91–107. doi:10.2307/1536346

Crenshaw, T. L., & Goldberg, J. P. (1996). *Sexual pharmacology*. New York, NY: W. W. Norton.

Critchley, H. D., Corfield, D. R., Chandler, M. P., Mathias, C. J., & Dolan, R. J. (2000). Cerebral correlates of autonomic cardiovascular arousal: A functional neuroimaging investigation in humans. *Journal of Physiology, 523*, 259–270. doi:10.1111/j.1469-7793.2000.t01-1-00259.x

Critchley, H. D., Nagai, Y., Gray, M. A., & Mathias, C. J. (2011). Dissecting axes of autonomic control in humans: Insights from neuroimaging. *Autonomic Neuroscience: Basic and Clinical, 161*, 34–42. doi:10.1016/j.autneu.2010.09.005

Crowley, W. R., Popolow, H. B., & Ward, O. B., Jr. (1973). From dud to stud: Copulatory behavior elicited through conditioned arousal in sexually inactive male rats. *Physiology and Behavior, 10*, 391–394. doi:10.1016/0031-9384(73)90328-4

Cutmore, T. R., & Zamble, E. (1988). A Pavlovian procedure for improving sexual performance of noncopulating male rats. *Archives of Sexual Behavior, 17*, 371–380. doi:10.1007/BF01541814

Darwin, C. (1859). *The origin of species*. London, England: A. L. Burt.

Devidze, N., Zhang, Q., Zhou, J., Lee, A. W., Pataky, S., Kow, L. M., & Pfaff, D. W. (2008). Presynaptic actions of opioid receptor agonists in ventromedial hypothalamic neurons in estrogen- and oil-treated female mice. *Neuroscience, 152*, 942–949. doi:10.1016/j.neuroscience.2008.01.033

Diamond, L. E., Earle, D. C., Heiman, J. R., Rosen, R. C., Perelman, M. A., & Harning, R. (2006). An effect on the subjective sexual response in premenopausal women with sexual arousal disorder by bremelanotide (PT-141), a melanocortin receptor agonist. *Journal of Sexual Medicine, 3*, 628–638. doi:10.1111/j.1743-6109.2006.00268.x

Dominguez, J. M., & Hull, E. M. (2010). Serotonin impairs copulation and attenuates ejaculation-induced glutamate activity in the medial preoptic area. *Behavioral Neuroscience, 124*, 554–557. doi:10.1037/a0020353

Domjan, M., & Hall, S. (1986). Determinants of social proximity in Japanese quail (*Coturnix coturnix japonica*): Male behavior. *Journal of Comparative Psychology, 100*, 59–67. doi:10.1037/0735-7036.100.1.59

Domjan, M., O'Vary, D., & Greene, P. (1988). Conditioning of appetitive and consummatory sexual behavior in male Japanese quail. *Journal of the Experimental Analysis of Behavior, 50*, 505–519. doi:10.1901/jeab.1988.50-505

Dornan, W. A., & Malsbury, C. W. (1989). Neuropeptides and male sexual behavior. *Neuroscience and Biobehavioral Reviews, 13*, 1–15. doi:10.1016/S0149-7634(89)80046-6

Drewett, R. F. (1973). Sexual behaviour and sexual motivation in the female rat. *Nature, 242*, 476–477. doi:10.1038/242476a0

Ellis, H. (1900). The analysis of the sexual impulse. *Alienist and Neurologist, 21*, 247–262.

Erskine, M. S. (1989). Solicitation behavior in the estrous female rat: A review. *Hormones and Behavior, 23*, 473–502. doi:10.1016/0018-506X(89)90037-8

Erskine, M. S., & Baum, M. J. (1982). Effects paced coital stimulation on termination of estrus and brain indoleamine levels in female rats. *Pharmacology, Biochemistry and Behavior, 17*, 857–861. doi:10.1016/0091-3057(82)90373-2

Everaerd, W. (1995). Information processing approach and the sexual response in human studies. In J. Bancroft (Ed.), *The pharmacology of sexual function and dysfunction* (pp. 175–184). Amsterdam, the Netherlands: Elsevier.

Everitt, B. J. (1990). Sexual motivation: A neural and behavioral analysis of the mechanisms underlying appetitive and copulatory responses of male rats. *Neuroscience and Biobehavioral Reviews, 14*, 217–232. doi:10.1016/S0149-7634(05)80222-2

Everitt, B. J., Fray, P., Kostarczyk, E., Taylor, S., & Stacey, P. (1987). Studies of instrumental behavior with sexual reinforcement in male rats (*Rattus norvegicus*): I. Control by brief visual stimuli paired with a receptive female. *Journal of Comparative Psychology, 101*, 395–406. doi:10.1037/0735-7036.101.4.395

Exton, M. S., Bindert, A., Kruger, T., Scheller, F., Hartmann, U., & Schedlowski, M. (1999). Cardiovascular and endocrine alterations after masturbation-induced orgasm in women. *Psychosomatic Medicine, 61*, 280–289.

Fedirchuk, B., Song, L., Downie, J. W., & Shefchyk, S. J. (1992). Spinal distribution of extracellular field potentials generated by electrical stimulation of pudendal and perineal afferents in the cat. *Experimental Brain Research, 89*, 517–520. doi:10.1007/BF00229876

Fernández-Guasti, A., & Rodríguez-Manzo, G. (2003). Pharmacological and physiological aspects of sexual exhaustion in male rats. *Scandinavian Journal of Psychology, 44*, 257–263. doi:10.1111/1467-9450.00343

Ferrari, F., Ottani, A., & Giuliani, D. (2000). Inhibitory effects of the cannabinoid agonist HU 210 on rat sexual behavior. *Physiology and Behavior, 69*, 547–554. doi:10.1016/S0031-9384(00)00214-6

Ferretti, A., Caulo, M., Del Gratta, C., Di Matteo, R., Merla, A., Montorsi, F., & Romani, L. (2005). Dynamics of male sexual arousal: Distinct components of brain activation revealed by fMRI. *NeuroImage, 26*, 1086–1096. doi:10.1016/j.neuroimage.2005.03.025

Ferster, C. B., & Skinner, B. F. (1957). *Schedules of reinforcement*. New York, NY: Appleton-Century-Crofts. doi:10.1037/10627-000

Fiorino, D. F., Coury, A., & Phillips, A. G. (1997). Dynamic changes in nucleus accumbens dopamine efflux during the Coolidge effect in male rats. *Journal of Neuroscience, 17*, 4849–4855.

Fisher, H. E., Aron, A., Mashek, D., Li, H., & Brown, L. L. (2002). Defining the brain systems of lust, romantic attraction, and attachment. *Archives of Sexual Behavior, 31*, 413–419. doi:10.1023/A:1019888024255

Foldes, P., & Buisson, O. (2009). The clitoral complex: A dynamic sonographic study. *Journal of Sexual Medicine, 6*, 1223–1231. doi:10.1111/j.1743-6109.2009.01231.x

Forbes, C. E., & Grafman, J. (2010). The role of the human prefrontal cortex in social cognition and moral judgment. *Annual Review of*

Neuroscience, 33, 299–324. doi:10.1146/annurev-neuro-060909-153230

French, D., Fitzpatrick, D., & Law, O. T. (1972). Operant investigation of mating preference in female rats. *Journal of Comparative and Physiological Psychology, 81*, 226–232. doi:10.1037/h0033535

Frohmader, K. S., Bateman, K. L., Lehman, M. N., & Coolen, L. M. (2010). Effects of methamphetamine on sexual performance and compulsive sexual behavior in male rats. *Psychopharmacology, 212*, 93–104. doi:10.1007/s00213-010-1930-8

Frye, C. A., & Rhodes, M. E. (2010). Fluoxetine-induced decrements in sexual responses of female rats and hamsters are reversed by 3α,5α-THP. *Journal of Sexual Medicine, 7*, 2670–2680. doi:10.1111/j.1743-6109.2010.01814.x

Gabella, G. (1995). Autonomic nervous system. In G. Paxinos (Ed.), *The rat nervous system* (2nd ed., pp. 81–103). New York, NY: Academic Press.

Garavan, H., Pankiewicz, J., Bloom, A., Cho, J. K., Sperry, L., Ross, T. J., . . . Stein, E. A. (2000). Cue-induced cocaine craving: Neuroanatomical specificity for drug users and drug stimuli. *American Journal of Psychiatry, 157*, 1789–1798. doi:10.1176/appi.ajp.157.11.1789

García-Horsman, S. P., Agmo, A., & Paredes, R. G. (2008). Infusions of naloxone into the medial preoptic area, ventromedial nucleus of the hypothalamus, and amygdala block conditioned place preference induced by paced mating behavior. *Hormones and Behavior, 54*, 709–716. doi:10.1016/j.yhbeh.2008.07.011

Gazzola, V., Spezio, M. L., Etzel, J. A., Castelli, F., Adolphs, R., & Keysers, C. (2012). Primary somatosensory cortex discriminates affective significance in social touch. *Proceedings of the National Academy of Sciences of the United States of America, 109*, E1657–E1666. doi:10.1073/pnas.1113211109

Georgescu, M., Cyr, D., & Pfaus, J. G. (2012). AMPA/kainate receptors in the ventromedial hypothalamus mediate the effects of glutamate on estrus termination in the rat. *Pharmacology Biochemistry and Behavior, 102*, 146–150. doi:10.1016/j.pbb.2012.04.001

Georgescu, M., Sabongui, A., Del Corpo, A., Marsan, L., & Pfaus, J. G. (2009). Vaginocervical stimulation induces Fos in glutamate neurons in the ventromedial hypothalamus: Attenuation by estrogen and progesterone. *Hormones and Behavior, 56*, 450–456. doi:10.1016/j.yhbeh.2009.07.014

Georgiadis, J. R., Farrell, M., Boessen, R., Denton, D., Gavrilescu, M., Kortekaas, R., & Egan, G. (2010). Dynamic subcortical blood flow during male sexual activity with ecological validity: A perfusion fMRI study. *NeuroImage, 50*, 208–216. doi:10.1016/j.neuroimage.2009.12.034

Georgiadis, J. R., Kortekaas, R., Kuipers, R., Nieuwenburg, A., Pruim, J., Reinders, A. A. T. S., & Holstege, G. (2006). Regional cerebral blood flow changes associated with clitorally induced orgasm in healthy women. *European Journal of Neuroscience, 24*, 3305–3316. doi:10.1111/j.1460-9568.2006.05206.x

Georgiadis, J. R., & Kringelbach, M. L. (2012). The human sexual response cycle: Brain imaging evidence linking sex to other pleasures. *Progress in Neurobiology, 98*, 49–81. doi:10.1016/j.pneurobio.2012.05.004

Georgiadis, J. R., Kringelbach, M. L., & Pfaus, J. G. (2012). Sex for fun: Bringing together human and animal neurobiology. *Nature Reviews Urology, 9*, 486–498. doi:10.1038/nrurol.2012.151

Gilman, D. P., & Westbrook, W. H. (1978). Mating preference and sexual reinforcement in female rats. *Physiology and Behavior, 20*, 11–14. doi:10.1016/0031-9384(78)90195-6

Giraldi, A., Marson, L., Nappi, R., Pfaus, J. G., Traish, A. M., Vardi, Y., & Goldstein, I. (2004). Physiology of female sexual function: Animal models. *Journal of Sexual Medicine, 1*, 237–253. doi:10.1111/j.1743-6109.04037.x

Giuliano, F., Pfaus, J. G., Srilatha, B., Hedlund, P., Hisasue, S., Marson, L., & Wallen, K. (2010). Experimental models for the study of female and male sexual function. *Journal of Sexual Medicine, 7*, 2970–2995. doi:10.1111/j.1743-6109.2010.01960.x

Giuliano, F., Rampin, O., & Allard, J. (2002). Neurophysiology and pharmacology of female genital sexual response. *Journal of Sex and Marital Therapy, 28*(Suppl. 1), 101–121. doi:10.1080/00926230252851230

Gizewski, E. R., Krause, E., Karama, S., Baars, A., Senf, W., & Forsting, M. (2006). There are differences in cerebral activation between females in distinct menstrual phases during viewing of erotic stimuli: A fMRI study. *Experimental Brain Research, 174*, 101–108. doi:10.1007/s00221-006-0429-3

Goldman-Rakic, P. S. (1987). Development of cortical circuitry and cognitive function. *Child Development, 58*, 601–622. doi:10.2307/1130201

Gorzalka, B. B., Hill, M. N., & Chang, S. C. (2010). Male-female differences in the effects of cannabinoids on sexual behavior and gonadal hormone function. *Hormones and Behavior, 58*, 91–99. doi:10.1016/j.yhbeh.2009.08.009

Gorzalka, B. B., Morish, A. D., & Hill, M. N. (2008). Endocannabinoid modulation of male sexual behavior. *Psychopharmacology, 198*, 479–486. doi:10.1007/s00213-007-0901-1

Gościński, I., Kwiatkowski, S., Polak, J., & Orlowiejska, M. (1997). The Kluver-Bucy syndrome. *Acta Neurochirurgica, 139*, 303–306. doi:10.1007/BF01808825

Graham, J. M., & Desjardins, C. (1980). Classical conditioning: Induction of luteinizing hormone and testosterone secretion in anticipation of sexual activity. *Science, 210*, 1039–1041. doi:10.1126/science.7434016

Graham, M. D., & Pfaus, J. G. (2010). Differential regulation of female sexual behaviour by dopamine agonists in the medial preoptic area. *Pharmacology Biochemistry and Behavior, 97*, 284–292. doi:10.1016/j.pbb.2010.08.012

Graham, M. D., & Pfaus, J. G. (2012). Differential effects of dopamine antagonists infused to the medial preoptic area on the sexual behavior of female rats primed with estrogen and progesterone. *Pharmacology Biochemistry and Behavior, 102*, 532–539. doi:10.1016/j.pbb.2012.06.020

Green, J. D., Clemente, C. D., & de Groot, J. (1957). Rhinencephalic lesions and behavior in cats: An analysis of the Kluver-Bucy syndrome with particular reference to normal and abnormal sexual behavior. *Journal of Comparative Neurology, 108*, 505–545. doi:10.1002/cne.901080308

Guo, G., Tong, Y., Xie, C. W., & Lange, L. A. (2007). Dopamine transporter, gender, and number of sexual partners among young adults. *European Journal of Human Genetics, 15*, 279–287. doi:10.1038/sj.ejhg.5201763

Guo, G., & Tong, Y. Y. (2006). Age at first sexual intercourse, genes, and social context: Evidence from twins and the dopamine D4 receptor gene. *Demography, 43*, 747–769. doi:10.1353/dem.2006.0029

Hajós, M., Gartside, S. E., Varga, V., & Sharp, T. (2003). In vivo inhibition of neuronal activity in the rat ventromedial prefrontal cortex by midbrain-raphe nuclei: Role of 5-HT1A receptors. *Neuropharmacology, 45*, 72–81. doi:10.1016/S0028-3908(03)00139-4

Halata, Z., & Munger, B. L. (1986). The neuroanatomical basis for the protopathic sensibility of the human glans penis. *Brain Research, 371*, 205–230. doi:10.1016/0006-8993(86)90357-4

Hallam, T. J., Spana, C., Earle, D. C., Shadiack, A. M., & Sharma, S. D. (2007). Melanocortins in the treatment of male and female sexual dysfunction. *Current Topics in Medicinal Chemistry, 7*, 1137–1144. doi:10.2174/156802607780906681

Hamani, C., Mayberg, H., Stone, S., Laxton, A., Haber, S., & Lozano, A. M. (2011). The subcallosal cingulate gyrus in the context of major depression. *Biological Psychiatry, 69*, 301–308. doi:10.1016/j.biopsych.2010.09.034

Hayward, S. C. (1957). Modification of sexual behavior of the male albino rat. *Journal of Comparative and Physiological Psychology, 50*, 70–73. doi:10.1037/h0046203

Heiman, J. R. (1977). Psychophysiological exploration of sexual arousal patterns in females and males. *Psychophysiology, 14*, 266–274. doi:10.1111/j.1469-8986.1977.tb01173.x

Heimer, L., & Larsson, K. (1967). Impairment of mating behavior in male rats following lesions in the preoptic area-anterior hypothalamic continuum. *Brain Research, 3*, 248–263. doi:10.1016/0006-8993(67)90076-5

Heinzel, A., Walter, M., Schneider, F., Rotte, M., Matthiae, C., Tempelmann, C., & Northoff, G. (2006). Self-related processing in the sexual domain: A parametric event-related fMRI study reveals neural activity in ventral cortical midline structures. *Social Neuroscience, 1*, 41–51. doi:10.1080/17470910600663137

Herbenick, D., Reece, M., Schick, V., Sanders, S. A., Dodge, B., & Fortenberry, J. D. (2010a). Sexual behavior in the United States: Results from a national probability sample of men and women, ages 14–94. *Journal of Sexual Medicine, 7*(Suppl. 5), 255–265. doi:10.1111/j.1743-6109.2010.02012.x

Herbenick, D., Reece, M., Schick, V., Sanders, S. A., Dodge, B., & Fortenberry, J. D. (2010b). Sexual behaviors, relationships, and perceived health status among adult women in the United States: Results from a national probability sample. *Journal of Sexual Medicine, 7*(Suppl. 5), 277–290. doi:10.1111/j.1743-6109.2010.02010.x

Hermans, E. J., Bos, P. A., Ossewaarde, L., Ramsey, N. F., Fernandez, G., & van Honk, J. (2010). Effects of exogenous testosterone on the ventral striatal BOLD response during reward anticipation in healthy women. *NeuroImage, 52*, 277–283. doi:10.1016/j.neuroimage.2010.04.019

Hoffmann, H. (2012). Considering the role of conditioning in sexual orientation. *Archives of Sexual Behavior, 41*, 63–71. doi:10.1007/s10508-012-9915-9

Hoffmann, H., Janssen, E., & Turner, S. L. (2004). Classical conditioning of sexual arousal in women and men: Effects of varying awareness and biological relevance of the conditioned stimulus. *Archives of Sexual Behavior, 33*, 43–53. doi:10.1023/B:ASEB.0000007461.59019.d3

Hollis, K. L., Cadieux, E. L., & Colbert, M. M. (1989). The biological function of Pavlovian conditioning: A mechanism for mating success in the blue gourami. *Journal of Comparative Psychology, 103*, 115–121. doi:10.1037/0735-7036.103.2.115

Honda, C. N. (1985). Visceral and somatic afferent convergence onto neurons near the central canal in the sacral spinal cord of the cat. *Journal of Neurophysiology, 53*, 1059–1078.

Hoon, P. W. (1984). Physiologic assessment of sexual response in women: The unfulfilled promise.

Clinical Obstetrics and Gynecology, 27, 767–780. doi:10.1097/00003081-198409000-00025

Hoon, P. W., Wincze, J. P., & Hoon, E. F. (1976). Physiological assessment of sexual arousal in women. *Psychophysiology, 13*, 196–204. doi:10.1111/j.1469-8986.1976.tb00097.x

Hoshina, Y., Takeo, T., Nakano, K., Sato, T., & Sakuma, Y. (1994). Axon-sparing lesion of the preoptic area enhances receptivity and diminishes proceptivity among components of female rat sexual behavior. *Behavioural Brain Research, 61*, 197–204. doi:10.1016/0166-4328(94)90160-0

Hoy, S. M., & Scott, L. J. (2010). Dapoxetione: In premature ejaculation. *Drugs, 70*, 1433–1443. doi:10.2165/11204750-000000000-00000

Hughes, A. M., Everitt, B. J., & Herbert, J. (1987). Selective effects of beta-endorphin infused into the hypothalamus, preoptic area and bed nucleus of the stria terminalis on the sexual and ingestive behaviour of male rats. *Neuroscience, 23*, 1063–1073. doi:10.1016/0306-4522(87)90181-3

Hughes, A. M., Everitt, B. J., & Herbert, J. (1990). Comparative effects of preoptic area infusions of opioid peptides, lesions and castration on sexual behaviour in male rats: Studies of instrumental behaviour, conditioned place preference and partner preference. *Psychopharmacology, 102*, 243–256. doi:10.1007/BF02245929

Hull, C. (1943). *Principles of behavior*. New York, NY: Appleton-Century-Crofts.

Hull, E. M., & Dominguez, J. M. (2007). Sexual behavior in male rodents. *Hormones and Behavior, 52*, 45–55. doi:10.1016/j.yhbeh.2007.03.030

Hull, E. M., Lorrain, D. S., Du, J., Matuszewich, L., Lunley, L. A., Putnam, S. K., & Moses, J. (1999). Hormone-neurotransmitter interactions in the control of sexual behavior. *Behavioural Brain Research, 105*, 105–116. doi:10.1016/S0166-4328(99)00086-8

Hull, E. M., Warner, R. K., Bazzett, T. J., Eaton, R. C., Thompson, J. T., & Scaletta, L. L. (1989). D2/D1 ratio in the medial preoptic area affects copulation of male rats. *Journal of Pharmacology and Experimental Therapeutics, 251*, 422–427.

Ishai, A. (2007). Sex, beauty and the orbitofrontal cortex. *International Journal of Psychophysiology, 63*, 181–185. doi:10.1016/j.ijpsycho.2006.03.010

Ismail, N., Girard-Bériault, F., Nakanishi, S., & Pfaus, J. G. (2009). Naloxone, but not flupenthixol, disrupts the development of conditioned ejaculatory preference in the male rat. *Behavioral Neuroscience, 123*, 992–999. doi:10.1037/a0017096

Ismail, N., Zhao, Y., & Pfaus, J. G. (2008). Context-dependent acquisition of copulatory behavior in the male rat: Role of female availability. *Behavioral Neuroscience, 122*, 991–997. doi:10.1037/a0012831

Iverson, S., Iverson, L., & Saper, C. B. (2000). The autonomic nervous system and the hypothalamus. In E. R. Kandel, J. H. Schwartz, & T. M. Jessel (Eds.), *Principles of neural science* (pp. 960–981). New York, NY: McGraw-Hill.

Jenkins, W. J., & Becker, J. B. (2003). Female rats develop conditioned place preference for sex at their preferred interval. *Hormones and Behavior, 43*, 503–507. doi:10.1016/S0018-506X(03)00031-X

Johnson, R. D., & Halata, Z. (1991). Topography and ultrastructure of sensory nerve endings of the glans penis of the rat. *Journal of Comparative Neurology, 312*, 299–310. doi:10.1002/cne.903120212

Johnston, R. E., Zahorik, D. M., Immler, K., & Zakon, H. (1978). Alterations of male sexual behavior by learned aversions to hamster vaginal secretion. *Journal of Comparative and Physiological Psychology, 92*, 85–93. doi:10.1037/h0077428

Jones, S. L., Ismail, N., King, L., & Pfaus, J. G. (2012). Effect of chronic administration of testosterone propionate with or without estradiol on the sexual behavior and plasma steroid levels of aged female rats. *Endocrinology, 153*, 5928–5939. doi:10.1210/en.2012-1578

Kalivas, P. W., & Stewart, J. (1991). Dopamine transmission in the initiation and expression of drug- and stress-induced sensitization of motor activity. *Brain Research Reviews, 16*, 223–244. doi:10.1016/0165-0173(91)90007-U

Kantorowitz, D. A. (1978). An experimental investigation of preorgasmic reconditioning and postorgasmic deconditioning. *Journal of Applied Behavior Analysis, 11*, 23–34. doi:10.1901/jaba.1978.11-23

Kaplan, H. S. (1974). *The new sex therapy*. New York, NY: Brunner/Mazel.

Kendrick, K. M., Hinton, M. R., Atkins, K., Haupt, M. A., & Skinner, J. D. (1998). Mothers determine sexual preferences. *Nature, 395*, 229–230. doi:10.1038/26129

Keysers, C., & Gazzola, V. (2009). Expanding the mirror: Vicarious activity for actions, emotions and sensations. *Current Opinion in Neurobiology, 19*, 666–671. doi:10.1016/j.conb.2009.10.006

King, R., Belsky, J., Mah, K., & Binik, Y. (2011). Are there different types of female orgasm? *Archives of Sexual Behavior, 40*, 865–875. doi:10.1007/s10508-010-9639-7

Kingsberg, S. A., Simon, J. A., & Goldstein, I. (2008). The current outlook for testosterone in the management of hypoactivę sexual desire disorder in postmenopausal women. *Journal of Sexual Medicine, 5*(Suppl. 4), 182–193. doi:10.1111/j.1743-6109.2008.00961.x

Kinsey, A. C., Pomeroy, W. B., & Martin, C. E. (1948). *Sexual behavior in the human male*. Philadelphia, PA: W. B. Saunders.

Kinsey, A. C., Pomeroy, W. B., Martin, C. E., & Gebhard, P. H. (1953). *Sexual behavior in the human female.* Philadelphia, PA: W. B. Saunders.

Kippin, T. E., Cain, S. W., & Pfaus, J. G. (2003). Estrous odors and sexually conditioned neutral odors activate separate neural pathways in the male rat. *Neuroscience, 117*, 971–979. doi:10.1016/S0306-4522(02)00972-7

Kippin, T. E., & Pfaus, J. G. (2001a). The development of olfactory conditioned ejaculatory preferences in the male rat: I. Nature of the unconditioned stimulus. *Physiology and Behavior, 73*, 457–469. doi:10.1016/S0031-9384(01)00484-X

Kippin, T. E., & Pfaus, J. G. (2001b). The nature of the conditioned response mediating olfactory conditioned ejaculatory preference in the male rat. *Behavioural Brain Research, 122*, 11–24. doi:10.1016/S0166-4328(01)00162-0

Kippin, T. E., Samaha, A.-N., Sotiropoulos, V., & Pfaus, J. G. (2001). The development of olfactory conditioned ejaculatory preferences in the male rat: II. Parametric manipulation of conditioning session number and duration. *Physiology and Behavior, 73*, 471–485. doi:10.1016/S0031-9384(01)00485-1

Kippin, T. E., Talianakis, S., Schattmann, L., Bartholomew, S., & Pfaus, J. G. (1998). Olfactory conditioning of sexual behavior in the male rat (*Rattus norvegicus*). *Journal of Comparative Psychology, 112*, 389–399. doi:10.1037/0735-7036.112.4.389

Kleitz-Nelson, H. K., Dominguez, J. M., & Ball, G. F. (2010). Dopamine release in the medial preoptic area is related to hormonal action and sexual motivation. *Behavioral Neuroscience, 124*, 773–779. doi:10.1037/a0021490

Klucken, T., Schweckendiek, J., Merz, C. J., Tabbert, K., Walter, B., Kagerer, S., & Stark, R. (2009). Neural activations of the acquisition of conditioned sexual arousal: Effects of contingency awareness and sex. *Journal of Sexual Medicine, 6*, 3071–3085. doi:10.1111/j.1743-6109.2009.01405.x

Koch, P. C., & Peters, R. H. (1987). Suppression of adult copulatory behaviors following LiCl-induced aversive contingencies in juvenile male rats. *Developmental Psychobiology, 20*, 603–611. doi:10.1002/dev.420200606

Komisaruk, B. R., Beyer-Flores, C., & Whipple, B. (2006). *The science of orgasm.* Baltimore, MD: Johns Hopkins University Press.

Komisaruk, B. R., Whipple, B., Crawford, A., Liu, W. C., Kalnin, A., & Mosier, K. (2004). Brain activation during vaginocervical self-stimulation and orgasm in women with complete spinal cord injury: fMRI evidence of mediation by the vagus nerves. *Brain Research, 1024*, 77–88. doi:10.1016/j.brainres.2004.07.029

Koukounas, E., & McCabe, M. P. (2001). Sexual and emotional variables influencing sexual response to erotica: A psychophysiological investigation. *Archives of Sexual Behavior, 30*, 393–408. doi:10.1023/A:1010261315767

Kow, L. M., Mobbs, C. V., & Pfaff, D. W. (1994). Roles of second-messenger systems and neuronal activity in the regulation of lordosis by neurotransmitters, neuropeptides, and estrogen: A review. *Neuroscience and Biobehavioral Reviews, 18*, 251–268. doi:10.1016/0149-7634(94)90028-0

Kranz, F., & Ishai, A. (2006). Face perception is modulated by sexual preference. *Current Biology, 16*, 63–68. doi:10.1016/j.cub.2005.10.070

Kringelbach, M. L. (2005). The human orbitofrontal cortex: Linking reward to hedonic experience. *Nature Reviews Neuroscience, 6*, 691–702. doi:10.1038/nrn1747

Krug, R., Pietrowsky, R., Fehm, H. L., & Born, J. (1994). Selective influence of menstrual cycle on perception of stimuli with reproductive significance. *Psychosomatic Medicine, 56*, 410–417.

Krug, R., Plihal, W., Fehm, H. L., & Born, J. (2000). Selective influence of the menstrual cycle on perception of stimuli with reproductive significance: An event-related potential study. *Psychophysiology, 37*, 111–122. doi:10.1111/1469-8986.3710111

Krüger, T., Exton, M. S., Pawlak, C., von zur Muhlen, A., Hartmann, U., & Schedlowski, M. (1998). Neuroendocrine and cardiovascular response to sexual arousal and orgasm in men. *Psychoneuroendocrinology, 23*, 401–411. doi:10.1016/S0306-4530(98)00007-9

Krüger, T. H., Schiffer, B., Eikermann, M., Haake, P., Gizewski, E., & Schedlowski, M. (2006). Serial neurochemical measurement of cerebrospinal fluid during the human sexual response cycle. *European Journal of Neuroscience, 24*, 3445–3452. doi:10.1111/j.1460-9568.2006.05215.x

Laan, E., Everaerd, W., & Evers, A. (1995). Assessment of female sexual arousal: Response specificity and construct validity. *Psychophysiology, 32*, 476–485. doi:10.1111/j.1469-8986.1995.tb02099.x

Laan, E., Everaerd, W., van der Velde, J., & Geer, J. H. (1995). Determinants of subjective experience of sexual arousal in women: Feedback from genital arousal and erotic stimulus content. *Psychophysiology, 32*, 444–451. doi:10.1111/j.1469-8986.1995.tb02095.x

Ladas, A. K., Whipple, B., & Perry, J. D. (1982). *The G-spot and other discoveries about human sexuality.* New York, NY: Holt, Rinehart, & Winston.

Laeng, B., & Falkenberg, L. (2007). Women's pupillary responses to sexually significant others during the hormonal cycle. *Hormones and Behavior, 52*, 520–530. doi:10.1016/j.yhbeh.2007.07.013

Lake Polan, M., Desmond, J. E., Banner, L. L., Pryor, M. R., McCallum, S. W., Atlas, S. W., . . . Arnow, B. A. (2003). Female sexual arousal: A behavioral analysis. *Fertility and Sterility, 80*, 1480–1487. doi:10.1016/S0015-0282(03)02210-6

Lalumière, M. L., & Quinsey, V. L. (1998). Pavlovian conditioning of sexual interests in human males. *Archives of Sexual Behavior, 27*, 241–252. doi:10.1023/A:1018686817316

Landauer, M. R., Wiese, R. E., & Carr, W. J. (1977). Responses of sexually experienced and naive male rats to cues from receptive vs. nonreceptive females. *Animal Learning and Behavior, 5*, 398–402. doi:10.3758/BF03209586

Landis, C. C., & Gullette, R. R. (1925). Studies of emotional reactions: III. Systolic blood pressure and inspiration-expiration ratios. *Journal of Comparative Psychology, 5*, 221–253. doi:10.1037/h0074346

Larsson, K. (1956). *Conditioning and sexual behavior in the male albino rat.* Uppsala, Sweden: Almqvist & Wiksells.

Lauber, A. H., Romano, G. J., Mobbs, C. V., Howells, R. D., & Pfaff, D. W. (1990). Estradiol induction of proenkephalin messenger RNA in hypothalamus: Dose-response and relation to reproductive behavior in the female rat. *Molecular Brain Research, 8*, 47–54. doi:10.1016/0169-328X(90)90008-2

Lawrence, G. J., & Keifer, S. W. (1987). Cessation of male rat copulatory behavior using illness as punishment: Facilitation with a novel odor. *Behavioral Neuroscience, 101*, 289–291. doi:10.1037/0735-7044.101.2.289

Lee, J. W., & Erskine, M. S. (1996). Vaginocervical stimulation suppresses the expression of c-Fos induced by mating in thoracic, lumbar and sacral segments of the female rat. *Neuroscience, 74*, 237–249. doi:10.1016/0306-4522(96)00103-0

Lenz, K. M., & McCarthy, M. M. (2010). Organized for sex-steroid hormones and the developing hypothalamus. *European Journal of Neuroscience, 32*, 2096–2104. doi:10.1111/j.1460-9568.2010.07511.x

Letourneau, E. J., & O'Donohue, W. (1997). Classical conditioning of female sexual arousal. *Archives of Sexual Behavior, 26*, 63–78. doi:10.1023/A:1024573420228

Levin, R. J. (2005). Sexual arousal—Its physiological roles in human reproduction. *Annual Review of Sex Research, 16*, 154–189.

Li, S.-C. (2003). Biocultural orchestration of developmental plasticity across levels: The interplay of biology and culture in shaping the mind and behavior across the life span. *Psychological Bulletin, 129*, 171–194. doi:10.1037/0033-2909.129.2.171

Lloyd, E. A. (2005). *The case of the female orgasm: Bias in the science of evolution.* Cambridge, MA: Harvard University Press.

Lodder, J., & Zeilmaker, G. H. (1976). Role of pelvic nerves in the postcopulatory abbreviation of behavioral estrus in female rats. *Journal of Comparative and Physiological Psychology, 90*, 925–929. doi:10.1037/h0077278

López, H. H. (2010). Cannabinoid-hormone interactions in the regulation of motivational processes. *Hormones and Behavior, 58*, 100–110. doi:10.1016/j.yhbeh.2009.10.005

López, H. H., & Ettenberg, A. (2001). Dopamine antagonism attenuates the unconditioned incentive value of estrous female cues. *Pharmacology Biochemistry and Behavior, 68*, 411–416. doi:10.1016/S0091-3057(00)00472-X

López, H. H., Webb, S. A., & Nash, S. (2009). Cannabinoid receptor antagonism increases female sexual motivation. *Pharmacology Biochemistry and Behavior, 92*, 17–24. doi:10.1016/j.pbb.2008.10.004

Lou, H. C., Gross, J., Biermann-Ruben, K., Kjaer, T. W., & Schnitzler, A. (2010). Coherence in consciousness: Paralimbic gamma synchrony of self-reference links conscious experiences. *Human Brain Mapping, 31*, 185–192.

Mackintosh, N. J. (1994). *The psychology of animal learning.* London, England: Academic Press.

Mah, K., & Binik, Y. M. (2002). Do all orgasms feel alike? Evaluating a two-dimensional model of the orgasm experience across gender and sexual context. *Journal of Sex Research, 39*, 104–113. doi:10.1080/00224490209552129

Malatesta, V. J., Pollack, R. H., Wilbanks, W. A., & Adams, H. E. (1979). Alcohol effects on the orgasmic-ejaculatory response in human males. *Journal of Sex Research, 15*, 101–107. doi:10.1080/00224497909551027

Mallick, H. N., Tandon, S., Jagannathan, N. R., Gulia, K. K., & Kumar, V. M. (2007). Brain areas activated after ejaculation in healthy young human subjects. *Indian Journal of Physiology and Pharmacology, 51*, 81–85.

Mani, S. K., Allen, J. M., Clark, J. H., Blaustein, J. D., & O'Malley, B. W. (1994). Convergent pathways for steroid hormone- and neurotransmitter-induced rat sexual behavior. *Science, 265*, 1246–1249. doi:10.1126/science.7915049

Mani, S. K., Mitchell, A., & O'Malley, B. W. (2001). Progesterone receptor and dopamine receptors are required in Delta-9-tetrahydrocannabinol modulation of sexual receptivity in female rats. *Proceedings of the National Academy of Sciences of the United States of America, 98*, 1248–1254.

Manzo, J., Cruz, M. R., Hernandez, M.-E., Pacheco, P., & Sachs, B. D. (1999). Regulation of noncontact erection in rats by gonadal steroids. *Hormones and Behavior, 35*, 264–270. doi:10.1006/hbeh.1999.1519

Marson, L. (1995). Central nervous system neurons identified after injection of pseudorabies virus into the rat clitoris. *Neuroscience Letters, 190*, 41–44. doi:10.1016/0304-3940(95)11495-I

Marson, L. (2009). Central nervous system control of sexual function in males and females. In C. C. Carson, R. S. Kirby, I. Goldstein, & M. G. Wyllie (Eds.), *Textbook of male erectile dysfunction* (2nd ed., pp. 73–88). New York, NY: Informa Healthcare.

Marson, L. (2011). Autonomic regulation of sexual function. In I. J. Llewellyn-Smith & A. J. M. Verberne (Eds.), *Central regulation of autonomic functions* (2nd ed., pp. 366–418). Oxford, England: Oxford University Press. doi:10.1093/acprof:oso/9780195306637.003.0020

Marson, L., Cai, R., & Makhanova, N. (2003). Identification of spinal neurons involved in the urethrogenital reflex in the female rat. *Journal of Comparative Neurology, 462*, 355–370. doi:10.1002/cne.10732

Marson, L., & Carson, C. C. (1999). Central nervous system innervation of the penis, prostate, and perineal muscles: A transneuronal tracing study. *Molecular Urology, 3*, 43–50.

Marson, L., & Foley, K. (2004). Identification of neural pathways involved in genital reflexes in the female: A combined anterograde and retrograde tracing study. *Neuroscience, 127*, 723–736. doi:10.1016/j.neuroscience.2004.04.063

Marson, L., & McKenna, K. E. (1996). CNS cell groups involved in the control of the ischiocavernosus and bulbospongiosus muscles: A transneuronal tracing study using pseudorabies virus. *Journal of Comparative Neurology, 374*, 161–179. doi:10.1002/(SICI)1096-9861(19961014)374:2<161::AID-CNE1>3.0.CO;2-0

Martínez-González, D., Bonilla-Jaime, H., Morales-Otal, A., Henriksen, S. J., Velázquez-Moctezuma, J., & Prospéro-Garcia, O. (2004). Oleamide and anandamide effects on food intake and sexual behavior of rats. *Neuroscience Letters, 364*, 1–6. doi:10.1016/j.neulet.2004.03.080

Mass, R., Hölldorfer, M., Moll, B., Bauer, R., & Wolf, K. (2009). Why we haven't died out yet: Changes in women's mimic reactions to visual erotic stimuli during their menstrual cycle. *Hormones and Behavior, 55*, 267–271. doi:10.1016/j.yhbeh.2008.06.007

Masters, W. H., & Johnson, V. E. (1966). *Human sexual response*. Boston, MA: Little, Brown.

Masters, W. H., Johnson, V. E., & Kolodny, R. C. (1983). *Sex and human loving*. Boston, MA: Little, Brown.

Matthews, T. J., Grigore, M., Tang, L., Doat, M., Kow, L.-M., & Pfaff, D. W. (1997). Sexual reinforcement in the female rat. *Journal of the Experimental Analysis of Behavior, 68*, 399–410. doi:10.1901/jeab.1997.68-399

Matuszewich, L., Ormsby, J. L., Moses, J., Lorrain, D. S., & Hull, E. M. (1995). Effects of morphiceptin in the medial preoptic area on male sexual behavior. *Psychopharmacology, 122*, 330–335. doi:10.1007/BF02246262

Mayberg, H. S. (1997). Limbic-cortical dysregulation: A proposed model of depression. *Journal of Neuropsychiatry and Clinical Neurosciences, 9*, 471–481.

McCarthy, M. M., Malik, K. F., & Feder, H. H. (1990). Increased GABAergic transmission in medial hypothalamus facilitates lordosis but has the opposite effect in preoptic area. *Brain Research, 507*, 40–44. doi:10.1016/0006-8993(90)90519-H

McClintock, M. K. (1984). Group mating in the domestic rat as a context for sexual selection: Consequences for the analysis of sexual behavior and neuroendocrine responses. *Advances in the Study of Behavior, 14*, 1–50. doi:10.1016/S0065-3454(08)60298-3

McConaghy, N. (1970). Subjective and penile plethysmograph responses to aversion therapy for homosexuality: A follow-up study. *British Journal of Psychiatry, 117*, 555–560. doi:10.1192/bjp.117.540.555

McConaghy, N. (1974). Penile volume responses to moving and still pictures of male and female nudes. *Archives of Sexual Behavior, 3*, 565–570. doi:10.1007/BF01541138

McGinnis, M. Y., & Vakulenko, M. (2003). Characterization of 50-kHz ultrasonic vocalizations in male and female rats. *Physiology and Behavior, 80*, 81–88. doi:10.1016/S0031-9384(03)00227-0

McIntosh, T. K., & Barfield, R. J. (1984). Brain monoaminergic control of male reproductive behavior: III. Norepinephrine and the post-ejaculatory refractory period. *Behavioural Brain Research, 12*, 275–281. doi:10.1016/0166-4328(84)90153-0

McKenna, K. E. (1999). Central nervous system pathways involved in the control of penile erection. *Annual Review of Sex Research, 10*, 157–183.

Meerts, S. H., & Clark, A. S. (2009). Artificial vaginocervical stimulation induces a conditioned place preference in female rats. *Hormones and Behavior, 55*, 128–132. doi:10.1016/j.yhbeh.2008.09.003

Mehrara, B. J., & Baum, M. J. (1990). Naloxone disrupts the expression but not the acquisition by male rats of a conditioned place preference response for an oestrous female. *Psychopharmacology, 101*, 118–125. doi:10.1007/BF02253728

Meisel, R. D., & Sachs, B. D. (1994). The physiology of male reproduction. In E. Knobil & J. D. Neil (Eds.), *The physiology of reproduction* (Vol. 2, pp. 3–105). New York, NY: Raven Press.

Melis, M. R., & Argiolas, A. (2011). Central control of penile erection: A re-visitation of the role of oxytocin and its interaction with dopamine and glutamic acid in male rats. *Neuroscience and Biobehavioral Reviews, 35*, 939–955. doi:10.1016/j.neubiorev.2010.10.014

Melis, M. R., Melis, T., Cocco, C., Succu, S., Sanna, F., Pillolla, G., . . . Argiolas, A. (2007). Oxytocin injected into the ventral tegmental area induces penile erection and increases extracellular dopamine in the nucleus accumbens and paraventricular nucleus of the hypothalamus of male rats. *European Journal of Neuroscience, 26*, 1026–1035. doi:10.1111/j.1460-9568.2007.05721.x

Melis, M. R., Succu, S., Mascia, M. S., & Argiolas, A. (2004). Antagonism of CB 1 receptors in the paraventricular nucleus of male rats induces penile erection. *Neuroscience Letters, 359*, 17–20. doi:10.1016/j.neulet.2004.01.025

Melis, M. R., Succu, S., Spano, M. S., & Argiolas, A. (2000). Effect of excitatory amino acid, dopamine, and oxytocin receptor antagonists on noncontact penile erections and paraventricular nitric oxide production in male rats. *Behavioral Neuroscience, 114*, 849–857. doi:10.1037/0735-7044.114.4.849

Mendelson, S. D., & Pfaus, J. G. (1989). Level searching: A new assay of sexual motivation in the male rat. *Physiology and Behavior, 45*, 337–341. doi:10.1016/0031-9384(89)90136-4

Mermelstein, P. G., & Becker, J. B. (1995). Increased extracellular dopamine in the nucleus accumbens and striatum of the female rat during paced copulatory behavior. *Behavioral Neuroscience, 109*, 354–365. doi:10.1037/0735-7044.109.2.354

Meston, C. M. (2000). Sympathetic nervous system activity and female sexual arousal. *American Journal of Cardiology, 86*(2, Suppl. 1), 30–34. doi:10.1016/S0002-9149(00)00889-4

Meston, C. M., & Frolich, P. F. (2001). Update on female sexual function. *Current Opinion in Urology, 11*, 603–609. doi:10.1097/00042307-200111000-00008

Meston, C. M., & Gorzalka, B. B. (1996). Differential effects of sympathetic activation on sexual arousal in sexually dysfunctional and functional women. *Journal of Abnormal Psychology, 105*, 582–591. doi:10.1037/0021-843X.105.4.582

Meston, C. M., Gorzalka, B. B., & Wright, J. M. (1997). Inhibition of subjective and physiological sexual arousal in women by clonidine. *Psychosomatic Medicine, 59*, 399–407.

Meston, C. M., Levin, R. J., Sipski, M. L., Hull, E. M., & Heiman, J. R. (2004). Women's orgasm. *Annual Review of Sex Research, 15*, 173–257.

Meston, C. M., Moe, I. V., & Gorzalka, B. B. (1996). Effects of sympathetic inhibition on receptive, proceptive, and rejection behaviors in the female rat. *Physiology and Behavior, 59*, 537–542. doi:10.1016/0031-9384(95)02102-7

Mesulam, M. M., & Mufson, E. J. (1982). Insula of the old world monkey: III. Efferent cortical output and comments on function. *Journal of Comparative Neurology, 212*, 38–52. doi:10.1002/cne.902120104

Min, K., Munarriz, R., Kim, N. N., Choi, S., O'Connell, L., Goldstein, I., & Traish, A. M. (2003). Effects of ovariectomy and estrogen replacement on basal and pelvic nerve stimulated vaginal lubrication in an animal model. *Journal of Sex and Marital Therapy, 29*(Suppl. 1), 77–84. doi:10.1080/713847131

Mitchell, J. B., & Gratton, A. (1991). Opioid modulation and sensitization of dopamine release elicited by sexually relevant stimuli: A high speed chronoamperometric study in freely behaving rats. *Brain Research, 551*, 20–27. doi:10.1016/0006-8993(91)90908-E

Mitchell, J. B., & Gratton, A. (1992). Mesolimbic dopamine release elicited by activation of the accessory olfactory system: A high speed chronoamperometric study. *Neuroscience Letters, 140*, 81–84. doi:10.1016/0304-3940(92)90687-3

Mitchell, J. B., & Stewart, J. (1990). Facilitation of sexual behaviors in the male rat associated with intra-VTA injections of opiates. *Pharmacology Biochemistry and Behavior, 35*, 643–650. doi:10.1016/0091-3057(90)90302-X

Mobbs, D., Marchant, J. L., Hassabis, D., Seymour, B., Tan, G., Gray, M., & Frith, C. D. (2009). From threat to fear: The neural organization of defensive fear systems in humans. *Journal of Neuroscience, 29*, 12236–12243. doi:10.1523/JNEUROSCI.2378-09.2009

Moll, A. (1897). *Untersuchungen über die libido sexualis* [Analysis of the sexual libido]. Berlin, Germany: Fischer's Medicin Buchhandlung.

Moll, A. (1912). *The sexual life of the child* (E. Paul, Trans.). New York, NY: MacMillan. (Original work published 1908)

Montorsi, F., Perani, D., Anchisi, D., Salonia, A., Scifo, P., Rigiroli, P., & Fazio, F. (2003). Brain activation patterns during video sexual stimulation following the administration of apomorphine: Results of a placebo-controlled study. *European Urology, 43*, 405–411. doi:10.1016/S0302-2838(03)00053-8

Moss, F. A. (1924). A study of animal drives. *Journal of Experimental Psychology, 7*, 165–185.

Mouras, H., Stoléru, S., Moulier, V., Pelegrini-Issac, M., Rouxel, R., Grandjean, B., & Bittoun, J. (2008). Activation of mirror-neuron system by erotic video clips predicts degree of induced erection: An fMRI study. *NeuroImage, 42*, 1142–1150. doi:10.1016/j.neuroimage.2008.05.051

Munarriz, R., Kim, S. W., Kim, N. N., Traish, A. M., & Goldstein, I. (2003). A review of the physiology and pharmacology of peripheral (vaginal and clitoral) female genital arousal in the animal model.

Journal of Urology, 170, S40–S45. doi:10.1097/01.ju.0000075352.03144.15

Nash, S., & Domjan, M. (1991). Learning to discriminate the sex of conspecifics in male Japanese quail (*Coturnix coturnix japonica*): Tests of "biological constraints." *Journal of Experimental Psychology: Animal Behavior Processes, 17*, 342–353. doi:10.1037/0097-7403.17.3.342

Navarro, M., Fernandez-Ruiz, J. J., de Miguel, R., Hernandez, M. L., Cebeira, M., & Ramos, J. A. (1993). An acute dose of delta 9-tetrahydrocannabinol affects behavioral and neurochemical indices of mesolimbic dopaminergic activity. *Behavioural Brain Research, 57*, 37–46. doi:10.1016/0166-4328(93)90059-Y

Nelson, R. J. (2005). *An introduction to behavioral endocrinology* (3rd ed.). Sunderland, MA: Sinauer Associates.

Nissen, H. W. (1929). The effects of gonadectomy, vasotomy, and injections of placental and orchic extracts on the sex behavior of the white rat. *Genetic Psychology Monographs, 5*, 455–550.

Oei, N. Y., Rombouts, S. A., Soeter, R. P., van Gerven, J. M., & Both, S. (2012). Dopamine modulates reward system activity during subconscious processing of sexual stimuli. *Neuropsychopharmacology, 37*, 1729–1737. doi:10.1038/npp.2012.19

Oldenburger, W. P., Everitt, B. J., & de Jonge, F. H. (1992). Conditioned place preference induced by sexual interaction in female rats. *Hormones and Behavior, 26*, 214–228. doi:10.1016/0018-506X(92)90043-U

Ossewaarde, L., van Wingen, G. A., Kooijman, S. C., Backstrom, T., Fernandez, G., & Hermans, E. J. (2011). Changes in functioning of mesolimbic incentive processing circuits during the premenstrual phase. *Social Cognitive and Affective Neuroscience, 6*, 612–620. doi:10.1093/scan/nsq071

Ovid. (1930). *The love books of Ovid being the Amores, Ars Amatoria, Remedia Amoris and Medicamina Faciei Femineae of publius Ovidius Naso.* Retrieved from http://www.sacred-texts.com/cla/ovid/lboo

Paick, J. S., & Lee, S. W. (1994). The neural mechanism of apomorphine-induced erection: An experimental study by comparison with electrostimulation-induced erection in the rat model. *Journal of Urology, 152*, 2125–2128.

Palace, E. M., & Gorzalka, B. B. (1990). The enhancing effects of anxiety on arousal in sexually dysfunctional and functional women. *Journal of Abnormal Psychology, 99*, 403–411. doi:10.1037/0021-843X.99.4.403

Papka, R. E., Williams, S., Miller, K. E., Copelin, T., & Puri, P. (1998). CNS location of uterine-related neurons revealed by trans-synaptic tracing with pseudorabies virus and their relation to estrogen receptor-immunoreactive neurons. *Neuroscience, 84*, 935–952. doi:10.1016/S0306-4522(97)00563-0

Parada, M., Abdul-Ahad, F., Censi, S., Sparks, L., & Pfaus, J. G. (2011). Context alters the ability of clitoral stimulation to induce a sexually-conditioned partner preference in the rat. *Hormones and Behavior, 59*, 520–527. doi:10.1016/j.yhbeh.2011.02.001

Parada, M., Chamas, L., Censi, S., Coria-Avila, G., & Pfaus, J. G. (2010). Clitoral stimulation induces conditioned place preference and Fos activation in the rat. *Hormones and Behavior, 57*, 112–118. doi:10.1016/j.yhbeh.2009.05.008

Parada, M., Vargas, E. B., Kyres, M., Burnside, K., & Pfaus, J. G. (2012). The role of ovarian hormones in sexual reward states of the female rat. *Hormones and Behavior, 62*, 442–447. doi:10.1016/j.yhbeh.2012.07.012

Paredes, R. G., & Alonso, A. (1997). Sexual behavior regulated (paced) by the female induces conditioned place preference. *Behavioral Neuroscience, 111*, 123–128. doi:10.1037/0735-7044.111.1.123

Paredes, R. G., & Martinez, I. (2001). Naloxone blocks place preference conditioning after paced mating in female rats. *Behavioral Neuroscience, 115*, 1363–1367. doi:10.1037/0735-7044.115.6.1363

Paredes, R. G., & Vazquez, B. (1999). What do female rats like about sex? Paced mating. *Behavioural Brain Research, 105*, 117–127. doi:10.1016/S0166-4328(99)00087-X

Parish, A. R., & De Waal, F. B. (2000). The other "closest living relative": How bonobos (Pan paniscus) challenge traditional assumptions about females, dominance, intra-and intersexual interactions, and hominid evolution. *Annals of the New York Academy of Sciences, 907*, 97–113.

Pars, H. G., & Howes, J. F. (1977). Potential therapeutic agents derived from the cannabinoid nucleus. *Advances in Drug Research, 11*, 97–189.

Pattij, T., Olivier, B., & Waldinger, M. D. (2005). Animal models of ejaculatory behavior. *Current Pharmaceutical Design, 11*, 4069–4077. doi:10.2174/138161205774913363

Pavlov, I. P. (1927). *Conditioned reflexes* (G. V. Anrep, Trans.). New York, NY: Dover.

Pazos, M. R., Núñez, E., Benito, C., Tolón, R. M., & Romero, J. (2005). Functional neuroanatomy of the endocannabinoid system. *Pharmacology Biochemistry and Behavior, 81*, 239–247. doi:10.1016/j.pbb.2005.01.030

Pehek, E. A., Thompson, J. T., Eaton, R. C., Bazzett, T. J., & Hull, E. M. (1988). Apomorphine and haloperidol, but not domperidone, affect penile reflexes in rats. *Pharmacology Biochemistry and Behavior, 31*, 201–208. doi:10.1016/0091-3057(88)90334-6

Perelman, M. A. (2006). A new combination treatment for premature ejaculation: A sex therapist's perspective. *Journal of Sexual Medicine, 3*, 1004–1012. doi:10.1111/j.1743-6109.2006.00238.x

Perper, T. (1985). *Sex signals: The biology of love.* Philadelphia, PA: ISI Press.

Peters, R. H. (1983). Learned aversions to copulatory behaviors in male rats. *Behavioral Neuroscience, 97*, 140–145. doi:10.1037/0735-7044.97.1.140

Peters, R. H., Koch, P. C., Blythe, B. L., & Sufka, K. J. (1988). Ultrasonic vocalizations in male rats following acquisition of copulation-illness associations. *Physiology and Behavior, 44*, 749–751. doi:10.1016/0031-9384(88)90056-X

Pfaff, D. W. (1980). *Estrogens and brain function.* Berlin, West Germany: Springer-Verlag. doi:10.1007/978-1-4613-8084-9

Pfaff, D. W. (1999). *Drive: Neurobiological and molecular mechanisms of sexual motivation.* Bradford, MA: MIT Press.

Pfaff, D. W., Kieffer, B. L., & Swanson, L. W. (2008). Mechanisms for the regulation of state changes in the central nervous system: An introduction. *Annals of the New York Academy of Sciences, 1129*, 1–7. doi:10.1196/annals.1417.031

Pfaff, D. W., Montgomery, M., & Lewis, C. (1977). Somatosensory determinants of lordosis in female rats: Behavioral definition of the estrogen effect. *Journal of Comparative and Physiological Psychology, 91*, 134–145. doi:10.1037/h0077305

Pfaff, D. W., Schwartz-Giblin, S., McCarthy, M. M., & Kow, L.-M. (1994). Cellular and molecular mechanisms of female reproductive behaviors. In E. Knobil & J. D. Neill (Eds.), *The physiology of reproduction* (2nd ed., pp. 107–220). New York, NY: Raven Press.

Pfaus, J., Giuliano, F., & Gelez, H. (2007). Bremelanotide: An overview of preclinical CNS effects on female sexual function. *Journal of Sexual Medicine, 4*, 269–279. doi:10.1111/j.1743-6109.2007.00610.x

Pfaus, J. G. (1999). Revisiting the concept of sexual motivation. *Annual Review of Sex Research, 10*, 120–156.

Pfaus, J. G. (2009). Pathways of sexual desire. *Journal of Sexual Medicine, 6*, 1506–1533. doi:10.1111/j.1743-6109.2009.01309.x

Pfaus, J. G., & Gorzalka, B. B. (1987). Opioids and sexual behavior. *Neuroscience and Biobehavioral Reviews, 11*, 1–34. doi:10.1016/S0149-7634(87)80002-7

Pfaus, J. G., & Heeb, M. M. (1997). Implications of immediate-early gene induction in the brain following sexual stimulation of female and male rodents. *Brain Research Bulletin, 44*, 397–407. doi:10.1016/S0361-9230(97)00219-0

Pfaus, J. G., Ismail, N., & Coria-Avila, G. A. (2010). Sexual motivation. In G. Koob, D. Thompson, & M. Le Moal (Eds.), *Encyclopedia of behavioral neuroscience* (Vol. 3, pp. 201–209). New York, NY: Elsevier. doi:10.1016/B978-0-08-045396-5.00205-0

Pfaus, J. G., Kippin, T. E., & Centeno, S. (2001). Conditioning and sexual behavior: A review. *Hormones and Behavior, 40*, 291–321. doi:10.1006/hbeh.2001.1686

Pfaus, J. G., Kippin, T. E., & Coria-Avila, G. (2003). What can animal models tell us about human sexual response? *Annual Review of Sex Research, 14*, 1–63.

Pfaus, J. G., Kippin, T. E., Coria-Avila, G. A., Gelez, H., Afonso, V. M., Ismail, N., & Parada, M. (2012). Who, what, where, when, (and maybe even why)? How the experience of sexual reward influences sexual desire, preference, and performance. *Archives of Sexual Behavior, 41*, 31–62. doi:10.1007/s10508-012-9935-5

Pfaus, J. G., Kleopoulos, S. P., Mobbs, C. V., Gibbs, R. B., & Pfaff, D. W. (1993). Sexual stimulation activates c-*fos* within estrogen concentrating regions of the female rat forebrain. *Brain Research, 624*, 253–267. doi:10.1016/0006-8993(93)90085-2

Pfaus, J. G., Manitt, C., & Coopersmith, C. B. (2006). Effects of pelvic, pudendal, or hypogastric nerve cuts on Fos induction in the rat brain following vaginocervical stimulation. *Physiology and Behavior, 89*, 627–636. doi:10.1016/j.physbeh.2006.07.022

Pfaus, J. G., Marcangione, C., Smith, W. J., Manitt, C., & Abillamaa, H. (1996). Differential induction of Fos in the female rat brain following different amounts of vaginocervical stimulation: Modulation by steroid hormones. *Brain Research, 741*, 314–330. doi:10.1016/S0006-8993(96)00985-7

Pfaus, J. G., Mendelson, S. D., & Phillips, A. G. (1990). A correlational and factor analysis of anticipatory and consummatory measures of sexual behavior in the male rat. *Psychoneuroendocrinology, 15*, 329–340. doi:10.1016/0306-4530(90)90058-H

Pfaus, J. G., & Pfaff, D. W. (1992). Mu-, delta-, and kappa-opioid receptor agonists selectively modulate sexual behaviors in the female rat: Differential dependence on progesterone. *Hormones and Behavior, 26*, 457–473. doi:10.1016/0018-506X(92)90014-M

Pfaus, J. G., & Phillips, A. G. (1991). Role of dopamine in anticipatory and consummatory aspects of sexual behavior in the male rat. *Behavioral Neuroscience, 105*, 727–743. doi:10.1037/0735-7044.105.5.727

Pfaus, J. G., & Pinel, J. P. J. (1989). Alcohol inhibits and disinhibits sexual behavior in the male rat. *Psychobiology, 17*, 195–201.

Pfaus, J. G., & Scepkowski, L. A. (2005). The biological basis for libido. *Current Sexual Health Reports, 2*, 95–100. doi:10.1007/s11930-005-0010-2

Pfaus, J. G., Shadiack, A., Van Soest, T., Tse, M., & Molinoff, P. (2004). Selective facilitation of sexual solicitation in the female rat by a melanocortin receptor agonist. *Proceedings of the National Academy of Sciences of the United States of America, 101*, 10201–10204. doi:10.1073/pnas.0400491101

Pfaus, J. G., Smith, W. J., Byrne, N., & Stephens, G. (2000). Appetitive and consummatory sexual behaviors of female rats in bilevel chambers. II. Patterns of estrus termination following vaginocervical stimulation. *Hormones and Behavior, 37*, 96–107. doi:10.1006/hbeh.1999.1562

Pfaus, J. G., Smith, W. J., & Coopersmith, C. B. (1999). Appetitive and consummatory sexual behaviors of female rats in bilevel chambers: I. A correlational and factor analysis and the effects of ovarian hormones. *Hormones and Behavior, 35*, 224–240. doi:10.1006/hbeh.1999.1516

Pfaus, J. G., Wilkins, M. F., DiPietro, N., Benibgui, M., Toledano, R., Rowe, A., & Castro-Couch, M. (2010). Inhibitory and disinhibitory effects of psychomotor stimulants and depressants on the sexual behavior of male and female rats. *Hormones and Behavior, 58*, 163–176. doi:10.1016/j.yhbeh.2009.10.004

Platek, S. M., & Singh, D. (2010). Optimal waist-to-hip ratios in women activate neural reward centers in men. *PLoS ONE, 5*, e9042. doi:10.1371/journal.pone.0009042

Poels, S., Bloemers, J., van Rooij, K., Goldstein, I., Gerritsen, J., van Ham, D., . . . Tuiten, A. (2012). Toward personalized sexual medicine (Part 2): Testosterone combined with a PDE-5 inhibitor increases sexual satisfaction in women with HSDD and FSAD, and a low sensitive system for sexual cues. *Journal of Sexual Medicine*. Advance online publication. doi:10.1111/j.1743-6109.2012.02983.x

Rachman, S. (1966). Sexual fetishism: An experimental analogue. *Psychological Record, 16*, 293–296.

Rachman, S., & Hodgson, R. J. (1968). Experimentally induced "sexual fetishism": Replication and development. *Psychological Record, 18*, 25–27.

Rada, R. T. (1975). Alcoholism and forcible rape. *American Journal of Psychiatry, 132*, 444–446.

Ranieri-Collins, S. (1995). Alcohol-related sexual assault. *Trends in Health Care, Law, and Ethics, 10*, 37–40.

Rauch, S. L., Whalen, P. J., Shin, L. M., McInerney, S. C., Macklin, M. L., Lasko, N. B., & Pitman, R. K. (2000). Exaggerated amygdala response to masked facial stimuli in posttraumatic stress disorder: A functional MRI study. *Biological Psychiatry, 47*, 769–776. doi:10.1016/S0006-3223(00)00828-3

Redouté, J., Stoléru, S., Gregoire, M. C., Costes, N., Cinotti, L., Lavenne, F., & Pujol, J. F. (2000). Brain processing of visual sexual stimuli in human males. *Human Brain Mapping, 11*, 162–177. doi:10.1002/1097-0193(200011)11:3<162::AID-HBM30>3.0.CO;2-A

Ritz, T., Thöns, M., Fahrenkrug, S., & Dahme, B. (2005). Airways, respiration, and respiratory sinus arrhythmia during picture viewing. *Psychophysiology, 42*, 568–578.

Robbins, T. W. (2007). Shifting and stopping: Fronto-striatal substrates, neurochemical modulation, and clinical implications. *Philosophical Transactions of the Royal Society of London Series B: Biological Sciences, 362*, 917–932. doi:10.1098/rstb.2007.2097

Robinson, T. E., & Berridge, K. C. (1993). The neural basis of drug craving: An incentive-sensitization theory of addiction. *Brain Research Reviews, 18*, 247–291. doi:10.1016/0165-0173(93)90013-P

Rodríguez-Manzo, G. (1999). Blockade of the establishment of the sexual inhibition resulting from sexual exhaustion by the Coolidge effect. *Behavioural Brain Research, 100*, 245–254. doi:10.1016/S0166-4328(98)00137-5

Rodríguez-Manzo, G., Asai, M., & Fernández-Guasti, A. (2002). Evidence for changes in brain enkephalin contents associated to male rat sexual activity. *Behavioural Brain Research, 131*, 47–55. doi:10.1016/S0166-4328(01)00371-0

Rodríguez-Manzo, G., & Fernández-Guasti, A. (1994). Reversal of sexual exhaustion by serotonergic and noradrenergic agents. *Behavioural Brain Research, 62*, 127–134. doi:10.1016/0166-4328(94)90019-1

Rodríguez-Manzo, G., & Fernández-Guasti, A. (1995a). Opioid antagonists and the sexual satiation phenomenon. *Psychopharmacology, 122*, 131–136. doi:10.1007/BF02246087

Rodríguez-Manzo, G., & Fernández-Guasti, A. (1995b). Participation of the central noradrenergic system in the reestablishment of copulatory behavior of sexually exhausted rats by yohimbine, naloxone, and 8-OH-DPAT. *Brain Research Bulletin, 38*, 399–404. doi:10.1016/0361-9230(95)02007-E

Rodríguez-Manzo, G., López-Rubalcava, C., & Fernández-Guasti, A. (1999). Anxiolytic-like effect of ejaculation under various sexual behavior conditions in the male rat. *Physiology and Behavior, 67*, 651–657. doi:10.1016/S0031-9384(99)00119-5

Room, P., Russchen, F. T., Groenewegen, H. J., & Lohman, A. H. (1985). Efferent connections of the prelimbic (area 32) and infralimbic (area 25) cortices: An anterograde tracing study in the cat. *Journal of Comparative Neurology, 242*, 40–55. doi:10.1002/cne.902420104

Rosen, R. C. (2000). Prevalence and risk factors of sexual dysfunction in men and women. *Current Psychiatry Reports, 2*, 189–195. doi:10.1007/s11920-996-0006-2

Rosen, R. C., & Beck, J. G. (1988). *Patterns of sexual arousal*. New York, NY: Guilford Press.

Rowland, D. L. (2010). Genital and heart rate response to erotic stimulation in men with and without premature ejaculation. *International Journal of Impotence Research, 22*, 318–324. doi:10.1038/ijir.2010.22

Rowland, D. L., Strassberg, D. S., de Gouveia Brzao, C. A., & Slob, A. K. (2000). Ejaculatory latency and control in men with premature ejaculation: An analysis across sexual activities using multiple sources of information. *Journal of Psychosomatic Research, 48*, 69–77. doi:10.1016/S0022-3999(99)00078-1

Rupp, H. A., James, T. W., Ketterson, E. D., Sengelaub, D. R., Janssen, E., & Heiman, J. R. (2009). Neural activation in the orbitofrontal cortex in response to male faces increases during the follicular phase. *Hormones and Behavior, 56*, 66–72. doi:10.1016/j.yhbeh.2009.03.005

Sachs, B. D., Akasofu, K., Citron, J. H., Daniels, S. B., & Natoli, J. H. (1994). Noncontact stimulation from estrous females evokes penile erection in rats. *Physiology and Behavior, 55*, 1073–1079. doi:10.1016/0031-9384(94)90390-5

Sachs, B. D., & Barfield, R. J. (1976). Functional analysis of masculine copulatory behavior in the rat. *Advances in the Study of Behavior, 7*, 91–154. doi:10.1016/S0065-3454(08)60166-7

Sachs, B. D., & Garinello, L. D. (1978). Interaction between penile reflexes and copulation in male rats. *Journal of Comparative and Physiological Psychology, 92*, 759–767. doi:10.1037/h0077498

Salimpoor, V. N., Benovoy, M., Longo, G., Cooperstock, J. R., & Zatorre, R. J. (2009). The rewarding aspects of music listening are related to degree of emotional arousal. *PLoS ONE, 4*, e7487. doi:10.1371/journal.pone.0007487

Sand, M., & Fisher, W. A. (2007). Women's endorsement of models of female sexual response: The nurses' sexuality study. *Journal of Sexual Medicine, 4*, 708–719. doi:10.1111/j.1743-6109.2007.00496.x

Saper, C. B., Scammell, T. E., & Lu, J. (2005). Hypothalamic regulation of sleep and circadian rhythms. *Nature, 437*, 1257–1263. doi:10.1038/nature04284

Sarlo, M., Palomba, D., Buodo, G., Minghetti, R., & Stegagno, L. (2005). Blood pressure changes highlight gender differences in emotional reactivity to arousing pictures. *Biological Psychology, 70*, 188–196. doi:10.1016/j.biopsycho.2005.01.005

Schiffer, B., Paul, T., Gizewski, E., Forsting, M., Leygraf, N., Schedlowski, M., & Kruger, T. H. (2008). Functional brain correlates of heterosexual paedophilia. *NeuroImage, 41*, 80–91. doi:10.1016/j.neuroimage.2008.02.008

Scott, J. C. (1930). Systolic blood-pressure fluctuations with sex, anger and fear. *Journal of Comparative Psychology, 10*, 97–114. doi:10.1037/h0073671

Segraves, R. T. (2008). Management of hypoactive sexual desire disorder. *Advances in Psychosomatic Medicine, 29*, 23–32. doi:10.1159/000126622

Selye, H. (1974). *Stress without distress.* Philadelphia, PA: Lippincott.

Sesack, S. R., & Pickel, V. M. (1992). Prefrontal cortical efferents in the rat synapse on unlabelled neuronal targets of catecholamine terminals in the nucleus accumbens septi and on dopamine neurons in the ventral tegmental area. *Journal of Comparative Neurology, 320*, 145–160. doi:10.1002/cne.903200202

Sescousse, G., Redouté, J., & Dreher, J. C. (2010). The architecture of reward value coding in the human orbitofrontal cortex. *Journal of Neuroscience, 30*, 13095–13104. doi:10.1523/JNEUROSCI.3501-10.2010

Shafik, A., Shafik, I., El Sibai, O., & Shafik, A. A. (2006). Oviductal motile response to penile cervical buffeting. *Archives of Gynecology and Obstetrics, 273*, 216–220. doi:10.1007/s00404-005-0065-3

Sherwin, B. B., Gelfand, M. M., & Brender, W. (1985). Androgen enhances sexual motivation in females: A prospective, crossover study of sex steroid administration in the surgical menopause. *Psychosomatic Medicine, 47*, 339–351.

Siegel, R. K. (1982). Cocaine and sexual dysfunction. *Journal of Psychoactive Drugs, 14*, 71–74. doi:10.1080/02791072.1982.10471912

Sinchak, K., & Micevych, P. E. (2001). Progesterone blockade of estrogen activation of mu-opioid receptors regulates reproductive behavior. *Journal of Neuroscience, 21*, 5723–5729.

Sinchak, K., Mills, R. H., Eckersell, C. B., & Micevych, P. E. (2004). Medial preoptic area delta-opioid receptors inhibit lordosis. *Behavioural Brain Research, 155*, 301–306. doi:10.1016/j.bbr.2004.05.001

Singer, I., & Singer, J. (1972). Peridocity of sexual desire in relation to time of ovulation in women. *Journal of Biological Sciences, 4*, 471–481.

Sipski, M., Alexander, C., Gomez-Marin, O., & Spalding, J. (2007). The effects of spinal cord injury on psychogenic sexual arousal in males. *Journal of Urology, 177*, 247–251. doi:10.1016/j.juro.2006.08.059

Skinner, B. F. (1938). *The behavior of organisms.* New York, NY: Appleton-Century-Crofts.

Slob, A. K., Ernste, M., & van der Werff ten Bosch, J. J. (1991). Menstrual cycle phase and sexual arousability in women. *Archives of Sexual Behavior, 20*, 567–577. doi:10.1007/BF01550955

Snowdon, C. T., Tannenbaum, P. L., Schultz-Darken, N. J., Ziegler, T. E., & Ferris, C. F. (2011). Conditioned sexual arousal in a nonhuman primate. *Hormones and Behavior, 59*, 696–701. doi:10.1016/j.yhbeh.2010.10.009

Stanislaw, H., & Rice, F. J. (1988). Correlation between sexual desire and menstrual cycle characteristics. *Archives of Sexual Behavior, 17*, 499–508. doi:10.1007/BF01542338

Stoléru, S., Fonteille, V., Cornélis, C., Joyal, C., & Moulier, V. (2012). Functional neuroimaging studies of sexual arousal and orgasm in healthy men and women: A review and meta-analysis. *Neuroscience and Biobehavioral Reviews, 36*, 1481–1509. doi:10.1016/j.neubiorev.2012.03.006

Succu, S., Mascia, M. S., Sanna, F., Melis, T., Argiolas, A., & Melis, M. R. (2006). The cannabinoid CB 1 receptor antagonist SR 141716A induces penile erection by increasing extra-cellular glutamic acid in the paraventricular nucleus of male rats. *Behavioural Brain Research, 169*, 274–281. doi:10.1016/j.bbr.2006.01.017

Tamm, L., Menon, V., & Reiss, A. L. (2002). Maturation of brain function associated with response inhibition. *Journal of the American Academy of Child and Adolescent Psychiatry, 41*, 1231–1238. doi:10.1097/00004583-200210000-00013

Taylor, K. S., Seminowicz, D. A., & Davis, K. D. (2009). Two systems of resting state connectivity between the insula and cingulate cortex. *Human Brain Mapping, 30*, 2731–2745. doi:10.1002/hbm.20705

Tiefer, L. (1969). Copulatory behavior of male *Rattus norvegicus* in a multiple-female exhaustion test. *Animal Behaviour, 17*, 718–721. doi:10.1016/S0003-3472(69)80018-7

Tiefer, L. (2004). *Sex is not a natural act, and other essays*. New York, NY: Westview Press.

Toates, F. (1992). *Motivational systems*. Cambridge, England: Cambridge University Press.

Tolman, D. L., & Diamond, L. M. (2001). Desegregating sexuality research: Cultural and biological perspectives on gender and desire. *Annual Review of Sex Research, 12*, 33–74.

Traish, A. M., Kim, N. N., Munarriz, R., Moreland, R., & Goldstein, I. (2002). Biochemical and physiological mechanisms of female genital sexual arousal. *Archives of Sexual Behavior, 31*, 393–400. doi:10.1023/A:1019831906508

Truitt, W. A., & Coolen, L. M. (2002). Identification of a potential ejaculation generator in the spinal cord. *Science, 297*, 1566–1569. doi:10.1126/science.1073885

Truitt, W. A., Shipley, M. T., Veening, J. G., & Coolen, L. M (2003). Activation of a subset of lumbar spinothalamic neurons after copulatory behavior in male but not female rats. *Journal of Neuroscience, 23*, 325–331.

Turley, W. A., Jr., & Floody, O. R. (1981). Delta-9-Tetrahydrocannabinol stimulates receptive and proceptive sexual behaviors in female hamsters. *Pharmacology Biochemistry and Behavior, 14*, 745–747.

Tzschentke, T. M. (2001). Pharmacology and behavioral pharmacology of the mesolimbic dopamine system. *Progress in Neurobiology, 63*, 241–320. doi:10.1016/S0301-0082(00)00033-2

Vachon, P., Simmerman, N., Zahran, A. R., & Carrier, S. (2000). Increases in clitoral and vaginal blood flow following clitoral and pelvic plexus nerve stimulations in the female rat. *International Journal of Impotence Research, 12*, 53–57. doi:10.1038/sj.ijir.3900480

Van der Linden, P. M. A. (2001). Supervisory attentional system in patients with focal frontal lesions. *Journal of Clinical and Experimental Neuropsychology, 23*, 225–239. doi:10.1076/jcen.23.2.225.1212

Van Furth, W. R., & Van Ree, J. M. (1996). Appetitive sexual behavior in male rats: 2. Sexual reward and level-changing behavior. *Physiology and Behavior, 60*, 1007–1012. doi:10.1016/0031-9384(96)00009-1

van Netten, J. J., Georgiadis, J. R., Nieuwenburg, A., & Kortekaas, R. (2008). 8–13 hz fluctuations in rectal pressure are an objective marker of clitorally-induced orgasm in women. *Archives of Sexual Behavior, 37*, 279–285. doi:10.1007/s10508-006-9112-9

Vasey, P. L., & Duckworth, N. (2006). Sexual reward via vulvar, perineal, and anal stimulation: A proximate mechanism for female homosexual mounting in Japanese macaques. *Archives of Sexual Behavior, 35*, 523–532. doi:10.1007/s10508-006-9111-x

Vasey, P. L., & Jiskoot, H. (2010). The biogeography and evolution of female homosexual behavior in Japanese macaques. *Archives of Sexual Behavior, 39*, 1439–1441. doi:10.1007/s10508-009-9518-2

Veening, J. G., & Coolen, L. M. (1998). Neural activation following sexual behavior in the male and female rat brain. *Behavioural Brain Research, 92*, 181–193. doi:10.1016/S0166-4328(97)00190-3

Vogt, B. A. (2005). Pain and emotion interactions in subregions of the cingulate gyrus. *Nature Reviews Neuroscience, 6*, 533–544. doi:10.1038/nrn1704

Vogt, B. A., & Pandya, D. N. (1987). Cingulate cortex of the rhesus monkey: II. Cortical afferents. *Journal of Comparative Neurology, 262*, 271–289. doi:10.1002/cne.902620208

Volman, I., Roelofs, K., Koch, S., Verhagen, L., & Toni, I. (2011). Anterior prefrontal cortex inhibition impairs control over social emotional actions. *Current Biology, 21*, 1766–1770.

von Krafft-Ebing, R. (1929). *Psychopathia sexualis* [Sexual psychopathy] (F. J. Rebman, Trans.). New York, NY: Physicians and Surgeons. (Original work published 1886)

Waldinger, M. D., Zwinderman, A. H., Olivier, B., & Schweitzer, D. H. (2005). Proposal for a definition of lifelong premature ejaculation based on epidemiological stopwatch data. *Journal of Sexual Medicine, 2*, 498–507. doi:10.1111/j.1743-6109.2005.00069.x

Wallen, K. (1995). The evolution of female sexual desire. In P. R. Abramson & S. D. Pinkerton (Eds.), *Sexual nature/sexual culture* (pp. 57–79). Chicago, IL: University of Chicago Press.

Wallen, K., Winston, L. A., Gaventa, S., Davis-DaSilva, M., & Collins, D. C. (1984). Periovulatory changes in female sexual behavior and patterns of ovarian steroid concentration in group-living rhesus monkeys. *Hormones and Behavior, 18*, 431–450. doi:10.1016/0018-506X(84)90028-X

Walter, M., Bermpohl, F., Mouras, H., Schiltz, K., Tempelmann, C., Rotte, M., & Northoff, G. (2008). Distinguishing specific sexual and general emotional effects in fMRI-subcortical and cortical arousal during erotic picture viewing. *NeuroImage, 40*, 1482–1494. doi:10.1016/j.neuroimage.2008.01.040

Walter, M., Witzel, J., Wiebking, C., Gubka, U., Rotte, M., Schiltz, K., & Northoff, G. (2007). Pedophilia is linked to reduced activation in hypothalamus and lateral prefrontal cortex during visual erotic stimulation. *Biological Psychiatry, 62*, 698–701. doi:10.1016/j.biopsych.2006.10.018

Warner, R. K., Thompson, J. T., Markowski, V. P., Loucks, J. A., Bazzett, T. J., Eaton, R. C., & Hull, E. M. (1991). Microinjection of the dopamine antagonist cis-flupenthixol into the MPOA impairs copulation, penile reflexes and sexual motivation in male rats. *Brain Research, 540*, 177–182. doi:10.1016/0006-8993(91)90505-P

Watson, J. B. (1919). *Psychology from the standpoint of a behaviorist*. Philadelphia, PA: Lippincott. doi:10.1037/10016-000

Weil, Z. M., Zhang, Q., Hornung, A., Blizard, D., & Pfaff, D. W. (2010). Impact of generalized brain arousal on sexual behavior. *Proceedings of the National Academy of Sciences of the United States of America, 107*, 2265–2270. doi:10.1073/pnas.0914014107

Wenger, M. A., Averill, J. R., & Smith, D. D. B. (1968). Autonomic activity during sexual arousal. *Psychophysiology, 4*, 468–478. doi:10.1111/j.1469-8986.1968.tb02788.x

Wenkstern, D., Pfaus, J. G., & Fibiger, H. C. (1993). Dopamine transmission increases in the nucleus-accumbens of male rats during their first exposure to sexually receptive female rats. *Brain Research, 618*, 41–46. doi:10.1016/0006-8993(93)90426-N

Whalen, R. E. (1966). Sexual motivation. *Psychological Review, 73*, 151–163. doi:10.1037/h0023026

Whalen, R. E., & Lauber, A. H. (1986). Progesterone substitutes: CGMP mediation. *Neuroscience and Biobehavioral Reviews, 10*, 47–53. doi:10.1016/0149-7634(86)90032-1

Whipple, B., & Komisaruk, B. R. (1985). Elevation of pain threshold by vaginal stimulation in women. *Pain, 21*, 357–367. doi:10.1016/0304-3959(85)90164-2

Wiedey, J., Alexander, M. S., & Marson, L. (2008). Spinal neurons activated in response to pudendal or pelvic nerve stimulation in female rats. *Brain Research, 1197*, 106–114. doi:10.1016/j.brainres.2007.12.071

Wieseler Frank, J. L., Hendricks, S. E., & Olson, C. H. (2000). Multiple ejaculations and chronic fluoxetine: Effects on male rat copulatory behavior. *Pharmacology Biochemistry and Behavior, 66*, 337–342. doi:10.1016/S0091-3057(00)00191-X

Winn, P. (1998). Frontal syndrome as a consequence of lesions in the pedunculopontine tegmental nucleus: A short theoretical view. *Brain Research Bulletin, 47*, 551–563. doi:10.1016/S0361-9230(98)00136-1

Woodworth, R. S. (1918). *Dynamic psychology*. New York, NY: Columbia University Press.

Yells, D. P., Prendergast, M. A., Hendricks, S. E., & Nakamura, M. (1994). Fluoxetine-induced inhibition of male rat copulatory behavior: Modification by lesions of the nucleus paragigantocellularis. *Pharmacology Biochemistry and Behavior, 49*, 121–127. doi:10.1016/0091-3057(94)90465-0

Young, L. J., & Wang, Z. (2004). The neurobiology of pair-bonding. *Nature Neuroscience, 7*, 1048–1054. doi:10.1038/nn1327

Zahorik, D. M., & Johnston, R. E. (1976). Taste aversions to food flavors and vaginal secretion in golden hamsters. *Journal of Comparative and Physiological Psychology, 90*, 57–66. doi:10.1037/h0077255

Zamble, E., Hadad, G. M., Mitchell, J. B., & Cutmore, T. R. H. (1985). Pavlovian conditioning of sexual arousal: First- and second-order effects. *Journal of Experimental Psychology: Animal Behavior Processes, 11*, 598–610. doi:10.1037/0097-7403.11.4.598

Zamble, E., Mitchell, J. B., & Findlay, H. (1986). Pavlovian conditioning of sexual arousal: Parametric and background manipulations. *Journal of Experimental Psychology: Animal Behavior Processes, 12*, 403–411. doi:10.1037/0097-7403.12.4.403

Zellner, D. A., Berridge, K. C., Grill, H. J., & Ternes, J. W. (1985). Rats learn to like the taste of morphine. *Behavioral Neuroscience, 99*, 290–300. doi:10.1037/0735-7044.99.2.290

Zimbardo, P. G. (1958). The effects of early avoidance training and rearing conditions upon the sexual behavior of the male rat. *Journal of Comparative and Physiological Psychology, 51*, 764–769. doi:10.1037/h0038548

CHAPTER 8

SEXUAL DESIRE AND PLEASURE

Lori A. Brotto and Kelly B. Smith

Depending on whom one asks, sexual desire may have many different meanings. It has been equated to desire for sexual activity, desire for sexual intimacy, and the feeling of wanting associated with thinking about an attractive partner. Colloquially, some refer to desire as *feeling horny*. Some experts favor a description that does not hinge on sexual behavior such as the "subjective awareness of desire for sexual satisfaction, irrespective of sexual activity."

Desire has not always been situated within the psychological literature. In the 4th century BC, the Greek philosopher Apicurus described the "pleasure principle" and desire as a natural human necessity. For those in ancient times, sexual desire led to an appreciation and admiration of physical beauty, and the latter led to everything else. Throughout much of the Middle Ages as well as in the 19th and early 20th centuries, there was much interest in the brain–body connection as it relates to sexual desire. French sexologist Marc-Andrè Raffalovich posited that sexuality was not localized in adolescents ages 8 to 11 but that later on, a boy's desires acquire a genital focus. Freud extended this view in the early 1900s and believed that children possessed "polymorphous perversity" wherein the entire body is predisposed to sexuality, which then leads them to experience sexual deviation. As adults, however, they learn to repress this latent capacity to enjoy pleasure all over the body. Through Freud's psychoanalysis, the notion that people are all driven toward pleasure by unconscious forces gained widespread acceptance. Over the years, with advancements in science, the notion of pleasure centers in the brain has received empirical support and attracted the attention of brain–behavior scientists (e.g., psychologists, neuroscientists; see Chapter 7, this volume).

In the *Diagnostic and Statistical Manual of Mental Disorders* (4th ed., text revision; *DSM–IV–TR;* American Psychiatric Association, 2000), the definition of desire can be inferred from a description of when desire is lacking. Hypoactive sexual desire disorder (HSDD) is defined as "persistently or recurrently deficient (or absent) sexual fantasies and desire for sexual activity" when "the judgment of deficiency or absence is made by the clinician, taking into account factors that affect sexual functioning, such as age and the context of the person's life" (American Psychiatric Association, 2000, p. 541). From this perspective, desire, therefore, is defined as sexual fantasies and desire for sexual activity. Because of criticisms of this presumed narrow view of desire, which simplifies the feeling to spontaneous sexual fantasies and cravings for sex, there has been a surge of academic interest in how desire is experienced, expressed, and defined. Although consensus is far from attained, there is general agreement that "in anyone's hands, sexual desire can be a slippery concept" (Levine, 2002, p. 39). Because we are academic clinicians who specialize in the area of women's sexuality, this chapter may be especially relevant to the clinician reader (see Volume 2, Chapter 4, this handbook). In considering the definition of desire, concerns about the impact of differing definitions on the individual must be kept in mind. For example, in the medical model, a loss of desire that leads to distress would entitle an

http://dx.doi.org/10.1037/14193-008
APA Handbook of Sexuality and Psychology: Vol. 1. Person-Based Approaches, D. L. Tolman and L. M. Diamond (Editors-in-Chief)

individual to certain treatment services that come with assigning a medical diagnosis. However, the cost to the individual comes in the form of pathologization and potential stigmatization from having a so-called mental illness. A more social constructionist perspective views people's need to define "high" and "low" desire as a by-product of the media, culture, and pharmaceutical interests and that labels such as HSDD should be abandoned (see Volume 2, Chapter 10, this handbook). Although this perspective is compelling, it has gained little traction in a world that has consistently viewed sexual desire within a more medical model (however, see Chapters 1 and 6, this volume).

Before American psychiatrist Helen Singer Kaplan (1979, 1995) shone a spotlight onto sexual desire, Masters and Johnson's (1966) human sexual response cycle (HSRC) consisted of a linear fixed sequence of stages of sexual response—namely, excitement, plateau, orgasm, and resolution. Desire was not considered in the HSRC because it was based on observed physiological responses in the context of sexual activity. Moreover, there was a single category of sexual dysfunction: Men with sexual difficulties were labeled as impotent; women, as frigid. It followed that treatment was also nonspecific; there was one treatment for all sexual complaints. In 1956, urologist James Semans separated "ejaculatory impotence" from the rest of the male sexual dysfunctions, which greatly aided in the development of treatment for what later came to be known as premature ejaculation. Some years later in the 1970s, orgasm was separated from the excitement phase for women (Kaplan, 1974). Because the separation of excitement from orgasm for men and women enhanced treatment specificity, this led Kaplan (and independently, Harold Lief, another American psychiatrist) to persuasively introduce sexual desire as the first phase of the HSRC model. The triphasic model, as it came to be known, consisted of a linear stepwise progression from desire to arousal to orgasm. Desire, therefore, was seen as a crucial first step in the progression of sexual excitement. According to Kaplan (1979), *sexual desire* was defined as

> specific sensations which move the individual to seek out, or become receptive to, sexual experiences. These sensations are produced by the physical activation of a specific neural system in the brain. When this system is active, a person is "horny," he may feel genital sensations, or he may feel vaguely sexy, interested in sex, open to sex, or even just restless. These sensations cease after sexual gratification, i.e., orgasm. When this system is inactive or under the influence of inhibitory forces, a person has no interest in erotic matters; he "loses his appetite" for sex and becomes "asexual." (p. 10)

Kaplan (1979) likened sexual desire to other drive states, including hunger and thirst. In this way, she viewed sexual desire as biologically driven—influenced by activation and inhibition of neural substrates. She also believed that all sexual dysfunctions were caused by a single factor, namely, anxiety (Kaplan, 1979, p. 24). Treatment of low desire was therefore designed to reduce sexual anxiety and allow patients to confront their unconscious and involuntary avoidance of sexual activity. In the same year as Kaplan was formulating her views on the definition of sexual desire, Harold Lief (1977) also contributed important new information about sexual desire and can be credited for introducing "inhibited sexual desire" into the *DSM–III.*

Levine, another American psychiatrist, has written extensively on the nature of sexual desire. In response to listening to how professionals, the lay public, patients, and society at large discuss desire, Levine (1987) noted that three features characterize sexual desire: (a) Desire precedes and accompanies sexual arousal; (b) desire is the psychobiological propensity to engage in sexual behavior; and (c) desire is the energy brought to sexual behavior. These features led Levine to define sexual desire as "the psychobiologic energy that precedes and accompanies arousal and tends to produce sexual behavior" (p. 36). Levine went further to note that desire is the mind's capacity to integrate drive, wish, and motive. *Drive* is the product of a neuroendocrine generator of sexual impulses and is testosterone dependent. It is indicated by increased sexual excitability and "endogenous or spontaneous manifestations of genital excitement" (p. 36), including genital tingling, erection, or lubrication; heightened perception of others' physical characteristics; erotic fantasies and dreams; and masturbation or partner-seeking behavior. According to Levine, however, drive is more subjective than it is behavioral and is thus a challenge for the clinician to assess. Levine noted that with older age, sexual *wish* might be the dictating force behind sexual behavior. Wishes might include "it makes them feel good physically" and "it makes them feel connected to another person and less alone"; there may also be wishes not to have sexual activity, including "feel emotionally unready" and "fear pregnancy." As sexual drive pushes in one direction (presumably, toward sexual activity), sexual wishes may temper this impulse as a result of moral, social, and danger factors. As such, one may experience high levels of sexual drive and excitability while having a wish not to engage in sexual activity (and vice versa). Sexual *motive* represents the most complex aspect of desire and is the willingness to have sexual activity and behave sexually. It integrates drive and wish, and Levine noted that sexual motive is generally preceded by one or more of the following: drive, a decision to be sexual, interpersonal behavior, voyeuristic experience (e.g., witnessing others' sexual excitement), and attraction. Sexual motives are most observable through human behavior, as Levine described sexual willingness as a behavior produced by psychological motivational processes. In considering one's motives for engaging in sex, even in the presence of strong desire, one must consider that there may be disincentives to sex at play (Meana, 2010). For example, if one assesses the sexual situation as risky, dangerous, or having the potential to have a longer term negative outcome, such disincentives may influence behavior without dampening desire.

In the realm of sexual fantasies, Levine (1987) further posited that a person might find himself or herself preoccupied with fantasies after an interaction with another person that excites his or her drive. Options in such a situation would be to wait for the drive to dissipate, displace the drive onto something else, masturbate, or engage in partnered sexual activity.

In subsequent considerations of desire, Levine (2002) further explored the intricacies of sexual desire on the basis of his in-depth clinical experiences. He noted that sexual desire is highly responsive to the social situation and can intensely increase at times of turmoil (e.g., divorce) and decrease at times of loss (e.g., death of a partner). He proposed a spectrum that reflects the fluctuating nature of sexual desire: aversion–indifference–interest–need–passion (Levine, 2002, p. 43). Esther Perel, in her 2006 book *Mating in Captivity,* addressed the paradox in long-term partnerships that as emotional stability increases, passion fades in a corresponding manner in both men and women, and these effects cannot be attributed solely to aging. Drawing on 20 years of clinical experience, Perel described passion as deriving from the unknown, risk, surprise, and playfulness. She stated that (sexual) excitement is interwoven with uncertainty and with people's willingness to embrace the unfamiliar rather than shield themselves from it. Contrast that now with the defining features of a long-term relationship: stability, certainty, safety, and comfort—all features that may be antithetical to the experience of erotic lust. Indeed, women in longer term relationships report fewer cues that effectively elicit their sexual desire than do women in shorter term relationships (Carvalheira, Brotto, & Maroco, 2011). In particular, those women in longer term relationships reported fewer romantic cues and fewer explicit cues that evoked their desire than women in shorter term relationships. These same cues, earlier on in the relationship, may have been very effective in evoking desire; however, over time and repeated exposure, they lose their erotic appeal. So what is the mechanism behind the loss of incentive value in these cues that previously elicited desire?

In the research previously discussed, no distinction has been made between the different ways in which men and women experience sexual desire. However, in more recent research, sex differences that may be influenced by both biology and culture have become of great interest to researchers. Sims and Meana (2010) carried out in-depth qualitative interviews with married women who had lost desire for their husbands as an exploration of women's explanations for their waning desire. They identified three major contributors. First was the institutionalization of the relationship, which was associated with the overavailability of sex that removed the excitement and anticipation that used to accompany planning for encounters. Moreover, sanctioning married sex, or even mandating it among some groups, removed the illicit aspects of unmarried sex. The second major contributor Sims and Meana identified was overfamiliarity and the loss of romance women identified as being a major contributor to their waning desire. Presex and sexual acts became overly familiar, almost routine, leading sex to be mechanical and proscripted. The third major factor identified was desexualized roles in light of competing priorities, multiple obligations and roles, and therefore feeling less desirable. Although the observed pattern of a diminution of desire over the course of a lasting relationship is a rather normative finding, even when a corresponding increase occurs in one's sense of relationship happiness, its loss nonetheless creates great turmoil in individuals and poses a challenging conundrum for the sexual and relationship therapist to address. Moreover, respondents in the study by Sims and Meana (2010) would surely have met criteria for HSDD, although several noted that a change in their partner or lifestyle would have resurrected their desire, leaving the clinician with the dilemma of whether to diagnose a sexual disorder in a situation in which time seems to be the culprit, not the individual.

Given that a large body of research has noted low levels of agreement between women's self-reported and physiological arousal (Chivers, Seto, Lalumière, Laan, & Grimbos, 2010; see also Chapter 5, this volume), thereby suggesting that women do not use feedback from genital arousal to inform subjective feelings of desire or arousal, it is unlikely that the waning of sexual interest with relationship duration affects women's physiological sexual response; however, this is an open question that remains to be tested.

HOW DO INDIVIDUALS ARTICULATE WHAT THEY WANT?

Kinsey, Pomeroy, and Martin (1948) can likely be credited for carrying out the first large-scale scientific study on sex. Although Kinsey's structured interview focused on sexual behaviors and practices, it ultimately revealed much about sexual desire, preferences, and attractions. Moreover, his structured interview and quantitative recording techniques that preserved respondents' anonymity profoundly shaped how sex research was carried out over the next several decades.

More recently, qualitative research has contributed significant new information to the understanding of sexual desire. Some have argued persuasively that with sexuality research in particular, qualitative methods provide an opportunity to explore desire in more depth and from multiple perspectives in a way that is not captured in studies using simple self-report questionnaires (see Chapter 6, this volume). Indeed, the most commonly used self-report measure of sexual functioning in women, namely the Female Sexual Function Index (FSFI; Rosen et al., 2000), has only two items that make up the Sexual Desire subscale: "Over the past 4 weeks, how often did you feel sexual desire or interest?" and "Over the past 4 weeks, how would you rate your level (degree) of sexual desire or interest?" Women are provided response options ranging from "almost always or always" to "almost never or never" and "very high" to "very low or none at all," respectively. A woman who experiences desire only during sexual activity with her partner, which occurs approximately two to three times per month, but rarely or never experiences desire in the rest of her day-to-day interactions, might therefore endorse "very low" and "almost never" given that desire happens only in the context of her (relatively infrequent) sexual interactions. Using the FSFI, therefore, this woman might be portrayed as having a sexual dysfunction, at least in the absence of a biopsychosocial interview, which would provide the additional nuance to allow the interviewer to understand that she experiences a satisfying level of sexual desire with her partner, despite the relative infrequency of their sex. A similar question, coding structure, and interpretation of the two desire items is found on the male counterpart to this questionnaire, the International Index of Erectile Function (Rosen et al., 1997), and a similar concern exists about labeling as dysfunctional a man who only feels sexual desire about half the time. Instead, a qualitative interview that allowed the individual to provide a narrative of how she or he experiences sexual desire might highlight its complexity and show that the individual's desire during sexual activity is reliable, pronounced, and experienced as satisfying. Although self-report questionnaires are often preferred, particularly in the context of clinical trials in which comparisons between large groups of individuals are necessary, they usually provide only a limited, and perhaps incomplete, picture of how sexual desire is experienced.

We use findings from three recent qualitative studies in women (Brotto, Heiman, & Tolman, 2009; Goldhammer & McCabe, 2011; Graham, Sanders, Milhausen, & McBride, 2004) and one qualitative study in men (Janssen, McBride, Yarber, Hill, & Butler, 2008) to illustrate some of the nuances in capturing how individuals experience sexual desire.

SEXUAL DESIRE IS EXPERIENCED AS PHYSIOLOGICAL, COGNITIVE, EMOTIONAL, OR INTERPERSONAL

Although sexual desire has traditionally been conceptualized as something felt within, with an obvious physiological counterpart, such as butterflies in one's stomach, heart palpitations, or other signs of autonomic arousal, the evidence is clear that desire may be experienced through a number of different modalities, perhaps even simultaneously. In one qualitative study of middle-aged women, half of whom had sexual arousal difficulties and the other half of whom did not, most women included references to nongenital physical aspects of their desire, cognitive referents, and emotional referents, in addition to genital signs of excitement (Brotto et al., 2009). In a more recent study that aimed to explore sexual desire among 40 women in committed heterosexual partnerships, the finding that sexual desire was experienced in a variety of ways was also apparent (Goldhammer & McCabe, 2011) and further challenged previous conceptualizations of sexual desire. In particular, Goldhammer and McCabe (2011) found that desire was an idiosyncratic experience. Some women experienced it physiologically (e.g., vaginal lubrication); for others, it was a cognitive (i.e., thinking) event; for some it was defined in regard to the interpersonal relationship; and for still others, it was purely emotional. Cognitive and emotional factors are of paramount importance to consider in the sexual desires of men and women (Carvalho & Nobre, 2010, 2011), and much more recent research has focused on distraction, attention, and mindfulness as they interact with sexual desire (discussed later).

IS SEXUAL DESIRE THE SAME AS SEXUAL FANTASY?

Interestingly, although fantasies about sex seem to be understood as a natural expression of one's sexual desire, most women in two recent qualitative studies did not associate sexual desire with sexual thoughts or fantasies (Brotto et al., 2009; Goldhammer & McCabe, 2011). Furthermore, sexual fantasy frequency has been found not to correlate with sexual satisfaction in women (Cain et al., 2003), which stands in contrast to stereotypical notions that one who has sexual desire also experiences lustful erotic fantasies. The finding that women often deliberately use fantasies as a way of boosting sexual arousal or orgasm (Beck, Bozman, & Qualtrough, 1991; Hill & Preston, 1996; Lunde, Larsen, Fog, & Garde, 1991; Regan & Berscheid, 1996) is also at odds with the *DSM–IV–TR* definition of HSDD, which requires lack of sexual fantasies for one to meet diagnostic criteria (American Psychiatric Association, 2000). That sexual fantasies may be relatively rare despite women reporting sexual desire suggests that those women who do not experience fantasies, or those who deliberately create sexual fantasies, should not be pathologized. Sex differences may exist in the experience of sexual fantasies, however. Men experience sexual urges more often and tend to have greater sexual imagery (Jones & Barlow, 1990).

SEX DIFFERENCES IN SEXUAL FANTASIES AND DESIRE

Sex differences likely exist in the content of sexual fantasies such that men are more likely to have fantasies for sexual activities in which they do not currently engage, whereas women may fantasize more about what their actual sexual behaviors entail (Hsu, Kling, Kessler, & Knapke, 1994). Sexual fantasies have been suggested as being more relevant to the sexual desire of men than of women (Brotto, 2010a). As far as sex differences in sexual desire, many have speculated for decades that these differences are the result of sex differences in testosterone. A fairly consistent finding is that of a relationship between testosterone and both sexual desire and erectile function in younger men (Bancroft, 2012). However, evidence as to the role of testosterone in women's sexual desire and arousal is conflicting. In part, this may be because women have only approximately 10% the level of plasma total testosterone that men have, leaving room for a greater influence of individual, interpersonal, and sociocultural factors. Testosterone levels rise during the follicular phase of the menstrual cycle, providing a naturalistic within-person observation as to the relationship between circulating testosterone levels, which are not found in men, and women's sexual desire. Sexual activities tend to be lowest during menstruation and rise as ovulation approaches, and sexual desire is highest during the follicular phase when women reach peak fertility (Hedricks, 1994; Stanislaw & Rice, 1988). Subjective sexual arousal to erotic films has shown a similar pattern (Slob, Bax, Hop, Rowland, & van der Werff ten Bosch, 1996), and frequency of sexual fantasies as well as arousability of those fantasies has been found to be highest at ovulation (Dawson, Suschinsky, & Lalumière, 2012). An event-related potential study confirmed that a greater valence of sexual stimuli is found at the time of peak fertility than during other phases of the menstrual cycle (Krug, Plihal, Fehm, & Born, 2000). This greater valence was a selective increase in sexual stimuli rather than a more general increase in emotional processing. However, other nonhormonal factors significantly contribute and may obscure any influence of ovulatory increases in testosterone on women's sexual desire. As well, gendered sexual socialization and societal expectations for men and women's sexuality influence sex differences in desire; we return to these ideas later in the chapter.

IS DESIRE DISTINCT FROM SEXUAL AROUSAL?

Kaplan (1977, 1979) and Lief (1977) can be credited for expanding on Masters and Johnson's (1966) linear HSRC model of excitement, plateau, orgasm, and resolution by arguing that an initial sexual desire phase was necessary to jump-start one toward experiencing sexual excitement. Thus, on the basis of Kaplan's persuasion, sexual desire and sexual arousal came to be defined, studied, and treated as separate constructs. However, the validity of separating sexual desire from arousal had never been verified (or tested, for that matter); instead, several studies began to document that at least for women, desire and arousal might be conflated, interchangeable, and even experienced as one and the same. In qualitative studies of young partnered women (Goldhammer & McCabe, 2011), middle-aged women with and without sexual arousal concerns (Brotto et al., 2009), and college students (Beck et al., 1991), women generally found it difficult to differentiate desire and arousal. Laboratory studies have also found significant overlap between desire and arousal evoked in response to sexual stimuli (Goldey & van Anders, 2012). Even among women seeking treatment for sexual concerns, validated measures of sexual functioning have shown a high degree of overlap between desire and arousal (Rosen et al., 2000). In fact, across a large number of studies, mean scores on validated measures of sexual desire correlated highly with scores on the arousal domain (e.g., Dennerstein, Lehert, & Burger, 2005, as reviewed by Brotto, Graham, Binik, Segraves, & Zucker, 2011; Graham, 2010).

On the basis of the finding of overlap between desire and arousal, a (controversial) proposal has been made to merge disorders of desire (HSDD) and arousal (female sexual arousal disorder) into one condition (sexual interest/arousal disorder; Brotto, 2010b; Graham, 2010), which is discussed later in the Diagnostic Dilemmas section.

For men, it is possible that sexual desire and arousal are experienced mostly as discrete entities, in particular when one considers that erectile functioning can often take place in the absence of sexual desire or any form of erotic cues (e.g., nocturnal erections). Testosterone has also been found to be more highly associated with men's sexual desire than their erectile functioning (Bancroft, 2012). In a study of male outpatients seeking treatment for erectile dysfunction, the majority did not experience impairments in their sexual desire, and no significant correlations were found between measures of sexual desire and measures of penile tumescence (Corona et al., 2004). However, a qualitative study of men suggested complexity in how men experienced desire and arousal, with several of the men expressing confusion over questions that attempted to separate desire from arousal (Janssen et al., 2008). Once erectile function was removed from consideration, it appeared that many men could not distinguish sexual desire from arousal. Also interesting was Janssen et al.'s (2008) finding that masturbation was often a method used to alleviate sexual tension and therefore often took place in the absence of sexual desire, whereas sexual desire and arousal for partnered sex were somewhat more complex. In an earlier study of college students, men also showed a significant correlation between sexual desire and subjective sexual arousal ($r = .44$; Beck et al., 1991). In a recent community sample of Portuguese men, attentional focus was a significant predictor of the strength of men's dyadic sexual desire, leading the authors to conclude that sexual desire and arousal overlap in men because both depend on attentional processes (Carvalho & Nobre, 2011).

Notably, for women, genital response and subjective desire and arousal often show a low degree of overlap; genital responding in women has been suggested as being reflexively and automatically elicited in response to sexual stimuli, even when those stimuli are not perceived by the woman as desired or arousing. In this way, the body becomes prepared for sexual activity and serves a protective function to prevent genital injury (Chivers, 2005). For example, women may experience genital response during highly distressing experiences such as sexual assault or rape (Levin & van Berlo, 2004; see also Chapter 12, this volume) or when exposed to threatening sexual stimuli (e.g., hearing depictions of nonconsensual sexual activity; Suschinsky & Lalumière, 2011). This preparation hypothesis offers an explanation for why genital response may occur in situations that are not at all associated with desire and suggests that subjective desire and physiological arousal may be experienced separately.

INCENTIVE MOTIVATION MODEL

What does the statement that desire and arousal overlap for men and women mean? This statement, which has appeared with increasing frequency in the literature over the past decade, suggests that desire and arousal may be aspects of the same sexual construct or, in other words, two sides of the same sexual coin. Although one can easily identify the distinction between awareness of physical responding (whether genital or nongenital) and awareness of cognitive and emotional sexual responding, this distinction does not rule out the possibility that all these experiences are part of a single sexual response mechanism. An incentive motivation perspective instead views sexual arousal and desire as an interplay between a sexual response system and effective incentives that excite the system (Toates, 2009). Data from a large number of studies conducted primarily in the Netherlands have supported sexual response as an incentive motivation and desire–arousal as an emotion (Everaerd, Both, & Laan, 2006; Everaerd & Laan, 1995; Janssen, Everaerd, Spiering, & Janssen, 2000; Laan & Everaerd, 1995). This model postulates that one's initial response to an effective sexual stimulus takes place outside of consciousness and renders the sexual system responsive to further effective sexual stimuli. Once attentional resources become activated in the processing of a given sexual stimulus, sexual arousal is subjectively experienced, leading one to become aware of one's own motivation to continue to attend to and process those stimuli, particularly as one becomes aware of one's own sexual needs. Implicit in this model is the notion that sexual arousal precedes desire. Moreover, the model maintains that all of desire is responsive to stimuli, even if an individual is unaware of the presence of those stimuli (Janssen et al., 2000; Laan & Both, 2008). In the incentive motivation model, desire and arousal might be phenomenologically separated on the basis that arousal represents the subjective experience of genital response, whereas desire reflects the subjective experience of a willingness to engage sexually (Laan & Both, 2008), but this distinction is mostly artificial. When there are problems with sexual desire and arousal, they may in part be due to a failure to activate the sexual system, because of, for example, hormonal factors, cognitive interference, or judgment. In addition, if the sexual incentives are insufficient to trigger sexual response, or if they lack or have lost sexual meaning, then sexual desire and arousal will not become triggered.

WHAT DOES ASEXUALITY TEACH US ABOUT DESIRE?

If having sexual desire is one method of allowing an individual to classify him- or herself as a sexual person (Levine, 2002, p. 41), then the complete lack of sexual desire and attraction raises new questions about sexual development and classification. Although a notable proportion of individuals report chronic low sexual desire that is bothersome or otherwise clinically significant (discussed in the section Sexual Desire Disorders later in this chapter), a smaller minority of individuals note a lifelong history of chronic lack of desire that they have no interest in changing and have absolutely no personal distress over. Kinsey et al. (1948) first quantified this group, which they labeled *Category X,* as the group of individuals who had no sociosexual contacts or reactions, and it represented approximately 1% of their participants. However, Kinsey et al. did little with those data at the time, and the term *asexual* did not appear until decades later. In Bogaert's (2004) analysis of 18,000 British residents in a national probability survey, 1.05% answered "yes" to the sexual attraction item "I have never felt sexually attracted to anyone at all." Bogaert's sample was more religious than the comparison group of sexual individuals, although in a more recent mixed-methods study, asexual individuals were more likely to report atheism (Brotto, Knudson, Inskip, Rhodes, & Erskine, 2010). Because the asexual individuals had relatively less education and were of a lower social class, Bogaert speculated that one possible mechanism underlying the development of asexuality might relate to early environmental differences between asexual and sexual individuals. Interestingly, 44% were in a relationship—a figure somewhat higher than that found by Brotto, Knudson, et al. (2010). During their qualitative interviews, those asexual individuals in a relationship noted that they continued to experience romantic attraction in terms of wanting closeness, security, and connection in a relationship; however, they had no sexual attraction for that close partner. Asexual individuals also defined their relationships according to their romantic attraction—for example, heteroromantic, homoromantic, panromantic, or asexual. Heterogeneity exists, however, even in the experiences of asexual individuals, in that some identified as aromantic asexuals, desiring neither sexual nor romantic attachments. In Diamond's (2003) biobehavioral model of love and desire, she posited that the processes underlying the development of sexual desire are distinct from those underlying the development of romantic attachment. Diamond's model also explains that one can fall in love regardless of the gender of the partner and is consistent with the narratives shared by this sample of asexual individuals (Brotto, Knudson, et al., 2010). Although sexual desire is a strong motivator for pair bonding, it facilitates, but is not required for, romantic attachment. In Tennov's (1979) study of 1,000 individuals, 61% of women and 35% of men reported experiencing infatuation with a partner despite not feeling the need to engage in sex. In her extensive review, Diamond summarized both human and nonhuman literature also supporting this finding. However, recent findings showing similar patterns of neural activation during the experience of sexual desire and love and that they may exist on the same spectrum (Cacioppo, Bianchi-Demicheli, Frum, Pfaus, & Lewis, 2012) have suggested that researchers have much to learn about the disjunction between sexual attraction and desire and romantic attraction by studying those who identify as asexual.

Further research on asexuality has shown that the lack of sexual desire is not distressing (Bogaert, 2004; Brotto, Knudson, et al., 2010; Brotto & Yule, 2011; Prause & Graham, 2007) and that asexual individuals see no reason to pursue treatment for their lack of sexual attraction. Critics of asexuality have challenged the position that a complete absence of sexual attraction is not aberrant and pathologized asexuality by positing that asexuality is an extreme form of HSDD. That asexual individuals are not personally distressed by their lack of attraction is part of their pathology, critics have maintained, because it highlights the ego-syntonic nature of their (lack of) attraction. However, this debate over the usefulness of distress, per se, in distinguishing individuals with HSDD from asexual individuals raises many questions about the nature of distress. According to the *DSM–IV–TR* (American Psychiatric Association, 2000), *distress* in the sexual dysfunctions nomenclature is considered a necessary criterion across the various sexual dysfunctions and is defined as "marked distress or interpersonal difficulty" (p. 541). Because one's asexuality might evoke discord in a relationship in which one partner is sexual and the other is asexual, it is no surprise that interpersonal difficulties may arise, and the asexual individual may inadvertently receive a diagnosis of HSDD as a result of her or his interpersonal distress. Some experts have proposed that in future editions of the *DSM,* a disclaimer be made in the text excluding asexual individuals from receiving a diagnosis of HSDD, even if interpersonal distress is present (Brotto, 2010a, 2010b).

One finding that critics of asexuality emphasize is that asexual individuals masturbate with about the same frequency as sexual individuals (Brotto, Knudson, et al., 2010). If *asexuality* is defined as the absence of sexual desire, what incentives are there driving masturbation, particularly with the frequency attained by those who do feel sexual desire? Interestingly, unlike the larger population of sexual individuals, asexual individuals describe the urge to masturbate as stemming from "a need to clean out the plumbing," in the same way that there is an impulse to scratch an itch. Furthermore, they deny that sexual fantasies are conjured up during masturbation, and they maintain that the activity is not experienced as sexual. Whether nonsexual motives are sufficient for sustaining the level of masturbation seen among asexual individuals despite a reported lack of any sexual desire or attraction is interesting and suggests that desire for masturbation might be rather independent from desire for partnered sexual interactions. It is possible, therefore, that asexuality is more about lack of attraction for partnered sex than it is about lack of attraction for all forms of sex, although this needs further exploration. These findings raise interesting questions about the extent to which the desire for masturbation is truly a sexual desire versus an urge, impulse, or nonsexual need.

In an attempt to address whether asexuality might relate to an underlying psychological process, Brotto and Yule (2011) compared physiological sexual arousal in asexual, homosexual, bisexual, and heterosexual women. Participants viewed erotic stimuli in a controlled laboratory environment while a vaginal photoplethysmograph measured vaginal pulse amplitude. No significant differences were found in genital response between any of the groups, with asexual women showing as robust a genital response as the other subgroups of sexual women. These findings suggest that the reported absence of sexual attraction and desire is not the result of impaired physiological sexual responding. That sexual desire can be discordant from physiological sexual arousal is a common feature of women's, but not necessarily men's, sexual response (Chivers et al., 2010). The sexual arousal patterns of asexual men remain to be studied. Taken together, the research on asexuality has suggested that sexual desire, or its lack, may not be reliably inferred from one's romantic attraction, sexual activity (masturbation frequency), and physiological sexual response.

A major limitation of the existing literature on asexuality is that participants were recruited based on self-identification as asexual (Hinderliter, 2009). The lack of a validated measure of asexuality that would capture the construct among those individuals who had not yet identified as asexual means that only individuals who have embraced the asexual identity have been studied, and this group may differ in important ways from those who experience no sexual attraction but who have not discovered an asexual community. The research findings on asexuality provide scientists with a lens through which they can further their understanding of the intricacies of sexual desire and behavior. Furthermore, understanding how asexual individuals experience lack of desire and attraction—from a psychological, sociocultural, and biomedical perspective—has the potential to contribute important new knowledge to the study of desire (see Chapter 25, this volume).

A DEVELOPMENTAL PERSPECTIVE

Some people hold a belief that youth is associated with high levels of sexual interest, when sexual desires become realized and actualized as individuals experience sexual activity for the first time. This notion that sexual desire is abundant, incessant, and resistant to life's conflicting demands and challenges pervades much of Western society. In Levine's (1987) discussion of the three components of sexual desire, namely drive, wish, and motive, he described drive as testosterone dependent, spontaneous, and occurring most potently in adolescents. He further noted that drive manifestations "force adolescents to come to grips with their sexual selves" (p. 37). How they experience this drive in their youth may affect their later sexual desires as adults. Individuals who cannot identify with the youthful desires portrayed in the media may feel betrayed by their body and mind and robbed of the opportunity to experience what, apparently, every youth around them experiences (see Volume 2, Chapter 12, this handbook).

Feeling sexual desire is considered a normative part of human development (unless one is asexual; see the preceding section); however, young girls do not receive the message that such feelings are normal. In reality, evidence has suggested that powerful social and patriarchal forces shape how young women experience their own sexual desire. At puberty, the young woman quickly discovers that her body has become an object for the pleasurable viewing of others, and she, in turn, learns to see herself in this objectified manner. Narratives of personal sexual pleasure are often missing from women's stories of desire (Thomson, 1995; Tolman, 2002), particularly those of women who have experienced a history of abuse (Tolman & Szalacha, 1999). A disembodied narrative is also prevalent in young women's stories such that women's privileging of their body (as an object for others' desire) is cut off from their own subjective feelings. Only when specifically asked about their experience of desire and pleasure will adolescent women discuss these concepts. Aware of the sexual double standard—where boys are entitled to experience and express sexual desire and girls are denied the same—most girls studied by Tolman and Higgins (1996) reported an inability to resist it.

How do these early experiences, in which young women lack sexual agency and men's sexual desires are privileged, shape sexual desire later on? Young women may not have expectations for their own sexual desire as a result of their socialization to meet the sexual needs of men or boys, which may have an impact on their experiences of desire and their future labeling of lack of desire as "disordered" (Tolman, 2001).

Although sexual script theory suggests that patterns of initiating sexual activity follow traditional gender roles such that men are the initiators of sexual activity and women are the restrictors of sexual activity (Gagnon, 1990), more recent evidence has illustrated a more nuanced view of this finding. In a recent study that examined 31 men and 32 women with a mean age of 20.4 years, all of whom monitored their daily sexual activities over 3 weeks using a structured diary, male initiation of sexual activity was more common than female initiation (Vannier & O'Sullivan, 2011). Most occasions of sexual activity involved indirect verbal initiation strategies (compared with direct verbal strategies; 57% vs. 45%, respectively), and nearly all sexual encounters involved some nonverbal initiation strategy. A nonverbal response to a partner's sexual initiation was the most common pattern, whether it was direct or indirect, and men were more likely than women to use an indirect nonverbal than a direct nonverbal response. Verbal responses to a partner's initiations were slightly less common than nonverbal responses, with no differences found between men and women. These findings collectively illustrate that young adults' desire to engage in sexual activity is expressed with fewer words than actions and may have implications for sexual communication more generally as one ages. Vannier and O'Sullivan (2011) also found no gender differences in receptivity to a partner's invitations, and responses tended to match the style of the initiation such that a nonverbal direct invitation was met with a nonverbal direct response.

Another feature of young adults' sexual desire and interactions is that sexual behavior can occur in the absence of desire. O'Sullivan and Allgeier (1998) defined such sexual compliance as instances in which the sexual activity itself is not wanted or desired, yet the individual freely consents to it. Sexual compliance exists in a relationship to maintain harmony and reflects the fact that occasionally one partner may make sacrifices for the good of the relationship. Vannier and O'Sullivan (2010) examined couples in a committed relationship and studied the characteristics of sexual compliance and how this might influence one's decision to assert one's needs in other ways, such as in the use of contraceptives. They also tested the relationship between compliance and type of sexual activity, according to its rating of intensity (e.g., intercourse vs. oral sex). Overall, participants expressed a high level of desire to engage in sexual activity, with no differences between men and women. Of the participants, 46% reported at least one occasion of sexual compliance, and those occasions of compliant sexual activity were rated as less enjoyable than those occasions that were desired sexually. In qualitative interviews, several participants noted that sexual compliance was part of an unspoken contract between them and their partners about maintaining sexual contact. The participants also noted that their lack of desire for sex during instances of sexual compliance was accounted for by feeling tired (58%), stressed (42%), or angry (17%). Most participants also noted that even though they began a sexual interaction out of compliance and not sexual desire, once the interaction continued and they experienced some sexual arousal, sexual desire for the activity itself significantly increased. This finding is reminiscent of the circular model of human sexual response articulated by Basson (2001a, 2002), in which the absence of sexual desire at the start of a sexual interaction may be quite normative, particularly for individuals in long-term relationships. Basson went on to note that once information processing allows for the experience of sexual arousal, further awareness of these sensations by the individual then opens the pathway toward feeling some sexual desire. The findings of Vannier and O'Sullivan (2010) and the model articulated by Basson (2001a, 2002) suggest that there is, perhaps, a developmental trajectory leading from sexually compliant experiences as a young person toward lack of spontaneous sexual desire as an adult. Only when the latter is associated with distress would it merit a sexual desire disorder label. Understanding the progression of sexual compliance over time and with relationship duration may be a fruitful area of study in the future, particularly because those experiences of sexual compliance were rated as less enjoyable (see Chapters 13, 14, and 16, this volume).

Although most research on the prevalence of sexual desire difficulties has focused on adults, a few studies have examined these complaints in younger samples. For example, a British national sample of men and women ages 16 to 44 found that 17% of male and 41% of female respondents in the youngest age group experienced low sexual desire (Mercer et al., 2003). In a sample of 171 late adolescent men and women with a mean age of 19.5 who completed validated surveys of sexual functioning, O'Sullivan and Majerovic (2008) found no gender differences in desire for sexual activity, although the men had a higher desire for masturbation than the women. Fifty-eight percent of the men reported not being interested in sex at some point in their lives, with the majority of men (86%) reporting that such lack of interest was only rarely or never a concern. Of women, 81% reported no sexual interest at some point, with 58.6% of women noting that such lack of interest was rarely a concern and 21.9% reporting that it was sometimes a concern. Only 1% of women reported that their lack of interest in sex was always a concern for them. An interesting finding was that compared with a slightly older sample of young adults with a mean age of 24.5 years, both younger women and younger men had significantly lower desire for masturbation, though the two age groups did not differ on levels of sexual pleasure or satisfaction.

At the other end of the developmental trajectory, there is also a commonly held belief that sexual desire fades with age and relationship duration (see Chapter 17, this volume). Partnered older individuals ($N = 1{,}009$ couples) from Brazil, Germany, Japan, Spain, and the United States completed a survey that assessed relationship happiness and sexual satisfaction (Heiman et al., 2011). For men, being in good health, viewing their partner's orgasm as important, kissing and cuddling often, and being touched by a partner often significantly predicted relationship happiness. None of these variables significantly predicted relationship happiness for women. Relationship duration significantly predicted relationship happiness for both men and women but in slightly different ways. For men, relationship happiness increased as duration increased. For women, relationship duration had a negative effect on relationship happiness in the first 1 to 15 years of the relationship, then positively influenced relationship happiness after that. In looking at predictors of sexual satisfaction, sexual functioning and frequency of sex significantly predicted sexual satisfaction for men and women. Also, for both men and women, relationship duration had a significant positive effect on sexual satisfaction, with a slightly stronger effect for women than for men (Heiman et al., 2011). Thus, despite data showing a decline in sexual desire (Witting et al., 2008) and a decline in sexual frequency (Klusmann, 2002) with age and relationship duration, relationship duration appears to be beneficial for long-term sexual satisfaction, both in men and in women (see Chapter 8, this volume).

PSYCHOLOGICAL MECHANISMS IN DESIRE

Psychological factors play a key role in the experience of desire and pleasure. A large number of psychological variables have been found to influence desire, including psychological disorders such as anxiety and depression, childhood abuse, perceived stress, and body image (see Brotto, Bitzer, Laan, Leiblum, & Luria, 2010; Brotto & Klein, 2010; and Meuleman & van Lankveld, 2005, for reviews). Psychological factors may predispose, precipitate, or maintain desire difficulties; for individuals who seek help for desire problems, a comprehensive assessment of such factors enables clinicians to select and guide appropriate treatment. With regard to psychological mechanisms underlying desire, cognitive–emotional factors and attentional processes have been studied and are highly relevant to the experience of desire.

Cognitive and emotional variables often contribute to the onset and maintenance of desire problems. Nobre (2009) recently proposed a conceptual model of female sexual desire difficulties on the basis of cognitive theory. This model is interactional and posits that specific cognitive–emotional variables interact with and influence sexual desire. Negative sexual beliefs are viewed as predisposing factors that set the stage for the activation of negative schemas (i.e., core beliefs that guide the interpretation of and meaning assigned to a situation); in turn, these schemas generate negative cognitions and emotional responses in a sexual situation that decrease the focus on erotic stimuli and impair sexual response and desire (see Nobre, 2009, for a more detailed description of the model's theoretical components). In testing this model, Nobre examined sexually conservative beliefs (e.g., "masturbation is not a proper activity for women"), thoughts of abuse (e.g., "[my partner] is abusing me"), thoughts of failure or disengagement (e.g., "I am not satisfying my partner"), lack of erotic thoughts, and guilt and anger as cognitive–emotional predictors of women's sexual desire. Having conservative beliefs, failure or disengagement thoughts, and a lack of erotic thoughts were significantly and directly related to women's experiencing lower levels of sexual desire. Additionally, the cognitive and emotional variables influenced desire indirectly; for example, one way in which guilt affected sexual desire was through the presence of failure or disengagement thoughts and the absence of erotic thoughts. This model underscores the important predisposing and maintaining role of cognitions and emotions in women's sexual desire difficulties.

Strong support has also been found for the importance of cognitive factors in men's sexual desire. A recent study conducted with Portuguese men recruited from the community compared medical factors (e.g., presence of medical conditions), psychological adjustment, relationship adjustment, and cognitive–emotional factors as predictors of male sexual desire (Carvalho & Nobre, 2011). Cognitions, particularly a lack of erotic thoughts during sexual activity, emerged as the best predictor of men's sexual desire. Again, these findings highlight the critical link between sexual desire and cognitive–emotional variables; such findings also suggest a key role for psychological treatment approaches that use cognitive strategies to help men and women who experience desire difficulties (see Volume 2, Chapter 4, this handbook).

Attention is another mechanism involved in desire and has long been implicated in the development and treatment of sexual difficulties. For example, sensate focus, a long-standing technique used in the treatment of low desire, is designed to focus one's attention on and promote enjoyment of nongenital and genital touch sensations (Kaplan, 1979). Moreover, as noted earlier, factors such as negative cognitions may decrease the focus on erotic stimuli during sexual activity, leading to dampened sexual response and desire. The role of attention in desire has also been investigated empirically in laboratory-based settings. Using a dot detection task to evaluate attention, Prause, Janssen, and Hetrick (2008) found that the amount of men's and women's attention that was captured by sexual stimuli predicted differences in participants' level of sexual desire. In this study, individuals with relatively higher levels of sexual desire were slower to detect dots that replaced sexual images; this finding suggested that participants with higher sexual desire perhaps attended to and were more engaged by the sexual stimuli and that attention directly contributes to the experience of sexual desire. Clinically, the findings also lend support to the possibility that altering one's attention may have an impact on desire. To this end, mindfulness, or nonjudgmental present-moment awareness, has been applied to helping women with desire difficulties (Brotto, Basson, & Luria, 2008); by helping women learn to focus and attend to their moment-by-moment experiences nonjudgementally, distractions may be reduced and desire and pleasure may increase (see Chapter 25, this volume).

SOCIAL CONTEXTS THAT INTERACT WITH DESIRE

Sexual desire is often shaped by context, including interpersonal and larger sociocultural contexts. Indeed, models of sexuality that emphasize context have increasingly emerged in the literature over the past 10 to 15 years. The "new view" of women's sexuality is one example of such a model (Tiefer, Hall, & Tavris, 2002; see Table 8.1). In the new view model, which was organized around the major causes of women's sexual problems, women can identify their own sexual problems, which Tiefer et al. (2002) defined as "discontent or dissatisfaction with any emotional, physical, or relational aspect of sexual experience" (p. 229). This view identifies sexual problems, such as desire difficulties, as stemming from any of the following four main and interrelated aspects of women's sexual lives: (a) sociocultural, political, and economic factors; (b) relationship or partner factors; (c) psychological factors; and finally (d) medical factors. (Examples of contributing factors within each of these categories are presented in Table 8.1.) The model also posits that there is no one "normal" sexual experience or response and that sexual difficulties cannot be addressed without regard to the relationship and context in which sex unfolds. The notion of "sexual plasticity," or the idea that desire can be shaped and changed by sociocultural context, has also received considerable attention in the literature (e.g., Baumeister, 2000; Diamond, 2008). Female sexuality is thought to be particularly "plastic" or "fluid" and responsive to context; as such, women may experience sexual desire and engage in sexual activities that "run counter to [their] overall [sexual] orientation" (Diamond, 2012, p. 3; see also Chapter 20, this volume). In this section, we review desire and pleasure in consideration of sociocultural messages regarding gender norms, socioeconomic variables, and relationship factors.

Gender Norms

Messages regarding norms and traditional roles for males and females are abundant in U.S. society—people receive such messages from a variety of sources, including families, social networks (e.g., school), and media representations. With regard to sexuality, heterosexual scripts that govern what is expected in a sexual situation are based on traditional and stereotyped gender roles. Not every individual adheres to such scripts, and sexual scripts have become more egalitarian over time (Katz & Farrow, 2000). From the perspective of traditional roles, however, males are expected to be dominant, initiate sexual activity (typically vaginal intercourse), and be ready and willing to engage in sexual activity at any time (Drew, 2003). Dominant discourse portrays male sexuality as predictable, autonomous, and performance oriented (McCarthy & McDonald, 2009). Females, in contrast, are expected to be more submissive or to refuse sexual advances. Moreover, heterosexual discourse positions intercourse as the most important sexual act (Drew, 2003; Katz & Farrow, 2000). Rigid gender roles may contribute to the experience of low desire. For example, men who adhere to traditional sexual scripts may experience low desire and avoidance of sexual activity if they are unable to perform perfectly

TABLE 8.1

A New View Classification of Women's Sexual Problems

General factor	Subfactor
Sexual problems due to sociocultural, political, or economic factors	A. Ignorance and anxiety due to inadequate sex education, lack of access to health services, or other social constraints: 1. Lack of vocabulary to describe subjective or physical experience. 2. Lack of information about human sexual biology and life-stage changes. 3. Lack of information about how gender roles influence men's and women's sexual expectations, beliefs, and behaviors. 4. Inadequate access to information and services for contraception and abortion, STD prevention and treatment, sexual trauma, and domestic violence. B. Sexual avoidance or distress due to perceived inability to meet cultural norms regarding correct or ideal sexuality, including: 1. Anxiety or shame about one's body, sexual attractiveness, or sexual responses. 2. Confusion or shame about one's sexual orientation or identity, or about sexual fantasies and desires. C. Inhibitions due to conflict between the sexual norms of one's subculture or culture of origin and those of the dominant culture. D. Lack of interest, fatigue, or lack of time due to family and work obligations.
Sexual problems relating to partner and relationship	A. Inhibition, avoidance, or distress arising from betrayal, dislike, or fear of partner, partner's abuse or couple's unequal power, or arising from partner's negative patterns of communication. B. Discrepancies in desire for sexual activity or in preferences for various sexual activities. C. Ignorance or inhibition about communicating preferences or initiating, pacing, or shaping sexual activities. D. Loss of sexual interest and reciprocity as a result of conflicts over commonplace issues such as money, schedules, or relatives, or resulting from traumatic experiences, e.g., infertility or the death of a child. E. Inhibitions in arousal or spontaneity due to partner's health status or sexual problems.
Sexual problems due to psychological factors	A. Sexual aversion, mistrust, or inhibition of sexual pleasure due to: 1. Past experiences of physical, sexual, or emotional abuse. 2. General personality problems with attachment, rejection, cooperation, or entitlement. 3. Depression or anxiety. B. Sexual inhibition due to fear of sexual acts or of their possible consequences, e.g., pain during intercourse, pregnancy, sexually transmitted disease, loss of partner, loss of reputation.
Sexual problems due to medical factors	Pain or lack of physical response during sexual activity despite a supportive and safe interpersonal situation, adequate sexual knowledge, and positive sexual attitudes. Such problems can arise from: A. Numerous local or systemic medical conditions affecting neurological, neurovascular, circulatory, endocrine or other systems of the body. B. Pregnancy, sexually transmitted diseases, or other sex-related conditions. C. Side effects of many drugs, medications, or medical treatments. D. Iatrogenic conditions.

Note. STD = sexually transmitted disease. From "Beyond Dysfunction: A New View of Women's Sexual Problems," by L. Tiefer, M. Hall, and C. Tavris, 2002, *Journal of Sex & Marital Therapy, 28*(Suppl. 1), pp. 225–232. Copyright 2002 by Taylor & Francis. Adapted with permission.

with intercourse (McCarthy & McDonald, 2009). As well, women may not necessarily pursue sexual pleasure for fear of negative repercussions (e.g., stigmatization; Richgels, 1992), and a primary focus on intercourse (instead of other sexual activities that may be more pleasurable for females) may lead to reduced desire in women. Notably, women who do not desire sexual intercourse may also be labeled as dysfunctional because of the centrality placed on intercourse in U.S. society (Drew, 2003).

Empirical investigations have examined links between gender norms and sexual desire and pleasure. When presented with a priming task, female college students were found to implicitly associate sex with submission (Sanchez, Kiefer, & Ybarra, 2006). Furthermore, the students who engaged in a higher number of submissive sexual behaviors reported less sexual arousability, with the term *arousability* referring to the ease with which subjective excitement occurs (Hoon & Chambless, 1998) and can act as a trigger for sexual desire (Basson, 2009). In addition, the amount of pleasure derived from sexual activity and intimacy has been found to be affected by the degree to which men and women believe it is important to conform to gender norms (Sanchez, Crocker, & Boike, 2005); specifically, basing self-esteem on the approval of others and feeling less autonomous during partnered sexual activities accounted for the relationship between gender norm conformity and pleasure. Sanchez et al. (2005) argued that individuals who conform to gender norms may feel pressure to perform certain roles to gain approval from others; this need for approval may then restrict one's feelings of freedom during sexual activity. Some interesting data have suggested that nontraditional gender roles can also be associated with less sexual desire: In one study, heterosexual men and women who identified with nontraditional gender roles reported less sexual desire than those with more traditional identity (Katz & Farrow, 2000). From a theoretical perspective, Katz and Farrow (2000) posited that people who identify with nontraditional roles may experience discomfort from sexual interactions that are governed by traditional sexual scripts.

Media (e.g., television, magazines) also play an influential role in disseminating information about gender roles and sexuality (Ward, 2003). Content analysis of popular magazines has indicated that sexual desire tends to be portrayed differently, and often stereotypically, for males versus females. For example, a recent analysis of magazine stories published from 2006 to 2008 that were directed at adolescent girls (e.g., stories in *CosmoGirl!*) found that sexual wanting was portrayed more often for boys than for girls in U.S. magazines, whereas a comparable gender difference was not found in Dutch magazines (Joshi, Peter, & Valkenburg, 2011). Unexpectedly, sexual pleasure was portrayed with similar frequency for boys and girls in these stories, with the authors suggesting that perhaps magazine coverage is shifting from the dominant sexual script that emphasizes male pleasure (see Chapter 25, this volume; Volume 2, Chapter 12, this handbook).

Socioeconomic Status

Some research has noted an association between desire and socioeconomic variables such as education. Using a national probability sample of more than 3,000 adults between the ages of 18 and 59, the National Health and Social Life Survey examined the prevalence of and risk factors related to sexual difficulties among individuals of various social groups (Laumann, Paik, & Rosen, 1999). Both men and women with fewer years of education reported experiencing less pleasure from sex. As well, women with less education were more likely to report low desire; in fact, female college graduates were approximately half as likely to experience low desire as women with less education. Economic position was also related to sexual difficulties in women, including problems with desire. Specifically, women with less income were at modest risk of experiencing sexual difficulties. This association between economic position and desire was not found for men. One interpretation of the link between socioeconomic variables and desire is that people of lower socioeconomic status may experience more stress, which, in turn increases the risk of having sexual difficulties. Additionally, better health status is related to desire, and having lower income can influence access to health care services and resources that may bolster emotional and physical health.

Research with adults ages 45 and older has also found that attitudes toward sexuality help to explain the relationship between education and desire (DeLamater & Sill, 2005). In particular, positive attitudes toward sex have been found to be associated with greater levels of sexual desire, and education may help foster such attitudes. As noted by DeLamater and Sill (2005) in reference to older adults, "Greater education may undermine the negative stereotypes of sexual expression by older persons" (p. 147). Finally, we should note that women with higher social status have also been found to experience lower frequency of desire; again, one hypothesis for this association links desire to stress, particularly work-related stress that may come with a higher socioeconomic position, putting strain on one's capacity for sexual desire (Eplov, Giraldi, Davidsen, Garde, & Kamper-Jørgensen, 2007).

Relational Context

Both theoretical and empirical work has increasingly highlighted the association between sexual desire and relationship factors, particularly in women (see Chapter 10, this volume). For example, Basson (e.g., 2001a) has proposed a model of human sexual response emphasizing the role that long-term intimacy between partners can play in motivating sexual behavior and triggering desire. This model recognizes that spontaneous desire may motivate one to be sexual but that multiple reasons exist for engaging in sexual activity. Reasons other than spontaneous sexual desire are often important for having sex with a partner and may include enrichment of emotional closeness and a desire to increase one's attractiveness to a partner (Basson, 2001a, 2003). This model underscores the importance of context in triggering responsive sexual desire, both the context of the relationship in which sexual activity occurs (e.g., positive feelings toward the partner) and the immediate sexual context (e.g., private and erotic environment).

Although originally designed as a model applicable to both men and women, Basson's model has been widely applied to understanding women's sexual response and highlights the important connection between relationship factors and sexual desire. From this perspective, women with low desire are not considered to have an innate dysfunction of sexual response; instead, a dearth of reasons to engage in sexual activity, a problematic context, or both are contributing factors in the experience of low desire (Basson & Brotto, 2009). Research with women and men has indicated that multiple factors, often those that are relationally based, may indeed lead to sexual desire. McCall and Meston (2006, 2007) have documented that love–emotional bonding cues (e.g., talking about the future with one's partner) and romantic–implicit cues (e.g., laughing with a partner) are some triggers of sexual desire in women, and a series of studies by Meston and Buss (2007) found that at least 237 distinct reasons why people engage in sex could be identified, with many of them being nonsexual.

Much research has also shown an association between sexual desire and relationship satisfaction. In one such study, higher marital satisfaction was significantly associated with higher levels of sexual desire for one's partner among married couples who were recruited from the community, as were higher levels of shared and mutual decision making (i.e., egalitarianism) in the relationship (Brezsnyak & Whisman, 2004). A large sample of women in Europe found that those with low desire were more likely to report both decreased sexual and relationship satisfaction than women who did not experience low desire (Dennerstein, Koochaki, Barton, & Graziottin, 2006). Although such studies have not indicated directionality, satisfaction may be both a causal factor and an outcome of desire in relationships (Brezsnyak & Whisman, 2004).

Relational factors other than satisfaction also seem to contribute to sexual desire. A recent qualitative study with married women who met criteria for HSDD found that overfamiliarity with their partner and institution of the relationship (e.g., deeroticizing effect of readily available sex) were viewed by women as dampening their desire (Sims & Meana, 2010). Longitudinal studies have also been conducted to understand desire and its link to relationship goals. For example, approach goals in a relationship—that is, goals that concentrate on pursuing positive relational experiences such as fun and growth—have been found to buffer against reductions in sexual desire over time; additionally, approach goals seem to buffer against the harmful effects of negative relationship events on desire (Impett, Strachman, Finkel, & Gable, 2008).

As evidenced by the predominant discussion in this section on women's desire, women tend to emphasize relationship factors in sexuality more so than men, and more research has been carried out on women's desire and relational factors (Peplau, 2003). For instance, Regan and Berscheid (1996) found that women were more likely than men to view interpersonal goals such as love, intimacy, and closeness as important for sexual desire, whereas men were more likely to view sexual activity or pleasure as goals. Of course, the consequent dangers of assuming static and universal gender differences must be kept in mind. A discrepancy in level of sexual desire, wherein the women in a heterosexual relationship may be more likely to experience less desire than their male partners, is also a common reason why couples seek treatment for problems with low desire.

PHYSIOLOGICAL AND NEUROBIOLOGICAL MECHANISMS INVOLVED IN DESIRE

Early research on sexual response was primarily biological and physiological in nature. Frank Beach (1956) challenged the purely vascular view of sexual response that predated his work and noted that *sexual drive* should be replaced by the term *sexual appetite* in recognition that it is a by-product of one's experience with little or no relation to biological or physiological needs. He proposed one of the earliest models of sexual motivation (on the basis of research with rodents), based on a two-factor theory: First, copulation was initiated by a sexual arousal mechanism that increased the male's sexual excitement in the presence of a sexual stimulus. Copulation was then maintained by the second factor, an intromission and ejaculation mechanism, which further modified the male's internal state. When Masters and Johnson carried out their research in the 1960s and 1970s, they focused on physiological responding as couples engaged in sexual activity (Masters & Johnson, 1966), and the groundwork for their HSRC model, composed of excitement, plateau, orgasm, and resolution, was entirely based on the physiological processes unfolding during sexual activity. Kaplan (1979), who introduced sexual desire to the HSRC model, equated sexual desire with other drive states that depend on a specific anatomical location in the brain and found that the need to seek out sexual stimuli (or be receptive to them) is produced by the physical activation of neural systems. She described inhibitory and activating centers involved in sexual desire located within the limbic system with extensive neural connections throughout the brain. In the decades since the influential thinking of Beach (1956), Masters and Johnson (1966), and Kaplan (1979), science has advanced considerably in terms of understanding the biological and physiological underpinnings of sexual desire and how these domains may interact with one another. Some of the initial speculations about a dual control mechanism have received some of the most extensive study and empirical support to date.

Although much of what is known today about the neurotransmitters involved in sexual desire is derived from research on rodents, there are parallels between the sexual behavior patterns in rodents and humans that allow rodents to be useful homologues to understanding human behavior (Pfaus, 2009; see Chapter 7, this volume). Bancroft and Janssen (2000; Bancroft, Graham, Janssen, & Sanders, 2009) proposed the dual control model, which reflects a balance of excitatory and inhibitory mechanisms and has three basic assumptions:

1. Neurobiological inhibition of sexual response is an adaptive pattern that reduces the likelihood of sexual response at inappropriate times;
2. Individuals vary in their propensity for sexual excitation and inhibition; and
3. Sexual stimulus effects are mediated by the psychological and neurophysiological characteristics of the individuals involved.

Both excitation and inhibition activate the autonomic nervous system, but the balance of excitation versus inhibition may dictate whether one may be prone to sexual difficulties (high inhibition, low excitation) or to sexual risk taking (high excitation, low inhibition). In the case of sexual desire, increased levels might be attributed to a more dominant excitatory system, whereas a decrease in sexual desire might be the result of a more dominant inhibitory process. Of course, these systems may wax and wane within and across individuals and over time.

Excitatory Mechanisms

Within the dual control model, dopamine, norepinephrine, melanocortin, and oxytocin systems in the hypothalamus and limbic system stimulate sexual arousal, attention, and behaviors toward sexual incentives. The ability to respond to sexual stimuli also depends on steroid hormone actions in specific brain regions as well as interactions of those hormones with receptor complexes. Whereas norepinephrine and oxytocin activation are involved in mechanisms of sexual arousal, dopamine and melanocortins are thought to be involved in the activation of sexual interest. Dopamine's excitatory actions have been borne out in studies that have found a facilitatory effect of dopamine agonists (chemicals that bind to a receptor and increase the actions or activities of that cell) on male rat sexual behavior and a sometimes indiscriminate increase in sexual desire seen among people taking Parkinson's drugs, which facilitate dopamine activity (as reviewed by Pfaus, 2009). Furthermore, dopamine antagonists (chemicals that bind to a receptor and block or decrease the activities of that cell), often used in the treatment of schizophrenia, can impair sexual response. Dopamine and steroids appear to interact such that estradiol and testosterone exert effects that facilitate dopamine's activities.

Norepinephrine is involved in the regulation of arousal and influences sympathetic tone. An agonist (clonidine) that reduces norepinephrine release has been found to significantly blunt both physiological and subjective sexual arousal to erotic stimuli (Meston, Gorzalka, & Wright, 1997). Because of the link between sexual arousal and motivation (Laan & Both, 2008), it is likely that decreased levels of noradrenergic activity may also play a role in reduced sexual desire.

Melanocortin agonists, interestingly, have been of great interest recently to pharmaceutical companies, which have found that the melanocortin agonist bremelanotide increases sexual desire and arousal in women (Diamond et al., 2006). Owing to concerns about safety and the (intranasal) mode of delivery, the company that manufactured bremelanotide has reformulated the mode of delivery for this agonist. New trials with women with low desire have been carried out, with the expectation by the company that this new formulation may be available for women who lack sexual interest in the years ahead.

Oxytocin cell bodies located in the hypothalamus are involved in the lordosis response of female rats and the ejaculation response of male rats. Anecdotal evidence from a single case study has suggested that intranasal administration of oxytocin significantly increased sexual desire in a male receiving the drug for treatment of anxiety (MacDonald & Feifel, 2012).

Inhibitory Mechanisms

According to Bancroft and Janssen's (2000) dual control model, inhibitory mechanisms are important for sexual decision making that involves risk. An underactive inhibitory system would predispose one to engage in sexual risk, whereas an overactive inhibitory system might make one vulnerable to having a sexual dysfunction. In a detailed review of the mechanisms involved in sexual inhibition in men, Bancroft (1999) noted that the limbic system plays a key role in the regulation of sexual behavior. Inhibitory chemicals include endogenous opioids, endocannabinoids, and serotonin, among others, and function to inhibit central excitatory mechanisms. The endogenous release of opioids that accompanies orgasm is known to significantly dampen sexual desire and arousal (Rodríguez-Manzo & Fernández-Guasti, 1995) by calming hypothalamic regions involved in sexual response. Opioid release is thought to be involved in the reward state that accompanies sexual pleasure, thereby reducing sexual desire. Observations about the clinical and therapeutic effects of cannabis have led researchers to examine more closely the role of the endocannabinoid system in the control of sexual response. The cannabinoid receptor Type 1 is distributed throughout the motor and limbic systems as well as the hypothalamus, and cannabinoid receptor Type 1 agonists have been found to impair sexually proceptive behaviors in female rats (Ferrari, Ottani, & Giuliani, 2000). There is also evidence in women that increases in erotica-induced subjective and physiological sexual arousal are significantly associated with decreases in endogenous cannabinoid levels (Klein, Hill, Chang, Hillard, & Gorzalka, 2012), making the endocannabinoid system a target for future drug development.

Considerable research has examined the role of serotonin in sexual response (Pfaus, 2009). Serotonin is involved in inhibiting the actions of dopamine. Disruptions in orgasmic functioning of men and women are common after treatment with serotonin-enhancing drugs, including the selective serotonin reuptake inhibitors (Clayton, 2010).

However, treatment with serotonergic drugs compared with placebo does not appear to affect sexual desire in nondepressed women (Reed et al., 2012).

When the excitatory system is activated, it blunts the inhibition system, yet in reality the excitatory and inhibitory systems act in concert to control sexual behavior. Pharmaceutical companies' programs of research align with the proposed theory of a hypofunctioning excitatory system and hyperfunctioning inhibitory system in their quest to find an effective pharmacologic cure for low desire. Although some empirical support has been found for some of these tested agents (e.g., bremelanotide, flibanserin), they have not been approved by the U.S. Food and Drug Administration because of a lack of long-term safety data (e.g., bremelanotide), lack of efficacy for the end points that the U.S. Food and Drug Administration required, and concern regarding potential adverse events (e.g., flibanserin).

In his sexual tipping point model, psychologist Perelman (2006) used the concepts of inhibition and excitation and applied them to understanding the etiology for and treatment of sexual difficulties. This model suggests that an individual has a tipping point (somewhat like a threshold), dynamic and not static, that integrates biological, psychological, and sociocultural influences to determine sexual response. In the case of an individual with low desire, organic and sociocultural factors may interfere with the response to previously effective sexual stimuli. The model provides an algorithm for care providers suggesting how pharmaceutical and psychological or psychosocial treatments might be properly timed and administered (see Volume 2, Chapter 5, this handbook). The administration of a drug alone may alter this threshold for response, so that psychological skills may be optimized.

What the dual control and sexual tipping point models offer is an algorithm that allows hypotheses about the mechanisms involved in sexual desire in men and women to be tested and frameworks for how sexual difficulties might be managed. Furthermore, these models stress the adaptive nature of sexual response to the context; specifically, the adaptive nature of sexual excitation would lead one to engage in sex for procreation or sexual reward and pleasure, whereas sexual inhibition would deter one from engaging in sex that may have negative outcomes (e.g., sexually transmitted infection, damaging effect on the relationship).

Hormones and Sexual Desire

According to the incentive motivation model of sexual response (Toates, 2009), the experience of sexual desire and arousal hinges on a sexually responsive system. The sex hormones estrogen and testosterone have received the most attention, although it is still not entirely clear exactly what role they play in sexual desire. Considerable work has focused on the role of estrogen in women's sexual response, particularly as women transition through menopause, when there is a sharp decline in serum estradiol. Estrogen-related menopausal changes include hot flashes, sleep disturbance, mood changes, vaginal atrophy, and vaginal dryness. Evidence of reduced vaginal blood flow has also been found when women are assessed with a vaginal photoplethysmograph (Laan & van Lunsen, 1997); however, when a woman is adequately sexually aroused, these reduced estrogens are thought to have little or no impact on vaginal blood flow. It is possible that the dryness and vaginal atrophy may negatively affect a woman's desire for sex (Dennerstein, Lehert, Burger, & Dudley, 1999).

One Australian prospective longitudinal study followed women transitioning through menopause and carried out annual hormonal assessments as well as face-to-face interviews with participants. Changes in androgens (total testosterone, free testosterone index, and dehydroepiandrosterone sulfate) were unrelated to any aspect of sexual functioning (Dennerstein, Randolph, Taffe, Dudley, & Burger, 2002). Using structural equation modeling to examine the relative effects of a variety of psychosocial factors and hormones on libido, "feelings for partner" was a much stronger predictor than were any of the hormones, including estrogen and testosterone (Dennerstein et al., 1999). Moreover, in a recent study comparing hormonal versus nonhormonal predictors of whether women had HSDD (verified by an in-depth clinical interview) versus a more severe form of HSDD that also included lack of responsive sexual desire, logistic regression analyses determined that hormone levels did not significantly predict group status, whereas three psychosocial factors—developmental history, psychiatric history, and psychosexual history—significantly predicted group membership (Brotto, Petkau, Labrie, & Basson, 2011). Specifically, those women who lacked both spontaneous and responsive sexual desire had a greater contribution of these psychosocial variables than women with HSDD alone. Psychiatric factors in particular emerged as the single greatest predictor when all hormonal and nonhormonal variables, age, and relationship duration were considered collectively.

These findings challenge the long-standing debate about the extent to which testosterone is the "hormone of desire." Evidence has been found that testosterone has a direct impact on sexual interest in men (Regan, 1999) and that reports of low desire significantly predict testosterone levels that fall below a certain threshold (Travison, Morley, Araujo, O'Donnell, & McKinlay, 2006), although findings have also shown that, among men with erectile dysfunction, testosterone levels did not differ between the subset of men with and without HSDD (Ansong & Punwaney, 1999; Corona et al., 2009). With menopause, the reduction in testosterone is less marked (compared with the sharp decline in estradiol). This decline in serum testosterone is due to the reduced peripheral conversion of androstenedione (secreted from the ovaries) to testosterone. Some reduction in testosterone also occurs as a result of less adrenal output of the testosterone precursor dehydroepiandrosterone. Complicating this picture is the fact that most testosterone production takes place intracellularly, where testosterone also exerts its effects. Because available assays only measure testosterone that has spilled into the serum, their accuracy in providing an estimate of androgens in any given woman is seriously questionable (Labrie et al., 2006).

Research that has examined the association between levels of testosterone and women's sexual desire has also been conflicting. Despite early studies suggesting that low desire was associated with low levels of testosterone, a large number of more recent studies have failed to find a significant difference in testosterone levels between women with and without low desire (as reviewed in Brotto, Bitzer, et al., 2010; Nappi et al., 2010). Thus, there are no available cut-offs that denote the separation from normal to problematically low sexual desire, nor is there any blood test for HSDD. Somewhat paradoxically, however, treatment of low desire with testosterone in women results in a statistically significant improvement in most women (Basson, 2010; Davis, Moreau, et al., 2008; Davis, Paplia, et al., 2008), but not all (Barton et al., 2007).

Perhaps some of the inconsistency in interpreting effects of testosterone on sexual desire stems from a failure to consider sociocultural and psychological interactions with testosterone. A recent study (van Anders, 2012) that had 196 men and women provide saliva samples of testosterone and measured solitary and partnered sexual desire found a significant correlation between testosterone and solitary desire, but not partnered desire, in women. Interestingly, testosterone was negatively correlated with partnered sexual desire only among women who had higher cortisol, suggesting, perhaps, stress-activated increases in testosterone. In contrast, testosterone was unrelated to either solitary or partnered sexual desire in men. Moreover, differences between men and women in sexual desire were not mediated by level of testosterone but by masturbation frequency, suggesting a more pronounced effect of behavioral and not hormonal variables in accounting for sex differences in desire.

DESIRE AND PLEASURE

In their qualitative study of women, Goldhammer and McCabe (2011) found that sexual desire might be related to a variety of different behaviors, depending on the context in which the desire was experienced. Women noted that their initiation of sexual behavior was not necessarily driven by sexual desire; rather, it was often influenced by a number of (sexual and nonsexual) factors, such as being aware that it had been too long since the last time the couple had sex. Moreover, women in at least one qualitative study reported the intrinsic pleasure of simply experiencing sexual desire, and it was not imperative to act on this desire (Brotto et al., 2009). Couples therapist Esther Perel (2006) viewed love and pleasure or eroticism as distinct, although in conventional discussions both experts and nonexperts may interchange the terms. She stated that the very factors that are important to a long-term, stable, and monogamous relationship (e.g., stability, understanding, compassion) may be the very same factors that douse the fire of sexual desire, the latter of which relies on novelty, excitement, and mystery (Perel, 2006). On the basis of this approach, desire and pleasure become fueled when space is introduced between partners, when the forbidden becomes pleasurable.

How do sexual desire and pleasure influence one another? Interestingly, neither is necessary for sexual activity to take place (Meston & Buss, 2007). Nonetheless, desire for sexual pleasure is an important sexual motive to consider. The domain of sexual fantasies, which represent a private mental experience with the goal, presumably, of eliciting pleasure, provides an opportunity to examine how pleasure and desire influence one another. Vance (1989) has written extensively about the dangers for women in experiencing sexual desire and pleasure. The expression of desire may lead to dangerous sexual encounters, and because pleasure and safety are at opposite ends of the dimension, the expression of pleasure, too, can be problematic for women. In a study of 85 men and 77 women, Zurbriggen and Yost (2004) examined themes of sexual desire and pleasure in participants' private fantasies. Whereas sexual pleasure and desire were correlated for men (mean $r = .43$), this association was much weaker for women (mean $r = .24$). Specifically, men were likely to mention desire and pleasure for themselves as well as their partners in their fantasies, whereas women were more likely to only mention pleasure and desire for themselves. The fact that orgasm is a more likely outcome of sexual activity for men than for women simply reinforces the nonoverlap between sexual desire and pleasure for women.

Is Wanting the Same as Liking?

There is evidence that wanting sex is not necessarily the same as liking sex. Most measures of sexual satisfaction confound sexual frequency, sexual liking, and sexual wanting. As noted by Toates (2009), the wanting of sex may differ between men and women, with women being more influenced by controlled and deliberate processes and men being more influenced by automatic processes. In a series of studies, Krishnamurti and Loewenstein (2012) developed and established the test–retest reliability and convergent, discriminant, and predictive validity of a 15-item partner-specific sexual liking and sexual wanting scale. They found that higher levels of partner-specific sexual liking were associated with more initiation on the part of the partner, but not necessarily with one's own initiation of sexual activity. They also found that higher levels of partner-specific sexual wanting were associated with higher levels of self-initiation. Their data suggest that sexual satisfaction (i.e., liking) might be entirely independent from feelings of sexual desire. The latter finding has also been supported in large epidemiological studies of women's sexual health, which have shown that sexual satisfaction might not hinge on a woman's level of sexual desire. Contemporary models of women's sexual response position sexual satisfaction as a critical outcome determining whether women will initiate or be receptive to sexual activity on a future occasion (Basson, 2001b, 2002, 2003). Although the definition of sexual satisfaction differs across studies, there is general agreement that sexual satisfaction has both personal and relational domains (Meston & Trapnell, 2005). Relational sexual satisfaction might include domains such as feeling safe, not lonely, and not distant from a partner, and individual aspects of sexual satisfaction might include feeling content, free of sexual tension, pleasantly indulged, relaxed, and happy (Philippsohn & Hartmann, 2009). One's level of sexual satisfaction depends on one's frame of reference, which includes one's own expectations and past experiences (Byers & Macneil, 2006). Therefore, a woman who does not expect to experience orgasm during a sexual encounter with a partner may be more sexually satisfied than a woman who occasionally does not experience orgasm but expects one. Recent population-based studies of sexual functioning in women have shown that a significant proportion of women are sexually satisfied even though they are experiencing some sexual difficulties (e.g., reduced sexual desire or arousal). In the Study of Women's Health Across the Nation, 70% of women reported thinking about sex less than once a week (a threshold that some might consider falling into the level of women with HSDD), but 86% of them remained sexually satisfied (Cain et al., 2003). Among 164 women seeking general medical care, 48.8% met the clinical threshold for sexual dysfunction on a validated measure of sexual functioning, although 80.5% reported feeling that they were sexually satisfied (Ferenidou et al., 2008). Not surprisingly, the most common sexual complaint was low desire. In using data from the National Health and Social Life Survey to explore individual, relational, and cultural sexual satisfaction in 1,035 mid-life women in a sexual relationship, women's health positively influenced their emotional satisfaction (Carpenter, Nathanson, & Kim, 2009; see also Chapter 21, this volume). Interestingly, relationship duration was not a predictor of sexual satisfaction in this study. Sexual fantasies and sexual satisfaction are also not correlated in women (Cain et al., 2003). Behavior might also be discordant with sexual satisfaction. Among 290 British women ages 18 to 75, 79% indicated being very satisfied with their current sex life despite the fact that 24% had not engaged in any sexual activity in the past 3 months (Dunn, Croft, & Hackett, 2000). The interesting counterpart to these findings is that a number of studies have found that a proportion of women without any overt sexual symptoms will still report being sexually dissatisfied (King, Holt, & Nazareth, 2007; Laumann et al., 2005; Lutfey, Link, Rosen, Wiegel, & McKinlay, 2009; Öberg, Fugl-Meyer, & Fugl-Meyer, 2004).

More recent research has examined the association between motives for engaging in sexual activity and sexual satisfaction. A series of studies carried out by Meston and Buss (2007) with 1,549 male and female university students (mean = age 19, range = 16–42 years) found 237 distinct reasons why men and women engaged in sexual activity. These reasons could be categorized into four broad clusters: physical, emotional, goal attainment, and insecurity, with many subfactors contained in each domain. The most common reasons provided for having sex included attraction, pleasure, affection, love, romance, emotional closeness, arousal, the desire to please, adventure, excitement, experience, connection, celebration, curiosity, and opportunity. When these theoretically derived motives for sex were examined as potential predictors of sexual satisfaction in men and women, what emerged was a common set of motives that significantly predicted satisfaction for both men and women. These motives included love and commitment, self-esteem, and resource motives such that those who had sex for love and commitment seemed to have more sexual satisfaction. Those who had sex to raise their self-esteem tended to have lower sexual satisfaction, as did those whose motives for sex included resource attainment. Additional motives for sex predicted sexual satisfaction for women but not men, and they included experience seeking, pleasure, and expression motives. This was the case even after controlling for sexual functioning, neuroticism, and sexual attitudes. The findings from this study suggest that sexual desire, or motivation for sex, may relate to a variety of nonsexual reasons and that having a particular type of motive for sex may predict sexual satisfaction. It is interesting to note that in this study desire-related motives did not emerge as significant predictors of sexual satisfaction.

It is also important to note that reasons for engaging in sexual activity may vary across different relational or situational contexts. For example, Meston and Buss (2007) noted that reasons for engaging in sex may differ across shorter versus longer term relationships. Although some relationship (e.g., "I wanted to intensify my relationship") and situational (e.g., "It was a romantic setting") reasons were endorsed, participants in the Meston and Buss study were broadly asked to report their reasons for engaging in sex.

CROSS-CULTURAL ISSUES IN SEXUAL DESIRE

Just as the HSRC model of Masters and Johnson (1966) has been criticized for espousing a gender-neutral model of sexual functioning that ignores potentially important differences between men and women (Tiefer, 1991), it can also be criticized for making the presumption of cross-cultural universality in sexual responding. There is a growing body of literature comparing sexual attitudes, practices, and difficulties between various cultural groups and, in particular, a small but emerging interest in cross-cultural differences in sexual desire.

In a sample of Latina women seeking outpatient care, 41.3% had low levels of overall sexual functioning that were significantly associated with treatment for anxiety or depression (Hullfish et al., 2009). Using the Changes in Sexual Functioning Questionnaire, Hullfish et al. (2009) found that the most prevalent issue was low desire, on which 94.3% of the Latina women fell below the clinical cut-off. Among aboriginal groups, a pervasive double standard exists whereby men are expected to behave aggressively and to be interested in sex alone and women are not expected to initiate sex or resist sex and are viewed as "letting" sexual encounters occur (Devries & Free, 2010). In exploring levels of sexual desire in these ethnocultural groups, it is imperative to consider that sexual desire, as a construct, may be experienced very differently in different groups (see Volume 2, Chapter 6, this handbook). Thus, the conclusions that one draws about group differences must be tempered with adequate cultural sensitivity and competence.

In the Study of Women's Health Across the Nation, 16,065 mid-life women ages 40 to 55 were studied cross-sectionally, and a smaller cohort were observed longitudinally. The goal of the study was to examine multiple aspects of sexual functioning across diverse ethnic groups as women transitioned through menopause. Among the 2,466 women who had sex in the past 6 months, the Caucasian, African American, and Hispanic women were more likely to find sex quite or extremely important compared to Chinese or Japanese women (Cain et al., 2003).

Regarding sexual desire, in the Global Study of Sexual Attitudes and Behaviors, the first large, multicountry survey of sexuality in older adults, 13,883 women and 13,618 men ages 40 to 80 were asked, "During the last 12 months have you ever experienced a lack of interest in having sex for a period of 2 months or more?" (Laumann et al., 2005). Women endorsing "yes" were then asked to rate its frequency as *occasionally, sometimes,* or *frequently*. Among the 9,000 women who had had sexual intercourse in the past year, 25.6% to 32.9% of women from Europe or North America noted lack of desire was a problem, whereas 43.4% from the Middle East and 34.8% to 43.3% from Asia endorsed this item. Among the 11,205 sexually active male respondents, 12.5% to 17.6% of men from Europe or North America and 21.6% from the Middle East endorsed this item, and 19.6% to 28.0% of men from Asia reported low desire. A recent study that compared Black (n = 251) and White (n = 544) partnered women on how women evaluated their sexual relationship and their own sexuality found that level of sexual interest significantly predicted a woman's evaluation of her own sexuality and found no differences between Black and White women (Bancroft, Long, & McCabe, 2011).

In samples of younger individuals studied, sexual desire was similarly lower among the East Asian male and female participants compared with Caucasian participants (Brotto, Chik, Ryder, Gorzalka, & Seal, 2005; Brotto, Woo, & Gorzalka, 2011; Brotto, Woo, & Ryder, 2007; Woo, Brotto, & Gorzalka, 2011, 2012). Evidence is also emerging that sex guilt specifically, or a "generalized expectancy for self-mediated punishment for violating or for anticipating violating standards of proper sexual conduct" (Mosher & Cross, 1971, p. 27), may mediate the association between culture and sexual desire (Brotto et al., 2011; Woo et al., 2011, 2012). This finding suggests that culture-linked attitudes, such as sex guilt, which become altered with the process of acculturation, may mediate changes in individuals' level of sexual desire. Of course, whether the experience of sexual desire is the same across cultures has never been examined closely and raises concern about the use of Western-derived measures of sexual desire with non-Western samples.

SEXUAL DESIRE DISORDERS

Those who experience difficulties with sexual desire are said to have a sexual desire disorder if their symptoms meet specific diagnostic criteria. Two types of sexual desire disorders are outlined in the sexual dysfunctions category of the *DSM–IV–TR* (American Psychiatric Association, 2000): sexual aversion disorder and HSDD. Defined as "persistent or recurrent extreme aversion to, and avoidance of, all (or almost all) genital sexual contact with a sexual partner" (American Psychiatric Association, 2000, p. 542), sexual aversion disorder is likely better conceptualized as an anxiety disorder than as a sexual dysfunction (see Brotto, 2010c, for a review). HSDD is defined by the criterion of "persistently or recurrently deficient (or absent) sexual fantasies and desire for sexual activity" (American Psychiatric Association, 2000, p. 541). To be diagnosed with sexual aversion disorder or HSDD using *DSM–IV–TR* criteria, an individual must also experience marked distress or interpersonal difficulty. Given that little empirical information is available regarding sexual aversion disorder, in this section we briefly review the prevalence, known etiology, and treatment of HSDD only.

Prevalence

Low desire is the most common sexual difficulty among women. Several studies have attempted to determine the prevalence rate of female low desire and HSDD; across studies, different methodologies have been used and variable rates have been documented (see Brotto, 2010b, for a review). Some research, for example, has tried to document the prevalence rate of low sexual desire only, whereas other research has assessed both low desire and related distress. One of the most cited studies that assessed sexual difficulties (related distress was not measured) in a U.S. sample is the National Health and Social Life Survey (Laumann et al., 1999). In this study, 27% to 32% of sexually active women between the ages of 18 and 59 reported that they had lacked desire for sex in the past year. A multicountry study of sexual problems was the Global Study of Sexual Attitudes and Behaviors, which included more than 13,000 women and men between the ages of 40 and 80 in 29 different countries (Laumann et al., 2005). Lack of interest in sex that lasted for 2 months or more in the past year was reported by approximately 26% to 43% of women across various geographic regions; the rate of frequent lack of interest in sex ranged from 5.4% of women in Northern Europe to 13.6% of women in East Asia. Also, lack of interest in sex was the most common sexual problem reported by women in the Global Study of Sexual Attitudes and Behaviors. When findings from these and various other studies (e.g., Bancroft, Loftus, & Long, 2003; Dennerstein et al., 2006; Fugl-Meyer & Sjogren Fugl-Meyer, 1999; Leiblum, Koochaki, Rodenberg, Barton, & Rosen, 2006; Mercer et al., 2003; Öberg et al., 2004; Shifren, Monz, Russo, Segreti, & Johannes, 2008; West et al., 2008; Witting et al., 2008) are considered together, low desire seems to affect approximately 20% to 30% of women across all ages (Brotto, Bitzer, et al., 2010).

However, when female HSDD is assessed—that is, when low desire is assessed in conjunction with distress—prevalence rates are typically reduced by half (Brotto, Bitzer, et al., 2010; Dennerstein et al., 2006; Leiblum et al., 2006; Shifren et al., 2008; West et al., 2008). For example, in a telephone interview study of 755 premenopausal, 552 naturally menopausal, and 637 surgically menopausal women between the ages of 30 and 70 in the United States, the estimated prevalence rate of low desire was 36.2% and the estimated prevalence rate of HSDD was 8.3% (ranging from 6.6% for naturally menopausal women to 12.5% for surgically menopausal women; West et al., 2008).

To date, rates of HSDD have not been documented in men. With regard to rates of low desire in men, the National Health and Social Life Survey found that 13% to 17% of sexually active men between the ages of 30 and 59 reported a lack of desire for sex in the past year; 14% of men ages 18 to 29 reported the same (Laumann et al., 1999). In the Global Study of Sexual Attitudes and Behaviors, approximately 13% to 28% of men reported a lack of interest in sex for 2 months or more in the past year, and the rate of frequent lack of interest in sex ranged from 1.3% of men in southern Europe to 3.1% of men in the Middle East (Laumann et al., 2005). Other studies have also examined prevalence rates of low desire in men but have not documented rates of low desire and related distress (e.g., Araujo, Mohr, & McKinlay, 2004; Eplov et al., 2007; Fugl-Meyer & Sjogren Fugl-Meyer, 1999; Mercer et al., 2003; Najman, Dunne, Boyle, Cook, & Purdie, 2003). Given that in women rates of low sexual desire accompanied by distress (i.e., HSDD) are lower than rates of low desire alone, Brotto (2010a) has proposed that HSDD may affect 1% to 20% of men.

Known Etiology

Numerous factors (biological, psychological, and social) have been implicated in the etiology of

HSDD, with the etiology often being multifactorial (Basson, Wierman, van Lankveld, & Brotto, 2010). For both men and women, biological factors related to low desire include specific medication use or chronic illness (we should note that to receive a diagnosis of HSDD according to *DSM–IV–TR* criteria, the reduced desire cannot be accounted for completely by the effects of substances or medical conditions). The selective serotonin reuptake inhibitors used to treat depression, for example, are commonly associated with reduced desire, as are antihypertensive and antiandrogen medications (see Basson & Brotto, 2009, and Maurice, 2007, for a review of other medications associated with low desire). Medical illnesses and related treatments (e.g., chemotherapy), fatigue, pain, psychological difficulties, incontinence, and immobility can also impair desire. Also, men with chronic illnesses (e.g., diabetes, renal disease) are at risk for hypogonadism (i.e., low levels of androgens), a symptom of which is reduced sexual desire (Wang et al., 2009). The relationship between sex hormones and desire is less clear in women; even though reduced estrogen and androgen levels, particularly testosterone, have been thought to play a role in women's low sexual desire, a recent study examining the role of androgens and sexual desire difficulties did not find testosterone deficits in women with HSDD (Basson, Brotto, Petkau, & Labrie, 2010). Menopause, in which estrogen production is decreased, has been linked to low desire (Dennerstein et al., 2006; Meston & Bradford, 2007).

Psychosocial factors play a large role in the onset and maintenance of HSDD for both men and women. For example, mental health difficulties, including the presence of mood and anxiety disorders, are strongly associated with low desire. A recent study conducted with 400 premenopausal women who were enrolled in the HSDD Registry for Women found that psychosocial factors were most likely to be perceived by women as contributing to their ongoing difficulties with desire; specifically, stress or fatigue was the most highly endorsed factor (reported by 60% of women), followed by dissatisfaction with physical appearance (reported by almost 41%; Maserejian et al., 2010). Relationship factors and social messages, such as those discussed earlier in this chapter, may also serve to precipitate and maintain desire difficulties (e.g., Basson, Wierman, et al., 2010; McCarthy & McDonald, 2009).

Treatment

Treatments for HSDD generally fall into the psychological or medical categories. Psychological treatments include sex therapy, cognitive–behavioral therapy (CBT), and mindfulness-based therapy, whereas medical treatments include hormonal agents and medications; these forms of treatment (psychological and medical) are sometimes used in conjunction in the management of low sexual desire (see Volume 2, Chapters 4 and 5, this handbook). Education is also an important component of treating desire difficulties. For example, education regarding responsive versus spontaneous desire and female sexual response is often helpful for women with low desire, as is discussion regarding normative decreases in desire with age (Basson, Wierman, et al., 2010). Before treatment, a comprehensive biopsychosocial assessment that gathers information regarding medical (e.g., use of medications), psychological (e.g., current mood and level of anxiety), social (e.g., relationship duration), and sexual history (e.g., presence of other sexual problems) is recommended for desire difficulties (Basson, Wierman, et al., 2010; McCarthy & McDonald, 2009). Notably, similar to research regarding prevalence and etiology, the sexual desire treatment literature has largely focused on women.

Psychological treatment. Psychological treatments are widely used to treat HSDD and have been evaluated in some studies; it is recognized, however, that randomized controlled trials are greatly needed in this area (Basson, Wierman, et al., 2010). Sex therapy techniques for HSDD include sensate focus exercises. In these exercises, partners take turns first touching and caressing nonsexual parts of each other's bodies and providing feedback about these experiences (genital touching and intercourse are disallowed during this stage); the exercises are designed to eventually include sexual touch and to promote enjoyment for both partners while decreasing demands for performance (Kaplan, 1979). A study using a modified sex therapy approach with 60 heterosexual couples in which the female partner experienced low sexual desire reported that approximately 57% of couples had a favorable outcome (defined as problem resolved or largely resolved) with regard to improved sexual functioning after treatment, and approximately 47% maintained these gains at 3-month follow-up (Hawton, Catalan, & Fagg, 1991). A 7-week treatment program for couples that emphasized sensate focus exercises documented that 65% of women with HSDD and 63% of men with HSDD had a successful treatment outcome; in this study, success was defined as resolution of the sexual problem with no development of new problems and the couple having engaged in weekly intercourse for the 3 final weeks of the program. Completion of the sensate focus exercises was significantly related to treatment success (Sarwer & Durlak, 1997).

CBT for HSDD focuses on the interaction between maladaptive thoughts (e.g., "I am a bad sexual partner"), feelings (e.g., guilt), and behaviors (e.g., avoiding physical affection with partner). Techniques used in CBT include cognitive restructuring (i.e., identification and challenge of maladaptive thoughts) and exercises such as communication skills training, with the premise that shifts in negative thinking will also produce changes in related feelings and behaviors. Although few controlled studies have evaluated CBT for HSDD, this treatment approach appears promising for treatment of female low desire (ter Kuile, Both, & van Lankveld, 2010). For example, a 12-week group CBT and sex therapy treatment for couples in which the female partner had HSDD resulted in improvement for 74% of women at the end of treatment and 64% of women at 3- and 12-month follow-up (Trudel et al., 2001). In addition, treated couples reported significant improvements in sexual and marital quality compared with wait-list control couples. CBT bibliotherapy (i.e., manualized self-help) for couples with sexual dysfunction, the majority of whom met *DSM–IV–TR* diagnostic criteria for HSDD, has also been empirically evaluated (van Lankveld, Everaerd, & Grotjohann, 2001). Although couples who received bibliotherapy reported significant improvements compared with wait-list controls, group differences for female participants were no longer found in the follow-up period.

Recently, mindfulness-based therapy has been tested for women with desire and arousal problems. Mindfulness is a practice that is described as "paying attention in a particular way: on purpose, in the present moment, and non-judgmentally" (Kabat-Zinn, 1994, p. 4). Mindfulness has its roots in Eastern spiritual practices but has increasingly been applied in Western health care for a variety of conditions. Mindfulness emphasizes nonjudgmental awareness of one's experiences (e.g., thoughts, feelings, physical sensations) and offers additional skills that can be used to complement CBT. Through mindfulness, for example, one can learn to be more engaged and present in activities, including sexual ones, which may ultimately serve to increase enjoyment of and desire for sexual activity (see Brotto & Woo, 2010, for a case example). On testing a three-session group mindfulness-based therapy for female desire or arousal difficulties, Brotto, Basson, and Luria (2008) found improvements in sexual desire, distress, and subjective arousal. Interestingly, women reported mindfulness to be the most effective aspect of the treatment. Similar results were found for women treated for cervical or endometrial cancer who had secondary sexual arousal disorder (Brotto, Heiman, et al., 2008); specifically, women reported improvements in sexual function, including desire, along with improvements in mood, mental health, and sexual distress after receiving MBCT. Given that both of these trials were uncontrolled, future research is needed to test MBCT interventions for low desire using randomized controlled trial methodology.

Biomedical treatment. Medical approaches for HSDD focus on hormonal and nonhormonal pharmacological treatments. For men with hypogonadism and corresponding low desire, testosterone supplementation can be effective for restoring sexual desire (Wang et al., 2009). Whether testosterone supplementation is beneficial for women with HSDD is not currently known, and a recent study did not find evidence of testosterone deficits in women with HSDD (Basson, Brotto, et al., 2010). However, testosterone has been thought to play a role in female sexual desire, and testosterone supplementation has a long history of being prescribed for women with low desire (Basson & Brotto, 2009). Most of the trials investigating this type of treatment for women's low desire have examined transdermal testosterone administered to surgically menopausal women. Although some benefits have been noted in such trials, the clinical significance of the findings has been questioned and research methodology critiqued (see Basson, 2009, and Meston & Bradford, 2007, for reviews). Another concern about testosterone supplementation in women is the lack of data regarding long-term safety. Current recommendations advise against the generalized treatment of women with testosterone (Wierman et al., 2006).

In addition to testosterone, a number of other pharmacological therapies have been proposed to treat low desire in women. These therapies include medications such as buproprion and flibanserin that were originally developed for treating depression. Flibanserin is a serotonin receptor type 5-HT_{1A} agonist and a 5-HT_{2A} antagonist (Moll & Brown, 2011; Stahl, Sommer, & Allers, 2011), and it selectively acts on monoamines in specific regions of the brain. For example, flibanserin decreases serotonin levels and increases dopamine and norephinephrine levels in the prefrontal cortex; given the inhibitory role of serotonin and excitatory roles of dopamine and norephinephrine in sexual desire, flibanserin may enhance desire through its actions on these monoamines (Stahl et al., 2011). In general, however, more randomized controlled trials are needed to adequately evaluate the efficacy of such medications for treating sexual difficulties (Moll & Brown, 2011), and currently, no treatments for HSDD in women have received U.S. Food and Drug Administration approval (Stahl et al., 2011). In fact, flibanserin was recently denied such approval because of a need for further data on the efficacy and safety of the drug for HSDD (the development of flibanserin for HSDD was subsequently discontinued by the pharmaceutical company; Meyer-Kleinmann, 2010; Moll & Brown, 2011). In sum, the effectiveness of medical treatments for female HSDD has not been widely established. If medical treatments for HSDD are considered, it is recommended that they be combined with psychological treatments for optimal results (Maclaran & Panay, 2011), and the importance of addressing psychological factors associated with HSDD has been emphasized in the literature (e.g., Basson, 2009).

CUTTING-EDGE ISSUES IN DESIRE RESEARCH

In the sections that follow we consider new, important, or cutting-edge issues in the study of sexual desire. We especially believe that functional magnetic resonance imaging (fMRI) and the use of mixed-methods designs (e.g., qualitative and quantitative methodologies integrated) offer promise for further decoding what is sexual desire.

Functional Magnetic Resonance Imaging

fMRI is a neuroimaging technique that measures blood flow and oxygenation changes in the brain in response to specific stimuli (e.g., images of a sexual partner; Ortigue, Bianchi-Demicheli, Patel, Frum, & Lewis, 2010). Recently, studies have started to apply fMRI technology to better understand the neural activation patterns associated with sexual desire. In such studies, individuals are typically shown both nonerotic and erotic pictures or videos while their neural responses to such stimuli are recorded using fMRI.

In one of the first fMRI studies to compare women with and without HSDD, video clips showing erotic, sport, and relaxation stimuli were presented on three different occasions to 16 young heterosexual women with HSDD and 20 women without sexual difficulties (Arnow et al., 2009). Both physiological arousal using a vaginal photoplethysmograph and mental arousal to the videos were also assessed during the fMRI sessions. Differences between women with and without HSDD were found in response to the erotic video clips; specifically, the women without sexual difficulties reported more mental arousal and demonstrated more activation in a brain region involved in the encoding and retrieval of memories (i.e., the entorhinal cortex). As suggested by Arnow et al. (2009), this increased activation may signal that women with HSDD encode and retrieve past erotic experiences differently than women without desire difficulties. On the basis of increased activation in the medial frontal gyrus and right inferior frontal gyrus of women with

HSDD, they also suggested that women with this condition assign more attention than women without sexual difficulties to monitoring or evaluating their responses to erotic stimuli, which likely interferes with sexual response. More important, this finding highlights the key role of attention in sexual desire and suggests a role for interventions that help women develop nonjudgmental awareness in the presence of erotic cues (e.g., mindfulness).

Both decreased and increased neural activation in women with HSDD were also demonstrated in a recent study comparing 13 sexually active women with HSDD with 15 controls (Bianchi-Demicheli et al., 2011). On viewing erotic and nonerotic pictures, women with HSDD showed less activation in areas of the brain that have been suggested by previous research to be involved in processing erotic stimuli. Additionally, women with HSDD showed more activation in some brain areas involved in higher order cognitive or social functions. The results were consistent with the hypothesis that women with HSDD allocate more attention to monitoring or evaluating their responses to erotic stimuli than women without sexual difficulties. Bianchi-Demicheli et al. (2011) also suggested that women with HSDD process visual stimuli in a manner that differs from that of women without desire difficulties—a manner that ultimately interferes with stimuli being experienced as erotic. Such research has provided initial information on neural mechanisms involved in female HSDD and provides exciting possibilities for future studies and clinical interventions designed to reduce low desire.

In sexually healthy men, fMRI research has found that a number of brain areas respond to visual erotic stimuli, including areas involved in attention (Mouras et al., 2003). Differential processing of sexual stimuli has been noted in men with HSDD using another imaging technique, positron emission tomography (Stoléru et al., 2003). To date, we are not aware of any fMRI research conducted with men with HSDD.

Mixed-Methods Designs

Mixed-methods research design refers to the integration of quantitative and qualitative methods in the same study. Using both types of methods can enrich a study by, for example, simultaneously enabling researchers to generalize the results and acquire greater understanding of the topic (Hanson, Creswell, Clark, Petska, & Creswell, 2005). Interest in mixed-methods design has increased substantially in recent years in the social and health sciences (Creswell, 2009). Although sexual desire has typically been studied using quantitative methods (e.g., use of validated questionnaires to measure desire), the use of qualitative methods has been advocated to gain understanding about the experiential aspects of desire (Tolman & Diamond, 2001; see Chapter 1, this volume).

Some studies have used a mixed-methods approach to understand how girls and women experience sexual desire. For example, Tolman and Szalacha (1999) used both qualitative and quantitative methods of analysis to examine interview data from 30 adolescent girls regarding their experiences with sexual desire and pleasure. The study was organized around three main research questions, each of which emerged in sequential order on the basis of findings from the previous question. Girls' descriptions of their sexual desire experiences were first analyzed qualitatively. Approximately two thirds of the girls reported experiencing sexual desire; however, differences were noted between girls from urban versus suburban schools with regard to how they responded to such desire. Urban girls spoke of sacrificing sexual pleasure as a way of protecting themselves from vulnerabilities and negative consequences (e.g., pregnancy, AIDS), whereas suburban girls described more sexual curiosity as well as internal conflict (e.g., conflict about feeling sexually curious in the face of cultural messages regarding women's sexuality).

Quantitative analyses subsequently examined the differences regarding the themes of perceived vulnerability and pleasure that emerged in girls' descriptions of their sexual desire. Overall, approximately 47% of the narratives contained vulnerability as the predominant theme, approximately 29% focused predominantly on pleasure, and the remaining narratives contained both themes equally. The narratives of suburban girls contained significantly more themes of pleasure than those of urban girls. However, further analyses indicated that suburban girls who had been sexually violated spoke significantly more about vulnerability than other suburban girls and had narratives that more closely resembled those of urban participants. Final qualitative analyses indicated that suburban girls who had not been sexually violated spoke about experiencing sexual desire and pleasure in both their minds and their bodies; in general, these descriptions differed from those of the other girls in the sample. Also, the final qualitative analyses identified a subset of urban girls who had experienced sexual violation but associated their sexual desire more with pleasure than with vulnerability.

Overall, Tolman and Szalacha's (1999) study highlighted the "dilemma of desire" (Tolman, 2002) experienced by many adolescent girls, in which girls' desire is associated with feeling vulnerable to negative consequences and their sexuality is considered a source of conflict and danger. The combined findings ultimately provided insight into female adolescent sexuality and highlighted the value of a mixed-methods research approach. As Tolman and Szalacha noted,

> Grounded in a method of data collection that gave girls an opportunity to interrupt the usual silence about their sexuality and using qualitative and quantitative methods to analyze these data, we learned far more about this aspect of female adolescent development than forcing a choice between qualitative and quantitative methods would have afforded. (p. 32)

Brotto et al. (2009) also used a narrative approach to understand the experience and meaning of sexual desire among women. Middle-aged women with or without sexual arousal difficulties ($n = 22$) completed individual qualitative interviews as well as two validated self-report measures of sexual functioning (i.e., the FSFI and the Brief Index of Sexual Functioning for Women). Findings from the self-report measures indicated that women with sexual arousal difficulties experienced poorer functioning in all aspects of sexual response (arousal, desire, lubrication, orgasm) and more pain with vaginal penetration in the preceding month; in addition, sexual activity with a partner was initiated by only two women in the control group during this time, and women with arousal difficulties reported significantly fewer sexual thoughts or fantasies than controls.

Despite the differences noted in sexual functioning on the questionnaires, however, all women in the narrative interviews described experiencing sexual desire in some form. More important, the descriptions of desire were quite similar between women with and without sexual difficulties. Nongenital physical sensations and cognitive–emotional experiences (e.g., feeling relaxed with a partner) were part of women's experiences with sexual desire, and both groups described several triggers for desire (e.g., physical touch by a partner; feeling desired by a partner). Interestingly, sexual fantasies were not present in women's narrative descriptions of their desire. Additionally, women identified several factors that inhibited desire. For example, thinking about their sexual difficulty inhibited desire for the women with arousal disorder, whereas partner factors such as depressed mood were identified more by women without sexual difficulties. Women in both groups also described emotional connection with a partner as a focus of their desire, and both groups were motivated to continue sexual activity once it began. This motivation was present even though women reported that they did not initiate the activity themselves or experience spontaneous desire when approached by their partner. Notably, some women in both groups had difficulty articulating their understanding of sexual desire, with careful reflection helping to clarify the meaning of desire.

Important implications arise out of such findings and highlight the value of using mixed-method research designs. In Brotto et al.'s (2009) study, for example, reliance on self-report data would have portrayed sexual desire as occurring with less frequency and intensity in women with arousal difficulties. Instead, however, by allowing women to reflect on and describe their unique experiences with desire, the narrative interviews demonstrated that desire is experienced by women with and without sexual difficulties and is often present (or dampened) in response to several factors. Such findings highlight the complexities of female desire and support a model that includes responsive (triggered) desire and accounts for contextual factors (e.g., Basson's, 2001a, 2001b, model of sexual response). In addition, these findings demonstrate that "what may be deemed a 'dysfunction' on a questionnaire item may not be a dysfunction in reality" (Brotto et al., 2009, p. 396). The FSFI (Rosen et al., 2000), for example, assesses desire using two items that quantify the frequency and overall level of a woman's desire; in this way, it is likely to generate a negative response from women with sexual difficulties and does not capture the varying definitions of desire that women themselves describe. In contrast, qualitative methods provide women with the opportunity to thoroughly depict their personal desire experiences and, in doing so, highlighted similarities between women with and without sexual difficulties.

Both of the studies described in this section captured rich data with the use of mixed methods. Such data would not have been obtained if they had relied only on self-report questionnaires or qualitative interviews. Mixed-methods designs have offered important insight into the lived experiences of women's desire, and the use of combined methods assist in the challenge to adequately define and conceptualize sexual desire.

DIAGNOSTIC DILEMMAS

Although the conceptualization of sexual desire in the *DSM–IV–TR* rests heavily on the HSRC model of Masters and Johnson (1966), Kaplan (1977, 1979), and Lief (1977), the definition's focus on desire for sexual activity and availability of fantasies as a *sin qua non* has been harshly criticized. For one, critics of Masters and Johnson's model have noted that this definition perpetuates the notion that sexual response occurs in linear stages, that desire always leads unidirectionally to arousal, and that the experiences of sexual response in men and women are equivalent (e.g., Basson, 2001a, 2001b; Tiefer, 1991). Moreover, this placement of sexual desire within an internal combustion framework that assumes that, like hunger and thirst, desire is an internally generated need that must be quenched is completely inaccurate (Laan & Both, 2008; Toates, 2009). The notion that sexual desire is spontaneous, that it floats freely within individuals and propels them toward sexual activity, is not supported by the evidence; instead, much more support exists for desire conceptualized within an incentive motivation model, which posits that all sexual desire is responsive to internally generated and external sexual cues and stimuli. For example, when Meston and Buss (2007) asked university students about the reasons for engaging in sex, "I was attracted to the person" was the top reason for both women and men. "I was horny," capturing, perhaps, Kaplan's notion of spontaneous desire, was in seventh place for both women and men (Meston & Buss, 2007). Indeed, when women themselves were presented with descriptions of prevailing models of sexual desire (i.e., Masters and Johnson's and Kaplan's linear model of desire leading to arousal and Basson's circular model of responsive desire), significant differences were found in how much women adopt the different models (Sand & Fisher, 2007). In fact, only those women with sexual difficulties, according to the FSFI (Rosen et al., 2000), were more likely to endorse Basson's circular model of responsive desire (Sand & Fisher, 2007); more recently, however, others have found no differences in models of desire adopted between women with and without sexual difficulties (Giles & McCabe, 2009).

An expanded conceptualization of sexual desire that captures the rich heterogeneity across individuals (Meana, 2010) has also been supported by studies that have probed individuals' narrative stories of sexual desire (see Chapter 6, this volume). For example, qualitative research, both in women (Brotto et al., 2009) and in men (Janssen et al., 2008), has suggested that desire and arousal, whether subjective arousal and excitement or physiological, are often experienced along with sexual desire. Interestingly, for at least some women, desire and arousal are interchangeable concepts, and individuals express conflation between definitions of desire and arousal (Brotto et al., 2009). As summarized by Graham (2010), responses on self-report questionnaires also show a significant positive correlation between desire and arousal domains (Graham, 2010), ranging from .52 to .85 when using the FSFI (Brotto, Graham, et al., 2011). Because of significant concerns about using an outdated model of sexual response that privileges spontaneous desire and assumes that desire for sexual activity captures sexual desire for all individuals throughout their lifetimes, a proposal has been made to undertake a significant overhaul of the definition of desire adopted in the *DSM–IV–TR* (Brotto, 2010b; Graham, 2010).

Whereas the *DSM–IV–TR* definition of HSDD focuses on persistent or recurrent deficiency in sexual fantasies and desire for sexual activity associated with distress, it has been criticized as inadequately capturing the experiences of women (Brotto, 2010b). Indeed, evidence has shown that women adopt different models of sexual response, with some noting that they enjoy the apparently spontaneous feelings of horniness that drive them to seek out a sexual partner, and others instead endorsing a model that emphasizes their receptivity to sexual activity on the basis of a variety of nonsexual motivations (Giles & McCabe, 2009; Sand & Fisher, 2007). Meana (2010) has also articulated that any future diagnostic system that is to adequately, accurately, and sensitively detect a desire disorder in women must account for the large interindividual variability in how desire is experienced and not lead to overpathologizing because of low threshold criteria. In an effort to approximate these goals, the Sexual Dysfunctions subworkgroup for the fifth edition of the *DSM* (*DSM–5*) proposed a number of changes, the most notable of which were (a) that a polythetic approach to desire disorder be adopted, (b) that desire and arousal be captured together within a larger sexual interest–arousal disorder spectrum, (c) that objective indicators for frequency and duration be adopted, and (d) that important information on contextual, personal, and interpersonal factors that may determine the desire expression be assessed and coded on a dimensional scale. The proposed criteria for sexual interest/arousal disorder have been published (Brotto, 2010b; Graham, 2010) and subsequently revised on the basis of feedback from the larger scientific and clinical communities. However, there has been no shortage of debate on the proposal for sexual interest/arousal disorder, and final criteria will not be available to the public until publication of the *DSM–5*.

One criticism relates to the lack of sufficient evidence that desire and arousal are necessarily overlapping or, according to the incentive motivation model, two sides of the same sexual coin. This argument notes that evidence of high degrees of correlation between two concepts is not grounds for merging them (see Chapter 4, this volume). This view also sees significant costs in "lumping" versus "splitting" in that diagnostic precision may be sacrificed. However, proponents of the effort to merge desire and arousal disorders have suggested that just as symptoms of desire and arousal have in the past been separately assessed in research and clinical settings, this will continue to be the case. Another concern relates to the potential negative impact on large-scale pharmaceutical trials that are nearing completion. Given past failures of testosterone and flibanserin to receive regulatory approval and ongoing expensive efforts to develop and validate drugs for the treatment of women's low desire, a significant concern exists that changing definitions of sexual dysfunction would have a direct and deleterious impact on drug development, which rests on which definition of dysfunction is adopted.

An entirely different criticism of the current diagnostic system has come from the feminist and social constructionist perspective, which has noted that the very context in which sexual dysfunction diagnoses are made is inherently problematic. By not recognizing the important impact of politics, inadequate sex education, lack of access to preventive health care services, culture, and unhealthy sexual messages, to name but a few, clinicians are likely to adopt a simplistic medical model view that assumes that sexual dysfunction is rooted in biological factors. Inadequate attention is given to the relational nature of sexuality; thus, to diagnose a sexual dysfunction in an individual is missing half the story. By equating sex with dancing and not with digestion, the inherent flaws in adopting a medical model of desire disorder are obvious. Moreover, this critical feminist perspective, such as is represented in the New View model, rejects the notion of multiple sexual dysfunctions divided up according to which aspect of function is impaired, and it instead argues that sexual problems should be categorized according to the factors that caused them (see Table 8.1). The advantages of the New View model are that it avoids defining any one particular pattern of experience; focuses on causation, which would guide treatment; and is sensitive to the important influence of sociocultural, political, and economic factors that influence sexual function. In terms of adoption for the *DSM–5*, however, which requires substantial empirical evidence to support any major changes in diagnostic nomenclature, the New View model has received only minimal empirical attention.

In a recent study that explored the extent to which the New View framework corresponded with women's accounts of their sexual difficulties, an open-ended questionnaire was administered to 49 women who were asked to describe their sexual difficulties in their own words (Nicholls, 2008). Qualitative analyses revealed that 67% of the difficulties could be captured using the New View framework at a subcategorical level. At a higher thematic level, 31% of categorized difficulties could not be categorized at a lower, subcategory level. Overall, 98% of the sexual issues could be classified under the New View scheme. In support of the critical position that the current *DSM–IV–TR* does not capture the relational nature of sexual experiences, Nicholls (2008) found that 65% of problems were classified as problems relating to partner or relationship and only 7% were problems resulting from medical factors. This is, to date, the only empirical test of the New View framework, and it must be borne in mind that women may adopt different theoretical models to account for their experiences of sexual desire (Sand & Fisher, 2007).

FUTURE DIRECTIONS FOR THE FIELD

Much remains unknown about the brain and sexual desire. Imaging studies are few and sometimes present conflicting findings that perhaps illustrate the pivotal roles for sociocultural and contextual factors in understanding desire. Within the study of central mechanisms, preliminary support has been found for the influence of the endocannabinoid system, which is a worthwhile area to explore. Many men and women suffer from personal and relational distress related to their lack of sexual desire. However, it is clear that a strictly pharmacological approach, at least in the case of women, may not capture the intricacies of desire. Good evidence has been found for the role of psychological treatments, including CBT and mindfulness-based therapy. However, the placebo response is also evident in this domain of study, and the extent to which benefits arise from the treatment itself, or from nonspecific factors such as having an empathic clinician, thinking about one's sexuality more, or the improved communication between a couple that may accompany participation in treatment, is unknown and is an important domain of future study. How desire is expressed among different ethnocultural groups has been almost completely ignored and is a major gap that future researchers should study. Further insight into the relative contributions of brain and body versus culture and psychology to desire, and more evidence for treatments to enhance sexual desire among those who mourn its loss, will ultimately shed light on one of the most puzzling unanswered questions, namely, what sexual desire is.

CONCLUSION

Desire has been and continues to be one of the most enigmatic of human sexual experiences. Although science has advanced markedly and allowed the field to better understand the biochemical, neurological, behavioral, psychological, and sociocultural aspects of sexual desire, much remains to be known. There has been abundant media attention focused on sexual desire and an intense pharmaceutical presence in the quest to find an elixir for low desire, and we expect even greater advances in the decade ahead of us. One certainty exists in understanding sexual desire: In anyone's hands, sexual desire is indeed a slippery concept.

References

American Psychiatric Association. (2000). *Diagnostic and statistical manual of mental disorders* (4th ed., text rev.). Washington, DC: Author.

Ansong, K. S., & Punwaney, R. B. (1999). An assessment of the clinical relevance of serum testosterone level determination in the evaluation of men with low sexual drive. *Journal of Urology*, *162*, 719–721. doi:10.1097/00005392-199909010-00023

Araujo, A. B., Mohr, B. A., & McKinlay, J. B. (2004). Changes in sexual function in middle-aged and older men: Longitudinal data from the Massachusetts Male Aging Study. *Journal of the American Geriatrics Society, 52*, 1502–1509. doi:10.1111/j.0002-8614.2004.52413.x

Arnow, B. A., Millheiser, L., Garrett, A., Lake Polan, M., Glover, G. H., Hill, K. R., . . . Desmond, J. E. (2009). Women with hypoactive sexual desire disorder compared to normal females: A functional magnetic resonance imaging study. *Neuroscience, 158*, 484–502. doi:10.1016/j.neuroscience.2008.09.044

Bancroft, J. (1999). Central inhibition of sexual response in the male: A theoretical perspective. *Neuroscience and Biobehavioral Reviews, 23*, 763–784. doi:10.1016/S0149-7634(99)00019-6

Bancroft, J. (2012). The behavioral correlates of testosterone. In E. Nieschlag & H. M. Behre (Eds.), *Testosterone: Action, deficiency, substitution* (pp. 87–122). Cambridge, England: Cambridge University Press.

Bancroft, J., Graham, C. A., Janssen, E., & Sanders, S. A. (2009). The dual control model: Current status and future directions. *Journal of Sex Research, 46*, 121–142. doi:10.1080/00224490902747222

Bancroft, J., & Janssen, E. (2000). The dual control model of male sexual response: A theoretical approach to centrally mediated erectile dysfunction. *Neuroscience and Biobehavioral Reviews, 24*, 571–579. doi:10.1016/S0149-7634(00)00024-5

Bancroft, J., Loftus, J., & Long, J. S. (2003). Distress about sex: A national survey of women in heterosexual relationships. *Archives of Sexual Behavior, 32*, 193–208. doi:10.1023/A:1023420431760

Bancroft, J., Long, J. S., & McCabe, J. (2011). Sexual well-being: A comparison of U.S. Black and White women in heterosexual relationships. *Archives of Sexual Behavior, 40*, 725–740. doi:10.1007/s10508-010-9679-z

Barton, D. L., Wender, D. B., Sloan, J. A., Dalton, R. J., Balcueva, E. P., Atherton, P. J., . . . Loprinzi, C. L. (2007). Randomized controlled trial to evaluate transdermal testosterone in female cancer survivors with decreased libido; North Central Cancer Treatment Group protocol N02C3. *Journal of the National Cancer Institute, 99*, 672–679. doi:10.1093/jnci/djk149

Basson, R. (2001a). Human sex-response cycles. *Journal of Sex & Marital Therapy, 27*, 33–43. doi:10.1080/00926230152035831

Basson, R. (2001b). Using a different model for female sexual response to address women's problematic low sexual desire. *Journal of Sex & Marital Therapy, 27*, 395–403. doi:10.1080/713846827

Basson, R. (2002). Rethinking low sexual desire in women. *BJOG, 109*, 357–363. doi:10.1111/j.1471-0528.2002.01002.x

Basson, R. (2003). Biopsychosocial models of women's sexual response: Applications to management of "desire disorders." *Sexual and Relationship Therapy, 18*, 107–115. doi:10.1080/1468199031000061308

Basson, R. (2009). Pharmacotherapy for women's sexual dysfunction. *Expert Opinion on Pharmacotherapy, 10*, 1631–1648.

Basson, R. (2010). Testosterone therapy for reduced libido in women. *Therapeutic Advances in Endocrinology and Metabolism, 1*, 155–164. doi:10.1177/2042018810379588

Basson, R., & Brotto, L. A. (2009). Disorders of sexual desire and subjective arousal in women. In R. Balon & R. T. Segraves (Eds.), *Clinical manual of sexual disorders* (pp. 119–159). Washington, DC: American Psychiatric Publishing.

Basson, R., Brotto, L. A., Petkau, J. A., & Labrie, F. (2010). Role of androgens in women's sexual dysfunction. *Menopause, 17*, 962–971. doi:10.1097/gme.0b013e3181d59765

Basson, R., Wierman, M. E., van Lankveld, J., & Brotto, L. A. (2010). Summary of the recommendations on sexual dysfunctions in women. *Journal of Sexual Medicine, 7*, 314–326. doi:10.1111/j.1743-6109.2009.01617.x

Baumeister, R. F. (2000). Gender differences in erotic plasticity: The female sex drive as socially flexible and responsive. *Psychological Bulletin, 126*, 347–374. doi:10.1037/0033-2909.126.3.347

Beach, F. A. (1956). Characteristics of masculine "sex drive." In M. R. Jones (Ed.), *Nebraska symposium on motivation* (Vol. 4, pp. 1–32). Lincoln: University of Nebraska Press.

Beck, J. G., Bozman, A. W., & Qualtrough, T. (1991). The experience of sexual desire: Psychological correlates in a college sample. *Journal of Sex Research, 28*, 443–456. doi:10.1080/00224499109551618

Bianchi-Demicheli, F., Cojan, Y., Waber, L., Recordon, N., Vuilleumier, P., & Ortigue, S. (2011). Neural bases of hypoactive sexual desire disorder in women: An event-related fMRI study. *Journal of Sexual Medicine, 8*, 2546–2559. doi:10.1111/j.1743-6109.2011.02376.x

Bogaert, A. F. (2004). Asexuality: Prevalence and associated factors in a national probability sample. *Journal of Sex Research, 41*, 279–287. doi:10.1080/00224490409552235

Brezsnyak, M., & Whisman, M. A. (2004). Sexual desire and relationship functioning: The effects of marital satisfaction and power. *Journal of Sex & Marital Therapy, 30*, 199–217. doi:10.1080/00926230490262393

Brotto, L. A. (2010a). The DSM diagnostic criteria for hypoactive sexual desire disorder in men. *Journal of Sexual Medicine, 7*, 2015–2030. doi:10.1111/j.1743-6109.2010.01860.x

Brotto, L. A. (2010b). The DSM diagnostic criteria for hypoactive sexual desire disorder in women. *Archives of Sexual Behavior, 39*, 221–239. doi:10.1007/s10508-009-9543-1

Brotto, L. A. (2010c). The DSM diagnostic criteria for sexual aversion disorder. *Archives of Sexual Behavior, 39*, 271–277. doi:10.1007/s10508-009-9534-2

Brotto, L. A., Basson, R., & Luria, M. (2008). A mindfulness-based group psychoeducational intervention targeting sexual arousal disorder in women. *Journal of Sexual Medicine, 5*, 1646–1659. doi:10.1111/j.1743-6109.2008.00850.x

Brotto, L. A., Bitzer, J., Laan, E., Leiblum, S., & Luria, M. (2010). Women's sexual desire and arousal disorders. *Journal of Sexual Medicine, 7*, 586–614. doi:10.1111/j.1743-6109.2009.01630.x

Brotto, L. A., Chik, H. M., Ryder, A. G., Gorzalka, B. B., & Seal, B. N. (2005). Acculturation and sexual function in Asian women. *Archives of Sexual Behavior, 34*, 613–626. doi:10.1007/s10508-005-7909-6

Brotto, L. A., Graham, C. A., Binik, Y. M., Segraves, R. T., & Zucker, K. J. (2011). Should sexual desire and arousal disorders in women be merged? A response to DeRogatis, Clayton, Rosen, Sand, and Pyke (2010). *Archives of Sexual Behavior, 40*, 221–225. doi:10.1007/s10508-010-9706-0

Brotto, L. A., Heiman, J. R., Goff, B., Greer, B., Lentz, G. M., Swisher, E., . . . Van Blaricom, A. (2008). A psychoeducational intervention for sexual dysfunction in women with gynecologic cancer. *Archives of Sexual Behavior, 37*, 317–329. doi:10.1007/s10508-007-9196-x

Brotto, L. A., Heiman, J. R., & Tolman, D. L. (2009). Narratives of desire in mid-age women with and without arousal difficulties. *Journal of Sex Research, 46*, 387–398. doi:10.1080/00224490902792624

Brotto, L. A., & Klein, C. (2010). Psychological factors involved in women's sexual dysfunctions. *Expert Review of Obstetrics and Gynecology, 5*, 93–104. doi:10.1586/eog.09.67

Brotto, L. A., Knudson, G., Inskip, J., Rhodes, K., & Erskine, Y. (2010). Asexuality: A mixed methods approach. *Archives of Sexual Behavior, 39*, 599–618. doi:10.1007/s10508-008-9434-x

Brotto, L. A., Petkau, J. A., Labrie, F., & Basson, R. (2011). Predictors of sexual desire disorders in women. *Journal of Sexual Medicine, 8*, 742–753. doi:10.1111/j.1743-6109.2010.02146.x

Brotto, L. A., & Woo, J. S. T. (2010). Cognitive-behavioral and mindfulness-based therapy for low sexual desire. In S. Leiblum (Ed.), *Treating sexual desire disorders: A clinical casebook* (pp. 149–164). New York, NY: Guilford Press.

Brotto, L. A., Woo, J. S. T., & Gorzalka, B. B. (2011). Differences in sexual guilt and desire in East Asian and Euro-Canadian men. *Journal of Sex Research, 49*, 594–602. doi:10.1080/00224499.2011.618956

Brotto, L. A., Woo, J. S. T., & Ryder, A. G. (2007). Acculturation and sexual function in Canadian East Asian men. *Journal of Sexual Medicine, 4*, 72–82. doi:10.1111/j.1743-6109.2006.00388.x

Brotto, L. A., & Yule, M. A. (2011). Physiological and subjective sexual arousal in self-identified asexual women. *Archives of Sexual Behavior, 40*, 699–712. doi:10.1007/s10508-010-9671-7

Byers, E. S., & Macneil, S. (2006). Further validation of the interpersonal exchange model of sexual satisfaction. *Journal of Sex & Marital Therapy, 32*, 53–69. doi:10.1080/00926230500232917

Cacioppo, S., Bianchi-Demicheli, F., Frum, C., Pfaus, J. G., & Lewis, J. W. (2012). The common neural bases between sexual desire and love: A multilevel kernel density fMRI analysis. *Journal of Sexual Medicine, 9*, 1048–1054. doi:10.1111/j.1743-6109.2012.02651.x

Cain, V. S., Johannes, C. B., Avis, N. E., Mohr, B., Schocken, M., Skurnick, J., . . . Ory, M. (2003). Sexual functioning and practices in a multi-ethnic study of midlife women: Baseline results from SWAN. *Journal of Sex Research, 40*, 266–276. doi:10.1080/00224490309552191

Carpenter, L. M., Nathanson, C. A., & Kim, Y. J. (2009). Physical women, emotional men: Gender and sexual satisfaction in midlife. *Archives of Sexual Behavior, 38*, 87–107. doi:10.1007/s10508-007-9215-y

Carvalheira, A., Brotto, L. A., & Maroco, J. (2011). Portuguese version of Cues for Sexual Desire Scale: The influence of relationship duration. *Journal of Sexual Medicine, 8*, 123–131. doi:10.1111/j.1743-6109.2010.01909.x

Carvalho, J., & Nobre, P. (2010). Predictors of women's sexual desire: The role of psychopathology, cognitive-emotional determinants, relationship dimensions, and medical factors. *Journal of Sexual Medicine, 7*, 928–937. doi:10.1111/j.1743-6109.2009.01568.x

Carvalho, J., & Nobre, P. (2011). Predictors of men's sexual desire: The role of psychological, cognitive-emotional, relational, and medical factors. *Journal of Sex Research, 48*, 254–262. doi:10.1080/00224491003605475

Chivers, M. L. (2005). A brief review and discussion of sex differences in the specificity of sexual arousal. *Sexual and Relationship Therapy, 20*, 377–390. doi:10.1080/14681990500238802

Chivers, M. L., Seto, M. C., Lalumière, M. L., Laan, E., & Grimbos, T. (2010). Agreement of self-reported and genital measures of sexual arousal in men and women: A meta-analysis. *Archives of Sexual Behavior, 39*, 5–56. doi:10.1007/s10508-009-9556-9

Clayton, A. H. (2010). The pathophysiology of hypoactive sexual desire disorder in women. *International Journal of Gynecology & Obstetrics, 110*, 7–11. doi:10.1016/j.ijgo.2010.02.014

Corona, G., Mannucci, E., Petrone, L., Giommi, R., Mansani, R., Fei, L., . . . Maggi, M. (2004). Psychobiological correlates of hypoactive sexual desire in patients with erectile dysfunction. *International Journal of Impotence Research, 16*, 275–281. doi:10.1038/sj.ijir.3901158

Corona, G., Mannucci, E., Ricca, V., Lotti, F., Boddi, V., Bandini, E., . . . Maggi, M. (2009). The age-related decline of testosterone is associated with different specific symptoms and signs in patients with sexual dysfunction. *International Journal of Andrology, 32*, 720–728. doi:10.1111/j.1365-2605.2009.00952.x

Creswell, J. W. (2009). Mapping the field of mixed methods research. *Journal of Mixed Methods Research, 3*, 95–108. doi:10.1177/1558689808330883

Davis, S., Papalia, M.-A., Norman, R. J., O'Neill, S., Redelman, M., Williamson, M., . . . Humberstone, A. (2008). Safety and efficacy of a testosterone metered-dose transdermal spray for treating decreased sexual satisfaction in premenopausal women: A randomized trial. *Annals of Internal Medicine, 148*, 569–577.

Davis, S. R., Moreau, M., Kroll, R., Bouchard, C., Panay, N., Gass, M., . . . Studd, J. (2008). Testosterone for low libido in postmenopausal women not taking estrogen. *New England Journal of Medicine, 359*, 2005–2017. doi:10.1056/NEJMoa0707302

Dawson, S. J., Suschinsky, K. D., & Lalumière, M. L. (2012). Sexual fantasies and viewing times across the menstrual cycle: A diary study. *Archives of Sexual Behavior, 41*, 173–183. doi:10.1007/s10508-012-9939-1

DeLamater, J. D., & Sill, M. (2005). Sexual desire in later life. *Journal of Sex Research, 42*, 138–149. doi:10.1080/00224490509552267

Dennerstein, L., Koochaki, P., Barton, I., & Graziottin, A. (2006). Hypoactive sexual desire disorder in menopausal women: A survey of Western European women. *Journal of Sexual Medicine, 3*, 212–222. doi:10.1111/j.1743-6109.2006.00215.x

Dennerstein, L., Lehert, P., & Burger, H. (2005). The relative effects of hormones and relationship factors on sexual function of women through the natural menopausal transition. *Fertility & Sterility, 84*, 174–180.

Dennerstein, L., Lehert, P., Burger, H., & Dudley, E. (1999). Factors affecting sexual functioning of women in the mid-life years. *Climacteric, 2*, 254–262. doi:10.3109/13697139909038085

Dennerstein, L., Randolph, J., Taffe, J., Dudley, E., & Burger, H. (2002). Hormones, mood, sexuality, and the menopausal transition. *Fertility and Sterility, 77*(Suppl. 4), 42–48. doi:10.1016/S0015-0282(02)03001-7

Devries, K. M., & Free, C. (2010). "I told him not to use condoms": Masculinities, femininities and sexual health of Aboriginal Canadian young people. *Sociology of Health and Illness, 32*, 827–842. doi:10.1111/j.1467-9566.2010.01242.x

Diamond, L. E., Earle, D. C., Heiman, J. R., Rosen, R. C., Perelman, M. A., & Harning, R. (2006). An effect on the subjective sexual response in premenopausal women with sexual arousal disorder by bremelanotide (PT-141), a melanocortin receptor agonist. *Journal of Sexual Medicine, 3*, 628–638. doi:10.1111/j.1743-6109.2006.00268.x

Diamond, L. M. (2003). What does sexual orientation orient? A biobehavioral model distinguishing romantic love and sexual desire. *Psychological Review, 110*, 173–192. doi:10.1037/0033-295X.110.1.173

Diamond, L. M. (2008). *Sexual fluidity: Understanding women's love and desire.* Cambridge, MA: Harvard University Press.

Diamond, L. M. (2012). The desire disorder in research on sexual orientation in women: Contributions of dynamical systems theory. *Archives of Sexual Behavior, 41*, 73–83.

Drew, J. (2003). The myth of female sexual dysfunction and its medicalization. *Sexualities, Evolution, and Gender, 5*, 89–96. doi:10.1080/14616660310001632563

Dunn, K. M., Croft, P. R., & Hackett, G. I. (2000). Satisfaction in the sex life of a general population sample. *Journal of Sex & Marital Therapy, 26*, 141–151. doi:10.1080/009262300278542

Eplov, L., Giraldi, A., Davidsen, M., Garde, K., & Kamper-Jørgensen, F. (2007). Sexual desire in a nationally representative Danish population. *Journal of Sexual Medicine, 4*, 47–56. doi:10.1111/j.1743-6109.2006.00396.x

Everaerd, W., Both, S., & Laan, E. (2006). The experience of sexual emotions. *Annual Review of Sex Research, 17*, 183–199.

Everaerd, W., & Laan, E. (1995). Desire for passion: Energetics of sexual response. *Journal of Sex & Marital Therapy, 21*, 255–263. doi:10.1080/00926239508414645

Ferenidou, F., Kapoteli, V., Moisidis, K., Koutsogiannis, I., Giakoumelos, A., & Hatzichristou, D. (2008). Presence of a sexual problem may not affect women's satisfaction from their sexual function. *Journal of Sexual Medicine, 5*, 631–639. doi:10.1111/j.1743-6109.2007.00644.x

Ferrari, F., Ottani, A., & Giuliani, D. (2000). Inhibitory effects of the cannabinoid agonist HU 210 on rat sexual behavior. *Physiology & Behavior, 69*, 547–554. doi:10.1016/S0031-9384(00)00214-6

Fugl-Meyer, A. R., & Sjogren Fugl-Meyer, K. (1999). Sexual disabilities, problems and satisfaction in 18–74 year old Swedes. *Scandinavian Journal of Sexology, 2*, 79–105.

Gagnon, J. H. (1990). The explicit and implicit use of the scripting perspective in sex research. *Annual Review of Sex Research, 1*, 1–43.

Giles, K. R., & McCabe, M. P. (2009). Conceptualizing women's sexual function: Linear vs. circular models of sexual response. *Journal of Sexual Medicine, 6*, 2761–2771. doi:10.1111/j.1743-6109.2009.01425.x

Goldey, K. L., & van Anders. S. M. (2012). Sexual arousal and desire: Interrelations and responses to three modalities of sexual stimuli. *Journal of Sexual Medicine, 9*, 2315–2329.

Goldhammer, D. L., & McCabe, M. P. (2011). A qualitative exploration of the meaning and experience of sexual desire among partnered women. *Canadian Journal of Human Sexuality, 20*, 19–29.

Graham, C. A. (2010). The DSM diagnostic criteria for female sexual arousal disorder. *Archives of Sexual Behavior, 39*, 240–255. doi:10.1007/s10508-009-9535-1

Graham, C. A., Sanders, S. A., Milhausen, R. R., & McBride, K. R. (2004). Turning on and turning off: A focus group study of the factors that affect women's sexual arousal. *Archives of Sexual Behavior, 33*, 527–538. doi:10.1023/B:ASEB.0000044737.62561.fd

Hanson, W. E., Creswell, J. W., Clark, V. L. P., Petska, K. S., & Creswell, J. D. (2005). Mixed methods research in counseling psychology. *Journal of Counseling Psychology, 52*, 224–235. doi:10.1037/0022-0167.52.2.224

Hawton, K., Catalan, J., & Fagg, J. (1991). Low sexual desire: Sex therapy results and prognostic factors. *Behaviour Research and Therapy, 29*, 217–224. doi:10.1016/0005-7967(91)90111-F

Hedricks, C. A. (1994). Female sexual activity across the human menstrual cycle: A biopsychosocial approach. *Annual Review of Sex Research, 5*, 122–172.

Heiman, J. R., Long, J. S., Smith, S. N., Fisher, W. A., Sand, M. S., & Rosen, R. C. (2011). Sexual satisfaction and relationship happiness in midlife and older couples in five countries. *Archives of Sexual Behavior, 40*, 741–753. doi:10.1007/s10508-010-9703-3

Hill, C. A., & Preston, L. K. (1996). Individual differences in the experience of sexual motivation: Theory and measurement of dispositional sexual motives. *Journal of Sex Research, 33*, 27–45. doi:10.1080/00224499609551812

Hinderliter, A. C. (2009). Methodological issues for studying asexuality. *Archives of Sexual Behavior, 38*, 619–621. doi:10.1007/s10508-009-9502-x

Hoon, E. F., & Chambless, D. (1998). Sexual Arousability Inventory (SAI) and Sexual Arousability Inventory—Expanded (SAI–E). In C. M. Davis, W. L. Yarber, R. Bauserman, G. Schreer, & S. L. Davis (Eds.), *Handbook of sexuality-related measures* (pp. 71–74). Thousand Oaks, CA: Sage.

Hsu, B., Kling, A., Kessler, C., & Knapke, K. (1994). Gender differences in sexual fantasy and behavior in a college population: A ten-year replication. *Journal of Sex & Marital Therapy, 20*, 103–118. doi:10.1080/00926239408403421

Hullfish, K. L., Pastore, L. M., Mormon, A. J. A., Wernecke, Y., Bovbjerg, V. E., & Clayton, A. H. (2009). Sexual functioning of Latino women seeking outpatient gynecologic care. *Journal of Sexual Medicine, 6*, 61–69. doi:10.1111/j.1743-6109.2008.01032.x

Impett, E. A., Strachman, A., Finkel, E. J., & Gable, S. L. (2008). Maintaining sexual desire in intimate relationships: The importance of approach goals. *Journal of Personality and Social Psychology, 94*, 808–823. doi:10.1037/0022-3514.94.5.808

Janssen, E., Everaerd, W., Spiering, M., & Janssen, J. (2000). Automatic processes and the appraisal of sexual stimuli: Toward an information processing model of sexual arousal. *Journal of Sex Research, 37*, 8–23. doi:10.1080/00224490009552016

Janssen, E., McBride, K. R., Yarber, W., Hill, B. J., & Butler, S. M. (2008). Factors that influence sexual arousal in men: A focus group study. *Archives of Sexual Behavior, 37*, 252–265. doi:10.1007/s10508-007-9245-5

Jones, J. C., & Barlow, D. H. (1990). Self-reported frequency of sexual urges, fantasies and masturbatory fantasies in heterosexual males and females. *Archives of Sexual Behavior, 19*, 269–279. doi:10.1007/BF01541552

Joshi, S. P., Peter, J., & Valkenburg, P. M. (2011). Scripts of sexual desire and danger in US and Dutch teen girl magazines: A cross-national content analysis. *Sex Roles, 64*, 463–474. doi:10.1007/s11199-011-9941-4

Kabat-Zinn, J. (1994). *Wherever you go, there you are: Mindfulness meditation in everyday life.* New York, NY: Hyperion.

Kaplan, H. S. (1974). *The new sex therapy: Active treatment of sexual dysfunctions.* New York, NY: Brunner & Mazel.

Kaplan, H. S. (1977). Hypoactive sexual desire. *Journal of Sex & Marital Therapy, 3*, 3–9. doi:10.1080/00926237708405343

Kaplan, H. S. (Ed.). (1979). *Disorders of sexual desire.* New York, NY: Brunner/Mazel.

Kaplan, H. S. (1995). *The sexual desire disorders.* New York, NY: Brunner/Mazel.

Katz, J., & Farrow, S. (2000). Heterosexual adjustment among women and men with non-traditional gender identities: Testing predictions from self-verification theory. *Social Behavior and Personality, 28*, 613–620. doi:10.2224/sbp.2000.28.6.613

King, M., Holt, V., & Nazareth, I. (2007). Women's views of their sexual difficulties: Agreement and disagreement with clinical diagnoses. *Archives of Sexual Behavior, 36*, 281–288. doi:10.1007/s10508-006-9090-y

Kinsey, A. C., Pomeroy, W. B., & Martin, C. E. (1948). *Sexual behavior in the human male*. Bloomington: Indiana University Press.

Klein, C., Hill, M. N., Chang, S. C., Hillard, C. J., & Gorzalka, B. B. (2012). Circulating endocannabinoid concentrations and sexual arousal in women. *Journal of Sexual Medicine, 9*, 1588–1601. doi:10.1111/j.1743-6109.2012.02708.x

Klusmann, D. (2002). Sexual motivation and the duration of partnership. *Archives of Sexual Behavior, 31*, 275–287. doi:10.1023/A:1015205020769

Krishnamurti, T., & Loewenstein, G. (2012). The Partner-Specific Sexual Liking and Sexual Wanting scale: Psychometric properties. *Archives of Sexual Behavior, 41*, 467–476.

Krug, R., Plihal, W., Fehm, H. L., & Born, J. (2000). Selective influence of the menstrual cycle on perception of stimuli with reproductive significance: An event-related potential study. *Psychophysiology, 37*, 111–122. doi:10.1111/1469-8986.3710111

Laan, E., & Both, S. (2008). What makes women experience desire? *Feminism & Psychology, 18*, 505–514. doi:10.1177/0959353508095533

Laan, E., & Everaerd, W. (1995). Determinants of female sexual arousal: Psychophysiological theory and data. *Annual Review of Sex Research, 6*, 32–76.

Laan, E., & van Lunsen, R. H. W. (1997). Hormones and sexuality in postmenopausal women: A psychophysiological study. *Journal of Psychosomatic Obstetrics & Gynecology, 18*, 126–133.

Labrie, F., Bélanger, A., Bélanger, P., Bérubé, R., Martel, C., Cusan, L., . . . Leclaire, J. (2006). Androgen glucuronides, instead of testosterone, as the new markers of androgenic activity in women. *Journal of Steroid Biochemistry and Molecular Biology, 99*, 182–188. doi:10.1016/j.jsbmb.2006.02.004

Laumann, E. O., Nicolosi, A., Glasser, D. B., Paik, A., Gingell, C., Moreira, E., & Wang, T. for the GSSAB Investigators' Group. (2005). Sexual problems among women and men aged 40–80 y: Prevalence and correlates identified in the Global Study of Sexual Attitudes and Behaviors. *International Journal of Impotence Research, 17*, 39–57. doi:10.1038/sj.ijir.3901250

Laumann, E. O., Paik, A., & Rosen, R. C. (1999). Sexual dysfunction in the United States: Prevalence and predictors. *JAMA, 281*, 537–544. doi:10.1001/jama.281.6.537

Leiblum, S. R., Koochaki, P. E., Rodenberg, C. A., Barton, I. P., & Rosen, R. C. (2006). Hypoactive sexual desire disorder in postmenopausal women: US results from the Women's International Study of Health and Sexuality (WISHeS). *Menopause, 13*, 46–56. doi:10.1097/01.gme.0000172596.76272.06

Levin, R. J., & van Berlo, W. (2004). Sexual arousal and orgasm in subjects who experience forced or non-consensual sexual stimulation—A review. *Journal of Clinical Forensic Medicine, 11*, 82–88. doi:10.1016/j.jcfm.2003.10.008

Levine, S. B. (1987). More on the nature of sexual desire. *Journal of Sex & Marital Therapy, 13*, 35–44. doi:10.1080/00926238708403877

Levine, S. B. (2002). Reexploring the concept of sexual desire. *Journal of Sex & Marital Therapy, 28*, 39–51. doi:10.1080/009262302317251007

Lief, H. I. (1977). Inhibited sexual desire. *Medical Aspects of Human Sexuality, 7*, 94–95.

Lunde, I., Larsen, G. K., Fog, E., & Garde, K. (1991). Sexual desire, orgasm, and sexual fantasies: A study of 625 Danish women born in 1910, 1936 and 1958. *Journal of Sex Education and Therapy, 17*, 111–115.

Lutfey, K. E., Link, C. L., Rosen, R. C., Wiegel, M., & McKinlay, J. B. (2009). Prevalence and correlates of sexual activity and function in women: Results from the Boston Area Community Health (BACH) survey. *Archives of Sexual Behavior, 38*, 514–527. doi:10.1007/s10508-007-9290-0

MacDonald, K., & Feifel, D. (2012). Dramatic improvement in sexual function induced by intranasal oxytocin. *Journal of Sexual Medicine, 9*, 1407–1410. doi:10.1111/j.1743-6109.2012.02703.x

Maclaran, K., & Panay, N. (2011). Managing low sexual desire in women. *Women's Health, 7*, 571–583. doi:10.2217/whe.11.54

Maserejian, N. N., Shifren, J. L., Parish, S. J., Braunstein, G. D., Gerstenberger, E. P., & Rosen, R. C. (2010). The presentation of hypoactive sexual desire disorder in premenopausal women. *Journal of Sexual Medicine, 7*, 3439–3448. doi:10.1111/j.1743-6109.2010.01934.x

Masters, W. H., & Johnson, V. E. (1966). *Human sexual response*. Boston, MA: Little, Brown.

Maurice, W. L. (2007). Sexual desire disorders in men. In S. R. Leiblum (Ed.), *Principles and practice of sex therapy* (4th ed., pp. 181–211). New York, NY: Guilford Press.

McCall, K., & Meston, C. (2006). Cues resulting in desire for sexual activity in women. *Journal of Sexual Medicine, 3*, 838–852. doi:10.1111/j.1743-6109.2006.00301.x

McCall, K., & Meston, C. (2007). Differences between pre- and postmenopausal women in cues for sexual desire. *Journal of Sexual Medicine, 4*, 364–371. doi:10.1111/j.1743-6109.2006.00421.x

McCarthy, B., & McDonald, D. (2009). Assessment, treatment, and relapse prevention: Male hypoactive sexual desire disorder. *Journal of Sex & Marital Therapy, 35*, 58–67. doi:10.1080/00926230802525653

Meana, M. (2010). Elucidating women's (hetero) sexual desire: Definitional challenges and content expansion. *Journal of Sex Research, 47*, 104–122. doi:10.1080/00224490903402546

Mercer, C. H., Fenton, K. A., Johnson, A. M., Wellings, K., Macdowall, W., McManus, S., . . . Erens, B. (2003). Sexual function problems and help seeking behaviour in Britain: National probability sample survey. *British Medical Journal, 327*, 426–427. doi:10.1136/bmj.327.7412.426

Meston, C., & Trapnell, P. (2005). Development and validation of a five-factor sexual satisfaction and distress scale for women: The Sexual Satisfaction Scale for Women (SSS-W). *Journal of Sexual Medicine, 2*, 66–81. doi:10.1111/j.1743-6109.2005.20107.x

Meston, C. M., & Bradford, A. (2007). Sexual dysfunctions in women. *Annual Review of Clinical Psychology, 3*, 233–256. doi:10.1146/annurev.clinpsy.3.022806.091507

Meston, C. M., & Buss, D. M. (2007). Why humans have sex. *Archives of Sexual Behavior, 36*, 477–507. doi:10.1007/s10508-007-9175-2

Meston, C. M., Gorzalka, B. B., & Wright, J. M. (1997). Inhibition of subjective and physiological sexual arousal in women by clonidine. *Psychosomatic Medicine, 59*, 399–407.

Meuleman, E. J. H., & van Lankveld, J. J. (2005). Hypoactive sexual desire disorder: An underestimated condition in men. *BJU International, 95*, 291–296. doi:10.1111/j.1464-410X.2005.05285.x

Meyer-Kleinmann, J. (2010). *Following regulatory feedback Boehringer Ingelheim decides to discontinue flibanserin development.* Retrieved from http://www.boehringer-ingelheim.ca/en/news/press_releases/2010/8_october_2010.html

Moll, J. L., & Brown, C. S. (2011). The use of monoamine pharmacological agents in the treatment of sexual dysfunction: Evidence in the literature. *Journal of Sexual Medicine, 8*, 956–970. doi:10.1111/j.1743-6109.2010.02190.x

Mosher, D. L., & Cross, H. J. (1971). Sex guilt and premarital sexual experiences of college students. *Journal of Consulting and Clinical Psychology, 36*, 27–32. doi:10.1037/h0030454

Mouras, H., Stoléru, S., Bittoun, J., Glutron, D., Pélégrini-Isaac, M., Paradis, A.-L., . . . Burnod, Y. (2003). Brain processing of visual sexual stimuli in healthy men: A functional magnetic resonance imaging study. *NeuroImage, 20*, 855–869. doi:10.1016/S1053-8119(03)00408-7

Najman, J. M., Dunne, M. P., Boyle, F. M., Cook, M. D., & Purdie, D. M. (2003). Sexual dysfunction in the Australian population. *Australian Family Physician, 32*, 951–954.

Nappi, R. E., Albani, F., Santamaria, V., Tonani, S., Martini, E., Terreno, E., . . . Polatti, F. (2010). Menopause and sexual desire: The role of testosterone. *Menopause International, 16*, 162–168. doi:10.1258/mi.2010.010041

Nicholls, L. (2008). Putting the new view classification scheme to an empirical test. *Feminism & Psychology, 18*, 515–526. doi:10.1177/0959353508096180

Nobre, P. J. (2009). Determinants of sexual desire problems in women: Testing a cognitive-emotional model. *Journal of Sex & Marital Therapy, 35*, 360–377. doi:10.1080/00926230903065716

Öberg, K., Fugl-Meyer, A. R., & Fugl-Meyer, K. S. (2004). On categorization and quantification of women's sexual dysfunctions: An epidemiological approach. *International Journal of Impotence Research, 16*, 261–269. doi:10.1038/sj.ijir.3901151

Ortigue, S., Bianchi-Demicheli, F., Patel, N., Frum, C., & Lewis, J. W. (2010). Neuroimaging of love: fMRI meta-analysis evidence toward new perspectives in sexual medicine. *Journal of Sexual Medicine, 7*, 3541–3552. doi:10.1111/j.1743-6109.2010.01999.x

O'Sullivan, L. F., & Allgeier, E. R. (1998). Feigning sexual desire: Consenting to unwanted sexual activity in heterosexual dating relationships. *Journal of Sex Research, 35*, 234–243. doi:10.1080/00224499809551938

O'Sullivan, L. F., & Majerovic, J. (2008). Difficulties with sexual functioning in a sample of male and female late adolescent and young adult university students. *Canadian Journal of Human Sexuality, 17*, 109–121.

Peplau, L. A. (2003). Human sexuality: How do men and women differ? *Current Directions in Psychological Science, 12*, 37–40. doi:10.1111/1467-8721.01221

Perel, E. (2006). *Mating in captivity: Reconciling the erotic and the domestic.* New York, NY: HarperCollins.

Perelman, M. A. (2006). A new combination treatment for premature ejaculation: A sex therapist's perspective. *Journal of Sexual Medicine, 3*, 1004–1012. doi:10.1111/j.1743-6109.2006.00238.x

Pfaus, J. G. (2009). Pathways of sexual desire. *Journal of Sexual Medicine, 6*, 1506–1533. doi:10.1111/j.1743-6109.2009.01309.x

Philippsohn, S., & Hartmann, U. (2009). Determinants of sexual satisfaction in a sample of German women. *Journal of Sexual Medicine, 6*, 1001–1010. doi:10.1111/j.1743-6109.2008.00989.x

Prause, N., & Graham, C. A. (2007). Asexuality: Classification and characterization. *Archives of Sexual Behavior, 36*, 341–356. doi:10.1007/s10508-006-9142-3

Prause, N., Janssen, E., & Hetrick, W. (2008). Attention and emotional responses to sexual stimuli and their relationship to sexual desire. *Archives of Sexual Behavior, 37*, 934–949. doi:10.1007/s10508-007-9236-6

Reed, S. D., Guthrie, K. A., Joffe, H., Shifren, J. L., Seguin, R. A., & Freeman, E. W. (2012). Sexual function in nondepressed women using escitalopram for vasomotor symptoms: A randomized controlled trial. *Obstetrics & Gynecology, 119*, 527–538. doi:10.1097/AOG.0b013e3182475fa4

Regan, P. C. (1999). Hormonal correlates and causes of sexual desire: A review. *Canadian Journal of Human Sexuality, 8*, 1–16.

Regan, P. C., & Berscheid, E. (1996). Beliefs about the state, goals, and objects of sexual desire. *Journal of Sex & Marital Therapy, 22*, 110–120. doi:10.1080/00926239608404915

Richgels, P. B. (1992). Hypoactive sexual desire in heterosexual women. *Women and Therapy, 12*, 123–135. doi:10.1300/J015V12N01_10

Rodríguez-Manzo, G., & Fernández-Guasti, A. (1995). Opioid antagonists and the sexual satiation phenomenon. *Psychopharmacology, 122*, 131–136. doi:10.1007/BF02246087

Rosen, R., Brown, C., Heiman, J., Leiblum, S., Meston, C., Shabsigh, R., . . . D'Agostino, R., Jr. (2000). The Female Sexual Function Index (FSFI): A multidimensional self-report instrument for the assessment of female sexual function. *Journal of Sex & Marital Therapy, 26*, 191–208. doi:10.1080/009262300278597

Rosen, R. C., Riley, A., Wagner, G., Osterloh, I. H., Kilpatrick, J., & Mishra, A. (1997). The International Index of Erectile Function (IIEF): A multidimensional scale for assessment of erectile dysfunction. *Urology, 49*, 822–830. doi:10.1016/S0090-4295(97)00238-0

Sanchez, D. T., Crocker, J., & Boike, K. R. (2005). Doing gender in the bedroom: Investing in gender norms and the sexual experience. *Personality and Social Psychology Bulletin, 31*, 1445–1455. doi:10.1177/0146167205277333

Sanchez, D. T., Kiefer, A. K., & Ybarra, O. (2006). Sexual submissiveness in women: Costs for sexual autonomy and arousal. *Personality and Social Psychology Bulletin, 32*, 512–524. doi:10.1177/0146167205282154

Sand, M., & Fisher, W. A. (2007). Women's endorsement of models of female sexual response: The nurses' sexuality study. *Journal of Sexual Medicine, 4*, 708–719. doi:10.1111/j.1743-6109.2007.00496.x

Sarwer, D. B., & Durlak, J. A. (1997). A field trial of the effectiveness of behavioral treatment for sexual dysfunctions. *Journal of Sex & Marital Therapy, 23*, 87–97. doi:10.1080/00926239708405309

Semans, J. H. (1956). Premature ejaculation: A new approach. *Southern Medical Journal, 49*, 353–358.

Shifren, J. L., Monz, B. U., Russo, P. A., Segreti, A., & Johannes, C. B. (2008). Sexual problems and distress in United States women: Prevalence and correlates. *Obstetrics & Gynecology, 112*, 970–978. doi:10.1097/AOG.0b013e3181898cdb

Sims, K. E., & Meana, M. (2010). Why did passion wane? A qualitative study of married women's attributions for declines in sexual desire. *Journal of Sex & Marital Therapy, 36*, 360–380. doi:10.1080/0092623X.2010.498727

Slob, A. K., Bax, C. M., Hop, W. C., Rowland, D. L., & van der Werff ten Bosch, J. J. (1996). Sexual arousability and the menstrual cycle. *Psychoneuroendocrinology, 21*, 545–558. doi:10.1016/0306-4530(95)00058-5

Stahl, S. M., Sommer, B., & Allers, K. A. (2011). Multifunctional pharmacology of flibanserin: Possible mechanism of therapeutic action in hypoactive sexual desire disorder. *Journal of Sexual Medicine, 8*, 15–27. doi:10.1111/j.1743-6109.2010.02032.x

Stanislaw, H., & Rice, F. J. (1988). Correlation between sexual desire and menstrual cycle characteristics. *Archives of Sexual Behavior, 17*, 499–508. doi:10.1007/BF01542338

Stoléru, S., Redouté, J., Costes, N., Lavenne, F., Bars, D. L., Dechaud, H., . . . Pujol, J. F. (2003). Brain processing of visual sexual stimuli in men with hypoactive sexual desire disorder. *Psychiatry Research: Neuroimaging, 124*, 67–86. doi:10.1016/S0925-4927(03)00068-4

Suschinsky, K. D., & Lalumière, M. L. (2011). Prepared for anything? An investigation of female genital arousal in response to rape cues. *Psychological Science, 22*, 159–165.

Tennov, D. (1979). *Love and limerence: The experience of being in love.* New York, NY: Stein & Day.

ter Kuile, M. M., Both, S., & van Lankveld, J. J. D. M. (2010). Cognitive behavioral therapy for sexual dysfunctions in women. *Psychiatric Clinics of North America, 33*, 595–610. doi:10.1016/j.psc.2010.04.010

Thomson, S. (1995). *Going all the way: Teenage girls' tales of sex, romance, and pregnancy*. New York, NY: Hill & Wang.

Tiefer, L. (1991). Historical, scientific, clinical and feminist criticisms of "the human sexual response cycle" model. *Annual Review of Sex Research, 2*, 1–23.

Tiefer, L., Hall, M., & Tavris, C. (2002). Beyond dysfunction: A new view of women's sexual problems. *Journal of Sex & Marital Therapy, 28*(Suppl. 1), 225–232. doi:10.1080/00926230252851357

Toates, F. (2009). An integrative theoretical framework for understanding sexual motivation, arousal, and behavior. *Journal of Sex Research, 46*, 168–193. doi:10.1080/00224490902747768

Tolman, D. L. (2001). Female adolescent sexuality: An argument for a developmental perspective on the new view of women's sexual problems. In E. Kaschak & L. Tiefer (Eds.), *A new view of women's sexual problems* (pp. 195–210). New York, NY: Haworth Press.

Tolman, D. L. (2002). *Dilemmas of desire: Teenage girls talk about sexuality*. Cambridge, MA: Harvard University Press.

Tolman, D. L., & Diamond, L. M. (2001). Desegregating sexuality research: Cultural and biological perspectives on gender and desire. *Annual Review of Sex Research, 12*, 33–74.

Tolman, D. L., & Higgins, T. (1996). How being a good girl can be bad for girls. In N. Maglin & D. Perry (Eds.), *Bad girls/good girls: Women, sex, and power in the nineties* (pp. 205–225). New Brunswick, NJ: Rutgers University Press.

Tolman, D. L., & Szalacha, L. A. (1999). Dimensions of desire: Bridging qualitative and quantitative methods in a study of female adolescent sexuality. *Psychology of Women Quarterly, 23*, 7–39. doi:10.1111/j.1471-6402.1999.tb00338.x

Travison, T. G., Morley, J. E., Araujo, A. B., O'Donnell, A. B., & McKinlay, J. B. (2006). The relationship between libido and testosterone levels in aging men. *Journal of Clinical Endocrinology & Metabolism, 91*, 2509–2513. doi:10.1210/jc.2005-2508

Trudel, G., Marchand, A., Ravart, M., Aubin, S., Turgeon, L., & Fortier, P. (2001). The effect of a cognitive-behavioral group treatment program on hypoactive sexual desire in women. *Sexual and Relationship Therapy, 16*, 145–164. doi:10.1080/14681990120040078

van Anders, S. M. (2012). Testosterone and sexual desire in healthy women and men. *Archives of Sexual Behavior, 41*, 1471–1484. doi:10.1007/s10508-012-9946-2

Vance, C. S. (1989). *Pleasure and danger: Exploring female sexuality*. London, England: Pandora.

van Lankveld, J. J. D. M., Everaerd, W., & Grotjohann, Y. (2001). Cognitive-behavioral bibliotherapy for sexual dysfunctions in heterosexual couples: A randomized waiting-list controlled clinical trial in the Netherlands. *Journal of Sex Research, 38*, 51–67. doi:10.1080/00224490109552070

Vannier, S. A., & O'Sullivan, L. F. (2010). Sex without desire: Characteristics of occasions of sexual compliance in young adults' committed relationships. *Journal of Sex Research, 47*, 429–439. doi:10.1080/00224490903132051

Vannier, S. A., & O'Sullivan, L. F. (2011). Communicating interest in sex: Verbal and nonverbal initiation of sexual activity in young adults' romantic dating relationships. *Archives of Sexual Behavior, 40*, 961–969. doi:10.1007/s10508-010-9663-7

Wang, C., Nieschlag, E., Swerdloff, R., Behre, H. M., Hellstrom, W. J., Gooren, L. J., . . . Wu, F. C. W. (2009). Investigation, treatment, and monitoring of late-onset hypogonadism in males: ISA, ISSAM, EAU, EAA, and ASA recommendations. *European Urology, 55*, 121–130. doi:10.1016/j.eururo.2008.08.033

Ward, L. M. (2003). Understanding the role of entertainment media in the sexual socialization of American youth: A review of empirical research. *Developmental Review, 23*, 347–388. doi:10.1016/S0273-2297(03)00013-3

West, S. L., D'Aloisio, A. A., Agans, R. P., Kalsbeek, W. D., Borisov, N. N., & Thorp, J. M. (2008). Prevalence of low sexual desire and hypoactive sexual desire disorder in a nationally representative sample of US women. *Archives of Internal Medicine, 168*, 1441–1449. doi:10.1001/archinte.168.13.1441

Wierman, M. E., Basson, R., Davis, S. R., Khosla, S., Miller, K. K., Rosner, W., & Santoro, N. (2006). Androgen therapy in women: An Endocrine Society clinical practice guideline. *Journal of Clinical Endocrinology & Metabolism, 91*, 3697–3710. doi:10.1210/jc.2006-1121

Witting, K., Santtila, P., Varjonen, M., Jern, P., Johansson, A., von der Pahlen, B., . . . Sandnabba, K. (2008). Female sexual dysfunction, sexual distress, and compatibility with partner. *Journal of Sexual Medicine, 5*, 2587–2599. doi:10.1111/j.1743-6109.2008.00984.x

Woo, J. S. T., Brotto, L. A., & Gorzalka, B. B. (2011). The role of sex guilt in the relationship between culture and women's sexual desire. *Archives of Sexual Behavior, 40*, 385–394. doi:10.1007/s10508-010-9609-0

Woo, J. S. T., Brotto, L. A., & Gorzalka, B. B. (2012). The relationship between sex guilt and sexual desire in a community sample of Chinese and Euro-Canadian women. *Journal of Sex Research, 49*, 290–298.

Zurbriggen, E. L., & Yost, M. R. (2004). Power, desire, and pleasure in sexual fantasies. *Journal of Sex Research, 41*, 288–300. doi:10.1080/00224490409552236

CHAPTER 9

SEXUAL DIVERSITY

Peggy J. Kleinplatz and Lisa M. Diamond

> Such a continuous and widely spread series [of sexual behaviors] raises a question as to whether the terms "normal" and "abnormal" belong in a scientific vocabulary. (Kinsey, Pomeroy, & Martin, 1948, p. 199)

How are we to understand the diversity in human sexual interest and expression? The question itself betrays the assumption that there is a correct or at least a normative sort of sexual interest or arousal pattern from which some people are said to diverge. When people speak of preferences for colors or music or movies, there is no assumption that blue is better than red or that rock is superior to bluegrass. It is acknowledged that some tastes are more common than others and that Angelina Jolie is especially popular at the box office; however, few would criticize those who prefer Meryl Streep, even though she does not sell as many tickets as Kristen Stewart. Some fans say that Katharine Hepburn remains an eternal favorite. Why then do mental health professionals and lay people try to classify sexual desires and behaviors? What is the meaning of this exercise?

Not long after the American Psychiatric Association removed homosexuality from the *Diagnostic and Statistical Manual of Mental Disorders* (2nd ed., 7th printing) in 1973, historian of sexuality Vern Bullough (1979) pointed out that continuing questions about the origins of homosexuality betrayed the belief that homosexuality was still perceived as both deviant and pathological. The evidence that people are still unable to see sexual diversity as akin to diverse tastes in movies is revealed by the continuing classification of unusual sexual interests in the *DSM* (reviewed in more depth in a separate section later in this chapter), as well as by the pop culture discourse. Our goal in this chapter is to provide an overview of the current state of psychological knowledge regarding alternative (or, in colloquial terms, kinky) sexual interests and practices. A comprehensive review of the behaviors deemed as paraphilic or of each and every type of alternative sexual practice (e.g., voyeurism, pedophilia, paraphilic infantilism, swinging) is beyond the scope of this chapter (for a detailed review of the paraphilias, see Laws & O'Donohue, 2008). Rather, we begin by highlighting the fundamental theoretical and ideological debates and assumptions that surround the topic of sexual diversity and review recent revisions to the *DSM* that make some of these debates and assumptions salient. We then turn to some of the more common forms of alternative sexual interest and behavior that the average clinician is likely to encounter (bondage and discipline, dominance and submission, and sadism and masochism [BDSM]; fetishes; polyamory; and same-sex interest among otherwise heterosexual individuals). We review what is known about these phenomena from a psychological perspective and also how they are appraised by the culture at large, particularly by the mainstream media. We conclude by discussing important issues facing clinicians treating clients with unusual (or non-normative) sexual interests and highlighting some of the most important areas for future research.

http://dx.doi.org/10.1037/14193-009
APA Handbook of Sexuality and Psychology: Vol. 1. Person-Based Approaches, D. L. Tolman and L. M. Diamond (Editors-in-Chief)

DEFINING DIVERSITY: THEORETICAL AND HISTORICAL CONSIDERATIONS

The problems in discussing sexual diversity are manifest when seeking relevant points of reference. Sexual diversity relative to what? Homogeneity? Iceland's population is relatively homogeneous compared with Toronto's heterogeneous society. Theoretically, matters of population demographics are statistical facts and value neutral. How one regards differences in composition is a value judgment. Canadians value diversity, as reflected by the government ministry devoted to promoting multicultural diversity rather than subscribing to a melting pot mentality. If one is a member of the Aryan Nation, this difference is crucial and should be identified and eradicated rather than either celebrated or amalgamated.

Do researchers define *sexual diversity* in relation to what is typical or in relation to what is considered "normal"? Is diversity merely a politically correct buzzword to camouflage a continuing professional interest in classifying deviance? Does the study of diversity simply entail the documentation of practices that are statistically uncommon, or does it move beyond this innocuous goal toward the more dubious aim of identifying and demarcating individuals and acts that are deemed psychologically or morally aberrant?

Aside from the meaning of the endeavor to classify sexual inclinations, distinguishing normal from "other" sexuality may not be feasible in and of itself. Orford (2001, p. 123) has written, "It is impossible to separate normal and abnormal sexual behaviour in other than an arbitrary way." Robert L. Spitzer (2005), a former editor of the *DSM*, has argued that the differences between normal and abnormal sexuality are not merely matters of diversity but of identifying bona fide disorders and, therefore, of treating them accordingly. For example, he maintained that the human eye was created for purposes of vision; accordingly, people who are blind (i.e., who possess eyes but cannot use them for their intended purpose) do not represent a variation in the spectrum of vision but have a disorder. By the same reasoning, individuals who have sexual organs but who become aroused by activities that do not promote normal pair bonding and reproduction (the activities for which human genitals were obviously intended) are similarly disordered and require treatment to help them use their genitals for the purpose designed by evolution (Spitzer, 2005, pp. 113–114). Spitzer stated explicitly that although essentialist arguments are not popular, it is self-evident that the use of the genitals for nonreproductive purposes is clearly evidence of psychopathology and not benign variation.

This line of reasoning is currently echoed in the proposed revisions for the fifth edition of the *DSM*, which presuppose that there is a normal sequence of copulatory and precopulatory sexual activities and that sexual patterns that deviate from this norm are paraphilic (Blanchard, 2009). Certainly, some of the practices listed in the current *DSM* (4th ed., text revision; *DSM–IV–TR;* American Psychiatric Association, 2000) as paraphilias (i.e., persistent motivation to pursue sexual objects and activities that deviate from social norms) are illegal activities (such as the pursuit of sex with underage children) rather than mental illnesses, which seems rather odd given that most sections of the *DSM–IV–TR* say little about behaviors (as opposed to mental or emotional states, impulses, inclinations, and so on) as distinguishing factors in psychopathology (Moser, 2001). In addition, not all paraphiliacs will ever act on their atypical desires. Many pedophiles, for example, never act on their sexual desires for children, and correspondingly, many, if not most, cases of child sexual abuse are committed by normal adults who never enter the criminal justice system (Finkelhor, 2008). A recent meta-analysis found that approximately 50% of child sex offenders are not pedophilic and experience their primary erotic arousal to other adults (Seto, 2008).

Thus, the further one delves into distinguishing between normal and abnormal sexuality on a conceptual level, the more apparent it becomes that sex itself or what counts as a sex act is not understood uniformly. As described by Laws and O'Donohue (2008) in their review of the paraphilia literature, "There are no well-corroborated accounts of the psychopathology involved in the paraphilias. In addition, too little is known about 'normal' sexuality and sexual development. Thus, again, there are gaps in what constructs ought to be measured" (p. 6).

There is a lack of conceptual clarity regarding the entire spectrum of sexuality, from problematic to normal to optimal.

Other attempts at defining atypical sexuality have sought to distinguish normal versus abnormal sexuality in presumably more objective terms, that is, via statistical data. The belief historically has been that by definition, uncommon desires are deviant. However, a recent German population sample found that 62.4% of men reported a pattern of sexual arousal that would qualify as one of the *DSM–IV–TR* paraphilias, indicating that the presence of "deviant" paraphilic desires may not be quite as deviant as previously believed (Ahlers et al., 2011). Any sex therapist can testify that the most common fantasies (and most fantasies are, by default, taboo) involve nonmonogamous sex (typically threesomes) and fantasies about forced sex (which, in most cases, do not appear to be about sexual coercion as much as they appear to be about being so sexually irresistible that Robert Pattinson or Katy Perry or both resolve to stop at nothing to seduce you).

In summary, the supposedly scientific project of reliably distinguishing normal from abnormal desires and practices (outside the context of illegal activities or those that harm other individuals) is, at best, unsuccessful. At worst, it is deeply biased. Allowing social values to determine what qualifies as an acceptable form of sexuality is certainly a common practice in society at large, and among many different subcultures and organized communities, but it should not be cloaked with a façade of scientific neutrality (see Volume 2, Chapter 6, this handbook).

THE *DIAGNOSTIC AND STATISTICAL MANUAL OF MENTAL DISORDERS*

Socially unacceptable sexuality has long been identified as pathological throughout the various editions of the *DSM*. Sexual behaviors and proclivities, from masturbation, oral sex, and nymphomania to rape and zoophilia, have been listed and subsequently withdrawn from *DSM* classification. The criteria for inclusion or exclusion have inevitably presupposed some conception of what normal sexuality means, although this conception has not been articulated explicitly. Mainstream psychology and sexology have little in the way of paradigms of normal sexuality outside the physiologically based human sexual response cycle model of sexual functioning, along with research on the sexual behaviors and attitudes of (mostly White and middle-class) college students. It is highly doubtful that these paradigms will be of value for understanding the full spectrum of sexual desires.

The silence surrounding what counts as normal will change with the *DSM–5* (American Psychiatric Association, 2012). Whereas previous editions of the *DSM* have defined the paraphilias as a list of eight atypical sexual behaviors (i.e., voyeurism, exhibitionism, fetishism, transvestic fetishism, sexual sadism, sexual masochism, frotteurism, pedophilia) and paraphilia not otherwise specified, the fifth edition will define the paraphilias in terms of deviation from the presumed norm: "Essentially, it defines paraphilias as erotic interests that are *not* focused on copulatory or precopulatory behaviors, or the equivalent behaviors in same-sex adult partners" (Blanchard, 2009). That is, Blanchard (2009) has proposed that rather than a list by concatenation, the *DSM–5* should list paraphilias by exclusion: "The term paraphilia denotes any intense and persistent sexual interest in genital stimulation or preparatory fondling with phenotypically normal, consenting adult human partners." These definitions focus explicitly on genital contact, sexual intercourse, and whatever leads up to them in the normal sequence of sexual activities and define as paraphilic whatever diverges in other directions.

Unlike previous editions, the *DSM–5* will explicitly distinguish between the existence of a paraphilia, to be ascertained by the clinician, and the presence of a "paraphilia disorder" to be diagnosed as pathological. The former would be the assessment of an interest per se, which would not necessarily be grounds for pathology, whereas the latter would involve the atypical interest plus distress and dysfunction, which would be necessary for diagnosing a disorder. (For a detailed review of the *DSM*'s historical treatment of the paraphilias and of the process by which the most recent round of revisions was drafted, see Kamens, 2011).

BDSM

The abbreviation BDSM is the combined shorthand for three (or four) combined terms: bondage and discipline, dominance and submission, sadism and masochism, and sometimes slave and master. The abbreviation represents the umbrella term for people interested in what is sometimes simply called *kink*. The core attributes of BDSM generally include power exchange, eroticizing of intense sensation, role play, consent, and some mutual definition of the activities as being sexual in nature or context, whether or not they involve genital contact (Weinberg, Williams, & Moser, 1984; see Chapter 25, this volume). *Power exchange* refers to the submissive, bottom, or slave giving control to the partner, referred to as the dominant, top, or master for the course of their B interactions or relationship. One can conceive of the top as taking charge of the bottom, taking care of the bottom, or alternately being served by him or her. Intense sensation involves what is described in the *DSM–IV–TR* as arousal to pain and imagined similarly by the lay public. The whips-and-chains stereotypes predominate here, but what is actually perceived as painful varies across individuals and contexts. Role play during BDSM activities may be quite subtle or overt and elaborate. Consent is a crucial aspect of BDSM relationships and scenes and is part of the credo of the BDSM world: "safe, sane, and consensual." Although partners may role play giving over total power (i.e., total power exchange; see Dancer, Kleinplatz, & Moser, 2006) to the other, it is prior and ongoing consent that differentiates BDSM from sexual assault. For example, practitioners of BDSM typically establish and use "safe words," that is, code words (e.g., *red, yellow, green*) to unambiguously signal to the partner a wish to slow down, change, or stop certain behaviors (whereas conventional words such as *stop* and *no* might be a part of the role play, making their meaning unclear when said in the middle of a sexual scene). This stands in marked contrast to sexual assault in which *no* really does mean "no." The shared understanding of roles, vocabulary, costumes, and use of props underscore the theatrical aspects of BDSM scenes. As such, the notion that they are sexual even though they may not involve genital contact highlights the extent to which BDSM play involves the primacy of mutually shared meanings, sometimes over observable behaviors.

Myths and Misinformation About BDSM

BDSM practices are diverse, and hence there exists no uniform set of common activities and associated intents. However, there are a number of common myths and misperceptions about BDSM—held by laypeople as well as clinicians—that we attempt to correct in the sections that follow.

Pain and suffering. A common oversimplification, echoed in the *DSM–IV–TR* (American Psychiatric Association, 2000, pp. 572–574), is that BDSM is about sexual arousal in direct response to pain, suffering, and humiliation, which is usually seen as evidence of psychopathology, given that pain is usually understood as the body's warning signal of incipient damage. Hence, those who seek it out intentionally are automatically viewed as mentally ill. However, people who are aroused by BDSM do not generally enjoy pain and do not typically become aroused by pain in nonsexual contexts. (For example, put them in a dentist's chair, and BDSM practitioners will generally feel no more arousal than the average dental patient.) They may, however, enjoy giving or receiving intense physical stimulation within a circumscribed erotic interaction, knowing that it will not exceed previously agreed-on limits, will not cause any actual injury, and will cease immediately at either partner's request. This illustration indicates that the experience of pain as desirable and arousing is a fundamentally contextual phenomenon for BDSM practitioners: It depends on the participants, the setting, the situation, and the psychological appraisal of both parties. Recent evidence for this assertion has come from psychophysiological research (Seto, Lalumière, Harris, & Chivers, 2012) showing that men who identify as sadists in the BDSM community show significantly greater genital arousal to stories depicting consensual sexual violence (e.g., mutually arousing hitting, whipping) than to stories depicting nonconsensual sexual violence (i.e., sexual assault). Notably, the very same pattern (greater sexual arousal to consensual than nonconsensual sexual violence) was found among men who did not identify as sadists. One of the notable findings of this study concerned the similarities between these groups: Overall, the primary difference between their patterns of genital arousal was that BDSM members were more aroused—although by only a small degree—by consensual sexual violence than by nonviolent (commonly called *vanilla*) consensual sex, whereas nonsadists were much more aroused by nonviolent consensual sex than by violent consensual sex. These findings, and specifically the critical role played by consent for both BDSM practitioners and nonpractitioners, should also serve as a reminder that the experience of pain or suffering is a contextual phenomenon for everyone. There are those who look at ballerinas and see only beauty and agility, but the bleeding and contorted feet endured routinely in the course of ballet training indicate that this suffering, too, is defined by its contextual framing. Athletic competition provides another salient example: The goals in boxing and football literally involve hitting or tackling one's opponents until they can no longer stand up, and yet these pursuits and the audiences for them are rarely accused of being sadistic or masochistic. The curious question, then, is why those who pursue painful and extreme physical experiences in a sexual context are pathologized and often criminalized, but those who enjoy and enthusiastically pursue other forms of painful and extreme experience, such as running ultra marathons (50–100 miles) or climbing mountains at altitudes and temperatures that potentially endanger one's life, are not generally sanctioned or are looked at askance (White, 2006).

If anything, the categories of acceptable and unacceptable forms of extreme physical experience ought to be reversed. After all, pleasurable stimulation (such as sexual arousal) elevates pain thresholds more than 80%, and the experience of orgasm can elevate pain thresholds more than 100% (Whipple & Komisaruk, 1985, 1988). Thus, what may look exceedingly painful may not be perceived as such during the heights of sexual passion. Furthermore, perceptions of pain depend heavily on appraisals of meaning. The pain of giving birth, for example, is experienced differently from the pain of cancer, especially when labor contractions are welcomed by women who understand that each one brings them closer to meeting their new baby. Glucklich (2001) pointed out that various Eastern and Christian religious traditions use the transformative power of pain for spiritual development.

Similarly, humiliation can only be understood in terms of subjective experience. The most common BDSM activities and interests, spanking and bondage, could easily be perceived by onlookers as degrading. However, the psychological themes that correspond to these activities are as innumerable and unique as the individuals who engage in such activities (Kleinplatz, 2006, 2012). For one individual, bondage and spanking may evoke feelings of erotic surrender; for another, they may represent and embody the trust that is reserved for only the most intimate relations; for others, they may speak to losing oneself in the moment by relinquishing all responsibility for sexual performance—or, indeed, they may signal rejection of conventional, goal-oriented sexual scripts in their entirety (Kleinplatz, 2006, 2012; Kleinplatz, Ménard, Paquet et al., 2009).

BDSM and escapism, affect dysregulation, and sexual addiction. Another myth about BDSM is that participants engage in it because they must, because they are unable to respond to conventional sexual relations. The *DSM–IV–TR* (American Psychiatric Association, 2000, p. 568) stated that one of the criteria for diagnosis was that the behaviors or fantasies were obligatory to produce arousal. However, research has indicated that paraphiliacs are generally able to respond to multiple kinds of sexual stimuli, conventional and otherwise (Langevin, Lang, & Curnoe, 1998). Recent research conducted by Seto (2011) on self-identified masochists found that these individuals' genital responses to auditory descriptions of vanilla sex were just as strong as the responses of nonmasochistic individuals. In essence, they differed from nonmasochists only in their potential for arousal to depictions of consensual masochistic sexual activity, not in their lack of arousal to conventional vanilla sexual activity (which was quite high).

Nonetheless, the belief remains that participants turn to BDSM because they are incapable of real interpersonal intimacy. Again, as stated in the *DSM–IV–TR* (American Psychiatric Association, 2000), "There is often impairment in the capacity for reciprocal, affectionate sexual activity" (p. 567). This definition seems ironic given that BDSM activities require high levels of authenticity, vulnerability, and trust as well as unusually effective communications skills (Kleinplatz, Ménard, Paquet et al., 2009), which are prerequisites for erotic intimacy (Kleinplatz, 2006, 2010).

BDSM arousal has been defined as one of the hallmarks of sexual addiction (Carnes, 1991), and participants are commonly assumed to use their sexual proclivities as a form of escapism (Baumeister, 1988), affect regulation, or self-medication. In addition, as with all addictions, the "addiction" to BDSM is presumed to be progressive, such that participants need increasingly intense BDSM activities over time. Four striking aspects of this line of thinking are questionable: First, given that all adults periodically use sexuality as a way of altering their feeling states, it makes little sense to pathologize the use of sex for emotion regulation. In fact, one might argue that if having sex does not improve your mood, make you feel special and intimate, or provide an oasis from the worlds of work and family responsibilities, you may not be doing it right! As for the arguments regarding progressive increases in BDSM practice, one can easily argue that increased participation in BDSM among satisfied practitioners is a straightforward reflection of the fact that they have found a form of sexual practice they find fulfilling and choose to repeat it (interestingly, few claims of addiction are leveled at individuals who repeatedly and increasingly pursue missionary-style penile–vaginal intercourse at the expense of all other forms of sexual practice). The same accusation of addiction could be leveled at individuals who regularly and selectively pursue any activity that gives them great pleasure, including television viewing, Internet use, exercise, or participation in yoga or religious retreats.

Second, as escapist and affect regulation activities go, consensual sexual activities—even when atypical—seem rather benign compared with addictions such as cigarette smoking and drug or alcohol abuse. Third, the notion that some purposes of sexuality should be singled out as evidence of psychopathology (i.e., pleasure or mood regulation versus reproduction or marital bonding) highlights the underlying belief that there is one and only one correct and healthy purpose for sex and that other uses are morally, culturally, and psychologically suspect. Fourth, it is apparent to clinicians that people use, misuse, and abuse all kinds of activities, from the commonplace (e.g., eating) to the extraordinary (ultramarathon running) as ways of avoiding themselves and others in potentially destructive ways. When these cases arise, it is important to treat the underlying psychopathology (e.g., depression, anxiety, obsessive–compulsive disorder) rather than pathologizing and attempting to control the specific form of behavior in which it happens to be manifest (see Volume 2, Chapter 4, this handbook).

BDSM and Psychopathology

Although the lay public and mental health professionals often assume that BDSM practitioners are inherently pathological, few BDSM practitioners report distress or seek treatment for paraphilias in general or BDSM in particular (Darcangelo, 2008; Hucker, 2008). Krueger (2010) reported that in more than 400 million visits to primary care physicians in the United States, not one case of sexual sadism or sexual masochism was diagnosed. Given the scarcity of patients, it is hard to rigorously test beliefs about psychopathology among BDSM practitioners. The small number of empirical investigations that have been conducted involved self-identified members of the BDSM community rather than clinical populations. Most notably, in 2006 Cross and Matheson tested the prevailing theories of BDSM as psychopathology, specifically that it is motivated by the desire for escape from self (Baumeister, 1988), as well as the notion that in relationships involving a male top and a female bottom, the men were necessarily misogynists. They compared BDSM practitioners with a control group using an extensive battery of psychometric tests (i.e., the Danger-Seeking, Stress, Social Potency and Authoritarianism subscales of the Dependent Personality Questionnaire; the Neuroticism subscale of the Eysenck Personality Inventory; the Symptom Checklist–90—Revised; the Social Personality Inventory; the Locus of Control Scale; and the Rosenberg Self-Esteem Scale). Cross and Matheson concluded there was "no support for the view that sadomasochism is an illness—our measures of mental illness did not differentiate sadomasochists from non-sadomasochists" (p. 159).

It is noteworthy that rather than being misogynists, male and female BDSM participants were more likely than the controls to be profeminist.

It may be time to consider alternate ways of understanding BDSM outside of models of psychopathology. Certainly, the descriptions by BDSM practitioners in the community literature suggest that their activities are experienced as life affirming, growth enhancing, and intensely erotic (Califia, 2002; Taormino, 2012; Thompson, 2004). The few clinical illustrations of BDSM couples in sex therapy have suggested that being true to one's own desires in a relationship can eventuate in profound self-knowledge and a sense of coming home and can be transformative (Kleinplatz, 2006).

FETISHES

The term *fetish* has two entirely different meanings depending on who is using the term and in what context. In the diagnostic sense, the term *fetish* is defined in the *DSM–IV–TR* as sexual arousal to inanimate objects or materials, for example, boots, diapers, rubber, or leather. Whereas the diagnosis of fetishism refers to arousal to an inanimate object per se, transvestic fetishism is defined as arousal while wearing the inanimate objects, that is, heterosexual male arousal to the act of cross-dressing. It is revealing that the *DSM–IV–TR* exclusion criteria for this diagnosis include being female or being a gay male. The diagnostic criteria for transvestic fetishism highlight the nature of current gender binaries and the narrow, rigid character of normal male sexuality as defined and reinforced by the mental health professions. (Although partialism has previously been considered a paraphilia akin to fetishism, those who identify as "leg men" or "tit men" would find the idea that they are mentally ill absurd. Their desires, after all, are the outgrowth of the predominant cultural sexual script for heterosexual men, which identifies certain female body parts—legs, breasts, and buttocks versus elbows, ankles, or necks—as particularly sexually appealing.)

By contrast, in the world of alternative sexualities, *fetish* is an adjective used to describe participation in a broad range of kinky (i.e., atypical) activities or events. Just as the terms *Black* and *queer* were used historically to denigrate minority groups and were later reappropriated by the groups in question to assert self-determination, so too has *fetish* been reclaimed by kink groups to depathologize and affirm sexual diversity. For example, the Internet home for all manner of alternative sexual expression is http://fetlife.com, is a social networking site for the kink world. As of August 2012, Fetlife listed 1,548,947 members, who shared 7,353,873 pictures and 55,173 videos, participated in 2,180,596 discussions in 45,712 groups, were going to 5,258 upcoming events, and were reading 742,556 blog posts. As it states on the opening page of the Fetlife website, "Welcome to kinky heaven!"

This choice of title highlights the power of language to shape sexual (and other) experience (see Chapter 1, this volume). Just as clinical jargon has been used to demarcate the turf of those who can and cannot diagnose and treat sexual psychopathology (e.g., paraphilias, nymphomania), participants in various sexual communities have rejected the medicalized hegemony represented by such terminology and sought greater influence over sexual discourse. For these reasons, clinicians working with clients who have atypical sexual interests should be prepared for the fact that clients might use a broad range of terms and descriptors with regard to their sexual interests and activities; there is no single glossary that can be used as a roadmap. For example, some BDSM practitioners might describe their interest in BDSM as a fetish or a kink, whereas others might not, and might disdain such language. Individuals who lack access to kinky communities might be completely unfamiliar with the shorthand terms used to describe their sexual practices, including even relatively widespread terms such as BDSM. Hence, the imperative is for clinicians to listen carefully to the client's own language use, jettison their own assumptions about the right way to classify or conceptualize different sexual practices, and allow clients a safe space to determine the meaning of their sexual practices for their own sense of identity and community.

SEXUAL DIVERSITY AND THE POPULAR IMAGINATION

Every now and again, a sadomasochistically themed book or movie makes its way into popular culture and ostensibly becomes a social phenomenon. For example, in the mid-1980s, the book and movie *9½ Weeks* (Barish, Damon, Kimmel, King, & Lyne, 1986); in 2002, the movie *Secretary* (Beardsley, Posner, Posner, Roban, & Shainberg, 2002); and in 2012, the book trilogy *50 Shades of Grey* (James, 2012a, 2012b, 2012c) each became enormously popular and created considerable media speculation about BDSM. In addition, in each instance the media fomented frenzy about why BDSM material should capture the popular imagination. Although widely interpreted as evidence of the nascent hunger for deviant sexual expression, these incidents may instead have provided an avenue for titillation while reinforcing heteronormative sexual and gender role norms (Khan, 2009a, 2009b; Weiss, 2006). The farther each storyline diverges from the hallmarks of conventionally gendered, vanilla, and heterosexual norms, the greater the necessity for corrective reaction. After all, mainstream culture cannot allow transgressive sex to stand as valid (Rubin, 2011).

All three of these popularized storylines (*9½ Weeks, Secretary, 50 Shades of Grey*) involve male dominant–female submissive relationships. Each revolves around the dawning realization on the part of the naïve female heroine that she is becoming captivated by a strong, successful, powerful man who means to entice her into erotic surrender. Each relationship has the potential to become increasingly sexually deviant, and therein lies the inevitable outcome. Either the sex must be tamed in the confines of marriage or the relationship is doomed. For example, as the male protagonist in *9½ Weeks* (Barish et al., 1986) increasingly tests the heroine's willingness to violate sexual norms—playtime is over—the heroine realizes the extent of the depravity and literally flees the relationship. It was one thing to star in a command striptease performance for her lover in the privacy of his well-appointed home; it was quite another to be duped into a dark, three-way sexual encounter with a female sex worker in a sleazy motel. In the end, the heroine reclaims her independence and the dominant male is left alone, seemingly desperate and pathetic.

Correspondingly, *Secretary* (Beardsley et al., 2002) and *50 Shades of Grey* (James, 2012c) are superficially about BDSM relationships but are better understood as old-fashioned love stories. Their narratives involve the capacity of heterosexual marital love to triumph over adversity. In these cases, the grand romance conquers even a history of psychopathology, which is portrayed as the original impetus for being drawn to sexually violent and degrading behavior. In *50 Shades of Grey,* the perky, virginal heroine is wildly attracted to the impossibly handsome and wealthy Mr. Grey, who tenders a contract to make her his sexual submissive. Before she can even sign the contract, the joys of vanilla intimacy so transform Mr. Grey that he relinquishes even the most innocuous symbols of BDSM play to make her his wife and mother to his children. The hook for her is that this man's idea of dominance entails taking care of her to the point of buying the safest car on the market for her and providing bodyguards to watch over her in case of the inevitable threats to the hyperrich. She becomes the most conventional of romance novel characters, swooning every time he looks at her and having instantaneous and convulsive orgasms every time he thrusts his penis into her vagina with no additional stimulation. She becomes his dependent, not his submissive.

This reproduction of heteronormativity (Rubin, 2011) is nothing if not a throwback to the 1950s: It is all too reminiscent of Doris Day–Rock Hudson vehicles in which the independent career woman takes on but ultimately succumbs to her business rival and playboy as they join in marriage (see Chapter 2, this volume). (For a particularly poignant and laughable illustration of these themes, listen to Doris Day singing "Should I Surrender" in *Lover Come Back* [Shapiro, Melcher, Arthur, & Mann, 1961].) The reason that we call attention to these popularized narratives, and the degree to which they tend to bolster rather than subvert mainstream norms regarding appropriate male and female sexual roles, is that they play an important role in the average individual's conceptualization of normal versus alternative sexual practices, the conditions under which they are pursued, and their broader meaning with respect to the participants' mental health. Although the popularity of these narratives may give the impression that society is becoming more open to and accepting of sexual diversity, this is not necessarily the case. It is important for psychologists to realize, and to communicate to their clients, that cultural messages that would appear, on the surface, to foster visibility and acceptance of kinky sexual practices often serve the opposite function. That is, they subtly reinforce the view that although normal individuals might temporarily dabble on the sexual wild side, the only individuals who consistently prefer alternative sexual practices such as BDSM to conventional, heteronormative, vanilla sex are fundamentally disordered. Even individuals who proudly embrace their kinks and who have found accepting communities of like-minded friends and partners are likely to struggle with these pervasive cultural messages and with the feelings of shame and social rejection that they are likely to encounter. Psychologists working with such clients should be prepared to critically engage and unpack these cultural messages to foster their clients' sense of self-worth and self-acceptance.

POLYAMORY AND NONMONOGAMY

When most individuals consider the notion of sexual diversity, they typically think of unconventional sexual practices, such as BDSM. However, another important form of sexual diversity is the pursuit of multiple concurrent sexual–romantic relationships, a practice commonly known as *polyamory*. *Polyamory* is conventionally defined as the practice of maintaining multiple, concurrent romantic–sexual relationships with the full knowledge and consent of all parties. This aspect of open knowledge and consent is what distinguishes polyamory from infidelity, and the existence of ongoing relationships incorporating emotional commitment as well as sexual behavior is what distinguishes polyamory from swinging (in which married or cohabitating couples periodically pursue sexual behavior with one another's partners over a limited span of time and in which no ongoing emotional relationship is desired or expected). The practice of maintaining multiple romantic–sexual relationships, sometimes codified as marriages (in which case they are technically defined as polygamous) and sometimes not, has a long history (reviewed in Anapol, 2010; Fisher, 1992), having been documented in ancient times across a range of countries and cultures, including Greece, Rome, Africa, India, China, Italy, and England, and more recently among the Oneida community of upstate New York in the early 19th century. Perhaps the most famous practitioners of religiously sanctioned polygamy were the members of the Church of Latter-Day Saints (commonly known as Mormons), although polygamy was discontinued as a sanctioned practice in 1890 (however, it continues to be practiced among some Mormon fundamentalists). As documented by Fisher (1992), the vast majority of human societies appear to have permitted the practice of multiple wives (although in some cases this practice was restricted to higher status members of the community), and as documented by Ryan and Jetha (2010), evidence regarding the evolution of the human species has strongly suggested that strict monogamy appears to be the exception rather than the norm. Hence, although the sexual revolution of the 1970s (and the Internet boom of the 1990s) sparked upsurges of interest in polyamory, accompanied by academic and popular writings and active community building, the practice appears to be as old as sex itself. The modern practice of polyamory is associated with political and philosophical challenges to the cultural privileging of monogamy, with its implicit condoning of sexual and emotional ownership, and practitioners often seek to establish more open and egalitarian forms of sexual and romantic partnership (Bettinger, 2006; Rust, 1996; Sheff, 2005). For some individuals, polyamory is an inherently individual practice representing an expression of their own desires for emotional and sexual intimacy. However, for other individuals polyamory is also an inherently political choice, reflecting attempts to live in concert with feminist, socialist, or lesbian/gay/bisexual critiques of conventional patriarchal dictates regarding marriage, family, monogamy, and property (Barker, 2005; Jamieson, 2004; Sheff, 2005; Weeks, 1991).

The development of the Internet has fostered pronounced increases in the visibility and openness of polyamory because individuals involved in polyamorous partnerships have found that the Internet makes it easier to find like-minded individuals, share social support, and develop a sense of community. Yet the overall population prevalence of polyamory remains unknown and difficult to estimate given that all studies of polyamorous individuals have involved nonrandom samples, often drawn from settings and websites specifically geared toward this population. One reliable finding that has emerged, however, concerns the diversity of the population with regard to sexual orientation. Individuals who practice polyamory are diverse in their sexual orientations, including heterosexuals, bisexuals, lesbian women, and gay men (Weitzman, 2006). However, some research has suggested that bisexual individuals appear disproportionately likely to openly claim and practice polyamory (Klesse, 2006; Rust, 1996), perhaps because the process of questioning restrictive cultural standards regarding exclusive heterosexuality and homosexuality commonly prompts bisexual individuals to question a broader range of cultural standards regarding the supposed moral and psychological preeminence of monogamy.

Another important finding regarding polyamory concerns the diversity of relationship forms that individuals pursue. Labriola (1999) identified three common models for polyamorous relationships: the primary–secondary model, the multiple primary partners model, and the multiple nonprimary relationships model. Research to date has indicated that the primary–secondary model, also known as hierarchical polyamory, is the most prevalent, at least among bisexuals and lesbians (Labriola, 1999; Rust, 1996; Weitzman, 2006). In this model, a couple views their relationship with each other as their primary bond and devotes the majority of their time, energy, and loyalty to this bond, but remains open to additional lovers (Weitzman, 2006). In the multiple primary partners model, an individual might have two partners, each of whom is considered to be of equal importance. In some cases, the two partners will also be involved with one another, thereby establishing a triadic relationship (Rust, 1996). Some of these arrangements are open, meaning that all of the participants are free to enter into additional outside relationships, and some are closed. Other forms that have been documented include V structures, in which a single individual has two partners who are not involved with one another, and broader poly webs or families, involving larger communities of individuals with overlapping, relatively fluid erotic and emotional ties to one another (Labriola, 1999). Notably, not all of the relationships in polyamorous dyads, triads, or families involve equivalent degrees of sexual intimacy, and in some cases individuals may have a sexual and romantic tie to one partner but a romantic and nonsexual tie to another (Klesse, 2006).

Polyamorous relationships clearly pose fundamental challenges to conventional mainstream notions about the nature and functioning of romantic relationships, all of which are based on the assumptions that monogamy is the most natural, normal, ethical, and healthy form of intimate relating (Ritchie & Barker, 2006; Rubin, 2011). Of course, similar challenges to the cultural privileging of monogamy (and the cultural privileging of coupled over single individuals, as articulated by DePaulo & Morris, 2005) are posed by all forms of nonmonogamy, whether or not they are explicitly undertaken and defined as polyamorous. For example, studies have long found that male–male couples are more likely than either male–female or female–female couples to develop open and honest agreements by which each party can pursue extradyadic sexual activity (Bonello, 2009; Solomon, Rothblum, & Balsam, 2004). Estimates vary from study to study, but some data have suggested that between one third and two thirds of male–male couples have openly nonmonogamous relationships (Bryant & Demian, 1994; Crawford et al., 2003; Davidovich, de Wit, & Stroebe, 2004; LaSala, 2004; Prestage et al., 2008). Sexual-minority men rate monogamy as less important to their relationship satisfaction and sexual satisfaction than do female–female and heterosexual couples (Blumstein & Schwartz, 1983; Kurdek, 1991), and studies comparing open to closed relationships have found no differences in satisfaction or stability (reviewed in Bonello, 2009).

What distinguishes open relationships from polyamory is that they are often undertaken for the specific purpose of sexual release and are not intended to lead to ongoing, emotionally intimate ties outside of the primary dyad. In fact, many couples develop clear rules about extradyadic sex that are specifically intended to avoid the inadvertent development of emotional attachment (Hoff & Beougher, 2010; Ramirez & Brown, 2010). For example, some couples only pursue extradyadic sex in the form of threesomes; other rules specify that mutual friends and former lovers are off limits or that new friendships or emotional connections cannot be formed with outside sexual partners; some couples agree not to discuss outside sexual partners with one another, whereas other couples specifically request that details be provided afterward (for more examples, see Hoff & Beougher, 2010). Hence, many couples explicitly claim that although the partnership is sexually nonmonogamous, it remains emotionally monogamous (Adam, 2006; LaSala, 2004).

As argued by Klesse (2006), one of the ways in which practitioners of polyamory have attempted to gain greater visibility and social legitimacy for their relationships has been to highlight distinctions between these forms of sexual nonmonogamy and polyamory (as well as distinctions between polyamory and swinging), emphasizing the fact that polyamorous relationships involve ongoing, committed, emotional partnerships rather than time-limited outlets for sexual release. This distinction is often highly relevant to practitioners of polyamory. However, this rhetorical strategy has been critiqued as essentially giving in to the regressive sex-negativity of conventional society, in which sexual behavior is only deemed socially legitimate when pursued as an expression of emotional intimacy rather than for the sake of pleasure in and of itself (Klesse, 2006). Along these lines, there remain active debates among practitioners of polyamory about what factors qualify an arrangement as polyamorous and the degree to which the individual motives of the participants (i.e., personal gratification and autonomy vs. personal-as-political social activism) matter. As summarized by Klesse, polyamorists seeking to distance themselves from swingers and couples in open relationships may inadvertently "hamper the potential of polyamory discourses for grounding a truly pluralistic sexual ethics that may embrace the diversity of non-monogamous sexual and intimate practices" (p. 566). Klesse and others have stated that instead of arguing that polyamory is fundamentally more mature and less focused on sex than nonmonogamy or swinging, polyamorists should focus instead on challenging society's denigration of all individuals who openly value and pursue sexual pleasure and expression for its own sake. The fact that so many practitioners of polyamory take pains to emphasize the difference between polyamory and promiscuity underscores the degree to which society continues to privilege a relative narrow range of sexual practices pursued within a narrow range of relational contexts involving a narrow range of gender combinations (Califia, 2000; Rubin, 2011).

This, in essence, is why we consider polyamory and other forms of nonmonogamy to be important components of sexual diversity and worth discussing in the context of the broader topic of alternative sexual practices. Individuals who pursue such arrangements continue to be treated as non-normative (and potentially pathological) by the culture at large, despite the fact that no empirical evidence for this assertion exists. However, just as unconventional practices such as BDSM have come to receive greater mainstream media attention (for better or worse), the same is true of polyamory and nonmonogamy (reviewed in Barker & Langdridge, 2010b). Perhaps the most notable example is a recent reality television series on the Showtime cable network, *Polyamory: Married and Dating* (Berman, Braun, Garcia, & Stein, 2012) that follows two different polyfamilies in southern California: One triad consists of a married male–female couple and their female girlfriend (whom they end up jointly marrying over the course of the series), and one foursome consists of two married couples who decide to live together. In both cases, all members of the polyfamily are sexually involved with one another, and all members have the option of pursuing additional romantic and sexual relationships outside of the family. On one hand, the series presents polyamory as a serious, thoughtful, positive relationship option and highlights the mutual love, respect, and commitment among the participants. On the other hand, every single episode includes considerable nudity and sexual activity, and the potential for these families to serve as sources of sexual titillation for the average monogamous viewer may be a greater priority (and considerably more likely to generate cable subscriptions) than the potential for these families to inspire broader questioning of hetero–monogamous–patriarchal norms. Yet, one truth that the series does make clear (along with many other mainstream cultural treatments of nonmonogamy) is the degree to which individuals pursuing such arrangements remain vulnerable to sexual stigmatization, at the hands of their own immediate families as well as society at large. This, again, renders them quite similar to other individuals with atypical sexual practices (and to gay, lesbian, and bisexual individuals) and exposes them to chronic stress and potential psychological distress. Clinicians whose clients practice polyamory or nonmonogamy must remain mindful of the negative cultural context in which such individuals negotiate their intimate lives and choices.

PERIODIC SAME-SEX ATTRACTIONS AND BEHAVIOR

The phenomenon of sexual orientation (i.e., a stable sexual predisposition to the same sex, the other sex, or both sexes) is addressed at length in Chapters 18 through 20 of this volume. A relevant topic with respect to sexual diversity is the phenomenon of same-sex interest and behavior among individuals who do not possess a same-sex orientation and who report that their general pattern of sexual arousal, fantasy, and attraction is to the other sex rather than the same sex. This phenomenon is far more common than many would assume. To provide just a few salient examples from recent representative survey data (see Chapter 20, this volume), nearly 80% of American women and men who report any incidence of same-sex attraction or behavior describe themselves as heterosexual, and the single most common type of individual reporting same-sex attractions—including 10% of American women and 3.9% of American men—is someone who considers him- or herself mostly heterosexual (Chandra, Mosher, Copen, & Sionean, 2011). Historically, such individuals have been treated with skepticism and suspicion by laypeople and scientists alike. They have been viewed as either closeted lesbian, gay, or bisexual individuals (who cling to a mostly heterosexual label to avoid the stigma associated with same-sex sexuality) or as confused or questioning "heteroflexibles" (Essig, 2000; Savage, 2002). The latter are seen as especially suspect: They are perceived as individuals who may have experienced sporadic same-sex fantasies or engaged in experimental same-sex contact (especially given the increased cultural visibility and acceptance of same-sex sexuality in the mainstream media) but who are not really gay or bisexual. Because such individuals have no place within conventional models of sexual orientation, which presume that there is no such thing as having just a few same-sex attractions, they have historically been excluded from psychological research on sexual orientation (reviewed in Diamond, 2008). As a result, relatively little is known about how they interpret their same-sex attractions.

A small number of interview studies conducted with these populations have indicated that they are well aware of their dubious status within both heterosexual and gay, lesbian, and bisexual communities: Many openly admit that they are not certain their sporadic experiences of same-sex sexuality are sufficient to count as evidence of a same-sex predisposition, but at the same time they are not sure how to reconcile these feelings with their overall heterosexuality (Diamond, 2008; Golden, 1996). These questions about the authenticity of one's same-sex sexuality harken back to a long-standing distinction between constitutional versus facultative same-sex sexuality (Bell, Weinberg, & Hammersmith, 1981). Constitutional same-sex sexuality has historically been attributed to a stable and enduring same-sex orientation, whereas facultative same-sex sexuality has been attributed to situational factors such as "play, exploration, lack of opposite-gender partners, hazing, initiation rituals, intoxication, sexual frustration, prostitution, boredom, opportunism, curiosity, and mistakes" (Muscarella, 1999, p. 9). For example, women who pursue same-sex activity in the safe and relatively tolerant environment of college but who resume exclusive heterosexual behavior afterward have been called "LUGs," or "lesbians until graduation" (Davis, 1999; Kyrakanos, 1998; Rimer, 1993).

The problem, however, is that no reliable basis exists on which to know what distinguishes between constitutional and facultative forms of same-sex sexuality (see also Savin-Williams, 2009). Whether this distinction even makes sense is unclear, especially for women, who are more likely than men to report sexual attractions to both sexes (vs. exclusive same-sex attractions). Women are more likely than men to show genital arousability to both men and women, regardless of self-identified sexual orientation, and women's sexual feelings appear to show a greater capacity for fluidity, flexibility, and change over time than men's (see Chapter 20, this volume). In fact, it is not even clear what might constitute the definitive test of constitutional same-sex sexuality for either women or men: What distribution of same-sex versus other-sex attractions is sufficient to move an individual from the heteroflexible or confused category to the bisexual or gay category, and over what span of time? Should one attend to the context in which these attractions emerged? After all, some individuals report that their first and only experience of same-sex desire took place in the context of a single relationship with a single individual, and such experiences are often discounted as evidence of repression or false consciousness (Diamond, 2008). The inconvenient reality (as noted by Kirkpatrick, 2000) is that social behaviors are always jointly determined by "a range of constitutional propensities interacting with a range of facultative opportunities" (p. 390), rendering the entire constitutional–facultative distinction (and, of course, its implied nature–nurture distinction) overly simplistic.

The end result is that both researchers and the culture at large have no neat category in which to place individuals who appear to be (and feel themselves to be) generally heterosexual but who periodically desire and enjoy same-sex contact. Their desires place them outside of the conventional criteria for both heterosexual and lesbian, gay, or bisexual individuals, making it difficult for them to find social support and acceptance, even within the broader sexual-minority community. Thus, although same-sex sexuality is generally treated with greater respect and acceptance than BDSM or fetishism, this acceptance is still predicated on the specific form that same-sex sexuality takes. Specifically, forms of same-sex sexuality that fundamentally mirror conventional monogamous heterosexuality in all ways save for the sex or gender of the preferred partner (i.e., same-sex desire channeled to a single partner in the context of an emotionally intimate and committed monogamous relationship) are granted social legitimacy. By contrast, forms of same-sex sexuality that challenge conventional models of fixed, stable sexual orientations (and which thereby suggest that anyone might be susceptible to deviant same-sex desires or behaviors) continue to be denigrated as indices of mental instability, confusion, developmental delay, promiscuity, or hypersexuality. Yet according to the existing data available from representative studies, heterosexually identified individuals with periodic same-sex attractions and fantasies are more numerous than lesbian, gay, and bisexual individuals, and hence more normative and less alternative than many would conventionally assume. Accordingly, it is critically important for clinicians not to assume that any experience of same-sex desire or behavior is a sign of latent homosexuality and instead to allow individuals to determine for themselves the role of same-sex sexuality in their lives and identity (see Chapter 19, this volume). Therapists must also remain mindful of the unique issues of self-doubt, stigma, internalized homophobia, and marginalization that are likely to face heterosexually identified individuals with periodic same-sex attractions. Such clients may present to therapists as sharing society's view that there is something abnormal about their particular pattern of desire and behavior or as sharing the view that their reluctance to claim a gay or bisexual label is indicative of deep-seated repression and self-denial. These individuals (as with all individuals with alternative sexual desires and practices) need a safe therapeutic space within which they can pursue their own process of meaning-making regarding their sexual desires.

CLINICAL IMPLICATIONS

Therapists' codes of ethics increasingly encourage them to develop cultural sensitivity, competence, and literacy: "Therapists who ignore cultural values, attitudes, and behaviors different from their own deprive themselves of crucial information and may tend to impose their own worldview and assumptions on clients in a misguided and harmful approach" (Pope & Vasquez, 2007, p. 227). Understanding sexual diversity in a clinically useful way means appreciating the role of the patient's sexuality from within his or her own worldview and experience (Nichols, 2006; Ribner, 2012), which entails learning enough about the client's proclivities and (where applicable) community to be nonjudgmental; it does not require expertise in every possible sexual interest but sufficient awareness so that the client is not forced to educate the therapist to be understood in context (Kolmes, Stock, & Moser, 2006; see Volume 2, Chapter 4, this handbook). Toward this end, we have included in the references a range of resources intended to be helpful to the mental health professional seeking reliable, up-to-date, and sensitively presented information on these issues (in particular, see Barker & Langdridge, 2010a; Beckmann, 2009; Karasic & Drescher, 2005; Kleinplatz & Moser, 2004, 2005a, 2005b, 2006; Laws & O'Donohue, 2008; Morin, 1995; Moser 1999, 2001; Moser & Kleinplatz, 2002, 2005a, 2005b, 2007; Nichols, 2006).

In working with sexual diversity, therapists need to be mindful of the role of stigma in the lives of "outsiders." Whether dealing with racial minorities, sexual minorities, individuals with disabilities, or individuals with unconventional sexual practices (including same-sex sexuality), psychotherapists should be sensitive to the fact that these populations have often internalized the suspicion, fear, ridicule, and outright prejudice that they have faced in society at large and that are bred in ignorance. In many cases, these experiences will lead clients to report distress over their sexuality. However, this reported distress does not mean that the sexual feelings themselves are the source of the problem (and hence pathological). Rather, it is crucial for therapists to assist their clients with differentiating between distress related to their sexual proclivities per se and distress arising from experiences of stigma, isolation, and social alienation (Division 44, 2000; Kleinplatz & Moser, 2004; Nichols, 2006). Realistically, in countries in which sexual minorities are forbidden to marry and to adopt children, it is quite rational for clients to fear giving in to atypical sexual desires. For example, BDSM practitioners have a long history of being declared mentally ill and losing custody of their children, security clearances, and jobs (Wright, 2006). Openly polyamorous communities are commonly threatened with allegations of child abuse. Yet the alternatives—remaining closeted about one's desires or attempting to deny and suppress them—can lead to medical, psychological, and quality-of-life problems (Moser, 1999).

Given the cultural taboo surrounding alternative sexual desires and practices, and given that many therapists may be entirely unfamiliar with issues of sexual diversity, it is all too easy for the clinician to become part of the problem when working with clients expressing alternative sexual desires and practices. Sexuality is intensely personal and is central to people's self-concepts. Therapists are people, first and foremost, and have been subject to the same social and cultural influences (and taboos) regarding sexuality as have their clients. Although psychologists are in general trained to be nonjudgmental, they receive disturbingly minimal coursework or a complete absence of training in dealing with human sexuality (S. Miller & Byers, 2009, 2010). The situation for physicians is, if anything, even worse, with many reporting considerable discomfort about discussing sexuality by the end of medical school (Frank, Coughlin, & Elon, 2008; Malhotra, Khurshid, Hendricks, & Mann, 2008; Shindel et al., 2010; see Volume 2, Chapter 5, this handbook). As such, when patients approach clinicians to discuss their own concerns involving alternate sexual practices, the professional's own immediate, visceral reactions—combined with a lack of knowledge about just what is normal versus pathological and hence how to address the clients' basic questions and concerns—may hamper comprehensive health care (Kolmes et al., 2006; Moser, 2009). For example, the polyamorous patient seeking safer-sex information may suddenly be subject to the physician's judgments about promiscuity. The consensually dominant–submissive couple may unexpectedly find themselves treated as though they presented a case of domestic abuse. It is noteworthy that guidelines for health professionals and the legal system distinguishing between consensual BDSM and abuse are available at https://ncsfreedom.org/component/k2/item/435-sm-vs-abuse-policy-statement.html. If clinicians are to be of help in dealing with atypical sexual proclivities, they must first take responsibility for their own countertransference reactions and deal with them via training, consultation, or supervision so that they do not distort the therapy process. As in all cases, when the therapist or physician is truly beyond his or her expertise or comfort zone, the ethical course of action is to refer to better qualified professionals.

To the extent that ignorance is often part of the problem, treatment for the consequences of stigma, including alienation and outright loneliness, can include bibliotherapy and community support. Community educational and social support networks used to be relatively scarce outside large cities. Fortunately, they are currently readily accessible via the Internet. It is valuable for therapists to be able to refer patients to appropriate resources that they know to contain accurate, reliable information. As indicated earlier, fetlife.com provides an excellent starting point to a wide range of informational and supportive resources for individuals with a broad range of alternative sexual interests. For those who prefer books on nonmonogamous or alternate sexualities, please see the resources listed in the References (Califia, 2002; M. Miller & Devon, 1995; Morin, 1995; Newmahr, 2011; Taormino, 2008, 2012; Thompson, 2004). In addition, for partners of individuals who have atypical sexual proclivities, the classic resource is Easton and Liszt's (2000) *When Someone You Love Is Kinky*.

DIRECTIONS FOR FUTURE RESEARCH

As reviewed in this chapter, much of the existing empirical research on alternative sexual practices was conducted to document (or disprove) potential problems associated with these practices. This bias reflects a larger bias within the sexology literature more generally, which has tended to emphasize problematic forms of sexuality. Within the developmental literature, this translates into an emphasis on the deleterious implications of adolescent sexuality that is too frequent, too early, or pursued with too many partners (see Chapter 13, this volume). Within the clinical literature, this bias translates into an emphasis on sexual dysfunctions or dyadic sexual problems, with the aim of moving couples to a state of normal sexual functioning as defined by the classic sexual response cycle (Masters & Johnson, 1966). Even within the sex education literature, the emphasis is on the prevention of undesirable side effects of sexuality, such as pregnancy, sexually transmitted infections, sexual abuse, and so forth. Hence, the mainstream sexology literature does not fully represent the entire spectrum of sexuality and instead remains clustered on the negative end of the continuum. It is within this unbalanced context that discussions of diverse, atypical sexual desires and practices tend to cast such desires and practices as fundamentally "other" and pathological. Hence, too little attention has been paid to the entire spectrum of sexual experience and too little focus has occurred on what makes certain sexual experiences beyond positive—that is, more than just not negative, but instead extraordinary and even optimal.

In considering directions for future research on sexual diversity, this is where we think researchers must begin. Historically, alternative sexual practices such as BDSM have been conceived of as behaviors that certain (deviant) individuals must undertake to achieve any sexual arousal and satisfaction. This view, of course, is belied by the self-reports of individuals with alternative forms of sexual expression who report seeking to enhance, heighten, and optimize their sexual expression. Yet the negative cast of most sexuality research has crowded out empirical attention to such motives and to the variety of strategies that some individuals pursue for the sake of seeking not simply satisfactory sex, but extraordinary sex.

An example of the direction in which we think research needs to head has been provided by Kleinplatz and colleagues (Kleinplatz, 2012; Kleinplatz & Ménard, 2007; Kleinplatz, Ménard, Paquet et al., 2009; Kleinplatz, Ménard, Paradis et al., 2009), who recently conducted a series of studies examining optimal sexuality in mainstream and marginalized groups, including older married people, and among self-identified members of sexual-minority groups from gay, lesbian, bisexual, and transgender individuals to kink to poly community members. Key informants, that is, individuals who reported having optimal sexual experiences, were interviewed about the nature of these experiences. Eight components were found that distinguished optimal sexual experiences from merely good or very good sex (Kleinplatz, Ménard, Paquet et al., 2009). Surprisingly, the components of these experiences were virtually identical, whether in the 80-year-old man who had been married for 55 years or the 22-year old poly domme (Kleinplatz, Ménard, Paradis, Campbell, & Dalgleish, in press). These components were (a) being present, focused, and embodied; (b) connection, alignment, and merger; (c) deep sexual and erotic intimacy; (d) extraordinary communication and deep empathy; (e) exploration, interpersonal risk taking, and fun; (f) authenticity, genuineness, and transparency; (g) vulnerability and surrender; and (h) transcendence and transformation.

That is, the qualities that make for intense erotic intimacy are universal among extraordinary lovers. They involve being embodied within, connected to one's partner or partners, and ready and willing to take interpersonal risks in the context of deep mutual empathy and (just) enough emotional safety. Although considerable differences may exist between the sexual behaviors of men and women, young and old people, and conventional and unconventional lovers at the problematic end of the continuum (or even when examining normal sexuality), these differences are not found when examining the high end of the spectrum. The focus on sexual behavior and activities seen in the literature on ordinary or problematic sexuality may not be relevant for understanding optimal sexuality or, indeed, for effecting optimal sexual experiences per se. Thus, one of the most important directions for future research involves more substantive, multimethod, intensive investigation of how both alternative and normative sexual desires and practices contribute to the upper end of the continuum of sexual experience, among different populations and at different stages of life.

Along the same lines, more research is needed on these questions from a developmental perspective. Kleinplatz and colleagues (Kleinplatz, 2006, 2012; Kleinplatz, Ménard, & Lawless, in press; Kleinplatz, Ménard, Paquet et al., 2009) found that to begin the journey toward optimal sexuality, individuals first had to jettison the sexual scripts acquired in the course of normal development to discover what was, in fact, sexually fulfilling for them. Unfortunately, this line of inquiry is rather different from most developmental research in sexology. Historically, developmental research on sexuality has focused on when adolescents begin to engage in different types of sexual behaviors (with different risk profiles regarding pregnancy and sexually transmitted infections), and little research has focused on how they interpret their experience of sexual pleasure, boredom, excitement, and disappointment and how they come to develop, refine, test, and revise their sexual repertoire. Although a clinical literature exploring the potential developmental etiology of various paraphilias exists (reviewed in Becker & Johnson, 2009; Gijs, 2008), nothing is known about the normative development of broad versus narrow sexual interests and practices and the degree to which this development is shaped by different intrapsychic, interpersonal, contextual, and cultural factors. For example, there has been intensive interest over the past decade in understanding the potential influence of Internet pornography (which is far more readily available than at any other time in history) on different aspects of adolescent sexual attitudes and behaviors (see Owens, Behun, Manning, & Reid, 2012, for a review; see also Volume 2, Chapter 1, this handbook). Yet little of this research has focused on adolescents' sexual tastes and their own subjective perceptions of what they do and do not want, how easy it is (or will be) to fulfill their desires, and the time course for the development and expression of their own personal sexual profiles.

Also missing is research on the interpersonal context of alternative sexual practices at all stages of life. Although it is common to think about alternative sexual interests and practices as properties of individuals, in actuality the vast majority of sexual behavior takes place within established romantic ties (Laumann, Gagnon, Michael, & Michaels, 1994; Willets, Sprecher, & Beck, 2004), such that Gagnon, Giami, Michaels, and Colomby (2001) have argued that living in a couple is the chief regulator of an individual's sexual conduct. Hence, perhaps the single most universal characteristic of the diverse range of individuals with unusual sexual interests and practices is the need, at some point in time, to communicate these interests with a partner and potentially negotiate similarities and differences between their respective sexual scripts. To put it simply, sex is not a natural act but rather one that necessitates communication, negotiation, and compromise. We know little about how individuals with diverse sexual interests manage these interests within new and established relationships and the extent to which partners gradually shape and potentially broaden one another's sexual interests over the course of time.

To investigate these processes, we need to bear in mind Simon and Gagnon's (1986; Gagnon, 1990) powerful notion of sexual scripts. Specifically, each partner in a relationship brings his or her own sexual attitudes, history, habits, fantasies, fears, and preferences to the dyad, where they interact with those of the other partner to create a unique erotic dynamic. Over time, couples develop a mutual sexual script specifying appropriate and desirable sexual behaviors, roles, and practices. By the time two individuals come together in a sustained partnership, they might have developed drastically different preferences and expectations regarding sexual practice, derived from their individual histories of parental socialization, social and community norms, cultural and religious beliefs, and idiosyncratic personal experiences. As their mutual sexual script evolves over the course of the relationship, each new element involves a delicate (and often implicit) process of negotiation. Once the script is in place, future introductions of variety and experimentation necessarily involve "a certain amount of transgression" (Bozon, 2001, p. 3), leaving each partner vulnerable to rejection or disapproval, but also containing the possibility that the less adventurous partner will, through this process, discover a new range of pleasurable activities and interests that have the potential to take the partner closer to her or his own experience of extraordinary or optimal sexuality.

Hence, there is nothing natural or automatic about an individual's or a couple's sex life. Even during the earliest stages of relationship development, when sexual activity is typically highest, partners' unfamiliarity with one another's preferences and their own self-consciousness create the possibility for anxiety. It can be especially challenging for individuals who know that their own tastes and preferences are outside the norm and who are worried that their own preferred sexual practices, positions, or styles might prove displeasing, uncomfortable, or both to the other. Achieving mutual sexual and relationship satisfaction requires open and honest communication, and yet research has suggested that it is difficult for many couples to achieve (reviewed in Byers, 2011). For example, one study found that even partners who had been together as long as 14 years had not completely disclosed their sexual desires and preferences to one another (MacNeil & Byers, 2009). As a result, misperceptions were common: Partners reported understanding only 62% of what their partner found pleasing and only 26% of what the partner found displeasing. This finding stands in stark contrast to the findings among extraordinary lovers who use "black belt" levels of communication—rather than what psychologists typically see as effective communication—to attain optimal sexual intimacy (Kleinplatz, 2010; Kleinplatz & Ménard, 2007; Kleinplatz, Ménard, & Campbell, in press; Kleinplatz, Ménard, Paquet et al., 2009).

Given the obvious gaps in current knowledge regarding the sexual dynamics of romantic relationships, one of the most promising directions for future research on sexual diversity is one suggested by Bozon (2001). Although he was speaking of normative sexual functioning, his recommendations are perhaps even more pertinent for individuals with alternative sexual practices. Specifically, he argued for greater focus on couples' sexual life histories, including a comprehensive, process-oriented perspective on how couples develop, maintain, and change their sexual scripts over the course of their relationship. He contrasted this approach with the conventional focus on sexual frequency and satisfaction, noting that conventional measures typically failed to reveal "trends in the meaning of sex, in sexual repertoire, in interaction between partners, in sexual difficulties, or in the dynamics of extradyadic relationships" (Bozon, 2001, p. 14). By treating diversity, variability, and change over time in sexual interests and practices as normative features of an individual's and a couple's life history, researchers have the potential to move beyond the historical tendency to pathologize sexual diversity. They can move instead toward research programs that consider a broader range of questions about how atypical sexual practices are discovered, disclosed, interpreted, experienced, and altered in the normative course of dyadic sexual functioning and the role that they play in both individual and couple functioning.

To provide just one example of how this might be manifest in research, columnist Dan Savage, who provides sex advice to individuals of all sexual orientations and with a wide range of sexual interests, routinely encourages his listeners to be (and to seek partners who are) *GGG,* which he defined as "good, giving, and game. . . . Think 'good in bed,' 'giving equal time and equal pleasure,' and 'game for anything—within reason'" (Savage, 2007, para. 16). The field of relationship science has developed a vast array of psychometric scales to measure a wide range of relationship constructs and phenomena (attachment security, relationship satisfaction, conflict tactics, propensity for violence, attitudes toward commitment and intimacy, relational maintenance strategies, motives for sexual contact, etc.); however, not a single one of these scales attempts to measure the degree to which partners are—or strive to be—game for one another's novel and potentially challenging sexual interests and preferences. The fact that this relatively straightforward notion, which would appear to have obvious benefits for individual-level and couple-level health and well-being, has barely registered on the radar of sexuality and relationship researchers, testifies to the continued marginalization of individuals with alternative sexual interests within the broader field of basic sexual and relationship functioning. Again, one recent exception is research that looks at the willingness, openness, and receptivity among extraordinary lovers, whether lesbian, gay, bisexual, transgender, kinky, or vanilla to dive in and explore sexually together to attain erotic bliss (Kleinplatz, Ménard & Campbell, in press).

CONCLUSION

Clearly, cultural change—within Western society at large as well as within the field of psychology—remains necessary. The forthcoming *DSM–5* (reviewed earlier) shows openness to the possibility that alternative sexual interests and practices might, in fact, be healthy and need not be associated with distress or psychopathology. However, controversy surrounding this proposed compromise position indicates that the societal default still involves pathologizing rather than embracing sexual diversity. For psychologists to make progress in studying the development, experience, and expression of the full range of sexual desires and practices, this default perspective must be replaced by a standpoint that honors and celebrates sexual diversity and variability and its contribution to healthy, vibrant, optimal sexual functioning over the life span.

References

Adam, B. D. (2006). Relationship innovation in male couples. *Sexualities, 9,* 5–26. doi:10.1177/1363460706060685

Ahlers, C. J., Schaefer, G. A., Mundt, I. A., Roll, S., Englert, H., Willich, S. N., & Beier, K. M. (2011). How unusual are the contents of paraphilias? Paraphilia-associated sexual arousal patterns in a community-based sample of men. *Journal of Sexual Medicine, 8,* 1362–1370. doi:10.1111/j.1743-6109.2009.01597.x

American Psychiatric Association. (1973). *Diagnostic and statistical manual of mental disorders* (2nd ed., 7th printing). Washington, DC: Author.

American Psychiatric Association. (2000). *Diagnostic and statistical manual of mental disorders* (4th ed., text revision). Washington, DC: Author.

American Psychiatric Association. (2012). DSM–5 *development: Proposed revisions to the paraphilias.* Retrieved from http://www.dsm5.org/ProposedRevision/Pages/proposedrevision.aspx?rid=187#

Anapol, D. (2010). *Polyamory in the 21st century: Love and intimacy with multiple partners.* Lanham, MD: Rowman & Littlefield.

Barish, K., Damon, M., Kimmel, S., King, Z. (Producers), & Lyne, A. (Director). (1986). *9½ weeks* [Motion picture]. Beverly Hills, CA: Metro-Goldwyn-Mayer.

Barker, M. (2005). This is my partner, and this is my . . . partner's partner: Constructing a polyamorous identity in a monogamous world. *Journal of Constructivist Psychology, 18,* 75–88. doi:10.1080/10720530590523107

Barker, M., & Langdridge, D. (2010a). *Understanding non-monogamies.* New York, NY: Routledge.

Barker, M., & Langdridge, D. (2010b). Whatever happened to non-monogamies? Critical reflections on recent research and theory. *Sexualities, 13,* 748–772. doi:10.1177/1363460710384645

Baumeister, R. F. (1988). Masochism as escape from self. *Journal of Sex Research, 25,* 28–59. doi:10.1080/00224498809551444

Beardsley, J., Posner, J., Posner, P. J., Roban, M. (Producers), & Shainberg, S. (Director). (2002).

Secretary [Motion picture]. Santa Monica, CA: Lions Gate Films.

Becker, J. V., & Johnson, B. R. (2009). Gender identity disorders and paraphilias. In J. A. Bourgeois, R. E. Hales, J. S. Young, & S. C. Yudofsky (Eds.), *The American Psychiatric Publishing board review guide for psychiatry* (pp. 425–435). Washington, DC: American Psychiatric Publishing.

Beckmann, A. (2009). *The social construction of sexuality and perversion: Deconstructing sadomasochism*. Basingstoke, England: Palgrave Macmillan. doi:10.1057/9780230244924

Bell, A. P., Weinberg, M. S., & Hammersmith, S. K. (1981). *Sexual preference: Its development in men and women*. Bloomington: Indiana University Press.

Berman, G., Braun, L., Garcia, N., Stein, E. (Executive Producers). (2012). *Polyamory: Married and dating*. New York, NY: Showtime Networks.

Bettinger, M. (2006). Polyamory and gay men: A family systems approach. In J. J. Bigner (Ed.), *An introduction to GLBT family studies* (pp. 161–181). New York, NY: Haworth Press.

Blanchard, R. (2009, April 3). *Paraphilias vs. paraphilic disorders, pedophilia vs. pedo- and hebephilia, and autogynephilic vs. fetishistic transvestism*. Paper presented at the annual meeting of the Society for Sex Therapy and Research, Arlington, Virginia.

Blumstein, P., & Schwartz, P. (1983). *American couples: Money, work, sex*. New York, NY: Morrow.

Bonello, K. (2009). Gay monogamy and extra-dyadic sex: A critical review of the theoretical and empirical literature. *Counselling Psychology Review, 24*, 51–65.

Bozon, M. (2001). Sexuality, gender, and the couple: A sociohistorical perspective. *Annual Review of Sex Research, 12*, 1–32.

Bryant, A. S., & Demian. (1994). Relationship characteristics of American gay and lesbian couples: Findings from a national survey. *Journal of Gay and Lesbian Social Services, 1*, 101–117. doi:10.1300/J041v01n02_06

Bullough, V. L. (1979). *Frontiers of sex research*. New York, NY: Prometheus Books.

Byers, E. S. (2011). Beyond the birds and the bees and was it good for you? Thirty years of research on sexual communication. *Canadian Psychology, 52*, 20–28.

Califia, P. (2000). *Public sex* (2nd ed.). San Francisco, CA: Cleis Press.

Califia, P. (2002). *Sensuous magic: A guide for adventurous couples*. Berkeley, CA: Cleis Press.

Carnes, P. (1991). *Don't call it love: Recovery from sexual addiction*. New York, NY: Bantam.

Chandra, A., Mosher, W. D., Copen, C., & Sionean, C. (2011). Sexual behavior, sexual attraction, and sexual identity in the United States: Data from the 2006–2008 National Survey of Family Growth (National Health Statistics Reports, No. 36). Hyattsville, MD: National Center for Health Statistics.

Crawford, I., Hammack, P. L., McKirnan, D. J., Ostrow, D., Zamboni, B. D., Robinson, B., & Hope, B. (2003). Sexual sensation seeking, reduced concern about HIV and sexual risk behaviour among gay men in primary relationships. *AIDS Care, 15*, 513–524. doi:10.1080/0954012031000134755

Cross, P. A., & Matheson, K. (2006). Understanding sadomasochism: An empirical examination of four perspectives. *Journal of Homosexuality, 50*, 133–166.

Dancer, P. L., Kleinplatz, P. J., & Moser, C. (2006). 24/7 SM slavery. *Journal of Homosexuality, 50*, 81–101. doi:10.1300/J082v50n02_05

Darcangelo, S. (2008). Fetishism: Psychopathology and theory. In D. R. Laws & W. O'Donohue (Eds.), *Sexual deviance: Theory, assessment, and treatment* (pp. 108–118). New York, NY: Guilford Press.

Davidovich, U., de Wit, J. B. F., & Stroebe, W. (2004). Behavioral and cognitive barriers to safer sex between men in steady relationships: Implications for prevention strategies. *AIDS Education and Prevention, 16*, 304–314. doi:10.1521/aeap.16.4.304.40398

Davis, A. (1999, October 25). Confessions of a LUG. *Flagpole Magazine Online*. Retrieved from http://www.alternet.org/story/1256/confessions_of_a_l.u.g.

DePaulo, B. M., & Morris, W. L. (2005). Singles in society and in science. *Psychological Inquiry, 16*, 57–83.

Diamond, L. (2008). *Sexual fluidity: Understanding women's love and desire*. Cambridge, MA: Harvard University Press.

Division 44/Committee on Lesbian, Gay, and Bisexual Concerns Joint Task Force on Guidelines for Psychotherapy with Lesbian, Gay, and Bisexual Clients. (2000). Guidelines for psychotherapy with lesbian, gay, & bisexual clients. *American Psychologist, 55*, 1440–1451.

Easton, E., & Liszt, C. A. (2000). *When someone you love is kinky*. San Francisco, CA: Greenery Press.

Essig, L. (2000, November 15). *Heteroflexibility*. Retrieved from http://dir.salon.com/mwt/feature/2000/11/15/heteroflexibility/index.html

Finkelhor, D. (2008). *Childhood victimization*. New York, NY: Oxford University Press. doi:10.1093/acprof:oso/9780195342857.001.0001

Fisher, H. E. (1992). *The anatomy of love: A natural history of mating, marriage, and why we stray*. New York, NY: W. W. Norton.

Frank, E., Coughlin, S. S., & Elon, L. (2008). Sex-related knowledge, attitudes, and behaviors of U.S. medical students. *Obstetrics and Gynecology, 112*, 311–319. doi:10.1097/AOG.0b013e3181809645

Gagnon, J. H. (1990). The implicit and explicit use of the scripting perspective in sex research. *Annual Review of Sex Research, 1*, 1–43.

Gagnon, J. H., Giami, A., Michaels, S., & Colomby, P. (2001). A comparative study of the couple in the social organization of sexuality in France and the United States. *Journal of Sex Research, 38*, 24–34. doi:10.1080/00224490109552067

Gijs, L. (2008). Paraphilia and paraphilia-related disorders: An introduction. In L. Incrocci (Ed.), *Handbook of sexual and gender identity disorders* (pp. 491–528). Hoboken, NJ: Wiley.

Glucklich, A. (2001). *Sacred pain: Hurting the body for the sake of the soul*. New York, NY: Oxford University Press.

Golden, C. (1996). What's in a name? Sexual self-identification among women. In R. C. Savin-Williams & K. M. Cohen (Eds.), *The lives of lesbians, gays, and bisexuals: Children to adults* (pp. 229–249). Fort Worth, TX: Harcourt Brace.

Hoff, C. C., & Beougher, S. C. (2010). Sexual agreements among gay male couples. *Archives of Sexual Behavior, 39*, 774–787. doi:10.1007/s10508-008-9393-2

Hucker, S. J. (2008). Sexual masochism: Assessment and treatment. In D. R. Laws & W. O'Donohue (Eds.), *Sexual deviance: Theory, assessment, and treatment* (pp. 264–271). New York, NY: Guilford Press.

James, E. L. (2012a). *Fifty shades darker*. New York, NY: Vintage Books.

James, E. L. (2012b). *Fifty shades freed*. New York, NY: Vintage Books.

James, E. L. (2012c). *Fifty shades of grey*. New York, NY: Vintage Books.

Jamieson, L. (2004). Intimacy, negotiated non-monogamy and the limits of the couple. In K. Duncombe, K. Harrison, G. Allan, & D. Marsden (Eds.), *The state of affairs* (pp. 35–57). Mahwah, NJ: Erlbaum.

Kamens, S. R. (2011). On the proposed sexual and gender identity diagnoses for *DSM–5*: History and controversies. *Humanistic Psychologist, 39*, 37–59. doi:10.1080/08873267.2011.539935

Karasic, D., & Drescher, J. (Eds.). (2005). *Sexual and gender diagnoses of the Diagnostic and Statistical Manual (DSM): A reevaluation*. Binghamton, NY: Haworth Press.

Khan, U. (2009a). Putting a dominatrix in her place: The representation and regulation of female dom/male sub sexuality. *Canadian Journal of Women and the Law, 21*, 143–175. doi:10.3138/cjwl.21.1.143

Khan, U. (2009b). A woman's right to be spanked: Testing the limits of tolerance of SM in the socio-legal imaginary. *Law and Sexuality: Review of Lesbian, Gay, Bisexual, and Transgender Legal Issues, 18*, 79–120.

Kinsey, A. C., Pomeroy, W. B., & Martin, C. E. (1948). *Sexual behavior in the human male*. Philadelphia: W. B. Saunders.

Kirkpatrick, R. C. (2000). The evolution of human homosexual behavior. *Current Anthropology, 41*, 385–413. doi:10.1086/300145

Kleinplatz, P. J. (2006). Learning from extraordinary lovers: Lessons from the edge. *Journal of Homosexuality, 50*, 325–348. doi:10.1300/J082v50n02_16

Kleinplatz, P. J. (2010). Lessons from great lovers. In S. Levine, S. Althof, & C. Risen (Eds.), *Handbook of clinical sexuality for mental health professionals* (2nd ed., pp. 57–72). New York, NY: Brunner-Routledge.

Kleinplatz, P. J. (2012). Is that all there is? A new critique of the goals of sex therapy. In P. J. Kleinplatz (Ed.), *New directions in sex therapy: Innovations and alternatives* (2nd ed., pp. 101–118). New York, NY: Routledge.

Kleinplatz, P. J., & Ménard, A. D. (2007). Building blocks toward optimal sexmuality: Constructing a conceptual model. *Family Journal, 15*, 72–78. doi:10.1177/1066480706294126

Kleinplatz, P. J., Ménard, A. D., & Campbell, M. (in press). Relational contributors to optimal sexual experiences. In A. C. Michalos (Ed.), *Encyclopedia of quality of life research*. New York, NY: Springer.

Kleinplatz, P. J., Ménard, A. D., & Lawless, S. (in press). Lessons about optimal sexual experiences from remarkable lovers. In A. C. Michalos (Ed.), *Encyclopedia of quality of life research*. New York, NY: Springer.

Kleinplatz, P. J., Ménard, A. D., Paquet, M.-P., Paradis, N., Campbell, M., Zuccarini, D., & Mehak, L. (2009). The components of optimal sexuality: A portrait of "great sex." *Canadian Journal of Human Sexuality, 18*, 1–13.

Kleinplatz, P. J., Ménard, A. D., Paradis, N., Campbell, M., Dalgliesh, T., Segovia, A., & Davis, K. (2009). From closet to reality: Optimal sexuality among the elderly. *Irish Psychiatrist, 10*, 15–18.

Kleinplatz, P. J., Ménard, A. D., Paradis, N., Campbell, M., & Dalgleish, T. L. (in press). Beyond sexual stereotypes: Revealing group similarities and differences in optimal sexuality. *Canadian Journal of Behavioural Science*.

Kleinplatz, P. J., & Moser, C. (2004). Towards clinical guidelines for working with BDSM clients. *Contemporary Sexuality, 38*(6), 1–4.

Kleinplatz, P. J., & Moser, C. (2005a). Is SM pathological? *Lesbian and Gay Psychology Review, 6*, 255–260.

Kleinplatz, P. J., & Moser, C. (2005b). Politics versus science: An addendum and response to Drs. Spitzer and Fink. *Journal of Psychology and Human Sexuality, 17*, 135–139.

Kleinplatz, P. J., & Moser, C. (Eds.). (2006). *Sadomasochism: Powerful pleasures.* New York, NY: Haworth.

Klesse, C. (2006). Polyamory and its "others": Contesting the terms of non-monogamy. *Sexualities, 9*, 565–583. doi:10.1177/1363460706069986

Kolmes, K., Stock, W., & Moser, C. (2006). Investigating bias in psychotherapy with BDSM clients. *Journal of Homosexuality, 50*, 301–324. doi:10.1300/J082v50n02_15

Krueger, R. B. (2010). The *DSM* diagnostic criteria for sexual sadism. *Archives of Sexual Behavior, 39*, 325–345.

Kurdek, L. A. (1991). Sexuality in homosexual and heterosexual couples. In K. McKinney & S. Sprecher (Eds.), *Sexuality in close relationships* (pp. 177–191). Hillsdale, NJ: Erlbaum.

Kyrakanos, J. (1998). LUGgin' It. *InsideOUT Magazine, 9.*

Labriola, K. (1999). Models of open relationships. *Journal of Lesbian Studies, 3*, 217–225. doi:10.1300/J155v03n01_25

Langevin, R., Lang, R. A., & Curnoe, S. (1998). The prevalence of sex offenders with deviant fantasies. *Journal of Interpersonal Violence, 13*, 315–327. doi:10.1177/088626098013003001

LaSala, M. C. (2004). Extradyadic sex and gay male couples: Comparing monogamous and nonmonogamous relationships. *Families in Society, 85*, 405–412.

Laumann, E. O., Gagnon, J. H., Michael, R. T., & Michaels, F. (1994). *The social organization of sexuality: Sexual practices in the United States.* Chicago, IL: University of Chicago Press.

Laws, D. R., & O'Donohue, W. T. (2008). Introduction. In D. R. Laws & W. O'Donohue (Eds.), *Sexual deviance: Theory, assessment, and treatment* (pp. 1–20). New York, NY: Guilford Press.

MacNeil, S., & Byers, E. S. (2009). Role of sexual self-disclosure in the sexual satisfaction of long-term heterosexual couples. *Journal of Sex Research, 46*, 3–14. doi:10.1080/00224490802398399

Malhotra, S., Khurshid, A., Hendricks, K. A., & Mann, J. R. (2008). Medical school sexual health curriculum and training in the United States. *Journal of the National Medical Association, 100*, 1097–1106.

Masters, W. H., & Johnson, V. E. (1966). *Human sexual response.* Boston, MA: Little, Brown.

Miller, M., & Devon, M. (1995). *Screw the roses, send me the thorns: The romance and sexual sorcery of sadomasochism.* Fairfield, CT: Mystic Rose Books.

Miller, S., & Byers, E. (2010). Psychologists' sexual education and training in graduate school. *Canadian Journal of Behavioural Science, 42*, 93–100. doi:10.1037/a0018571

Miller, S. A., & Byers, E. S. (2009). Psychologists' continuing education and training in sexuality. *Journal of Sex and Marital Therapy, 35*, 206–219. doi:10.1080/00926230802716336

Morin, J. (1995). *The erotic mind: Unlocking the inner sources of sexual passion and fulfillment.* New York, NY: HarperCollins.

Moser, C. (1999). *Health care without shame: A handbook for the sexually diverse and their caregivers.* Emeryville, CA: Greenery Press.

Moser, C. (2001). Paraphilia: A critique of a confused concept. In P. J. Kleinplatz (Ed.), *New directions in sex therapy: Innovations and alternatives* (pp. 91–108). Philadelphia, PA: Routledge.

Moser, C. (2009). When is an unusual sexual interest a mental disorder? *Archives of Sexual Behavior, 38*, 323–325. doi:10.1007/s10508-008-9436-8

Moser, C., & Kleinplatz, P. J. (2002). Transvestic fetishism: Psychopathology or iatrogenic artifact? *Netherlands Journal of Psychology, 52*(2), 16–17.

Moser, C., & Kleinplatz, P. J. (2005a). Does heterosexuality belong in the *DSM*? *Lesbian and Gay Psychology Review, 6*, 261–267.

Moser, C., & Kleinplatz, P. J. (2005b). *DSM–IV–TR* and the paraphilias: An argument for removal. *Journal of Psychology and Human Sexuality, 17*, 91–109.

Moser, C., & Kleinplatz, P. J. (2007). Themes of SM expression. In D. Langdridge & M. Barker (Eds.), *Safe, sane and consensual: Contemporary perspectives on SM* (pp. 35–54) Hampshire, England: MacMillan.

Muscarella, F. (1999). The homoerotic behavior that never evolved. *Journal of Homosexuality, 37*, 1–18. doi:10.1300/J082v37n03_01

Newmahr, S. (2011). *Playing on the edge: Sadomasochism, risk, and intimacy.* Bloomington: Indiana University Press.

Nichols, M. (2006). Psychotherapeutic issues with "kinky" clients: Clinical problems, yours and theirs. *Journal of Homosexuality, 50*, 281–300. doi:10.1300/J082v50n02_14

Orford, J. (2001). *Excessive appetites: A psychological view of addictions.* New York, NY: Wiley.

Owens, E. W., Behun, R. J., Manning, J. C., & Reid, R. C. (2012). The impact of Internet pornography on adolescents: A review of the research. *Sexual Addiction and Compulsivity, 19*, 99–122. doi:10.1080/10720162.2012.660431

Pope, K. S., & Vasquez, M. J. T. (2007). *Ethics in psychotherapy and counseling: A practical guide* (3rd ed.). San Francisco, CA: Jossey-Bass.

Prestage, G., Jin, F., Zablotska, I., Grulich, A., Imrie, J., Kaldor, J., . . . Kippax, S. (2008). Trends in agreements between regular partners among gay men in Sydney, Melbourne and Brisbane, Australia. *AIDS and Behavior, 12*, 513–520. doi:10.1007/s10461-007-9351-3

Ramirez, O. M., & Brown, J. (2010). Attachment style, rules regarding sex, and couple satisfaction: A study of gay male couples. *Australian and New Zealand Journal of Family Therapy, 31*, 202–213. doi:10.1375/anft.31.2.202

Ribner, D. S. (2012). Cultural diversity and sensitivity in sex therapy. In P. J. Kleinplatz (Ed.), *New directions in sex therapy: Innovations and alternatives* (2nd ed., pp. 161–174). New York, NY: Routledge.

Rimer, S. (1993, June 5). Campus lesbians step into unfamiliar light. *New York Times*, p. A2.

Ritchie, A., & Barker, M. (2006). "There aren't words for what we do or how we feel so we have to make them up": Constructing polyamorous languages in a culture of compulsory monogamy. *Sexualities, 9*, 584–601. doi:10.1177/1363460706069987

Rubin, G. (2011). *Deviations: A Gayle Rubin reader.* Durham, NC: Duke University Press.

Rust, P. C. R. (1996). Monogamy and polyamory: Relationship issues for bisexuals. In B. A. Firestein (Ed.), *Bisexuality: The psychology and politics of an invisible minority* (pp. 127–148). Thousand Oaks, CA: Sage.

Ryan, C., & Jetha, C. (2010). *Sex at dawn: The prehistoric origins of modern sexuality*. New York, NY: HarperCollins.

Savage, D. (2002, May 16). *Heteroflexible*. Retrieved from http://www.thestranger.com/seattle/SavageLove?oid=10764

Savage, D. (2007, March 1). *Right or wrong*. Retrieved from http://www.thestranger.com/seattle/SavageLove?oid=167448

Savin-Williams, R. C. (2009). How many gays are there? It depends. In D. A. Hope (Ed.), *Nebraska Symposium on Motivation: Vol. 54. Contemporary perspectives on lesbian, gay, and bisexual identities* (pp. 5–41). New York, NY: Springer.

Seto, M. C. (2008). *Pedophilia and sexual offending against children: Theory, assessment, and intervention.* Washington, DC: American Psychological Association. doi:10.1037/11639-000

Seto, M. C. (2011, August). *The self-reported and genital responses of self-reported male masochists.* Paper presented at the 37th annual meeting of the International Academy of Sex Research, Los Angeles, CA.

Seto, M. C., Lalumière, M. L., Harris, G. T., & Chivers, M. L. (2012). The sexual responses of sexual sadists. *Journal of Abnormal Psychology, 121*, 739–753. doi:10.1037/a0028714

Shapiro, S., Melcher, M., Arthur, R. (Producers), & Mann, D. (Director). (1961). *Lover come back* [Motion picture]. Universal City, CA: Universal Pictures.

Sheff, E. (2005). Polyamorous women, sexual subjectivity, and power. *Journal of Contemporary Ethnography, 34*, 251–283. doi:10.1177/0891241604274263

Shindel, A. W., Ando, K. A., Nelson, C. J., Breyer, B. N., Lue, T. F., & Smith, J. F. (2010). Medical student sexuality: How sexual experience and sexuality training impact U.S. and Canadian medical students' comfort in dealing with patients' sexuality in clinical practice. *Academic Medicine, 85*, 1321–1330. doi:10.1097/ACM.0b013e3181e6c4a0

Simon, W., & Gagnon, J. H. (1986). Sexual scripts: Permanence and change. *Archives of Sexual Behavior, 15*, 97–120. doi:10.1007/BF01542219

Solomon, S. E., Rothblum, E. D., & Balsam, K. F. (2004). Pioneers in partnership: Lesbian and gay male couples in civil unions compared with those not in civil unions and married heterosexual siblings. *Journal of Family Psychology, 18*, 275–286. doi:10.1037/0893-3200.18.2.275

Spitzer, R. L. (2005). Sexual and gender identity disorders: Discussion of questions for *DSM–V*. *Journal of Psychology and Human Sexuality, 17*, 111–116.

Taormino, T. (2008). *Opening up: A guide to creating and sustaining open relationships.* Berkeley, CA: Cleis Press.

Taormino, T. (2012). *The ultimate guide to kink: BDSM, role play, and the erotic edge.* Berkeley, CA: Cleis Press.

Thompson, M. (Ed.). (2004). *Leatherfolk: Radical sex, people, politics, and practice.* San Francisco, CA: Daedalus.

Weeks, J. (1991). Pretended family relationships. In *Against nature: Essays on history, sexuality, and identity* (pp. 134–156). London, England: Rivers Oram Press.

Weinberg, M. S., Williams, C. J., & Moser, C. (1984). The social constituents of sadomasochism. *Social Problems, 31*, 379–389. doi:10.2307/800385

Weiss, M. D. (2006). Mainstreaming kink: The politics of BDSM representation in U.S. popular media. *Journal of Homosexuality, 50*, 103–132. doi:10.1300/J082v50n02_06

Weitzman, G. (2006). Therapy with clients who are bisexual and polyamorous. *Journal of Bisexuality, 6*, 137–164. doi:10.1300/J159v06n01_08

Whipple, B., & Komisaruk, B. R. (1985). Elevation of pain thresholds by vaginal stimulation in women. *Pain, 21*, 357–367. doi:10.1016/0304-3959(85)90164-2

Whipple, B., & Komisaruk, B. R. (1988). Analgesia produced in women by genital self-stimulation. *Journal of Sex Research, 24*, 130–140. doi:10.1080/00224498809551403

White, C. (2006). The Spanner trials and the changing law on sadomasochism in the UK. *Journal of Homosexuality, 50*, 167–187. doi:10.1300/J082v50n02_08

Willets, M. C., Sprecher, S., & Beck, F. D. (2004). Overview of sexual practices and attitudes within relational contexts. In J. H. Harvey, A. Wenzel, & S. Sprecher (Eds.), *The handbook of sexuality in close relationships* (pp. 57–86). Mahwah, NJ: Erlbaum.

Wright, S. (2006). Discrimination of SM-identified individuals. *Journal of Homosexuality, 50*, 217–231. doi:10.1300/J082v50n02_10

CHAPTER 10

SEXUALITY IN THE CONTEXT OF RELATIONSHIPS

Emily A. Impett, Amy Muise, and Diana Peragine

Most dyadic sexual behavior occurs in the context of ongoing romantic relationships (see review by Willetts, Sprecher, & Beck, 2004); however, until relatively recently, scholars have devoted scant attention to linking what is known about human sexuality with what is known about close relationships. Thus, the study of sexuality and the science of relationships have developed as two rather distinct research traditions, each with their own journals, professional organizations, and academic conferences (Diamond, 2010). Scientists in these two traditions have amassed an incredible amount of data and made significant strides in advancing what is known about human sexuality and what is known about close relationships. A few landmark studies in each of these traditions are illustrative (see also Chapter 3, this volume). Beginning with research on sexuality, in the 1940s, Kinsey and colleagues (Kinsey, Pomeroy, & Martin, 1948; Kinsey, Pomeroy, Martin, & Gebhard, 1953) conducted in-depth interviews with 5,300 men and nearly 6,000 women regarding such topics as frequency of sexual behavior in marriage and same-sex behavior and attraction. In the 1990s, the first nationally representative study of sexuality was conducted. The National Health and Social Life Survey involved the collection of data from 3,432 participants and was specifically designed to investigate social and dyadic factors in human sexuality, such as sexual satisfaction, same-sex attraction, and partner matching on sexual preferences (Laumann, Gagnon, Michael, & Michaels, 1994). Turning to research on close relationships, in the 1970s the Boston Couples Study involved the random sampling of college students in 231 heterosexual dating relationships (e.g., Peplau, Rubin, & Hill, 1977). Some sexuality-related topics were covered, including sexual intimacy and sex role attitudes in relationships. In the 1980s, the American Couples Study provided extensive survey data from both members of thousands of married or cohabiting heterosexual, lesbian, and gay couples on such topics as negotiations in the bedroom, sexual initiation, and extradyadic sexual relationships (Blumstein & Schwartz, 1983).

Despite the tremendous growth of both of these fields in the past few decades, their growth as separate areas of scholarship means that fundamental questions about how sexual feelings, thoughts, and behaviors shape the development and maintenance of ongoing romantic relationships remain unanswered. Similarly, much is to be learned about how relationship processes influence and, in turn, shape sexuality. Our intention in writing this chapter is to discuss where psychology is in the study of sexuality and romantic relationships and to offer our thoughts about where it has yet to go. Because the literature on sexuality in relationship contexts has been pervaded by a focus on risk prevention and avoidance, we begin the chapter by presenting research on both the risks and the rewards of sexuality in the context of romantic relationships. Then, given the pervasive role of gender in shaping sexual interactions in ongoing romantic relationships and to provide a backdrop for the rest of our review, we discuss key male–female differences in three core aspects of sexuality: relational focus, sexual desire, and sexual

http://dx.doi.org/10.1037/14193-010
APA Handbook of Sexuality and Psychology: Vol. 1. Person-Based Approaches, D. L. Tolman and L. M. Diamond (Editors-in-Chief)

fluidity. Then, we discuss how sexuality is involved in the formation and development of romantic relationships, specifically focusing on the role of sexual attraction. We then turn to the role of sexuality in the maintenance of ongoing romantic relationships with an emphasis on attachment, sexual desire, and sexual satisfaction. Next, we review research on sexuality in the context of same-sex relationships as well as across the life span from adolescence to later adulthood. Finally, we consider the dark side of sexuality in romantic relationships, focusing on the topics of sexual aggression, extradyadic sex, and sexual jealousy. In each section of the chapter, we consider important directions for future research, and we conclude the chapter by discussing how several recent societal trends are changing the ways in which research on sexuality and relationships are conducted as well as the very ways in which sexuality is pursued and negotiated across relational contexts.

AVOIDING RISKS AND APPROACHING PLEASURE

A core conceptual issue in sexuality research in relational contexts reflects what has been—until relatively recently—a laser focus on risk avoidance and prevention. There are certainly good reasons to focus on preventing the risks associated with sex. For example, more than half of young women describe their first sexual experience as painful or disappointing (Thompson, 1990). Nearly half of all sexually active adolescents and young adults currently engage in unprotected sexual intercourse and put themselves at heightened risk for contracting sexually transmitted infections (Centers for Disease Control and Prevention, 2006). Among adults, lack of sexual desire for a romantic partner is one of the most common presenting problems at sex therapy clinics (Rosen, 2000). Most alarming is the fact that roughly half of newlyweds and those in long-term married relationships report having experienced sexual coercion at the hands of an intimate partner (Brousseau, Bergerson, Hébert, & McDuff, 2011; Panuzio & DiLillo, 2010). In short, the risks, dangers, and downsides of sex are incontrovertible.

Yet, to dwell on these and other negative outcomes of sex is at odds with several simple notions. Most people want to engage in sex, and one of the most commonly cited reasons for engaging in sex is powerful feelings of attraction and love for an intimate partner (Impett, Peplau, & Gable, 2005). Most people are moderately or highly satisfied with their sexual relationships, derive great pleasure from engaging in a broad range of sexually intimate behaviors, and can do so across the life span. Sexuality is a key factor in shaping happiness and satisfaction in relationships. For example, in a cross-national sample of individuals from 29 countries, the people who were most satisfied with their sex lives were often the happiest with their lives in general (Laumann et al., 2006). Moreover, those individuals who are more sexually satisfied tend to be more satisfied with their relationships (Brezsnyak & Whisman, 2004; Sprecher, 2002). Given that satisfying romantic and sexual relationships are vital components of psychological and physical health (Diamond & Huebner, 2012; Diener & Seligman, 2002; Uchino, Cacioppo, & Kiecolt-Glaser, 1996; see also Chapters 11 and 21, this volume), it is essential to understand the ways in which sexuality enables individuals and relationships to thrive and to integrate what is known about the incontrovertible risks of sex with the growing area of research on positive dimensions of sexuality across the life course (Diamond, 2006; Impett, Muise, & Breines, 2013).

ROLE OF GENDER

Because of the central relevance of gender to the study of sexuality in relational contexts, we discuss it at the outset of this chapter (see also Chapter 2, this volume). The overwhelming majority of research on how gender shapes sexuality in the context of relationships has focused on understanding core male–female differences. A century ago, sex experts asserted that men and women had strikingly different sexual natures. Psychologists were skeptical of this view and, beginning in the 1960s, focused on establishing similarities between men and women. For example, Masters and Johnson (1966) proposed a human sexual response cycle that was applicable to both men and women, although recent research has challenged the universality of this sexual response cycle, especially for women (Basson, 2001; Alperstein et al., 2001). In recent years, empirical research comparing men's and women's sexuality has flourished, leading psychologists to take stock of the available scientific evidence (see reviews by Peplau, 2003; Vohs, Catanese, & Baumeister, 2004). Our discussion of gender focuses on how three key gender differences—relational focus, sexual desire, and sexual fluidity—influence sexuality in the context of ongoing romantic relationships.

Relational Focus

One of the most consistent and robust gender differences in sexuality is women's greater tendency to emphasize relationships and commitment as a context for sexuality and men's greater tendency to separate sexuality from love and commitment. For example, men and women tend to differ in their definitions of sexual desire. In one illustrative study, more men (70%) than women (43%) believed that sexual desire was aimed at the physical act of sex (Regan & Berscheid, 1996). In contrast, more women (35%) than men (13%) cited love or emotional intimacy as the goal of sexual desire. Women's sexual fantasies are more likely to include a familiar partner, to include affection and commitment, and to describe the setting for a sexual encounter (see review by Leitenberg & Henning, 1995). In contrast, men's fantasies are more likely to involve strangers, anonymous partners, or multiple partners and to focus on specific sex acts or body parts. Compared with women, men tend to have more permissive attitudes toward casual sex (Peterson & Hyde, 2010). The term *sociosexual orientation* has been used to capture this intercorrelated set of sexual attitudes, preferences, and behaviors (see review by Simpson, Wilson, & Winterheld, 2004). Significant gender differences have reliably been found on measures of sociosexuality, both in the United States and in more than 50 other countries (Schmitt et al., 2003), although it is important to point out that the variability in sociosexuality that exists within each gender greatly exceeds that which exists between men and women (Simpson & Gangestad, 1991). In addition, recent research has suggested that men tend to report falling in love more quickly than do women (Harrison & Shortall, 2011). In addition, men's obsessive thoughts about a romantic partner make it difficult for them to control their sexual thoughts and behaviors (Bauermeister, Ventuneac, Pingle, & Parsons, 2012; Missildine, Feldstein, Punzalan, & Parsons, 2005), suggesting that the link between relationship factors and sexuality is not always stronger for women than for men.

The gender difference in emphasizing the relational aspects of sexuality has also been documented in samples of lesbians and gay men (see review by Peplau, Fingerhut, & Beals, 2004). Compared with gay men, lesbians have less permissive attitudes toward casual sex and are more likely to become sexually involved with partners who were first their friends. In fact, many lesbian and bisexual women have reported that they were never aware of their same-sex desires until they fell in love with a particular woman (Diamond, 2003). Gay men tend to report substantially more sex partners than either lesbians or heterosexuals and score significantly higher than other groups on measures of sociosexuality (Bailey, Gaulin, Agyei, & Gladue, 1994). Gay men in committed relationships are more likely than any other group to report that they have sex with partners outside their primary relationship and have open sexual arrangements (Blumstein & Schwartz, 1983; Peplau et al., 2004).

Several explanations have been posited for this gender difference in relational focus (see review by Diamond, 2004). One idea concerns the fact that women are more likely than men to have their first experiences of sexual arousal in the context of heterosexual dating relationships rather than in the context of solitary masturbation. Another explanation is that women have historically been socialized to restrict their feelings of sexual desire to the context of intimate relationships, whereas men have had more social license to engage in casual sex. Third, biological factors may also contribute to this difference, in particular, neurochemicals that mediate bonding processes in mammals, including oxytocin, vasopressin, and dopamine (Diamond, 2004; Hiller, 2004).

In a review of gender differences in sexuality, Conley, Moors, Matsick, Zeigler, and Valentine (2011) have suggested that differences in men's and women's attitudes and willingness to engage in casual sex are explained by perceptions of a casual partner's sexual prowess and anticipation of being stigmatized for engaging in a casual sex encounter. In a classic study by Clark and Hatfield (1989), men and women were propositioned for casual sex by confederates of the other sex. None of the women accepted the offer, whereas 70% of men agreed to casual sex with the female stranger who approached them. However, Conley (2010) provided evidence that the large gender difference in the acceptance of casual sex offers has less to do with the gender of the participants and more to do with the perceived personality characteristics of the proposer. Both men and women rated the female proposers of casual sex as more intelligent, successful, and sexually skilled than the male proposer. In a recent replication of the Clark and Hatfield (1989) study, Conley, Ziegler, and Moors (2012) found that when the proposed casual sex partner was someone attractive, known to the person, or perceived to have high sexual capabilities, a different pattern emerged. Gender differences in acceptance of a casual sex offer evaporated when participants considered offers from a very attractive person or someone familiar to them, such as a famous person. Women were also as likely as men to accept a casual sex offer if they believed that the person was a great lover and would provide them with a pleasurable sexual experience. Finally, women who anticipated being negatively labeled (e.g., called a slut) were less likely to have accepted both a recent real-life casual sex offer and a hypothetical casual sex offer.

Sexual Desire

Sexual desire has been defined as the drive or motivation to seek out sexual objects or to engage in sexual activities (Diamond, 2004; see also Chapter 8, this volume). In a comprehensive review of empirical research on the topic, Baumeister, Catanese, and Vohs (2001) concluded that—across a variety of markers or indicators of sexual desire—men tend to show more interest in sex than do women. For example, compared with women, men think about sex more often (Laumann et al., 1994) and report more frequent sex fantasies and feelings of desire (Leitenberg & Henning, 1995). Across the life span, men rate the strength of their own sex drive higher than do their female age mates. Men and women also differ in their preferred frequency of sex. When dating and married partners disagree about sexual frequency, men usually want to have sex more often than their female partners (McCabe, 1987; Smith et al., 2011). In heterosexual couples, actual sexual frequency may reflect a compromise between the desires of the male and female partners. In gay and lesbian relationships, in which sexual frequency is decided by partners of the same gender, lesbians report having sex less often than gay men or heterosexuals (Blumstein & Schwartz, 1983).

We should advance a word of caution in interpreting evidence of men's greater sexual desire. The gender difference in desire is particularly strong when considering men's and women's desires for solitary sexual activity, such as masturbation, or for sex with new and unfamiliar sexual partners (Oliver & Hyde, 1993). Although men have more sexual thoughts than women, they also think about food and sleep more than women, suggesting that men may have more thoughts about personal needs in general than do women (Fisher, Moore, & Pittenger, 2012). The gender difference in desire is much smaller in the beginning stages of relationships in which intimacy levels are rapidly increasing (Baumeister & Bratlavsky, 1999). Within the context of ongoing, intimate relationships, it is more accurate to describe women's sexual desire as more variable than men's (Leiblum, 2002). In addition, Wallen (1995) has suggested that it is important to distinguish between having an intrinsic interest in pursuing sex (proceptivity) and the capacity to become sexually aroused in response to situational or relationship cues (receptivity). Women's desire can be just as strong as men's when they are appropriately aroused (Tolman & Diamond, 2001) but may be more vulnerable to disruptions by such factors as hormonal fluctuations and relationship issues and concerns (Impett, Strachman, Finkel, & Gable, 2008; Leiblum, 2002). Gender differences in sexual desire in the context of ongoing romantic relationships still tend to exist, but they are relatively small in magnitude (e.g., Davies, Katz, & Jackson, 1999; Holmberg & Blair, 2009) or may be hard to detect given the higher relative variability in women's desire. Finally, as with all male–female comparisons, there are many exceptions to this general pattern, as research on highly sexual women has revealed (Blumberg, 2003; Wentland, Herold, Desmarais, & Milhausen, 2009).

Several explanations exist for the empirically documented gender differences in sexual desire. One explanation is primarily biological in nature and suggests that gender differences may be due to differences in levels of circulating androgens and estrogens (Bancroft, 1978; Udry, 1988). Indeed, evidence from the animal and human literatures extensively reviewed by Baumeister et al. (2001) has suggested that whereas androgens are responsible for the active initiation of sexual activity, estrogens are responsible for the acceptance of sexual activity. Another explanation for the gender difference focuses on the powerful social forces that restrict, limit, and control female sexual desire and cast girls and women in the role of sexual gatekeepers (Fine & McClelland, 2006). These messages are especially prominent in adolescence, a time when girls receive powerful messages that they do not want or need sexual activity as much as men and that sex is only appropriate in the context of committed or monogamous relationships (Tolman, 2006). These messages limit adolescent girls' ability to be aware of and to detect their own feelings of sexual arousal and may be responsible for the fact that many women report discrepancies between their degree of physiological arousal and their subjective feelings of arousal (Chivers, Rieger, Latty, & Bailey, 2005).

Regardless of their source, it is important to consider the implications of possible gender differences in desire for the successful maintenance of romantic relationships. One possible index of desire that may be especially important to consider is the desired frequency of sex. Research by McCabe (1987) demonstrated that across relationships of differing duration, whereas women reported that they were getting as much sexual intercourse as they wanted, men consistently reported wanting more sexual intercourse than they were currently getting. In a study of German university students in heterosexual relationships, Klusmann (2002) found that men were more likely than women to complain that their desired frequency of sex outpaced their actual frequency of sex, and this discrepancy grew larger with increased relationship length. In relationships characterized by overall differences in desire between male and female partners, a man may believe that he would be better off with a woman with a higher sex drive and, conversely, a woman may believe that she is inadequate or unable to fulfill her partner's sexual needs. Both of these perceptions may present considerable challenges for relationships, especially as couples try to maintain their relationships over the long haul (see review by Vohs et al., 2004). In heterosexual relationships in which men desire sex more frequently than their female partners, men tend to report lower sexual and relationship satisfaction (Smith et al., 2011). Moreover, some studies have shown that satisfaction with one's sex life in the context of relationships tends to be more important for men than for women. In a longitudinal study of romantic couples, Sprecher (2002) found that sexual satisfaction decreased over time for both men and women, but this effect was stronger for men. Furthermore, sexual dissatisfaction tends to predict relationship dissolution more strongly for men than for women in samples of dating couples (Sprecher, 2002) and married couples (Dzara, 2010), suggesting that couples may be more likely to break up or divorce when men are not happy with their sex lives.

Sexual Fluidity

Sexual fluidity (also called *erotic plasticity*) represents the extent to which an individual's sexual beliefs and behaviors can be altered by cultural, social, and situational factors. The original Kinsey et al. (1948, 1953) reports and Masters and Johnson's (1966) research on the human sexual response cycle suggested that women's sexual activity fluctuates more over time than men's. In a comprehensive review of research on the malleability of sexuality, Baumeister (2000) showed that women tend to exhibit more change in sexuality across time than men. For example, women change and adjust their sexual preferences more so than men over the course of a marriage (Ard, 1977). In her recent book, Diamond (2008) reviewed evidence suggesting that women exhibit greater changes in sexual orientation over time than do men (see Chapter 20, this volume). Baumeister (2000) also argued that social and cultural variables such as religion and education tend to have a stronger influence on women's sexuality. In addition, compared with men, women demonstrate a lower consistency between their sexual attitudes and their behaviors. One example of attitude–behavior consistency that differs quite markedly for men and women concerns patterns of sexual compliance or consensual unwanted sex (Impett & Peplau, 2003; O'Sullivan & Allgeier, 1998). These terms refer to situations in which one partner consents to sexual activity that he or she does not personally desire. In ongoing romantic relationships, women are roughly twice as likely as men to report engaging in undesired sex (see review by Impett & Peplau, 2003), and women in longer term relationships tend to be more sexually compliant than women in short-term relationships (Carvalheira, Brotto, & Leal, 2010). These results suggest that women may be relatively more likely than men to resolve a dilemma about undesired sex by taking their partner's welfare into account or by placing the relationship above their own sexual needs (Impett & Peplau, 2002).

The greater malleability of women's sexuality compared with the consistency and stability of men's sexuality over time has important implications for close relationships. Romantic relationships often involve a high degree of interdependence between partners, such that changes in one person's interests and preferences inevitably influence his or her partner (Rusbult & Van Lange, 2008). To the extent that women are more likely to change their sexual interests and preferences over time, these changes will influence their partner and the relationship. For example, in newly developing relationships, men and women tend to start out with high levels of desire. Although men tend to remain relatively high in sexual desire, women often report waning desire over the course of time in relationships (Baumeister & Bratlavsky, 1999). Thus, in the context of long-term intimate partnerships, men and women may find themselves in situations in which their levels of desire show decreasing correspondence—situations that may present challenges for the relationship.

In sum, research has pointed to three core gender differences in sexuality that have important implications for romantic relationships. Although the magnitude of these gender differences may be smaller in the context of ongoing relationships, in general women tend to place greater emphasis on relationships as an important context for sexual activity, report lower and more variable interest in or drive for sex, and demonstrate more fluidity in sexual interests and preferences over time than do men. An important direction for future research will be to focus on the implications of these differences for the quality and stability of intimate relationships. Qualitative methods are needed to understand how men and women experience their sexuality, and longitudinal methods would be ideal to investigate how gender shapes sexuality at different points in relationships and at different stages of the life span.

SEXUAL ATTRACTION

Before relationships are even formed and as they are initially developing, partners assess each other's romantic and sexual potential. In the 1960s and 1970s, research on close relationships focused on understanding initial romantic attraction. Much of this work was based on evolutionary perspectives and emphasized gender differences in partner preferences and mate selection. During the 1980s, with the growing influence of attachment theory, researchers shifted their focus from studying initial romantic attraction to studying relationship dynamics in ongoing romantic bonds (see Chapter 1, this volume). Yet in the past decade with the advent of speed dating, we have seen renewed focus on romantic attraction during real-life dating situations (Finkel, Eastwick, & Matthews, 2007). In this section, we review gender differences and similarities in partner preferences, consider individual differences in mating strategies, and discuss the disconnect between expressed partner preferences and actual mate selection.

Mate Preferences

Research on mate selection criteria, or the traits that people report desiring in a romantic partner, has largely focused on gender differences and suggested that men and women value different criteria in potential mates. Across 37 cultures, when asked to rank the qualities that are desired in a mate, women ranked dependability, stability, education, and intelligence more highly than men for a long-term partner, whereas men ranked physical appearance, health, and desire for a home and children more highly than women (Shackelford, Schmitt, & Buss, 2005). These gender differences in preferences for a long-term partner have been present across multiple generations. For example, in surveys of mate preferences conducted between 1939 and 1996, men consistently placed a higher premium on physical attractiveness, whereas women put greater importance on the financial stability of romantic partners (Buss, Shackelford, Kirkpatrick, & Larsen, 2001). Other studies on partner preferences have attempted to distinguish between necessary and "luxury" traits by giving people a "mate budget" and asking them to indicate which traits are necessities in a romantic partner. Men classified physical attractiveness as a necessity in a long-term partner, whereas women treated it as a luxury. The reverse pattern emerged for status and resources, with women viewing these qualities as necessities and men viewing them as luxuries (Li, Bailey, Kendrick, & Linsenmeier, 2002).

Although the mate selection literature has emphasized gender differences in partner preferences that persist across cohorts, cultures, and types of research methods, there are also important gender similarities. Although men ranked physical attractiveness higher than did women in Buss et al.'s (2001) cross-cohort study, it was nonetheless ranked only seventh of 18 possible characteristics. Similarly, women ranked financial stability as more important than did men, but it was only 11th on women's lists. In fact, for both men and women, the top four traits preferred in a long-term partner were dependability, emotional stability, pleasing disposition, and mutual attraction and love. With each successive cohort, physical attractiveness and financial prospects became more important for both sexes, with men in more recent years expressing a steeper rise in the importance of partner earning potential. Moreover, both men and women indicated that kindness and intelligence were necessities for a long-term partner (Li et al., 2002).

Gender differences are further attenuated when short-term partner preferences are considered. Both men and women name physical attraction as their top reason for considering casual sex and inquire first about physical attractiveness when screening for a one-night stand partner (Li & Kendrick, 2006). Several differences in mate preferences within gender have also been identified. Women consistently report valuing kindness and high social status in long-term partners (Li & Kendrick, 2006). However, when considering what they desire in short-term partners, some women prioritize long-term qualities such as social status, whereas others emphasize physical attractiveness at the expense of kindness and social status. A similar pattern tends to emerge for men (Li & Kendrick, 2006). For some men, short-term preferences diverge only slightly from long-term preferences, whereas for others, physical attractiveness is heavily prioritized in short-term relationships at the expense of kindness, social status, and creativity. As such, individual variation in mate selection criteria within gender is important to consider.

Individual differences in partner preferences and, by extension, mating strategies are at least partially explained by differences in *sociosexuality,* broadly defined as the extent to which a person desires uncommitted sexual activity (see review by Simpson et al., 2004). Individuals scoring high on measures of sociosexuality are more comfortable having sex outside of a committed relationship, prioritize physical attractiveness in romantic partners, and tend to be involved in relationships characterized by the rapid development of sexual intimacy and low levels of investment, love, and commitment. In contrast, individuals scoring low in sociosexuality tend to be more committed to maintaining their relationships, believe that love is necessary for sex, and prefer partners who place a premium on intimacy and commitment. Schmitt (2005) examined sociosexuality scores of men and women from 48 countries and found that men scored substantially higher than women. More recent research that has considered multiple dimensions of sociosexuality—including attitudes, behavior, and desire—has suggested that the desire dimension is driving the gender differences in sociosexuality, because men generally report greater desire for uncommitted sexuality than women, and women's desire scores are more consistent with their behavior than are men's (Penke & Asendorpf, 2008). For example, women who have positive attitudes toward uncommitted sexuality and a desire for sexual variety report a greater number of prior relationships, sex partners, and infidelities than men with similar attitudes and desires (Penke & Asendorpf, 2008). Consistent with this research, Penderson, Putcha-Bhagavatula, and Miller (2011) found that men and women do not differ in preferred number of sex partners, suggesting that individual differences may be more important than gender in considering partner preferences and mating strategies.

Mate Selection

In the past decade, research on interpersonal attraction has shifted in focus from self-reported preferences for hypothetical partners to real-life dating outcomes, allowing researchers to consider whether reported partner preferences translate into actual mate choices. Consistent with research on partner preferences, gender differences in romantic interest have been observed in online dating contexts. Men in high-income brackets enjoy greater online dating success, as measured by the number of first-contact e-mails received, whereas the effect of income on e-mail receipt is only moderate for women (Hitsch, Hortacsu, & Ariely, 2010). In the same way, women who include a photo in their online profile receive more than twice as many e-mails as women who do not post a photo and describe themselves as average in physical attractiveness. This effect is less pronounced for men (Hitsch et al., 2010; see also Volume 2, Chapter 3, this handbook).

Eastwick, Finkel, and Eagly (2011) examined whether gender differences in reported partner preferences also exist in face-to-face interactions. In a sample of undergraduates, participants reported gender-typical partner preferences, and these preferences predicted romantic interest after the assessment of a potential partner's profile. However, when participants actually met the subject of the profile, stated preferences failed to predict romantic interest. It appears that interest in hypothetical targets (e.g., viewed in online dating profiles or personal ads) is consistent with partner preferences, but in a face-to-face meeting, preferred qualities are reinterpreted to fit the traits displayed by the potential partner. For example, poor financial prospects can be reinterpreted as the product of a lazy, unmotivated lifestyle or the lot of a struggling but driven artist, depending on the context. The valence ascribed to target traits during face-to-face interactions dictates romantic attraction and, as a result, mate choice decisions after live interactions can deviate markedly from initial mate preferences.

Studies of romantic attraction in speed dating contexts have cast further doubt on the predictive validity of partner preferences. Eastwick and Finkel (2008) examined the mate preferences of undergraduates before a speed dating session and followed daters for 32 days. The data revealed no gender differences in partner preferences and no association between stated preferences and dating choices. For speed daters of both sexes, the physical attractiveness of a potential partner had the greatest bearing on romantic interest. Moreover, when women express an interest in a partner's earning potential or when men express an interest in good looks during a speed date, interaction troubles can follow (Korobov, 2011). By contrast, the expression of partner preferences that are resistant to traditional gender norms is more likely to result in mutual affiliation (Korobov, 2011). With regard to racial preferences, research by Fisman, Iyengar, Kamenica, and Simonson (2008) revealed that although speed daters expressed strong same-race preferences, nearly half of all matches are interracial. Speed dating studies have provided a unique opportunity to compare partner preferences and actual mate choices while retaining laboratory-like control and enhanced ecological validity. However, this approach may possibly prime short-term mating strategies, in which gender differences are muted to begin with, instead of providing evidence that both men and women place a premium on physical attractiveness for long-term partners (Eastwick & Finkel, 2008).

The question of whether speed dating choices merely reflect casual-sex partner selections has been addressed. In a sample of adults using commercial dating services who reported a greater interest in securing a long-term than a short-term partner, Asendorpf, Penke, and Back (2011) found that physical attraction was the main predictor of romantic interest for both men and women, consistent with the findings of Eastwick and Finkel (2008). Kurzban and Weeden (2005, 2007) compared reported partner preferences with actual mate choices in community samples of adults. Although men tended to specify a preferred body type and women were more likely to list cut-off points for education and income, these stated preferences deviated from actual mate choices. For both men and women, romantic interest in speed dating partners was determined almost exclusively by physically observable attributes such as attractiveness, body mass index, height, and age.

In contrast to evolutionary models of mate selection, the speed dating literature has suggested that men and women are more similar than different in the traits that influence their attraction to a romantic partner. Although gender differences in partner preferences have been found across cultures, stated preferences do not appear to dictate actual romantic interest. Instead, the willingness to pursue a relationship with an individual of the other sex is highly dependent on that individual's physical attractiveness. Consistent with research that has demonstrated an association between sexual priming and relationship goal pursuit (Gillath, Mikulincer, Birnbaum, & Shaver, 2008), the attraction literature has pointed to sexual attraction as the overarching factor that motivates people to pursue intimacy in a relationship context.

Although speed dating provides a unique window into real-life attraction, its generalizability has been contested because of the fast and formalized nature of speed dating events as well as an exclusive focus on heterosexual participants. Future research should examine the function of partner preferences in gay men's and lesbians' speed date selection as well as in relationships initiated outside of a speed dating context. Finally, longitudinal data are needed to determine the role of ideal partner preferences in mate retention and to clarify whether the same sexually charged variables that predict initial attraction also predict the transition from casual to committed mating and relating.

ATTACHMENT

Couples who stay together beyond the initial attraction phase will begin to develop an attachment bond, and attachment-related differences have implications for the maintenance of relationships. Although attachment and sexuality are distinct behavioral systems that evolved for different purposes and can be experienced separately (Diamond, 2003, 2004), long-term romantic partners typically function simultaneously as sexual partners and attachment figures (see reviews by Birnbaum, 2010; Gillath & Schachner, 2006). More than 2 decades ago, Hazan and Shaver (1987) argued that romantic relationships are made up of three distinct but related behavioral systems: sex, caregiving, and attachment. Since then, researchers have devoted considerable attention to understanding how these systems are related as well as how individual differences in attachment predict differences in the way that people experience romantic and sexual relationships. In this section, we discuss the extension of attachment theory to romantic relationships, review the literature linking attachment and sexuality, and discuss how attachment shapes sexual motivation (see Chapter 1, this volume).

Attachment in Romantic Relationships

Since the 1970s, attachment theory has been a leading perspective for understanding the bond between a child and a caregiver (e.g., Bowlby, 1979), and in the 1980s, this perspective was applied to romantic pair bonds (Hazan & Shaver, 1987). The same behaviors that are characteristic of infant–caregiver attachment—seeking and maintaining physical proximity, seeking comfort when needed, experiencing distress on separation, and viewing the attachment figure as a secure base—are directed toward a mate in adulthood (Hazan & Zeifman, 1999). There are important differences, however, between the parent–child bond and the bond between romantic partners. Most notably, adult attachments involve reciprocal caregiving as well as sexual attraction and mating (Shaver, Hazan, & Bradshaw, 1988). As such, romantic partnerships reflect an integration of the attachment, caregiving, and sexual systems.

Individual differences in attachment are best conceptualized along the two continuous dimensions of attachment anxiety and avoidance. An individual's position on the anxiety dimension reflects the extent to which he or she desires closeness with romantic partners but has heightened fears of rejection and abandonment. An individual's position on the avoidance dimension reflects the extent to which he or she feels uncomfortable with closeness in romantic relationships and strives for independence and emotional distance from partners (Mikulincer & Shaver, 2007). Low scores on both the anxiety and the avoidance dimensions reflect attachment security. An extensive body of research has shown that attachment anxiety and avoidance reliably predict differences in the way people experience romantic and sexual relationships (see review by Birnbaum, 2010). The bulk of the research on attachment in relationships has involved heterosexual samples, although similar prevalence rates of anxiety and avoidance and associations with relational and sexual outcomes have been identified among gay and lesbian individuals. One notable difference is that the attachment security of gays and lesbians is unrelated to their early relationships with parents but is instead predicted by self and peer acceptance, suggesting that for gay and lesbian individuals attachment security may be more strongly influenced by peer relationships than by early parenting (see review by Feeney & Noller, 2004).

Attachment and Sexuality in Relationships

Individual differences in adult romantic attachment influence how individuals experience and make meaning of their romantic and sexual relationships. Securely attached individuals generally have committed, stable, and satisfying romantic relationships and enjoy sex in the context of relationships (Birnbaum, Reis, Mikulincer, Gillath, & Orpaz, 2006; Simpson, 1990). Highly anxious individuals, however, tend to use sex to meet their needs for emotional intimacy and reassurance and are often preoccupied with relationship issues and overly concerned with their partner's sexual needs (Davis, Shaver, & Vernon, 2004; Schachner & Shaver, 2004). Although anxious individuals report greater sexual desire and are more likely to maintain passion over time (Davis et al., 2004), they report lower levels of sexual and marital satisfaction (Butzer & Campbell, 2008; Little, McNulty, & Russell, 2010). Interestingly, the romantic partners of anxiously attached individuals do not report lower levels of sexual satisfaction, a finding that may reflect the tendency for anxiously attached individuals to defer to a romantic partner's sexual needs (Butzer & Campbell, 2008; Impett & Peplau, 2002). Higher avoidance is also associated with lower levels of sexual satisfaction, reflecting avoidant individuals' greater discomfort with intimacy and closeness. Partners of more avoidant individuals are also less sexually satisfied, and their decreased sexual satisfaction detracts from feelings of relationship satisfaction (Butzer & Campbell, 2008; see also Volume 2, Chapter 4, this handbook).

The attachment and sexual systems not only influence one another but also contribute to the quality and stability of romantic relationships. For example, the influence that sexual experiences have on relationship satisfaction differs on the basis of an individual's attachment style. In a sample of married couples, the link between sexual and relationship satisfaction was stronger for people who were relatively more anxiously attached as well as for people who had anxiously attached partners (Butzer & Campbell, 2008). On days when anxiously attached individuals had more negative sexual experiences, their relationship satisfaction decreased, and on days when they had more positive sexual experiences, their relationship satisfaction increased. Conversely, the relationship satisfaction of avoidantly attached individuals was less influenced by their daily sexual experiences. Although avoidant individuals are not as affected by negative experiences, they are also less likely to reap the benefits of satisfying sexual experiences (Birnbaum et al., 2006). These findings highlight the tendency of anxiously attached individuals to use sex as a barometer for relationship satisfaction and the tendency of avoidant individuals to distance love from sex. Finally, this growing area of research on attachment and sexuality has also suggested that the frequency and quality of sexual interactions in a relationship may buffer against the negative impact of both attachment anxiety and avoidance on relationship quality. In a daily experience study, on days when partners reported more satisfying sex, anxiously attached individuals did not experience declines in their marital satisfaction, and among couples who reported more frequent sex, avoidance was not associated with lower marital satisfaction (Little et al., 2010).

Sexual fantasies can also provide a window into the interplay between attachment and sexuality in romantic relationships. In a study by Birnbaum (2007), people who scored high on attachment anxiety reported a greater number of sexual fantasies than those low in anxiety, and their fantasies were more likely to reflect desires for intimacy and representations of a partner as warm and affectionate. In contrast, highly avoidant people were more likely to report sexual fantasies that involved distance and alienation from a romantic partner. Moreover, on days when negative relational events occurred, attachment-related concerns were exacerbated in the fantasies of both anxious and avoidant partners, with anxious individuals fantasizing about being helpless and avoidantly attached individuals fantasizing about feeling self-sufficient and independent (Birnbaum, Mikulincer, & Gillath, 2011).

Researchers have demonstrated the utility of dyadic approaches to studying attachment and sexuality in relationships. For example, in one study, when husbands were high in attachment anxiety or avoidance, their wives reported lower levels of sexual desire and sexual communication 5 months later (Feeney & Noller, 2004). Brassard, Shaver, and Lussier (2007) found that avoidant men and women reported less frequent sex when their partner was more anxious, a finding that is likely the result of their partner's heightened desire for intimacy and their own need to avoid closeness in relationships. Having an anxious partner who constantly pursues intimacy may also make avoidant partners' distancing attempts more pronounced. Furthermore, some degree of matching between partners on attachment styles may be important in relationships. When both partners are highly anxious, sexual frequency tends to be high, but an anxious man partnered with a less anxious woman often results in less frequent sex (Brassard et al., 2007). The neediness and desire for closeness that is characteristic of anxious attachment seems to be better received by a more anxious than a less anxious partner.

If sex and attachment are interconnected, priming one system should motivate a person toward goals of the other system. In a recent study, compared with those primed with neutral pictures, individuals who were primed with erotic words and pictures showed a heightened desire to form and maintain romantic relationships (Gillath et al., 2008). In a review, Gillath and Schachner (2006) provided evidence for the interconnection between the attachment and sexual systems. When the sexual system is activated, people are motivated not only toward sexual behavior but also toward strengthening their current relationship; conversely, when the attachment system is activated, people are more interested in pursuing long-term, committed relationships than they are in pursuing short-term, casual relationships. Attachment avoidance, whether dispositional or primed, is associated with a desire for shorter term mating strategies, whereas attachment anxiety and security are associated with longer term mating strategies. In addition, when anxiously attached individuals are primed with security, they have a reduced desire for long-term partnerships, suggesting that attachment-related primes may remind anxious individuals of negative relational thoughts and experiences.

Attachment and Sexual Motives

In romantic relationships, partners may use sex to meet specific attachment-related needs, and therefore individual differences in anxiety and avoidance are associated with distinct motivations for engaging in sexual activity. Anxiously attached individuals tend to engage in sex to please a romantic partner, to express love, and to achieve emotional intimacy and are less likely to engage in sex in pursuit of physical pleasure (Davis et al., 2003, 2004; Impett, Gordon, & Strachman, 2008). Anxiously attached individuals are more likely to engage in *sexting*—sending sexually suggestive or propositioning text messages to their romantic partners—a behavior that is motivated by a desire to maintain their partner's interest and meet their needs for reassurance by eliciting a response from their partner (Weisskirch & Delevi, 2011). In contrast, because of fears of and discomfort with intimacy, avoidant individuals' sexual motives tend to focus on detaching sex and love. Avoidant attachment is associated with having sex to avoid negative relationship interactions and is negatively associated with having sex to express love for a partner (Impett, Gordon, & Strachman, 2008). Instead, avoidant people are more likely to have sex for self-enhancing reasons such as to pursue their own sexual pleasure (e.g., Schachner & Shaver,

2004). Attachment avoidance is also associated with a greater likelihood of engaging in extradyadic sex to reduce discomfort with a primary partner's desire for intimacy (Beaulieu-Pelletier, Philippe, LeCours, & Couture, 2011).

Sexual motives are also influenced by a partner's attachment style. Because avoidant individuals are relatively less likely to respond to a romantic partner's needs for intimacy, men and women with avoidant partners are more likely to engage in sex to pursue their own physical pleasure (Impett, Gordon, & Strachman, 2008). Research has also suggested that gender differences exist in the ways that men and women respond to an anxiously attached partner. Whereas women with more anxious partners are more likely to have sex to please their partners, men with more anxious partners are less likely to do so (Impett, Gordon, & Strachman, 2008). In general, women are more likely than men to have sex with their partners when they have little or no desire (Impett & Peplau, 2003) and may feel more obligated to meet their partner's needs, particularly when they are high in attachment anxiety (Impett & Peplau, 2002). Men's intimacy needs may be satiated by having an anxious partner, and therefore men may be less likely to comply with an anxious partner's sexual wishes or may be frustrated with their partner's constant demands for closeness (Impett, Gordon, & Strachman, 2008).

Relationship threats, such as rejection, uncertainty about a partner's love, and concerns that another person might be attempting to attract one's partner, can activate attachment-related goals. In one recent study, after thinking about a relationship threat (e.g., a partner considering a break up) versus a non–relationship threat (e.g., failing an exam), anxiously attached individuals reported fewer sexual motives focused on the pursuit of pleasure (Birnbaum, Weisberg, & Simpson, 2011). This finding suggests that relational threats may trigger anxious individuals to focus even less on their own sexual pleasure. In a study of individuals who reported on the content of their sexual fantasies after a relational threat, highly anxious individuals reported a heightened desire to satisfy a romantic partner's sexual needs, a strategy that was likely enacted to maintain the relationship (Birnbaum, Svitelman, Bar-Shalom, & Porat, 2008). In contrast, highly avoidant people further withdrew from their partners after a relationship threat and reported lower desires to engage in sex (Birnbaum et al., 2008). Interestingly, avoidant women, when threatened, were more likely to represent themselves as pleasing and affectionate toward their partner in their sexual fantasies, suggesting that in some situations women's greater relational orientation may supersede the impact of attachment (Birnbaum et al., 2008).

In sum, a growing body of research has shown important ways in which attachment and sexuality are linked in romantic relationships. More longitudinal research is needed to understand how attachment influences relational and sexual experiences over the course of romantic partnerships, and further research is needed on how partners' attachment styles interact to influence relational and sexual outcomes.

SEXUAL DESIRE

Sexual desire, defined as a motivational state that leads an individual to seek out opportunities to engage in sexual activities (Diamond, 2003, 2004; Gonzaga, Turner, Keltner, Campos, & Altemus, 2006), is another critical factor to consider in the maintenance of romantic relationships (see Chapter 8, this volume). Research on sexual desire has suggested that it involves both physical and cognitive aspects. Both men and women have reported gauging their levels of sexual desire via genital arousal (Beck, Bozman & Qualtrough, 1991), and some women have discussed desire as being sexual interest that is more thoughtful (Graham, Sanders, Milhausen, & McBride, 2004) and not necessarily indicative of a physical readiness for sex (Wood, Mansfield, & Koch, 2007). In this section, we consider how sexual desire changes over the course of a relationship, discuss the implications of partners having discrepancies in sexual desire, and review possible factors that may buffer against declines in sexual desire in relationships over time.

Sexual Desire Over the Course of a Relationship

Sexual desire has important implications for relationship maintenance. People who report higher levels of desire have fewer thoughts about leaving their current relationship and are less likely to be unfaithful to their partner or feel attracted to other people (Regan, 2000). Despite the associations between desire and relationship stability, there also seems to be a normative decline in desire over the course of a relationship, with sexual desire peaking in the early stages of a relationship and then decreasing over time (Sprecher & Regan, 1998). This decline occurs even if couples do not have children and when controlling for how satisfied they are in the relationship (Call, Sprecher, & Schwartz, 1995). Relationship duration has been shown to be a stronger predictor of sexual frequency than age (Johnson, Wadsworth, Welling & Fields, 1994), with one exemplary finding being that people who remarry later in life often report increased sexual frequency (Call et al., 1995). Researchers have suggested that declines in desire can be attributed to habituation to a romantic partner (see Chapters 7 and 13, this volume) and theorized that in long-term relationships, sex may be less rewarding than earlier in the relationship and therefore loses some of its importance (Call et al., 1995; Liu, 2000).

Whereas feelings of intimacy and closeness tend to increase over the course of a relationship, passion often declines. According to Baumeister and Bratlavsky (1999), passion is a function of changes in intimacy, meaning that long-term couples are at risk of declines in desire once the level of intimacy in a relationship is stable, even when levels of intimacy are high. In a recent empirical test of this theory in a 21-day diary study of established couples, daily increases in intimacy were associated with higher levels of passion, a greater probability of having sex, and greater sexual satisfaction (Rubin & Campbell, 2012). In-depth interviews with 22 women who reported high marital satisfaction but low sexual desire for their husbands revealed that the comfort and stability of long-term relationships contributes to the feeling that sex is less exciting (Simms & Meana, 2010). Other factors, such as the overfamiliarity of a long-term partner and the sexual repertoire and the desexualization of roles that often occurs in long-term relationships, such as shared household responsibilities and coparenting, also contribute to decreased desire (Simms & Meana, 2010). Changes in levels of desire in an established relationship may also be the result of changes in one or both partners' sexual functioning. Not surprisingly, when one partner experiences sexual difficulties, both partners report declines in sexual desire. Low levels of desire in women often co-occur with other sexual problems and with a partner's sexual dysfunction (McCabe & Goldhammer, 2012; see also Volume 2, Chapter 4, this handbook).

Discrepancies between actual and desired frequency of engaging in sex shape the quality of romantic relationships, and this association differs over the course of a relationship. In a study of 8,096 heterosexual dating couples, higher sexual desire, especially as reported by the female partner, was associated with increased relationship satisfaction for both partners, even when actual sexual frequency was lower than desired frequency (Willoughby & Vitas, 2012). However, in longer relationships, higher discrepancies between desired and actual frequency of sexual activity led male partners to feel less satisfied with their relationship and female partners to question the stability of their relationship. Therefore, higher desire than frequency may serve as a motivator for individuals to invest in a new relationship, but it may lead to negative consequences in more established relationships.

Family life stage and transition to parenthood have an impact on desire and sexual frequency in relationships. In a study using data from the National Survey of Families and Households, sexual frequency decreased during pregnancy and the initial postpartum period, especially when a couple was also parenting other children younger than age 4 (Call et al., 1995). The general pattern of desire during the transition to parenthood that has emerged in the literature is that women's desire declines over the course of pregnancy, especially during the third trimester, and remains low for the first few months postpartum (see review by Haugen, Schmutzer, & Wenzel, 2004). Men may experience similar declines over the course of their partner's pregnancy, although these declines are relatively less dramatic. Conversely, some women report increases in desire at various stages of their pregnancy, and many women may retain an interest in noncoital sexual activities, even if they desire less frequent intercourse. In a sample of 128 Iranian first-time parents, women's appearance concerns and fatigue were associated with lower levels of sexual desire, but high perceived intimacy among couples buffered against declines in marital satisfaction during the postpartum period (Nehzad & Goodarzi, 2011).

Ethnic differences in the experience of female sexual desire have been documented in the literature. The Global Study of Sexual Attitudes and Behaviors, which included more than 14,000 women and spanned 20 countries, revealed that low sexual desire or a lack of interest in sex is more common among East Asian than European and North American women (Laumann et al., 2005). In one study, Woo, Brotto, and Gorzalka (2011) found that East Asian women reported more sexual guilt and sexual conservatism than Caucasian women, and sexual guilt accounted for the association between ethnicity and sexual desire.

Recent qualitative research has suggested that over the course of a relationship, sexual desire becomes an increasingly partnered experience. Women in long-term relationships discuss their desire as being more responsive to their partner's initiation than spontaneous (Goldhammer & McCabe, 2011), and many couples equate the quality of their sexual relationship with the quality of their relationship as a whole (Elliott & Umberson, 2008). Some women, however, discuss declining desire despite high levels of relational satisfaction (Simms & Means, 2010). Further qualitative work in this area could offer insights into how couples manage desire discrepancies in their relationships and how desire and sexual motivation change over the course of a relationship. Because sexual desire and sexual frequency are not synonymous, the sexual motives of a partner with lower desire may have important implications for relationship quality. Longitudinal studies that consider the ebb and flow of desire over the course of a relationship are also warranted and could identify additional factors that contribute to declines over time.

Desire Discrepancies

In the context of a romantic relationship, perceptions of sexual compatibility, including the concordance between partners' levels of desire, have implications for relationship quality (Hurlbert, Apt, Hurlbert, & Pierce, 2000). Instead of conceptualizing an individual's sexual desire as high versus low, some researchers have begun to think about a person's sexual desire as relative to their partner's desire and have considered discrepancies in sexual desire between partners. For example, in a study of 36 lesbian and 33 heterosexual women, the majority of both lesbian (66%) and heterosexual (75%) participants reported desire discrepancies in their relationships (Matthews, Tartaro, & Hughes, 2003). Moreover, although men generally report higher sexual desire than women (see review by Baumeister et al., 2001), women are not always the partner with lower desire in heterosexual couples. In fact, Davies et al. (1999) found that men and women were relatively equally split on indicating which partner reported higher sexual desire in a sample of heterosexual couples.

In one study of desire discrepancies in dating couples, Mark and Murray (2012) found that larger desire differences between partners were associated with lower levels of sexual satisfaction for women (but not men) after controlling for relationship satisfaction and were associated with lower relationship satisfaction for men (but not women) after controlling for sexual satisfaction. Both perceived and actual desire discrepancies may influence women's relationship satisfaction; for men, perceived discrepancies affected relationship satisfaction, and this association was fully mediated by sexual satisfaction (Davies et al., 1999). Davies et al. (1999) also investigated whether these effects are due to similarity versus dissimilarity in partners' levels of desire or whether a specific pattern is important in terms of which partner is higher or lower in desire. Couples were categorized into three groups: women with lower desire than their partner, women with similar desire to their partner, and women with higher desire than their partner. Women with lower desire were significantly less satisfied than women in the other two groups, suggesting that the nature of the desire discrepancy is important for relational outcomes.

In a sample of 1,072 women in same-sex relationships, Bridges and Horne (2007) made an important distinction between problematic and nonproblematic desire discrepancies. When asking women about desire discrepancies in their relationship, they asked them to indicate whether they saw these discrepancies as problematic for their relationships. Women who reported that a desire discrepancy with their partner was problematic in their relationship had sex less frequently and felt less sexually satisfied than women who reported a nonproblematic desire discrepancy or no discrepancy with their partner. Therefore, a desire discrepancy may not necessarily be problematic in and of itself, but only to the extent that one or both members of the couple view it as problematic (see Chapter 20, this volume). Future research is needed to determine the extent to which desire discrepancies are perceived as problematic in heterosexual and gay male couples as well.

Buffering Against Declines in Sexual Desire

Although, on average, sexual desire tends to decline over time in long-term partnerships, research evidence has also suggested that sexual desire does not inevitably wane over the course of a relationship. From their review of the literature, Acevedo and Aron (2009) concluded that although the obsessive element of passionate love decreases over time, the romantic elements—including strong sexual desire—can be maintained in long-term relationships. Couples in long-term marriages report that sexual activity remains an important component of the relationship, albeit not as prominent as during the earlier stages of the relationship (Hinchliff & Gott, 2004).

Researchers have begun to investigate factors that promote the maintenance of desire in relationships. One line of research in particular has drawn on approach–avoidance theories of social motivation (see Gable & Impett, 2012, for a review). In the domain of sexuality, approach goals for sex represent desires to pursue positive outcomes such as one's own sexual pleasure, a partner's pleasure, or increased intimacy in the relationship (Cooper, Shapiro, & Powers, 1998). Avoidance goals, in contrast, represent desires to avert negative outcomes such as guilt associated with turning a partner down or increased conflict in the relationship. Research has shown that individuals who engage in sex for approach goals report increased desire during daily sexual interactions in their relationships and are more likely to sustain high levels of sexual desire for a partner over time, both in young dating couples (Impett, Strachman, et al., 2008) and in long-term cohabiting and married couples (Muise, Impett, Kogan, & Desmarais, 2012). One person's approach sexual goals are also associated with the partner's daily experiences, such that on days when one partner has sex to pursue approach goals, the other partner experiences more positive emotions, including feeling more loved by and affectionate toward their partner (Muise, Desmarais, Impett, & Milhausen, 2011). Moreover, engaging in novel activities with a partner creates opportunities for self-expansion and contributes to increased relationship satisfaction and less boredom in relationships (McKenna, 1989; McNeal & Aron, 1995). In this research, the link between exciting activities and increased satisfaction was stronger for couples who had been together longer, suggesting that self-expanding opportunities can help prevent against typical declines in passion in long-term couples.

Recent research using daily experience methods has suggested that sexual desire is responsive to changes in emotions and relationship quality within individuals and across partners. For example, in a 14-day daily experience study of college students in dating relationships, sexual desire was higher on days when people reported experiencing more frequent positive events and was lower on days with more frequent negative events (Impett, Strachman, et al., 2008). However, people who pursued sex for approach goals maintained high sexual desire even on days that would ordinarily be the most threatening to couples, such when they had disagreements with a partner. The link between approach goals and sexual desire in these studies was stronger for women than for men, consistent with research documenting that women's desire may be more fluid or responsive to situational cues than men's desire (Baumeister, 2000; Diamond, 2008). In a 56-day daily diary study, Ridley et al. (2006) documented considerable variation in patterns of desire in a sample of married couples and found that people's emotions and feelings about the relationship influenced their own and their partner's sexual desire. Specifically, on days when one partner experienced more positive emotions, both partners reported greater desire, and on days when one partner experienced more negative emotions, both partners experienced lower desire. Feelings of closeness and of equality between partners strengthened the link between positive emotions and desire, and on days when wives felt closer and more equal to their partners, the link between their husband's positive emotions and their own desire was strengthened (see Chapter 2, this volume). These findings highlight the utility of using dyadic daily experience methods to understand how the daily context of romantic relationships either enhances or detracts from sexual desire.

SEXUAL SATISFACTION

Whereas sexual desire provides the motivation or impetus for engaging in sexual activity, sexual satisfaction represents the extent to which people are satisfied or happy with their sexual experiences. Sexual satisfaction contributes to the quality of ongoing romantic relationships and to overall health and well-being (see Chapters 11 and 21, this volume). People who are the most satisfied with their sex lives are also the most satisfied with their relationships, and this is true for both dating and married couples (Brezsnyak & Whisman, 2004; Regan, 2000; Sprecher, 2002). In a multinational study of individuals from 29 countries, the individuals who were the most sexually satisfied were also the happiest with their lives in general (Laumann et al., 2006). A nationally representative survey revealed that the overwhelming majority of U.S. residents are extremely or very pleased with the physical (87%) and emotional (85%) aspects of their sex lives (Laumann & Michael, 2001). In this section, we discuss the well-documented association between sexual and relationship satisfaction, with a focus on exchange perspectives, and provide an overview of several established correlates and predictors of sexual satisfaction in relationships.

Sexual Satisfaction and Relationship Satisfaction

In dating and married couples across the life span, sexual and relationship satisfaction are closely linked (Byers, 2005; Sprecher, 2002). In a study of university students in dating relationships, changes in sexual satisfaction were positively associated with changes in relationship satisfaction, love, and commitment over 4 years (Sprecher, 2002). In a study that assessed sexual and relationship satisfaction over an 18-month period, changes in sexual and relational satisfaction were not directional but synchronous, and this finding was partly explained by the quality of communication in the relationship (Byers, 2005).

Much of the research on sexual satisfaction in relationships is grounded in exchange perspectives. Exchange perspectives consider such factors as the balance between rewards and costs, perceptions of equity and equality in relationships, and comparisons between what people expect and what they actually experience in their relationships (see review by Byers & Wang, 2004; see also Chapter 11, this volume). This research has shown that people tend to be most sexually satisfied when they experience high sexual rewards (e.g., feeling closer to a partner), experience fewer sexual costs (e.g., engaging in sexual activities that they do not enjoy), and perceive that both partners are relatively equal in sexual rewards and costs (Lawrance & Byers, 1995). Women are more likely than men to report sexual rewards that are focused on the partner or the relationship (e.g., how their partner treats them when they have sex) and to report sexual costs that focus on physical aspects of the sexual encounter (e.g., how easily they reach orgasm; Lawrance & Byers, 1995). In a sample of married couples, partners who perceived equitable treatment in their relationship were more sexually satisfied than partners who were either overbenefited or underbenefited, although overbenefited partners were more sexually satisfied than those who felt underbenefited (Hatfield, Greenberger, Traupmann, & Lambert, 1982). Finally, people who evaluate their rewards and costs more favorably than their expectations of how rewarding a sexual relationship should be are more sexually satisfied (see review by Byers & Wang, 2004).

Using the interpersonal exchange model of sexual satisfaction, Lawrance and Byers (1995) have shown that nonsexual aspects of a relationship are associated with sexual satisfaction. For example, in both dating and married couples, relationship satisfaction and its correlates (e.g., unresolved conflicts) are associated with sexual satisfaction (see review by Byers & Wang, 2004). General self-disclosure as well as disclosure of specific sexual likes and dislikes contribute to perceptions of rewards and costs in a relationship and therefore influence levels of sexual satisfaction (Byers & Demmons, 1999). Sexual self-disclosure is one factor that helps to maintain sexual satisfaction in long-term relationships (MacNeil & Byers, 2009).

Although sexual and relationship satisfaction are often tightly linked, research has also shown that one can occur without the other. Apt, Hurtbert, Pierce, and White (1996) used cluster analysis to identify distinct profiles of married women who varied in their sexual and relationship satisfaction. Whereas the most sexually satisfied women experienced the highest levels of relationship satisfaction and the most sexually dissatisfied women experienced the lowest levels, two of the groups evidenced clear discrepancies between their levels of sexual and relationship satisfaction. Some women reported being satisfied with their sex lives, but not with their relationship, whereas others reported relationship satisfaction without sexual satisfaction. As such, levels of relationship satisfaction are not sufficient to account for the experience of sexual satisfaction in all individuals. Nevertheless, research has shown that couples who enjoy positive, satisfying sexual relationships have more stable relationships than couples who are less sexually satisfied or who report sexual problems (e.g., Edwards & Booth, 1994; Sprecher, 2002). Future research should explore how the association between sexual satisfaction and relationship stability changes over time as intimate relationships progress through different stages and transitions.

Sexual Activity and Sexual Satisfaction

Although sexual satisfaction is not synonymous with sexual frequency, they are often linked. Both men and women report greater sexual satisfaction when their frequency of engaging in sex is high (e.g., Laumann et al., 1994), and this association has also been documented in non-Western countries such as China (Cheung et al., 2008) and Iran (Rahmani, Khoei, & Gholi, 2009). In fact, Norwegian couples indicated that having too little sex was the primary reason for reporting sexual dissatisfaction (Træen, 2010). Sexual frequency and sexual satisfaction are also positively correlated in samples of gay and lesbian individuals (Blumstein & Schwartz, 1983). This association is likely bidirectional, with satisfied couples pursuing sex more frequently and frequent sex leading to increases in sexual satisfaction (McNulty & Fisher, 2008). In a recent study of heterosexual couples in midlife and older adulthood conducted in five countries (Heiman, Long, Smith, Fisher, & Sand, 2011), affectionate behaviors such as kissing, cuddling, and caressing were associated with increased sexual satisfaction for both men and women. Contrary to common gender stereotypes, these associations were strongest for men. These behaviors were also significant predictors of men's (but not women's) general relationship satisfaction. Using data from the China Health and Family Life Survey, Parish, Luo, Stolzenberg, et al. (2007) found that knowledge of sexuality and more permissive sexual attitudes predicted greater sexual satisfaction in a sample of married and dating Chinese individuals living in urban areas, and this association was fully mediated by a greater variety of sexuality practices such as kissing, fondling, and oral sex. Similarly, among East Asian men living in North America, greater acculturation was associated with higher levels of sexual satisfaction, less sexual avoidance, and fewer sexual issues (Brotto, Woo, & Ryder, 2007). East Asian cultures consider sexuality a private issue, and therefore conversations about sexuality are thought to be taboo. Greater acculturation was associated with great sexual knowledge and more liberal attitudes about sex, which accounted for higher levels of sexual satisfaction and functioning.

Some studies have indicated that women report similar or higher levels of sexual satisfaction than men (Heiman et al., 2011; McNulty & Fisher, 2008). Over the course of a long-term relationship, women tend to report lower sexual satisfaction than men in the early stages of the relationship but higher sexual satisfaction later on in the relationship (Heiman et al., 2011). Sexual frequency may play a role. If men generally desire more frequent sex than women, women in heterosexual relationships may be having sex closer to their desired frequency than are their male partners. Indeed, ideal frequency is closer to actual frequency for women than for men (McNulty & Fisher, 2008). In general, physical aspects of sexual response are poor predictors of heterosexual women's sexual satisfaction; better predictors include their emotional well-being and the quality of their relationship with their partner (Bancroft, Loftus, & Long, 2003). However, in a study of middle-aged adults, sexual duration and frequency of sex and orgasm were significant predictors of sexual satisfaction for both men and women. Contrary to popular beliefs, however, physical aspects of sex were better predictors of women's satisfaction than relational factors, whereas relational aspects of sex were better predictors of men's satisfaction (Carpenter, Nathanson, & Kim, 2009). This research has suggested that the factors predicting women's satisfaction may be numerous, complex, and fluid across the life span (see Chapter 13, this volume).

Although physical sexual response (e.g., frequency of experiencing orgasm) is associated with sexual satisfaction (Laumann et al., 1994), it is important to note that sexual response is not sufficient for the experience of sexual satisfaction. Similarly, reporting a sexual issue (e.g., a problem with sexual response, sometimes termed *sexual dysfunction*) does not necessarily preclude having high sexual satisfaction, just as the absence of sexual issues does not inevitably mean that people are sexually satisfied (M. King, Holt, & Nazareth, 2007). In one study, 81% of women reported satisfaction with their sexual function, despite the fact that 70% of them reported at least one sexual problem (Ferenidou et al., 2008). In her research on optimal sexuality, Kleinplatz (2006; Kleinplatz et al., 2009) has argued that great sex has little to do with physical function but instead involves the critical factors of being present, connection, deep sexual and erotic intimacy, extraordinary communication, interpersonal risk taking and exploration, authenticity, vulnerability, and transcendence. An interesting finding was that orgasm, which is typically viewed as a standard indicator of sexual function, did not emerge in Kleinplatz's work as a key component of or even necessary to experience great sex.

Dyadic Approaches to Sexual Satisfaction

Dyadic approaches to understanding sexual satisfaction have also gained traction in recent research. In a study that validated a new scale for measuring sexual satisfaction, Stulhofer, Busko, and Brouillard (2010) found that sexual satisfaction has two main dimensions, one that is self or ego focused and reflects satisfaction with personal sensations and experiences and one that is partner or sexual activity focused and reflects satisfaction with a partner's sexual engagement. Men involved in long-term relationships in middle and later adulthood felt more satisfied with their relationships and their sex lives when they placed greater importance on their partner's reaching orgasm during sex (Heiman et al., 2011), indicating the role of the partner in individual reports of sexual satisfaction.

Exchange perspectives also demonstrate the utility of applying dyadic approaches to the study of sexual satisfaction. Men's and women's reports of their own sexual rewards and costs contribute to their partner's sexual satisfaction above and beyond their partner's own reports of rewards and costs (see review by Byers & Wang, 2004). Using the framework of the interpersonal exchange model of sexual satisfaction, Yucel and Gassanov (2010) demonstrated that sexual satisfaction in marriage was predicted by the interpersonal exchange of sexual rewards (e.g., frequency of sex, marital satisfaction) and costs (e.g., use of pornography, infidelity). Husbands and wives were more sexually satisfied when they had a partner who reported high marital satisfaction, had not experienced infidelity in the relationship, and had a partner who did not report solo use of pornography. It is important to point out that in this study, no negative impact was found when partners used pornography together, a finding that is consistent with other research that has found a positive association between viewing sexually explicit material with a partner and sexual satisfaction (Maddox, Rhoades, & Markman, 2011; see also Volume 2, Chapter 1, this handbook).

One person's feelings about a relationship contribute to both partners' experiences of relationship and sexual satisfaction. In a study of 198 couples, Bodenmann, Ledermann, and Bradbury (2007) found that people who reported higher levels of stress in their relationship, such as high levels of family responsibilities or conflict over the division of household tasks, had partners who were less sexually satisfied. In addition, when women report low levels of stress, marital satisfaction is not associated with frequency of sexual activity, and high levels of marital satisfaction buffer against declines in sexual activity during times of stress. Conversely, when men are relatively dissatisfied in their relationships, increased stress promotes sexual activity, suggesting that partners may become more sexually intimate during times of adversity (Bodenmann et al., 2007). Low levels of sexual satisfaction are associated with greater concerns with a partner's ability to provide support or commit to the relationship; however, one partner's feelings of sexual satisfaction seem to bolster the other partner's feelings of certainty about the relationship (Theiss & Nagy, 2010). One person's feelings about him- or herself can also contribute to both partners' feelings about the relationship. Women's feelings about their bodies are related to levels of sexual and relationship satisfaction (Koch, Mansfield, Thurau, & Carey, 2005; Pujols, Meston, & Seal, 2009), and among married heterosexual couples, both men and women feel more satisfied with their relationships to the extent that the woman in the relationship feels more sexually attractive (Meltzer & McNulty, 2010).

Sexual satisfaction has been conceptualized and measured in diverse ways (see review by Stulhofer et al., 2010), which partially accounts for some of the differences observed across studies. In the future, researchers would benefit from working toward a common definition that is multidimensional and considers the context in which sexual activity occurs. In addition, much of the research on sexual rewards and costs is based on individual perceptions. Given the dyadic nature of sexual satisfaction in relationships, research that assesses both partners' perceptions of sexual rewards and costs is warranted.

SEXUALITY IN SAME-SEX RELATIONSHIPS

We now turn our attention to sexuality in the context of the relationships of lesbians and gay men (see also Chapters 18 through 20, this volume). At the outset, it is important to point out that most lesbians and gay men want to have committed intimate partnerships (Bauermeister, 2012; Kaiser Family Foundation, 2001), and just as do heterosexual individuals (Laumann et al., 1994), the majority of gay men and lesbians report currently experiencing their sexuality within the context of an ongoing intimate relationship (Lever 1994, 1995). Despite the fact that most gay men and lesbians say that having legally sanctioned gay and lesbian marriages is very important to them (Kaiser Family Foundation, 2001), these relationships continue to develop within a climate of sexual prejudice (Herek, 2000). Negative social attitudes and unsupportive environments color the lives of lesbians and gay men and contribute to distinct sexual costs in intimate relationships (Maisel & Fingerhut, 2011). In one study, gay men and lesbians indicated that feelings of vulnerability and negative cultural and social attitudes detracted from their sexual relationships (Cohen, Byers, & Walsh, 2008). It will be essential for future research to investigate how living in a climate of prejudice and fear affects sexual minority couples' experiences of and feelings about their sexuality (see Chapter 6, this volume). What is known about sexuality in the relationships of sexual minority couples is primarily limited to the topics of sexual frequency, desire, and satisfaction as well as sexual exclusivity and sexual openness.

Sexual Frequency, Desire, and Satisfaction

Research comparing the frequency with which heterosexual and sexual minority couples engage in sexual activity has revealed three general trends. First, in the early stages of a relationship, gay couples tend to engage in sex more often than heterosexual and lesbian couples. For example, findings from the American Couples Study revealed that among couples who had been together for 2 years or less, two thirds of gay men reported having sex three or more times per week, compared with fewer than half of heterosexual couples and a third of lesbian couples (Blumstein & Schwartz, 1983). The relatively higher rates of engaging in sexual activity in gay couples may be influenced by a variety of factors, including men's relatively higher rates of sexual desire and comfort with sexual initiation (see reviews by Baumeister et al., 2001; Peplau, 2003).

A second trend concerns sexual frequency and desire over the course of a partnership. In heterosexual relationships, sexual frequency and desire tend to be highest in the beginning stages of relationships when partners are just getting to know each other and then decline over time (Klusmann, 2002; Michael, Gagnon, Laumann, & Kolata, 1994). This steady decline in sexual frequency is also present in gay and lesbian relationships (Blumstein & Schwartz, 1983; Christopher & Sprecher, 2000). Similar to heterosexual couples, the most sexually active gay and lesbian couples are those who have been together for 2 years or less (see review by Peplau et al., 2004).

A third pattern—but one that is highly controversial—is that lesbian couples tend to engage in sex less frequently than either heterosexual or gay male couples at different stages of relationships (Blumstein & Schwartz, 1983; Laumann et al., 1994). For example, in the American Couples study (Blumstein & Schwartz, 1983), lesbian couples engaged in sex less frequently than heterosexual or gay male couples, whether their relationships lasted less than 2 years or more than 10 years. Several recent studies, however, have not found differences in sexual frequency between women in lesbian versus heterosexual relationships (Matthews et al., 2003; Meana, Rakipi, Weeks, & Lykins, 2006). Because of these inconsistencies, some have suggested that biases in traditional conceptualizations of sexuality that equate sex with penile penetration may be at play in this research (Iasenza, 2002). Other possible explanations for possible lower sexual frequency in lesbian couples include gender socialization that encourages women to inhibit and repress sexual feelings, lower levels of sexual desire, and lower rates of sexual initiation (see review by Peplau et al., 2004; see also Chapter 20, this volume).

In addition to studying the frequency with which gay and lesbian couples engage in sex, researchers have also examined sexual satisfaction. Typically, gay and lesbian couples find their sexual relationships to be very rewarding (see review by Peplau et al., 2004). In general, research has revealed no substantial differences between heterosexual and gay and lesbian relationships in ratings of overall sexual satisfaction (Blumstein & Schwartz, 1983; Kurdek, 1991). Research has shown that lesbians tend to have orgasms more often during sexual interactions than do heterosexual women (Kinsey et al., 1953; Nichols, 2004), a finding that may stem from differences in knowledge and sexual techniques of women's partners or differences in the emotional qualities of sexual experiences. The correlates of sexual satisfaction for gay men and lesbians are similar to those found in heterosexual couples. In general, partners are more sexually satisfied to the extent that they engage in sex more frequently and are more satisfied with their relationships (Blumstein & Schwartz, 1983; Kurdek, 1991). The strength of the link between sexual and relationship satisfaction is similar in magnitude across different kinds of relationships (Holmberg & Blair, 2009). Internalized homophobia, or a gay and lesbian person's internalization of society's negative attitudes toward sexual minority individuals, is one factor that uniquely affects the sexual satisfaction of lesbians and gay men. Research with both gay men (Rosser, Metz, Bockting, & Buroker, 1997) and lesbians (Henderson, Lehavot, & Simoni, 2009) has shown that internalized homophobia detracts from both sexual and relationship satisfaction.

Sexual Exclusivity and Sexual Openness

One of the major differences between lesbian and gay male couples concerns norms and patterns of sexual exclusivity versus sexual openness in relationships (see review by Peplau et al., 2004). In lesbian relationships, monogamy tends to be the norm (Blumstein & Schwartz, 1983). For example, in a study of lesbians from Vermont who sought civil union status for their relationships, 92% of the women indicated that their relationship was sexually exclusive both in principle and in practice, and only 4% reported having sex with a person other than their partner since their relationship began (Campbell, 2002, as cited in Peplau et al., 2004).

Whereas monogamy tends to be the norm in lesbian relationships, gay male relationships are characterized by higher levels of sexual openness, perhaps a reflection of men's relatively more permissive attitudes toward casual sex (Peterson & Hyde, 2010). In the Campbell (2002, as cited in Peplau et al., 2004) study of Vermont civil unions, 83% of men characterized their relationships as sexually exclusive, and 61% of the sample reported being sexually exclusive since their relationship began. Other studies have found lower rates of sexual exclusivity among gay men (see review by Peplau et al., 2004). One consistent finding is that although many gay men begin their relationships with expectations of exclusivity, many either explicitly change their intentions or fail to live up to the standards they initially set (Blumstein & Schwartz, 1983; McWhirter & Mattison, 1984).

Because sexual exclusivity is not the norm in gay male relationships, partners tend to make agreements about the nature of their sexual relationship and their expectations for sexual behaviors that occur outside the relationship. In a large quantitative study of 566 gay couples, 45% had monogamous agreements, 47% had open agreements, and 8% reported discrepant agreements (Hoff, Beougher, Chakravarty, Darbes, & Neilands, 2010). Consistent with previous research (Blasband & Peplau, 1985; LaSala, 2004; Ramirez & Brown, 2010), couples with monogamous and open agreements reported similar levels of relationship satisfaction, suggesting that for gay couples, sexual openness does not diminish the quality of a primary partnership. In an in-depth qualitative follow-up study with 39 of these couples, Hoff and Beougher (2010) investigated the ways in which sexual agreements were negotiated. Negotiation typically involved one of three scenarios: clarifying an existing agreement or expectation, opening a monogamous agreement, or renegotiating an agreement after it had been broken. The men in this study acknowledged that having agreements to allow sex with outside partners had several benefits, including actualizing a nonheteronormative sexual identity and establishing boundaries that ultimately fostered a sense of trust and love between partners.

In sum, the picture painted of sexual minority couples is one of overwhelming similarity to heterosexual couples. Most gay and lesbian couples are quite satisfied with their sexual relationships, and relationship satisfaction and sexual satisfaction can both enhance and detract from one another. Frequency of sex and sexual desire tend to decrease over the course of time in relationships, a pattern to which no type of couple is immune. Whereas most lesbian relationships are sexually monogamous, gay male couples are more likely to be sexually open and to have explicit sexual agreements that regulate this openness. Currently, very little is known about sexuality among older lesbian and gay couples (Wierzalis, Barret, Pope, & Rankins, 2006). In addition, bisexual identity has been almost absent from the study of sexuality in the context of relationships. From in-depth interviews with bisexual men and women, researchers know that maintaining monogamous and open relationships that are satisfying and stable is possible (Edser & Shea, 2002; Gustavson, 2009). However, a survey of more than 700 people revealed that bisexual individuals experience unique challenges in finding a dating partner because they are often stigmatized as not desiring committed relationships (Andruff & Reissing, 2010). Future research that explores how bisexuality shapes couples' sexual and relational experiences is needed. In addition, lesbian, gay, and bisexual relationships may be altered as structural changes such as legal recognition continue to occur. Finally, as researchers explore diverse sexual identities, it is important to consider that sexuality exists alongside race, gender, class, and other identities. For example, M. R. Moore (2012) argued that despite the growing visibility of lesbian, gay, bisexual, and transgender sexualities, the majority of the research has been conducted with White, middle-class participants. Greater knowledge of how various identities intersect can help researchers better understand the diversity of sexual experiences. Future research is needed with more diverse samples as well as to investigate the link between sexual experiences and specific cultural norms, values, and attitudes.

SEXUALITY AND RELATIONSHIPS IN ADOLESCENCE AND EMERGING ADULTHOOD

Forming a healthy sexual identity is a key developmental task of adolescence (see review by Tolman & McClelland, 2011; see also Chapter 15, this volume). Research on adolescent sexuality is commonly organized around diminishing risks and negative outcomes (Ehrhardt, 1996), and historically very little has been known about positive dimensions of adolescents' sexual experiences, particularly those of adolescent girls. Investigations of adolescent sexuality have focused far more on tabulating the number and timing of youths' sexual behaviors than on understanding how sexuality develops in a relationship context (see review by Diamond & Savin-Williams, 2009). In this section, we consider recent research on adolescents' first sexual experiences, the varieties of sexual expression, and the pursuit of sexuality in alternative relationship contexts.

First Sexual Experiences

An individual's first sexual encounter symbolizes an important milestone or rite of passage in North America (e.g., O'Sullivan, Cheng, Harris, & Brooks-Gunn, 2007), yet most conceptualizations of first sexual experiences are quite negative. First sexual experiences are often referred to as *loss of virginity* and explored in reference to negative consequences such as risk and feelings of guilt (see reviews by Irvine, 2002; Levine, 2003). Initial sexual experiences lay an important foundation for sexual and relationship development, so it is especially important to highlight the positive aspects of these experiences. Indeed, the overwhelming majority of adolescents find their first sexual experience to be satisfying. For example, a study of more than 11,625 teens in England and Scotland showed that nearly three quarters were highly satisfied with their first sexual experience (Wight et al., 2008). Most adolescents pursue their first sexual experiences in the context of dating relationships (Manning, Longmore, & Giordano, 2000), although boys are more likely than girls to have their first sexual experiences with acquaintances or with girls whom they are "just dating" (see review by Diamond & Savin-Williams, 2009), a finding that reflects the broader gender difference in the extent to which men and women view relationships as an important motivator and context for sexuality (see review by Peplau, 2003).

Men consistently report more satisfying first sexual experiences than women (e.g., Carpenter, 2002; Wight et al., 2008). Feelings of guilt, shame, and regret about engaging in sexual activity, which are more common among women than men, are likely at play (Crockett, Bingham, Chopak, & Vicary, 1996; Higgins, Trussell, Moore, & Davidson, 2010). Nevertheless, focusing primarily on gender differences obscures the fact that many girls and women do indeed have pleasurable first sexual experiences, and many boys and men do not (Smiler, Ward, Caruthers, & Merriwether, 2005). A recent Canadian survey found that focusing on the emotional aspects of first intercourse, as opposed to physical satisfaction, reduced the gender discrepancy. Women reported less physical satisfaction than men, but equal levels of emotional satisfaction. Three quarters of both men and women reported having no regrets about first intercourse (Tsui & Nicoladis, 2004). It is important to note, however, that about half of the women reported pain at first intercourse (52%), and few reported having an orgasm (11%).

Some researchers have explored the relational factors that make first sexual experiences satisfying (Higgins et al., 2010; Smiler et al., 2005). For both men and women, relationship commitment and greater planning and intentionality predict having a better first sexual experience (Higgins et al., 2010; Smiler et al., 2005; Wight et al., 2008). The relationship context in which sexual activity occurs is also important. Several studies have shown that adolescents tend to find their first sexual experiences more satisfying when they occur in the context of healthy "steady" relationships (Donald, Lucke, Dunne, & Raphael, 1995; Weinberg, Lottes, & Shaver, 1995), although the relationship context appears to be more influential for women's than for men's sexual satisfaction. In addition, Carpenter (2002) reported that women whose first sexual experience was cunnilingus with another woman were more likely to describe the experience as physically pleasurable than women whose first experience was through sexual intercourse.

Varieties of Sexual Expression

Although most of the existing research on adolescent sexuality has focused on sexual intercourse, adolescents engage in other physically intimate behaviors such kissing, intimate touching, and oral sex more often than they have intercourse (Carver, Joyner, & Udry, 2003; Hensel, Fortenberry, & Orr, 2008). In one study, more than 80% of teens had engaged in noncoital, partnered sexual activities before age 16 (Bauserman & Davis, 1996). Several studies have shown that noncoital affectionate behaviors are positively correlated with relationship satisfaction and commitment (Rostosky, Galliher, Welsh, & Kawaguchi, 2000; Welsh, Haugen, Widman, Darling, & Grello, 2005).

Consistent with the more general focus on diminishing sexual risk taking and promoting safer sexual behavior among adolescents, much of the research on adolescent sexual behavior has focused on identifying the barriers to as well as the factors that promote consistent contraceptive and condom use (see review by Diamond & Savin-Williams, 2009). Given that condom use involves an interaction between two partners, it is essential to understand the relationship factors that promote or hinder participation in safe sex. Condom use tends to be more common with a new sexual partner and during the early weeks of relationships (Ku, Sonenstein, & Pleck, 1993; Manning et al., 2000). Research has shown that rates of condom use among adolescents tend to drop off dramatically, perhaps at less than 1 month of relationship duration (Fortenberry, Tu, Harezlak, Katz, & Orr, 2002). Condom use tends to be less likely in relationships marked by greater emotional intimacy and closeness (Hensel et al., 2008; B. Katz, Fortenberry, Zimet, Blythe, & Orr, 2000), consistent with findings in the literature on young adults (see review by Noar, Zimmerman, & Atwood, 2004).

Research with both adolescents and young adults has shown that different types of reasons for engaging in sex are associated with sexual risk-taking behaviors. For example, research by Cooper et al. (1998) has shown that having sex for enhancement reasons (e.g., to pursue physical pleasure) has been linked to an earlier age of first intercourse, more sexual partners and one-night stands, and a greater risk for acquiring sexually transmitted infections and unplanned pregnancies. Engaging in sex for intimacy reasons (e.g., to promote closeness with a partner) has also been associated with more frequent sex as well as less frequent and consistent condom use (Cooper et al., 1998; B. Katz et al., 2000). However, a study of British adolescents suggested that youths who engage in sex in pursuit of intimacy are more likely to discuss contraceptive use before first intercourse and to actually use it during their first sexual experience (Stone & Ingham, 2002), suggesting that pursuing sex for intimacy goals may enable young people to feel more comfortable discussing sexual topics at the beginning of their relationships.

Moving beyond a focus on sexual risk, some researchers have investigated links between sexual intercourse and the quality of adolescent romantic bonds. Sexual intercourse has complex links to romantic relationship quality (Fortenberry, Temkit, & Tu, 2005) and depends on such factors as the timing of intercourse and the relationship context. For example, in early adolescence engaging in sexual intercourse has been associated with being involved in poorer quality relationships characterized by lower relationship satisfaction and commitment (Welsh et al., 2005). However, engaging in sexual intercourse in a romantic relationship context later in adolescence has been associated with greater satisfaction and commitment. In early adolescence, sexual behavior may be more commonly motivated by desires to avoid losing the relationship or difficulties communicating about sexual behavior (O'Sullivan & Meyer-Bahlberg, 2003; Widman, Welsh, McNulty, & Little, 2006). As romantic relationships become more intimate, sexual behaviors may be one way in which partners express their growing commitment (Rostosky et al., 2000). In addition to age, sexual motivation has been shown to influence sexual experiences in adolescence. In a sample of girls ages 16 to 19, those who engaged in sex out of feelings of physical attraction or love were more likely than girls with lower approach goals to report that their most recent sexual experience was good, that they liked how their body felt, and that the experience made them feel closer to their partner (Impett & Tolman, 2006).

Alternative Sexual Relationships

Although the majority of adolescents and emerging adults have their first sexual experiences within the context of romantic relationships, there has been growing concern over young people engaging in alternative sexual arrangements that deviate from the conventional couple model of exclusive romantic involvement (Grello, Welsh, & Harper, 2006;

Grello, Welsh, Harper, & Dickson, 2003; Hughes, Morrison, & Asada, 2005; Manning et al., 2000; Paul & Hayes, 2002). Casual sexual relationships are no longer solely defined as a one-time sexual encounter; instead, casual sexual experiences can range from a one-time hook-up to an ongoing sexual relationship with a friend. In a focus group study, young people identified a variety of casual sex relationships, including one-night stands, one-time sexual encounters with a stranger or an acquaintance, friends-with-benefits (FWB) relationships, and the addition of sex to an existing friendship without a romantic commitment (Wentland & Reissing, 2011). In a nationally representative sample of sexually experienced adolescents ages 12 to 21, 70% to 85% reported engaging in intercourse with a casual sex partner in the previous year (Grello et al., 2006), most frequently with a friend (see also Manning, Giordano, & Longmore, 2006). In addition, FWB relationships have become common occurrences among college and university students, with 33% to 60% of undergraduate research participants reporting at least one experience of a FWB relationship (Owen & Fincham, 2011).

Although empirical work has suggested that adolescents whose first sexual experience took place in a casual rather than a romantic relationship are more likely to report depressive symptoms and delinquent behaviors (Grello et al., 2003; Monahan & Lee, 2008), these adolescents tend to report these problems both before and after the sexual experience, suggesting that casual sex is a correlate rather than a cause of adjustment problems. The associations between casual sex and poor adjustment tend to be stronger for women than for men (Grello et al., 2003, 2006), in part reflecting the influence of a double standard that stigmatizes women for engaging in casual sex (Crawford & Popp, 2003; Milhausen & Herold, 2001). Studies focusing specifically on young women have found that alternative relationships are frequently associated with shame, disappointment, regret, and sometimes sexual coercion (Caruthers, 2006; Hughes et al., 2005; Paul & Hayes, 2002). It is also important to point out that sex in the context of casual relationships has the potential to be as empowering as it might be damaging. Alternative sexual relationships may allow women in particular to break free of gender-stereotypical relationship roles. In terms of FWB relationships specifically, research has not supported the assertion that these relationships are emotionally damaging for young people (Eisenberg, Ackard, Resnick, & Neumark-Sztainer, 2009), and in fact Giordano, Manning, and Longmore (2006) suggested that these relationships may allow teens to seek sexual pleasure outside the confines of conventional relationships marked by power differentials between partners. In an in-depth qualitative study, Caruthers (2006) found that young adult women with one or two casual hook-ups did not have lower psychological or sexual well-being than did women who pursued sex within conventional dating relationships, and those young women who had periodic hook-ups were characterized by high sexual assertiveness and high sexual self-esteem.

In general, the majority of both men and women report more positive feelings about their FWB relationships such happiness, excitement, and desirability than they do negative feelings such as disappointment, confusion, or emptiness, with men being more likely than women to report positive outcomes (Owen & Fincham, 2011). University students have indicated that the main advantage of a FWB relationship is access to sex and companionship with a known and trusted friend without the commitment of a romantic relationship; however, there were also possible downsides, such as ruining the friendship or risking emotional pain if one person develops unreciprocated romantic feelings (Bisson & Levine, 2009; Weaver, MacKeigan, & MacDonald, 2011). Direct, honest communication about the nature of the relationship is thought to be one way to buffer against the negative consequences (Weaver et al., 2011), and those who worry about losing the friendship or are hoping for a committed relationship are more likely to experience negative emotions (Owen & Fincham, 2011). Nevertheless, FWB relationships have sexual health implications. Because of the established friendship, FWB relationships typically involve lower rates of condom use than other casual sex relationships, and individuals involved in FWB relationships may have additional sexual partners that are not always disclosed (VanderDrift, Lehmiller, & Kelly, 2012).

In future research, it will be important to understand the factors that account for the diversity of outcomes of pursuing different types of sexual relationships so that positive sexual development in adolescence and emerging adulthood can best be promoted. In addition, research that explores more nuanced motivations for pursuing ongoing casual sex relationships and that uses longitudinal and daily diary methods to understand how FWB relationships are managed and negotiated over time is warranted. Research on FWB relationships has also tended to rely on hypothetical scenarios or retrospective reports. Using daily experience and longitudinal methods, researchers can assess an individual's initial hopes, concerns, and expectations for the relationship, as well as aspects of his or her personality, and then track the development of sexual relationships over time. Such research could provide valuable information about who is most likely to experience positive or negative consequences of involvement in FWB relationships. Although Bisson and Levine (2009) suggested that a minority (10%) of FWB relationships develop into romantic relationships, it would be interesting to explore how the FWB arrangement affects a potential romance and the existing friendship between partners. Finally, although an extensive body of research has explored the influence of social class and race/ethnicity on sexual risk-taking behaviors in adolescence (e.g., Blum et al., 2000; Santelli, Lowry, Brener, & Robin, 2000), very little work has examined how these factors shape the development of different types of sexual relationships in adolescence, an important direction for future work.

SEXUALITY IN MIDDLE AND OLDER ADULTHOOD

Sexuality is an important component of romantic relationships throughout the life course (see Chapters 13 and 17, this volume). Although middle adulthood (typically defined as ages 45–59) and older adulthood (age 60 and older) have been associated with declines in sexual frequency, especially for women, these studies have often failed to discriminate between partnered and nonpartnered individuals (Araujo, Mohr, & McKinlay, 2004). Driven in part by the growing use of pharmaceuticals for male sexual dysfunction, much of the research on sexuality and aging reflects biological and medical perspectives that suggest that physical transformations, hormonal changes, and chronic illnesses reduce sexual activity and interest with age (Bacon et al., 2003; Corona et al., 2010; Lindau et al., 2007). The protective function of a positive partnership and reports of enhanced sexual experience in later-life relationships have largely been absent from the literature. In this section, we discuss sexual activity, sexual desire, and the association between sexual and relationship satisfaction in the context of relationships during middle and older adulthood.

Sexual Activity

Age-related changes in sexual interest and frequency can, at least partially, be accounted for by a person's relationship status—because the proportion of single individuals increases with age—and by the prevailing belief that real sex is penetrative sex. Women are more likely than men to lose their partners during older adulthood, because women tend to marry at younger ages than do men and have a longer life expectancy (Karraker, DeLamater, & Schwartz, 2011). Because the vast majority of sexual activity takes place within the context of marriage or long-term partnerships, opportunities for sexual activity tend to diminish with age, particularly for women (Gott & Hinchliff, 2003; Waite, Laumann, Das, & Philip, 2009). Couples in middle and older adulthood also report declines in sexual frequency, but these declines are only weakly predicted by age-related physical changes and the presence of illness (DeLamater & Moorman, 2007). Moreover, in a study of partnered individuals ages 57 to 85, the proportion of individuals who reported engaging in sexual intercourse in the past year declined with age, but the frequency of noncoital sexual activities such as kissing, caressing, and cuddling was not associated with age (Waite et al., 2009). Waite et al. (2009) found that partnered individuals who remained sexually active at older ages had fairly frequent sexual relations. Sexual frequency remained stable throughout the 65- to 75-year-old age range, with a modest decrease at older ages. In the oldest age bracket, 25% of individuals who had been sexually active in the past year reported engaging in intercourse at least once per week (Waite et al., 2009). This pattern reflects an age-related decrease in the proportion of couples remaining sexually active but does not suggest dramatic age-related declines in sexual frequency for all couples.

Despite these findings, physical functioning is an important factor to consider when studying sexuality and aging. Failure to meet expectations for intercourse leading to orgasm can lead to declines in sexual self-confidence, satisfaction, and, ultimately, avoidance of sexual activity (Kontula & Haavio-Mannila, 2009). The association between one's own health problems and partnered sexual activity is stronger for men than for women (Karraker et al., 2011; Kontula & Haavio-Mannila, 2009). Male health problems are overwhelmingly cited as the reason for sexual inactivity in relationships during older adulthood (Gott & Hinchliff, 2003). Despite recent advances in sexual enhancement drugs such as sildenafil (Viagra), many older adults would rather not trade the synchrony and sensual pleasures of natural aging for a medically aided return to penetrative sex (Potts, Grace, Vares, & Gavey, 2006; Vares, Potts, Gavey, & Grace, 2007). For aging couples fixated on penetrative sex, sexual frequency may decline even as desire is maintained. Consistent with reports that African American women older than age 35 display a strong preference for vaginal intercourse (Quadagno, Sly, Harrison, Eberstein, & Soler, 1998), Huang et al. (2009) found that African American women between the ages of 45 and 80 are less likely than Caucasian respondents to report weekly sexual activity despite a greater propensity to report at least moderate sexual desire. Couples who are able to move beyond the notion that intercourse is the primary or only mode of sexual expression and whose sex lives incorporate a broader repertoire of sexual behaviors seem better able to maintain or experience heightened sexual satisfaction in older adulthood (Hartmann, Philippsohn, Heiser, & Ruffer-Hesse, 2004; Hinchliff & Gott, 2008; Potts et al., 2006). For these couples, physical satisfaction with the relationship, sexual desire, and positive attitudes about sex are integral to remaining sexually active (DeLamater & Moorman, 2007).

An individual's sexual repertoire in later life is associated with his or her sexual activities and preferences across the life span. Woloski-Wruble, Oliel, Leefsma, and Hochner-Celnikier (2010) observed that current variety of sexual activity was predicted by sexual variety throughout the life course for women older than age 56, highlighting the importance of conducting longitudinal research on sexuality. These findings raise questions about the cross-sectional approach typical of aging research. If sexual activity is consistent across the life span, lower sexual activity in older age brackets may stem from cohort effects, rather than being a function of aging in and of itself. An important direction for future work will be to survey individuals who reached sexual maturity during or after the sexual revolution. Longitudinal data from this generation will be better poised to depict the sexual changes associated with aging than the cross-sectional data that are currently available.

Sexual Desire

Although research has indicated that the frequency of sexual activity often declines with age, feelings of sexual desire may be more likely to remain high. In a nationally representative U.S. study of partnered individuals in middle and older adulthood, no association was found between age and problems with sexual interest (Waite et al., 2009). Umidi, Pini, Ferrett, Vergani, and Annoni (2007) examined the impact of both aging and relationship context on sexual desire in single and married residents of Milan older than age 65. Taken together, levels of desire for sexual contact with a partner in this population were high, and gender discrepancies disappeared once singles were removed from the sample, with sexual desire reported by 91% and 89% of married men and women, respectively. In addition, ratings of the importance that people placed on affectivity and sexuality predicted levels of sexual desire. Similarly, Papaharitou et al. (2008) found that the majority of older adults in their sample who had married out of love and were still in love with their partners reported feeling sexual desire, flirting with their partner, and having regular sexual intercourse. For women, sexual desire becomes increasingly responsive to relationship factors with age.

In a sample of women ages 24 to 60, sexual desire, intimacy, and excitement declined with age and relationship duration, but mid-life and postmenopausal women exhibited increased synchrony between relationship satisfaction and sexual desire, arousal, and satisfaction (Birnbaum, Cohen, & Wertheimer, 2007). Feelings about intimacy in the relationship and behaviors such as eye contact, kissing, and caressing may become more important to sexual desire with age.

Sexual and Relationship Satisfaction

As in relationships at other stages of the life course, sexual and relationship satisfaction are associated in middle and older adulthood (DeLamater, Hyde, & Fong, 2008; Penhollow, Young, & Denny, 2009). Studies that have reported declining sexuality with age have often not distinguished between partner-specific and global measures of sexual satisfaction, which have been shown to have distinct correlates (Dundon & Rellini, 2010). Although factors such as psychological well-being and menopausal symptoms are linked to global sexual satisfaction, other factors such as relationship quality and emotional closeness to a partner are associated with partner-specific sexual satisfaction. Joint decision making on sexual matters may also contribute to sexual satisfaction for aging couples. In line with reports that Hispanic women older than age 35 are more likely than African American and Caucasian respondents to jointly decide on the timing and type of sex (Quadagno et al., 1998), Huang et al. (2009) found that Hispanic women between the ages of 45 and 80 enjoy greater sexual satisfaction than Caucasian respondents. In contrast to the idea that relational factors are more important to women's sexuality than to men's, partnered men in middle and late adulthood exhibit greater concordance between their relationship and sexual satisfaction than partnered women in the same age group (Heiman et al., 2011; Penhollow et al., 2009). In the same way, the proportion of partnered men reporting that they would not have sex without love increases in older age brackets while remaining stable for women (Waite et al., 2009). Finally, the importance of having a loving relationship with one's current partner is more closely tied to men's sexual satisfaction than to women's in the 40- to 59-year-old age range (Carpenter et al., 2009).

The shifting dynamics of sexual and relationship factors as couples age also provide the potential for improvements in sexuality in later life. Hartmann et al. (2004) examined the relation between age and sexuality for women across the life span and observed a higher correspondence between desired and actual frequencies of sexual activity for women older than age 45 than for younger women. In a study of more than 1,000 couples in the United States, Japan, Brazil, Germany, and Spain, Heiman et al. (2011) found that men's relationship happiness increased with relationship duration, and men in the 55- to 59-year-old age range were more likely to report experiencing heightened physical and emotional satisfaction with their sexual relationships than their younger counterparts. Similarly, men who reported more frequent kissing, hugging, touching, and caressing, as well as those who placed a premium on partner orgasm, expressed greater relationship happiness. For women, relationship duration was more closely tied to sexual satisfaction than to relationship satisfaction. Women in longer term relationships (i.e., those lasting 25–50 years) reported experiencing greater sexual satisfaction than men in long-term relationships as well as greater sexual satisfaction than women in relationships of 10 years or less (Heiman et al., 2011). Consistent with these findings, Carpenter et al. (2009) found that women ages 40 to 59 preferred longer sexual encounters than same-aged men and exhibited a greater link between bodily aspects of the sexual relationship (such as orgasm regularity, sexual frequency, and duration of the sexual encounter) and sexual satisfaction. Research framing late life as a period with potential for sexual growth and enhancement provides a unique counterpoint to the claim that physical aging detracts from partnered sexual activity.

In sum, although research on sexuality and relationship factors in middle and older adulthood has been limited, the emerging picture of the aging couple is not one of certain asexuality. Instead, this research has highlighted the protective effects of being involved in a positive, healthy partnership during a life stage when erotic and intimate aspects of relationship functioning become more deeply intertwined. Age-dependent biological changes that take place within the context of a close relationship and that are accompanied by an inclusive shift in sexual meaning-making represent opportunities for sexual growth and discovery. As survey data from older adults who were socialized during or after the "swinging '60s" become available, empirical evidence for sexual expansion during this life stage may be obtained.

DARK SIDE OF SEXUALITY

Romantic relationships can include sexual experiences that are positive, emotionally rewarding, and highly pleasurable at all stages of life, but they can also include negative emotions and risks of emotional and physical pain. In this section, we discuss sexual aggression, extradyadic sex (EDS), and sexual jealousy in the context of ongoing intimate relationships.

Sexual Aggression

In the same way that intimacy enhances the positive qualities of sex, the relational context may also influence the physical and psychological consequences of unwanted sexual behavior and other forms of sexual aggression (see Chapter 12, this volume). Still considered less serious and given less attention than nonpartnered assault, sexual aggression at the hands of an intimate partner is especially traumatic (Kirkwood & Cecil, 2001; Plichta & Falik, 2001; Temple, Weston, Rodriquez, & Marshall, 2007). It is also more prevalent than is widely believed, with 21% to 30% of undergraduates and 49% of newlyweds reporting sexual coercion in their current relationship (Brousseau et al., 2011; J. Katz & Myhr, 2008; Panuzio & DiLillo, 2010). Among long-term married couples, the prevalence of sexually aggressive behaviors is as high as 50% (Monson, Langhinrichsen-Rohling, & Taft, 2009). In heterosexual relationships, women are more commonly victimized than men (Brousseau et al., 2011), but Waldner-Haugrad and Gratch (1997) found no such gender differences in gay and lesbian relationships, with 52% of all individuals reporting at least one lifetime incident of sexual coercion. Rates are also affected by racial and ethnic differences, but individuals are often collapsed into White and non-White groups, concealing between-groups variation. Tjaden and Thoennes (2000) partitioned subjects into separate minority groups and found that data showing no significant difference between White and non-White subjects revealed higher rates of intimate partner rape for American Indian/Alaska Native individuals and lower rates for Asian/Pacific Islanders. Other researchers have reported exceptionally high rates of sexual aggression in African American couples. In a study by Ramisetty-Mikler, Caetano, and McGrath (2007), Black couples reported higher rates of both male- and female-perpetrated sexual aggression than White and Hispanic couples. Although Ramisetty-Mikler et al. speculated that greater bidirectional violence among Black couples may be an artifact of Black women's lower tolerance for partner violence because of their historical role as breadwinners and resultant willingness to defend themselves, it is difficult to ascertain whether cultural differences, willingness to report, or actual victimization are the cause of racial differences in sexual aggression.

Making broad interpretations of the existing data and comparing findings across studies is difficult because of inconsistencies in the ways in which sexual aggression is operationalized and measured. For instance, lower prevalence rates are found when aggression is narrowly conceptualized as the use of physical force (Russell, 1990). Verbal coercion has been neglected by sexual aggression researchers, but exerting social or emotional pressure on one's partner to obtain sex is just as reflective of wider relational problems as the use of physical force (J. Katz & Myhr, 2008). Moreover, people report lower rates of sexual victimization when polled about their current relationship than when they are asked about past relationships (Brousseau et al., 2011), and higher rates of marital rape are obtained when semistructured interviews rather than standard survey methods are used (Russell, 1990), suggesting that the types of methods that researchers use influence comfort with disclosing sensitive information about sexual experiences (see Chapter 4, this volume).

Sexual aggression within intimate relationships leads to greater and unique physical and psychological damage, compared with when the same acts are perpetrated by a stranger or acquaintance. First, revictimization is a hallmark of intimate partner sexual aggression. Compared with women raped by a stranger, victims of marital rape suffer greater proximity to the abuser and are more likely to sustain multiple sexual assaults (Mahoney, 1999). Second, the overlap between sexual, physical, and psychological aggression is greater when an intimate partner is the offender. For instance, people who suffer a combination of physical and sexual violence at the hands of an intimate partner tend to experience more unwanted sexual activity, more psychological aggression, and more severe partner abuse than victims of physical or sexual violence alone (J. Katz, Moore, & May, 2008). Finally, given the ties between revictimization, covictimization, and sexual aggression within intimate relationships, the psychological harm incurred from intimate partner aggression is especially severe. Across studies, women victimized by a partner are more likely to be diagnosed with depression, anxiety, and posttraumatic stress disorder than victims of nonintimate sexual aggression (Plichta & Falik, 2001; Temple et al., 2007).

The physical and psychological injuries associated with intimate partner sexual aggression have prompted relationship researchers to clarify the factors that place couples at risk for this behavior. J. Katz and Myhr (2008) identified three important correlates of sexual aggression in undergraduate dating relationships, including emotional abuse, monitoring behaviors, and general psychological aggression. Moreover, destructive verbal conflict patterns such as negative conflict engagement, withdrawal during conflict, and infrequent positive problem solving were associated with increased sexual aggression. Among married couples, correlates of unwanted sexual activity include the victim's belief that sex is a duty as well as female sexual dysfunction variables such as vaginal dryness, sexual pain, low arousal, and inorgasmia (Parish, Luo, Laumann, Kew, & Yu, 2007). In addition, relationship characteristics such as physical violence, inequity, an absence of daily intimacy and foreplay, and insensitivity to female sexual needs are associated with marital sexual aggression. In intimate relationships in which the man perceives himself to be of equal or greater desirability than his partner, men's perceptions of a relational threat, such as their partner's sexual infidelity, predict greater rates of sexual coercion. Finally, DeMaris (1997) examined whether the elevated sexual activity that is typical of violent marriages can be attributed to mutual hypersexuality or sexual extortion. Only husbands' violence predicted more frequent marital sex, lending support to the sexual extortion hypothesis.

The effects of intimate sexual aggression on sexual and relationship functioning are far reaching. Verbal sexual coercion in dating relationships is associated with lower levels of relationship satisfaction, sexual satisfaction, and sexual desire (J. Katz & Myrh, 2008). In a longitudinal study of newlywed couples, Panuzio and DiLillo (2010) found that higher rates of sexual coercion were associated with lower marital satisfaction 1 and 2 years later, regardless of the aggressor's gender. Consistent with these findings, victims of marital rape report more difficulties reaching orgasm and greater fear of sexuality than victims of marital violence alone (Shields, Resick, & Hanneke, 1990). In addition to sexual functioning problems, 88% of women who have been stalked and forced to have sex by an intimate partner report diminished sexual enjoyment, compared with 48% of women who have experienced a stalking-only relationship (Logan, Cole, & Shannon, 2007).

Just as many aspects of intimate relationships change with increased relationship duration and commitment, so too does sexual aggression. J. Katz and Myhr (2008) found that with increasing relationship duration, there is a shift from pestering dating partners for sex to verbal sexual coercion. In the same way, after sexual access has been established in a relationship, many men transition from using positive pressure tactics such as professing affection, paying their partner compliments, and promising to move the relationship forward to negative tactics such as threatening to leave the relationship and evoking feelings of guilt and obligation (Livingston, Buddie, Testa, & VanZile-Tamsen, 2004). Basile (2002) determined that although 10% of women report experiencing intimate partner rape in their lifetime, this number jumps to 13% when only married respondents are considered. Moreover, prevalence rates for all types of sexual coercion are greater for women victimized by a spouse than by another type of intimate partner. These findings suggest that, if anything, increased commitment and relationship duration amplify the constraints on leaving and promote rather than buffer partners from perpetrating or being the victims of sexual aggression.

In sum, victimization by an intimate partner constitutes an extraordinary breach of trust and security. This aspect of intimate partner sexual aggression, coupled with greater opportunities for revictimization and covictimization, amplifies the sexual, physical, and psychological symptoms of sexual coercion. Future studies should seek to dispel myths that intimate partner sexual aggression is not real rape and to identify how sexual coercion changes over the course of ongoing intimate relationships.

Extradyadic Sex

The central role of sex in ongoing relationships is underscored by the impact of nonconsensual extra dyadic sex (EDS) or infidelity on intimate relationships. A major source of relationship distress and dissolution, EDS is the most common antecedent of divorce and is frequently accompanied by depression and decrements in general psychological health for betrayed partners (Amato & Previti, 2003; Cano & O'Leary, 2000). Despite expectations for sexual exclusivity in more than 94% of ongoing relationships, 1% to 17% of cohabiting and married individuals report at least one lifetime incident of EDS, with prevalence rates ranging from 2% to 5% in any given year (Træen & Martinussen, 2008; Treas & Giesen, 2000; Whisman, Gordon, & Chatav, 2007; Whisman & Snyder, 2007). In undergraduate populations, EDS rates range from 19% to 21%, with as many as 51% of individuals reporting infidelity when the definition is expanded to encompass both sexual and emotional involvement with an extrapair partner (Brand, Markey, Mills, & Hodges, 2007; Mark, Janssen, & Milhausen, 2011). The disconnect between expectations for sexual exclusivity and the reality of EDS has been the focus of much research, but findings have varied across studies, and conclusions have been hampered by inconsistent and ambiguous definitions of extradyadic involvement. In the same way, the air of secrecy, guilt, and shame surrounding EDS makes it imperative to protect participants' anonymity. As a result, retrospective, cross-sectional designs that conflate the causes and consequences of EDS have dominated the literature, and longitudinal studies that provide detailed data on EDS but ensure anonymity are scarce.

Research undertaken to identify the factors that compel certain individuals to violate couple scripts for sexual exclusivity has focused on uncovering the demographic and personal characteristics that predispose individuals to engage in EDS as well as more proximal factors that provide individuals with direct incentives and opportunities for engaging in EDS. In terms of demographic and personal factors, research has shown that individuals who are low in religiosity, are more educated, and have higher income are relatively more likely than others to engage in EDS (Atkins, Baucom, & Jacobson, 2001). The influence of other factors such as age and relationship duration on EDS is less straightforward (DeMaris, 2009; Treas & Giesen, 2000). Findings on race and EDS are mixed, with some researchers reporting higher rates of EDS for African Americans than for individuals of other racial and ethnic groups (Treas & Giesen, 2000) and others reporting no between-race differences (Choi, Catania, & Dolcini, 1994). Wiederman's (1997) data suggested that the incidence of EDS in the past year is highest for African Americans, but that lifetime EDS does not differ between racial groups. One relatively consistent finding is that men have a greater desire to engage in EDS and hold more permissive attitudes toward EDS than women. Consistent with these gender differences in attitudes, some research has pointed to higher prevalence rates of EDS for men than for women (Atkins et al., 2001). Other studies have suggested that gender differences in the prevalence of EDS are shrinking or nonexistent, especially in younger cohorts (Brand et al., 2007; Mark et al., 2011). To address these inconsistencies, Treas and Giesen (2000) found that sex differences in EDS among married and cohabiting individuals were substantially reduced after accounting for sexual interest, sexual values, relationship satisfaction, and network ties to one's partner. These findings indicate that sex differences in EDS may be the product of attitudinal and relationship variables rather than reflecting the influence of gender per se.

In addition to demographic and personal characteristics, specific interpersonal circumstances seem to make EDS more likely. Low marital quality and female sexual unavailability during pregnancy represent proximal incentives for interested individuals to engage in EDS (DeMaris, 2009; Whisman et al., 2007). In addition, high-quality alternatives and time away from one's primary partner serve as proximal opportunities for EDS (Atkins et al., 2005; DeWall et al., 2011). DeMaris (2009) investigated the association between EDS and proximal and distal factors in a 20-year longitudinal study of married and cohabiting individuals. Although racial minority status, low religiosity, and marital duration predicted engaging in EDS, marital quality variables were uniquely associated with EDS and fully mediated the race–EDS link. Others have speculated that racial differences in EDS arise from ethnic differences in the gender ratio, with the shortage of single men in the Black community affording married men more opportunities to engage in EDS with single Black women (Wiederman, 1997). The intervening role of proximal variables in the link between intrapersonal characteristics and EDS was further clarified in three studies. In a study by Whisman et al. (2007), marital dissatisfaction accounted for the effects of low self-esteem on EDS. In a study by DeWall et al. (2011), avoidantly attached individuals were more likely to engage in EDS because of lower levels of commitment to their romantic relationships. Finally, in a study by DeMaris (2009), whereas EDS was not associated with relationship satisfaction, it was associated with spousal violence, proneness to divorce, marital instability, and time spent together, suggesting that specific relationship factors may contribute to EDS more than does the general quality of intimate relationships.

Research has also examined people's self-reported motivations for engaging in EDS. Individuals tend to emphasize relationship dissatisfaction as a major reason for their extradyadic involvement. In a study of undergraduates by Brand et al. (2007), boredom and dissatisfaction with a primary relationship, as well as being made to feel attractive by an extrapair individual, were among the most frequently reported reasons for pursuing EDS. Dissatisfaction with the primary relationship is cited more often by women than by men, suggesting that although prevalence rates do not differ by gender, motivations for engaging in EDS do (Blow & Hartnett, 2005; Brand et al., 2007). Among married and cohabiting men, EDS has been linked to the tendency to engage in regretful sexual behavior during negative emotional states, a high propensity for sexual excitation, high sexual inhibition stemming from fears of performance failure, and low regard for the consequences of EDS (Mark et al., 2011). The same sexual inhibition factors predict female EDS, along with low relationship happiness and low sexual compatibility (Mark et al., 2011). These findings point to the relatively larger role of relationship variables and mate-switching intentions in female than in male EDS.

Differences in EDS motivations are implicated in the outcome-related discrepancies of male- versus female-perpetrated EDS. Women who engage in EDS are more likely to reveal their extrapair involvement to their primary partner, initiate a break-up after EDS, and begin seeing their extrapair partner after relationship termination (Brand et al., 2007). Researchers have suggested that this gender difference signals a link between EDS attributions, forgiveness, and relationship dissolution. In a study by Hall and Fincham (2006), forgiveness after EDS predicted couple reconciliation, and attributions for EDS that were external, specific, and unstable led to forgiveness. Gender differences in attributions for EDS may detract from partner forgiveness after female EDS (Meston & Buss, 2007). As a result, relationship dissolution may be more likely in the case of female EDS resulting from a woman's possible intentions to switch mates and less forgiveness on the part of male partners. Future research should examine the combined effect of self-reported motivations for EDS and partner forgiveness on relationship dissolution.

Although relationship dissolution is the most common outcome of EDS, some couples persevere in the face of discovery of EDS. Reports of relationship improvement are rare, but enhanced marital closeness, increased assertiveness and self-care, a greater appreciation for good marital communication, and a higher value placed on family have been observed after infidelity (Charny & Parnass, 1995;

Olson, Russell, Higgins-Kessler, & Miller, 2002). By the same token, although couples attending therapy for infidelity problems report less time together, less enjoyment of time spent together, and more dishonesty, narcissism, and relationship instability at the outset of therapy, their relationship change is comparable to or faster than that of couples attending therapy for other reasons (Atkins, Eldridge, Baucom, & Christensen, 2005; Atkins, Yi, Baucom, & Andrew, 2005).

Research on long-term EDS is scarce, but the marital dynamic in cultures that tacitly condone male EDS provides insight into the effects of unaddressed infidelity on ongoing relationships. K. Moore (2010) gathered qualitative data on couple dynamics in Japanese marriages. Individuals older than age 60 reported sexless, siblinglike relationships, and individuals often attributed current marital celibacy to husband infidelity beginning early on in the relationship. Typically, this infidelity was not addressed. What followed was a breakdown in couple communication, growing distance between partners, female sexual unavailability, and the eventual loss of sexual ways of relating within the couple. These findings are consistent with reports that women react to partner EDS by distancing themselves from the marital relationship, whereas men more often respond with violence (Jankowiak, Nell, & Buckmaster, 2002).

Sexual Jealousy

Feelings of jealousy are one response to a perceived relationship threat, such as a partner's extradyadic behavior. Although jealousy can be seen as a sign of love and intent to preserve an important relationship (Bringle & Buunk, 1991), it is more often described as a negative emotion, one that has detrimental consequences for romantic relationships. In general, jealousy is associated with relational dissatisfaction and instability (Andersen, Eloy, Guerrero, & Spitzberg, 1995) as well as aggression toward a romantic partner (DeSteno, Valdesolo, & Bartlett, 2006).

An abundance of evidence has suggested that men are more likely than women to experience jealousy in response to sexual infidelity and that women are more likely than men to experience jealousy in response to emotional infidelity, findings that have been attributed to men's greater concern about parental certainty and women's greater concern about loss of resources (e.g., Buss, 2000; Buss, Larsen, Westen, & Semmelroth, 1992). One common criticism of these findings is that they are based on hypothetical forced-choice scenarios (DeSteno, 2010). When they are not forced to choose between emotional and sexual infidelity, men and women alike tend to rate both types of infidelity as jealousy provoking (DeSteno, Bartlett, Braverman, & Salovey, 2002; Lishner, Nguyen, Stocks, & Zillmer, 2008), suggesting that these two types of infidelity overlap and that both can be distressing for men and women. Research has also focused on gender differences in response to actual infidelity in romantic relationships. In one study (Kuhle, 2011), researchers analyzed 51 episodes of *Cheaters,* a reality show that captures actual infidelity experiences, and found that men were more likely than women to inquire about the sexual nature of the infidelity, such as asking their partners, "Did you have sex?" whereas women were more likely than men to inquire about the emotional nature of the infidelity, such as asking their partners, "Are you in love?"

A great degree of variability exists in the extent to which individuals experience jealousy in relationships and worry about relational threats (Pfeiffer & Wong, 1989). Miller and Maner (2009) found that gender differences in responses to sexual versus emotional infidelity were substantially more pronounced in individuals who were higher in chronic jealousy. Several individual differences also predict the experience of jealousy. Both men and women who have higher sex drives experience more sexual jealousy, and this association is stronger for men than for women (Burchell & Ward, 2011). Previous experience with sexual infidelity and higher levels of avoidant attachment predict increased sexual jealousy for men (Burchell & Ward, 2011). In general, avoidantly attached people are more distressed by sexual infidelities because of their discomfort with emotional closeness (Levy, Kelly, & Jack, 2006). In contrast, men and women who are higher in anxious attachment report higher levels of emotional jealousy (Knobloch, Solomon, & Cruz, 2001). In two studies of heterosexual couples, both self and partner personality characteristics were associated with jealousy. Highly neurotic and less agreeable individuals reported experiencing more jealousy, and those who were high in conscientiousness and who had conscientious partners worried less about a partner's infidelity but reacted more negatively to a partner's betrayal when it did occur (Dijkstra & Barelds, 2008).

In a study of individuals in dating and marital relationships, expression of jealousy was a stronger predictor of relationship satisfaction than jealousy experience. Partners who were able to express their feelings without placing blame on the partner were more satisfied than those who used accusatory, argumentative statements or who actively distanced from a partner (Andersen et al., 1995). Behavioral responses to jealousy can involve direct confrontations or more indirect behaviors such as ignoring one's partner (Guerrero, Andersen, Jorgensen, & Spitzberg, 1995) and engaging in partner surveillance or "snooping" behaviors. Guerrero and Afifi (1999) found that more intense and frequent experiences of jealousy predicted more partner surveillance (e.g., snooping or keeping close tabs on a partner). Among newlywed couples, a person was most likely to snoop if their partner was reluctant to share information with them and discuss their thoughts and feelings, and this was especially true for people who had low trust in their partners (Vinkers, Finkenauer, & Hawk, 2011). Because of the importance of jealousy responses for relationship quality, additional dyadic research on how couples manage jealousy in their relationships and qualitative research on how couples experience jealousy is warranted.

CONCLUSION

It is an exciting time for research on the psychology of sexuality and relationships, and much progress in these two fields of inquiry has been made. However, despite the growth of research in each of these topic areas as well as their wide appeal, we suggest that not enough of this work focuses on topics and questions truly at the intersection of the study of sexuality and relationships. With great eagerness, we look forward to future research on sexuality that considers the various contexts in which relationships are pursued and, similarly, research on close relationships that considers the central role of sexuality in the development and maintenance of intimate bonds.

A couple of recent societal trends are changing the ways in which sexuality is pursued and negotiated across relational contexts and, as such, lead to several critical directions for future research. First, the use of Internet technology and social media has outpaced the research on the influence of new media on relationships and sexuality (see Volume 2, Chapter 3, this handbook). Greater connectivity presents new opportunities such as connecting couples across geographical distance and providing new forums for sexual expression. A recent study documented that individuals who reported engaging in cybersex were more likely to engage in partnered online sexual activities than in online sexual activities without a partner (Shaughnessy, Byers, & Thornton, 2011), suggesting that Internet technology may create new opportunities for sexual exploration in relationships. In addition, online social networks can connect sexual minority youths and those living in rural areas and may provide an additional forum for coming out, social support, and connection (Gray, 2009; see Chapter 19, this volume). New media may also present new challenges for relationships, such as greater availability of alternate partners and access to relationship-relevant information (Muise, Christofides, & Desmarais, 2009), which may have implications for relationship satisfaction and stability. An important future direction will be to learn about the ways in which couples use the Internet and social media to benefit their sexual relationships and how they manage the new challenges that technology may bring.

A second societal change that has important implications for research on the intersection of sexuality and relationships concerns the growing racial and ethnic diversity in North American society. Although relationships in both adolescence and adulthood tend to be racially homogamous (Blackwell & Lichter, 2004), younger adults are most likely to participate in relationships that cross racial lines (Joyner & Kao, 2005), suggesting that the prevalence of multiracial and multiethnic couples will increase with time. Interracial sexual relationships that are formed in adolescence and young adulthood may influence the subsequent choice of partners later in life, as research has shown that women whose first sexual experience was with a partner of a different race are significantly more likely to be in interracial relationships as adults (R. B. King & Bratter, 2007). Moreover, relationship and sexual practices undoubtedly vary in important ways among racial and ethnic minorities and across the social class spectrum, and these diverse populations and patterns of intimacy present unique opportunities for new research that crosses traditional disciplinary boundaries.

Finally, the nature and process of forming intimate relationships have changed in important ways over the past several decades (see review by Sassler, 2010). The delay of marriage, relationship dissolution, and high divorce rates have all extended the amount of time that adults spend outside of formal marriage. In addition, the legal recognition of same-sex marriages and unions, as well as increased acceptance and visibility of alternative types of relationships such as polyamorous relationships (Barker & Langdridge, 2010), has increased the relationship options available. As a result, individuals have a variety of new types of intimate and sexual arrangements from which to choose, including short-term, casual sexual relationships; dating as a way to find long-term partners; and cohabitation as either a precursor to or a substitute for formal marriage. As the options for relational and sexual intimacy continue to expand, so too must our approaches to research on what we argue is one of the most dynamic and growing areas of research in psychology today.

References

Acevedo, B. P., & Aron, A. (2009). Does a long-term relationship kill romantic love? *Review of General Psychology, 13*, 59–65. doi:10.1037/a0014226

Alperstein, L., Ellison, C., Fishman, J. R., Hall, M., Handwerker, L., Hartley, H., . . . Tiefer, L. (2001). A new view of women's sexual problems. *Women and Therapy, 24*, 1–8.

Amato, P., & Previti, D. (2003). People's reasons for divorcing: Gender, social class, the life course, and adjustment. *Journal of Family Issues, 24*, 602–626. doi:10.1177/0192513X03024005002

Andersen, P. A., Eloy, S. V., Guerrero, L. K., & Spitzberg, B. H. (1995). Romantic jealousy and relational satisfaction: A look at the impact of jealousy experience and expression. *Communication Reports, 8*, 77–85. doi:10.1080/08934219509367613

Andruff, H., & Reissing, E. (2010). *What women think of relationships with bisexual men: An analysis of female attitudes toward bisexual male partners.* Paper presented at the 36th annual meeting of the Canadian Sex Research Forum, Toronto, Ontario, Canada.

Apt, C., Hurlbert, D. F., Pierce, A. P., & White, L. C. (1996). Relationship satisfaction, sexual characteristics, and the psychosocial well-being of women. *Canadian Journal of Human Sexuality, 5*, 195–210.

Araujo, A. B., Mohr, B. A., & McKinlay, J. B. (2004). Changes in sexual function in middle-aged and older men: Longitudinal data from the Massachusetts Male Aging Study. *Journal of the American Geriatrics Society, 52*, 1502–1509. doi:10.1111/j.0002-8614.2004.52413.x

Ard, B. N. (1977). Sex in lasting marriages: A longitudinal study. *Journal of Sex Research, 13*, 274–285. doi:10.1080/00224497709550985

Asendorpf, J., Penke, L., & Back, M. (2011). From dating to mating and relating: Predictors of initial and long-term outcomes of speed-dating in a community sample. *European Journal of Personality, 25*, 16–30. doi:10.1002/per.768

Atkins, D. C., Baucom, D. H., & Jacobson, N. S. (2001). Understanding infidelity: Correlates in a national random sample. *Journal of Family Psychology, 15*, 735–749. doi:10.1037/0893-3200.15.4.735

Atkins, D. C., Eldridge, K. A., Baucom, D. H., & Christensen, A. (2005). Infidelity and behavioral couple therapy: Optimism in the face of betrayal. *Journal of Consulting and Clinical Psychology, 73*, 144–150. doi:10.1037/0022-006X.73.1.144

Atkins, D. C., Yi, J., Baucom, D. H., & Andrew, C. (2005). Infidelity in couples seeking marital therapy. *Journal of Family Psychology, 19*, 470–473. doi:10.1037/0893-3200.19.3.470

Bacon, C. G., Mittleman, M. A., Kawachi, I., Giovannucci, E., Glasser, D. B., & Rimm, E. B. (2003). Sexual function in men older than 50 years of age: Results from the health professionals follow-up study. *Annals of Internal Medicine, 139*, 161–168.

Bailey, J. M., Gaulin, S., Agyei, Y., & Gladue, B. A. (1994). Effects of gender and sexual orientation on evolutionarily relevant aspects of human mating psychology. *Journal of Personality and Social Psychology, 66*, 1081–1093. doi:10.1037/0022-3514.66.6.1081

Bancroft, J. (1978). The relationships between hormones and sexual behavior in humans. In J. B. Hutchison (Ed.), *Biological determinants of sexual behavior* (pp. 493–519). Chichester, England: Wiley.

Bancroft, J., Loftus, J. L., & Long, J. S. (2003). Distress about sex: A national survey of women in heterosexual relationships. *Archives of Sexual Behavior, 32*, 193–208. doi:10.1023/A:1023420431760

Barker, M., & Langdridge, D. (2010). Whatever happened to non-monogamies? Critical reflections on recent research and theory. *Sexualities, 13*, 748–772. doi:10.1177/1363460710384645

Basile, K. C. (2002). Prevalence of wife rape and other intimate partner sexual coercion in a nationally representative sample of women. *Violence and Victims, 17*, 511–524. doi:10.1891/vivi.17.5.511.33717

Basson, R. (2001). Human sex-response cycles. *Journal of Sex and Marital Therapy, 27*, 33–43. doi:10.1080/00926230152035831

Bauermeister, J. A. (2012). Romantic ideation, partner-seeking, and HIV risk among young men who have sex with men. *Archives of Sexual Behavior, 41*, 431–440.

Bauermeister, J. A., Ventuneac, A., Pingle, E., & Parsons, J. T. (2012). Spectrums of love: Examining the relationship between romantic motivations and sexual risk among young gay and bisexual men. *AIDS and Behavior, 16*, 1549–1559. doi:10.1007/s10461-011-0123-8

Baumeister, R. F. (2000). Gender differences in erotic plasticity. *Psychological Bulletin, 126*, 347–374. doi:10.1037/0033-2909.126.3.347

Baumeister, R. F., & Bratlavsky, E. (1999). Passion, intimacy, and time: Passionate love as a function of change in intimacy. *Personality and Social Psychology Review, 3*, 49–67. doi:10.1207/s15327957pspr0301_3

Baumeister, R. F., Catanese, K. R., & Voh, K. D. (2001). Is there a gender difference in strength of sex drive? *Personality and Social Psychology Review, 5*, 242–273. doi:10.1207/S15327957PSPR0503_5

Bauserman, R., & Davis, C. (1996). Perceptions of early sexual experiences and adult sexual adjustment. *Journal of Psychology and Human Sexuality, 8*, 37–59. doi:10.1300/J056v08n03_03

Beaulieu-Pelletier, G., Philippe, F., LeCours, S., & Couture, S. (2011). The role of attachment avoidance in extradyadic sex. *Attachment and Human Development, 13*, 293–313. doi:10.1080/14616734.2011.562419

Beck, G. J., Bozman, A. W., & Qualtrough, T. (1991). The experience of sexual desire: Psychological correlates in a college sample. *Journal of Sex Research, 28*, 443–456. doi:10.1080/00224499109551618

Birnbaum, G., Cohen, O., & Wertheimer, V. (2007). Is it all about intimacy? Age, menopausal status, and women's sexuality. *Personal Relationships, 14*, 167–185. doi:10.1111/j.1475-6811.2006.00147.x

Birnbaum, G. E. (2007). Beyond the borders of reality: Attachment orientations and sexual fantasies. *Personal Relationships, 14*, 321–342. doi:10.1111/j.1475-6811.2007.00157.x

Birnbaum, G. E. (2010). Bound to interact: The divergent goals and complex interplay of attachment and sex within romantic relationships. *Journal of Social and Personal Relationships, 27*, 245–252. doi:10.1177/0265407509360902

Birnbaum, G. E., Mikulincer, M., & Gillath, O. (2011). In and out of a daydream: Attachment orientation, daily couple interactions, and sexual fantasies. *Personality and Social Psychology Bulletin, 37*, 1398–1410. doi:10.1177/0146167211410986

Birnbaum, G. E., Reis, H. T., Mikulincer, M., Gillath, O., & Orpaz, A. (2006). When sex is more than just sex: Attachment orientations, sexual experience, and relationship quality. *Journal of Personality and Social Psychology, 91*, 929–943. doi:10.1037/0022-3514.91.5.929

Birnbaum, G. E., Svitelman, N., Bar-Shalom, A., & Porat, O. (2008). The thin line between reality and imagination: Attachment orientations and the effects of relationship threats on sexual fantasies. *Personality and Social Psychology Bulletin, 34*, 1185–1199. doi:10.1177/0146167208319692

Birnbaum, G. E., Weisberg, Y. J., & Simpson, J. A. (2011). Desire under attack: Attachment orientations and the effects of relationship threat on sexual motivations. *Journal of Social and Personal Relationships, 28*, 448–468. doi:10.1177/0265407510381932

Bisson, M. A., & Levine, T. R. (2009). Negotiating a friends with benefits relationship. *Archives of Sexual Behavior, 38*, 66–73. doi:10.1007/s10508-007-9211-2

Blackwell, D. L., & Lichter, D. T. (2004). Homogamy among dating, cohabiting, and married couples. *Sociological Quarterly, 45*, 719–737. doi:10.1111/j.1533-8525.2004.tb02311.x

Blasband, D., & Peplau, L. A. (1985). Sexual exclusivity versus openness in gay male couples. *Archives of Sexual Behavior, 14*, 395–412. doi:10.1007/BF01542001

Blow, A. J., & Hartnett, K. (2005). Infidelity in committed relationships I: A methodological review. *Journal of Marital and Family Therapy, 31*, 183–216. doi:10.1111/j.1752-0606.2005.tb01555.x

Blum, R. W., Beuhring, T., Shew, M. L., Bearinger, L. H., Sieving, R. E., & Resnick, M. D. (2000). The effects of race/ethnicity, income, and family structure on adolescent risk behaviors. *American Journal of Public Health, 90*, 1879–1884. doi:10.2105/AJPH.90.12.1879

Blumberg, E. S. (2003). The lives and voices of highly sexual women. *Journal of Sex Research, 40*, 146–157. doi:10.1080/00224490309552176

Blumstein, P., & Schwartz, P. (1983). *American couples*. New York, NY: Pocket Books.

Bodenmann, G., Ledermann, T., & Bradbury, T. N. (2007). Stress, sex, and satisfaction in marriage. *Personal Relationships, 14*, 551–569. doi:10.1111/j.1475-6811.2007.00171.x

Bowlby, J. (1979). *The making and breaking of attachment bonds*. London, England: Tavistock.

Brand, R., Markey, C., Mills, A., & Hodges, S. (2007). Sex differences in self-reported infidelity and its correlates. *Sex Roles, 57*, 101–109. doi:10.1007/s11199-007-9221-5

Brassard, A., Shaver, P. R., & Lussier, Y. (2007). Attachment, sexual experience, and sexual pressure in romantic relationships: A dyadic approach. *Personal Relationships, 14*, 475–493. doi:10.1111/j.1475-6811.2007.00166.x

Brezsnyak, M., & Whisman, M. A. (2004). Sexual desire and relationship functioning: The effects of marital satisfaction and power. *Journal of Sex and Marital Therapy, 30*, 199–217. doi:10.1080/00926230490262393

Bridges, S. K., & Horne, S. G. (2007). Sexual satisfaction and desire discrepancy in same sex women's relationships. *Journal of Sex and Marital Therapy, 33*, 41–53. doi:10.1080/00926230600998466

Bringle, R. G., & Buunk, B. P. (1991). Extradyadic relationships and sexual jealousy. In K. McKinney & S. Sprecher (Eds.), *Sexuality and close relationships* (pp. 135–153). Hillsdale, NJ: Erlbaum.

Brotto, L. A., Woo, J. S. T., & Ryder, A. G. (2007). Acculturation and sexual function in Canadian East Asian men. *Journal of Sexual Medicine, 4*, 72–82. doi:10.1111/j.1743-6109.2006.00388.x

Brousseau, M. M., Bergerson, S., Hébert, M., & McDuff, P. (2011). Sexual coercion victimization and perpetration in heterosexual couples: A dyadic investigation. *Archives of Sexual Behavior, 40*, 363–372. doi:10.1007/s10508-010-9617-0

Burchell, J. L., & Ward, J. (2011). Sex drive, attachment style, relationship status and previous infidelity as predictors of sex differences in romantic jealousy. *Personality and Individual Differences, 51*, 657–661. doi:10.1016/j.paid.2011.06.002

Buss, D., Shackelford, T., Kirkpatrick, L., & Larsen, R. (2001). A half-century of mate preferences: The cultural evolution of values. *Journal of Marriage and the Family, 63*, 491–503. doi:10.1111/j.1741-3737.2001.00491.x

Buss, D. M. (2000). *The dangerous passion: Why jealousy is as necessary as love and sex*. New York, NY: Free Press.

Buss, D. M., Larsen, R. J., Westen, D., & Semmelroth, J. (1992). Sex differences in jealousy: Evolution, physiology, and psychology. *Psychological Science, 3*, 251–255. doi:10.1111/j.1467-9280.1992.tb00038.x

Butzer, B., & Campbell, L. (2008). Adult attachment, sexual satisfaction, and relationship satisfaction: A study of married couples. *Personal Relationships, 15*, 141–154. doi:10.1111/j.1475-6811.2007.00189.x

Byers, E. S. (2005). Relationship satisfaction and sexual satisfaction: A longitudinal study of individuals in long-term relationships. *Journal of Sex Research, 42*, 113–118. doi:10.1080/00224490509552264

Byers, E. S., & Demmons, S. (1999). Sexual satisfaction and sexual self-disclosure within dating relationships. *Journal of Sex Research, 36*, 180–189. doi:10.1080/00224499909551983

Byers, E. S., & Wang, A. (2004). Understanding sexuality in close relationships from the social exchange perspective. In J. H. Harvey, A. Wenzel, & S. Sprecher (Eds.), *The handbook of sexuality in close relationships* (pp. 203–234). Mahwah, NJ: Erlbaum.

Call, V., Sprecher, S., & Schwartz, P. (1995). The incidence and frequency of marital sex in a national sample. *Journal of Marriage and the Family, 57*, 639–652. doi:10.2307/353919

Cano, A., & O'Leary, K. (2000). Infidelity and separations predict major depressive episodes and symptoms of nonspecific depression and anxiety. *Journal of Consulting and Clinical Psychology, 68*, 774–781. doi:10.1037/0022-006X.68.5.774

Carpenter, L. M. (2002). Gender and the meaning and experience of virginity loss in the contemporary United States. *Gender and Society, 16*, 345–365. doi:10.1177/0891243202016003005

Carpenter, L. M., Nathanson, C. A., & Kim, Y. J. (2009). Physical women, emotional men: Gender and sexual satisfaction in midlife. *Archives of Sexual Behavior, 38*, 87–107. doi:10.1007/s10508-007-9215-y

Caruthers, A. S. (2006). *"Hookups" and "friends with benefits": Nonrelational sexual encounters as contexts of women's normative sexual development*. Unpublished doctoral dissertation, University of Michigan, Ann Arbor.

Carvalheira, A. A., Brotto, L. A., & Leal, I. (2010). Women's motivations for sex: Exploring the Diagnostic and Statistical Manual, fourth edition, text revision criteria for hypoactive sexual desire and female sexual arousal disorders. *Journal of Sexual Medicine, 7*, 1454–1463. doi:10.1111/j.1743-6109.2009.01693.x

Carver, K., Joyner, K., & Udry, J. R. (2003). National estimates of adolescent romantic relationships. In P. Florsheim (Ed.), *Adolescent romantic relations and sexual behavior: Theory, research, and practical implications* (pp. 23–56). Mahwah, NJ: Erlbaum.

Centers for Disease Control and Prevention. (2006). Youth risk behavior surveillance—United States, 2005. *MMWR Surveillance Summary, 55*(SS-5), 1–108. doi:10.1111/j.1746-1561.2006.00127.x

Charny, I., & Parnass, S. (1995). The impact of extramarital relationships on the continuation of marriages.

Journal of Sex and Marital Therapy, 21, 100–115. doi:10.1080/00926239508404389

Cheung, M. W. L., Wong, P. W. C., Liu, K. Y., Yip, P. S. F., Fan, S. Y., & Lam, T. (2008). A study of sexual satisfaction and frequency among Hong Kong Chinese couples. *Journal of Sex Research, 45*, 129–139. doi:10.1080/00224490801987416

Chivers, M. L., Rieger, G., Latty, E., & Bailey, J. M. (2005). A sex difference in the specificity of sexual arousal. *Psychological Science, 15*, 736–744. doi:10.1111/j.0956-7976.2004.00750.x

Choi, K., Catania, J., & Dolcini, M. (1994). Extramarital sex and HIV risk behavior among US adults: Results from the National AIDS Behavioral Survey. *American Journal of Public Health, 84*, 2003–2007. doi:10.2105/AJPH.84.12.2003

Christopher, F. S., & Sprecher, S. (2000). Sexuality in dating, marriage and other relationships: A decade review. *Journal of Marriage and the Family, 62*, 999–1017. doi:10.1111/j.1741-3737.2000.00999.x

Clark, R. D., & Hatfield, E. (1989). Gender differences in receptivity to sexual offers. *Journal of Psychology and Human Sexuality, 2*, 39–45.

Cohen, J. N., Byers, E. S., & Walsh, L. P. (2008). Factors influencing the sexual relationships of lesbians and gay men. *International Journal of Sexual Health, 20*, 162–176. doi:10.1080/19317610802240105

Conley, T. D. (2010). Perceived proposer personality characteristics and gender differences in acceptance of casual sex offers. *Journal of Personality and Social Psychology, 100*, 309–329. doi:10.1037/a0022152

Conley, T. D., Moors, A. C., Matsick, J. L., Zeigler, A., & Valentine, B. A. (2011). Women, men, and the bedroom: Methodological and conceptual insights that narrow, refine, and eliminate gender differences in sexuality. *Current Directions in Psychological Science, 20*, 296–300. doi:10.1177/0963721411418467

Conley, T. D., Ziegler, A., & Moors, A. C. (2012). Backlash from the bedroom: Stigma mediates gender differences in acceptance of casual sex offers. *Psychology of Women Quarterly*. Advance online publication. doi:10.1177/0361684312467169

Cooper, M. L., Shapiro, C. M., & Powers, A. M. (1998). Motivations for sex and risky sexual behavior among adolescents and young adults: A functional perspective. *Journal of Personality and Social Psychology, 75*, 1528–1558. doi:10.1037/0022-3514.75.6.1528

Corona, G., Lee, D., Forti, G., O'Connor, D., Maggi, M., O'Neil, T., . . . Wu, F. C.; EMAS Study Group. (2010). Age-related changes in general and sexual health in middle-aged and older men: Results from the European Male Ageing Study (EMAS). *Journal of Sexual Medicine, 7*, 1362–1380. doi:10.1111.j.1743-6109.2009.01601.x

Crawford, M., & Popp, D. (2003). Sexual double standards: A review and methodological critique of two decades of research. *Journal of Sex Research, 40*, 13–26. doi:10.1080/00224490309552163

Crockett, L. J., Bingham, C. R., Chopak, J. S., & Vicary, J. R. (1996). Timing of first sexual intercourse: The role of social control, social learning, and problem behaviour. *Journal of Youth and Adolescence, 25*, 89–111. doi:10.1007/BF01537382

Davies, S., Katz, J., & Jackson, J. L. (1999). Sexual desire discrepancies: Effects on sexual and relationship satisfaction in heterosexual dating couples. *Archives of Sexual Behavior, 28*, 553–567. doi:10.1023/A:1018721417683

Davis, D., Shaver, P. R., & Vernon, M. L. (2004). Attachment style and subjective motivations for sex. *Personality and Social Psychology Bulletin, 30*, 1076–1090. doi:10.1177/0146167204264794

Davis, D., Shaver, P. R., Widaman, K., Vernon, M., Follette, W. C., & Beitz, K. (2003). "I can't get no satisfaction": Insecure attachment, inhibited sexual communication, and sexual dissatisfaction. *Personal Relationships, 13*, 465–483. doi:10.1111/j.1475-6811.2006.00130.x

DeLamater, J., Hyde, J. S., & Fong, M. (2008). Sexual satisfaction in the seventh decade of life. *Journal of Sex and Marital Therapy, 34*, 439–454. doi:10.1080/00926230802156251

DeLamater, J., & Moorman, S. (2007). Sexual behavior in later life. *Journal of Aging and Health, 19*, 921–945. doi:10.1177/0898264307308342

DeMaris, A. (1997). Elevated sexual activity in violent marriages: Hypersexuality or sexual extortion? *Journal of Sex Research, 34*, 361–373. doi:10.1080/00224499709551904

DeMaris, A. (2009). Distal and proximal influences on the risk of extramarital sex: A prospective study of longer duration marriages. *Journal of Sex Research, 46*, 597–607. doi:10.1080/00224490902915993

DeSteno, D. (2010). Mismeasuring jealousy: A cautionary comment on Levy and Kelly (2010). *Psychological Science, 21*, 1355–1356. doi:10.1177/0956797610378688

DeSteno, D., Bartlett, M. Y., Braverman, J., & Salovey, P. (2002). Sex differences in jealousy: Evolutionary mechanism or artifact of measurement? *Journal of Personality and Social Psychology, 83*, 1103–1116. doi:10.1037/0022-3514.83.5.1103

DeSteno, D., Valdesolo, P., & Bartlett, M. Y. (2006). Jealousy and the threatened self: Getting to the heart of the green-eyed monster. *Journal of Personality and Social Psychology, 91*, 626–641. doi:10.1037/0022-3514.91.4.626

DeWall, C., Lambert, N., Slotter, E., Pond, R., Deckman, T., Finkel, E., Luchies, L., & Fincham, F. (2011). So far away from one's partner, yet so close to romantic alternatives: Avoidant attachment, interest in alternatives, and infidelity. *Journal of Personality and Social Psychology, 101*, 1302–1316. doi:10.1037/a0025497

Diamond, L. M. (2003). What does sexual orientation orient? A biobehavioral model distinguishing romantic love and sexual desire. *Psychological Review, 110*, 173–192. doi:10.1037/0033-295X.110.1.173

Diamond, L. M. (2004). Emerging perspectives on distinctions between romantic love and sexual desire. *Current Directions in Psychological Science, 13*, 116–119. doi:10.1111/j.0963-7214.2004.00287.x

Diamond, L. M. (2006). Introduction: In search of "good" sexual-developmental pathways for adolescent girls. *New Directions for Child and Adolescent Development, 2006*, 1–7. doi:10.1002/cd.158

Diamond, L. M. (2008). *Sexual fluidity: Understanding women's love and desire.* Cambridge, MA: Harvard University Press.

Diamond, L. M. (2010, July). *Where's the sex in relationship research? Where are the relationships in sex research?* Keynote address presented at the biennial meeting of the International Association for Relationship Research, Herzliya, Israel.

Diamond, L. M., & Huebner, D. M. (2012). Is good sex good for you? Rethinking sexuality and health. *Social and Personality Psychology Compass, 6*, 54–69. doi:10.1111/j.1751-9004.2011.00408.x

Diamond, L. M., & Savin-Williams, R. C. (2009). Adolescent sexuality. In R. M. Lerner & L. Steinberg (Eds.), *Handbook of adolescent psychology: Vol. 1. Individual bases of adolescent development* (pp. 479–523). Hoboken, NJ: Wiley.

Diener, E., & Seligman, M. E. P. (2002). Very happy people. *Psychological Science, 13*, 81–84. doi:10.1111/1467-9280.00415

Dijkstra, P., & Barelds, D. P. H. (2008). *Self and partner personality and responses to relationship threats. Journal of Research in Personality, 42*, 1500–1511. doi:10.1016/j.jrp.2008.06.008

Donald, M., Lucke, J., Dunne, M., & Raphael, B. (1995). Gender differences associated with young people's emotional reactions to sexual intercourse. *Journal of Youth and Adolescence, 24*, 453–464. doi:10.1007/BF01537191

Dundon, C., & Rellini, A. (2010). More than sexual function: Predictors of sexual satisfaction in a sample of women age 40–70. *Journal of Sex Medicine, 7*, 896–904. doi:10.1111/j.1743-6109.2009.01557.x

Dzara, K. (2010). Assessing the effect of marital sexuality on marital disruption. *Social Science Research, 39*, 715–724. doi:10.1016/j.ssresearch.2010.06.003

Eastwick, P., Finkel, E., & Eagly, A. (2011). When and why do ideal partner preferences affect the process of initiating and maintaining romantic relationships? *Journal of Personality and Social Psychology, 101*, 1012–1032. doi:10.1037/a0024062

Eastwick, P. W., & Finkel, E. J. (2008). The attachment system in fledgling relationships: An activating role for attachment anxiety. *Journal of Personality and Social Psychology, 95*, 628–647. doi:10.1037/0022-3514.95.3.628

Edser, S. J., & Shea, J. D. (2002). An exploratory investigation of bisexual men in monogamous, heterosexual marriages. *Journal of Bisexuality, 2*, 5–43. doi:10.1300/J159v02n04_02

Edwards, J. N., & Booth, A. (1994). Sexuality, marriage, and well-being: The middle years. In A. S. Rossi (Ed.), *Sexuality across the life course* (pp. 233–259). Chicago, IL: University of Chicago Press.

Ehrhardt, A. A. (1996). Our view of adolescent sexuality: A focus on risk behavior without the developmental context. *American Journal of Public Health, 86*, 1523–1525. doi:10.2105/AJPH.86.11.1523

Eisenberg, M. E., Ackard, D. M., Resnick, M. D., & Neumark-Sztainer, D. (2009). Casual sex and psychological health among young adults: Is having "friends with benefits" emotionally damaging? *Perspectives on Sexual and Reproductive Health, 41*, 231–237. doi:10.1363/4123109

Elliott, S., & Umberson, D. (2008). The performance of desire: Gender and sexual negotiation in long-term marriages. *Journal of Marriage and Family, 70*, 391–406. doi:10.1111/j.1741-3737.2008.00489.x

Feeney, J. A., & Noller, P. (2004). Attachment and sexuality in close relationships. In J. H. Harvey, A. Wenzel, & S. Sprecher (Eds.), *The handbook of sexuality in close relationships* (pp. 183–201). Mahwah, NJ: Erlbaum.

Ferenidou, F., Kapoteli, V., Moisidis, K., Koutsogiannis, I., Giakoumelos, A., & Hatzichristou, D. (2008). Presence of a sexual problem may not affect women's satisfaction from their sexual function. *Journal of Sexual Medicine, 5*, 631–639. doi:10.1111/j.1743-6109.2007.00644.x

Fine, M., & McClelland, S. I. (2006). Sexuality education and desire: Still missing after all these years. *Harvard Educational Review, 76*, 297–338.

Finkel, E., Eastwick, P., & Matthews, J. (2007). Speed-dating as an invaluable tool for studying romantic attraction: A methodological primer. *Personal Relationships, 14*, 149–166. doi:10.1111/j.1475-6811.2006.00146.x

Fisher, T. D., Moore, Z. T., & Pittenger, M. J. (2012). Sex on the brain? An examination of frequency of sexual cognitions as a function of gender, erotophilia, and social desirability. *Journal of Sex Research, 49*, 69–77. doi:10.1080/00224499.2011.565429

Fisman, R., Iyengar, S., Kamenica, E., & Simonson, I. (2008). Racial preferences in dating. *Review of Economic Studies, 75*, 117–132. doi:10.1111/j.1467-937x.2007.00465.x

Fortenberry, J. D., Temkit, M., & Tu, W. (2005). Daily mood, partner support, sexual interest, and sexual activity among adolescent women. *Health Psychology, 24*, 252–257. doi:10.1037/0278-6133.24.3.252

Fortenberry, J. D., Tu, W., Harezlack, J., Katz, B. P., & Orr, D. P. (2002). Condom use as a function of time in new and established adolescent sexual relationships. *American Journal of Public Health, 92*, 211–213.

Gable, S. L., & Impett, E. A. (2012). Approach and avoidance motives and close relationships. *Social and Personality Psychology Compass, 6*, 95–108.

Gillath, O., Mikulincer, M., Birnbaum, G. E., & Shaver, P. R. (2008). When sex primes love: Subliminal sexual priming motivates relationship goal pursuit. *Personality and Social Psychology Bulletin, 34*, 1057–1069. doi:10.1177/0146167208318141

Gillath, O., & Schachner, D. A. (2006). How do sexuality and attachment interrelate? Goals, motives, strategies. In G. S. Goodman & M. Mikulincer (Eds.), *Dynamics of romantic love: Attachment, caregiving, and sex* (pp. 121–147). New York, NY: Guilford Press.

Giordano, P. C., Manning, W. D., & Longmore, M. A. (2006). Adolescent romantic relationships: An emerging portrait of their nature and developmental significance. In A. C. Crouter & A. Booth (Eds.), *Romance and sex in adolescence and emerging adulthood: Risks and opportunities* (pp. 127–150). Mahwah, NJ: Erlbaum.

Goldhammer, D. L., & McCabe, M. P. (2011). A qualitative exploration of the meaning and experience of sexual desire among partnered women. *Canadian Journal of Human Sexuality, 20*, 19–29.

Gonzaga, G. C., Turner, R. A., Keltner, D., Campos, B., & Altemus, M. (2006). Romantic love and sexual desire in close relationships. *Emotion, 6*, 163–179. doi:10.1037/1528-3542.6.2.163

Gott, M., & Hinchliff, S. (2003). How important is sex in later life? The views of older people. *Social Science and Medicine, 56*, 1617–1628. doi:10.1016/S0277-9536(02)00180-6

Graham, C. A., Sanders, S. A., Milhausen, R. R., & McBride, K. R. (2004). Turning on and turning off: A focus group study of the factors that affect women's sexual arousal. *Archives of Sexual Behavior, 33*, 527–538. doi:10.1023/B:ASEB.0000044737.62561.fd

Gray, M. L. (2009). Negotiating identities/queering desires: Coming out online and the remediation of the coming-out story. *Journal of Computer-Mediated Communication, 14*, 1162–1189. doi:10.1111/j.1083-6101.2009.01485.x

Grello, C. M., Welsh, D. P., & Harper, M. S. (2006). No strings attached: The nature of casual sex in college students. *Journal of Sex Research, 43*, 255–267. doi:10.1080/00224490609552324

Grello, C. M., Welsh, D. P., Harper, M. S., & Dickson, J. W. (2003). Dating and sexual relationship trajectories and adolescent functioning. *Adolescent and Family Health, 3*, 103–112.

Guerrero, L. K., & Afifi, W. A. (1999). Toward a goal-oriented approach for understanding communicative responses to jealousy. *Western Journal of Communication, 63*, 216–248.

Guerrero, L. K., Andersen, P. A., Jorgensen, P. F., & Spitzberg, B. H. (1995). Coping with the green-eyed monster: Conceptualizing and measuring communicative responses to romantic jealousy. *Western Journal of Communication, 59*, 270–304.

Gustavson, M. (2009). Bisexuals in relationships: Uncoupling intimacy from gender ontology. *Journal of Bisexuality, 9*, 407–429. doi:10.1080/15299710903316653

Hall, J., & Fincham, F. (2006). Relationship dissolution following infidelity: The roles of attributions and forgiveness. *Journal of Social and Clinical Psychology, 25*, 508–522. doi:10.1521/jscp.2006.25.5.508

Harrison, M., & Shortall, J. (2011). Women and men in love: Who really feels it and says it first? *Journal of Social Psychology, 151*, 727–736. doi:10.1080/00224545.2010.522626

Hartmann, U., Philippsohn, S., Heiser, K., & Ruffer-Hesse, C. (2004). Low sexual desire in midlife and older women: Personality factors, psychosocial development, present sexuality. *Menopause, 11*, 726–741. doi:10.1097/01.ju. 0000164397.64370.d9

Hatfield, E., Greenberger, D., Traupmann, J., & Lambert, P. (1982). Equity and sexual satisfaction in recently married couples. *Journal of Sex Research, 18*, 18–31. doi:10.1080/00224498209551131

Haugen, E. N., Schmutzer, P. A., & Wenzel, A. (2004). Sexuality and the partner relationship during pregnancy and the postpartum period. In J. H. Harvey, A. Wenzel, & S. Sprecher (Eds.), *The handbook of sexuality in close relationships* (pp. 411–435). Mahwah, NJ: Erlbaum.

Hazan, C., & Shaver, P. (1987). Romantic love conceptualized as an attachment process. *Journal of Personality and Social Psychology, 52*, 511–524. doi:10.1037/0022-3514.52.3.511

Hazan, C., & Zeifman, D. (1999). Pair-bonds as attachments: Evaluating the evidence. In J. Cassidy & P. R. Shaver (Eds.), *Handbook of attachment theory and research* (pp. 336–354). New York, NY: Guilford Press.

Heiman, J. R., Long, S. J., Smith, S. N., Fisher, W. A., & Sand, M. S. (2011). Sexual satisfaction and relationship happiness in midlife and older couples in five countries. *Archives of Sexual Behavior, 40*, 741–753. doi:10.1007/s10508-010-9703-3

Henderson, A. W., Lehavot, K., & Simoni, J. M. (2009). Ecological models of sexual satisfaction among lesbian/bisexual and heterosexual women. *Archives of Sexual Behavior, 38*, 50–65. doi:10.1007/s10508-008-9384-3

Hensel, D. J., Fortenberry, J. D., & Orr, D. P. (2008). Variations in coital and noncoital sexual repertoire among adolescent women. *Journal of Adolescent Health, 42*, 170–176. doi:10.1016/j.jadohealth.2007.07.009

Herek, G. M. (2000). The psychology of sexual prejudice. *Current Directions in Psychological Science, 9*, 19–22. doi:10.1111/1467-8721.00051

Higgins, J. A., Trussell, J., Moore, N. B., & Davidson, J. K. (2010). Virginity lost, satisfaction gained? Physiological and psychological sexual satisfaction at heterosexual debut. *Journal of Sex Research, 47*, 384–394. doi:10.1080/00224491003774792

Hiller, J. (2004). Speculations on the links between feelings, emotions, and sexual behaviour: Are vasopressin and oxytocin involved? *Sexual and Relationship Therapy, 19*, 393–412. doi:10.1080/14681990412331297974

Hinchliff, S., & Gott, M. (2004). Intimacy, commitment, and adaptation: Sexual relationships within long-term marriages. *Journal of Social and Personal Relationships, 21*, 595–609. doi:10.1177/0265407504045889

Hinchliff, S., & Gott, M. (2008). Challenging social myths and stereotypes of women and aging: Heterosexual women talk about sex. *Journal of Women and Aging, 20*, 65–80. doi:10.1300/J074v20n01_06

Hitsch, G., Hortacsu, A., & Ariely, D. (2010). What makes you click? Mate preferences in online dating. *Quantitative Marketing and Economics, 8*, 393–427. doi:10.1007/s11129-010-9088-6

Hoff, C. C., & Beougher, S. C. (2010). Sexual agreements among gay male couples. *Archives of Sexual Behavior, 39*, 774–787. doi:10.1007/s10508-008-9393-2

Hoff, C. C., Beougher, S. C., Chakravarty, D., Darbes, L. A., & Neilands, T. B. (2010). Relationship characteristics and motivations behind agreements among gay male couples: Differences by agreement type and couple serostatus. *AIDS Care, 22*, 827–835. doi:10.1080/09540120903443384

Holmberg, D., & Blair, K. (2009). Sexual desire, communication, satisfaction, and preferences of men and women in same-sex versus mixed-sex relationships. *Journal of Sex Research, 46*, 57–66. doi:10.1080/00224490802645294

Huang, A., Subak, L., Thom, D., Eeden, S., Ragins, A., Kupperman, M., . . . Brown, S. (2009). Sexual functioning and aging in ethnically and racially diverse women. *Journal of the American Geriatrics Society, 57*, 1362–1368. doi:10.1111/j.1532-5415.2009.02353.x

Hughes, M., Morrison, K., & Asada, K. J. K. (2005). What's love got to do with it? Exploring the impact of maintenance rules, love attitudes, and network support of friends with benefits relationships. *Western Journal of Communication, 69*, 49–66. doi:10.1080/10570310500034154

Hurlbert, D. F., Apt, C., Hurlbert, M. K., & Pierce, A. P. (2000). Sexual compatibility and the sexual desire-motivation relation in females with hypoactive sexual desire disorder. *Behavior Modification, 24*, 325–347. doi:10.1177/0145445500243002

Iasenza, S. (2002). Beyond "lesbian bed death": The passion and play in lesbian relationships. *Journal of Lesbian Studies, 6*, 111–120. doi:10.1300/J155v06n01_10

Impett, E. A., Gordon, A., & Strachman, A. (2008). Attachment and daily sexual goals: A study of dating couples. *Personal Relationships, 15*, 375–390. doi:10.1111/j.1475-6811.2008.00204.x

Impett, E. A., Muise, A., & Breines, J. (2013). Because it feels good: Toward a positive psychology of sexuality. In M. Hojjat & D. Cramer (Eds.), *Positive psychology of love* (pp. 57–76). New York, NY: Oxford University Press.

Impett, E. A., & Peplau, L. A. (2002). Why some women consent to unwanted sex with a dating partner: Insights from attachment theory. *Psychology of Women Quarterly, 26*, 359–369. doi:10.1111/1471-6402.t01-1-00075

Impett, E. A., & Peplau, L. A. (2003). Sexual compliance: Gender, motivational, and relationship perspectives. *Journal of Sex Research, 40*, 87–100. doi:10.1080/00224490309552169

Impett, E. A., Peplau, L. A., & Gable, S. L. (2005). Approach and avoidance sexual motivation: Implications for personal and interpersonal well-being. *Personal Relationships, 12*, 465–482. doi:10.1111/j.1475-6811.2005.00126.x

Impett, E. A., Strachman, A., Finkel, E. J., & Gable, S. L. (2008). Maintaining sexual desire in intimate relationships: The importance of approach goals. *Journal of Personality and Social Psychology, 94*, 808–823. doi:10.1037/0022-3514.94.5.808

Impett, E. A., & Tolman, D. L. (2006). Adolescent girls' sexual experiences and sexual satisfaction. *Journal of Adolescent Research, 6*, 628–646. doi:10.1177/0743558406293964

Irvine, J. M. (2002). *Talk about sex: The battles over sex education in the United States*. Berkeley: University of California Press.

Jankowiak, W., Nell, M., & Buckmaster, A. (2002). Managing infidelity: A cross-cultural perspective. *Ethnology, 41*, 85–101.

Johnson, A. M., Wadsworth, J., Wellings, K., & Field, J. (1994). *Sexual attitudes and lifestyles*. London, England: Blackwell.

Joyner, K., & Kao, K. (2005). Interracial relationships and the transition to adulthood. *American Sociological Review, 70*, 563–581.

Kaiser Family Foundation. (2001). *Inside-OUT: A report on the experiences of lesbians, gays and bisexuals in America and the public's view on issues and policies related to sexual orientation*. Menlo Park, CA: Author.

Karraker, A., DeLamater, J., & Schwartz, C. (2011). Sexual frequency decline from mid to later life. *Journal of Gerontology, 66*, 502–512.

Katz, B. P., Fortenberry, J., Zimet, G. D., Blythe, M. J., & Orr, D. P. (2000). Partner-specific relationship characteristics and condom use among young people with sexually transmitted diseases. *Journal of Sex Research, 37*, 69–75. doi:10.1080/00224490009552022

Katz, J., Moore, J., & May, P. (2008). Physical and sexual covictimization from dating partners: A distinct type of intimate abuse? *Violence Against Women, 14*, 961–980. doi:10.1177/1077801208320905

Katz, J., & Myhr, L. (2008). Perceived conflict patterns and relationship quality associated with verbal sexual coercion by male dating partners. *Journal of Interpersonal Violence, 23*, 798–814. doi:10.1177/0886260507313949

King, M., Holt, V., & Nazareth, I. (2007). Women's views of their sexual difficulties: Agreement and disagreement with clinical diagnoses. *Archives of Sexual Behavior, 36*, 281–288. doi:10.1007/s10508-006-9090-y

King, R. B., & Bratter, J. L. (2007). A path toward interracial marriage: Women's first partners and husbands across racial lines. *Sociological Quarterly, 48*, 343–369.

Kinsey, A. C., Pomeroy, W. B., & Martin, C. E. (1948). *Sexual behavior in the human male*. Philadelphia, PA: W. B. Saunders.

Kinsey, A. C., Pomeroy, W. B., Martin, C. E., & Gebhard, P. H. (1953). *Sexual behavior in the human female*. Philadelphia, PA: W. B. Saunders.

Kirkwood, M., & Cecil, D. (2001). Marital rape: A student assessment of rape laws and the marital exemption. *Violence Against Women, 7*, 1234–1253. doi:10.1177/10778012010070110003

Kleinplatz, P. J. (2006). Learning from extraordinary lovers: Lessons from the edge. *Journal of Homosexuality, 50*, 325–348. doi:10.1300/J082v50n02_16

Kleinplatz, P. J., Menard, A. D., Paquet, M.-P., Paradis, N., Campbell, M., Zuccarino, D., & Mehak, L. (2009). The components of optimal sexuality: A portrait of "great sex." *Canadian Journal of Human Sexuality, 18*, 1–13.

Klusmann, D. (2002). Sexual motivation and the duration of partnership. *Archives of Sexual Behavior, 31*, 275–287. doi:10.1023/A:1015205020769

Knobloch, L. K., Solomon, D. H., & Cruz, M. G. (2001). The role of relationship development and attachment in the experience of romantic jealousy. *Personal Relationships, 8*, 205–224. doi:10.1111/j.1475-6811.2001.tb00036.x

Koch, P., Mansfield, P., Thurau, D., & Carey, M. (2005). "Feeling frumpy": The relationships between body image and sexual response changes in midlife women. *Journal of Sex Research, 42*, 215–23. doi:10.1080/00224490509552276

Kontula, O., & Haavio-Mannila, E. (2009). The impact of aging on human sexual activity and sexual desire. *Journal of Sex Research, 46*, 46–56. doi:10.1080/00224490802624414

Korobov, N. (2011). Mate-preference talk in speed-dating conversations. *Research on Language and Social Interaction, 44*, 186–209. doi:10.1080/08351813.2011.567102

Ku, L., Sonenstein, F. L., & Pleck, J. H. (1993). Young men's risk behaviors for HIV infection and sexually transmitted diseases, 1988 through 1991. *American Journal of Public Health, 83*, 1609–1615. doi:10.2105/AJPH.83.11.1609

Kuhle, B. X. (2011). Did you have sex with him? Do you love her? An in vivo test of sex differences in jealous interrogations. *Personality and Individual Differences, 51*, 1044–1047. doi:10.1016/j.paid.2011.07.034

Kurdek, L. A. (1991). Sexuality in homosexual and heterosexual couples. In K. McKinney & S. Sprecher (Eds.), *Sexuality in close relationships* (pp. 177–191). Hillsdale, NJ: Erlbaum.

Kurzban, R., & Weeden, J. (2005). HurryDate: Mate preferences in action. *Evolution and Human Behavior, 26*, 227–244. doi:10.1016/j.evolhumbehav.2004.08.012

Kurzban, R., & Weeden, J. (2007). Do advertised preferences predict the behavior of speed daters? *Personal Relationships, 14*, 623–632. doi:10.1111/j.1475-6811.2007.00175.x

LaSala, M. C. (2004). Extradyadic sex and gay male couples: Comparing monogamous and non-monogamous relationships. *Families in Society, 85*, 405–412.

Laumann, E. O., Gagnon, H. J., Michael, R. T., & Michaels, S. (1994). *The social organization of sexuality: Sexual practices in the United States*. Chicago, IL: University of Chicago Press.

Laumann, E. O., & Michael, R. T. (Eds.). (2001). *Sex, love, and health in America: Private choices and public policies*. Chicago, IL: University of Chicago Press.

Laumann, E. O., Nicolosi, A., Glasser, D. B., Paik, A., Gingell, C., Moreira, E., & Wang, T.; GSSAB Investigators' Group. (2005). Sexual problems among women and men aged 40–80 y: Prevalence and correlates identified in the Global Study of Sexual Attitudes and Behaviors. *International Journal of Impotence Research, 17*, 39–57.

Laumann, E. O., Paik, A., Glasser, D. B., Kang, J., Wang, T., Levinson, B., . . . Gingell, C. (2006). A cross-national study of subjective sexual well-being among older women and men: Findings from the global study of sexual attitudes and behaviors. *Archives of Sexual Behavior, 35*, 145–161. doi:10.1007/s10508-005-9005-3

Lawrance, K., & Byers, E. S. (1995). Sexual satisfaction in long-term heterosexual relationships: The interpersonal exchange model of sexual satisfaction. *Personal Relationships, 2*, 267–285. doi:10.1111/j.1475-6811.1995.tb00092.x

Leiblum, S. R. (2002). Reconsidering gender differences in sexual desire: An update. *Sexual and Relationship Therapy, 17*, 57–68. doi:10.1080/14681990220108027

Leitenberg, H., & Henning, K. (1995). Sexual fantasy. *Psychological Bulletin, 117*, 469–496. doi:10.1037/0033-2909.117.3.469

Lever, J. (1994, August 23). The 1994 Advocate survey of sexuality and relationships: The men. *Advocate*, pp. 18–24.

Lever, J. (1995, August 22). The 1995 Advocate survey of sexuality and relationships: The women. *Advocate*, pp. 22–30.

Levine, S. (2003). The nature of sexual desire: A clinician's perspective. *Archives of Sexual Behavior, 32*, 279–285. doi:10.1023/A:1023421819465

Levy, K. N., Kelly, K. M., & Jack, E. L. (2006). Sex differences in jealousy: A matter of evolution or attachment history? In M. Mikulincer & G. Goodman (Eds.), *Dynamics of romantic love: Attachment, caregiving, and sex* (pp. 128–145). New York, NY: Guilford Press.

Li, N., Bailey, J., Kendrick, D., & Linsenmeier, J. (2002). The necessities and luxuries of mate preferences: Testing the tradeoffs. *Journal of Personality and Social Psychology, 82*, 947–955. doi:10.1037/0022-3514.82.6.947

Li, N., & Kendrick, D. (2006). Sex similarities and differences in preferences for short-term mate: What, whether, and why? *Journal of Personality and Social Psychology, 90*, 468–489. doi:10.1037/0022-3514.90.3.468

Lindau, S., Schumm, P., Laumann, E., Levinson, W., Muircheartaigh, C., & Waite, L. (2007). A study of sexuality and health among older adults in the United States. *New England Journal of Medicine, 357*, 762–774. doi:10.1056/NEJMoa067423

Lishner, D. A., Nguyen, S., Stocks, E. L., & Zillmer, E. J. (2008). Are sexual and emotional infidelity equally upsetting to men and women? Making sense of forced-choice responses. *Evolutionary Psychology, 6*, 667–675.

Little, K. C., McNulty, J. K., & Russell, V. M. (2010). Sex buffers intimates against the negative implications of attachment insecurity. *Personality and Social Psychology Bulletin, 36*, 484–498. doi:10.1177/0146167209352494

Liu, C. (2000). A theory of marital sexual life. *Journal of Marriage and the Family, 62*, 363–374. doi:10.1111/j.1741-3737.2000.00363.x

Livingston, J., Buddie, A., Testa, M., & VanZile-Tamsen, C. (2004). The role of sexual precedence in verbal sexual coercion. *Psychology of Women Quarterly, 28*, 287–297. doi:10.1111/j.1471-6402.2004.00146.x

Logan, T., Cole, J., & Shannon, L. (2007). A mixed-methods examination of sexual coercion and degradation among women in violent relationships who do and do not report forced sex. *Violence and Victims, 22*, 71–94.

MacNeil, S., & Byers, S. (2009). Role of sexual self-disclosure in the sexual satisfaction of long-term heterosexual couples. *Journal of Sex Research, 46*, 3–14. doi:10.1080/00224490802398399

Maddox, A. M., Rhoades, G. K., & Markman, H. J. (2011). Viewing sexually-explicit materials alone or together: Associations with relationship quality. *Archives of Sexual Behavior, 40*, 441–448. doi:10.1007/s10508-009-9585-4

Mahoney, P. (1999). High rape chronicity and low rates of help-seeking among wife rape survivors in a nonclinical sample: Implications for research and practice. *Violence Against Women, 5*, 993–1016. doi:10.1177/10778019922181590

Maisel, N. C., & Fingerhut, A. W. (2011). California's ban on same-sex marriage: The campaign and its effects on gay, lesbian, and bisexual individuals. *Journal of Social Issues, 67*, 242–263. doi:10.1111/j.1540-4560.2011.01696.x

Manning, W. D., Giordano, P. C., & Longmore, M. A. (2006). Hooking up: The relationship contexts of "nonrelationship" sex. *Journal of Adolescent Research, 21*, 459–483. doi:10.1177/0743558406291692

Manning, W. D., Longmore, M. A., & Giordano, P. C. (2000). The relationship context of contraceptive use at first intercourse. *Family Planning Perspectives, 32*, 104–110.

Mark, K., Janssen, E., & Milhausen, R. (2011). Infidelity in heterosexual couples: Demographic, interpersonal, and personality-related predictors of extradyadic sex. *Archives of Sexual Behavior, 40*, 971–982. doi:10.1007/s10508-011-9771-z

Mark, K. P., & Murray, S. H. (2012). Gender differences in desire discrepancy as a predictor of sexual and relationship satisfaction in a college sample of heterosexual romantic relationships. *Journal of Sex and Marital Therapy, 38*, 198–215.

Masters, W. H., & Johnson, V. E. (1966). *Human sexual response.* Boston: Little, Brown.

Matthews, A. K., Tartaro, J., & Hughes, T. L. (2003). A comparative study of lesbian and heterosexual women in committed relationships. *Journal of Lesbian Studies, 7*, 101–114. doi:10.1300/J155v07n01_07

McCabe, M. P. (1987). Desired and experienced levels of premarital affection and sexual intercourse during dating. *Journal of Sex Research, 23*, 23–33. doi:10.1080/00224498709551339

McCabe, M. P., & Goldhammer, D. L. (2012). Demographic and psychological factors related to sexual desire among heterosexual women in a relationship. *Journal of Sex Research, 49*, 78–87. doi:10.1080/00224499.2011.569975

McKenna, C. (1989). *Marital satisfaction and sensation seeking in the first ten years of marriage: Self expansion versus boredom.* Unpublished doctoral dissertation, California Graduate School of Family Psychology, San Francisco.

McNeal, J. L., & Aron, A. (1995, June). *Exciting activities and relationship satisfaction: A comparison of married and dating couples.* Paper presented at the International Network Conference on Personal Relationships, Williamsburg, VA.

McNulty, J. K., & Fisher, T. D. (2008). Gender differences in response to sexual expectancies and changes in sexual frequency: A short-term longitudinal study of sexual satisfaction in newly married couples. *Archives of Sexual Behavior, 37*, 229–240. doi:10.1007/s10508-007-9176-1

McWhirter, D. P., & Mattison, A. M. (1984). *The male couple: How relationships develop.* Englewood Cliffs, NJ: Prentice-Hall.

Meana, M., Rakipi, R. S., Weeks, G., & Lykins, A. (2006). Sexual functioning in a nonclinical sample of partnered lesbians. *Journal of Couple and Relationship Therapy, 5*, 1–22.

Meltzer, A. L., & McNulty, J. K. (2010). Body image and marital satisfaction: Evidence for the mediating role of sexual frequency and sexual satisfaction. *Journal of Family, 24*, 156–164. doi:10.1037/a0019063

Meston, C. M., & Buss, D. M. (2007). Why humans have sex. *Archives of Sexual Behavior, 36*, 477–507. doi:10.1007/s10508-007-9175-2

Michael, R. T., Gagnon, J. H., Laumann, E. O., & Kolata, G. (1994). *Sex in America: A definitive survey.* New York, NY: Warner Books.

Mikulincer, M., & Shaver, P. R. (2007). *Attachment in adulthood—Structure, dynamics, and change.* New York, NY: Guilford Press.

Milhausen, R. R., & Herold, E. S. (2001). Reconceptualizing the sexual double standard. *Journal of Psychology and Human Sexuality, 13*, 63–83. doi:10.1300/J056v13n02_05

Miller, S. L., & Maner, J. K. (2009). Sex differences in response to sexual versus emotional infidelity: The moderating role of individual differences. *Personality and Individual Differences, 46*, 287–291. doi:10.1016/j.paid.2008.10.013

Missildine, W., Feldstein, G., Punzalan, J. C., & Parsons, J. T. (2005). S/he loves me, s/he loves me not: Questioning heterosexist assumptions of gender differences in sexual compulsivity and romantic obsession. *Sexual Addiction and Compulsivity, 12*, 1–12.

Monahan, K. C., & Lee, J. M. (2008). Adolescent sexual activity: Links between relational context and depressive symptoms. *Journal of Youth and Adolescence, 37*, 917–927. doi:10.1007/s10964-007-9256-5

Monson, C. M., Langhinrichsen-Rohling, J., & Taft, C. T. (2009). Sexual aggression in intimate relationships. In K. D. O'Leary & E. M. Woodin (Eds.), *Psychological and physical aggression in couples: Causes and interventions* (pp. 37–57). Washington, DC: American Psychological Association.

Moore, K. (2010). Sexuality and sense of self in later life: Japanese men's and women's reflections on sex and aging. *Journal of Cross-Cultural Gerontology, 25*, 149–163. doi:10.1007/s10823-010-9115-9

Moore, M. R. (2012). Intersectionality and the study of Black, sexual minority women. *Gender and Society, 26*, 33–39. doi:10.1177/0891243211427031

Muise, A., Christofides, E., & Desmarais, S. (2009). More information than you ever wanted: Does Facebook bring out the green-eyed monster of jealousy? *Cyberpsychology and Behavior, 12*, 441–444.

Muise, A., Desmarais, S., Impett, E., & Milhausen, R. R. (2011, September). *Approaching sexual desire in long-term couples: How approach and avoidance goals influence desire.* Paper presented at the 37th annual meeting of the Canadian Sex Research Forum, Vancouver, British Columbia, Canada.

Muise, A., Impett, E., Kogan, A., & Desmarais, S. (2012). Keeping the spark alive: Being motivated to meet a partner's sexual needs sustains sexual desire in long-term romantic relationships. *Social Psychological and Personality Science.* Advance online publication. doi:10.1177/1948550612457185

Nehzad, M. Z., & Goodarzi, A. M. (2011). Sexuality, intimacy, and marital satisfaction in Iranian first-time parents. *Journal of Sex and Marital Therapy, 37*, 77–88. doi:10.1080/0092623X.2011.547336

Nichols, M. (2004). Lesbian sexuality/female sexuality: Rethinking “lesbian bed death.” *Sexual and Relationship Therapy, 19*, 363–371. doi:10.1080/14681990412331298036

Noar, S. M., Zimmerman, R. S., & Atwood, K. A. (2004). Safer sex and sexually transmitted infections from a relationship perspective. In J. H. Harvey, A. Wenzel, & S. Sprecher (Eds.), *The handbook of sexuality in close relationships* (pp. 519–544). Mahwah, NJ: Erlbaum.

Oliver, M. B., & Hyde, J. S. (1993). Gender differences in sexuality: A meta-analysis. *Psychological Bulletin, 114*, 29–51. doi:10.1037/0033-2909.114.1.29

Olson, M., Russell, C., Higgins-Kessler, M., & Miller, R. (2002). Emotional processes following disclosure of an extramarital affair. *Journal of Marital and Family Therapy, 28*, 423–434. doi:10.1111/j.1752-0606.2002.tb00367.x

O’Sullivan, L. F., & Allgeier, E. R. (1998). Feigning sexual desire: Consenting to unwanted sexual activity in heterosexual dating relationships. *Journal of Sex Research, 35*, 234–243. doi:10.1080/00224499809551983

O’Sullivan, L. F., Cheng, M. M., Harris, K. M., & Brooks-Gunn, J. (2007). I wanna hold your hand: The progression of social, romantic, and sexual events in adolescent relationships. *Perspectives on Sexual and Reproductive Health, 39*, 100–107. doi:10.1363/3910007

O’Sullivan, L. F., & Meyer-Bahlburg, H. F. L. (2003). African-American and Latina inner-city girls’ reports of romantic and sexual development. *Journal of Social and Personal Relationships, 20*, 221–238. doi:10.1177/02654075030202006

Owen, J., & Fincham, F. D. (2011). Effects of gender and psychosocial factors on “friends with benefits” relationships among young adults. *Archives of Sexual Behavior, 40*, 311–320. doi:10.1007/s10508-010-9611-6

Panuzio, J., & DiLillo, D. (2010). Physical, psychological, and sexual intimate partner aggression among newlywed couples: Longitudinal prediction of marital satisfaction. *Journal of Family Violence, 25*, 689–699. doi:10.1007/s10896-010-9328-2

Papaharitou, S., Nakapoulou, E., Kirana, P., Giaglis, G., Moraitou, M., & Hatzchirou, D. (2008). Factors associated with sexuality in later life: An exploratory study of Greek married older adults. *Archives of Gerontology and Geriatrics, 46*, 191–201. doi:10.1016/j.archger.2007.03.008

Parish, W. L., Luo, Y., Laumann, E., Kew, M., & Yu, Z. (2007). Unwanted sexual activity among married women in urban China. *Journal of Sex Research, 44*, 158–171. doi:10.1080/00224490701263751

Parish, W. L., Luo, Y., Stolzenberg, R., Laumann, E., Farrer, G., & Pan, S. (2007). Sexual practices and sexual satisfaction: A population based study of Chinese urban adults. *Archives of Sexual Behavior, 36*, 5–20. doi:10.1007/s10508-006-9082-y

Paul, E. L., & Hayes, K. A. (2002). The casualties of casual sex: A qualitative exploration of the phenomenology of college students’ hook-ups. *Journal of Social and Personal Relationships, 19*, 639–661. doi:10.1177/0265407502195006

Penderson, W., Putcha-Bhagavatula, A., & Miller, L. (2011). Are men and women really that different? Examining sexual strategies theory (SST)’s key assumptions about sex-distinct mating mechanisms. *Sex Roles, 64*, 629–643. doi:10.1007/s11199-010-9811-5

Penhollow, T., Young, M., & Denny, G. (2009). Predictors of quality of life, sexual intercourse, and sexual satisfaction among active older adults. *American Journal of Health Education, 40*, 14–23.

Penke, L., & Asendorpf, J. (2008). Beyond global sociosexual orientations: A more differentiated look at sociosexuality and its effects on courtship and romantic relationships. *Journal of Personality and Social Psychology, 95*, 1113–1135. doi:10.1037/0022-3514.95.5.1113

Peplau, L. A. (2003). Human sexuality: How do men and women differ? *Current Directions in Psychological Science, 12*, 37–40. doi:10.1111/1467-8721.01221

Peplau, L. A., Fingerhut, A., & Beals, K. P. (2004). Sexuality in the relationships of lesbians and gay men. In J. H. Harvey, A. Wenzel, & S. Sprecher (Eds.), *The handbook of sexuality in close relationships* (pp. 349–370). Mahwah, NJ: Erlbaum.

Peplau, L. A., Rubin, Z., & Hill, C. T. (1977). Sexual intimacy in dating couples. *Journal of Social Issues, 33*, 86–109.

Peterson, J. L., & Hyde, J. S. (2010). A meta-analytic review of research on gender differences in sexuality, 1993–2007. *Psychological Bulletin, 136*, 21–38. doi:10.1037/a0017504

Pfeiffer, S. M., & Wong, P. T. P. (1989). Multidimensional jealousy. *Journal of Social and Personal Relationships, 6*, 181–196. doi:10.1177/026540758900600203

Plichta, S., & Falik, M. (2001). Prevalence of violence and its implications for women’s health. *Women’s Health Issues, 11*, 244–258. doi:10.1016/S1049-3867(01)00085-8

Potts, A., Grace, M., Vares, T., & Gavey, N. (2006). “Sex for life”? Men’s counter-stories on “erectile dysfunction,” male sexuality and ageing. *Sociology of Health and Illness, 28*, 306–329. doi:10.1111/j.1467-9566.2006.00494.x

Pujols, Y., Meston, C. M., & Seal, B. N. (2009). The association between sexual satisfaction and body image in women. *Journal of Sexual Medicine, 7*, 905–916. doi:10.1111/j.1743-6109.2009.01604.x

Quadagno, D., Sly, D., Harrison, D., Eberstein, I., & Soler, H. (1998). Ethnic differences in sexual decisions and behavior. *Archives of Sexual Behavior, 27*, 57–75. doi:10.1023/A:1018657825068

Rahmani, A., Khoei, E. M., & Gholi, L. A. (2009). Sexual satisfaction and its relation to marital happiness in Iranians. *Iranian Journal of Public Health, 38*, 77–82.

Ramirez, O. M., & Brown, J. (2010). Attachment style, rules regarding sex, and couple satisfaction: A study of gay male couples. *Australian and New Zealand Journal of Family Therapy, 31*, 202–213. doi:10.1375/anft.31.2.202

Ramisetty-Mikler, A., Caetano, R., & McGrath, C. (2007). Sexual aggression among White, Black, and Hispanic couples in the U.S.: Alcohol use, physical assault, and psychological aggression as its correlates. *American Journal of Drug and Alcohol Abuse, 33*, 31–43. doi;10.1080/00952990601082639

Regan, P. C. (2000). The role of sexual desire and sexual activity in dating relationships. *Social Behavior and Personality, 28*, 51–59.

Regan, P. C., & Berscheid, E. (1996). Beliefs about the state, goals, and objects of sexual desire. *Journal of Sex and Marital Therapy, 22*, 110–120.

Ridley, C. A., Cate, R. M., Collins, D. M., Reesing, A. L., Lucero, A. A., Gilson, M. S., & Almeida, D. M. (2006). The ebb and flow of marital lust: A relational approach. *Journal of Sex Research, 43*, 144–154. doi:10.1080/00224490609552309

Rosen, R. (2000). Prevalence and risk factors of sexual dysfunction in men and women. *Current Psychiatry Reports, 2*, 189–195. doi:10.1007/s11920-996-0006-2

Rosser, B. R. S., Metz, M. E., Bockting, W. O., & Buroker, T. (1997). Sexual difficulties, concerns, and satisfaction in homosexual men: An empirical study with implications for HIV prevention. *Journal of Sex and Marital Therapy, 23*, 61–73.

Rostosky, S. S., Galliher, R. V., Welsh, D. P., & Kawaguchi, M. C. (2000). Sexual behaviors and relationship qualities in late adolescent couples. *Journal of Adolescence, 23*, 583–597. doi:10.1006/jado.2000.0345

Rubin, H., & Campbell, L. (2012). Day-to-day changes in intimacy predict heightened relationship passion, sexual occurrence, and sexual satisfaction: A dyadic diary analysis. *Social Psychological and Personality Science, 3*, 224–231.

Rusbult, C. E., & Van Lange, P. A. M. (2008). Why we need interdependence theory. *Social and Personality Psychology Compass, 2*, 2049–2070. doi:10.1111/j.1751-9004.2008.00147.x

Russell, D. (1990). *Rape in marriage.* Bloomington: Indiana University Press.

Santelli, J. S., Lowry, R., Brener, N. D., & Robin, L. (2000). The association of sexual behaviors with socioeconomic status, family structure and race/ethnicity among US adolescents. *American Journal of Public Health, 90*, 1582–1588. doi:10.2105/AJPH.90.10.1582

Sassler, S. (2010). Partnering across the life course: Sex, relationships, and mate selection. *Journal of Marriage and the Family, 72*, 557–575. doi:10.1111/j.1741-3737.2010.00718.x

Schachner, D. A., & Shaver, P. R. (2004). Attachment dimensions and sexual motives. *Personal Relationships, 11*, 179–195. doi:10.1111/j.1475-6811.2004.00077.x

Schmitt, D. (2005). Sociosexuality from Argentina to Zimbabwe: A 48-nation study of sex, culture, and strategies of human mating. *Behavioral and Brain Sciences, 28*, 247–311. doi:10.1017/S0140525X05000051

Schmitt, D. P., Alcalay, L., Allik, J., Ault, L., Austers, I., Bennett, K. L., . . . Zupanèiè, A.; International Sexuality Description Project. (2003). Universal sex differences in the desire for sexual variety: Tests from 52 nations, 6 continents, and 13 islands. *Journal of Personality and Social Psychology, 85*, 85–104. doi:10.1037/0022-3514.85.1.85

Shackelford, T., Schmitt, D., & Buss, D. (2005). Universal dimensions of human mate preferences. *Personality and Individual Differences, 39*, 447–458. doi:10.1016/j.paid.2005.01.023

Shaughnessy, K., Byers, E. S., & Thornton, S. J. (2011). What is cybersex? Heterosexual students' definitions. *International Journal of Sexual Health, 23*, 79–89. doi:10.1080/19317611.2010.546945

Shaver, P., Hazan, C., & Bradshaw, D. (1988). Love as attachment. In R. J. Sternberg & M. L. Barnes (Eds.), *The psychology of love* (pp. 68–99). New Haven, CT: Yale University Press.

Shields, N. M., Resick, P. A., & Hanneke, C. R. (1990). Victims of marital rape. In R. T. Ammerman & M. Hersen (Eds.), *Treatment of family violence* (pp. 165–182). New York, NY: Wiley.

Simms, K. E., & Meana, M. (2010). Why did passion wane? A qualitative study of married women's attributes for declines in desire. *Journal of Sex and Marital Therapy, 36*, 360–380.

Simpson, J., & Gangestad, S. (1991). Individual differences in sociosexuality: Evidence for convergent and discriminant validity. *Journal of Personality and Social Psychology, 60*, 870–83. doi:10.1037/0022-3514.60.6.870

Simpson, J. A. (1990). Influence of attachment styles on romantic relationships. *Journal of Personality and Social Psychology, 59*, 971–980. doi:10.1037/0022-3514.59.5.971

Simpson, J. A., Wilson, C. L., & Winterheld, H. A. (2004). Sociosexuality and romantic relationships. In J. H. Harvey, A. Wenzel, & S. Sprecher (Eds.), *Handbook of sexuality in close relationships* (pp. 87–111). Mahwah, NJ: Erlbaum.

Smiler, A. P., Ward, M. L., Caruthers, A., & Merriwether, A. (2005). Pleasure, empowerment, and love: Factors associated with a positive first coitus. *Sexuality Research and Social Policy, 2*, 41–55.

Smith, A., Lyons, A., Ferris, J., Richters, J., Pitts, M., Shelley, J., & Simpson, J. M. (2011). Sexual and relationship satisfaction among heterosexual men and women: The importance of desired frequency of sex. *Journal of Sex and Marital Therapy, 37*, 104–115. doi: 10.1080/0092623X.2011.560531

Sprecher, S. (2002). Sexual satisfaction in premarital relationships: Associations with satisfaction, love, commitment, and stability. *Journal of Sex Research, 39*, 190–196. doi:10.1080/00224490209552141

Sprecher, S., & Regan, P. C. (1998). Passionate and companionate love in courting and young married couples. *Sociological Inquiry, 68*, 163–185. doi:10.1111/j.1475-682X.1998.tb00459.x

Stone, N., & Ingham, R. (2002). Factors affecting British teenagers' contraceptive use at first intercourse: The importance of partner communication. *Perspectives on Sexual and Reproductive Health, 34*, 191–197.

Stulhofer, A., Busko, V., & Brouillard, P. (2010). Development and bicultural validation of the new sexual satisfaction scale. *Journal of Sex Research, 47*, 257–268. doi:10.1080/00224490903100561

Temple, J., Weston, R., Rodriquez, B., & Marshall, L. (2007). Differing effects of partner and nonpartner sexual assault on women's mental health. *Violence Against Women, 13*, 285–297. doi:10.1177/1077801206297437

Theiss, J. A., & Nagy, M. E. (2010). Actor-partner effects in the associations between relationship characteristics and reactions to marital sexual intimacy. *Personal Relationships, 27*, 1089–1109. doi:10.1177/0265407510381254

Thompson, S. (1990). Putting a big thing into a little hole: Teenage girls' accounts of sexual initiation. *Journal of Sex Research, 27*, 341–361. doi:10.1080/00224499009551564

Tjaden, P., & Thoennes, N. (2000). *Extent, nature, and consequences of intimate partner violence: Findings from the National Violence Against Women Survey* (Report No. NCJ-181867). Washington, DC: National Institute of Justice.

Tolman, D. L. (2006). In a different position: Conceptualizing female adolescent sexuality development within compulsory heterosexuality. *New Directions for Child and Adolescent Development,* 112, 71–90. doi:10.1002/cd.163

Tolman, D. L., & Diamond, L. M. (2001). Desegregating sexuality research: Cultural and biological perspectives on gender and desire. *Annual Review of Sex Research, 12*, 33–74.

Tolman, D. L., & McClelland, S. I. (2011). Normative sexuality development in adolescence: A decade in review, 2000–2009. *Journal of Research on Adolescence, 21*, 242–255. doi:10.1111/j.1532-7795.2010.00726.x

Træen, B. (2010). Sexual dissatisfaction among heterosexual Norwegians in couple relationships. *Sexual and Relationship Therapy, 25*, 132–147.

Træen, B., & Martinussen, M. (2008). Extradyadic activity in a random sample of Norwegian couples. *Journal of Sex Research, 45*, 319–328. doi:10.1080/00224490802398324

Treas, J., & Giesen, D. (2000). Sexual infidelity among married and cohabiting Americans. *Journal of Marriage and the Family, 62*, 48–60. doi:10.1111/j.1741-3737.2000.00048.x

Tsui, L., & Nicoladis, E. (2004). Losing it: Similarities and differences in first intercourse experiences of men and women. *Canadian Journal of Human Sexuality, 13*, 95–106.

Uchino, B. N., Cacioppo, J. T., & Kiecolt-Glaser, J. K. (1996). The relationship between social support and physiological processes: A review with emphasis on underlying mechanisms and implications for health. *Psychological Bulletin, 119*, 488–531. doi:10.1037/0033-2909.119.3.488

Udry, J. R. (1988). Biological predispositions and social control in adolescent sexual behavior. *American Sociological Review, 53*, 709–722.

Umidi, S., Pini, M., Ferrett, M., Vergani, C., & Annoni, G. (2007). Affectivity and sexuality in the elderly: Often neglected aspects. *Archives of Gerontology and Geriatrics, 44*(Suppl. 1), 413–417. doi:10.1016/j.archger.2007.01058

VanderDrift, L. E., Lehmiller, J. J., & Kelly, J. R. (2012). Commitment in friends with benefits relationships: Implications for relationship and safe-sex outcomes. *Personal Relationships, 19,* 1–13. doi:10.1111/j.1475-6811.2010.01324.x

Vares, T., Potts, A., Gavey, N., & Grace, M. (2007). Reconceptualizing cultural narratives of mature women's sexuality in the Viagra era. *Journal of Aging Studies, 21*, 153–164. doi:10.1016/j.jaging.2006.08.002

Vinkers, C. D. W., Finkenauer, C., & Hawk, S. T. (2011). Why do close partners snoop? Predictors of intrusive behavior in newlywed couples. *Personal Relationships, 18*, 110–124.

Vohs, K. D., Catanese, K. R., & Baumeister, R. F. (2004). Sex in "his" versus "her" relationships. In J. H. Harvey, A. Wenzel, & S. Sprecher (Eds.), *The handbook of sexuality in close relationships* (pp. 455–474). Mahwah, NJ: Erlbaum.

Waite, L. J., Laumann, E. O., Das, A. S., & Philip, L. (2009). Sexuality: Measures of partnerships, practices, attitudes, and problems in the National Social Life, Health, and Aging Study. *Journals of Gerontology, Series B: Psychological Sciences and Social Sciences, 64*(Suppl. 1), i56–i66.

Waldner-Haugrad, L., & Gratch, L. (1997). Sexual coercion in gay/lesbian relationships: Descriptives and gender differences. *Violence and Victims, 12*, 87–98.

Wallen, K. (1995). The evolution of female sexual desire. In P. R. Abramson & S. D. Pinkerton (Eds.), *Sexual nature, sexual culture* (pp. 57–59). Chicago, IL: University of Chicago Press.

Weaver, A. D., MacKeigan, K. L., & MacDonald, H. A. (2011). Experiences and perceptions of young adults in friends with benefits relationships: A qualitative study. *Canadian Journal of Human Sexuality, 20*, 41–53.

Weinberg, M. S., Lottes, I. L., & Shaver, F. M. (1995). Swedish or American heterosexual college youth: Who is more permissive? *Archives of Sexual Behavior, 24*, 409–437.

Weisskirch, R., & Delevi, R. (2011). "Sexting" and adult romantic attachment. *Computers in Human Behavior, 27*, 1697–1701. doi:10.1016/j.chb.2011.02.008

Welsh, D. P., Haugen, P. T., Widman, L., Darling, N., & Grello, C. M. (2005). Kissing is good: A developmental investigation of sexuality in adolescent romantic couples. *Sexuality Research and Social Policy, 2*, 32–41. doi:10.1525/srsp.2005.2.4.32

Wentland, J. J., Herold, E. S., Desmarais, S., & Milhausen, R. R. (2009). Differentiating highly sexual women from less sexual women. *Canadian Journal of Human Sexuality, 18*, 169–182.

Wentland, J. J., & Ressing, E. (2011). Taking casual sex not too casually: Exploring definitions of casual sexual relationships. *Canadian Journal of Human Sexuality, 20*, 75–91.

Whisman, M., Gordon, K., & Chatav, Y. (2007). Predicting sexual infidelity in a population-based sample of married individuals. *Journal of Family Psychology, 21*, 320–324. doi:10.1037/0893-3200.21.2.320

Whisman, M., & Snyder, D. (2007). Sexual infidelity in a national survey of American women: Differences in prevalence and correlates as a function of method of assessment. *Journal of Family Psychology, 21*, 147–154. doi:10.1037/0893-3200.21.2.147

Widman, L., Welsh, D. P., McNulty, J. K., & Little, K. C. (2006). Sexual communication and contraceptive use in adolescent dating couples. *Journal of Adolescent Health, 39*, 893–899. doi:10.1016/j.jadohealth.2006.06.003

Wiederman, M. (1997). Extramarital sex: Prevalence and correlates in a national survey. *Journal of Sex Research, 34*, 167–174. doi:10.1080/00224499709551881

Wierzalis, E. A., Barret, B., Pope, M., & Rankins, M. (2006). Gay men and aging: Sex and intimacy. In D. Kimmel, R. Rose, & S. David (Eds.), *Lesbian, gay, bisexual and transgender aging: Research and clinical perspectives* (pp. 91–109). New York, NY: Columbia University Press.

Wight, D., Parkes, A., Strange, V., Allen, E., Bonell, C., & Henderson, M. (2008). The quality of young people's heterosexual relationships: A longitudinal analysis of characteristics shaping subjective experience. *Perspectives on Sexual and Reproductive Health, 40*, 226–237.

Willetts, M. C., Sprecher, S., & Beck, F. D. (2004). Overview of sexual practices and attitudes within relational contexts. In J. H. Harvey, A. Wenzel, & S. Sprecher (Eds.), *The handbook of sexuality in close relationships* (pp. 57–85). Mahwah, NJ: Erlbaum.

Willoughby, B. J., & Vitas, J. (2012). Sexual desire discrepancy: The effect of individual differences in desired and actual sexual frequency on dating couples. *Archives of Sexual Behavior, 41*, 477–486. doi:10.1007/s10508-011-9766-9

Woloski-Wruble, A., Oliel, Y., Leefsma, M., & Hochner-Celnikier, D. (2010). Sexual activities, sexual and life satisfaction, and successful aging in women. *Journal of Sexual Medicine, 7*, 2401–2410. doi:10.1016/S0022-5347(11)60266-8

Woo, S. T. J., Brotto, L. A., & Gorzalka, B. B. (2011). The role of sex guilt in the relationship between culture and women's sexual desire. *Archives of Sexual Behavior, 40*, 385–394. doi:10.1007/s10508-010-9609-0

Wood, J. M., Mansfield, P. K., & Koch, P. B. (2007). Negotiating sexual agency: Postmenopausal women's meaning and experience of sexual desire. *Qualitative Health Research, 17*, 189–200. doi:10.1177/1049732306297415

Yucel, D., & Gassanov, M. A. (2010). Exploring actor and partner correlates of sexual satisfaction among married couples. *Social Science Research, 39*, 725–738. doi:10.1016/j.ssresearch.2009.09.0022

CHAPTER 11

SEXUAL WELL-BEING

E. Sandra Byers and Uzma S. Rehman

Sexuality is an important aspect of most people's lives. Moreover, sexual well-being has consistently been shown to be robustly linked to positive individual and relationship outcomes. Indeed, it is one of the strongest predictors of relationship satisfaction and stability (Christopher & Sprecher, 2000; Karney & Bradbury, 1995; see also Chapter 10, this volume) as well as of overall psychological well-being and quality of life (Apt, Hurlbert, Pierce, & White, 1996; Davison, Bell, LaChina, Holden, & Davis, 2009; Laumann et al., 2006). But what is sexual well-being and does it differ from sexual (dis)satisfaction, sexual problems, and sexual difficulties? Certainly, individuals who report low sexual satisfaction are more likely to report sexual disorders or problems related to their sexual response, such as low sexual desire or arousal or orgasm difficulties (see Chapter 8, this volume). Thus, sexual well-being and sexual difficulties are associated with each other (Dunn, Croft, & Hackett, 2000; MacNeil & Byers, 1997). However, some individuals who do not have sexual problems report low sexual satisfaction; conversely, some individuals who experience a sexual problem or disorder report high sexual satisfaction. Furthermore, resolving a sexual problem or disorder does not necessarily increase sexual satisfaction. Thus, health and wellness in general, and sexual well-being in particular, are not simply the absence of distress, disease, symptoms, or dysfunction, just as happiness is not the absence of depression (Nosek et al., 1994; World Health Organization, 2006; see also Chapter 21, this volume).

In this chapter, we begin by providing a conceptual definition for sexual well-being. We then review research examining the role of individual factors and then interpersonal factors in sexual satisfaction; most of this research has not been based in theory. To underscore the importance of and need for theoretically informed research on sexual satisfaction, we review the interpersonal exchange models of sexual satisfaction (IEMSS; Lawrance & Byers, 1992) and examine available data in light of the key tenets of the IEMSS. Finally, we discuss how the IEMSS can be further developed, focusing specifically on research questions that will facilitate conceptual advancements in this field of study. Specifically, we provide examples of the types of theoretical questions that can enhance understanding of variation in sexual satisfaction as well as within-person changes in sexual satisfaction over time and outline the methods that are best suited to investigation of these questions. It is important to note that in general, research has found that most individuals who are in a romantic relationship report high sexual satisfaction (e.g., Lawrance & Byers, 1995; MacNeil & Byers, 2005, 2009; Purnine & Carey, 1997). Furthermore, even when studies using nonclinical samples have found that two groups differ significantly in their sexual satisfaction, the means indicate that the less satisfied group is still sexually satisfied overall, albeit less satisfied than the other group.

Order of authorship was determined alphabetically.

http://dx.doi.org/10.1037/14193-011
APA Handbook of Sexuality and Psychology: Vol. 1. Person-Based Approaches, D. L. Tolman and L. M. Diamond (Editors-in-Chief)

CONCEPTUALIZING SEXUAL WELL-BEING

Our conceptualization of the construct of sexual well-being is informed by theories and research in the area of subjective psychological well-being. Researchers examining subjective psychological well-being have tended to take one of two approaches (Ryff, 1989; Ryff & Keyes, 1995). The first approach has been to define psychological well-being in terms of the balance of positive and negative affect (Bradburn, 1969; McDowell, 2010; Ryff & Keyes, 1995). Individuals for whom positive feelings such as happiness predominate are seen as having high psychological well-being. When applied to the sexual domain, this approach would posit that an individual who has high sexual well-being would have a favorable balance between the positive and the negative feelings they experience with respect to their sexual life. The second approach has been to define psychological well-being in terms of overall life satisfaction, with satisfaction viewed as a cognitive component that is based on individuals' comparison of their views of their current situation and their ideals (McDowell, 2010; Ryff & Keyes, 1995). From this perspective, individuals' sexual well-being would be defined as their appraisal that their current sexual life compares favorably to how they would ideally like their sexual life to be.

Thus, it is important that any definition of sexual well-being takes both cognitions and affective factors into account. The definition of *subjective sexual satisfaction* proposed by Lawrance and Byers (1995) does just this. They defined sexual satisfaction as "an affective response arising from one's subjective evaluation of the positive and negative dimensions associated with one's sexual relationship" (p. 514). That is, sexual satisfaction is seen as a global emotional response that arises from cognitive appraisals and affective responses to various aspects of an individual's sexual life. In this chapter, we define *sexual well-being* in terms of subjective sexual satisfaction as conceptualized by Lawrance and Byers. Note that as a global emotional response, this definition encompasses satisfaction with specific aspects of a person's sexuality, sexual relationship, and sexual functioning such as their satisfaction with their sexual response, frequency of sexual activity, and enacted sexual script. Furthermore, this definition distinguishes sexual well-being from sexual health, which is a broader concept that includes physical, social, and psychological sexual well-being as well as the absence of disease, dysfunction, and sexual violence (World Health Organization, 2006).

Another important aspect of conceptualizations of psychological well-being that likely also applies to sexual well-being is that it involves both giving and receiving as well as positive relations with others (McDowell, 2010; Ryff, 1989). Most frequently, sexuality is an individual experience that occurs in a dyadic context. Thus, for most individuals sexual well-being and sexual satisfaction are inextricably linked to the experiences of the partner or partners. That is, an individual's sexual satisfaction is influenced by his or her partner's levels of satisfaction as well as by other partner and relationship characteristics (Byers & MacNeil, 2006; Henderson, Lehavot, & Simoni, 2009; Lawrance & Byers, 1995; Purnine & Carey, 1997). Lawrance and Byers's (1995) definition of sexual satisfaction places sexual satisfaction in the interpersonal or relational context in which sexual activity occurs (i.e., satisfaction with the sexual relationship) rather than as a characteristic of the individual. Thus, in this chapter, we distinguish the construct of sexual satisfaction from an individual's evaluation of sexual activity that does not involve another person (e.g., solitary masturbation; see Chapter 10, this volume).

ROLE OF INDIVIDUAL FACTORS IN SEXUAL SATISFACTION

Researchers have examined the relationships between a range of factors and sexual satisfaction as a way to identify characteristics that place individuals at risk for experiencing low sexual satisfaction. In the sections that follow, we review several of these factors.

Demographic Factors

A number of demographic variables have been investigated with the goal of better understanding factors that place certain individuals at greater risk of experiencing low sexual satisfaction. Little to no empirical support exists for a relationship between most of these variables and sexual satisfaction. Specifically, past research has failed to find an association between demographic characteristics such as race, education, income, or employment status and sexual satisfaction (see review by Rehman, Fallis, & Byers, 2013). However, some (but not all) researchers have found that age, gender, and sexual orientation are associated with sexual satisfaction. Thus, we consider only these demographic characteristics in greater detail.

Age. The literature on the association between age and sexual satisfaction has been characterized by inconsistent results. Some studies have found no relationship (e.g., Bancroft, Long, & McCabe, 2011; Dundon & Rellini, 2010; Tao & Brody, 2011); other studies have found that sexual satisfaction increases with age, at least for women (e.g., Trompeter, Bettencourt, & Barrett-Connor, 2012); and yet others have found that sexual satisfaction declines with age (e.g., Call, Sprecher, & Schwartz, 1995; Chao et al., 2011; Laumann et al., 2006; Pedersen & Blekesaune, 2003; Træen & Schaller, 2010). In general, the studies that have found a negative association between age and sexual satisfaction tend to be more methodologically rigorous in terms of sample size and use of representative sampling methods, resulting in higher levels of external validity. It is likely that lower levels of sexual satisfaction associated with increasing age are due to age-related declines in quality of health (Heiman, 2001; Laumann et al., 2006). Indeed, in their study of 27,500 men and women in 29 different countries, Laumann et al. (2006) found that age was no longer associated with sexual well-being after controlling for factors such as health. The link between age and sexual satisfaction can also be explained by habituation, the process by which individuals become less interested in sex through repeated exposure to the same partner over time. However, habituation alone is unlikely to explain the link between age and sexual satisfaction because many individuals experience declines in sexual frequency and sexual desire with age without a concomitant decline in sexual satisfaction (Trompeter et al., 2012). In addition, Heiman et al. (2011) found that for both men and women in midlife and older, longer relationship duration was associated with greater sexual satisfaction. In summary, although a greater number of studies have suggested that sexual satisfaction declines with age, the correlations are quite weak, and when other demographic variables are taken into account, age-related declines tend to disappear (see Chapters 8 and 17, this volume).

Gender. The data on gender differences in sexual satisfaction among heterosexual individuals are also highly variable and contradictory. However, there tends to be slightly more support for the position that men report higher levels of sexual satisfaction than do women. For example, Laumann et al. (2006) found that across different sociocultural contexts, men reported higher levels of sexual satisfaction overall than did women. Similarly, Petersen and Hyde (2010) concluded from their meta-analysis of research on gender differences in sexuality that men report greater sexual satisfaction. However, the overall effect size for this difference was small ($d = 0.17$). Some studies have examined the interaction between age and gender. These results have suggested that declines in sexual satisfaction tend to become greater for women, compared with men, beginning in late mid-life to early old age (e.g., Edwards & Booth, 1994; Laumann, Gagnon, Michael, & Michaels, 1994; see Chapter 2, this volume).

One explanation for the gender differences that have been found, at least in North America, is that they are a consequence of sampling. These studies were based on between-subjects comparisons rather than on couples—that is, they compared men and women who were not in a relationship with each other. Thus, they may reflect differences between the men and women who volunteered for these studies rather than differences in the experiences of men and women who are having sex with each other. MacNeil and Byers (2005, 2009) studied the sexual satisfaction of both members of Canadian heterosexual couples in dating and long-term relationships. They found that the male and female partners did not differ from each other in their sexual satisfaction. Similarly, Purnine and Carey (1997) reported similar levels of satisfaction for male and female partners in long-term relationships, although they did not test these differences statistically.

Another possible explanation for findings that men report higher sexual satisfaction than do women is that some of the measures used to assess sexual satisfaction include items that are more important to the sexual satisfaction of men than to the sexual satisfaction of women (Lawrance & Byers, 1995). That is, the gender differences that have been found in some studies may reflect the ways in which sexual satisfaction has been operationalized rather than men's and women's global appraisal of their sexual relationship.

Sexual orientation. Some past studies have examined whether heterosexual and sexual minority individuals differ in their levels of sexual satisfaction. Most studies that have included both men and women and have considered a variety of relationship types (heterosexual, lesbian, gay) have found no significant effects for men or women in mixed-sex versus same-sex relationships in overall sexual satisfaction (Blumstein & Schwartz, 1983; Holmberg & Blair, 2009; Holmberg, Blair, & Phillips, 2010; Kurdek, 1991; Kuyper & Vanwesenbeeck, 2011; Matthews, Tartaro, & Hughes, 2002). However, Henderson et al. (2009) found that heterosexual women reported significantly higher levels of sexual satisfaction than did lesbian and bisexual women, although the size of the difference was small. Similarly, Gil (2007) found that gay men reported significantly lower sexual satisfaction than did heterosexual men. However, different methods were used to recruit the two samples, making it difficult to know whether the results are true or an artifact of differing study methodologies. That is, the heterosexual men were all students in an introductory psychology class, whereas the gay sample included both students and men recruited from a gay support group. In conclusion, although the findings about the link between sexual orientation and sexual satisfaction are discrepant, the more methodologically rigorous studies have failed to find such an association (see Chapters 8 and 20, this volume).

Summary of the role of demographic factors in sexual satisfaction. For the most part, demographic factors have not been shown to be related to sexual satisfaction. The data on the link between age, gender, and sexual orientation and sexual satisfaction are characterized by discrepant findings. However, overall the research has suggested that sexual satisfaction declines with age; that men tend to experience higher levels of satisfaction than do women; and that heterosexual and sexual minority individuals do not differ in their sexual satisfaction. The discrepancies in the findings on the effects of age and gender on sexual satisfaction are most likely the result of methodological differences across studies. Indeed, the studies we reviewed here have focused on different populations, used a variety of different measures to assess sexual satisfaction, and varied in their data analytic methods (e.g., modeling sexual satisfaction dimensionally vs. categorically; see Chapter 6, this volume).

Personality, Affective, and Cognitive Factors

Researchers have examined the extent to which an individual's personality and cognitive–affective responses are associated with sexual satisfaction. In the sections that follow, we review the characteristics that have been investigated most thoroughly and propose potential mechanisms that might link personality and cognitive–affective factors to sexual satisfaction.

Personality factors. Most personality variables have not been found to be associated with sexual satisfaction. For instance, researchers have not found a significant association between four of the Big Five personality traits and sexual satisfaction. That is, conscientiousness (associated with being detail oriented, responsible, and industrious), agreeableness (associated with being cooperative, good natured, and helping others), openness to experience (associated with imagination and curiosity), and extraversion (associated with being outgoing, sociable, and confident) have not been found to be associated with sexual well-being (Donnellan, Conger, & Bryant, 2004). However, many researchers have shown that the fifth of the Big Five personality factors, neuroticism or the tendency to experience negative mood, is associated with lower sexual satisfaction (Costa, Fagan, Piedmont, Ponticas, & Wise, 1992; Davis et al.,

2006; Goldenberg et al., 2001; Heaven, Fitzpatrick, Craig, Kelly, & Sebar, 2000). Fisher and McNulty (2008) extended these findings by demonstrating that an individual's level of neuroticism predicted both his or her sexual satisfaction as well as declines in sexual satisfaction over time.

Constructs that are theoretically related to neuroticism, such as symptoms of depression and anxiety, have also been shown to be associated with lower levels of sexual satisfaction in both heterosexual individuals and sexual minority women (e.g., Henderson et al., 2009; Van Minnen & Kampman, 2000). Investigators have tended to examine the relationship between each of these variables (i.e., neuroticism, depressive symptoms, anxiety) and sexual satisfaction in isolation without taking into consideration the extensive overlap between these constructs. The issue of construct overlap is a pervasive problem in psychological research and is not limited to studies on sexuality (Judge, Erez, Bono, & Thoresen, 2002). In future studies, researchers need to identify whether these affective and personality tendencies have a common aspect, such as strong emotional reactivity, that leads to lower sexual satisfaction.

Attachment style. According to attachment theory, the type of relationship that infants have with their primary caregiver can affect their emotions, behaviors, and cognitions about their close relationships throughout their lives, particularly their romantic relationships (Bartholomew & Horowitz, 1991; Hazan & Shaver, 1987). Two broad categories of attachment styles exist: secure and insecure. Individuals with a secure attachment style tend to trust and rely on their partners for support; individuals with an insecure attachment style tend to experience anxiety or avoid intimacy in their relationships. More specifically, insecure individuals high in attachment anxiety tend to worry that their romantic partner will not be sufficiently available to them and fear being rejected. Insecure individuals high in attachment avoidance tend to distrust their partner and try to maintain independence from them.

Secure attachment style has been shown to predict a variety of positive sexual outcomes. Compared with other attachment styles, individuals who are high on attachment security are more likely to endorse positive attitudes toward touch and show more affection toward their partner (Brennan, Wu, & Love, 1998). In addition, secure attachment has been found to be associated with greater frequency of mutually initiated sexual contact and willingness to experiment sexually within the primary relationship (Hazan, Zeifman, & Middleton, 1994). On the basis of their review of the literature on attachment styles and sexuality, Feeney and Noller (2004) concluded that

> secure individuals' positive models of self and others foster a sense of confidence in the self as a sexual being, together with an appreciation of the intimate nature of sexual interactions. In other words, positive models of self and others are played out in attitudes and behaviors that promote active and satisfying sexual relationships. (p. 197)

In contrast, insecure patterns of attachment are generally associated with lower levels of sexual satisfaction (Brassard, Shaver, & Lussier, 2007; Butzer & Campbell, 2008; Davis et al., 2006). For example, Davis et al. (2006) found that both anxious and avoidant insecure attachment tendencies were associated with lower emotional and physical sexual satisfaction. These researchers also found that one of the mechanisms by which attachment style affected sexual satisfaction was through overall relationship satisfaction. That is, one way that attachment style affects relationships is by influencing the way that partners interact. For example, Scharfe and Bartholomew (1995) studied 128 established couples and found that individuals with secure attachment styles responded constructively during problem solving even in response to their partner's negative comments. In contrast, individuals with fearful attachment styles tended to avoid or withdraw from the discussion. Avoidance and withdrawal have both been shown to be associated with relationship distress (Gottman, 1994). As discussed later, relationship satisfaction is closely linked to sexual satisfaction (Lawrance & Byers, 1995; MacNeil & Byers, 2005, 2009; Purnine & Carey, 1997).

Sexual motives. *Sexual motives* refers to the reasons why people engage in sexual activity. Meston and Buss (2007) documented 237 distinct reasons for why people have sex that correspond to 13 general categories of motives. In a study involving 544 undergraduate students, not all of whom were in a romantic relationship, Stephenson, Ahrold, and Meston (2011) found that sexual satisfaction was positively associated with love and commitment motives and negatively associated with self-esteem and resources motives for both men and women. That is, people who more frequently engage in sexual activity to express their love and commitment to their partner are more sexually satisfied, whereas individuals who engage in sexual activity to attain resources (e.g., get a job) or to enhance their self-esteem are less sexually satisfied. For women, expression, pleasure, and experience-seeking motives were also associated with sexual satisfaction. Specifically, women who engaged in sexual activity more frequently for expression or pleasure motives were more sexually satisfied, and women who engaged in sexual activity to enhance their experience were less sexually satisfied. Unfortunately, the authors did not examine whether these findings were affected by the context in which sex occurred; thus, the extent to which these results apply to sexual activity with a romantic partner is not known. This is particularly problematic because some of the motives more likely apply to individuals who are in a relationship (e.g., love and commitment motives) and others more likely apply to individuals not in a relationship (e.g., resource attainment or experience enhancement motives). Nonetheless, even within relationships some motives (e.g., love and commitment) are likely to enhance sexual satisfaction, whereas other motives (e.g., duty and pressure) are likely to decrease sexual satisfaction (see also Chapter 10, this volume).

Body image. Concerns about body image are very common among North American women, even when sampling nonclinical populations (e.g., Cash, Phillips, Santos, & Hrabosky, 2004). Considerable work by feminist and other scholars has examined how dominant sociocultural values and media representations propagate women's feelings of discontentment and lack of acceptance of their body and appearance, which, in turn, may negatively affect their sexual well-being (e.g., Stice, 2002). Indeed, studies with college-age women have shown that poor body image is negatively associated with a number of dimensions of sexual well-being, including lower levels of sexual self-efficacy, lower sexual assertiveness, poorer sexual self-esteem, lower sexual frequency, lower sexual enjoyment, higher sexual anxiety, and more sexual problems (Ackard, Kearney-Cooke, & Peterson, 2000; Faith & Schare, 1993; Lowery et al., 2005; Pujols, Meston, & Seal, 2010; Weaver & Byers, 2006; Yamamiya, Cash, & Thompson, 2006). It is important to note that associations between body image and various sexual outcomes tend to remain significant, even after controlling for actual body size (Pujols et al., 2010; Weaver & Byers, 2006), thus suggesting that a woman's perception of her body size, rather than her actual body size, is what affects sexuality-related outcomes.

Most of the research on body image and sexual satisfaction has focused on women, with very little research examining the influence of men's body image on their sexual satisfaction. This focus is partly because women tend to have poorer body evaluations and report higher distress about their body image than do men (Cash & Deagle, 1997). However, some studies have demonstrated that men also report dissatisfaction with their bodies, although they are more concerned about body shape than body weight (Corson & Andersen, 2002). Holt and Lyness (2007) found that both men and women with more positive body image reported higher sexual satisfaction. Interestingly, they did not find that gender moderated this relationship, supporting the perspective that the influence of body image concerns on psychosexual outcomes is not limited to women. In a subsequent study, Penhollow and Young (2008) found that body image variables accounted for a significant amount of variation in women's and men's sexual satisfaction (see also Chapter 25, this volume).

Sexual cognitions. Individuals' thoughts during sexual activity—that is, whether they attend to their own and their partner's sexual pleasure (i.e., having erotic thoughts) or experience cognitive interference—are of particular relevance to sexual satisfaction (de Jong, 2010). *Cognitive interference* refers to nonerotic thoughts that distract the person from focusing on the erotic experience and may adversely affect sexual well-being, including sexual satisfaction (Barlow, 1986; Carvalho & Nobre, 2010; Dove & Widerman, 2000; Nobre & Pinto-Gouveia, 2008a, 2008b; Pujols et al., 2010; Purdon & Holdaway, 2006; Purdon & Watson, 2011). For example, Purdon and Watson (2011) found that men and women who had more frequent nonerotic thoughts and reported that these thoughts caused them greater anxiety reported lower sexual satisfaction. Purdon and Holdaway (2006) also noted that among university students, nonerotic thoughts most often relate to concerns about external consequences of the sexual activity, emotional consequences of the activity, body image (particularly for women), and concerns about performance (particularly for men). However, people can also have other types of distracting cognitions such as thoughts about life stressors (e.g., work), sexual abuse, morality and guilt, and dislike of the sexual activity. Masters and Johnson (1970) used the term *spectatoring* to describe one type of cognitive interference: a process by which an individual detaches himself or herself from the sexual experience and monitors and evaluates his or her performance (see also Pujols et al., 2010).

Potential mechanisms linking personality and cognitive–affective factors to sexual satisfaction. The tendencies to experience negative emotions, poor body image, insecure attachment style, and cognitive interference are associated with lower sexual satisfaction. These results, of course, do not identify the mechanisms by which these characteristics affect sexual satisfaction. One likely mechanism is that cognitive interference is not only directly linked to low sexual satisfaction but also mediates the relationships between sexual satisfaction and neuroticism, insecure attachment style, and poor body image. That is, cognitive interference in general, and the process of spectatoring in particular, can be triggered by a variety of different concerns in people with specific cognitive or attentional biases (de Jong, 2010; Wiegel, Scepkowski, & Barlow, 2007). In keeping with this view, Barlow (1986; see also Elliott & O'Donohue, 1997; Payne, Cheng, Govorun, & Stewart, 2005) has demonstrated that negative emotion (e.g., anxiety) leads some individuals (in this case, individuals with a sexual disorder) to focus on nonerotic thoughts, which, in turn, heightens the negative emotions, interfering with sexual responding. This process also likely plays an etiological role in low sexual satisfaction. That is, we suggest that a variety of negative, internal (e.g., poor body image, the tendency to experience negative emotions), relational (e.g., poor relationship quality, insecure attachment style), and contextual (e.g., work stress, history of sexual problems) triggers interfere with an individual's ability to be fully present during sexual activity. Instead, the individual focuses his or her attention on his or her concerns. Such cognitive interference, in turn, results in greater salience of negative aspects of the sexual relationship and lower salience of the positive aspects. If this occurs repeatedly over time, it may contribute to a more negative global appraisal of the sexual relationship and thus to lower sexual satisfaction.

A second potential mechanism to account for these relationships is that they affect couple interactions, the quality of the overall relationship, or both, which, in turn, affects sexual satisfaction. For example, in the Attachment Style section, we examined how couples' interaction style may be a mechanism that links attachment style to sexual satisfaction. We believe that how partners interact with each other may also be one mechanism explaining the associations between sexual satisfaction and some of the other personality, cognitive, and affective risk factors we have identified in this section (e.g., neuroticism, sexual motives). How couples interact and communicate is a dyadic mechanism that we explore in greater detail in the next section.

ROLE OF RELATIONSHIP FACTORS IN SEXUAL SATISFACTION

Researchers have increasingly begun to focus on the role of dyadic factors and processes, rather than individual factors, in sexual satisfaction. This focus is warranted because most sexual activity is affected by the interpersonal context in which it occurs.

Thus, to fully understand sexual satisfaction, it is important to examine partner qualities and contextual variables (DeLamater & Hyde, 2004). Indeed, the research to date on dyadic variables has borne out the importance of this level of analysis (Rehman et al., 2013). Most of this research has been done with mixed-sex couples; less is known about individuals in same-sex relationships.

Global Relationship Satisfaction

Across studies, robust and consistent evidence has suggested that individuals who report higher relationship satisfaction also report higher sexual satisfaction, and this finding has been replicated in many different samples, including sexual minority women (e.g., Byers, 2001; Byers, Demmons, & Lawrance, 1998; Cupach & Comstock, 1990; Haavio-Mannila & Kontula, 1997; Henderson et al., 2009; Kisler & Christopher, 2008; Lawrance & Byers, 1995). Because these data are correlational, they cannot inform us about the direction of the relationship between sexual and relationship satisfaction. Four studies have investigated how these variables are related to each other longitudinally. The research results have been inconsistent, with support found for a bidirectional association between relationship and sexual satisfaction (Henderson-King & Veroff, 1994); a causal relationship from relationship satisfaction to later sexual satisfaction but not vice versa (Sprecher, 2002); a causal relationship from initial sexual satisfaction to subsequent relationship satisfaction but not vice versa (Yeh, Lorenz, Wickrama, Conger, & Elder, 2006); and changes in relationship and sexual satisfaction occurring concurrently with limited evidence that higher relationship satisfaction leads to high sexual satisfaction or vice versa (Byers, 2005). In addition, Byers (2005) found some preliminary evidence that the two variables were causally linked for specific groups of participants only—that is, participants whose relationship satisfaction is decreasing and those whose sexual satisfaction is increasing. These results, and the inconsistencies in the findings of the various studies, suggest that the association between relationship and sexual satisfaction is complex, perhaps varying for individuals with specific characteristics or in different situations. Nonetheless, the data suggest that for at least some individuals, low or decreasing relationship satisfaction results in low sexual satisfaction.

The strong association between relationship and sexual satisfaction does not tell us what aspects of the dyadic context or which specific processes between partners serve to promote or suppress their sexual satisfaction. Thus, we now turn our attention to examining these factors.

Communication Skills

Intimate communication, both nonsexual and sexual, is important to the development and maintenance of satisfying romantic relationships, including sexual relationships (Byers, 2011; Cupach & Metts, 1991; MacNeil & Byers, 1997, 2005, 2009; Purnine & Carey, 1997). Both nonsexual and sexual communication contribute to feelings of intimacy and closeness and to overall relationship satisfaction. However, sexual communication can also help partners develop and maintain a mutually pleasurable sexual script (i.e., enacted sexual behaviors) and, thus, high sexual satisfaction (Davies, Katz, & Jackson, 1999; McCarthy & Bodner, 2005; Miller & Byers, 2004). This is because partners can and typically do differ from each other in their sexual preferences, and one or both partners' ideal or preferred sexual script may change over time (Laumann & Gagnon, 1995).

One type of communication that has received considerable attention in the area of sexual satisfaction and functioning, at least in mixed-sex couples, is self-disclosure. For example, in a systematic set of studies, Byers and colleagues (Byers & Demmons, 1999; MacNeil & Byers, 2005, 2009) have shed light on the role of sexual and nonsexual disclosure in sexual satisfaction. These researchers distinguished between nonsexual and sexual self-disclosure. *Nonsexual self-disclosure* refers to the degree to which the relationship is generally open and sharing; *sexual self-disclosure* refers to the degree to which an individual shares his or her sexual likes and dislikes with his or her intimate partner. Byers and colleagues found that individuals who disclose more about both the nonsexual and the sexual aspects of their relationship report higher relationship and sexual satisfaction (Byers & Demmons, 1999;

MacNeil & Byers, 2005, 2009) as well as fewer sexual concerns and problems (MacNeil & Byers, 1997). Unfortunately, little research has linked other types of sexual communication between partners, such as assertive or nonverbal sexual communication, to sexual satisfaction.

Sexual assertiveness is the ability to talk about sex with a partner, express sexual needs, initiate wanted sexual activities, and refuse unwanted sexual activities (Hurlbert, 2011). In new relationships and relationships that are not mutually monogamous, the ability to insist on safer sex practices may be another important aspect of sexual assertiveness (Morokoff et al., 1997). Ménard and Offman (2009) argued that there is a difference between disclosing sexual preferences and assertively making specific requests and initiating behaviors to enhance sexual pleasure. Indeed, it is difficult to imagine having a satisfying sexual relationship if one does not feel control over one's sexuality and free to express one's sexual needs. As Gagnon and Simon (1973) aptly stated, managing sexuality involves managing interpersonal relationships. Using a small sample recruited from the community, Ménard and Offman (2009) demonstrated that individuals who were more sexually assertive were also more sexually satisfied. Whitley and Poulsen (1975) found similar results in a sample of professional women. In certain groups, such as ethnic groups that favor traditional roles, women may be particularly discouraged from expressing their sexual needs and desires and thus might be particularly at risk for low sexual satisfaction. Indeed, Fahs and Swank (2011) found that lower status women were the most likely to report engaging in frequent, unsatisfying sex. Research is needed investigating the link between sexual assertive communication and sexual satisfaction in diverse ethnocultural groups.

Frequency of Sexual Activity

Many studies have demonstrated that individuals who report more frequent sexual activity also report higher sexual satisfaction (e.g., Bancroft et al., 2011; Christopher & Sprecher, 2000; Farr, Forssell, & Patterson, 2010; Heiman et al., 2011; Henderson et al., 2009; Yucel & Gassanov, 2010). Yucel and Gassanov (2010) speculated that a bidirectional relationship exists between sexual frequency and satisfaction. Specifically, they argued that couples who are not satisfied with their sexual relationship may consequently have sex less often; conversely, couples who have sex infrequently may feel less sexually satisfied as a result. One of the most consistent findings with regard to sexual frequency is that whereas couples' frequency of sexual activity decreases over time, no corresponding change in sexual satisfaction occurs (see review by Christopher & Sprecher, 2000). One possible explanation for this finding is that couples expect the frequency of sexual activity in their relationships to decrease over time and thus are not disappointed or dissatisfied when such changes occur as long as other aspects of the relationship remain positive. Another possibility is that sexual quality has a larger impact on sexual satisfaction in long-term relationships than does sexual frequency, and sexual quality remains high for most couples (Lawrance & Byers, 1995; MacNeil & Byers, 2009). That is, in keeping with our definition of sexual satisfaction as a global emotional response, sexual frequency is only one of a range of specific aspects of the sexual relationship that have an impact on sexual satisfaction. Indeed, Fahs and Swank (2011) showed that many women report low sexual satisfaction and high activity or, more often, high sexual satisfaction and low activity. In fact, they found that more women had a disjuncture than a match between sexual satisfaction and sexual activity. Unfortunately, they did not include men in their study.

It may also be that poor fit between partners in terms of their levels of sexual desire leads to declines in sexual satisfaction rather than low sexual frequency per se. We next examine the role of desire discrepancies and possible mechanisms by which desire discrepancies might lead to lower levels of sexual satisfaction.

Discrepancies in Sexual Desire and Desired Sexual Frequency

A discrepancy between partners in their level of sexual desire is the most common presenting difficulty for couples seeking sex therapy (Davies et al., 1999;

see Chapter 8, this volume; Volume 2, Chapter 4, this handbook). By *sexual desire,* we mean having an interest in sexual activity that leads the individual to seek out
sexual activity or be pleasurably receptive to the partner's initiation (Basson, 2007; Kaplan, 1995). Thus, a discrepancy in sexual desire results in one partner engaging in sexual activity less frequently than desired, the other partner engaging in sexual activity more frequently than desired, or both. In some of these cases, one individual meets the diagnostic criteria for hypoactive sexual desire disorder (American Psychiatric Association, 2000). However, in many of these cases an individual is identified by his or her partner as experiencing low desire because of the relationship context—that is, the individual experiences significantly lower desire than his or her partner does.

It is unlikely that for most couples, both partners have exactly the same level of desire. Nonetheless, Davies et al. (1999) demonstrated that perceiving one's own levels of sexual desire to be discrepant from one's partner's level of desire is associated with lower sexual satisfaction for both men and women. Smith et al. (2011) examined whether dissatisfaction with levels of sexual activity in the past 12 months was related to levels of sexual satisfaction using data from a population-based survey of 4,290 men and 4,366 women who ranged in age from 16 to 64 years. They divided the sample into three groups depending on whether respondents desired less, more, or the same frequency of sex with their partner as had occurred during the previous 12 months. It is important to note that although desire discrepancy and dissatisfaction with sexual frequency overlap conceptually, these two constructs are distinct. That is, some men and women engage in sexual behavior without experiencing sexual desire; conversely, sexual desire may not lead to sexual behavior regardless of the willingness of the partner (Hurlbert & Apt, 1994). Smith et al. (2011) found that men and women who reported being dissatisfied with the frequency of sex in their relationship had lower levels of sexual and relationship satisfaction than did men and women who were not dissatisfied with the frequency of sexual activity. For the most part, men who were dissatisfied with the frequency of sexual activity wanted sexual activity to be more frequent; among women who were dissatisfied, two thirds wanted sex more frequently and one third wanted sex less frequently.

Mechanisms by Which Discrepancies Between Partners Influence Sexual Satisfaction

It is unlikely that most couples have exactly the same level of sexual desire, want to engage in sexual activity with the exact same sexual frequency, and desire the exact same sexual script. Nonetheless, most couples report high sexual satisfaction (Lawrance & Byers, 1995). A worthwhile area of future inquiry is to investigate how dyadic processes, such as sexual communication, influence the impact of discrepant sexual scripts or sexual desire levels on sexual satisfaction. One mechanism that likely influences sexual satisfaction in a positive way is communication, specifically sexual self-disclosure and affective communication. Building on the theoretical work of Cupach and Metts (1991) and using couple-level data, Byers and colleagues (Byers & Demmons, 1999; MacNeil & Byers, 2005, 2009) identified two pathways linking self-disclosure with sexual satisfaction. First, they demonstrated that self-disclosure leads to higher relationship satisfaction, which in turn results in higher sexual satisfaction. Second, they demonstrated that sexual self-disclosure specifically facilitates the partner's understanding of the individual's sexual likes (but not his or her sexual dislikes), allowing the couple to develop a mutually pleasurable sexual script, thus increasing sexual satisfaction. That is, sexual self-disclosure helps couples to develop and maintain a sexually satisfying relationship by enhancing intimacy and facilitating couples in developing a mutual pleasurable sexual script that finds a middle ground for their discrepant interests.

Although Byers and colleagues (Byers & Demmons, 1999; MacNeil & Byers, 2005, 2009) found that self-disclosure of pleasing aspects of the sexual relationship is important for sexual satisfaction, self-disclosure of displeasing aspects did not enhance partner understanding. Indeed, greater partner understanding of the displeasing aspects of the sexual relationship was associated with a less enjoyable sexual script and lower sexual satisfaction, suggesting that self-disclosure about, and understanding of, negative aspects of the sexual relationship may follow a different path from that of positive aspects of the relationship. For example, partners may only communicate about these negative aspects when the negative aspects are high relative to the positive aspects of the sexual relationship—that is, they are already experiencing low sexual satisfaction. Alternatively, they may adopt negative communication patterns that result in decreased sexual satisfaction. Although they have not been investigated with respect to sexual satisfaction specifically, two types of negative interaction patterns identified by relationship researchers may be particularly useful in understanding how displeasing aspects of the sexual relationship in general and differences between partners in particular, if managed poorly, can lead to declines in sexual satisfaction over time for some couples.

One such negative interaction cycle is the demand–withdraw pattern (Sullaway & Christensen, 1983). In such an interaction, "one partner pressures the other through emotional demands, criticisms, and complaints, while the other retreats through withdrawal, defensiveness, and passive inaction" (Christensen & Heavey, 1990, p. 73). The degree to which this pattern occurs in response to a conflict in the relationship can be viewed as an index of the degree of polarization between partners on that particular topic of conflict (Rehman & Holtzworth-Munroe, 2006). Furthermore, spouses who engage in this type of interaction grow more polarized over time, increasing the chance of relationship dissolution (Gottman & Levenson, 1999). Indeed, sex therapists talk about couples developing and getting stuck in negative interaction patterns in which one partner constantly feels that he or she is asking, coercing, or demanding sex, and the other partner withdraws or refuses or gives in unhappily and reluctantly (McCarthy & Thestrup, 2008).

The second pattern that may be relevant is that of negative reciprocity, the tendency for partners to maintain or escalate negative communication once it has started (Gottman, 1979). In this pattern, both partners engage in escalating mutual attack and blame cycles. Unhappy couples are significantly more likely than happy couples to escalate their negative behaviors (Gottman & Levenson, 1986; Hooley & Hahlweg, 1989; Margolin & Wampold, 1981), which suggests that once they are in the midst of a negative exchange, they find it very difficult to pull out of that exchange. Here again, discrepancies in desire or differences in desired activities might lead couples to engage in often-repeated cycles of negative exchanges, where neither partner feels heard or understood but rather feels attacked and vilified. For example, the partner who does not want to engage in a particular sexual activity may be labeled as the prude while the other partner is likened to a sex addict. Often, demand–withdraw cycles and negative escalation can occur around the same conflict topics; in other instances, a couple may start off in one cycle and over time transition into the other pattern. In this way, the interaction pattern may be the mechanism that explains, at least in part, why some couples become distressed as a result of discrepancies between partners, whereas others do not. Both of these negative communication patterns have been linked to decreased relationship satisfaction (e.g., Christensen & Heavey, 1990; Gottman, 1979). Thus, it is likely that these patterns affect sexual satisfaction both through their negative impact on overall relationship well-being and by making it less likely that partners will successfully negotiate a mutually pleasurable sexual script that represents an acceptable compromise between their discrepant interests.

DIRECTIONS FOR FUTURE RESEARCH

Building on the Interpersonal Exchange Model of Sexual Satisfaction

As with many areas of sex research, much of the research on sexual satisfaction has proceeded atheoretically. However, on the basis of social exchange theory, Lawrance and Byers (1992, 1995) proposed the IEMSS as a framework for understanding sexual satisfaction within relationships. The IEMSS proposes that individuals are more sexually satisfied if (a) they experience a more favorable balance of sexual rewards and sexual costs in their relationship (i.e., if they experience high sexual rewards and low sexual costs); (b) this balance compares favorably with their expectations; (c) they perceive that their own and their partner's levels of sexual rewards and costs are approximately equal; and (d) they are more satisfied with the nonsexual aspects of the relationship. According to Thibaut and Kelley (1959), sexual rewards are exchanges between partners that are gratifying and pleasing to the individual; sexual costs are exchanges between partners that demand physical or mental effort or cause pain, embarrassment, anxiety, or other negative affect. Individuals may be similar in their overall appraisal of the balance of sexual rewards and costs in their sexual relationship, yet differ in the extent to which they find particular sexual exchanges (e.g., oral sex, sexual frequency, amount of affection expressed during sex, how easily they or their partner reach orgasm) rewarding or costly. Moreover, given that sexual satisfaction is seen as a global sentiment, the model proposes that an individual's sexual satisfaction is influenced by the history of exchanges in their relationship rather than by any specific sexual encounter or event. The IEMSS explicitly takes into account the interpersonal context of sexuality and emphasizes the role of both nonsexual aspects of the relationship and sexual exchanges in determining sexual satisfaction.

The IEMSS is the most well-researched theory of sexual satisfaction. A systematic and incremental body of research has demonstrated the validity of the IEMSS in predicting levels of sexual satisfaction in men and women, and these findings have been replicated with a number of different samples (Byers et al., 1998; Byers & MacNeil, 2006; Lawrance & Byers, 1995; Renaud, Byers, & Pan, 1996). In these studies, the model accounted for a large percentage of the variance in sexual satisfaction (between 58% and 79%). Nonetheless, to further enhance the understanding of sexual satisfaction, it is important to incorporate emerging findings, such as those we have reviewed, to further refine and develop the IEMSS.

In our opinion, the empirical evidence is not at the stage where we can propose specific changes to the IEMSS, either because the research has not been conducted or because there are contradictory findings. Thus, in this section, we identify key areas for future research. In doing so, we focus on identifying empirical questions that can serve as the groundwork for future theoretical developments in the study of sexual satisfaction in general and the development of the IEMSS in particular. Our suggestions fall into four general areas: incorporating stage of relationship into the IEMSS, incorporating factors that influence the components of the model into the IEMSS, incorporating partner effects into the IEMSS, and examining mechanisms affecting sexual satisfaction.

Incorporating stage of relationship into the IEMSS. The IEMSS is proposed as a general model for all couples regardless of relationship stage. However, the contribution of the four components to sexual satisfaction may possibly differ for individuals who are new to their relationship, in a short-term relationship, or in a committed, long-term relationship. Some evidence has supported the perspective that the components of the IEMSS exert different degrees of influence at different stages of a relationship. Byers and colleagues (Byers, 1999; Byers et al., 1998; Lawrance & Byers, 1995) found both similarities and differences between individuals in dating and in long-term relationships in Canada. Specifically, they found that sexual satisfaction was high in both couple types. They also found that the factors proposed by the IEMSS to influence sexual satisfaction predicted comparably high percentages of the variance in sexual satisfaction in both cohorts (79% for individuals in long-term relationships and 74% for dating couples). However, relationship satisfaction accounted for more variance in sexual satisfaction among daters than among individuals in long-term relationships. Conversely, compared with daters, sexual exchanges accounted for greater variance in sexual satisfaction in individuals in long-term relationships. An examination of the extent to which each of the components of the model contributes to sexual satisfaction for couples in other relationship stages (marriage, transition to parenthood, transition to the empty nest, retirement, etc.) would provide a more nuanced understanding of different predictors of sexual satisfaction at various relationship stages and life transition points.

It is also important to determine the extent to which sexual satisfaction itself and sexual exchanges vary over the course of the relationship or at different relationship stages, such as increases in commitment as signified by cohabitation or marriage. In a study of individuals in long-term relationships, Byers and MacNeil (2006) found that neither sexual satisfaction nor any of the IEMSS components (balance of rewards to costs, comparison level of rewards and costs, equality of rewards and costs) changed significantly over an 18-month period for either male or female participants, thus suggesting that neither sexual satisfaction nor sexual exchanges change rapidly or dramatically in long-term relationships (Christopher & Sprecher, 2000). In contrast, Sprecher (2001) assessed perceived sexual equity in a sample of young daters and found that both the men and the women tended to feel more sexually underbenefited over time. It may be that perceptions of the equity and equality of sexual exchanges tend to become less favorable in the early part of relationships but are more stable in long-term relationships. These results point to the importance of examining how relationship stage affects both sexual satisfaction and factors contributing to sexual satisfaction.

Prospective longitudinal studies are the methodology that is best suited to questions about the relative importance of the various components of the IEMSS to sexual satisfaction at various stages of a relationship and life transition. Because such studies can be prohibitively time consuming and costly, a more pragmatic approach is to conduct short-term longitudinal research. For example, researchers interested in the developmental course of relationships have focused on newlywed couples, because the greatest fluctuation in relationship satisfaction occurs over the first few years (Bramlett & Mosher, 2002). Moreover, relationship functioning in the early years of the marriage is strongly predictive of subsequent relationship happiness and stability (Huston, Caughlin, Houts, Smith, & George, 2001). Another opportunity is to study couples as they go through critical periods in their relationship such as parenthood.

Incorporating factors that influence the components of the model into the IEMSS. The IEMSS can be enriched by expanding the model to include factors that affect the components of the model (i.e., balance of sexual rewards to sexual costs, how rewards and costs compare with expectations, equality of rewards and costs, overall relationship quality) that are, in turn, hypothesized to affect sexual satisfaction. For example, although the model acknowledges individual differences in sexual rewards and costs, it is silent on factors that influence perceptions of sexual exchanges within the relationship. Many of the individual variables reviewed in this chapter, such as propensity toward negative affect, cognitions, sexual motives, body image, and attachment style likely influence perceptions of the level of sexual rewards and costs, how rewards and costs compare with expectations, and equality of sexual rewards and costs between partners. Although not part of the model per se, these factors also likely affect which specific sexual exchanges the individual finds rewarding or costly. Similarly, although the IEMSS identifies that sexual satisfaction is a result of dyadic process, it does not identify the dyadic process that leads to, for example, high relationship satisfaction or a favorable balance of sexual rewards to sexual costs. Yet, MacNeil and Byers (2005, 2009) have shown that communication within the relationship influences both relationship satisfaction and the balance of sexual rewards and costs.

Incorporating partner effects into the IEMSS. An important direction for future development of the IEMSS is to include partner effects in the model. *Partner effects* are defined as the effects of one partner's characteristics (e.g., dispositional characteristics, affective states, cognitive styles) on the other partner's outcomes (Cook & Kenny, 2005). The IEMSS is a contextual model, and the importance of partner variables is implied in the model. For example, the IEMSS includes perceptions of the partner's experience (i.e., perceived equality of rewards and costs) and the extent to which the partner's behavior affects the individual's perceptions of his or her own sexual rewards and costs. However, the IEMSS does not include specific partner effects, such as the partner's own experiences. Yet, for most people their partner's behavior and experiences, not just their perceptions of these experiences, constitute sexual rewards or sexual costs. In keeping with this view, using dyadic data, Byers and MacNeil (2006) have shown that sexual satisfaction is greatest for both men and women to the extent that both partners experience a favorable balance of sexual rewards and costs. Specifically they found that partner-reported favorable sexual exchanges added to the prediction of sexual satisfaction over and above both the individual's own experiences of these sexual exchanges and his or her perceptions of the equality between the individual's own and the partner's experiences. Another partner variable relevant to the IEMSS is partner relationship satisfaction. Not surprisingly, relationship satisfaction between partners tends to be significantly correlated but shares only 35% to 50% of their variance (e.g., Kenny & Ledermann, 2010). This finding suggests that partner relationship satisfaction is not redundant with own relationship satisfaction. Furthermore, a causal relationship may exist between relationship satisfaction and sexual exchanges that is not captured in the IEMSS. For example, it may be that high relationship satisfaction results in a more favorable balance of sexual rewards to costs. Conversely, a favorable balance of sexual rewards and costs may result in high relationship satisfaction. It is also possible that the relationship is reciprocal and incremental and thus that the current model represents the best configuration for these variables. Another partner variable that has been demonstrated to be related to sexual satisfaction is an understanding of one's partner's sexual preferences (MacNeil & Byers, 2005, 2009; Purnine & Carey, 1997). For example, Purnine and Carey (1997) showed that the partner's understanding of one's sexual preferences predicted both men's and women's sexual satisfaction (MacNeil & Byers, 2005, 2009).

Directly investigating partner effects in sexual satisfaction would also allow researchers to ask questions pertaining to the goodness of fit between partners. Specifically, by modeling Actor × Partner effects, researchers can start to ask questions about how an actor effect (e.g., partner A's perceptions of the equality between partners in their sexual rewards and costs on partner A's sexual satisfaction) is influenced by a partner variable (e.g., partner B's perception of the equality between partners in their sexual rewards and costs). It is possible, for example, that highest levels of sexual satisfaction occur only when both partners perceive the relationship to be equal on this dimension. Such an approach might also prove useful in furthering the understanding of the effects of perceived or actual discrepancies in sexual desire on sexual satisfaction. In short, there are many potential ways in which including partner effects can enhance the IEMSS and result in stronger prediction of sexual satisfaction. The methodological implications of examining partner effects are discussed next.

Examining mechanisms affecting sexual satisfaction. A critical area for future research is to propose specific mechanisms through which the variables that have been linked to sexual satisfaction exert their influence. Understanding these mechanisms is likely to have implications for interventions aimed at enhancing sexual satisfaction. In this chapter, we have proposed several mechanisms that we believe need to be investigated in future research. For example, we suggested that cognitive interference may be a mechanism by which risk factors such as poor body image, insecure attachment style, and neuroticism lead to lower levels of sexual satisfaction. Although these relationships have not been studied empirically, other important cognitive variables likely exist that mediate the relationships between the variables in the current IEMSS and in an expanded IEMSS, including expectations of how a particular sexual interaction will unfold, how a sexual partner might respond to requests for change in the couples' sexual repertoire, and attributions for partner's behavior pertaining to sex.

Couples' interaction style is another mechanism that needs to be incorporated into the IEMSS. For example, an unfavorable balance of sexual rewards and costs that arises from discrepancies between partners in level of desire or preferred sexual script may lead to lower levels of sexual satisfaction by affecting how partners interact with each other. Specifically, the manner in which couples negotiate or fail to negotiate such discrepancies is likely to influence sexual satisfaction. Individual risk factors may also influence sexual satisfaction through their impact on a couple's interaction style. For example, neuroticism may lead to polarizing and escalating patterns of interaction during conflict, leading to reduction in relationship satisfaction, one of the key factors posited to influence sexual satisfaction in the IEMSS.

Gathering Data From Both Members of a Dyad

One of the central points emphasized in this chapter is the need to expand thinking about sexuality and sexual satisfaction by better understanding the interpersonal context in which individual sexual lives are embedded. We have argued that a model of sexual satisfaction is incomplete if it ignores the quality of a couple's relationship and their patterns of interaction and disengagement. In emphasizing the importance of relationship characteristics, we do not mean to suggest that individual-level variables are unimportant. Rather, both of these levels of analysis are complementary and informative. That is, although individual-level analysis has been useful in identifying individual predictors associated with sexual satisfaction, including the individual's perceptions of his or her interaction with the partner, it does not fully capture dyadic processes within the couple. In addition, any one partner's report of the relationship is based on his or her own perception and may differ significantly from the other partner's report. Indeed, Byers and MacNeil (2006) found that male and female long-term partners differed significantly in their reports of their sexual satisfaction, balance of sexual rewards and cost, comparison level for sexual rewards and costs, and perceptions of the equality of sexual rewards.

Gathering data from only one partner prevents researchers from asking and answering many of the interesting questions that are of particular theoretical interest to researchers focusing on interdependence. Questions pertaining to fit between partners, reciprocal influences of one partner on the others, and how partner influences change over time fall into this category. Specific to the area of sexual satisfaction, researchers might be interested in investigating how discrepancies between partners in the balance of rewards and costs affect sexual satisfaction. To what extent does one partner's individual characteristics (e.g., neuroticism, attachment orientation) affect the other partner's experience of the sexual relationship or sexual satisfaction? Similarly, how does one partner's experience of a poor balance of sexual rewards and costs affect the other partner's experience of rewards and costs, comparison level, and sexual satisfaction over time? These questions can only be answered by gathering data from both partners. Although this approach has been taken in past studies (Byers & MacNeil, 2006; Purnine & Carey, 1997; Rehman, Rellini, & Fallis, 2011), the overwhelming majority of studies on sexuality gather data from only one partner.

One of the challenges faced by sexuality researchers is translating the concepts of interdependence between partners into methods of data collection and data analysis that allow them to capture this interdependence in their measurement strategies and data analytic methods. Sexuality research, including research on sexual satisfaction, has lagged behind other areas of dyadic research (e.g., research on romantic relationships) that have benefited greatly from methodological advancements in modeling dyadic data. Indeed, in terms of analyzing dyadic data, interdependent data points have been viewed in the past as a nuisance, and researchers "have developed strategies to sweep interdependence under the statistical rug" (Gonzalez & Griffin, 2012, p. 182). Gonzalez and Griffin (2012) also noted some of the common (but flawed) methods used by researchers to handle interdependent data, including averaging across both partners' reports, statistically partialing out interdependence, and dropping one dyad member's scores. Rather than using interdependent data to ask novel questions, these methods lead to loss of important information, diminished power, and the creation of constructs that may not be valid (e.g., pooling both partners' sexual satisfaction to get an average level of sexual satisfaction for the dyad). Fortunately, many statistical techniques have been explained in the literature, in accessible terms, that allow researchers to capitalize on their interdependent data rather than being constrained by it. Interested readers are encouraged to review techniques described by Gonzalez and Griffin (2012) and by Kenny, Kashy, and Cook (2006).

CONCLUSION

In this chapter, we have reviewed a number of key individual and dyadic variables that have been shown to be associated with sexual satisfaction. Unfortunately, much of the research in the area of sexual satisfaction has proceeded atheoretically. An exception to this is the IEMSS, a well-validated theory that provides a framework for understanding sexual satisfaction in relationships. In the final section of this chapter, we suggested a number of directions for future research that build on both the IEMSS and advances in dyadic data analysis. Adoption of these suggestions will enhance researchers' understanding of sexual satisfaction over the course of relationships and for individuals with different characteristics.

References

Ackard, D. M. D., Kearney-Cooke, A., & Peterson, C. B. C. (2000). Effect of body image and self-image on women's sexual behaviors. *International Journal of Eating Disorders, 28*, 422–429. doi:10.1002/1098-108X(200012)28:4<422::AID-EAT10>3.0.CO;2-1

American Psychiatric Association. (2000). *Diagnostic and statistical manual of mental disorders* (4th ed., text revision). Washington, DC: Author.

Apt, C., Hurlbert, D. F., Pierce, A. F., & White, L. C. (1996). Relationship satisfaction, sexual characteristics and the psychosocial well-being of women. *Canadian Journal of Human Sexuality, 5*, 195–210.

Bancroft, J., Long, J. S., & McCabe, J. (2011). Sexual well-being: A comparison of U.S. Black and White women in heterosexual relationships. *Archives of Sexual Behavior, 40*, 725–740. doi:10.1007/s10508-010-9679-z

Barlow, D. H. (1986). Causes of sexual dysfunction: The role of anxiety and cognitive interference. *Journal of Consulting and Clinical Psychology, 54*, 140–148. doi:10.1037/0022-006X.54.2.140

Bartholomew, K., & Horowitz, L. M. (1991). Attachment styles among young adults: A test of a four-category model. *Journal of Personality and Social Psychology, 61*, 226–244. doi:10.1037/0022-3514.61.2.226

Basson, R. (2007). Hormones and sexuality: Current complexities and future directions. *Maturitas, 57*, 66–70. doi:10.1016/j.maturitas.2007.02.018

Blumstein, P., & Schwartz, P. (1983). *American couples: Money, work, sex*. New York, NY: Morrow.

Bradburn, N. M. (1969). *The structure of psychological well-being*. Oxford, England: Aldine.

Bramlett, M. D., & Mosher, W. D. (2002). Cohabitation, marriage, divorce, and remarriage in the United States. *Vital and Health Statistics, 23*(22).

Brassard, A., Shaver, P. R., & Lussier, Y. (2007). Attachment, sexual experience, and sexual pressure in romantic relationships: A dyadic approach. *Personal Relationships, 14*, 475–493. doi:10.1111/j.1475-6811.2007.00166.x

Brennan, K. A., Wu, S., & Love, J. (1998). Adult romantic attachment and individual differences in attitudes toward physical contact in the context of adult romantic relationships. In J. A. Simpson & W. S. Rholes (Eds.), *Attachment theory and close relationships* (pp. 394–428). New York, NY: Guilford Press.

Butzer, B., & Campbell, L. (2008). Adult attachment, sexual satisfaction, and relationship satisfaction: A study of married couples. *Personal Relationships, 15*, 141–154. doi:10.1111/j.1475-6811.2007.00189.x

Byers, E. S. (1999). The interpersonal exchange model of sexual satisfaction: Implications for sex therapy with couples. *Canadian Journal of Counselling, 33*, 95–111.

Byers, E. S. (2001). Evidence for the importance of relationship satisfaction for women's sexual functioning. In E. Kaschak & L. Tiefer (Eds.), *A new view of women's sexual problems* (pp. 23–26). New York, NY: Haworth Press.

Byers, E. S. (2005). Relationship satisfaction and sexual satisfaction: A longitudinal study of individuals in long-term relationships. *Journal of Sex Research, 42*, 113–118. doi:10.1080/00224490509552264

Byers, E. S. (2011). Beyond the *birds and the bees* and *was it good for you?*: Thirty years of research on sexual communication. *Canadian Psychology/Psychologie Canadienne, 52*, 20–28. doi:10.1037/a0022048

Byers, E. S., & Demmons, S. (1999). Sexual satisfaction and sexual self-disclosure within dating relationships. *Journal of Sex Research, 36*, 180–189. doi:10.1080/00224499909551983

Byers, E. S., Demmons, S., & Lawrance, K. A. (1998). Sexual satisfaction within dating relationships: A test of the interpersonal exchange model of sexual satisfaction. *Journal of Social and Personal Relationships, 15*, 257–267. doi:10.1177/0265407598152008

Byers, E. S., & MacNeil, S. (2006). Further validation of the interpersonal exchange model of sexual satisfaction. *Journal of Sex and Marital Therapy, 32*, 53–69. doi:10.1080/00926230500232917

Call, V., Sprecher, S., & Schwartz, P. (1995). The incidence and frequency of marital sex in a national sample. *Journal of Marriage and the Family, 57*, 639–652. doi:10.2307/353919

Carvalho, J., & Nobre, P. (2010). Gender issues and sexual desire: The role of emotional and relationship variables. *Journal of Sexual Medicine, 7*, 2469–2478.

Cash, T. F., & Deagle, E. A. (1997). The nature and extent of body-image disturbances in anorexia nervosa and bulimia nervosa: A meta-analysis. *International Journal of Eating Disorders, 22*, 107–126. doi:10.1002/(SICI)1098-108X(199709)22:2<107::AID-EAT1>3.0.CO;2-J

Cash, T. F., Phillips, K. A., Santos, M. T., & Hrabosky, J. I. (2004). Measuring "negative body image": Validation of the Body Image Disturbance Questionnaire in a nonclinical population. *Body Image, 1*, 363–372. doi:10.1016/j.bodyim.2004.10.001

Chao, J.-K., Lin, Y.-C., Ma, M.-C., Lai, C.-J., Ku, Y.-C., Kuo, W.-H., & Chao, I.-C. (2011). Relationship among sexual desire, sexual satisfaction, and quality of life in middle-aged and older adults. *Journal of Sex and Marital Therapy*, *37*, 386–403. doi:10.1080/0092623X.2011.607051

Christensen, A., & Heavey, C. L. (1990). Gender and social structure in the demand–withdraw pattern of marital conflict. *Journal of Personality and Social Psychology, 59*, 73–81. doi:10.1037/0022-3514.59.1.73

Christopher, F. S., & Sprecher, S. (2000). Sexuality in marriage, dating, and other relationships: A decade review. *Journal of Marriage and the Family, 62*, 999–1017. doi:10.1111/j.1741-3737.2000.00999.x

Cook, W. L., & Kenny, D. A. (2005). The actor-partner interdependence model: A model of bidirectional effects in developmental studies. *International Journal of Behavioral Development, 29*, 101–109. doi:10.1080/01650250444000405

Corson, P., & Andersen, A. (2002). Body image issues among boys and men. In T. Cash & T. Pruzinsky (Eds.), *Body image: A handbook of theory, research, and clinical practice* (pp. 192–199). New York, NY: Guilford Press.

Costa, P. T., Fagan, P. J., Piedmont, R. L., Ponticas, Y., & Wise, T. N. (1992). The five-factor model of personality and sexual functioning in outpatient men and women. *Psychiatric Medicine, 10*, 199–215.

Cupach, W. R., & Comstock, J. (1990). Satisfaction with sexual communication in marriage: Links to sexual satisfaction and dyadic adjustment. *Journal of Social and Personal Relationships, 7*, 179–186. doi:10.1177/0265407590072002

Cupach, W. R., & Metts, S. (1991). Sexuality and communication in close relationships. In K. McKinney & S. Sprecher (Eds.), *Sexuality in close relationships* (pp. 93–110). Hillsdale, NJ: Erlbaum.

Davies, S., Katz, J., & Jackson, J. L. (1999). Sexual desire discrepancies: Effects on sexual and relationship satisfaction in heterosexual dating couples. *Archives of Sexual Behavior, 28*, 553–567. doi:10.1023/A:1018721417683

Davis, D., Shaver, P. R., Widaman, K. F., Vernon, M. L., Follette, W. C., & Beitz, K. (2006). "I can't get no satisfaction": Insecure attachment, inhibited sexual communication and sexual dissatisfaction. *Personal Relationships, 13*, 465–483. doi:10.1111/j.1475-6811.2006.00130.x

Davison, S. L., Bell, R. J., LaChina, M., Holden, S. L., & Davis, S. R. (2009). The relationship between self-reported sexual satisfaction and general well-being in women. *Journal of Sexual Medicine, 6*, 2690–2697. doi:10.1111/j.1743-6109.2009.01406.x

de Jong, T. (2010). Cognitive load theory, educational research, and instructional design; some food for thought. *Instructional Science, 38*, 105–134. doi:10.1007/s11251-009-9110-0

DeLamater, J., & Hyde, J. S. (2004). Conceptual and theoretical issues in studying sexuality in close relationships. In J. H. Harvey, A. Wenzel, & S. Sprecher (Eds.), *The handbook of sexuality in close relationships* (pp. 7–30). Mahwah, NJ: Erlbaum.

Donnellan, M. B., Conger, R. D., & Bryant, C. M. (2004). The Big Five and enduring marriages. *Journal of Research in Personality, 38*, 481–504. doi:10.1016/j.jrp.2004.01.001

Dove, N. L., & Widerman, M. W. (2000). Cognitive distraction and women's sexual functioning. *Journal of Sex and Marital Therapy, 26*, 67–78. doi:10.1080/009262300278650

Dundon, C. M., & Rellini, A. H. (2010). More than sexual function: Predictors of sexual satisfaction in a sample of women age 40–70. *Journal of Sexual Medicine, 7*, 896–904. doi:10.1111/j.1743-6109.2009.01557.x

Dunn, K. M., Croft, P. R., & Hackett, G. I. (2000). Satisfaction in the sex life of a general population sample. *Journal of Sex and Marital Therapy, 26*, 141–151. doi:10.1080/009262300278542

Edwards, J. N., & Booth, A. (1994). Sexuality, marriage, and well-being: The middle years. In A. S. Rossi (Ed.), *Sexuality, marriage, and well-being: The middle years* (pp. 233–259). Chicago, IL: University of Chicago Press.

Elliott, A. N., & O'Donohue, W. T. (1997). The effects of anxiety and distraction on sexual arousal in a nonclinical sample of heterosexual women. *Archives of Sexual Behavior, 26*, 607–624. doi:10.1023/A:1024524326105

Fahs, B., & Swank, E. (2011). Social identities as predictors of women's sexual satisfaction and sexual activity. *Archives of Sexual Behavior, 40*, 903–914. doi:10.1007/s10508-010-9681-5

Faith, M. S., & Schare, M. L. (1993). The role of body image in sexually avoidant behavior. *Archives of Sexual Behavior, 22*, 345–356. doi:10.1007/BF01542123

Farr, R. H., Forssell, S. L., & Patterson, C. J. (2010). Gay, lesbian and heterosexual adoptive parents: Couple and relationship issues. *Journal of GLBT Family Studies, 6*, 199–213. doi:10.1080/15504281003705436

Feeney, J. A., & Noller, P. (2004). Attachment and sexuality in close relationships. In J. H. Harvey, A.

Wenzel, & S. Sprecher (Eds.), *The handbook of sexuality in close relationships* (pp. 183–201). Mahwah, NJ: Erlbaum.

Fisher, T. D., & McNulty, J. K. (2008). Neuroticism and marital satisfaction: The mediating role played by the sexual relationship. *Journal of Family Psychology, 22*, 112–122. doi:10.1037/0893-3200.22.1.112

Gagnon, J. H., & Simon, W. (1973). *Sexual conduct: The social sources of human sexuality*. Chicago, IL: Aldine.

Gil, S. (2007). Body image, well-being and sexual satisfaction: A comparison between heterosexual and gay men. *Sexual and Relationship Therapy, 22*, 237–244. doi:10.1080/14681990600855042

Goldenberg, J. L., Pyszczynski, T., Greenberg, J., Solomon, S., Kluck, B., & Cornwell, R. (2001). I am *not* an animal: Mortality salience, disgust and the denial of human creatureliness. *Journal of Experimental Psychology: General, 130*, 427–435. doi:10.1037/0096-3445.130.3.427

Gonzalez, R., & Griffin, D. (2012). Dyadic data analysis. In H. Cooper (Ed.), *APA handbook of research methods in psychology: Vol. 3. Data analysis and research publication* (pp. 439–450). Washington, DC: American Psychological Association.

Gottman, J. (1979). Detecting cyclicity in social interaction. *Psychological Bulletin, 86*, 338–348. doi:10.1037/0033-2909.86.2.338

Gottman, J. M. (1994). An agenda for marital therapy. In S. Johnson & L. Greenberg (Eds.), *The heart of the matter: Perspectives on emotion in marital therapy* (pp. 256–293). New York, NY: Brunner-Mazel.

Gottman, J. M., & Levenson, R. W. (1986). Assessing the role of emotion in marriage. *Behavioral Assessment, 8*, 31–48.

Gottman, J. M., & Levenson, R. W. (1999). Dysfunctional marital conflict: Women are being unfairly blamed. *Journal of Divorce and Remarriage, 31*, 1–17.

Haavio-Mannila, E., & Kontula, O. (1997). Correlates of increased sexual satisfaction. *Archives of Sexual Behavior, 26*, 399–419. doi:10.1023/A:1024591318836

Hazan, C., & Shaver, P. (1987). Romantic love conceptualized as an attachment process. *Journal of Personality and Social Psychology, 52*, 511–524. doi:10.1037/0022-3514.52.3.511

Hazan, C., Zeifman, D., & Middleton, K. (1994, July). *Adult romantic attachment, affection, and sex.* Paper presented at the 7th International Conference on Personal Relationships, Groningen, the Netherlands.

Heaven, P. C. L., Fitzpatrick, J., Craig, F. L., Kelly, P., & Sebar, G. (2000). Five personality factors and sex: Preliminary findings. *Personality and Individual Differences, 28*, 1133–1141. doi:10.1016/S0191-8869(99)00163-4

Heiman, J. R. (2001). Sexual desire in human relationships. In W. Everaerd, E. Laan, & S. Both (Eds.), *Sexual appetite, desire and motivation: Energetics of the sexual system* (pp. 117–134). Amsterdam, the Netherlands: Royal Netherlands Academy.

Heiman, J. R., Long, J. S., Smith, S. N., Fisher, W. A., Sand, M. S., & Rosen, R. C. (2011). Sexual satisfaction and relationship happiness in midlife and older couples in five countries. *Archives of Sexual Behavior, 40*, 741–753. doi:10.1007/s10508-010-9703-3

Henderson, A. W., Lehavot, K., & Simoni, J. M. (2009). Ecological models of sexual satisfaction among lesbian/bisexual and heterosexual women. *Archives of Sexual Behavior, 38*, 50–65. doi:10.1007/s10508-008-9384-3

Henderson-King, D. H., & Veroff, J. (1994). Sexual satisfaction and marital well-being in the first years of marriage. *Journal of Social and Personal Relationships, 11*, 509–534. doi:10.1177/0265407594114002

Holmberg, D., & Blair, K. L. (2009). Sexual desire, communication, satisfaction, and preferences of men and women in same-sex versus mixed-sex relationships. *Journal of Sex Research, 46*, 57–66. doi:10.1080/00224490802645294

Holmberg, D., Blair, K. L., & Phillips, M. (2010). Women's sexual satisfaction as a predictor of well-being in same-sex versus mixed-sex relationships. *Journal of Sex Research, 47*, 1–11. doi:10.1080/00224490902898710

Holt, A., & Lyness, K. P. (2007). Body image and sexual satisfaction: Implications for couple therapy. *Journal of Couple and Relationship Therapy, 6*, 45–68. doi:10.1300/J398v06n03_03

Hooley, J. M., & Hahlweg, K. (1989). The cross-cultural consistency of marital communication. *Behavioral Assessment, 11*, 119–133.

Hurlbert, D. F. (2011). Hurlbert index of sexual desire. In T. D. Fisher, C. M. Davis, W. L. Yarber, & S. L. Davis (Eds.), *Handbook of sexuality-related measures* (3rd ed., pp. 525–530). New York, NY: Routledge.

Hurlbert, D. F., & Apt, C. (1994). Female sexual desire, response, and behavior. *Behavior Modification, 18*, 488–504. doi:10.1177/01454455940184006

Huston, T. L., Caughlin, J. P., Houts, R. M., Smith, S. E., & George, L. J. (2001). The connubial crucible: Newlywed years as predictors of marital delight, distress, and divorce. *Journal of Personality and Social Psychology, 80*, 237–252. doi:10.1037/0022-3514.80.2.237

Judge, T. A., Erez, A., Bono, J. E., & Thoresen, C. J. (2002). Are measures of self-esteem, neuroticism, locus of control, and generalized self-efficacy indicators of a common core construct? *Journal of Personality and Social Psychology, 83*, 693–710. doi:10.1037/0022-3514.83.3.693

Kaplan, F. H. (1995). Model-based representations of human sexual behavior. In P. R. Abramson & S. D. Pinkerton (Eds.), *Sexual nature/sexual culture* (pp. 353–370). Chicago, IL: University of Chicago Press.

Karney, B. R., & Bradbury, T. N. (1995). The longitudinal course of marital quality and stability: A review of theory, method and research. *Psychological Bulletin, 118*, 3–34. doi:10.1037/0033-2909.118.1.3

Kenny, D. A., Kashy, D. A., & Cook, W. (2006). *Dyadic data analysis*. New York, NY: Guilford Press.

Kenny, D. A., & Ledermann, T. (2010). Detecting, measuring, and testing dyadic patterns in the actor–partner interdependence model. *Journal of Family Psychology, 24*, 359–366. doi:10.1037/a0019651

Kisler, T. S., & Christopher, F. S. (2008). Sexual exchanges and relationship satisfaction: Testing the role of sexual satisfaction as a mediator and gender as a moderator. *Journal of Social and Personal Relationships, 25*, 587–602. doi:10.1177/0265407508090874

Kurdek, L. A. (1991). Sexuality in homosexual and heterosexual couples. In K. McKinney & S. Sprecher (Eds.), *Sexuality in close relationships* (pp. 177–191). Hillsdale, NJ: Erlbaum.

Kuyper, L., & Vanwesenbeeck, I. (2011). Examining sexual health differences between lesbian, gay, bisexual, and heterosexual adults: The role of sociodemographics, sexual behavior characteristics, and minority stress. *Journal of Sex Research, 48*, 263–274. doi:10.1080/00224491003654473

Laumann, E. O., & Gagnon, J. H. (1995). A sociological perspective on sexual action. In R. Parker & J. H. Gagnon (Eds.), *Conceiving sexuality: Approaches to sex research in a post-modern world* (pp. 183–213). New York, NY: Routledge.

Laumann, E. O., Gagnon, J. H., Michael, R. T., & Michaels, S. (1994). *The social organization of sexuality: Sexual practices in the United States*. Chicago, IL: University of Chicago Press.

Laumann, E. O., Paik, A., Glasser, D. B., Kang, J.-H., Wang, T., Levinson, B., & Gingell, C. (2006). A cross-national study of subjective sexual well-being among older women and men: Findings from the global study of sexual attitudes and behaviors. *Archives of Sexual Behavior, 35*, 143–159. doi:10.1007/s10508-005-9005-3

Lawrance, K., & Byers, E. S. (1992). Development of the interpersonal model of sexual satisfaction in long term relationships. *Canadian Journal of Human Sexuality, 1*, 123–128.

Lawrance, K., & Byers, E. S. (1995). Sexual satisfaction in long-term heterosexual relationship: The interpersonal exchange model of sexual satisfaction. *Personal Relationships, 2*, 267–285. doi:10.1111/j.1475-6811.1995.tb00092.x

Lowery, S. E., Kurpius, S. E. R., Befort, C., Blanks, E. H., Sollenberger, S., Nicpon, N. F., & Huser, L. (2005). Body image, self-esteem, and health-related behaviors among male and female first year college students. *Journal of College Student Development, 46*, 612–623. doi:10.1353/csd.2005.0062

MacNeil, S., & Byers, E. S. (1997). The relationship between sexual problems, communication and sexual satisfaction. *Canadian Journal of Human Sexuality, 6*, 277–283.

MacNeil, S., & Byers, E. S. (2005). Dyadic assessment of sexual self-disclosure and sexual satisfaction in heterosexual dating couples. *Journal of Social and Personal Relationships, 22*, 169–181. doi:10.1177/0265407505050942

MacNeil, S., & Byers, E. S. (2009). Role of sexual self-disclosure in the sexual satisfaction of long-term heterosexual couples. *Journal of Sex Research, 46*, 3–14. doi:10.1080/00224490802398399

Margolin, G., & Wampold, B. E. (1981). Sequential analysis of conflict and accord in distressed and nondistressed marital partners. *Journal of Consulting and Clinical Psychology, 49*, 554–567. doi:10.1037/0022-006X.49.4.554

Masters, W., & Johnson, V. (1970). *Human sexual inadequacy*. Boston, MA: Little, Brown.

Matthews, A. K., Tartaro, J., & Hughes, T. L. (2002). A comparative study of lesbian and heterosexual women in committed relationships. *Journal of Lesbian Studies, 7*, 101–114. doi:10.1300/J155v07n01_07

McCarthy, B., & Thestrup, M. (2008). Integrating sex therapy interventions with couple therapy. *Journal of Contemporary Psychotherapy, 38*, 139–149. doi:10.1007/s10879-008-9083-3

McCarthy, B. W., & Bodner, L. E. (2005). The equity model of sexuality: Navigating and negotiating the similarities and differences between men and women in sexual behaviour, roles and values. *Sexual and Relationship Therapy, 20*, 225–235. doi:10.1080/14681990500113229

McDowell, I. (2010). Measures of self-perceived well-being. *Journal of Psychosomatic Research, 69*, 69–79. doi:10.1016/j.jpsychores.2009.07.002

Ménard, D., & Offman, A. (2009). The interrelationships between sexual self-esteem, sexual assertiveness and sexual satisfaction. *Canadian Journal of Human Sexuality, 18*, 35–45.

Meston, C. M., & Buss, D. M. (2007). Why humans have sex. *Archives of Sexual Behavior, 36*, 477–507. doi:10.1007/s10508-007-9175-2

Miller, S. A., & Byers, E. S. (2004). Actual and desired duration of foreplay and intercourse: Discordance and misperceptions within heterosexual couples.

Journal of Sex Research, 41, 301–309. doi:10.1080/00224490409552237

Morokoff, P. J., Quina, K., Harlow, L. L., Whitmire, L., Grimley, D. M., Gibson, P. R., & Burkholder, G. J. (1997). Sexual Assertiveness Scale (SAS) for women: Development and validation. *Journal of Personality and Social Psychology, 73*, 790–804. doi:10.1037/0022-3514.73.4.790

Nobre, P. J., & Pinto-Gouveia, J. (2008a). Cognitions, emotions, and sexual response: Analysis of the relationship among automatic thoughts, emotional responses, and sexual arousal. *Archives of Sexual Behavior, 37*, 652–661. doi:10.1007/s10508-007-9258-0

Nobre, P. J., & Pinto-Gouveia, J. (2008b). Differences in automatic thoughts presented during sexual activity between sexually functional and dysfunctional men and women. *Cognitive Therapy and Research, 32*, 37–49. doi:10.1007/s10608-007-9165-7

Nosek, M., Howland, C., Young, M., Georgiou, D., Rintala, D., Foley, C., . . . Smith, Q. (1994). Wellness models and sexuality among women with physical disabilities. *Journal of Applied Rehabilitation Counseling, 25*, 50–58.

Payne, B. K., Cheng, C. M., Govorun, O., & Stewart, B. D. (2005). An inkblot for attitudes: Affect misattribution as implicit measurement. *Journal of Personality and Social Psychology, 89*, 277–293. doi:10.1037/0022-3514.89.3.277

Pedersen, W., & Blekesaune, M. (2003). Sexual satisfaction in young adulthood: Cohabitation, committed dating or unattached life? *Acta Sociologica, 46*, 179–193. doi:10.1177/00016993030463001

Penhollow, T., & Young, M. (2008). Predictors of sexual satisfaction: The role of body image and fitness. *Electronic Journal of Human Sexuality, 11*. Retrieved from http://www.ejhs.org/volume11/Penhollow.htm

Petersen, J. L., & Hyde, J. S. (2010). A meta-analytic review of research on gender differences in sexuality, 1993–2007. *Psychological Bulletin, 136*, 21–38. doi:10.1037/a0017504

Pujols, Y., Meston, C. M., & Seal, B. N. (2010). The association between sexual satisfaction and body image in women. *Journal of Sexual Medicine, 7*, 905–916. doi:10.1111/j.1743-6109.2009.01604.x

Purdon, C., & Holdaway, L. (2006). Non-erotic thoughts: Content and relation to sexual functioning and sexual satisfaction. *Journal of Sex Research, 43*, 154–162. doi:10.1080/00224490609552310

Purdon, C., & Watson, C. (2011). Non-erotic thoughts and sexual functioning. *Archives of Sexual Behavior, 40*, 891–902. doi:10.1007/s10508-011-9755-z

Purnine, D. M., & Carey, M. P. (1997). Interpersonal communication and sexual adjustment: The roles of understanding and agreement. *Journal of Consulting and Clinical Psychology, 65*, 1017–1025. doi:10.1037/0022-006X.65.6.1017

Rehman, U. S., Fallis, E., & Byers, E. S. (2013). Sexual satisfaction in heterosexual women. In D. Castañeda (Ed.), *An essential handbook of women's sexuality* (pp. 25–46). Santa Barbara, CA: Praeger.

Rehman, U. S., & Holtzworth-Munroe, A. (2006). A cross-cultural analysis of the demand-withdraw marital interaction: Observing couples from a developing country. *Journal of Consulting and Clinical Psychology, 74*, 755–766. doi:10.1037/0022-006X.74.4.755

Rehman, U. S., Rellini, A. H., & Fallis, E. (2011). The importance of sexual self-disclosure to sexual satisfaction and functioning in committed relationships. *Journal of Sexual Medicine, 8*, 3108–3115. doi:10.1111/j.1743-6109.2011.02439.x

Renaud, C., Byers, E. S., & Pan, S. (1996). Factors related to sexual satisfaction in mainland China. *Canadian Journal of Human Sexuality, 5*, 243–251.

Ryff, C. D. (1989). Happiness is everything, or is it? Explorations on the meaning of psychological well-being. *Journal of Personality and Social Psychology, 57*, 1069–1081. doi:10.1037/0022-3514.57.6.1069

Ryff, C. D., & Keyes, C. L. M. (1995). The structure of psychological well-being revisited. *Journal of Personality and Social Psychology, 69*, 719–727. doi:10.1037/0022-3514.69.4.719

Scharfe, E., & Bartholomew, K. (1995). Accommodation and attachment representations in young couples. *Journal of Social and Personal Relationships, 12*, 389–401. doi:10.1177/0265407595123004

Smith, T. W., Cribbet, M. R., Nealey-Moore, J. B., Uchino, B. N., Williams, P. G., MacKenzie, J., & Thayer, J. F. (2011). Matters of the variable heart: Respiratory sinus arrhythmia response to marital interaction and associations with marital quality. *Journal of Personality and Social Psychology, 100*, 103–119. doi:10.1037/a0021136

Sprecher, S. (2001). A comparison of emotional consequences of and changes in equity over time using global and domain-specific measures of equity. *Journal of Social and Personal Relationships, 18*, 477–501. doi:10.1177/0265407501184003

Sprecher, S. (2002). Sexual satisfaction in premarital relationships: Associations with satisfaction, love, commitment, and stability. *Journal of Sex Research, 39*, 190–196. doi:10.1080/00224490209552141

Stephenson, K. R., Ahrold, T. K., & Meston, C. M. (2011). The association between sexual motives and sexual satisfaction: Gender differences and categorical comparisons. *Archives of Sexual Behavior, 40*, 607–618. doi:10.1007/s10508-010-9674-4

Stice, E. (2002). Risk and maintenance factors for eating pathology: A meta-analytic review. *Psychological Bulletin, 128*, 825–848. doi:10.1037/0033-2909.128.5.825

Sullaway, M., & Christensen, A. (1983). Assessment of dysfunctional interaction patterns in couples. *Journal of Marriage and the Family, 45*, 653–660. doi:10.2307/351670

Tao, P., & Brody, S. (2011). Sexual behavior predictors of satisfaction in a Chinese sample. *Journal of Sexual Medicine, 8*, 455–460. doi:10.1111/j.1743-6109.2010.02129.x

Thibaut, J. W., & Kelley, H. H. (1959). *The social psychology of groups*. Piscataway, NJ: Transaction.

Træen, B., & Schaller, S. (2010). Subjective sexual well-being in a web sample of heterosexual Norwegians. *International Journal of Sexual Health, 22*, 180–194. doi:10.1080/19317611003776087

Trompeter, S. E., Bettencourt, R., & Barrett-Connor, E. (2012). Sexual activity and satisfaction in healthy community-dwelling older women. *American Journal of Medicine, 125*, 37–43. doi:10.1016/j.amjmed.2011.07.036

Van Minnen, A., & Kampman, M. (2000). The interaction between anxiety and sexual functioning: A controlled study of sexual functioning in women with anxiety disorders. *Sexual and Relationship Therapy, 15*, 47–57. doi:10.1080/14681990050001556

Weaver, A. D., & Byers, E. S. (2006). The relationships among body image, body mass index, exercise and sexual functioning in heterosexual women. *Psychology of Women Quarterly, 30*, 333–339. doi:10.1111/j.1471-6402.2006.00308.x

Whitley, M. P., & Poulsen, S. B. (1975). Assertiveness and sexual satisfaction in employed professional women. *Journal of Marriage and the Family, 37*, 573–581. doi:10.2307/350521

Wiegel, M., Scepkowski, L. A., & Barlow, D. H. (2007). Cognitive affective processes in sexual arousal and sexual dysfunction. In E. Janssen (Ed.), *The psychophysiology of sex* (pp. 143–165). Bloomington: Indiana University Press.

World Health Organization. (2006). *Defining sexual health: Report of a technical consultation on sexual health, 28–31 January 2002, Geneva.* Geneva, Switzerland: Author. Retrieved from http://www.who.int/reproductivehealth/topics/gender_rights/defining_sexual_health.pdf

Yamamiya, Y., Cash, T. F., & Thompson, J. K. (2006). Sexual experiences among college women: The differential effects of general versus contextual body images on sexuality. *Sex Roles, 55*, 421–427. doi:10.1007/s11199-006-9096-x

Yeh, H.-C., Lorenz, F. O., Wickrama, K. A. S., Conger, R. D., & Elder, G. H., Jr. (2006). Relationships among sexual satisfaction, marital quality, and marital instability at midlife. *Journal of Family Psychology, 20*, 339–343. doi:10.1037/0893-3200.20.2.339

Yucel, D., & Gassanov, M. (2010). Exploring actor and partner correlates of sexual satisfaction among married couples. *Social Science Research, 39*, 725–738. doi:10.1016/j.ssresearch.2009.09.002

CHAPTER 12

SEXUALITY AND SEXUAL VIOLENCE

Nicola Gavey and Charlene Y. Senn

The research literature from the wider field of sexual violence is vast. In this chapter, we introduce research on rape, sexual coercion, and unwanted sex and examine research on other areas of sexuality that collectively highlight the importance of attending to the connections and ambiguous boundaries between sexual violence on the one hand and "just sex" on the other.

We did not set out to duplicate efforts to review the myriad threads within this body of work (for recent reviews and collections, see Horvath & Brown, 2009; Koss, White, & Kazdin, 2011b; J. W. White, Koss, & Kazdin, 2011b). We focus specifically on the intersections and connections between sexual violence and sexuality. Even so, it is necessary to set some additional parameters around the scope of our discussion, in terms of both theoretical approach and the nature of the phenomena we address. Sexual violence is a complex issue that arguably persists for multiple reasons. Within psychology and other social sciences, multifactorial ecological models are currently favored for explaining the causes of sexual and other forms of interpersonal violence (e.g., Hamby, 2011; Heise, 1998; J. W. White, Koss, & Kazdin, 2011a) and conceptualizing harm, recovery, and prevention (e.g., Koss & Harvey, 1991; see also Harvey, 1996). Such models are also widely promoted by governmental, global, and local initiatives directed at sexual violence prevention and at violence prevention more generally (e.g., Carmody, 2009a; Centers for Disease Control and Prevention, 2009; World Health Organization, 2002). Although these approaches are useful for mapping factors at all levels of analysis that may contribute to and sustain sexual violence, our focus here is on elaborating in more depth one particular level of analysis: the gendered cultural norms and power relations that shape normative (hetero)sexuality (see Chapter 2, this volume). According to the feminist sociocultural framework organizing this chapter, these normative connections between gender, power, and sexuality provide a "cultural scaffolding" for sexual violence by men against women (e.g., Gavey, 2005) that helps to make sexual violence possible and, at the same time, helps obscure it in all but the most extreme and unusual forms (see Chapter 1, this volume). Paradigmatically, these gendered norms, and the sexual possibilities and imperatives they contribute to, take shape within heterosexuality, as we demonstrate in the chapter, although they may also be relevant to understanding sexual violence in other contexts, such as among men who have sex with men (e.g., Braun, Schmidt, Gavey, & Fenaughty, 2009).

In examining the intersections of sexual violence and sexuality through research evidence and wider cultural analysis, we show that sexual violence is not a clearly bounded and aberrant phenomenon that is separate from sexuality, but that it arises out of and sits alongside sexuality as usual. We do not therefore discuss in detail research that has sought to understand individual differences or pathologies

Authorship is alphabetical. We thank Deborah L. Tolman for careful editorial guidance. Charlene Y. Senn thanks doctoral students Dusty Johnstone and C. J. Chasin for their generosity in sharing their research syntheses on rape acknowledgment and unwanted but consensual sex.

http://dx.doi.org/10.1037/14193-012
APA Handbook of Sexuality and Psychology: Vol. 1. Person-Based Approaches, D. L. Tolman and L. M. Diamond (Editors-in-Chief)

that may increase the likelihood that particular men will perpetrate sexual violence or individual vulnerabilities that suggest particular women will be at higher risk than others. Although we recognize that such research may yield insights that are relevant to different kinds of questions, in this chapter we concentrate on research evidence and cultural analyses that demonstrate that sexually violent behavior is not as clearly demarcated from "normal" sexuality as one may like to think. Understanding the connections and intersections between sexual violence and everyday sexuality is important, we suggest, for informing theory, research, and practice in relation to sexuality, just as it is important for informing theory, research, and practice in relation to the problem of sexual violence. It allows us to better recognize the mundane workings of power in the realm of sex and sexuality, particularly gendered forms of power within heterosexual sex, and thereby to be sensitive to the nuance and complexity of questions to do with sexual choice and consent. It helps us to see the ways in which sexual choices are constrained and regulated, and it also forces us to recognize that sometimes these dynamics are actually forms of sexual violence.

In this chapter, we restrict our focus to sexual violence against women by men. Although anyone can be subject to sexual violence, and both women and men can be sexually aggressive, women disproportionately suffer the burden of sexual violence and men perpetrate the vast preponderance of sexual violence (e.g., Johnson & Dawson, 2011, Chapter 5; J. W. White et al., 2011b). Not only is this gendered pattern most common for sexual violence experienced by adults and adolescents, but it is widely regarded as a key constituent of gender-based violence (e.g., Heise, Ellsberg, & Gottmoeller, 2002) and violence against women (e.g., Koss, White, & Kazdin, 2011a; J. W. White et al., 2011b). Because our focus is on the connections between sexual violence and normative sexuality, we do not address childhood sexual abuse (see Chapter 14, this volume). Later in the chapter, we discuss research on rape, sexual coercion, unwanted sex, and one example of contemporary sexual practice that helps to flesh out understanding of the interplay between the most common forms of sexual violence and normative (hetero)sexuality. First, we set the scene with a definition of what we mean by sexual violence, followed by a brief discussion of the scope of the problem of sexual violence—in particular, its prevalence and its psychological impact.

SEXUAL VIOLENCE

Sexual violence and sexuality are not usually talked about in the same breath. Yet the lines between sexual seduction, persuasion, coercion, and violence can be slippery. Sexual violence is a widespread social problem that has been the subject of extensive research and theorizing in academic and activist communities for nearly 40 years. As with all forms of interpersonal violence, little agreement has been reached on the precise definition of *sexual violence* (e.g., Post, Biroscak, & Barboza, 2011). The term is used to refer to an inclusive range of sexual acts and experiences that are imposed, coerced, or forced onto a person of any age, including rape, attempted rape, sexual assault, sexual abuse, and sexual violation. Some forms of sexual violence involve physical violence or force, but not all forms do. What ties all these phenomena together is the sexual or sexualized act on or toward another without that person's consent (Gavey, in press).

It is important to recognize that although more specific terms such as *rape, sexual assault, sexual aggression, sexual violation, sexual victimization, sexual coercion,* and so on have precise meanings in different legal, social, and research situations, many of these terms are also used interchangeably in some contexts and have overlapping meanings. We use *sexual violence* to refer to the broadest range of these acts and experiences. When we use the more specific term *rape,* we are referring to the act of forced unwanted penetration of a person's vagina, anus, or mouth by a penis or some other body part (e.g., fingers) or object, or such acts perpetrated without a person's consent through the threat of force or through exploitation of a person's inability to consent because of some form of incapacitation (e.g., asleep, unconscious, or unable to act because of the effects of drugs or alcohol). Although the core features of this definition are the presence of force or threat of force against a person's will, the way that it has been interpreted has changed over time and still varies in different places. Increasingly, the term *rape* is used in a gender-neutral way, although in the past it was usually regarded as an act that was uniquely gendered, such that only women could be raped and only men could rape. Although terms such as *date rape* and *acquaintance rape* are used in common parlance as distinguished from *stranger rape,* in legal and research contexts these qualifiers refer only to the relationship of the perpetrator to the woman he has raped. The terms do not refer to any difference in the nature of the acts themselves. Later in the chapter when we discuss sexual coercion, we refer to a broad concept that includes a wide range of processes ranging from subtle pressure to physical force, although it is most useful in describing acts at the less obviously forced end of the continuum. Elsewhere in the chapter, we use other terms to match the specific language used in the material that we are discussing.

PREVALENCE OF SEXUAL VIOLENCE PERPETRATED BY MEN AGAINST WOMEN

For many years, sexual violence was considered to be rare by scholars (e.g., Deming & Eppy, 1981; Shorter, 1977) and within the context of a heterosexual relationship an oxymoron (e.g., Burkhart & Stanton, 1988). Research published in the 1980s, however, and replicated every decade since, has shown both that sexual victimization is much more common than was previously thought (e.g., Koss, Gidycz, & Wisniewski, 1987; Randall & Haskell, 1995; Russell, 1984; Tjaden & Thoennes, 2000; see Spitzberg, 1999 for a critical review) and that most acts of sexual violence and coercion are committed by men who are sexual partners (or former sexual partners) or otherwise known to the women they assault (e.g., Russell, 1982, 1984; Tjaden & Thoennes, 2000).

As findings about the high rates of sexual violence and coercion by men against women within acquaintance situations gained public attention, controversies regarding these estimates revolved around what is counted as rape or sexual violence (see Gavey, 2005, for a discussion). Some claimed that the problem was exaggerated because of improperly broad definitions of rape (e.g., Gilbert, as quoted in Hendrix, 1991, and Guttman, 1990, both cited in Koss, 1992). Researchers explained that these reactions were based on a misunderstanding and misrepresentation of the research, pointing out that research estimates of the prevalence of rape were based on definitions that were consistent with legal definitions (Koss, 1992; Muehlenhard, 1994). (See Fisher & Cullen, 2000; Fisher, Daigle, Cullen, & Turner, 2003; Koss, 1992; and Spitzberg, 1999, for more detailed discussions of measurement issues and Koss et al., 2007, for a more recent update.)

The best studies, of both general and college populations, have consistently found that between 18% and 25% of adult women have experienced attempted or completed rape (e.g., Koss et al., 1987; Laumann, Gagnon, Michael, & Michaels, 1994, Tjaden & Thoennes, 2000), although face-to-face interviews have obtained higher figures (Randall & Haskell, 1995; Russell, 1984). Studies of men from both community and college student populations have typically found that around one in 10 men admit to having engaged in acts that would legally be categorized as rape or attempted rape (Abbey & McAuslan, 2004; Senn, Desmarais, Verberg, & Wood, 2000; J. W. White & Smith, 2004), although in one community sample of single men the rate was closer to one in four (Abbey, Parkhill, BeShears, Clinton-Sherrod, & Zawacki, 2006).

When researchers included a wider continuum of sexual victimization, it was not uncommon to find as many as half or more of all women reporting having experienced some form of sexual coercion or sexual assault (Gavey, 1991a, 1991b; Koss et al., 1987). Research with men has also found that a significant number report having sexually pressured a woman when it was clear she did not want to have sex (Abbey & Jacques-Tiura, 2011; DeGue & DiLillo, 2004). Although rates are quite variable, more than half of the college men in Muehlenhard and Linton's (1987) study reported having had some form of sex with a woman when she had made it clear that she did not want to, and Senn et al. (2000) found that 27% of men from a community sample admitted to engaging in some degree of sexual coercion or sexual assault. More than 60% of the men in Abbey et al.'s (2006) community sample admitted to having committed acts that would be defined as sexual coercion, sexual assault, or rape.

Typically, only around 10% or fewer of the rapes and attempted rapes reported by women in these self-report studies are committed by strangers (e.g., Gavey, 1991a; Laumann et al., 1994; Russell, 1982, 1984). Several studies have found that somewhere between a half and nearly two thirds are perpetrated by men who are in some kind of romantic or sexual relationship with the woman (dates, boyfriends, husbands, etc.; e.g., Gavey, 1991a; Koss, 1988; Russell, 1982, 1984). Across a range of studies, it has been found that around 10% to 14% of married and cohabiting women have experienced rape by their husbands (E. K. Martin, Taft, & Resick, 2007; Russell, 1982), with one study finding that 37% had experienced some form of sexual victimization by a man who was their husband or partner at the time (Gavey, 1991a). When husbands are physically abusive, the percentage of women who have experienced marital rape rises to more than 40% (E. K. Martin et al., 2007).

EFFECTS OF SEXUAL VIOLENCE PERPETRATED BY MEN AGAINST WOMEN

Sexual violence is associated with a wide array of adverse psychological, social, health, and economic consequences for victim–survivors (S. L. Martin, Macy, & Young, 2011, provided a recent overview). Research detailing the nature and course of the psychological impact presents a complex picture. Since Burgess and Holmstrom's (1974) groundbreaking identification of a rape trauma syndrome, research has increasingly focused on the symptoms of posttraumatic stress disorder, which include forms of hyperarousal, traumatic "intrusions" such as flashbacks and nightmares, and psychological "constrictions" such as dissociation (Herman, 1998). Numerous studies have found an association between these kinds of distress and experiences of sexual violence such as rape and sexual assault (R. Campbell, Dworkin, & Cabral, 2009; Yuan, Koss, & Stone, 2006). Other forms of psychological distress associated with sexual violence include anxiety, depression (e.g., Frazier, 2003; Koss & Harvey, 1991), difficulties with sexuality and intimacy (e.g., Herman, 1998; Koss & Harvey, 1991), and disruption to one's values and sense of self (e.g., Gavey, 2007).

It is important to remember, however, that experiences of sexual violence are themselves diverse, with varying levels of physical force and violence, threat, fear, injury, and intimate betrayal. Even across one particular act such as rape, its exact nature and meaning can vary considerably as will its impact on women's lives (R. Campbell et al., 2009; Gavey, 2007; Womersley & Maw, 2009; Yuan et al., 2006). Although research overall has suggested that several common negative psychological consequences of rape exist, not all women who are raped experience them, and for many who do, the distress they experience decreases over time (e.g., Frazier, 2003; Koss & Figueredo, 2004; Koss & Harvey, 1991). At a broader cultural level, however, researchers have suggested that all women are adversely affected to some extent by living with the restrictions that fear of rape imposes on women's lives (e.g., Riger & Gordon, 1981; Senn & Dzinas, 1996).

RECENT HISTORICAL BEARINGS

Although a vast body of research and clinical literature on the harmful psychological impact of sexual violence is now available, the subject did not receive any serious professional or public recognition until the 1970s (e.g., Vigarello, 2001). This long silence is perhaps not surprising given that sexual violence has long held an uneasy and ambivalent place in Western societies, visible in the operation of rape laws and in general-public views about rape, both historically and to the present day. It is also seen through expert professional discourse and wider cultural views, norms, and values surrounding male and female sexuality. In the next sections of the chapter, we briefly discuss sexology, psychoanalysis, and the law to see how the complex relationship between sexuality and sexual violence has unfolded in these domains. We then discuss the dramatic shifts in understanding of sexual violence that began in the 1970s as a result of feminist scholarship and activism. Only at this time did sexual violence come to be seen as a social problem (for discussions, see Bevaqua, 2000; Gavey, 2005). After this section, we move on to discuss wider "rape-supportive" discourses still in circulation.

Western cultures have long endorsed a script for heterosexual sex that is male dominated and aggressive, clearly and explicitly evident in Havelock Ellis's (1899/1948) classic sexology from the turn of the 20th century. Heterosexual sex is depicted in highly gendered ways, as a performance choreographed around aggressive pursuit and coy surrender. Ellis (1948) instructed his readers that women instinctively "delight in roughness, violence, pain and danger," whereas men "delight in domination" (p. 32). It is natural, he suggested, for women to have to appear "to shun the male, to flee from his approaches—to even actually repel them" (p. 229). This "seeming reluctance of the female is not intended to inhibit sexual activity either in the male or in herself, but to increase it in both" (p. 229). These ideas were taken to a wider audience through Van de Velde's (1930) highly influential early sex manual *Ideal Marriage*. He advised his many readers that both women and men want to feel "the essential force of *maleness*" in the sexual act, "which expresses itself in a sort of violent and absolute *possession* of the woman" (p. 159). Both genders, he claimed, enjoy "a certain degree of male aggression and dominance—whether actual or apparent" (p. 159).

Both Ellis (1899/1948) and Van de Velde (1930) took care to emphasize that the man must be attentive to his female partner's arousal and feelings more generally, that it is "only within limits that a woman really enjoys the pain, discomfort, or subjection to which she submits" (Ellis, 1948, p. 101). This paternalistic advice for heterosexual sex, however, left much to the man's discretion and goodwill. He was in charge. Not only was aggression supposedly a natural and normal part of sex, according to the sexologists, but influential strands of psychoanalytic thinking cast femininity as inherently masochistic. Helene Deutsch went so far as to suggest that women fantasize about rape and secretly desire it (Albin, 1977; Brownmiller, 1975; S. S. M. Edwards, 1981). Together, these sexological and psychoanalytic claims created a backdrop that made it almost impossible for a woman's account of rape to be taken seriously regardless of the characteristics of the specific laws of her state or country. She could be dismissed as either lying completely (it was all a wishful fantasy) or trying to cover up or exploit the fact she had had consensual (unmarried) sex in a social context in which that was not proper feminine behavior.

These ideas found their way into the law accompanied by cautionary advice about how to regard rape accusations (e.g., Estrich, 1987; Schulhofer, 1998). As one legal scholar cautioned (quoting Freud in support): "Most women want their lovers to be at least somewhat aggressive and dominating. Some consciously or unconsciously want to be forced" (Weihofen, 1959, p. 210). Even if it was accepted that a woman was raped, she was not uncommonly blamed for provoking it (for a discussion, see Gavey, 2005). Sexology and psychoanalysis thus naturalized, reinforced, and authoritatively perpetuated stereotypes about rape, rape victims, and perpetrators in the course of their pronouncements on the nature of sexuality.

The first half of the 20th century was a time when men's voices still dominated in public life. As feminists later pointed out, the putative truths that were being posited in sexology (as well as in psychoanalytic writing) about a naturally sexually aggressive male and more submissive female could be seen to privilege a male point of view. Given the context of women's relative lack of autonomy within heterosexual marriage, these norms scripted sex as a site ripe for exploitation. The expert legitimation of these gendered sexual norms provided a lexicon for capturing any ambiguity around whether an act of aggressive sex was rape or a man acting out his natural role within the field of sex. It provided a logic of justification for a man's use of sexual force that could ultimately work to minimize and excuse rape (Gavey, 2005).

The influence of this logic could be seen with dramatic effect in the legal context of that time. "Real" rape (Estrich, 1987) that conformed to a narrow stereotype of aggravated stranger rape of "respectable" White women had long been regarded as a heinous crime, punishable by death (e.g., Hale, 1763, as cited in Taylor, 1987). Yet most other "simple" rapes that technically conformed to the letter of the law but involved victims, perpetrators, and circumstances that departed from the extralegal stereotype were, in practice, historically ignored or disregarded by the criminal justice system (Estrich,

1987). Even many cases of rape that conformed to the stereotypical script for "real" rape never resulted in convictions, because the standards required for proof were, in practice, very narrow. If they were believed at all that something took place, women were often held at least partially responsible for their fate (e.g., Backhouse, 2008). Their willingness (as a participant in even the most violent acts of sexual aggression) was assumed, unless there was proof of her utmost resistance, either corroboration or physical injuries consistent with a fight to the death (Backhouse, 2008; Estrich, 1987).

This treatment of women reporting rape in the criminal justice system is consistent with prejudicial assumptions about women's sexuality and the normative nature of male sexuality (Smart, 1995). Within rape trials, according to S. S. M. Edwards (1981), "a model of female sexuality as *agent provocateur*, temptress or seductress is set in motion" (p. 50). Until the introduction of relatively recent legal reform, women were able to be questioned directly about their past sexual behavior, with the effect that their character and credibility could be denigrated if found to have previously been "too sexual" (e.g., Backhouse, 2008; Estrich, 1987). Although any woman could be subject to this form of humiliation, the prejudicial treatment of women in the criminal justice system has historically been shaped according to judgments that are based on a woman's race or ethnicity, class, (dis) ability, neighborhood, poverty, and so on as well as her appearance and behavior (including drug and alcohol use; Backhouse, 2008; Jordan, 2004).

Rethinking Sexual Violence: Feminist Activism and Scholarship

The way people understand sexual violence began to shift dramatically in the 1970s. In opposition to the victim blaming and justificatory logic of popular understandings of sexual violence, which kept women silent and kept rape and sexual assault relatively hidden from public view, the women's movement created space for women to tell their side of the story (Bevacqua, 2000; Senn, 2000). Feminist activists and scholars began to realize that sexual violence was not just a private matter affecting a few unfortunate women but a major social problem touching the lives of many (Gavey, 2005). They argued that the normative gender relations of the time were thoroughly implicated in the maintenance and support of rape. "The act of rape," according to the New York Radical Feminists Manifesto, "is the logical expression of the essential relationship now existing between men and women" (Manhart & Rush, 1974, p. xvi), "not an isolated act that can be rooted out from patriarchy without ending patriarchy itself" (Griffin, 1977, p. 66). North American and other Anglo-Western societies were declared to be "rape cultures" because of the ways in which they actively tolerated rape while at the same time formally condemning it. A whole antirape movement gathered force to challenge the victim blaming that silenced women who had experienced rape and obstructed opportunities for seeking justice through the criminal justice system. This feminist activism was successful in lobbying for significant, albeit ultimately insufficient and flawed, legal reform (e.g., Caringella, 2009; Decker & Baroni, 2012; Easteal, 1998; Gotell, 2010; Schulhofer, 1998; Seidman & Vickers, 2004–2005; Tang 1998) as well as the establishment of support services for women who had been raped or sexually assaulted (Koss & Harvey, 1991).

Although rape myths and other rape-supportive claims continued to be put forward as facts, and the views of prominent social figures, such as police officers, politicians, and judges, were often unchanged (e.g., Jordan, 2004; Lees, 1993; van de Zandt, 1998), they no longer went unchallenged. For example, in the 1990s a New Zealand judge remarked, "The world would be a much less exciting place to live . . . if every man stopped the first time a woman said 'No'" (Quaintance, 1996). Public opinion had by this time changed sufficiently that his comments were met with widespread condemnation (Gavey, 2005). As recently as 2011, a similar case occurred in Canada, when a police officer addressing a university safety forum said, "I've been told I'm not supposed to say this—however, women should avoid dressing like sluts in order not to be victimized" (Rush, 2011, para. 10). This comment sparked an immediate and prolonged series of protests (i.e., "Slutwalks") organized by feminists in Toronto and subsequently around the world. In both cases, these men's authoritative assertions, which otherwise work to silence women (and others) who experience sexual violence or to trivialize their experiences, were called into question and met widespread public reprobation that would not have happened before the feminist antirape activism of the 1970s.

In the process of putting rape on the public agenda as a serious social issue (Bevacqua, 2000), it was politicized by bringing to light a "woman's point of view" (Gavey, 2005). Listening to women's accounts of their experiences of forced sex led feminists to reject the idea, implicit at the time, that rape could be sexy. Although it may have made sense to men to imagine the rape of women as a crime of passion or simply just an overly ardent act of lovemaking, it became clear that the experience of being subjected to forced unwanted sex was never sexy for the woman involved. It was instead humiliating and degrading (Brownmiller, 2000, cited in Lloyd, 2001), "an act of aggression in which the victim is denied her self-determination . . . an act of violence" (Griffin, 1977, p. 66). This second-wave feminist insistence that rape was about power, aggression, and violence was necessary, Brownmiller (2000, as cited in Lloyd, 2001) later explained, to counter the way that men "had romanticized rape and always presented scenarios of beautiful but just slightly unwilling, but really teasing victims" (p. 1553; see also Griffin, 1977; Piercy, 1985).

Rethinking Rape and Sex

Although feminists at this time called for a radical rethinking of rape, some went further, calling for critical attention to normative heterosexuality itself (e.g., MacKinnon, 1987). In going beyond Brownmiller's (1975) point that rape is an act of violence, they argued that not only is rape not sexy, but also a lot of what counts for sex is not sexy either (from a woman's point of view). Echoing sexologists from earlier in the century, they argued that heterosexuality is imbued with a dominance–submission dynamic and that power is enacted through sexual relations just as it is in other arenas of gender relations. Unlike the sexologists, however, they did not accept this characterization as natural, inevitable, or desirable. Instead they saw it as cause for concern that rape and sexual intercourse are not always automatically distinguishable from the point of view of women, men, or the law (e.g., Jackson, 1978; MacKinnon, 1983). A leading proponent of this view, MacKinnon (1987) insisted that it was essential to recognize that violence and coercion are not inherently absent from sex. From a woman's point of view, she argued, "sexuality in exactly these normal forms often *does* violate us" (p. 86). This assertion may, in fact, still sound like a radical proposition to many. Indeed, not all of the earlier feminist writers supported this analysis. Some were concerned that by emphasizing the normality of rape and sexual violence, the trauma experienced by victims of "real" violent rape is diluted and downplayed (e.g., Segal, 1987). Some were also cautious to avoid what could be seen as a blanket condemnation of heterosexual sex (e.g., Estrich, 1987).

After largely ignoring sexual violence for most of the 20th century, many psychologists and other social scientists soon came to agree with the feminist argument that rape was simply the end point on a continuum of heterosexual interactions in which male aggression and female passivity are integral to socially constructed gender roles and in which forms of coercion are normative (e.g., Berger & Searles, 1985; Burt, 1980; Clark & Lewis, 1977; Jackson, 1978; Kelly, 1987; Medea & Thompson, 1974; Russell, 1975, 1982, 1984; Weis & Borges, 1973). This recognition does not imply that all, or even most, heterosexual sex acts out this dominance–submission dynamic but rather that it is a familiar idealized pattern that is commonly treated as natural and normal and therefore is at the very least unremarkable. Researchers began to introduce a dimensional or continuum approach to their conceptualization of sexual violence to draw connections between a range of different nonconsensual sexual acts involving different levels of coercion or force (e.g., Finkelhor & Yllo, 1983, 1985; Kelly, 1987, 1988a, 1988b; Koss & Oros, 1982; Koss et al., 1987; Russell, 1982; see Kelly, 2012, for a retrospective reflection on the concept of a continuum of sexual violence).

Changes Within the Criminal Justice System

Accompanying these cultural shifts in understanding sexual violence have been changes in the criminal justice system's treatment of women reporting crimes of sexual violence. These changes have been evident in different ways, at different paces, in different parts of the world (e.g., Caringella, 2009; Easteal, 1998; Frank, Hardinge, & Wosick-Correa, 2009; Seidman & Vickers, 2004–2005). It is still the case that many reports of rape never proceed through the criminal justice system, often because of extralegal factors relating to the circumstances of the rape and judgments about the character of the victim (see Alderden & Ullman, 2012). It is still less likely that "simple" (Estrich, 1987) rapes will end up being prosecuted, and the chance of conviction for any act of rape is still very low (Alderden & Ullman, 2012; Caringella, 2009; see also Fine, 2012).

Until relatively recently, it was extremely difficult for a woman to even lay a complaint with the police if she knew the man who sexually assaulted her. If she was raped by her husband, it was impossible because in most jurisdictions, for most of the 20th century, rape of a wife was not legally possible. Not until late in the 20th century were these so-called marital exemptions removed from rape laws in most Western and many other countries. Even as late as the 1990s, some English lawmakers argued, in defense of retaining these exemptions, that women in effect rescind their right to decline sex with their husbands when they get married (Gavey, 2005; see also K. M. Edwards, Turchik, Dardis, Reynolds, & Gidycz, 2011). Sexual violence by husbands and intimate sexual partners continues to be minimized (e.g., Basile, 2002; Bennice & Resick, 2003). By 2002, 27 states in the United States still lacked what McMahon-Howard, Clay-Warner, and Renzulli (2009) referred to as "strong marital rape law" (p. 509). Nevertheless, it is well known that rape by husbands in particular can be just as or more violent than rape by strangers, especially within the context of domestic violence (e.g., Möller, Backstrom, Sondergaard, & Helstrom, 2012; Stermac, Del Bove, & Addison, 2001), and it is also more likely to be repeated (see Bennice & Resick, 2003, for a review). It is also clear that sexual violence by romantic and sexual partners in general can be harmful (e.g., see Bennice & Resick, 2003, and E. K. Martin et al., 2007, for reviews; Frazier & Seales, 1997; B. L. Katz, 1991; Koss, Dinero, Seibel, & Cox, 1988; Ullman, Filipas, Townsend, & Starzynski, 2006; Ullman & Siegel, 1993), even above and beyond the effects of physical partner violence (Bennice, Resick, Mechanic, & Astin, 2003). Even rape committed by intimate partners without explicit physical violence can be profoundly disruptive, including in ways that cause broader social and economic difficulties (Bennice & Resick, 2003) and in ways that are not easily measurable through the usual symptom checklists (Gavey, 2007; see also Chapter 10, this volume). One woman interviewed by Gavey (2007), for instance, described how in the "split second" of a nonviolent rape by her boyfriend, her whole life was changed because her identity, sense of value as a person, and moral compass were profoundly and adversely affected.

One of the reasons for this continued wide gap between the letter of the law and its application may be a concern by lawmakers and law enforcers about natural justice for men, given the perceived risk of innocent men being subject to false accusations and unjust punishment, a concern that dates back to the 17th-century English Chief Justice Sir Matthew Hale (Hale, 1763, as cited in Taylor, 1987). Supporting this concern is an extensive matrix of cultural presumptions, norms, and values about women and men, and sexuality and rape, that arguably allows this anxiety to prevail over and above a stronger and less ambiguous cultural stance against sexual violence.

ONGOING RAPE-SUPPORTIVE DISCOURSES

Critically examining legal and other social responses to sexual violence highlights the cultural ambivalence that exists around what rape is and where the boundaries are considered to lie between sexual violence seen as a crime and sexual pressure seen as an acceptable or tolerable part of sex itself (see Volume 2, Chapter 10, this handbook). From a feminist point of view, this ambivalence arises because rape, in all but the most egregious aggravated cases, arguably represents a flash point between what could be thought of as old and new cultural beliefs and values around gender and sexuality. In the contemporary modern context, women are formally accorded equal status in Western and many other societies (but not all). Formal legal and moral rhetoric has come to recognize that women have a right to autonomy and dignity that is equal to men's and that they should have as much right to control what happens to their own bodies as do men. From this point of view, rape is unambiguously wrong. However, the rights and values that this modern acceptance is pinned on arguably clash with less formally acceptable, yet still influential, vestiges of more traditional assumptions and values about gender differences that continue to some extent to shape popular commonsense understandings of gender relations (in varying degrees in different cultural, religious, and geopolitical contexts; see also Chapter 2, this volume; Volume 2, Chapters 9 and 13, this handbook). This clash, which is rarely acknowledged or articulated as such, is what explains the sometimes murky ground we can find ourselves on in making sense of coerced and forced sex and its relationship to sexuality. Gavey (2005) suggested that this underlay of contradictory values, norms, ideas, and practices forms a matrix of rape-supportive discourses that actually provide the "cultural scaffolding of rape."

Discourses

The notion of a discourse is rooted in Foucauldian social constructionist approaches (e.g., see Gavey, 1989, 2005) and has been widely used within feminist sociocultural research on sexuality and sexual violence. Discourses are sometimes described as regulated "system[s] of statements" (Henriques, Hollway, Urwin, Venn, & Walkerdine, 1984, p. 104; Hollway, 1983, p. 231; Parker, 1992, p. 5), although it is probably easier to imagine them as coherent patterns of meaning or sets of assumptions. At the same time, they are much more than this. Theoretically undergirding the concept of a discourse are the ideas that (a) these patterns of meaning are shared cultural resources rather than internal properties of an individual's mind and (b) they actively shape meaning and practice (see also Magnusson & Marecek, 2012). That is, they both enable and constrain one's ways of being and acting in, and understanding, the world. The concept of a discourse is thus very different from that of an attitude. While attitudes are properties of individuals, discourses are properties of cultures. Of course, multiple discourses are always in circulation at any one time and place that offer different ways of understanding aspects of one's personal and social worlds. Dominant discourses are those patterns of meaning that are hegemonic and seem most obvious and natural in a particular culture, time, and place. They flesh out and constitute people's taken-for-granted commonsense understandings about the nature of things, and in doing so are most influential in shaping the possibilities for identities, actions, and social and relational life more generally (e.g., Gavey, 1989). We come back to this concept later in the chapter.

Rape Myths

One way that social psychologists have made sense of the cultural scaffolding of rape is through exploring the form and extent of what are referred to as "rape myths" (Burt, 1980). Martha Burt (1980) proposed this concept to refer to "prejudicial, stereotyped, or false beliefs about rape, rape victims, and rapists" (p. 217). For example, the idea that many women secretly desire to be raped, that women who dress in revealing or sexualized clothing are "asking for trouble," that women who engage in consensual sex play and "let it get out of hand" only have themselves to blame if their partner then forces sex on them, and so on (Burt, 1980, p. 223). Burt's own and other research has shown high tolerance for such rape-supportive views, with reviews of the research finding them to be "widely and persistently held" (Lonsway & Fitzgerald, 1994, p. 134). Rape myths have been postulated to work to minimize, excuse, and justify sexual violence. In doing so, it has been suggested that they function to protect society "from confronting the reality and extent" of the problem (Lonsway & Fitzgerald, 1994, p. 136) and the need for social change (Z. D. Peterson & Muehlenhard, 2004).

Although people are less willing than they used to be to overtly blame the victim of a rape, research has suggested that many of the old myths continue to be influential in shaping ordinary understandings of rape (e.g., I. Anderson & Doherty, 2008; K. M. Edwards et al., 2011; McMahon, 2007, 2010; Weiss, 2009). For instance, women who have experienced rape continue to be held to account for the rape (I. Anderson & Doherty, 2008; Lea, 2007; McMahon,

2007, 2010), and a significant proportion hold themselves to account (Weiss, 2009). Those who report to the police still face a high chance of not being believed (Jordan, 2004), and those seeking formal support from community services and informal support from family and friends still sometimes receive negative hurtful responses (e.g., Ahrens, Campbell, Ternier-Thames, Wasco, & Sefl, 2007; R. Campbell, Wasco, Ahrens, Sefl, & Barnes, 2001).

Key categories of rape myths still in circulation relate in direct and indirect ways to implicit assumptions about male and female sexuality (Weiss, 2009), albeit in a more subtle form than they did in the past (Bohner, Eyssel, Pina, Siebler, & Viki, 2009; McMahon, 2007, 2010; McMahon & Farmer, 2011). In various ways they draw on old notions of female sexuality, on the one hand as dangerous and not to be trusted and on the other hand as delicate and sacred, in need of physical protection, and in both cases in need of moral regulation. At the same time, they reference the persistent idea of male sexuality as naturally constantly primed for action, easily triggered, and difficult (for him) to control once aroused beyond a certain point. So, for example, even some women who have been sexually assaulted make sense of the experience in ways that make excuses for the perpetrator by drawing on a vocabulary of male sexual aggression as natural: "He got carried away" (Weiss, 2009).

As Weiss (2009) noted, a good girl–bad girl dichotomy still operates, such that "good girls" are expected to actively anticipate and avoid any risks of sexual violence, whereas "bad girls" are held at least partly responsible for the sexual violence to which they are subjected. Thus, although the language of "chaste character" may no longer be used, it is not uncommon for people to believe that women whose sexual demeanor and history crosses an invisible line of feminine sexual respectability (i.e., too overtly sexualized in dress and behavior, too many sexual partners, sex outside of committed relationships, too much alcohol consumption) either secretly want to be raped, and enjoy it, or are at least somewhat to blame (e.g., K. M. Edwards et al., 2011; Weiss, 2009). This victim culpability is reinforced, as I. Anderson and Doherty (2008) have discussed, by powerful contemporary notions of the self-responsible neoliberal subject. This subject is held morally accountable, they argued, for being unable to keep herself safe from the unavoidable risks and hazards that life presents and by anticipating and avoiding them.

For groups of women who are racially marginalized, racist beliefs and actions may intersect with these rape myths to ensure an even worse situation (e.g., A. M. White, Strube, & Fisher, 1998). Some women, by virtue of ethnicity or race, are still more likely to be judged as implicitly always available for sex, which is sometimes seen to be coupled with a presumption that if they are raped they are undeserving of equal care or treatment (e.g., Razack, 1998). These cultural discourses and the racist practices they support are likely connected to the higher rates of violence against some groups of women, particularly, it has been shown in some contexts, indigenous women (e.g., Evans-Campbell, Lindhorst, Huang, & Walters, 2006; Tjaden & Thoennes, 2000). Within the United States, as Black feminist scholars have discussed, the institutionalized rape of Black women by White men during slavery—as well as the lynching of Black men for having sex with White women—and the ongoing racist legacies of these abuses, left a complex terrain of sometimes competing racial and sexual politics around rape, and challenges for the recognition of sexual violence against African American women (e.g., Collins, 2005; Crenshaw, 1993; Davis, 1990; A. M. White, 1999). Although rape myths are usually described in mainstream psychology as individual internal attributes, they can be seen from a more social perspective as elements of rape-supportive discourses that are properties of cultures rather than individuals (as we discuss in the next section). As suggested earlier, many influential rape myths are not formulated specifically or explicitly in relation to rape but are tied to conventional assumptions about masculine and feminine (hetero) sexuality. As we discuss in the next section, feminist critical psychologists and other scholars have discussed these notions in terms of the dominant discourses of heterosexuality, the familiar, culturally shared sets of assumptions that guide one's expectations for male and female sexuality (see Chapters 1 and 2, this volume).

THEORETICAL APPROACHES

Sexual violence is now widely accepted to be a pervasive and global problem. To explain its ubiquity across a continuum of sexually coercive and forceful acts, both sociocultural and biological theories have been suggested. Although they emphasize different levels of analysis for understanding sexual violence, both accept that it must be connected to normative features of human behavior or culture rather than simply a manifestation of individual pathology. In this section, we outline in more detail the feminist sociocultural approach. We then critically discuss the miscommunication hypothesis, which also draws on gendered cultural patterns to explain rape but in a way that is insufficiently attentive to the workings of power and the complexity of cultural norms that enable and constrain men's and women's ways of acting within a sexual encounter. Finally, we also briefly address an evolutionary approach.

Gender, Power, and the Cultural Conditions of Possibility for Sexual Violence

According to a feminist sociocultural approach, the normative gendered dynamics of heterosexuality actually shape the conditions of possibility for sexual violence. (Although most of the research we discuss applies to Western cultural norms, we do not claim that this is unique to Western cultures.) This is not to say that heterosexuality, even in its most conventional gendered forms, *is* sexual violence but that it provides normative desires, identities, and scripts that are gendered in ways that can be seen to lay the groundwork for sexual violence. Although there are exceptions (see, e.g., Vares, Potts, Gavey, & Grace, 2007), dominant portrayals and lived experiences of heterosexuality still tend to take for granted a relatively passive, responsive female sexuality and a more active and aggressive male sexuality (e.g., Gavey, 2005; Jozkowski & Peterson, 2012). Although these portrayals can be enacted in ways that contain no trace or threat of sexual violence, they can also be enacted in ways that quite easily slide from sexual initiation or seduction into sexual pressure and coercion. Thus, the boundaries between what is simply sex and what is a form of sexual violence (especially noncriminal forms) can be blurry. Moreover, one can argue that these dominant cultural norms for the gendered dynamics of heterosexual sex can provide a kind of camouflage for disguising violence in the midst of "sex," even sometimes criminal forms. At this point, we should say that we are bracketing off from our discussion forms of violent or "rough" sex that are consensual because they fall outside of our definition of sexual violence as something that is done to, or against, a person without his or her consent. Although there are relevant issues that could be discussed about consensual BDSM (bondage and discipline, dominance and submission, and sadomasochism), for instance, including different ways one might read it according to whether gendered patterns of dominance and submission conform to or depart from normative gendered patterns, these issues are beyond the scope of this chapter (see Chapters 9 and 25, this volume).

We have already introduced the concept of discourses, which refer to shared cultural patterns of meaning that shape the possibilities for how people can be and act in the world.

Hollway's (1984, 1989) early work on gender relations has been foundational in providing a discursive framework for thinking about the cultural organization of heterosexuality. She proposed that three dominant discourses provide a sociocultural template on which heterosexual relations are organized: *a male sexual drive discourse*, *a have/hold discourse*, and *a permissive sex discourse*. The male sexual drive discourse holds that the desire or "need" to have sex is a strong, almost overwhelming drive that exists in all healthy normal men and that men will go to great lengths to have sex. By contrast, through the have/hold discourse (which Hollway, 1989, named in relation to Christian marriage vows), women are depicted as comparatively asexual creatures for whom sex is a means to an end—that is, a monogamous heterosexual relationship and children. Hollway (1989) described how the male sexual drive discourse and the have/hold discourse work together in highly gender-differentiated ways to prescribe the normative form of heterosexual sex and relationships. According to this argument, both women's and men's sexuality are constructed through both discourses. The ongoing relevance of these discourses is addressed next.

Critical psychologists talk about discourses providing "subject positions" for people to take up that lay out specific possibilities for identity, behavior, and ways of making sense of the world (e.g., Henriques et al., 1984). Men are the subjects of the male sexual drive discourse; women are its objects. Within the terms of this discourse, women's role is to receive or reject men's sexual advances. So although they are not passive objects of the male sexual drive discourse, women's agency within this discursive context is limited to the extent of responding to (or perhaps anticipating) the man's needs and initiatives. That is, her actions are premised on the basis of meeting, or denying, his sexual pleasure rather than acting to advance her own. Of course, it is possible for women to resist a male sexual drive discourse, but it can never simply be a matter of stepping outside of it without the possibility of being marked by it. For example, within our culture the heterosexual woman who chooses to not have sex with her male partner when she does not feel like it herself enters a discursive space spiked with pejorative and potentially punitive consequences. Our language is filled with terms for the woman who sets firm sexual limits or is sexually uninterested: *ball-breaking, a cock teaser, frigid, cold bitch,* and *uptight,* for example. This vocabulary is widely understood and can be readily drawn on by women to police their own behavior and by others to insult women who do not toe the line. A whole other set of discursive resources is available for punishing and policing a woman whose sexuality is deemed excessive (particularly outside the confines of a monogamous heterosexual relationship). These are signaled through a different set of pejorative terms, such as *slut, slag, nympho, whore, ho, tart, loose,* and *easy*. These kinds of accusations—about both sexual excess and sexual insufficiency—are not trivial and are likely to have effects of constraining the way that women can act (Gavey, 2005). In fact, as seen earlier in the comments of police officers and judges, and as we discussed earlier in the section on rape myths, such constructions remain critical to social judgments of whether women are seen as legitimate rape victims.

Within this discursive weave, women's rewards in heterosexuality are not primarily sexual but are secondary gains related to relationships and family. Everyone is familiar with cultural tropes of women using their sexuality to variously "hook," "trap," or keep her man. Thus, women give (up) sex in return for love, commitment, and relationship, whereas men give (up) sexual freedom in return for a woman to look after them, sexually and in other ways.

This particular interlocking of a male sexual drive discourse and a have/hold discourse seems old-fashioned in the 21st century. Since at least the 1970s, women's rights to sexual pleasure have been staunchly argued and reiterated in the popular realm. Sex and marriage manuals have long promoted an active, competent, and "autonomous" sexuality for women outside of marriage (Weinberg, Swensson, & Hammersmith, 1983). The "permissive turn" that emerged in the 1960s has undoubtedly had an enormous influence on current heterosexual practice, bolstered, of course, by biotechnological developments such as the contraceptive pill. According to the terms of what Hollway (1984, 1989) called a permissive discourse, women were now assumed to be equally sexual, with natural drives and urges just like men. Many feminists, however, argued that the so-called sexual revolution was not all it was cracked up to be and the gender neutrality of permissive discourse was only a façade behind which a sexual double standard and gender inequality went on as usual (e.g., B. Campbell, 1980; Segal, 1983). Research has continued to find the sexual double standard alive and well (e.g., Crawford & Popp, 2003), with some researchers describing the dynamics of heterosexual sex between young men and women in particular "not, as it appears to be, masculinity-and-femininity in opposition: it *is* masculinity" (Holland, Ramazanoglu, Sharpe, & Thomson, 1998, p. 11) or, as Kalish and Kimmel (2011) have more recently described it in the context of U.S. college campuses, "guy's sex" (p. 138). Australian men interviewed by Mooney-Somers and Ussher (2010) oriented to gendered "truths" about the nature of heterosexual masculine sexuality, including a naturalized male desire for more (not necessarily better) sex. In a recent U.S. study, college students were asked to write narrative responses to questions about how they conceptualized, communicated, and interpreted sexual consent and nonconsent (Jozkowski & Peterson, 2012). They found both women and men adhered to traditional sexual scripts in which "men are expected to initiate sex and women are gatekeepers who determine if sex will actually occur" (Jozkowski & Peterson, 2012, p. 3). Tolman, Spencer, Rosen-Reynoso, and Porche (2003) found, in a study with younger U.S. teenagers, that both girls and boys "naturalized and normalized . . . male aggression and dominance" (p. 174). A small proportion of the men in Jozkowski and Peterson's (2012) study (around one in 10 for each category) indicated that they would use aggressive or deceptive tactics to indicate consent; as one man said, "Just stick it in and if she objects, pretend like I had done it by mistake" (p. 4).

The concept of *sexual scripts* (e.g., Simon & Gagnon, 1986) has been widely applied to understanding sexual behavior (Frith & Kitzinger, 2001), including sexual coercion (e.g., Byers, 1996; Frith & Kitzinger, 2001). Feminist scholars have suggested that reification of a traditional (hetero)sexual script may contribute to sexual coercion in a number of ways (see Byers, 1996, for summary). This traditional script portrays a picture of heterosexual practice that is similar to that conjured by the meeting of Hollway's (1984, 1989) dominant discourses of heterosexuality. Byers (1996) suggested it "legitimizes men's use of a variety of coercive and noncoercive influence strategies in attempting to overcome the woman's reluctance to engage in the sexual activity" (p. 10). At the most basic level, the notion of scripts as "a metaphor for conceptualizing the production of behaviour within social life" (Simon & Gagnon, 1986, p. 98) fits nicely with the sociocultural approach discussed above. However, according to Frith and Kitzinger (2001), the ways in which the notion of scripts are used within psychology are theoretically disparate and generally not consistent with a social constructionist approach. Often, they claimed, it is used in a way that implicitly resorts to cognitive constructs and thus is more "individualist and asocial" (Frith & Kitzinger, 2001, p. 213).

It Was Just a Miscommunication

Another cultural-level explanation for rape and sexual coercion of a woman by a man that has become popular over the past few decades is that it was simply a miscommunication rooted in fundamental differences in the ways in which women and men approach both sex and communication (see Beres, 2010; Crawford, 1995; Frith, 2009; McCaw & Senn, 1998). This idea emerges from the *two-cultures model* (Crawford, 1995), popularized by linguist Deborah Tannen and self-help author John Gray, which asserts and explains wider reaching difficulties in communication between the sexes as akin to cross-cultural communication (Crawford, 1995; Frith & Kitzinger, 1997). Claiming the existence of profound essential gender differences in communication style and goals, the model proposes that communication will inevitably be strained (Crawford, 1995). As applied to sexual violence, the model suggests that although a woman may have felt coerced into sexual activity, the man may have believed she was in fact consenting (McCaw & Senn, 1998). Attributions of miscommunication are usually applied in circumstances that fall outside the more extreme cases of violent stranger rape. They are used to attempt to explain those forms of sexual violence, usually by an intimate partner or acquaintance, in which there is no violent force or threat to harm and in which a woman's claims not to have consented are most often open to contestation. In other words, according to this idea sexual coercion and violence may be the result of a simple mistake rather than a willful disregard of the rights and feelings of one person by another. In depicting much of what is called sexual coercion or acquaintance rape as the result of everyday misunderstanding and miscommunication between men and women, the proposed solution is better communication (on the part of individual women) and enhanced sensitivity (on the part of individual men; for critical review, see Frith, 2009).

McCaw and Senn (1998) described three basic components of what they termed the *miscommunication hypothesis* for sexual coercion and acquaintance rape: (a) that men (mistakenly) overestimate women's interest in sex (with them), (b) that men interpret women's refusal as token and women commonly give token "no" responses, and (c) that women are reluctant to explicitly refuse men's coercive sexual advances. We present a brief summary of research that helps to unpack each of these components of the miscommunication model in turn.

Do men overperceive women's sexual interest? Abbey (1982) conducted the first research in this area with an ingenious study. Participants were randomly assigned to actor or observer roles in mixed-gender dyads. The male and female actors had a brief conversation on an assigned topic while unknown to them, the other dyad watched from another room. After the conversation, all four people rated the quality of the conversation and answered questions about each of the actors. In this way, the researchers could evaluate the actors' actual sexual interest in their conversation partners and compare it with their partner's ratings and the observers' perceptions. The findings were published in an article with the subtitle "Do Males Misperceive Females' Friendliness?" (Abbey, 1982). The answer, in a nutshell, was yes.

A review conducted by Lindgren, Parkhill, George, and Hendershot (2008) confirmed that after decades of replication and extension studies men appear "to perceive more sexuality in their own, other men's, and women's behavior" (p. 423) than do women, with few exceptions. Supporting the additional impact of a sexual double standard, certain behaviors, such as wearing more revealing clothing and carrying a condom, result in both men's and women's higher reported perceptions of women's, but not men's, interest in and willingness to engage in sex (see Lindgren et al., 2008). Gender differences in perceptions of sexual intent are most evident when the behaviors studied are mundane and not overtly sexual, that is, acts like making eye contact, complimenting someone, or having dinner with them, which are, of course, also behaviors associated with an interest in friendship and nonsexual affection as well as romantic or sexual relationships (e.g., Bondurant & Donat, 1999; see review in Lindgren et al., 2008). These findings together support the idea that men are in general more likely than women to overestimate women's sexual interest in them (and in other men).

However, it is difficult to tease out if and how men's reported misreading of women's lack of, or limited, sexual interest in them is related to sexual coercion. Some association does seem to exist, in that men who have sexually assaulted women in the past do report having misperceived women's sexual intentions more often than men who have not behaved in these ways (e.g., Zawacki, Abbey, Buck, McAuslan, & Clinton-Sherrod, 2003). What is not clear, however, is whether a tendency to genuinely misperceive sexual interest helps to explain coercive behavior or whether reported misperception represents a sense of entitlement that enables sexual coercion at the time or justifies it after the event. Several studies have found that men who report committing sexual assaults report having misperceived women's sexual interest and they also hold attitudes (e.g., hostile masculinity) and engage in other kinds of sexual behavior (e.g., have had a high number of casual sex partners) that have been associated with sexual violence perpetration (Abbey & Jacques-Tiura, 2011; Jacques-Tiura, Abbey, Parkhill, & Zawacki, 2007). Abbey and Jacques-Tiura (2011), using a representative community sample, replicated these aforementioned relationships but also asked men to provide more detail about one of the situations of sexual coercion they had reported. On the basis of the men's own descriptions, which included information that they knew that their actions were unwanted, Abbey and Jacques-Tiura concluded that men's misperception of women's sexual intentions was just one part of a constellation of self-serving "cognitive distortions" that enable perpetrators to justify their behavior. We draw particular attention to what these studies reveal about the cultural resources available to men for justifying coercive behavior rather than just individual properties that make some men more likely than others to draw on them. These findings in sum suggest that misperception of women's sexual interest does not provide the support for the miscommunication theory that is sometimes presumed.

Are women's "no"s routinely token, and do men perceive them as such? Sexual communication is not always straightforward. The idea that women do not always mean no when they say "no" has been taken up in law and sexology, as we have already discussed, and in popular culture (see Ehrlich & King, 1992) in ways that directly undermine the straightforward meaning of even a direct verbal "no" as a means for a woman to communicate nonconsent to sex. In a study of *token resistance* to sex,

Muehlenhard and Hollabaugh (1988) found that while around 60% of women said they had never said no when they meant yes, nearly 40% had done this on occasion. Some of the reasons given for providing a token "no" are consistent with the subject positions available for women within the dominant discourses of heterosexuality and traditional sexual scripts, for example, that the woman did not want to be seen as promiscuous, did not want to seem to be overly interested in sex, or was unsure about the man's feelings for her. The finding that some women do report having said no when they did not mean it was taken up by other researchers and the popular media as support for the miscommunication theory. Research has shown that both men and women believe that women commonly use token "no" responses (e.g., Muehlenhard & Hollabaugh, 1988). Later research showed that although women's use of the token "no" might seem to support gender stereotypes of women's coyness or manipulativeness or unwillingness to be direct, this behavior was actually not restricted to women; equal or higher numbers of men report having used token "no" responses (Krahé, Scheinberger-Olwig, & Kolpin, 2000; O'Sullivan & Allgeier, 1994; Muehlenhard & Rodgers, 1998).

Muehlenhard and her colleagues (Muehlenhard & Peterson, 2005; Muehlenhard & Rodgers, 1998) argued subsequently that the paradigm used for this research overestimated the extent to which women use a token "no" by failing to grasp the nuance of women's (and men's) experiences. When women were asked to describe in detail the kinds of experiences that were being counted as token resistance in quantitative surveys (i.e., saying no when they really wanted to and intended having sex), many were writing instead about situations in which they said no and meant no, even if they were ambivalent in their desire for sex (Muehlenhard & Rodgers, 1998). For instance, it is possible to feel aroused and physically desire sex but be unwilling because of concern about unwanted pregnancy (or some other reason). Other research, exploring women's and men's stories generated about a hypothetical situation in which a woman refuses a man's initiation of sexual activity but sexual intercourse happens later anyway, found a similar result. The small number of ostensibly token refusals that male and female participants created for their female characters were actually more commonly real "no"s that they were later willing to change to a "yes" in different circumstances (e.g., more privacy, presence of a condom, deeper trust in the relationship; Beres, Senn, & McCaw, 2009).

Although considerable caution seems warranted in interpreting what a reported token "no" actually represents, some limited evidence has shown that women's use (ever) of a token "no" is positively correlated with having experienced sexual violence (Krahé et al., 2000). Given that by definition, women were willing to have sex with a man during the situation in which they purportedly said no but meant yes, it is not clear how this is related to sexual victimization. One possibility, suggested by Krahé et al. (2000), is that men involved with women who have once used a token "no" may read a later no as encouragement to persist in their behavior. However, for this interpretation to hold true, we would need to know that the men who perpetrated the sexual violence were the same men who received the token "no." The picture is complicated by evidence from the same study that men's own reports of ever having used a token "no" in sexual situations and their belief that women have used a token "no" with them were both positively correlated with men's perpetration of sexual violence (Krahé et al., 2000). Thus, men who believe that women have used token resistance also seem to be likely to use it themselves and to be sexually aggressive. It is possible that men who perpetrate sexual violence buy into a view of sexual communication that is adversarial and dishonest, which affects both their own verbal communication and, similar to Abbey et al.'s (2006) findings on misperception of women's sexual intent, provides a justification for their sexually aggressive behavior.

Are women reluctant to refuse men's coercive sexual behavior? The answer to this question is somewhat complicated if one considers the full range of subtle coercion, including the fact that women (and men) sometimes consent to unwanted sex in circumstances in which they feel it is expected of them (as discussed later) and that the concepts of unwanted sex and coerced sex are not always clearly distinguished in the literature. Byers and Eastman (1979, as cited in Byers & Wilson, 1985), in a study of women's retrospective accounts, identified three responses as most typical in response to unwanted sexual advances by acquaintances, "a verbal negative, an excuse, and a message referring to the status of the relationship" (p. 377), for example, that she did not know him well enough. Many years later, Livingston, Buddie, Testa, and VanZile-Tamsen's (2004) large (1,000-plus women) retrospective study found that very few women (11%) said they did not use some type of resistance or refusal to have sex to which they explicitly did not want to consent. Of the women, 63% reported that they had explicitly refused the sex (Livingston et al., 2004). A study using hypothetical role plays also found that the most frequent response was a clear refusal (e.g., 92% used "unambiguous refusals" in role plays; Byers, Giles, & Price, 1987), but it is possible that this artificial context maximizes the chance of such verbal responses because women may be less constrained by the emotional investments and vulnerabilities that may factor into responding to real unwanted sexual advances. Sometimes women refuse sex with men by using strategies that are more indirect (e.g., Byers et al., 1987; Livingston et al., 2004). Women's feelings about the man and their desire to maintain relationships affect the use of these strategies (Muehlenhard, Andrews, & Beal, 1996). For example, Byers et al. (1987) asked women what influenced the strategies they used in their study role plays of refusals of unwanted sex. The most common consideration, expressed by 58% of the women, was their feelings for the man involved.

These studies' findings that women report more direct than indirect refusals appear to contradict the findings from studies using conversational analysis or discourse analytic approaches investigating how people usually consent to sex (e.g., Beres, 2010; Kitzinger & Frith, 1999). As we discuss next in a slightly different context, such studies (see also Hickman & Muehlenhard, 1999) suggest that people may not typically use explicit verbal messages to consent to sex they do want or to decline sex they do not (e.g., Beres, 2010). It seems, therefore, that the answer to the question of whether women are reluctant to refuse men's unwanted sexual behavior is both yes and no. These differences in conclusions may emerge from the different foci of the studies or the ways the questions are posed. In particular, there may be a distinct shift in how women respond when a situation escalates from unwanted sexual advances that they imagine they have some control over to how women respond to a situation more clearly regarded as directly coercive, threatening, or aggressive.

Would sexual assault stop or decrease if women used an unequivocal "no" in response to unwanted sexual advances and men heard it? Research informed by conversation analysis has shown that even the more subtle verbal and nonverbal strategies that women report using to communicate their unwillingness in sexual situations, including those that are sexually coercive, are likely to be perceived clearly as refusals by both men and women (Kitzinger & Frith, 1999; O'Byrne, Hansen, & Rapley, 2008; O'Byrne, Rapley, & Hansen, 2006). Conversation analysis has shown that these ways of saying no without always explicitly verbally saying "no" are identical to the types of refusals that are well understood in other aspects of people's daily lives (Kitzinger & Frith, 1999; O'Byrne et al., 2006, 2008). That is, people normally decline or refuse invitations through delicate conversational forms that routinely incorporate features such as hesitations, hedges, excuses, apologies, or even compliments (Kitzinger & Frith, 1999). Because these conversational forms are normative, and in fact directly verbally simply saying "no" would not be in most conversational contexts, these findings suggest that it is likely disingenuous or manipulative of a man to claim that he misunderstood a woman's attempts to signal no as he persisted and forced sex on her (Kitzinger & Frith, 1999; O'Byrne et al., 2006, 2008). This alternative explanation is also consistent with the findings discussed earlier, suggesting that men who have been sexually coercive and aggressive may be motivated to justify their behavior using explanations that reduce their responsibility (Abbey & Jacques-Tiura, 2011). The miscommunication theory serves as one discursive resource among others for them to draw on.

Moreover, if misunderstanding women's verbal and nonverbal behavior underlies men's persistence in sex that is not consensual, men with lower ability to read these cues should be the most likely to sexually coerce women. The research does not support this contention. Muehlenhard and Falcon's (1990) research found that men with the best social skills (i.e., "heterosocially skilled") were most likely to use verbal sexual coercion. In another study, when men were asked about how they would show their own consent for sex, a minority reported that they would try to trick women by engaging in sex acts they knew she was unlikely to want (e.g., anal sex) and then pretending they had made a mistake (13%) or would aggressively proceed without waiting for women to consent (14%; Jozkowski & Peterson, 2012). Studies have also found that it is not uncommon for men to show a willingness to persist in their attempts to engage in sexual behavior after women have clearly communicated their wish not to do so (e.g., average rating of "would probably stop" as the highest level of certainty for even women's "most verbally definite responses" [Byers et al., 1987]; an average rating of 31 out of 100 on a probability scale for continuing to attempt intercourse after a woman has clearly stated she is not willing to go beyond kissing [Muehlenhard et al., 1996]). These findings challenge the logic of the miscommunication theory.

As a framework for understanding acquaintance rape, miscommunication theory has survived despite critiques and the vulnerable support for its component assumptions (e.g., Beres, 2010; McCaw & Senn, 1998; Muehlenhard & Rodgers, 1998; O'Byrne et al., 2008). Theoretical approaches can and do have an impact on how seriously people consider sexual violence and what they think should be done about it (e.g., Dar-Nimrod, Heine, Cheung, & Schaller, 2011). As mentioned earlier, these ideas about communication have become very influential (Crawford, 1995; O'Byrne et al., 2008), including in the legal domain (Ehrlich, 2001). The theory is used by people to account for their own and others' experiences (e.g., O'Byrne et al., 2008) and to inform rape prevention recommendations and approaches (e.g., Krahé et al., 2000). Studies with young men and "experts" have shown that miscommunication discourse is used as a way of decreasing men's accountability for rape and holding women responsible while appearing on the surface less overtly victim blaming (Crawford, 1995; O'Byrne et al., 2008).

Similarly, researchers have found that a sizable number of women use the concept of miscommunication as a way of labeling their experiences of sexual violence (e.g., 38% of "unacknowledged victims" in Littleton, Axsom, & Grills-Taquechel, 2009). Fisher et al. (2003) argued that because the behaviors so labeled are consistent with legal definitions of rape, women "endure sexual victimization without a clear understanding that this conduct falls under the category of rape" (p. 569). This issue of how forced sex is labeled can have serious implications for women (see Women's Labels for Their Experiences section for more detail).

Beyond the critiques presented, then, the problem with the miscommunication theory is that it does still end up holding women responsible for rape as well as for rape prevention, and it draws attention away from the active role of men in committing rapes, and the gendered power relations within heterosexuality that continue to make rape possible (Beres, 2010; Crawford, 1995). O'Byrne et al. (2008) concluded that the miscommunication model should not be regarded "as a *basis* for rape prevention strategies but *as one of* the very rape myths that may serve, in practice, to promote, condone and exculpate coercive sexual behaviour" (p. 189).

It's in Our Genes

One other theory that is applied to understanding the connections between sexual violence and sexuality is evolutionary theory. Evolutionary explanations, which emerged in the late 1970s and gained prominence in 2000, pin the cause of rape on underlying differences that have evolved in male and female sexuality, related to differential investments in "offspring" and "reproductive success" (Vandermassen, 2011). This theory appears to agree with feminist claims that rape sits alongside heterosexual sexual practices rather than outside normative behavior but for very different reasons and with different conclusions. Evolutionary theory has been used to explain the origins and maintenance of men's sexual aggression, with some researchers (e.g., Thornhill & Palmer, 2000) portraying a biologically inherent aggressiveness to male sexuality. Claims of this kind have been widely critiqued by social and biological scientists and feminist scholars alike (e.g., Coyne & Berry, 2000; Lloyd, 2001; Travis, 2003; Ward & Siegert, 2002). Other researchers have attempted to integrate evolutionary and feminist approaches (see Vandermassen, 2011), often citing biological hypotheses as part of multifactorial ecological models (e.g., Malamuth, 1998; Malamuth, Linz, Heavey, Barnes & Acker, 1995). Given the complexity of teasing out possible points of connection and disjuncture between evolutionary and sociocultural approaches, further elaboration of this model is beyond the scope of this chapter (see Chapter 1, this volume).

In the next part of the chapter, we discuss research, first on rape and then on unwanted sex and sexual coercion, that collectively helps to further show the connections between sexual violence and sexuality.

RAPE

Although we now know that rape is in fact highly prevalent, it is still thought to be one of the most underreported of all violent crimes (e.g., Chen & Ullman, 2010). The proportion of women who report the rapes committed against them appears to have increased in many places (e.g., Clay-Warner & Burt, 2005; Kelly & Lovett, 2009); however, this increase is often not matched by a marked improvement in the rate of convictions (Kelly & Lovett, 2009; Lonsway & Archambault, 2012; Seidman & Vickers, 2004–2005). In the early prevalence studies, the great majority of women who had experienced rape or sexual assault did not report it to the police, and many never disclosed their experiences to anyone (Koss et al., 1987; Russell, 1984). Women who do not label their experiences as rape appear to be even less likely to disclose the experience to another person (e.g., Botta & Pingree, 1997; Layman, Gidycz, & Lynn, 1996) or report it to authorities (e.g., Botta & Pingree, 1997). To some extent, then, the problem is still likely to remain somewhat hidden in the context of sexuality research, clinical practice, and classrooms, despite far greater public and professional attention to the issue of sexual violence in recent decades. It is important for those working in these fields to overcome any tendency toward avoidance or minimization and at the same time not be limited by stereotypes in imagining the men who have perpetrated and the women who have been subject to sexual violence and how they understand their experience in relation to the broader context of social meanings around sexual violence.

Women Who Have Been Raped by Men

Any woman can be subjected to sexual violence, and therefore stereotypical impressions of the "rape victim" are likely to be highly misleading. At the same time, research has indicated that a woman's chances of experiencing rape are affected by the circumstances of her life. Women marginalized in relation to race and ethnicity, particularly indigenous women (Brownridge, 2009; Evans-Campbell et al., 2006); poverty (Brownridge, 2009); occupation (e.g., sex workers; Farley & Barkan, 1998; Shannon et al., 2009; Silbert, 1982); and disability (intellectual and physical; Powers, Hughes, & Lund, 2009) all appear to have higher rates of sexual assault by men, relative to women with race, class, and ability privilege (Abbey, Jacques-Tiura, & Parkhill, 2010; Brownridge, 2009). There are also some periods or stages in women's lives, such as the teenage and early adult years (Johnson & Dawson, 2011; Tjaden & Thoennes, 2000), when there is a higher likelihood of being sexually victimized. Tjaden and Thoennes (2000), for example, found that more than 50% of all women in the National Violence Against Women Survey who had experienced rape had been assaulted before they turned 18. Older women dating again after a marriage or long-term partnership has ended report similar levels of "unwanted advances" on dates as do younger dating women (Kalra, Wood, Desmarais, Senn, & Verberg, 1998), which may mean they would be as likely to encounter sexual aggression in such situations. Although the research in this area is still quite limited, it appears that lesbian women experience rape by men in adulthood as much as or possibly even more than do heterosexual women (for review, see Balsam, 2002; Balsam, Rothblum, & Beauchaine, 2005). Transgender women and men also experience high rates of sexual violence, with perpetrators most likely to be men who are known to them, predominantly family members or romantic and sexual partners (see Stotzer, 2009, for review; Cook-Daniels & Munson, 2010).

Women's Labels for Their Experiences

Not all women who have been subject to sexually violent acts that would meet a technical definition of rape regard themselves to be victims of rape. Best estimates of the prevalence of rape come from anonymous surveys (e.g., Koss et al., 1987) or face-to-face interviews done by trained female interviewers (e.g., Randall & Haskell, 1995; Russell, 1984). Rather than using the terms *rape* or *sexual assault,* researchers use operational definitions founded on behavioral descriptions of acts that would be consistent with legal definitions of rape in most jurisdictions (see Gavey, 2005, for a discussion of the methodological issues in relation to wider debates around victimization; see Koss et al., 2007, for a discussion of methodological issues). For example, in Koss's original research developing what is now, after numerous revisions (Koss et al., 2007), the gold standard for measuring the prevalence (or incidence, depending on time period used) of rape and sexual coercion (Sexual Experiences Survey), a woman would have been considered to have experienced rape if she checked an item that read "Have you had sexual intercourse when you didn't want to because a man threatened or used some degree of physical force (twisting your arm, holding you down, etc.) to make you?" (or one of two other items describing intercourse resulting from administration of alcohol or drugs or insertion of objects with force or threat of force [Koss et al., 1987, p. 167]; see Koss et al., 2007, for most recent version of the scale). When researchers use the label *rape* instead, the number of women who report having experienced it drops dramatically (Bondurant, 2001; Fisher et al., 2003; Gavey, 1991a, 1991b; Kahn, Jackson, Kully, Badger, & Halvorsen, 2003; Kahn, Mathie, & Torgler, 1994; Koss, 1988; Peterson & Muehlenhard, 2004; Post et al., 2011), as it does when they use the terms *sexual abuse* and *sexual assault* (Harned, 2004, 2005). Across a range of studies, anywhere from 40% to 70% of women whom researchers consider to have experienced rape do not themselves identify the experience as rape (Littleton, Rhatigan, & Axsom, 2007).

Koss (1985) referred to those women who endorse items that provide behavioral descriptions of acts that would legally count as rape in most jurisdictions but who do not identify or report what happened to them as rape as *hidden rape victims.* Subsequent researchers have used the term *unacknowledged rape victims* (e.g., Kahn et al., 1994, 2003; Layman et al., 1996). In an attempt to avoid suggesting that women who do not label their experiences as rape are wrong (and that the researchers are right), Z. D. Peterson and Muehlenhard (2011) have preferred to refer simply to *labelers* and *nonlabelers.*

Research has found that whether or not women label their experience rape relates to the characteristics of the rape itself (e.g., Littleton, Axsom, & Grills-Taquechel, 2009; Littleton, Radecki Breitkopf, & Berenson, 2008) and whether or not it matches stereotypical rape scripts (for what is believed to typically happen before, during, and after a rape, including who the actors are likely to be and how they would act during the rape; Z. D. Peterson & Muehlenhard, 2011). Women are more likely to label their experience rape when it is consistent with some aspects of the traditional stereotype of rape, for example, the rapist is a stranger, a weapon or other physical force is used, it occurs outside at night, and it leaves the woman with physical injuries (Bondurant, 2001; Kahn et al., 1994, 2003; see Littleton et al., 2007, for a review). Research with North American college women has found that those who do not label their experience as rape are more likely to have had experiences that fit more closely with the less stereotypical, albeit more typical, rape (e.g., Littleton, Axsom, & Grills-Taquechel, 2009; for a review, see Littleton et al., 2007). They are more likely to know the man who forced sex on them, to have been romantically involved with him, and to have had previous consensual sex with him. The rape itself is less likely to have involved physical force, injuries, and obvious forms of resistance, and she is more likely to have been drinking alcohol beforehand (Littleton et al., 2007). In short, in a context in which heterosexual sex is normatively patterned as male control and female submission, it can look more like bad sex than rape (Gavey, 2005; Z. D. Peterson & Muehlenhard, 2004, 2011).

As well as the match between the rape script that a woman holds and the circumstances of her experience, Z. D. Peterson and Muehlenhard (2011) suggested that whether a woman will conceptualize her experience as rape also depends on what she perceives the consequences of that characterization would be. For instance, for some women understanding their experience as rape might be helpful, because it could be associated with less self-blame; for others, it may be aversive, because it could be associated with feeling less in control and more upset by what happened. Z. D. Peterson and Muehlenhard (2011) also made the important point that neither the experience nor the label is necessarily dichotomous and fixed. That is, an experience may seem neither clearly rape nor clearly not-rape because it may fit to varying degrees with the script a woman holds for rape, which itself may change over time. When given the opportunity, many women may conceptualize their experiences in terms of a continuum ranging from clearly rape to not rape (Z. D. Peterson & Muehlenhard, 2004, 2011). Of the 77 women in Z. D. Peterson and Muehlenhard's (2011) study who had experiences meeting a legal definition of rape, many described their experience (by choosing any of the 24 labels provided) as "a bad sexual experience" (90.5% of those who had not labeled it as rape, and 100% of those who had labeled it as rape). None of the women described it as either a "normal sexual" or "pleasurable" experience (p. 565). A woman's understanding of an experience may change over time, as her circumstances or knowledge change, for example, as a result of conversations with friends with different views, experience of rape awareness education, or a change in social or relational investments (e.g., Harned, 2005; Z. D. Peterson & Muehlenhard, 2011). Z. D. Peterson and Muehlenhard (2011) gave the example of a woman who does not want to label an experience rape because she does not want to label her boyfriend a rapist, noting that the motivation to avoid calling it rape might disappear once the relationship ends.

Men Who Perpetrate Rape and Sexual Assault

Although early research on convicted rapists tended to support stereotypical portrayals of "the rapist" as abnormal (e.g., Groth & Burgess, 1977), many of these conclusions could not withstand the test of comparison with men identified as rapists who were not convicted or with control groups of college men (see Malamuth, 1981, for an early review). Research beginning in the 1980s and continuing to the present has shown that rape myth acceptance, hostility toward women, adversarial sexual beliefs, and sexual fantasies of men in colleges and universities are not as dissimilar to those of convicted rapists as one might expect if there were not some broader underlying connection to normative masculinities (Malamuth, 1981; Ryan, 2004; see also Volume 2, Chapter 1, this handbook).

Early research tried to estimate ordinary men's proclivity to rape through indirect methods designed to avoid social desirability factors that might preclude men admitting past acts of rape or sexual force (e.g., Malamuth, 1981, 1989). The now standard behaviorally-based approaches for obtaining self-report estimates of sexual violence perpetration (e.g., Koss & Gidycz, 1985; Koss & Oros, 1982) were not in wide use at the time. Men were asked how likely it was that they would personally commit rape or use sexual force (if they could be guaranteed of not getting caught and punished) in a situation similar to a hypothetical scenario that described forced sex but did not label it as such. (For reviews of this early work, see Malamuth, 1981, 1984, and Check & Malamuth, 1985). Although there was some variability across a variety of conditions in different studies (see Malamuth, 1981, for cross-study review), an average of 35% of all men in such studies indicated some likelihood that they would personally rape (i.e., 2 or higher on a 5-point scale ranging from *not at all likely* [1] to *very likely* [5]). About 20% of all men in these studies indicated an even higher likelihood (i.e., 3 or higher). When a more general category of *sexual force* was looked at, around 60% of men in these studies reported some likelihood of raping or using sexual force (e.g., Briere & Malamuth, 1983). Much of this research is now more than 3 decades old, but recent research has suggested that high levels of *rape proclivity* are not a thing of the past. As recently as 2010, Chapleau and Oswald found that fewer than half of the men in their sample reported that there was no chance they would engage in any of the behaviors described in five different acquaintance rape scenarios. Schewe, Adam, and Ryan (2009) found that 27% of the young college men in their study reported having been tempted to use force "to obtain sex" at least once in the past.

Self-reported rape proclivity does not necessarily translate into sexually aggressive behavior (e.g., Malamuth, 1988). Malamuth and his colleagues have been clear since the beginning of their work on rape proclivity that they were not suggesting that rape proclivity identifies potential rapists (Malamuth, 1989) or men who "are actually likely to rape" (Malamuth, Haber, & Feshbach, 1980, p. 134), although their critics have sometimes claimed that they do (e.g., Brannigan & Goldenberg, 1987, cited in Malamuth, 1989). Malamuth (1989) instead suggested that rape proclivity identifies an "attraction to sexual aggression" (p. 28). Early research did show an association between self-reported likelihood of raping and reports of having personally used force against women in sexual relationships (Malamuth, 1982, and Malamuth & Check, 1981, both cited in Malamuth, 1984; Murphy, Coleman, & Haynes, 1986; Petty & Dawson 1989), although Malamuth (1988) found these factors to be not strongly correlated. There does appear to be a connection between men's propensity to imagine they could engage in these acts and their adherence to rape-supportive discourses. Tieger (1981) found that those 20% of men in his sample who were classified as having a high likelihood of raping "believe that their own sexual aggression toward women would be well received and a normal response to the perceived seductive behavior on the part of the victim" (p. 156). Not surprisingly, rape proclivity has been found to be correlated with endorsement of rape myths (Bohner, Jarvis, Eyssel, & Siebler, 2005; Chapleau & Oswald, 2010), hostile sexism (Masser, Viki, & Power, 2006), adversarial sexual beliefs, sexual arousal to rape depictions, and laboratory aggression against female targets (see Malamuth, 1984, for early review).

Whether or not self-reported rape proclivity actually would predict rape or aggressive sexual behavior in any one man, it reflects gendered cultural values. Although the gap between imagining being able to rape and actually raping is a big one, the fact that so many men are willing to report that they could imagine themselves using sexual force does endorse feminist arguments that the building blocks of rape exist within or alongside normative heterosexuality rather than being the preserve of only an isolated deviant few. In support of this claim that gendered sexual styles consistent with rape are culturally normative, a recent study with university students in the United Kingdom showed that quotes from convicted rapists could only be distinguished from quotes from English "lad's mags" about 55% of the time (Horvath, Hegarty, Tyler, & Mansfield, 2012).

Several studies have found that the characteristics of men who self-report having raped are similar to those of men with high rape proclivity. They have shown relationships between certain attitudinal clusters (i.e., higher hostility toward women and stronger belief in rape myths); personal skills, abilities, and motivations (e.g., lesser ability to communicate emotions to sexual partners than other men), and behaviors (e.g., having or valuing higher numbers of sexual partners) and rape perpetration (e.g., Abbey & McAuslan, 2004; Abbey, Zawacki & Buck, 2005; Koss & Dinero, 1988; Koss, Leonard, Beezley, & Oros, 1985; Malamuth, Heavey, & Linz, 1993; Malamuth et al., 1995; Malamuth, Socklowskie, Koss, & Tanaka, 1991; Senn et al., 2000). According to Ryan (2004), the evidence has suggested that men who rape acquaintances without legal consequence, and who may regard themselves as "normal," share the same belief system as convicted sex offenders. They share in common not only rape-supportive beliefs but also, she suggested, "excessive sexual preoccupation, rape and/or seduction scripts and fantasies, and a self-definition embracing hypermasculinity and the power of men to dominate women sexually" (Ryan, 2004, p. 599). Other research has pointed to the role of heavy consumption of alcohol (Abbey, Parkhill, Jacques-Tiura, & Saenz, 2009) and pornography (Knight & Sims-Knight, 2009) in strengthening the association between attitudes such as hostility toward women or belief in rape myths and rape perpetration. Recent research has strengthened our understanding of the connections between individual men's attitudes toward rape, their rape proclivity and behavior, and broader cultural discourses. On an individual level, for example, researchers have demonstrated that bringing rape myths into a man's awareness increases his ratings of his rape proclivity (Bohner et al., 1998, 2005). This finding highlights the way in which rape-supportive discourse can act as a cultural resource that supports rape-supportive orientations. Bohner et al. (2005) found that this relationship is even stronger for men who have sexually coerced women in the past. Although research on individual differences enables some understanding of how men navigate different pathways in relation to a cultural scaffolding of rape, it would be a mistake to regard such differences as markers of individual pathology, which is itself the cause of sexual violence. The research has shown at the same time that such individual differences are embedded within and supported by more widely shared rape-supportive discourses.

Although empirically demonstrating cultural impact is difficult, a recent experimental study allowed examination of the impact of social norms about rape on men. Eyssel, Bohner, and Siebler (2006) told male participants (incorrectly) that other men like them on average gave high scores to each rape myth item. Under these circumstances, men's reports of their own likelihood of raping increased, above and beyond any influence of their prior rape myth beliefs. The flip side is that a positive social influence is also possible; men who were led to believe that other men did not subscribe to rape myths reported lower rape proclivity (Eyssel et al., 2006). Outside the laboratory, particularly masculine cultural contexts, such as sports teams, fraternities, and the military, have been associated with even higher levels of rape (including rapes by multiple perpetrators) than in the wider cultural context (Sanday, 1990; Schwartz & Dekeseredy, 1997; see Murnen & Kohlman, 2007, for a meta-analysis). These studies illuminate the importance of local sociocultural norms in shaping the acceptability of rape-supportive discourse and the likelihood that men will draw on it in articulating their views and justifying their behavior.

IN THE GRAY AREA BETWEEN SEXUAL VIOLENCE AND NORMATIVE HETEROSEXUAL SEX

At the same time as researchers such as Mary Koss (e.g., 1988) and Diana Russell (e.g., 1982) dramatically challenged the idea that rape was rare, two other important shifts happened in the way that rape was conceptualized. As already noted, the research showed that most rapes were committed by a man known to the woman he had raped, and often by a man who was romantically or sexually involved with her. The other significant shift, which we have already discussed, was the introduction of a dimensional or continuum approach to sexual violence (e.g., Finkelhor & Yllo, 1983, 1985; Kelly, 1987, 1988a, 1988b; Koss & Oros, 1982; Koss et al., 1987; Russell, 1982). Researchers took interest in a wider range of nonconsensual or forced sexual acts as well as in a broader range of coercive behaviors. For example, the Sexual Experiences Survey asked not only about forced unwanted "sex play" and intercourse but also about coerced unwanted sex play and intercourse (Koss & Oros, 1982). Attention was also drawn to the ways in which coercion can operate in the absence of force or the threat of force such that within relationships, for instance, women can feel pressured into having unwanted sex through subtle forms of interpersonal coercion (e.g., Finkelhor & Yllo, 1985). This type of coercion can involve pressure from a man that is subtle yet aggressively undermining as well as forms that simply wear down a woman's resistance, for example, through desperate pleading (e.g., Gavey, 1992, 2005). Women interviewed by Gavey (1992; an elaborated analysis is presented in Gavey, 2005) described giving into unwanted sex, despite not wanting to, out of pity or love or a need for sleep. Finkelhor and Yllo (1985) also identified what they called *social coercion,* whereby women would agree to unwanted sex because of the coercive pressures of expectation that come from dominant cultural norms, irrespective of the presence of any direct pressure from a sexual partner.

On the basis of her large-scale interview study of 930 women, Russell (1982) concluded that this sort of social coercion can lead women to "feel obligated to accommodate their husbands' sexual wishes no matter how repelled" (p. 356). Subsequent interview-based studies have shown that heterosexual coercion exists in both long-term, committed relationships and in casual encounters and that it can range from the seemingly mundane (an inconvenience) to the dangerous (violent forced sex; e.g., Basile, 1999; Bay-Cheng & Eliseo-Arras, 2008; Gavey, 1992, 2005). Although traditional norms may have left wives feeling obliged to have sex irrespective of their own desire (e.g., Gavey, 1992; Russell, 1982), contemporary norms may oblige women to have sex with their boyfriends because "good girlfriends say yes" (Bay-Cheng & Eliseo-Arras, 2008, p. 391; Gavey, 1992). Feminist scholars have described how these types of coercion are structured through the male sexual drive discourse, whereby a man can act out an ostensibly unstoppable sexual momentum, legitimated to some extent by the shared cultural presumptions made possible through this discourse (e.g., Gavey, 2005; Gavey, McPhillips, & Doherty, 2001).

Although a reasonably high proportion of men also report having had sex with a woman when they did not want to (Byers & O'Sullivan, 1998; Muehlenhard & Cook, 1988) and sometimes initiating sex in the absence of their own sexual desire (Vannier & O'Sullivan, 2010), the dynamics of this experience appear to be quite different for women and men. For instance, far fewer men than women report being extremely upset as a result of sexual coercion within a heterosexual dating context, and far fewer women than men report being not at all upset (O'Sullivan, Byers, & Finkelman, 1998).

Unwanted, Nonconsensual, and "Compliant" Sex: Sexual Coercion

Sexual coercion that takes place in the absence of direct threat or force raises questions of how to understand the gray area between sexual coercion and normative heterosexuality. It is possible to distinguish between dimensions of desire and consent, even though these have tended to be conflated in past discussions of sexual violence and coercion. It is possible to want sex (in the sense of physically desiring it, wishing for it, and feeling attracted and inclined toward it) and yet at the same time not be willing to have sex (for reasons to do with its meaning, risks, and consequences; Muehlenhard & Peterson, 2005; Z. D. Peterson & Muehlenhard, 2007). Thus, it is possible for nonconsensual sex to have been wanted at some level, just as it is possible for consensual sex to have been unwanted. How does one imagine the borders demarcating these practices and experiences in relation to sexual coercion? It seems clear that any sex that is nonconsensual is a form of sexual coercion, sexual assault, or rape. Muehlenhard and McCoy (1991), for instance, argued that "even if a man is certain that a woman's no really means yes, if she does mean no and he has sex with her, it is rape" (p. 460). There is more debate among scholars about how to think about unwanted but consensual sex.

It has long been recognized that women sometimes consent to, or at least passively allow, sex they do not want. In fact, women "lying back and thinking of England" is a cultural trope that fits directly with the part of the have/hold discourse that depicts women having more limited sexual desire than men and being willing to "give" sex to men in exchange for relationship security. Some researchers have conceptualized this kind of submission to unwanted sex as *sexual compliance* (O'Sullivan & Allgeier, 1998). J. Katz and Tirone (2010) noted two key ways in which researchers have made sense of this phenomenon. A more positive account, which is favored by some sexuality researchers, suggests that compliance within the context of relationships may be the outcome of an "implicit agreement between partners to remain sexually available to each another" (Vannier & O'Sullivan, 2010, p. 430). Vannier and O'Sullivan (2010) hypothesized that if done sparingly (and implicitly reciprocally), then this practice may be an acceptable form of compromise that functions to maintain relationships. Yet they also warned that it could be negative if this practice led to repeated engagement in undesired and unpleasurable sex.

However, it is not always possible to draw a sharp line between such an ambiguous notion of consensual compliance and more subtle forms of coercion (Gavey, 1992, 2005). The other key way that researchers have understood sexual compliance is more closely related to sexual coercion (J. Katz & Tirone, 2010) on a continuum of sexual violence.

Some theorists have questioned how meaningful the notion of consent ever is under conditions of inequality (e.g., MacKinnon, 1983; see also Pateman, 1980), whereas some research has shown that sometimes a woman may not even recognize a choice between consent and nonconsent (Gavey, 1992, 2005).

In studies of sexual compliance, it seems that participants sometimes describe sexual coercion when they are asked about sexual compliance, even when researchers make explicit attempts to exclude pressured sex (e.g., Vannier & O'Sullivan, 2010). One of the reasons for this slippage appears to be that past sexual coercion is connected explicitly by participants to their current sexual compliance. Vannier and O'Sullivan (2010) found in their diary study with U.S. college students that a significant proportion mentioned a previous occasion when their partner "used guilt or pressure to persuade them to engage in sexual activity" (p. 437). They speculated that this prior experience may have functioned to motivate participants to have sex they did not want, to avoid the negative consequences they had previously experienced, even when no pressure was applied on a subsequent occasion. J. Katz and Tirone's (2010) study provided compelling evidence for the suggestion that many women who have sex when they do not want to may do so on the basis of their past experience that refusing to have sex with their partner was followed by explicit sexual coercion. In their study, a woman was 7 times more likely to have engaged in sexual compliance if her partner had sexually coerced or sexually assaulted her previously. Other research has also documented this paradoxical situation whereby women appear to consent to unwanted sex to avoid being sexually coerced or raped (Basile, 1999; Gavey, 1992, 2005; Livingston et al., 2004). In such cases the terms *sexual compliance* and *unwanted sex* can be euphemistic because they are referring to sex that is not only unwanted but also directly pressured or even aggressively forced, but that a woman might insist is not sexual assault because she did not in her view communicate her lack of consent. Basile (1999) discussed this process of consenting to unwanted sex within a marital or other long-term relationship as *acquiescence*. One of the main types of acquiescence she found among the women she interviewed involved going along with sex for fear of repercussions if they did not. In some cases, in the context of relationships characterized by previous violence by the male partner, she argued it was "rape by acquiescence." Submission to forced, even violent, unwanted sex can also be experienced within more casual encounters. For instance, one woman in Gavey's (1992, 2005) study described aggressive unwanted sex with a virtual stranger that she said she "more or less consented" to, even though she felt she had no choice. Such findings highlight a tendency of women to minimize the coercion they experience. These dynamics highlight the complexity of the notion of consent and the need to consider it carefully in relation to the dynamics of power within any relationship as well as within gendered cultural norms, power relations, and sexual imperatives.

Women's Desire, Sexual Imperatives, and Sexual Violence

In drawing attention to the need to consider sexuality and sexual violence alongside each other, it is also important to draw critical attention to the contemporary gendered norms for (hetero)sexuality. Gavey (2005) has argued that the traditional gendered binary form of heterosexuality structures a normative dynamic for sex between men and women that provides the cultural building blocks for sexual violence. However, many feminist scholars have cautioned against reiterating and reinforcing this dynamic in representations of sexual violence, thereby inadvertently perpetuating the very norms of aggressive masculinity and passive femininity that can be seen to pattern men and women as ready-made rapists and victims (e.g., Cahill, 2001; Gavey, 2005; Marcus, 1992; McCaughey, 1997). This concern has led to scholarly attention to women's capacity for aggressive and violent resistance (e.g., Gavey, 2009; McCaughey, 1997) as well as an emphasis on recognizing women's active sexual desire, agency, and pleasure in the context of sexual violence prevention (e.g., Carmody, 2005, 2009b; Gavey, 1996, 2005; Senn, Gee, & Thake, 2011). Therefore, although closer attention needs to be paid to the gendered realities of sexual violence and coercion by those interested in sexuality in general (and vice versa), it is important to look toward possibilities that offer positive ways out of these problematic, narrow gendered norms for heterosexuality.

It is now more than 50 years since a "permissive turn" reimagined the possibilities for sexuality in many Western societies. In addition to the male sexual drive discourse and the have/hold discourse, Hollway (1984, 1989) identified a permissive discourse as the third dominant discourse shaping heterosexuality at the time. Social and technological changes in the 1960s opened up the possibilities for overhauling the restrictive moral limitations that prescribed where, when, and with whom sex was permissible for women. Although the promise of what sexual liberation held for women was often disappointing (see Gavey, 2005), claiming space for women's sexual desire, agency and exploration has been an important, albeit contested, item on the feminist agenda in many countries since the 1970s. Feminist scholars and activists remain interested in how best to promote diverse and egalitarian possibilities for women's sexuality—as both an end in itself and because it has increasingly been recognized as an important part of a sexual violence prevention agenda (e.g., Carmody, 2005, 2009b; Fine & McClelland, 2006; Gavey, 1996, 2005; Senn, 2011; Senn et al., 2011; Tolman, 2012)

What are the current possibilities for women's agency and empowerment in relation to sexuality, and how are these possibilities related to sexual coercion and sexual violence? In the next section, we look at one area of contemporary sex that holds contradictory opportunities for women—the realm of casual sex or "hooking up."

SEXUAL VIOLENCE AND SEXUALITY WITHIN CONTEMPORARY SEXUAL PRACTICE: THE EXAMPLE OF HOOKING UP

Casual sex has arguably been commonplace in many societies for several decades, although it has been suggested that hooking up may have replaced dating on North American college campuses and become the predominant organization of sexual activity (Bogle, 2008; Garcia, Reiber, Massey, & Merriwether, 2012; Kalish & Kimmel, 2011; see also Chapters 10 and 16, this volume). In Armstrong, England, and Fogarty's (2012) research with more than 14,000 college and university women, dating clearly existed side by side with hooking up (by their final year, 74% had at least one relationship of 6 months or more, and 69% had hooked up at least once). Hooking up is not necessarily a particularly frequent activity. Heldman and Wade's (2010) review demonstrated that across studies, only one quarter of students engage in 10 or more hook-ups across all their years of college, and in Armstrong et al.'s (2012) study the median number of hook-ups was three by senior year. No consensus exists about what activities constitute a hook-up. It will usually include kissing but may or may not involve a range of other activities, including intercourse (Bogle, 2008; Garcia et al., 2012; Heldman & Wade, 2010). The defining feature seems to be the lack of any presumption that it is part of or will lead on to a committed romantic relationship. Some research has suggested, however, that women's emotional investments and romantic hopes may far more commonly be part of the picture than the public discourse would suggest (Bogle, 2008; Garcia et al., 2012; Littleton, Tabernik, et al., 2009). Moreover, some research participants have used the term *hooking up* to describe a more traditional date (Littleton, Tabernik, et al., 2009), further complicating this term.

Hooking up is a contemporary sexual practice that invites debate. For some commentators, it can represent a new territory for agentic female sexual exploration and empowerment and for others it can be a site for disappointment, if not outright exploitation or even victimization. Given our claim that promoting affirmative opportunities for women's active sexuality is an essential part of preventing sexual violence, what does hooking-up sex offer? The early research has suggested that hook-ups may be neither a special site of female empowerment nor a site in which sexual violence is necessarily more likely. Some authors have highlighted the positive aspects of hooking up for women, such as the scope it offers for pleasure seeking (Kalish & Kimmel, 2011) and for disrupting a relationship imperative (Hamilton & Armstrong, 2009). Yet others have noted that the positive potential of heterosexual hook-ups may be tempered by the sexism that remains in contemporary sexual culture. On the basis of their longitudinal ethnographic research with a group of women in a university residence hall, Hamilton and Armstrong (2009) found that it was not uncommon for women in hook-ups to still be treated with disrespect, as disposable sex objects. Littleton, Tabernik, et al. (2009) found that 78% of college women who had hooked up reported having experienced "bad hook-ups," with a third of the women saying that more than half of their hook-ups could be characterized this way (p. 797). Women in this study characterized a typical (hypothetical) bad hook-up as including a wide range of features and consequences, such as unpleasant or unsatisfying sex, manipulation and disappointment, regret, shame, and embarrassment. More than half of all heterosexual women in a large-scale survey of more than 13,000 U.S. college student women said that they felt that the other person respected them less after having hooked up (Armstrong et al., 2012). Women in Armstrong et al.'s (2012) study were in general less likely to experience orgasm during hook-up sex than in relationship sex, and the rate of overall enjoyment was also lower than in relationship sex. The difference in likelihood of orgasm appeared to be due in part to the difference in sexual practices (less varied in hook-ups) and to what Armstrong et al. suggested is a new form of the sexual double standard in which neither women nor men in general pay high regard to the importance of women's pleasure during hook-ups.

Even where a sexist dynamic may not always be obvious, the constraints imposed by dominant heteronormative discourses can still dampen the opportunities for women to engage in heterosexual casual sex in ways that are satisfying and self-caring, as Beres and Farvid (2010) observed from their interviews with young women in separate studies in Canada and New Zealand (see also Moran & Lee, 2012; Chapter 11, this volume). It is also clear that women are still judged more negatively than men when engaging in certain sexual activities during a hook-up or if hooking up with too many different men, for example (Bogle, 2008; Hamilton & Armstrong, 2009; J. Katz, Tirone, & van der Kloet, 2012). That women can still face "slut stigma," as described by women in Hamilton and Armstrong's (2009) study, or consider the path home the next morning a "walk of shame" (Bogle, 2008), further reinforces the ongoing power of a sexual double standard (Crawford & Popp, 2003; see also Tolman, 2002) in which women's choices around sexuality are regulated and constrained to a greater extent than men's. Burns, Futch, and Tolman's (2011) interviews with girls and young women about their experiences of fellatio (not specifically in casual sexual encounters) suggested that a contemporary twist on the regulation of young women's sexuality might be their subjection to discourses of performance, where the risks they face are of being punitively judged as insufficiently knowledgeable and skilled rather than (or possibly as well as) being judged for a tarnished reputation. A particularly troubling aspect of this contradictory landscape in postfeminist, neoliberal times is that women are likely to attribute negative outcomes to what they characterize as their own personal failings and underestimate the extent to which their personal choices remain limited in the context of ongoing gender inequality, as Moran and Lee (2012, p. 16) pointed out on the basis of their interviews with Australian women about heterosexual "nonromantic sex." Bay-Cheng and Eliseo-Arras (2008) found a similar dynamic reported by women they interviewed about unwanted sex (not specifically in casual sexual encounters). They also noted that a neoliberal emphasis on personal responsibility led women to underplay even quite troubling experiences, which they interpreted as women avoiding conceptualizing what they experienced as having been victimizing. In doing so, these women did not articulate the role of a male partner's exploitation and sexist norms more generally in constraining their choices, even when this appeared to have been relevant according to their narratives.

Varying numbers of women, and some men, report having felt out of control and pressured into unwanted sex during hook-ups (Flack et al., 2007; E. L. Paul, McManus, & Hayes, 2000). Hook-ups can also be a site for more extreme forms of sexual violence (Littleton, Tabernik, et al., 2009). As Armstrong, Hamilton, and England (2010; Hamilton & Armstrong, 2009) point out, inequality also permeates relationships. The script for traditional dating remains influenced by gender stereotypes and offers men more power and control than women (Eaton & Rose, 2011). Thus, gendered power dynamics, inequality, and coercion that take place in hook-ups may actually be no worse than what some young women encounter in their relationships and, as Armstrong et al. (2010) pointed out, at least women do not become entrapped in hook-ups in the way that some women do in relationships with men who are coercive.

IMPLICATIONS

There are myriad possible implications for research and practice that arise from recognizing the connections between sexual violence and everyday (hetero) sexuality. In this section, we discuss two: First, we raise some general points in relation to considering how women who have experienced sexual violence are thought about and responded to; second, we discuss the implications for educational approaches to rape prevention.

Research and Practice With Women

Given the psychological and sociocultural complexities involved in conceptualizing an experience of forced sex as rape (Gavey, 2005; Kelly, 1988a; Z. D. Peterson & Muehlenhard, 2011), caution and care are required in making any assumptions about the experiences of the women with whom we work in our research, practice, and education roles (see Volume 2, Chapters 4, 6, and 13, this handbook). The master narratives most readily available for women to make sense of an experience of rape are not sophisticated and nuanced enough, McKenzie-Mohr and Lafrance (2011) would argue, to offer ways to both reject blame for rape and at the same time assert some sense of agency. McKenzie-Mohr and Lafrance's analysis of women's narrative accounts of rape suggests the importance of "listening for, and lingering in, the spaces where language fails" (p. 65). In doing so, it is important to take care not to minimize or overlook the possibility that women may have experienced distressing, forced unwanted sex, even though they may not call it rape or sexual assault. Research has suggested that unwanted sexual experiences (Harned, 2004), including those consistent with legal definitions of rape (Littleton & Henderson, 2009) but that are not described as rape (Littleton & Henderson, 2009) or as sexual abuse or sexual assault (Harned, 2004) by the woman, can nevertheless have potentially serious negative psychological impacts (Clements & Ogle, 2009; Harned, 2004; Littleton & Henderson, 2009). It is equally important to be aware of the pitfalls of imposing a label (such as *rape* or *trauma*) on a woman's experience when she herself does not see it in these terms. The complex ramifications of these labels may not always necessarily be in a woman's best interests because of the potential for limited prescriptive formulations that are still in some cases "othering" and stigmatizing (Gavey, 2007; Gavey & Schmidt, 2011; Marecek, 1999). In large part, women's reluctance may be a result of the unhelpful responses that they still too often receive when they disclose an experience of sexual violence. It has been found that those seeking support from community services sometimes receive negative responses that are akin to a "second rape" (e.g., R. Campbell et al., 2001; see also Ahrens et al., 2007). Indeed, one study on the effect of negative reactions from others highlighted how the reactions some women receive from others are so negative that they become silenced from further disclosures (Ahrens, 2006; for further discussion of these issues, see also Ullman, 2000, 2010, and Ullman, Filipas, Townsend, & Starzynski, 2007).

Although it is important, therefore, not to respond to disclosures of sexual violence with preconceived ideas, it is also important to be flexible enough in one's thinking and responding to recognize that some experiences women have that they may regard as "just sex" are exploitative, abusive, and unfair and may be profoundly insulting or hurtful. Some researchers have suggested that the perception of these experiences as "not rape" but rather as sex of some kind (L. Peterson 2008) may increase the likelihood that a woman will be sexually assaulted again (Littleton, Axsom, & Grills-Taquechel, 2009); it is more likely that the rapist was a boyfriend or partner and that the relationship is continuing (Kahn et al., 2003; Layman et al., 1996). In both ongoing sexual partnerships and casual sexual encounters, rape-supportive discourses may also provide a framework within which a woman's anger, indignation, and sadness at being subjected to sexual acts against her will may be difficult to honor as appropriate responses to mistreatment. For example, Weiss's (2009) research using National Crime Victimization Survey narratives found that one in five women who had been sexually victimized drew on rape myths to excuse or justify what had been done to them. These "social vocabularies" suggest that unwanted sex is normal, that men's sexual aggression is natural, and that it is the victim's fault. Notably, studies are beginning to identify the influence of neoliberal discourse that valorizes notions of personal freedom and individual choice as a factor that, alongside traditional gendered sexual norms, makes it difficult for women to acknowledge unwanted sex as victimizing (Bay-Cheng & Eliseo-Arras, 2008; Moran & Lee, 2012; see also Gavey, 2012).

Rape Prevention and Resistance Education

The prevention of rape and other forms of sexual violence is complicated and challenging. Since the 1990s, practitioners and researchers have made intensive efforts to design and evaluate educational programs aimed at preventing rape and sexual assault (for reviews, see L. A. Anderson & Whiston, 2005; Brecklin & Forde, 2001; Breitenbecher, 2000; Morrison, Hardison, Mathew, & O'Neil, 2004; Schewe, 2002; Yeater & O'Donohue, 1999). It is beyond the scope of this chapter to provide a comprehensive review of the sexual violence prevention literature or recommendations for prevention (see Lonsway et al., 2009). Instead, we focus briefly on how a feminist sociocultural analysis of the intersections and connections between sexual violence and sexuality might suggest that prevention education is approached somewhat differently. From this perspective, the problem of sexual violence has deep cultural roots, and sexual norms that remain highly gendered are part of the problem (e.g., Gavey, 2005; Littleton, 2011). Given how intertwined rape-supportive discourses are with traditional discourses about heterosexuality, it is perhaps not surprising that current rape prevention efforts have so far had only limited successes (e.g., see Lonsway et al., 2009, for a review for practitioners; Vladutiu, Martin, & Macy, 2011). Changing the very cultural conditions of possibility for sexual violence requires creating a social context that is less supportive of perpetrators, that is, reducing the cultural resources they can draw on to normalize, justify, and excuse their behavior. It also requires expanding the range of ways in which women can behave without reproach—sexually and, in self-defense, aggressively—so that their capacities to resist sexual violence are enhanced and so that they are less likely to be blamed if they are sexually victimized (in regard to arguments for women's physical resistance, see McCaughey, 1997). Any comprehensive effort toward sexual violence intervention aimed at producing this kind of society must include a gender analysis and a wider political engagement that challenges rape-supportive norms that persist as part of the cultural common sense about women, men, and sexuality in most places around the world. This is an incredibly difficult undertaking, because although education programs might call into question norms and values that support rape, these norms and values remain supported to some extent within the wider sociocultural context.

Most formal rape prevention education programs that are delivered to women and men together attempt to undermine rape-supportive discourses by presenting more accurate information about rape (e.g., that most rapes are perpetrated by acquaintances) and challenging rape myths (e.g., see reviews by Morrison et al., 2004; Vladutiu et al., 2011). This is a start, and most programs are effective in decreasing adherence to at least some rape-supportive myths in the short term but not in the longer term (e.g., Vladutiu et al., 2011). Programs have also often included brief discussions of gender role socialization and human sexuality (see Vladutiu et al., 2011) in recognition of the need to address sexism and normative heterosexual practices in discussions of rape. These have been short programs that often last only an hour; therefore, this discussion is cursory at best. Across all of these programs, however, there is little evidence of translation of these less rape-supportive views into reductions in sexual violence perpetration or victimization (Morrison et al., 2004).

In recent years, most programs for women have recognized that women have limited control over men's coercive sexual practices and therefore have focused on developing what women may be able to do to undermine a man's coercive advantages in certain situations or to stop or escape threatening and aggressive behavior. Most are described as rape risk reduction programs (e.g., Gidycz et al., 2001; Orchowski, Gidycz, & Raffle, 2008) but some are purposefully labeled *rape resistance programs* in an attempt to avoid any inadvertent suggestion that that women are responsible for men's behavior (e.g., Senn et al., 2011; Rozee & Koss, 2001). Both types of programs take a different approach from the programs discussed earlier. They focus specifically on the more prevalent acquaintance rape rather than stranger rape, not simply to highlight its relative prevalence as one fact in a myth-versus-fact exercise but instead as a background for the provision of all content and discussions so that assumptions about the separateness of rape from everyday life and relationships are challenged. These programs show, among other things, the connections between normative dating practices (e.g., man drives, man chooses the location for the date) and particular associated risks for women (e.g., isolation). Programs in this tradition have been effective beyond increasing knowledge about rape and reducing rape myth adherence in increasing women's reported self-protective behaviors in dating situations (Orchowski et al., 2008) and increasing their self-efficacy related to defending themselves successfully against possible future assault attempts by male acquaintances (Orchowski et al., 2008; Senn et al., 2011). Reductions in victimization (defined as the number of completed rapes in an interval after the intervention) have been somewhat more difficult to establish. In the early days of these programs, reductions in victimization were not evident or were found only for a subgroup of women, for example, for women with no history of sexual violence (e.g., K. A. Hanson & Gidycz, 1993). More recent programs, with more developed content addressing the cognitive and emotional barriers women face in recognizing and responding to acquaintance perpetrators (based substantially on the work of Nurius & Norris, 1996), have been more successful (Orchowski et al., 2008; Senn et al., 2011; see R. K. Hanson & Broom, 2005, for a meta-analysis). These latter programs tend to be based wholly or partially on Rozee and Koss's (2001) review of research relevant to rape prevention interventions and the long tradition of women's self-defense programs in the rape crisis and feminist communities (e.g., Bateman, 1978) and include self-defense training specifically targeted at male acquaintances (Gidycz, Rich, Orchowski, King, & Miller, 2006; Senn et al., 2011). There is, however, continued controversy over whether targeting women for education in this way is itself implicitly victim blaming (e.g., Carmody, 2003; Hollander, 2009). Although this criticism deserves careful consideration and attention (e.g., Senn, 2011), newer programs of this kind have been able to demonstrate that they reduce participants' woman-blaming explanations for the rapes of other women (Senn, Saunders, & Gee, 2008) and reduce their self-blame for sexual violence occurring to them after the intervention (Gidycz et al., 2006), thus interrupting rather than reinforcing rape-supportive discourse.

As noted earlier, some feminist scholars who emphasize the intersections of sexual violence and sexuality have argued for nuanced models of analysis and intervention to avoid inadvertently reinforcing the cultural scaffolding of sexual violence through uncritically reiterating, and in doing so contributing to a normalization of, depictions of an inherently aggressive male sexuality and an inherently passive or relatively asexual female sexuality. One implication of this for rape prevention education with women is the need to directly address and validate within programs the possibilities for active female sexual desire. Senn et al. (2011) have recently included emancipatory sexuality education (adapted from *Our Whole Lives;* Goldfarb & Casparian, 2000; Kimball, 2000) designed to build or enhance young women's sense of their own sexual entitlement and agency, in a sexual assault resistance program. This idea originated, in part, from the limited prior literature suggesting that gender-sensitive sexuality education may reduce rape-supportive attitudes and rape myths (e.g., Dallagher & Rosen, 1993) and in recognition that most rapes are committed by acquaintances, many within new or ongoing heterosexual relationships. Program content on sexuality attempts to increase women's sexual self-knowledge, their sexual self-efficacy, their ability to recognize what they want sexually, and their willingness to initiate sex they desire. The rationale is that this should reduce the delay between a woman's assessment that sexual behavior initiated by another person is unwanted and coercive and her taking action to protect herself if necessary or possible (Senn, 2011). There is preliminary support for the benefit of this approach (Senn et al., 2011). A randomized controlled trial to fully evaluate the enhanced program's effectiveness is in progress at three Canadian universities. However, no matter how promising such interventions may be, cultural norms related to differential evaluations of male and female sexuality, particularly the relationships between woman-blaming rape myths and pejorative judgments of sexually active women, remain a serious and highly entrenched obstacle to societal-level change (Littleton, 2011). Another approach, focused on promoting ethical sex in the service of sexual violence prevention, with both women and men, offers another promising direction for addressing naturalized inequality within (hetero) sexual relationships (e.g., Carmody, 2009b; see also Lamb, 2010, for promotion of sexual ethics teaching within sexuality education more generally).

Among the many prevention programs developed, very few (8% of those reviewed by Morrison et al., 2004) follow prevention guidelines for targeting men (see Flood, 2011, for a discussion of men's role in the prevention of violence against women more generally). Men's programs most commonly attempt to encourage individual men to take responsibility for their actions and help them to intervene with other men (Gidycz, Rich, & Marioni, 2002). Evaluations of these programs have suggested that they are usually effective at reducing rape-supportive attitudes and increasing knowledge about rape (see reviews by Brecklin & Forde, 2001; Breitenbecher, 2000; Flores & Hartlaub, 1998) but not at decreasing subsequent perpetration of sexual violence (for reviews, see Breitenbecher, 2000; Gidycz et al., 2002; and Lonsway et al., 2009; also see Tharp et al., 2011). One reason for the difficulty in developing prevention programs targeting men may be that the challenge to cultural norms related to heterosexuality and masculinity is too entrenched to be dealt with directly in short programs. A social norms approach (e.g., Fabiano, Perkins, Berkowitz, Linkenbach, & Stark, 2003) suggests that individual men may not personally endorse sexist and rape-supportive views to the extent that they believe other men do and that this misperception actually helps to foster a rape-supportive cultural environment through, for example, silencing male dissent. In education it is therefore crucial to distinguish between presenting descriptive norms (e.g., information about the prevalence of rape and about rape myths) and injunctive norms (i.e., what is being advocated as the right thing to do); otherwise, as L. A. Paul and Gray (2011) cautioned, education about descriptive norms alone may actually strengthen rape-supportive views and behaviors because their normality is inadvertently being reinforced.

Approaches designed to effect individual-level change, such as the ones discussed to this point, will always be limited in their capacity to prevent sexual violence. Multilevel ecological approaches (e.g., Casey & Lindhorst, 2009) that seek to go beyond change at the level of the individual and relationship and to target broader peer and community networks have the potential to change cultural norms in ways that are more egalitarian and foster more just and ethical sexual relations. Formal interventions that target both individuals and communities are still in their infancy and so have yet to be fully explored. Given how difficult it is to develop individual-level programs, and to evaluate them, this task will be challenging.

Bystander approaches to sexual violence prevention are perhaps furthest along in this movement toward multilevel ecological interventions. Bystander programs use social psychological theory to enable people to better recognize situations in which there is an elevated chance of sexual violence (e.g., when a man's behavior at a party suggests he is purposefully mixing a woman stronger and stronger drinks) and develop the skills and confidence that would enable them to intervene in helpful and safe ways. These programs also provide information about sexual violence that challenges woman-blame and rape myths to improve the support participants would be able to offer in the future to people who have been sexually victimized. These programs target individuals but at the same time also explicitly attempt to change the norms related to sexual violence within the communities in which they live, work, and study (e.g., Banyard, Moynihan, & Crossman, 2009; Banyard, Moynihan, & Plante, 2007; Burn, 2009; J. Katz, Heisterkamp, & Fleming, 2011). For example, Banyard et al. (2007) demonstrated that bystander education on sexual assault had positive outcomes similar to those found with other approaches to sexual assault prevention (i.e., decreases in rape myth acceptance and increases in knowledge) but additionally changed attitudes and beliefs related to intervening (e.g., bystander self-efficacy) and increased prosocial bystander behavior. Moreover, Banyard, Eckstein, and Moynihan (2010) showed that these effects are related to how the programs affect male and female students' perceptions that sexual violence is something they should care about and seek out further information on and that they can indeed make a difference by becoming involved in their community. A unique interactive performance-based intervention with a similar goal to increase prosocial behavior and empathy for rape survivors has also shown promise (Rich, 2010; Rodríguez, Rich, Hastings, & Page, 2006). Bystander approaches address people as members of a community who have the potential to proactively intervene to help stop sexual violence rather than as potential perpetrators with the hope of preventing it from happening in the first place. Nevertheless, bystander interventions could reduce levels of sexual violence if they produced a substantial enough community-level change through ripple effects on injunctive norms. This change would likely require dramatic increases in the number of people involved in the programs, perhaps through institutionalization. This is currently being attempted and assessed on one Canadian campus (Forrest & Senn, 2011, with an adapted version of Banyard, Plante, & Moynihan's 2005 Bringing in the Bystander program). Interventions that combine social norms and bystander approaches with groups of men, to shift perceptions about the cultural condoning of violence, have produced some positive results, including a reduction in men's perpetration of sexual violence across a 4-month period (Gidycz, Orchowski, & Berkowitz, 2011).

CONCLUSION

At first glance, sexuality and sexual violence might seem to be worlds apart. Sexual violence is a social problem that shows some of the worst aspects of humanity—aggressive abuses of power, exploitation, harm, and injustice. Sexuality, on the other hand, is often associated with some of the more virtuous and desirable aspects of human connection—love, care and intimacy, excitement, and pleasure. Yet sexuality and sexual violence are not in fact completely separate spheres. Although many everyday sexual acts, relationships, identities, and desires have little in common with the practice of sexual violence, mundane (hetero)sexual practice not uncommonly strays into the territory of sexual coercion and sexual violence. The ideals of an active, sexually driven or even forceful male and a passive, responsive, or even submissive female, which are still largely promoted as normal and natural within the commonsense logic of heteronormativity, form what can be described as a cultural scaffolding of rape (Gavey, 2005), a set of norms and aspirations that function to provide the cultural resources that enable sexual violence as well as a lens for denying and tolerating it. The boundaries between normative heterosexual practice and sexual violence can be blurry, even though this is by no means always the case. Recognizing the sexist terrain on which sexual relationships are grafted, constituted by pervasive unequal power relations between women and men, means that as researchers, practitioners, and educators we are compelled to think very carefully about how we understand choice and its limits in relation to the coercive pull of sexual norms.

There is a wealth of psychology and other social science research that highlights the persistent murky gray area between consensual sex and sexual violence, where the boundaries can be hard to discern, even in ostensibly more "modern" forms of sexual engagement, such as hooking up. This persistent difficulty in clarifying such a boundary is fueled by a more general and tenacious sexual imperative that takes shape in distinctly gendered ways. Recognizing that sexuality can be shaped by coercive power and even violence is necessary for fuller understandings of both sexuality and sexual violence.

References

Abbey, A. (1982). Sex differences in attributions for friendly behavior: Do males misperceive females' friendliness? *Journal of Personality and Social Psychology, 42*, 830–838. doi:10.1037/0022-3514.42.5.830

Abbey, A., & Jacques-Tiura, A. (2011). Sexual assault perpetrators' tactics: Associations with their personal characteristics and aspects of the incident. *Journal of Interpersonal Violence, 26*, 2866–2889. doi:10.1177/0886260510390955

Abbey, A., Jacques-Tiura, A., & Parkhill, M. R. (2010). Sexual assault among diverse populations of women: Common ground, distinctive features, and unanswered questions. In H. Landrine & N. Russo (Eds.), *Handbook of diversity in feminist psychology* (pp. 391–425). New York, NY: Springer.

Abbey, A., & McAuslan, P. (2004). A longitudinal examination of male college students' perpetration of sexual assault. *Journal of Consulting and Clinical Psychology, 72*, 747–756. doi:10.1037/0022-006X.72.5.747

Abbey, A., Parkhill, M. R., BeShears, R., Clinton-Sherrod, A. M., & Zawacki, T. (2006). Cross-sectional predictors of sexual assault perpetration in a community sample of single African American and Caucasian men. *Aggressive Behavior, 32*, 54–67. doi:10.1002/ab.20107

Abbey, A., Parkhill, M. R., Jacques-Tiura, A. J., & Saenz, C. (2009). Alcohol's role in men's use of coercion to obtain unprotected sex. *Substance Use and Misuse, 44*, 1329–1348. doi:10.1080/10826080902961419

Abbey, A., Zawacki, T., & Buck, P. O. (2005). The effects of past sexual assault perpetration and alcohol consumption on men's reactions to women's mixed signals. *Journal of Social and Clinical Psychology, 24*, 129–155. doi:10.1521/jscp.24.2.129.62273

Ahrens, C. E. (2006). Being silenced: The impact of negative social reactions on disclosure of rape. *American Journal of Community Psychology, 38*, 263–274. doi:10.1007/s10464-006-9069-9

Ahrens, C. E., Campbell, R., Ternier-Thames, N. K., Wasco, S. M., & Sefl, T. (2007). Deciding whom to tell: Expectations and outcomes of rape survivors' first disclosures. *Psychology of Women Quarterly, 31*, 38–49. doi:10.1111/j.1471-6402.2007.00329.x

Albin, R. S. (1977). Psychological studies of rape. *Signs: Journal of Women in Culture and Society, 3*, 423–435. doi:10.1086/493474

Alderden, M. A., & Ullman, S. E. (2012). Creating a more complete and current picture: Examining police and prosecutor decision-making when processing sexual assault cases. *Violence Against Women, 18*, 525–551. doi:10.1177/1077801212453867

Anderson, I., & Doherty, K. (2008). *Accounting for rape: Psychology, feminism and discourse analysis in the study of sexual violence.* London, England: Routledge.

Anderson, L. A., & Whiston, S. C. (2005). Sexual assault education programs: A meta-analytic examination of their effectiveness. *Psychology of Women Quarterly, 29*, 374–388. doi:10.1111/j.1471-6402.2005.00237.x

Armstrong, E. A., England, P., & Fogarty, A. C. K. (2012). Accounting for women's orgasm and sexual enjoyment in college hookups and relationships. *American Sociological Review, 77*, 435–462. doi:10.1177/0003122412445802

Armstrong, E. A., Hamilton, L., & England, P. (2010). Is hooking up bad for young women? *Contexts, 9*, 22–27. doi:10.1525/ctx.2010.9.3.22

Backhouse, C. (2008). *Carnal crimes: Sexual assault law in Canada, 1900–1975.* Toronto, Ontario, Canada: Osgoode Society for Canadian Legal History, Irwin Law.

Balsam, K. F. (2002). Traumatic victimization in the lives of lesbian and bisexual women: A contextual approach. *Journal of Lesbian Studies, 7*, 1–14. doi:10.1300/J155v07n01_01

Balsam, K. F., Rothblum, E. D., & Beauchaine, T. P. (2005). Victimization over the life span: A comparison of lesbian, gay, bisexual, and heterosexual siblings. *Journal of Consulting and Clinical Psychology, 73*, 477–487. doi:10.1037/0022-006X.73.3.477

Banyard, V., Moynihan, M., & Crossman, M. (2009). Reducing sexual violence on campus: The role of student leaders as empowered bystanders. *Journal of College Student Development, 50*, 446–457.

Banyard, V. L., Eckstein, R. P., & Moynihan, M. (2010). Sexual violence prevention: The role of stages of change. *Journal of Interpersonal Violence, 25*, 111–135. doi:10.1177/0886260508329123

Banyard, V. L., Moynihan, M. M., & Plante, E. G. (2007). Sexual violence prevention through bystander education: An experimental evaluation. *Journal of Community Psychology, 35*, 463–481. doi:10.1002/jcop.20159

Banyard, V. L., Plante, E. G., & Moynihan, M. M. (2005). *Rape prevention through bystander education: Bringing a broader community perspective to sexual violence prevention.* Retrieved from http://www.ncjrs.gov/pdffiles1/nij/grants/208701.pdf

Basile, K. C. (1999). Rape by acquiescence: The ways in which women "give in" to unwanted sex with their husbands. *Violence Against Women, 5*, 1036–1058.

Basile, K. C. (2002). Prevalence of wife rape and other intimate partner sexual coercion in a nationally representative sample of women. *Violence and Victims, 17*, 511–524. doi:10.1891/vivi.17.5.511.33717

Bateman, P. (1978). *Fear into anger: A manual of self-defense for women.* Chicago, IL: Nelson Hall.

Bay-Cheng, L. Y., & Eliseo-Arras, R. K. (2008). The making of unwanted sex: Gendered and neoliberal norms in college women's unwanted sexual experiences. *Journal of Sex Research, 45*, 386–397. doi:10.1080/00224490802398381

Bennice, J. A., & Resick, P. A. (2003). Marital rape: History, research, and practice. *Trauma, Violence, and Abuse, 4*, 228–246. doi:10.1177/1524838003004003003

Bennice, J. A., Resick, P. A., Mechanic, M., & Astin, M. (2003). The relative effects of intimate partner physical and sexual violence on posttraumatic stress disorder symptomatology. *Violence and Victims, 18*, 87–94. doi:10.1891/vivi.2003.18.1.87

Beres, M. (2010). Sexual miscommunication? Untangling assumptions about sexual communication between casual sex partners. *Culture, Health, and Sexuality, 12*, 1–14. doi:10.1080/13691050903075226

Beres, M., Senn, C. Y., & McCaw, J. (2009, August). *Taking "mis" out of miscommunication: Navigating desire differences in heterosex.* Paper presented at 117th Annual Convention of the American Psychological Association, Toronto, Ontario.

Beres, M. A., & Farvid, P. (2010). Sexual ethics and young women's accounts of heterosexual casual sex. *Sexualities, 13*, 377–393. doi:10.1177/1363460709363136

Berger, R. J., & Searles, P. (1985). Victim-offender interaction in rape: Victimological, situational, and feminist perspectives. *Women's Studies Quarterly, 13*(3–4), 9–15.

Bevacqua, M. (2000). *Rape on the public agenda: Feminism and the politics of sexual assault.* Boston, MA: Northeastern University Press.

Bogle, K. A. (2008). *Hooking up: Sex, dating and relationships on campus.* New York, NY: New York University.

Bohner, G., Eyssel, F., Pina, A., Siebler, F., & Viki, G. T. (2009). Rape myth acceptance: Cognitive, affective and behavioural effects of beliefs that blame the victim and exonerate the perpetrator. In M. Horvath & J. Brown (Eds.), *Rape: Challenging contemporary thinking* (pp. 17–45). Cullompton, England: Willan.

Bohner, G., Jarvis, C. I., Eyssel, F., & Siebler, F. (2005). The causal impact of rape myth acceptance on men's rape proclivity: Comparing sexually coercive and noncoercive men. *European Journal of Social Psychology, 35*, 819–828. doi:10.1002/ejsp.284

Bohner, G., Reinhard, M. A., Rutz, S., Sturm, S., Kerschbaum, B., & Effler, D. (1998). Rape myths as neutralizing cognitions: Evidence for a causal impact of anti-victim attitudes on men's self-reported likelihood of raping. *European Journal of Social Psychology, 28*, 257–268. doi:10.1002/(SICI)1099-0992(199803/04)28:2<257::AID-EJSP871>3.0.CO;2-1

Bondurant, B. (2001). University women's acknowledgement of rape: Individual, situational, and social factors. *Violence Against Women, 7*, 294–314.

Bondurant, B., & Donat, P. L. N. (1999). Perceptions of women's sexual interest and acquaintance rape: The role of sexual overperception and affective attitudes. *Psychology of Women Quarterly, 23*, 691–705. doi:10.1111/j.1471-6402.1999.tb00392.x

Botta, R. A., & Pingree, S. (1997). Interpersonal communication and rape: Women acknowledge their assaults. *Journal of Health Communication, 2*, 197–212. doi:10.1080/108107397127752

Braun, V., Schmidt, J., Gavey, N., & Fenaughty, J. (2009). Sexual coercion among gay and bisexual men in Aotearoa/New Zealand. *Journal of Homosexuality, 56*, 336–360. doi:10.1080/00918360902728764

Brecklin, L. R., & Forde, D. R. (2001). A meta-analysis of rape education programs. *Violence and Victims, 16*, 303–321.

Breitenbecher, K. H. (2000). Sexual assault on college campuses: Is an ounce of prevention enough? *Applied and Preventive Psychology, 9*, 23–52. doi:10.1016/S0962-1849(05)80036-8

Briere, J., & Malamuth, N. M. (1983). Self-reported likelihood of sexually aggressive behavior: Attitudinal vs. sexual explanations. *Journal of Research in Personality, 17*, 315–323. doi:10.1016/0092-6566(83)90023-5

Brownmiller, S. (1975). *Against our will: Men, women, and rape.* Harmondsworth, England: Penguin Books.

Brownridge, D. A. (2009). *Violence against women: Vulnerable populations.* New York, NY: Routledge.

Burgess, A. W., & Holmstrom, L. L. (1974). Rape trauma syndrome. *American Journal of Psychiatry, 131*, 981–986.

Burkhart, B. R., & Stanton, A. L. (1988). Sexual aggression in acquaintance relationships. In G. W. Russell (Ed.), *Violence in intimate relationships* (pp. 443–465). New York, NY: PMA.

Burn, S. M. (2009). A situational model of sexual assault prevention through bystander intervention. *Sex Roles, 60*, 779–792. doi:10.1007/s11199-008-9581-5

Burns, A., Futch, V., & Tolman, D. (2011). It's like doing homework. *Sexuality Research and Social Policy, 8*, 239–251. doi:10.1007/s13178-011-0062-1

Burt, M. R. (1980). Cultural myths and supports for rape. *Journal of Personality and Social Psychology, 38*, 217–230. doi:10.1037/0022-3514.38.2.217

Byers, E. S. (1996). How well does the traditional sexual script explain sexual coercion? Review of a program of research. *Journal of Psychology and Human Sexuality, 8*, 7–25. doi:10.1300/J056v08n01_02

Byers, E. S., Giles, B. L., & Price, D. L. (1987). Definiteness and effectiveness of women's responses to unwanted sexual advances: A laboratory investigation.

Basic and Applied Social Psychology, 8, 321–338. doi:10.1207/s15324834basp0804_5

Byers, E. S., & O'Sullivan, L. F. (1998). Similar but different: Men's and women's experiences of sexual coercion. In P. B. Anderson & C. Struckman-Johnson (Eds.), *Sexually aggressive women: Current perspectives and controversies* (pp. 144–168). New York, NY: Guilford Press.

Byers, E. S., & Wilson, P. (1985). Accuracy of women's expectations regarding men's responses to refusals of sexual advances in dating situations. *International Journal of Women's Studies, 8*, 376–387.

Cahill, A. J. (2001). *Rethinking rape*. Ithaca, NY: Cornell University Press.

Campbell, B. (1980). A feminist sexual politics: Now you see it, now you don't. *Feminist Review, 5*, 1–18. doi:10.1057/fr.1980.9

Campbell, R., Dworkin, E., & Cabral, G. (2009). An ecological model of the impact of sexual assault on women's mental health. *Trauma, Violence, and Abuse, 10*, 225–246. doi:10.1177/1524838009334456

Campbell, R., Wasco, S. M., Ahrens, C. E., Sefl, T., & Barnes, H. E. (2001). Preventing the "second rape": Rape survivors' experiences with community service providers. *Journal of Interpersonal Violence, 16*, 1239–1259. doi:10.1177/088626001016012002

Caringella, S. (2009). *Addressing rape reform in law and practice*. New York, NY: Columbia University Press.

Carmody, M. (2003). Sexual ethics and violence prevention. *Social and Legal Studies, 12*, 199–216. doi:10.1177/0964663903012002003

Carmody, M. (2005). Ethical erotics: Reconceptualizing anti-rape education. *Sexualities, 8*, 465–480. doi:10.1177/1363460705056621

Carmody, M. (2009a). *Conceptualising the prevention of sexual assault and the role of education* (ACSSA Issues No. 10). Melbourne, Australia: Australian Centre for the Study of Sexual Assault.

Carmody, M. (2009b). *Sex and ethics: Young people and ethical sex*. South Yarra, Australia: Palgrave Macmillan.

Casey, E. A., & Lindhorst, T. (2009). Toward a multilevel, ecological approach to the primary prevention of sexual assault: Prevention in peer and community contexts. *Trauma, Violence, and Abuse, 10*, 91–114. doi:10.1177/1524838009334129

Centers for Disease Control and Prevention. (2009). The social-ecological model: A framework for prevention. Retrieved from http://www.cdc.gov/violenceprevention/overview/social-ecologicalmodel.html

Chapleau, K. M., & Oswald, D. L. (2010). Power, sex, and rape myth acceptance: Testing two models of rape proclivity. *Journal of Sex Research, 47*, 66–78. doi:10.1080/00224490902954323

Check, J. V. P., & Malamuth, N. M. (1985). An empirical assessment of some feminist hypotheses about rape. *International Journal of Women's Studies, 8*, 414–423.

Chen, Y., & Ullman, S. E. (2010). Women's reporting of sexual and physical assaults to police in the National Violence Against Women Survey. *Violence Against Women, 16*, 262–279. doi:10.1177/1077801209360861

Clark, L., & Lewis, D. (1977). *Rape: The price of coercive sexuality*. Toronto, Ontario, Canada: Women's Educational.

Clay-Warner, J., & Burt, C. H. (2005). Rape reporting after reforms: Have times really changed? *Violence Against Women, 11*, 150–176. doi:10.1177/1077801204271566

Clements, C. M., & Ogle, R. L. (2009). Does acknowledgment as an assault victim impact postassault psychological symptoms and coping? *Journal of Interpersonal Violence, 24*, 1595–1614. doi:10.1177/0886260509331486

Collins, P. H. (2005). *Black sexual politics: African Americans, gender, and the new racism*. New York, NY: Routledge.

Cook-Daniels, L., & Munson, M. (2010). Sexual violence, elder abuse, and sexuality of transgender adults, age 50+: Results of three surveys. *Journal of GLBT Family Studies, 6*, 142–177.

Coyne, J. A., & Berry, A. (2000). Rape as adaptation: Is this contentious advocacy, not science? [Review of *A natural history of rape: Biological bases of sexual coercion*]. *Nature, 404*, 121–122. doi:10.1038/35004636

Crawford, M. (1995). *Talking difference: On gender and language*. London, England: Sage.

Crawford, M., & Popp, D. (2003). Sexual double standards: A review and methodological critique of two decades of research. *Journal of Sex Research, 40*, 13–26. doi:10.1080/00224490309552163

Crenshaw, K. (1993). Whose story is it, anyway? Feminist and antiracist appropriations of Anita Hill. In T. Morrison (Ed.), *Race-ing justice, en-gendering power: Essays on Anita Hill, Clarence Thomas, and the construction of social reality* (pp. 402–440). London, England: Chatto & Windus.

Dallager, C., & Rosen, L. A. (1993). Effects of a human sexuality course on attitudes toward rape and violence. *Journal of Sex Education and Therapy, 19*, 193–199.

Dar-Nimrod, I., Heine, S. J., Cheung, B. Y., & Schaller, M. (2011). Do scientific theories affect men's evaluations of sex crimes? *Aggressive Behavior, 37*, 440–449. doi:10.1002/ab.20401

Davis, A. Y. (1990). *Women, culture, and politics*. New York, NY: Vintage Books.

Decker, J. F., & Baroni, P. G. (2012). "No" still means "yes": The failure of the "non-consent" reform movement in American rape and sexual assault law. *Journal of Criminal Law and Criminology, 101*, 1081–1170.

DeGue, S., & DiLillo, D. (2004). Understanding perpetrators of nonphysical sexual coercion: Characteristics of those who cross the line. *Violence and Victims, 19*, 673–688. doi:10.1891/vivi.19.6.673.66345

Deming, M. B., & Eppy, A. (1981). The sociology of rape. *Sociology and Social Research, 65*, 357–380.

Easteal, P. (Ed.). (1998). *Balancing the scales: Rape, law reform and Australian culture.* Sydney, Australia: Federation Press.

Eaton, A. A., & Rose, S. (2011). Has dating become more egalitarian? A 35 year review using *Sex Roles. Sex Roles, 64*, 843–862. doi:10.1007/s11199-011-9957-9

Edwards, K. M., Turchik, J. A., Dardis, C. M., Reynolds, N., & Gidycz, C. A. (2011). Rape myths: History, individual and institutional-level presence, and implications for change. *Sex Roles, 65*, 761–773. doi:10.1007/s11199-011-9943-2

Edwards, S. S. M. (1981). *Female sexuality and the law.* Oxford, England: Martin Robertson.

Ehrlich, S. (2001). *Representing rape: Language and sexual consent.* London, England: Routledge. doi:10.4324/9780203459034

Ehrlich, S., & King, R. (1992). Gender-based language reform and the social construction of meaning. *Discourse and Society, 3*, 151–166. doi:10.1177/0957926592003002002

Ellis, H. (1948). *Studies in the psychology of sex* (3rd ed.). London, England: William Heinemann. (Original work published 1899)

Estrich, S. (1987). *Real rape.* Cambridge, MA: Harvard University Press.

Evans-Campbell, T., Lindhorst, T., Huang, B., & Walters, K. L. (2006). Interpersonal violence in the lives of urban American Indian and Alaska Native women: Implications for health, mental health, and help-seeking. *American Journal of Public Health, 96*, 1416–1422. doi:10.2105/AJPH.2004.054213

Eyssel, F., Bohner, G., & Siebler, F. (2006). Perceived rape myth acceptance of others predicts rape proclivity: Social norm or judgmental anchoring? *Swiss Journal of Psychology, 65*, 93–99. doi:10.1024/1421-0185.65.2.93

Fabiano, P. M., Perkins, H. W., Berkowitz, A., Linkenbach, J., & Stark, C. (2003). Engaging men as social justice allies in ending violence against women: Evidence for a social norms approach. *Journal of American College Health, 52*, 105–112. doi:10.1080/07448480309595732

Farley, M., & Barkan, H. (1998). Prostitution, violence, and posttraumatic stress disorder. *Women and Health, 27*, 37–49. doi:10.1300/J013v27n03_03

Fine, M. (2012). Troubling calls for evidence: A critical race, class and gender analysis of whose evidence counts. *Feminism and Psychology, 22*, 3–19. doi:10.1177/0959353511435475

Fine, M., & McClelland, S. (2006). Sexuality education and the discourse of desire: Still missing after all these years. *Harvard Educational Review, 76*, 297–338.

Finkelhor, D., & Yllo, K. (1983). Rape in marriage: A sociological view. In D. Finkelhor, R. J. Gelles, G. T. Hotaling, & M. A. Straus (Eds.), *The dark side of families: Current family violence research* (pp. 119–130). Beverly Hills, CA: Sage.

Finkelhor, D., & Yllo, K. (1985). *License to rape: Sexual abuse of wives.* New York, NY: Free Press.

Fisher, B. S., & Cullen, F. T. (2000). Measuring the sexual victimization of women: Evolution, current controversies, and future research (Measurement and Analysis of Crime and Justice, NCJ 185543). Rockville, MD: National Institute of Justice/NCJRS.

Fisher, B. S., Daigle, L. E., Cullen, F. T., & Turner, M. G. (2003). Acknowledging sexual victimization as rape: Results from a national-level study. *Justice Quarterly, 20*, 535–574. doi:10.1080/07418820300095611

Flack, W. F. J., Daubman, K. A., Caron, M. L., Asadorian, J. A., D'Aureli, N. R., Gigliotti, S. N., . . . Stine, E. R. (2007). Risk factors and consequences of unwanted sex among university students: Hooking up, alcohol, and stress response. *Journal of Interpersonal Violence, 22*, 139–157. doi:10.1177/0886260506295354

Flood, M. (2011). Involving men in efforts to end violence against women. *Men and Masculinities, 14*, 358–377. doi:10.1177/1097184X10363995

Flores, S. A., & Hartlaub, M. G. (1998). Reducing rape myth acceptance in male college students: A meta-analysis of intervention studies. *Journal of College Student Development, 39*, 438–448.

Forrest, A., & Senn, C. Y. (2011, June). *A curriculum initiative to institutionalize pro-social behaviour.* Invited Plenary Talk for the Addressing Sexual Violence: Changing Attitudes, Changing Lives Forum, Toronto, Ontario, Canada.

Frank, D. J., Hardinge, T., & Wosick-Correa, K. (2009). The global dimensions of rape-law reform: A cross-national study of policy outcomes. *American Sociological Review, 74*, 272–290. doi:10.1177/000312240907400206

Frazier, P. A. (2003). Perceived control and distress following sexual assault: A longitudinal test of a new model. *Journal of Personality and Social Psychology, 84*, 1257–1269. doi:10.1037/0022-3514.84.6.1257

Frazier, P. A., & Seales, L. M. (1997). Acquaintance rape is real rape. In M. Schwartz (Ed.), *Researching sexual violence against women: Methodological and personal perspectives* (pp. 54–64). Thousand Oaks: Sage.

Frith, H. (2009). Sexual scripts, sexual refusals and rape. In M. Horvath & J. Brown (Eds.), *Rape: Challenging contemporary thinking* (pp. 99–122). Cullompton, England: Willan.

Frith, H., & Kitzinger, C. (1997). Talk about sexual miscommunication. *Women's Studies International Forum, 20*, 517–528. doi:10.1016/S0277-5395(97)87415-8

Frith, H., & Kitzinger, C. (2001). Reformulating sexual script theory: Developing a discursive psychology of sexual negotiation. *Theory and Psychology, 11*, 209–232. doi:10.1177/0959354301112004

Garcia, J. R., Reiber, C., Massey, S. G., & Merriwether, A. M. (2012). Sexual hookup culture: A review. *Review of General Psychology, 16*, 161–176. doi:10.1037/a0027911

Gavey, N. (1989). Feminist poststructuralism and discourse analysis: Contributions to feminist psychology. *Psychology of Women Quarterly, 13*, 459–475. doi:10.1111/j.1471-6402.1989.tb01014.x

Gavey, N. J. (1991a). Sexual victimization among Auckland University students: How much and who does it? *New Zealand Journal of Psychology, 20*, 63–70.

Gavey, N. (1991b). Sexual victimization prevalence among New Zealand university students. *Journal of Consulting and Clinical Psychology, 59*, 464–466. doi:10.1037/0022-006X.59.3.464

Gavey, N. (1992). Technologies and effects of heterosexual coercion. *Feminism and Psychology, 2*, 325–351. doi:10.1177/0959353592023003

Gavey, N. (1996). Women's desire and sexual violence discourse. In S. Wilkinson (Ed.), *Feminist social psychologies: International perspectives* (pp. 51–65). Buckingham, England: Open University Press.

Gavey, N. (2005). *Just sex? The cultural scaffolding of rape.* New York, NY: Routledge.

Gavey, N. (2007). Rape, trauma, and meaning. In C. M. Elliott (Ed.), *Global empowerment of women: Responses to globalization and politicized religions* (pp. 233–246). New York, NY: Routledge.

Gavey, N. (2009). Fighting rape. In R. J. Heberle & V. Grace (Eds.), *Theorizing sexual violence* (pp. 96–124). New York, NY: Routledge.

Gavey, N. (2012, July). *Intimate intrusions of the neoliberal deceit.* Invited State of the Science address (Critical Psychology of Gender), 30th International Congress of Psychology, Cape Town, South Africa.

Gavey, N. (in press). Sexual violence. In T. Teo (Ed.), *Encyclopedia of critical psychology*. New York, NY: Springer.

Gavey, N., McPhillips, K., & Doherty, M. (2001). "If it's not on, it's not on"—or is it? Discursive constraints on women's condom use. *Gender and Society, 15*, 917–934. doi:10.1177/089124301015006008

Gavey, N., & Schmidt, J. (2011). "Trauma of rape" discourse: A double-edged template for everyday understandings of the impact of rape? *Violence Against Women, 17*, 433–456. doi:10.1177/1077801211404194

Gidycz, C. A., Lynn, S. J., Rich, C. L., Marioni, N. L., Loh, C., Blackwell, L. M., . . . Pashdag, J. (2001). The evaluation of a sexual assault risk reduction program: A multisite investigation. *Journal of Consulting and Clinical Psychology, 69*, 1073–1078. doi:10.1037/0022-006X.69.6.1073

Gidycz, C. A., Orchowski, L., & Berkowitz, A. D. (2011). Preventing sexual aggression among college men: An evaluation of a social norms and bystander intervention program. *Violence Against Women, 17*, 720–742. doi:10.1177/1077801211409727

Gidycz, C. A., Rich, C. L., & Marioni, N. L. (2002). Interventions to prevent rape and sexual assault. In J. Petrak & B. Hedge (Eds.), *The trauma of adult sexual assault: Treatment, prevention, and policy* (pp. 235–259). New York, NY: Wiley.

Gidycz, C. A., Rich, C. L., Orchowski, L., King, C., & Miller, A. K. (2006). The evaluation of a sexual assault self-defense and risk-reduction program for college women: A prospective study. *Psychology of Women Quarterly, 30*, 173–186. doi:10.1111/j.1471-6402.2006.00280.x

Goldfarb, E. S., & Casparian, E. M. (2000). *Our whole lives: Sexuality education for grades 10–12*. Boston, MA: Unitarian Universalist Association.

Gotell, L. (2010). Canadian sexual assault law: Neoliberalism and the erosion of feminist inspired law reform. In C. McGlynn & V. Munro (Eds.), *Rethinking rape law* (pp. 209–223). London, England: Routledge UK.

Griffin, S. (1977). Rape: The all-American crime. In D. Chappell, R. Geis, & G. Geis (Eds.), *Forcible rape: The crime, the victim, and the offender* (pp. 47–66). New York, NY: Columbia University Press.

Groth, A. N., & Burgess, A. W. (1977). Rape: A sexual deviation. *American Journal of Orthopsychiatry, 47*, 400–406. doi:10.1111/j.1939-0025.1977.tb01246.x

Hamby, S. (2011). The second wave of violence scholarship: Integrating and broadening theories of violence. *Psychology of Violence, 1*, 163–165. doi:10.1037/a0024121

Hamilton, L., & Armstrong, E. A. (2009). Gendered sexuality in young adulthood: Double binds and flawed options. *Gender and Society, 23*, 589–616. doi:10.1177/0891243209345829

Hanson, K. A., & Gidycz, C. A. (1993). Evaluation of a sexual assault prevention program. *Journal of Consulting and Clinical Psychology, 61*, 1046–1052. doi:10.1037/0022-006X.61.6.1046

Hanson, R. K., & Broom, I. (2005). The utility of cumulative meta-analysis: Application to programs for reducing sexual violence. *Sexual Abuse, 17*, 357–373.

Harned, M. S. (2004). Does it matter what you call it? The relationship between labeling unwanted sexual experiences and distress. *Journal of Consulting and Clinical Psychology, 72*, 1090–1099. doi:10.1037/0022-006X.72.6.1090

Harned, M. S. (2005). Understanding women's labeling of unwanted sexual experiences with dating partners. *Violence Against Women, 11*, 374–413. doi:10.1177/1077801204272240

Harvey, M. R. (1996). An ecological view of psychological trauma and trauma recovery. *Journal of Traumatic Stress, 9*, 3–23. doi:10.1002/jts.2490090103

Heise, L., Ellsberg, M., & Gottmoeller, M. (2002). A global overview of gender-based violence. *International Journal of Gynaecology and Obstetrics, 78*(Suppl. 1), S5–S14. doi:10.1016/s0020-7292(02)00038-3

Heise, L. L. (1998). Violence against women: An integrated, ecological framework. *Violence Against Women, 4*, 262–290. doi:10.1177/1077801298004003002

Heldman, C., & Wade, L. (2010). Hook-up culture: Setting a new research agenda. *Sexuality Research and Social Policy, 7*, 323–333. doi:10.1007/s13178-010-0024-z

Henriques, J., Hollway, W., Urwin, C., Venn, C., & Walkerdine, V. (1984). Changing the subject: Psychology, social regulation and subjectivity. London, England: Methuen.

Herman, J. L. (1998). *Trauma and recovery: From domestic abuse to political terror.* London, England: Pandora.

Hickman, S. E., & Muehlenhard, C. L. (1999). "By the semi-mystical appearance of a condom": How young women and men communicate sexual consent in heterosexual situations. *Journal of Sex Research, 36*, 258–272. doi:10.1080/00224499909551996

Holland, J., Ramazanoglu, C., Sharpe, S., & Thomson, R. (1998). *The male in the head: Young people, heterosexuality, and power.* London, England: Tufnell Press.

Hollander, J. A. (2009). The roots of resistance to women's self-defense. *Violence Against Women, 15*, 574–594. doi:10.1177/1077801209331407

Hollway, W. (1983). Heterosexual sex: Power and desire for the other. In S. Cartledge & J. Ryan (Eds.), *Sex and love: New thoughts on old contradictions* (pp. 124–140). London, England: Women's Press.

Hollway, W. (1984). Gender difference and the production of subjectivity. In J. Henriques, W. Hollway, C. Urwin, C. Venn, & V. Walkerdine (Eds.), *Changing the subject: Psychology, social regulation and subjectivity* (pp. 227–263). London, England: Methuen.

Hollway, W. (1989). *Subjectivity and method in psychology: Gender, meaning and science.* London, England: Sage.

Horvath, M., & Brown, J. (Eds.). (2009). *Rape: Challenging contemporary thinking.* Cullompton, England: Willan.

Horvath, M. A. H., Hegarty, P., Tyler, S., & Mansfield, S. (2012). "Lights on at the end of the party": Are lads' mags mainstreaming dangerous sexism? *British Journal of Psychology, 103*, 454–471. doi:10.1111/j.2044-8295.2011.02086.x

Jackson, S. (1978). The social context of rape: Sexual scripts and motivation. *Women's Studies International Quarterly, 1*, 27–38. doi:10.1016/S0148-0685(78)90311-1

Jacques-Tiura, A. J., Abbey, A., Parkhill, M. R., & Zawacki, T. (2007). Why do some men misperceive women's sexual intentions more frequently than others? *Personality and Social Psychology Bulletin, 33*, 1467–1480. doi:10.1177/0146167207306281

Johnson, H., & Dawson, M. (2011). *Violence against women in Canada: Research and policy perspectives* (pp. 93–122). Toronto, Ontario, Canada: Oxford University Press.

Jordan, J. (2004). *The word of a woman? Police, rape, and belief.* Basingstoke, England: Palgrave Macmillan. doi:10.1057/9780230511057

Jozkowski, K. N., & Peterson, Z. D. (2012). College students and sexual consent: Unique insights. *Journal of Sex Research.* Advance online publication. doi:10.1080/00224499.2012.700739

Kahn, A. S., Jackson, J., Kully, C., Badger, K., & Halvorsen, J. (2003). Calling it rape: Differences in experiences of women who do or do not label their sexual assault as rape. *Psychology of Women Quarterly, 27*, 233–242. doi:10.1111/1471-6402.00103

Kahn, A. S., Mathie, V. A., & Torgler, C. (1994). Rape scripts and rape acknowledgement. *Psychology of Women Quarterly, 18*, 53–66. doi:10.1111/j.1471-6402.1994.tb00296.x

Kalish, R., & Kimmel, M. (2011). Hooking up: Hot hetero sex or the new numb normative? *Australian Feminist Studies, 26*, 137–151. doi:10.1080/08164649.2011.546333

Kalra, M., Wood, E., Desmarais, S., Senn, C. Y., & Verberg, N. (1998). Exploring negative dating experiences and beliefs about rape among younger and older women. *Archives of Sexual Behavior, 27*, 145–153. doi:10.1023/A:1018630513681

Katz, B. L. (1991). The psychological impact of stranger versus nonstranger rape on victims' recovery. In A.

Parrot & L. Bechhofer (Eds.), *Acquaintance rape: The hidden crime* (pp. 251–269). New York, NY: Wiley.

Katz, J., Heisterkamp, H. A., & Fleming, W. M. (2011). The social justice roots of the Mentors in Violence prevention model and its application in a high school setting. *Violence Against Women, 17*, 684–702. doi:10.1177/1077801211409725

Katz, J., & Tirone, V. (2010). Going along with it: Sexually coercive partner behavior predicts dating women's compliance with unwanted sex. *Violence Against Women, 16*, 730–742. doi:10.1177/1077801210374867

Katz, J., Tirone, V., & van der Kloet, E. (2012, March 31). Moving in and hooking up: Women's and men's casual sexual experiences during the first two months of college. *Electronic Journal of Human Sexuality, 15*. Retrieved from http://mail.ejhs.org/volume15/Hookingup.html

Kelly, L. (1987). The continuum of sexual violence. In J. Hanmer & M. Maynard (Eds.), *Women, violence and social control* (pp. 46–60). Basingstoke, England: Macmillan.

Kelly, L. (1988a). How women define their experiences of violence. In K. Yllo & M. Bograd (Eds.), *Feminist perspectives on wife abuse* (pp. 114–132). Newbury Park, CA: Sage.

Kelly, L. (1988b). *Surviving sexual violence*. Cambridge, England: Polity.

Kelly, L. (2012). Standing the test of time? Reflections on the concept of the continuum of sexual violence. In J. M. Brown & S. L. Walklate (Eds.), *Handbook on sexual violence* (pp. xvii–xxvi). London, England: Routledge.

Kelly, L., & Lovett, J. (2009). *Different systems, similar outcomes? Tracking attrition in reported rape cases in eleven countries* [European briefing]. London, England: Child and Women Abuse Studies Unit.

Kimball, R. S. (2000). *Our whole lives: Sexuality for adults*. Boston, MA: Unitarian Universalist Association.

Kitzinger, C., & Frith, H. (1999). Just say no? The use of conversation analysis in developing a feminist perspective on sexual refusal. *Discourse and Society, 10*, 293–316. doi:10.1177/0957926599010003002

Knight, R. A., & Sims-Knight, J. (with S. Brown-McBride). (2009). *Using rapist risk factors to set an agenda for rape prevention* (Applied Research Forum). Harrisburg, PA: National Resource Center on Domestic Violence.

Koss, M. P. (1985). The hidden rape victim: Personality, attitudinal, and situational characteristics. *Psychology of Women Quarterly, 9*, 193–212. doi:10.1111/j.1471-6402.1985.tb00872.x

Koss, M. P. (1988). Hidden rape: Sexual aggression and victimization in a national sample of students in higher education. In A. W. Burgess (Ed.), *Rape and sexual assault II* (pp. 3–25). New York, NY: Garland.

Koss, M. P. (1992). Defending date rape. *Journal of Interpersonal Violence, 7*, 122–126. doi:10.1177/088626092007001010

Koss, M. P., Abbey, A., Campbell, R., Cook, S., Norris, J., Testa, M., . . . White, J. (2007). Revising the SES: A collaborative process to improve assessment of sexual aggression and victimization. *Psychology of Women Quarterly, 31*, 357–370. doi:10.1111/j.1471-6402.2007.00385.x

Koss, M. P., & Dinero, T. E. (1988). Predictors of sexual aggression among a national sample of male college students. *Annals of the New York Academy of Sciences, 528*, 133–147. doi:10.1111/j.1749-6632.1988.tb50856.x

Koss, M. P., Dinero, T. E., Seibel, C. A., & Cox, S. L. (1988). Stranger and acquaintance rape: Are there differences in the victim's experience? *Psychology of Women Quarterly, 12*, 1–24. doi:10.1111/j.1471-6402.1988.tb00924.x

Koss, M. P., & Figueredo, A. J. (2004). Change in cognitive mediators of rape's impact on psychosocial health across 2 years of recovery. *Journal of Consulting and Clinical Psychology, 72*, 1063–1072. doi:10.1037/0022-006X.72.6.1063

Koss, M. P., & Gidycz, C. A. (1985). Sexual experiences survey: Reliability and validity. *Journal of Consulting and Clinical Psychology, 53*, 422–423. doi:10.1037/0022-006X.53.3.422

Koss, M. P., Gidycz, C. A., & Wisniewski, N. (1987). The scope of rape: Incidence and prevalence of sexual aggression and victimization in a national sample of students in higher education. *Journal of Consulting and Clinical Psychology, 55*, 162–170. doi:10.1037/0022-006X.55.2.162

Koss, M. P., & Harvey, M. R. (1991). *The rape victim: Clinical and community interventions* (2nd ed.). Newbury Park, CA: Sage.

Koss, M. P., Leonard, K. E., Beezley, D. A., & Oros, C. J. (1985). Nonstranger sexual aggression: A discriminant analysis of the psychological characteristics of undetected offenders. *Sex Roles, 12*, 981–992. doi:10.1007/BF00288099

Koss, M. P., & Oros, C. J. (1982). Sexual Experiences Survey: A research instrument investigating sexual aggression and victimization. *Journal of Consulting and Clinical Psychology, 50*, 455–457. doi:10.1037/0022-006X.50.3.455

Koss, M. P., White, J. W., & Kazdin, A. E. (2011a). Violence against women and children: Perspectives and next steps. In M. P. Koss, J. W. White, & A. E. Kazdin (Eds.), *Violence against women and children, Vol. 2: Navigating solutions* (pp. 261–305). Washington, DC: American Psychological Association.

Koss, M. P., White, J. W., & Kazdin, A. E. (Eds.). (2011b). *Violence against women and children, Vol. 2: Navigating solutions.* Washington, DC: American Psychological Association.

Krahé, B., Scheinberger-Olwig, R., & Kolpin, S. (2000). Ambiguous communication of sexual intentions as a risk marker of sexual aggression. *Sex Roles, 42*, 313–337. doi:10.1023/A:1007080303569

Lamb, S. (2010). Toward a sexual ethics curriculum: Bring philosophy and society to bear on individual development. *Harvard Educational Review, 80*, 81–106.

Laumann, E. O., Gagnon, J. H., Michael, R. T., & Michaels, S. (1994). *The social organization of sexuality: Sexual practices in the United States.* Chicago, IL: University of Chicago Press.

Layman, M. J., Gidycz, C. A., & Lynn, S. J. (1996). Unacknowledged versus acknowledged rape victims: Situational factors and posttraumatic stress. *Journal of Abnormal Psychology, 105*, 124–131. doi:10.1037/0021-843X.105.1.124

Lea, S. J. (2007). A discursive investigation into victim responsibility in rape. *Feminism and Psychology, 17*, 495–514. doi:10.1177/0959353507083101

Lees, S. (1993). Judicial rape. *Women's Studies International Forum, 16*, 11–36. doi:10.1016/0277-5395(93)90077-M

Lindgren, K. P., Parkhill, M. R., George, W. H., & Hendershot, C. S. (2008). Gender differences in perceptions of sexual intent: A qualitative review and integration. *Psychology of Women Quarterly, 32*, 423–439. doi:10.1111/j.1471-6402.2008.00456.x

Littleton, H. (2011). Rape myths and beyond: A commentary on Edwards and colleagues (2011). *Sex Roles, 65*, 792–797. doi:10.1007/s11199-011-9982-8

Littleton, H., Axsom, D., & Grills-Taquechel, A. (2009). Sexual assault victims' acknowledgement status and revictimization risk. *Psychology of Women Quarterly, 33*, 34–42. doi:10.1111/j.1471-6402.2008.01472.x

Littleton, H., Radecki Breitkopf, C., & Berenson, A. (2008). Beyond the campus: Unacknowledged rape among low-income women. *Violence Against Women, 14*, 269–286. doi:10.1177/1077801207313733

Littleton, H., Tabernik, H., Canales, E. J., & Tamika, B. (2009). Risky situation or harmless fun? A qualitative examination of college women's bad hook-up and rape scripts. *Sex Roles, 60*, 793–804. doi:10.1007/s11199-009-9586-8

Littleton, H. L., & Henderson, C. E. (2009). If she is not a victim, does that mean she was not traumatized? Evaluation of predictors of PTSD symptomatology among college rape victims. *Violence Against Women, 15*, 148–167. doi:10.11771077801208329386

Littleton, H. L., Rhatigan, D. L., & Axsom, D. (2007). Unacknowledged rape. *Journal of Aggression, Maltreatment, and Trauma, 14*, 57–74. doi:10.1300/J146v14n04_04

Livingston, J. A., Buddie, A. M., Testa, M., & VanZile-Tamsen, C. (2004). The role of sexual precedence in verbal sexual coercion. *Psychology of Women Quarterly, 28*, 287–297. doi:10.1111/j.1471-6402.2004.00146.x

Lloyd, E. A. (2001). A natural history of rape: Biological bases of sexual coercion. *Michigan Law Review, 99*, 1536–1559. doi:10.2307/1290397

Lonsway, K. A., & Archambault, J. (2012). The "justice gap" for sexual assault cases: Future directions for research and reform. *Violence Against Women, 18*, 145–168. doi:10.1177/1077801212440017

Lonsway, K. A., Banyard, V. L., Berkowitz, A. D., Gidycz, C. A., Katz, J. T., Koss, M. P., . . . Ullman, S. E. (with Edwards, D.). (2009). *Rape prevention and risk reduction: Review of the research literature for practitioners.* Harrisburg, PA: National Online Resource Center on Violence Against Women.

Lonsway, K. A., & Fitzgerald, L. F. (1994). Rape myths in review. *Psychology of Women Quarterly, 18*, 133–164. doi:10.1111/j.1471-6402.1994.tb00448.x

MacKinnon, C. (1987). *Feminism unmodified: Discourses on life and law.* Cambridge, MA: Harvard University Press.

MacKinnon, C. A. (1983). Feminism, Marxism, method, and the state: Toward feminist jurisprudence. *Signs: Journal of Women in Culture and Society, 8*, 635–658. doi:10.1086/494000

Magnusson, E., & Marecek, J. (2012). *Gender and culture in psychology: Theories and practices.* Cambridge, England: Cambridge University Press. doi:10.1017/CBO9781139086318

Malamuth, N. M. (1981). Rape proclivity of males. *Journal of Social Issues, 37*, 138–157. doi:10.1111/j.1540-4560.1981.tb01075.x

Malamuth, N. M. (1984). Aggression against women: Cultural and individual causes. In N. Malamuth & E. Donnerstein (Eds.), *Pornography and sexual aggression* (pp. 19–52). Orlando, FL: Academic Press.

Malamuth, N. M. (1988). A multidimensional approach to sexual aggression: Combining measures of past behavior and present likelihood. *Annals of the New York Academy of Sciences, 528*, 123–132.

Malamuth, N. M. (1989). The Attraction to Sexual Aggression Scale: I. *Journal of Sex Research, 26*, 26–49. doi:10.1080/00224498909551491

Malamuth, N. M. (1998). An evolutionary-based model integrating research on the characteristics of sexually coercive men. In J. G. Adair, D. Belanger, & K. L. Dion (Eds.), *Advances in psychological science* (pp. 151–184). Hove, England: Psychology Press.

Malamuth, N., Haber, S., & Feshbach, S. (1980). Testing hypothesis regarding rape: Exposure to sexual violence, sex differences and the "normality" of rapists. *Journal of Research in Personality, 14*, 121–137. doi:10.1016/0092-6566(80)90045-8

Malamuth, N. M., Heavey, C. L., & Linz, D. (1993). Predicting men's antisocial behavior against women: The interaction model of sexual aggression. In N. M. Malamuth, C. L. Heavey, & D. Linz (Eds.), *Sexual aggression: Issues in etiology, assessment, and treatment* (pp. 63–97). Washington, DC: Taylor & Francis.

Malamuth, N. M., Linz, D., Heavey, C. L., Barnes, G., & Acker, M. (1995). Using the confluence model of sexual aggression to predict men's conflict with women: A 10-year follow-up study. *Journal of Personality and Social Psychology, 69*, 353–369. doi:10.1037/0022-3514.69.2.353

Malamuth, N. M., Socklowskie, R. J., Koss, M. P., & Tanaka, J. S. (1991). Characteristics of aggressors against women: Testing a model using a national sample of college students. *Journal of Consulting and Clinical Psychology, 59*, 670–681. doi:10.1037/0022-006X.59.5.670

Manhart, M. A., & Rush, F. (1974). New York radical feminists manifesto. In New York Radical Feminists, N. Connell & C. Wilson (Eds.), *Rape: The first sourcebook for women*. New York, NY: Plume/New American Library. (Original work published 1971)

Marcus, S. (1992). Fighting bodies, fighting words: A theory and politics of rape prevention. In J. Butler & J. W. Scott (Eds.), *Feminists theorize the political* (pp. 385–403). New York, NY: Routledge.

Marecek, J. (1999). Trauma talk in feminist clinical practice. In S. Lamb (Ed.), *New versions of victims: Feminist struggles with the concept* (pp. 158–182). New York, NY: New York University Press.

Martin, E. K., Taft, C. T., & Resick, P. A. (2007). A review of marital rape. *Aggression and Violent Behavior, 12*, 329–347. doi:10.1016/j.avb.2006.10.003

Martin, S. L., Macy, R. J., & Young, S. K. (2011). Health and economic consequences of sexual violence. In J. W. White, M. P. Koss, & A. E. Kazdin (Eds.), *Violence against women and children, Vol. 1: Mapping the terrain* (pp. 173–195). Washington, DC: American Psychological Association.

Masser, B., Viki, G. T., & Power, C. (2006). Hostile sexism and rape proclivity amongst men. *Sex Roles, 54*, 565–574. doi:10.1007/s11199-006-9022-2

McCaughey, M. (1997). *Real knockouts: The physical feminism of women's self-defense*. New York, NY: New York University Press.

McCaw, J., & Senn, C. Y. (1998). Perception of cues in conflictual dating situations: A test of the miscommunication hypothesis. *Violence Against Women, 4*, 609–624. doi:10.1177/1077801298004005006

McKenzie-Mohr, D., & Lafrance, M. (2011). Telling stories without the words: "Tightrope talk" in women's accounts of coming to live well after rape or depression. *Feminism and Psychology, 21*, 49–73. doi:10.1177/0959353510371367

McMahon, S. (2007). Understanding community-specific rape myths: Exploring student athlete culture. *Affilia, 22*, 357–370. doi:10.1177/0886109907306331

McMahon, S. (2010). Rape myth beliefs and bystander attitudes among incoming college students. *Journal of American College Health, 59*, 3–11. doi:10.108007448481.2010.483715

McMahon, S., & Farmer, G. L. (2011). An updated measure for assessing subtle rape myths. *Social Work Research, 35*, 71–81. doi:10.1093/swr/35.2.71

McMahon-Howard, J., Clay-Warner, J., & Renzulli, L. (2009). Criminalizing spousal rape: The diffusion of legal reforms. *Sociological Perspectives, 52*, 505–531. doi:10.1525/sop.2009.52.4.505

Medea, A., & Thompson, K. (1974). *Against rape: A survival manual for women: How to avoid entrapment and how to cope with rape physically and emotionally*. New York, NY: Farrar, Straus & Giroux.

Möller, A. S., Backstrom, T., Sondergaard, H. P., & Helstrom, L. (2012). Patterns of injury and reported violence depending on relationship to assailant in female Swedish sexual assault victims. *Journal of Interpersonal Violence, 27*, 3131–3148. doi:10.1177/0886260512441261

Mooney-Somers, J., & Ussher, J. M. (2010). Sex as commodity: Single and partnered men's subjectification as heterosexual men. *Men and Masculinities, 12*, 353–373. doi:10.1177/1097184X08322620

Moran, C., & Lee, C. (2012). Women's constructions of heterosexual non-romantic sex and the implications for sexual health. *Psychology and Sexuality*. Advance online publication. doi:10.1080/19419899.2012.715588

Morrison, S., Hardison, J., Mathew, A., & O'Neil, J. (2004). *An evidence-based review of sexual assault preventive intervention programs: Technical report*. Washington, DC: U.S. Department of Justice.

Muehlenhard, C. L. (1994). Are rape statistics exaggerated? A response to criticism of contemporary rape research. *Journal of Sex Research, 31*, 144–146. doi:10.1080/00224499409551742

Muehlenhard, C. L., Andrews, S. L., & Beal, G. K. (1996). Beyond "just saying no": Dealing with men's unwanted sexual advances in heterosexual dating contexts. *Journal of Psychology and Human Sexuality, 8*, 141–168. doi:10.1300/J056v08n01_10

Muehlenhard, C. L., & Cook, S. W. (1988). Men's self-reports of unwanted sexual activity. *Journal of Sex Research, 24*, 58–72. doi:10.1080/00224498809551398

Muehlenhard, C. L., & Falcon, P. L. (1990). Men's heterosocial skill and attitudes toward women as predictors of verbal sexual coercion and forceful rape. *Sex Roles, 23*, 241–259. doi:10.1007/BF00290046

Muehlenhard, C. L., & Hollabaugh, L. C. (1988). Do women sometimes say no when they mean yes? The prevalence and correlates of women's token resistance to sex. *Journal of Personality and Social Psychology, 54*, 872–879. doi:10.1037/0022-3514.54.5.872

Muehlenhard, C. L., & Linton, M. A. (1987). Date rape and sexual aggression in dating situations: Incidence and risk factors. *Journal of Counseling Psychology, 34*, 186–196. doi:10.1037/0022-0167.34.2.186

Muehlenhard, C. L., & McCoy, M. L. (1991). Double standard/double bind: The sexual double standard and women's communication about sex. *Psychology of Women Quarterly, 15*, 447–461. doi:10.1111/j.1471-6402.1991.tb00420.x

Muehlenhard, C. L., & Peterson, Z. D. (2005). Wanting and not wanting sex: The missing discourse of ambivalence. *Feminism and Psychology, 15*, 15–20. doi:10.1177/0959353505049698

Muehlenhard, C. L., & Rodgers, C. S. (1998). Token resistance to sex: New perspectives on an old stereotype. *Psychology of Women Quarterly, 22*, 443–463. doi:10.1111/j.1471-6402.1998.tb00167.x

Murnen, S. K., & Kohlman, M. H. (2007). Athletic participation, fraternity membership, and sexual aggression among college men: A meta-analytic review. *Sex Roles, 57*, 145–157. doi:10.1007/s11199-007-9225-1

Murphy, W. D., Coleman, E. M., & Haynes, M. R. (1986). Factors related to coercive sexual behaviour in a nonclinical sample of males. *Violence and Victims, 1*, 255–278.

Nurius, P. S., & Norris, J. (1996). A cognitive ecological model of women's response to male sexual coercion in dating. *Journal of Psychology and Human Sexuality, 8*, 117–139. doi:10.1300/J056v08n01_09

O'Byrne, R., Hansen, S., & Rapley, M. (2008). "If a girl doesn't say 'no'. . .": Young men, rape and claims of "insufficient knowledge." *Journal of Community and Applied Social Psychology, 18*, 168–193. doi:10.1002/casp.922

O'Byrne, R., Rapley, M., & Hansen, S. (2006). "You couldn't say 'no,' could you?": Young men's understandings of sexual refusal. *Feminism and Psychology, 16*, 133–154. doi:10.1177/0959-353506062970

Orchowski, L. M., Gidycz, C. A., & Raffle, H. (2008). Evaluation of a sexual assault risk reduction and self-defense program: A prospective analysis of a revised protocol. *Psychology of Women Quarterly, 32*, 204–218. doi:10.1111/j.1471-6402.2008.00425.x

O'Sullivan, L., & Allgeier, E. R. (1998). Feigning sexual desire: Consenting to unwanted sexual activity in heterosexual dating relationships. *Journal of Sex Research, 35*, 234–243. doi:10.1080/00224499809551938

O'Sullivan, L. F., & Allgeier, E. R. (1994). Dissembling a stereotype: Gender differences in the use of token resistance. *Journal of Applied Social Psychology, 24*, 1035–1055. doi:10.1111/j.1559-1816.1994.tb02372.x

O'Sullivan, L. F., Byers, E. S., & Finkelman, L. (1998). A comparison of male and female college students' experiences of sexual coercion. *Psychology of Women Quarterly, 22*, 177–195. doi:10.1111/j.1471-6402.1998.tb00149.x

Parker, I. (1992). *Discourse dynamics: Critical analysis for social and individual psychology*. London, England: Routledge.

Pateman, C. (1980). Women and consent. *Political Theory, 8*, 149–168.

Paul, E. L., McManus, B., & Hayes, A. (2000). Characteristics and correlates of college students' spontaneous and anonymous sexual experiences. *Journal of Sex Research, 37*, 76–88. doi:10.1080/00224490009552023

Paul, L. A., & Gray, M. J. (2011). Sexual assault programming on college campuses: Using social psychological belief and behavioral change principles to improve outcomes. *Trauma, Violence, and Abuse, 12*, 99–109. doi:10.1177/1524838010390710

Peterson, L. (2008). The not-rape epidemic. In J. Friedman & J. Valenti (Eds.), *Yes means yes: Visions of female sexual power and a world without rape* (pp. 209–220). Berkeley, CA: Seal.

Peterson, Z. D., & Muehlenhard, C. L. (2004). Was it rape? The function of women's rape myth acceptance and definitions of sex in labeling their own experiences. *Sex Roles, 51*, 129–144. doi:10.1023/B:SERS.0000037758.95376.00

Peterson, Z. D., & Muehlenhard, C. L. (2007). Conceptualizing the "wantedness" of women's consensual and nonconsensual sexual experiences: Implications for how women label their experiences with rape. *Journal of Sex Research, 44*, 72–88.

Peterson, Z. D., & Muehlenhard, C. L. (2011). A match-and-motivation model of how women label their nonconsensual sexual experiences. *Psychology of Women Quarterly, 35*, 558–570. doi:10.1177/0361684311410210

Petty, G. M., & Dawson, B. (1989). Sexual aggression in normal men: Incidence, beliefs, and personality characteristics. *Personality and Individual Differences, 10*, 355–362. doi:10.1016/0191-8869(89)90109-8

Piercy, M. (1985). Rape poem. In S. R. Sunday & E. Tobach (Eds.), *Violence against women: A critique of the sociobiology of rape* (p. ix). New York, NY: Gordian Press. (Original work published 1976)

Post, L. A., Biroscak, B., & Barboza, G. E. (2011). Prevalence of sexual violence. In J. White, M. P. Koss, & A. E. Kazdin (Eds.), *Violence against women and children, Vol. 1: Mapping the terrain* (pp. 101–123). Washington, DC: American Psychological Association. doi:10.1037/12307-005

Powers, L. E., Hughes, R. B., & Lund, E. M. (2009). *Interpersonal violence and women with disabilities: A research update.* Harrisburg, PA: National Resource Center on Domestic Violence/Pennsylvania Coalition against Domestic Violence.

Quaintance, L. (1996, July 5). Judge rebuked for comments, *New Zealand Herald,* p. 3.

Randall, M., & Haskell, L. (1995). Sexual violence in women's lives: Findings from the Women's Safety Project: A community-based survey. *Violence Against Women, 1,* 6–31. doi:10.1177/1077801295001 001002

Razack, S. H. (1998). *Looking White people in the eye: Gender, race, and culture in courtrooms and classrooms.* Toronto, Ontario, Canada: University of Toronto Press.

Rich, M. D. (2010). The interACT model: Considering rape prevention from a performance activism and social justice perspective. *Feminism and Psychology, 20,* 511–528. doi:10.1177/0959353510371366

Riger, S., & Gordon, M. T. (1981). The fear of rape: A study in social control. *Journal of Social Issues, 37,* 71–92. doi:10.1111/j.1540-4560.1981.tb01071.x

Rodríguez, J. I., Rich, M. D., Hastings, R., & Page, J. L. (2006). Assessing the impact of Augusto Boal's "Proactive performance": An embodied approach for cultivating prosocial responses to sexual assault. *Text and Performance Quarterly, 26,* 229–252. doi:10.1080/10462930600670614

Rozee, P. D., & Koss, M. P. (2001). Rape: A century of resistance. *Psychology of Women Quarterly, 25,* 295–311. doi:10.1111/1471-6402.00030

Rush, C. (2011, February 18). Cop apologizes for "sluts" remark at law school. *Toronto Star.* Retrieved from http://www.thestar.com/news/gta/2011/02/18/cop_apologizes_for_sluts_remark_at_law_school.html

Russell, D. E. H. (1975). *The politics of rape: The victim's perspective.* New York, NY: Stein & Day.

Russell, D. E. H. (1982). *Rape in marriage.* New York, NY: Collier Books.

Russell, D. E. H. (1984). *Sexual exploitation: Rape, child sexual abuse, and workplace harassment.* Beverly Hills, CA: Sage.

Ryan, K. M. (2004). Further evidence for a cognitive component of rape. *Aggression and Violent Behavior, 9,* 579–604. doi:10.1016/j.avb.2003.05.001

Sanday, P. R. (1990). *Fraternity gang rape.* New York, NY: New York University.

Schewe, P. A. (2002). Guidelines for developing rape prevention and risk reduction interventions. In P. A. Schewe (Ed.), *Preventing violence in relationships: Interventions across the life span* (pp. 107–136). Washington, DC: American Psychological Association. doi:10.1037/10455-005

Schewe, P. A. P., Adam, N. M., & Ryan, K. M. (2009). A qualitative analysis of the temptation to use force in sexual relationships. *Violence and Victims, 24,* 219–231. doi:10.1891/0886-6708.24.2.219

Schulhofer, S. J. (1998). *Unwanted sex: The culture of intimidation and the failure of law.* Cambridge, MA: Harvard University Press.

Schwartz, M. D., & Dekeseredy, W. S. (1997). *Sexual assault on the college campus: The role of male peer support.* Thousand Oaks, CA: Sage.

Segal, L. (1983). *Sensual uncertainty, or why the clitoris is not enough.* In S. Cartledge & J. Ryan (Eds.), *Sex and love* (pp. 30–47). London, England: Women's Press.

Segal, L. (1987). *Is the future female? Troubled thoughts on contemporary feminism.* London, England: Virago.

Seidman, I., & Vickers, S. (2004–2005). The second wave: An agenda for the next thirty years of rape law reform. *Suffolk University Law Review, 38,* 467–491.

Senn, C. Y. (2000). Violence. In L. Code (Ed.), *Routledge encyclopedia of feminist theories* (pp. 482–483). London, England: Routledge.

Senn, C. Y. (2011). An imperfect feminist journey: Reflections on the process to develop an effective sexual assault resistance programme for university women. *Feminism and Psychology, 21,* 121–137. doi:10.1177/0959353510386094

Senn, C. Y., Desmarais, S., Verberg, N., & Wood, E. (2000). Predicting coercive sexual behavior across the lifespan in a random sample of Canadian men. *Journal of Social and Personal Relationships, 17,* 95–113. doi:10.1177/0265407500171005

Senn, C. Y., & Dzinas, K. (1996). Measuring fear of rape: A new scale. *Canadian Journal of Behavioural Science/ Revue Canadienne des Sciences du Comportement, 28,* 141–144. doi:10.1037/0008-400X.28.2.141

Senn, C. Y., Gee, S., & Thake, J. (2011). Emancipatory sexuality education and sexual assault resistance: Does the former enhance the latter? *Psychology of Women Quarterly, 35,* 72–91. doi:10.1177/0361684310384101

Senn, C. Y., Saunders, K., & Gee, S. (2008). Walking the tightrope: Providing sexual assault resistance education for university women without victim blame. In S. Arcand, D. Damant, S. Gravel, & E. Harper (Eds.), *Violences faites aux femmes* (pp. 353–372). Quebec City, Quebec, Canada: Les Presses de Université du Québec.

Shannon, K., Kerr, T., Strathdee, S. A., Shoveller, J., Montaner, J. S., & Yndall, M. W. (2009). Prevalence and structural correlates of gender based violence among a prospective cohort of female sex workers. *BMJ, 339*, b2939. doi:10.1136/bmj.b2939

Shorter, E. (1977). On writing the history of rape. *Signs: Journal of Women in Culture and Society, 3*, 471–482. doi:10.1086/493478

Silbert, M. H. (1982). Prostitution and sexual assault: Summary of results. *International Journal for Biosocial Research, 3*, 69–71.

Simon, W., & Gagnon, J. (1986). Sexual scripts: Permanence and change. *Archives of Sexual Behavior, 15*, 97–120. doi:10.1007/BF01542219

Smart, C. (1995). *Law, crime and sexuality: Essays in feminism.* London, England: Sage.

Spitzberg, B. H. (1999). An analysis of empirical estimates of sexual aggression victimization and perpetration. *Violence and Victims, 14*, 241–260.

Stermac, L., Del Bove, G., & Addison, M. (2001). Violence, injury, and presentation patterns in spousal sexual assaults. *Violence Against Women, 7*, 1218–1233. doi:10.1177/10778010122183838

Stotzer, R. L. (2009). Violence against transgender people: A review of United States data. *Aggression and Violent Behavior, 14*, 170–179. doi:10.1016/j.avb.2009.01.006

Tang, K.-L. (1998). Rape law reform in Canada: The success and limits of legislation. *International Journal of Offender Therapy and Comparative Criminology, 42*, 258–270. doi:10.1177/0306624X9804200307

Taylor, J. (1987). Rape and women's credibility: Problems of recantations and false accusations echoed in the case of Cathleen Crowell and Gary Dotson. *Harvard Women's Law Journal, 10*, 59–116.

Tharp, A. T., DeGue, S., Lang, K., Valle, L. A., Massetti, G., Holt, M., & Matjasko, J. (2011). Commentary on Foubert, Godin, & Tatum (2010): The evolution of sexual violence prevention and the urgency of effectiveness. *Journal of Interpersonal Violence, 26*, 3383–3392. doi:10.1177/0886260510393010

Thornhill, R., & Palmer, C. T. (2000). *A natural history of rape: Biological bases of sexual coercion.* Cambridge, MA: MIT Press.

Tieger, T. (1981). Self-rated likelihood of raping and the social perception of rape. *Journal of Research in Personality, 15*, 147–158. doi:10.1016/0092-6566(81)90014-3

Tjaden, P., & Thoennes, N. (2000). *Full report of the prevalence, incidence, and consequences of violence against women: Findings from the National Violence Against Women Survey*. Washington, DC: U.S. Department of Justice, Office of Justice Programs.

Tolman, D. (2012). Female adolescents, sexual empowerment and desire: A missing discourse of gender inequity. *Sex Roles, 66*, 746–757. doi:10.1007/s11199-012-0122-x

Tolman, D. L. (2002). *Dilemmas of desire.* Cambridge, MA: Harvard University Press.

Tolman, D. L., Spencer, R., Rosen-Reynoso, M., & Porche, M. V. (2003). Sowing the seeds of violence in heterosexual relationships: Early adolescents narrate compulsory heterosexuality. *Journal of Social Issues, 59*, 159–178. doi:10.1111/1540-4560.t01-1-00010

Travis, C. B. (Ed.). (2003). *Evolution, gender, and rape.* Cambridge, MA: MIT Press.

Ullman, S. E. (2000). Psychometric characteristics of the social relations questionnaire: A measure of reactions to sexual assault victims. *Psychology of Women Quarterly, 24*, 257–271. doi:10.1111/j.1471-6402.2000.tb00208.x

Ullman, S. E. (2010). *Talking about sexual assault: Society's response to survivors.* Washington, DC: American Psychological Association. doi:10.1037/12083-000

Ullman, S. E., Filipas, H. H., Townsend, S. M., & Starzynski, L. L. (2006). The role of victim-offender relationship in women's sexual assault experiences. *Journal of Interpersonal Violence, 21*, 798–819. doi:10.1177/0886260506288590

Ullman, S. E., Filipas, H. H., Townsend, S. M., & Starzynski, L. L. (2007). Psychosocial correlates of PTSD symptom severity in sexual assault survivors. *Journal of Traumatic Stress, 20*, 821–831. doi:10.1002/jts.20290

Ullman, S. E., & Siegel, J. M. (1993). Victim-offender relationship and sexual assault. *Violence and Victims, 8*, 121–134.

Vandermassen, G. (2011). Evolution and rape: A feminist Darwinian perspective. *Sex Roles, 64*, 732–747. doi:10.1007/s11199-010-9895-y

Van de Velde, T. H. (1930). *Ideal marriage: Its physiology and technique* (S. Browne, Trans.). London, England: William Heinemann.

van de Zandt, P. (1998). Heroines of fortitude. In P. Easteal (Ed.), *Balancing the scales: Rape, law reform, and Australian culture* (pp. 124–142). Sydney, Australia: Federation Press.

Vannier, S. A., & O'Sullivan, L. F. (2010). Sex without desire: Characteristics of occasions of sexual compliance in young adults' committed relationships. *Journal of Sex Research, 47*, 429–439. doi:10.1080/00224490903132051

Vares, T., Potts, A., Gavey, N., & Grace, V. M. (2007). Reconceptualizing cultural narratives of mature women's sexuality in the Viagra era. *Journal of Aging Studies, 21*, 153–164. doi:10.1016/j.jaging.2006.08.002

Vigarello, G. (2001). *A history of rape: Sexual violence in France from the 16th to the 20th century*. Cambridge, England: Polity.

Vladutiu, C. J., Martin, S. L., & Macy, R. J. (2011). College- or university-based sexual assault prevention programs: A review of program outcomes, characteristics, and recommendations. *Trauma, Violence, and Abuse, 12*, 67–86. doi:10.1177/1524838010390708

Ward, T., & Siegert, R. (2002). Rape and evolutionary psychology: A critique of Thornhill and Palmer's theory. *Aggression and Violent Behavior, 7*, 145–168. doi:10.1016/S1359-1789(00)00042-2

Weihofen, H. (1959). Compensation for victims of criminal violence: A round table. *Journal of Public Law, 8*, 209–218.

Weinberg, M. S., Swensson, R. G., & Hammersmith, S. K. (1983). Sexual autonomy and the status of women: Models of female sexuality in U.S. sex manuals from 1950 to 1980. *Social Problems, 30*, 312–324. doi:10.2307/800356

Weis, K., & Borges, S. S. (1973). Victimology and rape: The case of the legitimate victim. *Issues in Criminology, 8*, 71–115.

Weiss, K. G. (2009). "Boys will be boys" and other gendered accounts: An exploration of victims' excuses and justifications for unwanted sexual contact and coercion. *Violence Against Women, 15*, 810–834. doi:10.1177/1077801209333611

White, A. M. (1999). Talking feminist talking black—Micromobilization processes in a collective protest against rape. *Gender and Society, 13*, 77–100. doi:10.1177/089124399013001005

White, A. M., Strube, M. J., & Fisher, S. (1998). A Black feminist model of rape myth acceptance: Implications for research and antirape advocacy in Black communities. *Psychology of Women Quarterly, 22*, 157–175. doi:10.1111/j.1471-6402.1998.tb00148.x

White, J. W., Koss, M. P., & Kazdin, A. E. (2011a). Conclusions and next steps. In J. W. White, M. P. Koss, & A. E. Kazdin (Eds.), *Violence against women and children, Vol. 1: Mapping the terrain* (pp. 287–310). Washington, DC: American Psychological Association.

White, J. W., Koss, M. P., & Kazdin, A. E. (Eds.). (2011b). *Violence against women and children, Vol. 1: Mapping the terrain*. Washington, DC: American Psychological Association.

White, J. W., & Smith, P. H. (2004). Sexual assault perpetration and reperpetration: From adolescence to young adulthood. *Criminal Justice and Behavior, 31*, 182–202. doi:10.1177/0093854803261342

Womersley, G., & Maw, A. (2009). Contextualising the experiences of South African women in the immediate aftermath of rape. *Psychology in Society, 38*, 40–60.

World Health Organization. (2002). *World report on violence and health: Summary*. Geneva, World Health Organization. Retrieved from http://www.who.int/violence_injury_prevention/violence/world_report/en/summary_en.pdf

Yeater, E. A., & O'Donohue, W. (1999). Sexual assault prevention programs: Current issues, future directions, and the potential efficacy of interventions with women. *Clinical Psychology Review, 19*, 739–771. doi:10.1016/S0272-7358(98)00075-0

Yuan, N. P., Koss, M. P., & Stone, M. (2006, March). *The psychological consequences of sexual trauma*. Harrisburg, PA: National Resource Center on Domestic Violence/Pennsylvania Coalition Against Domestic Violence. Retrieved from http://new.vawnet.org/Assoc_Files_VAWnet/AR_PsychConsequences.pdf

Zawacki, T., Abbey, A., Buck, P. O., McAuslan, P., & Clinton-Sherrod, A. M. (2003). Perpetrators of alcohol-involved sexual assaults: How do they differ from other sexual assault perpetrators and nonperpetrators? *Aggressive Behavior, 29*, 366–380. doi:10.1002/ab.10076

Part IV

SEXUALITY DEVELOPMENT

Chapter 13

LIFE-SPAN SEXUALITY THROUGH A SEXUAL HEALTH PERSPECTIVE

Devon J. Hensel and J. Dennis Fortenberry

In this chapter, we use *sexual health* as an organizing paradigm for a life course perspective on sexuality. *Sexual health* broadly refers to the functions of sex and sexuality in all stages of life, emphasizing enacted sexuality as a fundamental part of identity and a core element of health and well-being (Centers for Disease Control and Prevention, 2010; Pan American Health Organization & World Health Organization, 2000; World Health Organization [WHO], 2002). In distinguishing sexual health from sexuality, we refer to the ways in which the cultural, social, psychological, and biological constituents of sexuality are written into—and expressed by—individual bodies over a lifetime (see Chapter 25, this volume). Although not fully developed in this chapter, a sexual health perspective also allows us to explicitly link sexuality to more fundamental issues of sexual rights and sexual justice (see Volume 2, Chapters 8, 9, and 10, this handbook).

One challenge in undertaking a developmental approach to sexual health is appropriating a single working definition. Although several definitions have been used (W. M. Edwards & Coleman, 2004), the WHO (2002) has provided one of the most well-known and influential of these definitions, comprehensively outlining sexual health as

> a state of physical, emotional, mental and social well-being in relation to sexuality; it is not merely the absence of disease, dysfunction or infirmity. Sexual health requires a positive and respectful approach to sexuality and sexual relationships, as well as the possibility of having pleasurable and safe sexual experiences, free of coercion, discrimination and violence. (p. 11)

We use this definition in the current work, arguing that it both anchors and clarifies a life course understanding of sexual health in four important ways.

First, the sexual health perspective is multidimensional, organized, experienced, and expressed within an individual's beliefs and values, relationships, and behaviors as well as within larger contextual sociopolitical systems. This organization includes but, more importantly, transcends a limited focus on adverse outcomes (World Association of Sexuality, 2008; WHO, 2010). For example, decisions about contraceptive and condom use can reflect gender, class, and power dynamics or relationship-specific desires for intimacy and sexual pleasure (Higgins & Brown, 2008) in addition to concerns about preventing pregnancy or disease.

Second, the sexual health perspective emphasizes the ageless importance of sexuality, with different studies separately underscoring its salience during adolescence (Tolman & McClelland, 2011; see Chapter 15, this volume), early adulthood (Arnett, 2000; Boisard & Zimmer-Gembeck, 2011; Hensel, Newcamp, Miles, & Fortenberry, 2011; see Chapter 16, this volume), and later adulthood (Mulhall, King, Glina, & Hvidsten, 2008; Schick et al., 2010; see Chapter 17, this volume). Sex remains relevant in many relationships over many years and decades and as older relationships are replaced by newer relationships.

Third, sexual health embraces the continuity of sexuality, with movement in and out of different life stages bringing new experiences and new

http://dx.doi.org/10.1037/14193-013
APA Handbook of Sexuality and Psychology: Vol. 1. Person-Based Approaches, D. L. Tolman and L. M. Diamond (Editors-in-Chief)

developmental challenges in each stage (Pan American Health Organization & World Health Organization, 2000). For example, entering a new sexual relationship in early adulthood may carry with it different perceptions of sexual risk than new sexual relationships initiated in later adulthood.

Fourth, and perhaps most important, the sexual health perspective underscores the connectedness of sexuality, recognizing the interrelationships between early and later sexually related experiences. For example, although menarche and menopause are typically conceptualized as distinct, but separate, biological endpoints on a woman's reproductive continuum, emerging evidence has suggested that contextual effects, such as socioeconomic status and family structure, may influence the onset of both events in different ways (Mishra, Cooper, & Kuh, 2010). Likewise, the quality of an adolescent's relationship with his or her parents may have important long-term implications for the quality of the adolescent's relationship with future romantic or sexual partners.

These four characteristics of the sexual health perspective—multidimensionality, agelessness, continuity, and connectedness—articulate sexuality as a lifelong process, whereby participation in different types of experiences and behaviors provides important contexts of individual learning around sexuality at each life stage (Centers for Disease Control and Prevention, 2010; Fenton, 2010), with experiences in one stage linking to experiences in later stages (Jones & Barton, 2004; Nusbaum & Hamilton, 2002; Sandfort & Erhardt, 2004; WHO, 2007). Despite this broadened theoretical framework, only within the past decade has research on sexual health expanded out of an adult-age time frame and come to be viewed as a normative, and healthy, component of both adolescence and old age (e.g., DeLamater, 2012; Tolman & McClelland, 2011). An unfortunate consequence of this late-blooming inquiry is the lack of a cohesive, life-course view of sexual health, one that links development across the life stages.

Thus, in this chapter, we highlight the development of two core aspects of sexual health across the life course: partnering and sexual behavior. Although far from providing an exhaustive discussion of the entirety of life-span sexuality, in the absence of a compelling longitudinal model, we have purposefully focused this review by selecting meaningful threads that unite the life stages. These threads are important not only in their association to each other but also as constructs that highlight how sexuality changes within the unique developmental considerations in each stage. *Partnering* refers to the expectation, organization, and experience of sexuality in the context of interaction with significant others (Sassler, 2010; see Chapter 10, this volume). In this review, we describe how patterns of partnering change over the life course and how these changes influence the emotional, psychological, and behavioral orchestration of sexuality. *Sexual behaviors* describe the behavioral ways in which sexuality is expressed; in this review, these behaviors include, but are not limited to, partnered and nonpartnered behaviors as well as the absence of sexual behavior.

Comment is warranted regarding what we mean by *life stage*. We have chosen to describe partnering and sexual behavior within three life stages: adolescence, adulthood, and later life. We have chosen not to assign specific ages to these stages because considerable variability exists in the literature as to what constitutes the start and end of these periods. Rather, because sexuality is as much a social construct as an individual one, we use these socially meaningful intervals to point out how specific social changes within and between these stages contribute to an evolution in sexuality. Where appropriate, we point out how differences in specific ages associated with these stages (e.g., late adolescent vs. emerging adult or younger than 50 vs. older than 65) may add to understanding.

PARTNERING

In this section, we discuss partnering as a venue for sexual health across the life span. We purposely distinguish *partnering* from *partnership* as a means of capturing the ongoing variability in the timing, duration, and purpose of intimate relationships in relation to sexuality occurring in each life stage. One (or multiple) close relationships fulfill different needs, such as sex, intimacy, companionship, parenting, or self-actualization, at different points in time (Agnew, Arriaga, & Wilson, 2008), providing an ongoing understanding of one's self as a sexual person.

The past few decades have seen remarkable changes in the nature of intimate relationship formation as well as in the volume of empirical literature that describes these partnerships. Shifts in the timing and sequencing of relationship stages have expanded the way in which researchers consider relationships, moving from a framework that dichotomizes romantic attachments as either preceding or following heterosexual marriage to a framework acknowledging the many options for sexual partnering across the life course (Sassler, 2010). In industrialized societies, most individuals, across gender, race/ethnicity, sexual orientation, and other characteristics, can choose from casual, shorter term, or longer term relationships that may be monogamous or temporally concurrent or there may be a period in which an individual has no partner at all. For some, partnering may mean sharing a living situation as a precursor or as an alternative to marriage, and for others, partnering may mean maintaining separate residences.

An important aspect of a life-span perspective on partnering is that each partnership's form and content provide a context for the (re)learning and (re)organization of sexuality—and the experience of sexual health—during one's lifetime. The interpersonal interactions, individual or partner beliefs, and social norms that characterize each partnership provide a lens through which to view sexual health within the characteristics of each life stage. Changes in partnerships, both voluntary and involuntary, create opportunities for the new expression of old beliefs and behaviors. For example, in adolescence, the end of a relationship may mean the cessation of a brief coupling, whereas in adulthood or later life, the end of a relationship may mean the loss of a long-term partner through divorce or death. We suggest that although the terms we use to describe partnering phenomena may have different meanings across stages, their impact is equally felt and they are equally influential in sexual health in each life stage.

Moreover, partnering experiences in earlier stages inform the manner in which individuals perceive and experience partnerships in later life stages. For example, positive qualities of friendships and early romantic relationships in adolescence provide skills important to interpersonal emotion management in early adulthood (Simpson, Collins, Tran, & Haydon, 2007). Likewise, individuals entering into adulthood with a history of secure, nurturing partnerships may potentially be more willing and able to negotiate or accommodate a partner's preferences and desires, especially when making decisions about the relationship. To this end, in this section we review partnering patterns and transitions, describing the ways in which they both facilitate and constrain aspects of sexuality in adolescence, in adulthood, and in later life.

Adolescence

Adolescent relationships (and to some extent, emerging adult relationships) well exemplify development in the processes of partnering and sexual health because both are deeply entrenched in changes within an adolescent's social system. The first of these changes centers on diversification in a young person's patterns of interaction. In industrialized societies, interactions typically shift away from exclusively same-sex peer groups in preadolescence to concurrent same-sex and different-sex friendships in early and middle adolescence (Collins, 2003).

These shifts help facilitate the progression to later dyadic romantic relationships (Connolly, Craig, Goldberg, & Pepler, 2004). These close friendships provide lessons about the value of closeness, intimacy, and mutuality that are important in later romantic relationships (Furman & Shaffer, 2003). For example, positive same-sex friendship quality is linked to affection in (S. Shulman & Seiffge-Krenke, 2001) and quality of (Linder & Collins, 2005) romantic relationships. In middle adolescence, young people typically note increasing preoccupation with romantic feelings and emerging relationships, placing great emphasis on the role of these relationships in their lives (O'Sullivan, 2005). Finally, by late adolescence, many young people have experienced a serious romantic or sexual relationship (Carver, Joyner, & Udry, 2003; Collins, 2003). More recent work has also described how the number of uncommitted sexual relationships (or hook-ups) increase in late adolescence and emerging adulthood, particularly in the college population (e.g., Bogle, 2008).

Although much more is understood about the development of opposite-sex attraction in adolescence, knowledge about lesbian, gay, bisexual, and transgender (LGBT) youths in relationships is small but growing (see Chapter 19, this volume). Estimates of young men and young women reporting same-sex attraction, same-sex activity, or both vary widely (McCabe, Brewster, & Tillman, 2011; Pathela & Schillinger, 2010). Although the average age of a first serious same-sex relationship is 18 years (Floyd, 2002), many formative romantic experiences in adolescence involve both same- and opposite-sex partners (Collins, Welsh, & Furman, 2009). Developing literature has suggested that these choices can be separate from long-term identification with sexual orientation. For example, Lisa Diamond's (2008) work has suggested that sexuality is fluid between adolescence and adulthood, with fluctuations in same-sex and opposite-sex attraction, self-selected labels, and same-sex and opposite-sex sexual behaviors.

Partnering in adolescence also provides a context for first exposure to the types of experiences young people will need to manage sexual relationships later in life (Seiffge-Krenke, 2006). For example, earlier relationships contribute to the development of emotional skills in relationships, such as learning effective communication about one's needs (Stone & Ingham, 2002), negotiating conflict management (Giordano, Manning, & Longmore, 2010), managing verbal expressions of love and affection (O'Sullivan, 2005), balancing first explorations of sexual desire (Tolman, 2002), increasing intimacy and trust with questions around fidelity and relationship power (Bryan, Aiken, & West, 1997; Maticka-Tyndale, 1992; Wingood & DiClemente, 1998), and learning how to successfully end relationships (Giordano, Manning, Longmore, & Flanigan, 2012). At the same time, relationships provide for behavior experiences: behaviors such as hugging, kissing, hand-holding, and oral sex (Bay-Cheng, Robinson, & Zucker, 2009; Epstein, Calzo, Smiler, & Ward, 2009) emerge in early adolescent partnerships and become linked to more involved sexual behaviors (e.g., penile–vaginal intercourse) as a given relationship progresses or as a young person moves into subsequent relationships (O'Sullivan, Cheng, Harris, & Brooks-Gunn, 2007).

Some gender and racial/ethnic differences exist in the emergence of different emotional and behavioral skills. For example, young women often exhibit more confidence in navigating relationships than young men because the social dynamics contained in these relationships mimic those in prior friendships (Giordano et al., 2012). Young women appear to have more nuanced understanding of partnerships, ascribing different meanings to each relationship depending on the intent (e.g., sex only vs. long-term commitment) or the status of their partner (e.g., boyfriend vs. coparent; Nelson & Morrison-Beedy, 2008; Nelson, Morrison-Beedy, Kearney, & Dozier, 2011). Young men generally experience oral and vaginal sex earlier than female peers (Lammers, Ireland, Resnick, & Blum, 2000), and White adolescents typically have less sexual experience (e.g., ever having intercourse, numbers of partners) than ethnic minority peers (Santelli, Carter, Orr, & Dittus, 2009).

The partnering process remains important in emerging adulthood. This time frame, after secondary or high school, is commonly regarded as one in which individuals experience increased familial and legal autonomy yet have not yet reached other life transitions common in the mid- to late 20s (e.g., cohabitation, marriage, full-time employment). Giordano et al. (2012) additionally pointed out that emerging adulthood is also meaningful as a transition between adolescent relationships and the longer term partnerships observed among many adults. Their work illustrated that in the average span of 5 years, the movement out of teen dating relationships into early adult dating and early adult cohabiting relationships is marked by a decrease in communication awkwardness, greater confidence, increased sexual activity, and greater feelings associated with romantic love and other emotional rewards associated with the relationship (Giordano et al., 2012). Thus, compared with adolescent relationships, emerging adult relationships in this time frame reflect an increasing degree of investment and widening of skills accrued within early relationships. Reflecting on our earlier definition of sexual health, this means that accrual of emotional and behavioral experience contributes to higher levels of sexual health during the developmental transition from adolescence into adulthood.

A growing body of research has described the "friends with benefits" (FWB) relationship form, whereby adolescents and emerging adults regularly participate in sexual behaviors with friends. FWB combines attributes of both friendships and romantic relationships, joining the benefits of the psychological intimacy and trust afforded by a friendship with the sexual intimacy of a romantic relationship while avoiding the expectations of commitment or exclusivity often present in romantic relationships (Bisson & Levine, 2009; Hughes, Morrison, & Asada, 2005). FWB sexual activity also differs from hook-ups, or no-strings-attached sexual behavior (Bogle, 2008), which typically occurs once, usually between people who are strangers or acquaintances, but also without the expectations contained in a traditional romantic relationship (Paul & Hayes, 2002). Although FWB relationships are more often characterized as an emerging adult phenomenon (particularly among college students), they are also prevalent in adolescence and recognized by teenagers as distinctly different from romantic relationships and casual sex partners but not different from friendship except for sexual activity (Furman & Shaffer, 2011). The types of sexual behaviors shared in FWB encounters show wide variability, from kissing to manual–genital or oral–genital contact to penile–vaginal sex (Epstein et al., 2009; Furman & Shaffer, 2011; Olmstead, Pasley, & Fincham, 2012). These relationships may confer developmental benefits to sexuality compared with more committed relationships, such as providing a relatively safe and convenient environment to satisfy physical needs for sexual contact (Bisson & Levine, 2009). Some studies have suggested differences by class, particularly for emerging adult women, in perception of FWB relationships, suggesting that less privileged women, who are socialized into a faster track to adulthood, are less likely to endorse delaying commitment and participating in the hook-up culture (Hamilton & Armstrong, 2009). It is as yet unclear how long-term adult trajectories of sexuality differ among those with and without FWB experience in adolescence and emerging adulthood.

The diversity we have described is important in a life-course view of sexual health because the content of these experiences has important implications for positive sexuality in later life stages. For example, when controlling for parent and peer influences, adolescents with fewer partners and those with higher quality relationships were more likely to have higher quality emerging adult relationships (Collins & Madsen, 2006). Likewise, higher levels of depression in mid-adolescence are linked to greater relationship conflict and lower problem-solving skills in emerging adulthood (Vujeva, 2011). Moreover, better relationships in adolescence and emerging adulthood are linked to better long-term adult sexual health and well-being, including greater decision-making power (Cyranowski & Andersen, 1998), less sexual coercion (Abma, Driscoll, & Moore, 1998; Miller, Monson, & Norton, 1995; Nagy & DiClemente, 1995; Oliver & Hyde, 1993; Shrier, Pierce, Emans, & DuRant, 1998), higher condom use efficacy (Wingood & DiClemente, 2000), and lower unintended pregnancy (Fine, 1988).

In summary, partnering in adolescence contributes positively to both short- and long-term sexual health. Romantic relationships, which find their roots in early friendships, provide important venues for formative emotional and behavioral experiences. These experiences represent specific competencies around which subsequent partnerships are organized and evaluated.

Adulthood

Partnering in adulthood is fundamentally different from partnering in adolescence, not only in terms of relationship content, but also in terms of the benefits it provides to each member of the dyad. Compared with adolescent and emerging adult relationships, adult relationships are characterized by members' experience in prior relationships, longer relationship duration, and higher levels of commitment and interdependence (Miller & Benson, 1999). These types of positive, committed relationships are important for individuals' physical and mental well-being (Proulx, Helms, & Buehler, 2007; see also Chapter 11, this volume) in ways sometimes absent from adolescent relationships. Moreover, adolescents and emerging adults typically pursue partnerships with different goals than older single adults or previously married individuals (Sassler, 2010); for example, adolescents may choose partners on the basis of desire for sexual or intimate exploration or for the social status the relationship affords (Connolly & McIsaac, 2009), whereas adults may focus on a potential partner's emotional and financial compatibility for a long-term relationship (Barry, Madsen, Nelson, Carroll, & Badger, 2009), Finally, time horizons and desired ends also shape relationship behaviors among individuals of similar ages (Sassler, 2010). We describe these differences in more detail by evaluating two common relationship forms in this life stage: cohabitation and marriage.

Much of the past decade's literature has focused on the difference in the dynamics of cohabitation and marriage partnering forms. Concurrent with delay in the age at first marriage, cohabitation is an increasingly common partnering form, with differences in prevalence by completed education. One study of individuals in the United States has suggested that about two thirds of those with a high school education, compared with about 45% of those with some college, have lived with at least one romantic partner (Kennedy & Bumpass, 2008), with an average duration (14 months) shorter than that of several other Western countries (Heuveline & Timberlake, 2004). Many people use the cohabitation period as a barometer of marital compatibility, because slightly more than half of all cohabitations end in marriage (Goodwin, Mosher, & Chandra, 2010; Sassler, 2010). However, cohabitation is not an automatic precursor to marriage, suggesting that coresidence also emerges out of changes in employment or housing, out of convenience (Sassler, 2004), or in response to an unplanned pregnancy (Reed, 2006).

Some studies have shown that married couples typically fare better than cohabiting couples on a number of mental and social indicators (for a review, see Sassler, 2010). However, how sexuality emerges from within these typologies is far less clear. One might argue that because the very intent or focus in these relationships is different, one should also expect important differences in the ways individuals negotiate decisions about fertility, sexual behavior, and the like. For example, relationships formed around the intent to marry may have more forward-oriented communication, whereas more rapidly formed unions may preclude much discussion of the future (Smock, Manning, & Porter, 2005). In the long term, the impact of this difference may equip couples with a longer term orientation to have more frequent and more open communication about sexual preferences than couples whose focus is the here and now.

This sexual self-disclosure is a key element in long-term sexual satisfaction, because communication both enhances intimacy and closeness and allows partners to better understand each other's desires (Cupach & Metts, 1995). Among heterosexual couples in committed long-term relationships, better individual and partner sexual self-disclosure was associated with greater levels of sexual satisfaction (Rehman, Rellini, & Fallis, 2011). Likewise, another study of committed couples found that better sexual communication and better relationship quality were associated with better sexual satisfaction (Timm & Keiley, 2011). Moreover, relationship quality, inclusive of relationship happiness, is associated with significantly lower rates of relationship dissolution for both cohabiting and married couples (Yabiku & Gager, 2009). This hardiness can prove to be important: Although cohabiting couples typically report higher monthly sexual frequency than married couples (Michael, Gagnon, Laumann, & Kolata, 1994), other work has suggested they are also more likely to end the relationship when sexual frequency is low, perhaps because they lack the same resource set (e.g., stress management) as married couples (Yabiku & Gager, 2009).

Race/ethnicity and sexual orientation are also important contexts in which these resources are negotiated. For example, financial hardship has been associated with reduced relationship satisfaction, particularly among African Americans (Cutrona, Russell, Burzette, Wesner, & Bryant, 2011). Additionally, other work has noted that committed gay and lesbian couples have levels of relationship satisfaction and relationship resources comparable to those of heterosexual married couples (Kurdek, 1995). A clinical study suggested that same-sex couples have more quality interactions than married couples (Gottman et al., 2003), whereas other studies have found no difference between committed gay, lesbian, and married heterosexual couples (Julien, Chartrand, Simard,

Bouthillier, & Begin, 2003; Roisman, Clausell, Holland, Fortuna, & Elieff, 2008).

In summary, partnering in adulthood, although different in content and purpose than in adolescence or in later life, still has important implications for sexual health. Relationships in this life stage, which build on the experience of adolescence, lasting longer and involving more commitment than relationships in younger years, confer mental and physical health benefits to their members.

Later Life

In this section, we review the nascent literature describing partnering in later life (see Chapter 17, this volume). An important challenge around a body of knowledge in its infancy is the dearth of detail necessary to describe the dynamics of how sexuality is enacted within specific partnerships and how these choices may link back to earlier relationships. Although it is becoming clear that sexuality is a salient aspect of identity and well-being among those in their aging years, it is less clear how specific aspects of sexuality (such as sexual orientation or sexual desire) affect the ways in which people select and organize close relationships in this time frame.

An important focus for emerging research in this area will be to consider the impact of historical context on sexuality and partnering. For example, although those currently in adolescence and adults have come of age in a time of lessening negativity toward LGBT individuals and toward partnering forms that do not include marriage or children, individuals now reaching old age represent a generation who lived through times when same-sex desires or relationships and nonmarital or childless partnerships were stigmatized and, for the former, criminalized. Only since the 1960s, when the current elder cohort was already in mid-adulthood, have civil rights movement ideals encouraged the cultural acceptance of relationships that were not heterosexual or did not include traditional marriage or children (Fredriksen-Goldsen & Muraco, 2010; Park, 2002).

These patterns have considerably challenged what is known about the variety of partnering experiences in this cohort (DeLamater, 2012). Not surprisingly, several national and international studies have suggested that marriage remains the most common partnering type into later life (Kontula & Haavio-Mannila, 2009; Lindau et al., 2007; Waite, Laumann, Das, & Schumm, 2009), both overall and across different racial/ethnic groups (Calasanti & Kiecolt, 2007). Although some of the individuals in these marriages may be heterosexual, it is worth emphasizing that heterosexual marriage and same-sex preference are not necessarily independent. In several samples, approximately one third of the gay men older than age 55 (and as many as one half of lesbians in that age group) reported a previous marriage to an opposite-sex spouse (e.g., Herdt & McClintock, 2000), perhaps associated with common generational expectations earlier in life. Little is known, however, about how these marriages may have influenced their current relationship choices.

However, at the same time, because of longer life spans, the number of divorces and proportions of those never married, those entering or reentering (Calasanti & Kiecolt, 2007; King & Scott, 2005; Sassler, 2010), or those wanting to enter or reenter (Carr, 2004; Mahay & Lewin, 2007) intimate relationships in later life is increasing. Few aging individuals choose to cohabit: Studies from the United States and from Europe have suggested that establishing a joint residence accounts for less than 10% of men's or women's partnering patterns past age 65 (Kontula & Haavio-Mannila, 2009; Waite et al., 2009). In comparison to younger peers, older individuals who do choose to cohabit usually do so as an alternative, rather than as a precursor to, marriage or remarriage (Sassler, 2010), but typically report more equitable, happier, and more stable and harmonious relationships than do younger cohabiting couples (King & Scott, 2005). Such equity may have an important influence on how sexuality is (or is not) a part of these relationships; however, research has typically emphasized the declines in sexual function and desire during the later stages of life rather than seeking to understanding how changes in relationship forms may also enhance sexuality between dyad members (Kingsberg, 2000).

Recent work has also identified that many people in the later life stage are "living apart together" (LAT); that is, participating in an intimate relationship while maintaining separate residences. LAT relationships are viewed as a means of balancing a shared, intimate life with autonomy and independence in taking care of children or older parents (Haskey & Lewis, 2006), as a means of maintaining separate finances, or as a way of staying near family and friends instead of moving in with a partner (de Jong Gierveld & Hagestad, 2006). About 10% of men and women older than age 65 are reported to be in an LAT relationship (Kontula & Haavio-Mannila, 2009). LAT partnerships may also provide benefits for sexuality, allowing a connection between individuals without the stress of trying to legally integrate two lifestyles. Indeed, research has suggested that the healthiest relationships are those in which a couple is close but have autonomous and differentiated identities (Kingsberg, 2000).

Gender exerts an important influence on partnering during later life. Women are generally less likely to be part of a couple than men, particularly at the oldest end of the age spectrum (Heaphy, Yip, & Thompson, 2004; Kontula & Haavio-Mannila, 2009; Lindau et al., 2007; Waite et al., 2009). In Western countries, women typically live about 5 years longer than men (Austad, 2006; Waite et al., 2009); by age 85, this means there are two women for every one man (U.S. Census Bureau, 2010). Among heterosexuals, this shortage both reduces the number of monogamous partners available to women and shortens the amount of time a woman may be able to spend in a partnership (Karraker, DeLamater, & Schwartz, 2011; Sassler, 2010). Similar age difference patterns have been observed in older adults' same-sex relationships (Bennett & Gates, 2004)

Partnerships in later life confer similar benefits on sexuality as do those in earlier life stages. For example, some work has suggested that new relationships for women in later life can bring sexual satisfaction and emotional intimacy absent from earlier relationships (Hurd Clarke, 2006). Individuals may also choose nonmarital relationships as a means of obtaining the benefits of long-term physical or emotional intimacy without the sacrifices associated with partner caregiving (de Jong Gierveld & Hagestad, 2006). Individuals in LAT relationships perceive moderate to high levels of support from their partners but report less instrumental support than do those who are married or cohabiting (Hurd Clarke, 2006). Additionally, adults older than age 60 have reported seeking new relationships in later life specifically as a means of receiving emotional and sexual equality in relationships (Malta & Farquharson, 2012). A more specific description of sexual behavior within older relationships is detailed in the next section.

In summary, a young but developing body of literature has confirmed the changing face of partnering in the later life stage. Intimate relationships remain an important piece of sexual health in the 6th decade of life and beyond, with increasing numbers of individuals entering or reentering partnerships amid changes in expected longevity, marriage length, and prevalence of individuals who never marry. Commensurate with scholarship on relationships in the adolescent and adult life stages, later life relationships have been found to provide important benefits to their members. As this area of inquiry continues to grow, we hope research will illuminate additional details of the development of partnerships in this time frame, particularly with respect to mechanisms of partner selection and the long-term experience of those who are LGBT.

SEXUAL BEHAVIOR

In this section, we discuss another key venue of sexual health: sexual behavior. We begin by arguing that the past decade's research on sexual behavior, in regard to any point in the life span, has seen two important developments in consideration of the question "What is sex?" The first of these developments is a movement toward a more inclusive behavioral definition, one that transcends a traditional focus on penile–vaginal intercourse as sex to consider how different types of intimate contact with partners (e.g., kissing, hugging, holding hands, genital touching, oral sex, or penile–anal sex), nonpartnered behaviors (e.g., solo masturbation), and the absence of any behavior that may be considered sexual behavior. The second of these developments places emphasis on how a specific context helps to give rise to, organize, and assign meaning to specific behaviors. Within a life course perspective, these developments are key pieces to understanding how specific behaviors may be differently selected (or omitted) across life stages as a function of opportunities or constraints within a specific life stage. For example, limitations on sex in adolescence may be constructed around the desire to postpone sexual activity for a specific time or event (e.g., a serious relationship or for after marriage), or it may refer to the ways in which young people orchestrate intimate contact within the boundaries of parental supervision and curfews. In later life, the salience of limitation may be expressed in terms of declining physical health, especially after age 60. Likewise, sex may serve different interpersonal functions with different partners at different times in one's life, perhaps as a means of having a child or as a means of increasing intimacy in a relationship. To this end, we review the content, frequency, and meaning of specific behaviors, particularly as positioned within the social and historical framework of a specific life stage.

Absence of Sexual Behavior

We have purposefully chosen to use the term *absence* rather than one of the more often used cultural terms (e.g., *abstinence* or *celibacy*) as a means of highlighting the definitional ambiguity that occurs when one describes how people voluntarily or involuntarily opt out of sex. As we describe in more detail, even the term *absence* itself is somewhat misleading, assuming an all-or-none dichotomy rather than accurately describing how (and why) precisely which behaviors are (and are not) removed from a person's sexual repertoire.

An important pitfall of this oversimplification is the incorrect assumption of similarity between the absence of sexual behavior among adolescents, adults, and older adults and this absence among younger children (de Graaf & Rademakers, 2011; Rademakers, Rademakers, & Straver, 2003; see Chapter 14, this volume). For children, *absence* is an inappropriate concept because they have not yet developed cognitions about sex to make such decisions a relevant choice (Reynolds & Herbenick, 2003). However, absence in life stages beyond childhood is defined by behavioral choice, whether that choice is associated with an adolescent's views regarding the appropriate context of first sex or with how an older couple manages diminished desire or physical capacity.

During adolescence, particularly in the United States, the absence of sexual behavior is often couched in one of two applications of the word *abstinence*. As described in a review on abstinence (Santelli et al., 2006), in the behavioral sense, a perspective often used by developmental researchers and health researchers, *abstinence* refers to either the postponement of sex (often penile–vaginal) or refraining from sexual activity after its initiation. In contrast, as used by some government and religious institutions, abstinence is frequently defined in moral terms, using language such as *chastity* or *virginity* to describe the attitudes or commitments young people voluntarily make to postpone sex until marriage (Goodson, Buhi, & Dunsmore, 2006; Santelli et al., 2006). As described in more detail later, research has suggested that considerable variability exists in how adolescents themselves interpret and express these two definitions.

Culturally, the absence of sex is constructed differently in the adult and aging adult life stages. Among adults, because sexual activity is an expected component of long-term relationships (J. Edwards & Booth, 1994), its absence is scripted as an involuntary choice, particularly as an unintended side effect of different events, such as after childbirth (Pauls, Occhino, & Dryfhout, 2008) or in the management of different medical problems, such as HIV (Bogart et al., 2006) or cancer (Sadovsky et al., 2010). Conversely, even amid a growing understanding of the importance of sexuality in the latest parts of life (Bradford & Meston, 2007), stereotypes still invoke a presumed asexuality of old age in which the "natural" cessation of sexual activity is welcomed by individuals (Bradford & Meston, 2007; Hyde et al., 2010). As we suggest in this section, however, individuals themselves differ considerably in their evaluation of a cessation of sexual activity, the reasons why it happens, and the impact of this cessation on their understanding of sexuality.

One challenge in understanding the organization of sexual behavior is appropriating a clear definition for when sex does and does not occur, particularly in terms of accurately estimating behavior prevalence. This difficulty is especially the case in the adolescent stage. Indeed, most research has suggested that adolescents frequently report no oral, vaginal, or penile–anal sex (Hensel, Fortenberry, & Orr, 2008). As described earlier, however, most research describing any kind of absence of sexual behavior in adolescence has primarily been constructed around behavioral or moral definitions of *abstinence*. One qualitative study of adolescent men and women, primarily African American, at high risk for unintended pregnancy and sexually transmitted infection, showed that the majority of young people conceptualize abstinence in terms of the primary abstinence, meaning an absence of lifetime intercourse experience (Ott, Millstein, Ofner, & Halpern-Felsher, 2006). Other studies, however, have suggested that secondary abstinence (sexual experiences followed by periods without sexual activity) is a common phenomenon among some adolescents and emerging adults (Loewenson, Ireland, & Resnick, 2004). Many secondary abstainers still participate in other partnered sexual behaviors such as kissing, breast fondling, genital stimulation, and oral sex. Some gender differences exist in these patterns, with young women more likely than men to view vaginal sex as counting as sexual experience and White youths more likely than Black youths to view penile–anal sex as abstinence (Bersamin, Fisher, Walker, Hill, & Grube, 2007). Among a sample of university students, men were more likely to adopt a narrower definition of abstinence than female peers, including an absence of manual–genital stimulation (Byers, Henderson, & Hobson, 2009).

The focus on abstinence as a voluntary sexual behavior is additionally supported by abstinence pledge research. Research using the National Longitudinal Study of Youth found that although pledgers typically delayed first sex (defined as first penile–vaginal sex) 6 months longer than nonpledgers (Bearman & Brückner, 2001), almost a third of those with prior intercourse experience "reclaimed" sexual virginity by the subsequent wave (Rosenbaum, 2006). A qualitative study of young adults in the United States has supported this idea, noting that although most participants generally refuted the idea of secondary virginity, more women than men and more Latinos than Whites, Asians, or African Americans believed that it might be possible under some circumstances (Carpenter, 2011). Some research has speculated that young people are less likely to classify a behavior as counting as abstinence if they have an orgasm (Byers et al., 2009).

Both adolescents and emerging adults articulate benefits to primary and secondary abstinence, including social or health risk avoidance (Longmore, Eng, Giordano, & Manning, 2009; Morrison-Beedy, Carey, Côté-Arsenault, Seibold-Simpson, & Robinson, 2008; Ott, Pfeiffer, & Fortenberry, 2006) and commitment to self or one's morals (Morrison-Beedy et al., 2008; Ott et al., 2006c). Abstinence is also chosen by young people because of peer or parental pressure (Longmore et al., 2009) as well as to save their virginity for their future spouse (Abbott & Dalla, 2008). Younger adolescents have described abstinence as a normal aspect of a continuum that uses developmental readiness as a standard for motivated decisions for shifting from sexually abstinent activity to sexual activity (Ott, Pfeiffer, & Fortenberry, 2006). Middle and late adolescents combine conceptual ideas of abstinence, such as commitment and doing the right thing, with behavioral ideas of abstinence, including avoiding sexual activity (Forste & Haas, 2002; Goodson, Suther, Pruitt, & Wilson, 2003).

Similar definitional variability exists in the adult and aging adult life stages regarding what constitutes an absence of sex. For example, using a definition of "no vaginal intercourse," the National Survey of Sexual Health and Behavior (NSSHB) found that between 13% and 50% of adult women and between 15% and 40% of adult men in the United States were without sex in the past year (Herbenick et al., 2010c; Reece et al., 2010). In the same data, with the same definition, these proportions were higher in older age groups, with more women than men in the 60- to 69-year-old age group (58.1% vs. 46.3%) and in the 70-and-older age group (77.1% vs. 51.1%) reporting no vaginal intercourse in the past year (Herbenick et al., 2010b, 2010c; Reece et al., 2010; Schick et al., 2010). Alternatively, about 60% of a sample of 75- to 95-year-old men in Australia reported that they generally had no sexual activity in the past year (Hyde et al., 2010). Similar proportions of absence, with different definitions, have been seen in studies from several countries (Kontula & Haavio-Mannila, 2009; Lindau et al., 2007;

Michael et al., 1994; Nettleman, Ingersoll, & Ceperich, 2006; Palacios-Ceña et al., 2012; Waite et al., 2009).

An additional challenge arising from these varied definitions is understanding the perceptions of or motivations for the absence of sex in adult and aging individuals' lives. As suggested earlier, because sexual activity is an expected aspect of adult long-term relationships (J. Edwards & Booth, 1994), it is often presumed that the cessation of sex, or even irregular patterns of sex, are viewed as involuntary by different individuals. Emerging research, however, has supported the idea that in many adult relationships, sex is absent or erratic, with different evaluations of this absence depending on the member in question (Donnelly & Burgess, 2008). Moreover, only recently has the presumed asexuality of old given way to the recognition that sexuality remains an important component of relationships well into the latest parts of life (Hyde et al., 2010). Long-standing assumptions about sexual behavior and the aging process have typically described a "natural" decrease in sexual activity with increasing age, through which individuals voluntarily "sexually retire" (Gott, 2006) amid health issues, partnering changes, or both (for a review, see DeLamater, 2012). More recently, an exciting body of literature has emerged, confirming that although permanent or sporadic periods of sexual absence are a reality for some people, others integrate sexuality within the unique challenges of this life stage (DeLamater & Moorman, 2007; Gott & Hinchliff, 2003).

For example, declines in vaginal lubrication and elasticity of vaginal tissue in later life may make sexual activity uncomfortable for women, and erectile difficulty may make penile–vaginal intercourse more difficult for men (Trudel, Turgeon, & Piche, 2010). In either case, the use of sexual medications or the replacement of penile–vaginal intercourse with oral–genital sex may be possible. Additionally, common chronic illnesses in older age, as well as the medications used to treat them, can contribute to lower sexual desire, less sexual activity, or both in some men and women (DeLamater & Sill, 2005; Lindau & Gavrilova, 2010; Lindau et al., 2007; L. J. Smith, Mulhall, Deveci, Monaghan, & Reid, 2007). Likewise, caring for a spouse with a chronic condition such as Alzheimer's disease might influence one's sexual life to a greater extent depending on the level of stress introduced by the condition (Burgess, 2004). In response, some individuals may reprioritize the value placed on sex in light of different physical or mental challenges, whereas others adapt their sexual routine within the confines of these challenges (DeLamater & Moorman, 2007; Howard, O'Neill, & Travers, 2006; Kontula & Haavio-Mannila, 2009).

For individuals in either the adult or the aging adult life stage, partnering status and the dynamics of partnering have a major influence on the type and frequency of sexual abstinence. For example, the NSSHB, a cross-sectional survey of sexual behaviors and attitudes of individuals ages 14 to 94 years, has noted a decreased likelihood of any vaginal sex in the past year among unpartnered adult men and women in all age ranges, with the greatest discrepancies noted in the 30- to 39-year-old age range and, among those who were single, in the 60-and-older age range (Herbenick et al., 2010b, 2010c; Reece et al., 2010; Schick et al., 2010). Although the effects of partnership are similar across both life stages, the midlife shift may reflect a delay in first marriage or a transition between relationships, whereas the latter, particularly for aging women, is likely to reflect paucity in partner availability after the death of a spouse (Sassler, 2010). Within adult relationships, sexual activity may also temporarily cease during late pregnancy, immediately after childbirth, or both (De Judicibus & McCabe, 2002). Additionally, after menopause some women slow in their sexual activity, finding less interest in sex (Dillaway, 2005). Calling the absence of sex *celibacy* (broadly defined as the absence of intimate sexual contact), a qualitative study of married or long-term heterosexual couples in involuntarily celibate relationships (Donnelly & Burgess, 2008) has suggested within-relationship patterns of celibacy are variable, including a gradual slow down, an abrupt slow down, or little sexual activity ever. In this study, all participants identified negative outcomes from celibacy; those opting to remain in relationships despite the celibacy did so because of stronger nonsexual benefits (e.g., support and love), lack of alternative residence, or social proscription of relationship dissolution. In another study, short-term voluntary absence of sex among high-risk women was associated in one study with older age, no sexually transmitted infection or history of drug use, and not being married or pregnant (Nettleman et al., 2006).

In summary, we have suggested the importance of considering the absence of sex in the spectrum of sexual behaviors available to people across the life span. We highlighted the considerable definitional ambiguity around what is meant when people say they do not have sex, emphasizing that these meanings are constructed in ways illustrating both the characteristics unique to each life stage and the relationships in which the absence occurs. For adolescents, this absence is intimately intertwined with behavioral and moral descriptions of abstinence, particularly in terms of penile–vaginal sex. As young people themselves describe, however, wide variability exists in how individuals view precisely what this means, often substituting other behaviors. In contrast, adult relationships are often judged on the presence of sex, with its absence, irregularity, or periodic cessation viewed as something involuntarily chosen by members in a relationship. Finally, we note the shifting assumptions about the increasing absence of sex in the aging population, suggesting that individuals construct sexual lives around changing relationship forms and the limitations of physical and mental health.

Solo Masturbation

In this section, we discuss the organization of solo masturbation across the life span. We differentiate between masturbation that occurs with an individual by him- or herself and that which occurs with a partner. We do this as a means of illustrating how aspects of sexuality are enacted within specific behavioral opportunities and constraints.

Of all sexual behaviors, solo masturbation tends to be the most difficult to study because it carries a long history of stigmatization and association with immorality or pathology (Rye & Meaney, 2007). For the most part, the latter has lessened considerably, but many social and gender norms still proscribe masturbation, particularly among women (Gagnon & Simon, 1987; Pinkerton, Bogart, Cecil, & Abramson, 2003). Nevertheless, evidence has suggested that it is a widespread behavior across all life stages and is increasingly being endorsed as a means of promoting sexual development and sexual health (Coleman, 2003). For example, in contrast to partnered sexual behaviors, which may be orchestrated around a variety of different needs (e.g., emotional intimacy, reproduction, making money), solo masturbation may be a relatively easy way to focus solely on meeting one's personal sexual needs (Rye & Meaney, 2007). Moreover, solo masturbation has also increased in visibility as a safe-sex alternative when there is a risk of sexually transmitted infection or pregnancy (Coleman, 2003).

Most retrospective data have suggested that onset of masturbation occurs somewhere between ages 13 and 15 (Pinkerton, Cecil, Bogart, & Abramson, 2003), with reported frequencies from the NSSHB varying for young men between a few times a week to a few times per year, and the majority of young women (45.5%) masturbating a few times per year (Robbins et al., 2011). The majority of adults have lifetime experience with masturbation (Gerressu, Mercer, Graham, Wellings, & Johnson, 2008; Laumann, Gagnon, Michael, & Michaels, 2000; Pinkerton, Cecil, et al., 2003; A. M. A. Smith, Rosenthal, & Reichler, 1996). Data from the NSSHB for adults 18 to 59 years old have shown that about 60% of men and 40% of women solo masturbated in the past 90 days. Frequency of masturbation typically increases when people perceive social norms in support of it (Pinkerton, Cecil, et al., 2003). Although masturbation generally decreases with age, with the lowest past-90-days prevalence in the 70 and older age group (men, 35.8%; women, 16.1%), these data do show that a considerable proportion of people masturbate throughout their lives (Herbenick et al., 2010b; Reece et al., 2010). Other research in the aging population has generally supported these data (Kontula & Haavio-Mannila, 2009; Palacios-Ceña et al., 2012).

Solo masturbation may also have several important influences on developing sexuality, serving as an important means of learning about one's body and sexual responsiveness (Atwood & Gagnon, 1987; Kaestle & Allen, 2011). Work among late adolescent women has shown that individuals with negative masturbation experiences typically also had negative first sexual experiences with penile–vaginal sex, with only a minority of women (25%) finding masturbation enjoyable and rewarding (Hogarth & Ingham, 2009). Among emerging adult women, childhood and adolescent masturbation has been linked to positive later sexual experiences (Reynolds & Herbenick, 2003), better self-image (J. L. Shulman & Home, 2003), romantic and sexual relationship development, and positive sexual self-discovery (Kaestle & Allen, 2011). Young women with a history of masturbation and noncoital orgasmic responsiveness had higher levels of sexual subjectivity, felt more entitled to sexual pleasure through masturbation, were more efficacious in achieving pleasure, and reflected more on the sexual aspects of their lives than those who had never experienced a noncoital orgasm. Moreover, these women were more expressive in their intimate relationships and more resistant to gendered double standards (Horne & Zimmer-Gembeck, 2005). Less is known about this link in young or adult men.

Masturbation is also related to other sexual behavior across the lifetime, either in lieu of other behavior or in tandem with other behavior. For example, among young people, solo masturbation may serve as a method of sexual exploration for those not wishing to experience other types of sex. Likewise, masturbation may be one way of experiencing pleasure in the face of personal or partner health issues that prevent other sexual behaviors. For example, NSSHB data on people older than 65 have suggested that men in poor health reported a higher frequency of masturbation than men in good health (Schick et al., 2010); additionally, solo masturbation was highest across most age groups of adult men and women older than 18 years who did not have a partner (Herbenick et al., 2010b; Reece et al., 2010).

Moreover, solo masturbation may also occur as a prelude to sexual intercourse (Laumann et al., 2000) or as a follow-up to partnered sexual activities that were not sexually fulfilling (Das, 2007), or it may be introduced as part of an expanding set of dyadic sexual behaviors. For example, among 14- to 17-year-old adolescent men and women, those reporting masturbation in the past year also reported higher levels of giving and receiving oral sex, penile–vaginal intercourse, and penile–anal intercourse (Robbins et al., 2011). A study of postpartum women found that solo masturbation plays an important role in sexuality after birth, representing the behavior to which women returned most quickly and the behavior from which participants derived the most sexual pleasure as compared to partnered activities (Hipp, Kane Low, & van Anders, 2012).

In summary, we have suggested that although often overlooked as a relevant sexual behavior, solo masturbation is an important component of lifelong sexual health. Despite a history of social stigmatization, solo masturbation is widely reported in all life stages, serving developmental and exploratory functions in adolescence as well as substitutive and enhancement functions in adulthood and during later life. Although most research has focused on oral sex organized around the penis or vagina, emerging work has suggested that oral- and anal-focused sex are also components of people's sexual behavior set.

Oral Sex

As with many other sexual behaviors, the term *oral sex* can refer to one of a number of different practices and takes on different meanings depending on the context in which it occurs. Broadly speaking, oral sex invokes sexual contact involving genital stimulation—to the vagina, penis, or anus—by the use of the mouth, tongue, teeth, or throat (J. Edwards & Booth, 1994). Although many oral sexual behaviors are commonly practiced by individuals of different sexual orientations across all life stages (Rye & Meaney, 2007), research has most commonly focused on oral sex involving the vagina or penis. As we suggest in this section, the absence of shared meaning creates challenges for accurately estimating both the prevalence of oral sex across different life stages and disentangling the various motivations by which people choose it alone or in conjunction with other sexual behaviors (Hans, Gillen, & Akande, 2010).

Among adolescents, the prevalence, frequency, and timing of both behaviors differs with age (Brewster & Tillman, 2008). Retrospective data from the NHSSB (Fortenberry et al., 2010), which did not differentiate partner gender, and other data from the National Survey of Family Growth (NSFG; Copen,

Chandra, & Martinez, 2012), which focused on opposite-sex partners, have suggested that for young people receiving oral sex is more common than giving oral sex. Within both of these studies, however, notable gender patterns emerged, with fewer young women receiving oral sex (NHSSB, 13.2%; NSFG, 28.3%) than young men (NHSSB, 17.3%; NSFG, 35.1%) and more young women giving oral sex (NHSSB, 15.2%; NSFG, 27.4%) than young men (NHSSB, 11.7%; NSFG, 24.2%). Prospectively collected daily diary data collected from 14- to 17-year-old adolescent women suggested a pattern opposite that of the NHSSB and NSFG data: On days when any oral sex was reported, more days were associated with receiving oral sex than with giving oral sex (Hensel et al., 2008). A study of adolescent and emerging adult gays, lesbians, and bisexuals suggested the occurrence of both oral and oral–anal behaviors in the past 3 months (Schrimshaw, Rosario, Meyer-Bahlburg, & Scharf-Matlick, 2006). Another study of Australian male and female youths suggested very few adolescents report any oral sex with same-sex partners only or with opposite-sex and same-sex partners (VandeCreek, Peterson, & Bley, 2007). Little is known about oral–penile–anal sex in young people.

The NSSHB (Herbenick et al., 2010b; Reece et al., 2010) suggested that among adults ages 18 to 59 in the past 90 days, about a fifth of men received oral sex from a woman and fewer (10%–20%) gave oral sex to a woman. Fewer women (2%–23%) gave oral sex to men or received it (2%–15%) from men. In the same NSSHB data, more men than women older than age 50 had both given (37.1% vs. 25.8%) and received (39.3% vs. 23.6%) oral sex in the past 90 days (Schick et al., 2010). Estimates among men and women older than age 65 in Spain have suggested lower prevalence of oral sex, but similar gender patterns (Palacios-Ceña et al., 2012). Although data explicitly examining oral–anal prevalence in adults are scarce, one review (McBride & Fortenberry, 2010) suggested that 51% of adult men and 43% of adult women had participated in at least one act of oral–penile–anal sex.

Oral sex may serve different emotional, physical, and social functions across the life span. For example, oral sex is perceived as providing social status enhancement, with nearly one quarter of adolescents reporting elevated popularity as a reason to participate in oral sex (Brewster & Tillman, 2008; Cornell & Halpern-Felsher, 2006; Halpern-Felsher, Cornell, Kropp, & Tschann, 2005). Young people rate peers with oral sex experience as more popular than those without such experience (Bersamin et al., 2007; Prinstein, Meade, & Cohen, 2003). Teens often perceive oral–genital sex as more acceptable than penile–vaginal sex, with many adolescents anticipating experiencing it in the future (Halpern-Felsher et al., 2005). Some work has differentiated motivations in terms of giving or receiving oral sex. For example, in one study, although adolescent women believed that male partners prefer to receive fellatio over performing cunnilingus, they concurrently believed their male partners also desired, wanted, and enjoyed cunnilingus as much as they themselves did (Bay-Cheng & Fava, 2011).

In emerging adulthood, perceptions about oral sex appear to shift away from a social emphasis toward an emotional one. Women report significantly more emotional and love motivations for oral sex–only sexual encounters than do male peers (Vannier & O'Sullivan, 2010). Most college students rate oral sex as an intimate experience (Chambers, 2007); as confirmed in a qualitative study of college women (Backstrom, Armstrong, & Puentes, 2012), those with a positive evaluation of cunnilingus dually emphasized the emotional aspects of oral sex, particularly in its effectiveness in providing sexual pleasure and orgasm.

The prevalence and evaluation of oral sex is also strongly influenced by the type of relationship in which it happens. For example, in the context of casual relationships, oral sex is more likely to be perceived as less intimate, but also as less risky, than penile–vaginal sex (Dotson-Blake, Knoz, & Zusman, 2012). More emotional gain is typically expected from oral sex within the context of committed relationships (Vannier & O'Sullivan, 2012). Indeed, a sample of college women reported that because relationships create a context of emotional and physical comfort associated with sex, and because this comfort was central to their sexual enjoyment, committed or serious partnerships were therefore preferable to hook-ups for receiving or giving oral sex (Backstrom et al., 2012). Among those in the adult and aging adult life stages, across most age groups the likelihood of receiving oral sex and giving it, for both men and women, was more likely among those in a relationship (Herbenick et al., 2010b; Reece et al., 2010). Additionally, increased levels of physical health were associated with both oral sex types among men 50 to 59 years old (Reece et al., 2010).

Finally, some work has suggested that oral sex, as does masturbation, may have important relationships with other sexual behaviors. For example, some data have suggested that oral sex increases for young people as they also acquire experience with penile–vaginal sex (Lindberg, Jones, & Santelli, 2008). The relationship of oral sex to vaginal sex may differ by gender: Data from the NSFG have suggested that more young men (10.3%) than young women (9.8%) reported experiencing oral sex before initiating vaginal sex, whereas more young women (11.1%) than young men (8.4%) noted experiencing vaginal sex before oral sex (Copen et al., 2012). Hensel et al. (2008) found that adolescent women's daily diary reports of giving and receiving oral sex were likely to occur apart from, as well as in conjunction with, vaginal sex or penile–anal sex. One study of college women found little consensus as to whether women counted cunnilingus as sex or whether it was more or less intimate than vaginal sex (Backstrom et al., 2012). Moreover, having at least one act of oral–anal contact in the past 30 days was more likely among heterosexual men who had also engaged in penile–anal sex with their female partner (McBride & Fortenberry, 2010).

In summary, oral sex, which can be expressed in a variety of different forms, remains prevalent across the life span. Regarding the adolescent life stage, research has focused on understanding the perceived benefits young people associate with oral sex—as a means of increasing social standing or augmenting physical pleasure or, for some, as a substitute for penile–vaginal sex to maintain virginity. Moving into adulthood, this emphasis shifts to the emotional aspects of oral sex, with individuals integrating it to increase intimacy or as one behavior in a larger behavior set within relationships. For those in the aging adult life stage, oral sex also remains important, perhaps as a means of maintaining aspects of a sexual relationship as they face changes in physical health or partnership status.

Penile–Vaginal Sex

We begin this section by purposefully drawing attention to the phrases *penile–vaginal sex* and *vaginal sex.* Although these phrases are often used interchangeably among heterosexuals, referring to the insertion of a penis into a vagina, it is important to acknowledge that *vaginal sex* may mean something entirely different for women who have sex with women or for women who have sex with both men and women. For the latter groups, although some may have experienced penile–vaginal sex at some point in their lifetime, for many, *vaginal sex* may refer more broadly to stimulation of the vagina in ways that do not involve any penetration at all (Carpenter, 2001; Horowitz & Spicer, 2013; see Chapter 20, this volume). Where possible, we draw attention to these differences in the text that follows.

Perhaps more than any sexual behavior, penile–vaginal sex is socially scripted as the *sine qua non* of sexuality. That is, penile–vaginal sex is imbued with intense cultural significance (see Chapter 25, this volume; Volume 2, Chapter 6, this handbook), from its construction as the centerpiece of many young people's virginity; to its near-universal association, by heterosexuals and by those in same-sex relationships, with the definition of *having sex* (Horowitz & Spicer, 2013); to its placement as the expected focus of heterosexual sexual encounters (Simon & Gagnon, 2003). Penile–vaginal sex is enacted both within gender and relationship norms governing sexuality and also in deference to challenges associated with each life stage.

As described earlier in this section, although a number of behaviors can also be associated with loss of virginity, penile–vaginal intercourse has long been portrayed as the traditional way to lose one's virginity. In virtually every country, first penile–vaginal sex is constructed as a socially and sexually transformative moment, a rite of passage when young people transition from childhood into adulthood, from virgin to nonvirgin, and from sexually inexperienced to sexually experienced. Indeed, retrospective accounts of virginity loss among male and female college students have suggested that most heterosexuals define this transition through participation in penile–vaginal sex (Carpenter, 2001). In the same study, about two thirds of lesbian women and one gay man also reported penile–vaginal sex with an opposite-sex partner as a means to virginity loss, whereas one lesbian noted virginity loss through performing oral sex on another woman. In the context of adolescent development, first sex also symbolizes an important evolution in the ability to engage in romantic and sexual relationships (O'Sullivan et al., 2007).

Traditional sex and gender norms script this status change differently for young men and young women. Some work has suggested a loss–gain dichotomy in young people's narratives: First sex permits a young man to gain a step toward sexual power, whereas young women experience a loss of virginity, scripting them as passive participants in the sexual process (Holland, Ramazanoglu, Sharpe, & Thomson, 2010). Other studies have challenged this dichotomy, suggesting a more complex process by which young women can find agency balancing it with other negative aspects.

For example, a retrospective study of virginity loss among college students (Carpenter, 2002) found that heterosexual college women were particularly empowered if they viewed first sex as one step in a process toward greater sexual understanding of themselves and of a partner. Also using a sample of college students, Higgins, Trussell, Moore, and Davidson (2010) examined retrospective accounts of psychological and physical satisfaction at first sex among White and Black men and women, finding that higher psychological satisfaction was significantly linked to physiological satisfaction for both men and women across both racial groups. Moreover, although Black and White women's satisfaction was lower than that of their male counterparts, being in a committed relationship and experiencing less guilt were associated with increased psychological satisfaction for both groups. Sexual agency has been associated with intentions to engage in sexual activity among early adolescent women (O'Sullivan & Brooks-Gunn, 2005), with other work suggesting that some young women find it difficult to navigate away from social negativity even in the face of this agency (Tolman, 2002). An event-level analysis of adolescent women's mood and partner attitudes illustrates this balance, finding that sexual interest and partner support peaked on the day of first sex, with feelings of love peaking on the day before first sex (Tanner, Hensel, & Fortenberry, 2010). These findings lend support to the idea that first vaginal sex can be a both physically and emotionally positive experience for young women.

One consequence of a cultural emphasis on heterosexuality and penile–vaginal sex is that little is still known about early sexual experiences in LGBT groups. Young women who first have sex with other women appear to enjoy greater control over their first sexual experiences than women whose first partners are men; however, they face other challenges such as homophobic reactions from their parents or peers (Carpenter, 2002; Thompson, 1996). In a study of college men and women's retrospective accounts of virginity loss (Carpenter, 2002), a greater number of lesbian women and gay men (73%) than heterosexual men and women (46%) evaluated their virginity loss as one step in a developmental process toward sexual health. Conversely, half of heterosexual men and women but only a third of gay or lesbian youths viewed their virginity as a gift to their partner. Bisexual women and men vacillated in their views, with two thirds ever interpreting virginity as a gift and one third ever having perceived it as a step in a larger developmental process. Moreover, for many gay and bisexual participants, virginity loss was constructed as a developmental step because it closely intertwined with the process of coming out (see Chapter 19, this volume).

After first sex, most studies have suggested that vaginal sex is an uncommon event for young people. Estimates from the NSSHB suggested that 13.7% of boys and 16.0% of girls between ages 14 and 17 had vaginal sex in the past 90 days (Fortenberry et al., 2010). Diary data taken from primarily African American adolescent women residing in areas of high unintended pregnancy and sexually transmitted infection (Hensel et al., 2008) supported these patterns, showing that when sexual activity occurred, noncoital behaviors were more prevalent than vaginal sex. Prevalence of vaginal sex increased with age among adolescent men and women, with generally more boys reporting it than girls and slightly more occurring in boyfriend–girlfriend relationships (Fortenberry et al., 2010). These statistics contradict some risk framework assumptions about the frequency of adolescent sexual decision making (Fortenberry, 2005).

In the adult and aging adult stages, vaginal sex becomes the most commonly reported partnered sexual activity for men and women. In the United States, the percentage of men and women reporting this activity in the past 90 days peaks in the 25- to 29-year-old age group (men, 79.8%; women, 80.4%), occurring most frequently among those who had a partner, but declining with age (Herbenick et al., 2010c; Reece et al., 2010). In the aging adult life stage, in a population of Spanish adults, more than half of men and more than a third of women age 60 and older reported vaginal sex in the past year. Likewise, other work from the United States has suggested that 75% or more of men and women older than age 65 report they "usually or always" have vaginal sex (Waite et al., 2009).

Some research has informed parallel processes in LGBT individuals. With regard to quantity and type of sexual behavior, lesbian couples engage in less sex than do gay or heterosexual couples, but they engage in more nongenital sexual behavior, such as hugging, cuddling, and kissing than these two groups (James & Murphy, 1998). Other studies focusing on genital sexual activity have found that adult lesbians report the lowest frequency of sex compared with gay men and heterosexuals (Laumann et al., 2000).

Aside from the cultural emphasis on its place in the heterosexual sexual repertoire, there are a number of reasons why people choose to engage in vaginal sex, and these reasons can change, or remain equally important, across the life span. For example, vaginal sex may be a means of expressing or enhancing love and affection within a relationship. The frequency of vaginal sex increases over time in established relationships, often in tandem with relationship quality and sexual satisfaction, both in adolescent women's relationships (Sayegh, Fortenberry, Anderson, & Orr, 2005) and in early adult relationships (Rostosky, Galliher, Welsh, & Kawaguchi, 2000). Likewise, relationship satisfaction is significantly linked to a number of increased sexual behaviors, including vaginal intercourse, in the aging adult life stage (DeLamater & Moorman, 2007). For adults and aging adults, vaginal sex may increase in new partnerships or may decline as individuals in long-term relationships reprioritize other things over sex (Hinchliff & Gott, 2008). Vaginal sex may lessen after childbirth as time and sexual desire change (Pauls et al., 2008). Similarly, as couples find themselves moving from child rearing into becoming empty nesters, vaginal sex may resume as they spend more time together and worries about preventing pregnancy diminish after menopause (Dillaway, 2005).

Motivations for vaginal sex may also vary across the life span as well as with gender. For example, young women dually perceive higher pleasure (Halpern-Felsher et al., 2005) but more emotional consequences (Boekeloo & Howard, 2002) from vaginal sex than other types of sex. Similarly, in a study of adult men's and women's ratings of why people have sex, men rated physical reasons, such as stress reduction, and goal attainment, such as social status, more highly than women as motivations for sex (Meston & Buss, 2007). In the aging adult life stage, this focus may be much more emotional. A majority of men and women older than age 50 agreed that they "wouldn't have sex unless they were in love with their partner" and that "sex is essential to maintaining a relationship" (Waite et al., 2009, p. i60). This emotional connection may also increase physical satisfaction for those still sexually active in this life stage: Among men and women older than age 50, reported arousal levels significantly increased with age for men, and reports of orgasm increased for both men and women (Schick et al., 2010).

In summary, we have suggested the centrality of penile–vaginal sex in the cultural organization of sexual behaviors. For young people, vaginal sex is scripted as a major transitional event in (hetero)sexual development. Moreover, vaginal sex is an expected component of many long-term relationships in the adult and later life stages. We have illustrated the various reasons why individuals select vaginal sex, noting that these reasons ebb and flow with movement in and out of life stages and partnerships, but also with other life events, such as childbirth or changes in physical health.

Penile–Anal Sex

As with many other sexual behaviors described in this chapter, penile–anal sex has a long history of both cultural fascination and cultural stigma. As described in a recent review (McBride & Fortenberry, 2010), although social visibility of penile–anal sex has increased over the past decade, much of the existing research still focuses on men who have sex with men, rather than understanding how penile–anal sex may be chosen by heterosexual individuals and individuals of other sexual orientations as one piece in a larger sexual repertoire.

Within the larger cultural discomfort with penile–anal sex, literature describing it among young people is small but growing. A study of adolescents and young adults ages 15 to 21 in three U.S. cities found that 16% had reported it in the past 90 days (Lescano et al., 2009). One study of adolescents found that 10.9% of females and 11.1% of males reported any lifetime penile–anal sex experience, with Black adolescents less likely to report this experience than White adolescents and Hispanic males more likely than non-Hispanic White males to report this experience (Lindberg et al., 2008). The NSSHB data disagreed with these findings, with more female adolescents than male adolescents reporting past-90-day (female, 2.3%; male, 1.7%), past-year (female, 4.3%; male, 4.4%), or lifetime (female, 5.55%; male, 4.4%) experience with penile–anal sex, with similar patterns at most recent sexual event (Fortenberry et al., 2010). These same data also illustrated that among adolescent men, at last sexual event, 28.6% of penile–anal sex occurred with a male partner (Fortenberry et al., 2010).

These estimates among adolescents are considerably higher than reports of same-sex penile–anal sex in adult male populations (Herbenick et al., 2010a), although it has perhaps provided evidence of the fact that same-sex experimentation may peak in mid- to late adolescence (McCabe et al., 2011). More adults than adolescents report lifetime penile–anal sex: In the most recent NSFG, 35% of adult women and 40% of adult men, all ages 18 to 44 years, reported engaging in heterosexual anal intercourse in their lifetime (Mosher, Chandra, & Jones, 2005). Penile–anal sex typically occurs less often than vaginal sex, for both men and women (Herbenick et al., 2010b; Reece et al., 2010). Other work has shown that adult Whites are more likely than adult minority groups to engage in anal sex (Leichliter, 2008; Lescano et al., 2009), whereas other studies have demonstrated no association of penile–anal sex with race/ethnicity (Gorbach et al., 2009; Mosher et al., 2005). Penile–anal sex is least common in the aging adult life stage: Fewer than 5% of any men and women older than age 60 report any penile–anal sex in the past 90 days (Herbenick et al., 2010b; Reece et al., 2010), and its prevalence declines with age (Schick et al., 2010).

Reasons why people choose penile–anal sex can vary, with some patterns attributed to beliefs about how penile–anal sex compares with vaginal sex. Similar to perceptions of oral sex, most people are less likely to consider penile–anal sex as having sex (Sanders & Reinisch, 1999). In some instances, this perception may catalyze young and emerging adults to choose penile–anal sex out of the perception that it is a "safer" alternative to vaginal sex, posing no risk of pregnancy (Houston, Fang, Husman, & Peralta, 2007; Kaestle & Halpern, 2007). Penile–anal sex is more likely in young women when vaginal bleeding is present (Hensel, Fortenberry, & Orr, 2010), perhaps as a means of "not having sex" when menstruation norms proscribe vaginal sex.

Additionally, sexual relationship characteristics provide motivations for and perceptions of penile–anal sex. For example, among at-risk adolescents and emerging adults, imbalanced relationship power (e.g., a history of forced sex) is associated with more frequent penile–anal sex (Lescano et al., 2009). Qualitative work has suggested that among adult women, penile–anal sex occurs in the pursuit of one's own sexual pleasure, as an act of physical and emotional intimacy with one's partner, or in deference to one's partner's requests (Maynard, Carballo-Diéguez, Ventuneac, Exner, & Mayer, 2009). A sample of urban, ethnically diverse emerging adult men and women reinforced these results, describing penile–anal sex as a means of increasing sexual pleasure in serious relationships (Carter, Henry-Moss, Hock-Long, Bergdall, & Andes, 2010). Moreover, a study using daily diaries found that penile–anal sex is more likely among young women with greater sexual interest on a specific day (Hensel et al., 2008,

2010), whereas retrospective reports of a male partner's being in love (reciprocated or not) have been associated with penile–anal sex in young and emerging adult women (Kaestle & Halpern, 2007).

In terms of partnership type, a variety of studies (Fortenberry et al., 2010; McBride & Fortenberry, 2010; Misegades, Page-Shafer, Halperin, & McFarland, 2001) have suggested that penile–anal sex typically occurs more often in the context of main or exclusive relationships, perhaps as a means of reinforcing existing trust and intimacy or expanding one's sexual behavior repertoire. Another study noted that penile–anal sex with a casual partner was more likely among Puerto Ricans than among Blacks and among respondents ages 22 to 25 than ages 18 to 21, but noted no gender differences (Carter et al., 2010). In contrast, Leichliter (2008) found that penile–anal sex was more likely with a nonmonogamous sexual partner. Little to no qualitative research has examined heterosexual men's motivations for penile–anal sex, but a study of Black gay men found that younger and less masculine men wielded less power in relationships, making them more likely to be the receptive partner (Fields et al., 2012). Other qualitative work has challenged this idea (Hoppe, 2011), describing the different ways in which gay men understand sexual pleasure in specifically choosing a receptive role. For some men, pleasure was defined in terms of the mental or emotional pleasure of providing their partner physical pleasure; for others, it was the physical pleasure they themselves experienced from being a receptive partner. Finally, some men defined *sexual pleasure* as a combination of mental and physical pleasure from opting for a receptive role.

Behavioral patterns within relationships can also influence the occurrence of penile–anal sex. For example, among adolescent women, penile–anal sex is more likely when a young woman has also had penile–anal sex within the past week (Hensel et al., 2008, 2010). Among adult women, current reports of penile–anal sex are also linked to having engaged in recent penile–anal sex (Misegades et al., 2001). Moreover, some penile–anal sex practices take place around the occurrence of vaginal sex. For example, among both young men and young women, the likelihood of penile–anal sex increases as they move further in time from their first vaginal sex (Lindberg et al., 2008), perhaps reflecting increasing comfort with sexuality and desire to explore more sexual behavior. Among adolescent girls (Hensel et al., 2008, 2010) and adult women (Misegades et al., 2001), current penile–anal sex is linked to reporting vaginal sex on that same day, suggesting that individuals may integrate penile–anal sex into a larger set of sexual behavior choices. Among gay men, age is an especially prevalent factor in addition to partnership traits. One study in Australia reported that older men had a less extensive range of anal practices than younger men but switched more frequently between insertive and receptive roles with regular partners (Van de Ven, Rodden, Crawford, & Kippax, 1997). Several qualitative studies have shown that sexual intimacy is an especially important motivating factor for older gay men (Murray & Adam, 2001; Wierzalis, Barret, Pope, & Rankins, 2006).

In summary, we have suggested that despite cultural discomfort with the idea of penile–anal intercourse, adolescents, adults, and older adults do participate in penile–anal sex, both those in heterosexual relationships and those in same-sex relationships. Penile–anal sex can take on multiple meanings for individuals, used in some instances as substitute for vaginal sex, particularly under the assumption it is a safer alternative in terms of pregnancy risk, or in the event that one member of a dyad is experiencing menstruation. Penile–anal sex may also occur in conjunction with other sexual behaviors, such as vaginal sex, particularly as a means of expressing intimacy or sexual pleasure.

CONCLUSION

In this chapter, we have used sexual health as an organizing paradigm for a life-span perspective on sexuality. This paradigm pushes an understanding of sexuality beyond a simple focus on aspects of reproductive health or sexual function, positioning sexual health as a lifelong process by which sexuality remains a primary aspect of identity, as well as a core element in health and well-being, during every life stage. We have suggested that this life-span approach to sexual health necessarily engages the multiple dimensions in which sexuality is organized and acknowledges the salience of these dimensions from youth to old age, the continuity and change in these dimensions in the face of new experiences, and the connectedness of these dimensions, because past experiences inform current and future experiences. We have considered this perspective within the context of two important aspects of lifelong sexual development—partnering and sexual behavior. Although this chapter synthesizes only a small body of the available literature on both topics, we have forwarded the argument that the formation of important relationships, as well as the types of sexual behaviors that occur inside (and outside) of relationships, are two threads by which sexual health is expressed across different life stages.

In describing the contribution of partnering to sexual health across the life span, we began with the assertion that there have been incredible changes in both the nature of intimate relationship formation and the literature that describes them. We now have a better appreciation of how the partnering process varies in timing, sequence, and duration across life span, and more important, we have an emerging understanding of how each relationship creates a context for the (re)organization of sexuality. Relationships in adolescence represent diversification, not only in terms of their progression from friendship groups to later romantic dyads but also in terms of the formative sexual health skills they provide for future sexual health. We additionally described how romantic partnerships remain equally salient, as well as important to sexual health, in adulthood and in later life. A volume of literature has evaluated how committed relationships in adulthood are important sources of intimacy, communication, and sexual satisfaction in both heterosexual and same-sex couples. Likewise, emerging knowledge has suggested that aging individuals, much as their adult peers, choose a variety of relationship forms, deriving positive benefits from them.

We also presented evidence for an evolving view of how researchers think about what constitutes sex, as a means of thinking more broadly about the behavioral ways in which people choose to express their sexuality. Although much of the cultural discourse on sexual behavior places emphasis on penile–vaginal sex, we suggested that a life course perspective must recognize that people participate in many different types of intimate contact with partners, in ways that both include and exclude their genitals and in ways that may voluntarily or involuntarily exclude specific behaviors. Moreover, we forwarded the idea that behavior is inexorably linked to the context in which it is given meaning, with the same behavior assuming vastly different meanings at different points in time (see also Volume 2, Chapter 6, this handbook).

This summary has invoked only a small amount of the available research on partnering and sexual behavior. We suggest that amid a growing understanding of how partnering and sexual behavior differ across different life stages, the more important focus moving forward regards truly understanding the ways in which they are connected. For example, much remains to be learned about the dynamics of sexuality in the aging adult life stage. We know very little about varying motivations for sexual behavior, particularly how patterns vary as a function of race/ethnicity or sexual orientation. This information is important in being able to situate sexual health toward the end of life with sexual health in the beginning and middle points in life.

We also argue that a life span approach to sexuality opens up important possibilities to articulate what a lifelong developmental model of sexuality looks like. We advocate for research that pushes beyond arbitrary boundaries between life stages, explicitly modeling individual aspects of sexual health as they intersect with lifetime changes in relationships, new and old behaviors, and other biological and social characteristics. This research may include questions on how the content and nature of current experiences links to the ways in which people interpret and make decisions about future experiences, how individuals longitudinally balance positive aspects of sexuality with an understanding of risk management, how early sexual socialization influences individual beliefs and partnership events as individuals enter adulthood and old age, how old experiences become new again as individuals interpret them in new contexts, or how positive sexuality specifically links in the long and the short term to more global aspects of physical and mental health. We suggest that this more integrative, developmental approach is in fact a necessary step in encouraging research that normalizes and honors the importance of sexuality at all points during one's lifetime, not only as a defining characteristic of human identity but also as a core constituent of lifelong health and well-being.

References

Abbott, D. A., & Dalla, R. L. (2008). "It's a choice, simple as that": Youth reasoning for sexual abstinence or activity. *Journal of Youth Studies, 11*, 629–649. doi:10.1080/13676260802225751

Abma, J., Driscoll, A., & Moore, K. (1998). Young women's degree of control over first intercourse: An exploratory analysis. *Family Planning Perspectives, 30*, 12–18. doi:10.2307/2991518

Agnew, C. R., Arriaga, Z. B., & Wilson, J. E. (2008). Committed to what? Using the bases of relational commitment model to understand continuity and change in social relationships. In J. P. Forgas & J. Fitness (Eds.), *Social relationships: Cognitive, affective, and motivational processes* (pp. 147–164). New York, NY: Psychology Press.

Arnett, J. J. (2000). Emerging adulthood: A theory of development from the late teens through the twenties. *American Psychologist, 55*, 469–480. doi:10.1037/0003-066X.55.5.469

Atwood, J. D., & Gagnon, J. (1987). Masturbatory behavior in college youth. *Journal of Sex Education and Therapy, 13*, 35–42.

Austad, S. N. (2006). Why women live longer than men: Sex differences in longevity. *Gender Medicine, 3*, 79–92. doi:10.1016/S1550-8579(06)80198-1

Backstrom, L., Armstrong, E. A., & Puentes, J. (2012). Women's negotiation of cunnilingus in college hookups and relationships. *Journal of Sex Research, 49*, 1–12. doi:10.1080/00224499.2011.585523

Barry, C. M., Madsen, S. D., Nelson, L. J., Carroll, J. S., & Badger, S. (2009). Friendship and romantic relationship qualities in emerging adulthood: Differential associations with identity development and achieved adulthood criteria. *Journal of Adult Development, 16*, 209–222. doi:10.1007/s10804-009-9067-x

Bay-Cheng, L. Y., & Fava, N. M. (2011). Young women's experiences and perceptions of cunnilingus during adolescence. *Journal of Sex Research, 48*, 531–542. doi:10.1080/00224499.2010.535221

Bay-Cheng, L. Y., Robinson, A. D., & Zucker, A. N. (2009). Behavioral and relational contexts of adolescent desire, wanting, and pleasure: Undergraduate women's retrospective accounts. *Journal of Sex Research, 46*, 511–524. doi:10.1080/00224490902867871

Bearman, P. S., & Brückner, H. (2001). Promising the future: Virginity pledges and first intercourse. *American Journal of Sociology, 106*, 859–912. doi:10.1086/320295

Bennett, L., & Gates, G. J. (2004). *The cost of marriage inequality to children and their same sex parents*. Washington, DC: Human Rights Campaign.

Bersamin, M. M., Fisher, D. A., Walker, S., Hill, D. L., & Grube, J. W. (2007). Defining virginity and abstinence: Adolescents' interpretations of sexual behaviors. *Journal of Adolescent Health, 41*, 182–188. doi:10.1016/j.jadohealth.2007.03.011

Bisson, M. A., & Levine, T. R. (2009). Negotiating a friends with benefits relationship. *Archives of Sexual Behavior, 38*, 66–73. doi:10.1007/s10508-007-9211-2

Boekeloo, B. O., & Howard, D. E. (2002). Oral sexual experience among young adolescents receiving general health examinations. *American Journal of Health Behavior, 26*, 306–314. doi:10.5993/AJHB.26.4.7

Bogart, L. M., Collins, R. L., Kanouse, D. E., Cunningham, W., Beckman, R., Golinelli, D., & Bird, C. E. (2006). Patterns and correlates of deliberate abstinence among men and women with HIV/AIDS. *American Journal of Public Health, 96*, 1078–1084. doi:10.2105/AJPH.2005.070771

Bogle, K. (2008). *Hooking up: Sex, dating, and relationships on campus*. New York, NY: NYU Press.

Boisard, M.-A. L., & Zimmer-Gembeck, M. J. (2011). Sexual subjectivity, relationship status and quality, and same-sex sexual experience among emerging adult females. *Journal of Educational and Developmental Psychology, 1*, 54–64.

Bradford, A., & Meston, C. (2007). Senior sexual health: The effects of aging on sexuality. In L. VandeCreek, F. L. Peterson, & J. W. Bley (Eds.), *Focus on sexual health*. Sarasota, FL: Professional Resource Press.

Brewster, K. L., & Tillman, K. H. (2008). Who's doing it? Patterns and predictors of youths' oral sexual experiences. *Journal of Adolescent Health, 42*, 73–80. doi:10.1016/j.jadohealth.2007.08.010

Bryan, A. D., Aiken, L. S., & West, S. G. (1997). Young women's condom use: The influence of acceptance of sexuality, control over the sexual encounter, and perceived susceptibility to common STDs. *Health Psychology, 16*, 468–479. doi:10.1037/0278-6133.16.5.468

Burgess, E. O. (2004). Sexuality in midlife and later life couples. In J. Harvey, A. Wentzel, & S. Sprecher (Eds.), *The handbook of sexuality in close relationships* (pp. 437–454). Mahwah, NJ: Erlbaum.

Byers, E. S., Henderson, J., & Hobson, K. (2009). University students' definitions of sexual abstinence and having sex. *Archives of Sexual Behavior, 38*, 665–674. doi:10.1007/s10508-007-9289-6

Calasanti, T., & Kiecolt, K. J. (2007). Diversity among late-life couples. *Generations, 31*, 10–17.

Carpenter, L. (2011). Like a virgin . . . again? Secondary virginity as an ongoing gendered social construction. *Sexuality and Culture, 15*, 115–140. doi:10.1007/s12119-010-9085-7

Carpenter, L. M. (2001). The ambiguity of "having sex": The subjective experience of virginity loss in the United States. *Journal of Sex Research, 38*, 127–139. doi:10.1080/00224490109552080

Carpenter, L. M. (2002). Gender and the meaning and experience of virginity loss in the contemporary United States. *Gender and Society, 16*, 345–365. doi:10.1177/0891243202016003005

Carr, D. (2004). The desire to date and remarry among older widows and widowers. *Journal of Marriage and the Family, 66*, 1051–1068. doi:10.1111/j.0022-2445.2004.00078.x

Carter, M., Henry-Moss, D., Hock-Long, L., Bergdall, A., & Andes, K. (2010). Heterosexual anal sex experiences among Puerto Rican and Black young adults. *Perspectives on Sexual and Reproductive Health, 42*, 267–274. doi:10.1363/4226710

Carver, K., Joyner, K., & Udry, J. R. (2003). National estimates of adolescent romantic relationships. In P. Florsheim (Ed.), *Adolescent romantic relations and sexual behavior: Theory, research, and practical implications* (pp. 23–56). Mahwah, NJ: Erlbaum.

Centers for Disease Control and Prevention. (2010). *A public health approach for advancing sexual health in the United States: Rationale and options for implementation* (Meeting Report of an External Consultation). Atlanta, GA: Centers for Disease Control and Prevention, National Center for HIV/AIDS, Viral Hepatitis, STD, and TB Prevention.

Chambers, W. C. (2007). Oral sex: Varied behaviors and perceptions in a college population. *Journal of Sex Research, 44*, 28–42.

Coleman, E. (2003). Masturbation as a means of achieving sexual health. *Journal of Psychology and Human Sexuality, 14*, 5–16. doi:10.1300/J056v14n02_02

Collins, W. A. (2003). More than myth: The developmental significance of romantic relationships during adolescence. *Journal of Research on Adolescence, 13*, 1–24. doi:10.1111/1532-7795.1301001

Collins, W. A., & Madsen, S. D. (2006). Relationships in adolescence and young adulthood. In D. Perlman & A. Vangelisti (Eds.), *Handbook of personal relationships* (pp. 191–209). Cambridge, England: Cambridge University Press. doi:10.1017/CBO9780511606632.012

Collins, W. A., Welsh, D. P., & Furman, W. (2009). Adolescent romantic relationships. *Annual Review of Psychology, 60*, 631–652. doi:10.1146/annurev.psych.60.110707.163459

Connolly, J., Craig, W., Goldberg, A., & Pepler, D. (2004). Mixed-gender groups, dating, and romantic relationships in early adolescence. *Journal of Research on Adolescence, 14*, 185–207. doi:10.1111/j.1532-7795.2004.01402003.x

Connolly, J., & McIsaac, C. (2009). Adolescents' explanations for romantic dissolutions: A developmental perspective. *Journal of Adolescence, 32*, 1209–1223. doi:10.1016/j.adolescence.2009.01.006

Copen, C. E., Chandra, A., & Martinez, G. (2012). *Prevalence and timing of oral sex with opposite-sex partners among females and males aged 15–24 years: United States, 2007–2010* (National Health Statistics Reports, Vol. 56). Hyattsville, MD: National Center for Health Statistics.

Cornell, J. L., & Halpern-Felsher, B. L. (2006). Adolescents tell us why teens have oral sex. *Journal of Adolescent Health, 38*, 299–301. doi:10.1016/j.jadohealth.2005.04.015

Cupach, W., & Metts, S. (1995). The role of sexual attitude similarity in romantic heterosexual relationships. *Personal Relationships, 2*, 287–300. doi:10.1111/j.1475-6811.1995.tb00093.x

Cutrona, C. E., Russell, D. W., Burzette, R. G., Wesner, K. A., & Bryant, C. M. (2011). Predicting relationship stability among midlife African American couples. *Journal of Consulting and Clinical Psychology, 79*, 814–825. doi:10.1037/a0025874

Cyranowski, J. M., & Andersen, B. L. (1998). Schemas, sexuality, and romantic attachment. *Journal of Personality and Social Psychology, 74*, 1364–1379. doi:10.1037/0022-3514.74.5.1364

Das, A. (2007). Masturbation in the United States. *Journal of Sex and Marital Therapy, 33*, 301–317. doi:10.1080/00926230701385514

de Graaf, H., & Rademakers, J. (2011). The psychological measurement of childhood sexual development in Western societies: Methodological challenges. *Journal of Sex Research, 48*, 118–129. doi:10.1080/00224499.2011.555929

de Jong Gierveld, J., & Hagestad, G. N. (2006). Social integration in later life. *Research on Aging, 28*, 627–637. doi:10.1177/0164027506291871

De Judicibus, M. A., & McCabe, M. P. (2002). Psychological factors and the sexuality of pregnant and postpartum women. *Journal of Sex Research, 39*, 94–103. doi:10.1080/00224490209552128

DeLamater, J. (2012). Sexual expression in later life: A review and synthesis. *Journal of Sex Research, 49*, 125–141. doi:10.1080/00224499.2011.603168

DeLamater, J., & Moorman, S. M. (2007). Sexual behavior in later life. *Journal of Aging and Health, 19*, 921–945. doi:10.1177/0898264307308342

DeLamater, J. D., & Sill, M. (2005). Sexual desire in later life. *Journal of Sex Research, 42*, 138–149. doi:10.1080/00224490509552267

Diamond, L. M. (2008). Female bisexuality from adolescence to adulthood: Results from a 10-year longitudinal study. *Developmental Psychology, 44*, 5–14. doi:10.1037/0012-1649.44.1.5

Dillaway, H. E. (2005). Menopause is the "good old": Women's thoughts about reproductive aging. *Gender and Society, 19*, 398–417. doi:10.1177/0891243204271350

Donnelly, D. A., & Burgess, E. O. (2008). The decision to remain in an involuntarily celibate relationship. *Journal of Marriage and the Family, 70*, 519–535. doi:10.1111/j.1741-3737.2008.00498.x

Dotson-Blake, K. P., Knoz, D., & Zusman, M. E. (2012). Exploring social sexual scripts related to oral sex: A profile of college student perceptions. *Professional Counselor: Research and Practice, 2*, 1–11.

Edwards, J., & Booth, A. (1994). Sexuality, marriage and well-being: The middle years. In A. Rossi (Ed.), *Sexuality across the life course* (pp. 233–259). Chicago: University of Chicago.

Edwards, W. M., & Coleman, E. (2004). Defining sexual health: A descriptive overview. *Archives of Sexual Behavior, 33*, 189–195. doi:10.1023/B:ASEB.0000026619.95734.d5

Epstein, M., Calzo, J. P., Smiler, A. P., & Ward, L. M. (2009). "Anything from making out to having sex": Men's negotiations of hooking up and friends with benefits scripts. *Journal of Sex Research, 46*, 414–424. doi:10.1080/00224490902775801

Fenton, K. A. (2010). Time for change: Rethinking and reframing sexual health in the United States. *Journal of Sexual Medicine, 7*(Suppl. 5), 250–252. doi:10.1111/j.1743-6109.2010.02057.x

Fields, E. L., Bogart, L. M., Smith, K. C., Malebranche, D. J., Ellen, J., & Schuster, M. A. (2012). HIV risk and perceptions of masculinity among young Black men who have sex with men. *Journal of Adolescent Health, 50*, 296–303. doi:10.1016/j.jadohealth.2011.07.007

Fine, M. (1988). Sexuality, schooling, and adolescent females: The missing discourse of desire. *Harvard Educational Review, 58*, 29–53.

Floyd, F. J. S. T. S. (2002). Sexual orientation identity formation among gay, lesbian, and bisexual youths: Multiple patterns of milestone experiences. *Journal of Research on Adolescence, 12*, 167–191. doi:10.1111/1532-7795.00030

Forste, R., & Haas, D. W. (2002). The transition of adolescent males to first sexual intercourse: Anticipated or delayed? *Perspectives on Sexual and Reproductive Health, 34*, 184–190. doi:10.2307/3097728

Fortenberry, J. D. (2005). Adolescent sex and the rhetoric of risk. In D. Romer (Ed.), *Reducing adolescent risk: Towards an integrated approach* (pp. 293–300). Thousand Oaks, CA: Sage.

Fortenberry, J. D., Schick, V., Herbenick, D., Sanders, S. A., Dodge, B., & Reece, M. (2010). Sexual behaviors and condom use at last vaginal intercourse: A national sample of adolescents ages 14 to 17 years. *Journal of Sexual Medicine, 7*, 305–314. doi:10.1111/j.1743-6109.2010.02018.x

Fredriksen-Goldsen, K. I., & Muraco, A. (2010). Aging and sexual orientation: A 25-year review of the literature. *Research on Aging, 32*, 372–413. doi:10.1177/0164027509360355

Furman, W., & Shaffer, L. (2003). The role of romantic relationships in adolescent development. In P. Florsheim (Ed.), *Adolescent romantic relations and sexual behavior: Theory, research, and practical implications* (pp. 3–22). Mahwah, NJ: Erlbaum.

Furman, W., & Shaffer, L. (2011). Romantic partners, friends, friends with benefits, and casual acquaintances as sexual partners. *Journal of Sex Research, 48*, 554–564. doi:10.1080/00224499.2010.535623

Gagnon, J. H., & Simon, W. (1987). A sexual scripts approach. In J. H. Geer & W. T. O'Donoghue (Eds.), *Theories of human sexuality* (pp. 363–383). New York, NY: Plenum Press.

Gerressu, M., Mercer, C., Graham, C., Wellings, K., & Johnson, A. (2008). Prevalence of masturbation and associated factors in a British national probability survey. *Archives of Sexual Behavior, 37*, 266–278. doi:10.1007/s10508-006-9123-6

Giordano, P. C., Manning, W. D., & Longmore, M. A. (2010). Affairs of the heart: Qualities of adolescent romantic relationships and sexual behavior. *Journal of Research on Adolescence, 20*, 983–1013. doi:10.1111/j.1532-7795.2010.00661.x

Giordano, P. C., Manning, W. D., Longmore, M. A., & Flanigan, C. M. (2012). Developmental shifts in the character of romantic and sexual relationships from adolescence to young adulthood. In A. Booth, S. L. Brown, N. S. Landale, W. D. Manning, & S. M. McHale (Eds.), *Early adulthood in a family context* (Vol. 2, pp. 133–164). New York, NY: . doi:10.1007/978-1-4614-1436-0_9

Goodson, P., Buhi, E. R., & Dunsmore, S. C. (2006). Self-esteem and adolescent sexual behaviors, attitudes, and intentions: A systematic review. *Journal of Adolescent Health, 38*, 310–319. doi:10.1016/j.jadohealth.2005.05.026

Goodson, P., Suther, S., Pruitt, B. E., & Wilson, K. (2003). Defining abstinence: Views of directors, instructors, and participants in abstinence-only-until-marriage programs in Texas. *Journal of School Health, 73*, 91–96. doi:10.1111/j.1746-1561.2003.tb03579.x

Goodwin, P. Y., Mosher, W. D., & Chandra, A. (2010). *Marriage and cohabitation in the United States: A statistical portrait based on Cycle 6 (2002) of the National*

Survey of Family Growth. Washington, DC: National Center for Health Statistics.

Gorbach, P. M., Manhart, L. E., Hess, K. L., Stoner, B. P., Martin, D. H., & Holmes, K. K. (2009). Anal intercourse among young heterosexuals in three sexually transmitted disease clinics in the United States. *Sexually Transmitted Diseases, 36*, 193–198. doi:10.1097/OLQ.0b013e3181901ccf

Gott, M. (2006). Sexual health and the new ageing. *Age and Ageing, 35*, 106–107. doi:10.1093/ageing/afj050

Gott, M., & Hinchliff, S. (2003). How important is sex in later life? The views of older people. *Social Science and Medicine, 56*, 1617–1628. doi:10.1016/s0277-9536(02)00180-6

Gottman, J. M., Levenson, R. W., Gross, J., Frederickson, B. L., McCoy, K., Rosenthal, L., . . . Yoshimoto, D. (2003). Correlates of gay and lesbian couples' relationship satisfaction and relationship dissolution. *Journal of Homosexuality, 45*, 23–43. doi:10.1300/J082v45n01_02

Halpern-Felsher, B. L., Cornell, J. L., Kropp, R. Y., & Tschann, J. M. (2005). Oral versus vaginal sex among adolescents: Perceptions, attitudes, and behavior. *Pediatrics, 115*, 845–851. doi:10.1542/peds.2004-2108

Hamilton, L., & Armstrong, E. A. (2009). Gendered sexuality in young adulthood. *Gender and Society, 23*, 589–616. doi:10.1177/0891243209345829

Hans, J. D., Gillen, M., & Akande, K. (2010). Sex redefined: The reclassification of oral-genital contact. *Perspectives on Sexual and Reproductive Health, 42*, 74–78. doi:10.1363/4207410

Haskey, J., & Lewis, J. (2006). Living-apart-together in Britain: Context and meaning. *International Journal of Law in Context, 2*, 37–48. doi:10.1017/S1744552306001030

Heaphy, B., Yip, A. K. T., & Thompson, D. (2004). Ageing in a non-heterosexual context. *Ageing and Society, 24*, 881–902. doi:10.1017/S0144686X03001600

Hensel, D. J., Fortenberry, J. D., & Orr, D. P. (2008). Variations in coital and noncoital sexual repertoire among adolescent women. *Journal of Adolescent Health, 42*, 170–176. doi:10.1016/j.jadohealth.2007.07.009

Hensel, D. J., Fortenberry, J. D., & Orr, D. P. (2010). Factors associated with event level anal sex and condom use during anal sex among adolescent women. *Journal of Adolescent Health, 46*, 232–237. doi:10.1016/j.jadohealth.2009.06.025

Hensel, D. J., Newcamp, J., Miles, J. A., & Fortenberry, J. D. (2011). Picturing sexual spaces in everyday life: Exploring the construction of sexuality and sexual behavior among early adult women. *Sexuality Research and Social Policy, 8*, 267–281. doi:10.1007/s13178-011-0066-x

Herbenick, D., Reece, M., Schick, V., Sanders, S. A., Dodge, B., & Fortenberry, J. D. (2010a). An event-level analysis of the sexual characteristics and composition among adults ages 18 to 59: Results from a national probability sample in the United States. *Journal of Sexual Medicine, 7*, 346–361. doi:10.1111/j.1743-6109.2010.02020.x

Herbenick, D., Reece, M., Schick, V., Sanders, S. A., Dodge, B., & Fortenberry, J. D. (2010b). Sexual behavior in the United States: Results from a national probability sample of men and women ages 14–94. *Journal of Sexual Medicine, 7*, 255–265. doi:10.1111/j.1743-6109.2010.02012.x

Herbenick, D., Reece, M., Schick, V., Sanders, S. A., Dodge, B., & Fortenberry, J. D. (2010c). Sexual behaviors, relationships, and perceived health status among adult women in the United States: Results from a national probability sample. *Journal of Sexual Medicine, 7*, 277–290. doi:10.1111/j.1743-6109.2010.02010.x

Herdt, G., & McClintock, M. (2000). The magical age of 10. *Archives of Sexual Behavior, 29*, 587–606. doi:10.1023/A:1002006521067

Heuveline, P., & Timberlake, J. M. (2004). The role of cohabitation in family formation: The United States in comparative perspective. *Journal of Marriage and the Family, 66*, 1214–1230. doi:10.1111/j.0022-2445.2004.00088.x

Higgins, J. A., & Brown, I. (2008). Sexual needs, control, and refusal: How "doing" class and gender influences sexual risk taking. *Journal of Sex Research, 45*, 233–245. doi:10.1080/00224490802204415

Higgins, J. A., Trussell, J., Moore, N. B., & Davidson, J. K. (2010). Virginity lost, satisfaction gained? Physiological and psychological sexual satisfaction at heterosexual debut. *Journal of Sex Research, 47*, 384–394. doi:10.1080/00224491003774792

Hinchliff, S., & Gott, M. (2008). Challenging social myths and stereotypes of women and aging: Heterosexual women talk about sex. *Journal of Women and Aging, 20*, 65–81. doi:10.1300/J074v20n01_06

Hipp, L. E., Kane Low, L., & van Anders, S. M. (2012). Exploring women's postpartum sexuality: Social, psychological, relational, and birth-related contextual factors. *Journal of Sexual Medicine, 9*, 2330–2341. doi:10.1111/j.1743-6109.2012.02804.x

Hogarth, H., & Ingham, R. (2009). Masturbation among young women and associations with sexual health: An exploratory study. *Journal of Sex Research, 46*, 558–567. doi:10.1080/00224490902878993

Holland, J., Ramazanoglu, C., Sharpe, S., & Thomson, R. (2010). Deconstructing virginity—Young people's accounts of first sex. *Sexual and Relationship Therapy, 25*, 351–362. (Reprinted from *Sexual and Relationship Therapy, 15*, 221–232, 2000) doi:10.1080/14681994.2010.496970

Hoppe, T. (2011). Circuits of power, circuits of pleasure: Sexual scripting in gay men's bottom narratives. *Sexualities, 14*, 193–217. doi:10.1177/1363460711399033

Horne, S., & Zimmer-Gembeck, M. J. (2005). Female sexual subjectivity and well-being: Comparing late adolescents with different sexual experiences. *Sexuality Research and Social Policy, 2*, 25–40. doi:10.1525/srsp.2005.2.3.25

Horowitz, A. D., & Spicer, L. (2013). "Having sex" as a graded and hierarchical construct: A comparison of sexual definitions among heterosexual and lesbian emerging adults in the UK. *Journal of Sex Research, 50*, 139–150. doi:10.1080/00224499.2011.635322

Houston, A. M., Fang, J., Husman, C., & Peralta, L. (2007). More than just vaginal intercourse: Anal intercourse and condom use patterns in the context of "main" and "casual" sexual relationships among urban minority adolescent females. *Journal of Pediatric and Adolescent Gynecology, 20*, 299–304. doi:10.1016/j.jpag.2007.01.006

Howard, J. R., O'Neill, S., & Travers, C. (2006). Factors affecting sexuality in older Australian women: Sexual interest, sexual arousal, relationships and sexual distress in older Australian women. *Climacteric, 9*, 355–367. doi:10.1080/13697130600961870

Hughes, M., Morrison, K., & Asada, K. J. K. (2005). What's love got to do with it? Exploring the impact of maintenance rules, love attitudes, and network support on friends with benefits relationships. *Western Journal of Communication, 69*, 49–66. doi:10.1080/10570310500034154

Hurd Clarke, L. (2006). Older women and sexuality: Experiences in marital relationships across the life course. *Canadian Journal on Aging, 25*, 129–140. doi:10.1353/cja.2006.0034

Hyde, Z., Flicker, L., Hankey, G. J., Almeida, O. P., McCaul, K. A., Chubb, S. A. P., & Yeap, B. B. (2010). Prevalence of sexual activity and associated factors in men aged 75 to 95 years. *Annals of Internal Medicine, 153*, 693–702.

James, S., & Murphy, B. (1998). Gay and lesbian relationships in a changing social context. In C. Patterson & A. D'Augelli (Eds.), *Lesbian, gay, and bisexual identities in families: Psychological perspectives* (pp. 99–121). London, England: Oxford University Press.

Jones, R., & Barton, S. (2004). Introduction of history taking and principles of sexual health. *Postgraduate Medical Journal, 80*, 444–446. doi:10.1136/pgmj.2003.016873

Julien, D., Chartrand, E., Simard, M. C., Bouthillier, D., & Begin, J. (2003). Conflict, social support, and relationship quality: An observational study of heterosexual, gay male, and lesbian couples' communication. *Journal of Family Psychology, 17*, 419–428. doi:10.1037/0893-3200.17.3.419

Kaestle, C., & Allen, K. (2011). The role of masturbation in healthy sexual development: Perceptions of young adults. *Archives of Sexual Behavior, 40*, 983–994. doi:10.1007/s10508-010-9722-0

Kaestle, C. E., & Halpern, C. T. (2007). What's love got to do with it? Sexual behaviors of opposite-sex couples through emerging adulthood. *Perspectives on Sexual and Reproductive Health, 39*, 134–140. doi:10.1363/3913407

Karraker, A., DeLamater, J., & Schwartz, C. R. (2011). Sexual frequency decline from midlife to later life. *Journals of Gerontology, Series B: Psychological Sciences and Social Sciences, 66*, 505–512. doi:10.1093/geronb/gbr058

Kennedy, S., & Bumpass, L. (2008). Cohabitation and children's living arrangements: New estimates from the United States. *Demographic Research, 19*, 1663–1692. doi:10.4054/DemRes.2008.19.47

King, V., & Scott, M. E. (2005). A comparison of cohabiting relationships among older and younger adults. *Journal of Marriage and the Family, 67*, 271–285. doi:10.1111/j.0022-2445.2005.00115.x

Kingsberg, S. A. (2000). The psychological impact of aging on sexuality and relationships. *Journal of Women's Health and Gender-Based Medicine, 9*(Suppl. 1), 33–38. doi:10.1089/152460900318849

Kontula, O., & Haavio-Mannila, E. (2009). The impact of aging on human sexual activity and sexual desire. *Journal of Sex Research, 46*, 46–56. doi:10.1080/00224490802624414

Kurdek, L. A. (1995). Developmental changes in relationship quality in gay and lesbian cohabiting couples. *Developmental Psychology, 31*, 86–94. doi:10.1037/0012-1649.31.1.86

Lammers, C., Ireland, M., Resnick, M., & Blum, R. (2000). Influences on adolescents' decision to postpone onset of sexual intercourse: A survival analysis of virginity among youths aged 13 to 18 years. *Journal of Adolescent Health, 26*, 42–48. doi:10.1016/S1054-139X(99)00041-5

Laumann, E. O., Gagnon, J. H., Michael, R. T., & Michaels, S. (2000). *The social organization of sexuality: Sexual practices in the United States.* Chicago, IL: University of Chicago Press.

Leichliter, J. S. P. (2008). Heterosexual anal sex: Part of an expanding sexual repertoire? [Editorial]. *Sexually Transmitted Diseases, 35*, 910–911. doi:10.1097/OLQ.0b013e31818af12f

Lescano, C. M., Houck, C. D., Brown, L. K., Doherty, G., DiClemente, R. J., Fernandez, M. I., . . . Silver,

B. J. (2009). Correlates of heterosexual anal intercourse among at-risk adolescents and young adults. *American Journal of Public Health, 99*, 1131–1136. doi:10.2105/AJPH.2007.123752

Lindau, S. T., & Gavrilova, N. (2010). Sex, health, and years of sexually active life gained due to good health: Evidence from two US population based cross sectional surveys of ageing. *BMJ, 340*, c810. doi:10.1136/bmj.c810

Lindau, S. T., Schumm, L. P., Laumann, E. O., Levinson, W., O'Muircheartaigh, C. A., & Waite, L. J. (2007). A study of sexuality and health among older adults in the United States. *New England Journal of Medicine, 357*, 762–774. doi:10.1056/NEJMoa067423

Lindberg, L. D., Jones, R., & Santelli, J. S. (2008). Noncoital sexual activities among adolescents. *Journal of Adolescent Health, 43*, 231–238. doi:10.1016/j.jadohealth.2007.12.010

Linder, J. R., & Collins, W. A. (2005). Parent and peer predictors of physical aggression and conflict management in romantic relationships in early adulthood. *Journal of Family Psychology, 19*, 252–262. doi:10.1037/0893-3200.19.2.252

Loewenson, P. R., Ireland, M., & Resnick, M. D. (2004). Primary and secondary sexual abstinence in high school students. *Journal of Adolescent Health, 34*, 209–215. doi:10.1016/j.jadohealth.2003.05.002

Longmore, M. A., Eng, A. L., Giordano, P. C., & Manning, W. D. (2009). Parenting and adolescents' sexual initiation. *Journal of Marriage and Family, 71*, 969–982. doi:10.1111/j.1741-3737.2009.00647.x

Mahay, J., & Lewin, A. C. (2007). Age and the desire to marry. *Journal of Family Issues, 28*, 706–723. doi:10.1177/0192513X06297272

Malta, S., & Farquharson, K. (2012). The initiation and progression of late-life romantic relationships. *Journal of Sociology*. Advance online publication. doi:10.1177/1440783312442254

Maticka-Tyndale, E. (1992). Social construction of HIV transmission and prevention among heterosexual young adults. *Social Problems, 39*, 238–252. doi:10.2307/3096960

Maynard, E., Carballo-Diéguez, A., Ventuneac, A., Exner, T., & Mayer, K. (2009). Women's experiences with anal sex: Motivations and implications for STD prevention. *Perspectives on Sexual and Reproductive Health, 41*, 142–149. doi:10.1363/4114209

McBride, K. R., & Fortenberry, J. D. (2010). Heterosexual anal sexuality and anal sex behaviors: A review. *Journal of Sex Research, 47*, 123–136. doi:10.1080/00224490903402538

McCabe, J., Brewster, K. L., & Tillman, K. H. (2011). Patterns and correlates of same-sex sexual activity among U.S. teenagers and young adults. *Perspectives on Sexual and Reproductive Health, 43*, 142–150. doi:10.1363/4314211

Meston, C. M., & Buss, D. (2007). Why humans have sex. *Archives of Sexual Behavior, 36*, 477–507. doi:10.1007/s10508-007-9175-2

Michael, R. T., Gagnon, J. H., Laumann, E. O., & Kolata, G. (1994). *Sex in America: A definitive survey*. New York, NY: Little, Brown.

Miller, B. C., & Benson, B. (1999). Romantic and sexual relationships in adolescence. In W. Furman, B. Brown, & C. Feiring (Eds.), *The development of romantic relationships in adolescence* (pp. 99–121). Cambridge, England: Cambridge University Press.

Miller, B. C., Monson, B. H., & Norton, M. C. (1995). The effects of forced sexual intercourse on White female adolescents. *Child Abuse and Neglect, 19*, 1289–1301. doi:10.1016/0145-2134(95)00081-I

Misegades, L., Page-Shafer, K., Halperin, D., & McFarland, W. (2001). Anal intercourse among young low-income women in California: An overlooked risk factor for HIV? *AIDS, 15*, 534–535. doi:10.1097/00002030-200103090-00017

Mishra, G. D., Cooper, R., & Kuh, D. (2010). A life course approach to reproductive health: Theory and methods. *Maturitas, 65*, 92–97. doi:10.1016/j.maturitas.2009.12.009

Morrison-Beedy, D., Carey, M. P., Côté-Arsenault, D., Seibold-Simpson, S., & Robinson, K. A. (2008). Understanding sexual abstinence in urban adolescent girls. *Journal of Obstetric, Gynecologic and Neonatal Nursing, 37*, 185–195. doi:10.1111/j.1552-6909.2008.00217.x

Mosher, W. D., Chandra, A., & Jones, J. (2005). Sexual behavior and selected health measures: Men and women 15–44 years of age, United States, 2002. *Advance Data, 362*, 1–55.

Mulhall, J., King, R., Glina, S., & Hvidsten, K. (2008). Importance of and satisfaction with sex among men and women worldwide: Results of the global better sex survey. *Journal of Sexual Medicine, 5*, 788–795. doi:10.1111/j.1743-6109.2007.00765.x

Murray, J., & Adam, B. D. (2001). Aging, sexuality, and HIV issues among older gay men. *Canadian Journal of Human Sexuality, 10*, 75–90.

Nagy, S., & DiClemente, R. (1995). Adverse factors associated with forced sex among Southern adolescent girls. *Pediatrics, 96*, 944–946.

Nelson, L. E., & Morrison-Beedy, D. (2008). Sex partner type and condom use in African American adolescent mothers: A literature review. *Journal of Child and Adolescent Psychiatric Nursing, 21*, 213–219. doi:10.1111/j.1744-6171.2008.00140.x

Nelson, L. E., Morrison-Beedy, D., Kearney, M. H., & Dozier, A. (2011). Sexual partner type taxonomy use among urban Black adolescent mothers. *Canadian Journal of Human Sexuality, 20*, 1–10.

Nettleman, M., Ingersoll, K. S., & Ceperich, S. D. (2006). Characteristics of adult women who abstain from sexual intercourse. *Journal of Family Planning and Reproductive Health Care, 32*, 23–24. doi:10.1783/147118906775275226

Nusbaum, M. R. H., & Hamilton, C. D. (2002). The proactive sexual health history. *American Family Physician, 66*, 1705–1712.

Oliver, M. B., & Hyde, J. S. (1993). Gender differences in sexuality: A meta-analysis. *Psychological Bulletin, 114*, 29–51. doi:10.1037/0033-2909.114.1.29

Olmstead, S. B., Pasley, K., & Fincham, F. D. (2012). Hooking up and penetrative hookups: Correlates that differentiate college men. *Archives of Sexual Behavior*. Advance online publication. doi:10.1007/s10508-012-9907-9

O'Sullivan, L. F. (2005). The social and relationship contexts and cognitions associated with romantic and sexual experiences of early-adolescent girls. *Sexuality Research and Social Policy, 2*, 13–24. doi:10.1525/srsp.2005.2.3.13

O'Sullivan, L. F., & Brooks-Gunn, J. (2005). The timing of changes in girls' sexual cognitions and behaviors in early adolescence: A prospective, cohort study. *Journal of Adolescent Health, 37*, 211–219. doi:10.1016/j.jadohealth.2004.08.019

O'Sullivan, L. F., Cheng, M. M., Harris, K. M., & Brooks-Gunn, J. (2007). I wanna hold your hand: The progression of social, romantic and sexual events in adolescent relationships. *Perspectives on Sexual and Reproductive Health, 39*, 100–107. doi:10.1363/3910007

Ott, M. A., Millstein, S. G., Ofner, S., & Halpern-Felsher, B. L. (2006). Greater expectations: Adolescents' positive motivations for sex. *Perspectives on Sexual and Reproductive Health, 38*, 84–89. doi:10.1363/3808406

Ott, M. A., Pfeiffer, E. J., & Fortenberry, J. D. (2006). Perceptions of sexual abstinence among high-risk early and middle adolescents. *Journal of Adolescent Health, 39*, 192–198. doi:10.1016/j.jadohealth.2005.12.009

Palacios-Ceña, D., Carrasco-Garrido, P., Hernández-Barrera, V., Alonso-Blanco, C., Jiménez-García, R., & Fernández-de-las-Peñas, C. (2012). Sexual behaviors among older adults in Spain: Results from a population-based national sexual health survey. *Journal of Sexual Medicine, 9*, 121–129. doi:10.1111/j.1743-6109.2011.02511.x

Pan American Health Organization & World Health Organization. (2000). *Promotion of sexual health: Recommendations for action*. Retrieved from http://www.paho.org/english/hcp/hca/promotionsexualhealth.pdf

Park, K. (2002). Stigma management among the voluntarily childless. *Sociological Perspectives, 45*, 21–45. doi:10.1525/sop.2002.45.1.21

Pathela, P., & Schillinger, J. A. (2010). Sexual behaviors and sexual violence: Adolescents with opposite-, same-, or both-sex partners. *Pediatrics, 126*, 879–886. doi:10.1542/peds.2010-0396

Paul, E. L., & Hayes, K. A. (2002). The casualties of "casual" sex: A qualitative exploration of the phenomenology of college students' hookups. *Journal of Social and Personal Relationships, 19*, 639–661. doi:10.1177/0265407502195006

Pauls, R. N., Occhino, J. A., & Dryfhout, V. L. (2008). Effects of pregnancy on female sexual function and body image: A prospective study. *Journal of Sexual Medicine, 5*, 1915–1922. doi:10.1111/j.1743-6109.2008.00884.x

Pinkerton, S. D., Bogart, L. M., Cecil, H., & Abramson, P. R. (2003). Factors associated with masturbation in a collegiate sample. *Journal of Psychology and Human Sexuality, 14*, 103–121. doi:10.1300/J056v14n02_07

Pinkerton, S. D., Cecil, H., Bogart, L. M., & Abramson, P. R. (2003). The pleasures of sex: An empirical investigation. *Cognition and Emotion, 17*, 341–353. doi:10.1080/02699930302291

Prinstein, M. J., Meade, C. S., & Cohen, G. L. (2003). Adolescent oral sex, peer popularity, and perceptions of best friends' sexual behavior. *Journal of Pediatric Psychology, 28*, 243–249. doi:10.1093/jpepsy/jsg012

Proulx, C. M., Helms, H. M., & Buehler, C. (2007). Marital quality and personal well-being: A meta-analysis. *Journal of Marriage and Family, 69*, 576–593. doi:10.1111/j.1741-3737.2007.00393.x

Rademakers, J., Rademakers, M. J. C., & Straver, C. J. (2003). Body awareness and physical intimacy: An exploratory study. In J. Bancroft (Ed.), *Sexual development in childhood* (Vol. 1, pp. 121–126). Bloomington: Indiana University Press.

Reece, M., Herbenick, D., Schick, V., Sanders, S. A., Dodge, B., & Fortenberry, J. D. (2010). Sexual behaviors, relationships, and perceived health among adult men in the United States: Results from a national probability sample. *Journal of Sexual Medicine, 7*, 291–304. doi:10.1111/j.1743-6109.2010.02009.x

Reed, J. M. (2006). Not crossing the "extra line": How cohabitors with children view their unions. *Journal of Marriage and Family, 68*, 1117–1131. doi:10.1111/j.1741-3737.2006.00318.x

Rehman, U. S., Rellini, A. H., & Fallis, E. (2011). The importance of sexual self-disclosure to sexual satisfaction and functioning in committed relationships. *Journal of Sexual Medicine, 8*, 3108–3115. doi:10.1111/j.1743-6109.2011.02439.x

Reynolds, M. A., & Herbenick, D. (2003). The nature of childhood sexual experiences: Two studies 50 years apart. In J. Bancroft (Ed.), *Sexual development in childhood* (pp. 134–155). Bloomington: Indiana University Press.

Robbins, C. L., Schick, V., Reece, M., Herbenick, D., Sanders, S. A., Dodge, B., & Fortenberry, J. D. (2011). Prevalence, frequency, and associations of masturbation with partnered sexual behaviors among US adolescents. *Archives of Pediatrics and Adolescent Medicine, 165*, 1087–1093. doi:10.1001/archpediatrics.2011.142

Roisman, G. I., Clausell, E., Holland, A., Fortuna, K., & Elieff, C. (2008). Adult romantic relationships as contexts of human development: A multimethod comparison of same-sex couples with opposite-sex dating, engaged, and married dyads. *Developmental Psychology, 44*, 91–101. doi:10.1037/0012-1649.44.1.91

Rosenbaum, J. E. (2006). Reborn a virgin: Adolescents' retracting of virginity pledges and sexual histories. *American Journal of Public Health, 96*, 1098–1103. doi:10.2105/AJPH.2005.063305

Rostosky, S. S., Galliher, R. V., Welsh, D. P., & Kawaguchi, M. C. (2000). Sexual behaviors and relationship qualities in late adolescent couples. *Journal of Adolescence, 23*, 583–597. doi:10.1006/jado.2000.0345

Rye, B. J., & Meaney, G. J. (2007). The pursuit of sexual pleasure. *Sexuality and Culture, 11*, 28–51. doi:10.1007/BF02853934

Sadovsky, R., Basson, R., Krychman, M., Morales, A. M., Schover, L., Wang, R., & Incrocci, L. (2010). Cancer and sexual problems. *Journal of Sexual Medicine, 7*, 349–373. doi:10.1111/j.1743-6109.2009.01620.x

Sanders, S. A., & Reinisch, J. M. (1999). Would you say you "had sex" if . . .? *JAMA, 281*, 275–277. doi:10.1001/jama.281.3.275

Sandfort, T. G. M., & Erhardt, A. A. (2004). Sexual health: A useful public health paradigm or a moral imperative. *Archives of Sexual Behavior, 33*, 181–187. doi:10.1023/B:ASEB.0000026618.16408.e0

Santelli, J., Carter, M., Orr, M., & Dittus, P. (2009). Trends in sexual risk behaviors, by nonsexual risk behavior involvement, U.S. high school students, 1991–2007. *Journal of Adolescent Health, 44*, 372–379. doi:10.1016/j.jadohealth.2008.08.020

Santelli, J., Ott, M. A., Lyon, M., Rogers, J., Summers, D., & Schleifer, R. (2006). Abstinence and abstinence-only education: A review of U.S. policies and programs. *Journal of Adolescent Health, 38*, 72–81. doi:10.1016/j.jadohealth.2005.10.006

Sassler, S. (2004). The process of entering into cohabiting unions. *Journal of Marriage and Family, 66*, 491–505. doi:10.1111/j.1741-3737.2004.00033.x

Sassler, S. (2010). Partnering across the life course: Sex, relationships, and mate selection. *Journal of Marriage and Family, 72*, 557–575. doi:10.1111/j.1741-3737.2010.00718.x

Sayegh, M. A., Fortenberry, J. D., Anderson, J. G., & Orr, D. P. (2005). Effects of relationship quality on chlamydia infection among adolescent women. *Journal of Adolescent Health, 37*, 163e161–163e168.

Schick, V., Herbenick, D., Reece, M., Sanders, S. A., Dodge, B., Middlestadt, S. E., & Fortenberry, J. D. (2010). Sexual behaviors, condom use, and sexual health of Americans over 50: Implications for sexual health promotion for older adults. *Journal of Sexual Medicine, 7*, 315–329. doi:10.1111/j.1743-6109.2010.02013.x

Schrimshaw, E., Rosario, M., Meyer-Bahlburg, H., & Scharf-Matlick, A. (2006). Test–retest reliability of self-reported sexual behavior, sexual orientation, and psychosexual milestones among gay, lesbian, and bisexual youths. *Archives of Sexual Behavior, 35*, 220–229. doi:10.1007/s10508-005-9006-2

Seiffge-Krenke, I. (2006). Coping with relationship stressors: The impact of different working models of attachment and links to adaptation. *Journal of Youth and Adolescence, 35*, 24–38. doi:10.1007/s10964-005-9015-4

Shrier, L. A., Pierce, J. D., Emans, S. J., & DuRant, R. H. (1998). Gender differences in risk behaviors associated with forced or pressured sex. *Archives of Pediatrics and Adolescent Medicine, 152*, 57–63. doi:10.1001/archpedi.152.1.57

Shulman, J. L., & Home, S. G. (2003). The use of self-pleasure: Masturbation and body image among African American and European American women. *Psychology of Women Quarterly, 27*, 262–269. doi:10.1111/1471-6402.00106

Shulman, S., & Seiffge-Krenke, I. (2001). Adolescent romance: Between experience and relationships. *Journal of Adolescence, 24*, 417–428. doi:10.1006/jado.2001.0403

Simon, W., & Gagnon, J. H. (2003). Sexual scripts: Origins, influences and changes. *Qualitative Sociology, 26*, 491–497. doi:10.1023/B:QUAS.0000005053.99846.e5

Simpson, J. A., Collins, W. A., Tran, S., & Haydon, K. C. (2007). Attachment and the experience and expression of emotions in romantic relationships: A developmental perspective. *Journal of Personality and Social Psychology, 92*, 355–367. doi:10.1037/0022-3514.92.2.355

Smith, A. M. A., Rosenthal, D. A., & Reichler, H. (1996). High schoolers' masturbatory practices—Their relationship to sexual intercourse and personal characteristics. *Psychological Reports, 79*, 499–509. doi:10.2466/pr0.1996.79.2.499

Smith, L. J., Mulhall, J. P., Deveci, S., Monaghan, N., & Reid, M. C. (2007). Sex after seventy: A pilot study of sexual function in older persons. *Journal of Sexual Medicine, 4*, 1247–1253. doi:10.1111/j.1743-6109.2007.00568.x

Smock, P. J., Manning, W. D., & Porter, M. (2005). "Everything's there except money": How money shapes decisions to marry among cohabitors. *Journal of Marriage and Family, 67*, 680–696. doi:10.1111/j.1741-3737.2005.00162.x

Stone, N., & Ingham, R. (2002). Factors affecting British teenagers' contraceptive use at first intercourse: The importance of partner communication. *Perspectives on Sexual and Reproductive Health, 34*, 191–197. doi:10.2307/3097729

Tanner, A. E., Hensel, D. J., & Fortenberry, J. D. (2010). A prospective study of the sexual, emotional, and behavioral correlates associated with young women's first and usual coital events. *Journal of Adolescent Health, 47*, 20–25. doi:10.1016/j.jadohealth.2009.12.031

Thompson, S. (1996). *Going all the way: Teenage girls' tales of sex, romance, and pregnancy*. New York, NY: Farrar, Straus & Giroux.

Timm, T. M., & Keiley, M. K. (2011). The effects of differentiation of self, adult attachment, and sexual communication on sexual and marital satisfaction: A path analysis. *Journal of Sex and Marital Therapy, 37*, 206–223. doi:10.1080/0092623X.2011.564513

Tolman, D. L. (2002). *Dilemmas of desire: Teenage girls talk about sexuality*. Cambridge, England: Harvard University Press.

Tolman, D. L., & McClelland, S. I. (2011). Normative sexuality development in adolescence: A decade in review, 2000–2009. *Journal of Research on Adolescence, 21*, 242–255. doi:10.1111/j.1532-7795.2010.00726.x

Trudel, G., Turgeon, L., & Piche, L. (2010). Marital and sexual aspects of old age. *Sexual and Relationship Therapy, 25*, 316–341. doi:10.1080/14681991003750467

U.S. Census Bureau. (2010). *Population by age and sex, 2009*. Retrieved from http://www.census.gov/population/www/socdemo/age/age_sex_2009.html

VandeCreek, L., Peterson, F. L., & Bley, J. W. (2007). *Focus on sexual health*. Sarasota, FL: Professional Resource Press.

Van de Ven, P., Rodden, P., Crawford, J., & Kippax, S. (1997). A comparative demographic and sexual profile of older homosexually active men. *Journal of Sex Research, 34*, 349–360. doi:10.1080/00224499709551903

Vannier, S. A., & O'Sullivan, L. F. (2010). Sex without desire: Characteristics of occasions of sexual compliance in young adults' committed relationships. *Journal of Sex Research, 47*, 429–439.

Vannier, S. A., & O'Sullivan, L. F. (2012). Who gives and who gets: Why, when, and with whom young people engage in oral sex. *Journal of Youth and Adolescence, 41*, 572–582. doi:10.1007/s10964-012-9745-z

Vujeva, H. M. F. W. (2011). Depressive symptoms and romantic relationship qualities from adolescence through emerging adulthood: A longitudinal examination of influences. *Journal of Clinical Child and Adolescent Psychology, 40*, 123–135. doi:10.1080/15374416.2011.533414

Waite, L. J., Laumann, E. O., Das, A., & Schumm, L. P. (2009). Sexuality: Measures of partnerships, practices, attitudes, and problems in the National Social Life, Health, and Aging Study. *Journals of Gerontology, Series B: Psychological Sciences and Social Sciences, 64*(Suppl. 1), i56–i66. doi:10.1093/geronb/gbp038

Wierzalis, E. A., Barret, B., Pope, M., & Rankins, M. (2006). Gay men and aging: Sex and intimacy. In D. Kimmel, T. Rose, & S. David (Eds.), *Lesbian, gay, bisexual, and transgender aging: Research and clinical perspectives* (pp. 91–109). New York, NY: Columbia University Press.

Wingood, G. M., & DiClemente, R. J. (1998). Partner influences and gender-related factors associated with noncondom use among young adult African American women. *American Journal of Community Psychology, 26*, 29–51. doi:10.1023/A:1021830023545

Wingood, G. M., & DiClemente, R. J. (2000). Application of the theory of gender and power to examine HIV-related exposures, risk factors, and effective interventions for women. *Health Education and Behavior, 27*, 539–565. doi:10.1177/109019810002700502

World Association of Sexuality. (2008). *Sexual health for the millennium: A declaration and technical document synopsis*. Minneapolis, MN: World Association of Sexuality.

World Health Organization. (2002). *Defining sexual health: Report of a technical consultation on sexual health*. Retrieved from http://www.who.int/reproductive-health/publications/sexualhealth/index.html

World Health Organization. (2007). *Developing sexual health programmes: A conceptual framework for action*. Geneva, Switzerland: Author.

World Health Organization. (2010). *Measuring sexual health: Conceptual and practical considerations and related indicators*. Geneva, Switzerland: Author.

Yabiku, S. T., & Gager, C. T. (2009). Sexual frequency and the stability of marital and cohabiting unions. *Journal of Marriage and Family, 71*, 983–1000. doi:10.1111/j.1741-3737.2009.00648.x

Chapter 14

SEXUALITY IN CHILDHOOD

Sharon Lamb and Aleksandra Plocha

How does one know what is normative sexual development in childhood? Although Freud (1905/1975) boldly discussed the normative sexual lives of children, at least in terms of their unconscious lives, few following Freud have developed a theory of normative sexual development. Many scholars and sexuality educators have proclaimed that people are sexual from birth on, but because it is difficult to do research with children regarding their sexual thoughts, feelings, and behaviors, researchers rely on retrospective reports by older individuals as well as on observations by adults. Quite a bit of attention has been paid to children's sexuality via clinical reports and concerns regarding children who have been sexually abused. The emphasis has been on distinguishing normative play from sexual acting out. However, understanding children's normative sexual development from this vantage point can be problematic.

In this chapter, we review the evidence on childhood sexuality after first discussing theoretical perspectives and methodological approaches. We write from a postmodern perspective that contextualizes norms within ideologies and histories of sexuality (see Chapter 3, this volume), and so at the same time as we examine the research, we sometimes question the ways in which these norms have been established and suggest that they are fluid, even when presented as biological givens. We also write from a clinical perspective with regard to disordered and problematic behavior in hopes that this chapter will be of help to clinicians as well as scholars (see Volume 2, Chapter 4, this handbook). The effects of early sexualization through victimization, marketing, and media are also a part of this discussion of what is normative or expected within changing historical and cultural contexts (see Chapter 25, this volume).

THEORIES OF CHILDHOOD SEXUALITY

Freud was one of the first to write that people were born sexual creatures. Early on in his career, he made the discovery that childhood sexuality was connected to early sexual abuse experiences but, as Masson (1988) wrote, in response to enormous criticism from colleagues, he exchanged this theory for one in which the unconscious rather than experience played the most important role. In conjunction with what has come to be called *drive theory* (explaining instinctual sexual energy and the drive to release it), Freud (1905/1975) developed his theory of psychosexual stages. According to this theory, infants cathect to (invest libido in) various objects (actually, body parts) as they develop, first to the breast whereby sucking becomes the sexual act by which libido is discharged. Children develop through stages labeled *oral, anal, phallic, oedipal, latency,* and *genital.* In each of the first three stages, a different part of the body becomes the focus of sexual pleasure as well as release. Both the phallic phase (when the child's focus becomes the phallus) and the oedipal phase (when the child's focus becomes sexual feelings for the other-sex parent) have been met with criticism with regard to their privileging of the penis, and this criticism has come from within psychoanalytic theory as well as from without. The theory has also been criticized for its heterosexist bias

http://dx.doi.org/10.1037/14193-014
APA Handbook of Sexuality and Psychology: Vol. 1. Person-Based Approaches, D. L. Tolman and L. M. Diamond (Editors-in-Chief)

(see Chapter 18, this volume). Those who do research on childhood sexuality have also questioned the existence of a latency period whereby sexual drives, according to Freud, go underground (Friedrich, Grambsch, Broughton, Kuiper, & Beilke, 1991; Lamb, 2002, 2006; Okami, Weisner, & Olmstead, 2002). These theorists have suggested that these sexual impulses and behaviors go underground to the extent that they are hidden from parents and the culture, but that they continue.

Although Freud's (1905/1975) theory of sexual development has been widely criticized, his emphasis on sexual feelings, whether conscious or unconscious, was remarkable and brave. Ego psychologists such as Erik Erikson and object relations theorists such as Klein, Winnicott, and Fairbairn went on to deemphasize the sexual nature of these phases (Erikson, 1966; L. M. Flanagan, 2011). Erikson (1966) contextualized the stages of psychosexual development in their cultural context as expressions of crises in interpersonal growth throughout life. The object relations theorists emphasized the importance of attachment to a primary caregiver and the internalization of that relationship as a foundation for all future relationships, including sexual ones. Thus, although theories of interpersonal, relational, and intersubjective interactions arose from the work that followed Freud, something was lost in leaving behind a picture of the infant and child grappling with actual sexual feelings and thoughts, whether conscious or unconscious. That is, in focusing on the relationship, the idea of the child as a sexual being was no longer explored until recently, when Fonagy (2008) took up the charge. Object relations (psychoanalytic) theorists, Fonagy (2008) and Fonagy and Target (2006) described children's development of a sense of self through the ability to infer states of mind in themselves and in others. Representations of internal experiences such as arousal or sexual experiences become associated with certain affects on the basis of how a child's primary caregiver reflects or mirrors these experiences back to him or her. In Fonagy and Target's research, mothers reported that the way they responded to a baby's sexual arousal was to look away or ignore it. If a baby cannot find him- or herself in the other, the baby will not be able to control or understand his or her self states. This, Fonagy and Target warned, may intensify sexual arousal rather than help a child to manage it and may interfere with a child's ownership of these feelings, thereby making a state of arousal feel incongruent or alien.

Although Foucault's (1978) approach to sexuality is far too complex to explain in one or two paragraphs (see Chapter 1, this volume), this perspective is important to include for its emphasis on examining childhood sexuality in its historical context and exploring the ways in which discourse reveals ethics and ideology of the time. Foucault was interested in how repression is expressed and represented through discourse and how sexual pleasure manages to move people beyond repressive labels and practices. He described the medical and psychiatric establishment as regulating child sexuality as it does adult sexuality in order to predict damage and trauma, to support certain institutions as regulators, and to encourage self-surveillance in ways that confirm the power of these institutions. With regard to children, Foucault stated that the child is imagined as one who needs to be protected, setting up three intertwined groups: children as the innocents, psychiatrists as the establishment that defines trauma and harm, and dangerous adults who abuse children. For Foucault, pleasure was the only way out of this situation because pleasure undoes and undermines the regulated ways in which sex is permitted. In short, Foucault makes one think about how childhood sexuality is managed and what ideologies and discourse influence how it is viewed.

Theories that arose out of feminism, queer studies, and theories of gender tend to be postmodern (see Chapter 1, this volume). Fine (1988) translated Foucauldian analysis into a feminist analysis of discourse in sex education as it pertains to adolescent girls' development. Queer theory is concerned with the production of heteronormative identities (Rasmussen, 2006) by controlling discourses. Both Fine (1988) and Rasmussen (2006) argued that the discourse that surrounds sexuality controls who can be sexual and in what ways, marginalizing some forms of sexuality for various groups (e.g., adolescent girls or lesbian, gay, bisexual, and transgender youths).

Sexual script theory (Gagnon & Simon, 1973) is somewhat of a social learning theory that focuses on adults' sexual behavior and argues that individuals develop scripts for normative sexual behavior through observation and participation in culture (see Chapters 2 and 10, this volume). This theory is also supported by feminists who are social constructionists (Firth & Kitzinger, 2007). Relating this theory to childhood, one would argue either that children's scripts for sexual behavior are nonexistent or that their play involves practice of adult sexual scripts.

It is good to note that there are a few other "big" theories seeking to explain childhood sexuality that emphasize experience and culture, although anthropological studies have for some time contributed to an understanding of sexuality that is culture specific. Margaret Mead's (1961) early study marshaled a new way of questioning sexual development that took into account context and its relation to other cultural practices. She showed that the view of adolescence as stormy and sexually problematic did not exist in Samoa, where freedom for experimentation and a healthy attitude toward bodies and sex influenced a different kind of adolescence for girls growing up there in the 1940s. She wrote that among the Dobuans, "where the sex life of girls begins long before puberty, there is no initiation into tribal life and there is no cultural fear of menstruation. Among these people adolescence goes unremarked" (Mead, 1947, p. 7). Herdt's (1981, 1982) famous study of the ritualized homosexuality of boys in a culture in Papua New Guinea introduced the idea that people's perceptions of sexual orientation and of child sexual abuse are culturally and historically situated. In this culture, he found that masculinity, rather than homosexuality, was supported through the passing of the seed from men to young boys through fellatio.

There are collections of ethnographies that include childhood experiences and parenting practices that speak to the great cultural variety in sexual development and education around the globe (e.g., Martinson, 1994; see Chapter 6, this volume). A quick perusal of the many examples Janssen (2002) surveyed from the scholarly literature shows that masturbation by infants and children is common in some cultures for pleasure and amusement and that sexual play is often permitted until a certain age or as part of a certain ritual, for example, among the Zuni when boys get on top of girls and mimic adult intercourse.

Developmental theories tend to integrate biology and culture, nature and nurture; however, no one developmental perspective is used today to explain sexual development. Developmentalists generally look for the presence of certain behaviors and then for indications of change over time, whether in stages or gradually. They do not tend to question, as social constructionists do, why certain behaviors are considered sexual but not others. A common expectation is that biology provides the groundwork for sexual development, which culture then tweaks (e.g., Segal, Weisfeld, & Weisfeld, 1997). Thus, researchers look for the presence of hormones as well as for initial signs of activities and feelings associated with sex and sexuality. One focus of the developmental perspective is to look for the earliest showing of a sexual behavior. Another is to examine the sexual activity specific to a certain age group or developmental group, a grouping that would be considered established by biology, schooling, or traits that have some biological basis.

The biological perspective on childhood sexuality holds that biology and hormonal development are the driving forces behind sexual development (Buchanan, Eccles, & Becker, 1992) and sexual identity (Bailey, Dunne, & Martin, 2000; Byne, 2007; Weisfeld, 1999). Indeed, in Western societies, many ascribe to the belief that children are asexual and become sexual with the influx of hormones around age 12 (as can be seen by the absence of childhood sexuality sections in most major developmental textbooks, e.g., Belsky, 2010; Berger, 2010). Although hormones contribute to sexual changes in childhood and to the transition from childhood to adolescence, this narrow view of sexual drives, interests, thoughts, and feelings serves to reduce childhood sexual experiences, dismissing them as "just play," "experimentation," and "practice" (Lamb, 2002, 2006).

METHODS OF STUDYING CHILDHOOD SEXUALITY

Childhood sexuality is often studied as a gateway to adolescent sexuality (Martin, Luke, & Verduzco-Baker, 2007), but it deserves attention in its own right no matter how difficult it may be to obtain data in this area. Many sexual behaviors, at least in Western societies, are carried out in private and therefore difficult to study in standard ways. Attempts at quantitative work in this area have been reduced to (a) tabulating numbers of adults who remember and are willing to report their sexual activities as children (Lamb & Coakley, 1993; Leitenberg, Greenwald, & Tarran, 1989; Okami, Olmstead, & Abramson, 1997) and (b) describing observations by adults who have observed sexual behaviors in children (Fitzpatrick, Deehan, & Jennings, 1995; Freidrich, Fisher, Broughton, Houston, & Shafran, 1998; Thigpen, 2009). It goes without saying that the latter approach in particular provides, at best, a limited way of understanding what sexual behaviors exist in childhood and how those behaviors are exhibited. Instead, these types of studies inventory the kinds of sexual behaviors adults observe and are biased to the extent that adults need not only to see these behaviors to report them but also to recognize them as sexual, which is a subjective determination (de Graaf & Rademakers, 2011). Thus, the wording of questionnaires with regard to individual sexual behaviors does not always distinguish acts that are performed with sexual intention from acts that are not, for example, "undressing together" or "showing genitals" (Haugaard, 1996, p. 84) and "hugging and kissing" (Haugaard & Tilly, 1988, p. 215).

Although quantitative retrospective reports by adults are few, those that exist have lent credence to the belief that sexual behaviors occur throughout childhood, including middle childhood, the time psychoanalysts refer to as *latency*. Retrospective reports bear their own biases with regard to what is remembered, what is reported if remembered, and what is classified as sexual (de Graaf & Rademakers, 2011). Worries about sexual abuse of children as well as postchildhood experiences may lead adults to reinterpret memories of mutual play as abusive experiences (Lamb, 2002). At the same time, abusive experiences might also be remembered fondly as early sexual play and games because they were experienced that way or because they were reenvisioned as a means of coping with abuse (Lamb, 2002).

Qualitative research, generally consisting of interviews, enables researchers and clinicians to explore the meaning of childhood sexual games with individuals who report them and potentially offer insight into an individual's sexual experience at the time. This always occurs, however, through the distorted lens of memory, and the individual's current conceptualization of the experience (de Graaf & Rademakers, 2011). Qualitative questions aimed at understanding the thinking, feeling, and bodily responses of a child help to conceptualize and categorize such experiences as sexual while at the same time addressing what *sexual* means to people of different ages. Qualitative research can also help to define the wide (or narrow) range of sexual behaviors in childhood. As a starting point for such research, interviewing adults about their memories can establish what might have counted as sexual when the behavior occurred and what adults are now retrospectively counting as sexual behavior (Lamb, 2002).

Observations are another form of qualitative data (Kaeser, DiSalvo, & Moglia, 2000). Although they, as do survey data involving parents and teachers, limit findings to what is indeed observable, observations are still valuable (de Graaf & Rademakers, 2011). For younger children, observational reporting might be very helpful given that it is harder for them to keep secrets and hide their activities from the watchful eyes of those responsible for their well-being (e.g., preschool teachers observing sexual behavior). One quantitative study, however, did directly ask children about sexuality (Pluhar, DiIorio, Jennings, & Pines, 2005). Yet any account that says that sexual behavior declines after age 5 or 6 warrants suspicion; researchers should reinterpret such accounts to mean that sexual behavior is no longer observable after age 5 or 6.

ARE CHILDREN SEXUAL?

Research on the sexual behavior of children falls into three categories: (a) research that examines sexual interest of children, which usually attempts to trace the origins of certain adult preferences and practices; (b) research that reduces sexuality to acts such as masturbation or touching another child's genitals and aims to determine the presence and frequency of these acts; and (c) research that explores the narratives of childhood sexual experience primarily through memories. Although the first two foci are interesting, they tend to answer one or two questions to which many scholars already know the answers and so become primarily a project of documentation in which first times, numbers, and beginnings assume priority: Do children participate in sexual activity? If so, what kind? Some of these quantitative researchers also examine the extent to which childhood sexual experience influences adult experience (see Chapter 13, this volume). Research that explores the stories and memories of childhood sexuality aims to answer questions concerning how children are sexual and the meaning of their sexual practices.

Sexual Interest of Children

The research that examines the sexual interest of children appears to focus not on what makes children sexual but on the ages at which they begin to show sexual interest. This kind of research seems motivated by a desire to learn about what leads to adult preferences rather than about childhood sexuality in and of itself. John Money (1986) created a theory of the development of sexual arousal in which he described *love maps*. Working within a sexual scripts model, he defined love maps as schemas for preferred sexual objects and behaviors. His research indicated that the formation of love maps can occur as early as age 8.

Herdt and McClintock (2007) hypothesized that the advent of adrenal puberty, which occurs between the ages of 6 and 10, as opposed to gonadal puberty, which begins around the age of 11, is a source of adolescent sexual subjectivity, that is, the feelings, thoughts, and awareness of their own and others' sexuality, including feelings of attraction. They argued that attraction becomes stable and memorable around the age of 10 and that if one were to consult cross-cultural child development sources, one would see a much greater range and diversity of sexual development than observed in Western cultures. They supported this observation through data from a variety of cultures showing the age of 10 as an important age for puberty rites, sexualizing processes, and other indications that a child is newly perceived as a sexual person. Middle childhood is not a time of latency (as research reported in the next section has also confirmed) but a time in which psychophysiological arousal (including erotic feelings) produces "memorable and stable sexual attraction" (Herdt & McClintock, 2007, p. 184).

Those researchers who explore childhood sexual interest seem to be interested most frequently in the determination of heterosexual or homosexual (lesbian, gay, bisexual, and transgender) feelings. One study (Remafedi, Farrow, & Deisher, 1993) examined reports from 137 men regarding their first homosexual attraction, which was identified as falling between the ages of 9.27 and 10.66 years. Savin-Williams (1995) found that gay and bisexual adults reported feeling same-sex attraction at an average age of 8, although 30% recalled this feeling before elementary school (18% after puberty). Thus, the age range is very wide (see Chapter 19, this volume).

Although analyses of the sexual interests of children are rich in theory but lacking in data, there seems to be some agreement that sexual attraction begins before adolescence. While anthropologists Herdt and McClintock (2007) focused on the age of 10, it seems important to remember that gay and bisexual adults have offered memories of sexual attraction that come before elementary school. Whether these memories exist in heterosexual adults remains a question for research.

Sexual Behaviors of Children

As noted earlier, a significant portion of childhood sexuality research has focused on establishing the presence of sexual behaviors in childhood and then subsequently determining the frequency of these behaviors. Within this model, very little research has been done on childhood masturbation. Although de Graaf and Rademakers (2006) suggested that this paucity may be partly due to ingrained societal perceptions of childhood innocence and parental discomfort with childhood sexuality, it may also be explained by the fact that observing masturbation in children is difficult after they reach a certain age. When a child is young, researchers must rely on parental observation and interpretation of any act concerning touching the genitals as a form of masturbation.

Research on masturbation. Reports and research about sexual responsivity and masturbation have tended to define sex narrowly—as having to do with genitals, arousal, and, ultimately, orgasm. For example, Kinsey et al. (1953) reported orgasms in children as young as 7 months, and Rutter (1971) observed "orgasmic-like" responses in male infants as young as 5 months. In addition, infants seem to be born with the capacity for a physiological sexual response in the form of erections in male infants and vaginal lubrication in female infants (DeLamater & Friedrich, 2002; Martinson, 1976, 1994). To consider these responses to be sexual, however, is quite telling; furthermore, the very limitation of what constitutes physiological sexual response to these two potentially arbitrary genital responses betrays a bias with regard to what is meant by *sex*.

Perhaps more sexual than simple physiological responses, masturbation has been seen as an indication of early sexuality. Martinson (1994) reported adultlike masturbation in children as young as 2.5 years in both sexes. Although unable to estimate incidence, Kinsey et al. (1953) reported masturbation in female infants and girls ages 3 years and younger, with 23 observations of completed orgasm and one observation of masturbation in a 7-month-old. In presenting their survey research of parents and professionals, Friedrich et al. (1991) and Friedrich, Fisher, Broughton, Houston, and Shafran (1998) indicated that children of both genders normally touch themselves on their genitals between the ages of 2 and 9. In their review of literature on normal childhood sexuality, de Graaf and Rademakers (2006) cited Galenson's (1990) observations of sexual arousal in infants ages 15 to 19 months, which included flushing, quick breathing, and sweating. Brenot and Broussin (1996) observed that self-touch may occur even earlier, in utero.

Research on children's sexual behaviors with other children. Beyond studying arousal and masturbation, a number of researchers have examined other kinds of sexual behaviors in which children engage, albeit always using adults as reporters. In an early study, Friedrich et al. (1991) researched common sexual behaviors among 7- to 12-year-olds, those children presumed to be in latency. What was discovered, through surveying adults, was that sexuality during this age period was expressed through words, looking at nude pictures, trying to look at people undressing, and kissing nonfamily adults. In a later, very large study involving 1,114 children screened and rated by caregivers, Friedrich et al. (1998) found that sexual behaviors peaked at the age of 5 before dropping off. This finding is not surprising given that the assessment was of observable behaviors and in light of the fact that children between the ages of 5 and 8 become more interested in privacy (Money & Ehrhardt, 1972). Friedrich et al. (1998) also noted that the most common behaviors reported were touching one's own body parts at home or trying to watch others undress. Again, these limited findings seem all too expected when one considers that the results come from asking caregivers for their observations. Rather than assuming that these are the most commonly performed behaviors of young children, researchers should acknowledge that these are only the most commonly observed sexual acts. Friedrich et al. also found that mothers with more education reported more sexual behavior in their children and were more likely to believe that sexual behavior is normal. Again, it is not surprising that mothers who find sexual behavior to be normal are more willing to interpret what they see in their children as sexual and also report it to others.

Because many existing studies in this area have focused on predominantly White samples, Thigpen (2009) surveyed caregivers of 2- to 12-year-old African Americans to expand approaches to this question. Although the African American children were reported to engage in sexual behavior, their sexual behavior was not pronounced or elevated. Thigpen's findings were similar to those of Friedrich et al. (1998), but Thigpen encountered a lower level of reported masturbatory behavior that he argued might stem from lower levels of masturbation among African American adults. He also found that the frequency of sexual behavior did not decline or become covert when children approached adolescence, which may be because African American children begin sexual maturation earlier than White children.

Other studies have inquired about the sexual behavior adults have observed in children or about adult opinions regarding the sexual behavior of children. Sexual play with other children was reported by 36% of one sample of 233 parents in Ireland (Fitzpatrick et al., 1995). In research that surveyed teachers of 5- to 7-year-olds, Kaeser et al. (2000)

found that teachers observed verbal comments about sex and students attempting to touch or touching other students' genitals, butts, or breasts. Haugaard (1996) asked social workers and doctoral-level psychotherapists about the acceptability of various sexual acts between 4-year-old children and between 8-year-old children. Professionals found most acts acceptable for 4-year-olds (kissing, undressing together), with the exception of touching another child's genitals. With regard to 8-year-olds, 40% of the female professionals thought it was acceptable for two 8-year-olds to show each other their genitals, whereas only 25% of male professionals thought this. With regard to touching, 16% of female and 6% of male professionals thought this behavior was acceptable.

Some studies have arrived at questionable conclusions because of insufficient skepticism regarding survey data. For example, Rutter (1971), relying solely on caregiver reports, stated that children's interest in genitals increases between ages 2 and 5 and decreases between ages 6 and 12, when it then increases again. Today, one can guess, as was noted earlier, that the reported decrease may have more to do with what is observable than with what is true. He also observed that same-sex play occurs as a transient phase or isolated event in one of four children. Once again, looking back, researchers might now argue that same-sex play necessitated greater hiding or discretion because of homophobic concerns about same-sex sexual attraction (Lamb, 2006). Rutter (1971) and Kinsey et al. (1953) dismissed same-sex sexual play as transient, in the case of Rutter, or "casual and fruitless" (Kinsey et al., 1948, as cited in Martinson, 1994, p. 58), presumably because it did not relate to adult sexuality or had little to do with heterosexual development. As we describe in the next section, many of the imaginative games female children play with each other have a heterosexual storyline and so simultaneously promote and reflect same-sex and heterosexual practice and interest.

Pluhar et al. (2005), as noted earlier, directly asked children themselves about sexual behaviors. Of course, asking children may not be any more reliable a method than asking adults what they have observed. Given the cultural taboos regarding sexual play in childhood, many would most likely deny this sort of play or report only the most minimal of experiences. In their study of 377 urban children ages 6 to 12, 17% of the children surveyed had played games that involved boys and girls hugging or kissing each other; of 11- to 12-year-olds, 10% had "made out," 6% had touched a boy's penis, and 5% had touched a girl's vagina.

Taken together, this kind of research indicates a common interest in what children do, an interest that cannot be fully explored by surveying adults or by interviewing children. Yet having a few of these studies indicates what falls within the realm of possibility for children of all ages. The research by Pluhar et al. (2005) suggests that children exhibit sexual interest and participate in acts that are considered sexual, although touching someone's penis or vagina is considered part of a problematic sexual category.

Retrospective research on children's sexual behavior with other children. Haugaard (1996) asked more than 600 undergraduates to complete a survey regarding sexual experiences in childhood, and 59% of undergraduates recalled at least one sexual experience with another child (recall, however, that "undressing together" was counted as a sexual experience). He found that 38% reported a sexual experience before age 7, 39% between the ages of 7 and 10, and 35% at ages 11 and 12. More men than women reported at least one experience between the ages of 7 and 12. In another retrospective study with more than 1,000 undergraduates, also counting hugging and kissing as sexual encounters, he found that 42% remembered at least one.

Lamb and Coakley (1993) also used retrospective reporting to identify percentages of types of child sexual interpersonal behaviors. In their study of 128 undergraduate women, 85% had played some sexual game in childhood, a notably higher percentage than that obtained by those researchers who queried parents or teachers. In this study, about one quarter of participants had shown their genitals to another child; 15% had touched another child's genitals while clothed; 17% had touched another child's genitals while unclothed; 6% had used some object around the genitals in their play; and 4% had engaged in mouth–genital contact. Within their sample, cross-gender play was more likely to involve persuasion, manipulation, or coercion.

Beyond what children do and the frequency with which they do it, one additional question in which empirical researchers have expressed interest concerns the effects of such play. For example, researchers are interested in what the responses are of children who engage in such play and whether the play or sexual behavior in which children engage has some effect on adult development or, more specifically, on adult sexuality. In a survey of more than 1,000 undergraduates, Haugaard and Tilly (1988) examined positive and negative responses to sexual encounters with other children in childhood. Most of the experiences reported were heterosexual. As expected, those who experienced coercion reported less positive experiences. Those who played with friends or relatives viewed their sexual encounters as more positive. The type of sexual act involved in the encounter (e.g., sexual kissing, exposing of genitalia, fondling, oral sex, intercourse) was not, interestingly, associated with the response. That is, sexual encounters that involved genitals were not experienced as more or less positive than those that did not. The authors concluded that more than the extent of the sexual experience, the atmosphere surrounding the sexual experience was what had the greatest influence on the overall response to it.

With regard to effects in adulthood, Okami et al. (1997) found that having had a sexual experience with another child between the ages of 3 and 6 had no relation to long-term adjustment. Leitenberg, Detzer, and Srebnik (1993) asked college students to report on their masturbation experiences in childhood and adolescence. Having masturbation experiences was not related to adult sexual adjustment examined through measures of sexual functioning, sexual satisfaction, and frequency of sexual difficulties (see Chapters 8 and 11, this volume). Leitenberg et al. (1989) asked college students about their sexual activity with other children before age 13. Having sexual activity with other children during childhood appears to have little relation to later sexual behavior and adjustment. Okami et al. suggested that it may be futile to look at long-term effects and that researchers instead need to focus on the interaction between peers and the contexts in which they occur. Leitenberg et al. (1989) suggested that the mere absence or presence of sexual experience is too broad a category to show demonstrable impact, and future studies might investigate specific types of activity in this regard.

Sexual stories from childhood. The beauty of gathering stories from adults about their sexual experiences as children is that narratives provide not only a richer depiction of what occurred and in what context, but also provide insight into the affect and meaning of such events. As Lamb (2002) noted in her study of more than 100 women who were asked to look back on their sexual experiences and sexual play and games in childhood, the type of sexual behavior engaged in had very little to do with the affect associated with it. Although adults may differentiate between lesser and more serious sexual acts, a child, it appears, can feel every bit as guilty and stressed about something an adult might consider minor and feel positive and casual about something an adult might feel is fairly adult and substantially sexual. Of note in the examples in Lamb's book are those women who reported feeling a sexual thrill when simply touching bottom to bottom (butt to butt) at a sleepover and another woman who as a child simply laid down on the floor and pretended to be a glamorous dead woman clad in a slip in a story about detectives who entered a room to find a murdered woman. The "thrill" came when the detectives would say, "Isn't she beautiful?" Sexual feelings were conveyed by participants through the following kinds of remarks: "We did wondrous things with her," "It was very thrilling," "It was titillating and fun . . . it was a feeling," and "It was very, you know, intoxicating . . . very arousing" (Lamb, 2004, p. 378). Some even remarked, "I think I got sexually excited" (Lamb, 2004, p. 378).

To the extent that some of these games were not sexual by standards used by survey researchers to identify sexual behaviors and events, they demonstrate that what is considered sexual is highly fluid. These experiences are also a reminder of how narrow the definition of sexual is when it focuses on genital involvement, contributing to a cultural division between childhood sex and adult sex. Adult sex would purportedly involve more direct genital contact and nonimaginative interactions—not play or practice sex, but real sex. This theme of what was real and not real about the sex was something with which Lamb's (2002) participants had difficulty as well, tending to define play that had some arousal component to it as more real and adultlike.

Lamb (2002) categorized the sexual play of girls into themes. There were the "chase and kiss," "I'll show you mine if you show me yours," and "playing doctor" games, all of which are considered normative in childhood in that a public discourse about such games exists. However, the intensity of the feelings while playing these games, the seriousness of the games, the level of genital involvement, and the guilt feelings varied among girls. There were also games concerning Barbie dolls, games that mimicked adult experiences such as playing house or school with a sexual twist, going to a nightclub, or even pretending to be prostitutes.

The majority of the sexual play and games that Lamb's (2002, 2004) participants reported involved members of the same sex. Earlier research suggested that cross-sex games may involve more coercion and bullying (Lamb & Coakley, 1993). Lamb conjectured that the games she reported were likely same sex because in the United States today, children are sex segregated in their play after about the age of 6. Moreover, girls' friendships are known to have many intimate qualities (Rose, 1995). Nevertheless, the same-sex quality of the girls' games troubled girls and made them wonder at the time and in retrospect whether they were lesbians, particularly if their games produced sexual arousal. Some girls protected their heterosexuality, and thus their feelings of engaging in more normative behavior, by couching their sexual play in heterosexual scenarios ("You be the boy and I'll be the girl") and then switching roles (Lamb, 2004).

In her feminist analysis of this play, Lamb made the point that the more sexual the game felt to a girl, the more aroused she may have been during the game, the more likely she was to describe the game as wrong and to feel guilty about it, and the more likely she was to see herself as boylike. Girls who described themselves as very interested in sex in childhood saw themselves as different from other girls, and Lamb described this phenomenon as coming from a cultural understanding of girls as asexual or of femininity as embodying a passive sexuality. A girl who wanted sexual experiences was outside of the norm. One girl who saw herself as too interested in sex described her behavior as "very bizarre," explaining, "I was a girl and I shouldn't want that." When a girl's role in play was more assertive, when she did not play the ravished, courted, or pursued passive female, she would define her subjectivity as "male" or "weird."

Very few stories of boys' childhood sexual experiences have been collected. Those that have been tended to examine the way boys may have gotten themselves into trouble or categorized as sex offenders (P. Flanagan, 2010). Those researchers who examine boys' sexuality have primarily examined how hegemonic masculinity is expressed through sexual posturing at the end of childhood and beginning of adolescence. For example, Cohan (2009) observed "conquest" discourse among adolescent boys and an attitude that turned sex into something done "for the sake of the group" (p. 161). Research conducted in three coeducational schools in England to explore the response to sex education showed that 13- to 14-year-old boys ask questions about penis size, erections, and positions in sex and girls want to know more about the pressure to have sex and contraception (Forrest, 2010). A British ethnographic study found that boys ages 10 to 11 "performed" masculine sexuality through highly publicized heterosexual relationships, sexual harassment of girls, and public sex talk (Renold, 2007). These studies have focused on gender roles as much as actual sexuality and tended in this way to focus on problematic male sexuality rather than any joyful aspects of sex (Brown, Lamb, & Tappan, 2010).

The study of children's sexual experiences rarely includes the imaginative games that children play that incorporate sex, perhaps because the study of the sexual lives of children has been influenced by a framework that measures child sexuality against adult sexuality, marking progress through stages or steps toward a normative heterosexual, genital-involved sexuality that is imagined to be "adult." Instead, the scholar of childhood sexuality might do better to question the idea that play, practice, and experimentation are only the purview of childhood sex and whether arousal and "real sex" are the purview of adult sex.

INFLUENCES ON CHILDHOOD SEXUAL DEVELOPMENT

Several influences on childhood sexual development have been heavily researched, especially parental influences. Parents and their educational strategies, beliefs and attitudes, and parenting approaches have all become grist for the mill of understanding how children develop sexually. Quite a bit of research has also been done on the effects of sexual abuse on childhood sexuality as well as on later sexual well-being. Finally, the media have recently been investigated as an influence on children's sexual development since the American Psychological Association's (APA's) 2007 *Report of the APA Task Force on the Sexualization of Girls* (see Volume 2, Chapter 12, this handbook).

Parental Influence on Development and Expression of Sexuality

Parents, peers, and the media are perhaps the primary socializers of childhood sexuality (Martin et al., 2007). The literature regarding parental influence on the development and expression of sexuality has focused primarily on parent–child communication about sex, examining the content and process of the communication, factors predictive of communication, and behavioral outcomes (DiIorio, Pluhar, & Belcher, 2003). Very little, if any, research has focused on peer or sibling influence in childhood sexuality, although most of the stories and events described in both qualitative and quantitative research are stories of sexual activity between peers.

Americans consider parents the principal sexual educators of children (Pluhar, Jennings, & DiIorio, 2006). Parents tend to communicate more with older children (Grades 6–8) than with younger children (kindergarten–Grade 5; Byers, Sears, & Weaver, 2008). Self-efficacy (with regard to talking about sexual issues) and comfort seem to influence whether a parent will speak to a child about sex (Pluhar, DiIorio, & McCarty, 2008). Also, in one study (Byers et al., 2008), those who supported comprehensive sex education were more likely to encourage their children to ask questions or to discuss topics in greater detail than those who did not. Impediments to frank discussions about sex with children include parents' desire to preserve what they see as the innocence of childhood (DiIorio et al., 2003; Hutchinson & Cederbaum, 2011), embarrassment, lack of knowledge, and poor communication style (DiIorio et al., 2003).

Gender also makes a difference. In a study of 631 mothers of 3- to 6-year-olds, Martin and Luke (2010) found that mothers spoke more to their daughters than to their sons about relationships, reproduction, and the morality of sexual behavior. However, mothers did not differentiate between boys and girls with regard to communication about sexual abuse or pleasure (few talked about pleasure at all). Research has consistently indicated that mothers communicate more with daughters than with sons and fathers communicate more with sons than with daughters (DiIorio et al., 2003; King & Lorusso, 1997). Mother–daughter communication tends to be more reciprocal, or interactive, and mother–son communication tends to be more direct, or one-sided (Whalen, Henker, Hollingshead, & Burgess, 1996).

Martin (2009) also described mother–daughter communication as *heterosexualization*. Although she found that mothers did not talk about sex but rather about romance (a love-filled, monogamous, reproductive relationship), this discourse served to socialize 3- to 6-year-old daughters into heterosexuality. Of the mothers surveyed, 62% never mentioned gays or lesbians. From this survey, it appears that parents who do educate children about the possibility of being gay or lesbian do not do so in a way that discusses sex.

Gender of parent seems to be related to the frequency of and initiation of sex education with children. Both male and female adolescents have more frequent conversations with their mother than with their father (DiIorio, Kelley, & Hockenberry-Eaton, 1999). Depending on the topic, 1% to 16% of female adolescents had had a discussion with their father, whereas 7% to 30% of adolescent males had. With regard to discussions with mothers, as many as 60% of boys and 80% of girls discussed certain topics with their mothers. The conversations that male and female adolescents did have with their parents were similar, but the conversations with boys seemed to emphasize the consequences of sexually transmitted diseases, AIDS, and condom use, and the conversations with girls seemed to emphasize abstinence and normal development (DiIorio et al., 1999). Additional research has suggested that those fathers who discussed sex with their children generally discussed biology, the benefits of delaying sex, and potential negative consequences (Wilson, Dalberth, & Koo, 2010). A meta-analysis of work before 2003 showed that parental age and ethnicity, socioeconomic class, age, educational attainment, and level of religiosity have not been determined to be predictors of whether parent–child communication about sex occurred (DiIorio et al., 2003). The study examined 95 research studies from 1980 through 2002 and thus represented more than two decades of parental studies.

With regard to content, DiIorio et al. (2003), in their review of the literature, identified AIDS, sexually transmitted diseases, dating, menstruation, reproduction, birth control, and pregnancy as commonly discussed topics. Research from the 1990s showed that 70% of mothers said they had discussed AIDS with their school-age children (first, third, and fifth grades), whereas only 41% of mothers said their children asked them questions about AIDS (Sly et al., 1995; see Chapter 22, this volume). Sexual abuse appears to have been a popular topic, especially for parents with younger children (Pluhar et al., 2006), and changes in a child's body, especially in daughters, were seen as a natural cue to talk about sex (Pluhar et al., 2006, 2008). African American and Latina mothers reported that both body changes and an interest in boys were seen as signals to talk about sex (O'Sullivan, Meyer-Bahlburg, & Watkins, 2001). Parents of young children used media as a cue for initiating conversations, describing "teachable moments" (DiIorio et al., 2003). The earlier overall communication starts, the more likely it is to persist and develop further (Pluhar & Kuriloff, 2004).

Some researchers have noted that some content is consistently neglected in early talks about sex. For example, physical pleasure is neglected in conversations with girls (DiIorio et al., 2003; Downie & Coates, 1999). Also, some have indicated that girls receive mixed messages about sex (e.g., Philpy, 2007). Pluhar and Kuriloff (2004) discussed Ward and Wyatt's (1994) finding that White and Black women reported simultaneously receiving positive nonverbal messages and negative verbal messages.

Findings are mixed with regard to the effects of parent–child communication on future sexual activity, delaying sexual activity, and use of contraception (DiIorio et al., 2003), with some studies showing an effect and others not. The quality of the parental relationship is particularly important in early childhood, however, and seems to have an influence on adolescent sexual relationships (Pluhar et al., 2006). One study of college women showed that the greater amount of communication from one's mother, the more the daughter in college would see herself as sexually assertive and would have positive affect around sexuality (Barone & Wiederman, 1997). Amount of communication did not relate to sexual experience. Of note, those women who reported receiving greater communications with a negative emotional tone also reported having more sexual experience and more negative thoughts about sexuality. Barone and Wiederman (1997) found no relationship between mothers' perceived emotional tone and sexual comfort, assertiveness, and affect. Moore and Davidson (1999) also looked at the possible effects of parents as first sex-information sources on daughters' behavior and attitude and found that parents being the first source correlated with safer sexual behaviors and more positive sexual attitudes.

Sexual Abuse as an Influence on Childhood Sexuality

It is well known among clinicians that children who have been sexually abused exhibit higher levels of sexual behaviors (Browning & Laumann, 1997; Einbender & Friedrich, 1989; Friedrich, Trane, & Gully, 2005; Kendall-Tackett, Williams, & Finkelhor, 1993). Indeed, many of the studies that have examined normative sexual behavior in children have done so to differentiate problematic behavior from the norm (Friedrich et al., 1991, 2001; Friedrich & Grambsch, 1992), so much so that some have argued that "the vast majority of the extant research on sexuality and early childhood is tied to a social problem—childhood sexual abuse—while other aspects of sexuality in childhood are completely ignored" (Martin et al., 2007, p. 235). For example, Kendall-Tackett et al. (1993) looked across seven studies to find that 34% of sexually abused children had problems with sexual behavior; that is, they exhibited behavior that was developmentally inappropriate or potentially harmful to themselves or others. Gray, Pithers, Busconi, and Houchens (1999) found that 95% of sexually abused children had problem sexual behaviors. However, how do these rates compare with those of children who had not been sexually abused? Friedrich and Grambsch (1992) compared 880 children who had not been sexually abused with 276 who had and found that those who had been sexually abused were more likely to have touched another child's genitals, rubbed their bodies against other people, hugged a strange adult, or touched their genitals in public. Touching one's genitals in private did not distinguish one group from another. However, Drach, Wientzen, and Ricci (2001) found that of those children with sexual behavior problems, only 25% had been sexually abused. Those children identified with sexual behavior problems were more likely to have been sexually or physically abused as children (Letourneau, Schoenwald, & Sheidow, 2004). Clearly, not all children who were sexually abused develop sexual behavior problems. Hall, Matthews, and Pearce (1998) identified several variables predictive of sexual behavior problems among sexually abused children: sexual arousal during the abuse, use of sadism, and a history of physical and emotional abuse. Even more recently, Kellogg (2010) found that several factors contributed to whether a child who has been sexually abused will go on to develop sexual behavior problems. These factors include experiencing penetration, experiencing abuse by a family member, and experiencing abuse when the child was very young.

The Media as Influences on Childhood Sexuality

In the past decade, a number of journalists (Bloom, 2004; Dalton, 2005) and researchers (Attwood, 2006; Cook & Kaiser, 2004; Lamb & Brown, 2006; Levin & Kilbourne, 2008; Merskin, 2004) have pointed to what they have seen as early sexualization of children by marketers and the media. Since the *Report of the APA Task Force on the Sexualization of Girls* (APA, 2007), the primary focus has been on girls' early sexualization and the way the media invite girls to participate in what some have termed *raunch culture, pornographication,* and *striptease culture* (Levy, 2005; McNair, 1996, 2002; see Volume 2, Chapter 1, this handbook). One focus of this concern has been on media and marketing that promote to younger girls behaviors and products meant for older girls and adult women. Additional focus has been on their promotion of a narrow beauty ideal that equates becoming sexual with becoming sexy and on the overrepresentation of objectified female figures in the media that girls consume. Also, many have been concerned with the imposition of sexual looks on younger and younger girls, although little evidence of this was found in the research. Still, examples abound, such as the world of child beauty pageants in which girls wear adult-like clothing and makeup and are encouraged to flirt with the audience (Cookson, 2001), and magazine photo shoots that create an illusion of sexual maturity with certain poses, makeup, and lack of clothing (Cortese, 1999). It is important to note, however, that although scholars now know how exposure may produce earlier engagement in heterosexual intercourse (e.g., Martino et al., 2006), they still know little about how consumption of these materials can affect the sexual lives of children in childhood.

CONTROVERSIES REGARDING THE INNOCENCE OF CHILDREN

Considerable work relative to childhood sexuality has been done in two major areas: sexual behavior problems and the "innocence" of children. In the area of sexual behavior problems, clinicians and researchers are concerned with the trend toward labeling children with non-normative sexual interests and behaviors as sex offenders. In the area of the innocence of children, postmodern theorists have unpacked the idea of childhood sexual innocence and described how certain efforts to limit sexualization of children are somewhat misguided and aligned with repressive forces against sexual freedom.

In a time when sexual abuse is considered a more heinous crime than physical abuse or neglect (and when the general public believes that sex offenders are incurable), attention to children who act out sexually has been controversial. Juvenile sex offenders, as they are called in some states, are reported publicly on lists that developed as community notification became popular; 25 states have included juveniles on these lists (Jones, 2007).

Children exhibiting sexual behavior problems are a heterogeneous group (St. Amand, Bard, & Silovsky, 2008). The Task Force on Children With Sexual Behavior Problems provided a definition: "children ages 12 and younger who initiate behaviors involving sexual body parts (i.e., genitals, anus, buttocks, or breasts) that are developmentally inappropriate or potentially harmful to themselves or others" (Chaffin et al., 2008, p. 200). According to this report, these children are not younger versions of adult sex offenders, nor will they likely become adult sex offenders (Carpentier, Silovsky, & Chaffin, 2006), so it is inappropriate to treat them as such or provide adult sex offender treatments (Letourneau & Miner, 2005; St. Amand, Bard, & Silovsky, 2008). The etiology of these problems is not clearly understood (Chaffin et al., 2008) and may be multiply determined. Research has shown that children who have no history of sexual abuse demonstrate a wide range of sexual behavior problems (Chaffin et al., 2008). Conduct disorders may manifest as sexually problematic behavior toward other children (St. Amand et al., 2008). Risk factors are maltreatment, substandard parenting practices, exposure to sexually explicit media, living in a highly sexualized environment, and even exposure to family violence (Friedrich, Davies, Feher, & Wright, 2003). The Task Force on Children With Sexual Behavior Problems called for case-by-case interventions that look at the child in his or her home and social environment, stating that environment is typically more telling than individual characteristics regarding sexually problematic behavior (Chaffin et al., 2008).

The second controversy, which deserves more attention than can be accomplished in this chapter, is the controversial topic of how innocent children are. Hawkes and Egan (2008) reported that although childhood sexuality was already normalized in the 1920s and 1930s, it came under strict management by parents and experts so that it would not grow into a distorted form of adult sexuality through poor parenting. Robinson (2002) argued that current constructions of childhood suggest that children are too young and innocent to understand sex. She wrote that the "notion of 'childhood innocence' is mobilized to regulate children's knowledge" (p. 8). As the discussion of children who act out sexually demonstrates, those who do not conform to standards of childhood innocence can, on one hand, be demonized quite quickly. On the other hand, childhood sexual experiences are normalized by suggesting they are in some sense not "real" sex (Lamb, 2002, 2004).

Discussions about sexualization and the preservation of childhood innocence center around girlhood and, in this way, may further contribute to the long-established stereotypes of girls as more innocent than boys (Lamb, 2002). The worry is that girls in particular may be exposed to degrading, raunchy, and pornographic material (APA, 2007; Dines, 2010; Levin & Kilbourne, 2008) and that this exposure will contribute to a problematic development of sexuality and a narrow version of what sexuality is among these girls. Scholars such as Thompson (2010) and Renold (2006) have critiqued the bias against sexuality that those concerned about the loss of childhood innocence seem to make and argued that most people who are concerned do not classify other imitations of adult activities, such as playing with kitchen sets, as equally problematic. Thus, these critics believe that the present concern is really about the play as sexual, not that it crosses into adult areas. Those on the other side of this controversy have maintained that healthy sexual play is appropriate but that children may be incorporating into their play and ideas of sexuality a very narrow view, including the perception that the only thing of value about their sexuality is the extent to which they appear sexy to others (see Chapter 25, this volume).

CONCLUSIONS

In this chapter, we have presented both empirical research with regard to the presence and frequency of childhood sexual behaviors and narratives of childhood sexual experiences, controversies around childhood sexuality, and overarching constructions of childhood sexuality. We have dismissed, in part, biological understandings of sexuality that are based on hormones and puberty in order to examine the stories of childhood sexual experiences and the controversies around them. This has led to a number of questions. The following questions build on the most interesting discussions today, those that come out of discussions of sexualization, childhood innocence, and childhood deviance as well as those that come from a desire to understand childhood sexuality from the child's perspective. These questions should provide ample foundation for future research in this area:

1. How is childhood managed and who benefits from the management of childhood sexuality?
2. What are notions about childhood innocence based on, and why is innocence defined so specifically in terms of sexuality?
3. What are the themes and pleasures of boyhood sexuality?
4. How is heteronormativity conveyed in the management of childhood sexuality?
5. Who is defining sexual deviance within childhood and with what aims?

References

American Psychological Association, Task Force on the Sexualization of Girls. (2007). *Report of the APA Task Force on the Sexualization of Girls*. Washington, DC: Author. Retrieved from http://www.apa.org/pi/wpo/sexualization.html

Attwood, F. (2006). Sexed up: Theorizing the sexualization of culture. *Sexualities, 9*, 77–94. doi:10.1177/1363460706053336

Bailey, J. M., Dunne, M. P., & Martin, N. G. (2000). Genetic and environmental influences on sexual orientation and its correlates in an Australian twin sample. *Journal of Personality and Social Psychology, 78*, 524–536. doi:10.1037/0022-3514.78.3.524

Barone, N. M., & Wiederman, M. W. (1997). Young women's sexuality as a function of perceptions of maternal sexual communication during childhood. *Journal of Sex Education and Therapy, 22*, 33–38.

Belsky, J. (2010). *Experiencing the lifespan*. New York, NY: Worth.

Berger, K. S. (2010). *Invitation to the life span*. New York, NY: Worth.

Bloom, A. (2004, September). Sex and the 6-year-old girl. *O Magazine*, pp. 209–210.

Brenot, P., & Broussin, B. (1996). Orgasm in utero? *Sexologies, 5*(21), 15–16.

Brown, L. M., Lamb, S., & Tappan, M. (2010). *Packaging boyhood: Saving our sons from superheroes, slackers, and other media stereotypes*. New York, NY: St. Martin's Press.

Browning, C. R., & Laumann, E. O. (1997). Sexual contact between children and adults: A life course perspective. *American Sociological Review, 62*, 540.

Buchanan, C. M., Eccles, J. S., & Becker, J. (1992). Are adolescents victims of raging hormones? Evidence for activational effects of hormones. *Psychological Bulletin, 111*, 62–107.

Byers, E. S., Sears, H., & Weaver, A. (2008). Parents' reports of sexual communication with children in kindergarten to grade 8. *Journal of Marriage and Family, 70*, 86–96.

Byne, W. (2007). Biology and sexual minority status. In I. H. Meyer & M. E. Northridge (Eds.), *The health of sexual minorities: Public health perspectives on lesbian, gay, bisexual, and transgender populations* (pp. 65–90). New York, NY: Springer.

Carpentier, M. Y., Silovsky, J. F., & Chaffin, M. (2006). Randomized trial of treatment for children with sexual behavior problems: Ten-year follow-up. *Journal of Consulting and Clinical Psychology, 74*, 482–488.

Chaffin, M., Berliner, L., Block, R., Johnson, T., Friedrich, W. N., Louis, D., . . . Silovsky, J. F. (2008). Report of the ATSA Task Force on Children With Sexual Behavior Problems. *Child Maltreatment, 13*, 199–218. doi:10.1177/1077559507306718

Cohan, M. (2009). Adolescent heterosexual males talk about the role of male peer groups in their sexual decision-making. *Sexuality and Culture, 13*, 152–177.

Cook, D. T., & Kaiser, S. B. (2004). Betwixt and be tween: Age ambiguity and the sexualization of the female consuming subject. *Journal of Consumer Culture, 4*, 203–227.

Cookson, S. (Writer, Director). (2001). Living dolls: The making of a child beauty queen. In L. Otto (Producer), *American undercover*. New York, NY: Home Box Office.

Cortese, A. J. (1999). *Provocateur: Images of women and minorities in advertising*. New York, NY: Rowman & Littlefield.

Dalton, P. (2005, November 20). What's wrong with this outfit, Mom? *Washington Post*, pp. B1.

de Graaf, H., & Rademakers, J. (2006). Sexual development of prepubertal children. *Journal of Psychology and Human Sexuality, 18*, 1–21.

de Graaf, H., & Rademakers, J. (2011). The psychological measurement of childhood sexual development in Western societies: Methodological challenges. *Journal of Sex Research, 48*, 118–129.

DeLamater, J., & Friedrich, W. N. (2002). Human sexual development. *Journal of Sex Research, 39*, 10–14. doi:10.1080/00224490209552113

DiIorio, C., Kelley, M., & Hockenberry-Eaton, M. (1999). Communication about sexual issues: Mothers, fathers, and friends. *Journal of Adolescent Health, 24*, 181–189.

DiIorio, C., Pluhar, E., & Belcher, L. (2003). Parent-child communication about sexuality: A review of the literature from 1980–2002. *Journal of HIV/AIDS Prevention and Education for Adolescents and Children, 5*(3–4), 7–32. doi:10.1300/J129v05n03_02

Dines, G. (2010). *Pornland: How pornography has hijacked our sexuality*. Boston, MA: Beacon Press.

Downie, J., & Coates, R. (1999). The impact of gender on parent–child sexuality communication: Has anything changed? *Sexual and Marital Therapy, 14*, 109–121.

Drach, K. M., Wientzen, J., & Ricci, L. R. (2001). The diagnostic of sexual behavior problems in diagnosing sexual abuse in a forensic child abuse evaluation clinic. *Child Abuse and Neglect, 25*, 489–503.

Einbender, A. J., & Friedrich, W. N. (1989). Psychological functioning and behavior of sexually abused girls. *Journal of Consulting and Clinical Psychology, 57*, 155–7.

Erikson, E. H. (1966). Eight ages of man. *International Journal of Psychiatry, 2*, 281–307.

Fine, M. (1988). Sexuality, schooling, and adolescent females: The missing discourse of desire. *Harvard Educational Review, 58*, 29–53.

Firth, H., & Kitzinger, C. (2007). Reformulating sexual script theory. *Theory and Psychology, 11*, 209–232. doi:10.1177/0959354301112004

Fitzpatrick, C., Deehan, A., & Jennings, S. (1995). Children's sexual behaviour and knowledge: A community study. *Irish Journal of Psychological Medicine, 12*, 87–91.

Flanagan, L. M. (2011). Object relations. In J. Berzoff, L. M. Flanagan, & P. Hertz (Eds.), *Inside out and outside in: Psychodynamic clinical theory and psychopathology in contemporary multicultural contexts* (pp. 118–157). Lanham, MD: Rowman & Littlefield.

Flanagan, P. (2010). Making molehills into mountains: Adult responses to child sexuality and behaviour. *Explorations: An E-Journal of Narrative Practice, 1*, 57–69.

Fonagy, P. (2008). A genuinely developmental theory of sexual enjoyment and its implications for the psychoanalytic technique. *Journal of the American Psychoanalytic Association, 56*, 11–36, doi:10.1177/0003065107313025

Fonagy, P., & Target, M. (2006). The mentalization-based approach to self-pathology. *Journal of Personality Disorders, 20*, 544–576.

Forrest, S. (2010). "Big and tough": Boys learning about sexuality and manhood. *Sexual and Relationship Therapy, 25*, 219–233.

Foucault, M. (1978). *The history of sexuality*. New York, NY: Pantheon Books.

Freud, S. (1975). *Three essays on the theory of sexuality* (J. Strachey, Trans.). New York, NY: Basic Books. (Original work published 1905)

Friedrich, W. N., Davies, W. H., Feher, E., & Wright, J. (2003). Sexual behavior problems in preteen children: Developmental, ecological, and behavioral correlates. *Annals of the New York Academy of Sciences, 989*, 95–104.

Friedrich, W. N., Fisher, J., Broughton, D., Houston, M., & Shafran, C. (1998). Mayo Clinic study: Normative sexual behavior in children: A contemporary sample. *Pediatrics, 101*, e9.

Friedrich, W. N., Fisher, J. L., Dittner, C. A., Acton, R., Berliner, L., Butler, J., . . . Wright, J. (2001). Child sexual behavior inventory: Normative, psychiatric, and sexual abuse comparisons. *Child Maltreatreatment, 6*, 37–49. doi:10.1177/1077559501006001004

Friedrich, W. N., & Grambsch, P. (1992). Child sexual behavior inventory: Normative and clinical comparisons. *Psychological Assessment, 4*, 303–311.

Friedrich, W. N., Grambsch, P., Broughton, D., Kuiper, J., & Beilke, R. (1991). Normative sexual behavior in children. *Pediatrics, 88*, 456–464.

Friedrich, W. N., Trane, S. T., & Gully, K. J. (2005). Letter to the editor: Re: It is a mistake to conclude that sexual abuse and sexual behavior are not related. *Child Abuse and Neglect, 29*, 97–302.

Gagnon, J. H., & Simon, W. (1973). *Sexual conduct: The social sources of human sexuality.* Chicago, IL: Aldine.

Gray, A., Pithers, W. D., Busconi, A., & Houchens, P. (1999). Developmental and etiological characteristics of children with sexual behavior problems: Treatment implications. *Child Abuse and Neglect, 23*, 601–621.

Hall, D. K., Mathews, F., & Pearce, J. (1998). Factors associated with sexual behavior problems in young sexually abused children. *Child Abuse and Neglect, 22*, 1045–63.

Haugaard, J., & Tilly, C. (1988). Characteristics predicting children's responses to sexual encounters with other children. *Child Abuse and Neglect, 12*, 209–218.

Haugaard, J. J. (1996). Sexual behaviors between children: Professionals' opinions and undergraduates' recollections. *Families in Society, 77*, 81–89.

Hawkes, G. L., & Egan, R. D. (2008). Developing the sexual child. *Journal of Historical Sociology, 21*, 443–465. doi:10.1111/j.1467-6443.2008.00345.x

Herdt, G., & McClintock, M. (2007). The magical age of 10. In M. Tepper & A. F. Owens (Eds.), *Sexual health: Vol. 1. Psychological foundations* (pp. 183–203). Westport, CT: Praeger.

Herdt, G. H. (1981). *Guardians of the flutes: Idioms of masculinity*. New York, NY: McGraw-Hill.

Herdt, G. H. (1982). *Rituals of manhood: Male initiation in Papua New Guinea*. Berkeley: University of California Press.

Hutchinson, M., & Cederbaum, J. A. (2011). Talking to daddy's little girl about sex: Daughters' reports of sexual communication and support from fathers. *Journal of Family Issues, 32*, 550–572. doi:10.1177/0192513X10384222

Janssen, D. F. (2002, October). *Growing up sexually: World reference atlas and the scripting of sexual development*. Retrieved from http://www2.hu-berlin.de/sexology/gesund/archiv/gus/gus_afs.htm

Jones, M. (2007, July 22). How can you distinguish a budding pedophile from a kid with real boundary problems? *New York Times Magazine*. Retrieved from http://www.nytimes.com/2007/07/22/magazine/22juvenile-t.html

Kaeser, F., DiSalvo, C., & Moglia, R. (2000). Sexual behaviors of young children that occur in schools. *Journal of Sex Education and Therapy, 25*, 277–285.

Kellogg, N. (2010). Sexual behaviors in children: Evaluation and management. *American Family Physician, 82*, 1233–1238.

Kendall-Tackett, K. A., Williams, L. M., & Finkelhor, D. (1993). Impact of sexual abuse on children: A review and synthesis of recent empirical studies. *Psychological Bulletin, 113*, 164–80.

King, B. M., & Lorusso, J. (1997). Discussions in the home about sex: Different recollections by parents and children. *Journal of Sex and Marital Therapy, 23*, 52–60.

Kinsey, A. C., Martin, C. E., Gebhard, P. H., Pomeroy, W. B., Corner, G. W., & Yerkes, R. M. (1953). *Sexual behavior in the human female*. Philadelphia: W. B. Saunders.

Lamb, S. (2002). *The secret lives of girls: What good girls really do—Sex play, aggression, and their guilt*. New York, NY: Free Press.

Lamb, S. (2004). IV. Sexual tensions in girls' friendships. *Feminism and Psychology, 14*, 376–382.

Lamb, S. (2006). *Sex, therapy, and kids: Addressing their concerns through talk and play*. New York, NY: W. W. Norton.

Lamb, S., & Brown, L. M. (2006). *Packaging girlhood: Rescuing our daughters from marketers' schemes*. New York, NY: St. Martin's Press.

Lamb, S., & Coakley, M. (1993). Childhood sexual play and games: Differentiating play from abuse. *Child Abuse and Neglect, 17*, 515–26.

Leitenberg, H., Detzer, M. J., & Srebnik, D. (1993). Gender differences in masturbation and the relation of masturbation experience in preadolescence and/or early adolescence to sexual behavior and sexual adjustment in young adulthood. *Archives of Sexual Behavior, 22*, 87–98. doi:10.1007/BF01542359

Leitenberg, H., Greenwald, E., & Tarran, M. J. (1989). The relation between sexual activity among children during preadolescence and/or early adolescence and sexual behavior and sexual adjustment in young adulthood. *Archives of Sexual Behavior, 18*, 299–313. doi:10.1007/BF01541950

Letourneau, E., & Miner, M. (2005). Juvenile sex offenders: A case against the legal and clinical status quo. *Sexual Abuse: A Journal of Research and Treatment, 17*, 293–312. doi:10.1007/s11194-005-5059-y

Letourneau, E. J., Schoenwald, S. K., & Sheidow, A. J. (2004). Children and adolescents with sexual behavior problems. *Child Maltreatment, 9*, 49–61.

Levin, D., & Kilbourne, J. (2008). *So sexy so soon: The new sexualized childhood and what parents can do to protect their kids*. New York, NY: Ballantine.

Levy, A. (2005). *Female chauvinist pigs: Women and the rise of raunch culture*. New York, NY: Free Press.

Martin, K., & Luke, K. (2010). Gender differences in the ABC's of the birds and the bees: What mothers teach young children about sexuality and reproduction. *Sex Roles, 62*, 278–291.

Martin, K. A. (2009). Normalizing heterosexuality: Mothers' assumptions, talk, and strategies with young children. *American Sociological Review, 74*, 190–207.

Martin, K. A., Luke, K. P., & Verduzco-Baker, L. (2007). The sexual socialization of young children: Setting the agenda for research. *Advances in Group Processes, 24*, 231–259.

Martino, S. C., Collins, R. L., Elliott, M. N., Strachman, M. A., Kanouse, D. E., & Berry, S. H. (2006). Exposure to degrading versus nondegrading music lyrics and sexual behavior. *Pediatrics, 118*, e430–e441.

Martinson, F. M. (1976). Eroticism in infancy and childhood. *Journal of Sex Research, 12*, 251–262. doi:10.1080/00224497609550945

Martinson, F. M. (1994). *The sexual life of children*. Westport, CT: Greenwood.

Masson, J. (1988). *Against therapy: Emotional tyranny and the myth of psychological healing*. New York, NY: Atheneum.

McNair, B. (1996). *Mediated sex: Pornography and post-modern culture*. London, England: Arnold.

McNair, B. (2002). *Striptease culture: Sex, media and the democratization of desire*. London, England: Routledge.

Mead, M. (1947). *From the south seas: Studies of adolescence and sex in primitive societies*. New York, NY: Morrow.

Mead, M. (1961). *Coming of age in Samoa: A psychological study of primitive youth for Western civilization*. New York, NY: Morrow.

Merskin, D. (2004). Reviving Lolita? A media literacy examination of sexual portrayals of girls in fashion advertising. *American Behavioral Scientist, 48*, 119–129.

Money, J. (1986). *Lovemaps: Clinical concepts of sexual/erotic health and pathology, paraphilia, and gender transposition in childhood, adolescence, and maturity*. New York, NY: Irvington.

Money, J., & Ehrhardt, A. A. (1972). *Man and woman, boy and girl: Differentiation and dimorphism of gender identity from conception to maturity*. Oxford, England: Johns Hopkins University Press.

Moore, N. B., & Davidson, J. K. (1999). Parents as first sexuality information sources: Do they make a difference in daughters' sexual attitudes and behavior? *Journal of Sex Education and Behavior, 24*, 155–163.

Okami, P., Olmstead, R., & Abramson, P. R. (1997). Sexual experiences in early childhood: 18-year longitudinal data from the UCLA family lifestyles project. *Journal of Sex Research, 34*, 339–347.

Okami, P., Weisner, T., & Olmstead, R. (2002). Outcome correlates of parent-child bedsharing: An eighteen-year longitudinal study. *Journal of Developmental and Behavioral Pediatrics, 23*, 244–253.

O'Sullivan, L., Meyer-Bahlburg, H., & Watkins, B. (2001). Mother–daughter communication about sex among urban African American and Latino families. *Journal of Adolescent Research, 16*, 269–292.

Philpy, M. J. (2007). *Sexual binaries: An examination of mixed messages and teenage female sexuality in education and media*. New York, NY: Springer Verlag.

Pluhar, E. (2007). Childhood sexuality. In M. Tepper & A. F. Owens (Eds.), *Sexual health: Vol. 1. Psychological foundations* (pp. 155–181). Westport, CT: Praeger.

Pluhar, E., DiIorio, C., Jennings, T., & Pines, K. (2005, May 10). *"Sexual possibility situations" and progressive heterosexual behaviors among children ages 6–12*. Poster presented at the Annual Conference of the American Association of Sex Educators, Counselors and Therapists, Portland, OR.

Pluhar, E., Jennings, T., & DiIorio, C. (2006). Getting an early start: Communication about sexuality among mothers and children 6–10 years old. *Journal of HIV/AIDS Prevention in Children and Youth, 7*, 7–35. doi:10.1300/J499v07n01_02

Pluhar, E. I., DiIorio, C. K., & McCarty, F. F. (2008). Correlates of sexuality communication among mothers and 6–12-year-old children. *Child: Care, Health and Development, 34*, 283–290. doi:10.1111/j.1365-2214.2007.00807

Pluhar, E. I., & Kuriloff, P. (2004). What really matters in family communication about sexuality? A qualitative analysis of affect and style among African American others and adolescent daughters. *Sex Education, 4*, 304–321.

Rasmussen, M. (2006). Play school melancholia, and the politics of recognition. *British Journal of Sociology of Education, 27*, 473–487.

Remafedi, G., Farrow, J. A., & Deisher, R. W. (1993). Risk factors for attempted suicide in gay and bisexual youth. In L. D. Garnets & D. C. Kimmel (Eds.), *Psychological perspectives on lesbian and gay male experiences* (pp. 486–499). New York, NY: Columbia University Press.

Renold, E. (2006). "They won't let us play . . . unless you're going out with one of them": Girls, boys, and Butler's "heterosexual matrix" in the primary years. *British Journal of Sociology of Education, 27*, 489–509.

Renold, E. (2007). Primary school "studs": (De)constructing young boys' heterosexual masculinities. *Men and Masculinities, 9*, 275–297.

Robinson, K. (2002). Making the invisible visible: Gay and lesbian issues in early childhood education. *Contemporary Issues in Early Childhood, 3*, 415–434.

Rose, S. M. (1995). Women's friendships. In J. C. Chrisler & A. Huston Hemstreet (Eds.), *Variations on a theme: Diversity and the psychology of women* (pp. 79–105). Albany: State University of New York Press.

Rutter, M. (1971). Normal psychosexual development. *Journal of Child Psychology and Psychiatry, 11*, 259–283.

Savin-Williams, R. C. (1995). An exploratory study of pubertal maturation timing and self-esteem among gay and bisexual male youths. *Developmental Psychology, 31*, 56–64. doi:10.1037/0012-1649.31.1.56

Segal, N., Weisfeld, G., & Weisfeld, C. (1997). *Uniting psychology and biology: Integrative perspectives on human development*. Washington, DC: American Psychological Association.

Sly, D., Riehman, K., Wu, C., Eberstein, I., Quadagno, D., & Kistner, J. (1995). Early childhood differentials in mother-child AIDS-information interaction. *AIDS Education and Prevention, 7*, 337–354.

St. Amand, A., Bard, D. E., & Silovsky, J. F. (2008). Meta-analysis of treatment for child sexual behavior problems: Practice elements and outcomes. *Child Maltreatment, 13*, 145–166. doi:10.1177/1077559508315353

Thigpen, J. W. (2009). Early sexual behavior in a sample of low-income, African American children. *Journal of Sex Research, 46*, 67–79. doi:10.1080/00224490802645286

Thompson, K. (2010). Because looks can be deceiving: Media alarm and the sexualisation of childhood—do we know what we mean? *Journal of Gender Studies, 19*, 395–400. doi:10.1080/09589236.2010.533492

Weisfeld, G. (1999). *Evolutionary perspectives of human adolescence.* New York, NY: Basic Books.

Whalen, C. K., Henker, B., Hollingshead, J., & Burgess, S. (1996). Parent–adolescent dialogues about AIDS. *Journal of Family Psychology, 10*, 343–357.

Wilson, E., Dalberth, B., & Koo, H. (2010). "We're the heroes!": Fathers' perspectives on their role in protecting their preteenage children from sexual risk. *Perspectives on Sexual and Reproductive Health, 42*, 117–124.

CHAPTER 15

SEXUALITY IN ADOLESCENCE

Lucia F. O'Sullivan and Ashley E. Thompson

Adolescence is used in this chapter to characterize the period of development spanning childhood and adulthood. The term *adolescence* is derived from the Latin word *adolescere* and means "to grow into" adulthood (Gouws, Kruger, & Burger, 2000). It is often perceived as beginning at the onset of puberty (Al-Sahab, Ardern, Hamadeh, & Tamim, 2010; McDowell, Brody, & Hughes, 2007; Patton & Viner, 2007) and extends to the late teenage years, corresponding with most Western jurisdictions' legal age of adulthood or very early 20s. The term occasionally overlaps with the period capturing the transition between adolescence and adulthood, relatively newly referred to as "emerging adulthood" (Arnett, 2000), although issues directly relevant to the sexuality of young people in that phase of life are summarized in Chapter 16 of this volume.

Despite characterizing a relatively brief span of time in people's development, adolescence is probably the developmental period that has garnered the most research attention in the field of sexuality relative to all others, especially with regard to sexual health. The wealth of research on adolescent sexuality, however, is not evenly distributed across topics. Substantially more research has been conducted on factors predicting onset of sexual intercourse (Cavazos-Rehg et al., 2009; Haydon, Herring, Prinstein, & Halpern, 2012; Spriggs & Halpern, 2008; Vargas & Ponsoda, 2010; Zimmer-Gembeck & Helfand, 2008) and risk for pregnancy and sexually transmitted infection (STI; Cavazos-Rehg et al., 2010; Godeau et al., 2008; Lazarus et al., 2009) than on topics such as sexual pleasure, arousal, or satisfaction. How adolescent sexuality is defined, and the subsequent social value assigned to adolescent sexuality, reflects policy priorities and research attention (see Volume 2, Chapter 10, this handbook). Even the most cursory review has concluded that adolescent sexuality has been equated by the research, clinical, and policy collective with medical pathology and sociocultural deviance.

By extension, relatively little research has been conducted on normative trajectories of sexual development or the positive outcomes associated with sexual well-being (see Chapters 11 and 13, this volume). In particular, the dearth of information, until recently, on topics relating to normal adolescent sexual functioning, interest, arousal, pleasure, and satisfaction is astounding, as others have noted (e.g., Tolman & McClelland, 2011). Moreover, research on adolescents' sexual outcomes outweighs, by far, the scant research available on childhood sexuality, beyond that focused on childhood sexual abuse (see Chapters 14 and 25, this volume). In fact, this discrepancy belies a sociocultural preoccupation with "licentiousness," the temerity of youths for straying into adult domains, but perhaps most pointedly a deep discomfort with transitions from childhood to adulthood in positive, healthful, pleasure-based sexuality.

Viewing adolescent sexuality from a pathological or problem perspective reflects a strong need to preserve a view of children, and by extension adolescents, as innocent of and untainted by sexual thoughts, feelings, or experiences (Jackson, 1990). There is, of course, notable reluctance on the behalf of adults to extend adult privileges to adolescents in

http://dx.doi.org/10.1037/14193-015
APA Handbook of Sexuality and Psychology: Vol. 1. Person-Based Approaches, D. L. Tolman and L. M. Diamond (Editors-in-Chief)

other realms of life, such as alcohol use and driving, but sexual experiences appear to generate the most heightened moral sensitivities and concomitant efforts to control and suppress. For example, specific age limitations are aimed at prohibiting partnered sexual activity for adolescents in almost all jurisdictions of the world (English, 2002). Age limits also restrict adolescents' access to sexual material or media and even their participation in research. Being younger than the legal age of consent, adolescents are usually involved in research addressing their sexuality only if their parents have been fully informed of the research content and have consented to their child's participation. In special circumstances, youths are considered emancipated minors and are able to provide their own consent, but most of what is known about adolescent sexuality is produced with this constraint.

This structural feature of requiring parental involvement at the outset of any adolescent sexuality research necessarily limits the range and depth of topics addressed in the field. Adolescents are often reluctant to have their parents acknowledge or reflect on their children's sexual lives, fearing a loss of privacy, restrictions, or opposition from their parents. Notable efforts have been made at the institutional level, including ethical review boards, courts, and even political bodies, to hamper research on adolescent sexuality, citing their commitment to protecting public interests (e.g., Rind, 2008). Researchers also face considerable difficulty finding financial support for research on adolescent sexuality unless the proposed research purports to address some form of social ill.

Despite these significant obstacles, a sufficiently broad range of rigorous research summarizing what is known about adolescent sexuality to which researchers can refer is now available. To provide a conceptual framework for this section, we have adopted a biopsychosocial perspective to capture research addressing the physiological processes involved in the development of sexual interest and expression. We use this framework to summarize the cognitive, affective, and relational components of sexuality and the sociocultural, historical, political, and institutional forces that help to shape sexuality as a learned behavior (see Chapters 3 and 10, this volume; Volume 2, Chapters 12 and 13, this handbook). The majority of research on this topic has been generated by researchers at secondary institutions within Western cultures and as a result shapes conclusions on the basis of data obtained from primarily White, middle-class, able-bodied college students. Wherever possible, we describe what is known about diverse populations of youths in the sections that follow.

HISTORICAL CONTEXT

In recent decades, public policies in the United States and United Kingdom, less so in Canada and other European countries, have revolved around sexual abstinence. Although these programs have become very well established, they have also eliminated many adolescents' access to comprehensive sex information (Weiss & Bullough, 2004), and subsequently left them undereducated about essential issues relevant to their sexual lives (Santelli, 2008). Few issues in the field have proven so contentious. Abstinence-only education programs actually followed the onset of a general population-level and cross-cultural behavioral trend toward more conservative (less permissive) sexual behavior among youths, reflected in lower rates of pregnancy, fewer lifetime sexual partners, and more consistent contraceptive use (as discussed later). However, the 1990s found growing numbers of adolescents becoming infected or at risk for infection with HIV/AIDS. Other STIs, such as chlamydia and gonorrhea, became widespread among young adults and increasingly among adolescents as well. These serious concomitant public health issues have influenced public policy, education, and research agendas and have ultimately shaped our views of and research about adolescent sexuality.

Another important historical note that determines to some extent the information available on adolescent sexuality relates to the introduction of a remedy for male erectile dysfunction in 1998 (i.e., sildenafil [Viagra]). Since that time, researchers have noted an increased trend toward the medicalization of sex, including the sexual lives of girls and women (Tiefer, 1995, 2004). This trend toward medicalization has been reinforced in all domains of health, including sexual health, by the tremendous gains in financial and, thus, sociopolitical power of large pharmaceutical companies. Research on adolescent sexuality has reflected these cultural shifts, with many researchers embracing this new trend because of much-needed research funding. However, in the past decade or so, a burgeoning movement has begun to emphasize more positive components of adolescent sexuality (e.g., Bay-Cheng, 2005; Russell, 2005; Tolman & McClelland, 2011), "depathologize" the research generated from the public health perspective, and adopt a more progressive, integrated, rights-based approach to sexual development (see Volume 2, Chapter 8, this handbook).

NORMATIVE SEXUAL DEVELOPMENT

We review here the process of reaching sexual and reproductive maturity as well as the physiological processes and brain activity inherent to sexual response in partnered and solo sexual activities. Although individuals are sexual and capable of sexual response as children, and even prenatally, adolescence heralds remarkable, challenging, and often highly conspicuous changes across a range of domains in an individual's life, to which each person (and the people around them) must adjust. For some individuals, this adjustment proves easier than for others, as we discuss later, but for each individual, these transitions mark a change in status at the personal, interpersonal, and sociocultural levels. We use the term *normative* to refer to typical, common, age-appropriate, or developmentally expected, not pathological, trajectories in the progression toward sexual maturation.

Puberty

Pubertal development results in reproductive maturation in nearly all individuals (with some exceptions in cases of disorders of puberty). The process itself is biological, reflecting a complex series of neuroendocrine changes that set in motion some radical changes in hormonal activity, which in turn prompt development of reproductive organs and other physical changes in height, weight, muscle mass, and distribution of fat. These physical changes occur in a social context in which the individual's sexual status spurs social reactions from others and requires appraisal and reappraisal on the part of the individual regarding his or her developing body, feelings about the self, sexuality, and peer and family relations (e.g., Brooks-Gunn, Graber & Paikoff, 1994; Graber & Sontag, 2006).

Some of the social and emotional changes at puberty are attributed colloquially to raging hormones, and indeed hormones are central to the process of sexual development. Hormones are chemical products of the endocrine system and encompass either steroid or steroidlike hormones (e.g., androgens and estrogens), such as those produced by the gonads, or protein, peptide, or glycol-protein hormones, such as oxytocin and vasopressin (Halpern, 2006). Hormones have far-reaching effects on the body and its functioning, including the activity of glands, organs, neurotransmitters, and other hormones.

Hormonal activity during pubertal development has received considerable research attention, especially with regard to gonadal and adrenal steroids. A rapid increase in hormonal activity occurs that produces dramatic physical changes that propel an individual toward reproductive maturity. This surge in hormone activity does not mark the onset of sexual interest; many report experiencing sexual interest, arousal, and desire toward same-sex or other-sex individuals before puberty, often around age 10 when adrenal glands mature (Herdt & McClintock, 2000; Savin-Williams & Diamond, 2000), nor does it mark the onset of sexual activity. However, the external manifestations of pubertal development spurred by hormones, such as facial and axillary hair and muscle growth in boys and breast and hip development in girls, do make up a fairly public signal of sexual readiness that may prompt unanticipated or undesired sexual approaches from others.

Testosterone and estrogen are two central sex hormones that increase rapidly during pubertal development. Udry and his colleagues (Udry, 1985, 1988; Udry & Billy, 1987) have elucidated the role of gonadal steroids (e.g., testosterone) in the onset of partnered sexual activity for both boys and girls during pubertal development, a body of work that represents some of the few but valuable efforts to integrate both biological and psychosocial factors. Some of their research using saliva samples and weekly behavior checklists indicates that testosterone is more closely related to sexual activity for boys and less related or unrelated to sexual activity for girls, even though there are strong associations between sexual ideation, motivation, and testosterone levels (Halpern, Udry, & Suchindran, 1998; Udry, Talbert, & Morris, 1986). A longitudinal study of adolescent girls, however, linked pubertal changes in testosterone and transitions to intercourse (Halpern, Udry, & Suchindran, 1997). Hormone changes appear to contribute to sexual development at some level, but sexual development best reflects a wide and complex range of biological and psychosocial systems working in tandem (see Halpern, 2006). Even though pleasure-seeking behaviors are linked to the pubertal activation of the hypothalamo–pituitary–gonadal axis (e.g., Sato, Schulz, Sisk, & Wood, 2008), culture clearly moderates the expression of biological differences primarily through the socialization of gender roles and expectations regarding appropriate sexual behavior (e.g., Lam, Shi, Ho & Fan, 2002; see also Volume 2, Chapter 6, this handbook).

In Western cultures, puberty typically begins at age 10 or 11 for girls and is completed by ages 15 to 17, whereas it tends to start slightly later for boys, at age 12 or 13, and is typically completed by ages 16 to 18 (Coleman & Coleman, 2002). Some indexes of pubertal development are advanced among obese male and female adolescents; however, most indicate levels comparable to those of their nonobese counterparts (Denzer et al., 2007). Sexual minority boys report a slightly later onset of puberty, whereas sexual minority girls tend to report a slightly earlier onset of puberty (Savin-Williams & Ream, 2006). Average age of awareness of same-sex attractions is approximately 10, which is the same age for awareness of other-sex attractions, an age that is associated with maturation of the adrenal glands (adrenarche; Herdt & McClintock, 2000). First self-labeling as a sexual minority typically occurs between ages 14 and 21 (Perrin, 2002; see Chapter 19, this volume). This process of identifying with a sexual minority orientation appears to be occurring at younger ages than in previous generations (Floyd & Bakeman, 2006). Female adolescents seem to have more mobile or "fluid" sexual orientation than male adolescents (Diamond, 1998), with a larger proportion of female than male adolescents over time indicating an orientation other than completely heterosexual (e.g., Ott, Corliss, Wypij, Rosario, & Austin, 2011).

Menarche, or first menstruation, is often viewed as the onset of puberty for girls, but in fact it is one of the last events in girls' pubertal development. The extensive work of J. M. Tanner (e.g., Tanner, 1962, 1998) demonstrated that growth spurt, breast bud and genital development, growth of pubic and axillary hair, voice change, and changes in body curvature and fat distribution typically precede menarche. Yet menarche remains a pivotal point for girls and represents for many a symbol of a girl's reproductive maturity and adult female status. In one study, qualitative interviews with parents of girls age 10 to 13 revealed that menarche spurred a wide range of discussions about sexual propriety and (girls') responsibility to avoid pregnancy (O'Sullivan, Meyer-Bahlburg, & Watkins, 2001). Many parents begin to increase restrictions and prohibitions on girls' behavior and interactions at menarche because of heightened fears of pregnancy or sexual exploitation by others that are associated with this sociosexual milestone. Of note, it generally takes another 2 years from menarche before a girl's fertility becomes truly stable (Grumbach & Styne, 1998).

In recent years, considerable concern has been raised about the possibility of accelerated sexual development because of the decreasing age of menarche at the population level in past decades. Decreased age of menarche is a trend that is well established in most developed and many developing countries and is attributed primarily to improved living conditions and nutrition (Dixon-Mueller, 2008). However, there is little indication that menarche promotes onset of partnered sexual activities (James, Ellis, Schlomer, & Garber, 2012), although one extensive review of the research has indicated that earlier timing of girls' puberty relative to their peers was related to younger age at first intercourse, earlier onset of dating, and adolescent pregnancy (Ellis, 2004).

Interestingly, a review of the puberty literature indicates that no secular trend has been found among boys (Papadimitriou et al., 2011). It is somewhat more difficult to discern the onset of puberty among boys compared with girls, whose onset is marked by breast (bud) development (Tanner, 1962). Onset among boys is generally marked by testicular growth or volume and change in scrotal skin texture. The male equivalent of menarche is semenarche, which refers to a boy's first ejaculation, or oigarche, an event that is often noted in nocturnal emissions. Semenarche also connotes sexual maturity, but this aspect of sexual development appears to have far fewer emotional associations for adults than menarche among girls. In fact, in one study using interviews with 28 parents (15 mothers, 13 fathers), more than half (54%) of parents of sons ages 10 to 13 reported that they had never thought about their son's first ejaculation (Frankel, 2002).

Pubertal development during adolescence coincides with significant changes in cognitive, emotional, and social functioning. These changes include more abstract, hypothetical thinking, with new abilities to incorporate long-term perspectives, less egocentric thinking, and greater empathic identification with others (e.g., Larson, Clore, & Wood, 1999). Changes in social interactions with peers at times inundate adolescents with strong emotions, such as anger, self-consciousness, shame, and anxiety, at levels not previously experienced (Larson et al., 1999). Moreover, adolescents become better able to differentiate emotions (Nannis & Cowan, 1987), recognize that conflicting emotions can occur simultaneously (Harter & Buddin, 1987), gain skills in emotion regulation (McRae et al., 2012), and become capable of characterizing blended emotional states and attributing motivations to their behaviors (Fischer, Shaver, & Carnochan, 1990). Negative affective states, such as irritability and depression, increase during adolescence (e.g., Arnett, 1999), and middle adolescent girls report more negative daily mood and negative interpersonal events than younger adolescents (Flook, 2011).

Both girls and boys become increasingly dissatisfied with their body image around puberty (e.g., Graber, Peterson, & Brooks-Gunn, 1996) but also become more aware of the extent to which they are attracting sexual attention and are attracted sexually to others. Young people become more sensitive during puberty to others' appearance appraisals (e.g., Carlson Jones, 2004). Increased interactions during this time with mixed-gender groups appear related to higher rates of sexual harassment, sexual comments, and teasing (e.g., McMaster, Connolly, Pepler, & Craig, 2002) compared with rates in their earlier childhood years. Moreover, romantic interactions become more salient during late adolescence, with more time invested in romantic relationships (than with friendships and family relationships) compared with prepubertal adolescents (e.g., Zimmer-Gembeck, 1999).

The Brain and Physiological Response

The brain undergoes significant restructuring during adolescence, with many changes reflecting increased sensitivity to androgens (e.g., Sato et al., 2008). Sex differences in puberty-related maturation on human brain structures may be related to lasting sexual dimorphisms in the adult brain. Using physical sexual maturity and circulating testosterone as indexes of pubertal development (rather than age), researchers have found puberty-related maturation of the hippocampus, amygdala, and cortical gray matter volumes in more sexually mature adolescents and larger volumes in these structures overall for sexually mature boys than for girls (Bramen et al., 2011). These differences are noted in regions with high sex steroid hormone receptor densities.

Other research has found that among adolescents (ages 12–18), male adolescents had greater volumes of white matter than did female adolescents, whereas female adolescents had greater volumes and density in cortical regions than did male adolescents (Paus et al., 2010). White matter, which consists of glial cells and myelinated axons, regulates the coordination of communication between brain regions, whereas gray matter is more closely associated with cognitive processing. These differences are moderated by individual levels of the sex hormone testosterone (Sullivan et al., 2011). Thus, adolescence is a time of rapid change in neuroanatomy, yet it is not always clear how these changes translate into sexual response or behavior.

A substantial body of research before the 1990s documented sexual response at and prior to birth and in infancy (e.g., Calderone, 1983; C. S. Ford & Beach, 1963; Galenson & Riophe, 1974). For example, an ultrasound study revealed that male fetuses experience spontaneous erections and female fetuses are capable of orgasm (Giorgi & Siccardi, 1996). Although orgasms are possible at young ages, generally only girls can experience a sexual response cycle that resembles that of their adult counterparts. Boys become capable of ejaculation only once they reach puberty because this process is dependent on hormone production and maturation of internal reproductive structures. Because of the ethical and moral objections that would be raised in studying adolescents' sexual response, much of what is known about the brain and physiological response systems of adolescents has been extrapolated from studies of adults. There is a wealth of research on the impact of child and adolescent sexual abuse but, as might be expected, a dearth of studies on normal, uncoerced, and consensual sexual response. Some studies have assessed "deviant" sexual arousal among adolescents who have been caught for sexual offenses (e.g., Clift, Rajlic, & Gretton, 2009; Worling, 2012). However, it is unclear to what extent one can generalize from these studies. Sexual "readiness" is often interpreted as curiosity regarding (Smiler, 2008) or anticipation of sex (Forste & Haas, 2002). This body of work underscores how little is known about actual physiological responses involved in adolescents' sexual arousal and links to experiences of interest and desire (see Attraction, Desire, Interest, and Arousal section).

Sexual Self-Concept and Gender Role Socialization

To understand adolescent sexuality, it is important to examine how adolescents construct a sense of themselves as sexual people. Self-concept is a cognitive construct that is viewed as an organizational framework for interpreting experiences. It is generally viewed as being multifaceted in nature and consisting of an integration of dynamic core and peripheral concepts as well as idealized "possible selves" (see Markus & Nurius, 1986). Sexual self-concept is one of these peripheral concepts and is clearly relevant to understanding adolescent sexual behavior and motivations. In particular, *sexual self-concept* refers to "an individual's positive and negative perceptions and feelings about him- or herself as a sexual being" (Rostosky, Dekhtyar, Cupp, & Anderman, 2008, p. 277). The consolidation of one's sexual self-concept is considered an important developmental task in adolescence (e.g., Longmore, 1998).

Over the past few decades, a growth in research addressing adolescents' sexual self-concept has occurred, although almost all of it has centered on understanding girls' rather than boys' sense of themselves as sexual people. This work evolved from research on adult women (e.g., Andersen & Cyranowski, 1994; Snell, Fisher, & Miller, 1991) but expanded to include adolescents, usually in relation to intercourse attitudes, feelings about obtaining and using contraceptives, and past discussions about sex and contraception (e.g., Winter, 1988). Buzwell and Rosenthal (1996) identified five distinct styles of adolescents' sexual self-concepts in a study of 470 middle adolescent Australian youths (ages 15–17). These styles were sexually naïve (27%; a group with low sexual self-esteem, low sexual self-efficacy except in their perceived ability to refuse sex, and sexually anxious); sexually unassured (18%; a group with low sexual self-esteem, poor body-esteem, and low sexual self-efficacy but moderate levels of sexual interest); sexually competent (29%; a group with sexual self-esteem, positive body image, high sexual self-efficacy across all domains, and moderate sexual attitudes but some sexual anxiety); sexually adventurous (17%; a group with high sexual self-esteem and efficacy, high body image, sexual confidence across many domains, desire for sexual exploration, and low anxiety); and sexually driven (9%; a group with the highest scores on sexual self-esteem measures, body image, sexual self-efficacy, interest in exploring, sexual arousal, and the lowest sexual anxiety). As one might expect, differences were found in gender representation and sexual experience, with the latter groups containing more boys and more sexually experienced youths. The latter groups also reported higher levels of risk taking with both regular and casual partners.

Other researchers have conducted similar analyses and developed clusters of styles to characterize adolescents' sexual self-concept (e.g., O'Sullivan, Meyer-Bahlburg, & McKeague, 2006). Still others have explored important dimensions of sexual self-concept. One area that has received particular attention is femininity ideology and its links to sexual agency (e.g., Curtin, Ward, Merriwether, & Caruthers, 2011). Endorsement of femininity ideologies (or conventional views about femininity) are viewed as especially problematic in the field of sexual health because they have been associated with diminished sexual agency (i.e., a sense that one has power and control in sexual situations; Tolman, 2002a, 2002c). Researchers have found that young women who endorse femininity ideologies more strongly had lower levels of sexual assertiveness, poorer body esteem, and lower sexual risk knowledge and practice scores (Curtin et al., 2011; Impett, Schooler, & Tolman, 2006). Sexual self-concepts are believed to reflect quite closely the gender role socialization that an individual has experienced, that is, the lessons learned through social development that impart the roles, responsibilities, and obligations associated with being a woman or a man (Gagnon & Parker, 1995). Girls and boys are taught radically different lessons about their sexuality and sexual lives, almost entirely from a heterocentric perspective. Girls' socialization emphasizes the value of participation in and maintenance of interpersonal relationships (Breakwell & Millward, 1997) and romantic partnerships as the contexts for sexual expression (Fine, 1988; Thompson, 1994). Boys' socialization emphasizes sexual agency and the ability to pursue sexual opportunities with female partners wherever they arise. This fundamental difference in socialization positions young women and men from the outset in their approach and response to their developing sexuality.

Masturbation

Masturbation is a term that refers to the sexual stimulation of a person's genitals, by themselves or another, usually (but not always) to the point of orgasm. Adolescent boys consistently report higher rates of masturbation and more frequent masturbation than do adolescent girls (Robbins et al., 2011). One retrospective survey of adults indicated that 40% of women and 38% of men masturbated prepubertally, whereas the remainder recalled masturbating only postpubertally (43% and 61% of women and men, respectively) or not at all (Bancroft, Herbenick, & Reynolds, 2003). Masturbation appears to build on a foundation of touching or fondling one's genitals in childhood (Friedrich et al., 1992). In a U.S. national probability sample, adolescents ages 14 to 17 reported lifetime prevalence rates of masturbation. Results indicated that almost twice as many adolescent boys (80%) as adolescent girls (48%) reported solo masturbation (defined as "stimulated your body for sexual pleasure whether or not you had an orgasm"; Fortenberry et al., 2010). Yet masturbation rates for the prior 90 days were quite high and relatively similar for female and male adolescents: 37% and 43%, respectively. Rates increase each year for boys but remain relatively stable at approximately one third for each age among girls. However, we should emphasize that these rates are likely underestimates given the sensitivity of the topic.

It is important to bear in mind that fundamental differences exist in the morphological features of male and female genitals, making the two forms difficult to compare. Boys report learning early and easily (often accidentally) how to stimulate themselves sexually, whereas girls often indicate that they had to learn from secondary sources, such as books (e.g., Janssen, 2007). In line with this discrepancy is survey research that has shown that adolescent boys' first self- or partner-induced orgasm tends to occur around age 13 (typically from self-stimulation), and adolescent girls tends to occur 3 to 5 years later (typically from partnered sexual interactions; Janssen, 2007). Masturbation has been linked to numerous partnered sexual activities for both male and female adolescents (Robbins et al., 2011), suggesting that those who are more sexually oriented tend to find more sexual outlets overall. Knowing (or learning) how to masturbate is a central feature of sexual response in adults and a key feature of most sex therapies because it requires that individuals attend to the sensations most closely linked to their arousal.

Milestones

An individual's first experience of penile–vaginal intercourse is frequently viewed (usually incorrectly) as the onset of partnered sexual activities. It is becoming increasingly clear that young people engage in a range of "precoital" activities before they engage in first intercourse (e.g., Lindberg, Jones, & Santelli, 2008). Moreover, there are fairly predictable patterns in the acquisition of first sexual experiences, at least among Western young people, about whom we know the most. Generally, low-intimacy behaviors (e.g., extended kissing, holding hands, hugging) precede high-intimacy behaviors. Sexual touching and stimulation over clothes precedes sexual touching and stimulation under clothes while partially or completely naked. Non–genitally focused sexual activities generally precede genitally focused activities. In one interview study using U.S. national data, adolescents were asked to rank order the occurrence of partnered events that occurred in romantic relationships. The progression of sexual events among adolescents followed a fairly consistent sequence: kissing and holding hands, breast and chest fondling, manual genital contact, touching under or without clothes, touching genitals directly, oral sex, and penile–vaginal intercourse, followed by less common variations, such as anal sex (O'Sullivan, Mantsun, Harris, & Brooks-Gunn, 2007; see also Chapter 13, this volume).

Because most studies of adolescent sexuality development use samples of White, heterosexual youths from Western countries (see Thigpen, Pinkston, & Mayefsky, 2003), far less is known about the sequences of sexual, social, and interpersonal events in the partnerships of youths who fall outside this group. Research focusing on adolescent sexuality in more diverse samples is desperately needed. Although researchers are developing a fairly cogent picture of sexual events in these traditional research samples, there is reason to believe that notable variation occurs across major ethnic groups (O'Sullivan et al., 2007) and cross-culturally (Darroch, Landry, & Oslak, 1999) and likely across other subgroups as well.

Large-scale national surveys in Western countries have indicated that approximately 40% of 12- to 13-year-olds will report having held hands and one third will report having been kissed on the mouth (Waylen, Ness, McGovern, Wolke, & Low, 2010). Surveys have generally indicated that hugging, holding hands, and kissing are common among 12- to 13-year-old adolescents, whereas more genitally focused activities, such as oral sex and sexual intercourse, are relatively uncommon (T. Williams, Connolly, & Cribbie, 2008).

First oral sex is often reported as occurring within 6 months of vaginal intercourse (Lindberg et al., 2008; Ronis & O'Sullivan, 2011). A large U.S. national study has shown that the vast majority of younger adolescents (11–15 years) have not had sexual intercourse, but the odds of intercourse experience increase every year across adolescence (Herbenick et al., 2010). By ages 18 to 19, a majority (63%) have had intercourse experience. Approximately 50% will have first intercourse between ages 16 and 18 years, 15% will have first intercourse before age 16, and the remainder will engage in first intercourse at age 19 or older (e.g., Spriggs & Halpern, 2008). The average age of first heterosexual intercourse is 16.9 for boys and 17.4 for girls (Cavazos-Rehg et al., 2009). This age does not vary notably across Western cultures, although a lot of variation occurs within countries. For example, Asian adolescents report a later age for first intercourse than both Hispanic and American adolescents (Meston & Ahrold, 2010). Additionally, Caucasian American adolescents report a later age for first intercourse than both Hispanic American and African American adolescents (e.g., O'Donnell, Myint-U, O'Donnell, & Stueve, 2003). Rates vary significantly worldwide (see Dixon-Mueller, 2008, for an extensive review).

As Martin (1996) has argued, far more is known about the demographics of who is likely to or who is engaging in sexual interactions than is known of their actual experiences of first intercourse ("sex"). Many girls expect that sex will hurt and be painful and indicate that their primary emotion beforehand was nervousness despite notable curiosity and interest about sex as well (O'Sullivan & Hearn, 2008). Holland, Ramazanoglu, Sharpe, and Thomson's (2010) qualitative work described how first (hetero) sex is associated with notable ambivalence for young women. They contend with the excitement and curiosity of new experiences, often fueled by media depictions for those reporting heavy consumption of sexualized media (L'Engle, Brown, & Kenneavy, 2006), but also with managing loss. Boys' experiences tend to be more affirmative and help them to establish sexual and gender identity. In qualitative interviews, Martin (1996) found that girls tended to report hoping that sex would be romantic and pleasurable but fearing that it would be painful or lead to rejection. Boys generally reported anticipating sex, with some concerns about their performance and not being able to "do it right" (p. 166). Actual first experiences reflected missing agency on the part of girls ("it just happened") and frequently being pressured into sex by their male partners, whereas boys pursued sex more actively and reported feeling more grown up and independent as a result. In-depth interviews with girls by other researchers such as Tolman (2002a) and Thompson (1994) have reinforced many of these findings of reduced subjectivity.

Research has indicated that adolescents who are sexually active at earlier ages than their peers (i.e., early-onset youths) have different psychosocial and sexual profiles than their same-age, same-gender peers (Meschke, Zweig, Barber, & Eccles, 2000). According to the 2005 Youth Risk Behavior Survey, 47% of high school students reported ever having sexual intercourse, with 6% reporting having initiated their first sexual intercourse before age 13 (Cavazos-Rehg et al., 2009). Studies have indicated that those with an early sexual debut are more likely to have externalizing problems than their noninitiating peers (Price & Hyde, 2009), higher rates of sexual risk behaviors (Sandfort, Orr, Hirsch, & Santelli, 2008; Sneed, 2008), lower educational achievement (Spriggs & Halpern, 2008), and other poor interpersonal and social outcomes.

In large part because of sociocultural interests in delaying or suppressing adolescents' sexuality, far less is known about those who start their partnered sexual lives later (i.e., late-onset youths) than their peers. A strong inverse relationship does appear to exist between onset of partnered sexual activities and intelligence. That is, higher intelligence or high academic achievement are associated with postponement of a wide range of partnered sexual activities (e.g., Halpern, Joyner, Udry, & Suchindran, 2000; Laflin, Wang, & Barry, 2008), possibly because of a greater awareness of or sensitivity to messages about the possibility of negative health outcomes.

Overall, studies on adolescent sexual behavior have tended to privilege onset (Tolman, 2003) and neglect of other important questions, such as how frequently or consistently adolescents engage in these or other new sexual activities. Moreover, the research obsession with identifying predictor variables, especially in the study of first intercourse, has produced an artificially inflated perspective of causal pathways that reinforces concerns about "precipitating" factors. For example, researchers have identified such distal variables as hours of television viewing (Price & Hyde, 2009) and seasonality (Levin, Xu, & Bartkowski, 2002) as significant predictors of first intercourse. In short, researchers have produced a vast body of predictors that frequently lacks specificity and ultimately predicts a single event in an otherwise complex sexual life.

Sexual Contexts (Time, Space, Privacy)

For all the interest in determining which adolescents are having sex, getting pregnant, or infected, less information is available regarding the situational or contextual features of adolescents' sexual lives. Because most adolescent sexual activity is prohibited, youths typically face many constraints in terms of time, space, and privacy regarding their sexual lives. In-depth interviews have indicated that young people occasionally resort to public or semipublic spaces, including secluded areas in parks, rooftops and stairwells, and unsupervised parties held during school hours, to have sex (O'Sullivan & Meyer-Bahlburg, 2003). In the past 3 decades, changes have occurred in dating norms whereby early romantic and sexual exchanges typically occur now in mixed-peer groups rather than in solitary pairings (e.g., Connolly, Craig, Goldberg, & Pepler, 2004). Thus, sexual norms have evolved whereby young people split off from the group to engage in sexual activity nearby (Paikoff, 1995). A result of this lack of privacy is that young people often inadvertently (or purposefully) view others' sexual experiences—in some sense a means of learning how sex takes place but also, perhaps, of "normalizing" the activities of others.

A diary study of situational characteristics of adolescent girls' (ages 14–18) sexual encounters found that most sexual events that involved experiences of sexual intercourse (12% of occasions) did not take place in the after-school period (3:00–6:00 p.m.) when young people are often unsupervised but were more likely to occur during the evening hours (after 6:00 p.m.) and on weekends (Fortenberry et al., 2006). In Fortenberry et al.'s (2006) study, the first to our knowledge to gather such detailed information, homes of partners were the most common places for sex to occur, indicating that parents were likely present but not monitoring or prohibiting sexual activity. Afternoon sex usually occurred on vacation days rather than school days or weekends, and evening or night sex occurred more often on weekends than weekdays or vacation days. As time spent with a partner increased during a given day, odds of sex occurring that afternoon or evening for a sexually active adolescent increased five- to sixfold.

Well-Being

The sexual systems of the body are highly capable of producing pleasure and satisfaction, generating a sense of well-being in the process (see Chapter 11, this volume). Yet countervailing forces from socialization that equate sexual pleasure with guilt, shame, anxiety, and disappointment (especially among adolescents) are often equally as, if not more, powerful dynamics than those of pleasure. Despite innovative new approaches to understanding sexual health, such as the widely adopted definition of sexual health offered by the World Health Organization (Centers for Disease Control and Prevention, 2012), actually promoting sexual pleasure as an integral component of well-being has proven to be the most challenging element of a sexual health agenda (Hull, 2008). Adolescent girls, in particular, face considerable prohibitions against acknowledging their desire and enjoying sexual expression (Martin, 1996; Tolman, 2002b). Perhaps in response to Michelle Fine's (1988) powerful critique of a cultural framework that effectively silenced positive sexuality for girls, many researchers have accepted the challenge of investigating the factors that make up or predict "positive" sexuality for girls, so much so in fact that a wealth of research now addresses this topic.

In one study of sexual well-being, retrospective reports were collected from 1,986 young U.S. adults (ages 18–25) regarding their first vaginal intercourse experience (Higgins, Trussell, Moore, & Davidson, 2010). Approximately half of the women indicated that their first experience was not (31%) or else just slightly (21%) satisfying at the physiological level, compared with moderately (23%), considerably (18%), or extremely (7%) satisfying. Men had higher mean (recalled) satisfaction and reported that their first experiences were typically moderately (20%), considerably (31%), or extremely (34%) physiologically satisfying as compared with not (5%) or slightly (10%) satisfying in this sense. Similar patterns were found for psychological satisfaction with first intercourse. Recent research has suggested that the gender differences in first intercourse experiences may be age related (Walsh, Ward, Caruthers, & Merriwether, 2011). Gender differences found in self-reported experiences during first intercourse were less pronounced among older intercourse initiators than among younger initiators. The researchers attributed this trend to a number of likely factors, such as more integrated and positive sexual self-concepts among older girls, greater agency regarding the occurrence of first intercourse, or more extensive precoital sexual experience to enhance their experiences.

Girls' sexual experiences during adolescence may influence several aspects of overall well-being. We know that girls with more sexual experience appear to have greater self-esteem and happiness than girls with less sexual experience, two key indexes of general well-being (e.g., Horne & Zimmer-Gembeck, 2005). Girls with more sexual experience also have more positive sexual self-concepts (e.g., Impett & Tolman, 2006). In a survey of 116 adolescent girls (ages 12–19), both positive sexual self-concepts and "approach" sex motives (i.e., those that reflect actions to effect a positive outcome rather than avoid a negative outcome) were associated with sexual satisfaction among girls with intercourse experience (Impett & Tolman, 2006). This finding held true regardless of socioeconomic status, pubertal timing, and religiosity. Girls typically indicate that their most recent sexual experience was positive or satisfying (Impett & Tolman, 2006; O'Sullivan & Hearn, 2008).

Far less is known about the sexual well-being of adolescent boys. Boys tend to have higher levels of well-being overall, as indexed by higher self-esteem, greater expectations for success in life, and fewer feelings of alienation than girls (Gentile et al., 2009; McLean & Breen, 2009; Oliva, 1999). Male adolescents report greater satisfaction with their appearance after first intercourse than do female adolescents (Vasilenko, Ram, & Lefkowitz, 2011). More is known about sexual minority boys' well-being than about heterosexual boys' well-being, perhaps because of concerns associated with health disparities that sexual minority youth face as well as the internalized and overt stigma associated with their sexual orientation (Diamond & Lucas, 2004;

see also Chapter 20, this volume). However, little of this is related to their sexual well-being, specifically. Much more research is needed here.

Attitudes

Understanding adolescents' attitudes toward sexual behavior is essential for understanding the motives behind sexual activity, the choices made, and the reactions experienced after sexual activity. Moreover, examining individual differences, gender differences, and generational differences in attitudes toward sexual behavior among adolescents is also important to identify the possible influences that shape these attitudes as well as changes over time. In a U.S. study comparing five large data sets (Monitoring the Future, General Social Survey, International Social Science Project, Intergenerational Panel Study of Parents and Children, and the National Survey of Families and Households), researchers found trends in sexual attitudes from the 1960s through most of the 1990s indicating greater tolerance toward diversity and increased acceptance of divorce, premarital sex, unmarried cohabitation, and childbearing (Thornton & Young-DeMarco, 2001). Although people tend to believe that the genders differ notably in their sexual attitudes, with boys and men exhibiting more permissive or tolerant sexual attitudes than girls and women, researchers have found that this is not in fact the case. In a recent review of meta-analytic studies and large datasets from the United States, United Kingdom, and Australia that assessed the sexual attitudes of adolescents and adults (Petersen & Hyde, 2011), researchers found a small gender difference in general sexual attitudes indicating that men had somewhat more permissive attitudes than did women, but this difference was small and far smaller than it had been even a decade earlier. Although the results from the adolescent studies were not analyzed separately, it will be interesting to see in future generations whether this trend toward convergence in women's and men's sexual attitudes continues.

Although the gender difference in sexual attitudes appears to be disappearing, there are some areas in which girls and boys still report striking differences. For example, research on the reported outcomes of sexual activity is one topic area in which boys and girls differ. A comparison of data from the National Longitudinal Study of Adolescent Health revealed that girls perceived less positive outcomes relating to sex and reported more sex-related shame and guilt than boys (Cuffee, Hallfors, & Waller, 2007). Furthermore, cultural differences were also identified, with White boys experiencing more shame and guilt about sex than African American boys, although girls did not differ by race. In a more recent longitudinal study, researchers tracked the sexual behaviors and importance of abstinence, perceived peer norms, and family attitudes among female adolescents (ages 14–17) over 4 years (Akers et al., 2011). Although sexual behavior increased with age, the likelihood of engaging in new sexual behaviors was lower among those who perceived greater family disapproval of sexual experience. Girls' personal attitudes toward abstinence best predicted whether they transitioned to new sexual behaviors, even after controlling for perceived peer norms and family attitudes. In sum, it appears that the trend is toward greater tolerance in sexual attitudes overall, and there are relatively few discrepancies between female and male adolescent attitudes. The areas in which discrepancies emerge generally reflect the differential socialization and sexual experiences common to youths.

Norms

Despite the overwhelmingly large amount of research focusing on problematic aspects of adolescent sexuality, a fair body of research has accumulated that has focused on normative sexuality among adolescents, or what are typical or expected experiences among youths. These studies commonly address topics related to age of onset, sexual frequency, sexual activities, and occasionally partnership contexts. In particular, diary studies tracking sexual behavior over time have identified a range of sexual patterns, but most clear from these studies is that adolescents' sexual activity is usually fairly intermittent (e.g., Ott, Ofner, Tu, Katz, & Fortenberry, 2010). Some youths report first sexual experiences but then appear to have long stretches of relative inactivity, whereas others report steady rates over time, especially those youths in romantic relationships, or else rates steadily increase in frequency as experience and confidence grow. It is important to recognize that trajectories vary from the outset and that it is inappropriate to characterize all adolescents as sexually "activated" from the point of first experience (Tolman, 2002a). Interestingly, in one of the few studies examining sexuality within couples, the frequency of sexual intercourse was negatively correlated with relationship quality among younger adolescents (ages 14–17) but positively correlated with relationship quality among older adolescents (ages 17–21; Welsh, Haugen, Widman, Darling, & Grello, 2005).

Despite popular media claims of an oral sex "epidemic" (Parker-Pope, 2009), oral sex appears to be a regular component of adolescents' sexual repertoires, but by no means predominates. Data from the National Center for Health Statistics suggest that approximately 30% of 15-year-olds and 75% of 19-year-olds report having experienced (either given or received) oral sex with an opposite-gender partner (Mosher, Chandra, & Jones, 2005). Although oral sex among both girls and boys appears to be a normative behavior, most research to date has focused solely on girls' reports of fellatio, perhaps reflecting the marginalization of women's sexual pleasure (Bay-Cheng & Fava, 2011). Furthermore, prevalence estimates support this focus on fellatio, with young people often reporting having engaged in fellatio more often than cunnilingus (Vannier & O'Sullivan, 2012). In fact, this research has indicated that more than 90% of the sexual interactions reported by participants included fellatio; however, only 46% of all interactions included cunnilingus and almost never without a girl indicating that she had reciprocated with fellatio.

Although the lack of research on young women's experiences receiving oral sex can be worrisome, studies suggest that women often report positive motives for engaging in oral sex (both giving and receiving) as well as positive reactions to those experiences (Malacad & Hess, 2010; Vannier & O'Sullivan, 2012). Furthermore, the reasons for engaging in oral sex may differ among young women and men. For example, Chambers (2007) found that males were more likely than females to report receiving oral sex for their own pleasure (84 vs. 75%), whereas females were more likely than males (27% vs. 18%) to report receiving oral sex to please their partner. This disparity suggests that at least for some females, giving oral sex may be perceived as more desirable than receiving oral sex. These studies have typically been conducted using young adult populations and require the use of caution when applying them to adolescents. Future research needs to address adolescent populations to allow educators, health care providers, and counselors to develop strategies that are tailored to adolescent-specific oral sex experiences.

Anal intercourse is generally an infrequent sexual activity among heterosexual adolescents (Hensel, Fortenberry, & Orr, 2010), with a minority (10%) of 15- to 18-year-olds reporting ever having had anal sex (e.g., Lindberg et al., 2008). However, research has suggested that these numbers increase by the time that they reach young adulthood, with 30% of young adults in one study reporting having had anal intercourse at least once (Leichliter, Chandra, Liddon, Fenton, & Aral, 2007). Stigma associated with reports of both oral sex and anal intercourse may result in lower reported frequency, making it difficult to assess accurately among adolescents.

There has been considerable focus in the United States and United Kingdom on promoting sexual abstinence, often in the form of virginity pledges. A *virginity pledge* is an oral or written promise to refrain from sexual activity, usually until marriage, administered after a course offered through religious youth groups, schools, or large group events (Rosenbaum, 2009; see also Volume 2, Chapter 13, this handbook). Research findings have indicated that adolescents who take a pledge to remain sexually abstinent (a pledge that usually requires a promise to avoid all sexual activity until marriage) are more likely to be female, more religious, and to perceive that their friends or parents had more disapproving attitudes about their engagement in sexual behavior than nonpledgers (e.g., Bersamin, Walker, Waiters, Fisher, & Grube, 2005).

Despite the popularity of abstinence-based sexual education in the United States and the United Kingdom, research examining the effectiveness of virginity pledges has indicated that there are no differences in sexual activity between pledgers and nonpledgers (e.g., Bearman & Brückner, 2001;

Brückner & Bearman, 2005; Rosenbaum, 2009). In fact, in a recent analysis conducted in the United States comparing surveys of youths who had reported taking a virginity pledge with those who had not found that 5 years after the pledge, 82% of pledgers denied having taken a pledge (Rosenbaum, 2009). Moreover, the study also found that pledgers and nonpledgers did not differ in premarital sexual experiences, lifetime numbers of sexual partners, and age of first sex. However, fewer pledgers used contraception or condoms in the preceding year or contraceptives during their last occasion of sexual intercourse, indicating that preventive behaviors, but not sexual behaviors more generally, appeared to vary on the basis of sexual attitudes. A related study found that adolescents who abstain from all sex tend to have a lower socioeconomic status, fewer social or dating opportunities, and lower academic achievement levels (Woody, D'Souza, & Woody, 2000). Because both solo and partnered sexual activity are an integrated component of healthy sexual development, it seems misguided to try to have young people deny their sexuality. Regardless of efforts to quell sexual interest and expression, adolescence remains a period of life in which young people experiment sexually, gain confidence in their sexual interactions with others, and learn about their own sexual responses.

Unconventional Behavior and Patterns

Unconventional behavior and patterns are those that do not conform to trends characteristic of the vast majority of adolescents. Adolescents who begin their partnered sexual lives earlier than their peers may be viewed as engaging in unconventional (nonnormative) sexual behavior. A cross-cultural study comparing Finland, Scotland, France, Poland, and the United States found that early sexual initiation (before age 15) was linked to negative physical (e.g., headaches) and psychological symptoms (e.g., depression, loneliness) for girls, but not for boys (Madkour, Farhat, Halpern, Godeau, & Gabhainn, 2010). Another study linked (recalled) age of first intercourse with current sexual adjustment among 475 young adults (ages 18–29; Reissing, Andruff, & Wentland, 2012). Younger age of first intercourse among the women was associated with a less positive experience and more regret; however, a later age of first intercourse for women was associated with lower sexual self-efficacy and higher rates of current sexual aversion. For men, a younger age of first intercourse was associated with worse current sexual adjustment, whereas a later age of first intercourse was associated with higher levels of current sexual aversion. Being in a nonintact family, low parental supervision, antisocial behavior, high substance use, and a high proportion of other-sex friends have also been associated with earlier ages at first sexual intercourse (i.e., 13 or younger; Boislard & Poulin, 2011; Jamieson & Wade, 2011; Mendle et al., 2009; Olesen et al., 2012).

Adolescent girls in age-discrepant relationships in which they are involved with a male partner older than themselves report earlier onset of sexual activity, more sexual experience, less consistent use of contraception, and higher rates of pregnancy and infection (Darroch et al., 1999; Lee, Jennings, & Ellen, 2003). Likewise, adolescent boys (Grades 7–12) with older sexual partners had higher rates of sexual intercourse and pregnancy or STI histories (Loftus & Kelly, 2012). A recent study of gay and bisexual adolescent men (ages 14–22) found that having much older partners (vs. same-age or slightly older partners) was predictive of receptive anal sex under the influence of drugs or alcohol (Bruce, Harper, Fernández, & Jamil, 2012). Thus, this non-normative pattern of relationships appears to have links to sexual risk.

Survival sex is another form of unconventional behavior. This term refers to transactional or commercial sex or exchange of sex for payment of some kind, such as shelter, physical protection, or drugs (Leclerc-Madlala, 2003). Most research on this topic is conducted among homeless youths. Studies have suggested that a notable minority of youths (approximately 3%–10%), especially among homeless youths, report having exchanged sex for goods and resources, such as money, shelter, and gifts (e.g., Lavoie, Thibodeau, Gagné, & Hébert, 2010; Rice, Monro, Barman-Adhikari, & Young, 2010). Prevalence estimates among youths staying in shelters range from 9.5% to 19%, whereas estimates range from 10% to 54% among street youths (e.g., Walls & Bell, 2011). A survey of 1,625 homeless youths (ages 10–25) found that predictors of survival sex included being transgender, sexual minority, and older and having a past history (but not recent history) of alcohol and substance use and poor mental health (see Chapter 22, this volume).

Research among samples of African youths has indicated that sexual exchange is commonly a part of dating scripts. Qualitative interviews with late adolescent South African youths, for example, in a study that explored their views of sex, dating, and relationships found that the exchange of gifts or money was common as part of a negotiation regarding sex in heterosexual couples. They described these transactions whereby male partners provided gifts or clothes to the female partners, or helped cover household or schooling costs, as informal in nature but as signs of respect on behalf of the women (Harrison & O'Sullivan, 2010). Others have found this type of sexual exchange in other samples of typically economically impoverished groups but have also linked it to gender-based violence, thus reinforcing the inherent gender inequalities involved (e.g., Barnett & Maticka-Tyndale, 2011; Wamoyi, Fenwick, Urassa, Zaba, & Stones, 2011; Watt et al., 2012; see also Chapter 12, this volume).

In some countries, such as India, the majority of adolescent males' first sexual contact is with commercial sex workers (e.g., Sharma, Sharma, Dave, & Chauhan, 1996). Otherwise, research on commercial sex describes the experiences of youths in developing countries, such as Bangladesh, Indonesia, the Philippines, Nigeria, and Ethiopia, who are forced into sex work by parents to support their families (see Volume 2, Chapter 2, this handbook). However, one study of 815 Québec high school students found that 3% had bought and 4% had sold sexual services in their lifetimes (Lavoie et al., 2010). A larger study of 10,828 Norwegian students (ages 14–17) found that 1.4% had sold sexual services (Pedersen & Hegna, 2003). Sociodemographic variables do not typically predict who has sold sex, but adolescents with more problems relating to substance use, past sexual victimization, and conduct disorders are more likely to sell sex than those without such histories.

SEXUAL FUNCTIONING

Despite the abundance of research on rates of sexual activities among adolescents, predictors, and related outcomes, surprisingly little research has been done on the actual expression of sexuality within sexual encounters, whether solo or partnered. Building on a foundation of relatively poor sexual education, a reluctance of parents and other adults to impart sexual knowledge, and occasionally youths' easy access to questionable sources of information (see Sexual Socialization and Education section), adolescents often have a period of experiential learning that is required to master the mechanics of sexual interactions. Given the high rates of sexual dysfunction captured in surveys of adult populations, it is possible that many young people never acquire adequate sexual functioning in the first place (see Chapter 8, this volume; Volume 2, Chapter 5, this handbook).

Attraction, Desire, Interest, and Arousal

Although the development of sexual and romantic interest during adolescence is an essential developmental process, adolescent attraction is nearly absent from the literature. Studies have suggested that in comparison to adults, adolescents place a large amount of emphasis on popularity, social status, and physical attraction during partner selection (Carlson & Rose, 2007; de Bruyn & Cillessen, 2006; Dijkstra, Cillessen, Lindenberg, & Veenstra, 2010). Research has also established a relation between perceptions of aggression and attraction, namely, that adolescents of both genders report greater attraction to those who display more aggressive behaviors than to those who do not (e.g., Bukowski & Sippola, 2000). In addition, a recent study found that female adolescents who displayed high levels of aggression reported that they began dating at earlier ages than their less aggressive counterparts, and highly aggressive male adolescents reported having more total dating partners than did less aggressive male adolescents (Gallup, O'Brien, & Wilson, 2011).

Research has consistently reported that physical attractiveness is the most salient factor among adolescents in partner selection (e.g., Ha, Overbeek, & Engels, 2010; Regan & Joshi, 2003). Many studies have indicated that male adolescents place greater emphasis on physical appearance than do female adolescents (Ha et al., 2010). This greater emphasis on physical attractiveness by young men is consistent with studies among adults in which adult men report placing a greater emphasis on physical appearance than women. However, studies that have attempted to counteract the effects of socially desirable responding have found that physical appearance is the most salient factor for both genders (e.g., Sprecher, 1989). Studies have also made distinctions in preferences for attractiveness among differing relationship contexts (i.e., short- and long-term relationships). One study found that adolescents value physical appearance to a greater extent when evaluating a casual sex partner and intelligence and humor to a greater extent when evaluating a long-term romantic partner (Regan & Joshi, 2003).

The largely morality-based approach in society to adolescent sexuality tends to characterize youths as sexually innocent until such time as they are "corrupted" by the sexual attention of another, "raging hormones," or exposure to sexualized images or information. First awareness of sexual attraction occurs around age 10, often before the onset of puberty (Herdt & McClintock, 2000). It is difficult, however, to study sexual desire and arousal specifically among youths. There are the significant sociocultural and political obstacles mentioned earlier, but for girls in particular, there is the "missing discourse of desire" (Fine, 1988), indicating that the words and meanings of sexual desire are often impossible for youths to access, acknowledge, or experience and subsequently impossible for researchers to elicit in their surveys or interviews.

Related to research on attraction and desire has been work exploring adolescents' experiences of crushes. The term *crush* refers to a "target-specific liking for another person, characterized by unilateral physical or romantic attraction or sexual feelings and fantasies" (Bowker, Spencer, Thomas, & Gyoerkoe, 2012, p. 630). Crushes develop during early adolescence and are quite frequent among both adolescent boys and girls, with a recent study indicating that 56% of teens currently report experiencing feelings associated with having a crush (Bowker et al., 2012). Female adolescents report higher rates than do male adolescents. Although crushes are related to feelings of physical or romantic attraction, they are distinct from other-sex friendships and romantic relationships (Bowker et al., 2012; Furman & Collins, 2009). Crush nominations may certainly be reciprocated (as may feelings of attraction), but research has suggested that in most respects, crushes remain unidirectional (e.g., Bowker et al., 2012).

Flirting is another dimension of adolescents' sexual attraction and desire that has received some, albeit limited, research attention. Adolescents use flirting to express or elicit sexual attraction in ways that do not differ significantly from the ways in which adults flirt. One study found that adolescents tend to engage in a higher frequency of teasing and aggressive acts when flirting than adults. However, adolescents report using strategies that focus less on appearance enhancement than do adults (Eyre, Read, & Millstein, 1997). Some gender differences were noted in tactics used by adolescents to signal romantic and sexual interest: Male adolescents report using more coercive strategies (such as pressuring and lying) and strategies that signal social status (such as spending money), whereas female adolescents more frequently report using strategies that signal sexual interest (e.g., hinting at sex, flirting; Eyre et al., 1997).

Young people may have had few relevant social or psychological experiences to link with feelings of attraction (Bogaert, 2004), making these experiences difficult to recognize and acknowledge at first. Youths report pressure by peers to express romantic interests in others but often experience teasing or intrusive questioning from adults when they are known to be attracted to someone or to have a crush (O'Sullivan & Meyer-Bahlburg, 2003). Many learn to hide their earliest romantic and sexual interests for fear of being shamed or ridiculed.

Other studies have examined desire, arousal, and sexual response even more indirectly and often in creative ways to bypass the sociocultural restrictions on studying these topics. Such research includes studying Swedish adolescents' self-reports of arousal to pornography exposure (Löfgren-Mårtenson & Månsson, 2010), analyzing text messages for sexual content among U.S. youths (Underwood, Rosen, More, Ehrenreich, & Gentsch, 2012), and coding images and information in U.S. and Dutch teen magazines (Joshi, Peter, & Valkenburg, 2011), all in attempts to understand how young people incorporate or respond to sexual stimuli in their lives. For example, focus groups in Sweden revealed that adolescents use pornography as a stimulus for sexual arousal (as it is designed to do) and that male adolescents described using it because sexual desire was a frustrating need that required satisfaction (Löfgren-Mårtenson & Månsson, 2010). Adolescent boys typically report viewing pornography to get aroused and to masturbate; adolescent girls report viewing pornography out of curiosity or because a male partner enticed them to view it (e.g., Bleakley, Hennessy, & Fishbein, 2011; Wallmyr & Welin, 2006).

Studies that get closer to assessing adolescents' motives for sex often aim to capture associations with sexual risk outcomes, such as condom use (e.g., Cooper, Shapiro, & Powers, 1998; Stone & Ingham, 2002), rather than capturing the broad scope of motives linked to partnered sexual interactions. There are some notable exceptions. In a study tracking adolescents' experiences of positive and negative emotions around occasions of penile–vaginal intercourse (Shrier, Koren, Aneja, & de Moor, 2010), positive affect was shown to increase before sex occurred, peak at the point at which sex occurred, then return to baseline. Negative affect only showed declines after sex. Another study required 67 young people (ages 15–21) to answer questions about their most recent sexual events after being signaled randomly using handheld computer technology. Just "wanting" sex was the reason provided for 44% of the 234 sexual occasions reported over a 1-week period (Dawson, Shih, de Moor, & Shrier, 2008). This motive was more common than being in love (27%), external reasons (e.g., drunk, partner wanted it; 15%), or affect management (e.g., to feel less depressed, distract oneself, relax; 12%). In a diary study of 146 adolescent women (ages 14–17) tracked over 84 days, researchers found that two of the best predictors of intercourse on any given day were sexual interest and more positive mood (Fortenberry et al., 2005).

As an additional example of motives (and hence meaning) behind adolescents' participation in partnered sexual activities, Osorio et al. (2012) surveyed 8,495 high school students (ages 14–18) in the Philippines, El Salvador, and Peru. Participants indicated that the most common reason for first intercourse among girls was being in love or getting carried away by sexual arousal, whereas among boys feeling like it or getting carried away were most common. For both, wanting to know what sex was like and external pressure were also common reasons cited, whereas wanting to have fun, for social status, to maintain a relationship, or as a result of alcohol or drug use were quite uncommon reasons. A notable minority of youths, specifically one quarter of female and one-fifth of male adolescents (especially highly religious youths), expressed regret for having already had sexual relationships. The remainder indicated no regret whatsoever. Overall, sexual activity among adolescents appears to be a positive experience cross-culturally, with many adolescents reporting positive motives and reactions.

Very little is known about asexuality in the general population, that is, the lack of sexual attraction to anyone, and this is certainly true in studies of youths. We could find no studies on youths. However, analysis of a national probability sample of British residents (ages 16–59) found that approximately 1.05% of the population reported never having felt sexual attraction to anyone in their lifetime. Asexuality was more common among older people than among younger people, but distinct age categories were not analyzed (Bogaert, 2004). Bogaert (2004) argued that the results indicate a cohort effect or else reinterpretation (or dismissal) by adults of the sexual attractions that they experienced in youth. Although youths with physical or psychogenic disabilities are considered to have an essentially asexual status throughout their lives, they report normal levels of interest and activity (Brunnberg, Boström, & Berglund, 2009), calling into question assumptions about who does or should experience sexual interest and desire.

In a survey study of sexual functioning, high rates of sexual interest, desire, and arousal were reported in a sample of 171 late adolescents (ages 16–21; O'Sullivan & Majerovich, 2008). Few adolescents reported never having felt desire for kissing (one woman), foreplay (four men and two women), or intercourse (eight women and three men). Moreover, no gender differences were found in desire for these sexual activities, nor in measures of sexual pleasure and sexual satisfaction. Overall, young people reported high rates of interest and desire for sexual activity (see Chapter 8, this volume).

Myths and Misinformation

Although a great deal is known about the sources of information that adolescents access to learn about sexuality, more interesting in many respects is the misinformation that adolescents acquire, much of which is believed to shape their thoughts, feelings, and behaviors. Sexual myths are the exaggerated and unscientific beliefs relating to sex that individuals mistakenly take to be true (Kukulu, Gürsoy, & Sözer, 2009). In the past, peers have often been identified as a significant source of incorrect information for youths, especially in retrospective reports or qualitative investigations in which beliefs are deconstructed in groups (e.g., Kennedy & Roberts, 2009).

A notable body of literature has addressed rape-supportive attitudes or beliefs among youths, that is, the endorsement of beliefs that support men's right to sexual access to women by whatever means the men choose, including physically aggressive means (Burgess, 2007). Individuals who endorse rape myths tend to ascribe less responsibility to the perpetrator and more responsibility to the victim than do those who do not endorse such myths (e.g., Hammond, Berry, & Rodriguez, 2011; Suarez & Gadalla, 2010). Although much of the research on the endorsement of rape myths has focused on college students, prevention programs incorporating peer-education components also target secondary schools (Lanier, 2001). Some resistance is found to items such as "As long as people take precautions, they won't be raped" and "If someone is drunk or high, they can't be held responsible for their actions if they get too sexually aggressive" (e.g., P. Smith & Welchans, 2000). Higher levels of accurate sexual knowledge are linked to lower endorsement of rape myths among adolescents, even after taking into account academic performance and sex of participants (Mallet & Herbé, 2011).

Other areas of sexuality knowledge that reveal substantial errors among adolescent samples relate to pregnancy prevention and disease prevention (e.g., Hensel, Stupiansky, Herbenick, Dodge, & Reece, 2011). For example, a large survey of high school students revealed that overall knowledge about AIDS was high (mean percentage correct was 91.8%; Cohall et al., 2001). However, significant gaps in the knowledge were apparent, especially in relation to prevalence of common STIs, routes of transmission, recognition of symptoms, and potential health-related outcomes associated with exposure.

Media portrayals of sex in television, movies, music, and print have also been held responsible for perpetuating false ideas about sex, especially among Western youths, who report exceptionally high levels of media consumption (see Brown, 2002). A few studies of late have addressed the role of sexually explicit media as a source for adolescents of myths or misinformation about sex as well as mainstream media, such as television and magazines (see Volume 2, Chapter 12, this handbook). In short, adolescents garner considerable misinformation about sexuality in sociocultural contexts in which access to accurate, useful, and meaningful information is actively impeded.

Abilities

Much of the research in this field has made no distinctions on the basis of mental, emotional, or physical ability, and yet positive sexual functioning is well known to be in part dependent on the effective functioning and integration of a range of related systems. Research among adolescents is sparse, as it is among adults (e.g., McCabe, Cummins, & Deeks, 2000), and adolescents with disabilities are often deliberately excluded from studies of adolescent sexuality altogether (e.g. Maart & Jelsma, 2010). Most of the literature using adolescent samples has addressed sexuality among those with developmental disabilities generally (e.g., autism, fetal alcohol spectrum disorder) or with specific physical disabilities, such as chronic illness (e.g., cerebral palsy), genetic conditions (e.g., Down syndrome), or other physical conditions, such as spinal cord injuries or blindness.

Work in this area has tended to focus on educating youths with disabilities about their sexual development and prevention of sexual abuse, victimization, and other unwanted outcomes, such as unintended pregnancy (e.g., Valenti-Hein & Choinski, 2007). Youths with disabilities do appear to be at great risk of sexual abuse or victimization than youth who do not have disabilities (e.g., Cheng & Udry, 2002). However, by no means should their sexuality be characterized primarily in these terms. Although significant discomfort surrounds adolescent sexuality in general, it appears to be amplified for those with disabilities. A great deal of the literature, for instance, has focused on coping strategies for caretakers who need to address the sexual development or control the sexual expression or experiences of youths with disabilities.

Young people with disabilities are often considered to be asexual, sexually immature, or passive. Researchers have noted caregivers' resistance to allowing these youths opportunities for sexual expression (Brunnberg et al., 2009; Potgieter & Khan, 2005). There has been little discussion of the societal obstacles that contribute to functional limitations for those with disabilities or of ways in which the sexual lives of those with disabilities can be satisfying and fun; but that, of course, is true for much of the field of adolescence. Many of the studies have indicated that the sexual lives of adolescents with disabilities are not all that much different from those of adolescents without disabilities: They tend to start consensual sexual activity with partners somewhat later and have a little less sexual experience overall (Hellemans, Roeyers, Leplae, Dewaele, & Deboutte, 2010; Maart & Jelsma, 2010), but far more similarities than differences exist. They often report interest in marrying and having children, just as their counterparts without disabilities do, but they are much less likely to have sought or received information on sexual and reproductive functioning (e.g., Stevens, Steele, Jutai, & Kalnins, 1996).

In one study, researchers compared the sexual and romantic lives of youths with and without physical disabilities using data from a large U.S. national survey (Cheng & Udry, 2002). They found that youths with disabilities were as sexually experienced as their counterparts without disabilities (measured as percentages reporting sexual intercourse experience), despite generally greater social isolation. Youths with disabilities were less sure of their sexual orientation than were their counterparts without disabilities. The two groups did not differ in terms of sex and contraception attitudes, although boys with more severe disabilities had poorer knowledge scores.

The same researchers (Cheng & Udry, 2005) analyzed data from this national survey to compare adolescents with low and average cognitive abilities. In this case, they found that adolescents with low cognitive abilities had fewer romantic experiences and lower rates of sexual experience than those with average abilities. Moreover, boys with low cognitive abilities were more likely to report same-sex attraction (Cheng & Udry argued for more research to clarify why this association might exist), and among the sexually experienced youths, those with low cognitive abilities were less likely to use contraception and reported higher rates of risky sexual activity. In short, important discoveries remain to be made regarding the sexual lives of youths with disabilities. Those with chronic conditions are sexual beings and are entitled to lead positive sexual lives; however, intellectual, emotional, anatomical and physiological, and mobility impairments may pose obstacles to leading a healthy and satisfying sexual life.

Problems and Dysfunctions

Despite the strong interest in both adolescent problem behaviors and the high rates of sexual dysfunctions among adults (e.g., Laumann, Paik, & Rosen, 1999), almost no research exists on sexual dysfunctions among adolescents. Large prevalence surveys have occasionally incorporated late adolescents in their samples, but rates among adolescents are rarely analyzed separately from those of adults (e.g., Laumann et al., 1999; Mercer et al., 2003). A U.S. national sample assessed rates of sexual dysfunction in the preceding 1-year period among adults ages 18 to 59 (Laumann et al., 1999). Men and women in the 18- to 29-year-old age bracket reported the following rates of sexual problems: no sexual desire (14% for men, 32% for women, respectively), anorgasmia (inability to achieve orgasm; 7% and 26%), no sexual pleasure (10% and 27%), performance anxiety (19% and 16%), lack of sexual lubrication (arousal disorder; 19%, women only), and erectile problems (7%, men only). Unfortunately, rates among the late adolescents were obscured among those of the young adults. Another relevant study analyzed national survey data, including those from 233 women ages 18 to 24 (Fisher & Boroditsky, 2000). They found that 31% of these women were unable to have an orgasm during intercourse, 33% reported low sexual desire, and 22% reported physical pain during intercourse. Unfortunately, only three questions on problems in sexual functioning were incorporated into the study, and only women were surveyed.

Tolman (2001) has argued that "female adolescent sexual dysfunction is an oxymoron" (p. 197), but this argument could be extended to youths in general because in large part adolescents simply are expected to experience pain, discomfort, or lack of response in their sexual lives. Female adolescents who experience no interest or desire for sexual activity, who are unable to have an orgasm during intercourse, or who feel pain during sex and male adolescents who ejaculate faster than desired by himself or his partner, feel pain with insertion, or have trouble maintaining an erection would be more likely to be viewed as sexually inexperienced or inept rather than dysfunctional. In support of this view, the American Psychiatric Association's *Diagnostic and Statistical Manual of Mental Disorders* (4th ed., text revision; American Psychiatric Association, 2000), which catalogues dysfunctions and specifies the criteria for each across a range of domains actually has no age criteria for any of the sexual dysfunctions included in its issues. No published reports on rates of sexual problems, difficulties, or dysfunctions among youths exist to our knowledge. Of note, it is inappropriate in our view to describe sexual problems in terms of "dysfunctions" unless an individual has met all the criteria of a diagnosis and has reported marked distress—a standard feature of all sexual dysfunction diagnoses (see Volume 2, Chapters 4 and 5, this handbook). For young people in particular, the additional stigma associated with applying a psychiatric label to their experiences may be especially damaging. The constructs "problems" or "difficulties" better capture these experiences.

One study addressed sexual problems among young people ages 17 to 21 (O'Sullivan & Majerovich, 2008). As part of a larger study addressing the progression of sexual problems over time, 171 late adolescent men and women (ages 17–21) were surveyed regarding lifetime experiences of sexual difficulties. The percentages of men who indicated experiencing the following sexual difficulties "sometimes" or "always" were as follows: early ejaculation, 41.9%; performance anxiety, 32.6%; difficulty maintaining an erection, 23.1%; engaging in unwanted sexual activity, 18.7%; and inability to climax, 16.3%. Prevalence of sexual problems experienced "sometimes" or "always" among adolescent women were as follows: inability to climax, 52.1%; insufficient lubrication, 31.3%; performance anxiety, 31.2%; pain during intercourse, 25.8%; and lack of sexual pleasure, 11.2%. In addition, approximately half of the adolescent women had experienced pain inserting tampons (53.2%) or during pelvic exams (48.8%).

Landry and Bergeron (2011) also found that 20% of 251 sexually active adolescent girls (ages 12–19) reported pain during intercourse on at least 75% of the sexual occasions, results that mirror those found in population-based studies of women. Interviews with adolescent women (ages 14–20) about their reasons for continuing to have intercourse despite the considerable pain that they experienced revealed beliefs affirming their image of an ideal woman who is perceptive of and receptive to a (male) partner's sexual needs (Elmerstig, Mijma, & Berterö, 2008). Having sexual intercourse was a key component of being a normal woman, despite pain or discomfort, and themes of resignation, sacrifice, and guilt emerged through their stories.

Long-term (chronic) difficulties were uncommon among both female and male adolescents (O'Sullivan & Majerovich, 2008). Female adolescents reported higher lifetime rates than their male counterparts of the following: inability to orgasm, 87% versus 61%; pain during intercourse, 75% versus 33%; and lack of sexual interest, 81% versus 58%. An interesting finding was that when adolescents' rates were compared with those from a mixed sample of young adults and adults (ages 22–38), no differences in the mean number or types of sexual problems emerged. This finding indicates that the poor rate of sexual functioning noted in adulthood possibly stems in part from problems in sexual functioning that emerge during adolescence (see Chapter 13, this volume). This study provided rates of lifetime prevalence but little insight into the degree of distress associated with these problems.

Analyses of a second sample of 330 male and female sexually active youths (ages 16–21) indicated that 15% reported clinical levels of sexually related personal distress (O'Sullivan, Brotto, Byers, Majerovich,

& Wuest, 2012). Moreover, female adolescents revealed problems in desire, arousal and satisfaction, lubrication, orgasm, and genital pain that were midway between levels in adult women with sexual dysfunction and normal controls (Rosen et al., 2000). In addition, male adolescents' scores were midway between those of patients with erectile dysfunction and adult controls (Rosen et al., 1997). A substantial minority (18%) of the adolescent males were classified as having symptoms of premature ejaculation or possible premature ejaculation. We found no other studies that examined the range of sexual problems common among adolescents.

Sexual problems among adolescents that are secondary to other primary complaints, including gynecological or genitourinary problems or abnormalities (e.g., pelvic inflammatory disease, testicular cancer, endometriosis) or conditions requiring surgical treatments, such as congenital anomalies, ovarian cysts, or tumors (e.g., Greydanus & Matytsina, 2010), have received scant research attention. Other studies have provided less direct evidence of sexual problems among adolescents, such as reports of side effects associated with medications, such as selective serotonin reuptake inhibitors, antipsychotic medication, and long-term oral contraceptive use, or studies of adolescents' abuse of sildenafil (e.g., Peters, Johnson, Kelder, Meschack, & Jefferson, 2007). Given the overwhelming concerns expressed about adolescents' sexual activity and overall sexual health, it is surprising how little interest there appears to be in actual sexual functioning, or problems associated with sexual functioning, among adolescents (see Volume 2, Chapter 5, this handbook).

Alcohol and Substance Use in the Sexual Context

An abundance of research is available on alcohol and substance use among adolescents (e.g., Latimer & Zur, 2010), risk factors (e.g., Kelly et al., 2011), and related outcomes (e.g., Wells, Mihic, Tremblay, Graham, & Demers, 2008). However, less is known about alcohol and substance use in the sexual context except in relation to incidents of unprotected sexual intercourse (e.g., van Gelder, Reefhuis, Herron, Williams, & Roeleveld, 2011) or sexual violence and assault (e.g., McCauley et al., 2009).

Comparable to rates for sexual activity, more than half (69%) of high school students have consumed alcohol at some point (e.g., Poulin & Elliot, 2007), and many (38%) have reported lifetime use of marijuana (e.g., Elgar, Phillips, & Hammond, 2011). Alcohol consumption and substance use typically stem from adolescents' peer-group encounters and appear to be a routine part of their sexual experiences. The social shift in adolescence from same-sex peer interactions to mixed-sex group interactions often provides the context and opportunities for experimentation with dating relationships, sexual activity, and alcohol consumption. That is, adolescents tend to consume alcohol and connect with romantic and sexual partners in mixed-group settings that are unmonitored by adults. These behaviors are considered normative among adolescents (Hotton & Haans, 2004; Hussong, 2002).

Another parallel with sexual activity is that alcohol use among adolescents is usually framed solely as a risk activity among researchers, educators, and health care professionals (e.g., Maggs, 1997; Zufferey et al., 2007). Yet alcohol consumption during adolescence, even binge drinking, is usually associated with normal, developmental goals, such as interpersonal acceptance, competence, and confidence and reflects teens' movement toward adopting an adult identity. Preventive efforts often are aimed at "protecting against" sex initiation and alcohol, illicit drug, and tobacco use together (Schwartz et al., 2010), which pathologizes each of these behaviors. Regardless, alcohol consumption and drug use tend to be closely linked to adolescent sexual and dating contexts, with Western cultures showing closer concordance than non-Western cultures (e.g., Shell, Newman, & Xiaoyi, 2010).

In many Western countries, the use of sex, drugs, and alcohol has been positioned among younger adolescents as a means of rebellion, acting out, or breaking away from the family context (Ferguson & Meehan, 2010). However, rightly or wrongly, these behaviors clearly help youths to establish an adult identity: Sexual experience, as well as higher drug and alcohol use, are positively correlated with adolescents' subjective experience of age (Arbeau, Galambos, & Jansson, 2007). Moreover, alcohol consumption does not generally predict risky sexual practices alone, as is commonly believed, but instead predicts expectations for risky sexual outcomes (Fortenberry, Orr, Katz, Brizendine, & Blythe, 1997; Weinhardt & Carey, 2000). For example, Fortenberry et al. (1997) used diary methods with a sample of 82 adolescent women (ages 15–19). They found that the likelihood of using a condom when sober was the best predictor of condom use under the influence; risk behavior while drinking reflected typical or usual patterns of condom use. Other expectations reinforced in youth culture with regard to alcohol, substances, and sex include sexual enhancement and behavioral disinhibition (Kalichman, Simbayi, Cain, & Jooste, 2007), decreased nervousness (Leigh, 1990), and increased sexual responsiveness and availability among females (Goldman, Del Boca, & Darkes, 1999).

A meta-analysis comparing heterosexual and sexual minority youths revealed that sexual minority youths were almost twice as likely (odds ratio = 1.91) to report sex while intoxicated as their heterosexual peers (Herrick, Marshal, Smith, Sucato, & Stall, 2011). This difference may be related to the marginalized status of such youths, to the heterosexism they face on a daily basis, or both. Oddly, most studies have reported on odds of risky sexual behavior given substance or alcohol use histories or prevalence of alcohol or drug use at last sexual intercourse (e.g., Goodenow, Szalacha, Robin, & Westheimer, 2002, 2008) but few if any indexes of the co-occurrence of these activities among youths despite considerable qualitative research indicating that being drunk or high during sex is common (e.g., Tolman, 2002a). Goodenow et al. (2008) reported that approximately 22% of youths indicated that they had used alcohol or drugs at last sexual intercourse. We found only one study that provided self-reported rates of sex while high, and it used a sample of homeless or runaway youths (Moon et al., 2000). Rates of being high during sex in the prior 6 months for these youths were 44% for heterosexual females, 55% for heterosexual males, 73% for gay or bisexual males, and 89% for lesbian and bisexual females. It is unclear why studies of the co-occurrence of alcohol, substance use, and sexual activity are so rare given the social sanctions against each of these behaviors for youths, but this area clearly warrants additional research (see Chapter 21, this volume).

There are a few reports of sildenafil citrate (i.e., Viagra) abuse among teenage boys (e.g., Apodaca & Moser, 2011). Focus groups with 43 adolescent men (ages 18–19) who reported being current users indicated that they started using it around ages 15 to 16, mostly because of curiosity, peer pressure, and sexual enhancement (reported by a minority; Peters et al., 2007). Some reported partner coercion as a reason for using it. More than half indicated that their partner was a casual sexual partner and reported obtaining it from friends or stealing it from their father. Most reported few negative consequences of its use. In short, it is likely that alcohol and substance use represent activities characteristic of adolescents in their peer groups and symbolize for them their emerging adult identities. Thus, these activities will likely remain entwined with sexual activity for these reasons alone.

SEXUAL SOCIALIZATION AND EDUCATION

The process by which adolescents acquire sexual knowledge, attitudes, and values is known as sexual socialization (Schneewind, 2001). Sexual socialization is an essential aspect of sexual development during adolescence (e.g., Byers, Sears, & Weaver, 2008; Deptula, Henry, & Schoeny, 2010; L'Engle & Jackson, 2008). Adolescents acquire sexual information through a variety of formal and informal sources, including family, friends, mass media, and school- and clinic-based sexual education. Adolescent girls seek sexual information more actively than do their male counterparts (Lefkowitz, Boone, Sigman, & Kit-fong, 2002; Rosenthal & Feldman, 1999). Girls consult more sources, discuss a wider variety of sexual topics, and communicate with higher frequency with family and friends than do boys.

Communication and Exchanges With Family and Friends

The amount of research attention given to the role that family plays in sexual socialization among adolescents has increased in recent years (e.g., Hutchinson & Cederbaum, 2011; Martino, Elliott, Corona, Kanouse, & Schuster, 2008; Sneed, 2008). Improvements in adolescents' sexual health report card have been attributed to positive changes in family environments (such as improved parental education, reduced likelihood of being born to an adolescent mother) and positive trends in sexual norms (such as later age of first intercourse, reductions in partners; e.g., Manlove, Ikramullah, Mincieli, Holcombe, & Danish, 2009).

For most adolescents, parents are the earliest sources of information on positive sexual development (Lefkowitz & Stoppa, 2006; N. B. Moore & Davidson, 1999), suggesting that parents play a vital role in sexual knowledge transfer during adolescence. Although a large amount of research attention has been given to parent–adolescent sexual communication, most of the research has focused on mother–child communication, with a particular emphasis on mother–daughter discussions (e.g., Byers et al., 2008; DiIorio, Pluhar, & Belcher, 2003; Kapungu et al., 2010). The lack of research attention given to father–child communication likely reflects the frequency with which mothers discuss sexual topics with their children. Mothers simply talk to both sons and daughters about sexual topics more than do fathers (DiIorio et al., 2003; Jerman & Constantine, 2010; Swain, Ackerman, & Ackerman, 2006; Wilson & Koo, 2010).

Factors that influence parents' ability to discuss sexual topics with their teens include adolescent motivation, perceived outcomes, relationship quality, and perceived self-efficacy (Guilamo-Ramos, Jaccard, Dittus, & Collins, 2008; Jaccard, Dittus, & Gordon, 2000; Miller et al., 2009). In particular, parents are more likely to discuss sexual information if their teen is motivated to learn, the outcome of the discussion is positive, the parent and teen have a strong relationship, and the parent has high self-efficacy. Although research has commonly reported that close family relationships and parental involvement are also associated with more condom use, less exposure to risky situations, and later sexual onset in youths (e.g., Donenberg, Bryant, Emerson, Wilson, & Pasch, 2003; Teitelman, Ratcliffe, & Cederbaum, 2008), a body of research has also suggested that parent–child sexual communication does not influence the sex lives of youths. This area of research is exceedingly complex (see DiIorio et al., 2003, and Lefkowitz, 2002, for reviews).

The content of parent–adolescent sexual communication has been studied quite extensively. In particular, much of the work to date has focused on discussions about sex-related risks, with the most frequently discussed topics including STIs, pregnancy, abstinence, and contraceptives (Hadley et al., 2009). The range of topics being discussed between parents and adolescents is broad and differs between families (Martino et al., 2008). In fact, over time, parents are likely to cover a wide range of topics beyond risk and prevention, such as physical development, dating and romantic relationships, desire, sexual identity and orientation, and moral and religious aspects of sexuality (Lefkowitz & Stoppa, 2006).

Despite the large amount of research attention focusing on parents, little is known about the influence of siblings on adolescent sexual socialization, although some work has focused on the impact older siblings have on teens' sex lives (East & Jacobson, 2000; Kornreich, Hearn, Rodriguez, & O'Sullivan, 2003). Among these studies, the most common topic appears to be the age of sexual debut (Widmer, 1997; M. R. Moore & Chase-Lansdale, 2001), with results indicating that adolescents with older siblings tend to report an earlier age of first sexual intercourse than those without older siblings.

The focus on gender in work assessing the influence of older siblings indicates that adolescents with older brothers appear to adopt their brothers' views on the best age to become sexually active, whereas those with older sisters do not adopt their views to the same extent (Widmer, 1997). In addition, adolescents with older brothers have reported having lower levels of sexual interest and placing greater value on becoming a parent than have adolescents with older sisters (Kornreich et al., 2003). Conversely, adolescents with older sisters who are parents report more frequent intercourse than those without older sisters who are parents (East, Felice, & Morgan, 1993).

Although parents and siblings can be important sources of sexual information for adolescents, research has suggested that adolescents rely just as much, if not more, on peers as sources than parents (e.g., Epstein & Ward, 2008; Hampton, McWatters, Jeffery, & Smith, 2005). According to a public poll, nearly 45% of U.S. teenagers reported friends to be their main source of information about sex in comparison to 7% of teenagers who identified their parents as their main source for sex information (Stodghill, 1998). In addition, studies have demonstrated that peer influence remains a robust predictor of sexual onset and risky sexual behaviors during adolescence (e.g., Ali & Dwyer, 2011; Jaccard, Blanton, & Dodge, 2005; Whitaker & Miller, 2000).

The content of sex information received from peer groups tends to be much more sex positive and encouraging (less prohibitive or fear based) than most other sources available to adolescents (e.g., Epstein & Ward, 2008; Kehily, 2001). Adolescents report discussing a variety of sexual topics (e.g., sexual intercourse, HIV/AIDS, contraception, romantic relationships, and pregnancy) among their peer groups (DiIorio, Kelley, & Hockenberry-Eaton 1999), with topics related to sexual behaviors and techniques, dating, and STIs being the most frequently discussed (Lefkowitz, Boone, & Shearer, 2004). However, adolescents may be more skeptical of the information obtained from peers (e.g., Jones, Biddlecom, Hebert, & Mellor, 2011), and many report being well aware that they received incorrect information about contraception and pregnancy from peers or were lied to by friends about friends' own sexual experiences (Jones et al., 2011; Whitaker & Miller, 2000).

School- and Community-Based Sex Education

Dramatic sociocultural changes in the 1960s and 1970s that introduced the birth control pill, feminism, gay rights, and teen rebellion in many Western cultures served to remove sexual behavior from the confines of the marital context. However, by the 1980s, all movement toward providing comprehensive sex education, with nonjudgmental information regarding sexual health, contraception, and disease prevention, ended with the onset of the abstinence movement. Despite the limitations of these education and health programs, students continue to report trusting traditional sex information sources, such as school-based education, over Internet-based sources (Jones & Biddlecom, 2011). Historically, the vast majority of parents have been in favor of sex education in schools. Typically, there is little debate over the kind of sex education. An NPR/Kaiser/Kennedy School poll on sex education in the United States found that most parents want a wide range of topics to be covered (Kaiser Family Foundation, 2004). Most, however, did not want abstinence-only sex education in schools, even though the United States and United Kingdom in particular have spent a wealth of monies supporting abstinence-only programs across their countries.

The debate regarding the most appropriate form of sex education to provide has been considerable. Often the debate has centered on whether providing adolescents with information regarding contraception and disease prevention will spur them into sexual activity. However, the data are overwhelmingly clear—comprehensive sex education provides much-needed information when adolescents begin partnered sexual lives in terms of reduced risk, and it does not accelerate onset (see Santelli, Ott, Lyon, Rogers, & Summers, 2006). An in-depth analysis of a wide range of interventions and programs designed to prevent pregnancy and STIs has led researchers to conclude that the most effective efforts are those that are multidimensional in design and closely integrated prevention efforts into adolescents' lives while incorporating a range of influential contexts, such as clinical services, sex education programs, and youth development systems (Kirby, Crosby, Santelli & DiClemente, 2009; see Volume 2, Chapter 11, this handbook).

Other Sources of Sexual Information

Of the many sources that provide sexual information to adolescent boys and girls, the media generally rank among the top three avenues for obtaining sexual information, after peers and school-based sex education (Ward, 2003). Parents are preferred sources for youths, but parents typically do not provide sex information, according to their children's reports (Byers, 2011). Adolescents spend extraordinary numbers of their waking hours accessing these media, especially new technologies and TV, sources replete with a variety of sexual messages (e.g., Kunkel, Eyal, Finnerty, Biely, & Donnerstein, 2005; Roberts, Henriksen, & Foehr, 2009). A national survey in Canada of Internet use found that 97% of individuals ages 16 to 24 are online; 75% of them access the Internet every day (Statistics Canada, 2010). Among young people, the Internet is used for socializing more frequently than meeting others in person (67% use instant messenger systems daily with key friends, whereas 56% communicate daily with these friends in person; Quan-Haase, 2007). Research has shown that late adolescents typically use a minimum of two media channels most days to communicate with those in their offline social networks (e.g., Baym, Zhang, & Lin, 2004; see Volume 2, Chapter 3, this handbook). Between 25% and 70% of youths ages 10 to 17 reported using the Internet to seek information on sexual material, form or maintain romantic relationships, or engage in online sex (Brown & L'Engle, 2009).

Most of the studies assessing sexual content in the media have focused, to a large extent, on television (e.g., Ashby, Arcari, & Edmonson, 2006; R. L. Collins, 2005; Ward & Friedman, 2006). Studies have suggested that although television contains an abundance of sexual material, adolescents' exposure to sexual imagery through music lyrics and Internet content may be even more common than through television programs (see Roberts et al., 2009, for a review).

Despite the wide prevalence of and vast exposure to sexualized media, until recently little empirical evidence has demonstrated the extent of the impact the media have on adolescents' sexual socialization. Most research studies have found strong relationships between high media consumption and more permissive sexual attitudes, higher perceptions of the frequency of sexual activity, and greater levels of sexual experience (Brown et al., 2006; Roberts et al., 2009; see also Volume 2, Chapter 12, this handbook). Adolescents who have high diets of sexualized media might be those who seek such content and have more sexualized behavior in the first place; a third factor might account for the association between level of media consumption and sexual lives, or sexualized media might encompass models that are emulated by those who view such media the most (Steinberg & Monahan, 2011).

Media messages about sexuality tend to be "limited, unrealistic, and stereotypical" (Ward, Day, & Epstein, 2006, p. 57). In Ward et al.'s (2006) work, they argued that these messages feature a recreational or game-playing approach to sex in which men "score" and women are traded; adversarial relations between women and men, more generally; and a heavy emphasis on deception, manipulation, and dishonesty. Positive gains from media exposure may be sexual information unavailable from other more traditional sources, such as the information found in magazines and online sites, and diverse sexual models, increasingly true for sexual minority and transgender youths. Thus, there are concerns that adolescents are unable to keep in perspective the sexual and social reality of such material. More frequent exposure is linked to higher ratings of perceived reality associated with sexual media (Peter & Valkenburg, 2010), although an in-depth study of online pornography exposure, both wanted and unwanted, among 7,529 adolescents (ages 16–20) found no links with risky sexual outcomes (Luder et al., 2011; see Volume 2, Chapter 1, this handbook). Many youths find it difficult to avoid unwanted exposure to sexually explicit materials (Flood, 2007). Despite strong increases in sexual curiosity and a preoccupation with sexual matters, adolescents often lack the sexual experience, maturity, and critical thinking skills required to put such material in context (Thornburg & Lin, 2002).

ROMANTIC RELATIONSHIPS, INTIMATE EXCHANGE, AND PARTNERSHIPS

Romantic relationships are ongoing, voluntary interactions that are mutually acknowledged, characterized by intensity of experience, and marked by expressions of affection, including physical affection (W. A. Collins, 2003). During adolescence, a host of cognitive, biological, and interpersonal changes occur that facilitate the development of romantic relationships, such as improvements in communication skills and intimate exchange (e.g., S. Williams, Connolly, & Segal, 2001). Romantic relationships may be an especially important arena for interpersonal development because they provide opportunities to gain attributional insights, skills in emotion expression and regulation, and abilities to empathize and be intimate with another (W. A. Collins, 2003). Intimate relationships in adolescence are believed to influence the course of subsequent romantic relationships in adulthood (Erikson, 1968). In addition, they are critical to relatedness and autonomy—processes linked to secure attachment—and make up essential contexts for dating and sexual behavior (W. A. Collins & Sroufe, 1999).

Early romantic relationships may have later-life implications, but they are also important to study in their own right. Even though sexual behavior typically occurs in the context of romantic relationships, surprisingly little overlap has occurred in these areas of study. Romantic relationships are not synonymous with sexual relationships. Despite the complexity of this process, until recently little was known about the interpersonal contexts within which sexual behavior and its related affect are expressed (see Chapter 10, this volume).

Attachment, Intimacy, and Love

For a long period of time, the study of relationships among adolescents focused almost exclusively on platonic peer relationships. Little was known about romantic relationships or experiences before age 18, with the exception of a few select studies (e.g., Schofield, 1965). These relationships are often viewed as trivial, nominal, superficial, and not worthy of serious investigation (Furman & Collins, 2009). Some adolescents may have a great deal of experience with romantic relationships; others may have no experience at all. Some studies examined sexuality in adolescent romantic relationships, but most did so from a public health or risk perspective rather than a normative perspective. Primarily within the past 2 decades, the study of adolescent romantic relationships and experiences has flourished (e.g., Furman & Collins, 2009). The increased research attention to adolescent romantic relationships is essential because of the central role these relationships play in adolescents' lives.

Initiating and establishing relationships are major concerns among adolescents, resulting in considerable time spent thinking about past, present, or desired romantic relationships. Indeed, adolescents' self-esteem and self-worth are heavily influenced by relationship events (e.g., Tabares & Gottman, 2003), and being romantically involved is often accompanied by some of the most intense emotional highs and lows of adolescence (Larson et al., 1999). Furthermore, these relationships have long-term consequences and provide important developmental opportunities to become more emotionally competent and to acquire key relationship and communication skills that lay the groundwork for positive future relationships and commitment throughout adulthood (e.g., Diamond, Savin-Williams, & Dubé, 1999; Grover, 2008; Tabares & Gottman, 2003). Besides preparing for adulthood, relationship development also helps adolescents to develop a sense of identity (Larson et al., 1999), including a sexual identity (Furman & Shaffer, 2003).

After experiencing feelings of attraction to another, recognizing their attraction, and communicating their interest in connecting with desired others, adolescents begin to form romantic relationships. The definition of the term *romantic relationship* still remains somewhat ambiguous in its use among researchers, with little effort directed to operationally defining what the term means (Furman & Collins, 2009). Most studies have only asked participants to report on their romantic relationships, providing no definitions for their samples, whereas a select few have provided a brief description to participants (i.e., "when you like a guy [girl] and he [she] likes you back"; Giordano, Manning, & Longmore, 2006, p. 131). This lack of operationalization leaves some uncertainty surrounding what researchers have assessed in their studies of romantic relationships among adolescents and whether the constructs that they have assessed are valid.

During adolescence, the intensity of parental relationships begins to decrease (Bowlby, 1979), and adolescents begin to develop more intense relationships with peers, most frequently peers of the opposite sex (Ainsworth, 1989). In fact, many youths in middle to late adolescence report spending more time with romantic partners than with parents and family (e.g., Furman & Shaffer, 2003). Although, attachment theory originally only applied to the relationship between infants and children and parents, attachment theory was extended in the 1980s to romantic relationships (see Hazan & Shaver, 1987; Shaver & Hazan, 1988). Attachment is described throughout the literature as "the lasting psychological connectedness between human beings" (Bowlby, 1979, p. 194). The majority of romantic attachment literature has focused on adult relationships, and only recently has it extended to adolescent romantic relationship research (e.g., Tracy, Shaver, Albino, & Cooper, 2003).

Research has suggested that adolescents' attachment styles are similar to those of adults (i.e., secure, anxious, dismissive–avoidant, and fearful–avoidant; Bartholomew & Horowitz, 1991). Avoidant adolescents have been suggested to be least likely to have experience with romantic relationships and to report falling in love less often than nonavoidant adolescents; anxious adolescents, however, have reported falling in love more frequently than nonanxious adolescents; and securely attached adolescents were more likely to report frequent dating and participation in long-term relationships than avoidant adolescents, but not more than anxious adolescents (Tracy et al., 2003).

Intimacy research has also begun to flourish in the study of romantic relationships. *Intimacy* refers to the "quality of relationships characterized by commitment, feelings of closeness and trust, and self-disclosure" (Moss & Schwebel, 1993, p. 33). Intimacy is one of the most essential components of any romantic relationship. It helps adolescents to develop interpersonal skills and receive emotional support (Furman, 2002). Research has consistently suggested that intimacy significantly predicts relationship length and satisfaction among adolescent couples (e.g., Rostosky, Galliher, Welsh, & Kawaguchi, 2000). In addition, adolescents report intimacy as a primary motive for engaging in a variety of sexual behaviors (e.g., Gebhardt, Kuyper, & Greunsven, 2003; Ott, Millstein, Ofner, & Halpern-Felsher, 2006).

Using a narrative approach, one study found that young adults described their relationships during adolescence as merely a form of companionship in comparison to their trusting, stable, and supportive current adult relationships (Shulman & Kipnis, 2001). Interviews with Israeli adolescents found that younger adolescents reported relationship benefits of friendship and excitement more so than did their older adolescent counterparts, and adolescent girls reported attachment and security in their relationships to a larger extent than did adolescent boys (Shulman & Scharf, 2000). Perceptions of closeness, support, and attachment associated with romantic relationships appear to increase with age (Fraley & Davis, 1997).

According to researchers Hatfield and Walster (1978), passionate love is "a state of intense longing for union with another" (p. 9). Passionate love is most commonly felt during the early stages of relationships and can be described by the head-over-heels experiences of love. It has been theorized that at no other time throughout development is passionate love experienced more intensely than during adolescence (Hatfield, Brinton, & Cornelius, 1989). Yet there remains such a remarkable shortage of studies assessing love during adolescence despite its salience in all aspects of youth culture, especially movies and music. The few studies that have examined love experiences in adolescent samples are dated. One study of 195 early to middle adolescents (ages 12–16) found that a large proportion (71%) of the adolescents surveyed have had experience with some form of romantic partnership that lasted at least 1 month, and approximately 73% of these adolescents reported having been in love, although *in love* was not defined for participants (Montgomery & Sorell, 1998). In fact, the modal age of first falling in love was 12 years, with rates increasing at each successive age. By late adolescence, the majority of adolescents report having been in love (Hendrick & Hendrick, 1986). In fact, Hatfield, Schmitz, Cornelius, and Rapson (1988) found that adolescents of all ages report having passionate feelings for others and often labeled these feelings as *love*. Clearly, adolescents experience intense emotions, attach closely, and have intimate experiences within their romantic relationships, just as adults do. More research is needed to clarify the nature and range of experiences that occur among adolescents.

Dating, Socializing, Partnership Types, and Relationship Dissolution

Almost all adolescents express an interest in dating, and by late adolescence a majority have experienced an exclusive romantic relationship (e.g., Carver, Joyner, & Udry, 2003; O'Sullivan et al., 2007). In fact, dating relationships tend to be the context of first partnered sexual exchanges. Few adolescents report having sex before ever dating (e.g., Longmore, Manning, & Giordano, 2001), which is why, until recently, sexual activity outside of a relationship context has received so little research attention.

Data from a U.S. national survey (the National Longitudinal Study of Adolescent Health) have indicated that dating increases dramatically during these years, growing from 37% at age 12 to 53% at age 15 to 70% at 17 (Carver et al., 2003). Contrary to depictions of these relationships as transitory, if not ephemeral, a surprisingly large proportion of adolescents' romantic relationships last 11 months or more (20% for ages 14 or younger, 35% for ages 15–16, and 60% for ages 17–18). Most important, these relationships typically constitute a new and highly significant domain of both positive and negative emotion for adolescents. Most early to middle adolescents (83%) indicate that feelings of love in their relationships were reciprocated and describe patterns of frequent and ongoing exchange (Montgomery & Sorell, 1998).

The heterosexual relationships of young adults in the 1950s through 1970s were generally characterized by a fairly traditional dating script. This dating script involved increasing levels of familiarity and closeness acquired through exchanges in private settings, which culminated in the onset of progressively more intense sexual interactions, then marriage (Cate & Lloyd, 1992). More recently, adolescents report spending less time alone as couples at the start of a relationship and instead eventually pairing off romantically and sexually from informal groups of peers (e.g., Mongeau, Jacobsen, & Donnerstein, 2007; O'Sullivan & Meyer-Bahlburg, 2003). Of particular interest to researchers studying adolescents' intimate relationships have been recent changes in relationship structures, development, and understanding among youths of what makes up a typical or expected intimate relationship. Adolescent relationships in past decades involved romantic exchanges and demonstrations of commitment before more advanced sexual exchanges (Clark, Shaver, & Abrahams, 1999). However, recent research has documented trends in heterosexual relationships of the reverse, whereby romantic expression and commitment for some is built on a foundation of early and often advanced or highly intimate sexual exchanges. Still, most partnered sexual interactions first occur and continue to occur within committed relationships (e.g., de Graaf, van de Schoot, Woertman, Hawk, & Meeus, 2012; Giordano, Manning, & Longmore, 2010); this pattern remains by far the predominant trend in relationships at this time. However, researchers have documented a greater prevalence of sexual relationships without any expectations of or ultimately experiences of romantic connection (e.g., Grello, Welsh, & Harper, 2006).

There is now a substantial amount of research on these more casual forms of relationships and sexual exchanges, including studies on hooking up (e.g., Fortunato, Young, Boyd, & Fons, 2010; Manning, Giordano, & Longmore, 2006), friends with benefits (e.g., Lehmiller, VanderDrift, & Kelly, 2011), and one-night stands (e.g., Longmore et al., 2001). Analysis of U.S. national data have indicated that the majority of sexually active adolescents had sexual experiences outside of a romantic relationship (Manning, Longmore, & Giordano, 2005). Although casual sexual encounters have always been prevalent among a sizable proportion of adolescents (see Grello, Welsh, Harper, & Dickson, 2003), what is notable is the extent to which these casual forms are becoming more socially acceptable and possibly a dominant form of heterosexual interaction among young people (Bogle, 2007). For example, surveys have indicated that approximately 25% of the time, sexual intercourse first occurs with a friend, stranger, or someone the person is occasionally dating (Manning et al., 2005). Casual sex is less common among adolescents in research from Asian countries, but research from Australia and New Zealand shows trends in this respect that are similar to North American and Western European countries.

Some worry that sexual experiences that lack intimacy and commitment (i.e., nonromantic sexual interactions) may ultimately be psychologically harmful to adolescents and reduce opportunities for them to develop important skills relating to intimacy and communication (Manning et al., 2005). More casual sexual partnerships are certainly linked to higher rates of negative sexual health outcomes, including unplanned pregnancy and STIs (e.g., K. Ford, Woosung, & Lepkowski, 2001), but whether this type of partnership as a form of sexual expression and connection is inherently problematic is indeed unclear. Pursuit of causal exchanges, recreational sex, and concurrent partnerships might reflect young people's rejection of social expectations of monogamy, that is, sexual connection with one person at a time (Anderson, 2010). Nonromantic sexual interactions might help meet other important needs relating to sexual identity, drive, and experimentation. More research is certainly needed.

Infidelity, Extradyadic Sex, and Concurrent Sexual Partnerships

Exclusivity norms, that is, the view that sexual behavior is exclusive to a partnership, tend to predominate among dating, cohabiting, and married couples (e.g., Treas & Giesen, 2000). Use of social media introduces a whole new realm for infidelity. Although the HIV epidemic brought considerable research attention to the issue of infidelity and casual sex among young adults, especially among college students and gay men (e.g., Cerwonka, Isbell, & Hansen, 2000), relatively little is known about the issue of infidelity or concurrency (concurrent relationships) among adolescents. Data from a national U.S. survey compared the survey results of 4,707 adolescents who reported past experience of sexual intercourse (i.e., were sexually active; Kelley, Borawski, Flocke, & Keen, 2003). Adolescents were categorized as engaging in single (i.e., only one sexual relationship in the prior 18 months), sequential (i.e., two or more nonoverlapping relationships in the prior 18 months), or concurrent sexual partnerships (i.e., two or more overlapping relationships in the prior 18 months). Of the 4,707 adolescents, 65% were classified into single partnerships, 21% into sequential partnerships, and 14% into concurrent partnerships. Thus, a minority indicated that they had concurrent partnerships in the preceding 18 months, a rate that is higher than those found among married adults (i.e., 2%–6% of men and women; Luo, Cartun, & Snider, 2010; Treas & Giesen, 2000; Whisman & Snyder, 2007).

Although many studies have focused exclusively on occasions of intercourse, young people perceive that participation in a wide range of behaviors constitutes infidelity during dating (Randall & Byers, 2003), including extradyadic kissing and genital touching. Furthermore, when asked whether they had ever engaged in extended romantic kissing with a person other than a primary boyfriend or girlfriend, 19% of 330 adolescents (ages 13–17) indicated that they had (Ronis & O'Sullivan, 2011). A recent investigation suggested that many adolescents include online sexual activities, such as flirting or sexting, in their definitions of infidelity as well (Henline, Lamke, & Howard, 2007).

The most direct and comprehensive research on this topic to date was conducted by Feldman and Cauffman (1999a, 1999b) using a U.S. sample of 216 older adolescents and young adults (ages 18–24). The researchers surveyed participants about their four past relationships and asked them specifically about incidents of cheating, a term that was not defined. They found that 56% had experienced sexual infidelity on the part of a partner, 40% had been unfaithful themselves, and 28% reported both experiences, all while in a purportedly monogamous relationship (Feldman & Cauffman, 1999a). No gender differences were found. Those who had been unfaithful reported being motivated by sexual attraction, absence from their primary partner, or being under the influence of alcohol or substances. Less than half of the betrayals were never known to the betrayed partner; however, the majority of those discovered were a result of confessions. Betrayal was considered more acceptable if it occurred in a bad relationship or if there was strong sexual attraction to a new partner rather than vindictiveness on the part of the betrayer (Feldman & Cauffman, 1999b). Even so, research assessing attitudes toward betrayal has indicated that young people consistently express strong disapproval of sexual infidelity (Feldman, Cauffman, Jensen, & Arnett, 2000).

Individuals often do not know that their partner has other (concurrent) sexual partnerships. One study analyzed the sexual partnerships of 90 adolescent couples (ages 14–19). Both partners were interviewed separately about their own concurrency status and their perception of their partner's concurrency status. Among the male and female adolescents who believed that their partner had no other partners, 16% and 37% of their partners, respectively, reported having other partners (Lenoir, Adler, Borzekowski, Tschann, & Ellen, 2006). However, these participants were recruited from either primary care or STI clinics and thus may have had higher rates of concurrency than those in the general population. Even so, rates of concurrency appear to be high among adolescents, and there is reason to believe that the impact of betrayal may be extremely negative. A study of relationship trajectories among gay and bisexual African American youths reported considerable distress, low self-esteem, and disruptive behaviors (such as revenge sex) in response to partner infidelity (Eyre, Milbrath, & Peacock, 2007). Past research has also reported links between jealousy associated with sexual infidelity and teen dating violence (e.g., Giordano, Soto, Manning, & Longmore, 2010). Moreover, teens who reported experiencing violence in their romantic relationship also reported greater feelings of jealousy and more instances of cheating than those who did not experience such violence.

Little is known about the consequences of engaging in sexual activity outside of a primary relationship, although extradyadic sex is likely to be a precursor of relationship dissolution and partner change among adolescents just as it is among adults worldwide (e.g., Amato & Previti, 2003; Betzig, 1989). Whether extradyadic sexual contact or exchange occurred without the primary partner's prior consent is key to determining whether the behavior might be interpreted by the partner as cheating or infidelity (Luo et al., 2010). Studies have suggested that infidelity often results in relationship dissolution (e.g., Eyre et al., 2007; L. R. Williams & Hickle, 2011), which has been identified as one of the most distressing events reported among teens (Joyner & Udry, 2000; Monroe, Rohde, Seeley, & Lewinsohn, 1999). When relationships break up, it can be extremely traumatizing for youths, underscoring again the emotional involvement associated with these relationships (as with adults). Evidence is growing that a major cause of suicide among youths is the break up of a romantic relationship (Emanuele, 2008).

Sexually Explicit Material, Sexting, and Online Sexual Activity

In the past, adolescents accessed print pornography, videos, or late-night free-access cable to see sexually explicit material (Coopersmith, 2000; Sarracino & Scott, 2008). Because of the boom in free and easily accessible online pornography and the ubiquity of Internet use among youths, more traditional sources of sexually explicit media appear to be falling to the wayside. *Internet-based sexually explicit media* refers to "audio- and/or visual content on and from the Internet that depicts sexual activities in unconcealed ways, often with close-ups of (aroused) genitals and of oral, anal, and vaginal penetration" (Peter & Valkenburg, 2009a, p. 408). In an Australian survey, 84% of adolescent boys reported having viewed Internet sex sites at least once accidently (Flood, 2007). A U.S. national telephone survey of 1,500 Internet users (ages 10–17) found that 42% reported exposure to online pornography in the preceding year; 66% of these indicated that the exposure was accidental or unwanted (Wolak, Mitchell, & Finkelhor, 2007). Wanted exposure increased from 1% among 10- to 11-year-old boys to 26% among 14- to 15-year-old boys and 38% of 16- to 17-year-old boys. Girls report lower rates of wanted exposure: 2% to 5% of girls across ages 10 through 15 indicated that they had accessed sexual media intentionally. This figure increased to 8% among girls ages 16 to 17.

Despite the widespread availability of sexually explicit media to youths through new technologies, research addressing the impact of high exposure has only recently emerged. Some of the best research on this topic has been conducted by a Dutch research team led by Peter, Valkenburg, and colleagues. They found that adults use sexually explicit media more so than do adolescents, but in both groups, males, sensation seekers, and nonheterosexual individuals used it the most (Peter & Valkenburg, 2011b). They compared degree of exposure in the preceding 6-month period to semiexplicit and explicit content in both visual and audiovisual formats among 745 adolescents (ages 13–18) and found that exposure to sexually explicit audiovisual media, such as online movies, was significantly related to stronger endorsement of stereotypical beliefs that women are sexual objects meant for men's pleasure (Peter & Valkenburg, 2007). Other analyses of this database have indicated that more frequent exposure to online sexually explicit media was associated with greater sexual uncertainty (measured in terms of one's sexual self-concept and clarity about one's sexual beliefs and values) and stronger endorsement of more casual sex (Peter & Valkenburg, 2008), after controlling for multiple other factors. The longitudinal work showed that adolescents with high diets of sexually explicit media believed the interactions were more realistic than did their counterparts, viewed sex as serving physical purposes more than affectionate or relational purposes, had lower sexual satisfaction, and ultimately had greater sexual preoccupancy (Peter & Valkenburg, 2008, 2009a, 2009b, 2010), but interestingly did not show higher rates of sexual risk behavior (unlike a comparison group of male adults; Peter & Valkenburg, 2011a).

There has recently been a media storm relating to the frequency with which adolescents send, post, or receive sexual messages, photographs, or videos ("sexting") and the consequences associated with the unintended widespread distribution of this content (O'Keeffe & Clarke-Pearson, 2011). In some jurisdictions, individuals can be charged with possessing or distributing child pornography as a result (Ostrager, 2010). Despite the negative connotations surrounding sexting, young people are known to use sexually explicit content when communicating with peers. A 2008 study found that 20% of adolescents (ages 13–19) and 33% of young adults (ages 20–26) had sent nude or seminude photographs of themselves to another person via the Internet (National Campaign to Prevent Teen and Unplanned Pregnancy, 2009). In addition, 39% of adolescents and 59% of young adults had sent sexually explicit text messages.

Other online sexual activities include chatting online about sex with strangers or known others and communicating with or finding potential sexual partners online. In past decades, Internet use was not as widespread, so adolescents who used computer-mediated communication were more likely to be in contact with strangers than with those known to them, which has been a primary concern of parents about their children's online behavior (Eurobarometer, 2008) and has been fueled by media reports of online perpetrators targeting teenagers. However, trends in social media are such that adolescents mostly communicate with friends and acquaintances in their social networks (Statistics Canada, 2010).

Recent surveys have indicated that on average, about 50% of U.S. adolescents send an average of 50 text messages to friends and family per day (Lenhart, Ling, Campbell, & Purcell, 2010) and that overall they spend on average 7.4 hours online per day (Kaiser Family Foundation, 2010). Most adolescents are well informed about risky online behavior such as disclosing personal information (Liau, Khoo, & Peng Hwa, 2005). Even so, a recent Dutch study (Baumgartner, Valkenburg, & Peter, 2010) found that 17% of adolescents (ages 12–17) reported having engaged at least once in one of the following online risk activities: searching online for someone to talk with about sex, searching online for someone to have sex with, sending intimate photos or videos to someone online, and sending contact information to someone known exclusively online. This body of work has demonstrated that technology use is well integrated in the lives of adolescents, is a common form of communication and social exchange, and serves as a source for gathering sexual information, including information ostensibly intended for adults only (see Volume 2, Chapters 1 and 3, this handbook).

Cohabitation and Marriage

Age of first marriage has been increasing steadily for both women and men across many countries, including Canada, Japan, Russia, Italy, Germany, the United States, France, and the United Kingdom. For example, between 1972 and 2008 the average age of first marriage in Canada increased from 22.5 to 29.1 among women and 24.9 to 31.1 among men (Statistics Canada, 2012). U.S. data indicate that the median age of first marriage at this point is 28.4 for men and 26.5 for women (U.S. Census Bureau, 2009). Although rates of marriage among adolescents are low (usually less than 5% in developed countries), there was a slight increase in some Western countries during the 1990s, corresponding to more conservatism in sexual patterns and partnerships (Cohn, Passel, Wang, & Livingston, 2011). In developing countries, adolescent marriage rates are often high, with 15% of girls married before age 15 and 33% before age 18 (Population Council, 2007; UNICEF, 2005), even though there are clear links between early marriage and adverse outcomes, such as intimate partner violence, maternal and infant mortality, and poor education and employment opportunities (e.g., Jain & Kurz, 2007). Orphans and other disenfranchised youths are at risk for early marriage (and pregnancy) worldwide (e.g., Palermo & Peterman, 2009).

SEXUAL HEALTH OUTCOMES

Few areas in the field of human sexuality have received as much research attention as adolescents' sexual health outcomes. Adolescent health promotion is a complex, multidisciplinary, and dynamic field that captures some of the best research in public health and the clinical, social, and behavioral sciences. Accurately estimating the extraordinarily high intra- and interpersonal, social, economic, and medical costs to society (all societies) associated with adolescent morbidity and mortality is likely impossible (Hoffman, 2006), and few population-level health problems require such ambitious, comprehensive, and sustained effort (DiClemente, Santelli, & Crosby, 2009).

Contraception Use and Infection Prevention

Research on adolescents' contraception use has one of the longest histories of research, whereas disease prevention has one of the largest bodies of work behind it at this point, spurred in large part by recent STI epidemics among young people. Formal programs to improve pregnancy prevention efforts have often been stymied, and researchers have had difficulty developing an efficient, economical, and appealing program that has a sustained impact on rates. In one study, nonpregnant adolescent women (ages 14–19) who were recruited from large U.S. urban centers were tracked for 18 months (Sipsma, Ickovics, Lewis, Ethier, & Kershaw, 2011). One quarter (24%) indicated that they were ambivalent about or wanted to get pregnant in the preceding year. The desire to get pregnant proved the best predictor of actually getting pregnant: It doubled the risk of getting pregnant over the 18-month tracking period, especially among girls who were not in school. This finding supports the importance of examining the psychosocial factors associated with pregnancy risk; pregnancies are not simply unintended and a result of poor contraception use. Risk of pregnancy is generally clustered into family and social environments that are characterized by "some form of disadvantage, disorganization, or dysfunction" (Kirby, 2002, p. 482). Youths who are more strongly attached to their families and who endorse more strongly the standards of their parents, schools, or faiths tend to have fewer sexual risk and pregnancy outcomes (Kirby, 2002).

Of particular note, rates of consistent contraceptive use have improved so that the current generation of adolescents has one of the best records of use in decades, despite the moral panic and uneven media coverage surrounding this issue. Consistent condom use has steadily increased among adolescents over the past few decades (e.g., Wellings et al., 2001). Yet despite similarities in sexual onset and numbers of partners, European nations, Canada, Australia, and the United States vary significantly in terms of adolescent birth and STI rates (Darroch, Frost, & Singh, 2001; Madkour et al., 2010).

Internationally, contraception use has increased steadily over the past 30 years, with rates in the least developed regions typically approaching 60% of couples (UNFPA, 2012). Even in less developed regions, contraceptive use approaches 63% among partnered women of reproductive age. The most common forms continue to be hormone methods (typically oral contraceptives), condoms, and sterilization. In many countries, poverty and profound gender disparities in the ability to seek health care compromise women's capacity to plan their pregnancies. As a result, women residing in poverty-stricken countries are often unable to access effective contraceptive protection, although cultural factors and gender role norms also play significant roles in some contexts (see Chapter 23, this volume).

Condom use during penile–vaginal and anal intercourse has garnered the most research attention in this area. Condom use is a dual-protection method, meaning that it provides protection from both pregnancy and many STIs. A recent national study of 822 U.S. adolescents (ages 14–17) inquired about condom use during last vaginal intercourse and found that 80% of the adolescent boys' and 69% of the adolescent girls' most recent experience of penile–vaginal intercourse involved the use of a condom. The gender discrepancy might reflect different ages of sexual partners or a reporting bias. Moreover, the participants were not selected on the basis of dating each other so the discrepancy may also reflect trends in different dating pools. These rates are much higher than those found in U.S. national surveys just a few years earlier (Eaton et al., 2010).

Among 2,313 Canadian youths (ages 14–17), 74% and 61% of male and female adolescents, respectively, reported condom use at last intercourse (Gallupe, Boyce, & Fergus, 2009). Fewer than half (44%) of sexually active South African women (ages 15–24) reported condom use at last sex (MacPhail, Pettifor, Pascoe, & Rees, 2007), whereas 71% of adolescent and young adult Cambodian men (ages 15–24; Douthwaite & Sareoun, 2006) and 88% and 80% of French male and female adolescents (ages 13–19), respectively, reported condom use at most recent sexual intercourse (Advocates for Youth, 2012). Thus, rates vary significantly across samples of young people and countries (e.g., Santelli, Sandfort, & Orr, 2009). They also vary by activity: Condom use rates are higher for reports of anal intercourse than of penile–vaginal intercourse, and both rates are higher than those for oral sex. Overall, rates are higher among those having sex with casual sexual partners rather than committed sexual partners. Adolescents who have same-sex attractions, engage in same-sex sexual activity, or identify as a sexual minority (or nonheterosexual) youth report higher levels of sexual risk, pregnancy, forced sex, and poor health overall than their heterosexual counterparts (e.g., Halpern, 2011; Katz-Wise & Hyde, 2012). There may be many reasons for why these health disparities exist, but experiences and feelings of marginalization are very likely implicated (Bruce & Harper, 2011).

Partner influence, health beliefs, and social expectations are three key variables that influence condom use and consistency of condom use among young people. For example, fear of offending a partner, trust, the invisibility of many infections, gender roles for sexual interactions, magical thinking about one's ability to protect oneself, knowledge of partners' histories, communication with sexual partners, and concerns about social reputations or stigma are all related to condom use (e.g., Gallupe et al., 2009; Marston & King, 2006; O'Sullivan, Udell, Montrose, Antoniello, & Hoffman, 2010). In a study tracking young women's sexual behavior (ages 18–21) over a 3-month period, condom-protected intercourse was predicted by greater HIV knowledge, positive condom attitudes, higher condom use self-efficacy, stronger intentions to use condoms, lower rates of binge drinking and substance use, and lower psychological distress (Morrison-Beedy, Carey, Feng, & Tu, 2008).

As another example, researchers interviewed 269 adolescents (ages 15–19) with intercourse experience about their relationships and condom use consistency. They found that although 45% of the adolescents consistently used condoms, both negative relationship characteristics (conflict, partner's controlling behavior, mistrust, jealousy) and positive characteristics (love, enmeshment, self-disclosure) were negatively associated with consistent condom use (Manning, Flanigan, Giordano, & Longmore, 2009). Qualitative research on condom use has provided far greater insights into these dynamics in the past few decades. For example, interviews with young African American women (ages 14–17) explored how male partners occasionally use emotional manipulation, such as accusing a partner of having sex with someone else or of not trusting him sufficiently, to forego condoms (Teitelman, Tennille, Bohinski, Jemmott, & Jemmott, 2011). Many of the young women in the sample reported using self-silencing techniques when confronted with their partner's efforts to dissuade them from using condoms, meaning that the women suppressed their concerns or objections in response to partner resistance. Unfortunately, many young women perceive that they have little right to control aspects of their sexual encounters (Rickert, Sanghvi, & Wiemann, 2002). Other forms of interactions include "condom sabotage," whereby a male partner might surreptitiously remove the condom during sex.

Condom use is often abandoned fairly early in a relationship once one or both partners consider the relationship to be committed or monogamous (e.g., Matson, Adler, Millstein, Tschann, & Ellen, 2011). In one study of women's first and usual sexual interactions, condom use was found to be 9 times more likely at first intercourse than at later intercourse (A. E. Tanner, Hensel, & Fortenberry, 2010). Analyses of adolescents' sexual risk profiles over a 7-year period indicated that low condom use and multiple sexual partners during adolescence were linked to elevated infection rates, whereas high condom use coupled with risky sexual partnerships was not (Dariotis et al., 2008), attesting to the value of consistency in condom use overall for protecting sexual health. Condom breakage, slippage, or incorrect use is common among adults (e.g., Topping et al., 2011), although little is known about how well youths use condoms overall.

Pregnancy, Abortion, Childbearing, and Adoption

National health surveys across many countries closely track rates of pregnancy and childbearing among adolescent women, at least among those women who come in contact with health services. Estimates of abortion and adoption rates are less reliable, because many seek private services. Pregnancies can also result in spontaneous abortions (miscarriages) or stillbirths. Adolescent women are at higher risk than young adult women for these poor health outcomes because they generally have less access to health care before and during their pregnancies (see Chapter 21, this volume). In a study reviewing 838 Canadian adolescent pregnancies (mean age = 17 years) selected randomly from 13,554 pregnancies in a 5-year period, 1.8% ended in spontaneous abortion (including ectopic pregnancies), 61.3% ended in therapeutic abortion, none resulted in stillbirth, and 36.9% ended in delivery (Turnbull, Nguyen, Jamieson, & Palerme, 2011). Peak birth rates occurred in April–May and a trough occurred during December–January.

Despite media reports to the contrary, rates of adolescent pregnancy, abortion, childbearing, and adoption are actually significantly lower in most Western countries compared with past decades. In 2005, the U.S. adolescent pregnancy rate reached its lowest point (69.5 per 1,000 women ages 15–19) since its peak in 1990 (116.9 per 1,000; Guttmacher Institute, 2010). The U.S. 2006 abortion rate was 19.3 per 1,000 women, representing a significant drop from rates in the 1980s, and birthrates were 32% lower at 41.9 births per 1,000 women than the peak rate of 61.8 reached in 1991 (Guttmacher Institute, 2010). Other countries have also reported rates indicating similar trends in these sexual health outcomes among adolescents (Office for National Statistics, 2011; A. Smith, Rissel, Richters, Grulich, & de Visser, 2003; Statistics Canada, 2012). Although some have argued that birthrates have dropped only for nonminority women, this trend varies by study, and decreases are generally seen across all racial/ethnic groups. However, immigrant groups may show some increases in pregnancy and birth rates in other countries, such as the United Kingdom, France, and Germany.

Research has found strong associations (not causal relationships) between adolescent pregnancies and poor education and employment outcomes as well as mental health difficulties (Boden, Fergusson, & Horwood, 2008). Children born to adolescent mothers have lower rates of live births and poorer health status as infants, children, and beyond (D. A. Moore, Morrison, & Greene, 1997). Poverty, poor parental modeling, and lack of education and employment opportunities are also associated with adolescent pregnancy (M. R. Moore & Brooks-Gunn, 2002). Analysis of the National Longitudinal Study of Adolescent Health from 1994 through 2008 revealed that adolescent parents are more likely to be from economically impoverished families (National Campaign to Prevent Teen and Unplanned Pregnancy, 2009). Adolescent mothers also have higher rates of depression and substance use and less social support overall (Clemmens, 2001; de Paúl & Domenech, 2000; Reid & Meadows-Oliver, 2007).

A review of the literature would leave one with the impression that only adolescent girls can become parents; research on male adolescent parents is scant. Many studies have indicated that most men who father children by adolescent women tend to be somewhat (not significantly) older than their partners, come from similar socioeconomic backgrounds, and have similarly low education and employment opportunities (Bunting & McAuley, 2004). Many of the relationships between adolescent parents become strained and are terminated shortly after childbirth relative to other types of relationships.

It is important to note that adolescent pregnancy and parenting have been problematized in many societies, with the language of epidemiology and disease used to characterize it (UNICEF, 2001), and a growing and heated debate is now occurring in the literature regarding the construction of this health outcome as pathological (Kiely, 2012). Some have argued that adolescent pregnancy has been "framed as an epidemic scourge threatening ruin to our society" (Fortenberry, 2003, p. 293). Overall, it appears better to delay parenting until adulthood, although adulthood by no means guarantees the mental, physical, social, or financial resources required to parent effectively.

Sexually Transmitted Infections

More than 20 pathogens are transmissible through sexual interactions. Many of them (e.g., chlamydia, gonorrhea) are curable by appropriate antimicrobial treatment; however, this is not the case for viral forms. Despite the availability of effective treatment, bacterial STIs are still a major public health concern among adolescents internationally in large part because they are often asymptomatic and remain undiagnosed, but also because of the considerable stigma and shame associated with STIs.

In the United States, 48% of new STIs occur among individuals ages 15 to 24 (Weinstock, Berman, & Cates, 2004). Women, particularly adolescents, are especially vulnerable to infection, many of which remain asymptomatic, which increases the odds of transmission to others. The ratio of reported rates between young men and women for chlamydia, for example, is 1.0:2.0 in Canada, 1.0:1.5 in Australia, 1.0:1.0 in the United Kingdom, and 1.0:2.8 in the United States, although men show higher rates of gonorrhea and syphilis (Public Health Agency of Canada, 2009).

These infections pose a serious personal and public health problem and contribute to the increasing health care burdens of many countries. Some infections can adversely affect fertility and pregnancy by increasing risk of spontaneous abortions, stillbirths, endometritis, and vertical transmission to one's infant. Neonatal infections, such as gonococcal conjunctivitis, can also occur, which can in some cases lead to blindness; chlamydial pneumonia, which may lead to chronic respiratory disease; and herpes encephalitis. The psychological burden is also significant: An urban household sample of 594 sexually active young people (ages 15–24) revealed that level of STI-related stigma was associated with reduced odds of being screened (Cunningham, Kerrigan, Jennings, & Ellen, 2009). Focus groups with 1,948 rural youths (ages 15–17) in the United States indicated that foregone health care was closely related to barriers such as embarrassment about STIs (Elliott & Larson, 2004).

The magnitude of the STI burden is frequently unclear. STI surveillance systems exist in many countries, but the data are not always reliable or complete and are dependent on the quality of services offered, the extent to which people seek health care, and the complexity of the case (World Health Organization, 2012). However, international surveillance indicates that the highest rates of STIs are among urban men and women in their sexually most active ages (15–35 years; World Health Organization, 2012).

Sexual Health Interventions

Fortunately, a strong body of evidence-based research has explored the efficacy of the range of sexual health interventions targeting youths. These evaluations are of significance to researchers, practitioners, educators, and policymakers. Interventions generally take the form of programs designed for youths in school or community programs, and programs are typically expected to document their effectiveness as part of funding requirements. Behavior change is the gold standard for effectiveness, but many programs target changes in knowledge, intentions, or attitudinal components instead. More research is needed to understand cultural diversity in effective intervention planning and implementation. Many of the problems targeted in these interventions are inextricably linked to other societal problems, including poverty, marginalization, victimization, and substance abuse.

What is abundantly clear from this work is that these interventions appear to work best when tailored to specific subgroups of adolescents (e.g., sexual minority boys; African American girls; e.g., Sales, Milhausen, & DiClemente, 2006). In particular, an in-depth analysis of a wide range of disease and pregnancy interventions concluded that incorporating the overlapping spheres of an individual's life, including individual, relational, family, peer, community, and sociocultural, into prevention efforts, supplemented by traditional medical counseling, proved to be the most effective approach (Salazar, Santelli, Crosby, & DiClemente, 2009). No one method or trial stood out particularly, but the researchers emphasized the need to move away from an individual deficit model to examine the range of influences that sustain or counter sexual health decisions. Approaches that fail to recognize the integrated, multilevel developmental systems involved here typically yield few enduring successes in the promotion of healthy sexual lifestyles.

SUMMARY

Adolescence constitutes an essential period of exploration, experimentation, and evaluation, one that is full of trials and errors in the development of sexuality for most youths but one that most manage to navigate successfully. Although young people's sexual progression is a normal and essential component of being human, popular discourse has rendered it a singular act of deviance, irrationality, and immorality. Scholarship addressing adolescent sexuality has captured and reflected the dubiety regarding whether these questions ought to be examined at all. Many research areas, such as arousal, desire, pleasure, and satisfaction, have barely been explored at all relative to the surfeit of work scrutinizing the minutia surrounding first intercourse, pregnancy, childbearing, and infection. Studies of "risk" and "problem" behaviors have typically incorporated female or ethnic and sexual minority youths, whereas studies addressing normative patterns are most likely to use White, middle-class, able-bodied, heterosexual Western college student samples, further truncating researchers' perspective regarding negative and positive forms of sexuality. The fixation on penile–vaginal intercourse has reinforced views that this behavior is both the only "real" form of sex and also the most problem-laden form. Other sexual activities are proving more relevant to understanding the needs and interests of young people.

Certainly, a health paradigm aimed at reducing or eliminating negative health outcomes has been invaluable in many respects and remains critical in efforts designed to promote sexual health. Impossible to ignore, however, is that we still require an integrated, intelligible model of healthy, positive sexual development to which we can aspire. The term *health* evolved from *hale* and *whole*. Likewise, our metric should be more than the absence of disease or distress in an individual, group, or society; it should incorporate indexes of thriving, growth, well-being, and wellness (see Chapter 11, this volume). We argue here that we need to move away from the popular focus on health specifically, which has strong biological and medical connotations, to one that views individuals in terms of psychological, social, and physical well-being. Radical as this view might be, we also argue that much might be gained in scholarship by stepping aside from approaches advocating change, treatment, prediction, and control to an approach aimed at capturing subjective experiences, patterns and diversity, and long-term outcomes—the sexuality landscape, as it were—before expounding on efforts to alter the course of adolescents' sexual development.

In short, we need to take off the blindfold and embrace, rather than deny, the complexity of sexuality in the lives of adolescents. In the past decades of work on this topic, we have gained at a strictly information level but lost at the meaning level. Richer, more comprehensive accounts of adolescents' sexual and romantic lives are required now to flesh out this map, including elaborations of the emotional components, the time and spatial contexts in which actual sexual encounters occur, the relationship or partnership dynamics involved, and the meaning and significance that young people give to their range of experiences.

References

Advocates for Youth. (2012). *Adolescent sexual health in Europe and the U.S.* Retrieved from http://www.advocatesforyouth.org/component/content/article/419-adolescent-sexual-health-in-europe-and-the-us

Ainsworth, M. D. S. (1989). Attachments beyond infancy. *American Psychologist, 44*, 709–716. doi:10.1037/0003-066X.44.4.709

Akers, A. Y., Gold, M. A., Bost, J. E., Adimora, A. A., Orr, D. P., & Fortenberry, J. D. (2011). Variation in sexual behaviors in a cohort of adolescent females: The role of personal, perceived peer, and perceived family attitudes. *Journal of Adolescent Health, 48*, 87–93. doi:10.1016/j.jadohealth.2010.05.004

Ali, M. M., & Dwyer, D. S. (2011). Estimating peer effects in sexual behavior among adolescents. *Journal of Adolescence, 34*, 183–190. doi:10.1016/j.adolescence.2009.12.008

Al-Sahab, B., Ardern, C. I., Hamadeh, M. J., & Tamim, H. (2010). Age at menarche in Canada: Results from the National Longitudinal Survey of Children & Youth. *BMC Public Health, 10*, 736.

Amato, P. R., & Previti, D. (2003). People's reasons for divorcing: Gender, social class, the life course, and adjustment. *Journal of Family Issues, 24*, 602–626. doi:10.1177/0192513X03024005002

American Psychiatric Association. (2000). *Diagnostic and statistical manual of mental disorders* (4th ed., text revision). Washington, DC: Author.

Andersen, B. L., & Cyranowski, J. M. (1994). Women's sexual self-schema. *Journal of Personality and Social Psychology, 67*, 1079–1100. doi:10.1037/0022-3514.67.6.1079

Anderson, E. (2010). "At least with cheating there is an attempt at monogamy": Cheating and monogamism among undergraduate heterosexual men. *Journal of Social and Personal Relationships, 27*, 851–872. doi:10.1177/0265407510373908

Apodaca, T. R., & Moser, N. C. (2011). The use and abuse of prescription medication to facilitate or enhance sexual behavior among adolescents. *Clinical Pharmacology and Therapeutics, 89*, 22–24. doi:10.1038/clpt.2010.264

Arbeau, K. J., Galambos, N. L., & Jansson, S. M. (2007). Dating, sex, and substance use as correlates of adolescents' subjective experience of age. *Journal of Adolescence, 30*, 435–447. doi:10.1016/j.adolescence.2006.04.006

Arnett, J. J. (1999). Adolescent storm and stress, reconsidered. *American Psychologist, 54*, 317–326. doi:10.1037/0003-066X.54.5.317

Arnett, J. J. (2000). Emerging adulthood: A theory of development from the late teens through the twenties. *American Psychologist, 55*, 469–480. doi:10.1037/0003-066X.55.5.469

Ashby, S. L., Arcari, C. M., & Edmonson, M. B. (2006). Television viewing and risk of sexual initiation by young adolescents. *Archives of Pediatrics and Adolescent Medicine, 160*, 375–380. doi:10.1001/archpedi.160.4.375

Bancroft, J., Herbenick, D., & Reynolds, M. (2003). Masturbation as a marker of sexual development: Two studies 50 years apart. In J. Bancroft (Ed.), *Sexual development in childhood* (pp. 156–185). Bloomington: Indiana University Press.

Barnett, J. P., & Maticka-Tyndale, E. (2011). The gift of agency: Sexual exchange scripts among Nigerian youth. *Journal of Sex Research, 48*, 349–359.

Bartholomew, K., & Horowitz, L. M. (1991). Attachment styles among young adults: A test of a four-category model. *Journal of Personality and Social Psychology, 61*, 226–244. doi:10.1037/0022-3514.61.2.226

Baumgartner, S. E., Valkenburg, P. M., & Peter, J. (2010). Assessing causality in the relationship between adolescents' risky sexual online behavior and their perceptions of this behavior. *Journal of Youth and Adolescence, 39*, 1226–1239. doi:10.1007/s10964-010-9512-y

Bay-Cheng, L. Y. (2005). Left to their own devices: Disciplining youth discourse on sexuality education electronic bulletin boards. *Sexuality Research and Social Policy, 2*, 37–50.

Bay-Cheng, L. Y., & Fava, N. M. (2011). Young women's experiences and perceptions of cunnilingus during adolescence. *Journal of Sex Research, 48*, 531–542. doi:10.1080/00224499.2010.535221

Baym, N. K., Zhang, Y. B., & Lin, M. C. (2004). Social interactions across media: Interpersonal communication on the Internet, telephone, and face-to-face. *New Media and Society, 6*, 299–318. doi:10.1177/1461444804041438

Bearman, P. S., & Brückner, H. (2001). Promising the future: Virginity pledges and first intercourse. *American Journal of Sociology, 106*, 859–912. doi:10.1086/320295

Bersamin, M. M., Walker, S., Waiters, E. D., Fisher, D. A., & Grube, J. W. (2005). Promising to wait: Virginity pledges and adolescent sexual behavior. *Journal of Adolescent Health, 36*, 428–436. doi:10.1016/j.jadohealth.2004.09.016

Betzig, L. (1989). Causes of conjugal dissolution: A cross-cultural study. *Current Anthropology, 30*, 654–676. doi:10.1086/203798

Bleakley, A., Hennessy, M., & Fishbein, M. (2011). A model of adolescents' seeking of sexual content in their media choices. *Journal of Sex Research, 48*, 309–315. doi:10.1080/00224499.2010.497985

Boden, J. M., Fergusson, D. M., & Horwood, L. J. (2008). Early motherhood and subsequent life outcomes. *Journal of Child Psychology and Psychiatry, 49*, 151–160. doi:10.1111/j.1469-7610.2007.01830.x

Bogaert, A. F. (2004). Asexuality: Prevalence and associated factors in a national probability sample. *Journal of Sex Research, 41*, 279–287. doi:10.1080/00224490409552235

Bogle, K. A. (2007). The shift from dating to hooking up in college: What scholars have missed. *Social Compass, 2*, 775–788.

Boislard, M.-A. P., & Poulin, F. (2011). Individual, familial, friends-related and contextual predictors of early sexual intercourse. *Journal of Adolescence, 34*, 289–300. doi:10.1016/j.adolescence.2010.05.002

Bowker, J. C., Spencer, S. V., Thomas, K. K., & Gyoerkoe, E. A. (2012). Having and being an other-sex crush during early adolescence. *Journal of Experimental Child Psychology, 111*, 629–643. doi:10.1016/j.jecp.2011.11.008

Bowlby, J. (1979). *The making and breaking of affectional bonds.* London, England: Tavistock.

Bramen, J. E., Hranilovich, J. A., Dahl, R. E., Forbes, E. E., Chen, J., Toga, A. W., . . . Sowell, E. R. (2011). Puberty influences medial temporal lobe and cortical grey matter maturation differently in boys than girls matched for sexual maturity. *Cerebral Cortex, 21*, 636–646. doi:10.1093/cercor/bhq137

Breakwell, G. M., & Millward, L. J. (1997). Sexual self-concept and sexual risk-taking. *Journal of Adolescence, 20*, 29–41. doi:10.1006/jado.1996.0062

Brooks-Gunn, J., Graber, J. A., & Paikoff, R. L. (1994). Studying links between hormones and negative affect: Models and measures. *Journal of Research on Adolescence, 4*, 469–486. doi:10.1207/s15327795jra0404_2

Brown, J. D. (2002). Mass media influences on sexuality. *Journal of Sex Research, 39*, 42–45. doi:10.1080/00224490209552118

Brown, J. D., & L'Engle, K. L. (2009). X-rated: Sexual attitudes and behaviors associated with U.S. early adolescents' exposure to sexually explicit media. *Communication Research, 36*, 129–151. doi:10.1177/0093650208326465

Brown, J. D., L'Engle, K. L., Pardun, C. J., Guo, G., Kenneavy, K., & Jackson, C. (2006). Sexy media matter: Exposure to sexual content in music, movies, television, and magazines predicts Black and White adolescents' sexual behavior. *Pediatrics, 117*, 1018–1027. doi:10.1542/peds.2005-1406

Bruce, D., & Harper, G. W. (2011). Operating without a safety net: Gay male adolescents and emerging adults' experiences of marginalization and migration, and implications for theory of syndemic production of health disparities. *Health Education and Behavior, 38*, 367–378. doi:10.1177/1090198110375911

Bruce, D., Harper, G. W., Fernández, M. I., & Jamil, O. B. (2012). Age-concordant and age-discordant sexual behavior among gay and bisexual male adolescents. *Archives of Sexual Behavior, 41*, 441–448. doi:10.1007/s10508-011-9730-8

Brückner, H., & Bearman, P. (2005). After the promise: The STD consequences of adolescent virginity pledges. *Journal of Adolescent Health, 36*, 271–278. doi:10.1016/j.jadohealth.2005.01.005

Brunnberg, E., Boström, M. L., & Berglund, M. (2009). Sexuality of 15/16-year-old girls and boys with and without modest disabilities. *Sexuality and Disability, 27*, 139–153. doi:10.1007/s11195-009-9123-2

Bukowski, W. M., & Sippola, L. K. (2000). Variations in patterns of attraction to same- and other-sex peers during early adolescence. *Developmental Psychology, 36*, 147–154. doi:10.1037/0012-1649.36.2.147

Bunting, L., & McAuley, C. (2004). Teenage pregnancy and parenthood: The role of fathers. *Child and Family Social Work, 9*, 295–303. doi:10.1111/j.1365-2206.2004.00335.x

Burgess, G. H. (2007). Assessment of rape-supportive attitudes and beliefs in college men: Development, reliability, and validity of the Rape Attitudes and Beliefs Scale. *Journal of Interpersonal Violence, 22*, 973–993. doi:10.1177/0886260507302993

Buzwell, S., & Rosenthal, D. (1996). Constructing a sexual self: Adolescents' sexual self-perceptions and sexual risk-taking. *Journal of Research on Adolescence, 6*, 489–513.

Byers, E. S. (2011). Beyond the *birds and the bees* and *was it good for you?*: Thirty years of research on sexual communication. *Canadian Psychology/Psychologie Canadienne, 52*, 20–28. doi:10.1037/a0022048

Byers, E. S., Sears, H. A., & Weaver, A. D. (2008). Parents' reports of sexual communication with children in kindergarten to grade 8. *Journal of Marriage and Family, 70*, 86–96. doi:10.1111/j.1741-3737.2007.00463.x

Calderone, M. (1983). Fetal erection and its message to us. *SIECUS Report, 11*, 9–10.

Carlson, W., & Rose, A. J. (2007). The role of reciprocity in romantic relationships in middle childhood and early adolescence. *Merrill-Palmer Quarterly, 53*, 262–290. doi:10.1353/mpq.2007.0008

Carlson Jones, D. (2004). Body image among adolescent girls and boys: A longitudinal study. *Developmental Psychology, 40*, 823–835. doi:10.1037/0012-1649.40.5.823

Carver, K., Joyner, K., & Udry, J. R. (2003). National estimates of adolescent romantic relationships. In P. Florsheim (Ed.), *Adolescent romantic relations and sexual behavior: Theory, research, and practical implications* (pp. 23–56). Mahwah, NJ: Erlbaum.

Cate, R. M., & Lloyd, S. A. (1992). *Courtship.* Thousand Oaks, CA: Sage.

Cavazos-Rehg, P. A., Krauss, M. J., Spitznagel, E. L., Schootman, M., Bucholz, K. K., Peipert, J. F., . . . Beirut, L. J. (2009). Age of sexual debut among US adolescents. *Contraception, 80*, 158–162. doi:10.1016/j.contraception.2009.02.014

Cavazos-Rehg, P. A., Krauss, M. J., Spitznagel, E. L., Schootman, M., Peipert, J. F., & Cottler, L. B. (2010). Type of contraception method used at last intercourse and associations with health risk behaviors among US adolescents. *Contraception, 82*, 549–555. doi:10.1016/j.contraception.2010.05.007

Centers for Disease Control and Prevention. (2012). *Sexual health*. Retrieved from http://www.cdc.gov/sexualhealth

Cerwonka, E. R., Isbell, T. R., & Hansen, C. E. (2000). Psychosocial factors as predictors of unsafe sexual practices among young adults. *AIDS Education and Prevention, 12*, 141–153.

Chambers, W. C. (2007). Oral sex: Varied behaviors and perceptions in a college population. *Journal of Sex Research, 44*, 28–42. doi:10.1080/00224490709336790

Cheng, M. M., & Udry, J. R. (2002). Sexual behaviors of physically disabled adolescents in the United States. *Journal of Adolescent Health, 31*, 48–58. doi:10.1016/S1054-139X(01)00400-1

Cheng, M. M., & Udry, J. R. (2005). Sexual experiences of adolescents with low cognitive abilities in the U.S. *Journal of Developmental and Physical Disabilities, 17*, 155–172. doi:10.1007/s10882-005-3686-3

Clark, C. L., Shaver, P. R., & Abrahams, M. F. (1999). Strategic behaviors in romantic relationship initiation. *Personality and Social Psychology Bulletin, 25*, 709–722. doi:10.1177/0146167299025006006

Clemmens, D. (2001). The relationship between social support and adolescent mothers' interactions with their infants: A meta-analysis. *Journal of Obstetric, Gynecologic, and Neonatal Nursing, 30*, 410–420. doi:10.1111/j.1552-6909.2001.tb01560.x

Clift, R. J. W., Rajlic, G., & Gretton, H. M. (2009). Discriminative and predictive validity of the penile plethysmograph in adolescent sex offenders. *Sexual Abuse: A Journal of Research and Treatment, 21*, 335–362.

Cohall, A., Kassotis, J., Parks, R., Vaughan, R., Bannister, H., & Northridge, M. (2001). Adolescents in the age of AIDS: Myths, misconceptions, and misunderstandings regarding sexually transmitted diseases. *Journal of the National Medical Association, 93*, 64–69.

Cohn, D., Passel, J., Wang, W., & Livingston, G. (2011). *Barely half of U.S. adults are married—A record low*. Retrieved from http://www.pewsocialtrends.org/2011/12/14/barely-half-of-u-s-adults-are-married-a-record-low

Coleman, L., & Coleman, J. (2002). The measurement of puberty: A review. *Journal of Adolescence, 25*, 535–550. doi:10.1006/jado.2002.0494

Collins, R. L. (2005). Sex on television and its impact on American youth: Background and results from the RAND Television and Adolescent Sexuality study. *Child and Adolescent Psychiatric Clinics of North America, 14*, 371–385. doi:10.1016/j.chc.2005.02.005

Collins, W. A. (2003). More than myth: The developmental significance of romantic relationships during adolescence. *Journal of Research on Adolescence, 13*, 1–24. doi:10.1111/1532-7795.1301001

Collins, W. A., & Sroufe, L. A. (1999). Capacity for intimate relationships: A developmental construction. In W. Furman, B. B. Brown, & C. Feiring (Eds.), *The development of romantic relationships in adolescence* (pp. 125–147). New York, NY: Cambridge University Press.

Connolly, J., Craig, W., Goldberg, A., & Pepler, D. (2004). Mixed-gender groups, dating, and romantic relationships in early adolescence. *Journal of Research on Adolescence, 14*, 185–207. doi:10.1111/j.1532-7795.2004.01402003.x

Cooper, M. L., Shapiro, C. M., & Powers, A. M. (1998). Motivations for sex and risky sexual behavior among adolescents and young adults: A functional perspective. *Journal of Personality and Social Psychology, 75*, 1528–1558. doi:10.1037/0022-3514.75.6.1528

Coopersmith, J. (2000). Pornography, videotape, and the internet. *IEEE Technology and Society Magazine, 19*, 27–34. doi:10.1109/44.828561

Cuffee, J. J., Hallfors, D. D., & Waller, M. W. (2007). Racial and gender differences in adolescent sexual attitudes and longitudinal associations with coital debut. *Journal of Adolescent Health, 41*, 19–26. doi:10.1016/j.jadohealth.2007.02.012

Cunningham, S. D., Kerrigan, D. L., Jennings, J. M., & Ellen, J. M. (2009). Relationships between perceived STD-related shame and STD screening among a household sample of adolescents. *Perspectives on Sexual and Reproductive Health, 41*, 225–230. doi:10.1363/4122509

Curtin, N., Ward, M. L., Merriwether, M., & Caruthers, A. (2011). Femininity ideology and sexual health in young women: A focus on sexual knowledge, embodiment, and agency. *International Journal of Sexual Health, 23*, 48–62. doi:10.1080/19317611.2010.524694

Dariotis, J. K., Sonenstein, F. L., Gates, G. J., Capps, R., Astone, N. M., Pleck, J. H., . . . Zeger, S. (2008). Changes in sexual risk behavior as young men transition to adulthood. *Perspectives on Sexual and Reproductive Health, 40*, 218–225. doi:10.1363/4021808

Darroch, J. E., Frost, J. J., & Singh, S. (2001). *Teenage sexual and reproductive behavior in developed countries: Can more progress be made?* New York, NY: Alan Guttmacher Institute.

Darroch, J. E., Landry, D. J., & Oslak, S. (1999). Age differences between sexual partners in the United States. *Family Planning Perspectives, 31*, 160–167. doi:10.2307/2991588

Dawson, L. H., Shih, M., de Moor, C., & Shrier, L. (2008). Reasons why adolescents and young adults have sex: Associations with psychological characteristics and sexual behavior. *Journal of Sex Research, 45*, 225–232. doi:10.1080/00224490801987457 de Bruyn, E. H., & Cillessen, A. N. (2006). Popularity in early adolescence: Prosocial and antisocial subtypes. *Journal of Adolescent Research, 21*, 607–627. doi:10.1177/0743558406293966

de Graaf, H., van de Schoot, R., Woertman, L., Hawk, S. T., & Meeus, W. (2012). Family cohesion and romantic and sexual initiation: A three wave longitudinal study. *Journal of Youth and Adolescence, 41*, 583–592. doi:10.1007/s10964-011-9708-9

Denzer, C., Weibel, A., Muche, R., Karges, B., Sorgo, W., & Wabitsch, M. (2007). Pubertal development in obese children and adolescents. *International Journal of Obesity, 31*, 1509–1519. doi:10.1038/sj.ijo.0803691

de Paúl, J., & Domenech, L. (2000). Childhood history of abuse and child abuse potential in adolescent mothers: A longitudinal study. *Child Abuse and Neglect, 24*, 701–713. doi:10.1016/S0145-2134(00)00124-1

Deptula, D. P., Henry, D. B., & Schoeny, M. E. (2010). How can parents make a difference? Longitudinal associations with adolescent sexual behavior. *Journal of Family Psychology, 24*, 731–739. doi:10.1037/a0021760

Diamond, L. M. (1998). Development of sexual orientation among adolescent and young adult women. *Developmental Psychology, 34*, 1085–1095. doi:10.1037/0012-1649.34.5.1085

Diamond, L. M., & Lucas, S. (2004). Sexual-minority and heterosexual youths' peer relationships: Experiences, expectations, and implications for well-being. *Journal of Research on Adolescence, 14*, 313–340. doi:10.1111/j.1532-7795.2004.00077.x

Diamond, L. M., Savin-Williams, R. C., & Dubé, E. M. (1999). Sex, dating, passionate friendships, and romance: Intimate peer relations among lesbian, gay, and bisexual adolescents. In W. Furman, B. B. Brown, & C. Feiring (Eds.), *The development of romantic relationships in adolescence* (pp. 175–210). New York, NY: Cambridge University Press.

DiClemente, R. J., Santelli, J. S., & Crosby, R. A. (2009). Adolescent health: Understanding and preventing risk behaviors. In R. J. DiClemente, J. S. Santelli, & R. A. Crosby (Eds.), *Adolescent health: Understanding preventing risk behaviors* (pp. 549–559). San Francisco, CA: Jossey-Bass.

DiIorio, C., Kelley, M., & Hockenberry-Eaton, M. (1999). Communication about sexual issues: Mothers, fathers, and friends. *Journal of Adolescent Health, 24*, 181–189. doi:10.1016/S1054-139X(98)00115-3

DiIorio, C., Pluhar, E., & Belcher, L. (2003). Parent-child communication about sexuality: A review of the literature from 1980–2002. *Journal of HIV/AIDS Prevention and Education for Adolescents and Children, 5*, 7–32. doi:10.1300/J129v05n03_02

Dijkstra, J., Cillessen, A. N., Lindenberg, S., & Veenstra, R. (2010). Same-gender and cross-gender likeability: Associations with popularity and status enhancement: The TRAILS study. *Journal of Early Adolescence, 30*, 773–802. doi:10.1177/0272431609350926

Dixon-Mueller, R. (2008). How young is "too young"? Comparative perspectives on adolescent sexual, marital, and reproductive transitions. *Studies in Family Planning, 39*, 247–262. doi:10.1111/j.1728-4465.2008.00173.x

Donenberg, G. R., Bryant, F. B., Emerson, E., Wilson, H. W., & Pasch, K. E. (2003). Tracing the roots of early sexual debut among adolescents in psychiatric care. *Journal of the American Academy of Child and Adolescent Psychiatry, 42*, 594–608. doi:10.1097/01.CHI.0000046833.09750.91

Douthwaite, M. R., & Sareoun, L. Y. (2006). Sexual behaviour and condom use among unmarried young men in Cambodia. *AIDS Care, 18*, 505–513. doi:10.1080/13548500500221537

East, P., Felice, M., & Morgan, M. (1993). Sisters' and girlfriends' sexual and childbearing behavior: Effects on early adolescent girls' sexual outcomes. *Journal of Marriage and the Family, 55*, 953–963. doi:10.2307/352775

East, P. L., & Jacobson, L. J. (2000). Adolescent childbearing, poverty, and siblings: Taking direction from the new literature. *Family Relations: Interdisciplinary Journal of Applied Family Studies, 49*, 287–292. doi:10.1111/j.1741-3729.2000.00287.x

Eaton, D. K., Kann, L., Kinchen, S., Shanklin, S., Ross, J., Hawkins, J., . . . Wechsler, H. (2010). Youth risk behavior surveillance—United States, 2009. *MMWR: Surveillance Summaries, 59*, 1–142.

Elgar, F. J., Phillips, N., & Hammond, N. (2011). Trends in alcohol and drug use among Canadian adolescents, 1990–2006. *Canadian Journal of Psychiatry/Revue Canadienne de Psychiatrie, 56*, 243–247.

Elliott, B. A., & Larson, J. T. (2004). Adolescents in mid-sized and rural communities: Foregone care, perceived barriers, and risk factors. *Journal of Adolescent Health, 35*, 303–309.

Ellis, B. J. (2004). Timing of pubertal maturation in girls: An integrated life history approach. *Psychological Bulletin, 130*, 920–958. doi:10.1037/0033-2909.130.6.920

Elmerstig, E., Mijma, B., & Berterö, C. (2008). Why do young women continue to have sexual intercourse despite pain? *Journal of Adolescent Health, 43*, 357–363. doi:10.1016/j.jadohealth.2008.02.011

Emanuele, E. (2008). Of love and death: The emerging role of romantic disruption in suicidal behavior. *Suicide and Life-Threatening Behavior, 38*, 482. doi:10.1521/suli.2008.38.4.482

English, A. (2002). The health of adolescent girls: Does the law support it? *Current Women's Health Reports, 2*, 442–449.

Epstein, M., & Ward, L. (2008). "Always use protection": Communication boys receive about sex from parents, peers, and the media. *Journal of Youth and Adolescence, 37*, 113–126. doi:10.1007/s10964-007-9187-1

Erikson, E. H. (1968). *Identity: Youth and crisis*. New York, NY: Norton.

Eurobarometer. (2008). Towards a safer use of the internet for children in the EU: A parents' perspective (Flash Eurobarometer Series No. 248). Luxembourg: European Commission.

Eyre, S. L., Milbrath, C., & Peacock, B. (2007). Romantic relationships trajectories of African American gay/bisexual adolescents. *Journal of Adolescent Research, 22*, 107–131. doi:10.1177/0895904805298417

Eyre, S. L., Read, N. W., & Millstein, S. G. (1997). Adolescent sexual strategies. *Journal of Adolescent Health, 20*, 286–293. doi:10.1016/S1054-139X(96)00239-X

Feldman, S. S., & Cauffman, E. (1999a). Sexual betrayal among late adolescents: Perspectives of the perpetrator and the aggrieved. *Journal of Youth and Adolescence, 28*, 235–258. doi:10.1023/A:1021605532205

Feldman, S. S., & Cauffman, E. (1999b). Your cheatin' heart: Attitudes, behaviors, and correlates of sexual betrayal in late adolescents. *Journal of Research on Adolescence, 9*, 227–252. doi:10.1207/s15327795jra0903_1

Feldman, S. S., Cauffman, E., Jensen, L. A., & Arnett, J. J. (2000). The (un)acceptability of betrayal: A study of college students' evaluations of sexual betrayal by a romantic partner and betrayal of a friend's confidence. *Journal of Youth and Adolescence, 29*, 499–523. doi:10.1023/A:1005166627678

Ferguson, C. J., & Meehan, D. C. (2010). Saturday night's alright for fighting: Antisocial traits, fighting, and weapons carrying in a large sample of youth. *Psychiatric Quarterly, 81*, 293–302. doi:10.1007/s11126-010-9138-y

Fine, M. (1988). Sexuality, schooling and adolescent females: The missing discourse of desire. *Harvard Educational Review, 58*, 29–53.

Fischer, K. W., Shaver, P. R., & Carnochan, P. (1990). How emotions develop and how they organise development. *Cognition and Emotion, 4*, 81–127. doi:10.1080/02699939008407142

Fisher, W. A., & Boroditsky, R. (2000). Sexual activity, contraceptive choice, and sexual and reproductive health indicators among single Canadian women aged 15–29: Additional findings from the Canadian Contraceptive Study. *Canadian Journal of Human Sexuality, 9*, 79–93.

Flood, M. (2007). Exposure to pornography among youth in Australia. *Journal of Sociology, 43*, 45–60. doi:10.1177/1440783307073934

Flook, L. (2011). Gender differences in adolescents' daily interpersonal events and well-being. *Child Development, 82*, 454–461. doi:10.1111/j.1467-8624.2010.01521.x

Floyd, F. J., & Bakeman, R. (2006). Coming-out across the life course: Implications of age and historical context. *Archives of Sexual Behavior, 35*, 287–296. doi:10.1007/s10508-006-9022-x

Ford, C. S., & Beach, F. A. (1963). Development of sexual behavior in human beings. In R. Grinder (Ed.), *Studies in adolescence* (pp. 433–445). New York, NY: MacMillan.

Ford, K., Woosung, S., & Lepkowski, J. (2001). Characteristics of sexual partners of American adolescents and their association with use of condoms and other contraceptive methods. *Family Planning Perspectives, 33*, 100–105. doi:10.2307/2673765

Forste, R., & Haas, D. W. (2002). The transition of adolescent males to first sexual intercourse: Anticipated or delayed? *Perspectives on Sexual and Reproductive Health, 34*, 184–190. doi:10.2307/3097728

Fortenberry, J. D. (2003). Adolescent sex and the rhetoric of risk. In D. Romer (Ed.), *Reducing adolescent risk: Toward an integrated approach* (pp. 293–300). Thousand Oaks, CA: Sage. doi:10.4135/9781452233611.n31

Fortenberry, J. D., Katz, B. P., Blythe, M. J., Juliar, B. E., Tu, W., & Orr, D. P. (2006). Factors associated with time of day of sexual activity among adolescent women. *Journal of Adolescent Health, 38*, 275–281. doi:10.1016/j.jadohealth.2005.02.006

Fortenberry, J. D., Orr, D. P., Katz, B. P., Brizendine, E. J., & Blythe, M. J. (1997). Sex under the influence: A diary self-report study of substance use and sexual behavior among adolescent women. *Sexually Transmitted Diseases, 24*, 313–319. doi:10.1097/00007435-199707000-00001

Fortenberry, J. D., Schick, V., Herbenick, D., Sanders, S. A., Dodge, B., & Reece, M. (2010). Sexual behaviors and condom use at last vaginal intercourse: A national sample of adolescents ages 14 to 17 years. *Journal of Sexual Medicine, 7*, 305–314. doi:10.1111/j.1743-6109.2010.02018.x

Fortenberry, J. D., Temkit, M., Tu, W., Graham, C. A., Katz, B. P., & Orr, D. P. (2005). Daily mood, partner support, sexual interest, and sexual activity among adolescent women. *Health Psychology, 24*, 252–257. doi:10.1037/0278-6133.24.3.252

Fortunato, L., Young, A. M., Boyd, C. J., & Fons, C. E. (2010). Hook-up sexual experiences and problem behaviors among adolescents. *Journal of Child and Adolescent Substance Abuse, 19*, 261–278. doi:10.1080/1067828X.2010.488965

Fraley, R. C., & Davis, K. E. (1997). Attachment formation and transfer in young adults' close friendships and romantic relationships. *Personal Relationships, 4*, 131–144. doi:10.1111/j.1475-6811.1997.tb00135.x

Frankel, L. (2002). "I've never thought about it": Contradictions and taboos surrounding American males' experiences of first ejaculation (semenarche). *Journal of Men's Studies, 11*, 37–54. doi:10.3149/jms.1101.37

Friedrich, W. N., Grambsch, P., Damon, L., Hewitt, S. K., Koverola, C., Lang, R. A., . . . Broughton, D. (1992). Child sexual behavior inventory: Normative and clinical comparison. *Psychological Assessment, 4*, 303–311. doi:10.1037/1040-3590.4.3.303

Furman, W. (2002). The emerging field of adolescent romantic relationships. *Current Directions in Psychological Science, 11*, 177–180. doi:10.1111/1467-8721.00195

Furman, W., & Collins, W. A. (2009). Adolescent romantic relationships and experiences. In K. H. Rubin, W. Bukowski, & B. Laursen (Eds.), *Handbook of peer interactions, relationships, and groups* (pp. 341–360). New York, NY: Guilford Press.

Furman, W., & Shaffer, L. (2003). The role of romantic relationships in adolescent development. In P. Florsheim (Ed.), *Adolescent romantic relations and sexual behavior: Theory, research, and practical implications* (pp. 3–22). Mahwah, NJ: Erlbaum.

Gagnon, J. H., & Parker, R. G. (1995). Conceiving sexuality. In R. G. Parker & J. H. Gagnon (Eds.), *Conceiving sexuality: Approaches to sex research in a postmodern world* (pp. 3–16). New York, NY: Routledge.

Galenson, E., & Riophe, H. (1974). The emergence of genital awareness during the second year of life. In R. C. Friedman, R. M. Richart, & R. L. Van de Wiele (Eds.), *Sex differences in behavior* (pp. 32–38). New York, NY: Wiley.

Gallup, A. C., O'Brien, D. T., & Wilson, D. (2011). Intrasexual peer aggression and dating behavior during adolescence: An evolutionary perspective. *Aggressive Behavior, 37*, 258–267. doi:10.1002/ab.20384

Gallupe, O., Boyce, W. F., & Fergus, S. (2009). Non-use of condoms at last intercourse among Canadian youth: Influence of sexual partners and social expectations. *Canadian Journal of Human Sexuality, 18*, 27–34.

Gebhardt, W. A., Kuyper, L., & Greunsven, G. (2003). Need for intimacy in relationships and motives for sex as determinants of adolescent condom use. *Journal of Adolescent Health, 33*, 154–164. doi:10.1016/S1054-139X(03)00137-X

Gentile, B., Grabe, S., Dolan-Pascoe, B., Twenge, J. M., Wells, B. E., & Maitino, A. (2009). Gender differences in domain-specific self-esteem: A meta-analysis. *Review of General Psychology, 13*, 34–45. doi:10.1037/a0013689

Giordano, P. C., Manning, W. D., & Longmore, M. A. (2006). Adolescent romantic relationships: An emerging portrait of their nature and developmental significance. In A. C. Crouter & A. Booth (Eds.), *Romance and sex in adolescence and emerging adulthood: Risks and opportunities* (pp. 127–150). Mahwah, NJ: Erlbaum.

Giordano, P. C., Manning, W. D., & Longmore, M. A. (2010). Affairs of the heart: Qualities of adolescent romantic relationships and sexual behavior. *Journal of Research on Adolescence, 20*, 983–1013. doi:10.1111/j.1532-7795.2010.00661.x

Giordano, P. C., Soto, D. A., Manning, W. D., & Longmore, M. A. (2010). The characteristics of romantic relationships associated with teen dating violence. *Social Science Research, 39*, 863–874. doi:10.1016/j.ssresearch.2010.03.009

Giorgi, G., & Siccardi, M. (1996). Ultrasonographic observation of a female fetus' sexual behavior in utero. *American Journal of Obstetrics and Gynecology, 175*, 753.

Godeau, E., Gabhainn, S. N., Vignes, C., Ross, J., Boyce, W., & Todd, J. (2008). Contraceptive use by 15-year-old students at their last sexual intercourse: Results from 24 countries. *Archives of Pediatrics and Adolescent Medicine, 162*, 66–73. doi:10.1001/archpediatrics.2007.8

Goldman, M. S., Del Boca, F. K., & Darkes, J. (1999). Alcohol expectancy theory: The application of cognitive neuroscience. In K. E. Leonard & H. T. Blane (Eds.), *Psychological theories of drinking and alcoholism* (2nd ed., pp. 203–246). New York, NY: Guilford Press.

Goodenow, C., Szalacha, L. A., Robin, L. E., & Westheimer, K. (2002). AIDS-related risk among adolescent males who have sex with males, females, or both: Evidence from a statewide survey. *American Journal of Public Health, 92*, 203–210. doi:10.2105/AJPH.92.2.203

Goodenow, C., Szalacha, L. A., Robin, L. E., & Westheimer, K. (2008). Dimensions of sexual orientation and HIV-related risk among adolescent females: Evidence from a statewide survey. *American Journal of Public Health, 98*, 1051–1058. doi:10.2105/AJPH.2005.080531

Gouws, E., Kruger, N., & Burger, S. (2000). *The adolescent* (2nd ed.). Sandown, England: Heineman.

Graber, J. A., Peterson, A. C., & Brooks-Gunn, J. (1996). Pubertal processes: Methods, measures, and models. In J. A. Graber, J. Brooks-Gunn, & A. C. Peterson (Eds.), *Transitions through adolescence: Interpersonal domains and context* (pp. 223–253). Mahwah, NJ: Erlbaum.

Graber, J. A., & Sontag, L. M. (2006). Puberty and girls' sexuality: Why hormones are not the complete answer. *New Directions for Child and Adolescent Development, 112*, 23–38. doi:10.1002/cd.160

Grello, C. M., Welsh, D. P., & Harper, M. S. (2006). No strings attached: The nature of casual sex in college students. *Journal of Sex Research, 43*, 255–267. doi:10.1080/00224490609552324

Grello, C. M., Welsh, D. P., Harper, M. S., & Dickson, J. W. (2003). Dating and sexual relationship trajectories and adolescent functioning. *Adolescent and Family Health, 3*, 103–112.

Greydanus, D. E., & Matytsina, L. (2010). Female sexual dysfunction and adolescents. *Current Opinion in Obstetrics and Gynecology, 22*, 375–380. doi:10.1097/GCO.0b013e32833d9418

Grover, R. L. (2008). Riding the second wave of research on dating anxiety: Commentary on Chorney and Morris (2008). *Clinical Psychology: Science and Practice, 15*, 239–242. doi:10.1111/j.1468-2850.2008.00133.x

Grumbach, M. M., & Styne, D. M. (1998). Puberty: Ontogeny, neuroendocrinology, physiology, and disorders. In J. D. Wilson, D. W. Fostor, H. M. Kronenberg, & P. R. Larsen (Eds.), *Williams textbook of endocrinology* (pp. 1509–1625). Philadelphia, PA: W. B. Saunders.

Guilamo-Ramos, V., Jaccard, J., Dittus, P., & Collins, S. (2008). Parent–adolescent communication about sexual intercourse: An analysis of maternal reluctance to communicate. *Health Psychology, 27*, 760–769. doi:10.1037/a0013833

Guttmacher Institute. (2010). *U.S. teenage pregnancies, births, and abortions: National and state trends and trends by race and ethnicity.* Retrieved from http://www.google.com/ig?hl=en&source=iglk

Ha, T., Overbeek, G., & Engels, R. E. (2010). Effects of attractiveness and social status on dating desire in heterosexual adolescents: An experimental study. *Archives of Sexual Behavior, 39*, 1063–1071. doi:10.1007/s10508-009-9561-z

Hadley, W., Brown, L. K., Lescano, C. M., Kell, H., Spalding, K., DiClemente, R., & Donenberg, G. (2009). Parent–adolescent sexual communication: Associations of condom use with condom discussions. *AIDS and Behavior, 13*, 997–1004. doi:10.1007/s10461-008-9468-z

Halpern, C. T. (2006). Integrating hormones and other biological factors into a developmental systems model of adolescent female sexuality. *New Directions for Child and Adolescent Development, 112*, 9–22. doi:10.1002/cd.159

Halpern, C. T. (2011). Same sex attraction and health disparities: Do sexual minority youth really need something different for healthy development? *Journal of Adolescent Health, 48*, 5–6. doi:10.1016/j.jadohealth.2010.10.010

Halpern, C. T., Joyner, K., Udry, J. R., & Suchindran, C. (2000). Smart teens don't have sex (or kiss much either). *Journal of Adolescent Health, 26*, 213–225. doi:10.1016/S1054-139X(99)00061-0

Halpern, C. T., Udry, J. R., & Suchindran, C. (1997). Testosterone predicts initiation of coitus in adolescent females. *Psychosomatic Medicine, 59*, 161–171.

Halpern, C. T., Udry, J. R., & Suchindran, C. (1998). Monthly measures of salivary testosterone predict sexual activity in adolescent males. *Archives of Sexual Behavior, 27*, 445–465. doi:10.1023/A:1018700529128

Hammond, E. M., Berry, M. A., & Rodriguez, D. N. (2011). The influence of rape myth acceptance, sexual attitudes, and belief in a just world on attributions of responsibility in a date rape scenario. *Legal and Criminological Psychology, 16*, 242–252. doi:10.1348/135532510X499887

Hampton, M., McWatters, B., Jeffery, B., & Smith, P. (2005). Influence of teens' perceptions of parental disapproval and peer behavior on their initiation of sexual intercourse. *Canadian Journal of Human Sexuality, 14*, 105–121.

Harrison, A., & O'Sullivan, L. F. (2010). In the absence of marriage: Long-term concurrent partnerships, pregnancy, and HIV risk dynamics among South African young adults. *AIDS and Behavior, 14*, 991–1000. doi:10.1007/s10461-010-9687-y

Harter, S., & Buddin, B. J. (1987). Children's understanding of the simultaneity of two emotions: A five-stage developmental acquisition sequence. *Developmental Psychology, 23*, 388–399. doi:10.1037/0012-1649.23.3.388

Hatfield, E., Brinton, C., & Cornelius, J. (1989). Passionate love and anxiety in young adolescents. *Motivation and Emotion, 13*, 271–289. doi:10.1007/BF00995539

Hatfield, E., Schmitz, E., Cornelius, J., & Rapson, R. L. (1988). Passionate love: How early does it begin? *Journal of Psychology and Human Sexuality, 1*, 35–51. doi:10.1300/J056v01n01_04

Hatfield, E., & Walster, G. W. (1978). *A new look at love.* Lanham, MD: University Press of America.

Haydon, A. A., Herring, A. H., Prinstein, M. J., & Halpern, C. T. (2012). Beyond age at first sex: Patterns of emerging sexual behavior in adolescence and young adulthood. *Journal of Adolescent Health, 50*, 456–463. doi:10.1016/j.jadohealth.2011.09.006

Hazan, C., & Shaver, P. (1987). Romantic love conceptualized as an attachment process. *Journal of Personality and Social Psychology, 52*, 511–524. doi:10.1037/0022-3514.52.3.511

Hellemans, H., Roeyers, H., Leplae, W., Dewaele, T., & Deboutte, D. (2010). Sexual behavior in male adolescents and young adults with autism spectrum disorder and borderline/mild mental retardation. *Sexuality and Disability, 28*, 93–104. doi:10.1007/s11195-009-9145-9

Hendrick, C., & Hendrick, S. S. (1986). A theory and method of love. *Journal of Personality and Social Psychology, 50*, 392–402. doi:10.1037/0022-3514.50.2.392

Henline, B. H., Lamke, L. K., & Howard, M. D. (2007). Exploring perceptions of online infidelity. *Personal Relationships, 14*, 113–128. doi:10.1111/j.1475-6811.2006.00144.x

Hensel, D. J., Fortenberry, J. D., & Orr, D. P. (2010). Factors associated with event level anal sex and condom use during anal sex among adolescent women. *Journal of Adolescent Health, 46*, 232–237. doi:10.1016/j.jadohealth.2009.06.025

Hensel, D. J., Stupiansky, N. W., Herbenick, D., Dodge, B., & Reece, M. (2011). When condom use is not condom use: An event-level analysis of condom use behaviors during vaginal intercourse. *Journal of Sexual Medicine, 8*, 28–34. doi:10.1111/j.1743-6109.2010.02031.x

Herbenick, D., Reece, M., Schick, V., Sanders, S. A., Dodge, B., & Fortenberry, J. D. (2010). Sexual behavior in the United States: Results from a national probability sample of men and women ages 14–94. *Journal of Sexual Medicine, 7*, 255–265. doi:10.1111/j.1743-6109.2010.02012.x

Herdt, G., & McClintock, M. (2000). The magical age of 10. *Archives of Sexual Behavior, 29*, 587–606. doi:10.1023/A:1002006521067

Herrick, A. L., Marshal, M. P., Smith, H. A., Sucato, G., & Stall, R. D. (2011). Sex while intoxicated: A meta-analysis comparing heterosexual and sexual minority youth. *Journal of Adolescent Health, 48*, 306–309. doi:10.1016/j.jadohealth.2010.07.008

Higgins, J. A., Trussell, J., Moore, N. B., & Davidson, J. K. (2010). Virginity lost, satisfaction gained? Physiological and psychological sexual satisfaction at heterosexual debut. *Journal of Sex Research, 47*, 384–394. doi:10.1080/00224491003774792

Hoffman, S. D. (2006). *By the numbers—The public costs of teen childbearing*. Washington, DC: National Campaign to Prevent Teen Pregnancy.

Holland, J., Ramazanoglu, C., Sharpe, S., & Thomson, R. (2010). Deconstructing virginity—Young people's accounts of first sex. *Sexual and Relationship Therapy, 25*, 351–362. doi:10.1080/14681994.2010.496970

Horne, S., & Zimmer-Gembeck, M. J. (2005). Female sexual subjectivity and well-being: Comparing late adolescents with different sexual experiences. *Sexuality Research and Social Policy, 2*, 25–40. doi:10.1525/srsp.2005.2.3.25

Hotton, T., & Haans, D. (2004). Alcohol and drug use in early adolescence. *Statistics Canada Health Reports, 15*, 9–19.

Hull, T. H. (2008). Sexual pleasure and well-being. *International Journal of Sexual Health, 20*, 133–145. doi:10.1080/19317610802157234

Hussong, A. M. (2002). Differentiating peer contexts and risk for adolescent substance use. *Journal of Youth and Adolescence, 31*, 207–220. doi:10.1023/A:1015085203097

Hutchinson, M., & Cederbaum, J. A. (2011). Talking to daddy's little girl about sex: Daughters' reports of sexual communication and support from fathers. *Journal of Family Issues, 32*, 550–572. doi:10.1177/0192513X10384222

Impett, E. A., Schooler, D., & Tolman, D. L. (2006). To be seen and not heard: Femininity ideology and adolescent girls' sexual health. *Archives of Sexual Behavior, 35*, 129–142. doi:10.1007/s10508-005-9016-0

Impett, E. A., & Tolman, D. L. (2006). Late adolescent girls' sexual experiences and sexual satisfaction. *Journal of Adolescent Research, 21*, 628–646. doi:10.1177/0743558406293964

Jaccard, J., Blanton, H., & Dodge, T. (2005). Peer influences on risk behavior: An analysis of the effects of a close friend. *Developmental Psychology, 41*, 135–147. doi:10.1037/0012-1649.41.1.135

Jaccard, J., Dittus, P. J., & Gordon, V. V. (2000). Parent–teen communication about premarital sex: Factors associated with the extent of communication. *Journal of Adolescent Research, 15*, 187–208. doi:10.1177/0743558400152001

Jackson, S. (1990). Demons and innocents: Western ideas on children's sexuality in historical perspective. In M. E. Perry (Ed.), *Childhood and adolescent sexology* (pp. 23–49). New York, NY: Elsevier.

Jain, S., & Kurz, K. (2007). *New insights on preventing child marriage: A global analysis of factors and programs*. Washington, DC: International Center for Research on Women.

James, J., Ellis, B. J., Schlomer, G. L., & Garber, J. (2012). Sex-specific pathways to early puberty, sexual debut, and sexual risk taking: Tests of an integrated evolutionary-developmental model. *Developmental Psychology, 48*, 687–702.

Jamieson, L. K., & Wade, T. J. (2011). Early age of first sexual intercourse and depressive symptomatology among adolescents. *Journal of Sex Research, 48*, 450–460. doi:10.1080/00224499.2010.509892

Janssen, D. F. (2007). First stirrings: Cultural notes on orgasm, ejaculation, and wet dreams. *Journal of Sex Research, 44*, 122–134. doi:10.1080/00224490701263595

Jerman, P., & Constantine, N. A. (2010). Demographic and psychological predictors of parent–adolescent communication about sex: A representative statewide analysis. *Journal of Youth and Adolescence, 39*, 1164–1174. doi:10.1007/s10964-010-9546-1

Jones, R. K., & Biddlecom, A. E. (2011). Is the Internet filling the sexual health information gap for teens? An exploratory study. *Journal of Health Communication, 16*, 112–123. doi:10.1080/10810730.2010.535112

Jones, R. K., Biddlecom, A. E., Hebert, L., & Mellor, R. (2011). Teens reflect on their sources of contraceptive information. *Journal of Adolescent Research, 26*, 423–446. doi:10.1177/0743558411400908

Joshi, S. P., Peter, J., & Valkenburg, P. M. (2011). Scripts of sexual desire and danger in US and Dutch teen girl magazines: A cross-national content analysis. *Sex Roles, 64*, 463–474. doi:10.1007/s11199-011-9941-4

Joyner, K., & Udry, J. R. (2000). You don't bring me anything but down: Adolescent romance and depression. *Journal of Health and Social Behavior, 41*, 369–391. doi:10.2307/2676292

Kaiser Family Foundation. (2004). *Sex education in America.* Retrieved from http://www.kff.org/newsmedia/7015.cfm

Kaiser Family Foundation. (2010). *Generation M2: Media in the lives of 8- to 18-year olds.* Retrieved from http://www.kff.org/entmedia/mh012010pkg.cfm

Kalichman, S. C., Simbayi, L. C., Cain, D., & Jooste, S. (2007). Alcohol expectancies and risky drinking among men and women at high-risk for HIV infection in Cape Town South Africa. *Addictive Behaviors, 32*, 2304–2310. doi:10.1016/j.addbeh.2007.01.026

Kapungu, C. T., Baptiste, D., Holmbeck, G., Mcbride, C., Robinson-Brown, M., Sturdivant, A., & Paikoff, R. (2010). Beyond the "birds and the bees": Gender differences in sex-related communication among urban African-American adolescents. *Family Process, 49*, 251–264. doi:10.1111/j.1545-5300.2010.01321.x

Katz-Wise, S. L., & Hyde, J. S. (2012). Victimization experiences of lesbian, gay, and bisexual individuals: A meta-analysis. *Journal of Sex Research, 49*, 142–167. doi:10.1080/00224499.2011.637247

Kehily, M. (2001). Bodies in school: Young men, embodiment, and heterosexual masculinities. *Men and Masculinities, 4*, 173–185. doi:10.1177/1097184X01004002005

Kelley, S. S., Borawski, E. A., Flocke, S. A., & Keen, K. J. (2003). The role of sequential and concurrent sexual relationships in the risk of sexually transmitted diseases among adolescents. *Journal of Adolescent Health, 32*, 296–305. doi:10.1016/S1054-139X(02)00710-3

Kelly, A. B., Toumbourou, J. W., O'Flaherty, M., Patton, G. C., Homel, R., Connor, J. P., & Williams, J. (2011). Family relationship quality and early alcohol use: Evidence for gender-specific risk processes. *Journal of Studies on Alcohol and Drugs, 72*, 399–407.

Kennedy, B. L., & Roberts, S. T. (2009). Truths and myths that influence the sexual decision-making process among young multiethnic college women. *Archives of Psychiatric Nursing, 23*, 366–375. doi:10.1016/j.apnu.2008.10.007

Kiely, E. (2012). Teenage pregnancy: What's the problem? *Critical Social Policy, 32*, 153–155. doi:10.1177/0261018311425203b

Kirby, D. (2002). Antecedents of adolescent initiation of sex, contraceptive use and pregnancy. *American Journal of Health Behavior, 26*, 473–485. doi:10.5993/AJHB.26.6.8

Kirby, D., Crosby, R. A., Santelli, J. S., & DiClemente, R. J. (2009). Interventions to prevent pregnancy and sexually transmitted diseases, including HIV infection. In R. J. DiClemente, J. S. Santelli, & R. A. Crosby (Eds.), *Adolescent health: Understanding and preventing risk behaviors* (pp. 303–338). San Francisco, CA: Jossey-Bass.

Kornreich, J. L., Hearn, K. D., Rodriguez, G., & O'Sullivan, L. F. (2003). Sibling influence, gender roles, and sexual socialization of urban early adolescent girls. *Journal of Sex Research, 40*, 101–110. doi:10.1080/00224490309552170

Kukulu, K., Gürsoy, E., Sözer, G. A. (2009). Turkish university students' beliefs about sexual myths. *Sexuality and Disability, 27*, 49–59. doi:10.1007/s11195-009-9108-1

Kunkel, D., Eyal, K., Finnerty, K., Biely, E., & Donnerstein, E. (2005). *Sex on TV 4.* Menlo Park, CA: Kaiser Family Foundation.

Laflin, M. T., Wang, J., & Barry, M. (2008). A longitudinal study of adolescent transition from virgin to nonvirgin status. *Journal of Adolescent Health, 42*, 228–236. doi:10.1016/j.jadohealth.2007.08.014

Lam, T. H., Shi, H. J., Ho, L. M., & Fan, S. (2002). Timing of pubertal maturation and heterosexual behavior among Hong Kong Chinese adolescents. *Archives of Sexual Behavior, 31*, 359–366. doi:10.1023/A:1016228427210

Landry, T., & Bergeron, S. (2011). Biopsychosocial factors associated with dyspareunia in a community sample of adolescent girls. *Archives of Sexual Behavior, 40*, 877–889. doi:10.1007/s10508-010-9637-9

Lanier, C. A. (2001). Rape-accepting attitudes: Precursors to or consequences of forced sex. *Violence Against Women, 7*, 876–885. doi:10.1177/10778010122182802

Larson, R. W., Clore, G. L., & Wood, G. A. (1999). The emotions of romantic relationships: Do they wreak havoc on adolescents? In W. Furman, B. B. Brown, & C. Feiring (Eds.), *The development of romantic relationships in adolescence* (pp. 19–49). New York, NY: Cambridge University Press.

Latimer, W., & Zur, J. (2010). Epidemiologic trends of adolescent use of alcohol, tobacco, and other drugs. *Child and Adolescent Psychiatric Clinics of North America, 19*, 451–464. doi:10.1016/j.chc.2010.03.002

Laumann, E. O., Paik, A., & Rosen, R. C. (1999). Sexual dysfunction in the United States: Prevalence and predictors. *JAMA, 281*, 537–544. doi:10.1001/jama.281.6.537

Lavoie, F., Thibodeau, C., Gagné, M., & Hébert, M. (2010). Buying and selling sex in Québec adolescents: A study of risk and protective factors. *Archives of Sexual Behavior, 39*, 1147–1160. doi:10.1007/s10508-010-9605-4

Lazarus, J. V., Moghaddassi, M., Godeau, E., Ross, J., Vignes, C., Östergren, P., . . . Liljestrand, J. (2009). A multilevel analysis of condom use among adolescents in the European Union. *Public Health, 123*, 138–144. doi:10.1016/j.puhe.2008.10.014

Leclerc-Madlala, S. (2003). Transactional sex and the pursuit of modernity. *Social Dynamics: A Journal of African Studies, 29*, 213–233. doi:10.1080/02533950308628681

Lee, J. K., Jennings, J. M., & Ellen, J. M. (2003). Discordant sexual partnering: A study of high-risk adolescents in San Francisco. *Sexually Transmitted Diseases, 30*, 234–240. doi:10.1097/00007435-200303000-00012

Lefkowitz, E. S. (2002). Beyond the yes-no question: Measuring parent-adolescent communication about sex. In S. S. Feldman & D. A. Rosenthal (Eds.), *Talking sexuality: Parent-adolescent communication* (pp. 43–56). San Francisco, CA: Jossey-Bass. doi:10.1002/cd.49

Lefkowitz, E. S., Boone, T. L., & Shearer, C. L. (2004). Communication with best friends about sex-related topics during emerging adulthood. *Journal of Youth and Adolescence, 33*, 339–351. doi:10.1023/B:JOYO.0000032642.27242.c1

Lefkowitz, E. S., Boone, T. L., Sigman, M., & Kit-fong Au, T. (2002). He said, she said: Gender differences in mother-adolescent conversations about sexuality. *Journal of Research on Adolescence, 12*, 217–242. doi:10.1111/1532-7795.00032

Lefkowitz, E. S., & Stoppa, T. M. (2006). Positive sexual communication and socialization in the parent-adolescent context. In L. Diamond (Ed.), *New Directions for Child and Adolescent Development: Vol. 112. Rethinking positive adolescent female development* (pp. 39–56). San Francisco, CA: Jossey-Bass. doi:10.1002/cd.161

Lehmiller, J. J., VanderDrift, L. E., & Kelly, J. R. (2011). Sex differences in approaching friends with benefits relationships. *Journal of Sex Research, 48*, 275–284. doi:10.1080/00224491003721694

Leichliter, J. S., Chandra, A., Liddon, N., Fenton, K. A., & Aral, S. O. (2007). Prevalence and correlates of heterosexual anal and oral sex in adolescents and adults in the United States. *Journal of Infectious Diseases, 196*, 1852–1859. doi:10.1086/522867

Leigh, B. C. (1990). The relationship of sex-related alcohol expectancies to alcohol consumption and sexual behavior. *British Journal of Addiction, 85*, 919–928. doi:10.1111/j.1360-0443.1990.tb03722.x

L'Engle, K. L., Brown, J. D., & Kenneavy, K. (2006). Mass media are an important context for adolescents' sexual behavior. *Journal of Adolescent Health, 38*, 186–192. doi:10.1016/j.jadohealth.2005.03.020

L'Engle, K. L., & Jackson, C. (2008). Socialization influences on early adolescents' cognitive susceptibility and transition to sexual intercourse. *Journal of Research on Adolescence, 18*, 353–378. doi:10.1111/j.1532-7795.2008.00563.x

Lenhart, A., Ling, R., Campbell, S., & Purcell, K. (2010). *Teens and mobile phones.* Retrieved from http://pewinternet.org/Reports/2010/Teens-and-Mobile-Phones.aspx

Lenoir, C. D., Adler, N. E., Borzekowski, D. L. G., Tschann, J. M., & Ellen, J. M. (2006). What you don't know can hurt you: Perceptions of sex-partner concurrency and partner-reported behavior. *Journal of Adolescent Health, 38*, 179–185. doi:10.1016/j.jadohealth.2005.01.012

Levin, M. L., Xu, X., & Bartkowski, J. P. (2002). Seasonality of sexual debut. *Journal of Marriage and Family, 64*, 871–884. doi:10.1111/j.1741-3737.2002.00871.x

Liau, A. K., Khoo, A., & Peng Hwa, A. (2005). Factors influencing adolescents' engagement in risky Internet behavior. *CyberPsychology and Behavior, 8*, 513–520. doi:10.1089/cpb.2005.8.513

Lindberg, L. D., Jones, R., & Santelli, J. S. (2008). Noncoital sexual activities among adolescents. *Journal of Adolescent Health, 43*, 231–238. doi:10.1016/j.jadohealth.2007.12.010

Löfgren-Mårtenson, L., & Månsson, S. (2010). Lust, love, and life: A qualitative study of Swedish adolescents' perceptions and experiences with pornography. *Journal of Sex Research, 47*, 568–579. doi:10.1080/00224490903151374

Loftus, J., & Kelly, B. C. (2012). Short-term sexual health effects of relationships with significantly older females on adolescents boys. *Journal of Adolescent Health, 50*, 195–197. doi:10.1016/j.jadohealth.2011.04.014

Longmore, M. A. (1998). Symbolic interactionism and the study of sexuality. *Journal of Sex Research, 35*, 44–57. doi:10.1080/00224499809551916

Longmore, M. A., Manning, W. D., & Giordano, P. C. (2001). Preadolescent parenting strategies and teens' dating and sexual initiation: A longitudinal analysis. *Journal of Marriage and Family, 63*, 322–335. doi:10.1111/j.1741-3737.2001.00322.x

Luder, M.-T., Pittet, I., Berchtold, A., Akré, C., Michaud, P., & Surís, J. (2011). Associations between online pornography and sexual behavior among adolescents: Myth or reality? *Archives of Sexual Behavior, 40*, 1027–1035. doi:10.1007/s10508-010-9714-0

Luo, S., Cartun, M. A., & Snider, A. G. (2010). Assessing extradyadic behavior: A review, a new measure, and two new models. *Personality and Individual Differences, 49*, 155–163. doi:10.1016/j.paid.2010.03.033

Maart, S., & Jelsma, J. (2010). The sexual behavior of physically disabled adolescents. *Disability and Rehabilitation: An International Multidisciplinary Journal, 32*, 438–443.

MacPhail, C., Pettifor, A. E., Pascoe, S., & Rees, H. V. (2007). Contraception use and pregnancy among 15–24 year old South African women: A nationally representative cross-sectional survey. *BMC Medicine, 5*, 31. doi:10.1186/1741-7015-5-31

Madkour, A. S., Farhat, T., Halpern, C. T., Godeau, E., & Gabhainn, S. N. (2010). Early adolescent sexual initiation and physical/psychological symptoms: A comparative analysis of five nations. *Journal of Youth and Adolescence, 39*, 1211–1225. doi:10.1007/s10964-010-9521-x

Maggs, J. L. (1997). Alcohol use and binge drinking as goal-directed action during the transition to post-secondary education. In J. Schulenberg, J. L. Maggs, & K. Hurrelman (Eds.), *Health risks and developmental transitions during adolescence* (pp. 345–371). Cambridge, England: Cambridge University Press.

Malacad, B. L., & Hess, G. C. (2010). Oral sex: Behaviors and feelings of Canadian young females and implications for sex education. *European Journal of Contraception and Reproductive Health Care, 15*, 177–185. doi:10.3109/13625181003797298

Mallet, P., & Herbé, D. (2011). Does knowledge about sexuality prevent adolescents from developing rape-supportive beliefs? *Journal of Sex Research, 48*, 372–380. doi:10.1080/00224491003794048

Manlove, J., Ikramullah, E., Mincieli, L., Holcombe, E., & Danish, S. (2009). Trends in sexual experience, contraceptive use, and teenage childbearing: 1992–2002. *Journal of Adolescent Health, 44*, 413–423. doi:10.1016/j.jadohealth.2008.09.006

Manning, W. D., Flanigan, C. M., Giordano, P. C., & Longmore, M. A. (2009). Relationship dynamics and consistency of condom use among adolescents. *Perspectives on Sexual and Reproductive Health, 41*, 181–190. doi:10.1363/4118109

Manning, W. D., Giordano, P. C., & Longmore, M. A. (2006). Hooking up: The relationship contexts of "nonrelationship" sex. *Journal of Adolescent Research, 21*, 459–483. doi:10.1177/0743558406291692

Manning, W. D., Longmore, M. A., & Giordano, P. C. (2005). Adolescents' involvement in non-romantic sexual activity. *Social Science Research, 34*, 384–407. doi:10.1016/j.ssresearch.2004.03.001

Markus, H., & Nurius, P. (1986). Possible selves. *American Psychologist, 41*, 954–969. doi:10.1037/0003-066X.41.9.954

Marston, C., & King, E. (2006). Factors that shape young people's sexual behaviour: A systematic review. *Lancet, 368*, 1581–1586. doi:10.1016/S0140-6736(06)69662-1

Martin, K. A. (1996). *Puberty, sexuality and the self: Girls and boys at adolescence.* New York, NY: Taylor & Francis.

Martino, S. C., Elliott, M. N., Corona, R., Kanouse, D. E., & Schuster, M. A. (2008). Beyond the "big talk": The roles of breadth and repetition in parent-adolescent communication about sexual topics. *Pediatrics, 121*, e612–e618. doi:10.1542/peds.2007-2156

Matson, P. A., Adler, N. E., Millstein, S. G., Tschann, J. M., & Ellen, J. M. (2011). Developmental changes in condom use among urban adolescent females: Influence of partner context. *Journal of Adolescent Health, 48*, 386–390. doi:10.1016/j.jadohealth.2010.07.016

McCabe, M. P., Cummins, R. A., & Deeks, A. A. (2000). Sexuality and quality of life among people with physical disability. *Sexuality and Disability, 18*, 115–123. doi:10.1023/A:1005562813603

McCauley, J. L., Conoscenti, L. M., Ruggiero, K. J., Resnick, H. S., Saunders, B. E., & Kilpatrick, D. G. (2009). Prevalence and correlates of drug/alcohol-facilitated and incapacitated sexual assault in a nationally representative sample of adolescent girls. *Journal of Clinical Child and Adolescent Psychology, 38*, 295–300. doi:10.1080/15374410802698453

McDowell, M. A., Brody, D. J., & Hughes, J. P. (2007). Has age at menarche changed? Results from the National Health and Nutrition Examination Survey (NHANES) 1999–2004. *Journal of Adolescent Health, 40*, 227–231. doi:10.1016/j.jadohealth.2006.10.002

McLean, K. C., & Breen, A. V. (2009). Processes and content of narrative identity development in adolescence: Gender and well-being. *Developmental Psychology, 45*, 702–710. doi:10.1037/a0015207

McMaster, L. E., Connolly, J., Pepler, D., & Craig, W. M. (2002). Peer to peer sexual harassment in early adolescence: A developmental perspective. *Development and Psychopathology, 14*, 91–105. doi:10.1017/S0954579402001050

McRae, K., Gross, J. J., Weber, J., Robertson, E. R., Sokol-Hessner, P., Ray, R. D., . . . Ochsner, K. N. (2012). The development of emotion regulation: An fMRI study of cognitive reappraisal in children, adolescents and young adults. *Social Cognitive and Affective Neuroscience, 7*, 11–22. doi:10.1093/scan/nsr093

Mendle, J., Harden, K., Turkheimer, E., Van Hulle, C. A., D'Onofrio, B. M., Brooks-Gunn, J., . . . Lahey, B. B. (2009). Associations between father absence and age of first sexual intercourse. *Child Development, 80*, 1463–1480. doi:10.1111/j.1467-8624.2009.01345.x

Mercer, C. H., Fenton, K. A., Johnson, A. M., Wellings, K., Macdowall, W., McManus, S., . . . Erens, B. (2003). Sexual function problems and help seeking behavior in Britain: National probability sample survey. *British Medical Journal, 327*, 426–427. doi:10.1136/bmj.327.7412.426

Meschke, L. L., Zweig, J. M., Barber, B. L., & Eccles, J. S. (2000). Demographic, biological, psychological, and social predictors of timing of first intercourse. *Journal of Research on Adolescence, 10*, 315–338. doi:10.1207/SJRA1003_5

Meston, C. M., & Ahrold, T. (2010). Ethnic, gender, and acculturation influences on sexual behaviors. *Archives of Sexual Behavior, 39*, 179–189. doi:10.1007/s10508-008-9415-0

Miller, K. S., Fasula, A. M., Dittus, P., Wiegand, R. E., Wyckoff, S. C., & McNair, L. (2009). Barriers and facilitators to maternal communication with preadolescents about age-relevant sexual topics. *AIDS and Behavior, 13*, 365–374. doi:10.1007/s10461-007-9324-6

Mongeau, P. A., Jacobsen, J., & Donnerstein, C. (2007). Defining dates and first date goals: Generalizing from undergraduates to single adults. *Communication Research, 34*, 526–547. doi:10.1177/0093650207305235

Monroe, S. M., Rohde, P., Seeley, J. R., & Lewinsohn, P. M. (1999). Life events and depression in adolescence: Relationship loss as a prospective risk factor for first onset of major depressive disorder. *Journal of Abnormal Psychology, 108*, 606–614. doi:10.1037/0021-843X.108.4.606

Montgomery, M. J., & Sorell, G. T. (1998). Love and dating experience in early and middle adolescence: Grade and gender comparisons. *Journal of Adolescence, 21*, 677–689. doi:10.1006/jado.1998.0188

Moon, M. W., McFarland, W., Kellogg, T., Baxter, M., Katz, M. H., MacKellar, D., & Valleroy, L. A. (2000). HIV risk behavior of runaway youth in San Francisco: Age of onset and relation to sexual orientation. *Youth and Society, 32*, 184–201. doi:10.1177/0044118X00032002003

Moore, D. A., Morrison, D. R., & Greene, A. D. (1997). Effects on the children born to adolescent mothers. In R. A. Maynard (Ed.), *Kids having kids: Economic costs and social consequences of teen pregnancy* (pp. 145–180). Washington, DC: Urban Institute Press.

Moore, M. R., & Brooks-Gunn, J. (2002). *Adolescent parenthood.* In M. Bornstein (Ed.), *Handbook of parenting* (2nd ed., pp. 173–214). Mahwah, NJ: Erlbaum.

Moore, M. R., & Chase-Lansdale, P. L. (2001). Sexual intercourse and pregnancy among African American girls in high-poverty neighborhoods: The role of family and perceived community environment. *Journal of Marriage and Family, 63*, 1146–1157. doi:10.1111/j.1741-3737.2001.01146.x

Moore, N. B., & Davidson, J. R. (1999). Parents as first sexuality information sources: Do they make a difference in daughters' sexual attitudes and behavior? *Journal of Sex Education and Therapy, 24*, 155–163.

Morrison-Beedy, D., Carey, M. P., Feng, C., & Tu, X. M. (2008). Predicting sexual risk behaviors among adolescent and young women using a prospective diary method. *Research in Nursing and Health, 31*, 329–340. doi:10.1002/nur.20263

Mosher, W. D., Chandra, A., & Jones, J. (2005). *Sexual behavior and selected health measures: Men and women 15–44 years of age, United States, 2002.* Hyattsville, MD: National Center for Health Statistics.

Moss, B. F., & Schwebel, A. I. (1993). Defining intimacy in romantic relationships. *Family Relations, 42*, 31–37.

Nannis, E. D., & Cowan, P. A. (1987). Emotional understanding: A matter of age, dimension, and point of view. *Journal of Applied Developmental Psychology, 8*, 289–304. doi:10.1016/0193-3973(87)90005-0

National Campaign to Prevent Teen and Unplanned Pregnancy. (2009). *Socio-economic and family characteristics of teen childbearing.* Retrieved from http://www.thenationalcampaign.org/resources/pdf/SS/SS41_SocioEconomicFamilyCharacteristics.pdf

O'Donnell, L., Myint-U, A., O'Donnell, C., & Stueve, A. (2003). Long-term influence of sexual norms and attitudes on timing of sexual initiation among urban minority youth. *Journal of School Health, 73*, 68–75. doi:10.1111/j.1746-1561.2003.tb03575.x

Office for National Statistics. (2011). *Quarterly conceptions to women aged under 18, England and Wales.* Retrieved from http://www.ons.gov.uk/ons/publications/index.html?pageSize=50&newquery=teen&sortBy=pubdate&sortDirection=DESCENDING&content-type=publicationContentTypes

O'Keeffe, G. S., & Clarke-Pearson, K. (2011). The impact of social media on children, adolescents, and families. *Pediatrics, 127*, 800–804. doi:10.1542/peds.2011-0054

Olesen, T. B., Jensen, K. E., Nygård, M., Tryggvadottir, L., Sparén, P., Hansen, B., . . . Kjær, S. K. (2012). Young age at first intercourse and risk-taking behaviours—A study of nearly 65,000 women in four Nordic countries. *European Journal of Public Health, 22*, 220–224. doi:10.1093/eurpub/ckr055

Oliva, P. (1999). *School years: Young women, self-esteem and the confidence gap.* New York, NY: Doubleday.

Osorio, A., López-del Burgo, C., Carlos, S., Ruiz-Canela, M., Delgado, M., & de Irala, J. (2012). First sexual intercourse and subsequent regret in three developing countries. *Journal of Adolescent Health, 50*, 271–278. doi:10.1016/j.jadohealth.2011.07.012

Ostrager, B. (2010). SMS. OMG! LOL! TTYL: Translating the law to accommodate today's teens and the evolution from texting to sexting. *Family Court Review, 48*, 712–726. doi:10.1111/j.1744-1617.2010.01345.x

O'Sullivan, L. F., Brotto, L., Byers, E. S., Majerovich, J. A., & Wuest, J. (2012, February). *Problems in sexual functioning among adolescents and young adults*. Paper presented at the annual meeting of the International Society for the Study of Women's Sexual Health, Jerusalem, Israel.

O'Sullivan, L. F., & Hearn, K. D. (2008). Predicting first intercourse among urban early adolescent girls: The role of emotions. *Cognition and Emotion, 22*, 168–179. doi:10.1080/02699930701298465

O'Sullivan, L. F., & Majerovich, J. (2008). Difficulties with sexual functioning in a sample of male and female late adolescent and young adult university students. *Canadian Journal of Human Sexuality, 17*, 109–121.

O'Sullivan, L. F., Mantsun, M., Harris, K. M., & Brooks-Gunn, J. (2007). I wanna hold your hand: The progression of social, romantic and sexual events in adolescent relationships. *Perspectives on Sexual and Reproductive Health, 39*, 100–107. doi:10.1363/3910007

O'Sullivan, L. F., & Meyer-Bahlburg, H. L. (2003). African American and Latina inner-city girls' reports of romantic and sexual development. *Journal of Social and Personal Relationships, 20*, 221–238.

O'Sullivan, L. F., Meyer-Bahlburg, H. L., & McKeague, I. W. (2006). The development of the Sexual Self-Concept Inventory for early adolescent girls. *Psychology of Women Quarterly, 30*, 139–149. doi:10.1111/j.1471-6402.2006.00277.x

O'Sullivan, L. F., Meyer-Bahlburg, H. L., & Watkins, B. X. (2001). Mother-daughter communication about sex among urban African American and Latino families. *Journal of Adolescent Research, 16*, 269–292. doi:10.1177/0743558401163002

O'Sullivan, L. F., Udell, W., Montrose, V. A., Antoniello, P., & Hoffman, S. (2010). A cognitive analysis of college students' explanations for engaging in unprotected sexual intercourse. *Archives of Sexual Behavior, 39*, 1121–1131. doi:10.1007/s10508-009-9493-7

Ott, M. A., Millstein, S. G., Ofner, S., & Halpern-Felsher, B. L. (2006). Greater expectations: Adolescents' positive motivations for sex. *Perspectives on Sexual and Reproductive Health, 38*, 84–89. doi:10.1363/3808406

Ott, M. A., Ofner, S., Tu, W., Katz, B. P., & Fortenberry, J. D. (2010). Characteristics associated with sex after periods of abstinence among sexually experienced young women. *Perspectives on Sexual and Reproductive Health, 42*, 43–48. doi:10.1363/4204310

Ott, M. Q., Corliss, H. L., Wypij, D., Rosario, M., & Austin, S. B. (2011). Stability and change in self-reported sexual orientation identity in young people: Application of mobility metrics. *Archives of Sexual Behavior, 40*, 519–532. doi:10.1007/s10508-010-9691-3

Paikoff, R. L. (1995). Early heterosexual debut: Situations of sexual possibility during transition to adolescence. *American Journal of Orthopsychiatry, 65*, 389–401. doi:10.1037/h0079652

Palermo, T., & Peterman, A. (2009). Are female orphans at risk for early marriage, early sexual debut, and teen pregnancy? Evidence from sub-Saharan Africa. *Studies in Family Planning, 40*, 101–112. doi:10.1111/j.1728-4465.2009.00193.x

Papadimitriou, A., Douros, K., Kleanthous, K., Papadimitriou, D. T., Attilakos, A., & Fretzayas, A. (2011). Pubertal maturation of contemporary Greek boys: No evidence of a secular trend. *Journal of Adolescent Health, 49*, 434–436. doi:10.1016/j.jadohealth.2010.12.022

Parker-Pope, T. (2009, January 26). Well: The myth of rampant teenage promiscuity. *New York Times*. Retrieved from http://www.nytimes.com/2009/01/27/health/27well.html

Patton, G. C., & Viner, R. (2007). Pubertal transitions in health. *Lancet, 369*, 1130–1139. doi:10.1016/S0140-6736(07)60366-3

Paus, T., Nawaz-Khan, I., Leonard, G., Perron, M., Pike, G. B., Pitiot, A., . . . Pausova, Z. (2010). Sexual dimorphism in the adolescent brain: Role of testosterone and androgen receptor in global and local volumes of grey and white matter. *Hormones and Behavior, 57*, 63–75. doi:10.1016/j.yhbeh.2009.08.004

Pedersen, W., & Hegna, K. (2003). Children and adolescents who sell sex: A community study. *Social Science and Medicine, 56*, 135–147. doi:10.1016/S0277-9536(02)00015-1

Perrin, E. C. (2002). *Sexual orientation in child and adolescent health care*. New York, NY: Kluwer Academic/Plenum.

Peter, J., & Valkenburg, P. M. (2007). Adolescents' exposure to a sexualized media environment and their notions of women as sex objects. *Sex Roles, 56*, 381–395. doi:10.1007/s11199-006-9176-y

Peter, J., & Valkenburg, P. M. (2008). Adolescents' exposure to sexually explicit Internet material and sexual preoccupancy: A three-wave panel study. *Media Psychology, 11*, 207–234. doi:10.1080/15213260801994238

Peter, J., & Valkenburg, P. M. (2009a). Adolescents' exposure to sexually explicit Internet material and notions of women as sex objects: Assessing causality and underlying processes. *Journal of Communication, 59*, 407–433. doi:10.1111/j.1460-2466.2009.01422.x

Peter, J., & Valkenburg, P. M. (2009b). Adolescents' exposure to sexually explicit Internet material and sexual satisfaction: A longitudinal study. *Human Communication Research, 35*, 171–194. doi:10.1111/j.1468-2958.2009.01343.x

Peter, J., & Valkenburg, P. M. (2010). Processes underlying the effects of adolescents' use of sexually explicit Internet material: The role of perceived realism. *Communication Research, 37*, 375–399. doi:10.1177/0093650210362464

Peter, J., & Valkenburg, P. M. (2011a). The influence of sexually explicit Internet material on sexual risk behavior: A comparison of adolescents and adults. *Journal of Health Communication, 16*, 750–765. doi:10.1080/10810730.2011.551996

Peter, J., & Valkenburg, P. M. (2011b). The use of sexually explicit Internet material and its antecedents: A longitudinal comparison of adolescents and adults. *Archives of Sexual Behavior, 40*, 1015–1025. doi:10.1007/s10508-010-9644-x

Peters, R. J., Johnson, R. J., Kelder, S., Meschack, A. F., & Jefferson, T. (2007). Beliefs and social norms about sildenafil citrate (Viagra) misuse and perceived consequences among Houstonian teenage males. *American Journal of Men's Health, 1*, 208–212. doi:10.1177/1557988307303299

Petersen, J. L., & Hyde, J. S. (2011). Gender differences in sexual attitudes: A review of meta-analytic results and large datasets. *Journal of Sex Research, 48*, 149–165. doi:10.1080/00224499.2011.551851

Population Council. (2007). *Transitions to adulthood: Child marriage/married adolescents.* Retrieved from http://www.popcouncil.org/topics/youth_childmarriage.asp

Potgieter, C., & Khan, G. (2005). Sexual self-esteem and body image of South African spinal cord injured adolescents. *Sexuality and Disability, 23*, 1–20. doi:10.1007/s11195-004-2076-6

Poulin, C., & Elliot, D. (2007). *Student drug use survey in the Atlantic provinces 2007.* Retrieved from http://www.gov.ns.ca/hpp/publications/atl_tech_report_2007.pdf

Price, M. N., & Hyde, J. S. (2009). When two isn't better than one: Predictors of early sexual activity in adolescence using a cumulative risk model. *Journal of Youth and Adolescence, 38*, 1059–1071. doi:10.1007/s10964-008-9351-2

Public Health Agency of Canada. (2009). *Report on sexually transmitted infections in Canada: 2008.* Retrieved from http://www.phac-aspc.gc.ca/std-mts/report/sti-its2008/06-eng.php

Quan-Haase, A. (2007). University students' local and distant social ties: Using and integrating modes of communication on campus. *Information Communication and Society, 10*, 671–693. doi:10.1080/13691180701658020

Randall, H. E., & Byers, E. S. (2003). What is sex? Students' definitions of having sex, sexual partner, and unfaithful sexual behavior. *Canadian Journal of Human Sexuality, 12*, 87–96.

Regan, P. C., & Joshi, A. (2003). Ideal partner preferences among adolescents. *Social Behavior and Personality: An International Journal, 31*, 13–20. doi:10.2224/sbp.2003.31.1.13

Reid, V., & Meadows-Oliver, M. (2007). Postpartum depression in adolescent mothers: An integrative literature review. *Journal of Pediatric Health Care, 21*, 289–298. doi:10.1016/j.pedhc.2006.05.010

Reissing, E. D., Andruff, H. L., & Wentland, J. J. (2012). Looking back: The experience of first sexual intercourse and current sexual adjustment in young heterosexual adults. *Journal of Sex Research, 49*, 27–35. doi:10.1080/00224499.2010.538951

Rice, E., Monro, W., Barman-Adhikari, A., & Young, S. D. (2010). Internet use, social networking, and HIV/AIDS risk for homeless adolescents. *Journal of Adolescent Health, 47*, 610–613. doi:10.1016/j.jadohealth.2010.04.016

Rickert, V. I., Sanghvi, R., & Wiemann, C. M. (2002). Is lack of sexual assertiveness among adolescent and young adult women a cause for concern? *Perspectives on Sexual and Reproductive Health, 34*, 178–183. doi:10.2307/3097727

Rind, B. (2008). The Bailey affair: Political correctness and attacks on sex research. *Archives of Sexual Behavior, 37*, 481–484. doi:10.1007/s10508-008-9334-0

Robbins, C. L., Schick, V., Reece, M., Herbenick, D., Sanders, S. A., Dodge, B., & Fortenberry, J. D. (2011). Prevalence, frequency, and associations of masturbation with partnered sexual behaviors among us adolescents. *Archives of Pediatrics and Adolescent Medicine, 165*, 1087–1093. doi:10.1001/archpediatrics.2011.142

Roberts, D. F., Henriksen, L., & Foehr, U. G. (2009). *Adolescence, adolescents, and media.* In R. M. Lerner & L. Steinburg (Eds.), *Handbook of adolescent psychology: Vol. 2. Contextual influences on adolescent development* (3rd ed., pp. 314–344). New York, NY: Wiley.

Ronis, S., & O'Sullivan, L. F. (2011). A longitudinal analysis of predictions of male and female adolescents' transitions to intimate sexual behavior. *Journal of Adolescent Health, 49*, 321–323. doi:10.1016/j.jadohealth.2010.12.010

Rosen, R., Brown, C., Heiman, J., Leiblum, S., Meston, C., Shabsigh, R., . . . D'Agostino, R., Jr. (2000). The Female Sexual Function Index (FSFI): A multidimensional self-report instrument for the assessment of female sexual function. *Journal of Sex and Marital Therapy, 26,* 191–208. doi:10.1080/009262300278597

Rosen, R. C., Riley, A., Wagner, G., Osterloh, I. H., Kirkpatrick, J., & Mishra, A. (1997). The International Index of Erectile Function (IIEF): A multidimensional scale for assessment of erectile dysfunction. *Urology, 49,* 822–830. doi:10.1016/S0090-4295(97)00238-0

Rosenbaum, J. E. (2009). Patient teenagers? A comparison of the sexual behavior of virginity pledgers and matched nonpledgers. *Pediatrics, 123,* e110–e120. doi:10.1542/peds.2008-0407

Rosenthal, D. A., & Feldman, S. S. (1999). The importance of importance: Adolescents' perceptions of parental communication about sexuality. *Journal of Adolescence, 22,* 835–851. doi:10.1006/jado.1999.0279

Rostosky, S. S., Dekhtyar, O., Cupp, P. K., & Anderman, E. M. (2008). Sexual self-concept and sexual self-efficacy in adolescents: A possible clue to promoting sexual health? *Journal of Sex Research, 45,* 277–286. doi:10.1080/00224490802204480

Rostosky, S. S., Galliher, R. V., Welsh, D. P., & Kawaguchi, M. C. (2000). Sexual behaviors and relationship qualities in late adolescent couples. *Journal of Adolescence, 23,* 583–597. doi:10.1006/jado.2000.0345

Russell, S. T. (2005). Conceptualizing positive adolescent sexuality development. *Sexuality Research and Social Policy, 2,* 4–12.

Salazar, L. F., Santelli, J. S., Crosby, R. A., & DiClemente, R. J. (2009). Sexually transmitted disease transmission and pregnancy among adolescents. In R. J. DiClemente, J. S. Santelli, & R. A. Crosby (Eds.), *Adolescent health: Understanding and preventing risk behaviors* (pp. 275–302). San Francisco, CA: Jossey-Bass.

Sales, J. M., Milhausen, R. R., & DiClemente, R. J. (2006). A decade in review: Building on the experiences of past adolescent STI/HIV interventions to optimise future prevention efforts. *Sexually Transmitted Infections, 82,* 431–436. doi:10.1136/sti.2005.018002

Sandfort, T. G. M., Orr, M., Hirsch, J. S., & Santelli, J. (2008). Long-term health correlates of timing of sexual debut: Results from a national US study. *American Journal of Public Health, 98,* 155–161. doi:10.2105/AJPH.2006.097444

Santelli, J., Ott, M. A., Lyon, M., Rogers, J., & Summers, D. (2006). Abstinence-only education policies and programs: A position paper of the Society for Adolescent Medicine. *Journal of Adolescent Health, 38,* 83–87. doi:10.1016/j.jadohealth.2005.06.002

Santelli, J., Sandfort, T. G., & Orr, M. (2009). U. S./European differences in condom use. *Journal of Adolescent Health, 44,* 306. doi:10.1016/j.jadohealth.2008.12.017

Santelli, J. S. (2008). Medical accuracy in sexuality education: Ideology and the scientific process. *American Journal of Public Health, 98,* 1786–1792. doi:10.2105/AJPH.2007.119602

Sarracino, C., & Scott, K. M. (2008). *The porning of America.* Boston, MA: Beacon Press.

Sato, S. M., Schulz, K. M., Sisk, C. L., & Wood, R. I. (2008). Adolescents and androgens, receptors and rewards. *Hormones and Behavior, 53,* 647–658. doi:10.1016/j.yhbeh.2008.01.010

Savin-Williams, R. C., & Diamond, L. M. (2000). Sexual identity trajectories among sexual-minority youths: Gender comparisons. *Archives of Sexual Behavior, 29,* 607–627. doi:10.1023/A:1002058505138

Savin-Williams, R. C., & Ream, G. L. (2006). Pubertal onset and sexual orientation in an adolescent national probability sample. *Archives of Sexual Behavior, 35,* 279–286. doi:10.1007/s10508-006-9032-8

Schneewind, K. A. (2001). Socialization and education: Theoretical perspectives. In N. J. Smelser & P. B. Baltes (Eds.), *International encyclopedia of social and behavioral sciences* (pp. 14507–14513). Amsterdam, the Netherlands: Elsevier. doi:10.1016/B0-08-043076-7/02328-7

Schofield, M. G. (1965). *The sexual behaviour of young people.* London, England: Longman.

Schwartz, S. J., Phelps, E., Lerner, J. V., Huang, S., Brown, C. H., Lewin-Bizan, S., . . . Lerner, R. M. (2010). Promotion as prevention: Positive youth development as protective against tobacco, alcohol, illicit drug and sex initiation. *Applied Developmental Science, 14,* 197–211. doi:10.1080/10888691.2010.516186

Sharma, V., Sharma, A., Dave, S., & Chauhan, P. (1996). Sexual behavior of adolescent boys: A cause for concern. *Sexual and Marital Therapy, 11,* 147–151. doi:10.1080/02674659608404426

Shaver, P. R., & Hazan, C. (1988). A biased overview of the study of love. *Journal of Social and Personal Relationships, 5,* 473–501. doi:10.1177/0265407588054005

Shell, D. F., Newman, I. M., & Xiaoyi, F. (2010). The influence of cultural orientation, alcohol expectancies and self-efficacy on adolescent drinking behavior in Beijing. *Addiction, 105,* 1608–1615. doi:10.1111/j.1360-0443.2010.03006.x

Shrier, L. A., Koren, S., Aneja, P., & de Moor, C. (2010). Affect regulation, social context, and sexual intercourse in adolescents. *Archives of Sexual Behavior, 39,* 695–705. doi:10.1007/s10508-008-9394-1

Shulman, S., & Kipnis, O. (2001). Adolescent romantic relationships: A look from the future. *Journal of Adolescence, 24,* 337–351. doi:10.1006/jado.2001.0409

Shulman, S., & Scharf, M. (2000). Adolescent romantic behaviours and perceptions: Age-related differences and links with family and peer relationships. *Journal of Research on Adolescence, 10*, 99–118. doi:10.1207/SJRA1001_5

Sipsma, H. L., Ickovics, J. R., Lewis, J. B., Ethier, K. A., & Kershaw, T. S. (2011). Adolescent pregnancy desire and pregnancy incidence. *Women's Health Issues, 21*, 110–116. doi:10.1016/j.whi.2010.09.004

Smiler, A. P. (2008). "I wanted to get to know her better": Adolescent boys' dating motives, masculinity ideology, and sexual behavior. *Journal of Adolescence, 31*, 17–32. doi:10.1016/j.adolescence.2007.03.006

Smith, A., Rissel, C., Richters, J., Grulich, A., & de Visser, R. (2003). *Sex in Australia: Summary findings of the Australian Study of Health and Relationships.* Retrieved from http://www.slideshare.net/paigero/summary-findings-of-the-australian-study-of-health-and-relationships

Smith, P., & Welchans, S. (2000). Peer education: Does focusing on male responsibility change sexual assault attitudes? *Violence Against Women, 6*, 1255–1268. doi:10.1177/10778010022183622

Sneed, C. D. (2008). Parent-adolescent communication about sex: The impact of content and comfort on adolescent sexual behavior. *Journal of HIV/AIDS Prevention in Children and Youth, 9*, 70–83. doi:10.1080/10698370802126477

Snell, W. E., Jr., Fisher, T. D., & Miller, R. S. (1991). Development of the Sexual Awareness Questionnaire: Components, reliability and validity. *Annals of Sex Research, 4*, 65–92.

Sprecher, S. (1989). The importance to males and females of physical attractiveness, earning potential, and expressiveness in initial attraction. *Sex Roles, 21*, 591–607. doi:10.1007/BF00289173

Spriggs, A. L., & Halpern, C. T. (2008). Timing of sexual debut and initiation of postsecondary education by early adulthood. *Perspectives on Sexual and Reproductive Health, 40*, 152–161. doi:10.1363/4015208

Statistics Canada. (2010). *Canadian Internet use survey: Characteristics of individuals using the Internet* (Table 358-0124). Retrieved from http://www.statcan.gc.ca/tables-tableaux/sum-som/l01/cst01/comm35a-eng.htm

Statistics Canada. (2012). *Teenage pregnancy*. Retrieved from http://www.statcan.gc.ca/search-recherche/bb/info/3000020-eng.htm

Steinberg, L., & Monahan, K. C. (2011). Adolescents' exposure to sexy media does not hasten the initiation of sexual intercourse. *Developmental Psychology, 47*, 562–576. doi:10.1037/a0020613

Stevens, S. E., Steele, C. A., Jutai, J. W., & Kalnins, I. V. (1996). Adolescents with physical disabilities: Some psychosocial aspects of health. *Journal of Adolescent Health, 19*, 157–164. doi:10.1016/1054-139X(96)00027-4

Stodghill, R., II. (1998, June 15). Where'd you learn that? *Time Magazine*, pp. 52–59.

Stone, N., & Ingham, R. (2002). Factors affecting British teenagers' contraceptive use at first intercourse: The importance of partner communication. *Perspectives on Sexual and Reproductive Health, 34*, 191–197. doi:10.2307/3097729

Suarez, E., & Gadalla, T. M. (2010). Stop blaming the victim: A meta-analysis on rape myths. *Journal of Interpersonal Violence, 25*, 2010–2035. doi:10.1177/0886260509354503

Sullivan, E. V., Pfefferbaum, A., Rohlfing, T., Baker, F. C., Padilla, M. L., & Colrain, I. M. (2011). Developmental change in regional brain structure over 7 months in early adolescence. *NeuroImage, 57*, 214–224. doi:10.1016/j.neuroimage.2011.04.003

Swain, C. R., Ackerman, L. K., & Ackerman, M. A. (2006). The influence of individual characteristics and contraceptive beliefs on parent-teen sexual communications: A structural model. *Journal of Adolescent Health, 38*, 753.e9–753.e18.

Tabares, A., & Gottman, J. (2003). A marital process perspective of adolescent romantic relationships. In P. Florsheim (Ed.), *Adolescent romantic relations and sexual behavior: Theory, research, and practical implications* (pp. 337–354). Mahwah, NJ: Erlbaum.

Tanner, A. E., Hensel, D. J., & Fortenberry, J. D. (2010). A prospective study on the sexual, emotional, and behavioral correlates associated with young women's first and usual coital events. *Journal of Adolescent Health Care, 47*, 20–25. doi:10.1016/j.jadohealth.2009.12.031

Tanner, J. M. (1962). *Growth at adolescence.* Cambridge, MA: Blackwell.

Tanner, J. M. (1998). Sequence, tempo, and individual variation in growth and development of boys and girls aged twelve to sixteen. In R. E. Muuss & H. D. Porton (Eds.), *Adolescent behavior and society: A book of readings* (5th ed., pp. 34–46). New York, NY: McGraw-Hill.

Teitelman, A. M., Ratcliffe, S. J., & Cederbaum, J. A. (2008). Parent-adolescent communication about sexual pressure, maternal norms about relationship power, and STI/HIV protective behaviors of minority urban girls. *Journal of the American Psychiatric Nurses Association, 14*, 50–60. doi:10.1177/1078390307311770

Teitelman, A. M., Tennille, J., Bohinski, J. M., Jemmott, L. S., & Jemmott, J. B., III. (2011). Unwanted unprotected sex: Condom coercion by male partners and self-silencing of condom negotiation among adolescent girls. *Advances in Nursing Science, 34*, 243–259.

Thigpen, J. W., Pinkston, E. M., & Mayefsky, J. H. (2003). Normative sexual behavior of African American children. In J. Bancroft (Ed.), *Sexual development in childhood* (pp. 241–254). Bloomington: Indiana University Press.

Thompson, S. (1994). Teenage girls' narratives about sex. In A. S. Rossi (Ed.), *Sexuality across the life course* (pp. 209–232). Chicago, IL: University of Chicago Press.

Thornburg, D., & Lin, H. S. (2002). *Youth, pornography, and the Internet*. Washington, DC: National Academy Press.

Thornton, A., & Young-DeMarco, L. (2001). Four decades of trends in attitudes toward family issues in the United States: The 1960s through the 1990s. *Journal of Marriage and Family, 63*, 1009–1037. doi:10.1111/j.1741-3737.2001.01009.x

Tiefer, L. (1995). *Sex is not a natural act and other essays*. Boulder, CO: Westview Press.

Tiefer, L. (2004). Biological politics (read: propaganda) remains alive and well in sexology. *Feminism and Psychology, 14*, 436–441. doi:10.1177/0959353504044649

Tolman, D. L. (2001). Female adolescent sexuality: An argument for a developmental perspective on the new view of women's sexual problems. *Women & Therapy, 24*(1/2), 195–209. doi:10.1300/J015v24n01_21

Tolman, D. L. (2002a). *Dilemmas of desire: Teenage girls talk about sexuality*. Cambridge, MA: Harvard University Press.

Tolman, D. L. (2002b). Female adolescent sexuality: An argument for a developmental perspective on the new view of women's sexual problems. *Women and Therapy, 24*, 195–209. doi:10.1300/J015v24n01_21

Tolman, D. L. (2002c). Femininity as a barrier to positive sexual health for adolescent girls. In A. E. Hunter & C. Forden (Eds.), *Readings in the psychology of gender: Exploring our differences and commonalities* (pp. 196–206). Needham Heights, MA: Allyn & Bacon.

Tolman, D. L. (2003). Discussion paper. In J. Bancroft (Ed.), *Sexual development in childhood* (pp. 192–199). Bloomington: Indiana University Press.

Tolman, D. L., & McClelland, S. I. (2011). Normative sexuality development in adolescence: A decade in review, 2000–2009. *Journal of Research on Adolescence, 21*, 242–255. doi:10.1111/j.1532-7795.2010.00726.x

Topping, A. A., Milhausen, R. R., Graham, C. A., Sanders, S. A., Yarber, W. L., & Crosby, R. A. (2011). A comparison of condom use errors and problems for heterosexual anal and vaginal intercourse. *International Journal of STD and AIDS, 22*, 204–208. doi:10.1258/ijsa.2011.010259

Tracy, J. L., Shaver, P. R., Albino, A. W., & Cooper, M. (2003). Attachment styles and adolescent sexuality. In P. Florsheim & P. Florsheim (Eds.), *Adolescent romantic relations and sexual behavior: Theory, research, and practical implications* (pp. 137–159). Mahwah, NJ: Erlbaum.

Treas, J., & Giesen, D. (2000). Sexual infidelity among married and cohabitating Americans. *Journal of Marriage and the Family, 62*, 48–60. doi:10.1111/j.1741-3737.2000.00048.x

Turnbull, K., Nguyen, L. N., Jamieson, M. A., & Palerme, S. (2011). Seasonal trends in adolescent pregnancy conception rates. *Journal of Pediatric and Adolescent Gynecology, 24*, 291–293. doi:10.1016/j.jpag.2011.04.005

Udry, J. (1988). Biological predispositions and social control in adolescent sexual behavior. *American Sociological Review, 53*, 709–722. doi:10.2307/2095817

Udry, J., & Billy, J. O. (1987). Initiation of coitus in early adolescence. *American Sociological Review, 52*, 841–855. doi:10.2307/2095838

Udry, J. R. (1985). Androgenic hormones motivate serum sexual behavior in boys. *Fertility and Sterility, 43*, 90–94.

Udry, J. R., Talbert, L. M., & Morris, N. M. (1986). Biosocial foundations for adolescent female sexuality. *Demography, 23*, 217–230. doi:10.2307/2061617

Underwood, M. K., Rosen, L. H., More, D., Ehrenreich, S. E., & Gentsch, J. K. (2012). The Blackberry project: Capturing the content of adolescents' text messaging. *Developmental Psychology, 48*, 295–302. doi:10.1037/a0025914

UNFPA. (2012). *Reproductive health: Ensuring that every pregnancy is wanted.* Retrieved from http://www.unfpa.org/rh/planning.htm

UNICEF. (2001). *A league table of teenage births in rich nations* (Innocenti Report Card No. 3). Florence, Italy: Innocenti Research Centre.

UNICEF. (2005). *Early marriage: A harmful traditional practice: A statistical exploration.* New York, NY: Author.

U.S. Census Bureau. (2009). *Median age at first marriage for women.* Retrieved from http://factfinder2.census.gov/faces/nav/jsf/pages/index.xhtml

Valenti-Hein, D., & Choinski, C. (2007). Relationships and sexuality in adolescence and young adulthood. In A. Carr, G. O'Reilly, P. N. Walsh, & J. McEvoy (Eds.), *The handbook of intellectual disability and clinical psychology practice* (pp. 729–755). New York, NY: Routledge.

van Gelder, M. H. J., Reefhuis, J., Herron, A. M., Williams, M. L., & Roeleveld, N. (2011). Reproductive health characteristics of marijuana and cocaine users: Results from the 2002 national survey of family growth. *Perspectives on Sexual and Reproductive Health, 43*, 164–172. doi:10.1363/4316411

Vannier, S. A., & O'Sullivan, L. F. (2012). Who gives and who gets: Why, when, and with whom young people engage in oral sex. *Journal of Youth and Adolescence, 41*, 572–582. doi:10.1007/s10964-012-9745-z

Vargas, E., & Ponsoda, V. (2010). Sexual activity scale: A measure to predict the early onset of sexual intercourse. *Behavioral Psychology/Psicología Conductual, 18*, 591–611.

Vasilenko, S. A., Ram, N., & Lefkowitz, E. S. (2011). Body image and first sexual intercourse in late adolescence. *Journal of Adolescence, 34*, 327–335. doi:10.1016/j.adolescence.2010.04.005

Wallmyr, G., & Welin, C. (2006). Young people, pornography, and sexuality: Sources and attitudes. *Journal of School Nursing, 22*, 290–295. doi:10.1177/10598405060220050801

Walls, N. E., & Bell, S. (2011). Correlates of engaging in survival sex among homeless youth and young adults. *Journal of Sex Research, 48*, 423–436. doi:10.1080/00224499.2010.501916

Walsh, J. L., Ward, L., Caruthers, A., & Merriwether, A. (2011). Awkward or amazing: Gender and age trends in first intercourse experiences. *Psychology of Women Quarterly, 35*, 59–71. doi:10.1177/0361684310387781

Wamoyi, J., Fenwick, A., Urassa, M., Zaba, B., & Stones, W. (2011). "Women's bodies are shops": Beliefs about transactional sex and implications for understanding gender power and HIV prevention in Tanzania. *Archives of Sexual Behavior, 40*, 5–15. doi:10.1007/s10508-010-9646-8

Ward, L. (2003). Understanding the role of entertainment media in the sexual socialization of American youth: A review of empirical research. *Developmental Review, 23*, 347–388. doi:10.1016/S0273-2297(03)00013-3

Ward, L., & Friedman, K. (2006). Using TV as a guide: Associations between television viewing and adolescents' sexual attitudes and behavior. *Journal of Research on Adolescence, 16*, 133–156. doi:10.1111/j.1532-7795.2006.00125.x

Ward, L. M., Day, K. M., & Epstein, M. (2006). Uncommonly good: Exploring how mass media may be a positive influence on young women's sexual health and development. *New Directions for Child and Adolescent Development, 112*, 57–70. doi:10.1002/cd.162

Watt, M. H., Aunon, F. M., Skinner, D., Sikkema, K. J., Kalichman, S. C., & Pieterse, D. (2012). "Because he has bought for her, he wants to sleep with her": Alcohol as currency for sexual exchange in South African drinking venues. *Social Science and Medicine, 74*, 1005–1012. doi:10.1016/j.socscimed.2011.12.022

Waylen, A. E., Ness, A., McGovern, P., Wolke, D., & Low, N. (2010). Romantic and sexual behavior in young adolescents: Repeated surveys in a population-based cohort. *Journal of Early Adolescence, 30*, 432–443. doi:10.1177/0272431609338179

Weinhardt, L. S., & Carey, M. P. (2000). Does alcohol lead to sexual risk behavior? Findings from event-level research. *Annual Review of Sex Research, 11*, 125–157.

Weinstock, H., Berman, S., & Cates, W., Jr. (2004). Sexually transmitted diseases among American youth: Incidence and prevalence estimates, 2000. *Perspectives on Sexual and Reproductive Health, 36*, 6–10. doi:10.1363/3600604

Weiss, D., & Bullough, V. L. (2004). Adolescent American sex. *Journal of Psychology and Human Sexuality, 16*, 43–53. doi:10.1300/J056v16n02_04

Wellings, K., Nanchahal, K., Macdowall, W., McManus, S., Erens, B., Mercer, C. H., . . . Field, J. (2001). Sexual behavior in Britain: Early heterosexual experience. *Lancet, 358*, 1843–1850. doi:10.1016/S0140-6736(01)06885-4

Wells, S., Mihic, L., Tremblay, P. F., Graham, K., & Demers, A. (2008). Where, with whom, and how much alcohol is consumed on drinking events involving aggression? Event-level associations in a Canadian national survey of university students. *Alcoholism: Clinical and Experimental Research, 32*, 522–533. doi:10.1111/j.1530-0277.2007.00596.x

Welsh, D. P., Haugen, P. T., Widman, L., Darling, N., & Grello, C. M. (2005). Kissing is good: A developmental investigation of sexuality in adolescent romantic couples. *Sexuality Research and Social Policy, 2*, 32–41.

Whisman, M. A., & Snyder, D. K. (2007). Sexual infidelity in a national survey of American women: Differences in prevalence and correlates as a function of method of assessment. *Journal of Family Psychology, 21*, 147–154. doi:10.1037/0893-3200.21.2.147

Whitaker, D. J., & Miller, K. S. (2000). Parent-adolescent discussions about sex and condoms: Impact on peer influences of sexual risk behavior. *Journal of Adolescent Research, 15*, 251–273. doi:10.1177/0743558400152004

Widmer, E. D. (1997). Influence of older siblings on initiation of sexual intercourse. *Journal of Marriage and the Family, 59*, 928–938. doi:10.2307/353793

Williams, L. R., & Hickle, K. E. (2011). "He cheated on me, I cheated on him back": Mexican American and White adolescents' perceptions of cheating in romantic relationships. *Journal of Adolescence, 34*, 1005–1016. doi:10.1016/j.adolescence.2010.11.007

Williams, S., Connolly, J., & Segal, Z. V. (2001). Intimacy in relationships and cognitive vulnerability to depression in adolescent girls. *Cognitive Therapy and Research, 25*, 477–496. doi:10.1023/A:1005590720895

Williams, T., Connolly, J., & Cribbie, R. (2008). Light and heavy heterosexual activities of young Canadian adolescents: Normative patterns and differential predictors. *Journal of Research on Adolescence, 18*, 145–172. doi:10.1111/j.1532-7795.2008.00554.x

Wilson, E. K., & Koo, H. P. (2010). Mothers, fathers, sons, and daughters: Gender differences in factors associated with parent-child communication about sexual topics. *Reproductive Health, 7*, 31–39. doi:10.1186/1742-4755-7-31

Winter, L. (1988). The role of sexual self-concept in the use of contraceptives. *Family Planning Perspectives, 20*, 123–127. doi:10.2307/2135700

Wolak, J., Mitchell, K., & Finkelhor, D. (2007). Unwanted and wanted exposure to online pornography in a national sample of youth Internet users. *Pediatrics, 119*, 247–257. doi:10.1542/peds.2006-1891

Woody, J. D., D'Souza, H. J., & Woody, J. K. (2000). Adolescent non-coital sexual activity: Comparisons of virgins and non-virgins. *Journal of Sex Education and Therapy, 25*, 261–268.

World Health Organization. (2012). *Initiative for vaccine research (IVR): Sexually transmitted diseases.* Retrieved from http://www.who.int/vaccine_research/diseases/soa_std/en/index.html

Worling, J. (2012). The assessment and treatment of deviant sexual arousal with adolescents who have offended sexually. *Journal of Sexual Aggression, 18*, 36–63. doi:10.1080/13552600.2011.630152

Zimmer-Gembeck, M. J. (1999). Stability, change and individual differences in involvement with friends and romantic partners among adolescent females. *Journal of Youth and Adolescence, 28*, 419–438. doi:10.1023/A:1021612907073

Zimmer-Gembeck, M. J., & Helfand, M. (2008). Ten years of longitudinal research on U.S. adolescent sexual behavior: Developmental correlates of sexual intercourse, and the importance of age, gender and ethnic background. *Developmental Review, 28*, 153–224. doi:10.1016/j.dr.2007.06.001

Zufferey, A., Michaud, P., Jeannin, A., Berchtold, A., Chossis, I., van Melle, G., & Suris, J. C. (2007). Cumulative risk factors for adolescent alcohol misuse and its perceived consequences among 16 to 20 year old adolescents in Switzerland. *Preventive Medicine, 45*, 233–239. doi:10.1016/j.ypmed.2007.04.015

CHAPTER 16

SEXUALITY IN EMERGING ADULTHOOD

Carolyn T. Halpern and Christine E. Kaestle

> I'm cookie dough. I'm not done baking. I'm not finished becoming whoever the hell it is I'm gonna turn out to be. I make it through this, and the next thing, and the next thing, and maybe one day, I turn around and realize I'm ready. I'm cookies. And then, you know, if I want someone to enjoy warm, delicious, cookie me, then that's fine. That'll be then. When I'm done.—Buffy the Vampire Slayer, explaining why she was not yet ready for a committed long-term relationship (Whedon, 2003)

Just a few years before Buffy observed that she needed more time to bake, psychologist Jeffrey Arnett proposed that major shifts in demographic and economic trends, including earlier and nonmarital sexual initiation, increased number of sexual partners, and later entry into marriage and childbearing (Heck, Schoendorf, Ventura, & Kiely, 1997; Loh & Ram, 1990; Matthews & Hamilton, 2009; Thornton, 1988; Witwer, 1993), had profoundly affected the life course of young people (Arnett & Tanner, 2011a). Arnett (2000, 2011) argued that 18- to 29-year-old youths living in industrialized Western societies today inhabit a new stage of "emerging adulthood" in which they are no longer truly adolescents but do not yet have the financial or educational foundation to strike out as independent adults. Emerging adulthood is characterized not only by the delay of marriage, career, and parenthood but also by the deinstitutionalization and disruption of traditional normative sequences of such markers of adulthood (Arnett & Tanner, 2011a; Cherlin, 2004; Mouw, 2005; Rindfuss, 1991; Thornton, 1989). However, within the context of this heterogeneity, identity issues are theorized to consistently rise to the surface, and clarifying identity is possibly young people's primary developmental task at this stage as they explore the possibilities of the adult world (Arnett & Tanner, 2011a; Erikson, 1968).

Although the concept of emerging adulthood, and its utility, have been debated in various fields, its purported elements and focus on individual experimentation have been noted across decades and described widely using alternative terms and descriptions, including *not quite adults* (Settersten & Ray, 2010), *arrested adulthood* (Côté, 2000), *quarter life crisis* (A. Robbins & Wilner, 2001), *prolonged adolescence* (Erikson, 1968), *prolonged psychosocial moratorium* (Erikson, 1968; Hendry & Kloep, 2011), *youth* (Keniston, 1971), *novice phase* (Levinson, 1978), and *the transition to adulthood* (Settersten, Furstenberg, & Rumbaut, 2005). For the purposes of this chapter, we explore the potential application of the emerging adulthood perspective to sexuality during the late teens and into the 20s rather than debate the broader status and merit of emerging adulthood as a theoretical construct or

We greatly appreciate the assistance of Kelly L. Strutz, MPH, in organizing literature citations and proofreading manuscript drafts. Carolyn T. Halpern was partially supported by Eunice Kennedy Shriver National Institute of Child Health and Human Development Grant R01HD57046 (Carolyn T. Halpern, Principal Investigator) and by Carolina Population Center Grant 5 R24 HD050924, awarded to the Carolina Population Center at the University of North Carolina at Chapel Hill by the Eunice Kennedy Shriver National Institute of Child Health and Human Development.

http://dx.doi.org/10.1037/14193-016
APA Handbook of Sexuality and Psychology: Vol. 1. Person-Based Approaches, D. L. Tolman and L. M. Diamond (Editors-in-Chief)

a stage theory (Arnett, 2011). To date, the emerging adulthood framework has been extensively applied to questions in the domains of education, jobs, and financial independence, but its potential implications for understanding sexuality and sexual development have not yet been realized. For example, a recent (August 27, 2012) Web of Science citation search of the original article in which Arnett (2000) coined the term *emerging adulthood* and presented a theory of emerging adulthood yielded citations by 1,322 peer-reviewed articles; however, of those only 75 represented original research on sex or sexuality.

FEATURES OF EMERGING ADULTHOOD AND SEXUAL DEVELOPMENTAL TASKS

Arnett (2004) proposed five features that make emerging adulthood distinct: identity exploration, self-focus, feeling in between, age of possibilities, and instability. The opening cookie-dough metaphor from *Buffy the Vampire Slayer* captures these features by expressing a state of identity exploration that encompasses feeling in between but with an awareness of possibilities from a self-focused perspective. It describes a person awaiting further development before settling into a committed long-term romantic relationship. This time of experimentation may have important ramifications for self-development and life trajectories (Arnett, 2000; Martin & Smyer, 1990), as emerging adults "recenter" their interpersonal connections from dependency on parents to stable and intimate connections with other adults (Tanner, 2006).

In terms of sexuality, the broad theme of identity encompasses a variety of intraindividual psychosocial dimensions related to definitions, attitudes, values, and goals, whereas instability is more closely aligned with patterns of partnering and characteristics of relationships that may influence relationship quality and duration (see Chapter 10, this volume). For example, instability may reflect concerns about settling down and taking on enduring responsibilities. Alternatively, as individuals explore their personal and sexual identities, they may find that relationships that once seemed satisfying are no longer a good fit and may want to move on to other partners in the hopes of finding "the one." Havighurst (1948) proposed that among the developmental tasks of young adulthood (defined as ages 19–30) were the tasks of developing a stable partnership, learning to live with the partner, and establishing a family and an independent household. We suggest that an inherent tension exists between the exploratory and self-focused aspects of emerging adulthood and developmental tasks linked to increasing intimacy, seriousness, and commitment. Does the emerging adulthood framework imply that one must go through a number of relationships or sexual encounters before one can identify the right person and the right sexual space? Does sexual exploration in emerging adulthood ultimately contribute to better sexual health, or do instability and exploration impede later relationship stability and sexual satisfaction? Are there optimal amounts or types of exploration? Do these associations vary in relation to biopsychosocial categories such as gender, sexual orientation, socioeconomic class, or race/ethnicity?

In this chapter, we explore these questions by describing current patterns of partnering, sexual behavior, sexual attitudes and identity, and selected aspects of reproductive health. We rely primarily on research conducted since approximately 2004 to examine the intersection of emerging adulthood theoretical themes and the empirical literature.[1] We then bring together the themes in the emerging adult sexuality literature and theory and assess whether the construct of emerging adulthood can usefully inform a strategy for researching sexuality during this developmental period. Finally, we discuss some of the methodological issues in this literature and suggest future research directions.

CULTURAL CONTEXT FOR SEXUALITY IN EMERGING ADULTHOOD

It is surprising that the emerging adulthood framework, which on the face of it would seem to hold special relevance to sexuality, has to date only been modestly applied to sexual research. Recent demographic shifts in timing and sequence of marriage

[1]For a thorough summary of relevant research conducted before 2004, we refer readers to Lefkowitz and Gillen (2006).

and childbearing, some of the factors prompting the development of the construct of emerging adulthood, have been accompanied by profound changes in cultural attitudes about sex and romance, including greater acceptance of cohabitation (Cherlin, 2004; Seltzer, 2004; Thornton, 1988), premarital sex (Thornton, 1989; Treas, 2002), and diverse sexualities (Treas, 2002). Cultural change offers more sexual identity possibilities and pathways to consider and explore, and an increasingly sanctioned extended period of time for that exploration. During adolescence, most individuals start to explore recreational dating, fall in love, and, increasingly, initiate noncoital and coital sexual activity (Connolly, Craig, Goldberg, & Pepler, 2004; Regan, Durvasula, Howell, Ureño, & Rea, 2004; Roscoe, Diana, & Brooks, 1987). However, during emerging adulthood the focus shifts toward greater intimacy and seriousness (Arnett, 2000; Banker, Kaestle, & Allen, 2010; Cantor, Acker, & Cook-Flannagan, 1992; Montgomery, 2005). Although often exploratory and lacking enduring commitment, romantic relationships tend to last longer than they did during adolescence, and they may involve cohabitation as young people explore deeper levels of emotional and physical intimacy (Arnett, 2000; Thornton, 1988). In the emerging adulthood framework, through this culturally sanctioned search for a soul mate, emerging adults explore not only the kind of person they would like to be with in the long term but implicitly discover more about their own self-identity, including their sexual identity, through these experiences (Arnett, 2000; Barry, Madsen, Nelson, Carroll, & Badger, 2009; Cherlin, 2004; Zimmer-Gembeck & Petherick, 2006; see Chapters 19 and 20, this volume).

Changes in attitudes about sexual behavior, pace, and identity have been fueled partially by historic shifts in the structure of and access to the cultural environment. The digital revolution has provided today's youths with unprecedented access to diverse information and points of view and instant connectivity to the social world through the media devices that surround them and fill their hands and pockets and laps (Brown & Bobkowski, 2011; see Volume 2, Chapter 3, this handbook). The present media environment offers new opportunities for interaction and for seeking images and content that are driven by identity aspiration. Thus, the media facilitate sexual identity construction in novel ways (Brown & Bobkowski, 2011; Davis, 2010; Pempek, Yermolayeva, & Calvert, 2009; Steele, 1999). Both new and old media can be important sources of information and inspiration for developing sexual scripts because content is easily accessible and often explicit (Brown & Bobkowski, 2011; Buerkel-Rothfuss, Greenberg, & Brown, 1993; Ward, 2003).

Even though most sexual activity in emerging adulthood typically occurs in the context of romantic relationships (Furman & Shaffer, 2011), media depictions of sexuality generally involve little commitment on the part of couples and few negative reproductive health consequences such as sexually transmitted infection (STI) or unintended pregnancy, thus implicitly extolling the merits of exploration and change. Yet, the media also embody traditional gender roles and stereotypes and narratives depicting negative outcomes when gender roles are breached (Brown, 2002; Kunkel et al., 2007; Pardun, L'Engle, & Brown, 2005; Ward, 2002; Ward & Friedman, 2006), yielding mixed messages about normative and acceptable sexual scripts for young men and women. This conflicting content is important because longitudinal research has suggested that the sexual media content that is consumed by adolescents influences later sexual attitudes and behaviors as youths enter emerging adulthood (Brown & Bobkowski, 2011; Chandra et al., 2008; R. L. Collins et al., 2004; Peter & Valkenburg, 2008, 2011; see Volume 2, Chapter 12, this handbook).

The unprecedented amount of information and conflicting portrayals of sexual scripts encountered by emerging adults today are reflected in how they communicate and the language they use to describe their sexual and romantic experiences. Emerging adults use a large, diverse, and ever-evolving vocabulary to refer to romantic and sexual relationships (Banker et al., 2010; Furman & Hand, 2006; Surra, Boettcher-Burke, Cottle, West, & Gray, 2007), and the meaning of shifting labels may be unclear and confusing. The ideal relationship is often described in romanticized language, with emerging adults yearning for relationships they describe as true or deep or real, but there seems to be no agreed-on single label to distinguish such ideal relationships from less fulfilling or less committed ones (Banker et al., 2010).

Also, little agreement exists regarding what might seem to be a more concrete issue: what constitutes having had sex. Studies of college students have typically found that oral sex is not considered sex (Bogart, Cecil, Wagstaff, Pinkerton, & Abramson, 2000; Gute, Eshbaugh, & Wiersma, 2008; Pitts & Rahman, 2001). Furthermore, the definitions of nonromantic sexual relationship terms among emerging adults (such as *hook-ups* or *friends with benefits* [FWBs]) are also often unclear and ambiguous (Banker et al., 2010), and the type of sexual behavior that is likely to occur varies even within a given type of nonromantic encounter (Furman & Shaffer, 2011). In fact, young people often admit to great confusion over how to categorize their own relationship or how to talk to their partners about their relationship (Abbey, 1987; Banker et al., 2010; Bogle, 2008). This ambiguity in feelings toward sexual relations and discomfort in communicating with partners about expectations can lead to confusion and painful emotions (Banker et al., 2010; Eshbaugh & Gute, 2008).

In sum, emerging adulthood is thought to be characterized by exploration, instability, and self-focus, perhaps reflected in experimentation with risky behavior. In terms of sexual and romantic partnering, one might expect it to be manifested in an extended period of sexual exploration, perhaps with greater partner accumulation, and a fluidity in values and identity that is eventually integrated and stable. Indeed, studies have suggested that many emerging adults feel they should engage in a wide range of experiences before they settle down with adult responsibilities (Ravert, 2009), implying that what has often been deemed to be risky sexual behavior is more appropriately conceptualized as a normative developmental phenomenon (Haydon, McRee, & Halpern, 2011; Lam & Lefkowitz, 2012). If this pattern of sexuality does characterize emerging adulthood, it raises the question of whether greater exploration enhances the quality of sexual satisfaction and facilitates completion of Havighurst's (1948) tasks of achieving stable and happy partnerships and good reproductive health. If it does, then it suggests that periods of heterogeneous change may be developmentally useful for sexual health and development. Alternatively, instability and the lengthy sexual exploration that may result from a perceived need to find the right partner at the right time may actually impede achievement of committed relationships and satisfying sexual experiences. We turn now to a description of selected aspects of the literature on sexuality during emerging adulthood, with an eye toward findings that may suggest answers to questions about the implications of extended sexual exploration and postponement of commitment to sexual health. We start with a description of sexual patterns among contemporary emerging adults.

SEXUAL DEMOGRAPHY OF EMERGING ADULTS IN THE UNITED STATES

Today most Americans have sex before they marry. According to the 2002 National Survey of Family Growth (NSFG), 93% of respondents had had premarital sex by age 30 (Finer, 2007). Similarly, estimates from 2001 data from the National Longitudinal Study of Adolescent Health (Add Health) indicated that almost 90% of the 18- to 27-year-old respondents interviewed had had premarital sex (Halpern, Waller, Spriggs, & Hallfors, 2006). Thus, most emerging adults in the United States are sexually active, regardless of marital status. In this section, we use nationally representative data to describe broad patterns of sexual partnering, behavior, values, and identity and the implications of those patterns for reproductive health among emerging adults. For an overview of population patterns, we rely largely on the 2006–2010 NSFG (N = 22,682, response rate = 77%; Copen, Daniels, Vespa, & Mosher, 2012), a nationally representative multistage probability sample drawn from 85 areas across the United States, and Add Health, a prospective cohort study of a national probability sample of U.S. adolescents in Grades 7 to 12 in 1994 through 1995 (Harris et al., 2009). Four in-home Add Health interview waves have been completed to date, most recently in 2008 (Wave 4), when respondents were ages 24 to 32 (N = 15,701, response rate = 80%). Interviews conducted at Wave 3 when respondents were ages 18 to 26 also captured a portion of the emerging adulthood period.

Partnering: Marriage, Cohabitation, and Casual Sex Partners

In the sections that follow we describe patterns of partnering among emerging adults, with a focus on marriage, cohabitation, and casual sex partnering or "hook-ups." Overall, compared with past generations, today's emerging adults delay marriage longer, are more likely to cohabit before marriage, and are likely to have had at least one casual sexual experience.

Marriage. Dramatic but socioculturally uneven changes in marriage patterns have emerged over the past half century. In 1960, 68% of U.S. adults in their 20s were married; in 2008, only 28% were (Pew Research Center, 2010). This postponement is reflected in the median age at first marriage of 25.8 for women and 28.3 for men (Copen et al., 2012), compared with 23.9 for women and 26.1 for men in 1990 (U.S. Census Bureau, 2004). Data from the 2006–2010 NSFG indicated that the probability of first marriage by age 25 is 44% for women compared with 59% in 1995, a decrease of 25%. However, patterns vary by race/ethnicity. White women have the highest probability (48%) of first marriage by age 25, and Black women have the lowest (24%). The probability of first marriage by age 35 is 85% for Asians and 84% for Whites, followed by U.S.-born Hispanics (68%) and Black women (58%; Copen et al., 2012). Women with a high school diploma have a higher probability of first marriage by age 25 (53%) than women who have a bachelor's degree (37%). However, this probability reverses at older ages. By age 35, women with a bachelor's degree (84%) have a higher probability of marriage than women with a high school diploma (78%).

Relatively few men marry by age 25. Looking at the probability of first marriage by age 35, Asian (80%) and White (74%) men have the highest probabilities; Black (61%) and U.S.-born Hispanic (60%) men have the lowest. Unlike women, the probability of first marriage by age 35 is not significantly different between men with a bachelor's degree (73%) and those with a high school diploma (71%; Copen et al., 2012).

Divorce rates for men are estimated at 1% between the ages of 20 and 24 and 7.5% between the ages of 25 and 29. For women, respective estimates are higher at 2.6% and 11.9%. For those between the ages of 25 and 29, 15% of the ever-married men and 18.9% of the ever-married women have experienced a divorce (Kreider, 2005). Women and men who cohabit with their future spouse before first marriage are more likely to divorce than those who do not (Dush, Cohan, & Amato, 2003; Rodrigues, Hall, & Fincham, 2006; Teachman, 2003). However, that association is less evident in more recent cohorts (Manning & Cohen, 2012; Reinhold, 2010), suggesting the possibility of a weakening of this relationship (Copen et al., 2012).

Within this context of delayed marital timing, however, a significant minority of young adults report they would like to be married (about 20% of unmarried young men and about 30% of unmarried young women; Regnerus & Uecker, 2011). Emerging adults who are religious, who are in a romantic or sexual relationship, or who are cohabiting are more likely to want to be married. Moreover, analyses of data from the 1992 National Health and Social Life Survey, a national probability sample of 3,432 English-speaking Americans ages 18 to 59 (Laumann, Gagnon, Michael, & Michaels, 1994), suggest that when sexual interest and values, opportunities, type and satisfaction with primary relationship, and various demographic risk variables are taken into consideration, emerging adults are no more likely to show sexual infidelity than are older adults (Treas & Giesen, 2000), again suggesting valuing of commitment.

Cohabitation. The majority of young adults approve of nonmarital cohabitation (Axinn & Thornton, 2000), and many perceive living together as an appropriate way to "try out" a relationship (Thornton & Young-DeMarco, 2001). Cohabitation has almost doubled since 1990 (Pew Research Center, 2010), and it is increasingly the first coresidential union formed among young adults in the United States (Kennedy & Bumpass, 2008), contributing to the delay in first marriage.[2]

[2] However, if one considers entry into any marriage or cohabitation, then the timing of a first union occurs at roughly the same point in the life course as marriage did in the past (Bumpass, Sweet, & Cherlin, 1991).

Data from the 2006–2010 NSFG indicate that for women, 18.7% of 20- to 24-year-olds and 16.8% of 25- to 29-year-olds were currently cohabiting. For men, 15.0% of 20- to 24-year-olds and 19.5% of 25- to 29-year-olds were currently cohabiting (Copen et al., 2012). Wave 4 Add Health data also indicated that cohabitation is common among emerging adults, with about one in five men and women ages 24 to 32 residing with a nonmarital romantic partner at the time of the 2008 interview (our calculations). Racial/ethnic differences in the prevalence of cohabitation exist, as shown in Table 16.1. Black women are less likely than White women to cohabit at ages 18 to 19 but are approximately equally likely to cohabit at ages 20 to 29. Similarly, Black men are less likely than White men to cohabit up to age 24 but more likely between ages 25 and 29. In contrast, Latina women and Latino men are more likely than their non-Hispanic White counterparts to cohabit at all ages. Class differences are also evident. Individuals from lower income families, especially women, are more likely to transition to cohabitation (and marriage) earlier. Add Health data, for example, indicated that 33% of women in the lowest income quintile will cohabit by age 20, compared with 19% of women in the top income quintile (Meier & Allen, 2008). First cohabitations, on average, are shorter in duration than first marriages. For men who marry between ages 20 and 25, the marriage has a 78% probability of lasting 5 years; the parallel estimate for cohabitation is 14%. Figures for women are virtually identical at 79% and 14%, respectively (Goodwin, Mosher, & Chandra, 2010).

Qualitative data have suggested that emerging adults choose to cohabit for a variety of reasons, including finances, convenience, and in response to difficult relationships with parents. However, in contrast to survey reports (e.g., Thornton & Young-DeMarco, 2001), they do not necessarily see cohabitation as a trial to explore marriage and compatibility, nor do they tend to mention access to a sexual partner as an important reason to cohabit (Sassler, 2004). Individuals who transition to cohabitation rapidly, however, may be motivated to a greater extent by intense attraction (Sassler, 2004).

Casual sex partners and hook-ups. The literature on hooking up, or having intimate physical encounters without expectations of an ongoing relationship, is now relatively large. However, most work is based on college students, relies on convenience samples, focuses on differences between men and women (e.g., university-attending men are more likely to report engaging in casual sex than women; Owen & Fincham, 2011; Schwartz et al., 2011), and typically excludes examination of class, color, sexual orientation, and intersections with more traditional sexual paradigms shaped by institutions such as religion. Estimates of the prevalence of hook-up experience have varied, depending on the methodology used, but findings have ranged from two thirds to as many as 80% of North American college students reporting at least one hook-up experience at some point during college (Garcia, Reiber, Massey, & Merriwether, 2012; Heldman & Wade, 2010), and a quarter of college students who hook up will do so 10 or more times during their time in college (England, Schafer, & Fogarty, 2007). Estimates from the national Add Health sample have suggested that 71% of young adults ages 24 to 32, those with and without college experience, have had at least one hook-up, defined as having any type of sex with a male or female partner on one and only one occasion (Goldberg, Hussey, & Halpern, 2012). Of the work to date, most studies have examined correlates of hooking up, which include favorable attitudes about the behavior, greater alcohol use, and lower psychological well-being (e.g., Fielder & Carey, 2010a; Grello, Welsh, & Harper, 2006; Manning, Longmore, & Giordano, 2005; Owen, Rhoades, Stanley, & Fincham, 2010; Paul, McManus, & Hayes, 2000). Bogle (2008) suggested that the college campus enables casual sexual experimentation by its lack of personal supervision and easy access to peers. Alumni typically discontinue hooking up, probably because the change in context no longer supports the behavior. However, education level was not associated with the likelihood of a lifetime hook-up in the Add Health analysis (Goldberg et al., 2012).

As noted earlier regarding labels, there is ambiguity in what constitutes a hook-up, ranging from one-time encounters to regular encounters with friends. The sexual content of a hook-up also varies, with some not involving genital contact and

TABLE 16.1

Percentages of Women and Men Ages 18 to 29 Who Are Married or Cohabiting, by Age and Race/Ethnicity, National Survey of Family Growth Cycle 6, 2002

	Women (%)		Men (%)	
Age and race/ethnicity	Marriage	Cohabitation	Marriage	Cohabitation
18–19				
White	4.7	11.6	[a]	3.5
Black	[a]	4.7	[a]	[a]
Latino	9.2	13.5	[a]	3.9
Total	4.8	10.8	0.7	3.4
20–24				
White	23.4	15.2	16.3	12.8
Black	10.8	15.5	11.5	11.0
Latino	32.4	20.7	17.7	15.9
Total	23.1	15.7	15.4	13.4
25–29				
White	56.9	11.7	50.4	16.4
Black	31.4	11.0	26.9	21.3
Latino	48.6	19.3	41.6	21.9
Total	51.6	12.9	45.3	17.8

Note. From "Marriage and Cohabitation in the United States: A Statistical Portrait Based on Cycle 6 (2002) of the National Survey of Family Growth," by P. Y. Goodwin, W. D. Mosher, and A Chandra, 2010, *Vital and Health Statistics, 23*(28).
[a]Figure does not meet standards of reliability and precision.

approximately 40% ("most recent encounter") entailing vaginal intercourse (England et al., 2007). Some estimates for men are higher, with half of their most recent encounters involving vaginal sex (Paul et al., 2000). However, given suggestions that the past decade has seen significant change in the prevalence of oral and anal sex (Heldman & Wade, 2010) and the date differences in the conduct of these studies, whether actual sex differences occur in the context of hook-ups is not clear.

Just as adolescents may overestimate the number of their peers who are sexually active, university students may overestimate the prevalence, frequency, and intimate sexual content of campus hook-ups (Bogle, 2008; Freitas, 2008). Moreover, the meaning of hooking up to participants is not clear, given variations in research findings. Although most students report physical pleasure as a motivation (Garcia & Reiber, 2008), and even though there is a gender gap in pleasure as measured by orgasm (Armstrong, England, & Fogarty, 2012), some work has indicated that both men and women may see hooking up as a new strategy for starting relationships (England et al., 2007; Garcia & Reiber, 2008). Other work has suggested that hooking up may mean different things for young women and men, with women being more likely to anticipate a hook-up leading to a relationship (Grello et al., 2006). However, this does not mean that young men uniformly want a no-strings-attached relationship. Qualitative work has suggested that many men also see room in hook-ups for relational connection and have diverse motives for the activity. Few entirely adopt or reject nonrelational sex (Epstein, Calzo, Smiler, & Ward, 2009), and estimates have suggested that a majority of both young men and women in emerging adulthood would prefer a romantic relationship to a hook-up (Garcia et al., 2012).

In between one-time sexual encounters and committed relationships are longer arrangements for uncommitted sex, which have been termed *FWBs*, *booty calls*, and *fuck buddies*. One estimate has suggested that approximately 60% of undergraduates have been involved in booty-call relationships at some point (Bisson & Levine, 2009). These relationships appear to share features of both casual and more serious sexual relationships, and they may be appealing to both men and women for different reasons. They entail low emotional investment, possibly more appealing to men, yet offer an ongoing period of interaction that may allow for testing the waters, a feature likely of interest to women (Jonason, Li, & Richardson, 2011).

In some sense, hooking up or engaging in booty calls could be thought of as epitomizing the early adulthood period, reflecting the postponement of commitment and a new narcissism, and providing opportunities to explore sexual values and desires. Hooking up could serve to foster a sense of sexual competence and serve as a healthy outlet for sexual agency (Hamilton & Armstrong, 2009) via multiple encounters with diverse partners. We were unable to locate any studies that directly tested this hypothesis. However, studies have examined post–hook-up consequences such as positive and negative affect and physical health implications. Findings have suggested that high rates of impersonal sex (sexual behavior that is primarily concerned with and focused upon the sex act itself) may be associated with negative health correlates, especially for women (Schwartz et al., 2011). Hook-ups may also elevate the odds of contracting an STI, given a potentially greater number of unplanned sexual encounters (Heldman & Wade, 2010) and lower likelihood of condom use when sex has not been planned (Fielder & Carey, 2010b; Lewis, Granato, Blayney, Lostutter, & Kilmer, 2012; MacDonald & Hynie, 2008; Paul et al., 2000). However, implications for STIs may be more complex, because some work has suggested that a positive attitude toward casual sexual activity is associated with a greater likelihood of condom use (Lewis et al., 2012; see Chapter 23, this volume).

Relatively few studies have examined the potential mental health implications of casual sexual activity and whether implications vary across developmental periods. Both male and female students report varying degrees of post–hook-up emotional distress, such as feelings of isolation, regret, lower self-esteem, or depressive symptoms (Owen, Fincham, & Moore, 2011; Paul et al., 2000). In the small number of longitudinal studies that have been completed, findings have conflicted with regard to linkages between hooking up and psychological distress (e.g., Fielder & Carey, 2010a; Grello, Welsh, Harper, & Dickson, 2003), and there is variation in reports of positive and negative reactions. To date, findings have suggested that women may be more likely to respond negatively (e.g., Glenn & Marquardt, 2001; Grello et al., 2006; Owen et al., 2010). For example, Owen et al. (2010) found that almost half (49%) of young women endorsed negative adjectives after hooking up compared with only 26% of young men. However, other work with more nuanced measures of emotional reaction has found that both men and women had more positive than negative responses to the encounter (Owen & Fincham, 2011), and those with positive attitudes about hook-ups and sexual activity more generally showed the greatest positive affect (Lewis et al., 2012). The apparent moderating effect of sociosexual attitudes on condom use and post–hook-up affect further underscores the need for longitudinal research to assess immediate and longer term implications of casual sexual activity and the need for explicit consideration in these studies of sociosexuality and individuals' approval of and willingness to engage in uncommitted sexual relations (Simpson & Gangestad, 1991).

Given the lingering double standard regarding sexuality, it is reasonable to expect that the potential implications of hook-ups may vary for women and men depending on the context and outcomes under consideration. For example, some studies have found that women are more likely to report regret or feeling pressured to perform unwanted sex acts (Paul & Hayes, 2002). Women are judged negatively when they engage in multiple hook-ups, whereas men's status may increase (England et al., 2007; Glenn & Marquardt, 2001; Hamilton & Armstrong, 2009). Thus, women are much more likely to suffer in terms of reputational repercussions. The cultural message for women seems to be that casual sex is okay, but only to a point (Bogle, 2008). Clearly, traditional gender roles and femininity, which include proscriptions against women's initiating sexual relationships or asserting their needs and desires, conflict with the notion of young women's actively negotiating for safe and pleasurable sex and with female sexual agency in general (Curtin, Ward, Merriwether, & Caruthers,

2011; Tolman, 2002; see Chapter 25, this volume). Some evidence has suggested that endorsement of more traditional attitudes is linked not only to lower sexual agency but also to lower sexual knowledge (Curtin et al., 2011). An association may also exist between being in a committed relationship and sexual agency, although the direction—if causal—is not clear.

Attitudes About Partnering Types and Comparative Implications for Sexual and General Well-Being

Most young adults do not typically enter relationships with marriage intentions. During emerging adulthood, individuals may value the absence of relationship permanence, perhaps viewing stability as a potential constraint on career goals and viewing frequent change as a pathway to determining what they like and need in a relationship. The transition to university is associated with significant changes in attitudes and perceptions about sex, with students reporting being less judgmental and more open about the commonness of sexual behavior, perceiving these changes positively (Lefkowitz, 2005). Moreover, given cultural (e.g., media) representations of love and sexuality that emphasize flexibility and lack of permanence, young adults may envision settling down as sexless and just not much fun.

Nevertheless, relationship contexts of sexual involvement may affect whether emerging adults find their relationships to be satisfying and rewarding. Because mature romantic and sexual relationships take time to develop and require trust and reciprocity, casual encounters such as hook-ups may ultimately be counterproductive. Hooking up does not require deep, agentic exploration of the self or others. Where hooking up is the dominant script, it may offer just the illusion of actual choice (Bogle, 2008). Theoretically, the implications for more intimate relationships may vary for men and women. Good and Sherrod (1997) suggested that men's nonrelational and objectification view of sex, encouraged by media and aspects of male peer groups, is a "culturally prescribed psychosocial developmental stage" (p. 181) in which women are targets of desire to be pursued. Thus, as in the themes of emerging adulthood, a shift from nonrelational sex to intimate sexual relations represents a normative transition and a successful resolution of a developmental stage, at least for men. However, it is unclear whether this developmental resolution can be successful without engaging in relationship-building behaviors, which may be more common in a dating relationship that induces trust, commitment, and a dyadic identity that is more likely to promote interpersonal development (Paik, 2010).

Alternatively, linkages among sex, relationship type, and relationship quality may simply reflect a self-selection process. Young adults who are primarily interested in short-term sexual experiences, or who enter early adulthood with more sexual experience, may self-select into nonserious contexts of sexual involvement (Paik, 2010). Similarly, young adults who are interested in long-term relationships may be willing to invest in developing serious psychological and physical sexual intimacy.

Although associations may vary according to biological sex, outcomes, relationship quality, and other characteristics, evidence has suggested that marriage confers multiple emotional, physical, economic, and sexual intimacy benefits compared with cohabitation and singlehood (Gallo, Troxel, Matthews, & Kuller, 2003; Harris, Lee, & DeLeone, 2010; Kiecolt-Glaser & Newton, 2001; Williams & Umberson, 2004). Despite historical trends of marriage postponement, most emerging adults expect to marry eventually and believe that marriage and family are extremely important, though young women appear to support these values more than men (Johnston, Bachman, & O'Malley, 2007). Meier, Hull, and Ortyl (2009) used Wave 3 Add Health data (respondents ages 18–26 in 2001) to examine gender and sexual identity differences in value placed on romantic love ideology. They found that although there were some differences, the more striking pattern was the overall high ratings on the values of love, faithfulness, and lifelong commitment. Thus, despite intentions at the beginning of a relationship, most young adults are hoping for permanence. At this juncture, it is not clear whether change and relationship exploration enhance or detract from success in transition to relationship permanency and meaningful interpersonal connections.

Some evidence has linked extent of sexual experience and what has been termed *sexual subjectivity,* which includes sexual body-esteem, perceptions of entitlements to sexual desire and pleasure (from self and others), sexual self-efficacy (belief in one's ability to successfully accomplish sexual behavior), and sexual self-reflection (Horne & Zimmer-Gembeck, 2006). Much of the work has focused on sexual self-efficacy, and findings have suggested that more, and more diverse, sexual experiences are associated with greater sexual self-efficacy in both adolescent (Buzwell & Rosenthal, 1996) and late adolescent emerging adult samples (Zimmer-Gembeck, Ducat, & Boislard-Pepin, 2011). Twelve-month longitudinal data have also indicated that sense of sexual entitlement and efficacy increase with experience in the context of a romantic partnership. In the Zimmer-Gembeck et al. (2011) study, improvement was especially notable among women with no history of vaginal intercourse (regardless of other genital sexual experience) and among those who had their first coitus during the study period. The larger changes evident among women who had recently initiated sexual activity suggested that novel experiences prompt self-reflection and, in turn, personal growth. Whether such changes would continue through early adulthood is not clear (Zimmer-Gembeck et al., 2011).

More sexual interest and experience, and their apparent positive implications for sexual self-efficacy, may in turn enhance general sexual health and adjustment. Sexual self-efficacy has been positively linked in multiple studies to contraceptive use and general sexual adjustment among young men and women during emerging adulthood (Impett, Schooler, & Tolman, 2006; Reissing, Andruff, & Wentland, 2012; Reissing, Laliberte, & Davis, 2005). Conversely, sexual aversion may contribute to lower sexual self-efficacy (Reissing et al., 2005) through behavioral avoidance and therefore few opportunities for positive sexual experiences (Else-Quest, Hyde, & DeLamater, 2005). Older age at first vaginal intercourse is associated with more sexual problems later in life (Sandfort, Orr, Hirsch, & Santelli, 2008; Woo & Brotto, 2008), possibly a function of having fewer sexual experiences and less time for sexual development, leading to less sensuality, frequency, body awareness, and more sexual avoidance (Woo & Brotto, 2008). Thus, the timing and quality of the first sexual experience may precipitate positive or negative beliefs about sexuality, which in turn contribute to sexual interest and extent of sexual experience, facets that ultimately have the potential to enhance or detract from self-efficacy and perceptions of sexual competence (see Chapters 8 and 11, this volume).

As suggested in the findings of Zimmer-Gembeck et al. (2011), sexual self-esteem appears to be sensitive to situational and relational contexts. Among established couples in a Canadian study, sexual self-esteem among women was facilitated by a loving, open, stable relationship with a partner, whereas disrespect or lack of interest from a partner hindered sexual self-esteem (Heinrichs, MacKnee, Auton-Cuff, & Domene, 2009). Partnerships that embody close friendship may be especially supportive for such development, likely through more open communication (Bay-Cheng, Robinson, & Zucker, 2009). In contrast to the positive implications of sex in the context of close, stable relationships, some findings have suggested that casual encounters or hooking up may undermine aspects of sexual identity such as sexual self-efficacy. Detriments to efficacy could be a function of coercion or lack of control over sexual activity in the context of a hookup or of spontaneity and disinhibited behavior linked to alcohol use and sexual arousal (Downing-Matibag & Geisinger, 2009).

Because of persistent double standards for men and women, gender likely influences how relationship types and experiences relate to subjective experiences of sexuality. Traditional femininity ideologies (e.g., women as sexual gatekeepers or as sexually passive) have been linked to sexual agency among young women (Curtin et al., 2011). Specifically, femininity ideology has been tied to decreased sexual self-efficacy and sexual assertiveness (Caron, Davis, Halteman, & Stickle, 1993; Gavey & McPhillips, 1999; Tolman, 1999; Tolman, Impett, Tracy, & Michael, 2006; Tolman & Porche, 2000) as well as to negative experiences of sexual embodiment or comfort with one's body during sex (Curtin et al., 2011). For these reasons, some investigators have examined feminist ideologies as a counterinfluence, finding that endorsement of feminist perspectives is associated with young women's awareness of their sexual desire, sexual assertiveness, sexual self-efficacy, and sexual satisfaction (Schick, Zucker, & Bay-Cheng, 2008).

SEXUAL BEHAVIORS: ACTIVITY WITH PARTNERS, SEXUAL INEXPERIENCE, AND MASTURBATION

A wide range of sexual patterns exist among emerging adults in terms of solo versus partnered activity, number and sex of partners, and types and timing of sex acts experienced. Further, these patterns vary according to an individual's sex and racial/ethnic background as well as relationship contexts, and they have differential implications for relationship and sexual satisfaction.

Activity With Partners

Table 16.2 presents information about numbers and gender of sex partners and experience with different types of sexual activity for women participating in the 2006–2008 NSFG (Chandra, Mosher, Copen, & Sionean, 2011). Almost 13% of female 20- to 24-year-olds and 3% of female 25- to 29-year-olds reported no sexual contact with male partners. About a third of both age groups reported one or two partners. At the other extreme, 7% of 20- to 24-year-olds and 13% of 25- to 29-year-olds reported 15 or more lifetime sex partners. In the year before interview, higher percentages of 18- to 19-year-olds reported four or more other-sex partners; however, these figures do not control for marital status. Approximately 15% of women in their 20s reported a same-sex partner in the past 12 months,

TABLE 16.2

Sexual Behavior: 18- to 29-Year Old Women, National Survey of Family Growth, 2006–2008

Behavior	Ages 18–19 (%[b] [SE])	Ages 20–24 (% [SE])	Ages 25–29 (% [SE])
Lifetime other-sex partners[a]			
0	c	12.6 (3.4)	3.4 (1.1)
1	c	24.5 (1.7)	20.0 (1.9)
2	c	12.5 (1.6)	12.4 (1.5)
3–6	c	31.6 (2.8)	31.0 (2.3)
7–14	c	11.7 (1.2)	20.4 (2.)
15+	c	7.2 (1.2)	12.8 (1.7)
Median	c	2.6 (0.2)	3.6 (0.3)
No. other-sex partners, past 12 months (regardless of relationship status)			
1	36.6 (4.4)	57.8 (2.5)	82.3 (0.9)
2	12.3 (1.9)	14.1 (2.2)	5.4 (0.4)
3	4.0 (0.7)	4.6 (1.0)	1.7 (0.3)
4+	7.3 (1.5)	4.6 (0.9)	1.9 (0.3)
Any same-sex partners, past 12 months	c	15.2 (1.8)	14.3 (1.5)
Types of sexual behavior (other-sex partners)			
Vaginal	61.7(4.7)	85.0 (3.6)	95.2 (1.0)
Oral–genital	62.9 (4.7)	81.1 (3.3)	88.5 (1.6)
Anal	14.9 (2.1)	30.2 (2.4)	38.5 (2.4)
Any same-sex activity	11.9 (1.8)	15.8 (1.8)	15.0 (1.5)

Note. From *Sexual Behavior, Sexual Attraction, and Sexual Identity in the United States: Data From the 2006–2008 National Survey of Family Growth* (National Health Statistics Reports No. 36), by A. Chandra, W. D. Mosher, C. Copen, and C. Sionean, 2011, Hyattsville, MD: National Center for Health Statistics.
[a]Sex partner refers to oral, vaginal, or anal sex.
[b]Denominators based on all female respondents.
[c]Figures not reported.

and similar percentages reported any same-sex activity. Regarding sexual acts, the majority of all age groups had had vaginal sex: about 62% of 18- to 19-year-olds, 85% of 20- to 24-year-olds, and 95% of 25- to 29-year-olds. Prevalence of oral sex experience was similar, although among those older than age 19 it was somewhat less common than vaginal intercourse. Anal sex was less common; about 15% of 18- to 19-year-olds had experience with anal sex, rising to almost 39% among 25- to 29-year-olds.

Table 16.3 presents parallel information for men. Compared with women, similar percentages of men reported no other-sex partners. Somewhat lower percentages of men reported one or two other-sex partners compared with women, and greater percentages reported 15 or more lifetime partners, with 14% of 20- to 24-year-olds and almost a quarter of 25- to 29-year-olds reporting 15 or more lifetime other-sex sex partners. Greater percentages of men reported four or more other-sex partners in the past 12 months. These figures are consistent with earlier survey findings showing that men report more other-sex sexual partners than do women in the same age range (Chandra et al., 2011). Men are much less likely than women to report same-sex partners in the past 12 months (about 5% of the those ages 20–29, compared with 15% of women). Although there are some modest differences, similar percentages of men report experience with vaginal, oral–genital, and anal intercourse.

Bivariate comparisons indicate that age, marital or cohabiting status, educational attainment, and race/ethnicity are associated with numbers of partners. Overall patterns suggest that individuals who

TABLE 16.3

Sexual Behavior: 18- to 29-Year-Old Men, National Survey of Family Growth, 2006–2008

Behavior	Ages 18–19 (%[b] [SE])	Ages 20–24 (% [SE])	Ages 25–29 (% [SE])
Lifetime other-sex partners[a]			
0	[c]	14.4 (3.1)	3.8 (0.8)
1	[c]	19.1 (2.8)	11.8 (1.5)
2	[c]	8.0 (1.3)	8.9 (1.4)
3–6	[c]	26.1 (2.9)	29.5 (2.3)
7–14	[c]	18.1 (2.6)	22.9 (2.1)
15+	[c]	14.2 (2.3)	23.1 (1.6)
Median		4.1 (0.6)	5.7 (0.3)
No. other-sex partners, past 12 months (regardless of relationship status)			
1	33.9 (3.3)	49.8 (2.2)	68.6 (2.1)
2	15.1 (2.8)	12.2 (1.7)	9.7 (1.2)
3	7.4 (1.4)	6.8 (1.1)	4.0 (0.9)
4+	8.7 (1.7)	9.5 (1.5)	7.5 (1.2)
Any same-sex partners, past 12 months	[c]	4.6 (4.8)	4.8 (1.0)
Types of sexual behavior (other-sex partners)			
Vaginal	65.6 (3.5)	81.5 (3.6)	95.6 (0.9)
Oral–genital	69.8 (2.9)	80.1 (3.3)	90.5 (1.5)
Anal	16.6 (2.8)	31.9 (3.3)	42.5 (2.4)
Any same-sex activity	3.8 (1.2)	5.6 (1.1)	5.2 (1.1)

Note. From *Sexual Behavior, Sexual Attraction, and Sexual Identity in the United States: Data From the 2006–2008 National Survey of Family Growth* (National Health Statistics Reports No. 36), by A. Chandra, W. D. Mosher, C. Copen, and C. Sionean, 2011, Hyattsville, MD: National Center for Health Statistics.
[a]Sex partner refers to oral, vaginal, or anal sex.
[b]Denominators based on all male respondents.
[c]Figures not reported.

are older, married, and White report fewer other-sex partners (Chandra et al., 2011). Racial/ethnic patterns of sexual experience vary, depending on the behavior. Among women ages 20 to 24, non-Hispanic Whites were less likely to report vaginal intercourse than Hispanic (any race) and non-Hispanic Black women (80.6%, 91.2%, and 93.4%, respectively). For oral sex, Latinas were less likely to report experience (76.4%) than non-Hispanic White and non-Hispanic Black women (81.8% and 81.7%, respectively). Anal sex experience was similar across groups; approximately 30% of each racial/ethnic group reported anal intercourse. Race/ethnicity patterns also changed for same-sex experience; 17.3% of non-Hispanic Whites and 16.7% of non-Hispanic Black women, but only 9.4% of Latinas, reported same-sex encounters.

As with women, among men ages 20 to 24, non-Hispanic Whites were less likely to report vaginal intercourse than Hispanic (any race) and non-Hispanic Black men (78.5%, 94.6%, and 87.1% respectively). Latinos were more likely to report oral sex experience than non-Hispanic White and Black men (85.6%, 80.0%, and 81.0%, respectively). Latinos in this age range were also much more likely to report anal sex experience than White and Black peers (49.2%, 29.1%, and 26.6%, respectively). Non-Hispanic White men were most likely to report same-sex experience (5.9%) compared with 2.0% of Latinos and 4.5% of non-Hispanic Blacks. Chandra et al. (2011) reported that these figures were generally similar to those reported for the 2002 NSFG (Mosher, Chandra, & Jones, 2005).

Sex in Context

Population estimates do not reveal how sexual behavior during emerging adulthood may vary depending on its context. To date, only a modest literature has examined these issues. As suggested earlier, longer term relationships may allow for more experimentation in a context that is perceived as safe. Behavior may change within a relationship as it progresses over time and changes emotionally. In an analysis of 18- to 26-year-olds who participated in Wave 3 of Add Health and who were currently in a relationship of at least 3 months duration, Kaestle and Halpern (2007) found that 99% had had vaginal intercourse, 84% had experienced fellatio, 85% had experienced cunnilingus, and 23% had had anal sex in the context of that current relationship. Figures for men and women were very similar. However, the type of sexual activity reported varied, depending on the love pattern in the relationship. A wider range of activities was reported in couples with high levels of mutual love. Loving one's partner very much was also associated with providing and receiving oral sex. Relationship status also mattered; married and cohabiting couples were more likely to engage in sexual behavior beyond coitus, regardless of love pattern (see Chapter 10, this volume).

Sexual Satisfaction

Information about sexual satisfaction that focuses on the emerging adulthood years is also limited. Several studies of college students have found large gender differences in reports of satisfaction with first coitus. Twenty years ago, only about a quarter of college women reported physiological sexual satisfaction or psychological sexual satisfaction at first intercourse, compared with 81% and 67%, respectively, of college men (Darling, Davidson, & Passarello, 1992). Similar findings were reported in a more recent survey (Higgins, Trussell, Moore, & Davidson, 2010); 25% and 38% of young women experienced physiological and psychological sexual satisfaction at first intercourse, respectively, compared with 65% and 57% of men. A study of Canadian college students found that compared with their female counterparts, young male participants had significantly more positive affective reactions to their first sexual intercourse experience; 91.4% of men indicated that they had had a positive affective reaction to their first experience of sexual intercourse, but only 73% of women did (Reissing et al., 2012).

In one estimate, only 6% of women, but 62% of men, experience orgasm at first intercourse (Reissing et al., 2012). Individuals in longer relationships are more likely to report satisfaction than those in casual partnerships. Higgins et al. (2010), on the basis of a 2000 survey of never married self-identified heterosexual students who were 25 years or younger from four universities, found that most participants felt physiologically (84%) or psychologically (79%)

satisfied with their current sexual experiences. For women, orgasm frequency, vaginal intercourse frequency, planning for sexual activity, self-respect and comfort with their own sexuality, and involvement in an exclusive dating relationship were positively associated with physiological satisfaction in multivariate models. The same factors were associated with satisfaction for men, except for orgasm frequency and self-respect. In addition, lack of guilt, high self-esteem, and sexual agency (sexual decisions made by themselves) were predictive of physiological satisfaction in multivariate models. Predictors of psychological satisfaction were generally similar, although lack of guilt and self-esteem are important for women. Satisfaction was not significantly associated with a physical health factor, consistent condom use.

Other work, centered on emerging adults and older adults, has indicated that people in ongoing relationships have sex more frequently than those not in relationships and report greater satisfaction with their sex lives (Laumann et al., 1994; McGuire & Barber, 2010). These patterns confirm that individual, relationship, and cultural factors play a role in sexual health. They also suggest, as in Higgins et al. (2010), that characteristics of instability and nonexclusivity, as in hook-ups and other casual encounters, are less likely to promote sexual satisfaction, at least within the context of a given encounter (see Chapter 11, this volume).

Contraception and Abortion

Data from the NSFG have indicated that virtually all sexually experienced women have used some method of contraception. Among women in their 20s who are currently using contraception, about a quarter rely on oral contraception and 13% use condoms (Mosher & Jones, 2010). Three percent to 5% rely on withdrawal, and 3% to 5% (for each type) rely on injectables, intrauterine devices, or contraceptive rings. Fewer than 1% rely on periodic abstinence. Of women ages 25 to 29, approximately 10% rely on female sterilization and about 2% rely on male sterilization (Mosher & Jones, 2010). Of young women at risk of pregnancy,[3] 14% of 20- to 24-year-olds and 12% of 24- to 29-year-olds are not currently using a contraceptive despite estimates that only 4% to 6% of women in their 20s are actively pursuing pregnancy (Mosher & Jones, 2010). Consistent condom use tends to be low among emerging adults (Boyle & O'Sullivan, 2010), and young adults in committed relationships report especially low rates of consistent condom use (Anderson, 2003; van Empelen & Kok, 2006; Woolf & Maisto, 2008). Qualitative data have indicated that young adults who find sex to be a comfortable topic are not necessarily more likely to use condoms consistently than individuals who do not find it comfortable, suggesting that the broader communication context of a romantic pair may be important for developing skills in negotiating condom use in committed relationships (Boyle & O'Sullivan, 2010).

There are differences in female contraception by race/ethnicity. Among 20- to 24-year-olds, 19.1% of Whites, 28.6% of Blacks, and 53% of Hispanics who had premarital sex used no contraception at their first experience (Gavin et al., 2009). Between 36% and 68% of these racial/ethnic groups used a condom. Only 16.6% of Whites, 20.3% of Blacks, and 5.2% of Hispanic women used both a hormonal method and condoms (Gavin et al., 2009). Of never-married 20- to 24-year-old women who had sex during the 4 weeks before interview, fewer than a third of each racial/ethnic group reported always using condoms (Gavin et al., 2009). Among 20- to 24-year-old men, 15.9% of Whites, 19.8% of Blacks, and 34.9% of Hispanics who had premarital sex used no contraception at their first experience (Gavin et al., 2009). Among men, 67.0% of Whites, 77.1% of Blacks, and 56.8% of Hispanics reported condom use at first experience. Of never-married 20- to 24-year-old men who had sex during the previous 4 weeks, 34.4% of Whites, 55.7% of Blacks, and 38.7% of Hispanics reported always using condoms (Gavin et al., 2009).

Findings from a nationally representative probability sample of 1,800 unmarried men and women ages 18 to 29 (commissioned by the National Campaign to Prevent Teen and Unplanned Pregnancy) have indicated that regardless of gender or racial/ethnic group, almost nine of 10 emerging adults report that it is important for them to avoid

[3] Defined as current contraceptors and women who have had sex in the past 3 months but are not current contraceptors.

pregnancy at the present time; the same number believe that pregnancy should be planned (Kaye, Suellentrop, & Sloup, 2009). However, despite these attitudes, only about half of those who are sexually active contracept every time; 13% report that contraception is morally wrong. Among those who are currently in a sexual relationship and are not trying to get pregnant or cause a pregnancy, almost half use no contraception at all or contracept inconsistently. About a third of respondents who reported it was very important to avoid pregnancy right now said they would likely have unprotected sex in the next 3 months. A number of factors appear to account for this gap between desire and behavior. Thirty percent reported they knew little or nothing about condoms, 63% knew little or nothing about birth control pills, and 56% reported they had not heard of implants. This lack of knowledge is reflected in reports of fears about side effects of contraception including weight gain, infections, and serious disease (e.g., cancer), side effects that are not supported by clinical evidence. Almost four in 10 emerging adults believe that oral contraception is ineffective (i.e., odds of pregnancy within a year are 50% or greater on the pill) or that they themselves are infertile (Kaye et al., 2009). The latter belief reflects double the percentage who are actually likely to have impaired fecundity.

Differences in attitudes across racial/ethnic groups contribute to differences in contraceptive choices. For example, Hispanics (49%) and non-Hispanic Blacks (50%) are more likely than non-Hispanic Whites (34%) to express fatalistic attitudes about pregnancy, believing that birth control does not really matter (Kaye et al., 2009). They are also more suspicious of contraception, agreeing that "the government and public health institutions use poor and minority people as guinea pigs to try out new birth control methods" (40% of non-Hispanic Blacks and Hispanics). Hispanics are also more likely to believe that birth control is morally wrong (26% vs. 8%–11% of non-Hispanics). More than a third of Hispanic and non-Hispanic Black women believe that some types of birth control have serious side effects (e.g., infection, cancer) compared with about a quarter of non-Hispanic White women. Hispanic and non-Hispanic Black women are also more likely to believe they are infertile. Clearly, educational efforts targeted to youths are needed that present full and accurate information about contraception (Kaye et al., 2009; see Volume 2, Chapter 11, this handbook).

Emerging adults in longer term relationships may have reasons for foregoing effective contraception beyond inaccurate knowledge. Some may fear that requesting condom use could be interpreted by a partner as a lack of intimacy or a sign of infidelity (Gebhardt, Kuyper, & Greunsven, 2003). College students who are inconsistent condom users have given additional explanations for their behavior, explanations that often display fallacious logical arguments, such as a belief that the intimacy they have with their partner has protective qualities that make them invulnerable or that their very thoughts about their own invulnerability make them immune to risk (O'Sullivan, Udell, Montrose, Antoniello, & Hoffman, 2010; Wohl & Enzle, 2002). Alternatively, some inconsistent users simply minimize the severity of poor outcomes or ignore risks altogether (O'Sullivan et al., 2010). Mixed-methods research has suggested that the association between communication and consistent condom use is complex and that reported ease of communication about sexual topics is not necessarily related to condom use or negotiation of condom use. Rather, it may be more important to understand general communication with a partner and to build on that to develop skills in negotiating condom use in committed relationships (Boyle & O'Sullivan, 2010).

Recent national estimates have indicated that almost one fifth of all pregnancies in the United States end in abortion (Ventura, Abma, Mosher, & Henshaw, 2009). Women in the emerging adulthood period (here calculated as ages 20–29) account for the majority (56.9%) and also have the highest abortion rates of all age groups (29.4 and 21.4 abortions per 1,000 women ages 20–24 and 25–29 years, respectively), in contrast to 14.5 per 1,000 women ages 15 to 19 and 13.5 per 1,000 women ages 30 to 35 (Centers for Disease Control and Prevention [CDC], 2011a). The higher rates among women in their 20s are similar across racial/ethnic groups. Unmarried women account for most abortions, and this pattern is also consistent across race/ethnicity (estimates range from 64.5% to 89.5%).

Masturbation

Recent estimates from the National Survey of Sexual Health and Behavior have indicated that among 20- to 24-year-olds, 92% of men and 77% of women have masturbated (Herbenick et al., 2010). Implications of masturbation experience for healthy sexual development and quality of partnered sexual behavior are not known (Hogarth & Ingham, 2009). Obtaining the opportunity to learn about what one finds pleasurable via masturbation could facilitate healthy sexual identity development and perhaps more satisfying partnered relationships (Coleman, 2002).

Although masturbation normalization may begin in adolescence (Shapiro, 2008), this developmental task still continues to challenge individuals in emerging adulthood. Emerging adults report going through a process of trying to come to terms with the tension between masturbation's stigma and the pleasure it can bring (Kaestle & Allen, 2011). The continuation of development regarding acceptance and normalization of masturbation in emerging adulthood is supported by the fact that emerging adults may be more willing to report masturbation retrospectively than teenagers who are asked to report whether they currently masturbate (Coles & Stokes, 1985; Halpern, Udry, Suchindran, & Campbell, 2000). These patterns in willingness to report masturbation experience suggest masturbation is fundamentally different from other sexual activities, which are often reported more by teenagers than retrospectively by adults (Halpern, Udry et al., 2000). Masturbation may elicit greater feelings of guilt among adolescents (Coles & Stokes, 1985) that may lessen as emerging adults come to terms with how masturbation fits into healthy sexuality and self-discovery (Kaestle & Allen, 2011).

Gender appears to be important in whether emerging adults come to accept masturbation as normal, with differential sexual scripts contributing to the double standard (Coleman, 2002; Kaestle & Allen, 2011). Researchers have consistently found that men are more likely to report masturbating than women (Gerressu, Mercer, Graham, Wellings, & Johnson, 2008; Laumann et al., 1994; Pinkerton, Bogart, Cecil, & Abramson, 2002), and masturbation is still perceived as belonging to the masculine realm of appropriately pursuing pleasure as a sexual goal (Petersen & Hyde, 2010). In fact, compared with other sexual activities, the largest gender differences in reported behaviors are related to masturbation and in use of pornography (Petersen & Hyde, 2010; see Chapter 2, this volume; Volume 2, Chapter 1, this handbook).

Sexual Inexperience

Although there is literature on reasons why adolescents and young adults choose to have sex (e.g., Meston & Buss, 2007), relatively little work has been done on sexual inexperience in early adulthood. Analyses of Add Health data have indicated that about 3% of 24- to 32-year-olds are sexually inexperienced (defined as never having had vaginal, oral–genital, or anal sex; Haydon, Cheng, Herring, McRee, & Halpern, in press). Respondents who are younger, non-Hispanic Black or Hispanic (relative to non-Hispanic Whites), extraverted, early maturing (relative to average pubertal timing), and, not surprisingly, who have ever married or cohabited are less likely to be sexually inexperienced. Respondents who attend religious services weekly, are later maturing (compared with average pubertal timing), are obese, have below-average scores on a test of oral vocabulary (Add Health Picture Vocabulary Test, an abridged version of the Peabody Picture Vocabulary Test; Dunn, 1981), and report lack of interest in men or women are more likely to be inexperienced. However, inexperience is unrelated to biological sex, education achieved, physical disability, same-sex attraction, or sexual minority identity.

These findings suggest that emerging adults who are sexually inexperienced are a heterogeneous group. The strong associations between sexual inexperience and both lack of sexual interest and religiosity suggest that at least for some individuals, young adult celibacy represents either disinterest or personal choice. The association between religious attendance and sexual inexperience is consistent with a large body of research documenting delayed sexual involvement among highly religious individuals (Rostosky, Regnerus, & Wright, 2003; see Volume 2, Chapter 13, this handbook). To the extent that celibacy among these individuals is a religious choice supported by peer and community norms and expectations

(Adamcyzk, 2009; Regnerus, 2003; Smith, 2003), sexual inexperience during adulthood is likely a source of happiness rather than of frustration or distress. Other associations suggest lack of opportunity as a possible reason for inexperience. For example, current obesity is associated with a greater likelihood of sexual inexperience during young adulthood, indicating that associations between body mass index and delayed sexual involvement documented during both adolescence (Halpern, King, Oslak, & Udry, 2005) and emerging adulthood (Halpern et al., 2006) extend into later developmental periods as well. Similarly, the relationship between sexual inexperience and low cognitive ability confirms associations that have previously been observed among adolescents (Cheng & Udry, 2005; Halpern, Joyner, Udry, & Suchindran, 2000).

Sexual Orientation and Identity

Most theories explaining the development of sexual orientation or identity focus on linear progression through various stages of development (see Chapters 18, 19, and 20, this volume). Identity confusion experiences during adolescence are hypothesized to lead eventually to the assumption of a sexual minority identity, identity disclosure, and integration of private and public identity (Troiden, 1989). This perspective would clearly meld with the identity exploration themes of emerging adulthood. However, there is disagreement about whether sexual identity development entails distinct stages of invariant sequence or reflects a more fluid process, especially for women (Diamond, 2000). Fluid, nonlinear change in sexual identity may be particularly descriptive of emerging adults, for whom sexual experimentation is part of a broader pattern of exploration (Dickson, Paul, & Herbison, 2003). Overall, current research on sexual orientation identity dimensions has supported the general premise of emerging adulthood as a continued time of identity exploration and instability. Evidence has also suggested that sexual orientation and gender interact to influence relationship values (Meier et al., 2009); more research is needed to understand the intersection of sexual identity development and other characteristics.

SEXUAL HEALTH ISSUES: ASSAULT AND SEXUALLY TRANSMITTED INFECTIONS

Interest and research in positive sexuality, and the life experiences that can promote positive sexuality, is growing. However, injury and illness related to sexuality continue to place a heavy burden on emerging adults.

Sexual Assault

Rates of rape and sexual assault among individuals in late adolescence and early adulthood are more than twice those among older adults (2.2 per 1,000 for 16- to 19-year-olds and 2.1 per 1,000 for 20- to 24-year-olds compared with 0.8 per 1,000 among 35- to 49-year-olds). Rates are higher among women (4.5 per 1,000 and 3.7 per 1,000, respectively, for 16- to 19-year-olds, and 20- to 14-year-olds) and racial minorities (3.4 per 1,000 for Black 16- to 19-year-olds and 5.9 per 1,000 for Black 20- to 24-year-olds compared with 2.2 per 1,000 and 1.1 per 1,000 for Whites of parallel ages; U.S. Department of Justice, 2011). About 7% of 18- to 24-year-old women report that their first sexual intercourse was not voluntary; having a partner 3 or more years older increases the likelihood of involuntary sexual activity (Abma, Martinez, & Copen, 2010). The likelihood of sexual assault also appears to be increased by engagement in the hook-up culture. Although their sample size was small, Flack et al. (2007) found that among those who participate in the hook-up culture, about a quarter of women report being raped and three quarters report coerced sexual activity while engaging in a hook-up (see Chapter 12, this volume).

Sexually Transmitted Infection and HIV Risk

Young adults carry a high burden of STIs; in 2000, it was estimated that youths ages 15 to 24 accounted for 48% of all new cases of STIs in the United States, despite accounting for only 25% of the sexually active population (Weinstock, Berman, & Cates, 2004). Data from the 2010 CDC Sexually Transmitted Disease Surveillance report (CDC, 2011c) demonstrated that adolescents and young adults continue to be disproportionately represented among new cases of notifiable STIs and HIV within the past decade. Within this population, emerging adults are more at risk for having an STI than adults in their 30s; in 2008, about half of new cases of chlamydia (52%) and gonorrhea (49%), the most commonly reported notifiable diseases in the United States, were among young adults ages 20 to 29 (Kaiser Family Foundation 2011). Sexually active youths are at elevated risk of STIs because of behavioral, biological, and cultural factors (e.g., sexual risk taking, cervical immaturity, barriers to health care access). As we noted earlier, consistent condom use tends to be low among emerging adults. Moreover, the typical pattern of serial monogamy leads to inconsistent use patterns across partners, exacerbating the possibility of STIs (Boyle & O'Sullivan, 2010). Tendencies to discount the future (R. Robbins & Bryan, 2004) and to experience combinations of negative mood and high arousal (Leith & Baumeister, 1996) have also been linked to sexual risk taking.

Chlamydial infections in women, usually asymptomatic, can result in pelvic inflammatory disease, a major cause of infertility, ectopic pregnancy, and chronic pelvic pain. In 2010, young adults ages 15 to 24 had a chlamydia rate 4 times the national average. Cases were primarily concentrated among young women rather than men, with women ages 20 to 24 bearing the highest incidence of any age or gender subgroup (3,407.9 per 100,000; CDC, 2011c). Gonococcal infections are also a major cause of pelvic inflammatory disease and facilitate the transmission of HIV infection. In 2010, gonorrhea was most common among young women ages 15 to 19 and 20 to 24, though men ages 20 to 24 had the largest increase in cases between 2009 and 2010, with rates increasing by 6.2% (CDC, 2011c).

In contrast to chlamydia and gonorrhea, primary and secondary syphilis are much more common among young men than young women. Syphilis, a genital ulcerative disease, causes significant health complications if untreated and facilitates the transmission of HIV infection. In 2010, CDC surveillance data found a rate of syphilis among men ages 20 to 24 of 21.9 per 100,000, which was the highest rate reported for any age and sex group since 2008. This rate was almost 4 times the rate for women of the same age (4.5 per 100,000) and reflected an increase in incidence from the previous year, despite the fact that nationally, syphilis incidence decreased for the entire population (CDC, 2011c).

Persistent infection with high-risk human papillomavirus can lead to development of anogenital cancers such as cervical cancer. High-risk human papillomavirus is highest among 20- to 24-year-olds (Hariri et al., 2011). National Health and Nutrition Examination Survey data have suggested that unlike other STIs, genital herpes simplex virus is somewhat lower among 20- to 29-year-olds than among adults in their 30s and 40s (CDC, 2011c). Adolescents and young adults are also at a high risk for contracting HIV. In 2008, almost a third of new HIV cases were among 13- to 29-year-olds (Kaiser Family Foundation, 2011). In 2009, young adults ages 20 to 24 had the highest number of new cases of HIV of any age group (CDC, 2011b).

PREDICTORS OF SEXUAL PATTERNS

In addition to describing patterns of sexual attitudes, behaviors, and health in emerging adulthood, researchers are examining potential predictors of such patterns from earlier in life. Longitudinal studies have indicated that sociodemographic factors such as gender, race/ethnicity, and religiosity influence sexual behavior trajectories during emerging adulthood (Arnett, 2004; Fergus, Zimmerman, & Caldwell, 2007; Halpern et al., 2006). Physical factors such as disability, genetic polymorphisms, body mass index, and physical maturity relative to peers in adolescence have also been explored as possible predictors of sexual activity in emerging adulthood and examined for their health implications (Halpern, Kaestle, Guo, & Hallfors, 2007; Halpern et al., 2006; McRee, Haydon, & Halpern, 2010). For example, youths with physical disabilities are as sexually active as those without a disability (Blum, Kelly, & Ireland, 2001; Cheng & Udry, 2002; Surís, Resnick, Cassuto, & Blum, 1996), yet they may be less likely to receive sexuality education (Cheng & Udry, 2002) and may also be disadvantaged in some indicators of reproductive health care, such as regular receipt of pap smears, in emerging adulthood

(McRee et al., 2010; see Chapter 23, this volume). Research exploring psychological factors, such as body attitudes, has found negative attitudes to be associated with higher sexual aversion, which, in turn, may detract from sexual self-efficacy (the belief in one's capabilities to successfully accomplish behaviors and affective responses in a sexual context) and adjustment (Reissing et al., 2005). Positive sexual self-efficacy has been linked with better sexual adjustment and increased frequency of sexual activity among both women and men (Creti & Libman, 1989).

Family factors also influence later sexual relationships. The quality of parental relationships during adolescence is linked to the quality of sexual relationships in young adulthood (Conger, Cui, Bryant, & Elder, 2000; Joyner & Campa, 2006), and parental awareness and caring during emerging adulthood are associated with fewer sexual behaviors and risks (Wetherill, Neal, & Fromme, 2010). Greater levels of perceived awareness and caring by peers are also associated with lower sexual risk, although some combinations of factors, such as liberal sexual values and high levels of both parental awareness and caring and peer awareness and caring, are associated with a greater number of sexual partners and unsafe sexual behavior (Wetherill et al., 2010). The latter finding underscores the importance of simultaneously considering the systemic intersections of multiple psychosocial factors in predicting emerging adult sexual patterns. As another example, some studies have documented greater openness with parents in conversations about sex in the college years (Morgan, Thorne, & Zurbriggen, 2010), a pattern consistent with general relational development during emerging adulthood that includes increases in mutuality and disclosure (Grotevant & Cooper, 1985). Seeing this pattern in parent relationships would not necessarily be expected, and researchers have suggested that greater disclosure is dependent on both the parent and the young adult becoming more comfortable with open discussions (Morgan et al., 2010), underscoring the dyadic nature of parent–child relationships.

In addition to multiple determinants at a given time point, life-course theory posits that events and transitions that are widely separated by time are nevertheless connected; therefore, the later life course may reflect the influence of experiences that occurred perhaps decades earlier. Life-course analyses have examined trajectory and transition issues and hypothesized that the timing of when a transition takes place within a trajectory helps give it meaning (Elder, 1985). A life-course perspective can provide a valuable framework to explore the potential implications of early sexual experiences on resulting adaptations and subsequent sexual trajectories in emerging adulthood. For example, a history of sexual abuse during childhood is associated with higher numbers of sexual partners, an increased use of alcohol before sex, and more unprotected sex during emerging adulthood (Schacht et al., 2010; Schraufnagel, Davis, George, & Norris, 2010). A history of early sexual victimization is linked to poor sexual health outcomes in emerging adulthood as well (Haydon, Hussey, & Halpern, 2011; Trent, Clum, & Roche, 2007). Several studies have identified child sexual abuse as the strongest risk factor for adult sexual assault, with sexual revictimization being demonstrated consistently in a wide range of samples (Rich, Combs-Lane, Resnick, & Kilpatrick, 2004). More than one developmental trajectory is likely to link early sexual abuse and later sexuality, including processes of heightened or distorted sexuality or sexual preoccupation, sexual aversion and avoidance, and perhaps simultaneous preoccupation and aversion (Noll, Trickett, & Putnam, 2003). Trajectories may reflect stigma associated with childhood sexual victimization that is integrated into the self-concept, leading to the formation of compulsive replication of experiences learned from the abuse in later sexual experiences (Finkelhor & Brown, 1985).

The long-term impact of age at first intercourse on sexuality during emerging adulthood has also been examined. Age at first intercourse is often used as an indicator of sexual risk in adolescent populations and may potentially mark the beginning of a process in which earlier negative or positive social consequences accumulate over time to affect sexual activity patterns later in life. Among college students, women's descriptions of first sex are generally less positive than men's descriptions. However, for both men and women, first sex during early adolescence is often described as awkward and less positive compared with later first sex experiences (Walsh, Ward, Caruthers, & Merriwether, 2011). Concurrent partnerships are more common among those who report an earlier age of first sex (Adimora et al., 2002). Younger age at first intercourse is also associated with a greater likelihood of testing positive for an STI among late adolescents. However, the association becomes insignificant among young adults, suggesting that emerging adults who recently experienced first vaginal intercourse are at similar risk for STIs as those who started having sex years earlier (Kaestle, Halpern, Miller, & Ford, 2005). Interestingly, younger age at first intercourse has also been tied to positive outcomes, such as higher sexual adjustment among young women. First sexual intercourse experience is hypothesized to significantly impact current sexual adjustment by positively affecting beliefs about sexual self-efficacy (Reissing et al., 2005).

More recently, researchers have begun to move beyond examining only age at first sex to gain insight into patterns of sexuality in emerging adulthood. There is evidence of variation in the timing, sequencing, and spacing of initiating coital and noncoital behaviors (e.g., Halpern & Haydon, 2012; Lindberg, Jones, & Santelli, 2008; Song & Halpern-Felsher, 2011), suggesting the possibility of implications for later sexual behavior and health. However, only a couple of studies to date have examined associations between patterns of emerging sexual behavior and reproductive health outcomes. Analyses of a Dutch sample revealed diversity in emergent behavior, with some individuals experiencing gradual and linear sexual progressions (less intimate behaviors, such as kissing, precede more intimate behaviors, such as vaginal intercourse) and others showing nonlinear or tightly spaced progression (de Graaf, Vanwesenbeeck, Meijer, Woertman, & Meeus, 2009). Haydon, Herring, Prinstein, and Halpern (2012), using Add Health data, identified five classes of emergent sexual behavior. About half of the sample belonged to a class characterized predominately by initiation of vaginal sex first, an average age of initiation of approximately 16 years, and spacing of 1 year or more between initiation of the first and second behaviors. Classes characterized by postponement of sexual activity, initiation of only one type of behavior, or adolescent initiation of anal sex were substantially less common. Compared with the modal group described earlier, respondents who postponed sexual activity until early adulthood had lower odds of each of four outcomes: STI diagnoses (lifetime and past year), concurrent sexual partnerships, and exchanging sex for money (Haydon, Herring, & Halpern, 2012). Although greater variety of sexual experience generally predicted poorer reproductive health outcomes and greater sexual risk taking, early starters who initiated anal sex during adolescence only differed from the modal group in being more likely to report past-year concurrent partnerships (Haydon, Herring, & Halpern, 2012). These findings, as with those reported earlier for age at first vaginal sex and STIs in emerging adulthood, suggest that the implications of early and atypical patterns of sexual initiation do not necessarily extend into emerging adulthood. They also underscore the importance of context such as sexual networks because STI disparities by race persisted despite membership in the same latent classes (Haydon, Herring, & Halpern, 2012).

APPLYING THE CONCEPT OF EMERGING ADULTHOOD TO SEXUALITY RESEARCH

Examining larger scale trends in the sexual attitudes and behaviors of young adults documents the values and experiences that make up this time in the life course. We now turn to two questions. First, can the emerging adulthood concept help to structure and interpret the evidence we have detailed about sexual experiences in young adulthood? Second, does emerging adulthood as an idea help shape research to provide a better understanding of sexuality for this population?

Sexuality and the Emerging Adulthood Theory

The five themes of emerging adulthood discussed earlier in this chapter appear to reflect two superordinate factors (W. Collins & van Dulmen, 2006). The first superordinate factor is identity exploration (entailing self-focus, feeling in between, and testing possibilities), and the second superordinate factor is instability (for our purposes, most directly related to instability in relationships; W. Collins & van Dulmen, 2006). The overview of sexuality provided in this chapter could be thought of as a description of how emerging adults move through a variety of sexual developmental tasks and transitions related to identity exploration and instability. The overarching task to be achieved through these experiences is recentering, that is, realigning interpersonal and contextual connections by moving from those that reflect dependency to those that reflect permanency and independence on the basis of stable connections (Tanner, 2006).

Several patterns in the literature seem consistent with identity exploration. Masturbation, common by emerging adulthood, and attendant opportunities to learn about one's body, is a self-focused exploratory activity through which emerging adults may gain knowledge of their sexual preferences and develop a sense of sexual identity. Sexual experiences with a number of partners and, at least on the basis of studies of university students, participation in casual sex and hook-ups have become a large part of sexual development in emerging adulthood for many individuals. Exploratory relationships with same-sex partners are reported by substantial numbers of young adults, particularly women, as they develop their sexual identities. Evolving sexual norms of emerging adulthood may offer a more comfortable space for sexual minorities.

The long-term implications of these patterns for emotional health, sense of identity, and relationship quality have yet to be determined. Given persistent gender role differences in both perceptions and cultural acceptability of some behaviors, implications for well-being may be different for women and men. Women are socialized to be both the gatekeepers of sexual initiation and variety and the caretakers of their partners' needs, putting their partners' needs before their own. Findings regarding liking and participation in different types of sexual activities have suggested that these traditional gender differences remain. Although most young men and women like vaginal intercourse (92% of men and 87% of women ages 18–21 in current sexual partnerships), men are more likely to report liking fellatio (84%) than women are to report liking cunnilingus (75%). Women are also more likely than men to repeatedly engage in disliked activities (Kaestle, 2009). Participating in unwanted or strongly disliked sexual activities could indicate negative relationship characteristics such as dishonesty and dissatisfaction and could lead to shame or risky sexual behavior (Impett & Peplau, 2003; Kaestle, 2009; Kiefer & Sanchez, 2007; MacDonald & Hynie, 2008; see Chapters 10 and 11, this volume). Thus, the role of pleasure and gender in all types of sexual relationships merits more study.

Other themes in the literature have drawn attention to substantial relationship instability during emerging adulthood. Whether emerging adults are pairing up in hook-ups, more serious dating relationships, cohabitation, or marriage, a substantial minority accumulate a large number of sexual partnerships. The beginning, progression, and ending of each of these partnerships may represent a source of repeated instability as emerging adults attempt to recenter from their family of origin to intimate relationships. Furthermore, issues such as sexual assault, STIs, and unwanted pregnancy could also be thought of as major sources of instability as emerging adults attempt to develop their sexual selves.

Marriage or a long-term commitment to a romantic partner is a traditional marker of entry into adulthood and may be perceived as the end to sexual experimentation and instability (although one could clearly argue this point). As expected from an emerging adulthood perspective, fewer young adults have made these commitments compared with earlier cohorts, and the average age at first marriage is increasing. Life course theory proposes that the significance or effects of transitions can vary as a function of timing. An early marriage has different consequences than marriage at a later age (Glenn & Marquardt, 2001; Lehrer, 2008). Furthermore, traditional markers of adulthood, such as marriage, may not necessarily capture variation in autonomy and individuation. Evidence from nonrepresentative samples has suggested that the progression of individuals is quite variable, alternating between increasing and decreasing independence (Cohen, Kasen, Chen, Hartmark, & Gordon, 2003). Therefore, although historic marriage trends were part of the inspiration for emerging adulthood theory, marriage in and of itself cannot be accurately thought of as an end to emerging adulthood.

Themes in Emerging Adulthood Sexuality Research

Has the concept of emerging adulthood contributed to and shaped the understanding of sexuality during this developmental period? To begin to address this question, we examined the articles that reference Arnett's (2000) original emerging adulthood article. Sexual behavior approached from a health standpoint was by far the most common factor in the articles that referenced Arnett's germinal work, often with the word *risk* playing a prominent role in the title of the article (Fergus et al., 2007; Gillen, Lefkowitz, & Shearer, 2006; Grossbard, Lee, Neighbors, Hendershot, & Larimer, 2007; Moore & Davidson, 2006). To date, the particular focus has been on the sexual risk behaviors of men who have sex with men or other sexual minority groups (Agronick et al., 2004; Kubicek et al., 2008; O'Donnell et al., 2002; Warren et al., 2008), as well as on drug use and other health behaviors among sexual minority emerging adults (Kipke, Kubicek, et al., 2007; Kipke, Weiss, et al., 2007; Kipke, Weiss, & Wong, 2007; Kubicek et al., 2007). Measurement issues of orientation during emerging adulthood have also been discussed (Johnson et al., 2006; Thompson & Morgan, 2008; Worthington, Navarro, Savoy, & Hampton, 2008). A few researchers have also connected earlier experiences such as sexual debut (Armour & Haynie, 2007; Magnusson & Trost, 2006) or childhood sexual abuse (Murthi, Servaty-Seib, & Elliott, 2006; Schilling, Aseltine, & Gore, 2007) to one's trajectory through emerging adulthood, and some have explored the emotional contexts and motivations for dating and sexual activity (Kaestle & Halpern, 2007; Patrick, Maggs, & Abar, 2007; Zimmer-Gembeck & Petherick, 2006).

Various potential influences on sexuality during emerging adulthood have also been explored in articles referencing Arnett's (2000) emerging adulthood theory. A few researchers have used emerging adulthood as a framework to explore media effects on sexual attitudes using experimental methods (Eyal & Kunkel, 2008; Farrar, 2006; Ward, 2002), and specific types of media have been associated with sexual stereotypes (Kim & Ward, 2004) and with double standards in attitudes toward sex (Zurbriggen & Morgan, 2006). The connections between exposure to sexually objectifying media, body self-perceptions, and sexual self-concept have also been explored longitudinally (Aubrey, 2006, 2007). Other sources of influence on sexuality in emerging adulthood that have been examined include peers (Lefkowitz, Boone, & Shearer, 2004), religion (Davidson, Moore, Earle, & Davis, 2008; Lefkowitz, Gillen, Shearer, & Boone, 2004), and race (Davidson et al., 2008; Warren et al., 2008). This brief look suggests that much of the extant research explicitly linked to emerging adulthood is covering familiar ground.

Intersectionality, Context, and Sexuality in Emerging Adulthood

Efforts are increasing to simultaneously consider multiple facets of sexual behavior rather than examine only single behaviors in isolation. However, the literature on sexuality in emerging adulthood has yet to recognize and effectively incorporate intersectionality, the understanding that dimensions of culturally constructed categories work in concert (McCall, 2005; Purdie-Vaughns & Eibach, 2008; Shields, 2008). The intersection of multiple constructed categories contributes to systematic inequities in society and different experiences of development and identity through the life course. The assumption that variables make independent contributions to various outcomes and that one can assign independent values to causal factors has been criticized as an overly simplistic approach to developmental research (Gottlieb & Halpern, 2002). Because the existence of emerging adulthood is theoretically driven by major demographic and economic changes, synergistic interactions among various social categories may be particularly important in sexual identity exploration and therefore useful for an understanding of sexual satisfaction, preventive behavior, and health care access during emerging adulthood (Higgins, Mullinax, Trussell, Davidson, & Moore, 2011).

Categories such as socioeconomic class, race, ethnicity, gender, sexual orientation, and educational attainment all potentially affect the resources available to individuals as they enter emerging adulthood, the opportunities they will have for development, and the particular challenges and obstacles they face. Ethnicity and religion likely intersect in effects on sexuality (P. Collins, von Unger, & Armbrister, 2008; Fergus et al., 2007; James et al., 2011; Soet, Dudley, & Dilorio, 1999; Warren et al., 2008), possibly in different ways for men and women. For example, in a sample of college students, Ahrold, Farmer, Trapnell, and Meston (2011) found that female atheists and agnostics reported significantly more sexual fantasies than women with religious affiliations. However, religious group differences were not as strong in men. Moreover, the findings were complex, varying according to the sexual indicator and aspect of religion considered. For example, spirituality seemed to play a split role. In some cases, spirituality was associated with more conservative sexual fantasies and attitudes, whereas in others the opposite was true. These changes appeared to vary depending on the context of women's affiliation with an organized faith (Ahrold et al., 2011).

Critics of emerging adulthood theory have noted that although different groups may experience a delay in independence, some of them do so because they can afford to take extra time to explore roles and experiences, and others delay independent adulthood because they do not have the necessary resources and skills for independent living (Hendry & Kloep, 2011). Are those forced into delay by lack of resources having an emerging adulthood experience, or is emerging adulthood essentially synonymous with a college-track trajectory? Do fewer economic and social opportunities restrict an individual's sexual development and identity explorations?

This question is a difficult one to address because a large body of research on people this age has relied exclusively on college samples, often for practical reasons (Arnett, 2000). Young people from lower income families are more likely to cohabit or marry earlier and may lack some of the resources and opportunities to explore diverse sexualities and relationships during emerging adulthood (Meier & Allen, 2008). Arnett (1998; Arnett & Tanner, 2011b) has noted that people in their 20s from low socioeconomic status families are more likely to say that they had reached adulthood than those from higher brackets. However, he argued that although those from lower socioeconomic backgrounds may make marriage and parenthood transitions earlier than their peers in the middle and upper classes, they still experience a period of years between leaving secondary school and fully entering adult roles. In fact, Arnett (2004; Arnett & Tanner, 2011b) suggested that emerging adulthood may be even more important to youths from lower economic classes because it may facilitate new possibilities and opportunities for change in both love and work as individuals progress toward more stable commitments. Finding desirable partners may be more difficult, however, for youths who directly enter the workforce, because those settings tend to be more age heterogeneous (Meier & Allen, 2008). Thus, although they may share some common characteristics, the lives of emerging adults can presumably vary greatly depending on their social class background, educational attainment, and ethnicity (Arnett & Tanner, 2006; Côté, 2000). Researchers are just beginning to explore this heterogeneity in experiences and their implications for sexuality, often using qualitative techniques for in-depth investigations (Edin & Kefalas, 2005; Waters, 2011).

CONCLUSIONS

Emerging adulthood is characterized as a period of identity exploration, self-focus, and instability. Theoretically, these exploratory processes ultimately result in recentering, wherein an individual transitions from dependent connections toward commitment to an enduring romantic and sexual relationship. Sexuality, as a central facet of identity, is hypothesized to evolve throughout emerging adulthood as a consequence of new experiences and self-reflection. Our broad look at current sexual and partnering patterns in the United States suggests that general population patterns of types, timing, and numbers of partnering experiences reflect these themes, which is not surprising given the role of these demographic trends in the genesis of the construct of emerging adulthood.

The developmental qualities of these experiences, however, and their actual implications for sexual health and general well-being are less well documented, as is the potential for variation across different demographic segments of the population. Much of the research on sexuality during emerging adulthood that attempts to capture process, emotional salience, pleasure, and sexual identity has relied on small, selected samples, often reflecting primarily White college students from middle-class homes. Although rich in detail and insight, it is not likely that such reports can capture the full diversity of experience of youths from different backgrounds and living in different physical and social contexts. For example, it is not known whether the hook-up paradigm that seems so ubiquitous on college campuses is also a common experience among emerging adults who go directly into the workforce or who commute to technical or community college campuses. Such different settings may or may not foster and support a climate of sexual experimentation, and if they do, it is not clear whether the psychosocial consequences would be similar.

Achieving and maintaining healthy sexuality may be conceived as a developmental task that traverses all phases of the life course, beginning at infancy, when "we are conditioned for what our sexual life will be . . . [through] touch, attachment, and bonding" (Coleman, 2006, p. 8), through senescence (see Chapter 13, this volume). However, much of the research on emerging adult sexuality is cross-sectional, significantly limiting the capacity to capture developmental change and therefore to assess the utility of emerging adulthood themes for understanding and explaining the sexual life course of a given individual. Most work to date has examined only proximal associations (e.g., sexual behavior as associated with current religiosity, media use), not the developmental precedents of sexuality in emerging adulthood and the longer term implications for adult sexuality. Reliance on cross-sectional data also precludes opportunities to understand whether associations between sexual patterns and well-being reflect the effects of experience on the individual, the aspects of the individual and his or her background that lead to the selection of certain partnering types and experiences, or perhaps both.

In addition to addressing the limitations of selected samples and cross-sectional study designs, research on sexuality in emerging adulthood could be enriched through more widespread application of an integrative holistic perspective. Person-centered approaches, which simultaneously capture multiple personal and experiential dimensions and the implicit interactions among them, offer relatively manageable strategies for linking facets of sexuality with broader health and well-being and for illuminating nuances that might otherwise be missed. For example, on the basis of cluster analysis, McGuire and Barber (2010) found that two clusters of 20- and 21-year-old women, each characterized by high frequency of sexual activity, differed substantially in sexual risk taking and the importance attached to sex and therefore in related aspects of health. These findings suggest the limitations, and potential for misinterpretation, of simply examining linkages between isolated sexual measures, such as amount of experience or number of sexual encounters during emerging adulthood, and sexual health. It also raises the issue of examining sexuality in context, whether that context is a one-time encounter or a long-term committed relationship. The construct of emerging adulthood, with its emphasis on identity exploration and integration, could serve as a valuable framework for investigating the sexual pathways of diverse individuals if implemented with designs and measures that capture multiple sexual dimensions and the intersections of distinct cultural categories.

Despite increasing recognition of the need to balance the study of sexual risk with the study of positive sexuality, relatively few studies have successfully integrated these domains. As we noted earlier, little research has examined sexual satisfaction in emerging adulthood despite the importance of sexuality in this period of the life course. Closing this gap is particularly important for understanding the similarities and differences in how men and women experience sexuality during emerging adulthood in terms of behavioral and emotional responses to conflicting sexual scripts and of basic desire and pleasure. By furthering our understanding of the developmental processes underlying emerging adult sexuality, pleasure, and satisfaction on the one hand, we will also further the potential of public health efforts to promote safe sex practices and sexual health on the other.

References

Abbey, A. (1987). Misperceptions of friendly behavior as sexual interest: A survey of naturally occurring incidents. *Psychology of Women Quarterly, 11*, 173. doi:10.1111/j.1471-6402.1987.tb00782.x

Abma, J. C., Martinez, G. M., & Copen, C. E. (2010). Teenagers in the United States: Sexual activity, contraceptive use, and childbearing, National Survey of Family Growth 2006–2008. *Vital and Health Statistics, 23*(30).

Adamczyk, A. (2009). Socialization and selection in the link between friends' religiosity and the transition to sexual intercourse. *Sociology of Religion, 70*, 5–27. doi:10.1093/socrel/srp010

Adimora, A. A., Schoenbach, V. J., Bonas, D. M., Martinson, F. E., Donaldson, K. H., & Stancil, T. R. (2002). Concurrent sexual partnerships among women in the United States. *Epidemiology, 13*, 320–327. doi:10.1097/00001648-200205000-00013

Agronick, G., O'Donnell, L., Stueve, A., Doval, A. S., Duran, R., & Vargo, S. (2004). Sexual behaviors and risks among bisexually- and gay-identified young Latino men. *AIDS and Behavior, 8*, 185–197. doi:10.1023/B:AIBE.0000030249.11679.d0

Ahrold, T. K., Farmer, M., Trapnell, P. D., & Meston, C. M. (2011). The relationship among sexual attitudes, sexual fantasy, and religiosity. *Archives of Sexual Behavior, 40*, 619–630. doi:10.1007/s10508-010-9621-4

Anderson, J. E. (2003). Condom use and HIV risk among US adults. *American Journal of Public Health, 93*, 912–914. doi:10.2105/AJPH.93.6.912

Armour, S., & Haynie, D. (2007). Adolescent sexual debut and later delinquency. *Journal of Youth and Adolescence, 36*, 141–152. doi:10.1007/s10964-006-9128-4

Armstrong, E. A., England, P., & Fogarty, A. C. K. (2012). Accounting for women's orgasm and sexual enjoyment in college hookups and relationships. *American Sociological Review, 77*, 435–462. doi:10.1177/0003122412445802

Arnett, J. J. (1998). Learning to stand alone: The contemporary American transition to adulthood in cultural and historical context. *Human Development, 41*, 295–315. doi:10.1159/000022591

Arnett, J. J. (2000). Emerging adulthood: A theory of development from the late teens through the twenties. *American Psychologist, 55*, 469–480. doi:10.1037/0003-066X.55.5.469

Arnett, J. J. (2004). *Emerging adulthood: The winding road from the late teens through the twenties.* New York, NY: Oxford University Press.

Arnett, J. J. (2011). *Debating emerging adulthood: Stage or process.* New York, NY: Oxford University Press. doi:10.1093/acprof:oso/9780199757176.001.0001

Arnett, J. J., & Tanner, J. L. (Eds.). (2006). *Emerging adults in America: Coming of age in the 21st century.* Washington, DC: American Psychological Association. doi:10.1037/11381-000

Arnett, J. J., & Tanner, J. (2011a). In defense of emerging adulthood as a life stage: Rejoinder to Kloep's and Hendry's Chapters 4 and 5. In J. J. Arnett (Ed.), *Debating emerging adulthood: Stage or process* (pp. 121–134). New York, NY: Oxford University Press. doi:10.1093/acprof:oso/9780199757176.003.0007

Arnett, J. J., & Tanner, J. (2011b). Themes and variations in emerging adulthood across social classes. In J. J. Arnett (Ed.), *Debating emerging adulthood: Stage or process* (pp. 31–52). New York, NY: Oxford University Press. doi:10.1093/acprof:oso/9780199757176.003.0003

Aubrey, J. S. (2006). Exposure to sexually objectifying media and body self-perceptions among college women: An examination of the selective exposure hypothesis and the role of moderating variables. *Sex Roles, 55*, 159–172. doi:10.1007/s11199-006-9070-7

Aubrey, J. S. (2007). Does television exposure influence college-aged women's sexual self-concept? *Media Psychology, 10*, 157–181. doi:10.1080/15213260701375561

Axinn, W. G., & Thornton, A. (2000). The transformation in the meaning of marriage. In L. J. Waite, C. Bachrach, M. Hindin, E. Thomson, & A. Thornton (Eds.), *The ties that bind: Perspectives on marriage and cohabitation* (pp. 147–165). New York, NY: Aldine De Gruyter.

Banker, J. E., Kaestle, C. E., & Allen, K. R. (2010). Dating is hard work: A narrative approach to understanding sexual and romantic relationships in young adulthood. *Contemporary Family Therapy: An International Journal, 32*, 173–191. doi:10.1007/s10591-009-9111-9

Barry, C. M., Madsen, S. D., Nelson, L. J., Carroll, J. S., & Badger, S. (2009). Friendship and romantic relationship qualities in emerging adulthood: Differential associations with identity development and achieved adulthood criteria. *Journal of Adult Development, 16*, 209–222. doi:10.1007/s10804-009-9067-x

Bay-Cheng, L. Y., Robinson, A. D., & Zucker, A. N. (2009). Behavioral and relational contexts of adolescent desire, wanting, and pleasure: Undergraduate women's retrospective accounts. *Journal of Sex Research, 46*, 511–524. doi:10.1080/00224490902867871

Bisson, M. A., & Levine, T. R. (2009). Negotiating a friends with benefits relationship. *Archives of Sexual Behavior, 38*, 66–73. doi:10.1007/s10508-007-9211-2

Blum, R. W., Kelly, A., & Ireland, M. (2001). Health-risk behaviors and protective factors among adolescents with mobility impairments and learning and emotional disabilities. *Journal of Adolescent Health, 28*, 481–490. doi:10.1016/S1054-139X(01)00201-4

Bogart, L. M., Cecil, H., Wagstaff, D. A., Pinkerton, S. D., & Abramson, P. R. (2000). Is it "sex"? College students' interpretations of sexual behavior terminology. *Journal of Sex Research, 37*, 108–116. doi:10.1080/00224490009552027

Bogle, K. A. (2008). *Hooking up: Sex, dating, and relationships on campus*. New York, NY: New York University Press.

Boyle, A. M., & O'Sullivan, L. F. (2010). General and sexual communication in established relationships: An exploration of possible links to condom use among young adults. *Canadian Journal of Human Sexuality, 19*, 53–64.

Brown, J. D. (2002). Mass media influences on sexuality. *Journal of Sex Research, 39*, 42–45. doi:10.1080/00224490209552118

Brown, J. D., & Bobkowski, P. S. (2011). Older and newer media: Patterns of use and effects on adolescents' health and well-being. *Journal of Research on Adolescence, 21*, 95–113. doi:10.1111/j.1532-7795.2010.00717.x

Buerkel-Rothfuss, N. L., Greenberg, B. S., & Brown, J. D. (1993). Adolescents' and young adults' exposure to sexually oriented and sexually explicit media. In B. S. Greenberg, J. D. Brown, & N. L. Buerkel-Rothfuss (Eds.), *Media, sex, and the adolescent* (pp. 99–113). Cresskill, NJ: Hampton Press.

Bumpass, L. L., Sweet, J. A., & Cherlin, A. (1991). The role of cohabitation in declining rates of marriage. *Journal of Marriage and the Family, 53*, 913–927. doi:10.2307/352997

Buzwell, S., & Rosenthal, D. (1996). Constructing a sexual self: Adolescents' sexual self-perceptions and sexual risk-taking. *Journal of Research on Adolescence, 6*, 489–513.

Cantor, N., Acker, M., & Cook-Flannagan, C. (1992). Conflict and preoccupation in the intimacy life task. *Journal of Personality and Social Psychology, 63*, 644–655. doi:10.1037/0022-3514.63.4.644

Caron, S., Davis, C., Halteman, W., & Stickle, M. (1993). Predictors of condom-related behaviors among first-year college students. *Journal of Sex Research, 30*, 252–259. doi:10.1080/00224499309551709

Centers for Disease Control and Prevention. (2011a). Abortion surveillance—United States, 2007. *MMWR Surveillance Summaries, 60*(1), 1–39.

Centers for Disease Control and Prevention. (2011b). *HIV Surveillance Report 2009*. Atlanta, GA: Author.

Centers for Disease Control and Prevention. (2011c). *Sexually transmitted disease surveillance 2010*. Atlanta, GA: Author.

Chandra, A., Martino, S. C., Collins, R. L., Elliott, M. N., Berry, S. H., & Kanouse, D. E. (2008). Does watching sex on television predict teen pregnancy? Findings from a national longitudinal survey of youth. *Pediatrics, 122*, 1047–1054. doi:10.1542/peds.2007-3066

Chandra, A., Mosher, W. D., Copen, C., & Sionean, C. (2011). *Sexual behavior, sexual attraction, and sexual identity in the United States: Data from the 2006–2008 National Survey of Family Growth* (National Health Statistics Reports No. 36). Hyattsville, MD: National Center for Health Statistics.

Cheng, M. M., & Udry, J. R. (2002). Sexual behaviors of physically disabled adolescents in the United States. *Journal of Adolescent Health, 31*, 48–58. doi:10.1016/S1054-139X(01)00400-1

Cheng, M. M., & Udry, J. R. (2005). Sexual experiences of adolescents with low cognitive abilities in the US. *Journal of Developmental and Physical Disabilities, 17*, 155–172. doi:10.1007/s10882-005-3686-3

Cherlin, A. J. (2004). The deinstitutionalization of American marriage. *Journal of Marriage and the Family, 66*, 848–861. doi:10.1111/j.0022-2445.2004.00058.x

Cohen, P., Kasen, S., Chen, H. N., Hartmark, C., & Gordon, K. (2003). Variations in patterns of developmental transitions in the emerging adulthood period. *Developmental Psychology, 39*, 657–669. doi:10.1037/0012-1649.39.4.657

Coleman, E. (2002). Masturbation as a means of achieving sexual health. *Journal of Psychology and Human Sexuality, 14*(2–3), 5–16. doi:10.1300/J056v14n02_02

Coleman, E. (2006). The public health challenge. In *Defining sexual health: Report of a technical consultation on sexual health*, 28–31 January 2002 (p. 8). Geneva, Switzerland: World Health Organization.

Coles, R., & Stokes, G. (1985). *Sex and the American teenager*. New York, NY: Harper & Row.

Collins, P. Y., von Unger, H., & Armbrister, A. (2008). Church ladies, good girls, and locas: Stigma and the intersection of gender, ethnicity, mental illness, and sexuality in relation to HIV risk. *Social Science and Medicine, 67*, 389–397. doi:10.1016/j.socscimed.2008.03.013

Collins, R. L., Elliott, M. N., Berry, S. H., Kanouse, D. E., Kunkel, D., & Hunter, S. B. (2004). Watching sex on television predicts adolescent initiation of sexual behavior. *Pediatrics, 114*, e280–e289. doi:10.1542/peds.2003-1065-L

Collins, W. A., & van Dulmen, M. (2006). Friendships and romance in emerging adulthood: Assessing distinctiveness in close relationships. In J. J. Arnett & J. L. Tanner (Eds.), *Emerging adults in America: Coming of age in the 21st century* (pp. 219–234). Washington, DC: American Psychological Association. doi:10.1037/11381-009

Conger, R. D., Cui, M., Bryant, C. M., & Elder, G. H., Jr. (2000). Competence in early adult romantic relationships: A developmental perspective on family influences. *Journal of Personality and Social Psychology, 79*, 224–237. doi:10.1037/0022-3514.79.2.224

Connolly, J., Craig, W., Goldberg, A., & Pepler, D. (2004). Mixed-gender groups, dating, and romantic relationships in early adolescence. *Journal of Research on Adolescence, 14*, 185–207. doi:10.1111/j.1532-7795.2004.01402003.x

Copen, C. E., Daniels, K., Vespa, J., & Mosher, W. D. (2012). *First marriages in the United States: Data from the 2006–2010 National Survey of Family Growth* (National Health Statistics Reports No. 49). Hyattsville, MD: National Center for Health Statistics

Côté, J. E. (2000). *Arrested adulthood: The changing nature of maturity and identity*. New York, NY: New York University Press.

Creti, L., & Libman, E. (1989). Cognitions and sexual expression in the aging. *Journal of Sex and Marital Therapy, 15*, 83–101. doi:10.1080/0092623890 8403814

Curtin, N., Ward, L. M., Merriwether, A., & Caruthers, A. (2011). Femininity ideology and sexual health in young women: A focus on sexual knowledge, embodiment, and agency. *International Journal of Sexual Health, 23*, 48–62. doi:10.1080/19317611.201 0.524694

Darling, C. A., Davidson, J. K., & Passarello, L. C. (1992). The mystique of first intercourse among college youth: The role of partners, contraceptive practices, and psychological reactions. *Journal of Youth and Adolescence, 21*, 97–117. doi:10.1007/BF01536984

Davidson, J. K., Moore, N. B., Earle, J. R., & Davis, R. (2008). Sexual attitudes and behavior at four universities: Do region, race, and/or religion matter? *Adolescence, 43*, 189–220.

Davis, K. (2010). Coming of age online: The developmental underpinnings of girls' blogs. *Journal of Adolescent Research, 25*, 145–171. doi:10.1177/0743558409350503

de Graaf, H., Vanwesenbeeck, I., Meijer, S., Woertman, L., & Meeus, W. (2009). Sexual trajectories during adolescence: Relation to demographic characteristics and sexual risk. *Archives of Sexual Behavior, 38*, 276–282. doi:10.1007/s10508-007-9281-1

Diamond, L. M. (2000). Sexual identity, attractions, and behavior among young sexual-minority women over a 2-year period. *Developmental Psychology, 36*, 241–250. doi:10.1037/0012-1649.36.2.241

Dickson, N., Paul, C., & Herbison, P. (2003). Same-sex attraction in a birth cohort: Prevalence and persistence in early adulthood. *Social Science and Medicine, 56*, 1607–1615. doi:10.1016/S0277-9536(02)00161-2

Downing-Matibag, T. M., & Geisinger, B. (2009). Hooking up and sexual risk taking among college students: A health belief model perspective. *Qualitative Health Research, 19*, 1196–1209. doi:10.1177/ 1049732309344206

Dunn, L. M. (1981). *Peabody Picture Vocabulary Test—Revised: Manual for Forms L and M*. Circle Pines, NM: American Guidance Service.

Dush, C. M. K., Cohan, C. L., & Amato, P. R. (2003). The relationship between cohabitation and marital quality and stability: Change across cohorts? *Journal of Marriage and Family, 65*, 539–549. doi:10.1111/ j.1741-3737.2003.00539.x

Edin, K., & Kefalas, M. (2005). *Promises I can keep: Why poor women put motherhood before marriage*. Berkeley: University of California Press.

Elder, G. (1985). Perspectives on the life course. In G. Elder (Ed.), *Life course dynamics: Trajectories and transitions* (pp. 23–50). Ithaca, NY: Cornell University Press.

Else-Quest, N. M., Hyde, J. S., & DeLamater, J. D. (2005). Context counts: Long-term sequelae of premarital intercourse or abstinence. *Journal of Sex Research, 42*, 102–112. doi:10.1080/00224490509552263

England, P., Schafer, E. F., & Fogarty, A. C. K. (2007). Hooking up and forming romantic relationships on today's college campuses. In M. Kimmel (Ed.), *The gendered society reader* (3rd ed., pp. 531–593). New York, NY: Oxford University Press.

Epstein, M., Calzo, J. P., Smiler, A. P., & Ward, L. M. (2009). "Anything from making out to having sex:" Men's negotiations of hooking up and friends with benefits scripts. *Journal of Sex Research, 46*, 414–424. doi:10.1080/00224490902775801

Erikson, E. H. (1968). *Identity: Youth and crisis*. New York, NY: W. W. Norton.

Eshbaugh, E. M., & Gute, G. (2008). Hookups and sexual regret among college women. *Journal of Social Psychology, 148*, 77–90. doi:10.3200/ SOCP.148.1.77-90

Eyal, K., & Kunkel, D. (2008). The effects of sex in television drama shows on emerging adults' sexual attitudes and moral judgments. *Journal of Broadcasting and Electronic Media, 52*, 161–181. doi:10.1080/08838150801991757

Farrar, K. M. (2006). Sexual intercourse on television: Do safe sex messages matter? *Journal of Broadcasting and Electronic Media, 50*, 635–650. doi:10.1207/ s15506878jobem5004_4

Fergus, S., Zimmerman, M. A., & Caldwell, C. H. (2007). Growth trajectories of sexual risk behavior in adolescence and young adulthood. *American Journal of Public Health, 97*, 1096–1101. doi:10.2105/AJPH.2005.074609

Fielder, R. L., & Carey, M. P. (2010a). Predictors and consequences of sexual "hookups" among college students: A short-term prospective study. *Archives of Sexual Behavior, 39*, 1105–1119. doi:10.1007/s10508-008-9448-4

Fielder, R. L., & Carey, M. P. (2010b). Prevalence and characteristics of sexual hookups among first-semester female college students. *Journal of Sex and Marital Therapy, 36*, 346–359. doi:10.1080/0092623X.2010.488118

Finer, L. B. (2007). Trends in premarital sex in the United States, 1954–2003. *Public Health Reports, 122*, 73–78.

Finkelhor, D., & Brown, A. (1985). The traumatic impact of child sexual abuse: A conceptualization. *American Journal of Orthopsychiatry, 55*, 530–541. doi:10.1111/j.1939-0025.1985.tb02703.x

Flack, W. F., Jr., Daubman, K. A., Caron, M. L., Asadorian, J. A., D'Aureli, N. R., & Gigliotti, S. N. (2007). Risk factors and consequences of unwanted sex among university students: Hooking up, alcohol, and stress response. *Journal of Interpersonal Violence, 22*, 139–157. doi:10.1177/0886260506295354

Freitas, D. (2008). *Sex and the soul: Juggling sexuality, spirituality, romance, and religion on America's college campuses*. New York, NY: Oxford University Press.

Furman, W., & Hand, L. S. (2006). The slippery nature of romantic relationships: Issues in definition and differentiation. In A. C. Crouter & A. Booth (Eds.), *Romance and sex in adolescence and emerging adulthood: Risks and opportunities* (pp. 171–178). Mahwah, NJ: Erlbaum.

Furman, W., & Shaffer, L. (2011). Romantic partners, friends, friends with benefits, and casual acquaintances as sexual partners. *Journal of Sex Research, 48*, 554–564. doi:10.1080/00224499.2010.535623

Gallo, L. C., Troxel, W. M., Matthews, K. A., & Kuller, L. H. (2003). Marital status and quality in middle-aged women: Associations with levels and trajectories of cardiovascular risk factors. *Health Psychology, 22*, 453–463. doi:10.1037/0278-6133.22.5.453

Garcia, J. R., & Reiber, C. (2008). Hook-up behavior: A biopsychosocial perspective. *Journal of Social, Evolutionary, and Cultural Psychology, 2*, 192–208.

Garcia, J. R., Reiber, C., Massey, S. G., & Merriwether, S. G. (2012). Sexual hookup culture: A review. *Review of General Psychology, 16*, 161–176. doi:10.1037/a0027911

Gavey, N., & McPhillips, K. (1999). Heterosexual passivity as an obstacle to women initiating condom use. *Psychology of Women Quarterly, 23*, 349–367. doi:10.1111/j.1471-6402.1999.tb00366.x

Gavin, L., MacKay, A. P., Brown, K., Harrier, S., Ventura, S. J., & Kann, L. (2009). Sexual and reproductive health of persons aged 10–24 years—United States, 2002–2007. *MMWR Surveillance Summaries, 58*(6), 1–58.

Gebhardt, W. A., Kuyper, L., & Greunsven, G. (2003). Need for intimacy in relationships and motives for sex as determinants of adolescent condom use. *Journal of Adolescent Health, 33*, 154–164. doi:10.1016/S1054-139X(03)00137-X

Gerressu, M., Mercer, C. H., Graham, C. A., Wellings, K., & Johnson, A. M. (2008). Prevalence of masturbation and associated factors in a British national probability survey. *Archives of Sexual Behavior, 37*, 266–278. doi:10.1007/s10508-006-9123-6

Gillen, M. M., Lefkowitz, E. S., & Shearer, C. L. (2006). Does body image play a role in risky sexual behavior and attitudes? *Journal of Youth and Adolescence, 35*, 230–242. doi:10.1007/s10964-005-9005-6

Glenn, N., & Marquardt, E. (2001). *Hooking up, hanging out, and waiting for Mr. Right: College Women on dating and mating today*. New York, NY: Institute for American Values.

Goldberg, S., Hussey, J., & Halpern, C. T. (2012). *Adolescent predictors of lifetime hook-up occurrence among U.S. young adults.* Manuscript submitted for publication.

Good, G. E., & Sherrod, N. (1997). Men's resolution of non-relational sex across the lifespan. In R. Levant & G. Brooks (Eds.), *Men and sex: New psychological perspectives* (pp. 182–204). New York, NY: Wiley.

Goodwin, P. Y., Mosher, W. D., & Chandra, A. (2010). Marriage and cohabitation in the United States: A statistical portrait based on Cycle 6 (2002) of the National Survey of Family Growth. *Vital and Health Statistics, 23*(28).

Gottlieb, G., & Halpern, C. T. (2002). A relational view of causality in normal and abnormal development. *Development and Psychopathology, 14*, 421–435. doi:10.1017/S0954579402003024

Grello, C. M., Welsh, D. P., & Harper, M. S. (2006). No strings attached: The nature of casual sex in college students. *Journal of Sex Research, 43*, 255–267. doi:10.1080/00224490609552324

Grello, C. M., Welsh, D. P., Harper, M. S., & Dickson, J. W. (2003). Dating and sexual relationship trajectories and adolescent functioning. *Adolescent and Family Health, 3*, 103–112.

Grossbard, J. R., Lee, C. M., Neighbors, C., Hendershot, C. S., & Larimer, M. E. (2007). Alcohol and risky sex in athletes and nonathletes: What roles do sex motives play? *Journal of Studies on Alcohol and Drugs, 68*, 566–574.

Grotevant, H. D., & Cooper, C. R. (1985). Patterns of interaction in family relationships and the development of identity exploration in adolescence. *Child Development, 56*, 415–428. doi:10.2307/1129730

Gute, G., Eshbaugh, E. M., & Wiersma, J. (2008). Sex for you, but not for me: Discontinuity in undergraduate emerging adults' definitions of "having sex." *Journal of Sex Research, 45*, 329–337. doi:10.1080/00224490802398332

Halpern, C. J. T., Udry, J. R., Suchindran, C., & Campbell, B. (2000). Adolescent males' willingness to report masturbation. *Journal of Sex Research, 37*, 327–332. doi:10.1080/00224490009552055

Halpern, C. T., & Haydon, A. A. (2012). Sexual timetables for oral-genital, vaginal, and anal sex: Sociodemographic comparisons in a nationally representative sample. *American Journal of Public Health, 102*, 1221–1228. doi:10.2105/AJPH.2011.300394

Halpern, C. T., Joyner, K., Udry, J. R., & Suchindran, C. (2000). Smart teens don't have sex (or kiss much either). *Journal of Adolescent Health, 26*, 213–225. doi:10.1016/S1054-139X(99)00061-0

Halpern, C. T., Kaestle, C. E., Guo, G., & Hallfors, D. D. (2007). Gene-environment contributions to young adult sexual partnering. *Archives of Sexual Behavior, 36*, 543–554. doi:10.1007/s10508-006-9084-9

Halpern, C. T., King, R. B., Oslak, S. G., & Udry, J. R. (2005). Body mass index, dieting, romance, and sexual activity in adolescent girls: Relationships over time. *Journal of Research on Adolescence, 15*, 535–559. doi:10.1111/j.1532-7795.2005.00110.x

Halpern, C. T., Waller, M. W., Spriggs, A., & Hallfors, D. D. (2006). Adolescent predictors of emerging adult sexual patterns. *Journal of Adolescent Health, 39*, 926 e1–e10. doi:10.1016/j.jadohealth.2006.08.005

Hamilton, L., & Armstrong, E. A. (2009). Gendered sexuality in young adulthood: Double binds and flawed options. *Gender and Society, 23*, 589–616. doi:10.1177/0891243209345829

Hariri, S., Unger, E. R., Sternberg, M., Dunne, E. F., Swan, D., & Patel, S. (2011). Prevalence of genital human papillomavirus among females in the United States, the National Health and Nutrition Examination Survey, 2003–2006. *Journal of Infectious Diseases, 204*, 566–573. doi:10.1093/infdis/jir341

Harris, K. M., Halpern, C. T., Whitsel, E. A., Hussey, J., Tabor, J., & Entzel, P. (2009). *The National Longitudinal Study of Adolescent Health: Research design.* Retrieved from http://www.cpc.unc.edu/projects/addhealth/design

Harris, K. M., Lee, L., & DeLeone, F. Y. (2010). Marriage and health in the transition to adulthood: Evidence for African Americans in the Add Health Study. *Journal of Family Issues, 31*, 1106–1143. doi:10.1177/0192513X10365823

Havighurst, R. J. (1948). *Developmental tasks and education.* Chicago, IL: University of Chicago Press.

Haydon, A. A., Cheng, M. M., Herring, A. H., McRee, A. L., & Halpern, C. T. (in press). Like a virgin: Prevalence and predictors of adult sexual inexperience. Manuscript under review. *Archives of Sexual Behavior.*

Haydon, A. A., Herring, A. H., & Halpern, C. T. (2012). The association between patterns of emerging sexual behavior and reproductive health in young adulthood. *Perspectives on Sexual and Reproductive Health, 44*, 218–227.

Haydon, A. A., Herring, A. H., Prinstein, M. J., & Halpern, C. T. (2012). Beyond age at first sex: Patterns of emerging sexual behavior in adolescence and young adulthood. *Journal of Adolescent Health, 50*, 456–463. doi:10.1016/j.jadohealth.2011.09.006

Haydon, A. A., Hussey, J. M., & Halpern, C. T. (2011). Childhood abuse and neglect and the risk of STDs in early adulthood. *Perspectives on Sexual and Reproductive Health, 43*, 16–22. doi:10.1363/4301611

Haydon, A. A., McRee, A.-L., & Halpern, C. T. (2011). Risk-taking behavior. In B. B. Brown & M. J. Prinstein (Eds.), *Encyclopedia of adolescence: Vol. 1. Psychopathology and non-normative processes* (pp. 255–263). Oxford, England: Elsevier. doi:10.1016/B978-0-12-373951-3.00129-0

Heck, K. E., Schoendorf, K. C., Ventura, S. J., & Kiely, J. L. (1997). Delayed childbearing by education level in the United States, 1969–1994. *Maternal and Child Health Journal, 1*, 81–88. doi:10.1023/A:1026218322723

Heinrichs, K. D., MacKnee, C., Auton-Cuff, F., & Domene, J. R. (2009). Factors affecting sexual-self esteem among young adult women in long-term heterosexual relationships. *Canadian Journal of Human Sexuality, 18*, 183–199.

Heldman, C., & Wade, L. (2010). Hook-up culture: Setting a new research agenda. *Sexuality Research and Social Policy, 7*, 323–333. doi:10.1007/s13178-010-0024-z

Hendry, L., & Kloep, M. (2011). Lifestyles in emerging adulthood: Who needs stages anyway? In J. J. Arnett (Ed.), *Debating emerging adulthood: Stage or process* (pp. 77–108). New York, NY: Oxford University Press. doi:10.1093/acprof:oso/9780199757176.003.0005

Herbenick, D., Reece, M., Schick, V., Sanders, S. A., Dodge, B., & Fortenberry, J. D. (2010). Sexual behavior in the United States: Results from a national probability sample of men and women ages 14–94. *Journal of Sexual Medicine, 7*(Suppl. 5), 255–265. doi:10.1111/j.1743-6109.2010.02012.x

Higgins, J. A., Mullinax, M., Trussell, J., Davidson, J. K., & Moore, N. B. (2011). Sexual satisfaction and sexual health among university students in the United States. *American Journal of Public Health, 101*, 1643–1654. doi:10.2105/ajph.2011.300154

Higgins, J. A., Trussell, J., Moore, N. B., & Davidson, J. K. (2010). Virginity lost, satisfaction gained? Physiological and psychological sexual satisfaction at heterosexual debut. *Journal of Sex Research, 47*, 384–394. doi:10.1080/00224491003774792

Hogarth, H., & Ingham, R. (2009). Masturbation among young women and associations with sexual health: An exploratory study. *Journal of Sex Research, 46*, 558–567. doi:10.1080/00224490902878993

Horne, S., & Zimmer-Gembeck, M. J. (2006). The Female Sexual Subjectivity Inventory: Development and validation of a multidimensional inventory for late adolescents and emerging adults. *Psychology of Women Quarterly, 30*, 125–138. doi:10.1111/j.1471-6402.2006.00276.x

Impett, E. A., & Peplau, L. A. (2003). Sexual compliance: Gender, motivational, and relationship perspectives. *Journal of Sex Research, 40*, 87–100. doi:10.1080/00224490309552169

Impett, E. A., Schooler, D., & Tolman, D. L. (2006). To be seen and not heard: Femininity ideology and adolescent girls' sexual health. *Archives of Sexual Behavior, 35*, 129–142. doi:10.1007/s10508-005-9016-0

James, C. A., Hart, T. A., Roberts, K. E., Ghai, A., Petrovic, B., & Lima, M. D. (2011). Religion versus ethnicity as predictors of unprotected vaginal intercourse among young adults. *Sexual Health, 8*, 363–371. doi:10.1071/SH09119

Johnson, H. D., McNair, R., Vojick, A., Congdon, D., Monacelli, J., & Lamont, J. (2006). Categorical and continuous measurement of sex-role orientation: Differences in associations with young adults' reports of well-being. *Social Behavior and Personality: An International Journal, 34*, 59–76. doi:10.2224/sbp.2006.34.1.59

Johnston, L. G., Bachman, J. G., & O'Malley, P. M. (2007). *Monitoring the Future: A continuing study of American youth, 2005* (ICPSR 04536-v2). Ann Arbor: Inter-university Consortium for Political and Social Research, University of Michigan.

Jonason, P. K., Li, N. P., & Richardson, J. (2011). Positioning the booty-call relationship on the spectrum of relationships: Sexual but more emotional than one-night stands. *Journal of Sex Research, 48*, 486–495. doi:10.1080/00224499.2010.497984

Joyner, K., & Campa, M. (2006). How do adolescent relationships influence the quality of romantic and sexual relationships in young adulthood? In A. C. Crouter & A. Booth (Eds.), *Romance and sex in adolescence and emerging adulthood: Risks and opportunities* (pp. 93–102). Mahwah, NJ: Erlbaum.

Kaestle, C. E. (2009). Sexual insistence and disliked sexual activities in young adulthood: Differences by gender and relationship characteristics. *Perspectives on Sexual and Reproductive Health, 41*, 33–39. doi:10.1363/4103309

Kaestle, C. E., & Allen, K. R. (2011). The role of masturbation in healthy sexual development: Perceptions of young adults. *Archives of Sexual Behavior, 40*, 983–994. doi:10.1007/s10508-010-9722-0

Kaestle, C. E., & Halpern, C. T. (2007). What's love got to do with it? Sexual behaviors of opposite-sex couples through emerging adulthood. *Perspectives on Sexual and Reproductive Health, 39*, 134–140. doi:10.1363/3913407

Kaestle, C. E., Halpern, C. T., Miller, W. C., & Ford, C. A. (2005). Young age at first sexual intercourse and sexually transmitted infections in adolescents and young adults. *American Journal of Epidemiology, 161*, 774–780. doi:10.1093/aje/kwi095

Kaiser Family Foundation. (2011). *Sexual health of adolescents and young adults in the United States*. Menlo Park, CA: Author.

Kaye, K., Suellentrop, K., & Sloup, C. (2009). *The fog zone: How misperceptions, magical thinking, and ambivalence put young adults at risk for unintended pregnancy*. Washington, DC: National Campaign to Prevent Teen and Unplanned Pregnancy.

Keniston, K. (1971). *Youth and dissent: The rise of a new opposition*. New York, NY: Harcourt Brace Jovanovich.

Kennedy, S., & Bumpass, L. (2008). Cohabitation and children's living arrangements: New estimates from the United States. *Demographic Research, 19*, 1663–1692. doi:10.4054/DemRes.2008.19.47

Kiecolt-Glaser, J. K., & Newton, T. L. (2001). Marriage and health: His and hers. *Psychological Bulletin, 127*, 472–503. doi:10.1037/0033-2909.127.4.472

Kiefer, A. K., & Sanchez, D. T. (2007). Scripting sexual passivity: A gender role perspective. *Personal Relationships, 14*, 269–290. doi:10.1111/j.1475-6811.2007.00154.x

Kim, J. L., & Ward, L. M. (2004). Pleasure reading: Associations between young women's sexual attitudes and their reading of contemporary women's magazines. *Psychology of Women Quarterly, 28*, 48–58. doi:10.1111/j.1471-6402.2004.00122.x

Kipke, M. D., Kubicek, K., Weiss, G., Wong, C., Lopez, D., & Iverson, E. (2007). The health and health behaviors of young men who have sex with men. *Journal of Adolescent Health, 40*, 342–350. doi:10.1016/j.jadohealth.2006.10.019

Kipke, M. D., Weiss, G., Ramirez, M., Dorey, F., Ritt-Olson, A., & Iverson, E. (2007). Club drug use in Los Angeles among young men who have sex with men. *Substance Use and Misuse, 42*, 1723–1743. doi:10.1080/10826080701212261

Kipke, M. D., Weiss, G., & Wong, C. F. (2007). Residential status as a risk factor for drug use and HIV risk among young men who have sex with men. *AIDS and Behavior, 11*(2, Suppl.), 56–69. doi:10.1007/s10461-006-9204-5

Kreider, R. M. (2005). *Number, timing, and duration of marriages and divorces: 2001* (Current Population Reports, P 70-97). Washington, DC: U.S. Census Bureau.

Kubicek, K., Carpineto, J., McDavitt, B., Weiss, G., Iverson, E. F., Au, C. W., . . . Kipke, M. D. (2008). Integrating professional and folk models of HIV risk: YMSM's perceptions of high-risk sex. *AIDS Education and Prevention, 20*, 220–238. doi:10.1521/aeap.2008.20.3.220

Kubicek, K., McDavitt, B., Carpineto, J., Weiss, G., Iverson, E. F., & Kipke, M. D. (2007). Making informed decisions: How attitudes and perceptions affect the use of crystal, cocaine and ecstasy among young men who have sex with men. *Journal of Drug Issues, 37*, 643–672. doi:10.1177/00220426070 3700308

Kunkel, D., Eyal, K., Donnerstein, E., Farrar, K. M., Biely, E., & Rideout, V. (2007). Sexual socialization messages on entertainment television: Comparing content trends 1997–2002. *Media Psychology, 9*, 595–622. doi:10.1080/15213260701283210

Lam, C. B., & Lefkowitz, E. S. (2012). Risky sexual behaviors in emerging adults: Longitudinal changes and within-person variations. *Archives of Sexual Behavior*. Advance online publication. doi:10.1007/s10508-012-9959-x

Laumann, E. O., Gagnon, J. H., Michael, R. T., & Michaels, S. (1994). *The social organization of sexuality: Sexual practices in the United States.* Chicago, IL: University of Chicago Press.

Lefkowitz, E. S. (2005). "Things have gotten better": Developmental changes among emerging adults after the transition to university. *Journal of Adolescent Research, 20*, 40–63. doi:10.1177/0743558404271236

Lefkowitz, E. S., Boone, T. L., & Shearer, C. L. (2004). Communication with best friends about sex-related topics during emerging adulthood. *Journal of Youth and Adolescence, 33*, 339–351. doi:10.1023/B:JOYO.0000032642.27242.c1

Lefkowitz, E. S., & Gillen, M. M. (2006). "Sex is just a normal part of life": Sexuality in emerging adulthood. In J. J. Arnett & J. L. Tanner (Eds.), *Emerging adults in America: Coming of age in the 21st century* (pp. 235–255). Washington, DC: American Psychological Association. doi:10.1037/11381-010

Lefkowitz, E. S., Gillen, M. M., Shearer, C. L., & Boone, T. L. (2004). Religiosity, sexual behaviors, and sexual attitudes during emerging adulthood. *Journal of Sex Research, 41*, 150–159. doi:10.1080/00224490409552223

Lehrer, E. (2008). Age at marriage and marital instability: Revisiting the Becker–Landes–Michael hypothesis. *Journal of Population Economics, 21*, 463–484. doi:10.1007/s00148-006-0092-9

Leith, K. P., & Baumeister, R. F. (1996). Why do bad moods increase self-defeating behavior? Emotion, risk taking and self-regulation. *Journal of Personality and Social Psychology, 71*, 1250–1267. doi:10.1037/0022-3514.71.6.1250

Levinson, D. J. (1978). *The seasons of a man's life.* New York, NY: Knopf.

Lewis, M. A., Granato, H., Blayney, J. A., Lostutter, T. W., & Kilmer, J. R. (2012). Predictors of hooking up sexual behavior and emotional reactions among U.S. college students. *Archives of Sexual Behavior, 41*, 1219–1229. doi:10.1007/s10508-011-9817-2

Lindberg, L. D., Jones, R., & Santelli, J. S. (2008). Noncoital sexual activities among adolescents. *Journal of Adolescent Health, 43*, 231–238. doi:10.1016/j.jadohealth.2007.12.010

Loh, S., & Ram, B. (1990). Delayed childbearing in Canada: Trends and factors. *Genus, 46*, 147–161.

MacDonald, T. K., & Hynie, M. (2008). Ambivalence and unprotected sex: Failure to predict sexual activity and decreased condom use. *Journal of Applied Social Psychology, 38*, 1092–1107. doi:10.1111/j.1559-1816.2008.00340.x

Magnusson, C., & Trost, K. (2006). Girls experiencing sexual intercourse early: Could it play a part in reproductive health in middle adulthood? *Journal of Psychosomatic Obstetrics and Gynecology, 27*, 237–244. doi:10.1080/01674820600869006

Manning, W. D., & Cohen, J. (2012). Premarital cohabitation and marital dissolution: An examination of recent marriages. *Journal of Marriage and Family, 74*, 377–387. doi:10.1111/j.1741-3737.2012.00960.x

Manning, W. D., Longmore, M. A., & Giordano, P. C. (2005). Adolescents' involvement in non-romantic sexual activity. *Social Science Research, 34*, 384–407. doi:10.1016/j.ssresearch.2004.03.001

Martin, P., & Smyer, M. A. (1990). The experience of micro- and macroevents. A life span analysis. *Research on Aging, 12*, 294–310. doi:10.1177/0164027590123002

Matthews, T. J., & Hamilton, B. E. (2009). *Delayed childbearing: More women are having their first child later in life* (National Center for Health Statistics Data Brief No. 21). Hyattsville, MD: National Center for Health Statistics.

McCall, L. (2005). The complexity of intersectionality. *Signs, 30*, 1771–1800. doi:10.1086/426800

McGuire, J. K., & Barber, B. L. (2010). A person-centered approach to the multifaceted nature of young adult sexual behavior. *Journal of Sex Research, 47*, 301–313. doi:10.1080/00224490903062266

McRee, A. L., Haydon, A. A., & Halpern, C. T. (2010). Reproductive health of young adults with physical disabilities in the U.S. *Preventive Medicine, 51*, 502–504. doi:10.1016/j.ypmed.2010.09.006

Meier, A., & Allen, G. (2008). Intimate relationship development during the transition to adulthood: Differences by social class. *New Directions for Child and Adolescent Development, 2008*, 25–39. doi:10.1002/cd.207

Meier, A., Hull, K. E., & Ortyl, T. A. (2009). Young adult relationship values at the intersection of gender and sexuality. *Journal of Marriage and Family, 71*, 510–525. doi:10.1111/j.1741-3737.2009.00616.x

Meston, C. M., & Buss, D. M. (2007). Why humans have sex. *Archives of Sexual Behavior, 36*, 477–507. doi:10.1007/s10508-007-9175-2

Montgomery, M. J. (2005). Psychosocial intimacy and identity: From early adolescence to emerging adulthood. *Journal of Adolescent Research, 20*, 346–374. doi:10.1177/0743558404273118

Moore, N. B., & Davidson, J. K. (2006). College women and personal goals: Cognitive dimensions that differentiate risk-reduction sexual decisions. *Journal of Youth and Adolescence, 35*, 574–586. doi:10.1007/s10964-006-9041-x

Morgan, E. M., Thorne, A., & Zurbriggen, E. L. (2010). Longitudinal study of conversations with parents about sex and dating during college. *Developmental Psychology, 46*, 139–150. doi:10.1037/a0016931

Mosher, W. D., Chandra, A., & Jones, J. (2005). Sexual behavior and selected health measures: Men and women 15–44 years of age, United States, 2002. *Advance Data, 362*, 1–55.

Mosher, W. D., & Jones, J. (2010). Use of contraception in the United States: 1982–2008. *Vital and Health Statistics, 23*(29).

Mouw, T. (2005). Sequences of early adult transitions: A look at variability and consequences. In R. A. Settersten (Ed.), *On the frontier of adulthood: Theory, research, and public policy* (pp. 256–291). Chicago, IL: University of Chicago Press.

Murthi, M., Servaty-Seib, H. L., & Elliott, A. N. (2006). Childhood sexual abuse and multiple dimensions of self-concept. *Journal of Interpersonal Violence, 21*, 982–999. doi:10.1177/0886260506290288

Noll, J. G., Trickett, P. K., & Putnam, F. W. (2003). A prospective investigation of the impact of childhood sexual abuse on the development of sexuality. *Journal of Consulting and Clinical Psychology, 71*, 575–586. doi:10.1037/0022-006X.71.3.575

O'Donnell, L., Agronick, G., San Doval, A., Duran, R., Myint-U, A., & Stueve, A. (2002). Ethnic and gay community attachments and sexual risk behaviors among urban Latino young men who have sex with men. *AIDS Education and Prevention, 14*, 457–471. doi:10.1521/aeap.14.8.457.24109

O'Sullivan, L. F., Udell, W., Montrose, V. A., Antoniello, P., & Hoffman, S. (2010). A cognitive analysis of college students' explanations for engaging in unprotected sexual intercourse. *Archives of Sexual Behavior, 39*, 1121–1131. doi:10.1007/s10508-009-9493-7

Owen, J., & Fincham, F. D. (2011). Young adults' emotional reactions after hooking up encounters. *Archives of Sexual Behavior, 40*, 321–330. doi:10.1007/s10508-010-9652-x

Owen, J., Fincham, F. D., & Moore, J. (2011). Short-term prospective study of hooking up among college students. *Archives of Sexual Behavior, 40*, 331–341. doi:10.1007/s10508-010-9697-x

Owen, J. J., Rhoades, G. K., Stanley, S. M., & Fincham, F. D. (2010). "Hooking up" among college students: Demographic and psychosocial correlates. *Archives of Sexual Behavior, 39*, 653–663. doi:10.1007/s10508-008-9414-1

Paik, A. (2010). "Hookups," dating, and relationship quality: Does the type of sexual involvement matter? *Social Science Research, 39*, 739–753. doi:10.1016/j.ssresearch.2010.03.011

Pardun, C. J., L'Engle, K. L., & Brown, J. D. (2005). Linking exposure to outcomes: Early adolescents' consumption of sexual content in six media. *Mass Communication and Society, 8*, 75–91. doi:10.1207/s15327825mcs0802_1

Patrick, M. E., Maggs, J. L., & Abar, C. C. (2007). Reasons to have sex, personal goals, and sexual behavior during the transition to college. *Journal of Sex Research, 44*, 240–249. doi:10.1080/00224490701443759

Paul, E. L., & Hayes, K. A. (2002). The casualties of "casual" sex: A qualitative exploration of the phenomenology of college students' hookups. *Journal of Social and Personal Relationships, 19*, 639–661. doi:10.1177/0265407502195006

Paul, E. L., McManus, B., & Hayes, A. (2000). "Hookups": Characteristics and correlates of college students' spontaneous and anonymous sexual experiences. *Journal of Sex Research, 37*, 76–88. doi:10.1080/00224490009552023

Pempek, T. A., Yermolayeva, Y. A., & Calvert, S. L. (2009). College students' social networking experiences on Facebook. *Journal of Applied Developmental Psychology, 30*, 227–238. doi:10.1016/j.appdev.2008.12.010

Peter, J., & Valkenburg, P. M. (2008). Adolescents' exposure to sexually explicit Internet material, sexual uncertainty, and attitudes toward uncommitted sexual exploration: Is there a link? *Communication Research, 35*, 579–601. doi:10.1177/0093650208321754

Peter, J., & Valkenburg, P. M. (2011). The influence of sexually explicit Internet material and peers on stereotypical beliefs about women's sexual roles: Similarities and differences between adolescents and adults. *Cyberpsychology, Behavior, and Social Networking, 14*, 511–517. doi:10.1089/cyber.2010.0189

Petersen, J. L., & Hyde, J. S. (2010). A meta-analytic review of research on gender differences in sexuality, 1993–2007. *Psychological Bulletin, 136*, 21–38. doi:10.1037/a0017504

Pew Research Center. (2010). *The decline of marriage and rise of new families.* Washington, DC: Pew Research Center Social and Demographic Trends Project.

Pinkerton, S. D., Bogart, L. M., Cecil, H., & Abramson, P. R. (2002). Factors associated with masturbation in a collegiate sample. In W. O. Bockting & E. Coleman (Eds.), *Masturbation as a means of achieving sexual health* (pp. 103–122). New York, NY: Routledge.

Pitts, M., & Rahman, Q. (2001). Which behaviors constitute "having sex" among university students in the UK? *Archives of Sexual Behavior, 30*, 169–176. doi:10.1023/A:1002777201416

Purdie-Vaughns, V., & Eibach, R. (2008). Intersectional invisibility: The distinctive advantages and disadvantages of multiple subordinate-group identities. *Sex Roles, 59*, 377–391. doi:10.1007/s11199-008-9424-4

Ravert, R. D. (2009). "You're only young once": Things college students report doing now before it is too late. *Journal of Adolescent Research, 24*, 376–396. doi:10.1177/0743558409334254

Regan, P. C., Durvasula, R., Howell, L., Ureño, O., & Rea, M. (2004). Gender, ethnicity, and the developmental timing of first sexual and romantic experiences. *Social Behavior and Personality: An International Journal, 32*, 667–676. doi:10.2224/sbp.2004.32.7.667

Regnerus, M., & Uecker, J. (2011). *Premarital sex in America: How young Americans meet, mate, and think about marrying.* New York, NY: Oxford University Press.

Regnerus, M. D. (2003). Religion and positive adolescent outcomes: A review of research and theory. *Review of Religious Research, 44*, 394–413. doi:10.2307/3512217

Reinhold, S. (2010). Reassessing the link between premarital cohabitation and marital instability. *Demography, 47*, 719–733. doi:10.1353/dem.0.0122

Reissing, E. D., Andruff, H. L., & Wentland, J. J. (2012). Looking back: The experience of first sexual intercourse and current sexual adjustment in young heterosexual adults. *Journal of Sex Research, 49*, 27–35. doi:10.1080/00224499.2010.538951

Reissing, E. D., Laliberte, G. M., & Davis, H. J. (2005). Young women's sexual adjustment: The role of sexual self-schema, sexual self-efficacy, sexual aversion and body image. *Canadian Journal of Human Sexuality, 14*, 63–75.

Rich, C., Combs-Lane, A., Resnick, H., & Kilpatrick, D. (2004). Child sexual abuse and adult sexual revictimization. In L. Koenig, L. Doll, A. O'Leary, & W. Pequegnat (Eds.), *From child sexual abuse to adult sexual risk: Trauma, revictimization and intervention* (pp. 49–68). Washington, DC: American Psychological Association. doi:10.1037/10785-003

Rindfuss, R. R. (1991). The young adult years: Diversity, structural change, and fertility. *Demography, 28*, 493–512. doi:10.2307/2061419

Robbins, A., & Wilner, A. (2001). *Quarterlife crisis: The unique challenges of life in your twenties.* New York, NY: J. P. Tarcher/Putnam.

Robbins, R. N., & Bryan, A. (2004). Relationships between future orientation, impulsive sensation seeking, and risk behavior among adjudicated adolescents. *Journal of Adolescent Research, 19*, 428–445. doi:10.1177/0743558403258860

Rodrigues, A., Hall, J., & Fincham, F. (2006). What predicts divorce and relationship dissolution? In M. Fine & J. Harvey (Eds.), *Handbook of divorce and relationship dissolution* (pp. 85–112). Mahwah, NJ: Erlbaum.

Roscoe, B., Diana, M. S., & Brooks, R. H. (1987). Early, middle, and late adolescents' views on dating and factors influencing partner selection. *Adolescence, 22*, 59–68.

Rostosky, S. S., Regnerus, M. D., & Wright, M. L. (2003). Coital debut: The role of religiosity and sex attitudes in the Add Health Survey. *Journal of Sex Research, 40*, 358–367. doi:10.1080/00224490209552202

Sandfort, T. G., Orr, M., Hirsch, J. S., & Santelli, J. (2008). Long-term health correlates of timing of sexual debut: Results from a national US study. *American Journal of Public Health, 98*, 155–161. doi:10.2105/AJPH.2006.097444

Sassler, S. (2004). The process of entering into cohabiting unions. *Journal of Marriage and Family, 66*, 491–505. doi:10.1111/j.1741-3737.2004.00033.x

Schacht, R. L., George, W. H., Davis, K. C., Heiman, J. R., Norris, J., & Stoner, S. A. (2010). Sexual abuse history, alcohol intoxication, and women's sexual risk behavior. *Archives of Sexual Behavior, 39*, 898–906. doi:10.10.1007/s10508-009-9544-0

Schick, V. R., Zucker, A. N., & Bay-Cheng, L. Y. (2008). Safer, better sex through feminism: The role of feminist ideology in women's sexual well-being. *Psychology of Women Quarterly, 32*, 225–232. doi:10.1111/j.1471-6402.2008.00431.x

Schilling, E. A., Aseltine, R. H., & Gore, S. (2007). Young women's social and occupational development and mental health in the aftermath of child sexual abuse. *American Journal of Community Psychology, 40*, 109–124. doi:10.1007/s10464-007-9130-3

Schraufnagel, T. J., Davis, K. C., George, W. H., & Norris, J. (2010). Childhood sexual abuse in males and subsequent risky sexual behavior: A potential alcohol-use pathway. *Child Abuse and Neglect, 34*, 369–378. doi:10.1016/j.chiabu.2009.08.013

Schwartz, S. J., Waterman, A. S., Vazsonyi, A. T., Zamboanga, B. L., Whitbourne, S. K., Weisskirch, R. S., . . . Ham, L. S. (2011). The association of well-being with health risk behaviors in college-attending young adults. *Applied Developmental Science, 15*, 20–36. doi:10.1080/10888691.2011.538617

Seltzer, J. A. (2004). Cohabitation in the United States and Britain: Demography, kinship, and the future. *Journal of Marriage and Family, 66*, 921–928. doi:10.1111/j.0022-2445.2004.00062.x

Settersten, R. A., Furstenberg, F. F., & Rumbaut, R. G. (2005). *On the frontier of adulthood: Theory, research, and public policy.* Chicago, IL: University of Chicago Press.

Settersten, R. A., & Ray, B. (2010). *Not quite adults: Why 20-somethings are choosing a slower path to adulthood, and why it's good for everyone.* New York, NY: Delacorte Press.

Shapiro, T. (2008). Masturbation, sexuality, and adaptation: Normalization in adolescence. *Journal of the American Psychoanalytic Association, 56*, 123–146. doi:10.1177/0003065108315687

Shields, S. (2008). Gender: An intersectionality perspective. *Sex Roles, 59*, 301–311. doi:10.1007/s11199-008-9501-8

Simpson, J. A., & Gangestad, S. W. (1991). Individual differences in sociosexuality: Evidence for convergent and discriminant validity. *Journal of Personality and Social Psychology; 60*, 870–883. doi:10.1037/0022-3514.60.6.870

Smith, C. (2003). Theorizing religious effects among American adolescents. *Journal for the Scientific Study of Religion, 42*, 17–30. doi:10.1111/1468-5906.t01-1-00158

Soet, J. E., Dudley, W. N., & Dilorio, C. (1999). The effects of ethnicity and perceived power on women's sexual behavior. *Psychology of Women Quarterly, 23*, 707–723. doi:10.1111/j.1471-6402.1999.tb00393.x

Song, A. V., & Halpern-Felsher, B. L. (2011). Predictive relationship between adolescent oral and vaginal sex results from a prospective, longitudinal study. *Archives of Pediatrics and Adolescent Medicine, 165*, 243–249. doi:10.1001/archpediatrics.2010.214

Steele, J. R. (1999). Teenage sexuality and media practice: Factoring in the influences of family, friends, and school. *Journal of Sex Research, 36*, 331–341. doi:10.1080/00224499909552005

Surís, J. C., Resnick, M. D., Cassuto, N., & Blum, R. W. (1996). Sexual behavior of adolescents with chronic disease and disability. *Journal of Adolescent Health, 19*, 124–131. doi:10.1016/1054-139X(95)00282-W

Surra, C. A., Boettcher-Burke, T. M. J., Cottle, N. R., West, A. R., & Gray, C. R. (2007). The treatment of relationship status in research on dating and mate selection. *Journal of Marriage and Family, 69*, 207–221. doi:10.1111/j.1741-3737.2006.00354.x

Tanner, J. L. (2006). Recentering during emerging adulthood. In J. J. Arnett & J. L. Tanner (Eds.), *Emerging adults in America: Coming of age in the 21st century* (pp. 21–55). Washington, DC: American Psychological Association. doi:10.1037/11381-002

Teachman, J. D. (2003). Premarital sex, premarital cohabitations, and the risk of subsequent marital dissolution among women. *Journal of Marriage and Family, 65*, 444–455. doi:10.1111/j.1741-3737.2003.00444.x

Thompson, E. M., & Morgan, E. M. (2008). "Mostly straight" young women: Variations in sexual behavior and identity development. *Developmental Psychology, 44*, 15–21. doi:10.1037/0012-1649.44.1.15

Thornton, A. (1988). Cohabitation and marriage in the 1980s. *Demography, 25*, 497–508. doi:10.2307/2061317

Thornton, A. (1989). Changing attitudes toward family issues in the United States. *Journal of Marriage and the Family, 51*, 873–893. doi:10.2307/353202

Thornton, A., & Young-DeMarco, L. (2001). Four decades of trends in attitudes toward family issues in the United States: The 1960s through the 1990s. *Journal of Marriage and Family, 63*, 1009–1037. doi:10.1111/j.1741-3737.2001.01009.x

Tolman, D. L. (1999). Femininity as a barrier to positive sexual health for adolescent girls. *Journal of the American Medical Women's Association, 54*, 133–138.

Tolman, D. L. (2002). *Dilemmas of desire: Teenage girls talk about sexuality.* Cambridge, MA: Harvard University Press.

Tolman, D. L., Impett, E. A., Tracy, A. J., & Michael, A. (2006). Looking good, sounding good:

Femininity ideology and adolescent girls' mental health. *Psychology of Women Quarterly, 30*, 85–95. doi:10.1111/j.1471-6402.2006.00265.x

Tolman, D. L., & Porche, M. V. (2000). The Adolescent Femininity Ideology Scale: Development and validation of a new measure for girls. *Psychology of Women Quarterly, 24*, 365–376. doi:10.1111/j.1471-6402.2000.tb00219.x

Treas, J. (2002). How cohorts, education, and ideology shaped a new sexual revolution on American attitudes toward nonmarital sex, 1972–1998. *Sociological Perspectives, 45*, 267. doi:10.1525/sop.2002.45.3.267

Treas, J., & Giesen, D. (2000). Sexual infidelity among married and cohabiting Americans. *Journal of Marriage and the Family, 62*, 48–60. doi:10.1111/j.1741-3737.2000.00048.x

Trent, M., Clum, G., & Roche, K. M. (2007). Sexual victimization and reproductive health outcomes in urban youth. *Ambulatory Pediatrics, 7*, 313–316. doi:10.1016/j.ambp.2007.04.002

Troiden, R. R. (1989). The formation of homosexual identities. *Journal of Homosexuality, 17*, 43–74. doi:10.1300/J082v17n01_02

U.S. Census Bureau. (2004). Annual social and economic supplement: 2003 Current Population Survey (Current Population Reports, Series P20-553). Retrieved from http://www.census.gov/population/socdemo/hh-fam/tabMS-2.pdf

U.S. Department of Justice. (2011). *Criminal victimization in the United States, 2008 statistical tables.* Washington, DC: Office of Justice Programs, Bureau of Justice Statistics.

van Empelen, P., & Kok, G. (2006). Condom use in steady and casual sexual relationships: Planning, preparation and willingness to take risks among adolescents. *Psychology and Health, 21*, 165–181. doi:10.1080/14768320500229898

Ventura, S. J., Abma, J. C., Mosher, W. D., & Henshaw, S. K. (2009). Estimated pregnancy rates for the United States, 1990–2005: An update. *National Vital Statistics Reports, 58*(4).

Walsh, J. L., Ward, L. M., Caruthers, A., & Merriwether, A. (2011). Awkward or amazing: Gender and age trends in first intercourse experiences. *Psychology of Women Quarterly, 35*, 59–71. doi:10.1177/0361684310387781

Ward, L. M. (2002). Does television exposure affect emerging adults' attitudes and assumptions about sexual relationships? Correlational and experimental confirmation. *Journal of Youth and Adolescence, 31*, 1–15. doi:10.1023/A:1014068031532

Ward, L. M. (2003). Understanding the role of entertainment media in the sexual socialization of American youth: A review of empirical research. *Developmental Review, 23*, 347–388. doi:10.1016/s0273-2297(03)00013-3

Ward, L. M., & Friedman, K. (2006). Using TV as a guide: Associations between television viewing and adolescents' sexual attitudes and behavior. *Journal of Research on Adolescence, 16*, 133–156. doi:10.1111/j.1532-7795.2006.00125.x

Warren, J. C., Fernandez, M. I., Harper, G. W., Hidalgo, M. A., Jamil, O. B., & Torres, R. S. (2008). Predictors of unprotected sex among young sexually active African American, Hispanic, and White MSM: The importance of ethnicity and culture. *AIDS and Behavior, 12*, 459–468. doi:10.1007/s10461-007-9291-y

Waters, M. C. (2011). *Coming of age in America: The transition to adulthood in the twenty-first century.* Berkeley: University of California Press. doi:10.1525/california/9780520270923.001.0001

Weinstock, H., Berman, S., & Cates, W., Jr. (2004). Sexually transmitted diseases among American youth: Incidence and prevalence estimates, 2000. *Perspectives on Sexual and Reproductive Health, 36*, 6–10. doi:10.1363/3600604

Wetherill, R. R., Neal, D. J., & Fromme, K. (2010). Parents, peers, and sexual values influence sexual behavior during the transition to college. *Archives of Sexual Behavior, 39*, 682–694. doi:10.1007/s10508-009-9476-8

Whedon, J. (Writer & Director). (2003). Chosen [Television series episode]. In G. Berman, S. Gallin, F. R. Kuzui, K. Kuzui, M. Noxon, & J. Whedon (Executive Producers), *Buffy the vampire slayer.* Los Angeles, CA: United Paramount Network.

Williams, K., & Umberson, D. (2004). Marital status, marital transitions, and health: A gendered life course perspective. *Journal of Health and Social Behavior, 45*, 81–98. doi:10.1177/002214650404500106

Witwer, M. (1993). U.S. men and women now have highest mean age at marriage in this century, Census Bureau finds. *Family Planning Perspectives, 25*, 190–191. doi:10.2307/2135933

Wohl, M. J. A., & Enzle, M. E. (2002). The deployment of personal luck: Sympathetic magic and illusory control in games of pure chance. *Personality and Social Psychology Bulletin, 28*, 1388–1397. doi:10.1177/014616702236870

Woo, J. S., & Brotto, L. A. (2008). Age of first sexual intercourse and acculturation: Effects on adult sexual responding. *Journal of Sexual Medicine, 5*, 571–582. doi:10.1111/j.1743-6109.2007.00740.x

Woolf, S. E., & Maisto, S. A. (2008). Gender differences in condom use behavior? The role of power and partner type. *Sex Roles, 58*, 689–701. doi:10.1007/s11199-007-9381-3

Worthington, R. L., Navarro, R. L., Savoy, H. B., & Hampton, D. (2008). Development, reliability, and validity of the Measure of Sexual Identity Exploration and Commitment (MOSIEC). *Developmental Psychology, 44*, 22–33. doi:10.1037/0012-1649.44.1.22

Zimmer-Gembeck, M. J., Ducat, W. H., & Boislard-Pepin, M. A. (2011). A prospective study of young females' sexual subjectivity: Associations with age, sexual behavior, and dating. *Archives of Sexual Behavior, 40*, 927–938. doi:10.1007/s10508-011-9751-3

Zimmer-Gembeck, M. J., & Petherick, J. (2006). Intimacy dating goals and relationship satisfaction during adolescence and emerging adulthood: Identity formation, age and sex as moderators. *International Journal of Behavioral Development, 30*, 167–177. doi:10.1177/0165025406063636

Zurbriggen, E. L., & Morgan, E. M. (2006). Who wants to marry a millionaire? Reality dating television programs, attitudes toward sex, and sexual behaviors. *Sex Roles, 54*, 1–17. doi:10.1007/s11199-005-8865-2

CHAPTER 17

SEXUALITY IN AGING

Pepper Schwartz, Sarah Diefendorf, and Anne McGlynn-Wright

Men and women in the United States are living longer (National Center for Health Statistics, 2011). Between 2000 and 2007, life expectancy increased by 1 year for those over the age of 65 years (National Center for Health Statistics, 2011). With more total years and more healthy years (National Center for Health Statistics, 2011), the sex lives of individuals also may be extending. It is surprising, however, that an increase in life expectancy has not produced more research on the sexual experiences of older adults (Schick et al., 2010). The gap in the literature may exist for a number of reasons. First, there is a lack of large surveys focusing on individuals over 50 years of age. National studies on sexuality often have limited their population scope to people less than 50 years of age and have excluded aging populations (Herbenick et al., 2010b). When older individuals are included, they frequently are treated as one group—65 years and older. Second, a cultural stigma is associated with the topic. People do not like to talk about their grandparents' (or for that matter, their parents') sex lives. Many people, and it seems many researchers, would rather assume sex is not happening among the middle-aged, and certainly not among the elderly. Even though the 1948 Kinsey Report and subsequent research has shown quite a bit of sexual activity after age 50, there seems to be a lack of interest in either the causes or consequences of sexual behavior from middle age onward. Third, much of the current research on sexuality has been tied to understanding either fertility or disease and not much else. Because fertility is a less common issue among most people over 50 years in the United States, and disease profiles have been comparatively low in these age-groups, the National Institutes of Health have not made funding studies on the aged a priority.

These reasons go a long way to explain why, until very recently, little research has been conducted about the sex lives of older individuals. The lack of research has been frustrating to many medical and behavioral researchers and some writers, like Butler and Lewis, who described later life sexuality as surrounded by a "mythology fed by misinformation" (1993, p. 3; see also Wiley & Bortz, 1996). This chapter seeks to remove the mythical nature of the topic.

The discussion about sexuality and aging begins with the acknowledgment that being "older" has changed. Certainly, health issues still affect sexuality, and these problems can and should be taken into account (see Chapter 21, this volume). But the culture of how sexuality is experienced by people older than 50, 60, 70, and beyond is fundamentally different. First, sexual capability has expanded to later and later in the life cycle. The availability of prescription medications to enhance sexual performance and an increasing range of "sexual enhancement products" (e.g., vibrators, artificial lubricants, and herbal arousal concoctions), coupled with cultural messages that raise expectations for sexual activity in later life, aim to make sex in older age more possible, more enjoyable, and crucially, more acceptable (Schick et al., 2010). Second, the overall culture surrounding sex and sexuality in the United States has been changing rapidly. Those at

http://dx.doi.org/10.1037/14193-017
APA Handbook of Sexuality and Psychology: Vol. 1. Person-Based Approaches, D. L. Tolman and L. M. Diamond (Editors-in-Chief)

the leading edge of the baby boom (the so-called baby boomers) are now becoming eligible for Medicare, and the youngest of these have received their inevitable issue of the *AARP Magazine* (formerly the American Association of Retired Persons) with an announcement that they are now eligible for membership. Boomers, as we know, are quite a different cohort than the 65-year-olds who came before them. Boomers bring with them the values, ideals, and experiences of their youth, which fomented the sexual revolution, feminist movement, and the gay rights movement (which now has morphed into the lesbian, gay, bisexual, transgender, queer [LGBTQ] movement). Those 45 and older express relatively liberal views on sex and sexuality compared with past older cohorts (Fisher et al., 2010). Even the older generations have been affected by the revolutionary approaches to sexuality that began in the 1960s. Because we have a very large aging population and are seeing some significant changes in the beliefs and attitudes of these older age cohorts, it is important not to assume that any previous data about sexuality in old age are relevant for these men and women.

This chapter gives a brief overview of life-cycle effects on sexual attitudes and experiences, noting the biological, psychological, and sociocultural influences that cause, and are affected by, these changes. We begin this section with an overview of research on gender differences, and how gender differences emerge in nearly every aspect of sexual life and aging. In the second section, we will trace the demographic shifts and trends in types of relationship for older adults. The third section discusses the quality of sex among older adults, paying close attention to gender differences in satisfaction and frequency. The fourth section continues this discussion along lines of sexual orientation and relationship status, concluding this section with an analysis of how relationship factors affect the quality and frequency of sex. It also gives a brief overview of nonmonogamy in later life. The fifth section contains a discussion of the health concerns and sexual challenges older adults face. The sixth section provides an overview of sexual issues that become relevant among the extremely aged nearing the end of the life cycle. It discusses the ways sexuality is experienced in institutions, particularly in nursing homes.

SEXUALITY IN AGING: AN OVERVIEW

According to the 2010 census, the number of adults 45 years old and older climbed from just over 96 million in 2000 (or 34% of the overall population) to well over 120 million in 2010 (nearly 40% of the U.S. population; U.S. Census Bureau, 2010a). Furthermore, Cahill, South, and Spade (2000) predicted that approximately 1 to 2.8 million gay, lesbian, and bisexual individuals are over the age of 65, which is expected to increase to approximately 6 million by the year 2030. The expansion of the older adult population is the result of a decrease in mortality and an aging baby boom generation. This demographic reality has led to an increased interest in issues that affect those individuals at older ages—including an interest in the sexual lives of individuals at every stage of the life course. Despite major medical advances that help facilitate sexual functioning, we know relatively little about the role of sex in the lives of individuals after the age of 45. Furthermore, even less research has been done on how the sex lives of older adults vary by age, gender, racial or ethnic identity, sexual orientation, and a variety of other sociodemographic characteristics.

Sexual histories differ along the life course (see Chapter 13, this volume). There is no universal story of sexuality. General trends, however, may help capture some of the issues and events that individuals face as they advance through the life course. The following sections examine some of the sexual behaviors and attitudes of adults age 45 years and older.

Both academic and social commentaries about sexuality often ignore the oldest adult population. Newer studies, however, have begun to explore the sexual behaviors and attitudes of older adults and find that although the percent of individuals engaging in sexual practices may decrease with age (Carpenter, Nathanson, & Kim, 2006; Fisher et al., 2010; Laumann, Gagnon, Michael, & Michaels, 1994; Lindau et al., 2007; Wang, Lu, Chen, & Yu, 2008; Wylie & Kenney, 2010), older adults are still quite sexually active and sexually interested. The National Social Life, Health and Aging Project (NSHAP) interviewed a nationally representative group of 3,005 individuals ages 57–85 between 2005 and 2006. The study reported that almost 84% of men and 62% of women ages 57–64 engaged in sexual activity over the past year (Lindau et al., 2007). The AARP has reported similar findings with a sample of adults age 45 and older. The AARP report found that nearly half of the individuals surveyed engaged in kissing and hugging at least once a week over the past 6 months. Thirty-five percent of those interviewed reported sexual touching or caressing, and nearly a quarter of individuals reported having sexual intercourse at least once a week over the past 6 months (Fisher et al., 2010).

Despite the fact that a large number of older Americans are experiencing an active and healthy sexual life, it is also the case that multiple factors may lead to a decrease in sexual activity as individuals age. Numerous U.S. studies document that the number of individuals engaging in sexual activity decreases with age (DeLamater & Sill, 2005; Lindau et al., 2007; Herbenick et al., 2010b; Nusbaum, Lenahan, & Sadovsky, 2005), and some international studies draw the same conclusion (Binfa, Robertson, & Ransjo-Arvidson, 2009; Birnbaum, Cohen, & Wertheimer, 2007; Chao et al., 2011; Fraser, Maticka-Tyndale, & Smylie, 2004; Hinchliff, Gott, & Wylie, 2009; Kontula & Haavio-Mannila, 2009; Laganà & Maciel, 2010; Moore, 2010; Wang et al., 2008). Lindau et al. (2007) found that there is a 60% reduction in the odds of being sexually active for men ages 65–75 years compared with 57- to 64-year-olds. Women experience a nearly identical drop within the same time. By ages 75–85, the odds of having a sexual partner within the past year decrease by nearly 90% for both men and women (compared with 57- to 64-year-olds).

We cannot conclude, however, that a person who is sexually inactive considers sex unimportant. The majority of the older adult population is interested in getting or maintaining satisfying sexual relationships. According to the AARP, almost three quarters of individuals ages 45 and older considered a satisfying sexual relationship very or somewhat important (Fisher et al., 2010). Although many studies have noted that there is a decline in sexual interest over the life course, the decline does not appear to occur until individuals are well past their 50s. DeLamater and Sill (2005) reported that it is not until after age 75 that the majority of individuals indicate a lack of sexual desire, although psychological and physiological factors can contribute to a lack of desire at much earlier ages (Birnbaum et al., 2007; Brennan-Ing, Korpiak, & Seidel, 2011; Fraser et al., 2004; Hinchliff et al., 2009; Trudel, Villeneuve, Previllle, Boyer, & Frechette, 2010; Trudel, Turgeon, & Piche, 2010; Woloski-Wruble, Oliel, Leefsma, & Hochner-Celnikier, 2010; see Chapter 8, this volume). Although sexual desire may decrease with age, some of the decrease may be attributable to deeper psychological, environmental, and relationship issues. Interesting insights into the psychological, environmental, and relational issues that may cause decreases in desire may be gleaned by exploring gender differences in sexuality at older ages.

Gender Differences: Sexual Behavior and Sexual Attitudes

As we age, gender disparities in sexual behavior and attitudes grow among those who are sexually active. Gender differences may be caused by different life expectancies and changing life goals. For example, the number of women and men who have sexual partners declines with age; however, women, more than men, report the absence of a sexual partner (Carpenter et al., 2006; Fisher et al., 2010). Furthermore, as men and women age, this discrepancy in partner availability grows. AARP data indicate that in the United States, at 45–49 years 84% of men and 78% of women reported having a sexual partner in the past 6 months. After age 70, however, 63% of the men but only 34% of the women reported having a sexual partner. Lindau et al. (2007) reported a similar gender gap in sexual partners. Gender discrepancies in sexual partners also are seen in countries other than the United States. In a nationally representative sample of aging adults in Finland, Kontula and Haavio-Mannila (2009) found that the biggest gender difference among respondents is that women over the age of 60 are less likely than men to have a permanent sex partner. There are many possible reasons for these gendered disparities, including sexism, ageism, and other sociocultural factors (Carpenter et al., 2006; Wang et al., 2008). For example, in Taiwan women follow traditional cultural standards and select male partners older than themselves. Male partners generally pass on before their female counterparts, and women mourn the death for longer periods of time than seen in other areas (Kaiser, 1996; Wang et al., 2008). Both the biological and psychological factors for these gender disparities will be explained in the following paragraphs.

Some of these differences in sexual behavior between men and women may be explained, in part, by diverging sexual attitudes. As Fisher et al. (2010) reported, men are more likely than women to consider sex an important part of their life and think of sex more frequently. These disparities in gender and sexual importance may grow over time. For example, 91% of men, but only 73% of women, between the ages of 45 and 49 said that a satisfying sexual relationship was either very or somewhat important. As both men and women age, however, the importance assigned to sexual relationships decreases even further, with 80% of men and 39% of women saying that a sexual relationship is very or somewhat important (Fisher et al., 2010). Using data from the AARP's *Modern Maturity* Sexuality Survey (n = 1,384 ages 45 and older), DeLamater and Sill (2005) found a similar gender disparity in desire, which they suggested is related partially to women's decreased likelihood of an available sexual partner as they grow older. According to the authors, for women, having a sexual partner predicted desire (DeLamater & Sill, 2005), which is echoed in other findings (Basson, 2006). On the other hand, men's sexual desires do not appear tempered by the presence of available partners.

Many studies have attempted to explain both the emotional and psychological factors that contribute to gendered disparities in desire. Women might adjust their desire depending on opportunity (DeLamater & Sill, 2005) and "turn off" sexual desire as a coping mechanism after experiencing periods of time without a sexual partner. This strategy may even help prevent depression and frustration (Masters, Johnson, & Kolodny, 1994). Other studies employ sociocultural explanations for gendered disparities in desire. Drawing on ethnographic narratives of married women and men over the age of 60 in Japan, Moore (2010) found that men cite the source of their well-being in terms of a sustained sexual desire, whereas woman downplay their desire due to cultural norms of marital sexuality. In a qualitative study of Mexican American women living in the United States, Laganà and Maciel (2010) found that unmarried women who hold traditional beliefs about sexuality may not express sexual desire to others because of cultural pressures. The gendered differences we see in sexual behaviors and attitudes are produced by cultural, biological, psychological, and social contexts and will be a recurring theme in this chapter (see Chapter 2, this volume).

Biological Influences on Sexuality in Aging

Biological changes, including an increased number of health-related issues accompany older age and often disrupt sexual activity and interest. According to Lindau et al. (2007), individuals who identify as being in fair or poor health are less likely to be sexually active than individuals in good or excellent health. In fact, reporting being in poor or fair health (as opposed to good or excellent health) was associated with a nearly 80% decrease in the odds of being sexually active over the past year (Lindau et al., 2007). In addition, illness also may affect sexual desire for women but not men. DeLamater and Sill (2005) found that women who reported more illnesses were slightly more likely than healthier women to have lower sexual desire. The same relationship, however, was not found between men's illness and sexual desire. The ability for some individuals or groups to be able to withstand illness more than others can vary across cultures and race or ethnicity. For example, the AARP study showed that illness affected sexual frequency and desire in their general sample of respondents but not in their Hispanic sample (Fisher et al., 2010). This set of findings leads us to hypothesize that the impact of health may depend on the importance of sexuality to an individual before health becomes an issue. People may use health as an escape clause from sexuality if they are looking for one. In the AARP *Survey of Midlife and Older Adults* (Fisher et al., 2010), the Hispanic population actually reported worse health issues than the Caucasian sample, and yet poor health was less likely to affect their sex life.

Overall health and sexual problems generally appear to go hand in hand. Lindau et al. (2007)

found that individuals in poor or fair health were more likely to report multiple sexual problems than those in good or excellent health. The types of sexual problems that men and women report are different and appear to have a differing trajectory as well. Waite, Laumann, Das, and Schumm (2009) found that women between the ages of 57 and 85 reported similar sexual problems and did not differ on the basis of age. Women most consistently cited a lack of interest in sex as the number one reason for not engaging in sexual activity, followed by the inability to lubricate, and the inability to climax. Men, on the other hand, tended to have various sexual problems depending on their age. For example, the most common sexual problem cited by men was erection problems, followed by premature climax and lack of sexual interest. Issues with erectile function, however, tended to become more common as men aged, whereas premature climax tended to be more problematic for the younger group of older men. A lengthy discussion on the physical, relational, and psychological repercussions of these health issues can be found in the section Health Concerns and Sexual Challenges.

Psychological Aspects of Sexuality and Aging

Psychological factors play a major role in the sexual functioning of all adults, but feelings of self doubt and sexual unworthiness may be more acute among the 45 and older adult population. Cultural images that demean and denigrate aging bodies may affect sexual performance as much as physical conditions. In the United States, and in many countries, the pressure to conform to certain ideals of beauty spans all ages. For example, Laura Hurd Clarke (2010) interviewed older adult women in the United States about their bodies. Many of the women Clarke interviewed had internalized popular conceptions of beauty that required youthfulness and therefore were unable to appreciate their own bodies. Often times, older women who did not find their aging bodies attractive were less comfortable being sexual with their partners. The catalyst of this discontent, however, also may be the cultural messages that come through women's male partners. Margolin and White (1987) found that as men age, they become more critical and comment on the physical "declines" of their partner's body, and cite these physical changes as a reason for a loss of sexual desire in themselves. In contrast, some work has found that women do not become more body-conscious with age. A study of 20- to 84-year-old women found that body dissatisfaction remained stable across the age range, but habitual body monitoring, appearance anxiety, and self-objectification actually decreased with age (Tiggemann & Lynch, 2001).

Although societal ideals for men's and women's bodies are different, both men and women may experience shame as a result of sexual stereotyping and elevated standards of attractiveness (Sanchez & Kiefer, 2007). Testing whether body shame was related to sexual problems[1] and pleasure among heterosexual women and men ages 17 to 71 years, Sanchez and Kiefer (2007) found that although shame and self-consciousness were similar for women and men, women reported greater body image concerns[2] and more subsequent sexual problems than men. Most notably, women reported more problems with sexual arousal and orgasm. Sanchez and Kiefer concluded, as others had before them, that poor body image undermines sexual pleasure (Fredrickson & Roberts, 1997; Masters & Johnson, 1970). The authors found that age and relationship status were two demographic variables that most affected body image and capacity or frequency of orgasm (Sanchez & Kiefer, 2007). Although these studies cannot be compared directly, there seems to be ample evidence that both culture and gender put women at a greater risk for being dissatisfied with their body and thus at greater risk of experiencing insecurities about their sexuality or sex with a partner.

The impact of relationships, however, reaches beyond body image issues. Relationship status and the quality of a relationship is critical for predicting psychological well-being and sexual satisfaction (see

[1]*Sexual problems* are defined as difficulty with orgasm and becoming sexually aroused, and low levels of sexual pleasure, although acknowledging that not all men and women would consider these experiences problematic (Sanchez & Kiefer, 2007).

[2]However, lesbian women appear to be less susceptible to issues of body image (see Blumstein & Schwartz, 1983; Krakauer & Rose, 2002; Siever, 1994).

Chapter 10, this volume). Trudel et al. (2010) found that marital satisfaction, sexual satisfaction, and gender explain 14.2% of the variance of psychological distress among older couples. DeLamater and Moorman (2007) found that emotional well-being within a given kind of relationship affects both sexual desire and sexual activity. A positive attitude about sexuality, and a desire for sexual contact, coupled with a satisfying relationship, is strongly associated with greater frequency of sex (Blumstein & Schwartz, 1983; DeLamater & Moorman, 2007; Wang et al., 2008). Happy relationships do exist in the absence of sexual activity. As couples get older, sex (in its various forms) becomes less prioritized and its importance for relational happiness decreases (Kontula & Haavio-Mannila, 2009; Moore, 2010).

Our analysis is incomplete, however, if we look only at these issues in married or other kinds of couples. When we do look at older singles, however, several similarities emerge. In DeLamater and Sill's (2005) study of older adults, attitudes toward sex were found to be the number one predictor of sexual desire. Individuals who felt that sex was important to them were significantly more likely to have strong sexual desire. The authors conclude that negative attitudes toward sex are predictive of lower sexual desire and sum up their research with a call for sex-positive images for older Americans (DeLamater & Sill, 2005).

It is undoubtedly true, as Chao et al. have stated, "Sexual desire is a psychological state" (2011, p. 400). Emotional well-being affects sexual activity and satisfaction and vice versa. In a cross-sectional survey of elderly adults (over the age of 65) in Korea, Choi, Jang, Lee, & Kim (2011) found that those who felt very satisfied with their current sex life had significantly higher self-esteem than those who did not. Similarly, using data from the NSHAP, Ganong and Larson (2011) found that among adults ages 57–85, sexual activity that usually incorporates other forms of physical intimacy has a strong association with lower depression for both men and women.

The major 20th-century empiricists of sexology cite psychological factors such as fatigue, boredom, anxiety, and unsatisfying relationships as reasons for decline in sexual desire among individuals (Kinsey, Pomeroy, & Martin, 1948; Masters & Johnson, 1966). Anxiety is a particularly commonplace issue among older men when erectile function becomes problematic. For example, research on men's erectile dysfunction (ED) shows how inability to have a predictable or satisfying erection can lead to performance anxiety and subsequently, a loss of sexual desire (Moore, 2010; Starr & Weiner, 1981). Anxiety, however, is not just specific to men. In a study of 17 individuals at a psychosexual clinic in England, Hinchliff et al. (2009) found that women who experience sexual dysfunction also experience feelings of isolation and use words such as "abnormal" and "freak" to describe how they feel. The combination of socialcultural contexts that affect behavior and the individual-level, psychosexual processes are vital in understanding changes in sexuality as we age.

Social Aspects of Sexual Aging

In addition to a variety of physical and psychological determinants of sexual behavior and sexual attitudes, individuals are shaped by historical changes that altered the social and sexual landscapes of the United States and elsewhere. For example, men and women who came of age before the sexual revolution were likely to be influenced heavily by the gender and sexual conventions of their time. Both genders would have been told that sex before marriage was immoral and that women were the "gatekeepers" of sexual purity because their urges were not as strong as men's and therefore whatever happened was "their fault." These are not the messages delivered to most teenagers in the 21st century.[3] Thus, these, and other, cohort and period effects are worth noting. For example, in 2009, the AARP *Survey of Midlife and Older Adults* asked individuals 45 and older to respond to a variety of questions about sexual behaviors and attitudes. Only 22% of individuals surveyed agreed that people should have a sexual relationship if they are not married. Agreement with the statement, however, varied greatly by age. Americans who came of age before the sexual revolution of the 1960s, were more likely to say that individuals should not have sex if they are not married

[3]This is not true for participants in the Christian Courtship movement.

(Fisher et al., 2010). Obviously, changing attitudes have the potential for having a dramatic effect on an individual's sex life. For example, Carpenter et al. (2006) wrote that sexual conservatism, as measured by an individual's beliefs regarding premarital sex, can affect not only attitudes toward sex but also the opportunities for sexual activity as well. These beliefs may even affect differences in how older women and men behave in courtship. It appears that women who do not believe in premarital sex maintain this moral code before any marriage, whereas it appears that men tend to disregard this belief after a first marriage (Carpenter et al., 2006).

Keeping in mind how psychological, physical, and social aspects of aging affect sexual attitudes and behavior, the chapter now turns to an overview of sexuality and the aging process as it occurs within various types of relationships to observe and explain how different kinds of emotional commitments and institutional guidelines affect men's and women's sexual behavior and happiness.

DEMOGRAPHIC SHIFTS IN RELATIONSHIP STRUCTURES

It is not just biological, psychological, and sociocultural factors that must be taken into account when we look at the sexualities of older populations. Since the middle of the 20th century, a variety of social and economic factors have caused major changes to relationships and families. Marriage takes place later, divorce rates have climbed, cohabitation has seen a remarkable increase, and fertility has dropped (Lesthaeghe, 2010). Older adults, along with the rest of society, have witnessed these changes. Trends in remaining single, divorcing, and becoming widowed, which are tied inextricably to sexuality, have transmogrified over the past 50 years and vary by gender, race or ethnicity, and other sociodemographic characteristics.

Marriage

A combination of demographic facts shape the sexual lives of women and men. American men have a shorter life span than women and that creates a relatively smaller pool of eligible partners for older women, which continues to shrink as women age. The difference in the number of eligible partners is magnified by the propensity for men to marry younger women, especially at older ages where the age gap between men and their marriage partners is even greater (England & McClintock, 2009). This pattern creates an advantageous sex ratio for heterosexual men and creates both fewer opportunities and tougher competition for older heterosexual women who wish to enter into sexual relationships with men.

The sexual lives of African American women particularly are affected by lower marriage rates. Because of poverty, discrimination, and the additional vulnerabilities that occur among poor and disenfranchised communities, African American men have had a higher rate of incarceration, victimization, and serious health risks. These factors, and a variety of other factors, such as higher intermarriage rates among African American men than African American women, have reduced the number of available African American men as partners for African American women. According to Isen and Stevenson (2010), Black women are less likely than White women to become married. In 1990, 82% of 40-year-old Black women had been married versus 93% of 40-year-old White women. Over the next decade, the percentages stayed almost the same, with each group experiencing a 1% increase in marriage.

Although not being married does not exclude individuals from engaging in cohabiting or sexual relationships, lower marriage rates can correlate with sexual behavior. Using data from Canada's National Population Health Survey, Fraser et al. (2004) found that non-Caucasian women were less likely to report sexual activity. The authors posited that these lower rates reflect a preference for partners in their same racial or ethnic group and the fact that a smaller pool of these men decreased their ability to find what they considered suitable partners.

Although marriage does not provide the only entrance into sexual relationships, marriage continues to be one of the biggest predictors, although certainly not the only predictor, of rates of sexuality at older ages. A national Finnish study found that the most important determinant of frequency of sexual intercourse among their aging population was having a regular partner, which was, in most cases, a husband or a wife (Kontula & Haavio-Mannila, 2009). Marriage, of course, also can have negative effects on sexual frequency. Using data from the Quebec Health Survey of Older Adults (*n* = 508 couples), Trudel et al. (2010) found participants with low marital functioning had much poorer sexual functioning than those with more functional marriages. Wiley and Bortz (1996) found that regardless of gender, relationship problems were the single most important factor that affected individuals' sex lives. Furthermore, countless studies indicate that negative emotions, such as resentment and anger, create barriers to sexual intimacy within couples (Gottman, Coan, Swanson, & Carrere, 1998; Gottman & Levenson, 2000; Lief, 1977; LoPiccolo & Friedman, 1988; Schnarch, 2009, 2011; Wiley & Bortz, 1996; Zilbergeld & Ellison, 1980). These relationship factors may be even more crucial for nonheterosexual couples, who often face a social environment that, generally speaking, is less supportive than the social environments of their heterosexual coupled peers (Beals, Impett, & Peplau, 2002). Research, however, does indicate that the relationship between satisfaction and various emotional qualities in gay and lesbian relationships are similar to those found in heterosexual relationships (Gottman et al., 2003; see Chapter 20, this volume).

Although being single, divorced, or widowed is related to declines in sexual behavior, it does not preclude individuals from being sexually active. In fact, attitudes toward sexual relationships have changed dramatically over the past 10 years. The most recent AARP study found that the percentage of individuals over the age of 45 years who believe that unmarried individuals should not have sex has decreased from 41% in 1999 to 22% in 2009 (Fisher et al., 2010). The destigmatization of having sex outside of marriage and increased acceptance of having a sexual life throughout the life cycle, means that a variety of sexual behaviors and practices now are available to many aging individuals.

Divorce

Divorce rates have risen since the turn of the 20th century. Rates rose precipitously, however, starting at the end of the 1960s in the United States. Individuals who married after the 1950s were more likely to experience a divorce than those who were married during the 1950s. As Isen and Stevenson (2010) pointed out, however, the number rose considerably for those who married during the 1970s, to 37% of marriages ending in divorce for college-educated White females and 34% for college-educated White males. Although these rates have since plateaued and even fallen slightly; the fact remains that a large number of adults over the age of 45 years have experienced divorce.

Uncoupling, at least initially, is related to decreases in sexual behavior and sexual satisfaction (Blumstein & Schwartz, 1983; Laumann et al., 1994). For some of those leaving troubled marriages, however, the effect may be the opposite. Data from the AARP *Survey of Midlife and Older Adults* (*n* = 1670) indicate that divorce or separation had occurred among 13% of those who reported less satisfaction in their sex life compared with 10 years prior, but it was also true that 16% who had divorced or separated were among those who reported being more satisfied with their sex lives than they were 10 years ago (Fisher et al., 2010).

The increase in divorce made it pragmatic for society to reject marriage as the only appropriate context for sexual conduct. As divorce increased, stigma decreased, and older men and women reentered the dating market. Although some prized singlehood, the great majority of divorced men (and to a slightly lesser extent, divorced women) would pair again, either in another marriage or cohabitation. Sexual behavior was expected on the way to recoupling and, unlike the virginity standards that prevailed before the 1960s, extensive sexual behavior did not disqualify many from being "marriage material." That said, however, the goal of marriage was not universally embraced, and many women and men choose not to remarry. Isen and Stevenson (2010) reported that although one might expect an increase in remarriage to follow an increase in divorce rates, that is not the case. Such findings might be indicative of a growing group of older individuals who choose to cohabit instead of marrying again.

Cohabiting Adults

The number of individuals who cohabit has increased over the past few decades, and this is true among the older population as well as the population at large (Manning & Brown, 2009). Although the majority of individuals within the United States who cohabit are younger, a growing number of individuals over the age of 50 years are beginning to cohabit (U.S. Census Bureau, 2010b). The majority of older individuals who cohabit, according to Manning and Brown (2009) are divorced (nearly three quarters), whereas approximately 18% are widowed, and 11% have never been legally married.

In addition to having a different profile than younger cohabiters, who tend never to have been married, older cohabiters differ by both relationship quality and reasons for cohabiting. In a study comparing younger and older cohabiters, King and Scott (2005) found that those 50 years and older who cohabit spend more time together and seem to experience more enjoyable time together, as they report both fewer disagreements and fewer violent arguments. The authors also suggested that the purposes of cohabiting at older ages differ from the purposes of cohabiting at younger ages. Younger individuals tend to view cohabitation as a "trial marriage," whereas older individuals tend to view cohabitation as an alternative to marriage (King & Scott, 2005). In addition, despite the fact that marriage is in many cases "off the table," cohabiting older Americans have similar relationship satisfaction as their married counterparts (Brown & Kawamura, 2010).

There is also some new and persuasive indication that cohabiters actually have better sex lives than their married counterparts. Data show that individuals who are partnered but unmarried report higher rates of both sexual intercourse and sexual satisfaction than those who are married (Fisher et al., 2010). This is a partial departure from previous large-scale research in the area, which had found that committed couples, regardless of marriage or cohabitation status, have more sex than divorced or single people (Blumstein & Schwartz, 1983; Laumann et al., 1994). This change in numbers may be explained partially by the fact that the United States is seeing a significant rise in the numbers of people who choose to cohabit rather than marry. It also may mean that cohabitation is quite different after age 50 years than for younger people. It therefore may not present the stresses or unmet needs that cohabitation can entail among men and women who are younger in their careers, have young children, or are still of reproductive age and have reproductive goals that their fellow cohabiter does not share.

Widowed Adults

Manning and Brown (2009) reported that in 2008, nearly 20% of women between the ages of 65 and 69 years and less than 15% of men ages 65 to 79 years were widowed. At 85 years and older, this rate was substantially higher for both women and men (77% of women and 37% of men). For all men and women, but especially older men and women, loss of a partner affects quality of life in general and a sexual life specifically. This is no surprise, as research indicates a strong association between relationship satisfaction and sexual satisfaction (Blumstein & Schwartz, 1983; DeLamater & Moorman, 2007; Trudel et al., 2010). The death of a partner is associated with depression and feelings of sadness for both men and women, although there is some evidence that it is even more dramatic for women. Depression, in general, depresses sexual desire (Baldwin, 2001; Phillips & Slaughter, 2000). Feelings of loss also may affect sexual pleasure. Using data from the NSHAP (a nationally representative study conducted in the United States in 2005–2006), Laumann, Das, and Waite (2008) found that of men who had sex within the past year, widowed men were more likely to report a lack of sexual pleasure than married men. In addition, widowhood has found to be associated with anxiety for those who felt dependent on their deceased spouse (Carr et al., 2000). Given these demographic shifts in cohabitation, marriage and singlehood, the chapter now turns to see how these different life-style contexts affect the quality of sexual interaction among older heterosexual and homosexual populations.

QUALITY OF SEX AND SEXUALITY

The frequency of sexual contact is one measure of an individual's sexual life; the quality of those experiences interacts with, but also can be independent of, sexual frequency (see Chapters 6 and 11, this volume). Drawing heavily from the AARP's 2009 *Survey of Midlife and Older Adults* (AARP) and the

2009 *National Survey of Sexual Health and Behavior* (NSSHB), this section discusses the quality of sex lives during the latter half of the life course, nationally, and when possible, internationally. Available studies show that the quartile of life a person is in makes a big difference in the quality of her or his sex life, and thus this section distinguishes between healthy, middle-age adults ranging in age from 45 to 69 years and again among adults 70 years old and older. Second, this section traces these age-groups across four relationship categories: heterosexual singles, heterosexual couples, LGBTQ singles, and LGBTQ couples. Key differences in quality of sex life emerge along the lines of sexual orientation, relationship status, gender, age, health status, and race or ethnicity.

Bigger Picture: Quality of Sex Among Aging Adults

What characterizes the quality of sex lives of older adults? Although research is a bit unclear regarding what exact behaviors, conditions, and environments contribute to an individual's sexual satisfaction, the broad themes are fairly intuitive: satisfaction and happiness are correlated positively with mental and physical health (Schwartz & Young, 2009), and there seems to be a general correlation between relationship satisfaction and sexual satisfaction in both opposite-sex and same-sex couples (Blumstein & Schwartz, 1983; DeLamater & Moorman, 2007; Fisher et al., 2010; Schick et al., 2010; Trudel et al., 2010). More recently, however, the intersection of aging has been considered in regard to sexual satisfaction (see Carpenter et al., 2006; Laumann et al., 1994; Taylor & Gosney, 2011). Using both the AARP and NSSHB studies as starting points, this section provides an overview on sexual satisfaction and aging as influenced by a variety of demographic categories, especially gender.

Men

According to NSSHB data, reporting on experiences during their most recent partnered sexual event, 79% of men ages 50–59 reported "quite a bit" to "extremely" pleasurable sex. Only 3% of male respondents ages 50–59 reported "a little" pleasure during their last sexual experience. None of the respondents reported no pleasure at all. These numbers are very similar to those given by men between the ages of 60 and 69 years, with a slight increase in those reporting "a little" pleasure during their last sexual experience (up from 3% to 4%). For respondents ages 70–79 years, 68% of respondents still reported "quite a bit" to "extremely" pleasurable sex during their last partnered sexual event, but there is a notable increase in those reporting only "a little" pleasure—up from 4% to 16% (Schick et al., 2010, Table 5).

Other recent studies report more complicated findings. In their pre- and posttest surveys ($n = 158$, tests taken 6 months apart) surrounding a three-part instructional series on major topics involved with sexuality and aging, Wiley and Bortz (1996) found that 53% of men younger than 70 years old reported less enjoyment during sex now (as compared with 10 years prior), but only 43% of those older than 70 did so. Thirty-three percent of respondents older than 70 reported more enjoyment during sex now, as compared with 21% of the younger men (Wiley & Bortz, 1996). It may be that the younger men are comparing themselves to the height of their sexual prowess, whereas the older men already had accommodated to changes in their sexuality that happened during their 60s and thus had not felt there were noticeably greater losses in quality or ability since then. In any case, although men may report an increasing loss of pleasure during sexual events as they age, the majority of male respondents still report enjoyable sexual encounters.

Women

Data indicate that women may be sustaining sexual pleasure over the life course. More specifically, 69% of women ages 50–59 reported "quite a bit" to "extremely" pleasurable sex during their last partnered sexual event, with only 2% reporting "a little" pleasure—the latter on par with their male counterparts. The majority (66%) of respondents ages 60–69 still report quite a bit to extremely pleasurable sex. No respondents report little to no pleasure—with more clustering in the "moderate" pleasure category (16%). Interestingly, 70% of respondents ages 70–79 years report quite a bit to extremely pleasurable sex, with the other 30% of respondents reporting moderate pleasure (Schick et al.,

TABLE 17.1

2009 AARP Sexuality Survey Results: Sexual Satisfaction

		Sexual satisfaction					
		Extremely satisfied	Somewhat satisfied	Neither satisfied nor dissatisfied	Somewhat dissatisfied	Extremely dissatisfied	Total
Q 14: How satisfied are you with your sex life?		Row N %	Row N %	Row N %	Row N %	Row N %	Unweighted count
	Total	18%	25%	35%	15%	7%	1,092
Males	Age 45–49	32%	28%	19%	13%	8%	80
	Age 50–59	19%	31%	28%	14%	8%	197
	Age 60–69	13%	39%	21%	17%	10%	148
	Age 70+	5%	21%	32%	33%	9%	92
	Total	17%	31%	26%	18%	9%	517
Females	Age 45–49	19%	29%	24%	21%	6%	77
	Age 50–59	18%	22%	36%	16%	8%	201
	Age 60–69	18%	23%	42%	11%	5%	187
	Age 70+	17%	10%	66%	4%	3%	110
	Total	18%	21%	43%	13%	6%	575

From *Sex, Romance, and Relationships: AARP Survey of Midlife and Older Adults* (p. 37), by L. Fisher et al., 2010, Washington, DC: AARP. Copyright 2010 by AARP. Reprinted with permission.

2010). This finding is echoed by Wiley and Bortz (1996), who found that 78% of females over the age of 70 years reported more sexual enjoyment now as compared with 10 years ago.[4]

Women also experience sustained sexual satisfaction over the life course, with 18% of women ages 60–69 and 17% of women 70 years and older reporting extremely pleasurable sex (Table 17.1; see also Fisher et al., 2010). In contrast, 13% of men ages 60–69 years and only 5% of men ages 70 years and older report extreme satisfaction with their sex lives (Fisher et al., 2010). Therefore, it appears that although more men report more pleasurable sex in the younger age categories studied, women tend to report both more pleasurable sex and more satisfaction with their sex lives as they age. There appears to be an inverse correlation between pleasure of sexual event and age for men, but the opposite appears to be true for women.[5] Although there appears to be a gendered component to sexual pleasure over the life course, this pattern remains unexplained.

Characteristics of Sexual Events

NSSHB data indicate that respondents are not only engaging in pleasurable sex during the latter half of the life course but also that respondents frequently are engaging in a variety of sexual behaviors. Studies conducted using this data set found that over the past year, 63% of men and nearly 47% of women over the age of 50 reported masturbating (Schick et al., 2010). The majority of men in all age-groups reported masturbation during the past year with the exception of those ages 14–15 years and those 70 years and older (Herbenick et al., 2010b). Furthermore, solo masturbation was reported more commonly than most partnered sexual behaviors for those ages 50 years and older (Herbenick et al., 2010b). About two thirds of men and 45% of women reported frottage, oral sex, penile-vaginal intercourse, or anal intercourse within the past year. Furthermore, penile-vaginal intercourse is not unusual or sporadic. Of the respondents who reported penile-vaginal intercourse in the past year, about

[4]This study, however, had a small return rate for this age category, so these findings are not generalizable.

[5]The age category 80 years and older is also included in the NSSHB data set, but it was omitted because of very low *N* values for the purposes of this article. For more information, or to see the complete table, see Schick et al. (2010).

67% of the men and women also reported engaging in penile-vaginal intercourse a few times a month or more frequently (Schick et al., 2010). NSSHB data also indicate that this frequent behavior is also varied; 41 combinations of sexual behaviors were reported at participants' most recent sexual events (Herbenick et al., 2010a). Looking at the varied combinations of sexual behavior, it is clear that no single behavior or combination of behaviors constituted a majority of acts among respondents. Women ages 40–59 years were more likely to report engaging only in penile-vaginal intercourse during their last sexual event (Herbenick et al., 2010a).

Frequency of Sexual Events

In contrast to other studies that have suggested declines in the frequency of sexual behavior over time for older men and women (see Eisenberg, Shindel, Smith, Breyer, & Lipshultz, 2010; Waite et al., 2009), age was unrelated to the frequency of penile-vaginal intercourse for men in the NSSHB data (Schick et al., 2010). Surveying aging male participants from a men's lunch club in Northern California, Bortz, Douglas, Wallace, and Wiley (1999) found similarly high sexual behaviors among older men.[6] More than 75% of respondents were over the age of 70 years, and approximately 5% reported sex at least twice per week, and an additional 12% reported sex at least once per week. Sixty-four percent of respondents reported masturbation activity, 21% of whom reported masturbatory activity once a week (Bortz et al., 1999). Psychological differences among men may help explain who maintains sexual activity frequently or not at all. For example, a national study of sexual behaviors in Finland found that the frequency of sexual events for older men was strongly related to a man's high sexual esteem (self-rated; Kontula & Haavio-Mannila, 2009).

Women in the NSSHB study reported decreasing frequency of penile-vaginal intercourse over time. Beginning with the cohort in their 30s, increasing proportions of women reported having had no vaginal intercourse during the previous year; this was the case for nearly one third of the women ages 40–49 years, one half of women ages 50–59 years, and ultimately nearly four fifths of women ages 70 and older (Herbenick et al., 2010b). Woloski-Wruble et al. (2010) implemented a questionnaire study with a convenience sample of 127 women attending a menopause clinic in Israel and found that varied and more sexual activities in earlier life were predictive of more sexual activity—and more varied sexual activity—for women in later life. It is possible that as younger cohorts' perceptions of premarital sex become increasingly more liberal, we may see future older cohorts report more frequent sex than their predecessors. Overall, although sizeable portions of both men and women remain sexually active into their 80s (between 20% and 30%), age is related to a lower likelihood of sexual behaviors, solo and partnered (Schick et al., 2010). In some ways, older women may enjoy sex more than their male counterparts, but consider the context of older women's sexual lives: There are more unpartnered women than men, therefore reducing heterosexual women's opportunities for such partnered activities (Laganà & Maciel, 2010) and women suffer from the harsher standards (perceived and real) applied to women's bodies and sexual attractiveness as they age (Bancroft, Loftus, & Long, 2003; Birnbaum et al., 2007; Hinchliff et al., 2009; McQuaide, 1998).

Sexuality as Opportunity Versus Desire

Although not all aging adults are engaging in pleasurable and varied sexual activities, even those who report markedly declined sexual activity over the past 10 years wish they were participating in sexual activities more frequently (Wiley & Bortz, 1996). Surveying 158 older adults on sexuality and aging, Wiley and Bortz (1996) found that 60% of women and men, who were, on average, in their mid-60s, reported a decrease in their sex life, whereas 32% reported no change, and 8% of respondents reported an increase (Wiley & Bortz, 1996).

Respondents tend to view their sexual frequency of the past with nostalgia. In a longitudinal study, participants report that their current desired sexual frequency is on par with their sexual frequency from

[6]The majority of respondents were White and married. Findings may differ among older men outside of marriage, presuming more difficulty in having a consistent sexual partner.

10 years prior (Wiley & Bortz, 1996). For the majority of respondents, however, their desired sexual frequency is at odds with their actual frequency. Specifically, 92% of respondents reported their ideal sex life would include sex once per week, a desire that did not diminish among respondents over the age of 70 (Wiley & Bortz, 1996). Less than half of the respondents, however, reported sexual activity at least once per week (Wiley & Bortz, 1996). There is a gendered component to the gulf between desire and action as well; a larger percentage of men reported a decline in frequency (as compared with the past) than women. This divide also is reflected in findings that indicate that more men desired an increase in their sex life than women (Wiley & Bortz, 1996). As previously noted, however, this finding may be due to differences in opportunity for women and the ways in which women react to a lack of opportunity (Laganà & Maciel, 2010; Masters et al., 1994; Moore, 2010). DeLamater and Sill (2005) found that 78% of women who expressed low desire did not have a sexual partner. Men, on the other hand, maintained sexual desire even in the absence of a sexual partner. This may be explained by other research, which found that women often dismiss sexual desire because of lack of opportunity, whereas men may maintain said desire because of its cultural associations with masculinity (Moore, 2010; see Chapter 8, this volume).

Sexual behaviors vary across different age cohorts, and not surprisingly, shift and change over time. Masturbation is relatively more common in young and older individuals, and vaginal intercourse is more common than other sexual behaviors from early to late adulthood.

Although the majority of sexually active adults report varied sexual behaviors within age cohorts, research also indicates that sexual preferences change over time, across age cohorts, and in gendered ways (Table 17.2). Findings indicate that women report stable sexual preferences over time—that is, they report no significant differences in the importance of kissing, oral sex, manual or genital stimulation, intercourse, orgasm, loving and caring, and satisfying their partner. Loving and kissing were rated highly by women regardless of age (Wiley & Bortz, 1996). Men report significant changes in sexual preferences as compared with 10 years prior (Wiley & Bortz, 1996). Specifically, 10 years earlier, intercourse and orgasm were the highest ranked forms of sexual activity for men, rankings that

TABLE 17.2

Preferred Form of Sexual Activity 10 Years Ago and Currently

	Males					Females				
	10 years ago		Currently			10 years ago		Currently		
	$n = 47$		$n = 40$			$n = 36$		$n = 26$		
	M	*SD*	*M*	*SD*	*t*	*M*	*SD*	*M*	*SD*	*t*
Importance of kissing	4.26	1.90	4.31	2.03	1.00	3.02	1.75	3.30	1.87	< 1
Oral sex	5.70	1.65	5.27	1.79	2.17*	5.50	1.93	5.04	2.05	< 1
Manual/genital stimulation	4.57	1.58	4.30	1.87	1.00	4.50	1.90	3.96	2.12	< 1
Intercourse	2.72	1.59	3.23	1.73	2.56**	4.24	1.80	4.92	1.81	1.05
Orgasm	2.93	1.95	3.81	2.29	3.42***	3.94	1.76	3.78	1.79	< 1
Loving and caring	4.00	1.85	3.31	1.78	3.41***	2.62	1.68	2.39	1.64	1.35
Satisfying partner	3.22	1.74	3.11	1.67	< 1	4.08	1.86	4.11	1.55	1.12

Note. 1 = most important, 7 = least important. From "Sexuality and Aging—Useful and Successful," by D. Wiley and W. M. Bortz II, 1996, *The Journals of Gerontology, Series A: Biological Sciences and Medical Sciences*, *51*, p. M143. Copyright 1996 by the Gerontological Society of America. Reprinted with permission.

*$p < .05$; **$p < .01$; ***$p < .001$.

declined significantly across the decade. Both oral sex and "love preferences" (indicated as "loving and caring" in the survey) rose for men. These changes in preferred sexual activities may lend insight to the gendered gaps seen in both the reports of frequency of sexual activity and the measures of satisfaction and enjoyment related to these sexual activities.

With a broad overview of the sexual practices of aging adults in mind, it is important to note the following: first, the NSSHB was constructed in a way that gained access to aging adults living in communities. Because it can be assumed that a significant portion of the aging adult population in the United States is likely to be either hospitalized or living in a long-term care facility, these data are not generalizable to all aging adults in the United States (Herbenick et al., 2010b). A discussion on the intersections of sexuality and institutions, however, such as nursing homes, will follow. Furthermore, because of limitations of questions and no effort to oversample LGBTQ population or racial ethnic groups (besides an oversample of the Hispanic population in the AARP's 2009 survey; Fisher et al., 2010), current studies do not have enough data to report on minority groups (Herbenick et al., 2010b).[7] Finally, these numbers do not consider the situational or partner-related variables that influence sexual behavior and sexual health (Herbenick et al., 2010b), so we can only assume their impact on these numbers, on the basis of findings from other studies. The next section looks, specifically, at the intersections of sexuality and aging and different relationship statuses.

SEXUAL PARTNERS AND RELATIONSHIP TYPES

Although the NSSHB found that the majority of both men and women ages 50 and older report a relationship partner as their most recent sexual event partner, approximately 14% of men and 26% of women ages 50–59 years report a casual or dating partner, and 17% of men and just under 10% of women in this age-group report a friend. Some 11.3% of men and 7.1% of women ages 50–59 years report a new acquaintance as their most recent sexual event partner (Schick et al., 2010).[8]

Heterosexual Dating

In distinguishing singles from couples, we do not mean to imply that singles are not engaging with sexual partners. Although heterosexual singles may not have consistent access to a romantic or sexual partner, they report higher levels of sexual satisfaction than their married counterparts.[9] Specifically, 48% of dating singles report intercourse at least once a week, compared with 36% of those who are married (Fisher et al., 2010). Furthermore, 60% of dating singles are satisfied with their sex lives, whereas only 52% of married couples report sexual satisfaction (Fisher et al., 2010).

Heterosexual Singles

Of those age 45 and older, 88% of those single and not dating report no sex in the past 6 months, and only 19% of those single and dating report satisfaction with their sex lives (Fisher et al., 2010). Furthermore, as we might expect, reports indicate an inverse relationship between relationship status and both solo masturbation and penile-vaginal intercourse: Participants who identified as single reported a higher frequency of solo masturbation and a lower frequency of penile-vaginal intercourse (Schick et al., 2010). It is interesting that overall sexual satisfaction appears to be higher among dating singles than coupled heterosexuals, but it is important to look at these numbers in a gendered context. Men in every age-group over the age of 50 are significantly more likely to have a regular sex partner than women of the same age. This gap increases with age, because more women than men survive into their 60s, 70s, and 80s. For example, men age 70 and older are more than twice as likely to have a current or recent sexual partner than women of the same age (Fisher et al., 2010).

Finally, women are more likely to report orgasms if their most recent sexual partner was not their

[7]See the section on the LGBTQ population for an overview on the existing data.

[8]For full demographic make-up, including education, geographic location, income, working status, and health status, see Schick et al. (2010).

[9]Of course, one cannot assume that married individuals have consistent access to a romantic or sexual partner, either.

steady partner (Schick et al., 2010). This echoes findings from 40- to 80-year-old women in the Global Study of Sexual Attitudes and Behaviors (Laumann et al., 2006). Although aging women are less likely to have a sexual partner than men, they are more likely to experience more pleasurable sex if they are having sex outside of a relationship. This pleasure divide could be a result of many factors. Women who are sexually active in more casual or dating relationships may be recipients of more romantic gestures and the new, exciting aspects of relationships that often are abandoned or become rote in a long-term relationship. Furthermore, it is more likely that these casual relationships have more of a focus on sexuality than long-term relationships, which would be more likely to include other shared activities, like visiting grandchildren, as the result of a life built together. There may also be some self-selection process: Perhaps women who are pursuing sex outside of the confines of a relationship are more confident about their sexuality and body, and they may be more aware of what they need to receive pleasure—and more likely to ask for it (see Chapters 2 and 25, this volume).

Heterosexual Couples

As the baby boomers age, demographers predict that the portion of senior couples who cohabit (as opposed to marry) will increase dramatically in both the 2010 and 2020 census. The 2000 census data showed that unmarried partner households increased by 72% in a decade, a trend that is only expected to continue as baby boomers bring their more liberal attitudes and views toward sex and sexuality into old age. These views, coupled with higher divorce rates, higher life expectancies, and economic strain, combine to increase the number of aging couples that are sharing homes without the institutional ratification of marriage. It also can be assumed that these increasing numbers are capturing the growing LGBTQ population.

Although the cohabitating population is on the rise, married couples still represent the majority (more than 50%) in the large-scale data on the aging population (AARP & NSSHB reports). Much like the comparison between dating and married couples in terms of sexual satisfaction, data show that individuals who are partnered but unmarried report higher rates of both sexual intercourse and sexual satisfaction than those who are married (Fisher et al., 2010).

There is one notable exception to the disparity between couples along relationship status, however. The aging Hispanic population reports higher levels of satisfaction and sexual activity than the 45 and older population at large, controlling for relationship status. This is especially interesting because data indicate that the aging Hispanic population is also much more likely to report lower health and just as likely as the rest of the population to report that their sexual satisfaction is worse than it was 10 years ago (Fisher et al., 2010). Fifty-seven percent of the Hispanic population age 45 and older reports "extremely satisfied" or "somewhat satisfied" with their sex lives (Fisher et al., 2010). This population also reports many more romantic gestures toward their significant others, which may explain this divide. Aging Hispanic individuals are significantly more likely than the general population age 45 and older to report that they bring each other presents regularly (35% vs. 26%) and are also significantly more likely to set aside one day or evening a week to enjoy each other's company (Fisher et al., 2010). These findings are in line with other studies that show the connection between relationship satisfaction and sexual satisfaction (Blumstein & Schwartz, 1983; DeLamater & Moorman, 2007; Fisher et al., 2010; Schick et al., 2010; Trudel et al., 2010).

LGBTQ Singles and Couples

Our cultural presumption of heterosexuality as the most important kind of sexuality to study has skewed the amount and quality of information we have about sexual minorities. Large-scale research concerning LGBTQ couples and communities tend to be risk-focused (looking at issues regarding HIV transmission), resulting in a limited understanding of the complexity and diversity of LGBTQ individuals' sex lives (Rosenberger et al., 2011; see Chapters 9 and 20, this volume).

Recent data on the older LGBTQ population found that the majority (53%) report being single or unmarried, whereas 25% report a life partner (Brennan-Ing et al., 2011). Because gay marriage currently is legal in only seven states (at the time of this writing, several states are immersed in battles regarding the legalization of gay marriage), it is not surprising that just 4% report marriage. Furthermore, 62% report living alone, and 20% report living with a friend (Brennan-Ing et al., 2011), indicating a close peer network in later life that may not be as prevalent in the heterosexual community.

Gay Men

The NSSHB found that 9% of men and 2% of women 50 and older reported a same-sex partner during their most recent sexual event (Schick et al., 2010). Without oversampling this population, however, the small findings are not generalizable. There was a recent effort to do a version of the NSSHB for the bisexual and gay male identifying community, surveying men ages 45 and older who participated in one of two major websites for men who sought social or sexual interactions with other men. The researchers found that the most commonly reported behaviors during the most recent sex event were giving oral sex (75%) and kissing their sex partner on the mouth (74.8%). Anal sex play was the least common behavior, with just over 30% of men reporting engaging in receptive or insertive anal intercourse (Rosenberger et al., 2011). Although receptive anal intercourse was most commonly reported among the 18–24 age-group, it was the least commonly reported behavior among older age-groups. Furthermore, most men indicated that their most recent male-partnered sexual event occurred within the past 30 days, with the majority of these events occurring within the previous 7 days (Rosenberger et al., 2011). These men are just as—if not more—sexually active than their straight-identifying counterparts.

The type of partner with whom participants described engaging in sexual activity during their last male-partnered sexual event varied, with similar proportions of men indicating their partner was a boyfriend or significant other (18%), casual dating partner (19%), and finally, friend (17.3%; Rosenberger et al., 2011). Bisexual men were less likely than other respondents to report engaging in their most recent sexual event with a relationship partner, and this was particularly true among age categories 50–60 and 60 and older. One explanation for this finding could be that bisexual men are less likely to partner, or this pattern could be attributed to the stigma associated with bisexual men's engaging in sexual behavior with other men. It is also possible that the majority of bisexual men's partners are male even if they are married to a woman or in a committed heterosexual relationship. (Rosenberger et al., 2011).

By asking participants to rank their most recent sexual experience on a six-category ordinal scale (ranging from extreme arousal to not at all aroused), Rosenberger et al. (2011) found overall rates of arousal to be high, but, interestingly, found higher rates of arousal among older cohorts of men, with gay and bisexual identified men over the age of 60 years indicating the highest rates of arousal (80.8% and 84%, respectively). Although this age-group was not the most likely to report orgasm, 72% still did so. According to the authors, although it is easy to explain these higher rates of arousal with the addition and new prevalence of erectile medication, they argued that a more likely explanation is that this increased pleasure is due to increased maturity (Rosenberger et al., 2011).

Creating relationships and investing in them is part of this picture. It is telling to note that men were significantly more like to report orgasm if their sexual partner was a relationship partner ($p < .001$; Rosenberger et al., 2011). Although this finding did not hold for older women, the difference might be explained, at least in part, by dramatic changes in gay men's sexual patterns in middle and late age. The NSSHB indicates that loving and caring aspects of a relationship are more prioritized as men age.

Lesbians

In a large study of lesbian and bisexual women ages 18–59 in the United Kingdom, Bailey, Farquhar, and Whittaker (2003) found that oral sex, vaginal penetration with fingers, and mutual masturbation were the most commonly reported sexual practices between women (Bailey et al., 2003). Without controlling for age or relationship status, however, we cannot speculate as to how these sexual behaviors change over time or compare to peers, although some research in the area exists.

In a 1995 survey of 2,525 lesbian women ages 15–75 years old, Lever found that younger lesbians are more "adventurous" than older cohorts (defined by the use of strap-on dildos, bondage, or engagement in group sex; Lever, 1995). In comparison with heterosexual peers, research indicates that lesbians masturbate more frequently than heterosexual women (Laumann et al., 1994) and that lesbians have orgasms more easily (Kinsey, Pomeroy, Martin, & Gebhard, 1953). Other studies also found high rates of orgasms among lesbians (see review by Garnets & Peplau, 2006).

Although research on the frequency of sexual activity among lesbians is outdated, older studies found that the majority of lesbians reported sexual activity more than once a week (Blumstein & Schwartz, 1983; Peplau, Cochran, & Mays, 1997). A more recent study of African American lesbians found that the majority (47%) reported sexual activity one to three times a week (Peplau et al., 1997). The authors utilized an unrepresentative sample, however, so these findings are not generalizable. Blumstein and Schwartz (1983) looked at a temporal component to these rates of frequency, finding that sexual frequency in lesbian relationships declines significantly with age. Some research suggests that rates of frequency drop much faster than in heterosexual couples (Blumstein & Schwartz, 1983; Lever, 1995). The idea of "lesbian bed death" is heavily debated (see review by Garnets & Peplau, 2006), and research indicates that much like their heterosexual counterparts, lesbians are still engaging in sexual activity in midlife. Although older lesbians are less sexually active than younger lesbians, the majority remain sexually active with age-peer partners (Garnets & Peplau, 2006).

Lesbians generally report very positive feelings about their partners and also report high satisfaction with their relationships (Peplau & Spalding, 2000; Beals et al., 2002). The majority of lesbian relationships are monogamous (Campbell, 2002), although there may be some racial differences, with somewhat more nonmonogamy among African American lesbians (Peplau et al., 1997).

Garnets and Peplau (2006) compared single and paired lesbians and concluded that single lesbians may be at a greater advantage in the dating world than other women. They note multiple advantages, including the opportunity for partners in old age (because women tend to live longer than men), and the fact that lesbians tend to place less emphasis on youth or youthfulness when looking for a partner (Blumstein & Schwartz, 1983).

Clearly, more research is needed on the sexual lives of the older LGBTQ population. Until then, the following factors are especially important to consider when looking at the intersections of sexuality and aging in LGBTQ communities: potential for increased rates of partner loss because of HIV/AIDS, legal barriers for couples, and support networks for older LGBTQ individuals and relationships. Additionally, because of an almost complete lack of empirical data on older individuals or couples, the transgender and transexual population has been left invisible in this review (see Chapter 24, this volume).[10]

Nonmonogamies in Later Life

According to the most recent survey by the AARP, just under one in five individuals older than 45 reported having another sexual relationship during their current relationship. Twenty-one percent of men reported an outside relationship compared with half as many women (approximately 11%; Fisher et al., 2010). The AARP study indicated that the impact on sexual satisfaction in the primary relationship is different for the individual who has had the extrarelational affair and for the individual who has found out about an extrarelational affair. For those who had the affair, more than half reported that the outside sexual relationship had no impact on their sexual satisfaction in their primary relationship. In fact, a quarter of nonmonogamous partners said that the outside sexual relationship made the sexual satisfaction within their intimate relationship even better (Fisher et al., 2010).

Interestingly, the impact on people who find out about their partner's outside sexual experience was similar to the reports of their nonmonogamous partner. Nearly half said that the affair did not have an impact on their sexual satisfaction and slightly more than 20% claimed that the outside sexual behavior made their sexual satisfaction worse. This picture changes, however, when we look at gender differences. Women's sexual satisfaction in their primary

[10]For a study on sexual violence among older transgender adults, see Cook-Daniels and Munson (2010).

relationship dips much more than men's when their partner has gone outside the relationship. Thirty-nine percent of women but only 6% of men say that the affair made sexual satisfaction in the primary intimate relationship deteriorate.

Despite these differences, this negative impact on sexual satisfaction, as a result of sex outside the relationship, is much smaller than one might expect. In fact, when we compare the individuals who engaged in a sexual relationship outside of their primary relationship with individuals whose partner had an extrarelational relationship, we find that among those who engaged in outside sexual activity, more than 80% said that the affair either did not have an effect on sexual satisfaction or it made it better. Nearly 60% who found out about the extra relationship said it either had no impact on sexual satisfaction or made it better. This finding indicates an area in which further research is needed.

Finally, there appear to be differences by race and ethnicity as well. The Hispanic population is just as likely to report sexual activity outside of a committed relationship; however, they were more likely than the general population in this study to say that the sexual relationship had no effect on their current relationship (60% of the men vs. 49% of the women in the study; Fisher et al., 2010). Although studies on this topic for this age-group are rare in other countries, some data exist. Moore (2010) found that extramarital affairs among elders in Japan are couched in cultural understandings of masculinity, and the need for men to maintain their sense of masculinity in later life. Although wives may know about and have to accept these outside sexual experiences or affairs, Moore (2010) found that these affairs create feelings of mistrust and self-doubt among women.

The 2009 AARP study may make us wonder whether the same fidelity norms exist for older adult couples in the same way they exist for younger adult couples. Might older adult couples be affected less by outside sexual relationships? Could there be a modification of the norms of monogamy among some aging couples, or an increase in consensual nonmonogamous relationships? Do cohabiting couples differ from married ones? Do other racial and ethnic groups differ from the population at large? We do know that some same-sex couples differ from heterosexual couples in terms of having consensual nonmonogamy (Adam, 2006; Blasband & Peplau, 1985; Blumstein & Schwartz, 1983; Harry, 1984), but there are no large-scale empirical data to tell us whether these norms change as couples age or marry.[11] Data are insufficient on the evolution of norms in this consequential area of sexual behavior in long-term couples.

HEALTH CONCERNS AND SEXUAL CHALLENGES

Aging includes physical and emotional challenges. Physical changes cannot help but affect the sexual experiences of older adults. This section focuses on ED, lubrication issues, menopause, and finally, serious disease and disability to highlight the ways in which aging and physical and mental health status interact (see Chapter 21, this volume).

Lubrication, Loss of Desire, and Erectile Dysfunction

The NSSHB found that negligible numbers of aging adults experience pain during sex, but women do report difficulties with lubrication and men increasingly mention erection problems as age increases. Just over 50% of women report no difficulty with lubrication between the ages of 50 and 59 years, which drops to 18.8% between the ages of 70 and 79 (Schick et al., 2010). Even higher rates of individuals report no problems with sexual functioning in Finland (Kontula & Haavio-Mannila, 2009). Women who do report difficulties with sexual arousal, however, face emotional repercussions. Conducting in-depth interviews with women reporting sexual desire loss at a psychosexual clinic in England, Hinchliff et al. (2009) found that most of the participants equated their loss of sexual desire with their sense of selves as women. For example, the respondents used words such as "freak," "abnormal," and "odd" in discussing how different they felt in relation to other women. This sense of "otherness"

[11]See Adam (2006) for qualitative interviews on monogamy scripts at different stages of gay men's relationships.

was exacerbated by the ways in which respondents felt about their personal relationships. Respondents reported feelings of guilt and shame for not being able to sexually fulfill their partners' needs. Furthermore, feelings of isolation extended beyond intimate relationships; respondents felt isolated from family and friends because they did not feel comfortable discussing their loss of desire (and its subsequent emotional burdens) with others (Hinchliff et al., 2009).

Impotency issues are a major factor in the decline of sexual activity for men (Wiley & Bortz, 1996). It is estimated that 30 million men in the United States suffer from ED (Laumann, Paik, & Rosen, 1999), part of about 152 million worldwide who experience such problems with impotency (Aytac, McKinley, & Krane, 1999). Bortz et al. (1999), as well as every other study on the topic, found that this problem increases with age: 43% of those ages 55–64 years report erectile difficulty, whereas 64% of those 80 and older report problems.[12] The NSSHB found similar numbers (Schick et al., 2010). Wiley and Bortz (1996) found that 83% of men reported that achieving erections was presently more difficult than it was 10 years before, and 88% of those reporting such a decline said they were somewhat or very uncomfortable with this fact. Furthermore, a quarter of women reported this issue as being a problem in their relationship. The authors concluded that ED is a relationship issue as well as an individual problem. They caution therapists and other professionals to avoid thinking of this as only a male issue, but instead to approach it in the context of a relationship if the man in question has a partner (Wiley & Bortz, 1996; see Volume 2, Chapter 4, this handbook).

Researchers also wrote about secondary effects that occur when there are erectile problems. Some studies indicate that issues with ED can account for changes in sexual preferences and behavior. LoPiccolo (1991) noted that ED may cause couples to turn to other sexual activities because they no longer want to deal with being unsuccessful at intercourse. Certainly, many men (as individuals and who are in a couple) will use medication (on and off label) to try to remedy the issue. As Wiley and Bortz (1996) noted, however, not all couples navigate erectile problems in a positive way. Embarrassment, feelings of failure, and other sequella of changes in male sexual abilities can cause emotional problems in the sexual and nonsexual realms of a relationship. Male ED can trap a couple in patterns of negative anticipation, avoidance, and withdrawal. Sex therapists who work with couples on these issues often see patterns of anger, resentment, insecurity, blaming, and helplessness (Wiley & Bortz, 1996).

These psychological issues occur outside of coupled relationships as well. When men cannot produce an erection, many men feel intense and continuing performance anxiety (Trudel et al., 2010). These anxieties may cause men to seek advice from their doctor, but Hinchliff and Gott (2011) found that because of the perceived stigma surrounding sexual activities at older ages, men worry about seeking medical help and hesitate to bring the subject up (see Volume 2, Chapter 5, this handbook). Furthermore, the authors found that doctors are not likely to inquire about this potential issue even though it is likely to be a problem among older men. Wylie and Kenney (2010) noted embarrassment among both patients and doctors surrounding ED. Even when doctors are better informed about issues surrounding sexuality and aging, the older the patient, the less likely the doctor is to ask about his sexual life (Hinchliff & Gott, 2011).

Regardless of these impediments to treatment, many men still take steps to remedy problems with ED. Reporting on their most recent partnered sexual event, use of erectile medications seems to peak in the 60–69 age range (30%), dropping steadily on both sides of this cohort (Schick et al., 2010). Overall, just under 17% of individuals report use of erectile medication in the United States (Schick et al., 2010). Use of ED medication, however, is much higher among gay men over the age of 50. Nearly a quarter of men ages 50–59 (23.6%) and 35.7% of men 60 years of age and older report the use of ED drugs (Rosenberger et al., 2011).

The visit to the doctor about ED, and the stigma that inhibits asking a doctor about this issue has importance over and above helping men restore

[12]The AARP *Survey of Midlife and Older Adults* and the NSSHB found similar results.

their sexual self-confidence, increase their sexual pleasure, or ability to have intercourse. ED may be the harbinger of other, potentially life-threatening, health problems. Eardley et al. (2007) found an association between self-reported ED and diabetes, angina, and high cholesterol. Furthermore, men with diabetes were more likely to consider their ED to be "severe and permanent" (Eardley et al., 2007). Health problems interact in a variety of ways that can contribute, broadly, to declines in sexual health, frequency, and pleasure.

Menopause

By 2020, there will be as many women experiencing menopause in the United States as there will be women in their childbearing years (U.S. Census Bureau, 1998). As the numbers of older women increase in the United States, it becomes even more crucial to understand the various health issues (sexual and otherwise) that affect this population. Unfortunately for behavioral scientists, society relies on a heavily biomedical narrative to both describe and understand menopause as a life stage. Menopause is categorized by many researchers as a time in which hormonal changes result in a loss of reproductive capacity and subsequent diminishing sexual desire (Dennerstein, Dudley, & Burger, 2001; Mansfield, Koch, & Voda, 2000). Most gerontologists and other researchers interested in older populations, however, are moving away from research that relies solely on declining hormone levels and instead are turning to a more sociocultural perspective that emphasizes context (both intra- and interpersonal) as important to understanding menopausal and sexual experiences at midlife (Bancroft et al., 2003; Dennerstein et al., 2001; Dillaway, 2005; Hinchliff & Gott, 2011; Koch, Mansfield, Thurau, & Carey, 2005).

Dillaway (2005) has argued that menopause is better understood within the context of women's previous reproductive experiences, comparisons of menopause with other aging processes, and structural and ideological shifts that shape the meanings of reproduction and aging. Using self-rated attractiveness and self-reported sexual response changes, Koch et. al. (2005) found that among heterosexual middle-age women, women thought they were more attractive 10 years prior, regardless of menopausal status. Furthermore, the more a woman perceived herself as less attractive than before, the more likely she was to report decline in sexual desire or frequency of sexual activity (Koch et al., 2005). Without finding a link between menopause and self-perceived attractiveness, Koch et al. proposed that researchers should not concentrate on menopause as the critical predictor of continued female desire and arousal but rather would do well to look at factors associated with quality of life and relationships as well as more historical and sociocultural factors of ageism and sexism (Koch et al., 2005; Paquette & Raine, 2004). Other studies have found that these contextual factors tend to be important predictors of sexual satisfaction for women. For example, in a nationally representative sample of telephone interviews with women in the United States (n = 987 White and African American women), Bancroft et al. (2003) found that overall negative emotions and lack of emotional connection with a partner during sexual activity were the best predictors of sexual distress. In contrast, physical factors (such as vaginal lubrication, arousal, and orgasm) actually were poor predictors of sexual distress (Bancroft et al., 2003). Conducting research in the United Kingdom, Hinchliff and Gott (2011) found that changes in sexual activity at time of menopause are not due to perceived biological changes exclusively, but are due to relationship factors as well.

Psychological factors related to menopause also appear to correlate with race and ethnicity. Conducting focus groups with 30 women, grouped by ethnicity and menopausal status, Sampselle, Harris, Harlow, and Sowers (2002) found that Caucasian women tend to medicalize menopause and are more likely to have what doctors consider psychosomatic symptoms. African American and Latina women report more physical problems related to menopause (Green et al., 2010; Sampselle et al., 2002), but report happier and more upbeat feelings about the process, as they are more likely to see menopause as a stage of life rather than an end to their youth and attractiveness (Sampselle et al., 2002). Calasanti (2004) has argued for this happiness, stating that because of menopause, women are finally able to engage in sex the way they should have earlier in life—that is, engaging in sexual activity without the burdens of menstruation, contraception, or the threat of pregnancy. Thus, meanings of various sexualities may change over time because of changes in perception of gender norms or reproductive contexts; furthermore, these new meanings may induce women to feel young rather than old (Dillaway, 2005).

A good number of research studies have proposed that aging and menopause should be treated as distinct and separate processes; reproductive aging does not necessarily indicate mental or emotional aging (Dillaway, 2005). Others, however, have found a correlation between menopause and declines in sexual activity and functioning (Dennerstein et al., 2001). Clearly, a multidisciplinary approach to this topic is necessary. Thus, although the biomedical narratives of menopause carry weight in discussions of sexuality among aging women, more research is needed at both the micro level (relationship dynamics and quality of relationships) and macro level (role of ageism and sexism) to better understand the intersections of menopause, sexuality, and aging.

Overall Health Issues

The most recent AARP study on sexuality after 45 years found that healthy individuals generally are more satisfied with their sex lives than those who are not (Fisher et al., 2010). For example, among those who report an excellent health status, 42% report sex at least once a week and 54% report satisfaction with their sex lives (Fisher et al., 2010). In contrast, people who report a fair health status report less frequency and satisfaction: 19% report sex at least once a week and only 23% report satisfaction with their sex live (Fisher et al., 2010). Poor health was related to receiving and giving less oral sex and infrequent penile–vaginal intercourse. Participants with poor health reported more masturbation and frottage compared with respondents in good health (Schick et al., 2010). The correlation between sexual frequency and sexual behaviors has some international corroboration. For example, a national study in Taiwan found that one of the leading causes of the absence of sexual activity was health considerations (Wang et al., 2008).

Among individuals who report their sex lives were worse than 10 years prior, about one in three named personal health, more stress, and worse health of a partner as the main reasons for their decline in sexual satisfaction (Fisher et al., 2010). The flip side of this is that nearly one in four men and one in five women over 45 years state that better health would be the number one factor that would improve current satisfaction with their sex lives (Fisher et al., 2010). Health is a big category, however, and the challenges people face depend on their specific health problem. Some of the most challenging illnesses are degenerative diseases, particularly Alzheimer's disease (AD). In a study comparing couples in whom one individual has AD and couples in whom both individuals do not have AD, Wright (1998) found that fewer AD couples were sexually active, and they were much less affectionate than healthy couples. The author also noted that it is not just AD that drives less sexual frequency. The author noted that poor health (both mental and physical) of the caregiver also was related to less frequent sex (Wright, 1998).

INSTITUTIONS AND SEXUALITY IN LATER LIFE

Although national surveys tend to exclude men and women in nursing homes, data indicate that nursing home patients still are interested in sex and engaging in sexual activities, much like their community-dwelling counterparts. The intersection of sexuality and institutional living, however, brings up some specific issues about expressing sexual desire, and acting on it, when under institutional care and supervision.

Sex in Nursing Homes

Although sexual activity of a variety of forms occurs in nursing homes, professional caregivers in such settings are not always well equipped to discuss the topic—as seen, for example, in Hinchliff and Gott's (2011) study on patient–doctor discussions of ED (Ehrenfeld, Tabak, Bronner, & Bergman, 1997). Caregivers are in a difficult position. They are required to protect patients, but they also recognize that clients have the right to express sexual desires (Ehrenfeld et al., 1997). Some nursing homes may protect their client's privacy, but reviews of nursing homes reveal that many caregivers in nursing homes display negative attitudes toward the sexual needs of older people (Ehrenfeld et al., 1997; Hinrichs & Vacha-Haase, 2010). This lack of respect for the sexual rights of older people can be exacerbated in the case of the LGBTQ population. They are most likely to bear the brunt of negative attitudes because most caregivers rank heterosexual contact as more acceptable than homosexual contact (Hinrichs & Vacha-Haase, 2010). Ehrenfeld et al. (1997) proposed five reasons for these negative attitudes toward patients, regardless of sexual orientation:

> 1) caregivers believe sexual activity among hospitalized elderly people is immoral, unacceptable and goes against institution policy; 2) sex represents youth, pleasure, health, beauty and lust, all of which are incompatible with Alzheimer's patients, who are confused and lack understanding and energy; 3) caregivers find it difficult to speak objectively of patients' sexual problems with their families; 4) the caregivers themselves lack knowledge of the issue; and 5) caregivers hold the misguided belief that feeble-minded elderly patients do not need sex. (p. 256)

In addition, there seems to be a generational component to these attitudes: the younger the caregiver and the less their experience (less than 5 years working with elderly clients) the more likely the caretaker is to have more negative and restrictive attitudes toward sexual behavior in later life (Bouman, Arcelus, & Benbow, 2007). This is very unfortunate. Although these caretakers may believe that sexual desire and behavior is unseemly and unnecessary among the elderly, research indicates that the need for physical and emotional contact grows rather than decreases over time (Berman, 1987; Ehrenfeld et al., 1997; Naor, 2005), Clearly, assisted living facilities need to be better prepared to deal with their clients sexual needs. There has been more recent social change, however. Old-age homes for LGBTQ singles and couples have emerged in different parts of the United States (Frosch, 2011) and abroad (Tremlett, 2012). Some old-age homes prioritize sexual education and sexual rights for their inhabitants (Villarosa, 2002). Education about elder care and sexual rights has made a difference, but the progress is slow. The best that can be said is that some studies show that same-sex behaviors receive no better, but no worse, negative responses in long-term care facilities than heterosexual behaviors receive.

But even when sexual needs are included as part of residents' plan of care, this does not mean that attention has been paid to maintaining sexual and romantic aspects of their life (Roach, 2004). Residents' complaints include being upset about their loss of control over their private life and about the institution's lack of concern for their sexual and emotional needs (Bouman et al., 2007). Double-bed facilities are virtually nonexistent (Bouman et al., 2007), and the environmental design of buildings is an issue: Surveillance-friendly layouts decrease patient privacy (i.e., shared rooms, single beds, curtains for dividers, and unlockable doors (Bauer, 1999), contributing to a general lack of privacy that can make fulfillment of sexual needs difficult. When health professionals do discuss issues of sexuality, gerontologists stress that there is a need to broaden the framework of the discussion. For example, medications for ED help restore penetrative sex, but just having the medication is not enough. Many older adults also need actual advice, information, and counseling before they feel comfortable taking a pill.

There are a number of barriers to sexual expression in nursing homes, but interest in sexual activity is maintained by many older adults. Although there is often a shift from genital sex to other forms of physical intimacy as adults age (Bouman et al., 2007; Schick et al., 2010; Wiley & Bortz, 1996), illness, medication, and surgery are more likely to interfere with sexual functioning than aging alone (Nusbaum et al., 2005). Still, older adults in institutional environments have been found to be sexually interested despite their illnesses (Lemieux, Kaiser, Pereira, & Meadows, 2004; Moreira et al., 2005). Mulligan and Palguta (1991), conducting research on male residents of a Veterans Affairs Nursing Home, found that among those with partners, coitus was reported to occur at least monthly by 17%, and other forms of sexual activity (e.g., hugging, kissing) were practiced at least monthly by 73% of couples. Furthermore, age, the ability to function sexually, and frequency of intercourse correlated positively with sexual satisfaction (Mulligan & Palguta, 1991).

The Role of Medicine

In general, adults in their 70s and 80s take a cocktail of medications. Regardless of gender, older adults are more likely to be on prescription medications than younger adults (Fisher et al., 2010). On top of blood pressure, cholesterol pills, pain killers, blood thinners, sleeping pills, heart medications, antihypertension drugs, cancer drugs, and chemotherapy, about 10% of men over the age of 70 years and 3% of women take medications to help with sexual functioning—ED for men and vaginal dryness for women (Fisher et al., 2010). The issues to consider in this context include how many medications older people take, the dangers of one medication interacting toxically with another, and how any or all of these medications can hinder sex life.

AARP has found a minimal relationship between the role of medicine and sexuality in later life. When people who reported less sexual satisfaction were asked about changes that affected their sexual satisfaction over the past 10 years, less than 2% attribute that change to an increase in use of medication (Fisher et al., 2010). Furthermore, for those who report more satisfaction with their sex lives, 7% attribute the positive change to sexual drugs (Fisher et al., 2010). The role of medicine, broadly, and the role of ED medicine, more specifically, seems to be perceived as a minimal factor in the sex lives of aging adults. Many heart medications, diabetes medications, antipsychotics, antidepressants, and many other medicines, however, have a direct impact on the ability to be aroused, the ability to have an erection, and the ability to have an orgasm (Buffum, 1986; Eardley et al., 2007; Harrison et al., 1986; Masters et al., 1994; Schiavi, 1999). Drugs for high blood pressure represent the largest medication group responsible for sexual side effects (DeLamater & Sill, 2005). Understanding, and translating those risks—and looking for ameliorative alternatives—is an important issue for older men and women who would like to preserve their sexual life.

Sexually Transmitted Disease Rates

For the most part, older adult cohorts are not, and have not been, the targets of safe-sex campaigns. Although the sexual revolution brought awareness and openness to groups in slightly younger generations, research indicates that the vast majority of men and women over 50 years lack knowledge about sexual health and prophylactic measures in later life (Minichiello, Plummer, & Loxton, 2000).

As a result, the majority of sexually active men and women over 50 years do not, broadly speaking, practice safe sex (Fisher et al., 2010; Gott, Hinchliff, & Galena, 2004; Holden et al., 2005). Condom use does tend to be higher in situations that pose an increased risk (Gott et al., 2004), such as an unknown partner history, sexually transmitted infection (STI) or HIV status, or being a gay male (Brennan-Ing et al., 2011; Gott et al., 2004). Looking at men and women who have had sexual intercourse at least once a month in the past six months, the NSSHB found that half of single, dating men age 45 years and older report condom use rarely or not at all, whereas only 12% report consistent condom use (Fisher et al., 2010). From the same pool, more women reported condom use, with 32% of single, dating women reporting consistent use, and 29% reporting rare use to none at all (Fisher et al., 2010). Minkin (2010) suggested that the rapid increase in medications used for ED plays a role in the increased STIs seen among older women and men. Furthermore, some of the physical symptoms associated with menopause, such as vaginal dryness and the thinning of the vaginal mucosa, can facilitate the transmission of STIs (Minkin, 2010). The major impediment to safer sex among older adults is the widely held, and mistaken belief, that older individuals are at almost no risk of contracting an STI or sexually transmitted disease (STD; Goodroad, 2003). Because a potential pregnancy is no longer an issue, both heterosexual men and women are less fastidious than they would have been about using a prophylactic method. As a result, condom use drops significantly.

Survey data collected from 200 Chicago-area LGBTQ individuals with an average age of 60 years found that of those who participated in vaginal penetration during sexual activity, 44% reported always using condoms, and on the other end of the spectrum, 28% reported never using protection (Brennan-Ing et al., 2011). Similar rates of protection were found among those engaging in anal intercourse: 42% reported consistent condom use, whereas more than one third reported never using condoms during anal intercourse (Brennan-Ing et al., 2011). Similar percentages appear for taking protective measures with sex toys: 51% of respondents reported always taking precautions with sex toys, whereas 28% reported never taking precautions with sex toys (Brennan-Ing et al., 2011).

It follows then that recent data from the Centers for Disease Control and Prevention (CDC) found that reported cases of syphilis and chlamydia among people ages 55 and older increased 43% from 2005 to 2009 (Jameson, 2011). People are living longer, using sex-enhancing medicines, and having more sex in an era when dating and sex outside of marriage is acceptable. Unfortunately, this does not include the knowledge and the discipline needed to create safer sex for the individual or their partners. There is a serious need for sexual education among older populations and an increased awareness of the potential consequences of sexual activity. In addition, doctors and other members of the health community need to ensure that their patients are receiving the appropriate tests and screenings. Public health officials, commercial interests (such as condom companies), and gerontological professionals need to recognize that the majority of older people still have sexual desires and many are sexually active. Not only do older individuals still need to be able to have honest and clear conversations with medical staff about their sexual lives, but they also need age-appropriate messages that will help them enjoy sex without endangering their health or the health of their partners.

CONCLUSION

The demographic picture of the United States and, indeed, much of Canada and Europe is of a rapidly aging population. In particular, as the baby boomers age, they bring with them a unique set of values, beliefs, and experiences as a result of inventing and living through the sexual revolution, the feminist movement, and the LGBTQ movement. Although 21st-century older men and women, like aging adults of the past, face a complex mix of emotional, physical, and social issues that may hinder their ability and desire to participate in an active sex life, large numbers of people value their sexuality, have an active sexual life, and are intent on preserving that sexual life for as long as possible. Much of our knowledge about older men's and women's sexuality has been based on generations who came of age before the sexual revolution, the pill, and other technological advances. It is easy to forget that most of the research and clinical literature we rely on may not reflect modern cohort and period effects. For example, we talk about data pertaining to 70-year-olds, but we should remind ourselves that the oldest members of the baby boom are still in their 60s. Will they mirror the 70-year-olds in these present studies, or will they be much different because of their history and medical advances? We should be humble about our knowledge about sexual minorities and even more timid about conclusions about older people who belong to minority ethnic, racial, and religious groups. We know so little about the sexual lives of members of these groups. We also need to know much more about the differentiation of age-groups: Do we really know enough about how people feel about their sexuality in their 70s compared with their 60s? Do we have good models of successful and happy sex lives for both same- and opposite-sex couples in each of the decades past age 50 years?

The good news for researchers is that there is much to discover; the bad news for clinicians, therapists, doctors, caregivers, and older people is that we need much more information to attend to our own—and our clients—sexual and psychosexual needs as they proceed though what promises to be a much extended life cycle. In particular, new life styles, such as long-term cohabitation for older heterosexual men and women, and legal marriage for same-sex couples, will need to be studied so that older men and women can have support as they create new ways to be romantic and sexual. Furthermore, although large-scale, national studies provide a much better quantitative picture of what sexuality in the later parts of the life cycle looks like, these studies rely on individual's reports of their sexual behavior and therefore are inherently subjective.

Self-report data are useful, but we hope that more observational studies (such as ethnographies of nursing homes), in-depth interviews, psychiatric and clinical analysis, and perhaps video diaries can be used to get a clearer picture of the romantic and sexual context of everyday life among middle-age and older individuals and couples. Because most of the studies we have relied on are cross-sectional (with the exception of Wiley & Bortz, 1996), we cannot be sure how much of what we have uncovered about the intersections of sexuality and aging show causal relationships. Because of this, there is an even greater need for more descriptive qualitative data on the relational and social factors that affect sexual lives.

Finally, we were surprised at the paucity of psychological research on older men and women and their sexual lives. Perhaps the problem is that baby boomers are starting to retire, and this cohort has finally lost some of its fascination with its own life course. This seems unlikely; still, if there is any truth to this surmise, we would urge psychologists to refocus their research on the sexual issues and practices of people 50 years and older. The boomers always have been leaders of cultural change, and there is no indication this will cease to change as they enter each period of their lives.

References

Adam, B. (2006). Relationship innovation in male couples. *Sexualities, 9*, 5–26. doi:10.1177/1363460706060685

Aytac, I. A., McKinley, J. B., & Krane, R. J. (1999). The likely worldwide increase in erectile dysfunction between 1995 and 2025 and some possible policy consequences. *British Journal of Urology International, 84*, 50–56.

Bailey, J. V., Farquhar, C., & Whittaker, D. (2003). Sexual behavior of lesbians and bisexual women. *Journal of Sexual Transmission and Infection, 79*, 147–150. doi:10.1136/sti.79.2.147

Baldwin, D. S. (2001). Depression and sexual dysfunction. *British Medical Bulletin, 57*, 81–99. doi:10.1093/bmb/57.1.81

Bancroft, J., Loftus, J., & Long, J. S. (2003). Distress about sex: A national survey of women in heterosexual relationships. *Archives of Sexual Behavior, 32*, 193–208. doi:10.1023/A:1023420431760

Basson, R. (2006). Sexual desire and arousal disorders in women. *New England Journal of Medicine, 354*, 1497–1506. doi:10.1056/NEJMcp050154

Bauer, M. (1999). Their only privacy is between their sheets: Privacy and the sexuality of elderly nursing home residents. *Journal of Gerontological Nursing, 25*, 37–41.

Beals, K., Impett, E., & Peplau, L. A. (2002). Lesbians in love: Why some relationships endure and others end. *Journal of Lesbian Studies, 6*, 53–63. doi:10.1300/J155v06n01_06

Berman, M. S. (1987). *The anatomy of loving*. New York, NY: Columbia University Press.

Binfa, L., Robertson, E., & Ransjo-Arvidson, A. (2009). Chilean women's reflections about womanhood and sexuality during midlife in a Swedish or Chilean context. *Health Care for Women International, 30*, 1093–1110. doi:10.1080/07399330903276777

Birnbaum, G., Cohen, O., & Wertheimer, V. (2007). Is it all about intimacy? Age, menopausal status and women's sexuality. *Personal Relationships, 14*, 167–185. doi:10.1111/j.1475-6811.2006.00147.x

Blasband, D., & Peplau, L. (1985). Sexual exclusivity versus openness in gay couples. *Archives of Sexual Behavior, 14*, 395–412. doi:10.1007/BF01542001

Blumstein, P., & Schwartz, P. (1983). *American couples: money, work and sex*. New York, NY: William Morrow.

Bortz, W. M., II, Douglas, H., Wallace, D. H., & Wiley, D. (1999). Sexual function in 1,202 aging males: Differentiating aspects. *The Journals of Gerontology, Series A: Biological Sciences and Medical Sciences, 54*, M237–M241. doi:10.1093/gerona/54.5.M237

Bouman, W. P., Arcelus, J., & Benbow, S. M. (2007). Nottingham Study of Sexuality and Ageing (NoSSA II). Attitudes of care staff regarding sexuality and residents: A study in residential and nursing homes. *Sexual and Relationship Therapy, 22*, 45–61. doi:10.1080/14681990600637630

Brennan-Ing, M., Korpiak, S. E., & Seidel, L. (2011). *Health and psychosocial needs of LGBT older adults*. New York, NY: AIDS Community Research Initiative of America (ACRIA), ACRIA Center on HIV and Aging.

Brown, S., & Kawamura, S. (2010). Relationship quality among cohabitors and marrieds in older adulthood. *Social Science Research, 39*, 777–786. doi:10.1016/j.ssresearch.2010.04.010

Buffum, J. (1986). Pharmacosexology update: Prescription drugs and sexual function. *Journal of Psychoactive Drugs, 18*, 97–106.

Butler, R., & Lewis, M. (1993). *Sex and love after 60*. New York, NY: Ballantine Books.

Cahill, S., South, K., & Spade, J. (2000). *Outing age: Public policy issues affecting gay, lesbian, bisexual, and transgendered elders*. New York, NY: The Policy

Institute of the National Gay and Lesbian Task Force Foundation.

Calasanti, T. (2004). New directions in feminist gerontology: An introduction. *Journal of Aging Studies, 18*, 1–8. doi:10.1016/j.jaging.2003.09.002

Campbell, S. M. (2002, July). *Gay marriage: A descriptive study of civil unions in Vermont*. Poster presented at the International Conference on Personal Relationships, Halifax, Nova Scotia, Canada.

Carpenter, L., Nathanson, C., & Kim, Y. (2006). Sex after 40? Gender, ageism, and sexual partnering in midlife. *Journal of Aging Studies, 20*, 93–106. doi:10.1016/j.jaging.2005.06.003

Carr, D., House, J. S., Kessler, R. C., Ness, R. M., Sonnega, J., & Wortman, C. (2000). Marital quality and psychological adjustment to widowhood among older adults: A longitudinal analysis. *The Journals of Gerontology, Series B: Psychological Sciences and Social Sciences, 55*, S197–S207. doi:10.1093/geronb/55.4.S197

Chao, J. K., Lin, Y., Ma, M., Lai, C., Ku, Y., Kuo, W., & Chao, I. (2011). Relationship among sexual desire, sexual satisfaction, and quality of life in middle-aged and older adults. *Journal of Sex and Marital Therapy, 37*, 386–403. doi:10.1080/0092623X.2011.607051

Choi, K. B., Jang, S., Lee, M., & Kim, K. (2011). Sexual life and self-esteem in married elderly. *Archives of Gerontology and Geriatrics, 53*, e17–e20. doi:10.1016/j.archger.2010.08.011

Cook-Daniels, L., & Munson, M. (2010). Sexual violence, elder abuse and sexuality of transgender adults, age 50+: Results of three surveys. *Journal of GLBT Family Studies, 6*, 142–177. doi:10.1080/15504281003705238

DeLamater, J., & Moorman, S. (2007). Sexual behavior in later life. *Journal of Aging and Health, 19*, 921–945. doi:10.1177/0898264307308342

DeLamater, J. D., & Sill, M. (2005). Sexual desire in later life. *Journal of Sex Research, 42*, 138–149. doi:10.1080/00224490509552267

Dennerstein, L., Dudley, E., & Burger, H. (2001). Are changes in sexual functioning during midlife due to aging or menopause? *Fertility and Sterility, 76*, 456–460. doi:10.1016/S0015-0282(01)01978-1

Dillaway, H. E. (2005). Menopause is the "good old": Women's thoughts about reproductive aging. *Gender and Society, 19*, 398–417. doi:10.1177/0891243204271350

Eardley, I., Fisher, W., Rosen, R. C., Niederberger, C., Nadel, A., & Sand, M. (2007). The Multinational Men's Attitudes to Live Events and Sexuality study: The influence of diabetes on self-reported erectile function, attitudes and treatment-seeking patterns in men with erectile dysfunction. *International Journal of Clinical Practice, 61*, 1446–1453. doi:10.1111/j.1742-1241.2007.01460.x

Ehrenfeld, M., Tabak, N., Bronner, G., & Bergman, R. (1997). Ethical dilemmas concerning sexuality of elderly patients suffering from dementia. *International Journal of Nursing Practice, 3*, 255–259. doi:10.1111/j.1440-172X.1997.tb00110.x

Eisenberg, M. L., Shindel, A. W., Smith, J. F., Breyer, B. N., & Lipshultz, L. I. (2010). Socioeconomic, anthropomorphic, and demographic predictors of adult sexual activity in the United States: Data from the national survey of family growth. *Journal of Sexual Medicine, 7*, 50–58. doi:10.1111/j.1743-6109.2009.01522.x

England, P., & McClintock, E. A. (2009). The gendered double standard of aging in marriage markets. *Population and Development Review, 35*, 797–816. doi:10.1111/j.1728-4457.2009.00309.x

Fisher, L., Anderson, G., Chapagain, M., Montenegro, X., Smoot, J., & Takalkar, A. (2010). *Sex, romance and relationships: AARP Survey of Midlife and Older Adults*. Washington, DC: AARP.

Fraser, J., Maticka-Tyndale, E., & Smylie, L. (2004). Sexuality of Canadian women at midlife. *Canadian Journal of Human Sexuality, 13*, 171–187.

Fredrickson, B. L., & Roberts, T.-A. (1997). Objectification theory: Toward understanding women's lived experiences and mental health risks. *Psychology of Women Quarterly, 21*, 173–206. doi:10.1111/j.1471-6402.1997.tb00108.x

Frosch, D. (2011, October 28). Hard times for gay retirement havens. *New York Times*.

Ganong, K., & Larson, E. (2011). Intimacy and belonging: The association between sexual activity and depression among older adults. *Society and Mental Health, 1*, 153–172. doi:10.1177/2156869311431612

Garnets, L., & Peplau, L. A. (2006). Sexuality in the lives of aging lesbian and bisexual women. In D. Kimmel, T. Rose, & S. David (Eds.), *Lesbian, gay, bisexual and transgender aging: research and clinical perspectives* (pp.). New York, NY: Columbia University Press.

Goodroad, B. K. (2003). HIV and AIDS in people older than 50: A continuing concern. *Journal of Gerontological Nursing, 29*, 18–24.

Gott, M., Hinchliff, S., & Galena, E. (2004). General practitioner attitudes to discussing sexual health issues with older people. *Social Science and Medicine, 58*, 2093–2103. doi:10.1016/j.socscimed.2003.08.025

Gottman, J. M., Coan, J., Swanson, C., & Carrere, S. (1998). Predicting marital happiness and stability from newlywed interactions. *Journal of Marriage and Family, 60*, 5–22. doi:10.2307/353438

Gottman, J. M., & Levenson, R. W. (2000). The timing of divorce: Predicting when a couple will divorce over a 14-year period. *Journal of Marriage and Family, 62*, 737–745. doi:10.1111/j.1741-3737.2000.00737.x

Gottman, J. M., Levenson, R. W., Gross, J., Fredrickson, B., McCoy, K., Rosenthal, L., . . . Yoshimoto, D. (2003). Correlates of gay and lesbian couples' relationship satisfaction and relationship dissolution. *Journal of Homosexuality*, *45*, 23–43. doi:10.1300/J082v45n01_02

Green, R., Polotsky, A., Wildman, R., McGinn, A., Lin, J., Derby, C., . . . Santoro, N. (2010). Menopausal symptoms within a Hispanic cohort: SWAN, the Study of Women's Health Across the Nation. *Climacteric*, *13*, 376–384. doi:10.3109/13697130903528272

Harrison, W. M., Rabkin, M., Ehrhardt, M., Anke, J., Mc, S., Grath, J., . . . Quitkin, F. (1986). Effects of antidepressant medication on sexual function: A controlled study. *Journal of Clinical Psychopharmacology*, *6*, 144–149. doi:10.1097/00004714-198606000-00004

Harry, J. (1984). *Gay couples*. New York, NY: Praeger.

Herbenick, D., Reece, M., Schick, V., Sanders, S., Dodge, B., & Fortenberry, J. (2010a). An event-level analysis of the sexual characteristics and composition among adults ages 18 to 59: Results from a national probability sample in the United States. *Journal of Sexual Medicine*, *7*(Suppl. 5), 346–361. doi:10.1111/j.1743-6109.2010.02020.x

Herbenick, D., Reece, M., Schick, V., Sanders, S., Dodge, B., & Fortenberry, J. (2010b). Sexual behavior in the United States: Results from a national probability sample of men and women ages 14–94. *Journal of Sexual Medicine*, *7*(Suppl. 5), 255–265. doi:10.1111/j.1743-6109.2010.02012.x

Hinchliff, S., & Gott, M. (2011). Seeing medical help for sexual concerns in mid- and later life: A review of the literature. *Journal of Sex Research*, *48*, 106–117. doi:10.1080/00224499.2010.548610

Hinchliff, S., Gott, M., & Wylie, K. (2009). Holding onto womanhood: A qualitative study of heterosexual women with sexual desire loss. *Health: An Interdisciplinary Journal for the Social Study of Health, Illness, and Medicine*, *13*, 449–465. doi:10.1177/1363459309103917

Hinrichs, K. L., & Vacha-Haase, T. (2010). Staff perceptions of same-gender sexual contacts in long-term care facilities. *Journal of Homosexuality*, *57*, 776–789. doi:10.1080/00918369.2010.485877

Holden, C. A., McLachlan, R. I., Cumming, R., Wittert, G., Handelsman, D. J., de Kretser, D. M., & Pitts, M. (2005). Sexual activity, fertility, and contraceptive use in middle-aged and older men: Men in Australia, Telephone Survey (MATeS). *Human Reproduction*, *20*, 3429–3434. doi:10.1093/humrep/dei307

Hurd Clarke, L. (2010). *Facing age: Women growing older in anti-aging culture*. Toronto, Ontario, Canada: Rowman & Littlefield.

Isen, A., & Stevenson, B. (2010). *Women's education and family behavior: Trends in marriage, divorce, and fertility* (National Bureau of Economic Research Working Paper No. 15725). Cambridge, MA: National Bureau of Economic Research. Retrieved from http://www.nber.org/papers/w15725

Jameson, M. (2011, April 17). STD rates soar among aging individuals. *Orlando Sentinel*. Retrieved from http://www.cdcnpin.org/scripts/display/NewsDisplay.asp?NewsNbr=57598

Kaiser, F. E. (1996). Sexuality in the elderly. *Urologic Clinics of North America*, *23*, 99–109. doi:10.1016/S0094-0143(05)70296-2

King, V., & Scott, M. E. (2005). A comparison of cohabiting relationships among older and younger adults. *Journal of Marriage and Family*, *67*, 271–285. doi:10.1111/j.0022-2445.2005.00115.x

Kinsey, A. C., Pomeroy, W. B., & Martin, C. E. (1948). *Sexual behavior in the human male*. Bloomington: Indiana University Press.

Kinsey, A. C., Pomeroy, W. B., Martin, C. E., & Gebhard, P. H. (1953). *Sexual behavior in the human female*. Bloomington: Indiana University Press.

Koch, P. B., Mansfield, P., Thurau, D., & Carey, M. (2005). Feeling frumpy: The relationship between body image and sexual response changes in midlife women. *Journal of Sex Research*, *42*, 215–223. doi:10.1080/00224490509552276

Kontula, O., & Haavio-Mannila, E. (2009). The impact of aging on human sexual activity and sexual desire. *Journal of Sex Research*, *46*, 46–56. doi:10.1080/00224490802624414

Krakauer, I., & Rose, S. M. (2002). The impact of group membership on lesbians' physical appearance. *Journal of Lesbian Studies*, *6*, 31–44. doi:10.1300/J155v06n01_04

Laganà, L., & Maciel, M. (2010). Sexual desire among Mexican-American older women: A qualitative study. *Culture, Health and Sexuality*, *12*, 705–719. doi:10.1080/13691058.2010.482673

Laumann, E. O., Das, A., & Waite, L. J. (2008). Sexual dysfunction among older adults: Prevalence and risk factors from a nationally representative group of men and women 57–85 years of age. *Journal of Sexual Medicine*, *5*, 2300–2311.

Laumann, E. O., Gagnon, J. H., Michael, R. T., & Michaels, S. (1994). *The social organization of sexuality: Sexual practices in the United States*. Chicago, IL: University of Chicago Press.

Laumann, E. O., Paik, A., Glasser, D. B., Kang, J. H., Wang, T., Levinson, B., . . . Gingell, C. (2006). A cross-national study of subjective sexual well-being among older women and men: Findings from the global study of sexual attitudes and behaviors. *Archives of Sexual Behavior*, *35*, 143–159. doi:10.1007/s10508-005-9005-3

Laumann, E. O., Paik, A., & Rosen, R. C. (1999). Sexual dysfunction in the United States: Prevalence and predictors. *JAMA, 281*, 537–544. doi:10.1001/jama.281.6.537

Lemieux, L., Kaiser, S., Pereira, J., & Meadows, L. M. (2004). Sexuality in palliative care: Patient perspectives. *Palliative Medicine, 18*, 630–637. doi:10.1191/0269216304pm941oa

Lesthaeghe, R. J. (2010). *The unfolding story of the second demographic transition* (PSC Research Report No. 10-696). Ann Arbor, MI: Population Studies Center.

Lever, L. (1995, March 21). The 1995 Advocate survey of sexuality and relationships: The women. *Advocate (Boston, MA)*, 22–30.

Lief, H. (1977). What's new in sex research? Inhibited desire. *Medical Aspects of Human Sexuality, 2*, 944–994.

Lindau, S. T., Tessler, P., Schumm, E. O., Laumann, W., Levinson, C., O'Muircheartaigh, A., & Waite, L. J. (2007). A study of sexuality and health among older adults in the United States. *New England Journal of Medicine, 357*, 762–775. doi:10.1056/NEJMoa067423

LoPiccolo, J. (1991). Counseling and therapy for sexual problems in the elderly. *Clinics in Geriatric Medicine, 7*, 161–177.

LoPiccolo, J., & Friedman, J. (1988). Broad treatment of low sexual desire. In S. Lieblum & R. Rosen (Eds.), *Sexual desire disorders* (pp. 107–144). New York, NY: Guilford Press.

Manning, W. D., & Brown, S. L. (2009). *The demography of unions among older Americans: 1980–present.* Bowling Green, OH: National Center for Family and Marriage Research.

Mansfield, P. K., Koch, P. B., & Voda, A. (2000). Midlife women's attributes for their sexual response changes. *Health Care for Women International, 21*, 543–559. doi:10.1080/07399330050130322

Margolin, L., & White, L. (1987). The continuing role of physical attractiveness in marriage. *Journal of Marriage and Family, 49*, 21–27. doi:10.2307/352666

Masters, W., & Johnson, V. (1966). *Human sexual response*. Oxford, England: Little, Brown.

Masters, W., & Johnson, V. (1970). *Human sexual inadequacy*. Boston, MA: Little, Brown.

Masters, W., Johnson, V., & Kolodny, R. (1994). *Heterosexuality*. New York, NY: HarperCollins.

McQuaide, S. (1998). Women at midlife. *Social Work, 43*, 21–31. doi:10.1093/sw/43.1.21

Minichiello, V., Plummer, D., & Loxton, D. (2000). Knowledge and beliefs of older Australians about sexuality and health. *Australasian Journal on Ageing, 19*, 190–194. doi:10.1111/j.1741-6612.2000.tb00234.x

Minkin, M. J. (2010). Sexually transmitted infections and the aging female: Placing risks in perspective. *Maturitas, 67*, 114–116. doi:10.1016/j.maturitas.2010.05.003

Moore, K. L. (2010). Sexuality and sense of self in later life: Japanese men's and women's reflections on sex and aging. *Journal of Cross-Cultural Gerontology, 25*, 149–163. doi:10.1007/s10823-010-9115-9

Moreira, E. D., Brock, G., Glasser, D. B., Nicolosi, A., Laumann, E. O., Paik, A., . . . Gingell, C. (2005). Help-seeking behaviour for sexual problems: The Global Study of Sexual Attitudes and Behaviors. *International Journal of Clinical Practice, 59*, 6–16. doi:10.1111/j.1742-1241.2005.00382.x

Mulligan, T., & Palguta, R. F. (1991). Sexual interest, activity and satisfaction among male nursing home residents. *Archives of Sexual Behavior, 20*, 199–204. doi:10.1007/BF01541944

Naor, S. (2005, July). Love strong as death. A new perspective of love in the elderly. *Dorot, 8*, 28–31.

National Center for Health Statistics. (2011). *Health, United States, (2010): With special feature on death and dying*. Hyattsville, MD: Author.

Nusbaum, M. R. H., Lenahan, P., & Sadovsky, R. (2005). Sexual health in aging men and women: Addressing the physiologic and psychological sexual changes that occur with age. *Geriatrics, 60*, 18–23.

Paquette, M. C., & Raine, K. (2004). Sociocultural context of women's body image. *Social Science and Medicine. 59*, 1047–1058. doi:10.1016/j.socscimed.2003.12.016

Peplau, L. A., Cochran, S. D., & Mays, V. M. (1997). A national survey of the intimate relationships of African American lesbians and gay men: A look at commitment, satisfaction, sexual behavior, and HIV disease. In B. Greene (Ed.), *Psychological perspectives on lesbian and gay issues: Ethnic and cultural diversity among lesbians and gay men* (pp. 11–38). Newbury Park, CA: Sage.

Peplau, L. A., & Spalding, L. R. (2000). The close relationship of lesbians, gay men, and bisexuals. In C. Hendrick & S. S. Hendrick (Eds.), *Close relationships: A sourcebook* (pp. 111–124). Thousand Oaks, CA: Sage.

Phillips, R. L., & Slaughter, J. R. (2000). Depression and sexual desire. *American Family Physician, 62*, 782–786.

Roach, S. M. (2004). Sexual behaviour of nursing home residents: Staff perceptions and responses. *Journal of Advanced Nursing, 48*, 371–379. doi:10.1111/j.1365-2648.2004.03206.x

Rosenberger, J. G., Reece, M., Schick, V., Herbenick, D., Van Der Pol, B., Novak, D. S., & Fortenberry, J. D. (2011). Sexual behaviors and situational characteristics of most recent male partnered sexual event among gay and bisexually identified men in the United States. *Journal of Sexual Medicine, 8*, 3040–3050. doi:10.1111/j.1743-6109.2011.02438.x

Sampselle, C. M., Harris, V., Harlow, S., & Sowers, M. (2002). Midlife development and menopause in African American and Caucasian women. *Health Care for Women International, 23*, 351–363. doi:10.1080/0739933029008928

Sanchez, D. T., & Kiefer, A. (2007). Body concerns in and out of the bedroom: Implications for sexual pleasure and problems. *Archives of Sexual Behavior, 36*, 808–820. doi:10.1007/s10508-007-9205-0

Schiavi, R. (1999). *Aging and male sexuality*. Cambridge, England: Cambridge University Press. doi:10.1017/CBO9780511585098

Schick, V., Herbenick, D., Reece, M., Sanders, S., Dodge, B., Middlestadt, S., & Fortenberry, J. (2010). Sexual behaviors, condom use, and sexual health of Americans over 50: Implications for sexual health promotion for older adults. *Journal of Sexual Medicine*, 7(Suppl. 5), 315–329. doi:10.1111/j.1743-6109.2010.02013.x

Schnarch, D. (2009). *Passionate marriage: Keeping love and intimacy alive in committed relationships*. New York, NY: W. W. Norton & Co.

Schnarch, D. (2011). *Intimacy and desire: Awaken the passion in your relationship*. New York, NY: Beaufort Books.

Schwartz, P., & Young, L. (2009). Sexual satisfaction in committed relationships. *Sexuality Research and Social Policy*, *6*, 1–17. doi:10.1525/srsp.2009.6.1.1

Siever, M. D. (1994). Sexual orientation and gender as factors in socioculturally acquired vulnerability to body dissatisfaction and eating disorders. *Journal of Consulting and Clinical Psychology*, *62*, 252–260. doi:10.1037/0022-006X.62.2.252

Starr, B., & Weiner, M. B. (1981). *The Starr–Weiner report on sex and sexuality in the mature years*. New York, NY: Stein & Day.

Taylor, A., & Gosney, M. (2011). Sexuality in older age: Essential considerations for healthcare professionals. *Age and Ageing*, *40*, 538–543. doi:10.1093/ageing/afr049

Tiggemann, M., & Lynch, J. E. (2001). Body image across the life span in adult women: The role of self-objectification. *Developmental Psychology*, *37*, 243–253. doi:10.1037/0012-1649.37.2.243

Tremlett, G. (2012, January 2). Spain's first gay retirement home passes its first hurdle. *Guardian (London, England)*.

Trudel, G., Turgeon, L., & Piche, L. (2010b). Marital and sexual aspects of old age. *Sexual and Relationship Therapy*, *25*, 316–341. doi:10.1080/14681991003750467

Trudel, G., Villeneuve, L., Preville, M., Boyer, R., & Frechette, V. (2010a). Dyadic adjustment, sexuality and psychological distress in older couples. *Sexual and Relationship Therapy*, *25*, 306–315. doi:10.1080/14681991003702583

U.S. Census Bureau. (1998). *Statistical abstract of the United States: The national data book*. Washington, DC: Author.

U.S. Census Bureau. (2010a). *Age and sex composition: 2010*. Retrieved from http://2010.census.gov/2010census/data

U.S. Census Bureau. (2010b). *Families and living arrangements*. Retrieved from http://www.census.gov/population/www/socdemo/hh-fam.html

Villarosa, L. (2002, June 4). At elders' home, each day is Valentine's Day. *New York Times*.

Waite, L. J., Laumann, E. O., Das, A., & Schumm, L. P. (2009). Sexuality: Measures of partnerships, practices, attitude, and problems in the National Social Life, Health, and Aging Study. *The Journals of Gerontology, Series B: Psychological Sciences and Social Sciences, 64*(Suppl. 1), i56–i66.

Wang, T., Lu, C., Chen, I., & Yu, S. (2008). Sexual knowledge, attitudes, and activity of older people in Taipei, Taiwan. *Journal of Clinical Nursing, 17*, 443–450.

Wiley, D., & Bortz, W. M., II. (1996). Sexuality and aging—useful and successful. *The Journals of Gerontology, Series A: Biological Sciences and Medical Sciences*, *51*, M142–M146. doi:10.1093/gerona/51A.3.M142

Woloski-Wruble, A. C., Oliel, Y., Leefsma, M., & Hochner-Celnikier, D. (2010). Sexual activities, sexual and life satisfaction and successful aging in women. *Journal of Sexual Medicine, 7*, 2401–2410.

Wright, L. K. (1998). Affection and sexuality in the presence of Alzheimer's disease: A longitudinal study. *Sexuality and Disability*, *16*, 167–179.

Wylie, K., & Kenney, G. (2010). Sexual dysfunction and the ageing male. *Maturitas, 65*, 23–27. doi:10.1016/j.maturitas.2009.10.018

Zilbergeld, B., & Ellison, C. R. (1980). Desire discrepancies and arousal problems in sex therapy. In S. Leiblum & L. A. Pervlin (Eds.), *Principles and practice of sex therapy* (pp. 65–101). New York, NY: Guilford Press.

Part V

SAME-SEX SEXUALITY

CHAPTER 18

THEORIES AND ETIOLOGIES OF SEXUAL ORIENTATION

Margaret Rosario and Eric W. Schrimshaw

The purpose of this chapter is to understand what is meant by "sexual orientation" and to consider what might explain sexual orientation. In the process of such examination, we come to understand not only same-sex sexuality but also other-sex sexuality. In essence, there is no better way to understand any phenomenon than by means of contrast.

DEFINITIONS OF TERMS RELATED TO SEXUAL ORIENTATION

Sexual orientation is related or occasionally conflated with other terms. Consequently, it is important to define those terms. Although not necessarily identical, the definitions we provide are comparable to those offered by others (Shively & De Cecco, 1977; Zucker, 2008).

Sex

The *sex* of the individual refers to the individual's biological sex as male or female, which is based on the appearance of the external genitalia during utero or at birth. Agreement is presumed between the external markers of sex (genitalia, secondary sexual characteristics that begin appearing around puberty) and internal markers of sex (sex organs, chromosomal sex, relative concentrations of sex hormones). Although relatively infrequent, evidence emerges indicating discrepancies between and among internal and external biological markers of sex (e.g., Becker et al., 2008). Even when there is no discrepancy and one has no difficulty invoking the terms *boy/man* or *girl/woman* to describe one's sex, there may be a discrepancy between one's sex and one's gender identity (see Chapters 2, 19, 20, and 24, this volume).

Gender Identity

Gender identity refers to the individual's inchoate sense of self as girl/woman or boy/man. Correspondence usually exists between one's gender identity and one's assigned sex at birth. This correspondence is not perfect, however, even when there is no doubt of the external genitalia or any alternative biological explanation for the discrepancy. In such a case, one is a transgendered individual who may choose to chemically or surgically transition as much as possible (or desired) to the other sex (i.e., the sex that matches the gender identity; see Chapter 24, this volume).

Gender

Masculine or feminine *gender* refers to the behaviors, attitudes, or traits that are associated in a particular culture and time with the roles or characteristics assigned or considered more typical of men or women (see Chapter 2, this volume). Although the linkage does not imply an underlying biological basis or correspondence, such a link often is made across cultures. A particular behavior or characteristic is judged normative or even intrinsic to one but not the other sex. Such behaviors and characteristics are considered stereotypically "masculine" or "feminine," and one may speak of "gender conformity" or "gender nonconformity" (Bell, Weinberg, & Hammersmith, 1981). Nevertheless, not all behaviors or characteristics may be categorized as masculine or feminine by the culture; some may be androgenous (S. L. Bem, 1974).

http://dx.doi.org/10.1037/14193-018
APA Handbook of Sexuality and Psychology: Vol. 1. Person-Based Approaches, D. L. Tolman and L. M. Diamond (Editors-in-Chief)

Sexual Identity Development

Sexual identity development as lesbian, gay, bisexual, or heterosexual is a long-term process that probably begins early in life and undoubtedly has unconscious elements. Subsumed into two processes, *sexual identity development* involves identity formation and its integration with other aspects of the self (Rosario, Schrimshaw, & Hunter, 2011). For purposes of this chapter, sexual identity (i.e., self-identification as, for example, lesbian or gay) and sexual identity development are not the same. Indeed, what the individual calls him- or herself may not match his or her sexual identity development (see Chapters 19 and 20, this volume).

Definition of Sexual Orientation

Sexual orientation usually is considered a multidimensional construct. The aspects of sexual orientation, however, are not necessarily concordant. The dimensions of sexual orientation may differ on the basis of the specific theoretical or practical concerns of an investigation (see Chapters 19 and 20, this volume).

Sexual Attraction

At its most basic level, *sexual orientation* refers to the sex to which one is physically attracted; thus, it pivots on the sex of the object relative to the sex of the subject. The attractions are toward the same sex, the other sex, or both sexes. In addition, there may be no attractions toward either sex.

Sexual attraction refers to the extent to which sexual fantasies, erotic arousal, and sexual desires (the latter is also known in the literature as "sexual attractions") focus on either, both, or neither sex. The various dimensions of sexual attraction are concordant. Indicators of the sexes that individuals find desirable, are aroused by when viewing erotica, or focus on in their sexual fantasies are highly correlated and load strongly on a single factor (Rosario, Schrimshaw, Hunter, & Braun, 2006).

Sexual attraction encompasses the internal component of sexual orientation. As such, sexual attraction is independent of whatever pressure may be applied by any external force (e.g., family, religion, culture) for one to be attracted to one or the other sex. Sexual attraction also is independent of whatever efforts may be exerted by the individual to divert attraction to the other sex. Sexual attraction is not under the control of the individual. It is a reality that the individual learns about (and, in many cases, begins to accept and work through) during her or his sexual identity development. The only control an individual may exert over his or her attractions is deciding whether to accept the attractions and act on them.

Data from the 2006–2008 National Survey of Family Growth (NSFG), a household-based probability sample of the U.S. population, indicate that among those ages 18–44 years, approximately 1% of men and women are attracted only to the same sex (Chandra, Mosher, Copen, & Sionean, 2011). The survey found, however, that more women than men are attracted to both sexes (2.8% vs. 0.5%) and, consequently, fewer women than men are attracted only to the other sex (83% vs. 94%).[1]

Sexual Behavior

Sexual involvement with the object of one's sexual attractions is expected, although it is not guaranteed. Many factors determine sexual behavior besides sexual attraction. They include societal or religious injunctions and sanctions that reduce the settings offering opportunities to meet potential partners as well as penalize any such behavior. Even without such restrictions, the availability of potential sex partners is a factor. If few partners are available, sexual behavior is likely to be attenuated. If none are available for an extended time, sex with a partner at odds with one's attraction may occur, as happens for heterosexual individuals in sex-segregated settings, such as single-sex boarding schools (Johnson, Wadsworth, Wellings, & Field, 1994). The factors disrupting the link between sexual attraction and behavior (and subsequent relationship formation) may include self-negation, meaning refusal to have sexual relations with the object of one's attraction. This situation may occur for same-sex behavior for some individuals, given internalization by the individual of society's stigmatization of

[1]The percentages do not sum to 100% because we exclude for ease of presentation the following categories: mostly same sex, mostly other sex, and unsure.

homosexuality (Bauermeister et al., 2010; J. Brown & Trevethan, 2010). Nevertheless, as compared with factors that may attenuate sexual behavior, other factors may facilitate it. Sexual experimentation is likely to be elevated during adolescence because adolescence is a developmental period characterized by identity exploration both cognitively and behaviorally and in many domains, including the sexual domain (Erikson, 1968; see Chapter 15, this volume).

Given the potential contextual contingencies affecting sexual behavior, some scholars exclude it from the definition of sexual orientation (Sell, 1996). Others, however, do include it along with sexual attraction (Gonsiorek, Sell, & Weinrich, 1995; Laumann, Gagnon, Michael, & Michaels, 1994; Shively & De Cecco, 1977). The components of sexual attraction and behavior often are measured independently. One notable exception is Kinsey, Pomeroy, and Martin's (1948) work, as they used both sources of information from their intensive interviews to rate their participants along the famous Kinsey scale ranging from exclusively heterosexual (0) to exclusively homosexual (6).

Population data from the full sample of 2006–2008 NSFG, ages 15–44 years, indicate that more women than men report a history of same-sex behavior (12.5% vs. 5.2%), although a history of other-sex behavior is 89% among both sexes (Chandra et al., 2011). The disparity in same-sex behavior is even greater among young people ages 15–24 years (13.4% for women vs. 4.0% for men). The overall prevalence findings for the United States (9.2% for same-sex behavior) are not necessarily comparable with those of other locations. For comparison, 5.1% of a national household probability sample of New Zealanders age 16 and older reported a history of same-sex behavior (Wells, McGee, & Beautrais, 2011). Comparable figures were reported in a household probability sample of Britons (Hayes et al., 2012).

Sexual Identity

Sexual identity refers to self-identification as straight, lesbian, gay, bisexual, asexual or any variant or synonym (e.g., queer). Sexual identity sometimes is considered distinct from sexual orientation. How one self-identifies is a complex function of how one perceives, situates, and evaluates one's internal and external experiences in the time, culture, and settings in which one finds oneself. Many factors external to one's sexual attraction may bear directly and strongly on self-identification and may have little to do with the individual's sexual attraction. Thus, it may take some time for an individual to explore and determine his or her sexual identity; in fact, there may even be a time, especially during adolescence, when the individual is unsure of his or her sexual identity (Hatzenbuehler, Wieringa, & Keyes, 2011; Ott, Corliss, Wypij, Rosario, & Austin, 2011; Wells et al., 2011; see Chapter 16, this volume). Regardless, as with sexual behavior, many investigators include self-identification in their definition of sexual orientation (e.g., Laumann et al., 1994), but others do not (e.g., Gonsiorek et al., 1995; Kinsey et al., 1948).

Prevalence data from the 2006–2008 NSFG (Chandra et al., 2011) indicate that, of respondents ages 18–44 years, fewer women than men self-identified as homosexual, lesbian, or gay (1.1% vs. 1.7%) or as heterosexual (93.7% vs. 95.7%), but more women than men identified as bisexual (3.5% vs. 1.1%). In the New Zealand household survey, 1.4% of the population age 16 and older self-identified as homosexual or bisexual (Wells et al., 2011). As far as we know, one report is available on asexuality, indicating that 1.1% of a national probability sample of Britons identified as asexual (Bogaert, 2004). Of the asexual individuals (n = 195), 138 (70.8%) were women.

Romantic Relationship

More recently, some have begun to consider involvement in romantic relationships as a marker of sexual orientation (Wells et al., 2011; Worthington & Reynolds, 2009), in which the ability to form an intimate relationship with a representative of the sex to which one is attracted proves decisive. Many factors unrelated to one's sexual attraction, however, may affect romantic relationships. The stability and duration of such a relationship undoubtedly varies with development (i.e., the ages of the partners involved), the partners' reciprocity of affection, and the extent to which both partners have worked through unresolved issues pertaining to their sexuality. The level of mental health and functioning of each partner affects the stability and duration of an intimate relationship (Kernberg, 1995), as might other resources brought by the partners to the relationship (e.g., socioeconomic means). Furthermore, the degree of tolerance for the relationship expressed by others, ranging from friends and family to societal policies, also may bear on the relationship. Given the multiple and nonpsychosexual exigencies affecting romantic relationships, the likelihood that such relationships will serve as a prevalent marker of sexual orientation seems relatively low. Nevertheless, the establishment of a stable, mutually satisfying sexual and romantic relationship could be considered the ultimate indication of commitment to and integration of one's sexual orientation for all individuals, but especially for homosexual and bisexual individuals in same-sex relationships, given the obstacles such couples must overcome. More generally, given the acknowledged psychological benefits of having a romantic relationship, it would be anticipated that same-sex individuals in romantic relationships would demonstrate a variety of health advantages (Bauermeister et al., 2010; J. Brown & Trevethan, 2010; Frost & Meyer, 2009; see Chapter 10, this volume).

Given that relatively little research has employed romantic relationships as an indicator of sexual orientation, we will say no more about romantic relationships as a possible constituent of sexual orientation. Instead, we will concentrate on the other potential markers of sexual orientation, specifically sexual attraction, behavior, and identity.

Multiple Dimensions of Sexual Orientation

Differences in the definition of sexual orientation are both theoretical and practical in origin. A researcher interested in internal dynamics and their consequences naturally would be drawn to sexual attraction. A researcher whose interests concern how social forces shape and constrain the individual or group might gravitate to self-identification. These two theoretical foci track to the paradigms of essentialism and social constructionism, respectively (for details, see DeLamater & Hyde, 1998; Laumann et al., 1994; see Chapter 1, this volume). Diversity also exists in the definition of sexual orientation for practical reasons having to do with some dimensions proving more consequential for a subject matter than others. For example, sexual behavior is critical for researchers who study the acquisition of sexually transmitted infections, whereas other dimensions are less relevant (see Chapter 23, this volume). For another example, sexual attraction is important for those who study substance use or overweight-related health concerns among sexual-minority women, as will be discussed later in this chapter (see also Chapter 21, this volume).

Given the multiple dimensions of sexual orientation and the fact that theoretical or practical concerns determine the dimensions selected by any investigator, we have chosen to focus on the dimension of sexual attraction to either, both, or neither sex. Unlike sexual activity and self-identification, sexual attraction is unaffected by external conditions and individual control. We underscore that our definition does not exclude sexual behavior. We also understand that others may want to include self-identification in their definition or investigations; in fact, we have done so in our own work (Rosario et al., 2006). All that we affirm is that certain precepts should be considered when deciding on the scope of sexual orientation for one's investigation. The indicator(s) of sexual orientation theoretically should be guided or determined by the outcome under investigation (e.g., sexual behavior for sexual transmitted infections). The addition of more components must be weighed against what is gained at the expense of parsimony. The addition of more than one component also raises practical matters, such as how, if at all, the components are to be combined and what is to be done with inconsistencies among the components. Discordance exists among the components of sexual orientation, which is unsurprising given our earlier discussion.

Laumann et al. (1994) conducted a careful examination of concordance among same-sex sexual attraction (i.e., what they called "desire" and which consisted of being attracted to the same sex or finding the idea of sex with the same sex appealing), behavior, and identity in their national probability sample of the U.S. population, ages 18–59 years. Of the women who reported any adult same-sex sexuality (8.6% of the female sample), concordance among desire, behavior, and identity was only 15%. For the

10.1% of the men who reported any adult same-sex sexuality, comparable concordance was only 24%. With respect to discordance, 59% of the women and 44% of the men reported just same-sex desire (i.e., desire but no behavior or identity), the aspect of sexual orientation with the highest frequency (see Laumann et al., 1994, pp. 299 and 301, for more details). Discordance also has been found in more recent population surveys, such as the 2006–2008 NSFG (Chandra et al., 2011, p. 31, Tables 14 and 15). In this survey, 9.0% of the women and 3.2% of the men, ages 18–44 years, who identified as heterosexual had a history of sexual behavior with the same sex (see Chapter 20, this volume).[2]

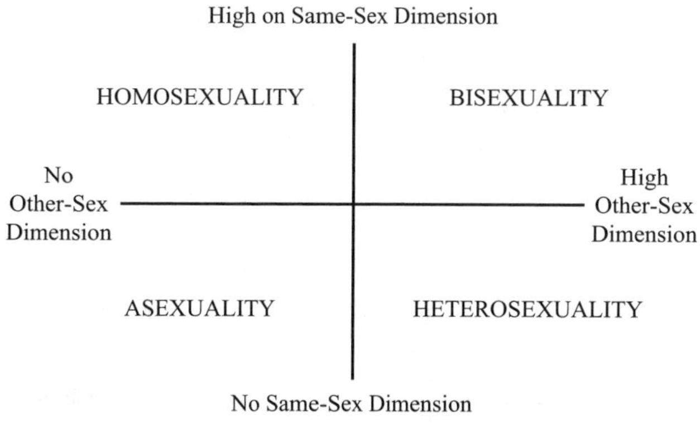

FIGURE 18.1. The two-dimensional model of sexual orientation. From "Theories of Sexual Orientation," by M. D. Storms, 1980, *Journal of Personality and Social Psychology, 38,* p. 784. Copyright 1980 by the American Psychological Association.

Conceptual Implications of Sexual Orientation

Our conception of sexual orientation draws on the work of Shively and De Cecco (1977). They proposed that sexual orientation varies along two dimensions, one being heterosexuality and the other homosexuality. For each aspect of sexual orientation (e.g., sexual attraction), one focuses on the degree of heterosexuality for one dimension and on the degree of homosexuality for the other dimension, with each dimension varying from not at all heterosexual (or homosexual) to being very heterosexual (or homosexual). Unfortunately, the relations between the two dimensions were not made clear. In addition, conflation of sexual orientation and self-identification is possible given that the response scales focus either on "heterosexuality" or "homosexuality."

Storms (1980) proposed two orthogonal dimensions, in which one focuses on same-sex sexual fantasies and the other on other-sex sexual fantasies, which we represent pictorially (Figure 18.1). The four resulting quadrants capture the four possible outcomes of orientation as homosexual, heterosexual, bisexual, and asexual; the latter refers to no sexual fantasies. Storms found, as hypothesized, that self-identified lesbians and gay men reported high levels of homoerotism and low levels of heteroerotism, heterosexual men and women reported the opposite pattern, and bisexual individuals reported high levels of both homo- and heteroerotism. There were no self-identified asexual individuals perhaps because the asexual identity was not made available to the sample ($n = 185$).

Bisexuality. The uniqueness of the perspectives proposed by Storms (1980) primarily concerns bisexuality and asexuality. Bisexuality is regarded as a distinct orientation, with high levels of both homoerotism and heteroerotism in terms of sexual attraction. This perspective differs from that of Kinsey et al. (1948), in which bisexuality contains an amalgam of both, but not, for example, high amounts of both. Kinsey et al. (1948) conceptualized sexual orientation along a single dimension from

[2]The concordance data provoke a number of questions or comments. First, concordance among dimensions of sexual orientation is more common among men than women. Why? Responding that women are more fluid than men merely reframes the empirical observation. A potential explanation has been offered (Diamond, 2006) that concerns woman's arousal to non-specific rather than sex-specific sexual stimuli and for which there is some empirical support (Chivers, Seto, & Blanchard, 2007; Peterson, Janssen, & Laan, 2010), although not unanimously (Chivers et al., 2007; Peterson et al., 2010; Rullo, Strassberg, & Isreal, 2010). Second, discordance is elevated in men and women particularly among those who report only same-sex attractions. What does this mean and how does an individual who is attracted to the same sex go about a presumably heterosexual life? What is psychically going on with this person? Third, the approximately 9% of women and 3% of men who identify as heterosexual but have a history of same-sex behavior possibly suggests a floor for experimentation, which differs from what the literature uses. The literature tends to classify any same-sex behavior as a marker of homosexual or bisexual behavior, but should it? What if an individual had one same-sex experience as a young person or even a brief same-sex relationship while in college, but nothing since; moreover, his or her attractions are toward the other sex and identity is heterosexual. Experimentation also should not be considered a marker of heterosexual or bisexual orientation. It may be that some lesbian and gay individuals at one point had penile-vaginal sex and even brief heterosexual relationships as ways of confirming whether they actually were lesbian or gay. Now that population data are available, more finely calibrated algorithms may be generated to account for sexual activity beyond just experimentation.

exclusive homosexuality to exclusive heterosexuality. Bisexuality is in the middle of the scale—that is, less than either extreme, a compromise or average of the two extremes.

The high levels of homoerotism and heteroerotism in sexual attraction expected for bisexual individuals say nothing about the individuals' sexual behavior with respect to the number of partners or the relative number of same- to other-sex partners. In addition, having a bisexual orientation does not mean that one is involved concurrently with both a male and female partner. The extent to which bisexual individuals may have concurrent partners remains to be determined and compared with concurrent partnerships among lesbian and gay individuals as well as heterosexual individuals. Nevertheless, bisexual individuals, as a group, have more sexual partners over some extended time than their same-sex heterosexual or homosexual peers, as evidence on men indicates (Hightow et al., 2006; Jeffries, 2011; Mercer, Hart, Johnson, & Cassell, 2009). This would be expected, provided bisexuals had relatively equal desire for both sexes as well as competing desire for the sex with which they were not involved. Greater variability in the number of partners, however, is observed among bisexual individuals (Hightow et al., 2006; Jeffries, 2011; Mercer et al., 2009), perhaps because their emotional commitment and sexual satisfaction with their partners should vary, as they do for heterosexual and homosexual individuals. Bisexual individuals raise interesting questions for which further research is greatly needed among both female and male bisexuals.

Asexuality. Storms (1980) posited asexuality as a possible sexual orientation, in which little, if any, sexual attraction is felt toward either men or women. This orientation is now receiving serious consideration, although its possible existence has been known for some time. Kinsey et al. (1948) had proposed a category for such individuals, although it was not included in the Kinsey scale. Clinicians (Kernberg, 1995) also have been aware of asexual individuals (see Volume 2, Chapter 4, this handbook).

Bogaert (2006b) has maintained that asexuality means absence of sexual attraction. An asexual person, however, may be involved in an intimate relationship (Bogaert, 2004; Brotto, Knudson, Inskip, Rhodes, & Erskine, 2010) and may engage in sexual behavior, even if minimal (Prause & Graham, 2007).

Equally important is the very definition of "sexual attraction" with respect to asexuality, especially in light of our definition of sexual attractions as including sexual fantasies, erotic arousal, and sexual desire. According to Bogaert (2004), "sexual attraction" refers to being attracted to one, both, or neither sex (i.e., what, among the constituents of sexual attraction, we refer to as sexual desire). Prause and Graham (2007) used self-identification as asexual and subjective reports of desire and arousal. The asexual women and men reported less desire and lower arousal than nonasexual men and women. Brotto and Yule (2011) examined self-reports and physiological arousal to viewing an erotic film, using a vaginal probe to assess genital congestion. Erotic arousal to the film was apparent among the asexuals both by self-report and vaginal photoplethysmography. Nevertheless, and as one would expect, the asexual women reported less sexual desire than the heterosexual, bisexual, and homosexual women.

Currently, it seems as if the defining characteristic of asexuality is little, if any, sexual desire because arousal does exist, as does some attenuated level of sexual activity at least for some individuals. The existence, characteristics, and effects of sexual fantasies in asexual individuals remain to be assessed. In general, more detailed examination concerning the psychosexuality of asexual individuals is needed.

Even with such research, a more basic question must be addressed: Is asexuality an orientation or a marker or consequence of psychopathology? It is always difficult to raise such issues, but they must be confronted. The fact that some individuals may identify as something akin to asexual or have experiences that closely relate to notions of asexuality does not make asexuality an orientation. The possibility of asexuality, as proposed by Storms (1980), is ultimately a logical deduction that may be divorced from any biological or psychological grounding. Certainly, clinical work with individuals who might identify or be classified by others as asexual suggests confounding with psychopathology (Kernberg, 1995). In addition, research with community samples of asexual individuals confirms overlap with psychopathology for some (Brotto et al., 2010). Nevertheless, we are keenly aware that the issue of psychopathology is a delicate one, given it was once raised about both homosexual and bisexual individuals. Unfolding theoretical and empirical research brought an end to the question. Whether asexuality will enjoy the same outcome remains to be determined. Regardless, this determination can be made only by forthrightly and dispassionately examining the possible confounding of psychopathology and asexuality. More thought and research are required about asexuality.

All sexual orientations. Figure 18.1 contains two important messages. The simplest one concerns classification into four sexual orientations. Categorization is familiar. Both in the general population and scientific community, a preference continues for thinking about and conducting investigations by classifying individuals into sexual-orientation groups. The number of groups has expanded over the years, for example, the focus on asexuality is relatively new. In addition, subclassifications are now investigated within quadrants. Thus, research on "mostly" (as compared with "completely," "entirely," or "exclusively") heterosexual or homosexual orientations (e.g., Ott et al., 2011; Thompson & Morgan, 2008; Vrangalova & Savin-Williams, 2012) calls for increased sensitivity to differences within categories (DeLuzio Chasin, 2011). The potential difficulty with the classification approach is that there is no theoretical end to classification. One can continue to slice the population into finer units of analysis. In fact, this can be done down to the absurdity of the *N* of 1. Might an alternative perspective enhance our understanding of sexual orientation?

The most valuable message contained in Figure 18.1 concerns the vectors rather than the quadrants. One can accept the complete dimensionality of each vector and focus on the conditional relation between the dimensions, examining the intersection of the two dimensions without arbitrarily categorizing the dimensions. We have no idea what would be learned by adhering to this new approach. It is, however, certainly the case that classification of continuous data necessarily involves loss of information. Consequently, it is unknown how much nuance or subtlety of information has been lost by means of classification. In addition, the suggested approach would cease to privilege heterosexuality. The classification scheme invariably leads to a comparison of sexual-minority groups (e.g., lesbians, gays, bisexuals) to heterosexuals, positioning heterosexuality as the standard from which deviations are tracked. As important as that may be in some circumstances (e.g., health disparities), equally important and conspicuously neglected are potential differences among sexual minorities. A vector approach would force one to think about such possibilities and, thus, potentially generate new hypotheses or questions. Finally, the vector approach would turn our gaze away from groups to focus on degree or extent of attraction in all its possibilities. The result should be a literature more relative in its characterization (e.g., "As same-sex desire increases relative to increasing [or decreasing] other-sex desire, one finds . . . "). The conditional relation (or interaction) between the two vectors would indicate the extent to which knowledge of one vector is essential to understanding the relation between the other vector and some outcome.

Change and Sexual Orientation

Sexual orientation may change over time. Freud (1905/1953), as far as we know, was the first to appreciate this possibility. Klein, Sepekoff, and Wolf (1985) were more specific, proposing that the past may differ from the present, as might one's ideal (potential future) orientation. Evidence of change is apparent during adolescence and the subsequent developmental period of emerging adulthood (approximately ages 18–25 years).

Adolescence and emerging adulthood mark the time when individuals usually become aware of their sexual orientation and sometimes investigate their orientation by means of experimentation. Indeed, different patterns or trajectories of change in sexual orientation have been found among young people (Dickson, Paul, & Herbison, 2003; Ott et al., 2011; Rosario et al., 2006; Savin-Williams & Ream, 2007). The data indicate that bisexuality may be a transitional identity to either homosexuality or heterosexuality for some young people as well as a consistent identity for other youth (Ott et al., 2011; Rosario et al., 2006). Youth who are unsure or uncertain of their identity predominantly transition to a heterosexual identity (Ott et al., 2011). Change in identity over time does not covary with sex, being equally prevalent among both sexes (Ott et al., 2011). Sex dimorphism, however, is apparent in other ways. Over time, the number of young women attracted to both sexes increased and those attracted just to men decreased over the first three waves of the National Longitudinal Survey of Adolescent Health (Add Health) of individuals in the United States (Savin-Williams & Ream, 2007). For the young men in this study, an increase in the numbers attracted to women was apparent over time and was attributed to the decreased number attracted to neither sex during early adolescence. Consequently, 85% of the women and 94% of the men identified as heterosexual by emerging adulthood. Nevertheless, geographic differences need to be considered, given data from New Zealand follow a different pattern (Dickson et al., 2003). Findings for current sexual attraction to the same or both sexes between Add Health and New Zealand were 12.9% and 16.4% for the women and 5.3% and 5.6% for the men, respectively (see Volume 2, Chapter 6, this handbook).

Change is not restricted to adolescents and emerging adults. Adults also may change. Such change is examined prospectively by tracking individuals over time or retrospectively by asking them to report on their past. The former methodology is the stronger of the two because it eliminates recall bias. Therefore, we disregard the retrospective reports (Calzo, Antonucci, Mays, & Cochran, 2011; Kinnish, Strassberg, & Turner, 2005) in favor of prospective studies.

Change in sexual identity was apparent in waves four and five of Add Health; the young people were in early adulthood (n = 28.5 years old) at wave four (Savin-Williams, Joyner, & Rieger, 2012). There was a decrease in the numbers who identified as completely heterosexual, with the decrease being greater for the women (85.6% to 80.2%) than the men (94.2% to 93.6%); for women, the greatest increase was to mostly heterosexual (10.8% to 15.8%). Overall, the greatest change was in the bisexual identities. For example, of the bisexuals who changed, 61.2% of the women and 47.3% of the men transitioned toward heterosexuality. The National Survey of Midlife Development in the United States (MIDUS) of middle-age individuals, specifically its first and second waves, which spanned approximately 10 years, indicated that women who were either lesbian or bisexual were significantly more likely to change their identity than were heterosexual women and to do so about equally to each of the other identities (Mock & Eibach, 2012). Bisexual men also were more likely to change their identity than heterosexual men and to do so equally in both directions. Sex differences indicated that more homosexual women than homosexual men were likely to change their identity. With respect to attractions or behaviors, only one research team, as far as we know, has investigated change, but this change was investigated only among women and in a convenience sample unlike the previous probability samples (Diamond, 2008). Over five waves of data, beginning when the women were in emerging adulthood, lesbians experienced a significant decline in same-sex attractions over time, but they experienced less change in their attractions than bisexual or unlabeled women. In addition, more lesbians engaged in same-sex than other-sex sexual behavior, followed by the unlabeled women, and ending with the bisexual women who were the least likely to have same-sex activity relative to other-sex activity.

In summary, change occurs particularly in women and in the nonexclusive homosexual and heterosexual categories at least with respect to identity (see Chapter 19, this volume). Change is usually to a proximal rather than a more distal category (Ott et al., 2011; Savin-Williams et al., 2012). Too little is known about change in sexual attraction or sexual behavior. Although change in adolescence and emerging adulthood is understandable, change in adulthood contradicts the prevailing view of consistency in sexual orientation. Why change occurs in the orientation of adults remains to be empirically examined and must be considered along with possible cohort effects that may be unique to the generation captured by MIDUS. Women are more likely to be sexual minorities than are men, and sexual-minority women are more likely to be bisexual.

Before leaving the section on the definition of sexual orientation, we emphasize that sexual orientation continues to be examined categorically. In addition, there is an implicit premise that sexual orientation is fixed or unchanging, except perhaps during adolescence when the young person discovers and experiments with his or her orientation or when undergoing treatment to change sexual orientation (although the validity of such change is problematic, as will be discussed later). We highlight the biases of sexual orientation as fixed because they characterize the forthcoming literature review.

THEORETICAL PERSPECTIVES FOR UNDERSTANDING SEXUAL ORIENTATION

Sexual orientation is varied, composed of groupings known by various names (e.g., heterosexual, homosexual, lesbian or gay, bisexual), and those names have changed over time (Sell, 1997). Nevertheless, the existence of varied sexual orientations has until quite recently focused primarily on homosexuality and heterosexuality. The aim has been to understand the existence of homosexuality relative to that of heterosexuality and, by so doing, understand heterosexuality.

Sexual orientation as homosexual and heterosexual has existed over time and throughout periods of civilization, from eras of enlightenment and great strides in the arts and sciences (e.g., the Golden Era) to periods marked by the opposite (e.g., the Middle Ages). The reach of sexual orientations extends to non-Western cultures and traverses the scale from underdeveloped and developed societies (e.g., United Nations High Commissioner for Human Rights, 2011). In addition, diversity in sexual orientation has existed, regardless of reactions to some of its manifestations. The environment external to the individual may be nurturing and reinforcing of an orientation. The same environment may be hostile to another orientation, seeking to eliminate it or, at minimum, cast it as forbidding, illegitimate, and inferior to the privileged pattern. Nevertheless, the survival of an orientation under such toxic conditions suggests an underlying force motivating it.

Something internal and powerful must account for sexual orientations. Consequently, one might suspect that the sexual orientations must serve an evolutionary function(s) to substantiate their existence. In addition to evolution, three other etiological explanations are possible. First, other subfields of biology may account for the variety of orientations. Second, the explanation may be ontological, found in environmental conditions experienced during critical developmental times that leave a lasting impression on the individual, directing his or her subsequent development along a particular pathway. Here, for example, one might find family dynamics between the child and his or her significant others that prove pivotal. Third, a conditional relation may exist between biology and environment that explains the full range of orientations. This explanation is not unlike the one characterizing the growing field of epigenetics, in which genes may have no effect unless activated by environmental conditions. The conditional relation that may hold promise for our concern involves biological factors by environmental factors of family dynamics.

Biological Etiology of Sexual Orientation

Evolution. It seems unlikely that a behavioral set of characteristics survives over time and settings if it does not serve an evolutionary purpose. Heterosexuality ensures reproduction and, thus, survival of the species. Homosexuality does not, if it excludes any other-sex contact. Discussion of homosexuality from an evolutionary perspective often implies exclusive same-sex focus. From this premise, the necessity is to consider an explanation that acknowledges the existence of homosexuality throughout the ages and reconciles that fact with its implied lack of reproductive fitness. The implication, however, may be wrong. Lesbians and gays may reproduce; at minimum, many report a history of opposite-sex partners (Johnson et al., 1994; Laumann et al., 1994). Although, as a group, fewer homosexuals may have been pregnant (Bauer, Jairam, & Baidoobonso, 2010) or had children than heterosexuals (Bogaert & Friesen, 2002; Schwartz, Kim, Kolundzija, Rieger, & Sanders, 2010), their level of reproduction may have been sufficient to avoid nature's extinction of homosexuality. We admit this is speculative, but speculation is often the rule rather than the exception when discussing evolutionary explanations for homosexuality.

Two other points about evolution to bear in mind as specific theories are discussed in the following paragraphs. Evolutionary explanations refer to the adaptations made by our ancestors during the development of the human species in the settings and environments in which they lived. They neither pertain to the challenges encountered by us in modern times nor to our solutions to these challenges. Second, there may be more than one way for evolutionary needs to be met and there may be more than one evolutionary aim. In other words, as important as reproduction is for the survival of the species, there may be direct and indirect pathways to such fitness as well as alternative survival strategies.

Kin selection hypothesis. E. O. Wilson (1975, 1978) offered an evolutionary perspective for the survival of homosexuality that was premised on reproductive fitness and homosexuality being exclusively same-sex focused and, thus, unable to contribute to the species' survival. He proposed that reproductive fitness was maintained, albeit indirectly rather than directly: Homosexual individuals lavish their resources on their family of origin, ultimately ensuring the reproductive fitness of siblings by enhancing the survival of nieces and nephews.

The empirical literature has been unsupportive of the kin selection hypothesis. An examination in the United States not only failed to support the hypothesis but also found that heterosexual men were more likely to support family members than were homosexual men (Bobrow & Bailey, 2001). In a British sample, no significant differences were found between the homosexual and heterosexual men in terms of their familial affinity and support (Rahman & Hull, 2005). The hypothesis also was not supported in the more collectivist culture of Japan, in which altruism would be expected to be elevated relative to its prevalence in Euro-centric nations (Vasey & VanderLaan, 2012). A review of the historical and cross-cultural data also provided little support for the kin selection hypothesis (Kirkpatrick, 2000), as did a review of the cross-species literature (Muscarella, 1999). In fact, the latter suggested that animals provided support to their same-sex sexual partners (Muscarella, 1999), a finding that could generalize to (at least current) humans.

As with many evolutionary explanations, the kin selection hypothesis cannot be tested directly because we have no equivalent of a fossil record to assess what our homosexual ancestors did. Data on current humans are based on challenges, settings, and norms currently in force, which may have differed from those experienced by our ancestors. For example, we know that lesbian and gay individuals currently tend to migrate to large cities, leaving behind their birthplaces (Laumann et al., 1994). They may do this to limit exposure to prejudice and discrimination, to find romantic partners, or to become part of a gay community. Whatever the reasons for the migration, such places were not available in ancestral times. In addition, it is unclear how homosexuality was perceived and evaluated in ancestral times. The general negative esteem in which homosexuality is held in the twenty-first century may not have been shared universally by our ancestors. Irrespective of these considerations, there is a basic weakness with the kin selection hypothesis. If Wilson's (1975, 1978) theory is correct that reproductive fitness indirectly accrues to the relatives of those who do not reproduce, why does nature not privilege asexuality over homosexuality? Even in ancestral times, homosexual individuals might have channeled some or all of their resources to their partners, something that asexual individuals may have been less likely to do.

Balance selection hypothesis. Related to the kin selection hypothesis is the balance selection hypothesis (Hamer & Copeland, 1994). It proposes that the diminished reproductive fitness of homosexual men is counterbalanced by having more siblings and other relatives, particularly on the maternal side, who are fertile. The hypothesis has been supported (e.g., Iemmola & Camperio Ciani, 2009; Rahman et al., 2008; Schwartz et al., 2010), although not unanimously (Blanchard, 2012). Its applicability to lesbians remains to be determined.

The alliance or affiliation hypothesis. As important as reproduction may be, it is but one among survival strategies. Survival may be ensured through other ways, including the formation of alliances or affiliations that provide safety and security. It is hypothesized that same-sex relationships facilitated survival of the individual. And, by so doing, they indirectly increased the likelihood that the individual might subsequently reproduce (Kirkpatrick, 2000; Muscarella, 2000).

Support exists for the alliance or affiliation hypothesis. The evidence is impressive among nonhuman primates (for reviews, see Kirkpatrick, 2000; Muscarella, 2000; Sommer & Vasey, 2006). For example, female rhesus macaques form such alliances in the face of social instability (Kapsalis & Johnson, 2006). Female bonobos use such relationships to control male bonobos (Parish, 1994). The strongest bonds between male olive baboons have been found among those in male–male alliances (Smuts & Watanabe, 1990). Past and current human societies have been reviewed that lend support to the hypothesis (Kirkpatrick, 2000). On the basis of the nonhuman primate literature, scenarios are offered about how our female and male ancestors may have used the alliance or affiliation strategy to survive (Muscarella, 2000).

The alliance hypothesis is biased toward bisexuality, given it proposes that alliances allow for the necessary survival to reproduce at some later time. It is certainly true that the ability to survive during ancestral times must have been a pressing concern. Without enhanced probability of survival, the likelihood of reproduction would have been curtailed.

Hypothesis of equilibrium reproductive economics of homosexuality. It is unclear whether same-sex sexuality facilitated survival or whether homosexuality served some other evolutionary function not directly connected to the individual. If the latter is true, then one is speaking of the hypothesis of balance polymorphism (Hutchinson, 1959), in which same-sex behavior exists to service some other trait that is under positive evolutionary selection. Hutchinson did not specify the trait under positive selection for homosexuality, but Miller (2000) did. On the basis of genetics, Miller argued that personality traits typical of male homosexuals (e.g., sensitivity, kindness) enhance the reproductive success of heterosexual men when the latter share those traits to lesser degree because women are attracted to men with feminine qualities. A similar argument was made for lesbianism, with traits of focal interest identified as the ability to be more assertive in acquiring a mate and securing necessary resources for herself and any potential offspring. In essence, female and male homosexuals have too many alleles for particular traits that, in fewer numbers, increase another individual's reproductive fitness. The alleles are maintained because the likelihood of homosexuality is more than compensated by the likelihood of enhanced fitness in others. Miller (2000) reviewed a great deal of literature indirectly supporting his hypothesis and implicating prenatal hormonal effects, which will be discussed in a subsequent section. More recent investigations also are supportive (for a meta-analysis, see Lippa, 2005, 2008b).

Sexual pleasure or desire hypothesis. An alternative perspective targets sexual pleasure or desire (Vasey, 2000). Primates want to enhance their sexual pleasure. Same-sex behavior provides such pleasure. The same-sex behavior has no evolutionary importance until such time as it serves some function(s) with fitness implications, such as those of affiliation or alliance that enhance survival. Accordingly, same-sex behavior is an "exaptation" (Gould & Vrba, 1982), meaning a characteristic originally serving no evolutionary purpose subsequently is enlisted into such a role, given its positive implications for fitness.

The pleasure or desire hypothesis has several strengths. First, it is parsimonious, making fewer inferences about the motives that drive behavior than previously mentioned hypotheses. Second, the literature supporting the affiliation or alliance hypothesis, by extension, also supports the desire hypothesis, as does other literature in which social motives underlying same-sex behavior are less clear or absent (e.g., Yamagiwa, 2006).

Conclusion. This subsection ends with three general comments. First, we have provided a review of the major evolutionary theories concerning same-sex behavior. There are additional, more nuanced hypotheses of the mentioned theories (for reviews, see Kirkpatrick, 2000; Vasey & Sommer, 2006). Second, all evolutionary theories are speculative. Even when there is supporting evidence from all possible sources—throughout known history, across the full development spectrum from the most to the least developed societies (and any other societal strata), and in other species—the empirical literature is too removed, given it is based on relatively current conditions. The required data are unavailable, given the fitness and survival challenges of interests are those faced by our ancestral predecessors in the environments in which they lived. We simply have no idea of the role of same-sex sexuality in those times or how such sexuality was perceived or lived by our ancestors. Third, regardless of the evolutionary hypothesis under discussion, one fact exists: If same-sex sexuality has an evolutionary purpose for humans, nature has left a written record in the genetic code.

Genetics

Genetic influences can be determined by multiple routes. The simplest concerns whether homosexuality or bisexuality is familial. In other words, is there a concentration of same-sex orientation in families?

Familial studies. For some time, it has been known that same-sex orientation runs in families (Bailey & Benishay, 1993; Schwartz et al., 2010). In addition, the likelihood of familial same-sex orientation is elevated among same-sex members (e.g., a lesbian is more likely to have a lesbian or bisexual sister than a gay or bisexual brother) and among first-degree than more distant relatives (Pattatucci & Hamer, 1995). More elegant genetic studies involve twins and adopted siblings and account for both genetic and environmental influences; the latter compose shared and nonshared experiences among the siblings. Genetic influences would be most apparent among monozygotic twins who would show the most elevated rates of same-sex orientation. They would be followed by dizygotic twins in terms of rates of same-sex orientation, with singletons having the lowest levels of concordance among biological siblings. Finally, adopted siblings would have the lowest rates of same-sex orientation because, lacking any genetic material in common, they should have no more same-sex orientation concordance than what would be expected by the distribution of same-sex orientation in the population.

The empirical literature supports the genetic hypothesis. Concordance rates for same-sex orientation range from 48% to 66% among monozygotic twins (Bailey & Pillard, 1991; Bailey, Pillard, Neale, & Agyei, 1993; Whitam, Diamond, & Martin, 1993), 16% to 30% among dizygotic twins (Bailey & Pillard, 1991; Bailey et al., 1993; Whitan et al., 1993), 9% to 14% among singletons (Bailey & Pillard, 1991; Bailey et al., 1993), and 6% to 11% among adoptive siblings (Bailey & Pillard, 1991; Bailey et al., 1993). The concordance rates are similar for men and women, for example, 48% of female monozygotic twins and 52% of male monozygotic twins are concordant on same-sex orientation (Bailey & Pillard, 1991; Bailey et al., 1993). In addition, across monozygotic and dizygotic twins, genetic factors accounted for 48% of the variance of sexual orientation as assessed by sexual attraction; no significant gender differences were found in heritability (Zietsch, Verweij, Bailey, Wright, & Martin, 2011), in which the latter refers to genetic influences independent of shared or unshared environmental influences. Nevertheless, the convenience samples involved in these studies may have biased results. Rather than recruiting lesbian, gay, and bisexual probands by means of advertisements in gay publications, as all the cited studies did, more representative samples would enhance confidence in the concordance rates.

Findings from more representative samples of the population support the genetic hypothesis, although, as one would expect, at diminished levels than the noted studies. The implicated effect sizes are noticeable, although they are generally nonsignificant because of statistical power. In a study using a volunteer national twin registry in Australia, the concordance rates for monozygotic twins were 20% for men and 24% for women, with smaller rates for dizygotic twins (Bailey, Dunne, & Martin, 2000). The rates between the monozygotic and dizygotic twins, however, did not differ significantly and the heritability or genetic estimates did not differ significantly from zero. A study using a national probability sample of the U.S. population found concordance rates of 32% and 13% for monozygotic and same-sex dizygotic twins, respectively (Kendler, Thornton, Gilman, & Kessler, 2000). These rates were not significantly different from each other, however, and the heritability estimates, although ranging from 0.28 to 0.65, were not significantly different from zero. Another study recruited cases from the Swedish registry of twins (Långström, Rahman, Carlström, &

Lichtenstein, 2010). Concordance rates for monozygotic and dizygotic twins were similar (e.g., 0.22 and 0.17 for female probands, respectively) and the heritability estimates were 0.39 for the men and 0.19 for the women. All statistics were nonsignificant, however, except for a study of twins from the Central Population Registry of Finland (Alanko et al., 2010). In a study of monozygotic and dizygotic twins, Alanko et al. (2010) found significant heritability estimates for homosexuality of 0.45 for women and 0.50 for men.

The low power inherent in many studies examining heritability effects among representative samples is a function of a relatively small population in the country under study and the low prevalence in any population of both same-sex orientation and twins. When these factors are combined (i.e., multiplied), the number of concordant pairs is greatly attenuated. Therefore, future research should consider combining national samples of twins across countries to boost power, generate more reliable estimates, and provide a more adequate test of the genetic hypothesis by means of familial analyses.

Genome studies. The genetic hypothesis ultimately is based on identifying a gene(s) linked to homosexuality. Initial steps in this direction have been taken (Hamer, Hu, Magnuson, Hu, & Pattatucci, 1993). As suggested earlier, Hamer et al. found that gay men were more likely to have gay brothers. They also were more likely to have more gay male relatives who descended from the maternal line (maternal uncles and sons of maternal aunts). The latter implicates maternal inheritance, regardless of whether the index case was raised with the relative (gay male sibling) or not (e.g., maternal uncle). Linkage was found to markers on the X chromosome, specifically the Xq28 region, in 33 of 40 sibling pairs ($p < .001$). Thus, Xq28 seems to be the region where the gene contributing to homosexuality is to be found in the very specific sample used: gay men with gay male siblings (Kinsey scale ratings of 5 or 6, in which 6 is exclusive homosexuality), no more than one lesbian relative, and no suggestion of father-to-son transmission of homosexuality. A follow-up study by the same laboratory confirmed the earlier results for gay male siblings in a new sample using the same inclusion criteria (Hu et al., 1995). It failed, however, to generalize the findings to men for whom the inclusion criteria were relaxed and to lesbian siblings using the comparable original inclusion criteria. Another study from a different laboratory failed to support the findings for gay men, regardless of whether the same inclusion criteria as Hamer et al. (1993) were used (Rice, Anderson, Risch, & Ebers, 1999). Consequently, more data are needed to replicate the findings by Hamer et al. (1993) with gay male siblings and to examine their generalizability to lesbian siblings.

The model by Hamer et al. (1993) is based on maternal transmission and, thus, is limited to the X chromosome. The complexity of homosexuality, however, may involve maternal and paternal transmission. It also may extend beyond the sex-linked chromosomes to the autosomes. A full genome scan of gay male siblings ($M = 5.7$ on Kinsey scales) was performed (Mustanski et al., 2005). Regions on chromosomes 7, 8, and 10 were identified and potential candidate genes were suggested. Evidence was not found for linkage to Xq28, but, according to the authors, resolution insensitivity may have been responsible for the null findings.

Another genetic approach. The study of genetics minimally requires a keen observational sense of phenomenon that may be under natural control, an ability to eliminate alternative (nurture) explanations, and the capability to quantify observed or actual probabilities and compare them with random or expected probabilities. On the basis of these principles, it has been argued that hair-whorl rotation on a man's scalp is related to both handedness (Klar, 2003) and sexual orientation (Klar, 2004) by a genetic pathway. Specifically, a clockwise hair whorl is related to being right-handed and heterosexual; a counterclockwise hair whorl to left-handedness and homosexuality. Empirical research finds that hair whorl and handedness are related (Klar, 2003), as are hair whorl and being homosexual as compared with heterosexual (Klar, 2004). Other investigations, however, have not replicated the relation between hair whorl and sexual orientation in men (Rahman, Clarke, & Morera, 2009; Schwartz et al., 2010).

Conclusion. Examination of genetic explanations for homosexuality is in its infancy. Familial studies would benefit greatly from larger sample sizes to generate adequate statistical power. The lack of significant findings in more representative samples of the population cannot be taken as evidence against genetic underpinnings, given the sizes of the effects.

The search has begun for potential genes accounting for homosexuality. Much more work is needed in this area. Wherever possible, it should be guided by a priori hypotheses to be theoretically grounded and reduce Type I error. Possible candidates on the basis of such reasoning are available (Zheng & Cohn, 2011). Some candidate genes have been tested and found to be nonsignificant (DuPree, Mustanski, Bocklandt, Nievergelt, & Hamer, 2004; Macke et al., 1993). In addition, there may be more than one genetic pathway to homosexuality. For some gay men, but not all, the gene(s) may be found on Xq28. For lesbians, too little work has been done to reach any conclusions.

Hormonal Effects

Hormonal effects constitute still another route by which sexual orientation may be determined. Ellis and Ames (1987) were the first to propose that homosexuality may be a function of atypical sex hormones during fetal development that affect subsequent development along a nonnormative pathway. As early as 1959, it was known that experimentally increasing testosterone during the fetal development of female guinea pigs resulted in masculinized genitalia at birth and male-gendered behavior during mating (Phoenix, Goy, Gerall, & Young, 1959). Subsequent work is based on this initial theoretical and empirical foundation, addressing the organizational and activational effects of sex hormones (for reviews, see Bao & Swaab, 2011; LeVay, 2011; Savic, García-Falgueras, & Swaab, 2010). The organizational effects refer to sex differences that are fixed or irreversible. The activational effects refer to sex differences in differentiated tissue that last so long as the hormone is present.

Hormonal effects prove critical during three periods of development. Each period is first reviewed for the general purpose of hormonal effects. This introduction is followed by specific implications of hormonal effects for sexual orientation for each period.

General purpose of hormonal effects during three developmental periods. The first impact of prenatal hormones occurs during the first few months of development. Sexual development begins with the genes of the sex chromosomes, which bring about the female and male gonads of ovaries and testes, respectively. This gonadal differentiation leads to sex differences in secretions of testosterone from the testes. Thus, without testes, the female pattern continues to unfold. Feminization is nature's default pattern of development that proceeds unless countervailing, masculinizing agents appear (e.g., Hines, 2011; McCarthy & Arnold, 2008), a fact that has been known for some time (for a review, see Sherfey, 1966).

Testes are necessary but insufficient for male development. Androgen sex hormones will be critical for the formation of the male fetus. The hormones must be directed at their proper target, at the right time, and in the right concentrations for male development to continue. Any disruptions will reverse the pattern back to the female template. Testosterone by means of dihydrotestosterone proves critical for formation of the penis, prostate, and scrotum during the first few months of pregnancy. Resistance to testosterone attributed to malfunctioning androgen receptors ensures the female pattern takes over. Although structural or morphological development may occur as expected, other ways exist by which atypical development may occur. In other words, there are different ways by which prenatal hormones affect development, with implications for sexual orientation.

A second phase of sexual development involves the brain and occurs during the second trimester of pregnancy. Testosterone entering the brain is converted to estradiol by the aromatase enzyme. Estradiol both masculinizes and defeminizes the brain. Regions affected include the hypothalamus, particularly the sexually dimorphic nucleus of the preoptic area (SDN-POA), later known as the interstitial nucleus of the anterior hypothalamus 1 (INAH1; Allen, Hines, Shryne, & Gorski, 1989; Swaab & Fliers, 1985). Differences also were found in INAH2 and INAH3, but not in INAH4 (Allen et al., 1989) or the suprachiasmatic nucleus (SCN; Swaab, Fliers, &

Partiman, 1985). These areas are expected to be larger in men than women. The sex difference in volume and cell number appears later in life, however, for example, after approximately age 4 years for SDN-POA (Swaab, Gooren, & Hofman, 1995). Consequently, environmental and psychological processes may intervene to influence sexual differentiation of the brain structures (Swaab et al., 1995). This may explain why sex differences have not always been found in the volume of some of these structures (LeVay, 1991; Swaab & Hofman, 1988, 1990).

As important as structure may be, function is as, if not, more important. These areas of the brain are involved in sexual behavior and the stress-coping process. Other brain structures undergoing sexual differentiation include, for example, the human anterior commissure (Allen & Gorski, 1991) and cortex (Goldstein et al., 2001). The affected brain regions have implications for sex differences in neurocognitive and emotional functioning as well as for psychopathology.

There is still a third phase of sexual differentiation. It coincides with puberty and the release of various hormones from the hypothalamus and the pituitary gland (Spear, 2007). Sexual maturation occurs, risk-taking increases, and identity concerns become prominent. This is the time when many individuals become aware of their unfolding sexual orientation.

With this brief overview of hormonal effects on sexual differentiation, we broach what is known about sexual orientation. The hypotheses are that sexual-orientation disparities exist within each sex, with the homosexuals displaying an atypical sexual pattern. The hypotheses pertain to homosexuals and heterosexuals; bisexuals usually are not considered. It is unclear what is done with bisexuals in studies, however, given the definition or operationalization of sexual orientation often is described insufficiently.

Implications for sexual orientation of prenatal hormonal effects during the first trimester of pregnancy. The first trimester is a critical phase in which organizational effects take place. Two conditions exemplify the impact of hormonal effects for sexual orientation during this developmental period.

Congenital adrenal hyperplasia. There is an enzyme defect that results in an overproduction of adrenal androgens. The condition, congenital adrenal hyperplasia (CAH), occurs in both sexes, but attention is particularly focused on girls. CAH has masculinizing effects in girls. Girls with CAH show a clear preference for male toys, activities, and playmates (Berenbaum & Snyder, 1995; Meyer-Bahlburg et al., 2004) as well as decreased interest in female-typical behaviors, such as in babies or playing with dolls (Leveroni & Berenbaum, 1998); nevertheless, their gender identity is female (Berenbaum & Bailey, 2003; Meyer-Bahlburg et al., 2004). CAH women, as compared with controls, are more socially detached and engage in less verbal aggression (Helleday, Edman, Ritzén, & Siwers, 1993), but they engage in more physical aggression than controls (Berenbaum & Resnick, 1997). Although one study disagrees (Titus-Ernstoff et al., 2003), the evidence indicates that CAH women are less likely to be exclusively heterosexual than controls (Hines, Brook, & Conway, 2004; Meyer-Bahlburg, Dolezal, Baker, & New, 2008; Zucker et al., 1996).

Diethlystilbestrol. The condition CAH is a natural occurrence. There is one accidental experimental situation that occurred during 1938 to 1971 when women were prescribed diethlystilbestrol (DES), starting in the 7th or 8th week of pregnancy and continuing throughout the pregnancy (*Physicians' Desk Reference to Pharmaceutical Specialties and Biologicals*, 1961), to reduce the likelihood of a miscarriage. DES was banned in 1971 by the U.S. Food and Drug Administration when it learned that DES elevated the risk of adenocarcinoma, a rare cancer, in female offspring (Schrager & Potter, 2004). Since then, a variety of adverse health outcomes have been associated with DES (Hoover et al., 2011). DES is a synthetic estrogen that reaches into and affects the brain, acting similar to estradiol (Meyer-Bahlburg et al., 1995). Because estradiol is androgenic, it has been hypothesized and confirmed that women exposed to DES in utero are more likely to be lesbian or bisexual than non-DES-exposed controls (Meyer-Bahlburg et al., 1995).

Implications for sexual orientation of prenatal hormonal effects on the brain during the second trimester of pregnancy. The impact of prenatal hormones on sexual differentiation is of great interest. Indirect markers of that early hormonal environment are targets of attention, as are any characteristics potentially linked to sexual differentiation of the brain (e.g., cognitive capabilities). We emphasize it is the prenatal hormonal state rather than any subsequent hormonal condition that is of concern.

Finger-length ratios (2D:4D). Finger-length ratios are one such indirect marker because they are related negatively to the ratio of testosterone to estrogen in amniotic fluid (Lutchmaya, Baron-Cohen, Raggatt, Knickmeyer, & Manning, 2004). Of particular interest is the ratio of the second (index) to fourth (ring) digit (2D:4D). This ratio is especially sex dimorphic (McFadden & Shubel, 2002), with lower ratios associated with higher levels of testosterone relative to estrogen, as the following twin studies indicate. Among dizygotic twins, women of opposite-sex twins have a lower 2D:4D ratio than women of same-sex twins (van Anders, Vernon, & Wilbur, 2006), which indicates androgen exposure by female twins to their male twins' testosterone. The finding has been replicated (Voracek & Dressler, 2007), but not by everyone (Hiraishi, Sasaki, Shikishima, & Ando, 2012; Medland, Loehlin, & Martin, 2008).

In humans, both testosterone and estrogen are implicated during the early months of pregnancy, with the 2D:4D disparity most marked in the right hand (Manning, 2011; McFadden & Shubel, 2002). Experimental work with mice confirms that the ratio of androgen to estrogen is determinant of the 2D:4D ratio, especially in the right paw (Zheng & Cohn, 2011). Moreover, the 2D:4D ratio occurs in a narrow window of prenatal development that also coincides with sexual differentiation of the brain (Zheng & Cohn, 2011).

The 2D:4D hypotheses are that heterosexual men have a lower ratio than heterosexual women, given the greater quantity of testosterone to estrogen among men. Lesbians have a lower 2D:4D ratio than heterosexual women. Homosexual men have a higher 2D:4D ratio than heterosexual men.

Although there are some null findings among women (Collaer, Reimers, & Manning, 2007; P. A. Hall & Schaeff, 2008; Lippa, 2003), the evidence generally indicates that lesbians have lower 2D:4D ratios than heterosexual women, supporting the hypothesis of greater exposure to testosterone by lesbians during fetal development (Kraemer et al., 2006; McFadden & Shubel, 2002; Rahman, 2005; Rahman & Wilson, 2003b; Williams et al., 2000; see McFadden et al., 2005, for a combined analysis of some of these and other studies). Indeed, a meta-analysis found a significant effect size between sexual orientation and 2D:4D for the right hand (Hedge's g [comparable to Cohen's *d*] = 0.29; 95% confidence interval [*CI*] = 0.06, 0.51) and left hand (Hedge's g = 0.23; 95% *CI* = 0.04, 0.43; Grimbos, Dawood, Burriss, Zucker, & Puts, 2010).

Three additional studies command particular mention. One study (van Anders & Hampson, 2005) found no significant difference between sexual-minority and heterosexual women in the 2D:4D ratio. The null finding was due to the variability in the sexual-minority group, however, given the negative correlations found between Kinsey ratings on sexual experience or fantasy and 2D:4D. These more subtle findings underscore the importance of degree or extent of homosexuality in the 2D:4D ratio. The second study (W. M. Brown, Finn, Cooke, & Breedlove, 2002a) found variability in the 2D:4D ratios of lesbians, such that *butches* (i.e., more masculine and gender nonconforming) had lower ratios than *femmes* (i.e., more feminine and gender conforming) on the right hand. This study provides more nuanced support for the hypothesis and suggests that potential null findings might arise if, as suggested, femmes are more similar to heterosexual women in digit ratio and more femmes are included in a study. The third study (L. S. Hall & Love, 2003) ruled out the possibility of genetic effects by studying monozygotic twins. It found that lesbians had lower 2D:4D ratios than heterosexual co-twins and no significant ratio differences were found when the twins were concordant on sexual orientation. The finding that sexual-minority women have lower 2D:4D ratios than heterosexual monozygotic twins has been replicated (Hiraishi et al., 2012).

The evidence for men is less consistent. As expected, studies found that homosexual men have higher 2D:4D ratios than heterosexual men (Collaer et al., 2007; P. A. Hall & Schaeff, 2008; Lippa, 2003; Hassan & Rahman, 2007; Manning, Churchill, & Peters, 2007; McFadden & Shubel, 2002), including a study of monozygotic twins (Hiraishi et al., 2012). Other studies found no significant differences (Kraemer et al., 2006; Voracek, Manning, & Ponocny, 2005; Williams et al., 2000). In addition, some studies found the reverse: hypermasculinity among the homosexual men relative to the heterosexual men (Rahman, 2005; Rahman & Wilson, 2003b; Robinson & Manning, 2000). A meta-analysis, consequently, found a trivial and nonsignificant effect size on the right hand (Hedge's $g = -0.02$; 95% $CI = -0.12, 0.12$) and similar findings for the left hand (Grimbos et al., 2010).

The inconsistent findings for the men and women, specifically nonsignificant findings, may be a function of the following considerations. First, differences in 2D:4D should be expected among same-sex homosexuals, bisexuals, and heterosexuals, with the greatest difference between the homosexuals and heterosexuals. Bisexuals should be intermediate between these extremes, but whether they differ from homosexuals or heterosexuals is an empirical question that depends on their bias toward one or the other extreme. Results from the BBC Internet survey indicate that the mean 2D:4D ratios of bisexual and heterosexual women are identical and higher than those of lesbians, although nonsignificantly given power (Manning et al., 2007). In this same study, the mean 2D:4D ratios of gay and bisexual men were essentially identical and significantly greater than those of heterosexual men. To the extent one may generalize from this sample, the findings indicate that studies with women need to be particularly sensitive to the numbers of bisexual women, as they will attenuate results if they are aggregated with the lesbians into a single group. This is no small matter because there are more bisexual women than lesbians (Chandra et al., 2011). In addition, the butch–femme phenomenon among lesbians must be considered (W. M. Brown et al., 2002a).

Second, the hand involved in the 2D:4D measurement is important, given prenatal testosterone is more sexually dimorphic in the right than the left hand (Lutchmaya et al., 2004; Manning, Bundred, Newton, & Flanagan, 2003; McFadden & Shubel, 2002). In other words, the hypothesized 2D:4D sexual-orientation differences should be most strongly apparent on the right than the left hand. Given this has not always been found (e.g., Hiraishi et al., 2012), measurement of both hands should continue to be taken.

Third, unexpected findings may be a function of geography, although possible reasons for such effects are unknown. An examination of digit-ratio studies on homosexual and heterosexual men found lower 2D:4D ratios for heterosexuals than homosexuals in the United States (Voracek et al., 2005), as expected. The opposite occurred in European studies, however, in which the homosexual men had lower 2D:4D ratios. The latter finding was attributed to the heterosexuals: The European heterosexuals had higher ratios than the U.S. heterosexuals. The homosexual men on both continents did not differ significantly.

More generally, ethnic or racial differences in 2D:4D ratios have been found (Manning et al., 2007). Although a meta-analysis of 2D:4D studies found that sexual-orientation differences between sexual-minority and heterosexual women were stronger in Europe than North American, race proved more important than geography (North America vs. Europe) for men (Grimbos et al., 2010): White sexual-minority men had lower 2D:4D ratios (more masculine) than heterosexual men. As samples of sexual-minority men became less White, however, the ratio for the sexual-minority men became greater than that of the heterosexual men.

Fourth, specific to homosexual men, the null findings between them and heterosexual men may be attributed to the curvilinear relation that has been found in 2D:4D ratios, indicating both hypo- and hypermasculinity among homosexual men. We will return to the possibility of hypo- and hypermasculinity among homosexual men after reviewing some other pertinent information.

Fifth, actual measurement of the 2D:4D ratio is a complicated matter. Measurement has varied greatly from, for example, having participants measure their fingers (e.g., Manning et al., 2007) to investigators measuring participants' fingers (e.g., McFadden & Shubel, 2002) as well as other measurement strategies (e.g., photocopies of the hands). Obviously, poor measurement would attenuate results.

Gender nonconformity. Signs of prenatal hormonal effects should be and are apparent behaviorally.

Gender nonconformity refers to behaviors or characteristics that are socially or culturally considered typical of the other sex (Bell et al., 1981). Gender nonconformity is related to homosexuality, as reviews of the literature have demonstrated (Bailey & Zucker, 1995; Zucker, 2008). Indeed, gender nonconformity among lesbian, gay, and bisexual individuals appears early in life, given retrospective reports (D'Augelli, Grossman, & Starks, 2008); is evident in adulthood (Lippa, 2002); and extends into old age (Clark, Armstrong, & Bonacore, 2005). Childhood gender nonconformity is related to adults' self-ratings as masculine and feminine and to their occupational careers (Lippa, 2008a).

Two sets of studies require special mention. One study rated home videos of homosexual and heterosexual women and men during their childhood for gender nonconforming behaviors (Rieger, Linsenmeier, Gygax, & Bailey, 2008). The male and female homosexuals engaged in more gender nonconforming behaviors as children than the heterosexuals. In addition, there was a relation between gender nonconformity in childhood (as per the home videos) and adult gender nonconformity (as per self-ratings and observations by others). The other studies involved twins and suggested that gender nonconformity, in addition to or rather than being a function of prenatal hormonal effects, may have a genetic component (Alanko et al., 2010; Bailey et al., 2000). Both studies found stronger relations between gender nonconformity and homosexuality among monozygotic twins than among dizygotic same-sex twins. For example, the Alanko et al. (2010) study, which was population based, found stronger and significant intraclass correlations among monozygotic twins (0.56 and 0.53 for male and female homosexuals, respectively), but not among dizygotic same-sex twins (0.27 and 0.07 for male and female homosexuals, respectively). These two sets of studies suggest that gender nonconformity among homosexuals may have a strong biological underpinning that has been underappreciated until now.

Cognitive functioning. Another marker of prenatal hormonal effects concerns the sex bias in certain cognitive abilities that is apparent at early ages and attributed to sexual differentiation of the brain, although the role of practice and socialization cannot be discounted. Women outperform men in verbal fluency, perceptual speed, and memory for object location; men do better in spatial tasks (Halpern, 1992; Kimura, 1999; Voyer, Voyer, & Bryden, 1995). Even in a comparable task, sex differences may exist in the approach or solution to the task. For example, navigational strategies differ for spatial location. Women use landmarks to identify a location and men rely on Euclidean and directional distances (e.g., Dabbs, Chang, Strong, & Milun, 1998; Saucier et al., 2002). Given these sex differences and the hormonal hypothesis for sexual orientation, it follows that homosexual men should differ from heterosexual men, such that the former are biased toward the female pattern; similarly, homosexual women should differ from heterosexual women, being biased toward the male pattern.

The findings are inconsistent for verbal tasks. One study confirmed the expected hypotheses for multiple markers of verbal fluency, even after controlling for age and intelligence quotient (IQ; Rahman, Abrahams, & Wilson, 2003). Another study found that homosexual men and heterosexual women were similar and outperformed heterosexual men in the digit-symbol test of the Wechsler Adult Intelligence Scale—Revised (WAIS–R; Rahman, Wilson, & Abrahams, 2004c). The lesbians and heterosexual women did not differ significantly, although the effect size (Cohen's $d = 0.26$) favored the enhanced performance of the heterosexual women on the task. For spatial memory, in which women outperform men, homosexual men and heterosexual women did not differ significantly on remembering the location of objects, and they outperformed heterosexual men in this task (Hassan & Rahman, 2007). Similar results were found in another study (Rahman et al., 2003). This study also included lesbians, who differed from heterosexual women in the expected male direction ($p < .05$), although the finding was considered nonsignificant by the researchers. In this study, moreover, no significant differences by sexual orientation, sex, or their interaction were found in recalling or recognizing objects. Similarly, no significant differences by sexual orientation, sex, or their interaction were found in another study of verbal fluency (Neave, Menaged, & Weightman, 1999). This study, however, found a significant sexual orientation-by-sex interaction in making verbal associations, indicating that homosexual men excelled over heterosexual men.

Findings for spatial abilities (e.g., mental rotation, water-level test, judging line orientation) are similar to verbal abilities in that they do not consistently support the hormonal hypothesis. Moreover, inconsistencies are found in the same study. The findings generally indicate that homosexual men and heterosexual women do not differ significantly from each other, but heterosexual men perform better (Neave et al., 1999; Rahman & Koerting, 2008; Sanders & Ross-Field, 1986). When lesbians are included in studies, they generally do not differ significantly from heterosexual women (Neave et al., 1999; Rahman, Andersson, & Govier, 2005; Rahman & Koerting, 2008; Rahman & Wilson, 2003a; Wegesin, 1998). When differences do occur, lesbians outperform heterosexual women, in keeping with the hypothesis (Collaer et al., 2007; Peters, Manning, & Reimers, 2007; Rahman & Koerting, 2008; Rahman & Wilson, 2003a; van Anders & Hampson, 2005).

Reasons for the inconsistent cognitive findings are unclear, given the studies generally control for IQ, age, and other covariates that may confound findings. It is lesbians who are at odds with the hypothesis. Differences are expected between them and heterosexual women, but null findings are common. The nonsignificant findings may be a function of butch–femme differences. If the butch–femme phenomenon is attributed to hormonal effects, femmes would be more similar to heterosexual women than would be butch lesbians, who would be more similar to heterosexual men. No relation has been found, however, between identifying as butch–femme and cognitive abilities (Rahman, Wilson, & Abrahams, 2004a). The lack of findings may be due to measurement, given the difficulty in validly assessing the butch–femme phenomenon (Rosario, Schrimshaw, Hunter, & Levy-Warren, 2009). Alternatively, the degree of same-sex sexuality may be operative. Sexual-minority women include many more bisexual than lesbian women (Chandra et al., 2011), and the bisexual women may account for inconsistent findings.

There are other potential methodological explanations for the lack of significant difference between the homosexual and heterosexual women. Most of the cognitive literature is based on the research of Rahman and colleagues. In addition, most of their research, with two exceptions (Rahman & Koerting, 2008; Rahman et al., 2005), appears to be based on the same sample of participants (Rahman et al., 2003; Rahman & Wilson, 2003a; Rahman, Wilson, & Abrahams, 2003, 2004a, 2004b, 2004c). Thus, replication is needed in additional samples and by other independent researchers.

Otoacoustic emissions. Other potential markers of prenatal hormonal effects have received some attention. Otoacoustic emissions (OAEs) are sounds that originate in the cochlea and enhance one's hearing capabilities. OAEs are elevated in women relative to men, and the disparity is attributed to prenatal hormones. Consequently, sexual-minority individuals are hypothesized to shift away from their own sex in the direction of the opposite sex. The hypothesis concerning OAEs has been extended to include auditory-evoked potentials (AEPs), which are electrical potentials in the brain in response to sounds of clicks. There is general support for the hypothesis that homosexual and bisexual women are more masculinized than heterosexual women, although homosexual men are hypermasculinized rather than hypomasculinized (McFadden, 2002). Findings, however, are not consistently significant (Loehlin & McFadden, 2003). Clearly, more research is needed before we can adequately evaluate the hypothesis that prenatal hormonal effects link hearing and sexual orientation.

Relations among markers of prenatal hormonal effects. It seems reasonable to expect relations among the various markers of prenatal hormonal effects. The few available studies generally support the hypothesis. A lower 2D:4D ratio has been found in women with CAH relative to non-CAH women (W. M. Brown, Hines, Fane, & Breedlove, 2002b). Similarly, a lower ratio has been found in butch as compared with femme lesbians (W. M. Brown et al., 2002a). With respect to spatial abilities, a lower 2D:4D ratio has been related to line judgments (Collaer et al., 2007) and mental rotation (Peters et al., 2007) among samples of homosexual and heterosexual women and men. No significant relations, however, were found between spatial abilities and 2D:4D ratios of homosexual and heterosexual women by another research team (van Anders & Hampson, 2005). In addition, 2D:4D and otoacoustic emissions generally were not related significantly (McFadden & Shubel, 2003). Despite the few null findings, the significant findings concerning 2D:4D ratios and a wide range of hypothesized prenatal hormonal effects on sexual orientation are prevalent and noteworthy.

Implications for sexual orientation of the third phase of sexual differentiation: puberty. Sex differences are apparent in pubertal timing and development of secondary sex characteristics, given the increase of sex hormones released during adrenarche and puberty. Girls undergo puberty at younger ages than boys and they are lighter in weight and shorter in height than boys (Underwood & Van Wyk, 1992). Therefore, one would expect sex atypical patterns for homosexual women and men, provided hormonal effects associated with puberty exist. Homosexual women would be expected to reach puberty at a later age and to be heavier and taller than heterosexual women. Homosexual men would be expected to attain puberty at an earlier age and to be lighter and shorter than heterosexual men. Puberty is also the time when sex-dimorphic behavior problems (some that may have been apparent during childhood) become (more) apparent.

Pubertal timing. The empirical findings for pubertal timing, at best, are mixed. No significant differences were found between exclusive lesbians and exclusive heterosexual women, defined either by attractions or sexual activity, on age at menarche in a national probability sample of Britons (Bogaert & Friesen, 2002). Another national sample of Britons confirmed the nonsignificant findings on pubertal age for women (Bogaert, 2010), as did national probability samples of U.S. adult (Bogaert, Friesen, & Klentrou, 2002) and adolescent (Savin-Williams & Ream, 2006) populations. With respect to men, no significant findings supported the pubertal timing hypothesis between homosexual and heterosexual adolescents on markers of puberty (Savin-Williams & Ream, 2006). Another study, however, found that homosexual men, in keeping with the sex atypical pattern, experienced puberty at younger ages than heterosexual men (Bogaert et al., 2002). More studies are needed, including studies conducted outside the United States and Great Britain, before conclusions can be reached concerning the link between pubertal timing and sexual orientation.

Weight and height. The issue of weight and height, or their combination by means of body mass index (BMI), has received considerable attention, but most of the research is irrelevant for our purposes. The limited but pertinent findings generally agree that homosexual women have a higher BMI than heterosexual women, as the sex atypical hypothesis would predict. In a U.S. national sample of young people, lesbian and bisexual women as compared with heterosexual women were heavier, and the difference was apparent in adolescence (Austin et al., 2009). A Danish study, however, did not support the hypothesis of weight differences in puberty because women who married women were heavier at birth than women who married men, suggesting that the weight disparity was possibly attributed to prenatal rather than pubertal hormones (Frisch & Zdravkovic, 2010). The remaining and prevalent studies have no bearing on the hypothesis because they focus on sexual-orientation disparities in adulthood and not on BMI differences during adolescence (i.e., puberty). Given the ability of weight to be manipulated by diet or exercise, it is irrelevant whether sexual-orientation disparities in weight or BMI exist in studies of adult women in the United States (Boehmer, Bowen, & Bauer, 2007; Jun et al., 2012; Martin & Nguyen, 2004; Valanis et al., 2000) or do not exist, as in two different national British samples of adult women with respect to height and weight (Bogaert, 2010; Bogaert & Friesen, 2002). In all fairness, most of these studies and those that followed on men were designed and conducted to examine health disparities by sexual orientation rather than potential weight differences linked to pubertal hormones.

For adolescent men, the hormonal hypothesis is not supported because gay and bisexual boys were heavier rather than lighter during early and middle adolescence relative to heterosexual boys (Austin et al., 2009). From the perspective of the hormonal hypothesis during puberty, it matters not at all that these gay and bisexual boys became thinner than heterosexual peers during late adolescence. In fact, the totality of the findings supports a social or cultural hypothesis in which young men may become sensitive to and strive to achieve low weight as they become involved in the weight-conscious gay male community. Clearly, such a hypothesis is irrelevant for understanding weight differences in puberty, but it may explain weight differences in late adolescence and beyond. The adult literature does not resolve the conflict because it does not probe into the weight of participants during their adolescence. The literature finds that adult gay and bisexual men are generally thinner than male heterosexual peers (Bogaert, 2010; Brennan, Ross, Dobinson, Veldhuizen, & Steele, 2010; Deputy & Boehmer, 2010), although some findings are nonsignificant (Bogaert & Friesen, 2002) and others show a higher prevalence of homosexual men being overweight or obese (Guadamuz et al., 2012).

Height is a less ambiguous test of the hormonal hypothesis because it cannot be easily manipulated. Homosexual men are shorter than heterosexual men (Bogaert, 2010). The hormonal effect may occur prenatally, at least for some men, rather than during puberty, however, because the Danish study found that men who married men were more likely than men who married women to be shorter in length at birth (Frisch & Zdravkovic, 2010).

These findings for men when paired with some of the nonsignificant findings or curvilinear findings of the prenatal section may have important implications. There may be at least two subpopulations of homosexual men. One group consists of relatively feminized men as evident by, for example, higher 2D:4D ratios (e.g., McFadden & Shubel, 2002) and shorter stature (Frisch & Zdravkovic, 2010) relative to heterosexual men. Another group consists of hypermasculinized men as evident by lower 2D:4D ratios (e.g., Rahman, 2005; Robinson & Manning, 2000) and larger penile size (Bogaert & Hershberger, 1999) relative to heterosexual men. The differences between the two groups may be comparable to differences between butch and femme lesbians (e.g., W. M. Brown et al., 2002a). The complexities of understanding these groups are evident in the different developmental periods when hormonal effects occurred (e.g., prenatal for 2D:4D, pubertal for height). Those complexities are likely to increase as bisexuals are considered. In addition, it will be necessary to cross the equivalent of butch or femme among men by sexual orientation as gay or bisexual, if one may generalize from female homosexuals and bisexuals (Rosario et al., 2009). Despite these considerations, a complication remains to be addressed that pertains to the link between hormonal effects and hypermasculinization among homosexual and bisexual men.

Psychological distress. There are markers of psychological distress that become apparent during puberty and, therefore, may have implications for sexual orientation. The literature finds that externalizing symptomatology or risk-taking (e.g., substance use) is elevated among boys relative to girls, with the difference becoming apparent around puberty and increasing thereafter into emerging adulthood (for a meta-analysis, see Byrnes, Miller, & Schafer, 1999). On the other hand, internalizing symptoms, such as depressive symptomatology, become more prevalent among girls than boys beginning around puberty (for a meta-analysis, see Hyde, Mezulis, & Abramson, 2008). Given the hormonal hypothesis, one expects that lesbian and bisexual female youths are biased toward the male pattern, and gay and bisexual male youths are biased toward the female pattern on psychological distress. These differences should persist into adulthood.

The hormonal hypothesis is supported for substance use, particularly for lesbian and bisexual female youths. They report higher levels of substance use than female heterosexuals, whereas gay and bisexual male adolescents, by comparison, are not as dissimilar from male heterosexuals (e.g., Corliss et al., 2010; Needham, 2012; Rosario, Hunter, & Gwadz, 1997; Russell, Driscoll, & Truong, 2002). In addition, a meta-analysis (Marshal et al., 2008) confirmed the difference between lesbian and bisexual female adolescents and female heterosexual peers (Cohen's $d = 5.02$) and found a relatively smaller, but substantial, effect size between the sexual-minority and heterosexual boys (Cohen's $d = 3.29$). Another meta-analysis involving youths and adults (King et al., 2008) found that the disparities persist into adulthood and qualitatively worsen, especially for lesbian and bisexual women who are at elevated risk for past-year substance use disorder relative to heterosexual women (relative risk [*RR*] = 3.42, 95% *CI* = 1.97, 5.92); similar comparisons between gay and bisexual men and heterosexual men were nonsignificant (*RR* = 1.25; 95% *CI* = 0.90, 1.75). Furthermore, the hormonal effect on substance use is greater for butch than femme lesbian or bisexual female youths, as one would hypothesize (Rosario, Schrimshaw, & Hunter, 2008). Finally, substance use is not the only externalizing symptoms for which hormonal effects are found. More homosexual than heterosexual women gamble, whereas fewer homosexual than heterosexual men gamble (Hershberger & Bogaert, 2005).

Support for the hormonal hypothesis with respect to internalizing symptoms is not forthcoming. Although a meta-analysis did find sexual-orientation disparities in suicidality and depressive symptomatology among youths, these sexual-orientation differences did not vary by sex (Marshal et al., 2011), as would be expected by the hormonal hypothesis. Another meta-analysis involving youths and adults similarly did not find that sexual-orientation disparities in suicidality or symptoms of depression or anxiety varied by sex (King et al., 2008).

Conclusion. Much research has been devoted to prenatal hormonal effects that may inform sexual orientation directly or indirectly by means of the hormonal cascade attending adrenarche and puberty. There is relatively strong evidence that lesbianism may be attributed to elevated testosterone during prenatal development. Moreover, the effect is more pronounced in butch than femme lesbians and in lesbians as compared with bisexual women. The findings for men suggest a curvilinear relation of hypomasculinity and hypermasculinity underlying gay and bisexual male orientation. The argument has a flaw, however, and it concerns hypermasculinity. Subgroups of men known to be exposed to excess testosterone or the equivalent prenatally are not more likely to be homosexual than controls. Men with CAH, who were exposed to excess testosterone, were no more likely than non-CAH men to engage in childhood gender nonconforming behaviors, and they were equally likely to report a heterosexual sexual orientation (Hines et al., 2004). Similarly, men exposed to DES prenatally did not differ on heterosexuality from non-DES-exposed controls (Meyer-Bahlburg, Ehrhardt, Whitehead, & Vann, 1987; Titus-Ernstoff et al., 2003). Consequently, the hypothesis of prenatal hormonal effects for understanding the etiology of homosexuality and bisexuality among men, at least with respect to hypermasculinity, is problematic (see also Chapter 20, this volume).

Maternal Immunological Effects and Male Homosexuality

An alternative to genetic and hormonal effects has been proposed to explain the epidemiological finding that homosexual men have more older brothers than do heterosexual men (e.g., Blanchard & Bogaert, 1996; Blanchard & Ellis, 2001; Bogaert, 2003; Rahman et al., 2009; Robinson & Manning, 2000; Schwartz et al., 2010; Williams et al., 2000). A meta-analysis of findings indicated that the effect occurs even when the family size is approximately identical between homosexual and heterosexual men and after controlling for numbers of older sisters and younger brothers and sisters (Blanchard, 2004). It occurs irrespective of the amount of time reared with biological or nonbiological male and female siblings (Bogaert, 2006a). The effect also is independent of maternal and paternal ages (Blanchard, 2004).

The phenomenon, labeled the fraternal birth order (FBO) effect because it has not been found in women (e.g., Bogaert, 1997, 2000, 2006a), is noticeable. A meta-analysis has found that the odds of a man being homosexual increases from 2% when he has no older brothers to 6% given four older brothers, on the basis of a population prevalence rate of male homosexuality of 2% (Blanchard, 2001). The attributable fraction represents the difference in the prevalence of homosexuality among men with varying numbers of older brothers to the prevalence of homosexuality when there are no older brothers. It has been found to be 24% when there is only one older brother (Blanchard, 2001) in a sample of homosexual men recruited from a gay-focused organization and a gay pride parade event (Blanchard & Bogaert, 1996); in other words, the homosexuality of approximately one in four men was attributed to having one older brother. The attributable fraction, furthermore, increased in curvilinear fashion as the number of older brothers increased (Cantor, Blanchard, Paterson, & Bogaert, 2002; see Blanchard, 2004, Figure 3). The population-attributable fraction aggregates across the attributable fractions for varying numbers of older brothers. On the basis of combined national probability samples from Great Britain and the United States, the population attributable fraction was found to be 28.6% (95% *CI* = 14.8%, 48.0%; Blanchard & Bogaert, 2004), indicating that the sexual orientation of slightly more than one of four homosexual men is due to having one or more older brothers.

The FBO effect occurs prenatally in all likelihood. Findings indicate that male infants with older brothers weigh less than male infants with older sisters (Blanchard & Ellis, 2001; Côté, Blanchard, & Lalumière, 2003) and homosexual men with older brothers weigh less at birth than heterosexual men with older brothers (Blanchard & Ellis, 2001).

The FBO effect has been attributed to the maternal immune hypothesis (Blanchard, 2004; Blanchard & Bogaert, 1996; Blanchard & Klassen, 1997). In essence, a woman's immune system responds negatively to male fetuses, detecting and responding to the minor histocompatibility antigens linked to the fetus' Y chromosome (i.e., H–Y antigens). The maternal immune hypothesis extends the immune system's memory for foreign objects to propose that each additional male fetus potentiates the maternal immune response regardless of whether the fetus develops to term or is lost through miscarriage or abortion (Ellis & Blanchard, 2001). Furthermore, it is hypothesized that fetal exposure to the maternal H–Y antibodies affects the future man's sexual behavior. This could occur by altering the typical sexual differentiation of the brain along a more female pathway, provided the H–Y antibodies are able to cross into the brain. Alternative pathways also are possible (for a discussion, see Blanchard, 2004). Finally, given the H–Y antigen is expressed only by male fetuses, there is no immune response against female fetuses.

Review of evidence supporting the maternal immune hypothesis exists (Blanchard & Klassen, 1997; Bogaert & Skorska, 2011). Potential explanations for why homosexual men may have younger heterosexual brothers also are available (Blanchard, 2004). Regardless, the FBO effect has not been unanimously supported (Francis, 2008; McConaghy et al., 2006; Rahman et al., 2004a). The supporting and nonsupporting evidence for the FBO effect suggests some other factor(s) may be playing an important modifying role. In fact, even Blanchard recently modified his hypothesis regarding the FBO effect along these lines.

Recent investigations have found that FBO and handedness interact (Blanchard, Cantor, Bogaert, Breedlove, & Ellis, 2006; Blanchard & Lippa, 2008; Bogaert, 2006a; Bogaert, Blanchard, & Crosthwait, 2007). Specifically, the FBO effect occurs among right-handed homosexual men; among non-right-handed (left-handed or ambidextrous) men, the number of older brothers is not significantly related to homosexuality. Even greater complexity has been found empirically, in which the FBO effect exists among moderately right-hand homosexual men, but not among those who are non-right-handed or extremely right-handed (Bogaert, 2007). Possible reasons for the recent findings have been suggested (Blanchard, 2008a, 2008b). Some reasons are not parsimonious and require additional assumptions and speculations. Among the plausible candidates are that non-right-handed fetuses either are not sensitive to the mother's anti–male antibodies or the mother of such fetuses do not produce anti–male antibodies (Blanchard, 2008b). Regardless of the outcome for the maternal immune hypothesis, the issue of handedness involves another etiological hypothesis for homosexuality.

Biological Instability Explaining Homosexuality

It has been proposed that genetic mutations or environmental stress experienced during the second trimester of pregnancy may result in atypical neurodevelopment either directly or by means of epigenetic (i.e., genetic by environmental) effects (Lalumière, Blanchard, & Zucker, 2000). Such neurodevelopment is assessed indirectly by means of fluctuating asymmetry, meaning deviations from symmetry. Although most of the research on fluctuating asymmetry has occurred among animals, in which experimentation has been prevalent, observations in humans have been noted with respect to handedness; dermatoglyphics (i.e., skin ridges on the palms, fingers, toes, and soles); length of fingers and toes; and width of wrists, elbows, knees, and ankles. Deviations from moderate right-handedness (e.g., left-handedness or extreme right-handedness) are considered a marker of fluctuating asymmetry in neurodevelopment (Lalumière et al., 2000). Dermatoglyphics are under genetic control, but pharmaceuticals, other drugs (e.g., alcohol), infections, or other insults experienced by the mother during the fetus' early neurodevelopment may modify the fetus' skin ridges in a pattern that deviates from symmetry (e.g., Qazi, Masakawa, McGann & Woods, 1980; Wright, Parker, & Mavalwala, 1972). A similar situation holds for length and width of various digits and joints (e.g., Furlow, Prewitt, Gangestad, & Thornhill, 1997; Gangestad, Bennett, & Thornhill, 2001).

The hypothesis is that homosexuality is associated with fluctuating asymmetry, such as non-right-handedness. There is some support for the hypothesis, although the hypothesis may be conflated with the hormonal effects during prenatal development, as will be discussed after this review. A meta-analysis of handedness studies (Lalumière et al., 2000) found that homosexual women were almost twice as likely to be non-right-handed than were heterosexual women ($OR = 1.91$; 95% $CI = 1.52, 2.40$) and homosexual men were 34% more likely to be non-right-handed than heterosexual men ($OR = 1.34$; 95% $CI = 1.24, 1.45$). Across the sexes, the odds of homosexuals being non-right-handed relative to heterosexuals was 1.39 (95% $CI = 1.29, 1.50$).

Confirming evidence for fluctuating asymmetry generally exists for homosexual women relative to heterosexual women, although one investigative team found no significant difference between homosexual and heterosexual women on total ridge count or fluctuating asymmetry Mustanski, Bailey, & Kaspar, 2002). More homosexual women than heterosexual women evidenced fluctuating asymmetry on a composite measure and on five of the seven markers of asymmetry (P. A. Hall & Schaeff, 2008). Most particularly, a study of monozygotic twins, which therefore controlled for genetic perturbations, found that in twins discordant for sexual orientation, the lesbians had a lower total ridge count than their heterosexual co-twins (L. S. Hall, 2000), which, in the case of monozygotic twins, means the lesbians experienced some insult or the heterosexual co-twins experienced some event that increased their fetal size.

The findings for fluctuating asymmetry among men are generally inconsistent. No difference had been found between homosexual and heterosexual men on total ridge count, but more homosexual men have been found to have leftward ridge asymmetry, which is more typical of women than men (J. A. Y. Hall & Kimura, 1994). In addition, homosexual men were more likely to be asymmetrical on a composite measure and on four of the seven measures in the composite (P. A. Hall & Schaeff, 2008). Others, however, have not found significant differences between homosexual and heterosexual men on total ridge count or fluctuating asymmetry (Forastieri et al., 2002; Mustanski et al., 2002).

There are several issues or concerns with the hypothesis of biological instability. First, biological instability occurs contemporaneously with hormonal effects during the second trimester of pregnancy. Therefore, it is difficult to disentangle from hormonal effects. Mustanski et al. (2002) attempted to do so by being finely attuned to both hypotheses. They argued that the hormonal hypothesis posits gender atypicality among homosexuals: Lesbians (like heterosexual men) are more likely to be, for example, non-right-handed than heterosexual women, whereas gay men (like heterosexual women) are less likely to be non-right-handed than heterosexual men. The biological instability hypothesis posits that female and male homosexuals are more likely to be non-right-handed than same-sex heterosexual peers. They found that lesbians were more likely to be non-right-handed than heterosexual women, but there were no differences on other markers of fluctuating asymmetry. Rahman (2005) also compared the hypotheses. Although he found that male and female homosexuals had lower 2D:4D ratios, there were no significant differences by sexual orientation or its interaction with sex on a composite of nine bilateral body measurements.

Clearly, more research is needed that compares the hypotheses of hormonal effects and fluctuating asymmetry and, in the process, considers what we do know. The empirical literature suggests that development for female and male homosexuals may differ. As mentioned earlier, main effects may best describe lesbian development, such that, for example, more testosterone increases the probability of lesbianism. Moderating relations may best characterize male homosexual development, such as too little prenatal testosterone for some men or the FBO effect occurring only for right-handed men.

Second, the meaning of "biological instability" is unclear. Although individuals may differ on their total ridge count, for example, what importance does this have for a practical marker of instability, such as mental or physical well-being or some other form of adaptation? Does the morphological finding have any functional significance? It is true that more left-handed individuals have accidents than right-handed individuals (Coren & Previc, 1996; MacNiven, 1994), but the disparity may be a function of appliances and other manmade objects that are designed for right-handed persons rather than to some innate vulnerability elevating the likelihood of such outcomes. We agree with others (McCormick, Witelson, & Kingstone, 1990) that the focus of research should expand to include the meaning or function of any sexual differentiation that is found.

Summary

Research on potential biological mechanisms underlying homosexuality and bisexuality is in its infancy. Given the existence of same-sex behavior through known time and cultures and across species, some evolutionary function seems necessary to explain its existence. Indeed, the fact the behavior among humans persists even under trying circumstances only underscores the imprimatur of nature attached to the behavior. Evolutionary hypotheses have been proposed and some have garnered more support than others. We will never know whether any of these hypotheses correctly explains homosexuality unless we stumble on some equivalent of a fossil record. We reemphasize that to understand homosexuality from an evolutionary perspective demands that we understand homosexuality in the ancestral environment and not from the perspective of "recent" or current situations and settings.

There is an alternative. The existence of an evolutionary explanation for homosexuality, whatever it may be, must be etched into the genome. Careful thought will be required to narrow on potential genes, particularly given that our current knowledge indicates that humans have more than 23,000 protein-coded genes. Hamer et al. (1993) focused on the region where the "gay" gene might be located. Consequently, we are far from identifying potential genes that may explain not just male homosexuality but also female homosexuality. Until then, we can continue to pursue family studies, specifically twin studies, to tract and quantify genetic contributions. Those contributions appear to be substantial, given genetic heritability estimates of approximately 40% to 50% for both sexes.

In addition to genetic contributions, sexual differentiation of the fetus and brain by hormones provides another means for understanding homosexuality and heterosexuality. The evidence indicates that female homosexuality is linked to exposure to elevated levels of testosterone. Moreover, the extent of homosexuality (i.e., from bisexuality to exclusive lesbianism) varies with the exposure level, as does the butch–femme phenomenon. The evidence for men is generally inconsistent, except with respect to lower levels of prenatal testosterone among some men. Male homosexuality also seems to be explained by the FBO effect or to more nuanced effects involving, for example, the conditional effect of handedness on the relation between FBO and homosexuality.

ENVIRONMENTAL ETIOLOGY OF SEXUAL ORIENTATION

As important as biology may be for understanding homosexuality and heterosexuality, the environment plays a critical role. Twin studies, as reviewed previously, demonstrate that approximately 40–50% of homosexuality is attributed to genetics. Even if this amount is augmented by some quantity for nongenetic biological effects, such as those concerning hormonal effects during prenatal development, a noticeable amount still might remain to be explained. That explanation would be attributed to the environment, either directly or in interaction with genetics. We now turn to environmental explanations.

Psychoanalytic Effects

Freud's (1905/1953) psychoanalytic theory cannot be properly understood without appreciating that he had been trained as a scientist. He was aware of the medical and scientific developments of the day, including the relatively recent evolutionary theory of Darwin, and he anchored his unfolding theory in biology. He was well read in other epistemologies, for example, literature. Like any scientist, Freud wanted to understand the phenomenon he studied in the most parsimonious way possible and by ruling out alternative or rival explanations. He was also a man of his time, trained to practice medicine in an extremely patriarchal and heterosexist time.

Freud (1905/1953) premised an original bisexuality to human development. The premise harkens back to Plato's (1993) notion in *The Symposium*, as articulated by Aristophanes, of unity of male and female before the cleavage into components. Those components, for Plato, correspond with the various sexual orientations, in which the individual searches for the missing part, meaning the man or the woman who completes or renders the individual whole once again. Thus, for example, the lesbian searches for the woman and the female heterosexual for the man who completes them.

From the original bisexual matrix, according to Freud (1905/1953), the sexual orientations unfold. The particular orientation that emerges depends on which aspect of the original bisexuality is repressed. Consequently, all human beings are potentially capable of bisexuality, but the extent of repression determines the degree of homosexuality and heterosexuality, ranging from the equality of bisexuality to the exclusivity of one or the other extreme.

The explanation for the sexual orientations is the Oedipus complex, a psychodrama involving the subject and the two significant others (mother and father) and occurring between approximately ages 3–6 years. Freud (1923/1961) used the adjectives "positive" and "negative" to describe the complex. The positive complex refers to the complex that leads to heterosexuality and the negative refers to the complex that gives rise to homosexuality.

The Oedipus complex involves two intertwined processes. The first concerns which significant other the child selects as the love object. If it is the parent of the same sex, the child will be homosexual; if the child selects the parent of the opposite sex, the child will be heterosexual. Vacillation between the significant others as love objects determines the degree of homosexuality or heterosexuality. Occurring simultaneously with the love object is the object of identification. If the child identifies with the same-sex parent, heterosexuality results; with the opposite-sex parent, homosexuality. Freud (1923/1961) anticipated the hormonal findings discussed earlier. He stated that the identification process is contingent on the child's degree of masculinity and femininity.

The Oedipus complex is a drama of the first love. It involves the gamut of emotions. It also is the foundation for the superego, which develops out of the identification process. The superego is the part of the psyche that stands in contrast and opposition to the id (libido and aggression). The superego contains all the rules and regulations and rigidities by which the individual's life will be ruled to some extent. Playing referee between the antithetical and waging factions of the id and superego, as well as dealing with the external world, is the ego. Consequently, one finds in the Oedipus complex the explanation for the compulsion that characterizes each sexual orientation, in which the individual is driven toward one or both sexes, regardless of canon strictures, lay laws, or other opprobrium that may be experienced internally or externally. The Oedipus complex ends in its repression, with the child entering a latency period marked by asexuality. At puberty, the child becomes aware of the results of the Oedipus complex by means of discovering the sex to which she or he is attracted.

The Oedipus complex is a parsimonious explanation for complex phenomena. It intuitively makes sense that the original love object affects one's subsequent sexual partners. The complex, however, does have some difficulties. It is easy to understand why a girl becomes a lesbian and why a boy becomes a heterosexual man; both are born into a relationship with the mother. It is unclear how a heterosexual woman or a homosexual man comes about. They need to transfer their love to the father. Freud provides explanations for the transference, but they are not particularly convincing (for a more thorough discussion, see Schrut, 1994): Penis envy drives the girl to the father (Freud, 1925/1961). For the boy, several pathways to homosexuality exist, for example, awareness that the mother is castrated turns the boy away from women and toward men, or an erotic fixation on the mother faithfully binds the boy to her (Freud, 1910/1957; see also Freud, 1905/1953, 1914/1957).

Regardless, the Oedipus complex makes clear that a heterosexual woman always should be much closer to the possibility of bisexuality than a heterosexual man. This suggests that women are more fluid than men with respect to sexual orientation, as others have argued (e.g., Baumeister, 2000) and shown (Chivers, Rieger, Latty, & Bailey, 2004) because nearly every female infant is born into a relationship with the mother as primary love object (i.e., a lesbian relationship). This reality naturally leads to the hypothesis that more women are sexual minorities than men, as the empirical literature confirms (e.g., Chandra et al., 2011).

For men, biological factors in some algorithmic combination with psychodynamic factors may account for homosexuality. The maternal immune hypothesis (in which the mother reacts negatively to each successive male fetus) and psychoanalytic notions of transference of the love object to the father would seem to fit best. From another literature, we empirically know that a woman's psychological and physiological states affect her fetus, meaning the fetus is responsive to those effects (Monk, Myers, Sloan, Ellman, & Fifer, 2003; for a literature review, see Kinsella & Monk, 2009). The effects, moreover, are enduring in that they affect the fetus' subsequent temperament as an infant (Werner et al., 2007). Therefore, the maternal immune response may predispose the male fetus away from the mother, given her rejection of him, and, consequently, turn him toward the only alternative love object, the father. For the same reasons, the maternal immune response may potentiate the allure of the father during the Oedipal vacillation between the significant others as love objects.

Behaviorist Explanations

Unlike biological or psychodynamic explanations for homosexuality, behaviorist explanations propose that heterosexuality or homosexuality is learned; there is nothing inherent or essential determining sexual orientation. D. J. Bem (1996) offered a behaviorist theory to account for sexual orientation that relies on basic learning principles.

The theory of exotic-becomes-erotic (D. J. Bem, 1996) depends critically on gender conformity. A child who is gender conforming prefers same-sex playmates, making the opposite sex an exotic species. Another child who is gender nonconforming in behaviors feels different from same-sex peers and prefers other-sex peers as playmates; over time, the felt difference with the same-sex peers makes those peers exotic. At some point, physiological arousal occurs in response to whichever sex is exotic. Sexual attraction to the exotic sex follows.

The theory rests on numerous assumptions along each link of its causal chain, as the following examples make clear. The theory presumes that all future homosexuals are gender nonconforming as children, which is as correct as saying that no future heterosexual women were ever tomboys. The exotic association also is confusing because it does not explain, for example, why boys who will be heterosexual do not find effeminate boys exotic and, thus, arousing. Importantly, it is unclear what is meant by "arousal" and why and how it is paired with the sex that behaves in a manner opposed to the child's gendered behavior. In essence, the connections among the theory's parts are inadequate. Finally, as far as we know, no empirical evidence supports the theory.

Irrespective of D. J. Bem's (1996) theory, other behaviorists have considered the possibility of conditioning homosexuality (Hoffmann, 2012). Although theoretical possibilities are considered, neither an explicit theory nor pertinent data are provided as to how classical conditioning brings about sexual-minority individuals. Complementary data, however, are available that argue against learning perspectives. Sexual-minority individuals who strive to become heterosexual expose themselves to various interventions in the hopes of accomplishing their aim. The interventions are based on classical and operant principles. The efforts are unsuccessful even among the highly motivated individuals who pursue such interventions (for reviews, see American Psychological Association, 2009; Beckstead, 2012).

Although behaviorism may not have a direct effect on sexual orientation, it is possible that operant principles (i.e., learning by means of reinforcement and punishment), may moderate the relation between biological determinants and sexual orientation, such that the relation may be stronger in some environments versus others. Lippa and Tan (2001) examined sexual-orientation disparities in gender-nonconforming behaviors and personality characteristics by ethnic and racial background. They argued that lesbian and gay men from more gender-polarized cultures (Latinos and Asians) would be more gender atypical in their behaviors and personality traits than peers from a less gender-polarized culture (White Americans) relative to same-sex heterosexuals from the respective cultural groups. Their hypotheses were confirmed. Asian and Latino lesbian and gay men were more atypical than same-sex heterosexuals than was the case between White lesbian and gay men and same-sex heterosexuals. This suggests that experiences in the socialization process more strongly differentiated Latino and Asian than White lesbians and gay men from their respective same-sex heterosexual peers. Consequently, the relations between biological predisposing factors and sexual orientation may depend on operant principles, in which reinforcements or punishments differ among subpopulations nested in the sexual orientations (e.g., Asian as compared with White lesbians; see Chapter 19, this volume; Volume 2, Chapter 6, this handbook).

Consequences of Sexual Orientation

Socialization (or operant principles) may play an important role in the study of sexual orientation in other ways. The alternative perspective differs from the one we have pursued, which concerns the determinants of sexual orientation and modifiers of the relations between hypothesized determinants and sexual orientation. Instead, the alternative perspective targets the consequences of sexual orientation for health and other adaptational outcomes as well as the mediators of any relations between sexual orientation and outcomes. It maintains that there will be important consequences for individuals subject to the punishment that is likely to be experienced by those who are or are perceived to be homosexual or bisexual (Herek, Gillis, Cogan, & Glunt, 1997; Meyer, 2003; Rosario, Schrimshaw, Hunter, & Gwadz, 2002). Although we cannot do justice to the scope of this alternative perspective in the allotted space, we provide a brief sense of this body of research.

Lesbians, gays, and bisexuals have elevated rates of internalizing and externalizing psychological symptomatology than heterosexuals (for meta-analyses, see King et al., 2008; Marshal et al., 2011). Experiences of victimization (e.g., physical assault, verbal abuse, discrimination) are more prevalent among lesbians, gays, and bisexuals than heterosexuals (for a meta-analysis, see Katz-Wise & Hyde, 2012). Therefore, it is unsurprising that victimization has been related to elevated symptomatology among lesbians, gay, and bisexuals relative to heterosexuals in representative samples of the population (Bontempo & D'Augelli, 2002; Hughes, McCabe, Wilsnack, West, & Boyd, 2010; Roberts, Austin, Corliss, Vandermorris, & Koenen, 2010; Russell & Joyner, 2001), as has an unsupportive environment (Eisenberg & Resnick, 2006; Goodenow, Szalacha, & Westheimer, 2006; Hatzenbuehler, 2011). A dramatic demonstration of the impact of victimization on health was made available by using the National Epidemiological Survey on Alcohol and Related Conditions. The longitudinal study (Hatzenbuehler, McLaughlin, Keyes, & Hasin, 2010) assessed change in psychiatric diagnoses before and after implementation of constitutional state laws banning same-sex marriages, and it controlled for potential confounders of psychiatric disorders. Lesbians, gays, and bisexuals residing in states that implemented anti–gay marriage laws experienced significant increases in rates of any mood disorder ($OR = 1.67$, 95% $CI = 1.01, 2.77$) and comordid disorders ($OR = 2.00$, 95% $CI = 1.22, 3.28$) than did lesbian, gay, and bisexual peers living in states without such laws; for the latter, no significant change in rates of disorders occurred over time.

Actual or anticipated victimization may affect other important aspects of individuals' lives, including their acceptance and integration of their sexual identity, relationships with others, and their involvement in health risk behaviors, such as sexual risk behaviors. In addition, these processes vary with ethnic and racial backgrounds. For example, although lesbian, gay, and bisexual youth of Black, Latino, and White backgrounds do not differ on attaining psychosexual milestones of sexual attraction, behavior, and identity, Black youth have integrated their lesbian, gay, or bisexual identity to a lesser extent than White peers (Rosario, Schrimshaw, & Hunter, 2004). Another study also found no significant differences among ethnic or racial groups in attaining psychosexual milestones, but individuals of minority ethnic and racial backgrounds were less likely to have disclosed their lesbian, gay, or bisexual status to others (Grov, Bimbi, Nanín, & Parsons, 2006). Still another study underscored the importance of identity integration (Crawford, Allison, Zamboni, & Soto, 2002). It found that the integration of Black and gay identities was related to, for example, higher self-esteem, life satisfaction, and self-efficacy regarding HIV prevention efforts.

Summary of the Phenomena of Sexual Orientation

Sexual orientation is a multidimensional construct, although every theoretician and researcher is able to choose as many as the full menu allows or as little as one among the three dimensions: attractions to either or neither sex, sexual activity with either or neither sex, and sexual identity as lesbian or gay, bisexual, heterosexual, asexual, or any related identity. Some dimensions have subparts. Attractions consist of sexual fantasies, erotic arousal, and sexual desires. Sexual activity requires a focus on behavior with women and with men. In addition to this complexity, sexual orientation may change over time. This is most likely to occur for sexual activity and self-identification. It also is most likely to occur during adolescence and emerging adulthood when the young person is discovering and exploring his or her sexual orientation.

Despite any exploration that occurs, there is a strong biological foundation for sexual orientation. A genetic component exists for sexual orientation in men and women. In addition, prenatal hormones have an effect in sexual-minority women and the effect is stronger among butch than femme women and among lesbian than bisexual women. The FBO effect plays a role in sexual-minority men and, thus, the maternal immune hypothesis requires serious consideration. Biological explanations, however, do not entirely explain sexual orientation.

Psychoanalytic contingencies are evident as main effects or in interaction with biological factors. Main effects seem to be particularly likely for sexual-minority women and conditional relations for sexual-minority men. A joint program of research by psychoanalysts and biologically oriented scientists may prove fruitful.

Behaviorist explanations for directly understanding sexual orientation are inadequate because they a priori dismiss biological explanations. Operant principles by means of socialization, however, may moderate the relation between biological explanations and sexual orientation. Operant principles also hold promise for understanding some of the potential poor health and adaptational consequences of sexual orientation in light of society's continued stigmatization of homosexuality.

Whether the theoretician or empirical researcher focuses on the etiology or consequences of sexual orientation, it is certainly true that much more research needs to be done before we understand the full scope and implications of sexual orientation for ourselves and other species. Such understanding ultimately means learning about one of our most profound and meaningful identities. It is coming to know who we are.

FUTURE RESEARCH DIRECTIONS

Although a great deal of work has been done to understand the origins of sexual orientation, more remains to be done and especially as knowledge of the human genome continues to increase. We encourage theoretical work that identifies potential candidate genes that may account for homosexuality. The work of Hamer et al. (1993) has served as a model of the approach to emulate. They generated and argued for an a priori hypothesis regarding the chromosomal area where the "gay" gene should be found and followed with hypothesis testing. We do not underestimate the challenges attending such theoretical work as we strongly encourage its pursuit. With more than 23,000 protein-coded genes in the human genome, a priori hypothesis generation will be critical and difficult. As this effort unfolds, work should continue on family studies examining genetic effects by means of twin and adopted siblings. It is essential that such studies have sufficient power to properly test null hypotheses of no heritability effects. This can be achieved by pooling samples over national borders. These studies also can be expanded beyond testing for heritability effects to include examination of prenatal hormonal effects, such as 2D:4D ratios and cognitive functioning. A pool of scientists representing genetics and various psychological disciplines would form a strong investigative team with the potential to expand our understanding of sexual orientation (see Chapter 19, this volume).

Differences among homosexual, bisexual, and heterosexual individuals need to be considered and preferably examined along with differences along the butch–femme continuum both in women and men. There may be subgroups of homosexuals, for example. The data we reviewed suggest that butch and femme lesbians may differ on prenatal hormonal markers (e.g., W. M. Brown et al., 2002a). Butch and femme lesbians and femme bisexual women have been found to differ on markers of sexual orientation (Rosario et al., 2009). Butch and femme lesbians are similar on sexual attraction and lifetime numbers of male and female partners, but they differ from bisexual women, as one would expect. Differences between lesbians and bisexual women are found on some aspects of sexual identity development (e.g., internalized homonegativity), but not others, in which the butch–femme distinction seems important. Femme lesbians and femme bisexual women do not differ on degree of comfort with others knowing about their homosexuality or bisexuality, but butch lesbians are much more comfortable in this respect than either of these groups (Rosario et al., 2009). It is unknown whether similar findings exist among homosexual and bisexual men because, as far as we know, no comparable data are available on men. In general, for men and women by butch and femme gender status, and by homosexual and bisexual sexual orientation (2×2×2), much more data are needed on gender nonconformity and other markers of prenatal hormonal effects. Such work must be highly sensitive to measurement issues, given the negativity attending gender nonconforming identities among some homosexuals (Rosario et al., 2009).

The issue of plasticity or change in sexual orientation needs to be considered. As we said earlier, one should expect change during adolescence and emerging adulthood as young people explore their sexual orientation. Change during adulthood is more difficult to understand, given the general expectation that sexual orientation is relatively fixed. It may be that change occurs in specific subpopulations or under certain conditions. Representative data on the U.S. population indicate that change usually occurs to nearby rather than more distant sexual-orientation categories and it is much more prevalent among the nonexclusive orientations, which include the groups that are bisexual to some extent or other (Savin-Williams et al., 2012). Bisexuality may inherently be a more flexible orientation than either homosexuality or heterosexuality, with individuals varying on the extent to which they are attracted to one or the other sex. Although bisexuals, as a group, may be highly attracted to both sexes (Storms, 1980), they may be somewhat biased in one or the other direction as individuals. In addition, their bias may change over time, as representative samples have found (Mock & Eibach, 2012; Savin-Williams et al., 2012). What may explain the bias requires careful thought and exploration as well as samples that minimize selection biases.

Related to plasticity of sexual orientation is the hypothesis of sex difference. Women are hypothesized to be more plastic than men. This may be true for most women, but not all. In fact, the data suggest, as the genetic and prenatal hypotheses would suggest, that lesbians differ from bisexual and heterosexual women in this respect. They are predominantly aroused by their own sex (Chivers et al., 2004, 2007; Rieger & Savin-Williams, 2012). Heterosexual women (Chivers et al., 2004, 2007) or bisexual and heterosexual women are aroused by both sexes (Rieger & Savin-Williams, 2012). In other words, the plasticity of sexual arousal attributed to women applies to those women who are not lesbians. Therefore, it is essential that researchers recruit sufficient cases to ensure that lesbian and bisexual women are not combined into a single sample. Such a sexual-minority sample could generate findings that are not true of either group and that mislead our understanding.

The role of the environment must be considered. We already have suggested as much when warning of the measurement sensitivity required when assessing the butch–femme phenomenon. The environment also may play an important role in identifying as homosexual, bisexual, heterosexual, or comparable synonyms. The pressure in certain cultures or settings to be heterosexual may lead to a higher prevalence of bisexual identity (or behavior) for some as a compromise between the external pressure and internal dynamics; thus, a lower prevalence of homosexuality might be found than otherwise might be the case. In-depth studies of individuals whose sexual attraction may be strongly biased toward the same sex, but whose behavior or identity deviates in the other direction may shed light on potential tensions between external pressures and internal dynamics. A careful examination of such individuals' symptomatic profiles also is suggested because the price for the discordance may be steep.

Despite the magnitude of the literature covered herein, the conclusion is that we are in the early stages of understanding sexual orientation. It is complicated in every way, with multiple groupings within each major sexual-orientation category subdivided in known (e.g., sex, butch and femme) and perhaps unknown ways. For example, Hamer et al. (1993) found the location of the "gay" gene in the Xq28 region of the X chromosome, but only in some gay men. Taken together, these findings suggest that there are multiple homosexualities or multiple pathways to homosexuality across the sexes. Identifying and confirming the multiple pathways and sexual-orientation categories constitute the task before the scientific community. The result of the endeavor, if successful, will be to understand the spectrum of sexual orientation and, in the process, to understand who we are.

References

Alanko, K., Santtila, P., Harlaar, N., Witting, K., Varjonen, M., Jern, P., . . . Sandnabba, N. K. (2010). Common genetic effects of gender atypical behavior in childhood and sexual orientation in adulthood: A study of Finnish twins. *Archives of Sexual Behavior, 39*, 81–92. doi:10.1007/s10508-008-9457-3

Allen, L. S., & Gorski, R. A. (1991). Sexual dimorphism of the anterior commissure and massa intermedia of the human brain. *Journal of Comparative Neurology, 312*, 97–104. doi:10.1002/cne.903120108

Allen, L. S., Hines, M., Shryne, J. E., & Gorski, R. A. (1989). Two sexually dimorphic cell groups in the human brain. *Journal of Neuroscience, 9*, 497–506.

American Psychological Association. (2009). *Report of the American Psychological Association's Task Force on Appropriate Therapeutic Responses to Sexual Orientation.* Washington, DC: Author. Retrieved from http://www.apa.org/pi/lgbt/resources/therapeutic-response.pdf

Austin, S. B., Ziyadeh, N. J., Corliss, H. L., Haines, J., Rockett, H. R., Wypij, D., & Field, A. E. (2009). Sexual orientation disparities in weight status in adolescence: Findings from a prospective study. *Obesity, 17*, 1776–1782. doi:10.1038/oby.2009.72

Bailey, J. M., & Benishay, D. S. (1993). Familial aggregation of female sexual orientation. *American Journal of Psychiatry, 150*, 272–277.

Bailey, J. M., Dunne, M. P., & Martin, N. G. (2000). Genetic and environmental influences on sexual orientation and its correlates in an Australian twin sample. *Journal of Personality and Social Psychology, 78*, 524–536. doi:10.1037/0022-3514.78.3.524

Bailey, J. M., & Pillard, R. C. (1991). A genetic study of male sexual orientation. *Archives of General Psychiatry, 48*, 1089–1096. doi:10.1001/archpsyc.1991.01810360053008

Bailey, J. M., Pillard, R. C., Neale, M. C., & Agyei, Y. (1993). Heritable factors influence sexual orientation in women. *Archives of General Psychiatry, 50*, 217–223. doi:10.1001/archpsyc.1993.01820150067007

Bailey, J. M., & Zucker, K. J. (1995). Childhood sex-typed behavior and sexual orientation: A conceptual analysis and quantitative review. *Developmental Psychology, 31*, 43–55. doi:10.1037/0012-1649.31.1.43

Bao, A.-M., & Swaab, D. F. (2011). Sexual differentiation of the human brain: Relation to gender identity, sexual orientation and neuropsychiatric disorders. *Frontiers in Neuroendocrinology, 32*, 214–226. doi:10.1016/j.yfrne.2011.02.007

Bauer, G. R., Jairam, J. A., & Baidoobonso, S. M. (2010). Sexual health, risk behaviors, and substance use in heterosexual-identified women with female sex partners: 2002 US National Survey of Family Growth. *Sexually Transmitted Diseases, 37*, 531–537. doi:10.1097/OLQ.0b013e3181d785f4

Bauermeister, J. A., Johns, M. M., Sandfort, T. G. M., Eisenberg, A., Grossman, A. H., & D'Augelli, A. R. (2010). Relationship trajectories and psychological well-being among sexual minority youth. *Journal of Youth and Adolescence, 39*, 1148–1163. doi:10.1007/s10964-010-9557-y

Baumeister, R. F. (2000). Gender differences in erotic plasticity: The female sex drive as socially flexible and responsive. *Psychological Bulletin, 126*, 347–374. doi:10.1037/0033-2909.126.3.347

Becker, J. B., Berkley, K. J., Geary, N., Hampson, E., Herman, J. P., & Young, E. A. (Eds.). (2008). *Sex differences in the brain: From genes to behaviors*. New York, NY: Oxford University Press.

Beckstead, A. L. (2012). Can we change sexual orientation? *Archives of Sexual Behavior, 41*, 121–134. doi:10.1007/s10508-012-9922-x

Bell, A. P., Weinberg, M. S., & Hammersmith, S. K. (1981). *Sexual preference: Its development in men and women*. Bloomington: Alfred C. Kinsey Institute of Sex Research, Indiana University.

Bem, D. J. (1996). Exotic becomes erotic: A developmental theory of sexual orientation. *Psychological Review, 103*, 320–335. doi:10.1037/0033-295X.103.2.320

Bem, S. L. (1974). The measurement of psychological androgyny. *Journal of Consulting and Clinical Psychology, 42*, 155–162. doi:10.1037/h0036215

Berenbaum, S. A., & Bailey, J. M. (2003). Effects of gender identity of prenatal androgens and genital appearance: Evidence from girls with congenital adrenal hyperplasia. *Journal of Clinical Endocrinology and Metabolism, 88*, 1102–1106. doi:10.1210/jc.2002-020782

Berenbaum, S. A., & Resnick, S. M. (1997). Early androgen effects on aggression in children and adults with congenital adrenal hyperplasia. *Psychoneuroendocrinology, 22*, 505–515. doi:10.1016/S0306-4530(97)00049-8

Berenbaum, S. A., & Snyder, E. (1995). Early hormonal influences on childhood sex-typed activity and playmate preferences: Implications for the development of sexual orientation. *Developmental Psychology, 31*, 31–42. doi:10.1037/0012-1649.31.1.31

Blanchard, R. (2001). Fraternal birth order and the maternal immune hypothesis of male homosexuality. *Hormones and Behavior, 40*, 105–114. doi:10.1006/hbeh.2001.1681

Blanchard, R. (2004). Quantitative and theoretical analyses of the relation between older brothers and homosexuality in men. *Journal of Theoretical Biology, 230*, 173–187. doi:10.1016/j.jtbi.2004.04.021

Blanchard, R. (2008a). Review and theory of handedness, birth order, and homosexuality in men. *Laterality, 13*, 51–70. doi:10.1080/13576500701710432

Blanchard, R. (2008b). Sex ratio of older siblings in heterosexual and homosexual, right-handed and non-right-handed men. *Archives of Sexual Behavior, 37*, 977–981. doi:10.1007/s10508-006-9119-2

Blanchard, R. (2012). Fertility in the mothers of first-born homosexual and heterosexual men. *Archives of Sexual Behavior, 41*, 551–556. doi:10.1007/s10508-011-9888-0

Blanchard, R., & Bogaert, A. F. (1996). Homosexuality in men and number of older brothers. *American Journal of Psychiatry, 153*, 27–31.

Blanchard, R., & Bogaert, A. F. (2004). Proportion of homosexual men who owe their sexual orientation to fraternal birth order: An estimate based on two national probability samples. *American Journal of Human Biology, 16*, 151–157. doi:10.1002/ajhb.20006

Blanchard, R., Cantor, J. M., Bogaert, A. F., Breedlove, S. M., & Ellis, L. (2006). Interaction of fraternal birth order and handedness in the development of male homosexuality. *Hormones and Behavior, 49*, 405–414. doi:10.1016/j.yhbeh.2005.09.002

Blanchard, R., & Ellis, L. (2001). Birth weight, sexual orientation and the sex of preceding siblings. *Journal of Biosocial Science, 33*, 451–467. doi:10.1017/S0021932001004515

Blanchard, R., & Klassen, P. (1997). H-Y antigen and homosexuality in men. *Journal of Theoretical Biology, 185*, 373–378. doi:10.1006/jtbi.1996.0315

Blanchard, R., & Lippa, R. A. (2008). The sex ratio of older siblings in non-right-handed homosexual men. *Archives of Sexual Behavior, 37*, 970–976. doi:10.1007/s10508-006-9107-6

Bobrow, D., & Bailey, J. M. (2001). Is male homosexuality maintained via kin selection? *Evolution and Human Behavior, 22*, 361–368. doi:10.1016/S1090-5138(01)00074-5

Boehmer, U., Bowen, D. J., & Bauer, G. R. (2007). Overweight and obesity in sexual-minority women: Evidence from population-based data. *American Journal of Public Health, 97*, 1134–1140. doi:10.2105/AJPH.2006.088419

Bogaert, A. F. (1997). Birth order and sexual orientation in women. *Behavioral Neuroscience, 111*, 1395–1397. doi:10.1037/0735-7044.111.6.1395

Bogaert, A. F. (2000). Birth order and sexual orientation in a national probability sample. *Journal of Sex Research, 37*, 361–368. doi:10.1080/00224490009552059

Bogaert, A. F. (2003). Number of older brothers and sexual orientation: New tests and the attraction/behavioral distinction in two national probability samples. *Journal of Personality and Social Psychology, 84*, 644–652. doi:10.1037/0022-3514.84.3.644

Bogaert, A. F. (2004). Asexuality: Prevalence and associated factors in a national probability sample. *Journal of Sex Research, 41*, 279–287. doi:10.1080/0022 4490409552235

Bogaert, A. F. (2006a). Biological versus nonbiological older brothers and men's sexual orientation. *Proceedings of the National Academy of Sciences of the United States of America, 103*, 10771–10774. doi:10.1073/pnas.0511152103

Bogaert, A. F. (2006b). Toward a conceptual understanding of asexuality. *Review of General Psychology, 10*, 241–250. doi:10.1037/1089-2680.10.3.241

Bogaert, A. F. (2007). Extreme right-handedness, older brothers, and sexual orientation in men. *Neuropsychology, 21*, 141–148. doi:10.1037/0894-4105.21.1.141

Bogaert, A. F. (2010). Physical development and sexual orientation in men and women: An analysis of NATSAL-2000. *Archives of Sexual Behavior, 39*, 110–116. doi:10.1007/s10508-008-9398-x

Bogaert, A. F., Blanchard, R., & Crosthwait, L. E. (2007). Interaction of birth order, handedness, and sexual orientation in the Kinsey interview data. *Behavioral Neuroscience, 121*, 845–853. doi:10.1037/0735-7044.121.5.845

Bogaert, A. F., & Friesen, C. (2002). Sexual orientation and height, weight, and age of puberty: New tests from a British national probability sample. *Biological Psychology, 59*, 135–145. doi:10.1016/S0301-0511 (01)00131-4

Bogaert, A. F., Friesen, C., & Klentrou, P. (2002). Age of puberty and sexual orientation in a national probability sample. *Archives of Sexual Behavior, 31*, 73–81. doi:10.1023/A:1014083218773

Bogaert, A. F., & Hershberger, S. (1999). The relation between sexual orientation and penile size. *Archives of Sexual Behavior, 28*, 213–221. doi:10.1023/A:1018780108597

Bogaert, A. F., & Skorska, M. (2011). Sexual orientation, fraternal birth order, and the maternal immune hypothesis: A review. *Frontiers in Neuroendocrinology, 32*, 247–254. doi:10.1016/j.yfrne.2011.02.004

Bontempo, D. E., & D'Augelli, A. R. (2002). Effects of at-school victimization and sexual orientation on lesbian, gay, or bisexual youths' health risk behaviors. *Journal of Adolescent Health, 30*, 364–374. doi:10.1016/S1054-139X(01)00415-3

Brennan, D. J., Ross, L. E., Dobinson, C., Veldhuizen, S., & Steele, L. S. (2010). Men's sexual orientation and health in Canada. *Canadian Journal of Public Health, 101*, 225–228.

Brotto, L. A., Knudson, G., Inskip, J., Rhodes, K., & Erskine, Y. (2010). Asexuality: A mixed-method approach. *Archives of Sexual Behavior, 39*, 599–618. doi:10.1007/s10508-008-9434-x

Brotto, L. A., & Yule, M. A. (2011). Physiological and subjective sexual arousal in self-identified asexual women. *Archives of Sexual Behavior, 40*, 699–712. doi:10.1007/s10508-010-9671-7

Brown, J., & Trevethan, R. (2010). Shame, internalized homophobia, identity formation, attachment style, and connection to relationship status in gay men. *American Journal of Men's Health, 4*, 267–276. doi:10.1177/1557988309342002

Brown, W. M., Finn, C. J., Cooke, B. M., & Breedlove, S. M. (2002a). Differences in finger length ratios between self-identified 'butch' and 'femme' lesbians. *Archives of Sexual Behavior, 31*, 123–127. doi:10.1023/A:1014091420590

Brown, W. M., Hines, M., Fane, B. A., & Breedlove, S. M. (2002b). Masculinized finger length patterns in human males and females with congenital adrenal hyperplasia. *Hormones and Behavior, 42*, 380–386. doi:10.1006/hbeh.2002.1830

Byrnes, J. P., Miller, D. C., & Schafer, W. D. (1999). Gender differences in risk taking: A meta-analysis. *Psychological Bulletin, 125*, 367–383. doi:10.1037/0033-2909.125.3.367

Calzo, J. P., Antonucci, T. C., Mays, V. M., & Cochran, S. D. (2011). Retrospective recall of sexual orientation identity development among gay, lesbian, and bisexual adults. *Developmental Psychology, 47*, 1658–1673. doi:10.1037/a0025508

Cantor, J. M., Blanchard, R., Paterson, A. D., & Bogaert, A. F. (2002). How many gay men owe their sexual orientation to fraternal birth order? *Archives of Sexual Behavior, 31*, 63–71. doi:10.1023/A:1014031201935

Chandra, A., Mosher, W. D., Copen, C., & Sionean, C. (2011). *Sexual behavior, sexual attraction, and sexual identity in the United States: Data from the 2006–2008 National Survey of Family Growth* (National Health Statistics Reports, no. 36, 1–36). Hyattsville, MD: National Center for Health Statistics.

Chivers, M. L., Rieger, G., Latty, E., & Bailey, J. M. (2004). A sex difference in the specificity of sexual arousal. *Psychological Science, 15*, 736–744. doi:10.1111/j.0956-7976.2004.00750.x

Chivers, M. L., Seto, M. C., & Blanchard, R. (2007). Gender and sexual orientation differences in sexual response to sexual activities versus gender of actors in sexual films. *Journal of Personality and Social Psychology, 93*, 1108–1121. doi:10.1037/0022-3514.93.6.1108

Clark, M. A., Armstrong, G., & Bonacore, L. (2005). Measuring sexual orientation and gender expression among middle-aged and older women in a cancer screening study. *Journal of Cancer Education, 20*, 108–112. doi:10.1207/s15430154jce2002_12

Collaer, M. L., Reimers, S., & Manning, J. T. (2007). Visuospatial performance on an internet line judgment task and potential hormonal markers: Sex, sexual orientation, and 2D:4D. *Archives of Sexual Behavior, 36,* 177–192. doi:10.1007/s10508-006-9152-1

Coren, S., & Previc, F. H. (1996). Handedness as a predictor of increased risk of knee, elbow, or shoulder injury, fractures and broken bones. *Laterality, 1,* 139–152.

Corliss, H. L., Rosario, M., Wypij, D., Wylie, S. A., Frazier, A. L., & Austin, S. B. (2010). Sexual orientation and drug use in a longitudinal cohort study of U.S. adolescents. *Addictive Behaviors, 35,* 517–521. doi:10.1016/j.addbeh.2009.12.019

Côté, K., Blanchard, R., & Lalumière, M. L. (2003). The influence of birth order on birth weight: Does the sex of preceding siblings matter? *Journal of Biosocial Science, 35,* 455–462. doi:10.1017/S0021932003004553

Crawford, I., Allison, K. W., Zamboni, B. D., & Soto, T. (2002). The influence of dual-identity development on the psychosocial functioning of African-American gay and bisexual men. *Journal of Sex Research, 39,* 179–189. doi:10.1080/00224490209552140

Dabbs, J. M., Chang, E. L., Strong, R. A., & Milun, R. (1998). Spatial ability, navigation strategy, and geographic knowledge among men and women. *Evolution and Human Behavior, 19,* 89–98. doi:10.1016/S1090-5138(97)00107-4

D'Augelli, A. R., Grossman, A. H., & Starks, M. T. (2008). Gender atypicality and sexual orientation development among lesbian, gay, and bisexual youth. *Journal of Gay and Lesbian Mental Health, 12,* 121–143.

DeLamater, J. D., & Hyde, J. S. (1998). Essentialism vs. social constructionism in the study of human sexuality. *Journal of Sex Research, 35,* 10–18. doi:10.1080/00224499809551913

DeLuzio Chasin, C. J. D. (2011). Theoretical issues in the study of asexuality. *Archives of Sexual Behavior, 40,* 713–723. doi:10.1007/s10508-011-9757-x

Deputy, N. P., & Boehmer, U. (2010). Determinants of body weight among men of different sexual orientation. *Preventive Medicine, 51,* 129–131. doi:10.1016/j.ypmed.2010.05.010

Diamond, L. M. (2006). The evolution of plasticity in female-female desire. *Journal of Psychology and Human Sexuality, 18,* 245–274. doi:10.1300/J056v18n04_01

Diamond, L. M. (2008). Female bisexuality from adolescence to adulthood: Results from a 10-year longitudinal study. *Developmental Psychology, 44,* 5–14. doi:10.1037/0012-1649.44.1.5

Dickson, N., Paul, C., & Herbison, P. (2003). Same-sex attraction in a birth cohort: Prevalence and persistence in early adulthood. *Social Science and Medicine, 56,* 1607–1615. doi:10.1016/S0277-9536(02)00161-2

DuPree, M. G., Mustanski, B. S., Bocklandt, S., Nievergelt, C., & Hamer, D. H. (2004). A candidate gene study of CYP19 (aromatase) and male sexual orientation. *Behavior Genetics, 34,* 243–250. doi:10.1023/B:BEGE.0000017870.77610.52

Eisenberg, M. E., & Resnick, M. D. (2006). Suicidality among gay, lesbian, and bisexual youth: The role of protective factors. *Journal of Adolescent Health, 39,* 662–668. doi:10.1016/j.jadohealth.2006.04.024

Ellis, L., & Ames, M. A. (1987). Neurohormonal functioning and sexual orientation: A theory of homosexuality/heterosexuality. *Psychological Bulletin, 101,* 233–258. doi:10.1037/0033-2909.101.2.233

Ellis, L., & Blanchard, R. (2001). Birth order, sibling sex ratio, and maternal miscarriages in homosexual and heterosexual men and women. *Personality and Individual Differences, 30,* 543–552. doi:10.1016/S0191-8869(00)00051-9

Erikson, E. H. (1968). *Identity: Youth and crisis.* New York, NY: Norton.

Forastieri, V., Pinto Andrade, C., Lima, V., Souza, A., Santana Silva, M., Niño el-Hani, C., . . . Flores, R. Z. (2002). Evidence against a relationship between dermatoglyphic asymmetry and male sexual orientation. *Human Biology, 74,* 861–870. doi:10.1353/hub.2003.0002

Francis, A. M. (2008). Family and sexual orientation: The family-demographic correlates of homosexuality in men and women. *Journal of Sex Research, 45,* 371–377. doi:10.1080/00224490802398357

Freud, S. (1953). Three essays on the theory of sexuality. In *Standard edition of the complete psychological works of Sigmund Freud* (Vol. 7, pp. 135–243). London, England: Institute of Psycho-Analysis. (Original work published 1905)

Freud, S. (1957). Leonardo Da Vinci and a memory of his childhood. In *Standard edition of the complete psychological works of Sigmund Freud* (Vol. 11, pp. 59–137). London, England: Institute of Psycho-Analysis. (Original work published 1910)

Freud, S. (1957). On narcissism. In *Standard edition of the complete psychological works of Sigmund Freud* (Vol. 14, pp. 67–102). London, England: Institute of Psycho-Analysis. (Original work published 1914)

Freud, S. (1961). The ego and the id. In *Standard edition of the complete psychological works of Sigmund Freud* (Vol. 19, pp. 12–66). London, England: Institute of Psycho-Analysis. (Original work published 1923)

Freud, S. (1961). Some psychical consequences of the anatomical distinction between the sexes. In *Standard edition of the complete psychological works of Sigmund Freud* (Vol. 19, pp. 243–258). London, England: Institute of Psycho-Analysis. (Original work published 1925)

Frisch, M., & Zdravkovic, S. (2010). Body size at birth and same-sex marriage in young adulthood. *Archives of Sexual Behavior, 39*, 117–123. doi:10.1007/s10508-008-9408-z

Frost, D. M., & Meyer, I. H. (2009). Internalized homophobia and relationship quality among lesbians, gay men, and bisexuals. *Journal of Counseling Psychology, 56*, 97–109. doi:10.1037/a0012844

Furlow, F. B., Prewitt, T. A., Gangestad, S. W., & Thornhill, R. (1997). Fluctuating asymmetry and psychometric intelligence. *Proceedings of the Royal Society of London, 264*, 823–829. doi:10.1098/rspb.1997.0115

Gangestad, S. W., Bennett, K., & Thornhill, R. (2001). A latent variable model of developmental instability in relation to men's sexual behavior. *Proceedings of the Royal Society of London, 268*, 1677–1684. doi:10.1098/rspb.2001.1675

Goldstein, J. M., Selidman, L. J., Horton, N. H., Makris, N., Kennedy, D. N., Caviness, V. S., Jr., . . . Tsuang, M. T. (2001). Normal sexual dimorphism of the adult human brain assessed by in vivo magnetic resonance imaging. *Cerebral Cortex, 11*, 490–497. doi:10.1093/cercor/11.6.490

Gonsiorek, J. C., Sell, R. L., & Weinrich, J. D. (1995). Definition and measurement of sexual orientation. *Suicide and Life-Threatening Behavior, 25*(Suppl.), 40–51.

Goodenow, C., Szalacha, L., & Westheimer, K. (2006). School support groups, other school factors, and the safety of sexual minority adolescents. *Psychology in the Schools, 43*, 573–589. doi:10.1002/pits.20173

Gould, S. J., & Vrba, E. S. (1982). Exaptation—a missing term in the science of form. *Paleobiology, 8*, 4–15.

Grimbos, T., Dawood, K., Burriss, R. P., Zucker, K. J., & Puts, D. A. (2010). Sexual orientation and the second to fourth finger length ratio: A meta-analysis in men and women. *Behavioral Neuroscience, 124*, 278–287. doi:10.1037/a0018764

Grov, C., Bimbi, D. S., Nanín, J. E., & Parsons, J. T. (2006). Race, ethnicity, gender, and generational factors associated with the coming-out process among gay, lesbian, and bisexual individuals. *Journal of Sex Research, 43*, 115–121. doi:10.1080/00224490609552306

Guadamuz, T. E., Lim, S. H., Marshal, M. P., Friedman, M. S., Stall, R. D., & Silvestre, A. J. (2012). Sexual, behavioral, and quality of life characteristics of healthy weight, overweight, and obese gay and bisexual men: Findings from a prospective cohort study. *Archives of Sexual Behavior, 41*, 385–389. doi:10.1007/s10508-011-9859-5

Hall, J. A. Y., & Kimura, D. (1994). Dermatoglyphic asymmetry and sexual orientation in men. *Behavioral Neuroscience, 108*, 1203–1206. doi:10.1037/0735-7044.108.6.1203

Hall, L. S. (2000). Dermatoglyphic analysis of total finger ridge count in female monozygotic twins discordant for sexual orientation. *Journal of Sex Research, 37*, 315–320. doi:10.1080/00224490009552053

Hall, L. S., & Love, C. T. (2003). Finger-length ratios in female monozygotic twins discordant for sexual orientation. *Archives of Sexual Behavior, 32*, 23–28. doi:10.1023/A:1021837211630

Hall, P. A., & Schaeff, C. M. (2008). Sexual orientation and fluctuating asymmetry in men and women. *Archives of Sexual Behavior, 37*, 158–165. doi:10.1007/s10508-007-9282-0

Halpern, D. F. (1992). *Sex differences in cognitive abilities* (2nd ed.). Hillsdale, NJ: Erlbaum.

Hamer, D. H., & Copeland, P. (1994). *The science of desire: The search for the gay gene and the biology of behavior*. New York, NY: Simon & Schuster.

Hamer, D. H., Hu, S., Magnuson, V. L., Hu, N., & Pattatucci, A. M. L. (1993). A linkage between DNA markers on the X chromosome and male sexual orientation. *Science, 261*, 321–327. doi:10.1126/science.8332896

Hassan, B., & Rahman, Q. (2007). Selective sexual-orientation-related differences in object location memory. *Behavioral Neuroscience, 121*, 625–633. doi:10.1037/0735-7044.121.3.625

Hatzenbuehler, M. L. (2011). The social environment and suicide attempts in lesbian, gay, and bisexual youth. *Pediatrics, 127*, 896–903. doi:10.1542/peds.2010-3020

Hatzenbuehler, M. L., McLaughlin, K. A., Keyes, K. M., & Hasin, D. S. (2010). The impact of institutional discrimination on psychiatric disorders in lesbian, gay, and bisexual populations: A prospective study. *American Journal of Public Health, 100*, 452–459. doi:10.2105/AJPH.2009.168815

Hatzenbuehler, M. L., Wieringa, N. F., & Keyes, K. M. (2011). Community-level determinants of tobacco use disparities in lesbian, gay, and bisexual youth: Results from a population-based study. *Archives of Pediatrics and Adolescent Medicine, 165*, 527–532. doi:10.1001/archpediatrics.2011.64

Hayes, J., Chakraborty, A. T., McManus, S., Bebbington, P., Brugha, T., Nicholson, S., & King, M. (2012). Prevalence of same-sex behavior and orientation in England: Results from a national survey. *Archives of Sexual Behavior, 41*, 631–639. doi:10.1007/s10508-011-9856-8

Helleday, J., Edman, G., Ritzén, E. M., & Siwers, B. (1993). Personality characteristics and platelet MAO activity in women with congenital adrenal hyperplasia (CAH). *Psychoneuroendocrinology, 18*, 343–354. doi:10.1016/0306-4530(93)90010-I

Herek, G. M., Gillis, J. R., Cogan, J. C., & Glunt, E. K. (1997). Hate crime victimization among lesbian, gay, and bisexual adults: Prevalence, psychological correlates, and methodological issues. *Journal of Interpersonal Violence, 12*, 195–215. doi:10.1177/088626097012002003

Hershberger, S. L., & Bogaert, A. F. (2005). Male and female sexual orientation differences in gambling. *Personality and Individual Differences, 38*, 1401–1411. doi:10.1016/j.paid.2004.09.002

Hightow, L. B., Leone, P. A., MacDonald, P. D. M., McCoy, S. I., Sampson, L. A., & Kaplan, A. H. (2006). Men who have sex with men and women: A unique risk group for HIV transmission on North Carolina college campuses. *Sexually Transmitted Diseases, 33*, 585–593. doi:10.1097/01.olq.0000216031.93089.68

Hines, M. (2011). Prenatal endocrine influences on sexual orientation and on sexually differentiated childhood behavior. *Frontiers in Neuroendocrinology, 32*, 170–182. doi:10.1016/j.yfrne.2011.02.006

Hines, M., Brook, C., & Conway, G. S. (2004). Androgen and psychosexual development: Core gender identity, sexual orientation, and recalled childhood gender role behavior in women and men with congenital adrenal hyperplasia (CAH). *Journal of Sex Research, 41*, 75–81. doi:10.1080/00224490409552215

Hiraishi, K., Sasaki, S., Shikishima, C., & Ando, J. (2012). The second to fourth digit ratio (2D:4D) in a Japanese twin sample: Heritability, prenatal hormone transfer, and association with sexual orientation. *Archives of Sexual Behavior, 41*, 711–724. doi:10.1007/s10508-011-9889-z

Hoffmann, H. (2012). Considering the role of conditioning in sexual orientation. *Archives of Sexual Behavior, 41*, 63–71. doi:10.1007/s10508-012-9915-9

Hoover, R. N., Hyer, M., Pfeiffer, R. M., Adam, E., Bond, B., Cheville, A. L., . . . Troisi, R. (2011). Adverse health outcomes in women exposed in utero to diethylstilbestrol. *New England Journal of Medicine, 365*, 1304–1314. doi:10.1056/NEJMoa1013961

Hu, S., Pattatucci, A. M. L., Patterson, C., Li, L., Fulker, D. W., Cherny, S. S., . . . Hamer, D. H. (1995). Linkage between sexual orientation and chromosome Xq28 in males but not in females. *Nature Genetics, 11*, 248–256. doi:10.1038/ng1195-248

Hughes, T., McCabe, S. E., Wilsnack, S. C., West, B. T., & Boyd, C. J. (2010). Victimization and substance use disorders in a national sample of heterosexual and sexual minority women and men. *Addiction, 105*, 2130–2140. doi:10.1111/j.1360-0443.2010.03088.x

Hutchinson, G. E. (1959). A speculative consideration of certain possible forms of sexual selection in man. *American Naturalist, 93*, 81–91. doi:10.1086/282059

Hyde, J. S., Mezulis, A. H., & Abramson, L. Y. (2008). The ABCs of depression: Integrating affective, behavioral, and cognitive models to explain the emergence of the gender difference in depression. *Psychological Review, 115*, 291–313. doi:10.1037/0033-295X.115.2.291

Iemmola, F., & Camperio Ciani, A. (2009). New evidence of genetic factors influencing sexual orientation in men: Female fecundity increase in the maternal line. *Archives of Sexual Behavior, 38*, 393–399. doi:10.1007/s10508-008-9381-6

Jeffries, W. L., IV. (2011). The number of recent sex partners among bisexual men in the United States. *Perspectives on Sexual and Reproductive Health, 43*, 151–157. doi:10.1363/4315111

Johnson, A. M., Wadsworth, J., Wellings, K., & Field, J. (1994). *Sexual attitudes and lifestyles*. London, England: Blackwell Scientific.

Jun, H.-J., Corliss, H. L., Nichols, L. P., Pazaris, M. J., Spiegelman, D., & Austin, S. B. (2012). Adult body mass index trajectories and sexual orientation: The Nurses' Health Study II. *American Journal of Preventive Medicine, 42*, 348–354. doi:10.1016/j.amepre.2011.11.011

Kapsalis, E., & Johnson, R. L. (2006). Getting to know you: Female-female consortships in free-ranging rhesus monkeys. In V. Sommer & P. L. Vasey (Eds.), *Homosexual behaviour in animals: An evolutionary perspective* (pp. 220–237). New York, NY: Cambridge University Press.

Katz-Wise, S. L., & Hyde, J. S. (2012). Victimization experiences of lesbian, gay, and bisexual individuals: A meta-analysis. *Journal of Sex Research, 49*, 142–167. doi:10.1080/00224499.2011.637247

Kendler, K. S., Thornton, L. M., Gilman, S. E., & Kessler, R. C. (2000). Sexual orientation in a U.S. national sample of twin and nontwin sibling pairs. *American Journal of Psychiatry, 157*, 1843–1846. doi:10.1176/appi.ajp.157.11.1843

Kernberg, O. F. (1995). *Love relations: Normality and pathology*. New Haven, CT: Yale University Press.

Kimura, D. (1999). *Sex and cognition*. Cambridge, MA: MIT Press.

King, M., Semlyesn, J., Tai, S. S., Killaspy, H., Osborn, D., Popelyuk, D., & Nazareth, I. (2008). A systematic review of mental disorder, suicide, and deliberate self harm in lesbian, gay, and bisexual people. *BMC Psychiatry, 8*, 70–86. doi:10.1186/1471-244X-8-70

Kinnish, K. K., Strassberg, D. S., & Turner, C. W. (2005). Sex differences in the flexibility of sexual orientation: A multidimensional retrospective assessment. *Archives of Sexual Behavior, 34*, 173–183. doi:10.1007/s10508-005-1795-9

Kinsella, M. T., & Monk, K. (2009). Impact of maternal stress, depression and anxiety on fetal neurobehavioral development. *Clinical Obstetrics and Gynecology, 52*, 425–440. doi:10.1097/GRF.0b013e3181b52df1

Kinsey, A. C., Pomeroy, W. B., & Martin, C. E. (1948). *Sexual behavior in the human male.* Philadelphia, PA: W. B. Saunders.

Kirkpatrick, R. C. (2000). The evolution of human homosexual behavior. *Current Anthropology, 41*, 385–413. doi:10.1086/300145

Klar, A. J. S. (2003). Human handedness and scalp hair-whorl direction develop from a common genetic mechanism. *Genetics, 165*, 269–276.

Klar, A. J. S. (2004). Excess of counterclockwise scalp hair-whorl rotation in homosexual men. *Journal of Genetics, 83*, 251–255. doi:10.1007/BF02717894

Klein, F., Sepekoff, B., & Wolf, T. J. (1985). Sexual orientation: A multi-variable dynamic process. Journal of Homosexuality. *Journal of Homosexuality, 11*, 35–49. doi:10.1300/J082v11n01_04

Kraemer, B., Noll, T., Delsignore, A., Milos, G., Schnyder, U., & Hepp, U. (2006). Finger length ratio (2D:4D) and dimensions of sexual orientation. *Neuropsychobiology, 53*, 210–214. doi:10.1159/000094730

Lalumière, M. L., Blancharch, R., & Zucker, K. J. (2000). Sexual orientation and handedness in men and women: A meta-analysis. *Psychological Bulletin, 126*, 575–592. doi:10.1037/0033-2909.126.4.575

Långström, N., Rahman, Q., Carlström, E., & Lichtenstein, P. (2010). Genetic and environmental effects on same-sex sexual behavior: A population study of twins in Sweden. *Archives of Sexual Behavior, 39*, 75–80. doi:10.1007/s10508-008-9386-1

Laumann, E. O., Gagnon, J. H., Michael, R. T., & Michaels, S. (1994). *The social organization of sexuality: Sexual practices in the United States.* Chicago, IL: University of Chicago Press.

LeVay, S. (1991). A difference in hypothalamic structure between heterosexual and homosexual men. *Science, 253*, 1034–1037. doi:10.1126/science.1887219

LeVay, S. (2011). *Gay, straight, and the reason why: The science of sexual orientation.* New York, NY: Oxford University Press. doi:10.1007/s11199-011-9997-1

Leveroni, C. L., & Berenbaum, S. A. (1998). Early androgen effects on interest in infants: Evidence from children with congenital adrenal hyperplasia. *Developmental Neuropsychology, 14*, 321–340. doi:10.1080/87565649809540714

Lippa, R. A. (2002). Gender-related traits of heterosexual and homosexual men and women. *Archives of Sexual Behavior, 31*, 83–98. doi:10.1023/A:1014035302843

Lippa, R. A. (2003). Are 2D:4D finger-length ratios related to sexual orientation? Yes for men, no for women. *Journal of Personality and Social Psychology, 85*, 179–188. doi:10.1037/0022-3514.85.1.179

Lippa, R. A. (2005). Sexual orientation and personality. *Annual Review of Sex Research, 16*, 119–153.

Lippa, R. A. (2008a). The relation between childhood gender nonconformity and adult masculinity-femininity and anxiety in heterosexual and homosexual men and women. *Sex Roles, 59*, 684–693. doi:10.1007/s11199-008-9476-5

Lippa, R. A. (2008b). Sex differences and sexual orientation differences in personality: Findings from the BBC Internet survey. *Archives of Sexual Behavior, 37*, 173–187. doi:10.1007/s10508-007-9267-z

Lippa, R. A., & Tan, F. D. (2001). Does culture moderate the relationship between sexual orientation and gender-related personality traits? *Cross-Cultural Research, 35*, 65–87. doi:10.1177/106939710103500104

Loehlin, J. C., & McFadden, D. (2003). Otoacoustic emissions, auditory evoked potentials, and traits related to sex and sexual orientation. *Archives of Sexual Behavior, 32*, 115–127. doi:10.1023/A:1022496207882

Lutchmaya, S., Baron-Cohen, S., Raggatt, P., Knickmeyer, R., & Manning, J. T. (2004). 2nd to 4th digit ratios, fetal testosterone and estradiol. *Early Human Development, 77*, 23–28. doi:10.1016/j.earlhumdev.2003.12.002

Macke, J. P., Hu, N., Hu, S., Bailey, M., King, V. L., Brown, T., . . . Nathans, J. (1993). Sequence variation in the androgen receptor gene is not a common determinant of male sexual orientation. *American Journal of Human Genetics, 53*, 844–852.

MacNiven, E. (1994). Increased prevalence of left-handedness in victims of head trauma. *Brain Injury, 8*, 457–462. doi:10.3109/02699059409150997

Manning, J. T. (2011). Resolving the role of prenatal sex steroids in the development of digit ratio. *Proceedings of the National Academy of Sciences of the United States of America, 108*, 16143–16144. doi:10.1073/pnas.1113312108

Manning, J. T., Bundred, P. E., Newton, D. J., & Flanagan, B. F. (2003). The 2nd to 4th digit ratio and variation in the androgen receptor gene. *Evolution and Human Behavior, 24*, 399–405. doi:10.1016/S1090-5138(03)00052-7

Manning, J. T., Churchill, A. J. G., & Peters, M. (2007). The effects of sex, ethnicity, and sexual orientation on self-measured digit ratio (2D:4D). *Archives of Sexual Behavior, 36*, 223–233. doi:10.1007/s10508-007-9171-6

Marshal, M. P., Dietz, L. J., Friedman, M. S., Stall, R., Smith, H. A., McGinley, J., . . . Brent, D. A. (2011). Suicidality and depression disparities between sexual minority and heterosexual youth: A meta-analytic review. *Journal of Adolescent Health, 49*, 115–123. doi:10.1016/j.jadohealth.2011.02.005

Marshal, M. P., Friedman, M. S., Stall, R., King, K. M., Miles, J., Gold, M. A., . . . Morse, J. Q. (2008). Sexual orientation and adolescent substance use: A meta-analysis and methodological review. *Addiction, 103*, 546–556. doi:10.1111/j.1360-0443.2008.02149.x

Martin, J. T., & Nguyen, D. H. (2004). Anthropometric analysis of homosexuals and heterosexuals: Implications for hormone exposure. *Hormones and Behavior, 45*, 31–39. doi:10.1016/j.yhbeh.2003.07.003

McCarthy, M. M., & Arnold, A. P. (2008). Sex differences in the brain: What's old and what's new. In J. B. Becker, K. J. Berkley, N. Geary, E. Hampson, J. P. Herman, & E. A. Young (Eds.), *Sex differences in the brain: From genes to behavior* (pp. 15–33). New York, NY: Oxford University Press.

McConaghy, N., Hadzi-Pavlovic, D., Stevens, C., Manicavasagar, V., Buhrich, N., & Vollmer-Conna, U. (2006). Fraternal birth order and ratio of heterosexual/homosexual feelings in women and men. *Journal of Homosexuality, 51*, 161–174. doi:10.1300/J082v51n04_09

McCormick, C. M., Witelson, S. F., & Kingstone, E. (1990). Left-handedness in homosexual men and women: Neuroendocrine implications. *Psychoneuroendocrinology, 15*, 69–76. doi:10.1016/0306-4530(90)90048-E

McFadden, D. (2002). Masculinization effects in the auditory system. *Archives of Sexual Behavior, 31*, 99–111. doi:10.1023/A:1014087319682

McFadden, D., Loehlin, J. C., Breedlove, S. M., Lippa, R. A., Manning, J. T., & Rahman, Q. (2005). A reanalysis of five studies on sexual orientation and the relative length of the 2nd and 4th fingers (the 2D:4D ratio). *Archives of Sexual Behavior, 34*, 341–356. doi:10.1007/s10508-005-3123-9

McFadden, D., & Shubel, E. (2002). Relative lengths of fingers and toes in human males and females. *Hormones and Behavior, 42*, 492–500. doi:10.1006/hbeh.2002.1833

McFadden, D., & Shubel, E. (2003). The relationship between otoacoustic emissions and relative lengths of fingers and toes in humans. *Hormones and Behavior, 43*, 421–429. doi:10.1016/S0018-506X(03)00014-X

Medland, S. E., Loehlin, J. C., & Martin, N. G. (2008). No effects of prenatal hormone transfer on digit ratio in a large sample of same- and opposite-sex dizygotic twins. *Personality and Individual Differences, 44*, 1225–1234. doi:10.1016/j.paid.2007.11.017

Mercer, C. H., Hart, G. J., Johnson, A. M., & Cassell, J. A. (2009). Behaviourally bisexual men as a bridge population for HIV and sexually transmitted infections? Evidence from a national probability survey. *International Journal of STD and AIDS, 20*, 87–94. doi:10.1258/ijsa.2008.008215

Meyer, I. H. (2003). Prejudice, social stress, and mental health in lesbian, gay, and bisexual populations: Conceptual issues and research evidence. *Psychological Bulletin, 129*, 674–697. doi:10.1037/0033-2909.129.5.674

Meyer-Bahlburg, H. F. L., Dolezal, C., Baker, S. W., Carlson, A. D., Obeid, J. S., & New, M. I. (2004). Prenatal adrogenization affects gender-related behavior but not gender identity in 5–12-year-old girls with congenital adrenal hyperplasia. *Archives of Sexual Behavior, 33*, 97–104. doi:10.1023/B:ASEB.0000014324.25718.51

Meyer-Bahlburg, H. F. L., Dolezal, C., Baker, S. W., & New, M. I. (2008). Sexual orientation in women with classical or non-classical congenital adrenal hyperplasia as a function of degree of prenatal androgen excess. *Archives of Sexual Behavior, 37*, 85–99. doi:10.1007/s10508-007-9265-1

Meyer-Bahlburg, H. F. L., Ehrhardt, A. A., Rosen, L. R., Gruen, R. S., Veridiano, N. P., Vann, F. H., & Neuwalder, H. F. (1995). Prenatal estrogens and the development of homosexual orientation. *Developmental Psychology, 31*, 12–21. doi:10.1037/0012-1649.31.1.12

Meyer-Bahlburg, H. F. L., Ehrhardt, A. A., Whitehead, E. D., & Vann, F. H. (1987). Sexuality in males with a history of prenatal exposure to diethylstilbestrol (DES). In American Cancer Society, *Proceedings of the workshop on psychosexual and reproductive issues affecting patients with cancer* (pp. 79–82). New York, NY: American Cancer Society.

Miller, E. M. (2000). Homosexuality, birth order, and evolution: Toward an equilibrium reproductive economics of homosexuality. *Archives of Sexual Behavior, 29*, 1–34. doi:10.1023/A:1001836320541

Mock, S. E., & Eibach, R. P. (2012). Stability and change in sexual orientation identity over a 10-year period in adulthood. *Archives of Sexual Behavior, 41*, 641–648. doi:10.1007/s10508-011-9761-1

Monk, C., Myers, M. M., Sloan, R. P., Ellman, L. M., & Fifer, W. P. (2003). Effects of women's stress-elicited physiological activity and chronic anxiety on fetal heart rate. *Journal of Developmental and Behavioral Pediatrics, 24*, 32–38. doi:10.1097/00004703-200302000-00008

Muscarella, F. (1999). The homoerotic behavior that never evolved. *Journal of Homosexuality, 37*(3), 1–18. doi:10.1300/J082v37n03_01

Muscarella, F. (2000). The evolution of homoerotic behavior in humans. *Journal of Homosexuality, 40*, 51–77. doi:10.1300/J082v40n01_03

Mustanski, B. S., Bailey, J. M., & Kaspar, S. (2002). Dermatoglyphics, handedness, sex, and sexual orientation. *Archives of Sexual Behavior, 31*, 113–122. doi:10.1023/A:1014039403752

Mustanski, B. S., DuPree, M. G., Nievergelt, C. M., Bocklandt, S., Schork, N. J., & Hamer, D. H. (2005). A genomewide scan of male sexual orientation. *Human Genetics, 116*, 272–278. doi:10.1007/s00439-004-1241-4

Neave, N., Menaged, M., & Weightman, D. R. (1999). Sex differences in cognition: The role of testosterone and sexual orientation. *Brain and Cognition, 41*, 245–262. doi:10.1006/brcg.1999.1125

Needham, B. L. (2012). Sexual attraction and trajectories of mental health and substance use during the transition from adolescence to adulthood. *Journal of Youth and Adolescence, 41*, 179–190. doi:10.1007/s10964-011-9729-4

Ott, M. Q., Corliss, H. L., Wypij, D., Rosario, M., & Austin, S. B. (2011). Stability and change in self-reported sexual orientation identity in young people: Application of mobility metrics. *Archives of Sexual Behavior, 40*, 519–532. doi:10.1007/s10508-010-9691-3

Parish, A. R. (1994). Sex and food control in the 'uncommon chimpanzee': How bonobo females overcome a phylogenetic legacy of male dominance. *Ethology and Sociobiology, 15*, 157–179. doi:10.1016/0162-3095(94)90038-8

Pattatucci, A. M. L., & Hamer, D. H. (1995). Development and familiality of sexual orientation in females. *Behavior Genetics, 25*, 407–420. doi:10.1007/BF02253370

Peters, M., Manning, J. T., & Reimers, S. (2007). The effects of sex, sexual orientation, and digit ratio (2D:4D) on mental rotation performance. *Archives of Sexual Behavior, 36*, 251–260. doi:10.1007/s10508-006-9166-8

Peterson, Z. D., Janssen, E., & Laan, E. (2010). Women's sexual responses to heterosexual and lesbian erotica: The role of stimulus intensity, affective reaction, and sexual history. *Archives of Sexual Behavior, 39*, 880–897. doi:10.1007/s10508-009-9546-y

Phoenix, C. H., Goy, R. W., Gerall, A. A., & Young, W. C. (1959). Organizing action of prenatally administered testosterone propionate on the tissues mediating mating behavior in the female guinea pig. *Endocrinology, 65*, 369–382. doi:10.1210/endo-65-3-369

Physicians' desk reference to pharmaceutical specialties and biologicals (15th ed.). (1961). Oradell, NJ: Medical Economics.

Plato. (1993). *The symposium and the phaedrus: Plato's erotic dialogues.* Albany, NY: State University Press.

Prause, N., & Graham, C. A. (2007). Asexuality: Classification and characterization. *Archives of Sexual Behavior, 36*, 341–356.

Qazi, Q. H., Masakawa, A., McGann, B., & Woods, J. (1980). Dermatologyphic abnormalities in the fetal alcohol syndrome. *Teratology, 21*, 157–160.

Rahman, Q. (2005). Fluctuating asymmetry, second to fourth digit length ratios and human sexual orientation. *Psychoneuroendocrinology, 30*, 382–391.

Rahman, Q., Abrahams, S., & Wilson, G. D. (2003). Sexual-orientation-related differences in verbal fluency. *Neuropsychology, 17*, 240–246.

Rahman, Q., Andersson, D., & Govier, E. (2005). A specific sexual-orientation-related difference in navigational strategy. *Behavioral Neuroscience, 119*, 311–316.

Rahman, Q., Clarke, K., & Morera, T. (2009). Hair whorl direction and sexual orientation in human males. *Behavioral Neuroscience, 123*, 252–256.

Rahman, Q., Collins, A., Morrison, M., Orrells, J. C., Cadinouche, K., Greenfield, S., & Begum, S. (2008). Maternal inheritance and familial fecundity factors in male homosexuality. *Archives of Sexual Behavior, 37*, 962–969.

Rahman, Q., & Hull, M. S. (2005). An empirical test of the kin selection hypothesis for male homosexuality. *Archives of Sexual Behavior, 34*, 461–467.

Rahman, Q., & Koerting, J. (2008). Sexual-orientation-related differences in allocentric spatial memory tasks. *Hippocampus, 18*, 55–63.

Rahman, Q., & Wilson, G. D. (2003a). Large sexual-orientation-related differences in performance on mental rotation and judgment of line orientation tasks. *Neuropsychology, 17*, 25–31.

Rahman, Q., & Wilson, G. D. (2003b). Sexual orientation and the 2nd to 4th finger length ratio: Evidence for organizing effects of sex hormones or developmental instability. *Psychoneuroendocrinology, 28*, 288–303.

Rahman, Q., Wilson, G. D., & Abrahams, S. (2003). Sexual orientation related differences in spatial memory. *Journal of International Neuropsychological Society, 9*, 376–383.

Rahman, Q., & Wilson, G. D., Abrahams, S. (2004a). Biosocial factors, sexual orientation and neurocognitive functioning. *Psychoneuroendocrinology, 29*, 867–881.

Rahman, Q., Wilson, G. D., & Abrahams, S. (2004b). Developmental instability is associated with neurocognitive performance in heterosexual and homosexual men, but not in women. *Behavioral Neuroscience, 118*, 243–247.

Rahman, Q., Wilson, G. D., & Abrahams, S. (2004c). Performance differences between adult heterosexual and homosexual men on the digit-symbol substitution subtest of the WAIS–R. *Journal of Clinical and Experimental Neuropsychology, 26*, 141–148.

Rice, G., Anderson, C., Risch, N., & Ebers, G. (1999). Male homosexuality: Absence of linkage to microsatellite markers at Xq28. *Science, 284*, 665–667.

Rieger, G., Linsenmeier, J. A. W., Gygax, L., & Bailey, J. M. (2008). Sexual orientation and childhood gender nonconformity: Evidence from home videos. *Developmental Psychology, 44*, 46–58.

Rieger, G., & Savin-Williams, R. C. (2012). The eyes have it: Sex and sexual orientation differences in pupil dilation patterns. *PLos One,* 7(8), 1–10.

Roberts, A. L., Austin, S. B., Corliss, H. L., Vandermorris, A. K., & Koenen, K. C. (2010). Pervasive trauma exposure among US sexual orientation minority adults and risk of posttraumatic stress disorder. *American Journal of Public Health, 100*, 2433–2441.

Robinson, S. J., & Manning, J. T. (2000). The ratio of 2nd to 4th digit length and male homosexuality. *Evolution and Human Development, 21*, 333–345.

Rosario, M., Hunter, J., & Gwadz, M. (1997). Exploration of substance use among lesbian, gay, and bisexual youth: Prevalence and correlates. *Journal of Adolescent Research, 12*, 454–476.

Rosario, M., Schrimshaw, E. W., & Hunter, J. (2004). Ethnic/racial differences in the coming-out process of lesbian, gay, and bisexual youths: A comparisons of sexual identity development over time. *Cultural Diversity and Ethnic Minority Psychology, 10*, 215–228.

Rosario, M., Schrimshaw, E. W., & Hunter, J. (2008). Butch/femme differences in substance use and abuse among young lesbian and bisexual women: Examination and potential explanations. *Substance Use and Misuse, 43*, 1002–1015.

Rosario, M., Schrimshaw, E. W., & Hunter, J. (2011). Different patterns of sexual identity development over time: Implications for the psychological adjustment of lesbian, gay, and bisexual youths. *Journal of Sex Research, 48*, 3–15.

Rosario, M., Schrimshaw, E. W., Hunter, J., & Braun, L. (2006). Sexual identity development among lesbian, gay, and bisexual youths: Consistency and change over time. *Journal of Sex Research, 43*, 46–58.

Rosario, M., Schrimshaw, E. W., Hunter, J., & Gwadz, M. (2002). Gay-related stress and emotional distress among gay, lesbian, and bisexual youths: A longitudinal examination. *Journal of Consulting and Clinical Psychology, 70*, 967–975.

Rosario, M., Schrimshaw, E. W., Hunter, J., & Levy-Warren, A. (2009). The coming-out process of young lesbian and bisexual women: Are there butch/femme differences in sexual identity development? *Archives of Sexual Behavior, 38*, 34–49.

Rullo, J. E., Strassberg, D. S., & Isreal, E. (2010). Category-specificity in sexual interest in gay men and lesbians. *Archives of Sexual Behavior, 39*, 874–879.

Russell, S. T., Driscoll, A. K., & Truong, N. (2002). Adolescent same-sex romantic attractions and relationships: Implications for substance use and abuse. *American Journal of Public Health, 92*, 198–202.

Russell, S. T., & Joyner, K. (2001). Adolescent sexual orientation and suicide risk: Evidence from a national study. *American Journal of Public Health, 91*, 1276–1281.

Sanders, G., & Ross-Field, L. (1986). Sexual orientation and visuo-spatial ability. *Brian and Cognition, 5*, 280–290.

Saucier, D. M., Green, S. M., Leason, J., MacFadden, A., Bell, Sc., & Elias, L. J. (2002). Are sex differences in navigation caused by sexually dimorphic strategies or by differences in the ability to use the strategies? *Behavioral Neuroscience, 116*, 403–410.

Savic, I., García-Falgueras, A., & Swaab, D. F. (2010). Sexual differentiation of the human brain in relation to gender identity and sexual orientation. *Progress in Brain Research, 186*, 41–62.

Savin-Williams, R. C., Joyner, K., & Rieger, G. (2012). Prevalence and stability of self-reported sexual orientation identity during young adulthood. *Archives of Sexual Behavior, 41*, 103–110.

Savin-Williams, R. C., & Ream, G. L. (2006). Pubertal onset and sexual orientation in an adolescent national probability sample. *Archives of Sexual Behavior, 35*, 279–286.

Savin-Williams, R. C., & Ream, G. L. (2007). Prevalence and stability of sexual orientation components during adolescence and young adulthood. *Archives of Sexual Behavior, 36*, 385–394.

Schrager, S., & Potter, B. E. (2004). Diethylstilbestrol exposure. *American Family Physician, 69*, 2395–2400.

Schrut, A. (1994). The Oedipus complex: Some observations and question s regarding its validity and universal existence. *Journal of the American Academy of Psychoanalysis, 22*, 727–751.

Schwartz, G., Kim, R. M., Kolundzija, A. B., Rieger, G., & Sanders, A. R. (2010). Biodemographic and physical correlates of sexual orientation in men. *Archives of Sexual Behavior, 39*, 93–109.

Sell, R. L. (1996). The Sell assessment of sexual orientation: Background and scoring. *Journal of Lesbian, Gay and Bisexual Identity, 1*, 295–310.

Sell, R. L. (1997). Defining and measuring sexual orientation. *Archives of Sexual Behavior, 26*, 643–658.

Sherfey, M. J. (1966). The evolution and nature of female sexuality in relation to psychoanalytic theory. *Journal American Psychoanalytic Association, 14*, 28–127.

Shively, M. G., & De Cecco, J. P. (1977). Components of sexual identity. *Journal of Homosexuality, 3*, 41–48.

Smuts, B. B., & Watanabe, J. M. (1990). Social relationships and ritualized greetings in adult male baboons (*papio cynocephalus anubis*). *International Journal of Primatology, 11*, 147–172.

Sommer, V., & Vasey, P. L. (Eds.). (2006). *Homosexual behaviour in animals: An evolutionary perspective* (pp. 3–42). New York, NY: Cambridge University Press.

Spear, L. (2007). The developing brain and adolescent-typical behavior patterns: An evolutionary perspective. In D. Romer & E. F. Walker (Eds.), *Adolescent psychopathology and the developing brain: Integrating brain and prevention science.* (pp. 9–30). New York, NY: Oxford University Press.

Storms, M. D. (1980). Theories of sexual orientation. *Journal of Personality and Social Psychology, 38*, 783–792.

Swaab, D. F., & Fliers, E. (1985). A sexually dimorphic nucleus in the human brain. *Science, 228*, 1112–1115.

Swaab, D. F., Fliers, E., & Partiman, T. S. (1985). The suprachiasmatic nucleus of the human brain in relation to sex, age, and senile dementia. *Brain Research, 342*, 37–44.

Swaab, D. F., Gooren, L. J. G., & Hofman, M. A. (1995). Brain research, gender, and sexual orientation. *Journal of Homosexuality, 28*, 283–301.

Swaab, D. F., & Hofman, M. A. (1988). Sexual differentiation of the human hypothalamus: Ontogeny of the sexually dimorphic nucleus of the preoptic area. *Developmental Brain Research, 44*, 314–318.

Swaab, D. F., & Hofman, M. A. (1990). An enlarged suprchiasmatic nucleus in homosexual men. *Brain Research, 537*, 141–148.

Thompson, E. M., & Morgan, E. M. (2008). "Mostly straight" young women: Variations in sexual behavior and identity development. *Developmental Psychology, 44*, 15–21.

Titus-Ernstoff, L., Perez, K., Hatch, E. E., Troisi, R., Palmer, J. R., . . . Hoover, R. (2003). Psychosexual characteristics of men and women exposed prenatally to diethylstilbestrol. *Epidemiology, 14*, 155–160.

Underwood, L. E., & Van Wyk, J. J. (1992). Normal and aberrant growth. In J. D. Wilson & D. W. Forster (Eds.), *Williams textbook of endocrinology* (8th ed., pp. 1079–1138). Philadelphia, PA: W. B. Suanders.

United Nations High Commissioner for Human Rights. (2011). *Discriminatory laws and practices and acts of violence against individuals based on their sexual orientation and gender identity.* Retrieved from http://www2.ohchr.org/english/bodies/hrcouncil/docs/19session/a.hrc.19.41_english.pdf

Valanis, B. G., Bowen, D. J., Bassford, T., Whitlock, E., Charney, P., & Carter, R. A. (2000). Sexual orientation and health: Comparisons in the Women's Health Initiative sample. *Archives of Family Medicine, 9*, 843–853.

van Anders, S. M., & Hampson, E. (2005). Testing the prenatal androgen hypothesis: Measuring digit ratios, sexual orientation, and spatial abilities in adults. *Hormones and Behavior, 47*, 92–98.

van Anders, S. M., Vernon, P. A., & Wilbur, C. J. (2006). Finger-length ratios show evidence of prenatal hormone-transfer between opposite-sex twins. *Hormones and Behavior, 49*, 315–319.

Vasey, P. L. (2000). Commentary to Kirkpatrick (2000). *Current Anthropology, 41*, 402–403.

Vasey, P. L., & Sommer, V. (2006). Homosexual behaviour in animals: Topics, hypotheses and research trajectories. In V. Sommer & P. L. Vasey (Eds.), *Homosexual behaviour in animals: An evolutionary perspective* (pp. 3–42). New York, NY: Cambridge University Press.

Vasey, P. L., & VanderLaan, D. P. (2012). Sexual orientation in men and avuncularity in Japan: Implications for the kin selection hypothesis. *Archives of Sexual Behavior, 41*, 209–215.

Voracek, M., & Dressler, S. G. (2007). Digit ratio (2D:4D) in twins: Heritability estimates and evidence for a musculinized trait expression in women from opposite-sex pairs. *Psychological Reports, 100*, 115–126.

Voracek, M. Manning, J. T., & Ponocny, I. (2005). Digit ratio (2D:4D) in homosexual and heterosexual men from Austria. *Archives of Sexual Behavior, 34*, 335–340.

Voyer, D., Voyer, S., & Bryden, M. P. (1995). Magnitude of sex differences in spatial abilities: A meta-analysis and consideration of critical variables. *Psychological Bulletin, 117*, 250–270.

Vrangalova, Z., & Savin-Williams, R. C. (2012). Mostly heterosexual and mostly gay/lesbian: Evidence for new sexual orientation identities. *Archives of Sexual Behavior, 41*, 85–101.

Wegesin, D. J. (1998). A neuropsychologic profile of homosexual and heterosexual men and women. *Archives of Sexual Behavior, 27*, 91–108.

Wells, J. E., McGee, M. A., & Beautrais, A. L. (2011). Multiple aspects of sexual orientation: Prevalence and sociodemographic correlates in a New Zealand national survey. *Archives of Sexual Behavior, 40*, 155–168.

Werner, E. A., Myers, M. M., Fifer, W. P., Cheng, B., Fang, Y., Allen, R., & Monk, C. (2007). Prenatal predictors of infant temperament. *Developmental Psychobiology, 49*, 474–484.

Whitam, F. L., Diamond, M., & Martin, J. (1993). Homosexual orientation in twins: A report on 61 pairs and three triplet sets. *Archives of Sexual Behavior, 22*, 187–206.

Williams, T. J., Pepitone, M. E., Christensen, S. E., Cooke, B. M., Huberman, A. D., . . . Breedlove, S. M. (2000). Finger-length ratios and sexual orientation. *Nature, 404*, 455–456.

Wilson, E. O. (1975). *Sociobiology: The new synthesis.* Cambridge, MA: Belknap.

Wilson, E. O. (1978). *On human nature.* Cambridge, MA: Harvard University Press.

Worthington, R. L., & Reynolds, A. L. (2009). Within-group differences in sexual orientation and identity. *Journal of Counseling Psychology, 56*, 44–55.

Wright, H. T., Parker, C. E., & Mavalwala, J. (1972). Unusual dermatoglyphic findings associated with Tomegliac Inclusion Disease in infancy. *California Medicine, 116*, 14–20.

Yamagiwa, J. (2006). Playful encounters: The development of homosexual behaviour in male mountain gorillas. In V. Sommer & P. L. Vasey (Eds.), *Homosexual behaviour in animals: An evolutionary perspective* (pp. 273–293). New York, NY: Cambridge University Press.

Zheng, Z., & Cohn, M. J. (2011). Developmental basis of the new sexually dimorphic digit ratio. *Proceedings of the National Academy of Sciences, 108*, 16289–16294.

Zietsch, B. P., Verweij, K. J. H., Bailey, J. M., Wright, M. J., & Martin, N. G. (2011). Sexual orientation and psychiatric vulnerability: A twin study of neuroticism and psychoticism. *Archives of Sexual Behavior, 40*, 133–142.

Zucker, K. J. (2008). Reflections on the relation between sex-typed behavior in childhood and sexual orientation in adulthood. *Journal of Gay and Lesbian Mental Health, 12*, 29–59.

Zucker, K. J., Bradley, S. J., Oliver, G., Blake, J., Fleming, S., & Hood, J. (1996). Psychosexual development of women with congenital adrenal hyperplasia. *Hormones and Behavior, 30*, 300–318.

CHAPTER 19

DEVELOPMENT OF SEXUAL ORIENTATION AND IDENTITY

Brian Mustanski, Laura Kuper, and George J. Greene

Understanding the development of both sexual orientation and identity requires an appreciation of the complexity of these two constructs and the challenges in their scientific study. As with the scientific study of many phenomena, sexual orientation is a construct that has become more difficult to define as it has become better studied (see Chapter 18, this volume). The evolution of research on sexual orientation has led to more recent appreciation of the fact that it may be a strikingly different phenomenon in men and women and that models developed on the basis of the study of men may not fit the phenomena in women. The relatively recent inclusion of adolescents in research on sexual orientation has begun to increase appreciation for the intersection of developmental processes within sociotemporal settings and the complexity of disentangling the two (see Chapter 15, this volume). Within the developmental framework, the study of fluidity and stability recently has come to the foreground. These exciting scientific developments have called into question old assumptions and have highlighted the need to apply new methods. This chapter places these developments into context by describing the history of research on sexual orientation, defining the construct and how it is measured, reviewing studies of its etiology and development, integrating theory and empirical findings, and ending with some recommendations for future research directions.

HISTORICAL BACKGROUND OF SEXUAL ORIENTATION RESEARCH

Although a thorough review of the history of research on sexual orientation and identity development is beyond the scope of this chapter, a few influential events will be reviewed as they provide an important backdrop for contextualizing the subsequent sections (for a more comprehensive review, see Institute of Medicine, 2011). Over time, a complex and dynamic interplay among social, cultural, and political forces have unfolded to influence both the experiences of individuals who are now considered lesbian, gay, and bisexual (LGB) as well as the research and clinical perspectives on these populations (Bleys, 1996). Accounts of individuals participating in same-sex sexual acts or romantic partnerships and experiencing what historians have inferred were same-sex attractions have been documented across a wide range of cultures and historical periods (Blackwood, 1986; see Chapter 3, this volume).

The birth of the modern field of same-sex sexuality research typically is traced back to the late 1800s, at which point researchers developed an interest in classifying forms of "sexual deviance." Within this early work, individuals who experienced same-sex attractions were viewed through an inversion model. When early work was largely unable to differentiate homosexuals on the basis of immediate physical

During the writing of this chapter Dr. Mustanski was supported by a Scholars Award from the William T. Grant Foundation on the sexual health of LGBT youth. Drs. Mustanski and Greene were supported by grants from the National Institutes of Health (NIH) for research on the health of young gay and bisexual men (R21MH095413, R01DA025548). The views expressed in this chapter are those of the authors and not necessarily those of the William T. Grant Foundation or the NIH.

http://dx.doi.org/10.1037/14193-019
APA Handbook of Sexuality and Psychology: Vol. 1. Person-Based Approaches, D. L. Tolman and L. M. Diamond (Editors-in-Chief)

features, individuals experiencing same-sex attraction were reconceptualized as possessing a cross-sex "essence" and often were referred to as third or intermediate sex (Doan & Bland, 1998; Hirschfeld, 2000; Ulrichs, 1994). Although such initial frameworks were limited, scholars have argued that the birth of this field established sexual orientation as a fundamental aspect of one's identity and facilitated the gradual emergence of social and political organizing over the ensuing decades. It was not until the work of Freud (1905/1953), however, that the sex of the individual to whom one is attracted became the defining characteristic of one's sexual orientation. Previously, gender role, gender expression, and sexual role (e.g., "passive" vs. "active" partner) were conflated into a single dimension. Around this time, the unique experiences of those whose felt gender identity conflicted with that associated with their birth sex increasingly was recognized as transsexual (and later as part of a larger transgender spectrum; see Chapter 24 this volume). The work of sex researcher Alfred Kinsey and colleagues (Kinsey, Pomeroy, & Martin, 1948; Kinsey, Pomeroy, Martin, & Gebhard, 1953) was particularly influential as the first large-scale study demonstrating that same-sex attractions and behavior are relatively common variations in sexuality and best represented dimensionally (e.g., the Kinsey scale ranged from 0 to 6, with 0 indicating exclusive heterosexuality and 6 indicating exclusive homosexuality).

Despite the dissenting perspectives of several researchers (e.g., H. Ellis & Symonds, 1897; Ulrichs, 1994), homosexuality primarily was seen as a form of mental illness for much of the twentieth century, and same-sex behavior was largely illegal. Inclusion of homosexuality as a personality disturbance in the first edition of the *Diagnostic and Statistical Manual for Mental Disorders* (American Psychiatric Association, 1952) further supported the discriminatory practices of many employers as well as the largely ineffective attempts of physicians and psychologists to cure homosexuality (e.g., through castration, electroshock treatment, aversive conditioning; Chauncey, 1993). Nearly 20 years later, with the rise of the gay rights movement (Armstrong & Crage, 2006; D'Emilio, 1983) and influenced by the groundbreaking research of Hooker (1957), which failed to find differences among heterosexual and homosexual men in psychological adjustment or psychopathology, the American Psychiatric Association removed homosexuality from the second edition of the *Diagnostic and Statistical Manual for Mental Disorders* (American Psychiatric Association, 1974). In their review of psychological perspectives on LGB populations, Hammack, Mayers, and Windell (2011) cited the mid-1970s as a major shift in the field from a "sickness" toward "species" script. They associate this "species" script with the development of several new lines of research centered on understanding the unique experiences and adjustment of same-sex–attracted individuals within the context of widespread social prejudice. Since then, the American Psychological Association (APA; 2009) also has released a position statement that describes same-sex attractions, behavior, and partnerships as normal variations in human sexuality, and explicitly condemns the use of therapeutic techniques aimed at changing an individual's sexual orientation.

Beginning in the 1980s, the disproportional impact of HIV/AIDS on gay and bisexual men represented another critical period of lesbian, gay, bisexual, transgender (LGBT) history. The onset of this epidemic cut short the lives of many men, permanently altering social networks and traumatizing noninfected LGBT individuals who often served as primary caretakers in the face of unsupportive families (Levine, Nardi, & Gagnon, 1997). The ensuing decades also witnessed the development of an organizational infrastructure aimed at providing social support, treatment, and prevention-oriented services to LGBT communities (Epstein, 1996). Relationships between LGBT communities, health providers, and researchers were forged, leading to the development of treatments significantly lengthening the life expectancy of HIV-positive individuals. Despite these efforts, men who have sex with men (MSM), particularly those of color and those in younger age-groups, continue to remain at much greater risk for contracting HIV/AIDS than the general public (Centers for Disease Control and Prevention, 2010). Combating these disparities has remained a central focus of research within the fields of psychology and public health (see Chapter 22, this volume), as has addressing physical and mental health disparities more generally (Institute of Medicine, 2011).

From the 1990s to the present, many LGBT activist groups have focused attention on legal reform efforts, typically surrounding hate crime legislation, legalization of same-sex marriage, and inclusion in the military (see Volume 2, Chapter 10, this handbook). For example, a handful of states have passed laws legalizing same-sex marriage and an additional handful have enacted laws providing similar or more limited rights through civil unions. In 1996, just before the start of these efforts, the U.S. Congress passed the Defense of Marriage Act that defined marriage as a union of one man and one woman. Subsequently, more than half of all states reacted to this movement by enacting laws or constitutional provisions that defines marriage similarly. Despite these laws, social views toward LGB individuals have shifted significantly, particularly within the past decade. Results from a 2011 Gallup poll, which conducts phone interviews with a randomly selected, representative sample of U.S. adults, indicated that support for same-sex marriage is at an all-time high of 53% (Newport, 2011). This figure was significantly higher for those identifying as a Democrat or Liberal and for those within the youngest age bracket (18 to 34 years).

This focus, however, has remained controversial within LGBT communities. Legal scholars in particular have raised concerns over the effectiveness of this almost-exclusive reliance on a legal rights framework, particularly in its ability to effect change for those who are multiply oppressed. Within the field of psychology, Hammack et al. (2011) noted another major shift beginning in the 1990s that is actively recasting sexual desire away from a "species" script and toward a "subject" script. Similar to the political and legal reform efforts focused on identity-based organizing, they argue that the field of psychology generally has reified rather than challenged the dominant socially constructed categories of sexual difference by implicitly or explicitly assuming that such categories are largely fixed and ahistorical. As influenced by queer theory, however, this move toward a "subject" script has begun to challenge the ontological reality and stability of such categories and more fully contextualized the experience of sexual minorities through consideration of social, cultural, and historical factors. This tension is visible throughout this chapter, and readers should keep in mind this historical background as they consider the current state and future directions of the field (see Chapter 1, this volume).

DEFINING SEXUAL ORIENTATION AND IDENTITY

In defining the constructs of sexual orientation and identity, it is useful then to apply the fundamental concept of a nomological network, proposed by Cronbach and Meehl (1955) as a means to establish construct validity. This approach is critical when defining a theoretical construct that cannot be measured directly and precisely. A nomological network is a representation of the concepts of interest, their observable manifestations and measurement operationalization, and theoretical propositions specifying interrelationships among and between them. Beliefs about the core elements of the nomological network of sexual orientation and their interrelationships vary among researchers. Although myriad components of sexual orientation have been proposed, most frequently included and studied are sexual attractions, identity labels, and sexual behavior. Less frequently, but sometime included, are components of social and lifestyle preferences (Klein, Sepekoff, & Wolf, 1985). More recently, components of romance and affection have been included (Diamond, 2003c, 2005a). Approaches to assess these components of sexual orientation have continued to evolve as newer measurement technologies, such as neuroimaging, psychophysiology, and implicit associations, have been applied to the study of sexual orientation (see Chapter 5, this volume). According to Cronbach and Meehl (1955), learning more about a theoretical construct is a matter of "elaborating the nomological network in which it occurs, or of increasing the definiteness of the components" (p. 290). Early in the study of this construct, the network will be limited with few connections, but as research comes to support or refute elements of the network, the nomological network will come into greater clarity. In the case of sexual orientation, this requires greater specification of the core components and how they are interrelated and measured (see Chapter 4, this volume).

A Nomological Network for Sexual Orientation

Figure 19.1 illustrates a simple nomological network for sexual orientation, with core components of self-identification, sexual behavior, romantic attraction, and sexual attractions. The first three of these components are measured through self-report. Self-identification is assessed by asking questions like, "Do you identify as heterosexual, gay, lesbian, or bisexual?" and corresponds to socially constructed identity categories that continue to evolve. Sexual behavior aspects of sexual orientation can be assessed by asking questions like, "Do you have sex with men, women, or both?" and can be measured with units such as the number or percentage of same-sex partners. Romantic orientation might be assessed by asking, "Who do you fall in love with?" or "Who would you want to be in a romantic relationship with?" and could be measured with units such as the number of percentage of past same-sex partners or a Likert scale of romantic attractions to men versus women or two Likert scales—one for men and one for women. Sexual attractions essentially index the gender that produces sexual arousal, which includes physiological, affective, and cognitive components (Janssen, Everaerd, Spiering, & Janssen, 2000). It can be measured with self-report, but also through genital arousal patterns (Chivers, Seto, Lalumiere, Laan, & Grimbos, 2010) and possibly through patterns of brain activation measured by neuroimaging (Stoleru & Mouras, 2007), by viewing time of erotic images, and through implicit association measures (Mustanski, Chivers, & Bailey, 2002; see Chapters 8 and 9, this volume).

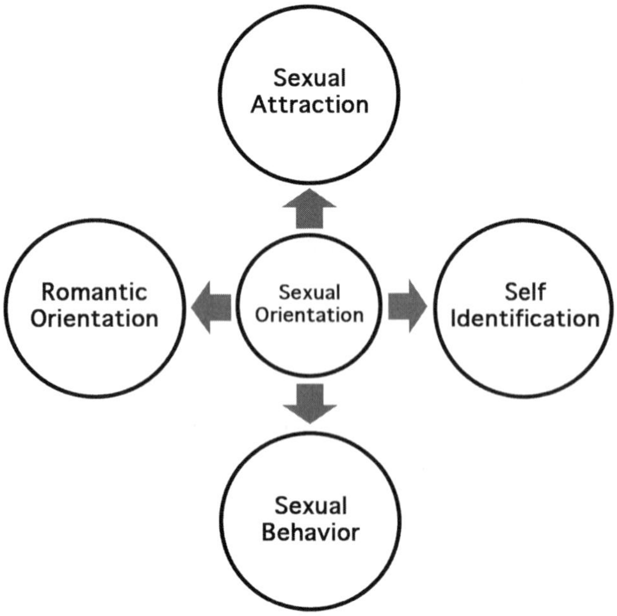

FIGURE 19.1. Nomological network of sexual orientation.

The relationships between constructs within the nomological network currently are not well defined and likely vary in men and women. Some have argued that male sexual orientation operates as a stable "compass" reliably directed by sexual arousal toward one gender or the other (Bailey, 2009). In this model, the components fall in line with sexual attractions at the top of the hierarchy for men, with sexual behavior stemming from these attractions, and finally self-identification as a product of labeling behaviors and attractions. The relevance of romantic orientation rarely is discussed for men. Women's sexual orientation has been characterized by discrepancies among these components; for example, in some women, attractions may be present for both men and women, sexual behavior might only be with men, romantic attractions may be toward women, and no labels are adopted. Women's sexual orientation has also been described as "fluid" across the life course (Diamond, 2012), meaning that the patterns may change and evolve across development (see Chapter 13, this volume). In this conceptualization, one component does not dominate in defining sexual orientation, but rather they each are relatively independent dimensions that must be considered in terms of their stability and change over time. In considering this model, we highlight that these are group-level trends, and many women are highly stable and consistently same sex or opposite sex in the dimensions of their orientation and men also experience their orientation as fluid. Some individuals do not experience their potential partners' gender as an important component of their sexual attraction.

Sexual Orientation, Bisexuality, and Gender Identity

The issues of variability and fluidity in sexual orientation highlight additional areas of complexity: distinctions between bisexuality and homosexuality. In their groundbreaking study on the topic, Weinberg, Williams, and Pryor (1994) described bisexuality as a nonexclusive preference for one sex over the other and noted that this may manifest as concurrent attractions to both sexes or variation over time as individuals move into and out of different environments and relationships. As described by Diamond (2012), oscillations between same-sex and other-sex desires would appear to be more common among individuals who consistently are attracted to both men and women, whereas less substantial oscillation may be characteristic of exclusively gay, exclusively lesbian, or heterosexual individuals.

There is also complexity in the relationship between the development of sexual orientation and gender identity. Gender identity refers to a person's basic sense of being male, female, or of indeterminate sex, and individuals who transcend or cross norms for their biological sex are identified as transgender or gender variant (APA, Task Force on Gender Identity and Gender Variance, 2009). Transgender people may have any sexual orientation—not just gay as sometimes is assumed—and to varying degrees, they experience their gender identity and their sexual orientation as distinct phenomena (Bockting, Benner, & Coleman, 2009; Kuper, Nussbaum, & Mustanski, 2011; see also Chapter 24, this volume).

MEASUREMENT OF SEXUAL ORIENTATION

As highlighted by the Institute of Medicine (2011), the operationalization and measurement of sexual orientation is an important challenge facing scholars in the field. Definitions of sexual orientation and theoretical frameworks for understanding sexual orientation abound in the literature. As such, there are a commensurate number of methods to operationalize the construct, ranging from single-item measures to multidimensional scales and physiologic assessments.[1] Studies vary in which components of sexual orientation are measured and often differ in operational definitions of these dimensions.

Single-Item Measures

Single-item measures of sexual orientation are common in large, population-based studies in which item inclusion comes at a premium. These scales tend to assess sexual orientation identity, but they may vary depending on the context of the study and the study's research goals. To illustrate, in health disparities research, the construct of identity is often more appropriate than other dimensions of sexual orientation because it identifies an individual's location in relationship to disparity groups. Although the design and construction of these types of scales seem straightforward, they often are rife with challenges and often lead to missing data and misclassification of sexual identity because of the salience and fluidity of sexual identity of some groups over others. To address these challenges, and to improve the estimates of the LGB population, researchers developed and evaluated a sexual identity question for the National Health Interview Survey (NHIS; Miller & Ryan, 2011). Rigorous testing involved 386 in-depth cognitive interviews as well as analysis of data from the 2002 and 2006 National Survey of Family Growth. For administration with women, for example, the NHIS first asks if they think of themselves as Lesbian or Gay, Straight (not lesbian or gay), Bisexual, Something else, or Don't know. For those who select the latter two options, separate follow-up questions aim to clarify item comprehension, response error, use of alternate labels, and transgender identity among other variables. The survey also provides an open-ended option for unique responses to the identity question (for a full description of scale development and sample items, see Miller & Ryan, 2011).

Multiple-Item Measures

In a review of sexual orientation measures, Sell (2007) outlined measurement tools, including the Kinsey Scale (Kinsey et al., 1948), Klein Scale (Klein et al., 1985), Shively and de Cecco Scale (Shively & de Cecco, 1977), Sell Assessment (Sell, 1996), and Friedman Measure of Adolescent Sexual Orientation (Friedman et al., 2004). The most frequently used among these is the Kinsey Scale (Kinsey et al., 1948)—a bipolar scale that assesses sexual orientation on a continuum between "exclusive heterosexuality" and "exclusive homosexuality." Across

[1]Reviews of other methods of sexual orientation assessment such as cognitive measures, phallomentric assessment of gender preference, and vaginometry are beyond the scope of this review.

single- and multi-item measurement tools, fundamental challenges are associated with measuring sexual orientation: confounding psychological and behavioral components of sexual orientation, assessing homosexuality and heterosexuality on a single continuum, determining the relative importance of both homosexual and heterosexual dimensions of sexual orientation, increasing respondent burden and decreasing practicality in measuring multiple dimensions of sexual orientation, inadequately examining validity and reliability, and having limited ability to assess variance in sexual orientation over time and among diverse groups.

In theory, assessing multiple variables should capture sexual orientation more accurately. As such, researchers have suggested the use of multiple methods to measure sexual orientation. For example, analysis of data from the 2002 National Survey of Family Growth (n = 6,356) revealed discordant health outcomes for women according to their classification on the basis of sexual orientation identity, attraction, and sex of sex partners (Bauer & Jairam, 2008). The researchers recommended collecting information for both sexual orientation identity and behavior to avoid having to use one measure as a proxy for the other (Bauer & Jairam, 2008). Despite efforts to assess sexual orientation as a multidimensional construct, no single measure is recommended for use across studies. Questions concerning sexual attraction, sexual behavior, and sexual orientation identity are not equally important in all studies and must be considered in the context of the study. For example, sexual behavior may be more important for studies of sexually transmitted infections because it is behaviors—not identity—that lead to infection. Ideally, which combination of these dimensions is used in research is informed by a particular study's research goals. With the general lack of agreement on the definition of sexual orientation, there is a parallel lack of consensus on the methods to operationalize the construct. The absence of standardized measures contributes to the variability of population estimates and can make comparisons across studies difficult, particularly for efforts to enumerate LGBT populations and assess their health. For recommendations on tools to assess dimensions of sexual orientation, an online, open-access clearinghouse for sexual orientation identity data and measures is available at http://www.gaydata.org.

BIOLOGICAL PROCESSES IN THE DEVELOPMENT OF SEXUAL ORIENTATION

When considering the evidence of biological processes in the development of sexual orientation, the term *biological* frequently is misunderstood and misused. To be clear, all human behaviors are enacted by the brain and thus in some sense are biological (see Chapter 7, this volume). Similarly, much of the interest in the biological basis of sexual orientation stems from desire to prove one side of a false dichotomy between nature and nurture. Rather than asking if sexual orientation is biological, it is more fruitful to consider how differences in sexual orientation may emanate from differences in biological processes (Mustanski & Bailey, 2003). In the past two decades, a number of reviews have been published on the role of biological processes in the development of sexual orientation (Mustanski et al., 2002; Rahman & Wilson, 2003), including articles focused on hormones (Gooren, Fliers, & Courtney, 1990; Hines, 2011), genetic factors (Bailey & Pillard, 1995; Ngun, Ghahramani, Sanchez, Bocklandt, & Vilain, 2011), and neuroscience (Savic, Garcia-Falgueras, & Swaab, 2010; Swaab, 2008) as well as with a specific focus on women (Peplau, Sparlding, Conley, & Veniegas, 1999) and gender-variant identities (Veale, Clarke, & Lomax, 2010). Included in such reviews are studies that explored genetic, neuroanatomic, endocrine, and morphological differences on the basis of sexual orientation.

In contrast to the frameworks that emphasize the role of social and contextual factors in the development of sexual orientation, perspectives that highlight the role of biological processes place little to no emphasis on the experience of being LGB and instead focus on etiological mechanisms that contribute to the development of sexual orientation (Mustanski et al., 2002; Rahman & Wilson, 2003). A further difference is the general tendency of biologically oriented studies to conceptualize sexual orientation as a stable trait rather than a dynamic and socially bound construct. We next describe research on specific biological processes in the development of sexual orientation.

Genetic Influences

Research hypothesizing genetic influences on sexual orientation began more than 60 years ago, motivated by the idea that gay men are genetically female (Lang, 1937, 1940). Techniques for identifying the sex chromosomes discredited this hypothesis (Pare, 1956). Without evidence for clear chromosomal abnormalities among homosexual subjects, researchers turned to three other methods for exploring the genetic nature of sexual orientation: (a) family studies, to explore the frequency and pattern of the familiality of homosexuality; (b) twin and adoption studies, to partition the population variance in sexual orientation into genetic and environmental components; and (c) molecular genetics studies, to identify specific genes that influence an individual's sexual orientation.

The bulk of the research on genetic influences has focused on family and twin studies. The median rate of homosexuality in brothers of gay men is approximately 9% (Bailey & Pillard, 1995), a figure above recent population base rates of homosexuality (Laumann, Gagnon, Michael, & Michaels, 1994). Female homosexuality also appears to run in families, although estimates of homosexuality among sisters of lesbians vary widely, ranging from 6% to 25% (Bailey & Pillard, 1995). Although both male and female homosexuality appears to run in families, it remains unclear whether it runs in the *same* families. Family studies cannot disentangle whether a trait's familiality is due to genetic or common environmental effects because siblings not only share common genes but also usually share their rearing environment. Twin studies allow for variance in a trait within a population to be partitioned into heritable effects and for influences to be explained by the shared and nonshared sibling environment. Although the concordance rates for twins vary on the basis of ascertainment method and population, several studies using rigorous population-based sampling methods consistently have shown evidence for the heritability of sexual orientation (Mustanski et al., 2002).

There has been limited molecular genetics research on sexual orientation. Hamer, Hu, Magnuson, Hu, and Pattatucci (1993) reported that male homosexuality was more often represented on the mother's side of the family versus the father's side. A linkage scan reported in the same article showed significant linkage of male homosexuality to the X-chromosome region Xq28. Three attempted replications of this linkage study have been reported, two finding the same effect (Hu et al., 1995; Sanders et al., 1998) and one reporting a failure to replicate (Rice, Anderson, Risch, & Ebers, 1999). A genomewide linkage scan of gay brother pairs showed suggestive linkage to loci on chromosome 7 and 8 (Mustanski et al., 2005). A maternal origin effect was found on chromosome 10, with significant linkage for maternally transmitted genes but no paternal contribution. This result suggested the presence of a maternally expressed, paternally silenced imprinted gene for sexual orientation in this region. The exact genes of effect within this putative region have yet to be identified, although there has been a recent publication of an association between a genetic variant in the same chromosome 7 region reported by Mustanski et al. in a Chinese sample of men (Wang et al., 2011).

Hormonal Influences

The most influential and widely used theory about the origins of homosexuality implicates sex-atypical androgen action (L. Ellis & Ames, 1987). The earliest research on the relationship between sex hormones and human sexual orientation tested the hypothesis that some gay men had decreased levels of circulating testosterone, but no such differences were found (Meyer-Bahlburg, 1984). Additionally, experimental manipulations of male androgen levels appear to affect the magnitude of the libido, rather than the direction of the sexual orientation (Barahal, 1940). Results from research on activational hormone effects in women has been less consistent, with two studies finding lesbians to have higher levels of testosterone than heterosexual women (Gartrell, Loriaux, & Chase, 1977; Loraine, Adamopoulos, Kirkham, Ismail, & Dove, 1971), and two other studies finding no differences (Dancey, 1990; Downey, Ehrhardt, Schiffman, Dyrenfurth, & Becker, 1987). Two studies compared two putative subtypes of lesbian women: those who either self-identify or were rated as "butch" and those who were "femme" (Pearcey, Docherty, & Dabbs, 1996; Singh, Vidaurri, Zambarano, & Dabbs, 1999). *Butch* is a colloquial term used to refer to a masculine woman, and *femme* is the term used for a more feminine lesbian woman. Both studies found significant differences in salivary testosterone levels among lesbian women, but these studies must be interpreted with caution because of their failure to consistently control for the phase of the menstrual cycle and their reliance on indirect measures of plasma hormone levels. Thus, research exploring the activational role of hormones on adult sexual orientation seems to suggest no effect in men and the need for additional research examining hormone levels in butch and femme lesbian women and heterosexual women.

Another route through which hormones could influence sexual orientation is through prenatal, organizational action. A now-classic paper by Phoenix, Goy, Gerall, and Young (1959), which demonstrated differential organizational and activational influences of sex hormones, initiated this line of research. In this study, Phoenix et al. injected pregnant guinea pigs with testosterone during gestation and castrated them after birth. At birth, the treated female offspring had masculinized external genitalia that were nearly identical to those of normal male offspring. When the offspring were sexually mature, they were injected with various doses of estrogen. Compared with female controls, the prenatally treated females demonstrated reproductive behaviors (i.e., lordosis, mounting) that were comparable to male controls and significantly different than female controls. Thus, Phoenix et al. found that testosterone, when administered during sensitive periods of development, has a masculinizing action on neuronal tissue involved in mating behavior.

Because of the ethical issues in experimentally manipulating prenatal hormones in humans, much of the research in this area is based on individuals with disorders of sexual development (DSD) or from situations in which women have been prescribed hormones during pregnancy. These studies provide information on the consequences of dramatic alterations in hormones prenatally for the development of sexual orientation. Information has come from rare studies in which hormones have been measured during early development and a larger number of studies that have related physical characteristics that are thought to serve as proxy measures for prenatal hormone exposure.

The most extensively studied DSD is congenital adrenal hyperplasia (CAH; New & Josso, 1988), a rare genetic disorder that results in overproduction of androgens by the adrenal gland. In girls, this can result in masculinization of the female genitals and is believed to have similar effects on the development of brain structures related to gender and sexual orientation. At least 10 studies have been published on the sexual orientation of girls and women with CAH in comparison with female controls. The conclusion from these studies is that women with CAH are less likely to be exclusively or almost exclusively heterosexual than are other women (for a detailed review of these studies, see Hines, 2011). Similar results have been found in studies of women who were exposed prenatally to masculinizing hormones (e.g., diethylstilbestrol; Hines, 2011).

Some research also has investigated the influence of early androgen deficiency on sexual orientation in men, but fewer data are available because of the greater rarity of these DSD. Androgen insensitivity syndrome (AIS) is a genetic disorder in which the testes produce normal amounts of androgens but because of deficiency in the ability of androgen receptors to respond to androgens, the affected individual appears female at birth (Wisniewski et al., 2000). These genetically male (i.e., XY) individuals typically are assigned and reared as girls with no suspicion of the underlying disorder or the Y chromosome. When menstruation fails to occur, the disorder usually is diagnosed because of the lack of female reproductive structures. Sexual orientation in XY women with AIS appears not to differ from that of XX women in the general population (Hines, 2011). Two studies examined genetic variation in genes related to hormone pathways in men. A candidate gene study on the human androgen receptor gene (Macke et al., 1993) and one on the aromatase gene (CYP19; DuPree, Mustanski, Bocklandt, Nievergelt, & Hamer, 2004) found no evidence that variations in these genes played a role in variations in sexual orientation, but they likely were underpowered given the sample sizes needed to detect genetic effects.

Several physical characteristics that are thought to develop as a result of prenatal androgen exposure have been explored in relation to sexual orientation. The relation between sexual orientation and these characteristics is hypothesized to be the result of nonspecific effects of prenatal sex-atypical hormonal action. That is, if sexual orientation is related to perturbations in prenatal hormone environments, then the effects of these perturbations should be observable in sexually dimorphic traits other than sexual orientation. Much of this research has focused on the ratio of the length of the second digit of the hand to the length of the fourth digit (2D:4D). This ratio is larger in women than in men and it has been proposed that this sex difference develops under the control of androgenic hormones prenatally (for evidence to the contrary see Hickey et al., 2010). The relationship between sexual orientation and 2D:4D has been inconsistent and controversial (McFadden et al., 2005), but a recent meta-analysis of studies on the topic found that heterosexual women had higher left- and right-hand 2D:4D ratios than did lesbians, but it found no difference between heterosexual and gay men (Grimbos, Dawood, Burriss, Zucker, & Puts, 2010).

Neuroanatomical Differences

Similar to research on prenatal hormones that was based on testing sexual orientation effects that mirrored sex differences, research on structural differences in the brain on the basis of sexual orientation largely has focused on regions known to have a sex difference. Neuroanatomical differences have been reported for three brain regions on the basis of sexual orientation in human males. First, the arginine vasopressin neuronal population of the suprachiasmatic nucleus in the hypothalamus was found to be 1.7 times larger in gay versus heterosexual men, and contained 2.1 times as many cells (Swaab & Hoffman, 1990). Second, on the basis of the reported sex differences in several interstitial nuclei of the anterior hypothalamus (Allen, Hines, Shryne, & Gorski, 1989), LeVay (1991) measured these regions in the autopsied brains of 19 gay men who died of AIDS, 16 presumably heterosexual men (6 died of AIDS), and 6 presumably heterosexual women (1 died of AIDS). A heterosexual orientation was presumed in those brains that were not specifically provided by deceased individuals who were known to be gay on the basis of medical records. Sex differences were observed in the third interstitial nucleus of the anterior hypothalamus (INAH-3), which also was found to be smaller in gay men and more similar in size to female controls. Subsequently, Byne et al. (2001) reported a nonsignificant trend toward INAH-3 occupying a smaller volume in gay men ($N = 14$) than in heterosexual men ($N = 34$), with no difference in the number of neurons within the nucleus. A comparable sexual orientation effect has been observed in male sheep (Roselli, Larkin, Resko, Stellflug, & Stormshak, 2004). And third, the anterior commissure (AC) is a fibrous tract located within the hypothalamus, which connects the two hemispheres of the brain. The putative increased size of the AC in females has been posited as an explanation for the modest decrease in functional cerebral lateralization (FCL) possibly found in women (Allen & Gorski, 1991). Some evidence for sexual orientation differences in FCL have been shown to exist, and thus research on this structure seems theoretically appropriate. Allen and Gorski (1992) examined the ACs of 30 gay men, 30 presumably heterosexual men, and 30 presumably heterosexual women, matched for age. The gay men in their sample had ACs that were 34% larger than those of the heterosexual men. Lasco, Jordan, Edgar, Petito, and Byne (2002), however, failed to find any variation in the size of the AC with sexual orientation in a sample of 120 participants. Recently, Savic and Lindstrom (2008) found a possible relationship between the difference in AC size and the sex-atypical hemispheric asymmetries observed in homosexual men and women.

Functional scanning also has revealed brain differences in relation to sexual orientation. Most notably, a series of studies have explored the influence of putative pheromones on sexual orientation by means of PET scanning (Berglund, Lindstrom, & Savic, 2006; Savic, Berglund, & Lindstrom, 2005; Savic & Lindstrom, 2008). These studies found that putative pheromones primarily excreted by men stimulated the hypothalamus of heterosexual women and homosexual men in the same way. Heterosexual men, however, were not stimulated by a male scent, suggesting that pheromones may be a contributing factor in determining partner choice. Comparing heterosexual and lesbian women revealed that lesbians reacted to putative pheromones in a sex-atypical way. This pattern of results suggests the possibility that brain response to pheromones may play a role in patterning sexual orientation in humans, but experience and exposure also could explain the pattern. Very few of these neuroanatomical studies have included lesbian women or bisexuals, but some recent studies have included female-to-male transsexuals (Bao & Swaab, 2010).

Fraternal Birth-Order Effects

Perhaps the most replicated finding in sexual orientation research is that gay men are born later in their sibships compared with heterosexual men. Furthermore, recent studies have clarified that this effect primarily is due to older brothers who increase the probability of homosexuality in later born males by 33% (Blanchard, 1997; Blanchard & Bogaert, 1996). Numerous studies in diverse samples have found that gay men had significantly more older brothers compared with heterosexual men, but they did not have a greater number of older sisters, once the number of older brothers has been controlled (for a review, see Bogaert & Skorska, 2011). In subsequent research, Bogaert demonstrated that biological older brothers increase the odds of homosexuality, even if these older brothers were reared in a different household than a younger gay brother (Bogaert, 2006). This study also demonstrated that nonbiological siblings (e.g., adopted or older stepbrothers) had no effect on men's sexual orientation. This suggests that that the fraternal birth order effect operates during prenatal life, not as a result of experiences during childhood or adolescence. Classic genetic effects cannot explain these results because purely genetic phenomena do not show birth-order effects, although epigenomic effects resulting from the prenatal environment may be possible. Blanchard and Bogaert (1996) have hypothesized that a maternal immune response, provoked by male fetuses, becomes stronger with each male pregnancy, thereby allowing the mother's immune system to act as the meter by which fraternal birth order is recorded. For a detailed explanation of the maternal immune hypothesis, see the review by Bogaert and Skorska (2011).

DEVELOPMENTAL PRECURSORS OF SEXUAL ORIENTATION

Besides directly observing and studying biological processes, another way to understand the relative influence of social and biological factors in the development of sexual orientation is by identifying correlates of sexual orientation that may exist developmentally before social influences or may differ in the extent to which they are biologically or socially determined. For example, if markers of sexual orientation are identified very early in development, it would suggest that the process of sexual orientation differentiation also begins very early in development. If an early social experience is correlated with later sexual orientation, it would suggest experience plays a role.

Childhood Gender Nonconformity

Childhood gender nonconformity (CGNC) remains the most frequently studied developmental precursor to sexual orientation. The pioneering studies of Green (1987) were the first to document evidence of this relationship. Green's studies followed into adulthood a group of boys who were referred to clinical settings because of gender atypical behavior, and discovered these boys were more likely than a group of comparison boys to identify as gay or bisexual. Since then, a number of both prospective and retrospective studies of males and females have found a robust correlation between CGNC and adult sexual orientation (Bailey & Zucker, 1995; Cohen, 2002; Skidmore, Linsenmeier, & Bailey, 2006). Most often cited in support of this relationship is a review of 48 retrospective studies conducted by Bailey and Zucker (1995). They found that effect sizes representing the relationship between CGNC and sexual orientation were large for both men and women, but larger for men. According to the authors, they are "the largest effect sizes ever reported in the realm of sex-dimorphic behaviors" (Bailey & Zucker, 1995, p. 49). In these studies, CGNC is defined most frequently by self or parental ratings of toy and activity preference. Most studies measuring CGNC also include ratings of imagined roles or role models, preference for rough and tumble play or competitive athletics, or preference for male or female friends. Measures of cross-dressing and stated gender identity occasionally are included. Other studies have demonstrated that on average, gay and lesbian adults continue to view themselves as more gender nonconforming through adulthood (Lippa, 2005, 2008). Experimental research further suggests that in adulthood, this gender nonconformity is visible to others and commonly relied on as a marker of sexual orientation (Rieger, Linsenmeier, Gygax, & Bailey, 2008; Rieger, Linsenmeier, Gygax, Garcia, & Bailey, 2010). Population-based longitudinal studies have found that levels of masculinity and femininity remain fairly stable across the life span and that these rates of stability appear similar to those of personality traits measured longitudinally (Helson & Moane, 1987; Helson & Wink, 1992).

Although some research suggests a linear relationship between CGNC and degree of same-sex attraction (e.g., Dunne, Bailey, Kirk, & Martin, 2000), other studies have suggested that certain components of CGNC may be differentially predictive of later sexual orientation. For example, in her studies of lesbian and heterosexual tomboys, Carr (2005, 2007) found that although both groups of participants shared a tendency to "accept masculinity" in childhood (which was subsequently linked to experiences of gender in adulthood), "rejecting femininity" was more closely linked to lesbianism. Another study found that CAH among girls, which is associated with greater androgenization, was strongly linked to toy and activity preference, whereas playmate preference was weakly associated and existed independent of toy and activity preference (Berenbaum & Snyder, 1995). Therefore, some components of CGNC may be more related to subsequent sexual orientation than others.

Important methodological issues must be kept in mind when considering the association between CGNC and sexual orientation. In general, most research studies of CGNC are a decade or more old (e.g., those cited in Bailey & Zucker, 1995), utilize nonrepresentative samples (e.g., primarily White, gay men), employ differing recruitment strategies (e.g., recruiting LGB participants at bars), and may reflect a participant bias that could artificially inflates differences. That is, LGB participants may overreport CGNC given its centrality in dominant perspectives on the origins of same sex sexuality. Taking a feminist, constructivist perspective, Gottschalk (2003b) further challenged the theoretical assumptions underpinning research on CGNC, namely the assumption that essential gender differences exist independently of the highly gender dichotomized society.

Gender nonconformity is also less predictive of female sexual orientation. Bailey and Zucker's (1995) review suggested that among females who are as gender nonconforming as the typical lesbian is in childhood, only 6% subsequently identify as lesbian in adulthood. Several studies also suggested that roughly half of females considered themselves to be tomboys in adolescence, which generally is viewed as more socially acceptable than femininity in boys (Hyde, Rosenberg, & Behrman, 1977; Plumb & Cowan, 1984). More broadly, research demonstrating differences in women's experience of erotic attraction (see Chapter 20, this volume), as well as capacity for fluidity and situational responsiveness, call into question models of sexual orientation that historically have been developed to reflect the experiences of gay men. Of the same-sex attracted women in a study conducted by Diamond (1998), three fourths failed to indicate at least one of the following markers: childhood indicators of difference, awareness of attractions prior to questioning, and stability of attractions (see Chapter 20, this volume). At the same time, population-based studies of twins have found some evidence of overlap in the genetic influences on childhood gender conformity, adult gender identity, and adult sexual orientation, particularly among women (Bailey, Dunne, & Martin, 2000).

Bem (1996, 2000) proposed a theory, termed exotic becomes erotic (EBE), which attempts to provide a theoretical explanation for this observed relationship between CGNC and sexual orientation. Bem (1996, 2000) argued that that CGNC and associated differences in temperament lead children to view same-sex others as more unfamiliar or exotic and that this nonspecific autonomic arousal is transformed into an erotic, romantic attraction as development progresses. Bem (2000) demonstrated that within a twin sample, the genetic influence on sexual orientation is fully mediated by CGNC. He also cited evidence that most gay men and lesbians report feeling different, often on a gender-related basis, from their same-sex peers during both childhood and adolescence (Bell, Weinberg, & Hammersmith, 1981; Newman & Muzzonigro, 1993). Although less direct support exists to suggest these feelings of differentness result in increased arousal, experimental evidence demonstrates that generalized physiological arousal can increase erotic arousal (White, Fishbein, & Rutstein, 1981; Wolchik et al., 1980).

Although Bem argued that feeling different on a specifically gender-related basis is central, in their critique of EBE theory, Peplau, Garnets, Spalding, Conley, and Veniegas (1998) emphasized that this variable was not predictive of future sexual orientation in the original study (i.e., Bell et al., 1981) cited by Bem (1996). In a response paper, Bem (1998) argued that this association was significantly weakened by the author's failure to differentiate between gay and bisexual participants, although the model's ability to predict bisexual orientation thus remains problematic. Peplau et al. (1998) also introduced additional cross-cultural research that fails to support a relationship between sex segregation and rates of homosexuality, which Bem (1996) initially drew on to provide support for an association between exoticism and erotic attraction development. Although EBE theory situates CGNC as a causal mechanism in the development of same-sex attractions, a biological perspective also may be used to argue that both are expressions of the similar underlying predisposition (i.e., both are correlated but not causally related).

Pubertal Timing

In addition to the hormonal, genetic, and older brother effects associated with biological contributions, pubertal timing also has been studied as another potential developmental precursor to sexual orientation development. These findings remain somewhat mixed, are primarily limited to male samples, may be affected by sampling or reporting bias, and are complicated by variations in measurement technique (e.g., age of first orgasm, age of first sexual fantasy or behavior, physical growth, and change in secondary sex characteristics; Bogaert & Blanchard, 1996; Savin-Williams, 1995). Nonetheless, in the only study utilizing a national probability sample, Bogaert, Friesen, and Klentrou (2002) did find a younger age of puberty for gay men, as measured by voice change or growth of pubic hair, but they failed to find an association between age of puberty and sexual orientation among women, as measured by menarche, which is the best validated marker of pubertal timing.

Researchers have suggested that variations in age of puberty among LGB individuals reflect nonspecific or generalized effects of prenatal hormones on development, which manifest in a variety of physical, psychological, and behavioral differences (Bogaert & Blanchard, 1996). More specifically, early hormonal feminization of gay and bisexual males shifts these individuals toward a more female typical, and thus younger, average age of puberty onset. Although this theory follows that lesbian and bisexual females would experience a later age of puberty onset, Bogaert et al.'s (2002) findings may reflect sex differences in the biological influences thought to underlie differences in sexual orientation.

Taking a different approach, Storms (1981) proposed a classic and social learning theory model of erotic orientation development on the basis of this premise of earlier sexual maturation among LGB individuals. This theory suggests erotic attraction is directly influenced by the peer context. Individuals who undergo puberty at earlier ages do so within an environment in which socialization is focused on same-sex peer groups, leading to a LGB orientation. As development processes, interaction with other-sex peers increases and the social environment becomes more facilitative of heterosexuality. Most individuals undergo puberty at this time, leading them to develop a heterosexual orientation. This theory suffers many of the methodological shortcomings of EBE theory, and unlike EBE theory, has not been subject to any empirical research. As with EBE theory, whether pubertal timing and sexual orientation development are causally related or whether they represent differential manifestations of a common underlying predisposition has yet to be determined.

Sexual Abuse

Much has been written about the association between childhood sexual abuse and subsequent homosexuality. Indeed, studies using varying methodologies have reported a correlation between different types of child abuse and varying components of a homosexual sexual orientation, including data from clinical samples and case studies, surveys of MSM, and cross-sectional surveys (reviewed in Purcell, Patterson, & Spikes, 2007; H. W. Wilson & Widom, 2010). Not all studies, however, have found this pattern of results. Furthermore, some evidence suggests that the relationship may be stronger among men than women. The largest reviews of the literature in this area indicated that MSM report rates of childhood sexual abuse that are approximately three times higher than that of the general male population (Purcell, Malow, Dolezal, & Carballo-Dieguez, 2004). One of the most methodologically rigorous studies in this area used a prospective longitudinal case-control design that involved following abused and matched nonabused children into adulthood 30 years later. It found that men with documented histories of childhood sexual abuse had 6.75 times greater odds than controls of reporting ever having same-sex sexual partners (H. W. Wilson & Widom, 2010). To help control for possible confounding factors, the authors conducted post hoc analyses controlling for number of lifetime sexual partners and sex work, but the association remained. The effect in women was smaller (odds ratio = 2.11) and a statistical trend ($p = .09$).

A number of theories have been offered to explain the association between childhood sexual abuse and adult homosexuality. One perspective is that sexual abuse causes homosexuality (e.g., Cameron & Cameron, 1995), and this case often is made in the context of proposing that psychological treatment for abuse can "reorient" an LGB individual's sexual orientation toward heterosexuality. Because most sexual perpetrators are male, this perspective requires different mechanisms in men and women. As Gartner (1999) described, boys who are sexually abused by an older male may perceive the abuse as an indication that they are gay. On the other hand, it has been speculated that women who are sexually abused may develop an aversion toward sex with men and feel more comfortable in intimate relationships with other women (Marvasti & Dripchak, 2004). Why boys and girls would have such differing reactions to sexual abuse by an older male has not been well articulated. Another version of the causal hypothesis is that the experience of sexual abuse may result in uncertainty regarding sexual orientation and greater experimentation with both same- and opposite-sex relationships, regardless of ultimate sexual orientation (Gartner, 1999; Gilgun & Reiser, 1990).

An alternative perspective is that a child's sexual orientation precedes the abuse and this sequence could be manifested in a number of ways. First, it is possible that youth who are exploring their sexual identity are more likely to be present in situations in which they are at risk for being sexually abused (Holmes & Slap, 1998), although this is not meant to imply agency on the part of the child regarding the abuse. Second, adolescent males who are exploring their sexual identity may seek out and engage in sex with other men. Given the limited number of adolescent males who may be available partners, these young men may seek out sex with older "out" partners, and some of these encounters may be coercive in nature. Third, it is possible that some of the childhood characteristics that are more often found among gay men (e.g., gender nonconformity) may increase the likelihood that they will be sought out by adult perpetrators of sexual abuse. And, importantly, it is possible that LGB individuals are more likely to report abuse, yet they are as likely as adult heterosexual men to experience it.

Any potential theory for this association must be able to explain why the rate of childhood sexual abuse is higher than homosexuality (Pereda, Guilera, Forns, & Gomez-Benito, 2009). In other words, many sexually abused children do not go on to have a homosexual orientation. Conversely, most LGB individuals do not report a history of sexual abuse, and therefore if there is a relationship, it must have important moderators that have not yet been articulated. Overall, these associative or potentially causal links are not well understood and are in need of further research.

DEVELOPMENTAL STUDY OF SEXUAL ORIENTATION

Patterns of sexual orientation development have been understudied and are difficult to observe because of large and poorly measured cohort effects (Martin & D'Augelli, 2009). There have only been a handful of longitudinal studies that have assessed sexual orientation from adolescence into adulthood. A substantial confound in research on the development of sexual orientation is the fact that the social change that has resulted in greater acceptance of LGBT individuals cannot be disentangled from developmental patterns in traditional longitudinal designs (Mustanski, 2011). For example, if researchers follow a cohort of 16-year-olds for several years and observe increasing same-sex attractions across development, is this pattern caused by a developmental change or the fact that society became more accepting of homosexuality during that same period? To rigorously answer that question would require a multiple cohort longitudinal design in which societal and developmental changes can be disentangled, but as of yet no such study has been published. Similarly, adolescence is the developmental period during which sexual attractions emerge and, just like their heterosexual peers, the initiation of sexual behavior is synchronized with biological changes connected with puberty (Savin-Williams, 1995). Although the steps subsequent to the expression of same-sex attractions once were theorized to be linear, staged milestones (i.e., coming out to self, same-sex behavior, public identification, romantic relationships, etc.), empirical data from longitudinal studies of the unfolding and stability of sexual orientation have questioned the linearity and universality assumptions.

Development of Sexual Identity

Sexual orientation identity development generally is conceptualized as a process of becoming aware of one's same sex attractions, incorporating such experiences into one's overall sense of self, and "coming out" to others. Beginning in the 1970s, psychologists took an interest in developing models to capture this process. These models borrow themes from prior work within the field of psychosocial or ego development, for which notable theorists, such as Erikson (1959/1994), have proposed similar stages. Early homosexual identity development models tend to view identity development as a trajectory of mastering successive developmental tasks. Models vary, however, in the extent to which they adopt an individual versus interpersonal focus, with newer perspectives highlighting how individual experiences become shaped by larger sociocultural influences.

Stage-Sequential Perspectives The mastery of developmental tasks, such as the achievement of cognitive and behavioral milestones in the integration of an LGB identity, has been of particular interest (Drasin et al., 2008). Prevailing questions include: Are there distinct developmental milestones? What is the sequence of these developmental markers? How do the stages of development and their sequential ordering vary among diverse nonheterosexual populations in varied sociocultural and historical contexts? Pooling across sexual orientation development research, four primary psychosexual milestones typically are measured: (a) age of initial awareness of same-sex sexual attraction; (b) age of first same-sex sexual activity; (c) age of deciding that one is gay or self-labeling; and (d) age of first disclosure that one is gay.

Research on the timing of sexual orientation milestones among LGB populations has suggested that the occurrence of these markers tend to follow a stage-sequential model. In general, age ranges for achieving the four primary milestones across subgroups (i.e., sex and race/ethnicity) are as follows:

- *7–12 years of age* for initial awareness of same-sex sexual attraction (D'Augelli, 2002; D'Augelli, Hershberger, & Pilkington, 1998; Diamond, 1998; Dubé & Savin-Williams, 1999; Herdt & Boxer, 1993; Maguen, Floyd, Bakeman, & Armistead, 2002; Rosario, Meyer-Bahlburg, Hunter, & Exner, 1996; Savin-Williams, 1995)
- *13–18 years of age* for initiating same-sex sexual activity (Diamond, 1998; Dubé & Savin-Williams, 1999; Floyd & Stein, 2002; Herdt &

Boxer, 1993; Maguen et al., 2002; Rosario et al., 1996; Savin-Williams, 1995, 1998)

- *14–18 years of age* for self-identifying that one is gay (D'Augelli, 2002; D'Augelli et al., 1998; Diamond, 1998; Dubé & Savin-Williams, 1999; Rosario et al., 1996)
- *15–19 years of age* for first disclosing to someone else that one is gay, lesbian, or bisexual (D'Augelli, 2002; D'Augelli, Grossman, & Starks, 2008; D'Augelli et al., 1998; Dubé & Savin-Williams, 1999; Maguen et al., 2002)

Among the prominent stage-sequential theorists, Cass (1984) and Troiden (1979) proposed similar, widely cited identity development models that take an individual, psychological adjustment perspective and emphasize resolution of internal conflict. During the early stages of both models, defensive strategies predominate, as individuals deny, minimize, or disassociate from first experiences of same-sex desire. Such reactions were seen as a way for individuals to manage the discomfort associated with the potential implications of their attractions, which stemmed from an internalization of the culture's negative views toward homosexuality. As individuals began to acknowledge the possibility of being homosexual, they further question their attractions and seek out information, eventually coming into contact with others in the LGB community. This contact allows for the comparison of experiences, facilitates participation in identity-confirming same-sex behavior and relationships, and helps to foster a more positive view of homosexuality. Cass (1984) proposed that this shift toward self-acceptance typically is accompanied by a stage of identity pride during which individuals associate most strongly with LGB others and tend to emphasize their homosexual identity while devaluing non-LGB others. During any one of these stages, however, individuals may enter into a transient or permanent identity foreclosure if attempts toward positive identity development are met with particularly influential negative reactions. Lastly, during identity synthesis or commitment, an individual's homosexual identity becomes effectively incorporated as one aspect of the individual's overall sense of self (Cass, 1984; Troiden, 1979).

While acknowledging the role of these internal processes, other models such as Coleman's (1981) model have placed greater emphasis on interpersonal contexts and interactions that occur during the process of identity development. During early exploration, Coleman (1981) argued that others' reactions to initial disclosures are critical, as positive reactions can bolster one's developing self-concept and further the process. Although first sexual experiences can serve a similar role, he cautioned that individuals may experience a heightened interest or pressure to "make up for lost time," which can result in one's emerging self-concept becoming overly tied to the amount or outcome of sexual activity. Similarly, when engaging in first romantic relationships, he posited an individual's internalization of negative societal views may play out within the relationship as a tendency toward being self-defeating. Previous experiences of rejection or isolation may lead individuals to seek relationships of an unsustainable or unbalanced level of intensity, or they may lead individuals to be overly sensitized to feelings of jealousy or perceived negative reactions from partners. In the final stage of identity integration, Coleman (1981) described individuals as both able to maintain a healthy relationship and able to put negative reactions of others into perspective. In contrast to such stage models, D'Augelli et al. (1998) proposed a model that also focuses on interpersonal context, but it does not assume a fixed progression between steps. In this model, proposed processes can occur concurrently or independently. The six stages include exiting heterosexuality, developing a personal LGB identity, developing an LGB social identity, becoming an LGB offspring, developing an LGB intimacy status, and entering an LGB community.

The majority of such models utilized qualitative interviews to inform the selection and description of stages, but few models have been tested empirically beyond these initial samples. One notable exception is the model proposed by Cass (1984). In her original paper, Cass developed two quantitative measures to reflect the proposed characteristics of each stage, which she administered to an additional sample of 178 LGB adults. Discriminant analysis distinguished all six stages, although Cass acknowledged that the first two stages and the last two stages were most similar, suggesting four stages may be more appropriate. Relatively few respondents (30%) were in the first three stages of the model, which also limited her ability to draw conclusions. An additional instrument, *The Gay Identity Questionnaire*, was developed to measure Cass's six stages and tested by Brady and Busse (1994); it later was readministered by Halpin and Allen (2004) and Johns and Probst (2004). Both studies also found relatively few respondents were in initial stages (1–3) or the identity pride stage (5). These researchers suggested that a two-stage model of unintegrated versus integrated identity appears to best match the data. Unfortunately, the cross-sectional design of such studies is a major limitation, as is the fundamental difficulty of recruiting individuals at early stages of identity development.

Since their inception, a number of additional criticisms of stage models also have accumulated, and research has demonstrated that these processes are more nonlinear and dynamic than suggested by the stages typically proposed (e.g., Diamond, 1998; Mosher, 2001). Others have argued that these models can be seen as overly prescriptive, particularly in that they appear to assume one's degree of maturity on the basis of where one is in the process. Both of these critiques apply particularly to individuals experiencing attraction to both males and females. For a variety of reasons, some individuals temporarily may identify as bisexual before identifying as gay or lesbian. For some individuals, however, bisexuality is a stable, enduring identity, which may be arrived at early on in development or following periods of identifying as heterosexual or lesbian or gay (Fox, 1995). Bias or prejudice directed specifically at bisexual individuals appears to exist both within the larger society as well as lesbian and gay communities. This has led researchers to suggest that such individuals may feel "caught" between communities (Dodge & Sandfort, 2007; M. D. E. Meyer, 2003; Mustanski, Garofalo, & Emerson, 2010). A bisexual identity development model proposed by Weinberg et al. (1994) suggests that such individuals may experience unique distress or confusion surrounding the relationship between their attractions to each sex as well as the possibility or legitimacy of a specifically bisexual identity. The lack of social support for this identity, combined with fluctuations in attractions over time, and, for some, the inability to act on attractions, led the authors to conclude that a period of "continued uncertainty" was common. T. Brown (2002) proposed a similar set of stages, but replaced this latter stage with a process (rather than goal-orientated) stage of "identity maintenance." He also identified important gender differences in these processes, such a differential social stigma experienced by men and women and the interactions that occur between one's gender identity and sexuality.

Given these stage-based models were developed to represent the experiences of individuals surveyed by researchers, they are also inevitably historically and culturally bound. Although various identity development models do acknowledge social pressures, they have been criticized for failing to address fundamental limits on ways of identifying and making meaning imposed by society. For example, in some cultures or communities, one's sexuality is primarily defined by one's role within sexual activity regardless of the partner's sex or, alternatively, by one's role within the family regardless of outside sexual activity. Identities or social roles that combine aspects of one's sexual activity or attractions and gender expression exist in a number of cultures (e.g., two spirit identities within Native American communities, L. B. Brown, 1997; see Volume 2, Chapter 6, this handbook). Within the United States, in addition to increasing social acceptance and legal recognition of the rights of sexual minority individuals, LGB characters increasingly are represented in television and film, and the Internet has evolved to become an important source of information, support, and community (Magee, Bigelow, Dehaan, & Mustanski, 2011). Together, these shifts suggest that individuals coming out in the twenty-first century are less likely to experience feelings of secrecy, isolation, and internal distress than those in earlier generations. On the other hand, experiences of LGB-related victimization continue to remain commonly reported (Mays & Cochran, 2001).

Sociocultural Approaches

More recently, researchers have begun to develop socioculturally informed approaches to provide alternative perspectives on how individuals come to make meaning of their experiences of sex, gender, and sexuality. These approaches draw of the social ecological perspectives initially articulated by Bronfenbrenner (1977) who viewed individuals as embedded within multiple layers of the larger social structure. They also incorporate life-course or lifespan perspectives that highlight how individuals' experiences vary as a function of both their age and generational cohort (e.g., Elder & Shanahan, 2007). For example, Sandfort (2005) discussed how the masculinization of gay male culture that took place in the 1970s and 1980s, coupled with the emergence of macho and leathermen stereotypes, shaped the way gay men experienced and expressed their identities. In her research, Gottschalk (2003a) found lesbian women who formed their identities prior to the feminist movement (1950s–1970s) or following the resurgence of conservatism and biological studies of sexual orientation (1980s–1990s) endorsed biological theories of sexual orientation. They placed emphasis on CGNC, along with other early markers, as evidence of the innateness of their sexuality. For lesbians coming out during the rise of feminism (1970s–1980s), CGNC often was conceptualized as a rejection of sex stereotypes and resentment of boys' relative freedom, and these women were more likely to indicate that they chose lesbianism.

More broadly, Cohler and Hammack (2007) have proposed the existence of two main contemporary gay narratives that individuals draw on when attempting to make meaning of their experiences. The first narrative of "struggle and success" parallels the early identity development models previously reviewed. This perspective compliments the earlier work of Monteflores and Schultz (1978), who proposed that identity development involves a process of "recasting the past," or reexamining and reinterpreting previous experiences from new perspective in order to provide continuity to one's current experience. Along with others (e.g., Rust, 1996, 2003), they highlighted how coming out can disrupt one's existing sense of self, and thus the connections one makes between the past, present, and future. This process also may involve renegotiating of cultural norms, expectations, and values, as these are typically oriented toward heterosexuals.

In contrast, the second narrative of "emancipation" has emerged more recently and is associated with the depathologization of same sex sexuality, as reflected in the greater fluidity and diversity of self-identification visible in some more recent samples of adolescents. In particular, Savin-Williams (2011) has suggested that many contemporary youth appear to be confronting the need to identify with a sexual orientation label and challenging the assumption that one's sexual orientation is a fundamental aspect of oneself. This has been accompanied by an increase in alterative identities such as "queer" and "pansexual" or the general tendency to reject the use of any label. This newer narrative appears particularly applicable to women's experiences of sexuality, as articulated within the work of Diamond (1998, 2005b). How widespread such perspectives are remains unknown, although Savin-Williams argued that they will continue to increase over time in line with larger sociocultural shifts. To illustrate, one survey of 2,560 California high school students collected from 2003 to 2005 found that the majority of sexual minority youth (71%) endorsed traditional sexual orientation identities (i.e., LGB), whereas 13% indicated they were questioning, 6% identified as queer, and 9% indicated other responses that reflected ambivalence, resistance, or fluidity in identity (Russell, Clarke, & Clary, 2009).

From a sociocultural perspective, studies with generational cohorts of LGB populations tend to suggest that more recent samples of LGB individuals are reaching psychosocial milestones at earlier ages than more historic cohorts (Dank, 1971; Drasin et al., 2008; Dubé & Savin-Williams, 1999; Grov, Bimbi, Nanin, & Parsons, 2006; Skerven & de St. Aubin, 2006). In one of the earliest reports of cohort differences in milestone achievement, men younger than 30 years of age self-identified as gay at earlier ages then men older than the age of 30 (Dank, 1971). In a national magazine survey of 2,402 gay men (Drasin et al., 2008), researchers found that younger cohorts reported awareness of same-sex attraction, having sex with other males, and coming out at an earlier age than older cohorts. Similarly, research on lesbian sexual identity development examined history, age, and cohort effects for 10 milestones in two samples of women—one collected in 1979 and another in 2003 to 2004 (Skerven & de St. Aubin, 2006). Among the milestones studied, there were significant differences in more than half of the markers, including awareness of being attracted to other women and self-identifying as a lesbian. These shifts in ages toward earlier attainment of psychosexual milestones have been attributed to greater availability of information and supportive role models (Herdt & Boxer, 1993) as well as a decrease in stigma associated with homosexuality (Grov et al., 2006). In light of these findings, longitudinal research that examines developmental experiences over time is essential for building sophisticated models of sexual orientation that take into account the diversity and complexity of experiences over the life course.

In several subsequent papers, Hammack and colleagues (Hammack & Cohler, 2011; Hammack, Thompson, & Pilecki, 2009) presented and analyzed a handful of same-sex attracted individuals' life-course narratives. Together, these highlight diversity of trajectories, and associated intracohort variability, that has resulted from the widespread availability of multiple narratives. They also demonstrate how individuals draw on aspects of both narratives as a function of their experiences within multiple contexts (e.g., family or peer rejection) as well as their access to these narratives. As a whole, these socioculturally informed approaches attempt to explicate how individuals' experiences are shaped by the characteristics, structure, and functioning of multiple, temporally dynamic settings (e.g., home, school, religion) that are embedded within the larger social structure (Horn, Kosciw, & Russell, 2009). The studies we have mentioned have begun to explicate LGB individual's experiences in relation to one or several of these contexts, but more comprehensive approaches are needed.

Intersectionality Approaches

In addition to the tendency to obscure individual variability by focusing on the typical experiences of groups of participants, most early models of sexual orientation identity development were further limited by sampling mostly adult White males. A small but growing literature has begun to apply an intersectionality perspective to describe the experiences of racial and ethnic minority LGB individuals. Coined by Crenshaw (1989), the intersectionality perspective emerged from feminist scholarship, as well as critical race theories, and aims to understand social inequality on the basis of such dimensions as gender, race, sexual orientation, and social class among other categories (Bowleg, 2008; Cole, 2009; Davis, 2008). Intersectionality documents the existence of social hierarchies and examines how distinctive social power relations mutually construct each other (Bowleg, 2008; P. H. Collins, 1998). In the examination of social inequalities on the basis of race, gender, and sexual orientation, the Institute of Medicine (2011) outlined four guiding principles. First, the full spectrum of social and historical experience needs to be taken into account within and between groups with respect to diverse social classifications. Second, race and gender are socially constructed and the experiences of minority group members are understood in relation to unequal control and access to resources. Third, institutional practices and policies contribute to unequal treatment and influence the economic and social status of groups. And fourth, the representations (i.e., depictions) of individuals and social groups are fundamentally linked to historical, social, political, structural, and geographic factors.

The intersectionality approach has been applied to the analysis of dual identity experiences, multiple minority stress experiences, and resiliency (e.g., Bowleg, Huang, Brooks, Black, & Burkholder, 2003; M. D. E. Meyer, 2003). In relation to sexual orientation development, the intersectionality perspective reveals that the experience of being lesbian, gay, or bisexual (e.g., self-identification, disclosure, identity-behavior concordance) tends to vary by the racial or ethnic group with which one identifies as well as by such other factors as socioeconomic status (Chae & Ayala, 2010; Herek, Norton, Allen, & Sims, 2010; Ross, Essien, Williams, & Fernandez-Esquer, 2003).

Other factors, including internalized homophobia, perceptions of rejection, and limited availability of support resources, have been hypothesized to delay the timing of identity labeling (Manalansan, 1996) and disclosure (Savin-Williams, 1996) among racially and ethnically diverse youth. The research in this area is mixed, however. Some investigators have reported that there are no significant differences in the timing of psychosexual milestones or in sexual identity formation among African American, Asian, Latino, and White youth (Grov et al., 2006; Rosario et al., 1996), whereas others have found distinct racial and ethnic differences in the timing of certain milestones. For example, in a combined sample of published research on gay and bisexual males (Dubé & Savin-Williams, 1999), Latinos reported awareness of same-sex attraction earlier than African American and White youth. Similarly, Asian Americans reported later initiation with a same-sex partner than the other three groups. In terms of the sequencing of milestones, groups tended to diverge from the prevailing stage-sequential model. White and Latino youth were almost equally likely to progress through either the identity-centered sequence or sex-centered pattern of development, whereas the majority of African American males tended to engage in same-sex behavior before labeling their sexual identity (Dubé & Savin-Williams, 1999), thus potentially reflecting African American males' reluctance to identify themselves as gay or bisexual (Manalansan, 1996).

In general, the processes of racial or ethnic and sexual orientation development may occur concurrently or at different periods of the life span and may interact or occur independently. J. F. Collins (2000) proposed a model of identity formation whose stages of questioning, suppression, exploration, and acceptance can be applied to both racial and ethnic and sexual orientation identity. In a qualitative study with African American and Latino male adolescents, Jamil, Harper, and Fernandez (2009) also identified similar themes that cut across both ethnic and sexual identity development, including awareness and exploration of differences. These authors noted, however, important differences in these processes, which, although occurring simultaneously, rarely were referenced together by participants. For example, racial and ethnic identity development was discussed as a process of becoming aware of one's heritage in the context of family and cultural activities, and sexual orientation identity development was discussed as a more private, individual process.

Additional researchers have highlighted the cultural conflicts such individuals experience as racial and ethnic minority individuals within LGB communities, and as LGB individuals within racial and ethnic minority communities (Parks, Hughes, & Matthews, 2004; B. D. M. Wilson & Miller, 2002). Combining an intersectional and ecological approach, P. A. Wilson (2008) outlined many interactive and dynamic influences present within the social networks (e.g., family socialization), communities (e.g., racial, gender, and religious norms), and social structures (e.g., generational and cultural shifts) of African American men who are primarily attracted to other men. P. A. Wilson highlighted how these influences, although experienced idiosyncratically, may cause conflicts in the identity development process of such men to predispose them toward bisexual sexual behavior. Taking a slightly different perspective, researchers such as I. H. Meyer (2010) have challenged the assumption that possessing a positive racial and ethnic and sexual minority identity creates an internal tension. They, along with other researchers studying resiliency (Bowleg et al., 2003), have suggested that individuals may draw from experiences and associated coping resources developed in reference to one aspect of one's identity and apply these to another aspect.

Although much of the intersectionality research has focused on the experiences of racial and ethnic minorities, several researchers have attempted to develop models of identity development that center on the experiences of women. Early work by Sophie (1985) reconceptualized the process as more flexible and nonlinear than early stage models, and the work of McCarn and Fassinger (1996) distinguished between the processes of developing an individual and group identity. In a subsequent study, Swann and Anastas (2003) found that the stages identified by McCarn and Fassinger (1996) did not fit with the experiences of adolescent same-sex attracted females. They instead proposed phases of exploring identity possibilities, managing stigma, and consolidating one's identity. Although these perspectives are largely consistent with stage-sequential models, research with lesbians and bisexual women highlight deviations from these models (Diamond, 1998, 2000; Grov et al., 2006; Rosario et al., 1996; Savin-Williams & Diamond, 2000). In considering the ages of milestone achievement, women tend to report awareness of attraction to the same sex and self-identification at older ages than do men (Diamond, 1998; Rosario et al.,

1996; Savin-Williams & Diamond, 2000). The order in which various milestones are achieved also may differ by gender (Diamond, 1998, 2000; Savin-Williams & Diamond, 2000). For example, in one study, women reported that self-identification as a lesbian or bisexual occurred before initiating sexual activity (Savin-Williams & Diamond, 2000). This identity-centered sequence of development among women (in contrast to a sex-centered pattern among men) reflects the importance of a sense of identity over sexual activities (Dubé, 2000).

Researchers adopting intersectional approaches also have highlighted the importance of considering other aspects one's experience or social status including class, economic status, religion, and disability status (Fassinger & Arseneau, 2007). In addition to influencing one's experience of their sexuality, these characteristics are thought to shape the contexts individuals come into contact with and the resources available to them during the identity development process. Thus far, no theoretical models have been proposed for how this process unfolds similarly or differently across such characteristics. Although the handful of studies we reviewed have, to varying degrees, begun to apply intersectional principles to research with diverse groups, more research is needed to fully develop this field. In general, controversies have emerged about whether intersectionality is a theory, a heuristic device, or a method for conducting feminist analysis (Davis, 2008). Scholars also have debated which categories (and how many) should be included in intersectional analysis and whether categories should be used at all. There are further disagreements on the focus and scope of intersectionality but a general consensus that intersectionality would benefit from a broadly accepted definition and a methodology explicating how, where, and when it should be applied (Davis, 2008). As articulated by Cole (2009), translating the theoretical insights of intersectionality into a research paradigm requires a reconceptualization of the meaning and consequences of social categories.

Differential Developmental Trajectories Approach

This approach draws on intersectionalist frameworks to further explicate the types of variance that exist within and across groups of LGBT and heterosexual individuals (Savin-Williams & Cohen, 2004). The differential development trajectories (DDT) perspective captures the experiences of youth, but it also can be applied to adults. The first tenant of this perspective highlights the shared uniqueness of LGBT individuals' experiences, which result from shared biological, social, and historical influences. This framework also highlights differences that occur across LGBT individuals, which emerge through intersections with other aspects of the self and variations across contexts. Together, these tenants call for research examining *when and where*, *why*, and, *how* similarities and differences that emerge across groups of LGBT individuals. This tenant speaks to the importance of integrating LGBT development within the larger field of developmental research, which also has been advocated for by Diamond (2003a). The analysis of gender differences in the age and sequence of achieving developmental milestones underscores how biological and environmental variables interact with personal characteristics to produce divergent pathways of identity development (Cass, 1996). Examining sexual orientation development trajectories among women and men, Savin-Williams and Diamond (2000) reported that gay males, similar to their heterosexual counterparts, began their sexual careers shortly after pubertal onset. Increases in androgen levels were strongly associated with increases in sexual motivation and with sexual initiation. For males, a desire for sex was hypothesized to be sufficient motivation for pursuing sexual activity. In contrast, few females reported pursuing sex on the basis of sexual motivation alone; social and emotional contexts influence the timing of same-sex sexual behavior among lesbian and bisexual women. Because of the diversity and complexity of human experience, each individual LGBT person possesses a somewhat unique, idiosyncratic experience. The last tenant of the DDT approach cautions against the use of mean differences or general descriptions of groups to understand any one individual's experience.

Longitudinal Research on Developmental Trajectories

To paint a saturated picture of the development of sexual orientation and gender identity ideally would require multiple diverse cohorts of children followed across the life span with developmentally sensitive measurement of sexual orientation, gender identity and expression, and related phenomena (e.g., childhood gendered behaviors, psychosexual milestones). Multiple generations ideally would be studied because it would allow for disaggregation of social changes from developmental processes.

Ideally, analyses of these data would incorporate theories from developmental science such as proposed in Savin-Williams' (2011) DDT framework, which highlighted the fact that there can be multiple distinct trajectories (rather than assuming a universal developmental pattern), that individuals can reach an adult homosexual orientation via multiple developmental pathways (i.e., equifinality), that LGBT youth have aspects of similarity and dissimilarity with their heterosexual peers, and that development is unlikely to be linear. No such studies exist as of yet, but the closest approximation to this idea design comes in the form of a handful of longitudinal studies with various follow-up lengths of time in diverse sets of populations—all of which have been focused on sexual orientation rather than gender identity.

One of the primary focus areas of longitudinal research on sexual orientation has been the stability versus fluidity of various components of sexual orientation. The study with the youngest sample of LGBT youth to date, explored changing orientation labels among racially diverse sexual minority youth (ages 14–21) in New York City over 12 months (Rosario, Schrimshaw, Hunter, & Braun, 2006). They found most youth remained consistent in their identity label, but 30–40% of bisexual youth shifted to a gay or lesbian label during the year, and 7% shifted from gay or lesbian to bisexual; only 2–3% of youth shifted to a "straight" identity label. Youth who consistently identified as gay or lesbian reported sexual attractions and behavior that were more same-sex oriented than those who transitioned. Inconsistent with research on slightly older samples, female youth were less likely to change their sexual orientation label than males. Limitations of this study included the relatively brief time period, small sample ($n = 156$), and wide age range at enrollment. A larger study of racially diverse LGBT adolescents reported that nearly three quarters of participants indicated that they previously adopted a different identity label (in most cases, heterosexual or bisexual), but fewer youth reported a change in the sex of their attractions (Mustanski, Newcomb, Heinz, Birkett, & Ashbeck, 2011). Over 30 months of longitudinal follow-up and five waves of assessment of sexual attractions, the study found that youth increased in their same-sex attractions over time. Girls and bisexually identified youth were more likely to report attractions to both sexes at younger ages, but over time, they particularly increased in their levels of same-sex attraction.

Taking advantage of the much larger, population-based National Longitudinal Survey of Adolescent Health, which assed sexual orientation three times over 6 years, Savin-Williams and Ream (2007) found youth with a nonheterosexual orientation in any dimension were less likely than exclusively heterosexual youth to remain consistent in their attractions and behavior over time. They also found, however, that as some LGB youth shifted to opposite-gender attractions, behavior, or heterosexual self-labels, a larger number of heterosexual youth shifted to same- or both-gender attractions and behaviors, keeping the overall prevalence similar across time.

By far, the longest longitudinal study of its kind was conducted by Diamond (1998, 2000, 2003b, 2005b, 2008) and described trajectories of 89 young adult women's attractions, identity labels, and behaviors. She found relative consistency in sexual attractions, but more than two thirds changed labels and behavior over the course of 10 years, with a small number of young women dropping a lesbian or bisexual label for a heterosexual identity, but far more of them switching between lesbian and bisexual, or shifting to "unlabeled." Contrary to the belief by some that sexual orientation labels become fixed in adulthood, longitudinal studies of adults have similarly documented fluidity, although more so in women and those who identify as bisexual (Dickson, Paul, & Herbison, 2003; Pattatucci & Hamer, 1995; Stokes, Damon, & McKirnan, 1997; Stokes, McKirnan, & Burzette, 1993; Weinberg et al., 1994). Upon consideration of the fluidity in sexual orientation in women, (Diamond, 2012) has called for increased attention to variability in sexual orientation as an important marker in addition to overall tendency for attractions to men, women, or both (see Chapter 20, this volume).

Natural variation in sexual attractions over time does not indicate that sexual orientation can be changed intentionally by the individual or through some kind of "therapeutic" process. Although there has been some debate about the potential effectiveness of putative interventions to change sexual orientations (see Spitzer, 2003, and accompanying editorials), major mental health professional organizations have published statements that this is not possible and potentially harmful (American Psychiatric Association, 2000; APA, 2009).

SUMMARY AND CONCLUSION

This chapter approached sexual orientation and identity development from a number of different perspectives and focused on prevailing theoretical frameworks. Although growing rapidly within the past several decades, many gaps exist in the literature, which is further bounded by significant methodological limitations of existing scholarship. Although the theoretical perspectives that were integrated throughout this review provide a valuable lens into the complexities of same-sex attraction and desire, behavior, and identity, researchers historically have tended to focus exclusively on either biological or sociocultural influences, and many have focused more narrowly on a particular developmental period (Tolman & Diamond, 2001). Nonetheless, although much more research is needed to explain the degree of influence and specific mechanisms of action underlying the development of sexual orientation identity, Hammack's (2005) life-course approach integrates biological and sociocultural influences and is a strong reflection of the current state of the field. Therefore, the chapter ends with a discussion of this approach.

Life-Course Development of Human Sexual Orientation: An Integrative Paradigm

In this theoretical framework (Hammack, 2005), biological differences serve as a predisposing force "to respond affectively and intimately to members of the same sex" (p. 277), although he has positioned such responsiveness on a continuum. This biological predisposition then becomes reflected in sexual desire and subsequently is experienced and understood by individuals, as influenced by their sociocultural positioning. Drawing on previous work by Diamond (2003c), Hammack distinguished affectional bonding from sexual desire, acknowledging that they may occur independently or concurrently. The extent to which this distinction is made, and how it is reflected upon, differs across gender and culture. For example, within Western society, close affectional relationships between young females are seen as culturally normative, whereas similar relations among young boys may prompt questioning of sexual orientation (see Chapter 10, this volume).

In terms of social and cognitive development, one's sense of self, or one's *subjectivity*, develops most prominently in adolescence. This process occurs simultaneously with the internalization of cultural patterns of identity and meaning-making. Hammack (2005) introduced the notion of a *cultural press* to explain the Western process of "coming out." As one becomes aware of one's sexual desire within this internalized sociocultural system, a *motivational force* develops, propelling internalization and outward identification with a sexual orientation identity consistent with this system. Although the form and function of the cultural press likely varies on the basis of other factors (e.g., race and gender), the process also entails an integration of sexual orientation identity into one's overall life narrative, which is shaped by the sociocultural possibilities available to do so (e.g., institutional policies, access to resources). Hammack (2005) also has highlighted the role of individual agency in the ways in which individuals reflect on and react to such influences.

The life-course perspective offered by Hammack (2005) presented a biosocial, historical framework for sexual identity development and also acknowledged DDTs, particularly along the lines of gender and ethnicity. With the overarching goal to articulate a theory of sexual orientation in cultural context, adaptations of Hammack's theory are needed to account for divergent trajectories. More comprehensive approaches would examine how individuals' experiences are shaped by the characteristics (e.g., structure, function) of multiple and temporally dynamic settings (e.g., home, school, community) that are embedded within larger sociocultural systems. In particular, examinations of social ecology from an intersectional perspective would highlight the full spectrum of social and historical experiences of diverse populations to document the existence of social hierarchies and power relations that impact development. In this light, social identities may be understood in relation to institutional practices and policies, as well as unequal control and access to resources, that interact with the developmental trajectories of sexual minorities (see Volume 2, Chapter 10, this handbook). Furthermore, as articulated by Diamond (2005c), future research should address "*which* ecological factors interact with *which* biological processes, under *what* conditions, with *what* outcomes, in *which* individuals, at *which* ages, and—most importantly—*through which mechanisms*" (p. 294).

Future Research Directions

Longitudinal research that examines developmental experiences over time is essential for building sophisticated models of sexual orientation that take into account the diversity and complexity of experiences over the life course. A paucity of longitudinal research has assessed sexual orientation from adolescence into adulthood. Attaining a comprehensive understanding of the development of sexual orientation ideally would require multiple cohorts of children followed across the life span with developmentally sensitive measurement of sexual orientation, gender identity and expression, and related phenomena (e.g., biological processes, childhood gendered behaviors, psychosexual milestones). To disaggregate the effect of sociohistorical changes on developmental processes, multiple generations would need to be studied. A significant challenge to this longitudinal approach would be the ability to recruit large enough samples that would yield sufficient subgroups of individuals reporting same-sex attraction, desire, behavior, and identity. Additionally, recruiting individuals at early stages of identity development may pose significant barriers to this research design.

On the basis of the literature reviewed in this chapter, and framed by the life-course perspective, specific areas for future investigation include the following: (a) research that charts the development of sexual orientation in varying racial and sociocultural groups and in a variety of genders; (b) molecular genetics research on sexual orientation which has already shown genetic linkages to sexual orientation (Hamer et al., 1993; Hu et al., 1995; Mustanski et al., 2005; Sanders et al., 1998; Wang et al., 2011); (c) neuroanatomical and psychophysiological research with women and bisexuals; (d) studies on childhood gender nonconformity in relation to female sexual orientation (Bailey & Zucker, 1995; Bailey et al., 2000; Diamond, 1998); (e) research examining associations between gender identity and sexual orientation, particularly among transgender individuals (Bockting et al., 2009; Kuper et al., 2011); and (f) measurement of sexual orientation as a construct that is nonlinear, dynamic, fluid, and historically and culturally bound.

Conclusion

Reflecting on the interaction between biological and sociocultural processes, sexual orientation development is best represented as a continuous, life-long process. Over the course of life, individuals experience the following: (a) changes or fluctuations in sexual attractions, behaviors, and romantic partnerships; (b) the need to negotiate coming out across contexts; and (c) sociocultural changes (e.g., societal views of LGBT individuals). Additionally, many individuals who experience same-sex attraction or engage in same-sex behavior do not identify as lesbian, gay, or bisexual. For example, several studies of youth suggest that many of the individuals acknowledging same-sex attractions or reporting a history of same-sex sexual activity do not endorse a sexual minority identity (Remafedi, Resnick, Blum, & Harris, 1992; Savin-Williams & Ream, 2007). Unfortunately, across theoretical frameworks and models of sexual orientation, most past research has not included such individuals.

This review of the development of sexual orientation and identity concludes by reminding readers that despite the common assertions to the contrary and popular interest in this research, the ontogeny and stability of sexual orientation do not have clear moral, legal, or policy consequences (Mustanski & Bailey, 2003). Whether an individual's sexual orientation is or is not influenced by biological processes, is stable or fluid, or is adolescent or adult in expression, variability in sexual orientation should be respected as a natural form of diversity.

References

Allen, L. S., & Gorski, R. A. (1991). Sexual dimorphism of the anterior commissure and massa intermedia of the human brain. *Journal of Comparative Neurology, 312*, 97–104. doi:10.1002/cne.903120108

Allen, L. S., & Gorski, R. A. (1992). Sexual orientation and the size of the anterior commissure in the human brain. *Proceedings of the National Academy of Sciences of the United States of America, 89*, 7199–7202. doi:10.1073/pnas.89.15.7199

Allen, L. S., Hines, M., Shryne, J. E., & Gorski, R. A. (1989). Two sexually dimorphic cell groups in the human brain. *Journal of Neuroscience, 9*, 497–506.

American Psychiatric Association. (1952). *Diagnostic and statistical manual of mental disorders*. Washington, DC: Author.

American Psychiatric Association. (1974). *Diagnostic and statistical manual of mental disorders* (2nd ed.). Washington, DC: Author.

American Psychiatric Association. (2000). *Position statement: Therapies focused on attempts to change sexual orientation (reparative or conversion therapies)*. Washington, DC: Author.

American Psychological Association. (2009). *Report of the task force on appropriate therapeutic responses to sexual orientation*. Washington, DC: Author.

American Psychological Association, Task Force on Gender Identity and Gender Variance. (2009). *Report of the task force on gender identity and gender variance*. Washington, DC: Author.

Armstrong, E. A., & Crage, S. M. (2006). Movements and memory: The making of the Stonewall myth. *American Sociological Review, 71*, 724–751. doi:10.1177/0003 12240607100502

Bailey, J. M. (2009). What is sexual orientation and do women have one? In D. A. Hope (Ed.), *Contemporary perspectives on lesbian, gay, and bisexual identities* (pp. 43–63). New York, NY: Springer Science + Business Media.

Bailey, J. M., Dunne, M. P., & Martin, N. G. (2000). Genetic and environmental influences on sexual orientation and its correlates in an Australian twin sample. *Journal of Personality and Social Psychology, 78*, 524–536. doi:10.1037/0022-3514.78.3.524

Bailey, J. M., & Pillard, R. C. (1995). Genetics of human sexual orientation. *Annual Review of Sex Research, 6*, 126–150.

Bailey, J. M., & Zucker, K. J. (1995). Childhood sex-typed behavior and sexual orientation: A conceptual analysis and quantitative review. *Developmental Psychology, 31*, 43–55. doi:10.1037/0012-1649.31.1.43

Bao, A. M., & Swaab, D. F. (2010). Sex differences in the brain, behavior, and neuropsychiatric disorders. *Neuroscientist, 16*, 550–565. doi:10.1177/10738584 10377005

Barahal, H. S. (1940). Testosterone in psychotic male homosexuals. *Psychiatric Quarterly, 14*, 319–330. doi:10.1007/BF01573190

Bauer, G. R., & Jairam, J. A. (2008). Are lesbians really women who have sex with women (WSW)? Methodological concerns in measuring sexual orientation in health research. *Women and Health, 48*, 383–408. doi:10.1080/03630240802575120

Bell, A. P., Weinberg, M. S., & Hammersmith, S. K. (1981). *Sexual preference: Its development in men and women*. Bloomington: Indiana University Press.

Bem, D. J. (1996). Exotic becomes erotic: A developmental theory of sexual orientation. *Psychological Review, 103*, 320–335. doi:10.1037/0033-295X.103.2.320

Bem, D. J. (1998). Is EBE theory supported by the evidence? Is it androcentric? A reply to Peplau et al. (1998). *Psychological Review, 105*, 395–398. doi:10.1037/0033-295X.105.2.395

Bem, D. J. (2000). Exotic becomes erotic: Interpreting the biological correlates of sexual orientation. *Archives of Sexual Behavior, 29*, 531–548. doi:10.1023/A:1002050303320

Berenbaum, S. A., & Snyder, E. (1995). Early hormonal influences on childhood sex-typed activity and playmate preferences: Implications for the development of sexual orientation. *Developmental Psychology, 31*, 31–42. doi:10.1037/0012-1649.31.1.31

Berglund, H., Lindstrom, P., & Savic, I. (2006). Brain response to putative pheromones in lesbian women. *Proceedings of the National Academy of Sciences of the United States of America, 103*, 8269–8274. doi:10.1073/pnas.0600331103

Blackwood, E. (1986). *Anthropology and homosexual behavior*. New York, NY: Haworth Press.

Blanchard, R. (1997). Birth order and sibling sex ration in homosexual versus heterosexual males and females. *Annual Review of Sex Research, 8*, 27–67.

Blanchard, R., & Bogaert, A. F. (1996). Homosexuality in men and number of older brothers. *American Journal of Psychiatry, 153*, 27–31.

Bleys, R. (1996). *The geography of perversion: Male to male sexual behavior outside the west and the ethnographic imagination, 1750–1918*. New York: New York University Press.

Bockting, W., Benner, A., & Coleman, E. (2009). Gay and bisexual identity development among female-to-male transsexuals in North America: Emergence of a transgender sexuality. *Archives of Sexual Behavior, 38*, 688–701. doi:10.1007/s10508-009-9489-3

Bogaert, A. F. (2006). Biological versus nonbiological older brothers and men's sexual orientation. *Proceedings of the National Academy of Sciences of the United States of America, 103*, 10771–10774. doi:10.1073/pnas.0511152103

Bogaert, A. F., & Blanchard, R. (1996). Physical development and sexual orientation in men: Height, weight and age of puberty differences. *Personality and Individual Differences, 21*, 77–84. doi:10.1016/0191-8869(96)00045-1

Bogaert, A. F., Friesen, C., & Klentrou, P. (2002). Age of puberty and sexual orientation in a national probability sample. *Archives of Sexual Behavior, 31*, 73–81. doi:10.1023/A:1014083218773

Bogaert, A. F., & Skorska, M. (2011). Sexual orientation, fraternal birth order, and the maternal immune hypothesis: A review. *Frontiers in Neuroendocrinology, 32*, 247–254. doi:10.1016/j.yfrne.2011.02.004

Bowleg, L. (2008). When Black + lesbian + woman ≠ Black lesbian woman: The methodological challenges of qualitative and quantitative intersectionality research. *Sex Roles, 59*, 312–325. doi:10.1007/s11199-008-9400-z

Bowleg, L., Huang, J., Brooks, K., Black, A., & Burkholder, G. (2003). Triple jeopardy and beyond: Multiple minority stress and resilience among Black lesbians. *Journal of Lesbian Studies, 7*, 87–108. doi:10.1300/J155v07n04_06

Brady, S., & Busse, W. J. (1994). The Gay Identity Questionnaire: A brief measure of homosexual identity formation. *Journal of Homosexuality, 26*, 1–22. doi:10.1300/J082v26n04_01

Bronfenbrenner, U. (1977). Toward an experimental ecology of human development. *American Psychologist, 32*, 513–531. doi:10.1037/0003-066X.32.7.513

Brown, L. B. (1997). Women and men, not-men and not-women, lesbians and gays: American Indian gender style alternatives. In L. B. Brown (Ed.), *Two spirit people: American Indian lesbian women and gay men* (pp. 5–20). New York, NY: Harrington Park Press. doi:10.1300/J041v06n02_02

Brown, T. (2002). A proposed model of bisexual identity development that elaborates on experiential differences of women and men. *Journal of Bisexuality, 2*, 67–91. doi:10.1300/J159v02n04_05

Byne, W., Tobet, S., Mattiace, L., Lasco, M. S., Kemether, E., Edgar, M. A., . . . Jones, L. B. (2001). The interstitial nuclei of the human anterior hypothalamus: An investigation of variation within sex, sexual orientation and HIV status. *Hormones and Behavior, 40*, 86–92. doi:10.1006/hbeh.2001.1680

Cameron, P., & Cameron, K. (1995). Does incest cause homosexuality? *Psychological Reports, 76*, 611–621. doi:10.2466/pr0.1995.76.2.611

Carr, C. L. (2005). Tomboyism or lesbianism? Beyond sex/gender/sexual conflation. *Sex Roles, 53*, 119–131. doi:10.1007/s11199-005-4286-5

Carr, C. L. (2007). Where have all the tomboys gone? Women's accounts of gender in adolescence. *Sex Roles, 56*, 439–448. doi:10.1007/s11199-007-9183-7

Cass, V. (1996). Sexual orientation identity formation: A Western phenomenon. In R. P. Cabaj & T. S. Stein (Eds.), *Textbook of homosexuality and mental health* (pp. 227–251). Washington, DC: American Psychiatric Association.

Cass, V. C. (1984). Homosexual identity formation: Testing a theoretical model. *Journal of Sex Research, 20*, 143–167. doi:10.1080/00224498409551214

Centers for Disease Control and Prevention. (2010). *HIV and AIDS among gay and bisexual men.* Atlanta, GA: Author.

Chae, D. H., & Ayala, G. (2010). Sexual orientation and sexual behavior among Latino and Asian Americans: Implications for unfair treatment and psychological distress. *Journal of Sex Research, 47*, 451–459. doi:10.1080/00224490903100579

Chauncey, G., Jr. (1993). The postwar sex crime panic. In W. Graebner (Ed.), *True stories from the American past* (pp. 160–178). New York, NY: McGraw-Hill.

Chivers, M. L., Seto, M. C., Lalumiere, M. L., Laan, E., & Grimbos, T. (2010). Agreement of self-reported and genital measures of sexual arousal in men and women: A meta-analysis. *Archives of Sexual Behavior, 39*, 5–56. doi:10.1007/s10508-009-9556-9

Cohen, K. M. (2002). Relationships among childhood sex-atypical behavior, spatial ability, handedness, and sexual orientation in men. *Archives of Sexual Behavior, 31*, 129–143. doi:10.1023/A:1014043504661

Cohler, B. J., & Hammack, P. L. (2007). The psychological world of the gay teenager: Social change, narrative, and "normality." *Journal of Youth and Adolescence, 36*, 47–59. doi:10.1007/s10964-006-9110-1

Cole, E. R. (2009). Intersectionality and research in psychology. *American Psychologist, 64*, 170–180. doi:10.1037/a0014564

Coleman, E. (1981). Developmental stages of the coming out process. *Journal of Homosexuality, 7*, 31–43. doi:10.1300/J082v07n02_06

Collins, J. F. (2000). Biracial-bisexual individuals: Identity coming of age. *International Journal of Sexuality and Gender Studies, 5*, 221–253. doi:10.1023/A:1010137025394

Collins, P. H. (1998). It's all in the family: Intersections of gender, race, and nation. *Hypatia, 13*, 62–82. doi:10.1111/j.1527-2001.1998.tb01370.x

Crenshaw, K. (1989). Demarginalizing the intersection of race and sex: A Black feminist critique of antidiscrimination doctrine, feminist theory, and antiracist politics. *University of Chicago Legal Forum, 14*, 538–554.

Cronbach, L. J., & Meehl, P. E. (1955). Construct validity in psychological tests. *Psychological Bulletin, 52*, 281–302. doi:10.1037/h0040957

Dancey, C. P. (1990). Sexual orientation in women: An investigation of hormonal and personality variables. *Biological Psychology, 30*, 251–264. doi:10.1016/0301-0511(90)90142-J

Dank, B. M. (1971). Coming out in the gay world. *Psychiatry: Journal for the Study of Interpersonal Processes, 34*, 180–197.

D'Augelli, A. R. (2002). Mental health problems among lesbian, gay, and bisexual youths ages 14 to 21. *Clinical Child Psychology and Psychiatry, 7*, 433–456. doi:10.1177/1359104502007003039

D'Augelli, A. R., Grossman, A. H., & Starks, M. T. (2008). Families of gay, lesbian, and bisexual youth: What do parents and siblings know and how do they react? *Journal of GLBT Family Studies, 4*, 95–115. doi:10.1080/15504280802084506

D'Augelli, A. R., Hershberger, S. L., & Pilkington, N. W. (1998). Lesbian, gay, and bisexual youth and their families: Disclosure of sexual orientation and its consequences. *American Journal of Orthopsychiatry, 68*, 361–371. doi:10.1037/h0080345

Davis, K. (2008). Intersectionality as buzzword: A sociology of science perspective on what makes a feminist theory successful. *Feminist Theory, 9*, 67–85. doi:10.1177/1464700108086364

D'Emilio, J. (1983). *Sexual politics, sexual communities.* Chicago, IL: University of Chicago Press.

Diamond, L. M. (1998). Development of sexual orientation among adolescent and young adult women. *Developmental Psychology, 34*, 1085–1095. doi:10.1037/0012-1649.34.5.1085

Diamond, L. M. (2000). Sexual identity, attractions, and behavior among young sexual-minority women over a 2-year period. *Developmental Psychology, 36*, 241–250. doi:10.1037/0012-1649.36.2.241

Diamond, L. M. (2003a). New paradigms for research on heterosexual and sexual-minority development. *Journal of Clinical Child and Adolescent Psychology, 32*, 490–498. doi:10.1207/S15374424JCCP3204_1

Diamond, L. M. (2003b). Was it a phase? Young women's relinquishment of lesbian/bisexual identities over a 5-year period. *Journal of Personality and Social Psychology, 84*, 352–364. doi:10.1037/0022-3514.84.2.352

Diamond, L. M. (2003c). What does sexual orientation orient? A biobehavioral model distinguishing romantic love and sexual desire. *Psychological Review, 110*, 173–192. doi:10.1037/0033-295X.110.1.173

Diamond, L. M. (2005a). From the heart or the gut? Sexual-minority women's experiences of desire for same-sex and other-sex partners. *Feminism and Psychology, 15*, 10–14. doi:10.1177/0959353505049697

Diamond, L. M. (2005b). A new view of lesbian subtypes: Stable versus fluid identity trajectories over an 8-year period. *Psychology of Women Quarterly, 29*, 119–128. doi:10.1111/j.1471-6402.2005.00174.x

Diamond, L. M. (2005c). Toward greater specificity in modeling the ecological context of desire. *Human Development, 48*, 291–297. doi:10.1159/000086873

Diamond, L. M. (2008). Female bisexuality from adolescence to adulthood: Results from a 10-year longitudinal study. *Developmental Psychology, 44*, 5–14. doi:10.1037/0012-1649.44.1.5

Diamond, L. M. (2012). The desire disorder in research on sexual orientation in women: Contributions of dynamical systems theory. *Archives of Sexual Behavior, 41*, 73–83. doi:10.1007/s10508-012-9909-7

Dickson, N., Paul, C., & Herbison, P. (2003). Same-sex attraction in a birth cohort: Prevalence and persistence in early adulthood. *Social Science and Medicine, 56*, 1607–1615. doi:10.1016/S0277-9536(02)00161-2

Doan, L., & Bland, L. (1998). *Sexology uncensored: The documents of sexual science.* Chicago, IL: University of Chicago Press.

Dodge, B., & Sandfort, T. G. (2007). A review of mental health research on bisexual individuals when compared to homosexual and heterosexual individuals. In B. A. Firestein (Ed.), *Becoming visible: Counseling bisexuals across the life span* (pp. 28–51). New York, NY: Columbia University Press.

Downey, J., Ehrhardt, A. A., Schiffman, M., Dyrenfurth, I., & Becker, J. (1987). Sex hormones in lesbian and heterosexual women. *Hormones and Behavior, 21*, 347–357. doi:10.1016/0018-506X(87)90019-5

Drasin, H., Beals, K. P., Elliott, M. N., Lever, J., Klein, D. J., & Schuster, M. A. (2008). Age cohort differences in the developmental milestones of gay men. *Journal of Homosexuality, 54*, 381–399. doi:10.1080/00918360801991372

Dubé, E. M. (2000). The role of sexual behavior in the identification process of gay and bisexual males. *Journal of Sex Research, 37*, 123–132. doi:10.1080/00224490009552029

Dubé, E. M., & Savin-Williams, R. C. (1999). Sexual identity development among ethnic sexual-minority male youths. *Developmental Psychology, 35*, 1389–1398. doi:10.1037/0012-1649.35.6.1389

Dunne, M. P., Bailey, J. M., Kirk, K. M., & Martin, N. G. (2000). The subtlety of sex-atypicality. *Archives of*

Sexual Behavior, 29, 549–565. doi:10.1023/A:1002002420159

DuPree, M. G., Mustanski, B. S., Bocklandt, S., Nievergelt, C., & Hamer, D. H. (2004). A candidate gene study of CYP19 (aromatase) and male sexual orientation. *Behavior Genetics, 34*, 243–250. doi:10.1023/B:BEGE.0000017870.77610.52481149[pii]

Elder, G. H., & Shanahan, M. J. (2007). The life course and human development. *Handbook of Child Psychology*. doi:10.1002/9780470147658.chpsy0112

Ellis, H., & Symonds, J. A. (1897). *Sexual inversion*. Bedford Row, England: Wilson and Macmillan.

Ellis, L., & Ames, M. A. (1987). Neurohormonal functioning and sexual orientation: A theory of homosexuality/heterosexuality. *Psychological Bulletin, 101*, 233–258.

Epstein, S. (1996). *Impure science: AIDS, activism, and the politics of knowledge*. Berkeley, CA: University of California Press.

Erikson, E. (1994). *Identity and the life cycle*. New York, NY: Norton. (Original work published 1959)

Fassinger, R. E., & Arseneau, J. R. (2007). "I'd rather get wet than be under that umbrella": Differentiating the experiences and identities of lesbian, gay, bisexual, and transgender people. In K. J. Bieschke, R. M. Perez & K. A. DeBord (Eds.), *Handbook of counseling and psychotherapy with lesbian, gay, bisexual, and transgender clients* (2nd ed., pp. 19–49). Washington, DC: American Psychological Association.

Floyd, F. J., & Stein, T. S. (2002). Sexual orientation identity formation among gay, lesbian, and bisexual youths: Multiple patterns of milestone. *Journal of Research on Adolescence, 12*, 167–191. doi:10.1111/1532-7795.00030

Fox, R. C. (1995). Bisexual identities. In A. R. D'Augelli & C. J. Patterson (Eds.), *Lesbian, gay, and bisexual identities over the life span: Psychological perspectives* (pp. 48–86). New York, NY: Oxford University Press.

Freud, S. (1953). Three essays on the theory of sexuality. In J. Strachey (Ed.), *The standard edition of the complete psychological works of Sigmund Freud* (Vol. 7, pp. 123–243). London, England: Hogarth Press. (Original work published 1905)

Friedman, M. S., Silvestre, A. J., Gold, M. A., Markovic, N., Savin-Williams, R. C., Huggins, J., & Sell, R. L. (2004). Adolescents define sexual orientation and suggest ways to measure it. *Journal of Adolescence, 27*, 303–317. doi:10.1016/j.adolescence.2004.03.006

Gartner, R. B. (1999). Sexual victimization of boys by men: Meanings and consequences. *Journal of Gay and Lesbian Psychotherapy, 3*, 1–33. doi:10.1300/J236v03n02_01

Gartrell, N. K., Loriaux, D. L., & Chase, T. N. (1977). Plasma testosterone in homosexual and heterosexual women. *American Journal of Psychiatry, 134*, 1117–1120.

Gilgun, J. F., & Reiser, E. (1990). The development of sexual identity among men sexually abused as children. *Families in Society, 71*, 515–523.

Gooren, L., Fliers, E., & Courtney, K. (1990). Biological determinants of sexual orientation. *Annual Review of Sex Research, 1*, 175–195.

Gottschalk, L. (2003a). From gender inversion to choice and back changing perceptions of the aetiology of lesbianism over three historical periods. *Women's Studies International Forum, 26*, 221–233. doi:10.1016/s0277-5395(03)00052-9

Gottschalk, L. (2003b). Same-sex sexuality and childhood gender non-conformity: A spurious connection. *Journal of Gender Studies, 12*, 35–50. doi:10.1080/0958923032000067808

Green, R. (1987). *The "sissy boy syndrome" and the development of homosexuality*. New Haven, CT: Yale University Press.

Grimbos, T., Dawood, K., Burriss, R. P., Zucker, K. J., & Puts, D. A. (2010). Sexual orientation and the second to fourth finger length ratio: A meta-analysis in men and women. *Behavioral Neuroscience, 124*, 278–287. doi:10.1037/a0018764

Grov, C., Bimbi, D. S., Nanin, J. E., & Parsons, J. T. (2006). Race, ethnicity, gender, and generational factors associated with the coming-out process among gay, lesbian, and bisexual individuals. *Journal of Sex Research, 43*, 115–121. doi:10.1080/00224490609552306

Halpin, S. A., & Allen, M. W. (2004). Changes in psychosocial well-being during stages of gay identity development. *Journal of Homosexuality, 47*, 109–126.

Hamer, D., Hu, S., Magnuson, V., Hu, N., & Pattatucci, A. M. (1993). A linkage between DNA markers on the X chromosome and male sexual orientation. *Science, 261*, 321–327. doi:10.1126/science.8332896

Hammack, P. L. (2005). The life course development of human sexual orientation: An integrative paradigm. *Human Development, 48*, 267–290. doi:10.1159/000086872

Hammack, P. L., & Cohler, B. J. (2011). Narrative, identity, and the politics of exclusion: Social change and the gay and lesbian life course. *Sexuality Research and Social Policy, 8*, 162–182. doi:10.1007/s13178-011-0060-3

Hammack, P. L., Mayers, L., & Windell, E. P. (2011). Narrative, psychology, and the politics of sexual identity in the United States: From "sickness" to "species" to "subject." *Psychology and Sexuality*. doi:10.1080/19419899.2011.621131

Hammack, P. L., Thompson, E. M., & Pilecki, A. (2009). Configurations of identity among sexual minority youth: Context, desire, and narrative. *Journal of*

Youth and Adolescence, 38, 867–883. doi:10.1007/s10964-008-9342-3

Helson, R., & Moane, G. (1987). Personality change in women from college to midlife. *Journal of Personality and Social Psychology, 53*, 176–186.

Helson, R., & Wink, P. (1992). Personality change in women from the early 40s to the early 50s. *Psychology and Aging, 7*, 46–55.

Herdt, G. H., & Boxer, A. (1993). *Children of Horizons: How gay and lesbian teens are leading a new way out of the closet* (Uncorrected page proof. ed.). Boston, MA: Beacon Press.

Herek, G. M., Norton, A. T., Allen, T. J., & Sims, C. L. (2010). Demographic, psychological, and social characteristics of self-identified lesbian, gay, and bisexual adults in a US probability sample. *Sex Res Social Policy, 7*, 176–200. doi:10.1007/s13178-010-0017-y

Hickey, M., Doherty, D. A., Hart, R., Norman, R. J., Mattes, E., Atkinson, H. C., & Sloboda, D. M. (2010). Maternal and umbilical cord androgen concentrations do not predict digit ratio (2D:4D) in girls: A prospective cohort study. *Psychoneuroendocrinology, 35*, 1235–1244. doi:10.1016/j.psyneuen.2010.02.013

Hines, M. (2011). Prenatal endocrine influences on sexual orientation and on sexually differentiated childhood behavior. *Frontiers in Neuroendocrinology, 32*, 170–182. doi:10.1016/j.yfrne.2011.02.006

Hirschfeld, M. (2000). *The homosexuality of men and women* (2nd ed., M. A. Lombardi-Nash, Trans.). Buffalo, NY: Prometheus Books.

Holmes, W. C., & Slap, G. B. (1998). Sexual abuse of boys: Definition, prevalence, correlates, sequelae, and management. *JAMA, 280*, 1855–1862. doi:10.1001/jama.280.21.1855

Hooker, E. (1957). The adjustment of the male overt homosexual. *Journal of Projective Techniques, 21*, 18–31.

Horn, S. S., Kosciw, J. G., & Russell, S. T. (2009). Special issue introduction: New research on lesbian, gay, bisexual, and transgender youth: Studying lives in context. *Journal of Youth and Adolescence, 38*, 863–866. doi:10.1007/s10964-009-9420-1

Hu, S., Pattatucci, A., Patterson, C., Li, L., Fulker, D., Cherny, S., . . . Hamer, D. (1995). Linkage between sexual orientation and chromosome Xq28 in males but not females. *Nature Genetics, 11*, 248–256.

Hyde, J. S., Rosenberg, B. G., & Behrman, J. A. (1977). Tomboyism. *Psychology of Women Quarterly, 2*, 73–75. doi:10.1111/j.1471-6402.1977.tb00574.x

Institute of Medicine. (2011). *The health of lesbian, gay, bisexual, and transgender people: Building a foundation for better understanding*. Washington, DC: National Academies Press.

Jamil, O. B., Harper, G. W., & Fernandez, M. I. (2009). Sexual and ethnic identity development among gay-bisexual-questioning (GBQ) male ethnic minority adolescents. *Cultural Diversity and Ethnic Minority Psychology, 15*, 203–214. doi:10.1037/a0014795

Janssen, E., Everaerd, W., Spiering, M., & Janssen, J. (2000). Automatic processing and the appraisal of sexual stimuli: Toward an information processing model of sexual arousal. *Journal of Sex Research, 37*, 8–23.

Johns, D. J., & Probst, T. M. (2004). Sexual minority identity formation in an adult population. *Journal of Homosexuality, 47*, 81–90. doi:10.1300/J082v47n02_05

Kinsey, A. C., Pomeroy, W. B., & Martin, C. E. (1948). *Sexual behavior in the human male*. Bloomington: Indiana University Press.

Kinsey, A. C., Pomeroy, W. B., Martin, C. E., & Gebhard, P. H. (1953). *Sexual behavior in the human female*. Philadelphia, PA: W. B. Saunders.

Klein, F., Sepekoff, B., & Wolf, T. J. (1985). Sexual orientation: A multi-variable dynamic process. *Journal of Homosexuality, 11*, 35–49.

Kuper, L. E., Nussbaum, R., & Mustanski, B. (2011). Exploring the diversity of gender and sexual orientation identities in an online sample of transgender individuals. *Journal of Sex Research, 49*, 244–254. doi:10.1080/00224499.2011.596954

Lang, T. (1937). *Weiterer Beitrag zur Frage nach der genetischen Bedingtheit der Homosexualitaet* [Further contribution to the question of the genetic determination of homosexuality]. *Zeitschrift fuer die Gesamte Neurologie und Psychiatrie, 157*, 557–574.

Lang, T. (1940). Studies in the genetic determination of homosexuality. *Journal of Nervous and Mental Disease, 92*, 55–64.

Lasco, M. S., Jordan, T. J., Edgar, M. A., Petito, C. K., & Byne, W. (2002). A lack of dimorphism of sex or sexual orientation in the human anterior commissure. *Brain Research, 936*, 95–98. doi:10.1016/S0006-8993(02)02590-8

Laumann, E. O., Gagnon, J. H., Michael, R. T., & Michaels, S. (1994). *The social organization of sexuality: Sexual practices in the United States*. Chicago, IL: University of Chicago Press.

LeVay, S. (1991). A difference in hypothalamic structure between heterosexual and homosexual men. *Science, 253*, 1034–1037.

Levine, M. P., Nardi, P. M., & Gagnon, G. H. (1997). *In changing times: Gay men and lesbians encounter HIV/AIDS*. Chicago, IL: University of Chicago Press.

Lippa, R. A. (2005). Sexual orientation and personality. *Annual Review of Sex Research, 16*, 119–153.

Lippa, R. A. (2008). Sex differences and sexual orientation differences in personality: Findings from the BBC Internet survey. *Archives of Sexual Behavior, 37*, 173–187. doi:10.1007/s10508-007-9267-z

Loraine, J. A., Adamopoulos, D. A., Kirkham, K. E., Ismail, A. A. A., & Dove, G. A. (1971). Patterns of hormone excretion in male and female homosexuals. *Nature, 234*, 552–555. doi:10.1038/234552a0

Macke, J. P., Hu, N., Hu, S., Bailey, M., King, V. L., Brown, T., . . . Nathans, J. (1993). Sequence variation in the androgen receptor gene is not a common determinant of male sexual orientation. *American Journal of Human Genetics, 53*, 844–852.

Magee, J. C., Bigelow, L., Dehaan, S., & Mustanski, B. S. (2011). Sexual health information seeking online: A mixed-methods study among lesbian, gay, bisexual, and transgender young people. *Health Education and Behavior, 39*, 276–289. doi:10.1177/1090198111401384

Maguen, S., Floyd, F. J., Bakeman, R., & Armistead, L. (2002). Developmental milestones and disclosure of sexual orientation among gay, lesbian, and bisexual youths. *Journal of Applied Developmental Psychology, 23*, 219–233. doi:10.1016/s0193-3973(02)00105-3

Manalansan, M. F. (1996). Double minorities: Latino, Black, and Asian men who have sex with men. In R. C. C. K. M. Savin-Williams (Ed.), *The lives of lesbians, gays, and bisexuals: Children to adults* (pp. 393–415). Orlando, FL: Harcourt Brace.

Martin, J. I., & D'Augelli, A. R. (2009). Timed lives: Cohort and period effects in research on sexual orientation and gender identity. In W. Meezan & J. I. Martin (Eds.), *Handbook of research with lesbian, gay, bisexual, and transgender populations* (pp. 190–207). New York, NY: Routledge.

Marvasti, J. A., & Dripchak, V. L. (2004). The trauma of incest and child sexual abuse: Psychobiological perspective. In J. A. Marvasti (Ed.), *Psychiatric treatment of victims and survivors of sexual trauma: A neuro-biopsychological approach* (pp. 3–17). Springfield, IL: Charles C Thomas.

Mays, V. M., & Cochran, S. D. (2001). Mental health correlates of perceived discrimination among lesbian, gay, and bisexual adults in the United States. *American Journal of Public Health, 91*, 1869–1876. doi:10.2105/ajph.91.11.1869

McCarn, S. R., & Fassinger, R. E. (1996). Revisioning sexual minority identity formation: A new model of lesbian identity and its implications for counseling and research. *Counseling Psychologist, 24*, 508–534.

McFadden, D., Loehlin, J. C., Breedlove, S. M., Lippa, R. A., Manning, J. T., & Rahman, Q. (2005). A reanalysis of five studies on sexual orientation and the relative length of the 2nd and 4th fingers (the 2D:4D ratio). *Archives of Sexual Behavior, 34*, 341–356.

Meyer, I. H. (2010). Identity, stress, and resilience in lesbians, gay men, and bisexuals of color. *Counseling Psychologist, 38*, 442–454. doi:10.1177/0011000009351601

Meyer, M. D. E. (2003). Looking toward the intersexions: Examining bisexual and transgender identity formation from a dialectical theoretical perspective. *Journal of Bisexuality, 3*, 151–170. doi:10.1300/J159v03n03_11

Meyer-Bahlburg, H. F. L. (1984). Psychoendrocrine research on sexual orientation. Current Status and future options. In G. J. DeVries, J. P. C. D. Bruin, H. M. B. Uylings & M. A. Corner (Eds.), *Progress in brain research* (Vol. 61, pp. 375–398). Amsterdam, the Netherlands: Elsevier.

Miller, K., & Ryan, J. M. (2011). *Design, development, and testing of the NHIS Sexual Identity Question.* Hyattsville, MD: National Center for Health Statistics.

Monteflores, C., & Schultz, S. J. (1978). Coming out: Similarities and differences for lesbians and gay men. *Journal of Social Issues, 34*, 59–72. doi:10.1111/j.1540-4560.1978.tb02614.x

Mosher, C. M. (2001). The social implications of sexual identity formation and the coming-out process: A review of the theoretical and empirical literature. *Family Journal: Counseling and Therapy for Couples and Families, 9*, 164–173.

Mustanski, B. (2011). Ethical and regulatory issues with conducting sexuality research with LGBT adolescents: A call to action for a scientifically informed approach. *Archives of Sexual Behavior, 40*, 673–686. doi:10.1007/s10508-011-9745-1

Mustanski, B., Newcomb, M., Heinz, A., Birkett, M., & Ashbeck, A. (2011). *Sex differences in developmental trajectories of sexual attractions among LGBT youth.* Paper presented at the annual meeting of the International Academy of Sex Research, Los Angeles, CA.

Mustanski, B. S., & Bailey, J. M. (2003). A therapist's guide to the genetics of human sexual orientation. *Sexual and Relationship Therapy, 18*, 429–436.

Mustanski, B. S., Chivers, M. L., & Bailey, J. M. (2002). A critical review of recent biological research on human sexual orientation. *Annual Review of Sex Research, 13*, 89–140.

Mustanski, B. S., Dupree, M. G., Nievergelt, C. M., Bocklandt, S., Schork, N. J., & Hamer, D. H. (2005). A genomewide scan of male sexual orientation. *Human Genetics, 116*, 272–278. doi:10.1007/s00439-004-1241-4

Mustanski, B. S., Garofalo, R., & Emerson, E. M. (2010). Mental health disorders, psychological distress, and suicidality in a diverse sample of lesbian, gay, bisexual, and transgender youths. *American Journal of Public Health, 100*, 2426–2432. doi:AJPH.2009.178319[pii]10.2105/AJPH.2009.178319

New, M. I., & Josso, N. (1988). Disorders of gonadal differentiation and congenital adrenal hyperplasia. *Endocrinology and Metabolism Clinics of North America, 17*, 339–366.

Newman, B. S., & Muzzonigro, P. G. (1993). The effect of traditional family values on the coming out process of gay male adolescents. *Adolescence, 28*, 213–226.

Newport, F. (2011). For first time, majority of Americans favor legal gay marriage. Retrieved from http://www.gallup.com/poll/147662/first-time-majority-americans-favor-legal-gay-marriage.aspx

Ngun, T. C., Ghahramani, N., Sanchez, F. J., Bocklandt, S., & Vilain, E. (2011). The genetics of sex differences in brain and behavior. *Frontiers in Neuroendocrinology, 32*, 227–246. doi:10.1016/j.yfrne.2010.10.001

Pare, C. M. B. (1956). Homosexuality and chromosomal sex. *Journal of Psychosomatic Research, 1*, 247–251.

Parks, C. A., Hughes, T. L., & Matthews, A. K. (2004). Race/ethnicity and sexual orientation: Intersecting identities. *Cultural Diversity and Ethnic Minority Psychology, 10*, 241–254. doi:10.1037/1099-9809.10.3.241

Pattatucci, A. M. L., & Hamer, D. H. (1995). Development and familiarity of sexual orientation in females. *Behavior Genetics, 25*, 407–420.

Pearcey, S. M., Docherty, K. J., & Dabbs, J. M., Jr. (1996). Testosterone and sex role identification in lesbian couples. *Physiology and Behavior, 60*, 1033–1035.

Peplau, L. A., Garnets, L. D., Spalding, L. R., Conley, T. D., & Veniegas, R. C. (1998). A critique of Bem's "Exotic Becomes Erotic" theory of sexual orientation. *Psychological Review, 105*, 387–394.

Peplau, L. A., Sparlding, L. R., Conley, T. D., & Veniegas, R. C. (1999). The development of sexual orientation in women. *Annual Review of Sex Research, 10*, 71–99.

Pereda, N., Guilera, G., Forns, M., & Gomez-Benito, J. (2009). The prevalence of child sexual abuse in community and student samples: A meta-analysis. *Clinical Psychology Review, 29*, 328–338. doi:10.1016/j.cpr.2009.02.007

Phoenix, C. H., Goy, R. W., Gerall, A. A., & Young, W. C. (1959). Organizing action of prenatally administered testosterone propionate on the tissues mediating mating behavior in the female guinea pig. *Endocrinology, 65*, 369–382.

Plumb, P., & Cowan, G. (1984). A developmental study of destereotyping and androgynous activity preferences of tomboys, nontomboys, and males. *Sex Roles, 10*, 703–712. doi:10.1007/bf00287381

Purcell, D. W., Malow, R. M., Dolezal, C., & Carballo-Dieguez, A. (2004). Sexual abuse of boys: Short- and long-term associations and implications for HIV prevention. In L. J. Koenig, L. S. Doll, A. O'Leary & W. Pequegnat (Eds.), *From child sexual abuse to adult sexual risk: Trauma, revictimization, and intervention* (pp. 93–114). Washington, DC: American Psychological Association.

Purcell, D. W., Patterson, J. D., & Spikes, P. S. (2007). Childhood sexual abuse experienced by gay and bisexual men: Understanding the disparities and interventions to help eliminate them. In R. J. Wolitski, R. Stall & R. O. Valdiserri (Eds.), *Unequal opportunity: Health disparities affecting gay and bisexual men in the United States* (pp. 72–96). New York, NY: Oxford University Press.

Rahman, Q., & Wilson, G. D. (2003). Born gay? The psychobiology of human sexual orientation. *Personality and Individual Differences, 34*, 1337–1382.

Remafedi, G., Resnick, M., Blum, R., & Harris, L. (1992). Demography of sexual orientation in adolescents. *Pediatrics, 89*, 714–721.

Rice, G., Anderson, C., Risch, N., & Ebers, G. (1999). Male homosexuality: Absence of linkage to microsatellite markers at Xq28. *Science, 284*, 665–667.

Rieger, G., Linsenmeier, J. A. W., Gygax, L., & Bailey, J. M. (2008). Sexual orientation and childhood gender nonconformity: Evidence from home videos. *Developmental Psychology, 44*, 46–58. doi:10.1037/0012-1649.44.1.46

Rieger, G., Linsenmeier, J. A. W., Gygax, L., Garcia, S., & Bailey, J. M. (2010). Dissecting "gaydar": Accuracy and the role of masculinity-femininity. *Archives of Sexual Behavior, 39*, 124–140. doi:10.1007/s10508-008-9405-2

Rosario, M., Meyer-Bahlburg, H. F. L., Hunter, J., & Exner, T. M. (1996). The psychosexual development of urban lesbian, gay, and bisexual youths. *Journal of Sex Research, 33*, 113–126. doi:10.1080/00224499609551823

Rosario, M., Schrimshaw, E. W., Hunter, J., & Braun, L. (2006). Sexual identity development among gay, lesbian, and bisexual youths: Consistency and change over time. *Journal of Sex Research, 43*, 46–58.

Roselli, C. E., Larkin, K., Resko, J. A., Stellflug, J. N., & Stormshak, F. (2004). The volume of a sexually dimorphic nucleus in the ovine medial preoptic area/anterior hypothalamus varies with sexual partner preference. *Endocrinology, 145*, 478–483. doi:10.1210/en.2003-1098

Ross, M. W., Essien, E. J., Williams, M. L., & Fernandez-Esquer, M. E. (2003). Concordance between sexual behavior and sexual identity in street outreach samples of four racial/ethnic groups. *Sexually Transmitted Diseases, 30*, 110–113.

Russell, S. T., Clarke, T. J., & Clary, J. (2009). Are teens "post-gay"? Contemporary adolescents' sexual identity labels. *Journal of Youth and Adolescence, 38*, 884–890. doi:10.1007/s10964-008-9388-2

Rust, P. C. (1996). Managing multiple identities: Diversity among bisexual women and men. In B. A. Firestein (Ed.), *Bisexuality: The psychology and politics of an invisible minority* (pp. 53–83). Thousand Oaks, CA: Sage.

Rust, P. C. (2003). Finding a sexual identity and community: Therapeutic implications and cultural assumptions in scientific models of coming out. In L. D. Garnets & D. C. Kimmel (Eds.), *Psychological perspectives on lesbian, gay, and bisexual experiences* (pp. 227–269). New York, NY: Columbia University Press.

Sanders, A. R., Cao, Q., Zhang, J., Badner, J. A., Goldin, L. R., & Guroff, J. J. (1998). *Genetic linkage study of male homosexual orientation.* Paper presented at the annual meeting of the American Psychiatric Association, Toronto, Ontario, Canada.

Sandfort, T. G. M. (2005). Sexual orientation and gender: Stereotypes and beyond. *Archives of Sexual Behavior, 34*, 595–611. doi:10.1007/s10508-005-7907-8

Savic, I., Berglund, H., & Lindstrom, P. (2005). Brain response to putative pheromones in homosexual men. *Proceedings of the National Academy of Sciences of the United States of America, 102*, 7356–7361. doi:10.1073/pnas.0407998102

Savic, I., Garcia-Falgueras, A., & Swaab, D. F. (2010). Sexual differentiation of the human brain in relation to gender identity and sexual orientation. *Progress in Brain Research, 186*, 41–62. doi:10.1016/B978-0-444-53630-3.00004-X

Savic, I., & Lindstrom, P. (2008). PET and MRI show differences in cerebral asymmetry and functional connectivity between homo- and heterosexual subjects. *Proceedings of the National Academy of Sciences of the United States of America, 105*, 9403–9408.

Savin-Williams, R. C. (1995). An exploratory study of pubertal maturation timing and self-esteem among gay and bisexual male youths. *Developmental Psychology, 31*, 56–64. doi:10.1037/0012-1649.31.1.56

Savin-Williams, R. C. (1996). Ethnic- and sexual-minority youth. In R. C. Savin-Williams (Ed.), *The lives of lesbians, gays, and bisexuals: Children to adults* (pp. 152–165). Orlando, FL: Harcourt Brace.

Savin-Williams, R. C. (1998). The disclosure to families of same-sex attractions by lesbian, gay, and bisexual youths. *Journal of Research on Adolescence, 8*, 49–68. doi:10.1207/s15327795jra0801_3

Savin-Williams, R. C. (2011). Identity development among sexual-minority youth. In S. J. Schwartz, K. Luyckx, & V. Vignoles (Eds.), *Handbook of identity theory and research* (pp. 671–689). New York, NY: Springer.

Savin-Williams, R. C., & Cohen, K. M. (2004). Homoerotic development during childhood and adolescence. *Child and Adolescent Psychiatric Clinics of North America, 13*, 529–549. doi:10.1016/j.chc.2004.02.005

Savin-Williams, R. C., & Diamond, L. M. (2000). Sexual identity trajectories among sexual-minority youths: Gender comparisons. *Archives of Sexual Behavior, 29*, 607–627. doi:10.1023/a:1002058505138

Savin-Williams, R. C., & Ream, G. L. (2007). Prevalence and stability of sexual orientation components during adolescence and young adulthood. *Archives of Sexual Behavior, 36*, 385–394.

Sell, R. L. (1996). The Sell Assessment of Sexual Orientation: Background and scoring. *Journal of Gay, Lesbian, and Bisexual Identity, 1*, 295–310.

Sell, R. L. (2007). Defining and measuring sexual orientation for research. In I. H. Meyer & M. E. Northridge (Eds.), *The health of sexual minorities: Public health perspectives on lesbian, gay, bisexual, and transgender populations* (pp. 355–374). New York, NY: Springer Science + Business Media.

Shively, M. G., & de Cecco, J. P. (1977). Components of sexual identity. *Journal of Homosexuality, 3*, 41–48. doi:10.1300/J082v03n01_04

Singh, D., Vidaurri, M., Zambarano, R. J., & Dabbs, J. M., Jr. (1999). Lesbian erotic role identification: Behavioral, morphological, and hormonal correlates. *Journal of Personality and Social Psychology, 76*, 1035–1049.

Skerven, K., & de St. Aubin, E. (2006). Lesbian self-development in context: Cohort analysis at two points in history. *Research in Human Development, 3*, 251–269. doi:10.1207/s15427617rhd0304_5

Skidmore, W. C., Linsenmeier, J. A. W., & Bailey, J. M. (2006). Gender nonconformity and psychological distress in lesbians and gay men. *Archives of Sexual Behavior, 35*, 685–697. doi:10.1007/s10508-006-9108-5

Sophie, J. (1985). A critical-examination of stage theories of lesbian identity development. *Journal of Homosexuality, 12*, 39–51.

Spitzer, R. L. (2003). Can some gay men and lesbians change their sexual orientation? 200 participants reporting a change from homosexual to heterosexual orientation. *Archives of Sexual Behavior, 32*, 403–417.

Stokes, J. P., Damon, W., & McKirnan, D. J. (1997). Predictors of movement toward homosexuality: A longitudinal study of bisexual men. *Journal of Sex Research, 34*, 304–312.

Stokes, J. P., McKirnan, D., & Burzette, R. (1993). Sexual behavior, condom use, disclosure of sexuality, and stability of sexual orientation in bisexual men. *Journal of Sex Research, 30*, 203–213.

Stoleru, S., & Mouras, H. (2007). Brain functional imaging studies of sexual desire and arousal in human males. In E. Janssen (Ed.), *The psychophysiology of sex* (pp. 3–34). Bloomington: Indiana University Press.

Storms, M. D. (1981). A theory of erotic orientation development. *Psychological Review, 88*, 340–353. doi:10.1037//0033-295x.88.4.340

Swaab, D. F. (2008). Sexual orientation and its basis in brain structure and function. *Proceedings of the National Academy of Sciences of the United States of America, 105*, 10273–10274. doi:10.1073/pnas.0805542105

Swaab, D. F., & Hoffman, M. A. (1990). An enlarged suprachiasmatic nucleus in homosexual men. *Brian Research, 537*, 141–148.

Swann, S. K., & Anastas, J. W. (2003). Dimensions of lesbian identity during adolescence and young adulthood. *Journal of Gay and Lesbian Social Services: Issues in Practice, Policy and Research, 15*, 109–125. doi:10.1300/J041v15n01_08

Tolman, D. L., & Diamond, L. M. (2001). Desegregating sexuality research: Cultural and biological perspectives on gender and desire. *Annual Review of Sex Research, 12*, 33–74.

Troiden, R. R. (1979). Becoming homosexual: Model of gay identity acquisition. *Psychiatry-Interpersonal and Biological Processes, 42*, 362–373.

Ulrichs, K. H. (1994). *The riddle of "man-manly" love: The pioneering work on male homosexuality*. Buffalo, NY: Prometheus Books.

Veale, J. F., Clarke, D. E., & Lomax, T. C. (2010). Biological and psychosocial correlates of adult gender-variant identities: New findings. *Personality and Individual Differences, 49*, 252–257. doi:10.1016/j.paid.2010.03.045

Wang, B., Zhou, S., Hong, F., Wang, J., Liu, X., … Ma, X. (2011). Association analysis between the tag SNP for sonic hedgehog rs9333613 polymorphism and male sexual orientation. *Journal of Andrology, 33*, 951–954. doi:10.2164/jandrol.110.012849

Weinberg, M. S., Williams, C. J., & Pryor, D. W. (1994). *Dual attraction: Understanding bisexuality*. New York, NY: Oxford University Press.

White, G. L., Fishbein, S., & Rutstein, J. (1981). Passionate love and the misattribution of arousal. *Journal of Personality and Social Psychology, 41*, 56–62.

Wilson, B. D. M., & Miller, R. L. (2002). Strategies for managing heterosexism used among African American gay and bisexual men. *Journal of Black Psychology, 28*, 371–391. doi:10.1177/009579802237543

Wilson, H. W., & Widom, C. S. (2010). Does physical abuse, sexual abuse, or neglect in childhood increase the likelihood of same-sex sexual relationships and cohabitation? A prospective 30-year follow-up. *Archives of Sexual Behavior, 39*, 63–74. doi:10.1007/s10508-008-9449-3

Wilson, P. A. (2008). A dynamic-ecological model of identity formation and conflict among bisexually-behaving African-American men. *Archives of Sexual Behavior, 37*, 794–809. doi:10.1007/s10508-008-9362-9

Wisniewski, A. B., Migeon, C. J., Meyer-Bahlburg, H. F., Gearhart, J. P., Berkovitz, G. D., Brown, T. R., & Money, J. (2000). Complete androgen insensitivity syndrome: Long-term medical, surgical, and psychosexual outcome. *Journal of Clinical Endocrinology and Metabolism, 85*, 2664–2669.

Wolchik, S. A., Beggs, V. E., Wincze, J. P., Sakheim, D. K., Barlow, D. H., & Mavissakalian, M. (1980). The effect of emotional arousal on subsequent sexual arousal in men. *Journal of Abnormal Psychology, 89*, 595–598.

CHAPTER 20

GENDER AND SAME-SEX SEXUALITY

Lisa M. Diamond

One of the most important developments in research on same-sex sexuality over the past several decades has been the increasing awareness of the way in which sexuality manifests itself differently in men versus women, at all stages of the life course. During the first wave of rigorous psychological research on sexual orientation in the 1970s and 1980s, it was common for researchers to discuss "gay men and lesbians" as if they were a single, coherent group, differentiated only by biological sex. Research since that time, however, has revealed pervasive differences in the development, expression, and phenomenology of same-sex sexuality in men and women. In light of these findings, some have argued that female and male sexual orientation may have fundamentally different origins, mechanisms, and manifestations (Bailey, 2009; Chivers, Rieger, Latty, & Bailey, 2004; Hyde, 2005b; Mustanski, Chivers, & Bailey, 2002). Yet the full extent of—and underlying reasons for—these differences remains to be fully specified. This chapter provides a comprehensive review of research documenting gender differences in same-sex sexuality over the life course and discusses potential explanations for these differences. Although I am mindful of the cautions raised by Hyde (Hyde, 2005a; see also Chapter 2, this volume) regarding the overemphasis and inflation of gender differences at the expense of noting the pervasive similarities between men and women, same-sex sexuality is a phenomenon in which women's unique experiences historically have gone underinvestigated, and in which our newfound appreciation of gender differences is productively challenging current scientific models of sexual orientation for both men and women. Accordingly, I devote more attention to female same-sex sexuality than to male same-sex sexuality in this chapter to correct for the historical inattention to women's experiences and to call attention to important discoveries about female same-sex sexuality that have the potential to change the way we think about male sexuality as well. Toward this end, this chapter concludes by highlighting some of the most important directions for future research, which include a more nuanced approach to the sexuality of men as well as women.

Given that Chapters 18 and 19 of this volume provide comprehensive coverage of basic definitional and measurement issues regarding sexual orientation as well as foundational theoretical and empirical work on the phenomena of same-sex sexuality, this chapter does not reiterate this background information. It begins, instead, by highlighting the dominant model of sexual orientation that emerged from early research conducted on gay men to clarify the key domains in which women differ. Two issues of terminology, however, bear clarification. First, the term *sexual minorities* is used in this chapter to refer to individuals with same-sex attractions and behavior, in order to include the entire population of individuals with these experiences (whereas the term *gay/lesbian/bisexual* refers only to individuals who adopt those specific sexual identities). Research conducted with representative samples indicates that the majority of individuals with same-sex attractions and behavior do not self-identify as gay, lesbian, bisexual (Chandra, Mosher,

http://dx.doi.org/10.1037/14193-020
APA Handbook of Sexuality and Psychology: Vol. 1. Person-Based Approaches, D. L. Tolman and L. M. Diamond (Editors-in-Chief)

Copen, & Sionean, 2011; Laumann, Gagnon, Michael, & Michaels, 1994; Savin-Williams & Ream, 2007). Some continue to identify as heterosexual, whereas others maintain no identity label at all. Historically, such individuals have been excluded from psychological research on sexual orientation (reviewed in Diamond, 2008b), yet their experiences are critical for understanding the phenomenon of same-sex sexuality in all of its manifestations. This chapter, however, does use the descriptors *lesbian*, *gay*, and *bisexual* when summarizing studies or research traditions that specifically recruited research participants on the basis of their lesbian, gay, or bisexual identification.

Second, this chapter generally refers to *same-sex sexuality* rather than sexual orientation. As reviewed eloquently in Chapters 18 and 19 of this volume, the construct of sexual orientation denotes a multifaceted sexual predisposition for the same sex, the other sex, or both sexes, encompassing sexual attractions, fantasies, affectional feelings, behavior, and so on. Statements about an individual's sexual orientation are therefore statements about his or her general pattern of sexual attraction, behavior, etc. Statements about same-sex sexuality, however, make no presumptions about an individual's general pattern of attraction or behavior. Like the construct of sexual orientation, same-sex sexuality has multiple manifestations, which might occur entirely on their own or in combination with one another, including same-sex attractions, same-sex sexual contact, same-sex love relationships, same-sex fantasies, and arousability to same-sex images. By using the broad umbrella term *same-sex sexuality* instead of sexual orientation, we can capture and analyze this phenomenon without making presumptions about individuals' underlying sexual predispositions. This is particularly important when studying women, given that (as will be reviewed) women appear more likely than men to experience sexual attractions and behaviors that sometimes run counter to their overall orientation.

THE MALE MODEL OF SEXUAL ORIENTATION

With the exception of Kinsey's seminal research on women (Kinsey, Pomeroy, Martin, & Gebhard, 1953), much of the foundational research that supports current understandings of sexual orientation was conducted with predominantly or exclusively male samples, given that openly identified gay or bisexual men historically have been easier to sample (Sell & Petrulio, 1996). Originally, this was not considered a substantive problem, given that sexual orientation implicitly was presumed to operate similarly for women and men (Adler, 1967; De Cecco, 1981; Futuyma & Risch, 1983–1984; Storms, 1980). The model of sexual orientation that emerged from this research was rigidly categorical, yielding two fundamental types of people: homosexuals and heterosexuals. This dichotomy has its roots in the historical view of homosexuality as a form of pathology, with an associated cluster of signs and symptoms (Block, 1909; Forel, 1908; Krafft-Ebing, 1882).

Although modern researchers no longer consider sexual orientation to be a sickness, they generally consider it to be a "master status," a trait that emerges early in life, remains relatively stable, and exerts a uniform pressure on a wide range of associated experiences (e.g., sexual attraction, arousal, behavior, fantasy, identification). To summarize from the 2011 Institute of Medicine Report on the health of sexual-minority populations, sexual orientation is taken to represent "an enduring pattern of or disposition to experience sexual or romantic desires for, and relationships with, people of one's same sex, the other sex, or both sexes" (Institute of Medicine, 2011, p. 27).

This standard model of sexual orientation ably captures most men's experiences with same-sex sexuality, but it proves less successful in capturing the full range of women's experiences of same-sex sexuality, for the following reasons (each of which is reviewed in depth throughout this chapter). First, whereas the standard model views sexual orientation as an inborn trait that begins to express itself early in life, women show more variability than men in the timing of their first same-sex attractions and behaviors. In some cases, women's first experiences of same-sex sexuality occur relatively late in life, directly contrary to the standard model. Second, whereas the standard model views exclusive homosexuality to be the prototypical form of same-sex sexuality, women are substantially more likely to experience nonexclusive (or "bisexual") patterns of attraction and behavior than exclusive same-sex attractions and behavior. Third, whereas the standard model presumes that sexual orientation is a fixed and stable trait, women show more change over time in their patterns of attraction, identity, and behavior. Fourth, whereas the standard model presumes that sexual orientations are fundamentally "about" sexual desire and fundamentally "about" gender, many women grant a relatively greater role for their *affectional* feelings in shaping their erotic desires and choices, and some of these women report that these affectional considerations outweigh criteria such as gender. In other words, they report that their desires are triggered by "the person, not their gender," whereas the standard model presumes that "gender of partner" is perhaps the single most important partner characteristic circumscribing an individuals' capacity for sexual desire. Fifth, and finally, women's sexuality appears to be more "fluid" or "plastic" than men's, meaning that it is highly sensitive to social and interpersonal influences, and hence it is more prone to such phenomena as long-term variability and inconsistency across domains. Because of women's propensity for fluidity, their underlying sexual predispositions appear to have less deterministic influences on their life-course pattern of sexual attraction and behavior than is the case for men.

The following sections review the empirical evidence for each of these key gender differences, highlighting their potential explanations and implications, and concluding with a discussion of key directions for future research.

Developmental Trajectories

Some of the earliest evidence for distinct gender differences in same-sex sexuality emerged from research on its initial expression and development during late childhood and adolescence. As reviewed in Chapter 19 of this volume, a considerable body of research has focused on developing stage-sequential psychological models of the "coming-out" process, through which individuals first became aware of their same-sex attractions; first explored same-sex contact; and eventually adopted a gay, lesbian, or bisexual identity. Most of these models mark the onset of sexual identity development as the individual's first awareness of same-sex attractions, presumed to occur in late childhood or early adolescence (although sometimes preceded by childhood "feelings of differentness" or gender-atypical behaviors). The next stage involves a period of testing and exploration, during which youths seek information about gay, lesbian, and bisexual individuals and communities and may begin experimenting with same-sex sexual contact. Succeeding stages of identity development entail adopting a sexual-minority label, disclosing this sexual identity to others, becoming involved in a same-sex romantic relationship, and embracing one's sexual identity within a larger social context (e.g., the political arena).

As reviewed in Chapter 19 of this volume, stage-sequential models of identity development have been critiqued strongly over the years for their overly prescriptive nature, for their rigid (and often untested) assumptions regarding "healthy" development, for their insensitivity to sources of sociocultural variation, and for their inapplicability to bisexuals (reflecting the fact that bisexually identified individuals generally were excluded from the research samples on which the models generally were developed and validated). Perhaps more important, the very notion of "prototypical" pathways of sexual identity development has become increasingly suspect, as researchers have collected increasingly rigorous data—from increasingly diverse samples—on *variation* in developmental trajectories. For example, although it once was thought that all sexual minorities experienced the emergence of their same-sex attractions before adolescence, we now know that this is not always the case. Rather, sexual minorities show a wide range of different developmental histories, with different ages and contexts for the classic "milestones" of first same-sex attractions, first conscious sexual questioning, first same-sex contact, and first self-identification (Dubé & Savin-Williams, 1999; Floyd & Bakeman, 2006; Rosario, Schrimshaw, & Hunter, 2008, 2011; Rosario, Schrimshaw, Hunter, & Levy-Warren, 2009; Savin-Williams, 2001).

Yet some of the largest and most notable deviations from conventional coming-out models have been documented among lesbians and bisexual women (Diamond, 1998; Golden, 1987; Kitzinger & Wilkinson, 1995; Rust, 1993; Sophie, 1985–1986). This perhaps is to be expected, given that many of these models were derived from exclusively or predominantly male samples (typically drawn from community support groups for self-identified lesbian, gay, and bisexual teens). The most consistent gender differences involved later ages of first awareness, same-sex contact, or identification (D'Augelli & Hershberger, 1993; Grov, Bimbi, Nanin, & Parsons, 2006; Herdt & Boxer, 1993; Herek, Norton, Allen, & Sims, 2010; Maguen, Floyd, Bakeman, & Armistead, 2002; Rosario et al., 1996). Although most of these studies (with the notable exception of Herek et al., 2010) involve relatively small and unrepresentative samples, the consistency of gender differences is notable. Because the magnitude of gender differences in identity milestones varies from study to study, and because some studies find subgroups of women whose patterns resemble that of their male counterparts (Rosario et al., 2008; Savin-Williams & Diamond, 2000), it is more accurate to conclude that women show greater variability in the timing of sexual identity development, than to conclude that they are uniformly "later." In addition to variability in timing, women show greater variability than do men in the sequencing of different stages, the length of time between successive stages, and the overall duration of the process, with some women pausing and then revisiting identity questioning multiple times, rather than moving inexorably toward the adoption of a lesbian, gay, or bisexual label (Eliason, 1996; Savin-Williams & Diamond, 2000; Sophie, 1985–1986; Weinberg, Williams, & Pryor, 1994).

Perhaps most striking, however, are the many cases of women who report no adolescent awareness of same-sex attractions at all, and instead begin experiencing these attractions in mid- to late-adulthood (Blumstein & Schwartz, 1977; Cassingham & O'Neil, 1993; Charbonneau & Lander, 1991; Kitzinger & Wilkinson, 1995). Historically, such long delays in awareness were attributed to repression and latency. For example, writing in the 1970s about the late-life lesbian transitions they observed among their own research participants, Saghir and Robins (1973) attributed these cases to "dormancy" in women's underlying homosexuality. Yet over the years, studies probing the antecedents and phenomenology of such late-life transitions have suggested that the dormancy model is not always accurate. Loewenstein (1984–1985), for example, concluded from her research on more than 700 women that those reporting late-life same-sex "passions" were undergoing a genuine emergence of novel same-sex desires. Similarly, Kitzinger and Wilkinson (1995) interviewed 80 lesbians whose first sexual questioning took place in adulthood rather than adolescence. More than two thirds of these women had been married; the average age of their first same-sex experience was 18, and the average age of first lesbian identification was 34. Although some women described themselves as having suppressed their lesbianism for many years, others experienced the transition to same-sex sexuality as a sudden transformation, described in terms of "rebirth," a "quantum leap," a "conversion experience," or "emerging from a chrysalis" (Kitzinger, 1995, p. 100).

Notably, the context for these transformative experiences was often an intimate emotional relationship with a specific woman, and this pattern emerges in adolescence as well. Whereas young men typically emphasize an awareness of explicit same-sex arousal or attraction when describing the factors that triggered or sustained their process of sexual identity questioning, women tend to place greater emphasis on romantic and affectional feelings for same-sex friends (Diamond, 2000a, 2002; Golden, 1987; Savin-Williams, 1998; Savin-Williams & Diamond, 2000). Some women report experiencing emotional attractions to women before ever experiencing physical attractions for women, or describe their sexual feelings as developing out of a singular emotional attachment (Blumstein & Schwartz, 1990; Cassingham & O'Neil, 1993; Diamond, 2008b; Rose, Zand, & Cimi, 1993; Walsh, 2010; Weinberg et al., 1994). Other women emphasize ideological factors and social reference groups as triggering or supporting their identity questioning (Blumstein & Schwartz, 1990; Cass, 1990; Esterberg, 1994; Nichols, 1990; Rust, 1993, 1995; Silber, 1990). This is often the case for "political lesbians," who typically report that they chose to orient their lives around women for social and political reasons and then found their sexual desires following suit (Golden, 1987, 1994; Kitzinger & Wilkinson, 1995; Silber, 1990; Whisman, 1993, 1996).

The notion that same-sex sexual orientations express themselves uniformly early in development, in the form of clear-cut same-sex desires, is inaccurate. Although there is variability in both men and women regarding the developmental unfolding of same-sex sexuality, this variability appears to be particularly large among women.

Nonexclusive Attractions

Among the most well-documented gender differences regarding same-sex sexuality is the fact that women's sexual attractions, behaviors, and patterns of genital arousal are more likely to be nonexclusive (i.e., directed to both sexes, in varying degrees) than to be exclusively directed to the same sex (I use the term *nonexclusive* instead of *bisexual* because the latter term tends to connote equal degrees of attraction to each sex, whereas *nonexclusive* better captures the experiences of individuals who may be predominantly—but not exclusively—drawn to one sex or the other). This fact runs directly counter to the conventional model of sexual orientation, reviewed earlier, which posits that sexual orientation has only two forms: exclusive homosexuality and exclusive heterosexuality. Reflecting this view, researchers studying the nature of sexual orientation historically have excluded individuals claiming nonexclusive patterns of attraction, sometimes for the sake of methodological clarity and sometimes because such individuals simply were not considered to be "real" homosexuals (Burr, 1996; Rust, 2000; Whisman, 1993, 1996).

Yet numerous surveys using large, random, representative samples have shown that men and women reporting sexual attractions to both men and women (to varying degrees) outnumber those reporting exclusive same-sex attractions (Chandra et al., 2011; Hayes et al., 2012; Laumann et al., 1994; Mosher, Chandra, & Jones, 2005; Savin-Williams, 2006). For example, one large-scale representative study of American adults (Mosher et al., 2005) found that 6% of American men and nearly 13% of American women reported attractions to both sexes, whereas 1.5% of men and 0.8% of women were attracted exclusively to the same sex (the same basic pattern emerged in Chandra et al., 2011). In Wave 4 of the National Longitudinal Study of Adolescent Health (during which participants were in early adulthood), 6.4% of men and nearly 20% of women reported a nonheterosexual orientation, and of these individuals, only 5% of women and 26% of men reported being exclusively homosexual. Similar results have been found internationally: A random sample of British adults found that 5.2% of men and 6% of women reported a nonheterosexual orientation, and of these individuals, only 10% of the women and 20% of the men described their orientation as exclusively homosexual (Hayes et al., 2012). In a large cohort study of New Zealanders (Dickson, Paul, & Herbison, 2003), 5.6% of men and 16.4% of women reported some degree of same-sex attraction at age 26, and of these individuals, 5% of the women and 21% of the men described their orientation as exclusively homosexual. A follow-up study (Dickson, Roode, Cameron, & Paul, 2013) found that at age 32, 4.9% of men and 14.7% of women reported same-sex attractions, and at age 38 these percentages were 6.4% for men and 12.4% for women. Among those with same-sex attractions, 27% of men and 5% of women reported exclusive same-sex attractions at age 32, and at age 38 these figures were 23% for men and 7% for women. Hence, directly contrary to the conventional wisdom that individuals with exclusive same-sex attractions represent the prototypical "type" of sexual-minority individual, and that those with bisexual patterns of attraction are infrequent exceptions, the opposite is true: Individuals with nonexclusive patterns of attraction are indisputably the "norm," and those with exclusive same-sex attractions are the exception.

Perhaps more notably, however, the proportion of women with nonexclusive attractions far exceeds the proportion of men with nonexclusive attractions. In the studies by Mosher et al. (2005) and Chandra et al. (2011), the proportion of women with nonexclusive patterns of attraction is double the proportion of men with nonexclusive attractions. In the studies by Dickson et al. (2003, 2013), the proportion of women with nonexclusive attractions was more than triple the proportion of men with nonexclusive attractions, and in the study by Savin-Williams et al. (2012) using the Adolescent Health data set, the proportion of women with nonexclusive attractions was four times larger than the proportion of men with nonexclusive attractions. Hence, the long-standing tendency for researchers to ignore the experiences of sexual-minority individuals with nonexclusive attractions, and focus instead on the (rather small and unrepresentative) subset of sexual minorities with exclusive same-sex attractions, has misrepresented the experiences of women to a substantially greater degree than it has misrepresented the experiences of men.

The specific distribution of attractions to same-sex versus other-sex partners also reveals notable gender differences. In every large-scale representative study reviewed thus far, the single largest group of individuals with same-sex attractions report predominant—but not exclusive—*other-sex* attractions. We might think of such individuals as "Kinsey 1s" or "mostly straight" (following Thompson & Morgan, 2008). On the Kinsey scale, 0 represents exclusive heterosexuality and 6 represents exclusive same-sex sexuality. Hence, individuals who consider themselves "Kinsey 1s" can be viewed as possessing the minimum degree of same-sex attraction that nonetheless rules out complete heterosexuality. What is particularly interesting about the prevalence of these individuals from study to study is that they historically have been treated with the most skepticism and denigration from scientists and laypeople alike. To some degree, this reflects appropriate scientific skepticism about measurement, given the inherent ambiguity in self-reported, single-item measures of same-sex attraction (see Chapter 19, this volume).

The problem, however, is that this vaguely defined category of "mostly, but not completely, straight" women clearly represents the majority of women with same-sex attractions. In Mosher et al.'s study (2005), for example, fully 10% of American women described their attractions as "mostly other-sex," whereas only 3.4% endorsed "both sexes," "only same-sex," or "mostly same-sex." Among men, this difference was not as stark (3.9% endorsing "mostly other-sex" compared with 3.2% endorsing the other categories). Similar gender differences have emerged from other studies. Fergusson, Horwood, Ridder, and Beautrais (2005) found in a large New Zealand birth cohort that 12% of women but only 4–5% of men described their attractions as predominantly other-sex and described their identity as "mostly heterosexual." In a random, representative survey of American adolescents, nearly 11% of young women described their romantic attractions as "mostly heterosexual but somewhat attracted to people of the same sex," whereas only about 4% of male adolescents endorsed this description (Udry & Chantala, 2006). In Laumann et al.'s 1994 study, women with "mostly heterosexual" attractions accounted for 62% of all women reporting any same-sex attractions, whereas men with mostly heterosexual attractions accounted for 40% of those with any same-sex attractions. In the Adolescent Health data reported by Savin-Williams et al. (2012), "mostly heterosexual" individuals accounted for 80% of women but 55% of men with same-sex attractions. In a sample of nearly 2000 Montréal high school students, more than 9% described their sexual identity as either "unsure" or "heterosexual with same-sex attraction," and 69% of these students were female. In one of the only systematic studies of "mostly straight" individuals, Thompson and Morgan (2008) found that although "mostly straight" women show diverse patterns of current and prior attractions and behavior, they nonetheless appear to represent a distinct subtype of nonheterosexual women, with erotic profiles falling somewhere between bisexuality and exclusive heterosexuality.

One distinguishing characteristic of this group appears to be their maintenance of a heterosexual identity label despite open acknowledgement of same-sex attraction (and sometimes same-sex behavior), resulting in stark discrepancies among the domains of identity, attraction, and behavior. Importantly, such discrepancies are relatively common. In fact, the most recent representative survey indicates that 78% of women reporting any same-sex attractions or behavior and 72% of men reporting any same-sex attractions or behavior do not identify as lesbian, gay, or bisexual (Chandra et al., 2011). Approximately half of the women in this group and more than a third of the men in this group are individuals who describe their attractions as "mostly opposite-sex."

Studies employing in-depth qualitative interviews help to reveal why this pattern exists (Diamond, 2008b; Golden, 1996). Individuals who are mostly—but not exclusively—attracted to the opposite sex often doubt whether their sporadic same-sex attractions are enough to "count" as nonheterosexual, given that the dominant cultural model of sexual orientation posits only two categories of sexual orientation—exclusive homosexuality and exclusively heterosexuality—neither of which represents their experiences. Even the "bisexual" label seems a poor fit, given that many individuals assume (albeit incorrectly) that bisexuality must entail roughly equal degrees of attraction to both men and women. Furthermore, bisexuality continues to be widely dismissed in the culture at large as a "false" or "transitional" identity. Accordingly, individuals with "mostly straight" patterns of attraction generally find that none of the available identity labels represents their experiences, and many conclude as a result that their same-sex attractions may represent a transient aberration, perhaps attributable to confusion or curiosity, rather than an important component of their overall sexual disposition.

Such experiences are substantially more likely to occur among women than among men, considering that three times as many women as men describe their attractions as "mostly opposite sex" (12% of women vs. 4% of men; Mosher et al., 2005). Hence, the fact that more women than men report discordance among the domains of attraction, behavior, and identity (see in Chapter 18, this volume) is partly attributable to the fact that many more women than men report a form of same-sex sexuality—"mostly heterosexual"—which is particularly hard to reconcile with the available cultural models of homosexuality or bisexuality.

Nonspecific Sexual Arousal

The research reviewed on nonexclusive attractions relies on self-report measures, and such data have obvious limitations (see Chapter 18, this volume). Notably, the same basic finding—that women are more likely to show sexual attraction to both sexes than to the same-sex exclusively—has emerged from studies using psychophysiological assessments of genital sexual arousal. Research by Chivers and her colleagues (Chivers & Bailey, 2005; Chivers et al., 2004; Chivers, Seto, & Blanchard, 2007) consistently has found patterns of "nonspecific" genital arousal in women (i.e., patterns of sexual arousal that do not appear to target one gender or the other), in contrast to the gender-specific patterns of sexual arousal detected in men. The methodology for these studies involves continuous measurement of blood flow to the genitals (a well-validated marker of sexual arousal) while participants view erotic film clips. Participants also indicated their *subjective* experience of arousal with continuous ratings during the video presentation. Chivers' initial study (Chivers et al., 2004) compared four different groups: self-identified gay men, self-identified heterosexual men, self-identified lesbian women, and self-identified heterosexual women. Respondents viewed videos of women having sex with women, men having sex with men, and men having sex with women. The results showed that gay men were most physiologically and subjectively aroused by the male videos, whereas heterosexual men were most physiologically and subjectively aroused by the female videos. In other words, both their genital responses and their subjective responses were highly gender specific. Women's self-reported subjective responses showed a similar pattern: Lesbians reported more arousal to the female videos and heterosexual women reported more arousal to the male videos. Their genital responses, however, showed a completely different pattern: Regardless of women's self-described sexual orientation, they showed roughly equivalent genital responses to the male and female sexual stimuli. In other words, their genital responses were nonspecific with respect to gender. Importantly, this was not equally true for each and every woman: On average, lesbians showed somewhat greater gender specificity (i.e., greater genital arousal to the female than to the male videos) than did the heterosexual women, but not nearly as much as the heterosexual and gay men. It also bears emphasizing that women did show specificity with regard to their self-reported arousal, meaning that women's genital and subjective responses often diverged from one another, a finding that has emerged consistently across different studies (reviewed in Chivers, Seto, Lalumiere, Laan, & Grimbos, 2010), although the specific degree of divergence varies widely from woman to woman (Rellini, McCall, Randall, & Meston, 2005).

Since publication of Chivers' first study, the results have been replicated numerous times using both photoplethysmography (Chivers & Bailey, 2005; Chivers et al., 2007; Chivers & Timmers, 2012; Peterson, Janssen, & Laan, 2010) and measures of visual attention to sexual stimuli, such as looking time and eye tracking (Hamann, Herman, Nolan, & Wallen, 2004; Lykins, Meana, & Strauss, 2008; Rullo, Strassberg, & Israel, 2010; Rupp & Wallen, 2007; Tsujimura et al., 2009), consistently demonstrating that women show less category specificity than do men but that lesbian-identified women show greater category specificity than do heterosexual women. Furthermore, Chivers' follow-up research has contributed greatly to our understanding of this basic phenomenon by elucidating that women do show different patterns of genital response to different types of sexual stimuli, but the key feature that triggers greater genital response is simply greater sexual activity, regardless of the gender (or species) of the actors involved (Chivers & Bailey, 2005). Specifically, women show greater genital responses to depictions of partnered sexual activity than to masturbation, and greater responses to masturbation than to solitary nude exercise, regardless of whether the individuals depicted are their preferred sexual targets (i.e., men for heterosexual women, and women for lesbian women). Men also show greater genital responses to stimuli that involve greater levels of sexual activity, but only if the stimuli depict their preferred sexual targets. Another notable finding to emerge from this body of work is that women's "nonspecificity" with regard to genital response extends beyond gender. Women also show genital (but not subjective) arousal to depictions of nonhuman primate sexual activity (Chivers & Bailey, 2005; Chivers et al., 2007) and depictions of sexual coercion (Suschinsky & Lalumiere, 2011; Suschinsky, Lalumiere, & Chivers, 2009).

Of course, genital or neurobiological measures do not necessarily provide "truer" measures of sexual orientation than do individuals' own subjective reports, but the correspondence between the findings of genital "nonspecificity" and the findings regarding nonexclusivity in women's self-reported attractions is striking: Regardless of whether they identify as gay, lesbian, or bisexual, women appear to possess a greater propensity to experience sexual attraction and arousal for both sexes than do men. Why might this be the case? Chivers et al. (2007) have noted that Goy and Goldfoot (1975) indicated more than 30 years ago that in many different mammalian species, bisexuality is an intrinsically dimorphic trait that develops (through prenatal hormonal pathways) in either the male or the female of a species, but never both. This suggests the provocative possibility that in humans, women are "the more bisexual sex," whereas males are more likely to be exclusively heterosexual or homosexual (see also Bailey, 2009; Rieger, Bailey, & Chivers, 2005). Numerous cultural factors might produce the very same phenomenon, such as the greater cultural acceptability of female–female intimacy more generally (reviewed in Diamond, 2003b), but the animal data suggest the possibility that there might also be a biological component to this gender differences. We revisit the potential implications of this notion toward the end of the chapter.

Change Over Time

Historically, researchers have presumed that sexual orientation represents a fixed and longitudinally stable trait (reviewed in Diamond, 2008b). Although this appears to be true for most individuals, research on sexual minorities has long documented that many recall having undergone notable shifts in their patterns of sexual attractions, behaviors, or identities over time (Golden, 1996; Kinnish, Strassberg, & Turner, 2005; Kitzinger & Wilkinson, 1995; Weinberg et al., 1994). Retrospective reports of change have obvious shortcomings, and much more reliable data on the phenomenon of change has come from a number of small-scale prospective studies conducted with community-based samples (Diamond, 2000b, 2003a, 2005b, 2008a, 2008b; Pattatucci & Hamer, 1995; Rosario,

Schrimshaw, Hunter, & Braun, 2006; Stokes, Damon, & McKirnan, 1997; Stokes, McKirnan, & Burzette, 1993). In recent years, however, a number of studies tracking longitudinal change in sexuality using large-scale, population-based samples have been published (Dickson et al., 2003; Ott, Corliss, Wypij, Rosario, & Austin, 2011; Savin-Williams & Ream, 2007), making it possible to draw more definitive conclusions about this phenomenon than was previously possible. Because this literature is reviewed in both Chapters 18 and 19 of this volume, this summary will focus only on the primary findings and patterns regarding gender differences in the propensity for change.

Some of the earliest data on longitudinal change in same-sex sexuality were collected by Pattatucci and Hamer (1995), who collected 18-month follow-up data from 175 lesbian, bisexual, and heterosexual women recruited from lesbian, gay, and bisexual organizations. The authors averaged respondents' Kinsey ratings of sexual attraction, fantasy, and behavior and found that over the 18-month assessment period, about 20% changed their Kinsey classification (usually to an adjacent category). Rosario et al. (2006) followed a more ethnically diverse group of 156 urban sexual-minority youth over the same time period (18 months) and found that 28% changed sexual identity categories. Longer follow-ups were conducted by Weinberg et al. (1994), who assessed change over a 5-year interval among, gay, lesbian, bisexual, and heterosexual men and women; approximately two thirds reported changes of one Kinsey point or more in their sexual attractions, and 85% reported changes of one point or more in their sexual behavior. My own longitudinal research has found that over a 10-year period, approximately two thirds of sexual-minority women changed their sexual identity labels, with between 25% and 30% changing labels within each 2–3 year period (Diamond, 2008b). Women with nonexclusive patterns of attractions were significantly more likely to undergo changes in identity than women with predominant or exclusive same-sex attractions, and over the entire 10-year period, women were more likely to switch to identities involving nonexclusive attractions and behavior (i.e., bisexual and "unlabeled" identities) than to switch to identities involving exclusive attractions and behavior (i.e., lesbian or heterosexual identities).

This would appear to suggest that over time, women's changes in sexual identity take the form of broadened patterns of attraction, behavior, and identification, with lesbian-identified women shifting away from exclusive same-sex sexuality, heterosexually identified (or "mostly" heterosexually identified) women shifting toward greater (but still nonexclusive) same-sex sexuality, and bisexually identified women shifting in either direction, but staying in a nonexclusive range. Do the more recent and reliable large-scale studies of prospective change bear this out? Similarly, do the prospective studies confirm the results of retrospective studies documenting larger and more frequent changes in women than in men?

Beginning with the question of gender, all of the large-scale prospective studies find greater longitudinal change in sexual attraction, behavior, or identity among women than men, and particularly of sexual-minority women (in all studies, heterosexually identified individuals show greater stability than nonheterosexuals, although the stability of female heterosexuals is consistently lower than the stability of male heterosexuals). For example, Dickson et al. (2003) sampled a cohort of approximately 1,000 New Zealanders born in the early 1970s. Of participants who reported any same-sex attractions at age 21, 35% of the men and 55% underwent a major shift in their attractions by age 26 (the three categories they could endorse were "occasional attraction to the same sex," "major attraction to the same sex," and "only attracted to the opposite sex"). Additionally, of the individuals who described themselves as "only attracted to the opposite sex" at 21, 12% of women but only 2% of men shifted to one of the same-sex attraction categories by age 26. Similar patterns (greater change in women than among men) have been found in every other large-scale prospective study of same-sex sexuality that has been published, on samples ranging from adolescence to early adulthood (Mock & Eibach, 2012; Ott et al., 2011; Savin-Williams, Joyner, & Rieger, 2012; Savin-Williams & Ream, 2007). The other gender differences that prove consistent across these studies are (a) greater overall prevalence of same-sex attraction and behavior among women than among men overall, and (b) greater nonexclusivity in women's than men's attractions and behaviors.

THE DIRECTION OF CHANGE: INCREASING NONEXCLUSIVITY AMONG WOMEN

Perhaps most intriguing is the specific pattern of change shown by women versus men. As noted earlier, the patterns of change detected in smaller scale studies suggest that women increasingly gravitate toward nonexclusive patterns of attraction and identity over time (importantly, this pattern cannot be detected by simply classifying changes as "toward same sex" vs. "toward other sex"). Rather, we need to know the specific combination of "starting category" and "ending category" so that we can determine whether individuals are moving toward greater nonexclusivity (which would include both lesbian and heterosexual transitions toward bisexuality, despite the fact that the former change represents greater other-sex sexuality and the latter change represents greater same-sex sexuality) or toward greater exclusivity.

In the study by Dickson et al. (2003), men were equally likely to transition to the "occasional same-sex attraction" category as they were to transition to the "only opposite-sex" or "major same-sex" attraction category. Women, in sharp contrast, were twice as likely to transition to the "occasional same-sex category" as to the "only opposite-sex" or "major same-sex" attraction categories. Although this study does not differentiate between exclusive and nonexclusive forms of "major" same-sex sex attraction, it supports the notion that women's changes are more likely to involve movement toward nonexclusivity than exclusivity.

Similar findings emerge from Savin-Williams et al.'s (2012) analyses of Waves 3 and 4 of the National Longitudinal Study of Adolescent Health study, which included a sample of more than 12,000 youth ranging in age from 24 to 34 years of age. They found that of the youth who described themselves as mostly heterosexual, bisexual, or homosexual at Wave 3, 50% of women and 43% of men changed their identity category by Wave 4. Of the youth making identity changes, the adoption of a nonexclusive identity (bisexual or mostly heterosexual) was twice as likely among women as among men (25% vs. 12%, respectively), whereas the adoption of an exclusive homosexual identity was more than twice as likely among men as among women (20% vs. 8%). The same pattern also was found by Ott et al. (2011), who examined changes in a large prospective cohort study of more than 13,000 youths. They found that between the ages of 13 and 23, the percentage of women adopting nonexclusive identity labels (bisexual or mostly heterosexual) increased by nearly 10%, representing more than a three fold increase (from 4.6% to 14.4%), whereas the percentage adopting "mostly or completely homosexual" identities increased by a single percentage point (from 0% to 1%). In contrast, among men, there was an 11-fold increase in the percentage of men identifying as mostly or completely homosexual, from 0.3% to 3.5%, but only a twofold increase in the percentage identifying as bisexual or mostly heterosexual (from 2.8% to 5.9%). Again, the pattern is clear: Men start out with more exclusive patterns of same-sex sexuality than do women, and over time, they tend to become more exclusive. Women start out with more nonexclusive patterns of same-sex sexuality, and over time, they tend to become even more nonexclusive. The fact that these findings have been replicated consistently in numerous large-scale studies using different sampling frames and assessing men and women at different ages is particularly striking.

These studies reveal little about the reasons for these changes. Although large-scale population-based studies have the advantage of representativeness, they provide relatively little information about process and phenomenology. In my own small-scale longitudinal study, I directly asked participants for the specific reasons behind each of their identity changes. The answers (summarized in Diamond, 2008b) were surprisingly consistent and concord with the results of Golden's (1987, 1996) retrospective interview research. First, women reported that the more time went by, the more aware they became of their own capacity for nonexclusive attractions and behavior. These realizations were particularly stark among the women who initially had identified as lesbian in their late teens or early twenties, and who often found themselves unexpectedly involved with men in later years, either as casual one-night-stands or as significant emotional attachments. Second, some women reported that as time went by, they came to believe that their sexual attractions had less to do with gender, and more to do with the specific chemistry or emotional attachment that they happened to develop with specific individuals, male or female. These individuals increasingly chafed against conventional labels such as "gay and lesbian" or "bisexual," which treat "preferred partner gender" as the key defining characteristic of one's sexual identity, and they often stopped labeling their sexuality altogether (except to assert that they assuredly were not heterosexual). Such phenomenological reports are notable for their consistency with Chivers and colleagues' psychophysiological studies of "nonspecific" genital responding (Chivers et al., 2004; Chivers et al., 2007; Chivers & Timmers, 2012). Whereas Chivers' findings suggest that "gender of partner" is not the primary dimension of importance when it comes to eliciting women's *genital* arousal, the interview data collected by Golden (1987, 1996) and Diamond (2008b) have suggested that "gender of partner" is not the primary dimension of importance when it comes to eliciting women's *subjective* arousal, attraction, and infatuation. Rather, women appear more sensitive than men to the role of *interpersonal relationships and emotional feelings,* as described in the next section.

The Relationship Context of Female Same-Sex Sexuality

As noted in the discussion of developmental trajectories, women generally place more emphasis than do men on the role of specific, emotionally intimate relationships in triggering their first awareness of same-sex sexuality. Yet importantly, the salience of specific intimate relationships extends far beyond women's initial experiences of same-sex desire, and appears to characterize their patterns of same-sex sexuality more broadly. Blumstein and Schwartz (1990) criticized conventional models of sexual orientation for failing to represent the experiences of women "whose fundamental sexual desire seems to be produced within the context of a relationship, rather than by an abstract preference for women or men" (p. 356). They concluded that these women's sexuality was less focused on physical, bodily characteristics and more frequently was triggered by love, admiration, affection, and companionship. A number of other studies over the years have found that although some women identify as lesbian or bisexual on the basis of their sexual desires and fantasies (similar to the experiences of men), many other women report that their identification as lesbian or bisexual was based more heavily on their emotional attachments to women, which sometimes were described as more intense and motivating than their sexual desires (Blumstein & Schwartz, 1990; Diamond, 2006b; Esterberg, 1994; Gramick, 1984; Nichols, 1987; Savin-Williams, 1998; Vance & Green, 1984; Weinberg et al., 1994). Other women report that their desires are not so much directed toward women at all but rather toward "the person and not their gender" (Blumstein & Schwartz, 1990; Cassingham & O'Neil, 1993; Diamond, 2002, 2006b; Golden, 1987).

Perhaps the starkest example of such a situational, interpersonally based sexual response is found in the phenomenon of "relationship-specific" desires, or cases in which the emotional intensity of a particular relationship is described as spilling over into novel same-sex desires, albeit restricted to the relationship in question (Blumstein & Schwartz, 1990; Cass, 1990; Cassingham & O'Neil, 1993; Diamond, 2000a, 2003b, 2006b). Even after decades of otherwise-satisfying heterosexual marriages, the process of developing an intense affectional bond with a specific, singular female friend often provides the sole motivation for a woman's late-life transition to same-sex sexuality (Cass, 1990; Cassingham & O'Neil, 1993; Diamond, 2008b; Kitzinger & Wilkinson, 1995; Penelope & Wolfe, 1989; Stanley & Wolfe, 1980; Walsh, 2010). For example, more than three fourths of the women interviewed by Kitzinger and Wilkinson (1995) reported that a sexual or emotional relationship with a particular woman sparked their transition to lesbianism. This occurs cross-culturally as well: Blackwood (1985) noted that strong affectional relationships between co-wives in some polygamous societies often transitioned to erotic contact over time.

Despite the fact that such cases of relationship-specific and emotionally triggered desires have cropped up consistently across historical, anthropological, and psychological research, both scientists and laypeople have tended to doubt their authenticity. After all, traditional, organismic models of sexual development dictate that there is no such thing as having "just some" sexual desires for "just one" emotionally significant friend (Blumstein & Schwartz, 1990). Sexual orientations are supposed to represent generalized sexual predispositions, such that attractions to *anyone* of the same sex should signal an underlying tendency to be attracted to *everyone* of the same sex, emotional bonds notwithstanding. Hence, it is assumed tacitly that given enough time and self-reflection, such individuals eventually will conclude that they have been attracted to women "all along."

Yet findings from my own longitudinal research suggest otherwise. Over 10 years of observation, 11 of the 89 sexual-minority women that I interviewed reported that their first experience of same-sex desires was sparked by an intense affectional bond to a single woman. Over the ensuing 10 years, none of these women retracted their initial accounts and decided that they must have been broadly attracted to women all along. Rather, they continued to perceive the initial onset of their same-sex sexuality as a single, emotionally significant same-sex bond that gradually gave rise to same-sex sexual desire. In interpreting these women's reports, it is important to remember that all women—regardless of sexual orientation—have been exposed to traditional cultural norms, which posit that female sexual desire and expression is socially acceptable only within the context of a longstanding, exclusive, romantic relationship, ideally a marriage (Gagnon & Simon, 1973). Men, in contrast, typically are granted considerably more latitude in their sexual behavior and grow up exposed to cultural messages that claim that it is perfectly normal and expected for men to experience intense sexual desires outside of any relational context (reviewed in Shibley-Hyde & Durik, 2000; Tolman & Diamond, 2001). Furthermore, female socialization practices often focus on fostering communal orientations in women, which might reinforce women's perceptions that their sexual desires are interpersonally based (Andersen, Cyranowski, & Aarestad, 2000).

Hence, the fact that women are more likely than men to report same-sex desires springing from same-sex emotional attachments may be partly attributable to the manner in which men and women are socialized to experience and interpret their sexual desires. Yet it is unlikely that cultural pressures are the sole reason for this gender difference. Rather, a growing body of research coming out of dynamic systems theory (reviewed in Diamond, 2007; Fausto-Sterling, 2012) suggests that emotionally based same-sex attractions might in fact represent authentic cases of *emergence*, in which dynamic, ongoing interactions among the biosocial processes underlying sexual desire and emotional attachment give rise to truly novel forms of thought, affect, and behavior (Fogel & Thelen, 1987; Lewis, 2000), in this case same-sex desires. Hence, both cultural and biological factors might interact to facilitate relationship-specific same-sex desires among women.

Unfortunately, one of the chief difficulties for understanding how exactly such transformative experiences take place, and their underlying psychological and biological processes, is the lack of basic research on the mechanisms through which different components of sexual and affectional experience (arousal, desire, attraction, love, infatuation, motivation, fantasy) relate to and mutually influence one other, both at a single moment in time and also as they develop and change over the life course (Chivers & Bailey, 2007; Chivers et al., 2010; Diamond, 2008b; Igartua, Thombs, Burgos, & Montoro, 2009; Laan & Janssen, 2007; Laumann et al., 1994; Savin-Williams & Ream, 2007; Suschinsky et al., 2009). Yet research on the underlying neurobiology of mammalian affiliation provides some promising directions for future study, suggesting a potential biological basis for the role of emotional attachment in triggering sexual desires. Specifically, although the biobehavioral systems underlying the formation of emotional attachments are distinct from those underlying sexual desire (Aron et al., 2005; Fisher, Aron, Mashek, Li, & Brown, 2002), there are nonetheless powerful neurobiological interconnections between them (reviewed in Cacioppo, Bianchi-Demicheli, Frum, Pfaus, &

Lewis, 2012; Cacioppo, Bianchi-Demicheli, Hatfield, & Rapson, 2012; Diamond, 2003b; Diamond & Dickenson, 2012; Ortigue, Bianchi-Demicheli, Patel, Frum, & Lewis, 2010). For example, several of the neurochemicals known to mediate attachment formation—most notably oxytocin, vasopressin, and dopamine—also mediate sexual behavior, and these neurochemicals often show hormone-dependent, gender-specific patterns of functioning (Carter, 1992; Carter & Keverne, 2002). Additionally, there is overlap in some of the brain regions involved in sexual desire and romantic love, most notably the caudate, insula, putamen, and anterior cingulate cortex (ACC). Given that the putamen and the caudate are both associated with motivational states and reward, their joint relevance for both sexual desire and romantic love likely reflects the fact that love and desire both involve strong motivation to seek the love object (albeit for different rewards: proximity in the case of romantic love, and sexual activity in the case of desire). The joint relevance of the rostral ACC for both love and sexual desire is also notable, given that this region of the ACC has been found by Walter et al. (2008) to be particularly sensitive to the *emotional valence* of sexual stimuli. Altogether, the fact that these regions prove relevant for both love and desire provides potential neurobiological pathways through which each type of experience might influence the other (Diamond & Dickenson, 2012).

Hence, the development of novel sexual desires in the context of emotional bonds might be interpreted to indicate that under certain circumstances, neurobiologically mediated links between love and desire reorganize to produce emergent, relationship-specific desires. For this to occur, however, it seems that we must assume some degree of "openness" in women's sexual phenomenology more generally—that is, a general readiness to respond and reorganize in response to opportunistic factors, such as the formation of an intense emotional attachment. Such a heightened sensitivity has been described as *female sexual fluidity*, and it may provide a productive starting point for developing a comprehensive explanatory model for all of the differences reviewed thus far in this chapter between male and female same-sex sexuality.

Female Sexual Fluidity

One potential explanation for the fact that women show greater propensity for change in same-sex sexuality than men, that they have more nonexclusive attractions and nonspecific patterns of genital arousal, and that their sexual desires are more sensitive to interpersonal and situational influences is that women's sexuality is fundamentally more "fluid" than men's, meaning that women show more "situation-dependent flexibility in sexual responsiveness" (Diamond, 2003b, 2006a, 2008b). Such flexibility would make it possible for some women to experience desires for either men or women under certain circumstances, regardless of her overall sexual orientation. In other words, although women—like men—appear to be born with generalized sexual predispositions, these orientations may not provide the "last word" on their sexual attractions and experiences over the life span. Instead, women of all orientations appear capable of variation in their erotic and affectional feelings over time, as they encounter different situations, relationships, and life stages.

The notion that some women's same-sex sexuality appears to be flexible and situation-dependent has long circulated in the empirical literature (Blumstein & Schwartz, 1990; Dixon, 1984, 1985; Goode & Haber, 1977); historically, however, such cases have been considered exceptional rather than normative and have not been considered to provide useful information about the phenomenon of sexual orientation. After all, researchers have long distinguished between *constitutional* same-sex sexuality, supposedly attributable to a stable and enduring same-sex orientation, and *facultative* same-sex sexuality, which is instead attributable to transient situational factors, such as "play, exploration, lack of opposite-gender partners . . . and mistakes" (Muscarella, 1999, p. 9). According to this view, the sudden onset of same-sex desire and behavior in a woman who falls in love with her female best friend is simply casual experimentation or curiosity and is not to be taken seriously. It is for this reason that many women who pursued same-sex activity in the safe and relatively tolerant environment of college, but resumed exclusive heterosexual behavior afterward, have been derided as "LUGs," or "lesbians until graduation" (Davis, 1999; Kyrakanos, 1998;

Rimer, 1993). In a similar fashion, women who consider themselves "mostly heterosexual" have long been dismissed as going through an "experimental phase," despite increasing evidence for the legitimacy of this sexual orientation category (Thompson & Morgan, 2008; Vrangalova & Savin-Williams, 2012).

In recent years, scholars have come to take women's capacity for sexual fluidity more seriously as a phenomenon with wide-ranging implications for our scientific understanding of female sexuality and sexual orientation more generally. Baumeister (2000) was the first to synthesize the accumulating strands of evidence for female sexual variability into a comprehensive argument for gender differences in "erotic plasticity." He reviewed the extensive psychological, historical, and sociological evidence on gender differences in sexuality and argued that women's sexuality is more variable than men's with respect to overall drive, desired partner characteristics, preferred sexual acts and practices, and consistency between attitudes and behaviors. The key difference between Baumeister's notion of erotic plasticity and the term *sexual fluidity* is that the latter term typically is used to refer to variability in same-sex versus other-sex desire and behavior, whereas Baumeister's "plasticity" refers to variability in all aspects of sexual behavior and responding. Whether sexual fluidity and erotic plasticity represent two distinct types of variability or whether fluidity is best considered a "subtype" of broader erotic plasticity remains an open empirical question.

Sexual fluidity provides a possible explanation for the fact that women historically have been more likely than men to ascribe a role for choice, circumstance, chance, and change in their experiences of same-sex sexuality over the life course (Golden, 1996; Whisman, 1996). Gagnon (1990), for example, observed over many years of research on female and male sexuality that women's participation in same-sex sexuality sometimes appeared to come about in direct response to situational factors, often in an unpredictable fashion. Beginning with the feminist movement of the 1970s and extending decades afterward, researchers have observed that women's immersion in feminist politics, coupled with the development of strong same-sex friendships and exposure to lesbian-gay-bisexual peers, often proved to be powerful triggers for new and unexpected same-sex attractions and fantasies (Cass, 1990; Golden, 1987, 1994; Shuster, 1987). The contemporary context provides an altogether different set of gender-specific contexts that provide potential triggers for same-sex sexuality. In particular, the past decade has witnessed a notable increase in television and film portrayals of both bisexual women as well as heterosexually identified women engaging in same-sex behavior, often with few negative social consequences (reviewed in Diamond, 2005a; Meyer, 2010; Thompson, 2007), and some have argued that this has produced a newfound cultural context in which it is now more acceptable—and sometimes encouraged, in certain contexts—for young women to engage in experimental same-sex context (Fahs, 2009; Yost & McCarthy, 2012).

If female sexuality is, in fact, differentially sensitive to such cultural influences, then one would expect to find that (a) more contemporary women than men engage in same-sex behavior despite reporting exclusive other-sex attractions; and (b) the total number of women reporting some degree of same-sex attraction and behavior (especially in the "mostly heterosexual" range) should have increased over the past several decades, whereas similar changes should not be observable among men. In fact, both propositions are true. Recent representative survey data indicate that more than twice as many women as men report engaging in same-sex behavior despite adopting a heterosexual identity or describing their sexual attractions as exclusively heterosexual (Chandra et al., 2011; McCabe, Brewster, & Harker Tillman, 2011; Mosher et al., 2005). As for cohort effects, Appleby (2012) analyzed 14 waves of General Social Survey data collected between 1988 and 2010, comparing rates of same-sex behavior in successive cohorts of women and men. The General Social Survey uses a nationally representative area probability sample, and it began asking questions about same-sex sexual behavior in 1988. Since that time, these questions have been asked of more than 33,000 individuals. Appleby found a strong linear cohort effect for all measures of same-sex sexual behavior among women (i.e., ever having a same-sex partner since age 18, having a majority of same-sex partners since age 18, having any same-sex partners in the past year, having any same-sex partners in the past 5 years) but not among men. For example, among women born before 1946, only 2% reported having at least one same-sex partner since age 18. Yet this rate rises linearly with each successive birth cohort, reaching a peak of 9% among women born between 1975 and 1992. The same linear pattern was detected for each type of same-sex behavior outcome assessed. These findings strongly support the notion of women's greater sexual flexibility and sensitivity to situational and interpersonal influences.

Important questions still remain regarding the magnitude and source of gender differences in fluidity (Shibley-Hyde & Durik, 2000). Blumstein and Schwartz (1990), for example, echoing a widely held view, have argued that "there are few absolute differences between male and female sexuality. What differences we observed are primarily the result of the different social organization of women's and men's lives in various cultural contexts" (p. 307). Other researchers, similarly, have argued that the appearance of a distinctively female capacity for fluidity might simply be an artifact of female sexual socialization. For example, the pervasive social and cultural forces that have long controlled and suppressed female sexuality may distort women's awareness of their own sexual feelings and identities, channeling them rigidly toward heterosexuality with few opportunities to express and experiment with same-sex desires (Baumeister & Twenge, 2002; Fine, 1988; Laumann & Mahay, 2002; Tolman & Diamond, 2001; Ussher, 1993; Welles, 2005). Consequently, the appearance of greater sexual fluidity in women might simply be attributable to the fact that the greater cultural repression of female sexuality leaves more room for life-course variability as women move into and out of environments that provide more license for them to act on their desires. Clearly, the pervasive nature of social and cultural influences on both female and male sexuality complicates our task of identifying the magnitude and source of gender differences in sexual orientation and in sexual fluidity. With this in mind, we conclude with a discussion of some of the most promising and important areas for future research.

DIRECTIONS FOR FUTURE RESEARCH: DEEPER INTO GENDER

As gender differences in same-sex sexuality have been documented repeatedly in ever larger, more diverse, and more representative samples (Chandra et al., 2011; Dickson et al., 2003; Igartua et al., 2009; Laumann et al., 1994; Mosher et al., 2005; Ott et al., 2011; Savin-Williams et al., 2012; Savin-Williams & Ream, 2007), researchers increasingly have rejected the presumption that female and male sexual orientation are "two sides of the same coin" and have argued instead that female sexual orientation has fundamentally unique mechanisms and manifestations (Chivers et al., 2004; Diamond, 2008b; Hyde, 2005b; Mustanski et al., 2002). How, then, might we begin the task of developing new scientific models of female same-sex sexuality and sexual orientation?

One provocative possibility suggested by Bailey (2009) is that women might not have sexual orientations (to the degree that one defines sexual orientation as a fixed, gender-specific pattern of sexual arousal). This notion provides a compelling (if rather sweeping) explanation of the extant data on women's propensity for nonexclusive and fluid sexual attractions and concords with Goy and Goldfoot's (1975) observation that many mammalian species have one "bisexual" (or "unoriented") sex. At the same time, however, the extant data (reviewed earlier) indicates that there is considerable variation regarding women's specific degrees of sexual nonexclusivity and nonspecificity. If women have no sexual orientation, then why do some women seem so much more "oriented" than others? Bailey's (2009) resolution to this problem was to argue that the vast majority of women (i.e., heterosexual and bisexual women) lack a sexual orientation and that lesbians (who appear to have more gender-oriented patterns of desire) represent an exception.

But there might be a way to revise models of sexual orientation to account for both "oriented" and "unoriented" women. Specifically, we might investigate the possibility that female sexual orientation is composed of two orthogonal dimensions: One dimension represents the degree of "genderedness" of a woman's desires (i.e., the degree to which a woman's desires are oriented to one gender over the other); the second dimension represents the direction of this targeting (same sex vs. other sex). Hence, the appropriate question to ask when assessing a woman's sexual orientation might not be "Are you a heterosexual, lesbian, or bisexual?" as currently is presumed, but instead the first question to ask is "Does the partner's gender matter?" (*gender* denoting, in this case, the potential partner's observable "presentation" as male vs. female). Second, if the partner's gender matters, which gender is preferred? Historically, scientific conceptualizations of sexual orientations have focused only on the second question, assuming that the answer to the first question was uniformly "yes." Yet the experiences of women who claim to be attracted to "the person, not the gender" suggest that we might revisit this assumption. For some women, sexuality might be "gender neutral," in which case a host of other factors (emotional intimacy, sex drive, mood, personality similarity or difference) might determine which partners she finds most attractive and the sexual encounters she finds most appealing. Weinberg et al. (1994) have argued that this type of gender neutrality might represent a subtype of bisexuality. Specifically, they noted that a subset of their bisexually identified respondents appeared to possess an "open gender schema," meaning that they responded sexually to a broad range of traits and partner characteristics regardless of gender.

Importantly, not all individuals with "gender-neutral" patterns of attraction characterize themselves as bisexual (Diamond, 2008b; Savin-Williams, 2005). To the contrary, some explicitly reject conventional sexual identity labels, or they adopt alternative labels such as "queer" or "pansexual" to better represent the gender-neutral nature of their attractions (Berenson, 2002; Bower, Gurevich, & Mathieson, 2002; Hollander, 2000; Horner, 2007; Savin-Williams, 2005). This raises the inevitable question of why some women experience their nonexclusive attractions as gender neutral, whereas others do not. We know remarkably little about the gradual "gendering" of children's erotic impulses more generally (Gagnon, 1990). Although children engage in both solitary self-stimulation and partnered sex play from an early age (reviewed in Diamond & Savin-Williams, 2009), "gender of partner" does not appear to emerge as a discernable preference until 9 or 10 years of age (McClintock & Herdt, 1996). As Gagnon (1990) argued,

> During the ages of 12 to 17 the gender aspects of the "who" in the sexual scripts that are being formed are not fixed. . . A deeper complication is that it is not obvious whether it is the gender aspects of the "who" that have provoked the nascent desire or even if the desire is linked to a "who" at all. (p. 199)

Perhaps then, an orientation toward person-centered attractions represents a more substantiated form of this gender neutrality, in which our sexual scripts remain fundamentally "open" with regard to the "gender aspects of the 'who'." Notably, Liben and Bigler (2008) have argued that there is considerable variation in children's degree of "gender salience" (i.e., the degree to which they reflexively attend to gender more generally) and that children with low levels of gender salience may be less likely to exhibit a rigidly homosexual or heterosexual orientation. According to this framework, "low gender salience" (as an individual difference dimension) might facilitate the development of an "open gender schema" with regard to sexual desires.

Another (albeit speculative) possibility is that most individuals begin life with a relatively open gender schema, which comes to be increasingly gender targeted as a function of normative gender socialization (toward greater "gender saliency," in Liben and Bigler's, 2008, terms) and especially during sexual maturation (as a function of the individuals' underlying sexual orientation). Perhaps for males, then, the most common deviation from the standard heterosexual pathway is the substitution of a same-sex orientation for the standard other-sex orientation. Perhaps for females, the most common deviation from the standard heterosexual pathway is the failure of a gender-based orientation to develop. In such cases, women's patterns of sexual arousal might remain fundamentally nonspecific, and their patterns of conscious, subjective attraction might come to depend on a host of nongendered cues, such as emotional intimacy, and personality.

This need not suggest that all women with same-sex attractions follow such a trajectory. Lesbians with relatively exclusive same-sex attractions might follow a developmental trajectory more similar to gay men (i.e., the development of a same-sex orientation rather than the failure of a gender-based orientation to develop). Several studies suggest that lesbians are qualitatively distinct from both bisexual and heterosexual women in that they show more male-typical patterns of "gender specificity" (i.e., consistent and exclusive "targeting" toward one gender) and stability in their sexual arousal and attractions (Chivers & Bailey, 2007; Chivers et al., 2007; Diamond, 2005b; Diamond & Wallen, 2011; Suschinsky et al., 2009). Perhaps, then, there may be four forms of sexual orientation in women, with different underlying causes and developmental trajectories: heterosexual, bisexual, lesbian, and "nongendered." Women in the latter group might resemble women in any of the other groups at different stages of the life course, depending on a variety of cultural, situational, and interpersonal circumstances. This may be why "Kinsey 1s" who identify as heterosexual are not necessarily "lying" to themselves or to others when they profess their heterosexuality. As Chivers et al. (2007) have cautioned, we cannot presume that a woman with a nonspecific pattern of sexual arousal is fundamentally bisexual; making such a simplistic and erroneous presumption "overlooks the complexity and multidimensionality of female sexuality" (p. 1119).

Importantly, although the foregoing discussion of "nongendered" attractions and orientations has focused on women's experiences, it might apply equally well to many men's experiences, and further investigation of this possibility is an important direction for future research. Although the research reviewed earlier on sexual fluidity suggests that women have a greater propensity for sexual plasticity than do men, and that's men's same-sex sexuality tends to manifest itself in a more stable, "categorical" fashion (Bailey, 2009), we simply do not have enough data on this question to support firm conclusions. Certainly, the representative survey data reviewed earlier (Chandra et al., 2011; Hayes et al., 2012; Laumann et al., 1994; Mosher et al., 2005; Savin-Williams, 2006) indicate that although women are more likely than men to report nonexclusive (or "bisexual") patterns of attraction, nonexclusive attractions are more common than exclusive same-sex attractions among both men and women. Hence, despite the ongoing debate over whether male bisexuals "really exist" at the level of genital arousal to same-sex and other-sex stimuli (Rieger, Bailey, & Chivers, 2005), they certainly do exist at the level of self-reported same-sex and other-sex attractions, even though most of the men reporting these nonexclusive patterns of attraction consider themselves to be heterosexual, as reviewed previously (see also Morgan, Steiner, & Thompson, 2010; Vrangalova & Savin-Williams, 2012). Even the research on genital arousal increasingly has suggested more complex patterns of arousal among men than conventionally have been assumed. After an initial study that appeared to suggest that men claiming bisexual patterns of attraction actually tended to show relatively exclusive patterns of genital arousal to either same-sex or other-sex stimuli (Rieger et al., 2005), more recent studies using different inclusion criteria for bisexually identified men, and different experimental methodologies, have found support for bisexual patterns of genital arousal (Cerny & Janssen, 2011; Rosenthal, Sylva, Safron, & Bailey, 2011, 2012). Hence, we can no longer conclude that men's sexuality is rigid and categorical, whereas women's sexuality is variable and fluid. Rather, both men and women appear to have some propensity for sexual variability. It is possible that the factors that drive and structure this variability might be quite different for men versus women and that these factors are distributed differently within the overall population. Yet to answer these important, basic questions, we need to begin asking men more nuanced and multifaceted questions about variability in sexual experience and expression over the life course, and we need rigorous longitudinal data that systematically assesses variation over time in identity, behavior, and attraction. If anything, the evidence reviewed in this chapter regarding the distinctive features of female same-sex sexuality should prompt us to revisit our assumptions about male sexuality as well and to ensure that future research on same-sex sexuality in both men and women takes an inclusive approach that seeks to capture and explain all of its complex manifestations.

CONCLUSION

Of all of the preconceptions about sexual orientation that scientific research has challenged and revised over the years, among the most important is the presumption that female and male sexual orientation are parallel phenomena, with the same origins and outcomes. To the contrary, women's greater propensity for nonexclusive, fluid patterns of attraction suggests the possibility that that the underlying determinants of female same-sex sexuality may be quite different from those for men, requiring different explanatory models. A great deal of basic science remains to be done before we can draw rigorous conclusions about the extent and bases of the gender differences reviewed in this chapter. Substantive investigation of these gender differences has the potential to make enormous contributions to our broader understanding of sexuality and sexual orientation, largely by prompting us to reconsider many of our longstanding assumptions about these phenomena, and to consider new sets of questions: What sorts of experiences "count" as sexual desires? What is the difference between gender-based erotic preferences and other forms of erotic preferences? What is the relationship between genital arousal and subjective desire, and how might their underlying mechanisms develop and unfold differently in women and men with different sexual predispositions? What factors drive the long-term developmental course of sexual predispositions and learned preferences? Wrestling with these questions undoubtedly will lead to more accurate scientific models of sexuality for both men and women.

References

Adler, K. A. (1967). Life style, gender role, and the symptom of homosexuality. *Journal of Individual Psychology, 23*, 67–78.

Andersen, B. L., Cyranowski, J. M., & Aarestad, S. (2000). Beyond artificial, sex-linked distinctions to conceptualize female sexuality: Comment on Baumeister (2000). *Psychological Bulletin, 126*, 380–384. doi:10.1037/0033-2909.126.3.380

Appleby, K. (2012). *Same-sex sexual behavior in America.* Unpublished doctoral dissertation, University of Oregon, Eugene.

Aron, A., Fisher, H., Mashek, D. J., Strong, G., Li, H., & Brown, L. L. (2005). Reward, motivation, and emotion systems associated with early-stage intense romantic love. *Journal of Neurophysiology, 94*, 327–337. doi:10.1152/jn.00838.2004

Bailey, J. M. (2009). What is sexual orientation and do women have one? In D. A. Hope (Ed.), *Nebraska Symposium on Motivation: Vol. 54. Contemporary perspectives on lesbian, gay, and bisexual identities* (pp. 43–63). Lincoln: University of Nebraska Press.

Baumeister, R. F. (2000). Gender differences in erotic plasticity: The female sex drive as socially flexible and responsive. *Psychological Bulletin, 126*, 347–374. doi:10.1037/0033-2909.126.3.347

Baumeister, R. F., & Twenge, J. M. (2002). Cultural suppression of female sexuality. *Review of General Psychology, 6*, 166–203. doi:10.1037/1089-2680.6.2.166

Berenson, C. (2002). What's in a name? Bisexual women define their terms. *Journal of Bisexuality, 2*, 9–21. doi:10.1300/J159v02n02_02

Blackwood, E. (1985). Breaking the mirror: The construction of lesbianism and the anthropological discourse on homosexuality. *Journal of Homosexuality, 11*, 1–17. doi:10.1300/J082v11n03_01

Block, I. (1909). *The sexual life of our time.* London, England: Heinemann.

Blumstein, P., & Schwartz, P. (1977). Bisexuality: Some social psychological issues. *Journal of Social Issues, 33*, 30–45. doi:10.1111/j.1540-4560.1977.tb02004.x

Blumstein, P., & Schwartz, P. (1990). Intimate relationships and the creation of sexuality. In D. P. McWhirter, S. A. Sanders, & J. M. Reinisch (Eds.), *Homosexuality/heterosexuality: Concepts of sexual orientation* (pp. 307–320). New York, NY: Oxford University Press.

Bower, J., Gurevich, M., & Mathieson, C. (2002). (Con) tested identities: Bisexual women reorient sexuality. *Journal of Bisexuality, 2*, 23–52. doi:10.1300/J159v02n02_03

Burr, C. (1996). *A separate creation: The search for the biological origins of sexual orientation.* New York, NY: Hyperion.

Cacioppo, S., Bianchi-Demicheli, F., Frum, C., Pfaus, J. G., & Lewis, J. W. (2012). The common neural bases between sexual desire and love: A multilevel kernel density fMRI analysis. *Journal of Sexual Medicine* [online first, February 12, 2012]. DOI: 10.1111/j. 1743–6109.2012.02651.x.

Cacioppo, S., Bianchi-Demicheli, F., Hatfield, E., & Rapson, R. (2012). Social neuroscience of love.

Clinical Neuropsychiatry: Journal of Treatment Evaluation, 9, 3–13.

Carter, C. S. (1992). Oxytocin and sexual behavior. *Neuroscience and Biobehavioral Reviews, 16*, 131–144. doi:10.1016/S0149-7634(05)80176-9

Carter, C. S., & Keverne, E. B. (2002). The neurobiology of social affiliation and pair bonding. In J. Pfaff, A. P. Arnold, A. E. Etgen, & S. E. Fahrbach (Eds.), *Hormones, brain, and behavior* (Vol. 1, pp. 299–337). New York, NY: Academic Press. doi:10.1016/B978-012532104-4/50006-8

Cass, V. (1990). The implications of homosexual identity formation for the Kinsey model and scale of sexual preference. In D. P. McWhirter, S. A. Sanders, & J. M. Reinisch (Eds.), *Homosexuality/heterosexuality: Concepts of sexual orientation* (pp. 239–266). New York, NY: Oxford University Press.

Cassingham, B. J., & O'Neil, S. M. (1993). *And then I met this woman.* Freeland, WA: Soaring Eagle.

Cerny, J. A., & Janssen, E. (2011). Patterns of sexual arousal in homosexual, bisexual, and heterosexual men. *Archives of Sexual Behavior, 40*, 687–697. doi:10.1007/s10508-011-9746-0

Chandra, A., Mosher, W. D., Copen, C., & Sionean, C. (2011, March). Sexual behavior, sexual attraction, and sexual identity in the United States: Data from the 2006–2008 National Survey of Family Growth. *National Health Statistics Reports, 3*, 1–36.

Charbonneau, C., & Lander, P. S. (1991). Redefining sexuality: Women becoming lesbian in midlife. In B. Sang, J. Warshow, & A. J. Smith (Eds.), *Lesbians at midlife: The creative transition* (pp. 35–43). San Francisco, CA: Spinsters.

Chivers, M. L., & Bailey, J. M. (2005). A sex difference in features that elicit genital response. *Biological Psychology, 70*, 115–120. doi:10.1016/j.biopsycho.2004.12.002

Chivers, M. L., & Bailey, J. M. (2007). The sexual psychophysiology of sexual orientation. In E. Janssen (Ed.), *The psychophysiology of sex* (pp. 458–474). Bloomington: Indiana University Press.

Chivers, M. L., Rieger, G., Latty, E., & Bailey, J. M. (2004). A sex difference in the specificity of sexual arousal. *Psychological Science, 15*, 736–744. doi:10.1111/j.0956-7976.2004.00750.x

Chivers, M. L., Seto, M. C., & Blanchard, R. (2007). Gender and sexual orientation differences in sexual response to sexual activities versus gender of actors in sexual films. *Journal of Personality and Social Psychology, 93*, 1108–1121. doi:10.1037/0022-3514.93.6.1108

Chivers, M. L., Seto, M. C., Lalumiere, M. L., Laan, E., & Grimbos, T. (2010). Agreement of self-reported and genital measures of sexual arousal in men and women: A meta-analysis. *Archives of Sexual Behavior, 39*, 5–56. doi:10.1007/s10508-009-9556-9

Chivers, M. L., & Timmers, A. D. (2012). Effects of gender and relationship context in audio narratives on genital and subjective sexual response in heterosexual women and men. *Archives of Sexual Behavior, 41*, 185–197. doi:10.1007/s10508-012-9937-3

D'Augelli, A. R., & Hershberger, S. L. (1993). Lesbian, gay, and bisexual youth in community settings: Personal challenges and mental health problems. *American Journal of Community Psychology, 21*, 421–448. doi:10.1007/BF00942151

Davis, A. (1999, October 25). Confessions of a LUG. *Flagpole Magazine Online.*

De Cecco, J. P. (1981). Definition and meaning of sexual orientation. *Journal of Homosexuality, 6*, 51–67. doi:10.1300/J082v06n04_04

Diamond, L. M. (1998). Development of sexual orientation among adolescent and young adult women. *Developmental Psychology, 34*, 1085–1095. doi:10.1037/0012-1649.34.5.1085

Diamond, L. M. (2000a). Passionate friendships among adolescent sexual-minority women. *Journal of Research on Adolescence, 10*, 191–209. doi:10.1207/SJRA1002_4

Diamond, L. M. (2000b). Sexual identity, attractions, and behavior among young sexual-minority women over a two-year period. *Developmental Psychology, 36*, 241–250. doi:10.1037/0012-1649.36.2.241

Diamond, L. M. (2002). "Having a girlfriend without knowing it": The relationships of adolescent lesbian and bisexual women. *Journal of Lesbian Studies, 6*, 5–16. doi:10.1300/J155v06n01_02

Diamond, L. M. (2003a). Was it a phase? Young women's relinquishment of lesbian/bisexual identities over a 5-year period. *Journal of Personality and Social Psychology, 84*, 352–364. doi:10.1037/0022-3514.84.2.352

Diamond, L. M. (2003b). What does sexual orientation orient? A biobehavioral model distinguishing romantic love and sexual desire. *Psychological Review, 110*, 173–192. doi:10.1037/0033-295X.110.1.173

Diamond, L. M. (2005a). "I'm straight, but I kissed a girl": The trouble with American media representations of female-female sexuality. *Feminism and Psychology, 15*, 104–110. doi:10.1177/0959353505049712

Diamond, L. M. (2005b). A new view of lesbian subtypes: Stable vs. fluid identity trajectories over an 8-year period. *Psychology of Women Quarterly, 29*, 119–128. doi:10.1111/j.1471-6402.2005.00174.x

Diamond, L. M. (2006a). The evolution of plasticity in female-female desire. *Journal of Psychology and Human Sexuality, 18*, 245–274. doi:10.1300/J056v18n04_01

Diamond, L. M. (2006b). How do I love thee? Implications of attachment theory for understanding same-sex love and desire. In M. Mikulincer & G. Goodman (Eds.), *Dynamics of romantic love: Attachment, caregiving, and sex* (pp. 275–292). New York, NY: Guilford Press.

Diamond, L. M. (2007). A dynamical systems approach to female same-sex sexuality. *Perspectives on Psychological Science, 2*, 142–161. doi:10.1111/j.1745-6916.2007.00034.x

Diamond, L. M. (2008a). Female bisexuality from adolescence to adulthood: Results from a 10 year longitudinal study. *Developmental Psychology, 44*, 5–14. doi:10.1037/0012-1649.44.1.5

Diamond, L. M. (2008b). *Sexual fluidity: Understanding women's love and desire.* Cambridge, MA: Harvard University Press.

Diamond, L. M., & Dickenson, J. A. (2012). The neuroimaging of love and desire: Review and future directions. *Clinical Neuropsychiatry: Journal of Treatment Evaluation, 9*, 39–46.

Diamond, L. M., & Savin-Williams, R. C. (2009). Adolescent sexuality. In R. M. Lerner & L. Steinberg (Eds.), *Handbook of adolescent psychology* (3rd ed., pp. 479–523). New York, NY: Wiley. doi:10.1002/9780470479193.adlpsy001015

Diamond, L. M., & Wallen, K. (2011). Sexual-minority women's sexual motivation around the time of ovulation. *Archives of Sexual Behavior, 40*, 237–246. doi:10.1007/s10508-010-9631-2

Dickson, N., Paul, C., & Herbison, P. (2003). Same-sex attraction in a birth cohort: Prevalence and persistence in early adulthood. *Social Science and Medicine, 56*, 1607–1615. doi:10.1016/S0277-9536(02)00161-2

Dickson, N., Roode, T., Cameron, C., & Paul, C. (2013). Stability and change in same-sex attraction, experience, and identity by sex and age in a New Zealand birth cohort. *Archives of Sexual Behavior, 13*(2). doi:10.1007/s10508-012-0063-z

Dixon, J. K. (1984). The commencement of bisexual activity in swinging married women over age thirty. *Journal of Sex Research, 20*, 71–90. doi:10.1080/00224498409551207

Dixon, J. K. (1985). Sexuality and relationship changes in married females following the commencement of bisexual activity. *Journal of Homosexuality, 11*, 115–133. doi:10.1300/J082v11n01_10

Dubé, E. M., & Savin-Williams, R. C. (1999). Sexual identity development among ethnic sexual-minority male youths. *Developmental Psychology, 35*, 1389–1398. doi:10.1037/0012-1649.35.6.1389

Eliason, M. J. (1996). An inclusive model of lesbian identity assumption. *Journal of Gay, Lesbian, and Bisexual Identity, 1*, 3–19.

Esterberg, K. G. (1994). Being a lesbian and being in love: Constructing identities through relationships. *Journal of Gay and Lesbian Social Services, 1*, 57–82. doi:10.1300/J041v01n02_04

Fahs, B. (2009). Compulsory bisexuality? The challenges of modern sexual fluidity. *Journal of Bisexuality, 9*, 431–449. doi:10.1080/15299710903316661

Fausto-Sterling, A. (2012). *Sex/gender: Biology in a social world.* New York, NY: Routledge.

Fergusson, D. M., Horwood, L. J., Ridder, E. M., & Beautrais, A. L. (2005). Sexual orientation and mental health in a birth cohort of young adults. *Psychological Medicine, 35*, 971–981. doi:10.1017/S0033291704004222

Fine, M. (1988). Sexuality, schooling, and adolescent females: The missing discourse of desire. *Harvard Educational Review, 58*, 29–53.

Fisher, H. E., Aron, A. P., Mashek, D. J., Li, H., & Brown, L. L. (2002). Defining the brain systems of lust, romantic attraction, and attachment. *Archives of Sexual Behavior, 31*, 413–419. doi:10.1023/A:1019888024255

Floyd, F. J., & Bakeman, R. (2006). Coming-out across the life course: Implications of age and historical context. *Archives of Sexual Behavior, 35*, 287–296. doi:10.1007/s10508-006-9022-x

Fogel, A., & Thelen, E. (1987). Development of early expressive and communicative action: Reinterpreting the evidence from a dynamic systems perspective. *Developmental Psychology, 23*, 747–761. doi:10.1037/0012-1649.23.6.747

Forel, A. (1908). *The sexual question: A scientific, psychological, hygienic, and sociological study* (C. F. Marshall, Trans.). New York, NY: Physicians & Surgeons Book Company.

Futuyma, D. J., & Risch, S. J. (1983–1984). Sexual orientation, sociobiology, and evolution. *Journal of Homosexuality, 9*, 157–168. doi:10.1300/J082v09n02_10

Gagnon, J. H. (1990). Gender preference in erotic relations: The Kinsey Scale and sexual scripts. In D. P. McWhirter, S. A. Sanders, & J. M. Reinisch (Eds.), *Homosexuality/heterosexuality: Concepts of sexual orientation* (pp. 177–207). New York, NY: Oxford University Press.

Gagnon, J. H., & Simon, W. (1973). *Sexual conduct: The social sources of human sexuality.* Chicago, IL: Aldine.

Golden, C. (1987). Diversity and variability in women's sexual identities. In L. P. C. Boston (Ed.), *Lesbian psychologies: Explorations and challenges* (pp. 19–34). Urbana: University of Illinois Press.

Golden, C. (1994). Our politics and choices: The feminist movement and sexual orientation. In B. Greene & G. M. Herek (Eds.), *Lesbian and gay psychology: Theory, research, and clinical applications* (pp. 54–70). Thousand Oaks, CA: Sage.

Golden, C. (1996). What's in a name? Sexual self-identification among women. In R. C. Savin-Williams & K. M. Cohen (Eds.), *The lives of lesbians, gays, and bisexuals: Children to adults* (pp. 229–249). Fort Worth, TX: Harcourt Brace.

Goode, E., & Haber, L. (1977). Sexual correlates of homosexual experience: An exploratory study of college women. *Journal of Sex Research, 13*, 12–21. doi:10.1080/00224497709550956

Goy, R. W., & Goldfoot, D. A. (1975). Neuroendocrinology: Animal models and problems of human sexuality. *Archives of Sexual Behavior, 4*, 405–420. doi:10.1007/BF01541724

Gramick, J. (1984). Developing a lesbian identity. In T. Darty & S. Potter (Eds.), *Women-identified women* (pp. 31–44). Palo Alto, CA: Mayfield.

Grov, C., Bimbi, D. S., Nanin, J. E., & Parsons, J. T. (2006). Race, ethnicity, gender, and generational factors associated with the coming-out process among gay, lesbian, and bisexual individuals. *Journal of Sex Research, 43*, 115–121. doi:10.1080/00224490609552306

Hamann, S., Herman, R. A., Nolan, C. L., & Wallen, K. (2004). Men and women differ in amygdala response to visual sexual stimuli. *Nature Neuroscience, 7*, 411–416. doi:10.1038/nn1208

Hayes, J., Chakraborty, A. T., McManus, S., Bebbington, P., Brugha, T., Nicholson, S., & King, M. (2012). Prevalence of same-sex behavior and orientation in England: Results from a national survey. *Archives of Sexual Behavior, 41*, 631–639. doi:10.1007/s10508-011-9856-8

Herdt, G., & Boxer, A. M. (1993). *Children of Horizons: How gay and lesbian teens are leading a new way out of the closet.* Boston, MA: Beacon Press.

Herek, G. M., Norton, A. T., Allen, T. J., & Sims, C. L. (2010). Demographic, psychological, and social characteristics of self-identified lesbian, gay, and bisexual adults in a US probability sample. *Sexuality Research and Social Policy, 7*, 176–200. doi:10.1007/s13178-010-0017-y

Hollander, G. (2000). Questioning youths: Challenges to working with youths forming identities. *School Psychology Review, 29*, 173–179.

Horner, E. (2007). Queer identities and bisexual identities: What's the difference? In B. A. Firestein (Ed.), *Becoming visible: Counseling bisexuals across the lifespan* (pp. 287–296). New York, NY: Columbia University Press.

Hyde, J. S. (2005a). The gender similarities hypothesis. *American Psychologist, 60*, 581–592. doi:10.1037/0003-066X.60.6.581

Hyde, J. S. (2005b). The genetics of sexual orientation. In J. S. Hyde (Ed.), *Biological substrates of human sexuality* (pp. 9–20). Washington, DC: American Psychological Association. doi:10.1037/11196-002

Igartua, K., Thombs, B. D., Burgos, G., & Montoro, R. (2009). Concordance and discrepancy in sexual identity, attraction, and behavior among adolescents. *Journal of Adolescent Health, 45*, 602–608. doi:10.1016/j.jadohealth.2009.03.019

Institute of Medicine. (2011). *The health of lesbian, gay, bisexual, and transgender people: Building a foundation for better understanding.* Washington, DC: The National Academies Press.

Kinnish, K. K., Strassberg, D. S., & Turner, C. W. (2005). Sex differences in the flexibility of sexual orientation: A multidimensional retrospective assessment. *Archives of Sexual Behavior, 34*, 173–183. doi:10.1007/s10508-005-1795-9

Kinsey, A. C., Pomeroy, W. B., Martin, C. E., & Gebhard, P. H. (1953). *Sexual behavior in the human female.* Philadelphia, PA: W. B. Saunders.

Kitzinger, C. (1995). Social constructionism: Implications for lesbian and gay psychology. In A. R. D'Augelli & C. Patterson (Eds.), *Lesbian, gay, and bisexual identities over the lifespan* (pp. 136–161). New York, NY: Oxford University Press. doi:10.1093/acprof:oso/9780195082319.003.0006

Kitzinger, C., & Wilkinson, S. (1995). Transitions from heterosexuality to lesbianism: The discursive production of lesbian identities. *Developmental Psychology, 31*, 95–104. doi:10.1037/0012-1649.31.1.95

Krafft-Ebing, R. (1882). *Psychopathia sexualis* (M. E. Wedneck, Trans.). New York, NY: Putnams.

Kyrakanos, J. (1998). LUGgin' It. *InsideOUT Magazine, 9.*

Laan, E., & Janssen, E. (2007). How do men and women feel? Determinants of subjective experience of sexual arousal. In E. Janssen (Ed.), *The psychophysiology of sex* (pp. 278–290). Bloomington: Indiana University Press.

Laumann, E. O., Gagnon, J. H., Michael, R. T., & Michaels, F. (1994). *The social organization of sexuality: Sexual practices in the United States.* Chicago, IL: University of Chicago Press.

Laumann, E. O., & Mahay, J. (2002). The social organization of women's sexuality. In G. M. Wingood & R. J. DiClemente (Eds.), *Handbook of women's sexual and reproductive health* (pp. 43–70). New York, NY: Academic/Plenum. doi:10.1007/978-1-4615-0689-8_4

Lewis, M. D. (2000). The promise of dynamic systems approaches for an integrated account of human development. *Child Development, 71*, 36–43. doi:10.1111/1467-8624.00116

Liben, L. S., & Bigler, R. S. (2008). Developmental gender differentiation: Pathways in conforming and nonconforming outcomes. *Journal of Gay and Lesbian Mental Health, 12*, 95–112.

Loewenstein, S. F. (1984–1985). On the diversity of love object orientations among women. *Journal of Social Work and Human Sexuality, 3*, 7–24. doi:10.1300/J291v03n02_02

Lykins, A. D., Meana, M., & Strauss, G. P. (2008). Sex differences in visual attention to erotic and non-erotic stimuli. *Archives of Sexual Behavior, 37*, 219–228. doi:10.1007/s10508-007-9208-x

Maguen, S., Floyd, F. J., Bakeman, R., & Armistead, L. (2002). Developmental milestones and disclosure of sexual orientation among gay, lesbian, and bisexual youths. *Journal of Applied Developmental Psychology, 23*, 219–233. doi:10.1016/S0193-3973(02)00105-3

McCabe, J., Brewster, K. L., & Harker Tillman, K. (2011). Patterns and correlates of same-sex sexual activity among U.S. teenagers and young adults. *Perspectives on Sexual and Reproductive Health, 43*, 142–150. doi:10.1363/4314211

McClintock, M. K., & Herdt, G. (1996). Rethinking puberty: The development of sexual attraction. *Current Directions in Psychological Science, 5*, 178–183. doi:10.1111/1467-8721.ep11512422

Meyer, M. D. E. (2010). Representing bisexuality on television: The case for intersectional hybrids. *Journal of Bisexuality, 10*, 366–387. doi:10.1080/15299716.2010.521040

Mock, S. E., & Eibach, R. P. (2012). Stability and change in sexual orientation identity over a 10-year period in adulthood. *Archives of Sexual Behavior, 41*, 641–648. doi:10.1007/s10508-011-9761-1

Morgan, E. M., Steiner, M. G., & Thompson, E. M. (2010). Processes of sexual orientation questioning among heterosexual men. *Men and Masculinities, 12*, 425–443. doi:10.1177/1097184X08322630

Mosher, W. D., Chandra, A., & Jones, J. (2005). *Sexual behavior and selected health measures: Men and women 15—44 years of age, United States, 2002* (Advance data from Vital and Health Statistics, No. 362). Hyattsville, MD: National Center for Health Statistics.

Muscarella, F. (1999). The homoerotic behavior that never evolved. *Journal of Homosexuality, 37*, 1–18. doi:10.1300/J082v37n03_01

Mustanski, B. S., Chivers, M. L., & Bailey, J. M. (2002). A critical review of recent biological research on human sexual orientation. *Annual Review of Sex Research, 13*, 89–140.

Nichols, M. (1987). Lesbian sexuality: Issues and developing theory. In L. P. C. Boston (Ed.), *Lesbian psychologies* (pp. 97–125). Urbana: University of Illinois Press.

Nichols, M. (1990). Lesbian relationships: Implications for the study of sexuality and gender. In J. C. Gonsiorek & J. D. Weinrich (Eds.), *Homosexuality: Research implications for public policy* (pp. 350–364). Newbury Park, CA: Sage.

Ortigue, S., Bianchi-Demicheli, F., Patel, N., Frum, C., & Lewis, J. W. (2010). Neuroimaging of love: FMRI meta-analysis evidence toward new perspectives in sexual medicine. *Journal of Sexual Medicine, 7*, 3541–3552. doi:10.1111/j.1743-6109.2010.01999.x

Ott, M. Q., Corliss, H. L., Wypij, D., Rosario, M., & Austin, S. B. (2011). Stability and change in self-reported sexual orientation identity in young people: Application of mobility metrics. *Archives of Sexual Behavior, 40*, 519–532. doi:10.1007/s10508-010-9691-3

Pattatucci, A. M. L., & Hamer, D. H. (1995). Development and familiality of sexual orientation in females. *Behavior Genetics, 25*, 407–420. doi:10.1007/BF02253370

Penelope, J., & Wolfe, S. J. (1989). *The original coming out stories*. Freedom, CA: Crossing Press.

Peterson, Z. D., Janssen, E., & Laan, E. (2010). Women's sexual responses to heterosexual and lesbian erotica: The role of stimulus intensity, affective reaction, and sexual history. *Archives of Sexual Behavior, 39*, 880–897. doi:10.1007/s10508-009-9546-y

Rellini, A. H., McCall, K. M., Randall, P. K., & Meston, C. M. (2005). The relationship between women's subjective and physiological sexual arousal. *Psychophysiology, 42*, 116–124. doi:10.1111/j.1469-8986.2005.00259.x

Rieger, G., Bailey, J. M., & Chivers, M. L. (2005). Sexual arousal patterns of bisexual men. *Psychological Science, 16*, 579–584. doi:10.1111/j.1467-9280.2005.01578.x

Rimer, S. (1993, June 5). Campus lesbians step into unfamiliar light. *New York Times*, p. A2.

Rosario, M., Meyer-Bahlburg, H. F., Hunter, J., Exner, T. M., Gwadz, M., & Keller, A. M. (1996). The psychosexual development of urban lesbian, gay, and bisexual youths. *Journal of Sex Research, 33*, 113–126. doi:10.1080/00224499609551823

Rosario, M., Schrimshaw, E. W., & Hunter, J. (2008). Predicting different patterns of sexual identity development over time among lesbian, gay, and bisexual youths: A cluster analytic approach. *American Journal of Community Psychology, 42*, 266–282. doi:10.1007/s10464-008-9207-7

Rosario, M., Schrimshaw, E. W., & Hunter, J. (2011). Different patterns of sexual identity development over time: Implications for the psychological adjustment of lesbian, gay, and bisexual youths. *Journal of Sex Research, 48*, 3–15. doi:10.1080/00224490903331067

Rosario, M., Schrimshaw, E. W., Hunter, J., & Braun, L. (2006). Sexual identity development among lesbian, gay, and bisexual youths: Consistency and change over time. *Journal of Sex Research, 43*, 46–58. doi:10.1080/00224490609552298

Rosario, M., Schrimshaw, E. W., Hunter, J., & Levy-Warren, A. (2009). The coming-out process of young lesbian and bisexual women: Are there butch/femme differences in sexual identity development? *Archives of Sexual Behavior, 38*, 34–49. doi:10.1007/s10508-007-9221-0

Rose, S., Zand, D., & Cimi, M. A. (1993). Lesbian courtship scripts. In E. D. Rothblum & K. A. Brehony (Eds.), *Boston marriages* (pp. 70–85). Amherst: University of Massachusetts Press.

Rosenthal, A. M., Sylva, D., Safron, A., & Bailey, J. M. (2011). Sexual arousal patterns of bisexual men revisited. *Biological Psychology, 88*, 112–115. doi:10.1016/j.biopsycho.2011.06.015

Rosenthal, A. M., Sylva, D., Safron, A., & Bailey, J. M. (2012). The male bisexuality debate revisited: Some bisexual men have bisexual arousal patterns. *Archives of Sexual Behavior, 41*, 135–147. doi:10.1007/s10508-011-9881-7

Rullo, J. E., Strassberg, D. S., & Israel, E. (2010). Category-specificity in sexual interest in gay men and lesbians. *Archives of Sexual Behavior, 39*, 874–879. doi:10.1007/s10508-009-9497-3

Rupp, H. A., & Wallen, K. (2007). Sex differences in viewing sexual stimuli: An eye-tracking study in men and women. *Hormones and Behavior, 51*, 524–533. doi:10.1016/j.yhbeh.2007.01.008

Rust, P. C. R. (1993). Coming out in the age of social constructionism: Sexual identity formation among lesbians and bisexual women. *Gender and Society, 7*, 50–77. doi:10.1177/089124393007001004

Rust, P. C. R. (1995). *Bisexuality and the challenge to lesbian politics: Sex, loyalty, and revolution.* New York: New York University Press.

Rust, P. C. R. (2000). Criticisms of the scholarly literature on sexuality for its neglect of bisexuality. In P. C. R. Rust (Ed.), *Bisexuality in the United States: A reader and guide to the literature* (pp. 5–10). New York, NY: Columbia University Press.

Saghir, M. T., & Robins, E. (1973). *Male and female homosexuality: A comprehensive investigation.* Baltimore, MD: Williams & Wilkins.

Savin-Williams, R. C. (1998). "*. . . And then I became gay": Young men's stories.* New York, NY: Routledge.

Savin-Williams, R. C. (2001). A critique of research on sexual-minority youths. *Journal of Adolescence, 24*, 5–13. doi:10.1006/jado.2000.0369

Savin-Williams, R. C. (2005). *The new gay teenager.* Cambridge, MA: Harvard University Press.

Savin-Williams, R. C. (2006). Who's gay? Does it matter? *Current Directions in Psychological Science, 15*, 40–44. doi:10.1111/j.0963-7214.2006.00403.x

Savin-Williams, R. C., & Diamond, L. M. (2000). Sexual identity trajectories among sexual-minority youths: Gender comparisons. *Archives of Sexual Behavior, 29*, 607–627. doi:10.1023/A:1002058505138

Savin-Williams, R. C., Joyner, K., & Rieger, G. (2012). Prevalence and stability of self-reported sexual orientation identity during young adulthood. *Archives of Sexual Behavior, 41*, 103–110. doi:10.1007/s10508-012-9913-y

Savin-Williams, R. C., & Ream, G. L. (2007). Prevalence and stability of sexual orientation components during adolescence and young adulthood. *Archives of Sexual Behavior, 36*, 385–394. doi:10.1007/s10508-006-9088-5

Sell, R. L., & Petrulio, C. (1996). Sampling homosexuals, bisexuals, gays, and lesbians for public health research: A review of the literature from 1990 to 1992. *Journal of Homosexuality, 30*, 31–47. doi:10.1300/J082v30n04_02

Shibley-Hyde, J. S., & Durik, A. M. (2000). Gender differences in erotic plasticity—Evolutionary or sociocultural forces? Comment on Baumeister (2000). *Psychological Bulletin, 126*, 375–379. doi:10.1037/0033-2909.126.3.375

Shuster, R. (1987). Sexuality as a continuum: The bisexual identity. In L. P. C. Boston (Ed.), *Lesbian psychologies* (pp. 56–71). Urbana: University of Illinois Press.

Silber, L. J. (1990). Negotiating sexual identity: Non-lesbians in a lesbian feminist community. *Journal of Sex Research, 27*, 131–139. doi:10.1080/00224499009551547

Sophie, J. (1985–1986). A critical examination of stage theories of lesbian identity development. *Journal of Homosexuality, 12*, 39–51. doi:10.1300/J082v12n02_03

Stanley, J. P., & Wolfe, S. J. (1980). *The coming out stories.* Watertown, MA: Persephone Press.

Stokes, J. P., Damon, W., & McKirnan, D. J. (1997). Predictors of movement toward homosexuality: A longitudinal study of bisexual men. *Journal of Sex Research, 34*, 304–312. doi:10.1080/00224499709551896

Stokes, J. P., McKirnan, D., & Burzette, R. (1993). Sexual behavior, condom use, disclosure of sexuality, and stability of sexual orientation in bisexual men. *Journal of Sex Research, 30*, 203–213. doi:10.1080/00224499309551704

Storms, M. D. (1980). Theories of sexual orientation. *Journal of Personality and Social Psychology, 38*, 783–792. doi:10.1037/0022-3514.38.5.783

Suschinsky, K. D., & Lalumiere, M. L. (2011). Prepared for anything? An investigation of female genital arousal in response to rape cues. *Psychological Science, 22*, 159–165. doi:10.1177/095679761 0394660

Suschinsky, K. D., Lalumiere, M. L., & Chivers, M. L. (2009). Sex differences in patterns of genital sexual arousal: Measurement artifacts or true phenomena? *Archives of Sexual Behavior, 38*, 559–573. doi:10.1007/s10508-008-9339-8

Thompson, E. M. (2007). Girl friend or girlfriend?: Same-sex friendship and bisexual images as a context for flexible sexual identity among young women. *Journal of Bisexuality, 6*, 47–67. doi:10.1300/J159v06n03_04

Thompson, E. M., & Morgan, E. M. (2008). "Mostly straight" young women: Variations in sexual behavior and identity development. *Developmental Psychology, 44*, 15–21. doi:10.1037/0012-1649.44.1.15

Tolman, D. L., & Diamond, L. M. (2001). Desegregating sexuality research: Combining cultural and biological perspectives on gender and desire. *Annual Review of Sex Research, 12*, 33–74.

Tsujimura, A., Miyagawa, Y., Takada, S., Matsuoka, Y., Takao, T., Hirai, T., . . . Okuyama, A. (2009). Sex differences in visual attention to sexually explicit videos: A preliminary study. *Journal of Sexual Medicine*. England: Wiley-Blackwell.

Udry, J. R., & Chantala, K. (2006). Masculinity-femininity predicts sexual orientation in men but not in women. *Journal of Biosocial Science, 38*, 797–809. doi:10.1017/S002193200500101X

Ussher, J. M. (1993). The construction of female sexual problems: Regulating sex, regulating woman. In J. M. Ussher & C. D. Baker (Eds.), *Psychological perspectives on sexual problems: New directions in theory and practice* (pp. 9–40). New York, NY: Routledge.

Vance, B. K., & Green, V. (1984). Lesbian identities: An examination of sexual behavior and sex role acquisition as related to age of initial same-sex encounter. *Psychology of Women Quarterly, 8*, 293–307. doi:10.1111/j.1471-6402.1984.tb00638.x

Vrangalova, Z., & Savin-Williams, R. C. (2012). Mostly heterosexual and mostly gay/lesbian: Evidence for new sexual orientation identities. *Archives of Sexual Behavior, 41*, 85–101. doi:10.1007/s10508-012-9921-y

Walsh, C. (Ed.). (2010). *Dear John, I love Jane: Women write about leaving men for women*. Berkeley, CA: Seal Press.

Walter, M., Bermpohl, F., Mouras, H., Schiltz, K., Tempelmann, C., Rotte, M., . . . Northoff, G. (2008). Distinguishing specific sexual and general emotional effects in fMRI-subcortical and cortical arousal during erotic picture viewing. *NeuroImage, 40*, 1482–1494. doi:10.1016/j.neuroimage.2008.01.040

Weinberg, M. S., Williams, C. J., & Pryor, D. W. (1994). *Dual attraction: Understanding bisexuality*. New York, NY: Oxford University Press.

Welles, C. E. (2005). Breaking the silence surrounding female adolescent sexual desire. *Women and Therapy, 28*, 31–45. doi:10.1300/J015v28n02_03

Whisman, V. (1993). Identity crisis: Who is a lesbian anyway? In A. Stein (Ed.), *Sisters, sexperts, queers: Beyond the lesbian nation* (pp. 47–60). New York, NY: Penguin.

Whisman, V. (1996). *Queer by choice: Lesbians, gay men, and the politics of identity*. New York, NY: Routledge.

Yost, M. R., & McCarthy, L. (2012). Girls gone wild? Heterosexual women's same-sex encounters at college parties. *Psychology of Women Quarterly, 36*, 7–24. doi:10.1177/0361684311414818

Part VI

SEXUAL BODIES/EMBODYING SEXUALITY

CHAPTER 21

SEXUALITY AND HEALTH

William H. George, Jeanette Norris, Hong V. Nguyen, N. Tatiana Masters, and Kelly Cue Davis

Sexuality is a primal and essential facet of being human that intersects with many aspects of our experience, especially health. Sexual functioning and sexual health are indispensable both to our quality of life and to the continuation of our species. This chapter examines the deleterious and beneficial associations between sexuality and both physical and mental health. The topic of sexuality and health is extraordinarily broad and overlaps to some degree with practically every other chapter in this volume. It is also a topic rife with seemingly self-evident but contested definitions, tacit assumptions, and ambiguous coverage boundaries. Therefore, our treatment of the topic begins with explicit statements about definitions, assumptions, and coverage.

DEFINITIONS

To begin examining sexuality and health, three pertinent constructs necessitate definition: health, sexuality, and sexual health. In accordance with the conceptual and practical importance of these constructs, considerable attention has been devoted to defining these terms. Although there have been cycles of contemplation, consensus building, and criticism (e.g., Coleman, 2007; Larson, 1996), the World Health Organization (WHO) has set forth the most widely accepted and enduring definitions (Edwards & Coleman, 2004). These definitions, while not definitive or immune from criticism and debate, do provide useful framing to our discussion of sexuality and health.

After World War II, at a time when the health of individuals and societies was an overwhelming global concern, the WHO defined *health* as "a state of complete physical, mental and social well-being and not merely the absence of disease or infirmity" (WHO, 1946, p. 100). Despite considerable criticism (e.g., Larson, 1996), this definition of health remains the conventional wisdom, and it set the stage for defining sexual health.

An initial definition of *sexual health*—"the integration of the somatic, emotional, intellectual and social aspects of sexual being, in ways that are positively enriching and that enhance personality, communication and love" (WHO, 1975, p. 6)—heralded subsequent international meetings and debates aimed at further developing and refining this definition. Early meetings recognized a need to posit an understanding of sexuality as a fundamental part of an understanding of sexual health. This definition of *sexuality* was articulated in a WHO technical document:

> [Sexuality is] an integral part of the personality of everyone: man, woman, and child. It is a basic need and an aspect of being human that cannot be separated from other aspects of life. Sexuality is not synonymous with sexual intercourse, it is not about whether we have orgasms or not, and it is not the sum total of our erotic lives. These may be part of our sexuality but equally they may not. Sexuality is so much more: it is in the energy that motivates us to find love, contact, warmth and intimacy; it is expressed in the way we feel, move, touch and are touched; it is about being sensual as well as being sexual. Sexuality influences thoughts, feelings, actions and interactions and thereby our mental and physical health. (Langfeldt & Porter, 1986, p. 5)

http://dx.doi.org/10.1037/14193-021
APA Handbook of Sexuality and Psychology: Vol. 1. Person-Based Approaches, D. L. Tolman and L. M. Diamond (Editors-in-Chief)

Having adopted this definition of sexuality as a precursor to revising the definition of sexual health, and in the context of subsequent definitions debated by stakeholders including sex education and sexology organizations and the U.S. Surgeon General's Office, the WHO (2010) presented this working definition of sexual health:

> A state of physical, emotional, mental and social well-being related to sexuality; it is not merely the absence of disease, dysfunction or infirmity. Sexual health requires a positive and respectful approach to sexuality and sexual relationships as well as the possibility of having pleasurable and safe sexual experiences, free of coercion, discrimination, and violence. For sexual health to be attained and maintained, the sexual rights of all persons must be respected, protected and fulfilled. (p. 3)

Two additional definitions also are warranted at the outset. Sexual functioning can be defined as a normative sexual response, including sexual desire, sexual excitement and arousal, orgasm, and resolution. Sexual dysfunctions are defined as disturbances in sexual desire and in the psychophysiological changes that characterize the sexual response cycle and cause marked distress and interpersonal difficulty. These disturbances may include difficulties in sexual desire, interest, arousal, and orgasm, and pain during sexual activity (see Chapters 8 and 11, this volume).

Assumptions

The definition of sexual health and its evolution highlight important assumptions that underpin our approach to sexuality and health in this chapter. First, the definition of sexual health is not fixed. As a "working definition," it is dynamic and subject to modifications over time as our conceptualizations change. Second, considerations of sexuality and health are not restricted to biological processes and functions, but also encompass attention to psychological and social domains, which are interwoven inextricably with experiences of biological sexual processes and functions. Third, considerations of sexuality and health are not restricted to illness, disease, and dysfunction, but they also embody sexual wellness and beneficence—that is, the idea that positive sexual health benefits overall well-being. Fourth, it is assumed that experiences of sexual coercion, abuse, exploitation, violence, and oppression undermine positive sexual health. Fifth, sexual pleasure, feeling loved, and loving are understood to be essential motivational aspects of positive sexual health. Finally, the freedom from being discriminated against on the basis of aspects of one's sexuality and the right to pursue positive sexual health are to be respected at individual, interpersonal, and societal levels (see Chapters 12 and 25, this volume; Volume 2, Chapters 8 and 10, this handbook). These definitions and assumptions frame our approach to this chapter.

Coverage

The objectives of this chapter are to review basic issues and research findings pertaining to major domains of the intersection between sexuality and health. Three broad domains traditionally associated with health problems will be addressed: physical health syndromes, mental health syndromes, and sexually transmitted infections and diseases. Substance use is highly associated with sexual behavior and there is a wide-ranging body of literature. The literature on alcohol and sexuality is extensive and well developed and will be an important domain of coverage of psychoactive drugs and sex. Although the literature is much less extensive, the association between sexuality and other psychoactive drugs also will be covered. Literature pertaining to comorbidity of substance use disorders and sexual disorders also will be covered in these sections. Finally, much of the aforementioned coverage concentrates on health problems, whether medical disorders or problematic sexual outcomes of substance use. As is evident in our definitions and assumptions, however, an important element of our approach to this chapter is the recognition that sexuality is largely a positive force in the human experience and as such has many beneficial and salutary associations with health. Thus, a fifth domain of coverage will be the health benefits of sex. We will conclude with a summary of our coverage and suggestions for future research, implications for health care providers, and theory development.

CHRONIC PHYSICAL ILLNESSES AND SEXUALITY

As life expectancy in the United States continues to rise, these increased longevity rates are coupled with greater rates of chronic illnesses, such as heart disease, cancer, diabetes, arthritis, and stroke (National Center for Health Statistics, 2007). Some reports estimate that 133 million Americans (or almost one out of every two adults) have at least one chronic illness (Partnership for Solutions, 2004). Because improvements in medical treatments are allowing individuals with chronic illnesses to live longer, the focus of treatment eventually shifts from enabling survival to improving quality of life (Basson, Rees, Wang, Montejo, & Incrocci, 2010; Verschuren, Enzlin, Dijkstra, Geertzen, & Dekker, 2010).

Although sexual functioning and well-being is a critical aspect of living a healthy life (World Association for Sexual Health, 2008), the impact of chronic illness on sexuality often is overlooked in both research studies (Verschuren et al., 2010) and clinical practice (Anderson & Wolf, 1986; Barsky, Friedman, & Rosen, 2006; Nusbaum, Hamilton, & Lenahan, 2003; see also Volume 2, Chapter 4, this handbook). Given the increasing numbers of people living with one or more chronic illnesses, a better understanding of the ways in which sexual function and well-being may be affected by chronic physical illness is warranted. Covering the effects of specific illnesses on sexuality is beyond the scope of this chapter; rather, this chapter presents issues and concerns regarding sexual function and well-being that may emerge within a variety of chronic illnesses and provides some specific examples to elucidate these generalities.

Physiological Effects of Chronic Illness on Sexual Function

Chronic illnesses can have both direct and indirect physiological effects on sexual functioning throughout the sexual response cycle (Nusbaum et al., 2003). Direct effects refer to the organic alteration of physiological sexual processes or anatomy such that sexual functioning is disrupted (Verschuren et al., 2010; see also Chapter 7, this volume). Examples of direct physiological effects include the inability to achieve orgasm because of the disruption of neural transmission between the brain and genitals in cases of spinal cord injury or diabetes-related peripheral neuropathy (Clayton & Ramamurthy, 2008) and sexual dysfunction caused by vascular abnormalities commonly found in cardiovascular diseases like hypertension (Manolis & Doumas, 2008; Perez, Gadgil, & Dizon, 2009). Indirect physiological effects refer to physical changes or symptoms of an illness that although not directly impairing physiological sexual processes, nonetheless may have a negative impact on sexual functioning (Verschuren et al., 2010). For example, arthritic symptoms such as immobility and pain and Parkinsonian symptoms of muscle rigidity and bradykinesia may increase the difficulty of performing certain sexual behaviors (Bronner & Vodusek, 2011; Clayton & Ramamurthy, 2008).

In addition to these physiological effects of the illnesses themselves, the treatments for chronic illnesses can have iatrogenic effects on sexual functioning and well-being (Sadovsky et al., 2010; Verschuren et al., 2010). First, prescribed medications result in problems in sexual functioning for some patients. As an example, many beta-blockers and diuretics, often used to treat hypertension, are associated with an increased risk of sexual dysfunction (Manolis & Doumas, 2008; Perez et al., 2009). Another prominent example—to be discussed in more detail later—involves antidepressant medications, such as selective serotonin reuptake inhibitors (SSRIs), which have been associated with anorgasmia and loss of desire. Because medication-induced sexual dysfunction is a common cause of drug therapy nonadherence (Manolis & Doumas, 2008; Perez et al., 2009), care must be taken to prescribe medications that have fewer deleterious sexual side effects. Second, surgical procedures also may have negative effects on sexual functioning. For example, many cancer treatments may involve the total or partial surgical removal of the affected area, including ovaries, breasts, the uterus, the prostate, testes, and the penis. Surgical treatment of prostate cancer may result not only in erectile dysfunction (ED) but also in loss of sexual desire and decreased general sexual satisfaction. Similarly, surgery for gynecological cancers, like radical hysterectomies, may result in decreased sexual desire, potentially through the loss of ovarian hormones (Sadovsky et al., 2010). Although increased odds of survival are the main goal of surgical cancer treatments, there is increasingly an emphasis on the development and use of surgical techniques that not only improve survival odds but also minimize their negative effects on patients' sexual functioning (Sadovsky et al., 2010). Third, cancer patients must cope with the negative sexual side effects of both radiation and chemotherapies. In women, for example, chemotherapy may result in an earlier onset of menopause, and radiation may cause vaginal narrowing and shortening (Sadovsky et al., 2010).

Psychological Effects of Chronic Illness on Sexual Function

For many individuals, living with a chronic physical illness can result in psychological reactions, in both themselves and their sexual partners, that can impair sexual functioning and well-being above and beyond any physiological effects of the illness itself. These reactions may range from normal adjustment and grief reactions to problematic or even psychopathological reactions, such as a major depressive episode (Verschuren et al., 2010). Importantly, such reactions may change significantly over time, given the progression of the illness. That is, illnesses or injuries that are relatively stable (e.g., traumatic brain injury) may involve one initial period of adjustment followed by continued coping. Illnesses that entail a progression of deterioration (e.g., multiple sclerosis) require continual adjustment to increased symptoms and functional impairment over time (Verschuren et al., 2010). As such, one-time assessments of psychological reactions to chronic illness may not be sufficient. Health care providers continually must evaluate patients' adjustment to their illnesses, particularly as changes in the disease progression occur (Sadovsky et al., 2010).

Once patients have been informed of their diagnosis of a serious chronic illness, concerns of survival are likely paramount. As concerns over survival recede and symptom management stabilizes, however, other issues pertinent to sexual well-being may come to the forefront (Steinke, 2005). Adjustment to living with a chronic physical illness often involves "adapting one's sense of self to include an altered and impaired body" (Anderson & Wolf, 1986, p. 170). The extent to which one's sexual identity may be altered by a chronic illness depends not only on the illness itself but also on the importance a particular individual places on body image, sexual intimacy and fulfillment, and their current relationship status (Barsky et al., 2006; Steinke, 2005; see also Chapter 25, this volume). For some patients, sexual concerns will be relatively unimportant. For others, sexual issues may be a critical intervention target for improving the patient's quality of life. As with the physiological effects of chronic illness, these psychological effects may result from the disease itself or from the treatment of the disease.

One concern of many patients and their partners is that sexual activity may exacerbate the physical symptoms of the illness (e.g., pain, shortness of breath) or may precipitate the recurrence of an episodic problem (e.g., heart attack, stroke; Basson et al., 2010; Nusbaum et al., 2003). Many couples may avoid any and all sexual activity to cope with this worry. Although consideration of the patient's risk level is important, few, if any, chronic illnesses require a complete restriction of all sexual activity (Nusbaum et al., 2003; Steinke, 2005). Providing the patient and his or her partner with information about any sexual activity guidelines specific to the illness, and discussing any warning signs to be aware of when engaging in sexual activity, may alleviate these concerns and allow the couple to incorporate a healthy level of sexual activity back into their lives (Nusbaum et al., 2003; Steinke, 2005).

Changes in physical functioning potentially detrimental to sexual functioning are also a primary concern of many chronic illness patients. For example, illnesses with symptoms of urinary incontinence may increase fears of having an "accident" during intercourse, particularly for women (Bronner & Vodusek, 2011; Clayton & Ramamurthy, 2008). Concerns about the wearing of insulin pumps, ostomy bags, or catheters may decrease sexual interest and spontaneity (Clayton & Ramamurthy, 2008; Perez et al., 2009). Other bodily control concerns during intercourse include symptoms like drooling and muscle spasticity as well as difficulties in controlling aspects of the sexual act itself, such as lubrication and erections (Clayton & Ramamurthy, 2008). Such threats to personal control over bodily functions and movement may lead to the avoidance of sexual activity (Anderson & Wolf, 1986; Verschuren et al., 2010).

Perhaps one of the largest areas of concern for individuals coping with chronic illness and its effects on sexuality is body image and appearance. Many chronic illnesses and their treatments can result in negative changes in appearance that can have devastating effects on one's sexual self-esteem and sexual identity. Women diagnosed with lupus, for example, report that the changes in their appearance caused by the disease were the most influential factor in their avoidance of sexual contact. The skin rashes, weight gain, hair loss, and other physical appearance changes caused by lupus and its treatments instilled in some women a feeling of being "unlovable," often leading to fears of being abandoned by their partners (Karlen, 2002). For cancer patients, in addition to the detrimental effects of fatigue and nausea, radiation and chemotherapy treatments often result in changes in physical appearance, like alopecia and weight loss, which can devalue one's sense of sexual attractiveness to others (Anderson & Wolf, 1986; Sadovsky et al., 2010). Surgical treatments for a variety of illnesses, particularly those that visibly affect physical features associated with sex (e.g., mastectomy), may result in disfigurements that challenge one's sexual self-esteem. The reaction of one's sexual partner to these changes in physical appearance, however, can have a dramatic impact on whether the relationship suffers as a result (Scott & Kayser, 2009).

Sexual Partnerships

The establishment of a new intimate or sexual relationship can be particularly difficult for individuals with chronic physical illness. Fear of rejection as well as hesitancy about disclosing personal medical information to an unfamiliar person may make it difficult for some individuals to pursue new partners (Sadovsky et al., 2010). Some individuals have noted that their illness forced them to reprioritize the characteristics they desired in a partner, and as such, found new intimate partners who better suited their new lifestyles (Karlen, 2002).

For individuals already in a sexual partnership, the diagnosis of a chronic physical illness may pose serious challenges to their relationship with their partner. In addition to the effects of disease on the ill partner, the healthy partner will have his or her own reactions to and ability to cope with having a partner with a chronic illness. How the partnership fares with chronic illness will depend on the preexisting psychological health of both partners and their relational skills and dynamics (Verschuren et al., 2010). Because of the importance of the partner's response to chronic illness in the sexual well-being of the couple, it is advisable for health care practitioners to assess illness-related sexual problems with the couple together as well as with each partner individually (Basson et al., 2010; Nusbaum et al., 2003).

Diagnosis of a chronic illness may necessitate many changes within an intimate partnership, which may stress the relationship. The couple may have to terminate engagement in previously enjoyable activities, may be required to drastically alter future life plans, may have to adapt to the financial ramifications of a costly illness, and must adjust to living "medicalized" lives (Basson et al., 2010; Hughes, Hertlein, & Hagey, 2011; Sadovsky et al., 2010). Coping with feelings of grief and loss over these changes, as well as feelings of powerlessness over the illness, may place a strain on the relationship.

Additionally, the balance of power within the relationship may change, such that the healthy partner takes on a more powerful caregiver role, while the ill partner assumes a more dependent patient role (Verschuren et al., 2010). The ill partner may fear becoming a burden to his or her partner and may feel guilt or shame over relationship problems (sexual and otherwise) created by the illness; meanwhile, the healthy partner may feel anxious, responsible for the ill partner, or resentful about the amount of care he or she requires (Basson et al., 2010; Hughes et al., 2011). These concerns may result in the partners not fully sharing their emotions with one another in an attempt to protect the other person and avoid burdening him or her further (Verschuren et al., 2010).

Importantly, while coping with chronic illness may serve as a stressor within a partnership, it also may allow for the relationship to grow and deepen, both emotionally and sexually, over time (Karlen, 2002; Verschuren et al., 2010). Indeed, although negative sexual and relationship changes are often a focus of both research and treatment, some patients experience positive sexual changes as a result of their chronic illness, including strengthened intimate relationships (Karlen, 2002). For example, the healthy partner may come to enjoy the role of caregiver as it creates a sense of importance and feeling needed by their loved one. Moreover, the development of a chronic illness also may serve to focus the couple on their most important life values and goals, thereby shifting their priorities in a positive way (Karlen, 2002; Verschuren et al., 2010). Because adapting to a chronic illness provides this opportunity for growth, and because healthy sexual functioning and sexual well-being can be an important part of physical recovery (Sadovsky et al., 2010), care providers should consider shifting the emphasis of treatment from a deficit model approach to one that focuses on empowering the patient and his or her partner to approach the changes in their sexual relationship in an adaptive way through greater flexibility in coping (Barsky et al., 2006) and increased agency and communication (Hughes et al., 2011). Couple-based interventions have shown promise in this regard (Scott & Kayser, 2009).

Developmental Life-Span Issues

When considering the effects of chronic physical illness on sexuality, it is important to bear in mind how these effects may shift in relevance according to both physiological and psychological developmental stages. Children who develop a chronic physical illness may experience delayed sexual development and puberty, limited social activities with their peers, and a lack of access to sexual education, particularly education that entails a discussion of the effects of illness on developing sexuality (Finnegan, 2004; Sadovsky et al., 2010; Valencia & Cromer, 2000). Despite these issues, many studies have found no differences in the sexual activity levels of chronically ill and healthy adolescents (Valencia & Cromer, 2000).

Fertility concerns may be of particular importance to individuals diagnosed with a chronic illness earlier in the life span. Depending on the illness, younger adults may have concerns about their illness (or its treatment) impairing their ability to reproduce (Anderson & Wolf, 1986; Finnegan, 2004; Hughes et al., 2011; Sadovsky et al., 2010). For those who are able to conceive, doing so may result in a high-risk pregnancy, which may be coupled with concerns about their ability to care for a child given their own illness and the likelihood of the child inheriting their illness (Anderson & Wolf, 1986; Finnegan, 2004). Moreover, some forms of contraception pose health risks to some chronically ill individuals, further complicating reproductive concerns (Anderson & Wolf, 1986; Finnegan, 2004).

Older adults who already may be struggling with age-related sexual dysfunction may find these difficulties exacerbated by the development of a chronic illness (Hughes et al., 2011). Because their partners also may be older and dealing with their own health concerns, maintaining an active healthy sex life may be especially challenging. Furthermore, conversing about sexual concerns may be particularly difficult for some older adults (Steinke, 2005). Because of these various concerns, health care providers should be sensitive to developmental issues when discussing sexual concerns with chronically ill patients.

Summary

Sexual problems attributed to chronic illness are both common and complex. Because sexual functioning is an important contributor to quality of life even for those individuals living with chronic physical illness, multidisciplinary research and treatment efforts that address the heterogeneity of the effects of chronic illness on sexuality are essential. Further empirical and clinical advancements in this area could greatly enhance the sexual well-being of the chronically ill and their sexual partners.

MENTAL ILLNESSES AND SEXUALITY

Like physical illnesses, mental illness can have repercussions that affect sexuality. Mental illnesses include disorders characterized by disturbances in cognitive, emotional, or behavioral functioning at a level sufficient to create significant distress or disability. The literature linking mental disorders and sexuality is vast, far exceeding the scope of this chapter. This section reviews prominent trends that have emerged. It appears that most mental disorders have some impact on sexuality, if not directly, then indirectly because of their pharmaceutical treatments—for example, schizophrenia medications (e.g., Baggaley, 2008). Certain disorders, however, are especially associated with sexual functioning or sexual risk-taking and have received considerable research attention, including mood disorders and developmental disabilities. Substance use disorders also have been researched, but they will be considered in a later section on the effects of psychoactive drugs on sexuality.

Mood Disorders and Sexuality

Extensive empirical evidence attests to comorbidity between mood disorders—particularly depression (e.g., see reviews by Hartmann, 2007; Michael & O'Keane, 2000) and anxiety disorders (e.g., see reviews by Norton & Jehu, 1984; Seto, 1992)—and sexual dysfunctions.

Depression. Overall, in keeping with the understanding that sexuality is a primary source of positive experience, decreased sexual activity and enjoyment is associated with depressive mood and symptomology and vice versa. There is also evidence of increased sexual activity during depressive episodes, however, potentially indicative of pursuing reassuring emotional comfort (Michaels & O'Keane, 2000). Also, increased sexual interest has been reported among patients diagnosed with bipolar I disorder, which is associated with manic episodes (e.g., Mazza et al., 2011).

For depression, the comorbidity pattern is reflected across the sexual response cycle, such that disorders involving sexual arousal, sexual desire, and orgasm are more common among individuals diagnosed with depression than among controls (e.g., Dell'Osso et al., 2009). Likewise, depressive symptoms are common among individuals diagnosed with sexual disorders (e.g., Schnatz, Whitehurst, & O'Sullivan, 2010; see also Chapter 8, this volume). Additionally, among nonclinical samples, there is evidence that problems with sexual functioning co-occur with depressive symptoms among medical students (e.g., Shindel, Eisenberg, Breyer, Sharlip, & Smith, 2011; J. F. Smith, Breyer, Eisenberg, Sharlip, & Shindel, 2010). Among male medical students, depressive symptoms were associated with ED (e.g., J. F. Smith et al., 2010). Among female medical students, depressive symptoms were associated with worse orgasmic function and with interference with one's sex life due to stress or lack of a partner (e.g., Shindel et al., 2011). Similarly, among college students assessed on a daily basis, depressive symptoms were related negatively to the quantity and quality of sexual contact (Kashdan et al., 2011). Furthermore, the relationship between depression and sexual functioning appears to be moderated by gender among both clinical and nonclinical samples, although not consistently so (e.g., Kashdan et al., 2011; Laurent & Simons, 2009). For instance, survey data have shown that depressive symptoms are associated with reduced sexual desire among women but not necessarily among men (see review by Laurent & Simons, 2009). Daily diary data have shown that depressive symptoms were associated with lower feelings of connectedness to their partner during sex among women, but greater feelings of connectedness among men (e.g., Kashdan et al., 2011).

The true nature of the depression and sexual functioning association is not well understood. For instance, very little is known about premorbid sexual functioning in individuals suffering from depressive symptomatology. Also, because most studies are descriptive and correlational, we have gleaned little insight into causal direction, that is, whether depression lowers sexual functioning or whether lowered sexual functioning leads to depression.

It has been hypothesized generally that worsening mood leads to worsening sexual functioning (Laurent & Simons, 2009). Several experimental studies have investigated this hypothesis by utilizing mood induction procedures. Among women, experimentally induced happy mood resulted in more subjective sexual arousal than sad mood (ter Kuile, Both, & van Uden, 2010). Similarly, a cognitively induced positive schema resulted in greater positive mood and sexual arousal than a negative schema; and this was true for sexually healthy and dysfunctional women (Middleton, Kuffel, & Heiman, 2008) and for depressed and nondepressed women (Kuffel & Heiman, 2006). Likewise with men, experimentally induced negative affect has resulted in diminished sexual arousal (Meisler & Carey, 1991; Mitchell, DiBartolo, Brown, & Barlow, 1998; Wolchik et al., 1980). These experimental findings clearly indicate that worsening mood—either increased negative affect or decreased positive affect—has a causal impact lowering some if not all indicators of sexual arousal and sexual desire.

Similarly, some animal research is also consistent with this directional causal impact. Anhedonia, which often is associated with severe depression, is the general inability to experience pleasure from activities usually found enjoyable. In experimentation with rats, a model of depression characterized by "anhedonia-resembling behavior" induced by olfactory bulbectomy led to sexual deficits indicative of reduced arousal and desire (e.g., Wang et al., 2007; see also Chapter 7, this volume).

Interestingly, across several of the human experiments on mood and sexual arousal discussed earlier, it emerged that changes in positive mood appear more influential on sexual arousal than changes in negative mood. Consistent with this trend, Peterson and Janssen (2007) exposed men and women to erotic films, some of which involved negative content, and found that changes in positive mood were more predictive of sexual arousal than changes in negative mood. Moving from the laboratory to the natural world, a similar trend emerged in a daily dairy study of middle-age community women showing that positive mood on one day predicted more physical affection and sexual activity with a partner the following day (Burleson, Trevathan, & Todd, 2007). Yet, a daily diary study of adolescent women showed that same-day negative mood predicted less coital activity (Fortenberry et al., 2005). Overall, however, it appears generally that higher positive mood improves sexual functioning and lower positive mood diminishes it, consistent with the idea that depression and depressive mood negatively affect sexual functioning (Nobre & Pinto-Gouveia, 2006, 2008a, 2008b).

The reverse notion that sexual arousal and activity improves mood has received less research attention. Limited experimental evidence suggests that experiencing sexual arousal can improve mood on a short-term basis (e.g., Heiman, 1980; Meisler & Carey, 1991). Furthermore, the daily diary study of women showed "that mood-enhancing effects of sexual behavior and physical affection may remain active for at least an entire day and night" (Burleson et al., 2007, p. 365). Nevertheless, research has been insufficient to demonstrate and understand potential mood-enhancing effects of sexual arousal and activity for individuals suffering from depression disorders. More generally, among the broader population, it appears that frequent sexual intercourse is associated with improved mental health (e.g., Brody, 2010).

Antidepressant treatment. An unequivocal clinical and empirical trend regarding depression and sexuality is that treatment with antidepressant medications debilitates sexual functioning in many patients and that these sexual dysfunction effects of antidepressants undermine treatment compliance. The literature evaluating the effects of antidepressant medications on sexual functioning is vast and has been reviewed extensively (e.g., see reviews by Garnock-Jones & McCormack, 2010; Kennedy & Rizvi, 2009; Montejo, Majadas, Rizvi, & Kennedy, 2011; Schweitzer, Maguire, & Ng, 2009; Taylor, 2006; Werneke, Northey, & Bhugra, 2006). Generally, the evidence indicates that most antidepressant drugs are associated with sexual dysfunction to some degree. SSRIs and serotonin and norepinephrine reuptake inhibitors (SNRIs) have been prescribed widely and have received considerable research evaluation regarding sexual functioning. SSRIs and SNRIs affect sexual functioning adversely by increasing serotonin activity, which has been shown to have inhibitory effects on libido, ejaculation, and orgasm. Other recent antidepressants such as Bupropion and agomelatine do not increase serotonin activity and appear to have fewer sexual dysfunction side effects than SSRIs and SNRIs. Further research is needed to clarify variability in terms of which medications are more or less contributory to sexual dysfunction and disruptive of treatment compliance. In any case, clinical management of patients undergoing antidepressant medication treatment necessitates regularly monitoring for the possibility of adverse sexual effects and the potential utility of switching medications and coprescribing sexual dysfunction medications.

In treating major depressive disorder, it has now become well established that antidepressant medications, cognitive behavior therapy, and interpersonal psychotherapy constitute gold standards (e.g., DeRubeis et al., 2005; Stewart & Harkness, 2012). Furthermore, the cumulative evidence indicates that cognitive therapy is as efficacious as antidepressant medications (e.g., DeRubeis, Siegle, & Hollon, 2008) and that medications are superior to placebo only among patients suffering severe depression (e.g., Fournier et al., 2010). Given this evidence base, for many patients undergoing mild to moderate depression, nonpharmaceutical psychological treatments for depression provide a viable alternative to antidepressant medications and are not associated with iatrogenic effects on sexual functioning (Hoyer, Uhmann, Rambow, & Jacobi, 2009). Again, clinical management of depressed patients should be accompanied by regularly monitoring for adverse sexual effects with an eye toward evaluating the utility of either switching medications, coprescribing sexual dysfunction medications, or switching to cognitive therapy (see Volume 2, Chapter 4, this handbook).

Depression and sexual risk-taking. In addition to sexual functioning, depressive disorders have been associated with sexual risk-taking. The evidence has been mixed, however, with some studies showing depression related to increased sexual risk (e.g., Shrier et al., 2009; Sikkema et al., 2010) and with other studies (e.g., Meade et al., 2011) and a meta-analysis (e.g., Crepaz & Marks, 2001) showing no relationship. Researchers have suggested the possibility of a curvilinear relationship in which

> mild depression may be associated with increased sexual risk-taking (possibly as a coping mechanism for managing negative affect) and severe depression may be associated with decreased sexual activity (loss of interest in sex is a common symptom of depression, and sexual dysfunction is a common side-effect of many antidepressant medications). (Meade et al., 2011, p. 1832)

Further research is needed to understand the link between depression and sexual risk.

Anxiety. Anxiety and anxiety disorders, like depression, also have been associated with sexuality. Although there has been extensive and systematic research on the relationship between state anxiety and sexual functioning, particularly sexual arousal (e.g., see reviews by Barlow, 1986; Beck & Barlow, 1984; Norton & Jehu, 1984; Seto, 1992; Wiegel, Scepkowski, & Barlow, 2007), the research linking anxiety disorders with sexual functioning and sexual dysfunction has been less well developed (Laurent & Simons, 2009).

Generally, there is evidence of comorbidity between anxiety-related disorders and sexual difficulties; however, the findings are not consistent. With respect to generalized anxiety disorder, there is evidence that high trait anxiety is associated with premature ejaculation in men and with desire, arousal, and orgasmic problems in women (Dunn, Croft, & Hackett, 1999). Bradford and Meston (2006), however, found no relationship between trait anxiety and subjective sexual arousal in women. With respect to social anxiety and social phobia, evidence for comorbidity also is mixed. Some studies show evidence of a link (e.g., McCabe & Cobain, 1998), some do not (e.g., Líndal & Stefánsson, 1993; Stefánsson, Líndal, Björnsson, & Güdmundsdóttir, 1994), and some yield mixed results, and gender is often a moderating factor. For instance, Munoz and Stravynski (2010) investigated people with social phobias and found that men were less sexually active than controls; but women were equally active as nonphobic controls. Evidence also is mixed with respect to panic disorder depending in part on co-occurrence with depression (Mercan et al., 2006; Van Minnen & Kampman, 2000). Finally, evidence also is mixed on the comorbidity of sexual problems among individuals suffering from posttraumatic stress disorder (PTSD; e.g., Arbanas, 2010). Interestingly, with PTSD, it appears that the relation of sexual problems may depend on the nature of the original trauma (e.g., sexual assault) and on the specific PTSD symptom cluster, with emotional numbing being more related to sexual problems than hyperarousal (Nunnink et al., 2010). Overall, comorbidity between anxiety disorders and sexual disorders is variable depending on several factors, including gender, the particular anxiety disorder, and phases of the sexual response cycle. Laurent and Simons (2009) summarized that generalized anxiety disorder seemed associated with all phases of the sexual response cycle; that obsessive compulsive and panic disorder primarily were associated with arousal disorders and sexual aversion; that social phobias have been associated with most phases of the response cycle; and that PTSD has been related to sexual aversions, premature ejaculation, and ED. In any case, it is clear that because anxiety disorders can affect the creation and maintenance of intimate sexual relationships and that many pharmacological treatments negatively affect sexual functioning, considerably more research is needed to understand such moderating factors and to better clarify patterns of comorbidity.

Historically, an important aspect of the work on anxiety and sexual function has been theoretical assertions that sexual conflicts (and Freudian defenses against them) underlie anxiety disorders or, conversely, that heightened anxiety underlies sexual problems (e.g., W. H. Masters & Johnson, 1970). Although the former has been dismissed largely in mainstream psychology research, the latter has been the subject of extensive theorizing and research (e.g., van den Hout & Barlow, 2000). An initial challenge to the claim that sexual arousal and anxiety arousal were mutually inhibitory (Hoon, Wincze, & Hoon, 1977) sparked a stream of experimentation by Barlow and colleagues as well as others evaluating the effects of state anxiety on sexual arousal. Contrary to the original theorizing, it emerged that heightened state anxiety increases sexual arousal or has no effect. Furthermore, the effects depend on the context of the anxiety source, whether individuals are sexually functional or dysfunctional, cognitive attributions, and attentional focus. Briefly, Barlow's model of sexual dysfunction posits a positive feedback loop for sexually functional individuals, whereby anxiety can amplify sexual arousal, and a negative feedback loop for dysfunctional individuals, whereby anxiety associated with performance demands can distract from adequate cognitive processing of erotic cues and thereby interfere with arousal (e.g., see Barlow, 1986; Wiegel et al., 2007). Although this appears to be true for both men and women, more research has been conducted with men, and it appears that attentional and affective processes among sexually dysfunctional men are especially characterized by performance concerns (Wiegel et al., 2007).

Summary. Mood research indicates that generally reduced positive affect is associated with decreased sexual activity and functioning and heightened state anxiety is associated with increased sexual arousal or no effect. Comorbidity data generally show that mood disorders are associated with sexual dysfunctions, although there is notable inconsistency in these findings and the linkage appears to be stronger with depression than anxiety. Nevertheless, the overlap among comorbidity trends, basic research data, and theoretical frameworks are sufficiently compelling to suggest a proposal for an integrative model of internalizing psychopathology, which encompasses depression, anxiety, and sexual dysfunction, as a latent diagnostic entity based on emphasizing fear and distress as central nucleic features (Laurent & Simons, 2009). Clearly, more empirical and conceptual work is warranted on the connection between mood and sexual disorders.

Developmental/Intellectual Disability and Sexual Health

Developmental/intellectual disabilities (D/ID) are mental impairments that occur before adulthood. People with a diagnosis of D/ID may have less than average intellectual functioning along with significant limitations in communication skills, mobility, self-care, self-direction, social and/or interpersonal skills, use of community resources, functional academic skills, work, leisure, health, and safety (American Psychiatric Association, 2000). D/ID may be associated with a variety of specific disorders, such as Down syndrome or autism, but it is diagnosed based on intellectual and functional skill levels, and the level of severity is variable.

People with D/ID are sexual beings who engage in sexual activities (see Chapter 25, this volume). However, society often views the sexual behaviors of disabled persons as deviant or misperceives disabled persons as asexual, or believes they lack the capacity for engaging in responsible and healthy sexual behaviors. These misconceptions marginalize people with D/ID, decrease efforts to provide sexual education to this population, and place these individuals at risk for sexual victimization and sexually transmitted infections (STIs). Furthermore, these erroneous beliefs also may affect the attitudes of family members, caregivers, and medical providers, which in turn can affect the sexual functioning of people with D/ID. This section examines sexuality among individuals with D/ID as well as barriers to healthy sexual functioning in this population.

Sexuality of people with D/ID. Individuals with D/ID frequently engage in sexual activities. A national survey of 46 state residential facilities for individuals with D/ID showed that 63% of the facilities reported that sexual relations between patients occur sometimes or often (Gust, Wang, Grot, Ransom, & Levine, 2003). Another study assessing the sexuality of individuals with D/ID showed that these individuals engage in conventional sexual behavior, such as kissing, intercourse, and masturbation, and have relational needs, such as hugging and having an intimate partner (Siebelink, de Jong, Taal, & Roelvink, 2006). Seventy-five percent of the sample had experienced kissing and 51% had experienced intercourse. Male participants reported more sexual needs and experiences than did females, in particular regarding masturbation, watching pornography, and prostitution. Furthermore, those who had more sexual knowledge had more positive attitudes about sex, and those with more positive attitudes had more sexual experiences and needs. These findings indicate that individuals with D/ID are not asexual; in fact, they have sexual needs and often engage in sexual behaviors to satisfy those needs.

Barriers to sexual functioning. Mass involuntary sterilization of people with D/ID has been legally mandated and performed throughout history (reviewed in Stinson, Christian, & Dotson, 2002). The goals of the Eugenics movement were to prevent individuals with D/ID from passing on their disabilities to future generations and to "protect" them against unplanned pregnancies, sexual exploitation, and sexually transmitted diseases. This practice was not only unethical and harmful but also did not protect individuals with D/ID from these risks. Although research indicates that social views of sexuality and reproduction in people with D/ID have improved over time (Cuskelly & Bryde, 2004), continued misconceptions and stereotypes significantly affect the sexual rights and functioning of individuals with D/ID (see Volume 2, Chapter 8, this handbook).

Misconceptions about people with D/ID being asexual or incapable of responsible and healthy sexual behavior may have led to a lack of communication and education regarding sex from families, caretakers, and providers. A qualitative study examining mothers' attitudes about the sexuality of their children with D/ID showed that they generally perceived their children as not being interested in sex or as having limited opportunities to engage in sexual behavior with another person (Pownall, Jahoda, Hastings, & Kerr, 2011). Thus, mothers did not discuss sexual issues with their D/ID children, or they did so in a limited fashion. These mothers were reliant on their children's schools for sex education; however, they believed that schools do not do an adequate job of tailoring sex education to their children's special needs. Thus, it appears that individuals with D/ID may not be getting adequate sexual education at home or at school.

Limited knowledge and education about sex may put people with D/ID at risk for sexual victimization, STIs, and unwanted pregnancies. Although individuals with D/ID have been shown to have some knowledge about male and female body parts and menstruation, their knowledge about sexual diseases, safe sex practices, contraception, and pregnancy and their ability to perceive sexually dangerous situations have been shown to be relatively low (Galea, Butler, Iacono, & Leighton, 2004). Inaccurate "knowledge" also can be a problem; for example, Leutar & Mihokovic (2007) showed that although 95.8% of sampled individuals with D/ID reported knowing that pregnancy can result from no contraception use, 54.2% also believed that pregnancy can result from eating a watermelon; and 29.2% believed that it can result from kissing. Incorrect beliefs and a dearth of knowledge regarding sexuality may impair sexual functioning as well as put these individuals at risk for STIs and victimization.

Regarding STIs, a review by Servais (2006) showed that people with D/ID have low contraceptive use and are at high risk for pregnancy and STIs. Gust et al. (2003) showed that 5.2% of administrators from 49 state residential facilities reported at least one D/ID client with a sexually transmitted disease in the past year. A qualitative study examining D/ID women's perceptions about their sexuality showed that two of the eight women interviewed had a sexually transmitted disease, yet only one of them was able to identify that it was an STI and understood how it was acquired (Dotson, Stinson, & Christian, 2003). The lack of knowledge about STIs, modes of transmission, and safe sex practices among individuals with D/ID poses significant risk for contracting and transmitting STIs.

Individuals with D/ID are at high risk for sexual victimization. A study utilizing national data on sexual victimization in Taiwan showed that in 2007, the rate of sexual assault in people with D/ID was almost 14 times that of the general population (Lin, Yen, Kuo, Wu, & Lin, 2009). Although rates of reported sexual abuse among individuals with D/ID are high, they still may underrepresent the actual numbers. Individuals with D/ID may not be aware of their sexual rights and the inappropriateness or illegality of sexual behaviors perpetrated against them, or if they are aware, they may not have the capacity to report the abuse. Gust et al. (2003) showed that sexual abuse was discovered 55% of the time because of witnesses, medical evidence, or reasons other than victim disclosure. Without medical evidence or witnesses, sexual abuse may go largely unnoticed and unreported in this population.

Factors that may increase the risk for sexual victimization in individuals with D/ID include being dependent on others for care, social isolation, vulnerable settings, lack of mobility, lack of knowledge about appropriate sexual behavior, lack of ability to communicate and disclose the abuse, and increased risk of manipulation (reviewed in Di Giulio, 2003; Servais, 2006). Nosek, Foley, Hughes, and Howland (2001) found that individuals with D/ID may be isolated in settings such as special education classrooms or residential facilities, which segregate them from the larger community and make them vulnerable to sexual perpetrators. Often times, individuals with D/ID depend on their perpetrators for daily care. This further traps the victims and limits their access to help and escape. Thus, it is imperative for more research to be done to inform effective programs targeting the prevention of sexual victimization in populations with D/ID.

The issues surrounding sexual health among individuals with D/ID are varied and complex. Individuals with D/ID are sexual beings; they have sexual needs; and they engage in sexual behaviors. This population, however, faces multiple barriers to sexual health, including a lack of knowledge of safe sex practices, contraception, and sexual victimization. This lack of knowledge increases these individuals' risk of STIs, unwanted pregnancy, and sexual victimization. The research reviewed suggests that programs aimed at promoting sexual health in this population should focus on sex education. This includes education of family members, caretakers, and providers about the sexual health of individuals with D/ID and how to communicate with these individuals about their sexual functioning. Furthermore, because of the high risk for sexual victimization in this population, education about their vulnerability should be disseminated to residential facilities, clinics, hospitals, and schools to foster the prevention and detection of sexual abuse.

SEXUALLY TRANSMITTED INFECTIONS AND SEXUAL FUNCTIONING

STIs are associated with serious physical and psychological distress that may significantly affect sexual functioning (Graziottin & Serafini, 2009). Individuals diagnosed with an STI may find themselves worried about how the diagnosis will affect their health as well as the cost and consequences of treatment options. Furthermore, because of the stigmatized nature of STIs, individuals may experience feelings of shame, anxiety, sadness, and fear associated with negative social judgment and its potential effects on their current and future interpersonal relationships. STIs may cause unpleasant and painful physical symptoms and result in comparable unpleasant and painful treatments. This section will focus on the physical impact of STIs themselves and of their treatment (particularly HIV treatment) on sexual functioning. It also will focus on the psychological impact of STIs on sexual functioning as it relates to anxiety, depression, stigma, and interpersonal relationships.

Physical Impact on Functioning

STIs can produce an array of physical symptoms. Ironically, some medical treatments for STIs and their related symptoms can, in turn, produce additional physical symptoms. Therefore, in considering the physical impact of STIs on sexual functioning it is important to distinguish physical STI symptoms from physical symptoms that are a consequence of STI treatment.

Physical symptoms of STIs. STIs can have physically debilitating and painful symptoms that affect sexual functioning. For example, genital herpes may cause the development of inflamed and painful blisters on the genital skin; human papilloma virus (HPV) may cause genital warts, which may result in disfiguring of the genital area and bleeding; and chlamydia trachomatis may cause lower abdominal pain, dyspareunia, abnormal vaginal bleeding, and vaginal discharge (Centers for Disease Control and Prevention [CDC], 2010). A study assessing 998 women attending an STI clinic showed that individuals who were diagnosed with chlamydia reported more pain during intercourse and less sexual satisfaction than those with a common bacteria/yeast infection or no diagnosis (Cai et al., 2011). Physical symptoms of STIs also may cause cosmetic concerns, which may decrease sexual desire and arousal. People with physical symptoms of STIs often report feeling unattractive, shameful, and self-conscious (Newton & McCabe, 2008b). Although there are many more STIs and associated painful physical symptoms, these few examples illustrate that having these physical symptoms may significantly hinder sexual arousal and desire as well as make sexual activities painful.

Physical symptoms as a consequence of STI treatment. The physical consequences of treatment for STIs have been associated with sexual dysfunction. Treatments for HPV and genital warts may involve surgical, laser, or chemical therapies that usually are painful and may cause scarring (CDC, 2010). Filiberti et al. (1993) showed that 57% of patients reported sexual impairment after engaging in HPV treatment.

Untreated HIV infection can result in AIDS neuronal degeneration that can result in a range of neurocognitive impairments (McArthur, Brew, & Nath, 2005). In severe cases, AIDS-related cognitive impairments can result in dementia and can be accompanied by a range of affective disorders and by hypersexuality (e.g., Guay, 2008).

Highly active antiretroviral therapy (HAART) for HIV also has been associated with sexual dysfunction. HAART treatments that contain protease inhibitors have the most research indicating their association with sexual dysfunction (Schrooten et al., 2001). Moreno-Pérez et al. (2010) showed that longer exposure to protease inhibitors leads to lower erectile functioning, orgasmic functioning, and sexual desire. Lipodystrophy, a commonly studied side effect of HAART due to its psychological and physical impact on sexual functioning, is a fat distribution problem that results in fat loss in the limbs, buttocks, and face and accumulation of fat in the abdomen, back of the neck, and breast. Patients with HIV-related lipodystrophy have been found to be at risk for poor body image and sexual dysfunction (Sadeghi-Nejad, Wasserman, Weidner, Richardson, & Goldmeier, 2010). Furthermore, because symptoms of lipodystrophy are physically apparent and may reveal HIV status, individuals with this illness also have reported feeling stigmatized and sexually marginalized.

In contrast with the research showing the negative effect of HAART on sexual functioning, other studies have shown that CD4+ cell levels, viral load titres, and being treated with HAART are not associated with sexual dysfunction (Bouhnik, Préau, Schiltz, Obadia, & Spire, 2008; Wilson et al., 2010). It has been proposed that the association between HAART and sexual dysfunction is mediated by age such that older adults are more likely to be at risk for sexual dysfunction due to comorbid health problems such as hypercholesterolemia, diabetes, and hypertension. Thus, because HAART has lengthened the life span of AIDS patients, they are experiencing an increase of sexual dysfunction because of old age. Conflicting findings suggest more research is needed to determine whether there is a causal relationship between HAART and sexual dysfunction.

Psychological Impact on Functioning

Sexual dysfunction appears to be common in individuals with STIs. A nationally representative survey of 1,812 HIV-positive individuals living in France showed that the rate of sexual dysfunction in this sample is as high as 33% (Bouhnik et al., 2008). In comparison with the general population, sexual dysfunction occurs more frequently among individuals who have been diagnosed with an STI (Sadeghi-Nejad et al., 2010). Individuals diagnosed with an STI, including HIV, chlamydia, genital HPV, and herpes, are more likely to report a lack of libido, sexual difficulties, and multiple sexual problems than those without an STI diagnosis (Cai et al., 2011; Graziottin & Serafini, 2009; Wilson et al., 2010).

Reports of anxiety and depression are prevalent among those who have been diagnosed with an STI. In a U.S. sample of 2,864 HIV-infected individuals, 50% reported having anxiety and depression (Bing et al., 2001). Having multiple sexual problems is associated with major depression, and more HIV-positive men than HIV-negative men report having both major depression and sexual problems (Mao et al., 2009). Concerns about health status and treatment options as well as the impact of the STI on interpersonal relationships are frequently the source of these feelings and may contribute to sexual dysfunction.

Individuals diagnosed with an STI often experience shame and stigma associated with the infection, which may significantly affect feelings of sexuality and desirability. A qualitative study investigating stigma, mental health, and sexual behavior among individuals living with genital herpes and HPV genital warts showed that the stigma of having an STI made them feel depressed, damaged, and unworthy of having a relationship (Newton & McCabe, 2008b). In a follow-up quantitative study, these researchers compared those who had HPV and genital herpes with those who had no STI diagnosis and found that individuals with STIs reported significantly higher levels of sexual anxiety, sexual monitoring, fear of sex, and sexual depression as well as significantly lower levels of sexual optimism and sexual satisfaction than those with no STI diagnosis (Newton & McCabe, 2008a). Studies on HIV/AIDS populations also have shown the negative impact of stigma on sexual functioning. Bouhnik et al. (2008) showed that experiencing HIV discrimination from friends, relatives, sexual partners, coworkers, or health care providers was significantly associated with sexual dysfunction.

Concerns about disclosure and transmission within sexual relationships also are associated with sexual dysfunction among those living with an STI. Fear of disclosing STI status to a sexual partner is a common stressor reported by those living with an STI. Some individuals have reported slowing down or even ending their sexual relationship to delay or avoid disclosure (Newton & McCabe, 2008a). Not disclosing an STI to a current sexual partner has been associated with anxiety about sex, low sexual self-esteem, and sexual depression (Newton & McCabe, 2008a). Fear of transmitting the infection to a current sexual partner also may restrict sexual activities, cause conflict and tension within the relationship, and impair sexual functioning. A study assessing sexual satisfaction in men living with HIV showed that 59.4% reported a lack of interest in sex, 47.1% reported arousal problems, 52% reported having difficulties in sexual relationships, 66.7% reported fear of infecting sexual partners, and 71.4% reported low-self-esteem about interpersonal relationships (Jacobson, 2007). The research shows that many individuals living with STIs experience considerable amounts of emotional suffering brought on by stigma and discrimination as well as internalized shame, a sense of diminished self-worth, and relationship difficulties. Together, these psychological stressors put individuals living with an STI at risk for sexual dysfunction.

USE OF PSYCHOACTIVE DRUGS AND SEXUAL HEALTH

This section presents information concerning relationships among psychoactive substances used recreationally and aspects of sexual health, including sexual functioning and sexual risk-taking. The drugs to be discussed include (a) central nervous systems (CNS) depressants—specifically, alcohol, opioids (such as, heroin and methadone), and gamma hydroxybutyrate (GHB); (b) stimulants—specifically, cocaine, amphetamine, methamphetamine, and derivatives, such as MDMA or ecstasy; (c) sedatives or hypnotics—specifically, marijuana (also referred to as cannabis or THC). It also discusses ED medications, such as sildenafil (Viagra). It focuses on these drugs because they are currently some of the most widely used recreational drugs (National Institute on Drug Abuse [NIDA], 2011a). Although this coverage is not comprehensive, the section reviews those drugs for which empirical information was available regarding their sexual effects.

Several factors complicate understanding how these drugs affect sexuality. For instance, many users chronically ingest more than one drug, often simultaneously, making it difficult to disentangle effects of any particular substance. In addition, studies of drug use rely almost entirely on self-reports, which are subject to memory distortion, or even, in some cases, deliberate misrepresentation. Self-reports are garnered largely through retrospective cross-sectional surveys, although more recent studies employ prospective longitudinal designs. Nevertheless, the lack of randomized experimental designs largely precludes the ability to draw causal inferences about drug effects. Furthermore, with the exception of alcoholic beverages, there are no standard dosage amounts for many recreationally used substances, making the task of discerning causal effects even more challenging. This is especially true if the direction or magnitude of a drug's effects varies at different dosages. Individuals' tolerance and other variables related to drug-taking history may contribute to divergent findings across studies. Researchers frequently employ a variety of different measures from one another, making it hard to compare findings across studies. In some cases, what appear to be drug effects may be confounded by factors such as poverty and lack of access to health care; disentangling these issues can be all but impossible. Finally, some drugs may be understudied, especially for specific populations; thus, generalizing beyond one group that has received research attention may not be appropriate. Nevertheless, despite gaps in the literature, some patterns have emerged about how recreationally used substances may affect sexual functioning, including interest, arousal, ability to experience orgasm, erectile issues, and painful intercourse as well as sexual risk-taking.

CNS Depressants

Psychoactive substances classified as CNS depressants inhibit the function of the central nervous system, slowing brain activity and affecting judgments, perceptions, emotions, and motor behavior. Alcohol is the most widely used CNS depressant and, as such, has received extensive research attention with regard to sexuality.

Alcohol and sexual health. The near-ubiquitous pairing of alcohol with sexuality in Western culture suggests that drinking systematically co-occurs with or influences sexual responding, and thus sexual health. Of course, alcohol consumption does not always result in sexual activity. When drinking is associated with sexual activity, the nature of that association can be correlational, causal, or entirely spurious owing to third variable influences. Also, a person's motives for drinking and expectations about alcohol's sexual effects may play important roles in determining alcohol's real-world effects on sexuality. To be clear, available science indicates that acute alcohol intoxication can in fact exert a short-term causal impact on aspects of sexual functioning (see reviews by George & Gilmore, 2013; George & Stoner, 2000) and sexual risk-taking (see reviews by Hendershot & George, 2007; Rehm, Shield, Joharchi, & Shuper, 2012), and much of the research has been oriented toward explaining the nature of these effects. This section reviews literature on alcohol's effects on processes and outcomes related to (a) sexual functioning, including sexual arousal, sexual desire, and orgasm; and (b) sexual risk-taking, including willingness to engage in unprotected intercourse with a new partner.

Regarding alcohol and sexual health, it is important to distinguish between acute versus chronic use. Acute use refers to the amount of alcohol consumed in a particular drinking episode and the resultant sexual effects in that index episode. Acute use is operationalized in surveys as retrospective self-reports of the amount consumed before or during sexual events. In experiments, acute consumption is operationalized by having research participants come into a controlled laboratory setting and ingest beverages containing predetermined dosages of alcohol designed to result in precisely targeted blood alcohol concentrations (BACs). Chronic alcohol consumption refers to the amount of alcohol consumed habitually over time and is operationalized based on research participants' retrospective reporting.

Alcohol and sexual functioning. Several aspects of sexual functioning are affected by alcohol consumption. We will focus on sexual functioning and sexual dysfunctions in relation to sexual arousal, sexual desire, and orgasm.

Alcohol and men's sexual arousal. Regarding men's chronic alcohol consumption, it had become established that chronic high alcohol consumption indicative of alcohol dependence was linked with impaired erectile functioning and associated sexual dysfunctions in men, such as hypoactive sexual desire and either early or delayed ejaculation (e.g., O'Farrell, Choquette, Cutter, & Birchler, 1997; Ponizovsky, 2008). Similarly, among samples of men seeking treatment for ED, moderate to high alcohol use was associated with worse sexual function (e.g., Boddi et al., 2010; Dachille et al., 2008). Perhaps because of such findings obtained with alcoholic and sexually dysfunctional men and because of findings associating acute alcohol intoxication with attenuated erectile response (e.g., see reviews by Crowe & George, 1989; George & Stoner, 2000), it was presumed that chronic consumption of low and moderate amounts of alcohol also had deleterious effects on erectile functioning for all men. This presumption was in spite of survey findings and ample anecdotal evidence indicating that modest alcohol consumption was associated with enhanced sexual functioning. Two review papers, however, evaluating numerous population-based studies examining the effects of chronic alcohol consumption on erectile functioning have indicated that consuming low to moderate alcohol amounts actually offered some protection against experiencing ED (Cheng, Ng, Chen, & Ko, 2007; Chew, Bremner, Stuckey, Earle, & Jamrozik, 2009). This conclusion suggests that chronic drinking becomes a problem for erectile responding only at high levels of consumption. Overall, recent evidence has ushered a shift in our understanding of chronic alcohol consumption and erectile functioning, from appraising all consumption as deleterious to recognizing nondeleterious effects—and perhaps even protective effects—for low to moderate consumption.

Acute alcohol attenuation of erectile responding. There has been a similar shift in understanding acute alcohol consumption effects on erectile functioning. Although it once seemed conclusive that moderate to high doses of alcohol administered acutely attenuated men's erectile responding, recent research has illuminated more qualifying parameters on this so-called attenuation effect.

Approximately two dozen laboratory experiments have been conducted examining the effects of acute alcohol consumption on erectile responding. Evidence of an attenuation effect—alcohol reduces erection magnitude—initially was established based on findings published in 1976 (Briddell & Wilson, 1976; Farkas & Rosen, 1976; Rubin & Henson, 1976). In these pioneering experiments, young men were administered alcoholic or nonalcoholic drinks and presented with explicit sexual stimuli while erectile responding was assessed using a strain gauge to measure erection magnitude. The findings revealed that except at very low dosages, alcohol attenuated erectile response. Intoxicated men showed less erection magnitude than sober men. Another early study showed that alcohol also increased the amount of time it took to achieve orgasm. After this pioneering work, alcohol-induced attenuation of erectile responding was corroborated (Wilson, Lawson, & Abrams, 1978; Wilson, Niaura & Adler, 1985; Wormith, Bradford, Pawlak, Borzecki, & Zohar, 1988) and became axiomatic.

Two aspects of this attenuation effect were noteworthy. First, it cohered with what were understood to be the attenuating effects of chronic alcohol consumption. Thus, the scientific conclusion seemed unambiguous: Both chronic drinking and acute (except for very low dosages) drinking undermine erectile performance. This conclusion contradicted the lore about alcohol disinhibiting men's sexual responding. Second, in light of the then-emerging work on alcohol expectancy effects, the attenuation effect seemed to contribute to a narrative that resolved the old Shakespearean paradox about alcohol and sex: "Lechery, sir, it [drink] provokes, and unprovokes: it provokes the desire, but it takes away the performance" (Macbeth, 2.3.32). Specifically, it seemed that alcohol's salutary—"it provokes"—effects were attributable to its psychological expectancy properties, whereas its deleterious—"it unprovokes"—effects were attributable to its pharmacological properties.

The role of alcohol expectancies on men's postdrinking erectile response was identified with experiments using the balanced placebo design (Marlatt & Rohsenow, 1980), a method for evaluating the independent and interactive influences of alcohol's physiological and psychological or expectancy effects (George, Gilmore, & Stappenbeck, 2012). Two properties of drinking are manipulated systematically in the laboratory: expected alcohol content (expectancy) and actual alcohol content. Research subjects either (a) expect alcohol/receive alcohol, (b) expect alcohol/receive none, (c) expect no alcohol/receive none, or (d) expect no alcohol/receive alcohol. Use of drink "look/taste alikes" and limiting dosage to a low level make the deception necessitated in groups two and four possible. Landmark experiments showed that men in the expect alcohol conditions exhibited greater erectile response compared with men in the expect no alcohol conditions, and actual alcohol content was inconsequential (e.g., Wilson & Lawson, 1976).

This expectancy enhancement effect seemed clear: Men who think they are drinking alcohol report and exhibit more erectile arousal than men who do not. The effect seemed best attributed to the self-fulfilling prophecy explanation, whereby men who believe alcohol increases sexual arousal are more likely to experience heightened arousal after drinking than men who do not believe (George, Stoner, Norris, Lopez, & Lehman, 2000). The expectancy enhancement effect was a breakthrough in that the effect of "drink" on men's arousal could now be seen as consistent with the general sexual disinhibition outcomes conventionally understood as commonplace. Because people drink real drinks in the real world outside of the laboratory, there was an explanatory problem: Pharmacologically driven attenuation remained unreconciled with anecdotal lore and empirical trends attesting to postdrinking sexual enhancement. This led to reexamination of the attenuation effect.

Critics noted that the attenuation effect was not universal (e.g., George & Stoner, 2000; Langevin et al., 1985), and it emerged that attenuation effects were occurring in less than half of the relevant experiments. Also, in a study evaluating the highest BAC investigated to date (0.15%), alcohol attenuation of erectile arousal was not evident among men during sleep (Morlet et al., 1990). Furthermore, methodological problems that may have contributed to attenuation effects were identified (George, Norris, & Schacht, 2003).

In more recent experiments, these methodological problems were corrected. Using young community men, George et al. (2006) evaluated the effects of two BAC levels (0.08% and 0.10%) and of instructions to either maximize or suppress arousal while viewing an erotic film. At the lower BAC, alcohol did not attenuate genital arousal. Alcohol interacted, however, with arousal instructions to influence arousal onset. Sober men instructed to maximize arousal became aroused more quickly than did sober men instructed to suppress it. Intoxicated men did not show this effect, suggesting that alcohol lessened their ability to control the onset of their arousal. At the higher BAC, alcohol did have an attenuating effect on men's peak genital arousal, but no effect on other erectile measures. Two other studies evaluated the effects of different alcohol dosages during exposure to erotic stimuli, and no alcohol attenuation effects were detected (George et al., 2009; Prause, Staley, & Finn, 2011).

Contrary to earlier findings, these recent findings indicate that relatively high dosages of alcohol have a limited impact on men's erectile responding, with only certain types of arousal attenuation emerging and only at very high doses (George et al., 2009; Prause et al., 2011). These findings pose a challenge for the view that acute heavy drinking diminishes erectile performance. Furthermore, alcohol's attenuating effects on erectile functioning appear to be more context dependent than previously recognized, for example, upon the instructional demand to maximize versus suppress arousal. Generally, it now appears that there is little basis to view alcohol as necessarily interfering with sexual response for sexually functional men. It may be that the attenuation effect holds true only at higher degrees of intoxication, much higher than 0.10%, which—although relatively rare in laboratory experimentation—may be common in men's real-life encounters.

That said, an important consideration is whether the blood alcohol level is ascending or descending. In all of the noted studies, except the sleep study, investigators sought to assess alcohol's effects on the ascending limb or peak portions of the blood alcohol curve, whose effects involve euphoric mood and stimulation. Less is known about alcohol effects during the descending limb, which is characterized by dysphoric mood and fatigue. In the one study dedicated to examining alcohol's genital arousal effects on the descending limb, an attenuating effect was evident at a moderate dosage, but again only in a confined way (George et al., 2008). Men who received alcohol (target peak BAC = 0.08%) exhibited less genital arousal than no-alcohol controls, but only when instructed to maximize arousal and only on one of three erectile measures. This finding indicated again that attenuation effects may be more limited than previously thought and also that the threshold for attenuation effects may be somewhat lower on the descending than on the ascending limb of the alcohol curve. The latter point is consistent with the idea that the descending limb could be especially prone to potentiate alcohol attenuation effects because of the dysphoria and fatigue associated with descending blood alcohol. A potential implication of this finding is that in circumstances in which men are deliberately exerting a conscious effort to become maximally aroused, alcohol likely undermines peak erectile response for quite some time after drinking has ended and intoxication subsides. An interesting twist to these findings was that intoxicated men instructed to suppress their arousal exhibited more genital arousal than intoxicated men instructed to maximize their arousal. By implication, in circumstances in which men deliberately are trying to resist becoming aroused, being on the descending alcohol limb may hamper their effectiveness. Reduced effectiveness at suppressing arousal in conjunction with alcohol's tendency to heighten risk-taking could result in an increased likelihood of pursuing sexual activity in circumstances, such as disease-risk situations, in which sexual pursuit should be curtailed. Alcohol and disease risk will be discussed in further detail later.

A noteworthy limitation in this experimentation is that all but two of the studies reported (George et al., 2008; Morlet et al., 1990) investigated alcohol's effects under conditions of short-term acute administration on the ascending limb of the BAC curve. Thus, although there has been considerable research devoted to understanding alcohol's moderate-to-high dose (0.04–0.10) effects within an hour or so after drinking, very little is known about alcohol's effects at greater acute doses over longer periods of time—say hours after heavy drinking.

Acute episodic erectile failure. There are clinical and anecdotal reports of men experiencing erectile failure during episodes of excessive drinking. Phrases such as "whisky dick" and "brewer's droop" have emerged colloquially to characterize this phenomenon. Although the causal mechanism clearly would seem to be physiological, there are significant implications for sexual health. First, frequent episodes of alcohol-induced erectile failure may signal the presence or development of alcohol abuse or alcohol dependence disorders and could serve as a prompt for seeking addiction evaluation and treatment. Second, even a single episode can contribute to the development of an erectile disorder. Specifically, if the episode is not accurately attributed to alcohol, and instead is misattributed to psychological concerns about virility, sexual potency, or partner issues, then a recurrent pattern of erectile failure can develop and persist. Although initially caused by physiological processes, this pattern can become psychogenic in nature. For instance, subsequent alcohol-free sexual encounters can become characterized by partner conflict and performance anxiety about repeated erectile failure, both of which can drive emotional and cognitive distractibility that, in turn, disrupt normal erectile responding (e.g., Barlow, 1986). Third, whether it occurs sporadically or chronically, episodic erectile failures can have adverse effects on relationship stability, thereby undermining psychological, as well as sexual, health. Under these circumstances, alcohol moderation or abstinence and psychological or pharmacological treatment for erectile disorder may be advised.

Alcohol and ED medications. A final note about alcohol and erectile functioning concerns medications used to treat erectile disorder. There is growing evidence that medications such as Viagra (Sildenafil) and Cialis (Tadalafil) often are used in conjunction with alcohol, both legally and illicitly (Bechara, Casabé, De Bonis, Helien, & Bertolino, 2010). Among men diagnosed as suffering erectile disorder, alcohol dependence, or both, these medications appear to improve sexual functioning. Among sexually functioning nonalcoholic men, these medications often are used recreationally during drinking episodes, a pattern that has been especially observed in research findings with gay men (e.g., Holt, 2009). Little is known empirically about the interactive effects on sexual functioning of consuming alcohol with these drugs, and research is warranted.

Alcohol and women's sexual arousal. The few survey studies that have examined sexual arousal and alcohol use in women have had mixed findings. In a daily log study, alcohol was found to have no effect on arousal (Harvey & Beckman, 1986). In another diary study, however, it was found that alcohol use was related to increased sexual arousal during the post- and intermenstrual phases of the menstrual cycle (Lindman, Koskelainen, & Eriksson, 1999). A recent study classifying women into abstainer, light, and moderate drinking groups reported that drinking was unrelated to genital vascularization and lubrication and that moderate drinking was associated with lower depression and elevated sexual activity and orgasm (Battaglia et al., 2011). Impairment of sexual arousal has been related to alcohol dependency (for a review, see Sobczak, 2009a). Premenopausal alcoholic women who were abstinent even less than a year, however, have shown improvement in their ability to become sexually aroused (Gavaler et al., 1993).

As of 2012, approximately 16 experiments have examined acute alcohol intoxication effects on self-reported sexual arousal. The majority, specifically 13 out of 16, have found that alcohol intoxication increased self-reported arousal in women. The effect of alcohol has been more pronounced with higher dosages, but the effect was present in a variety of doses. In addition, the effect has been shown with a variety of different stimuli including erotic films, vignettes, and slides. One explanation for alcohol's effect on increasing self-reported sexual arousal in women is alcohol expectancy theory. As noted, this theory suggests a self-fulfilling prophecy whereby individuals who hold the belief that alcohol increases sexual arousal are more likely to perceive that alcohol enhances sexual arousal in alcohol-involved sexual situations than those who do not hold that belief. A second explanation for increased self-reported sexual arousal may be alcohol myopia theory, which asserts that alcohol-induced cognitive impairment constricts the range of cues one is capable of attending to in a situation. Alcohol myopia theory therefore would posit that intoxicated individuals may focus more intently on salient sexual cues such as erotic stimuli than sober individuals and consequently would experience themselves as more aroused. A third possible explanation for the increase in self-reported sexual arousal when intoxicated may be mediated by testosterone, which has been associated with heightened sexual feelings. A study of Finnish women found that alcohol increased testosterone levels, depending on different phases of the menstrual cycle and on oral contraception use (Eriksson, Fukunaga, & Lindman, 1994). For women not using oral contraceptives, the increase was evident during the ovulatory phase; for women using oral contraceptives, it was evident during days 17–20 of the cycle. These findings suggest that alcohol's effects on self-reported arousal may be related to testosterone in women. These potential explanations for how low to moderate dosages of alcohol can enhance women's self-reported sexual arousal warrant further research (see Chapter 8, this volume).

Nevertheless, regardless of the explanation, it seems clear that low to moderate dosages of alcohol result in women feeling and reporting more sexual arousal than if they were sober. Paradoxically, it seems that this effect can occur concurrently while alcohol actually is attenuating genital arousal. That is, in some experiments, women reported postdrinking increases in sexual arousal; yet, they also exhibited alcohol-induced decreases in physiologically measured genital arousal (e.g., George et al., 2009). This paradox is not surprising given the low agreement generally between women's self-report and genital measures across all sexual arousal studies (not just alcohol studies). In a review of studies examining the correspondence between self-report versus genital arousal, self-report and genital measures correlated substantially lower for women ($r = .26$) than for men ($r = .66$) (Chivers, Seto, Lalumiere, Laan, & Grimbos, 2010). Therefore, although paradoxical, it is not contradictory empirically that alcohol can have opposite effects on women's self-reported versus genital arousal.

Experiments evaluating alcohol's effects on genital arousal typically use a vaginal photoplethysmograph as measurement. Of 10 such experiments that have been reported to date, six (George et al., 2009; George et al., 2011, Study 2; Gilmore et al., 2010; Malatesta, Pollack, Crotty, & Peacock, 1982; Wilson & Lawson, 1976; 1978) found that alcohol attenuated women's genital arousal and four (George et al., 2011, Study 1; Prause et al., 2011; Schacht et al., 2007, 2010) found no evidence of attenuation. In an illustrative study with women between the ages of 21 and 35 years, the effects of two BACs (0.08% and 0.10%) were evaluated in the context of instructions to control arousal by either maximizing or suppressing it while viewing an erotic film (George et al., 2011). At the lower BAC, which is widely recognized as substantially intoxicating in that it is the legal criterion for drunk driving and is widely associated with generalized impairment, alcohol did not attenuate genital arousal.

Furthermore, women exhibited greater genital arousal under conditions of being instructed to maximize arousal than to suppress arousal. These findings were interesting in demonstrating that despite being intoxicated and despite the generally low correspondence between subjective and genital arousal, women were able to exert control over their genital arousal. At the 0.10% BAC, however, alcohol-attenuated women's genital arousal and no arousal control was evident. Thus, it seems clear that alcohol can attenuate women's genital arousal, and this effect is most evident at very high dosages. As noted, the mechanisms responsible for this attenuation effect have not been identified clearly. It has been presumed that the mechanisms are strictly physiological. This has not been established, however, and psychological mechanisms have not been ruled out.

Looking across both the self-report and genital assessment studies, it appears reasonable to contend that until the blood alcohol concentration exceeds 0.08%, women are likely to exhibit an arousal response pattern characterized by enhanced self-reported sexual arousal, no alcohol-induced diminution in genital arousal, and an effective capability to control their arousal response volitionally. These considerations suggest that women's postdrinking sexual responses are subject to considerable variability and are not dictated by physiological imperatives or limits. This variability apparently decreases at higher dosages, however, at which point it appears that intoxication effects may become less conducive to positive sexual responding and experience. Potentially, physiology related to high alcohol levels may overwhelm the sexuality-related response systems.

Alcohol, sexual interest, desire, and orgasm. Research on alcohol use and sexual interest and desire is limited. The few studies that have examined these relationships among women consist predominantly of descriptive surveys. Most studies have found that alcohol is related to increased sexual desire among nonclinical samples (e.g., Beckman, 1979; Harvey & Beckman, 1986; Woods, Mitchell, & Julio, 2010). An illustrative study specifically examined red wine intake in Italian women and found that women who reported moderate daily red wine intake also reported higher levels of sexual desire compared with women who did not drink alcohol (Mondaini et al., 2009). According to a recent review (Sobczak, 2009a), findings concerning the relationship between alcohol consumption and other aspects of sexual functioning are mixed. In some studies, women reported increased sexual activity after drinking, whereas in other studies, women reported having less sex when drinking. This review also concluded that heavy alcohol use is related to impaired sexual functioning, including lowered sexual interest, desire, and satisfaction; lack of orgasm and lubrication, as well as painful intercourse. Wilsnack, Klassen, Schur, and Wilsnack (1991) found in a longitudinal study that the most consistent predictor of women's problem drinking was sexual dysfunction. On the positive side, Gavaler et al. (1993) found that among premenopausal alcoholic women, being abstinent for less than a year had beneficial effects on sexual desire and ability to achieve orgasm. Among postmenopausal women, Gavaler, Rizzo, Rossaro, and Van Thiel (1994) found that alcoholic women's satisfaction with their sex lives improved after at least a year of abstinence.

Among women in treatment for alcohol or other drug use disorders, a history of child or adult sexual assault has been related to various types of sexual dysfunction (Wilsnack, Plaud, Wilsnack, & Klassen, 1997), including painful intercourse (Sutherland, Fantasia, & McClain, in press). Evidence suggests that women with a history of sexual trauma often use alcohol or other drugs to disconnect from in-the-moment sexual experiences (Sanjuan, Langenbucher, & Labouvie, 2009; Sobczak, 2009b; see also Chapter 12, this volume). Thus, sexual dysfunction and alcohol abuse likely have a reciprocal relationship.

Research on alcohol use and orgasm is also limited. Approximately 25% of women report problems with orgasm that rise to a clinical level. Overall, there is little research on alcohol and orgasm in women. The available studies, although few, examining the relationship between alcohol and orgasm have found that alcohol is related to more inconsistent orgasms or fewer orgasms overall in women (e.g., Johnson et al., 2004). One experiment examining the effect of acute alcohol on orgasms in women found that latency to orgasm was longer and subjective intensity of orgasm was decreased for women with higher BACs (Malatesta et al., 1982); however, higher BACs also were associated with greater sexual arousal. Another experiment examining the effect of acute alcohol on orgasms in men found increased orgasm latency after alcohol, increasing linearly with BAC level (0.03%, 0.06%, 0.09%) (Malatesta, Pollack, Wilbanks, & Adams, 1979). The authors noted, however, that this effect "may be viewed as a beneficial consequence" because "sexual intercourse would be prolonged for both partners" (p. 106).

Alcohol and STI/HIV-related sexual risk-taking. STIs, especially HIV/AIDS, remain a grave health threat and new infections are predominantly attributable to sexual contact, both among gay men and heterosexuals (CDC, 2012). The primary behaviors placing an individual at risk of disease include having unprotected anal or vaginal intercourse, doing so with multiple partners, and doing so with partners of unknown infection status. Risks are greater with new and casual partners than with established partners. Established partners also may pose risks, however, if involved in intravenous drug use or extradyadic sexual activity. Therefore, among sexually active individuals, consistent condom use and avoidance of partners of unknown risk status provide the greatest protection against STIs and HIV. Among factors associated with inconsistent condom use and sexual partnering, alcohol intoxication is prominent. If alcohol could be shown and understood to play a nonspurious role in risk-taking, then targeting alcohol use as an avenue of risk reduction would be indicated. Consequently, the association between alcohol and sexual risk-taking has been the subject of considerable research using a variety of methodological approaches.

The key question has been: Does alcohol contribute to sexual risk-taking? Global and situational covariation surveys have shown that alcohol is associated with increased risk, in that individuals who drink to intoxication use condoms less frequently overall than those who do not (e.g., Cooper, 2002; Dingle & Oei, 1997; Donovan & McEwan, 1995; Halpern-Felsher, Millstein, & Ellen, 1996; Leigh & Morrison, 1991). Event-level and daily diary studies (e.g., Leigh et al., 2008), however, have demonstrated that this relationship does not persist when individuals report on their intoxication and condom use during specific sexual events. These mixed findings have highlighted the complexity of alcohol's involvement in sexual risk-taking, underscoring the importance of moderating contextual factors, such as the risk level and relationship status of sexual partners (Cooper, 2002; Leigh, 2002; Weinhardt & Carey, 2000; see also Chapter 22, this volume). Theory-building longitudinal work by Cooper (2010) supported the idea that contextual and relationship factors, in conjunction with individual characteristics, affect the relationship between alcohol and unprotected sex. Still survey methods remain limited in their capacity to capture and explain alcohol-related condom use behavior in real time and, therefore, should be complemented by data from basic behavioral experiments.

Researchers using experimental methods have addressed a question that is more basic and at the same time more complex: Is alcohol capable of exerting a causal impact on sexual risk-taking, and, if so, how can this causation best be explained? Despite earlier ambiguity in survey data about alcohol's causal role, it is now well established through rigorous experiments that alcohol can and does have a causal impact on sexual risk behaviors (e.g., see review by Rehm et al., 2012).

At least eight independent investigative teams (e.g., Abbey et al., 2005; Cho & Span, 2010; Fromme, D'Amico, & Katz, 1999; George et al., 2009; MacDonald, Zanna, & Fong, 1996; Maisto, Carey, Carey, Gordon, & Schum, 2004; Monahan, Murphy, & Miller, 1999; Prause et al., 2011) have now conducted more than two dozen alcohol and sexual risk experiments. With little exception (e.g., Kruse & Fromme, 2005), these experiments have supported the hypothesis that rising alcohol intoxication increases the likelihood of unprotected intercourse with new and casual partners (see reviews by George & Stoner, 2000; Hendershot & George, 2007; Rehm et al., 2012) and stress several points. First, there is independent replication using a variety of protocols showing clear evidence of causal influences. Second, despite the pragmatic and ethical constraints on analogizing and studying sex in the laboratory, investigators have succeeded in developing protocols that credibly assess risky sex likelihood and pertinent constructs. Third, these researchers have identified in-the-moment processes and reactions that immediately precede sexual decision making and have demonstrated the theoretical importance of these constructs. Fourth, simultaneous consideration of distal and proximal determinants has advanced identification, isolation, and evaluation of mediating and moderating mechanisms.

Finally, these findings almost uniformly support the utility of alcohol myopia theory (Steele & Josephs, 1990) as the best framework to understand postdrinking sexual risk-taking. This support is best illustrated in experiments showing that (a) alcohol effects increase with dosage (e.g., George et al., 2009), which would not be predicted from an alcohol expectancy explanation; (b) alcohol affects risk indirectly via relevant subjective states, including sexual arousal (Davis et al., 2009; George, et al., 2009; Norris, Stoner, Hessler, Zawacki, Davis et al., 2009; Prause et al., 2011), perceived sexual potential (Norris, Stoner, Hessler, Zawacki, George et al., 2009; Purdie et al., 2011), positive mood and sexual desire (George et al., in press), and perceived intoxication (Davis et al., 2009); and (c) alcohol focuses the drinker cognitively on impelling cues in the situation (Norris, Stoner, Hessler, Zawacki, George et al., 2009) and a weighted composite of impelling–inhibiting cognitions has been shown to mediate alcohol's effects (Davis, Hendershot, George, Norris, & Heiman, 2007; MacDonald, MacDonald, Zanna, & Fong, 2000). In sum, the available science warrants the conclusion that alcohol can and does increase the likelihood of sexual risk-taking by attuning intoxicated participants to internal states congruent with being motivated toward sexual gratification. Alcohol's capacity to focus the drinker myopically on impelling cues despite extant risks in a sexual encounter fosters unsafe sex.

In addition, several variables may function as cofactors in alcohol-involved sexual situations. Sexual sensation-seeking (e.g., Maisto et al., 2004), alcohol expectancies (e.g., Maisto et al., 2004), relationship factors (Zawacki et al., 2009; Zawacki, 2011), and sexual victimization history (Schacht et al., 2010; Stoner et al., 2008) also have predicted sexual risk-taking in alcohol experiments. Victimization history has proven to be a particularly important cofactor. In heat-of-the-moment (HOTM) experiments utilizing second-person ("this is you") eroticized scenarios with heavy-episodic-drinking women at elevated risk of HIV/STI infection, both a history of sexual victimization and acute alcohol intoxication affected intentions to have unprotected sex. These effects were mediated by positive mood and sexual desire (George et al., in press). A second study also indicated that these effects were mediated by anticipating that the male partner would respond negatively to condom insistence and by a willingness to abdicate to his desire for unprotected sex (N. T. Masters et al., in press).

In HOTM experiments with heavy-episodic-drinking men, childhood sexual abuse and acute intoxication increased aggressive unprotected sexual intentions (i.e., intentions to proceed to have unprotected sexual intercourse with an unwilling partner). These effects were indirect via their sense of sexual entitlement, perceptions of the woman's sexual arousal, and likelihood of employing condom use–resistance tactics (Davis et al., 2012). In another

HOTM experiment, alcohol's effects on men's aggressive unprotected sexual intentions were moderated by alcohol-aggression expectancies and mediated by sexual-aggression congruent emotions and motivations (Davis, 2010). Furthermore, whether BAC is ascending (as in the earlier portion of a drinking episode) or descending (as in the later portion of a drinking episode) has been shown to moderate alcohol's effects on sexual risk (Davis et al., 2009).

Overall, research shows that in addition to alcohol's effects on sexual functioning, some of which are salutary, it is clear that alcohol constitutes a threat to sexual health through its effects on risk-taking. These effects in the real world are complicated by a host of dispositional, contextual, and situational factors. Basic behavioral experiments and especially HOTM experiments, however, have shown repeatedly that acute intoxication increases men's and women's willingness to have unprotected sex and have identified several important moderators and mediators, which are largely consistent with relevant theoretical frameworks, such as alcohol myopia theory and the cognitive mediation model (Norris, Masters, & Zawacki, 2004). Further research is warranted in elucidating these in-the-moment sexual risk-taking processes and behaviors and in gleaning insights that could be useful for augmenting extant preventative interventions and developing newer ones aimed at mitigating alcohol-induced sexual risk-taking.

GHB and sexual health. GHB is a CNS depressant that is used recreationally. Figures for use in the general population are not available. The 2010 Monitoring the Future Survey (Johnston, O'Malley, Bachman, & Schulenberg, 2011), however, found that 1.4% of 12th-grade students had used GHB in the past year. In a large multicity survey of club drug users (Shacham & Cottler, 2010), 10% reported lifetime GHB use. Although it is not clear how widely it is used, GHB often is employed to heighten sexual desire, lower sexual inhibitions (Lee & Levounis, 2008; Stein et al., 2011), and make sex more pleasant (Shacham & Cottler, 2010). Long-term and negative sexual effects have not been systematically investigated; however, users have reported feeling "too sexual" and dependent on the drug to have sex (Lee & Levounis, 2008). GHB has been tied to sexual risk-taking, such as having unprotected sex (Lee & Levounis, 2008). Understanding its particular effects is difficult because it is often used in combination with other drugs, such as methamphetamine and MDMA (Fisher, Reynolds, Ware, & Napper, 2011; Lee & Levounis, 2008). Fisher et al. (2011) found that GHB commonly was used in conjunction with both meth and ED drugs, thus making it a risk factor for engaging in unsafe sexual practices.

Opioids

Opioids include such drugs as heroin, oxycodone, and oxycontin (time-release form of oxycodone; NIDA, 2009). Interestingly, in 2010, oxycodone use in the United States—0.7% of the population, or nearly 2 million people—greatly exceeded that of heroin, which was used by 0.2% of U.S. residents ages 12 or older (approximately 600,000 people) (National Survey on Drug Use and Health [NSDUH]; Substance Abuse and Mental Health Services Administration [SAMHSA], 2011). Methadone and buprenorphine are synthetic opiate medications used to treat heroin addiction (NIDA, 2010). Because their mechanisms and effects are similar, these drugs will be discussed collectively.

Opiates' sexual effects appear to depend on dosage used, as well as level of addiction, in both men and women. Initially or at low doses, heroin may increase sexual desire, enjoyment, and satisfaction; however, over the long term, addicts report decreased sexual interest, arousal, and ability to experience orgasm (Frohmader, Pitchers, Balfour, & Coolen, 2010; Palha & Esteves, 2002; Rawson et al., 2002). Sexual dysfunction in some cases can serve as a motivation for seeking drug treatment (Palha & Esteves, 2002). Despite its detrimental effects on sexual functioning, drug use also is associated with increasing men's desire for sex. In one study, women being treated with methadone reported that using drugs increased their partners' demands for sex as well as their verbal and physical abuse if they tried to refuse. These women also stated that their own use rendered them unable to resist forced sex and that they often turned to drugs to cope with the effects of having forced sex (El-Bassel, Gilbert, & Rajah, 2003).

Although limited, there are findings indicating that sexual dysfunctions are more prevalent among men treated for heroin use than among men in the general population. Among Italian heroin and cocaine users undergoing treatment, ED was more prevalent than among general population men, and premature ejaculation was highly prevalent before initiating drug use (La Pera et al., 2003, 2008). On the basis of these findings, the investigators posited the "La Pera hypothesis" that sexual disorders lead some men to begin using heroin and other drugs as a self-medication strategy.

Heroin use also has been associated with sexual risk-taking (Frohmader et al., 2010; Raj, Saitz, Cheng, Winter, & Samet, 2007; Sánchez, Comerford, Chitwood, Fernandez, & McCoy, 2002). In particular, heroin use has been associated with having multiple partners, decreased condom use, and contracting STIs, including HIV. Rawson et al. (2002) reported, however, that only 7% of female and 4% of male heroin addicts in their study reported having risky sex when high. Nevertheless, the combination of high-risk sexual practices and injection as heroin's typical mode of ingestion greatly elevates heroin users' likelihood of HIV infection.

Stimulants

Stimulants are a class of drugs that elevate mood, increase feelings of well-being, and increase energy and alertness (NIDA, 2011b). They include methamphetamine, methylphenidate, cocaine, and MDMA. All of these drugs have been associated with sexual functioning and risk-taking.

Methamphetamine. NSDUH statistics reveal that in 2010 nearly 1 million people in the United States (0.4% of the population) used methamphetamine. According to recent reviews (Frohmader et al., 2010; Halkitis, 2009), both male and female users report heightened sexual desire, arousal, and pleasure. In men, however, chronic use results in an inability to achieve full erection and delayed ejaculation, a condition known colloquially as "crystal dick."

Sexual effects of methamphetamine have been most closely examined in gay men because of its relationship to risky sex and concomitant increased risk for HIV transmission. These studies have found that meth use is related to anonymous unprotected sex, increased number of partners, and extreme high-risk behaviors, such as group sex (Halkitis, 2009; Schilder, Lampinen, Miller, & Hogg, 2005). It is common for meth to be coadministered with a variety of other drugs, such as marijuana, GHB, cocaine, ecstasy, and Viagra, and similar relationships between multidrug use and high-risk sex have been found (Semple, Strathdee, Zians, & Patterson, 2009). A longitudinal study of gay men also found a strong positive relationship for HIV-positive men between methamphetamine use over time and frequency of unprotected anal receptive sex with casual partners (Halkitis, Mukherjee, & Palamar, 2009).

Sexual risk-taking among methamphetamine users is less well studied in heterosexuals than in gay men. Nevertheless, a recent review (Halkitis, 2009) reports relationships between the use of the drug and sexual risk behaviors, such as increased unprotected anal sex and number of sex partners, among heterosexual women. Similarly, among heterosexual men, studies have shown relationships between methamphetamine use and the likelihood of having multiple female partners, casual or anonymous female partners, drug-injecting female partners, exchanging money or drugs for sex, and decreased condom use (Halkitis, 2009).

Methylphenidate. Methylphenidate is a relatively weak stimulant most often prescribed for attention-deficit/hyperactivity disorder (ADHD; Frohmader et al., 2010). Its use in this context can produce sexual side effects. One clinical case study reports multiple erections and hypersexual behavior, both apparently linked to methylphenidate treatment for ADHD, in a male child and a male adolescent (Coskun & Zoroglu, 2009). Another notes compulsive masturbation and hypersexuality in a female child being treated for ADHD with methylphenidate (Bilgiç, Gürkan, & Türkoğlu, 2007). Both conclude that health care providers who prescribe the drug should be aware of these potential side effects and how they may complicate medication compliance.

Paradoxically, methylphenidate's unwanted sexual side effects have also gained attention as useful intended effects with the potential to treat sexual dysfunction associated with antidepressant medication. A clinical case study describes 4 adults taking SSRIs for depression and related conditions (Bartlik, Kaplan, & Kaplan, 1995). Low doses of psychostimulants (including methylphenidate), administered to treat co-occurring conditions (e.g., ADHD), resulted in enhanced arousal and orgasmic sensation among women and improved erectile strength among men. Two surveys of psychiatrists regarding their strategies for treating SSRI-related sexual dysfunction (Balon & Segraves, 2008; Perlis et al., 2002) suggest that prescribing methylphenidate is quite common and is viewed as moderately effective. However, both studies emphasize that the drug's utility can only be firmly established with formal controlled trials. Only one such randomized, double-blind, placebo-controlled trial has tested methylphenidate's effects on sexual dysfunction associated with antidepressant use (Pae et al., 2009). Sixty men and women with treatment-resistant major depression had their preexisting antidepressant medication supplemented with extended release methylphenidate or a placebo for 4 weeks. Placebo and experimental groups' mean scores on a sexual dysfunction measure were not different at baseline. Sexual dysfunction scores decreased by 20% during the study period among the experimental group (versus by 2.6% among the control group), but this group difference was not statistically significant. However, the small sample may not have allowed detection of modest effects.

Another study experimentally examined methylphenidate's effects on sexual desire (Volkow et al., 2007) and found that it was associated with increased desire. In a within-subjects design, male control subjects and cocaine abusers both rated their sexual desire higher when given methylphenidate than when given a placebo. The authors concluded that increasing sexual desire is one mechanism through which stimulant use can lead people to engage in sexually risky behavior.

Cocaine. Cocaine has been associated with increased sexual arousal among occasional and short-term users (Frohmader et al., 2010; Kim, Galanter, Castaneda, Lifshutz, & Franco, 1992) as well as increased sex drive and pleasure among long-term users in treatment (Rawson, Washton, Domier, & Reiber, 2002). Chronic use, however, appears to lead to decreased sexual desire, satisfaction, enjoyment, and orgasm intensity in both men and women as well as an inability to achieve orgasm and ejaculatory problems in men (Cocores, Miller, Pottash, & Gold, 1988; Frohmader et al., 2010; Kim et al., 1992). There appear to be strong gender differences in cocaine's effects on sexual interest and functioning. Rawson et al. (2002) found that male cocaine abusers were much more likely than female abusers to report heightened sex drive, pleasure, sexual obsession, enhanced performance, and likelihood of having sex. In a qualitative study of female drug abusers (El-Bassel et al., 2003), some women who had found sex unpleasant earlier in their lives reported that crack and heroin made it enjoyable and reduced its discomfort. They also reported, however, that even though crack in particular made them feel sexy, they did not want to have sex while taking it. These women also reported that crack increased their partners' desire for sex even though it simultaneously impeded their performance, a situation that led to conflict.

Cocaine use has been related to sexual risk-taking (Rawson et al., 2002), such as condom nonuse in men who have sex with men (McNall & Remafedi, 1999) and unprotected insertive anal intercourse with partners of unknown HIV status among HIV-negative gay men (Halkitis et al., 2009). Despite its detrimental sexual effects in chronic users, some increase their sexual activity, which leads to an increased number of sex partners and STIs (Kim et al., 1992).

MDMA. MDMA or ecstasy (4-methylenedioxy-methamphetamine) has become known as a "club drug" because of its use in nightclubs and other social settings. Many users report enhanced feelings of closeness, intimacy, and sensual pleasure, which are not necessarily associated with sex (Frohmader et al., 2010; Schilder et al., 2005). In a study of men and women who used MDMA before sex, Zemishlany, Aizenberg, and Weizman (2001) found that most participants reported experiencing increased sexual desire and satisfaction, but a substantial number reported delayed, but more intense, orgasms. Most women reported enhanced lubrication; however, equal numbers of men reported positive and negative erectile effects. In a large-scale study of recreational drug users, heavy MDMA users reported high rates of loss of sexual interest and pleasure (Parrott, Milani, Parmar, & Turner, 2001). These individuals, however, also had the highest rates of polydrug use in general; thus, it is not possible to attribute sexual effects solely to MDMA. In a study of regular MDMA users, Degenhardt (2005) found more similarities than differences in sexual risk behavior when comparing heterosexual and homosexual men and women. For instance, having unprotected sex and sharing needles did not differ across the groups. Both gay men and lesbians, however, were more likely to have sex while on drugs, a higher number of sex partners, and more injection drug use than were heterosexuals. Gay and bisexual men also reported higher rates of hepatitis C and HIV than heterosexual men (see Chapter 19, this volume).

Sedatives and Hypnotics: Marijuana

Marijuana and its related drug hashish are classified as sedatives and hypnotics; they are the most commonly used recreational drug in the United States besides alcohol. According to the NSDUH (SAMHSA, 2011), in 2010, approximately 11% of those 12 years of age or older (more than 29 million people) have used marijuana.

Several studies have provided evidence of consistent effects of marijuana on sexual functioning in both men and women. In their recent review, Gorzalka, Hill, and Chang (2010) noted that at low doses, women generally report enhanced sexual desire, pleasure, responsiveness, orgasmic quality, and sexual satisfaction. Only one study, based on global associations between lifetime use of substances and lifetime experience of sexual dysfunction (Johnson, Phelps, & Cottler, 2004), has reported negative effects, which included painful sex and inhibited orgasm. Positive effects appear to be dose dependent with more positive effects at low doses. Across several studies, men have reported increased sexual pleasure, arousal, satisfaction, and quality of orgasm (Gorzalka et al., 2010) after using marijuana. Both self-reports (Gorzalka et al., 2010; A. M. A. Smith et al., 2010) and one plethysmography study (Aversa et al., 2008), however, indicate that marijuana use may increase ED. Both positive and negative effects appear to depend on chronicity of use and dose at time of use. That is, long-term users and those who ingest a large dose report decreased positive effects and more erectile problems than light users.

Sexual risk-taking related specifically to marijuana use has not been well studied. In a population-based study of Australian adults, A. M. A. Smith et al. (2010) found relationships between cannabis use and sexual risk-related outcomes. Although there was no association between cannabis intake and condom use, increased number of sex partners over the previous year was related to frequency of cannabis use. In addition, among women, daily use was associated with increased reports of STI infection. Kingree and Phan (2002) found in a study of juvenile detainees that among boys and girls who were 14 years old or younger at the time of their most recent sexual event, lack of condom use was related to using marijuana within 3 hours before the event. With so little research to rely on, it is not possible to draw firm conclusions about the relationship between marijuana use and sexual risk-taking. Global association studies, such as A. M. A. Smith et al. (2010), leave open the possibility of third variable influences. Kingree and Phan's (2002) study points to the possibility that the relationship may be limited to particular high-risk groups or the very young. Further research will need to provide answers to these questions.

Erectile Dysfunction Medications

Millions of prescriptions have been written for ED medications since their introduction in 1998 (Food and Drug Administration, 1998). Besides treating ED per se, men seeking treatment for substance abuse have reported using these drugs for general enhancement of their sexual experience, including increased desire, sensation, ability to delay ejaculation, and have multiple orgasms in the same encounter as well as more intense orgasms (Horvath, Calsyn, Terry, & Cotton, 2007). ED drugs often are used in conjunction with recreational drugs, such as methamphetamine, cocaine, MDMA, and GHB (Fisher et al., 2011; Harte & Meston, 2011; Horvath et al., 2007; Pantalone, Bimbi, & Parsons, 2008), especially among gay men (Fisher et al., 2011). Gay men have reported using ED drugs to prolong sex and to maintain an erection with a condom (Pantalone et al., 2008) and to prevent erection problems caused by methamphetamine (Semple et al., 2009).

The association between the use of ED drugs and sexual risk-taking among gay men may depend on both their motivation for using the drug and their HIV status. Compared with non-ED drug users, gay men who use ED drugs appear more likely to have unprotected anal insertive sex (Pantalone et al., 2008). In addition Fisher et al. (2011) found that gay men who used ED drugs in conjunction with methamphetamine reported more anal insertive sex than those who used neither drug. Furthermore, Pantalone et al. (2008) found an association between HIV-negative gay men's use of ED drugs for countering other drug and alcohol effects and "barebacking" (i.e., having unprotected sex). HIV-negative gay men who used ED drugs to maintain an erection with a condom reported almost no unprotected anal intercourse with serodiscordant partners. Nevertheless, gay men who use ED medications, especially in conjunction with a recreational drug, are more likely than nonusers to report a higher incidence of STIs overall (Fisher et al., 2011; Pantalone et al., 2008) and HIV in particular (Fisher et al., 2011; Prestage et al., 2009).

Although ED drugs have important medical purposes, their use, especially in conjunction with recreational drugs, has been associated with sexual risk-taking and acquisition of STIs. This pattern of usage may not be causal—that is, it is not possible to determine that taking ED drugs along with another recreational drug directly leads to having unprotected sex. Rather, it may point to a group of high-risk individuals who, before taking these drugs, intend to have unprotected sex. It is noteworthy that at least some gay men use ED drugs to protect themselves. Prevention interventions need to capitalize on this motivation in their efforts to increase condom use.

HEALTH BENEFITS OF SEX

Sexuality is associated with both physical and psychosocial health benefits, with the term psychosocial health used here to refer to aspects of well-being beyond the physiological (e.g., mental, emotional, and social). The physical health benefits of sex include positive effects on overall, cardiovascular, immune system, and reproductive health. We review this science as well as critiques of the "sex for health" concept and literature in the following sections. After this summary of sex's physical health benefits, we turn to a discussion of sex's less concrete but equally important benefits to psychosocial health.

Physical Health Benefits

Research on sex's potential benefits to physical health, not surprisingly, has occurred primarily in the disciplines of epidemiology and medicine. It has used mostly cross-sectional and longitudinal survey methods; these methods sometimes are complemented by physiological tests or medical record review. The samples studied are most often midlife and older adults, both men and women. One major review differentiated among the health benefits of different sexual activities, concluding that penile–vaginal intercourse, but not other types of sex such as masturbation, was associated with health benefits in a number of realms (Brody, 2010). The majority of these studies define *sex* as any partnered heterosexual behavior, but several assess frequency of orgasm achieved by any method, while others measure sexual satisfaction, however it is attained.

Sex and overall good health. A population-based cross-sectional survey of midlife and older U.S. men and women found that those in very good or excellent health were more likely to be sexually active than similar-age peers. Among sexually active participants, reports of frequent sex (among men) and of a self-rated good quality sex life (among both men and women) were associated with better health (Lindau & Gavrilova, 2010). Another study focused on aging U.S. women with disabilities; among women who lived with their spouses, higher reported sexual satisfaction was linked to a lower risk of developing a new disability (Onder et al., 2003).

Sex and the cardiovascular and immune systems. Multiple medical and epidemiologcal studies, most of them in men, have documented associations between sex and better cardiovascular health. Two longitudinal survey studies of a cohort of older adult men in Wales demonstrated physical health benefits of sex. In one, men who reported higher orgasmic frequency across their lifetimes had lower mortality risk from all causes after age, social class, blood pressure, cholesterol, heart disease at baseline, and smoking were taken into account (G. D. Smith, Frankel, & Yarnell, 1997). In the other, more frequent vaginal intercourse had no association with greater risk of stroke, but it was associated with a lower risk of heart attack (Ebrahim et al., 2002). A similarly designed study of U.S. adult men found that men with a lower frequency of sexual activity of any type were more likely both to have cardiovascular disease and to die from it (Hall, Shackelton, Rosen, & Araujo, 2010).

Relationships between sex and blood pressure, and between sex and immune response, have been documented in both men and women. A small study asked Scottish adults to record their sexual behavior for 2 weeks, and then exposed them to stress and measured their blood pressure. Blood pressure was less reactive to stress in people who recently had vaginal intercourse than in those who had not or who had engaged in other types of sex (Brody, 2006). A small survey of male and female U.S. college students showed that the group members who reported frequent sex had higher levels of salivary immunoglobulin—associated with better immune health—than did groups with lower sexual frequency (Charnetski & Brennan, 2004).

Sex and the reproductive system. Sex also appears to be linked to better reproductive health in both women and men. Two studies provide information on the beneficial effects of sex on women's reproductive health (see Chapter 23, this volume). A large case-control retrospective survey study of U.S. women documented more intercourse and more orgasms during menstruation, over their sex lives to date, among women who did not have endometriosis than among those who did, after accounting for the effects of pregnancy history, intrauterine device use, smoking, and other relevant factors (Meaddough, Olive, Gallup, Perlin, & Kliman, 2002). In a small case-control study of both women and their male partners, Dutch women who had preeclampsia—which involves an immune reaction to the fetus—during their pregnancies were less likely to report a history of oral sex with the fathers of their babies than were controls. A substance present in male partners' semen was the likely mechanism of women being protected from preeclampsia through prior immune desensitization (Koelman et al., 2000).

There is also evidence of the positive effects of sex on men's reproductive functioning. A very large longitudinal study surveyed a cohort of older U.S. men about their ejaculatory frequency at different points across their life spans to date. After controlling for age and various cancer risk factors, the men with the highest ejaculatory frequency had a decreased risk of prostate cancer (Leitzmann, Platz, Stampfer, Willett, & Giovannucci, 2004).

Such findings indicate clearly that sex can improve reproductive health on a literal level in terms of the physiological effects of sexual behavior. Additionally, on a more metaphorical level, the role sex plays in people's worldviews may have an indirect beneficial effect on their reproductive health. The connection between sexuality and the prevention of STIs and HIV may seem obvious. Aspects of sexuality, such as pleasure and emotional intimacy, frequently are overlooked in public health interventions to prevent negative sexual health outcomes, such as STIs and unwanted pregnancy (Higgins & Hirsch, 2007).

There is some evidence that attention to the "sexy parts" of sex can enhance sexual health promotion. Studies show that foregrounding eroticism in STI/HIV risk reduction education may help people to reliably adopt safer sex practices such as condom use (Khan, Hudson-Rodd, Saggers, Bhuiyan, & Bhuiya, 2004; Philpott, Knerr, & Boydell, 2006). Conversely, ignoring the role of pleasure in sex can diminish, particularly for women, use of both contraception and sexual STI/HIV risk reduction techniques (Higgins & Hirsch, 2007). Even variable ideas about the role of sex in one's future have different associations with sexual health behavior. Youth who are open to the idea of eventually having sex, and who do not rule out the possibility by taking a virginity pledge, are more likely to use contraceptives or condoms when they do have their first intercourse (Bearman & Bruckner, 2001), thereby decreasing their risk of unwanted pregnancy and STIs (see Chapter 15, this volume).

Critique of "sex for health" studies. Medical and epidemiological research on the health benefits of sex, such as that reviewed thus far, receives abundant coverage in the popular press (Gupta, 2011). On the one hand, such material frequently is oversimplified or misrepresented. Media coverage rarely if ever acknowledges scientific studies' limitations (e.g., purely correlational, carried out with samples providing limited generalizability, addressing only certain sexual behaviors and not others). This coverage also has the potential to cause social or emotional harm to those individuals whose sexuality is made invisible or delegitimized by it, such as people who do not engage in coital, monogamous, or heterosexual sex (Bay-Cheng, 2006; Gupta, 2011). On the other hand, popular press coverage of scientific studies on the health benefits of sex may produce its own benefits by normalizing sex on a societal level and increasing at least some individuals' perception of their own sexuality's legitimacy (see Volume 2, Chapter 12, this handbook).

Psychosocial Health Benefits

In addition to the physical benefits it can offer, sex also can be associated with aspects of well-being beyond the physiological. We refer to this mental, emotional, and social well-being with the umbrella term *psychosocial health*. Former Surgeon General of the United States David Satcher (2001) acknowledged sexuality's role in psychosocial health when he described it as a "fundamental part of human life" (p. ii).

Sex—potentially hedonistic, expressive, spiritual, and playful—has been cherished for its inherent capabilities throughout human history. This value, however, has been documented predominantly in art rather than in academic literature. Poetry and song lyrics compare the beloved to essentials like light, air, and food and delineate the lengths to which people will go for passion. This essential and beneficent aspect of sexuality is tricky to capture, but it is undeniably part of its importance to many people's psychosocial health. The all-permeating sensation of rightness that can result from a good sexual experience is experienced as a powerful element of well-being (see Chapters 11 and 12, this volume).

Beyond its capability to contribute directly to psychosocial health, sex also can contribute to well-being indirectly through its association with relationships. In short, sex appears to be important to intimate relationships, and intimate relationships are important to human happiness (Diamond & Huebner, 2012). A review of the literature on sexual and relationship satisfaction (Sprecher & Cate, 2004) concluded that, overall, sexual satisfaction is associated with relationship satisfaction among both married and dating couples as well as among both heterosexual and same-sex couples. Sexual satisfaction also appears to be linked with other relationship quality indicators, such as people's perceptions of love and commitment (see Chapter 10, this volume).

Sprecher and Cate (2004), however, have drawn several caveats from their review. First, although sexual satisfaction appears to be an important contributor to relationship satisfaction and stability, it is nonetheless only one contributor, and how sexual satisfaction is conceptualized is key to understanding its links to relationship satisfaction. Second, the studies reviewed cannot demonstrate the direction of influences: Sexual satisfaction may precede relationship satisfaction, follow from it, or indeed, mutually and reciprocally influence it such that cause and effect cannot be determined accurately.

A recent study sheds some light on the first of these issues by exploring both sexual frequency and sexual satisfaction. For both men and women, sexual frequency was associated with sexual satisfaction among midlife and older committed heterosexual couples in multiple countries. Sexual satisfaction, in turn, was associated with relationship satisfaction, but sexual frequency was not. In other words, it was not how often a couple had sex, but rather their level of satisfaction with the sex they did have, that was linked to their happiness in the relationship (Heiman et al., 2011).

Another study employed longitudinal data to temporally order the associations between satisfaction with sex and satisfaction with a relationship. The use of cross-lagged models allowed researchers to demonstrate that sexual satisfaction preceded relationship satisfaction. Among midlife heterosexual couples in long relationships, women and men who reported being sexually satisfied were more likely to report being happy in their marriages and satisfied with their relationships at later time points.

Marital happiness and relationship satisfaction also were shown to predict relationship stability (Yeh, Lorenz, Wickrama, Conger, & Elder, 2006).

Taken together, this work indicates that in addition to being a part of psychosocial health in and of itself, sexual satisfaction also can be one key to the satisfying relationships that are key to human happiness (for a review, see Myers, 2000). Indeed, the link between committed, enduring sexual relationships and human health and happiness is one of health psychology's most solid findings in recent decades (Diamond & Huebner, 2012).

CONCLUSION

Sexuality and health is an extraordinarily broad topic that touches on numerous aspects of human functioning and well-being. As such, comprehensive coverage exceeds the scope of any one chapter and warrants its own encyclopedic volume. This chapter provided a broad overview of basic issues and research findings pertaining to major domains of the intersection between sexuality and health. It focused specifically on how sexuality intersects with physical health syndromes, mental health syndromes, STIs, alcohol use and abuse, substance use and abuse, and beneficial health effects. Among physical health symptoms, it is clear that a variety of chronic illnesses can have deleterious effects on sexuality, fostering sexual problems, effects that, in turn, can further erode quality of life and challenge intimate partnerships. The heterogeneity of these influences makes it exceedingly difficult to draw meaningful conclusions and chart future research directions. Generally speaking, much of the research to date has been largely descriptive and, as such, suggests a greater need for theory development aimed at identifying and delineating key psychological mechanisms that could be useful in better explaining the role of physical illnesses in sexual difficulties and in formulating interventions aimed at mitigating these effects. Nevertheless, a clear clinical implication at present is that health service providers who treat physical illnesses should consider assessing sexual issues and difficulties as indicators of disease impact and overall quality of life. Among mental health syndromes, research and theory has been valuable in highlighting the bidirectional influences of mood fluctuations and sexual functioning and in specifying that cognitive processes play an important role. It seems clear that a phenomenological experience characterized by psychic distress is a common element for both mood disorders and sexual difficulties. Indeed, some have suggested that changes in sexual functioning may function as diagnostic indicators of mood disorders and further research is needed to determine the utility of advancing an integrative internalizing syndrome reflecting correlated difficulties involving depression, anxiety, and sexuality (e.g., Laurent & Simons, 2009). In the case of developmental disabilities, while the research is still largely cross-sectional and descriptive, it seems that policy implications loom large because of the lack of standardized information about the sexual lives, difficulties, and risks associated with these populations. Overall, further research and theory development in all of these areas certainly are warranted.

There has been considerable research on substance use and abuse and sexuality. In particular, much has been learned demonstrating that alcohol—the most widely used substance—is reliably associated with sexual functioning and risk-taking, and also regarding explanations for how these effects unfold. With regard to other recreational substances, the research remains largely descriptive and future work aimed at specifying and explaining the nature of these effects is warranted. Given the apparent surge in recreational use of erectile medications, much work is needed in describing this trend and, in particular, tracking combined use of these drugs with other substances.

Finally, a focus on sexuality and health preordains greater attention to negatives than positives. Important health benefits, however, are associated with sexuality. Spotlighting and harnessing these positives of sexuality as a force for physical, psychological, and spiritual well-being can be as important a boon to overall health and wellness as mitigating the negatives.

References

Abbey, A., Saenz, C., & Buck, P. O. (2005). The cumulative effects of acute alcohol consumption, individual differences and situational perceptions on sexual decision making. *Journal of Studies on Alcohol, 66*, 82–90.

American Psychiatric Association. (2000). *Diagnostic and statistical manual of mental disorders* (4th ed., text revision). Washington, DC: Author.

Anderson, B. J., & Wolf, F. M. (1986). Chronic physical illness and sexual behavior: Psychological issues. *Journal of Consulting and Clinical Psychology, 54*, 168–175. doi:10.1037/0022-006X.54.2.168

Arbanas, G. (2010). Does post-traumatic stress disorder carry a higher risk of sexual dysfunctions? *Journal of Sexual Medicine, 7*, 1816–1821. doi:10.1111/j.1743-6109.2010.01704.x

Aversa, A., Rossi, F., Francomano, D., Bruzziches, R., Bertone, C., Santiemma, V., & Spera, G. (2008). Early endothelial dysfunction as a marker of vasculogenic erectile dysfunction in young habitual cannabis users. *International Journal of Impotence Research, 20*, 566–573. doi:10.1038/ijir.2008.43

Baggaley, M. (2008). Sexual dysfunction in schizophrenia: Focus on recent evidence. *Human Psychopharmacology: Clinical and Experimental, 23*, 201–209. doi:10.1002/hup.924

Balon, R., & Segraves, R. T. (2008). Survey of treatment practices for sexual dysfunction(s) associated with anti-depressants. *Journal of Sex & Marital Therapy, 34*(4), 353–365. doi: 10.1080/00926230802096390

Barlow, D. H. (1986). Causes of sexual dysfunction: The role of anxiety and cognitive interference. *Journal of Consulting and Clinical Psychology, 54*, 140–148. doi:10.1037/0022-006X.54.2.140

Barsky, J. L., Friedman, M. A., & Rosen, R. C. (2006). Sexual dysfunction and chronic illness: The role of flexibility in coping. *Journal of Sex and Marital Therapy, 32*, 235–253. doi:10.1080/00926230600575322

Bartlik, B. D., Kaplan, P., & Kaplan, H. S. (1995). Psychostimulants apparently reverse sexual dysfunction secondary to selective serotonin re-uptake inhibitors. *Journal of Sex & Marital Therapy, 21*, 264–271.

Basson, R., Rees, P., Wang, R., Montejo, A. L., & Incrocci, L. (2010). Sexual function in chronic illness. *Journal of Sexual Medicine, 7*, 374–388. doi:10.1111/j.1743-6109.2009.01621.x

Battaglia, C., Battaglia, B., Mancini, F., Nappi, R. E., Paradisi, R., & Venturoli, S. (2011). Moderate alcohol intake, genital vascularization, and sexuality in young, healthy, eumenorrheic women. A pilot study. *Journal of Sexual Medicine, 8*, 2334–2343. doi:10.1111/j.1743-6109.2011.02310.x

Bay-Cheng, L. Y. (2006). The social construction of sexuality: Religion, medicine, media, schools, and families. In M. M. Burnette & R. D. McAnulty (Eds.), *Sex and sexuality: Vol. 1. Sexuality today: Trends and controversies* (pp. 203–228). Westport, CT: Praeger.

Bearman, P. S., & Bruckner, H. (2001). Promising the future: Virginity pledges and first intercourse. *American Journal of Sociology, 106*, 859–912. doi:10.1086/320295

Bechara, A., Casabé, A., De Bonis, W., Helien, A., & Bertolino, M. V. (2010). Recreational use of phosphodiesterase type 5 inhibitors by healthy young men. *Journal of Sexual Medicine, 7*, 3736–3742. doi:10.1111/j.1743-6109.2010.01965.x

Beck, J. G., & Barlow, D. H. (1984). Current conceptualizations of sexual dysfunction: A review and an alternative perspective. *Clinical Psychology Review, 4*, 363–378. doi:10.1016/0272-7358(84)90017-5

Beckman, L. (1979). Reported effects of alcohol on the sexual feelings and behavior of women. *Journal of Studies on Alcohol, 40*, 272–282.

Bilgiç, A., Gürkan, K., & Türkoğlu, S. (2007). Excessive masturbation and hypersexual behavior associated with methylphenidate. *Journal of the American Academy of Child & Adolescent Psychiatry, 46*(7), 789–790.

Bing, E. G., Burnam, M. A., Longshore, D., Fleishman, J. A., Sherbourne, C. D., London, A. S., . . . Shapiro, M. (2001). Psychiatric disorders and drug use among human immunodeficiency virus-infected adults in the United States. *Archives of General Psychiatry, 58*, 721–728. doi:10.1001/archpsyc.58.8.721

Boddi, V., Corona, G., Monami, M., Fisher, A. D., Bandini, E., Melani, C., . . . Maggi, M. (2010). Priapus is happier with Venus than with Bacchus. *Journal of Sexual Medicine, 7*, 2831–2841. doi:10.1111/j.1743-6109.2010.01887.x

Bouhnik, A. D., Préau, M., Schiltz, M., Obadia, Y., & Spire, B. (2008). Sexual difficulties in people living with HIV in France–Results for a large representative sample of outpatients attending French hospitals (ANRS-EN12-VESPA). *AIDS and Behavior, 12*, 670–676. doi:10.1007/s10461-007-9355-z

Bradford, A., & Meston, C. M. (2006). The impact of anxiety on sexual arousal in women. *Behaviour Research and Therapy, 44*, 1067–1077. doi:10.1016/j.brat.2005.08.006

Briddell, D. W., & Wilson, G. T. (1976). Effects of alcohol and expectancy set on male sexual arousal. *Journal of Abnormal Psychology, 85*, 225–234. doi:10.1037/0021-843X.85.2.225

Brody, S. (2006). Blood pressure reactivity to stress is better for people who recently had penile-vaginal intercourse than for people who had other or no sexual activity. *Biological Psychology, 71*, 214–222. doi:10.1016/j.biopsycho.2005.03.005

Brody, S. (2010). The relative health benefits of different sexual activities. *Journal of Sexual Medicine, 7*, 1336–1361. doi:10.1111/j.1743-6109.2009.01677.x

Bronner, G., & Vodusek, D. B. (2011). Management of sexual dysfunction in Parkinson's disease. *Therapeutic Advances in Neurological Disorders, 4*, 375–383. doi:10.1177/1756285611411504

Burleson, M. H., Trevathan, W. R., & Todd, M. (2007). In the mood for love or vice versa? Exploring the relations among sexual activity, physical affection, affect and stress in the daily lives of mid-aged women. *Archives of Sexual Behavior, 36*, 357–368. doi:10.1007/s10508-006-9071-1

Cai, T., Mondaini, N., Migno, S., Meacci, F., Boddi, V., Gontero, P., . . . Bartoletti, R. (2011). Genital Chlamydia trachomatis infection is related to poor sexual quality of life in young sexually active women. *Journal of Sexual Medicine, 8*, 1131–1137. doi:10.1111/j.1743-6109.2010.02194.x

Centers for Disease Control and Prevention. (2010). Sexually transmitted diseases treatment guidelines. *Morbidity and Mortality Weekly Report, 59*(RR-12), 1–110.

Charnetski, C. J., & Brennan, F. X. (2004). Sexual frequency and salivary immunoglobulin A (IgA). *Psychological Reports, 94*, 839–844. doi:10.2466/pr0.94.3.839-844

Cheng, J. Y., Ng, E. M., Chen, R. Y., & Ko, J. S. (2007). Alcohol consumption and erectile dysfunction: Meta-analysis of population-based studies. *International Journal of Impotence Research, 19*, 343–352. doi:10.1038/sj.ijir.3901556

Chew, K. K., Bremner, A., Stuckey, B., Earle, C., & Jamrozik, K. (2009). Alcohol consumption and male erectile dysfunction: An unfounded reputation for risk? *Journal of Sexual Medicine, 6*, 1386–1394. doi:10.1111/j.1743-6109.2008.01115.x

Chivers, M. L., Seto, M. C., Lalumiere, M. L., Laan, E., & Grimbos, T. (2010). Agreement of self-reported and genital measures of sexual arousal in men and women: A meta-analysis. *Archives of Sexual Behavior, 39*, 5–56. doi:10.1007/s10508-009-9556-9

Cho, Y. H., & Span, S. A. (2010). The effect of alcohol on sexual risk-taking among young men and women. *Addictive Behaviors, 35*, 779–785. doi:10.1016/j.-addbeh.2010.03.007

Clayton, A., & Ramamurthy, S. (2008). The impact of physical illness on sexual dysfunction. *Advances in Psychosomatic Medicine, 29*, 70–88. doi:10.1159/000126625

Cocores, J. A., Miller, N. S., Pottash, A. C., & Gold, M. S. (1988). Sexual dysfunction in abusers of cocaine and alcohol. *American Journal of Drug and Alcohol Abuse, 14*, 169–173. doi:10.3109/00952999809001544

Coleman, E. (2007). Sexual health: Definitions and construct development. In M. S. Tepper & A. E. Owens (Eds.), *Sexual health: Vol. 1. Psychological foundations* (pp. 1–15). Westport, CT: Praeger.

Cooper, M. L. (2002). Alcohol use and risky sexual behavior among college students and youth: Evaluating the evidence. *Journal of Studies on Alcohol, 14*, 101–117.

Cooper, M. L. (2010). Toward a person × situation model of sexual risk-taking behaviors: Illuminating the conditional effects of traits across sexual situations and relationship contexts. *Journal of Personality and Social Psychology, 98*, 319–341. doi:10.1037/a0017785

Coskun, M., & Zoroglu, S. (2009). A report of two cases of sexual side effects with OROS methylphenidate. *Journal of Child and Adolescent Psychopharmacology, 19*(4), 477–479.

Crepaz, N., & Marks, G. (2001). Are negative affective states associated with HIV sexual risk behaviors? A meta-analytic review. *Health Psychology, 20*, 291–299. doi:10.1037/0278-6133.20.4.291

Crowe, L. C., & George, W. H. (1989). Alcohol and human sexuality: Review and integration. *Psychological Bulletin, 105*, 374–386. doi:10.1037/0033-2909.105.3.374

Cuskelly, M., & Bryde, R. (2004). Attitudes towards the sexuality of adults with an intellectual disability: Parents, support staff, and a community sample. *Journal of Intellectual and Developmental Disability, 29*, 255–264. doi:10.1080/13668250412331285136

Dachille, G., Lamuraglia, M., Leone, M., Pagliarulo, A., Palasciano, G., Salerno, M. T., & Ludovico, G. M. (2008). Erectile dysfunction in patients with alcohol consumption. *Alcoholism: Journal on Alcoholism and Related Addictions, 44*(2), 95–105.

Davis, K. C. (2010). The influence of alcohol expectancies and intoxication on men's aggressive unprotected sexual intentions. *Experimental and Clinical Psychopharmacology, 18*, 418–428. doi:10.1037/a0020510

Davis, K. C., George, W. H., Norris, J., Schacht, R. L., Stoner, S. A., Hendershot, C. S., & Kajumulo, K. F. (2009). Effects of alcohol and blood alcohol concentration limb on sexual risk-taking intentions. *Journal of Studies on Alcohol and Drugs, 70*, 499–507.

Davis, K. C., Hendershot, C. S., George, W. H., Norris, J., & Heiman, J. R. (2007). Alcohol's effects on sexual decision making: An integration of alcohol myopia and individual differences. *Journal of Studies on Alcohol and Drugs, 68*, 843–851.

Davis, K. C., Schraufnagel, T. J., Jacques-Tiura, A. J., Norris, J., George, W. H., & Kiekel, P. (2012). Childhood sexual abuse and acute alcohol effects on men's sexual aggression intentions. *Psychology of Violence, 2*, 179–193. doi:10.1037/a0027185

Degenhardt, L. (2005). Drug use and risk behaviour among regular ecstasy users: Does sexuality make a difference? *Culture, Health and Sexuality, 7*, 599–614. doi:10.1080/13691050500349875

Dell'Osso, L., Carmassi, C., Carlini, M., Rucci, P., Torri, P., Cesari, D., . . . Maggi, M. (2009). Sexual dysfunctions and suicidality in patients with bipolar disorder and unipolar depression. *Journal of Sexual Medicine, 6*, 3063–3070. doi:10.1111/j.1743-6109.2009.01455.x

DeRubeis, R. J., Hollon, S. D., Amsterdam, J. D., Shelton, R. C., Young, P. R., Salomon, R. M., . . . Gallop, R. (2005). Cognitive Therapy vs Medications in the Treatment of Moderate to Severe Depression. *Archives of General Psychiatry, 62*, 409–416. doi:10.1001/archpsyc.62.4.409

DeRubeis, R. J., Siegle, G. J., & Hollon, S. D. (2008). Cognitive therapy versus medication for depressions: Treatment outcomes and neural mechanisms. *Nature Reviews Neuroscience, 9*, 788–796. doi:10.1038/nrn2345

Diamond, L. M., & Huebner, D. M. (2012). Is good sex good for you? Rethinking sexuality and health. *Social and Personality Psychology Compass, 6*, 54–69. doi:10.1111/j.1751-9004.2011.00408.x

Di Giulio, G. (2003). Sexuality and people living with physical or developmental disabilities: A review of key issues. *Canadian Journal of Human Sexuality, 12*, 53–68.

Dingle, G. A., & Oei, T. P. S. (1997). Is alcohol a cofactor of HIV and AIDS? *Psychological Bulletin, 122*, 56–71. doi:10.1037/0033-2909.122.1.56

Donovan, C. & McEwan, R. (1995). A review of the literature examining the relationship between alcohol use and HIV-related sexual risk-taking in young people. *Addiction, 90*, 319–328. doi:10.1111/j.1360-0443.1995.tb03780.x

Dotson, L. A., Stinson, J., & Christian, L. (2003). People tell me I can't have sex. *Women and Therapy, 26*, 195–209. doi:10.1300/J015v26n03_02

Dunn, K. M., Croft, P. R., & Hackett, G. I. (1999). Association of sexual problems with social, psychological, and physical problems in men and women: A cross sectional population survey. *Journal of Epidemiology and Community Health, 53*, 144–148. doi:10.1136/jech.53.3.144

Ebrahim, S., May, M., Ben Shlomo, Y., McCarron, P., Frankel, S., Yarnell, J., & Smith, G. D. (2002). Sexual intercourse and risk of ischaemic stroke and coronary heart disease: The Caerphilly study. *Journal of Epidemiology and Community Health, 56*, 99–102. doi:10.1136/jech.56.2.99

Edwards, W. M., & Coleman, E. (2004). Defining sexual health: A descriptive overview. *Archives of Sexual Behavior, 33*, 189–195. doi:10.1023/B:ASEB.0000026619.95734.d5

El-Bassel, N., Gilbert, L., & Rajah, V. (2003). The relationship between drug abuse and sexual performance among women on methadone: Heightening the risk of sexual intimate violence and HIV. *Addictive Behaviors, 28*, 1385–1403. doi:10.1016/S0306-4603(02)00266-6

Eriksson, C. J., Fukunaga, T., & Lindman, R. (1994). Sex hormone response to alcohol. *Nature, 369*, 711. doi:10.1038/369711a0

Farkas, G. M., & Rosen, R. C. (1976). Effect of alcohol on elicited male sexual response. *Journal of Studies on Alcohol, 37*, 265–272.

Filiberti, A., Tamburini, M., Stefanon, B., Merola, M., Bandieramonte, G., Ventafridda, V., & De Palo, G. (1993). Psychological aspects of genital human papillomavirus infection: A preliminary report. *Journal of Psychosomatic Obstetrics and Gynaecology, 14*, 145–152. doi:10.3109/01674829309084437

Finnegan, A. (2004). Sexual health and chronic illness in childhood. *Paediatric Nursing, 16*, 32–36.

Fisher, D. G., Reynolds, G. L., Ware, M. R., & Napper, L. E. (2011). Methamphetamine and Viagra use: Relationship to sexual risk behaviors. *Archives of Sexual Behavior, 40*, 273–279. doi:10.1007/s10508-009-9495-5

Fortenberry, J. D., Temkit, M., Tu, W., Graham, C. A., Katz, B. P., & Orr, D. P. (2005). Daily mood, partner support, sexual interest, and sexual activity among adolescent women. *Health Psychology, 24*, 252–257. doi:10.1037/0278-6133.24.3.252

Fournier, J. C., De, C., Rubeis, R. J., Hollon, S. D., Dimidjian, S., Amsterdam, J. D., . . . Fawcett, J. (2010). Antidepressant drug effects and depression severity: A patient-level meta-analysis. *JAMA, 303*, 47–53. doi:10.1001/jama.2009.1943

Frohmader, K. S., Pitchers, K. K., Balfour, M. E., & Coolen, L. M. (2010). Mixing pleasures: Review of the effects of drugs on sex behavior in humans and animal models. *Hormones and Behavior, 58*, 149–162. doi:10.1016/j.yhbeh.2009.11.009

Fromme, K., D'Amico, E. J., & Katz, E. C. (1999). Intoxicated sexual risk taking: An expectancy or cognitive impairment explanation? *Journal of Studies on Alcohol, 60*, 54–63.

Galea, J., Butler, J., Iacono, T., & Leighton, D. (2004). The assessment of sexual knowledge in people with intellectual disability. *Journal of Intellectual and Developmental Disability, 29*, 350–365. doi:10.1080/13668250400014517

Garnock-Jones, K. P., & McCormack, P. L. (2010). Escitalopram: A review of its use in the management of major depressive disorder in adults. *CNS Drugs, 24*, 769–796. doi:10.2165/11204760-000000000-00000

Gavaler, J. S., Rizzo, A., Rossaro, L., & Van Thiel, D. H. (1994). Sexuality of alcoholic postmenopausal women: Effects of duration of alcohol abstinence.

Alcoholism: Clinical and Experimental Research, 18, 269–271. doi:10.1111/j.1530-0277.1994.tb00013.x

Gavaler, J. S., Rizzo, A., Rossaro, L., Van Thiel, D. H., Brezza, E., & Deal, S. R. (1993). Sexuality of alcoholic women with menstrual cycle function: Effects of duration of alcohol abstinence. *Alcoholism: Clinical and Experimental Research, 17*, 778–781. doi:10.1111/j.1530-0277.1993.tb00840.x

George, W. H., Davis, K. C., Masters, N. T., Jacques-Tiura, A. J., Heiman, J. R., Norris, J., . . . Andrasik, M. P. (in press). Sexual victimization, alcohol intoxication, sexual–emotional responding, and sexual risk in women. *Archives of Sexual Behavior*.

George, W. H., Davis, K. C., Norris, J., Heiman, J. R., Schacht, R. L., Stoner, S. A., & Kajumulo, K. F. (2006). Alcohol and erectile response: The effects of high dosage in the context of demands to maximize sexual arousal. *Experimental and Clinical Psychopharmacology, 14*, 461–470. doi:10.1037/1064-1297.14.4.461

George, W. H., Davis, K. C., Norris, J., Heiman, J. R., Schacht, R. L., Stoner, S. A., . . . Kajumulo, K. F. (2011). Women's sexual arousal: Effects of high alcohol dosages and self-control instructions. *Hormones and Behavior, 59*, 730–738. doi:10.1016/j.yhbeh.2011.03.006

George, W. H., Davis, K. C., Norris, J., Heiman, J. R., Stoner, S. A., Schacht, R. L., . . . Kajumulo, K. F. (2009). Indirect effects of acute alcohol intoxication on sexual risk-taking: The roles of subjective and physiological sexual arousal. *Archives of Sexual Behavior, 38*, 498–513. doi:10.1007/s10508-008-9346-9

George, W. H., Davis, K. C., Schraufnagel, T., Norris, J., Heiman, J. R., Schacht, R. L., . . . Kajumulo, K. F. (2008). Later that night: Descending alcohol intoxication and men's sexual arousal. *American Journal of Men's Health, 2*, 76–86. doi:10.1177/1557988307313549

George, W. H., & Gilmore, A. K. (2013). Alcohol's effects on sexual arousal and sexual functioning. In P. Miller (Ed.), *Principles of addiction* (pp. 339–347). London, England: Elsevier.

George, W. H., Gilmore, A. K., & Stappenbeck, C. A. (2012). Balanced Placebo Design: Revolutionary impact on addictions research and theory. *Addiction Research and Theory, 20*, 186–203. doi:10.3109/16066359.2012.680216

George, W. H., Norris, J., & Schacht, R. L. (2003, March 10). *Men's genital sexual arousal and alcohol intoxication: A critical re-appraisal.* Paper presented at the 16th annual meeting of the World Congress of Sexology, Havana, Cuba.

George, W. H., & Stoner, S. A. (2000). Understanding acute alcohol effects on sexual behavior. *Annual Review of Sex Research, 11*, 92–124.

George, W. H., Stoner, S. A., Norris, J., Lopez, P. A., & Lehman, G. L. (2000). Alcohol expectancies and sexuality: A self-fulfilling prophecy analysis of dyadic perceptions and behavior. *Journal of Studies on Alcohol, 61*, 168–176.

Gilmore, A. K., Schacht, R. L., George, W. H., Otto, J. M., Davis, K. C., Heiman, J. R., & Kajumulo, K. F. (2010). Assessing women's sexual arousal in the context of sexual assault history and acute alcohol intoxication. *Journal of Sexual Medicine, 7*(6), 2112–2119. doi:10.1111/j.1743-6109.2010.01786.x

Gorzalka, B. B., Hill, M. N., & Chang, S. C. H. (2010). Male-female differences in the effects of cannabinoids on sexual behavior and gonadal hormone function. *Hormones and Behavior, 58*, 91–99. doi:10:1016/j.yhbeh.2009.08.009

Graziottin, A., & Serafini, A. (2009). HPV infection in women: Psychosexual impact of genital warts and intraepithelial lesions. *Journal of Sexual Medicine, 6*, 633–645. doi:10.1111/j.1743-6109.2008.01151.x

Guay, D. R. P. (2008). Inappropriate sexual behaviors in cognitively impaired older individuals. *American Journal of Geriatric Pharmacotherapy, 6*, 269–288. doi:10.1016/j.amjopharm.2008.12.004

Gupta, K. (2011). "Screw health": Representations of sex as a health-promoting activity in medical and popular literature. *Journal of Medical Humanities, 32*, 127–140. doi:10.1007/s10912-010-9129-x

Gust, D. A., Wang, S. A., Grot, J., Ransom, R., & Levine, W. C. (2003). National survey of sexual behavior and sexual behavior policies in facilities for individuals with mental retardation/developmental disabilities. *Mental Retardation, 41*, 365–373. doi:10.1352/0047-6765(2003)41<365:NSOSBA>2.0.CO;2

Halkitis, P. N. (2009). Methamphetamine, sex, sexuality, and sexual risk taking. In P. N. Halkitis (Ed.), *Methamphetamine addiction: Biological foundations, psychological factors, and social consequences* (pp. 69–81). Washington, DC: American Psychological Association. doi:10.1037/11883-005

Halkitis, P. N., Mukherjee, P. P., & Palamar, J. J. (2009). Longitudinal modeling of methamphetamine use and sexual risk behaviors in gay and bisexual men. *AIDS and Behavior, 13*, 783–791. doi:10.1007/s10461-008-9432-y

Hall, S. A., Shackelton, R., Rosen, R. C., & Araujo, A. B. (2010). Sexual activity, erectile dysfunction, and incident cardiovascular events. *American Journal of Cardiology, 105*, 192–197. doi:10.1016/j.amjcard.2009.08.671

Halpern-Felsher, B. L., Millstein, S. G., Ellen, J. M. (1996). Relationship of alcohol use and risky sexual behavior: A review and analysis of findings. *Journal of Adolescent Health, 19*, 331–336. doi:10.1016/S1054-139X(96)00024-9

Harte, C. B., & Meston, C. M. (2011). Recreational use of erectile dysfunction medications in undergraduate men in the United States: Characteristics and associated risk factors. *Archives of Sexual Behavior, 40*, 597–606. doi:10.1007/s10508-010-9619-y

Hartmann, U. (2007). Depression and sexual dysfunction. *Journal of Men's Health and Gender, 4*, 18–25. doi:10.1016/j.jmhg.2006.12.003

Harvey, S. M., & Beckman, L. J. (1986). Alcohol consumption, female sexual behavior and contraceptive use. *Journal of Studies on Alcohol, 47*, 327–332.

Heiman, J. R. (1980). Female sexual response patterns: Interactions of physiological, affective, and contextual cues. *Archives of General Psychiatry, 37*, 1311–1316. doi:10.1001/archpsyc.1980.01780240109013

Heiman, J. R., Long, J. S., Smith, S. N., Fisher, W. A., Sand, M. S., & Rosen, R. C. (2011). Sexual satisfaction and relationship happiness in midlife and older couples in five countries. *Archives of Sexual Behavior, 40*, 741–753. doi:10.1007/s10508-010-9703-3

Hendershot, C. S., & George, W. H. (2007). Alcohol and sexuality research in the AIDS era: Trends in publication activity, target populations and research design. *AIDS and Behavior,* 11, 227–237. doi:10.1007/s10461-006-9130-6

Higgins, J. A., & Hirsch, J. S. (2007). The pleasure deficit: Revisiting the "sexuality connection" in reproductive health. *International Family Planning Perspectives, 33*, 133–139. doi:10.1363/3313307

Holt, M. (2009). "Just take Viagra": Erectile insurance, prophylactic certainty, and deficit correction in gay men's accounts of sexuopharmaceutical use. *Sexualities, 12*, 746–764. doi:10.1177/1363460709346112

Hoon, P. W., Wincze, J., & Hoon, E. (1977). A test of reciprocal inhibition: Are anxiety and sexual arousal in women mutually inhibitory? *Journal of Abnormal Psychology, 86*, 65–74. doi:10.1037/0021-843X.86.1.65

Horvath, K. J., Calsyn, D. A., Terry, C., & Cotton, A. (2007). Erectile dysfunction medication use among men seeking substance abuse treatment. *Journal of Addictive Diseases, 26*, 7–13. doi:10.1300/J069v26n04_02

Hoyer, J., Uhmann, S., Rambow, J., & Jacobi, F. (2009). Reduction of sexual dysfunction: Byproduct of cognitive-behavioural therapy for psychological disorders? *Sexual and Relationship Therapy, 24*, 64–73. doi:10.1080/14681990802649938

Hughes, A., Hertlein, K. M., & Hagey, D. W. (2011). A MedFT-informed sex therapy for treating sexual problems associated with chronic illness. *Journal of Family Psychotherapy,* 22, 114–127. doi:10.1080/08975353.2011.577689

Jacobson, J. (2007). Informing our psychosexual practice for treating erectile dysfunction in gay and bisexual men living with HIV: A response to the 2006 NHS Greater Glasgow HIV needs assessment report. *Sexual and Relationship Therapy,* 22, 397–414. doi:10.1080/14681990701391277

Johnson, S. D., Phelps, D. L., & Cottler, L. B. (2004). The association of sexual dysfunction and substance use among a community epidemiological sample. *Archives of Sexual Behavior, 33*, 55–63. doi:10.1023/B:ASEB.0000007462.97961.5a

Johnston, L. D., O'Malley, P. M., Bachman, J. G., & Schulenberg, J. E. (2011). *Monitoring the Future national survey results on drug use, 1975–2010: Vol. 2. College students and adults ages 19–50*. Ann Arbor: Institute for Social Research, University of Michigan. Retrieved from http://monitoringthefuture.org/pubs/monographs/mtf-vol2_2010.pdf

Karlen, A. (2002). Positive sexual effects of chronic illness: Case studies of women with lupus (SLE). *Sexuality and Disability, 20*, 191–208. doi:10.1023/A:1021497816364

Kashdan, T. B., Adams, L., Savostyanova, A., Ferssizidis, P., McKnight, P. E., & Nezlek, J. B. (2011). Effects of social anxiety and depressive symptoms on the frequency and quality of sexual activity: A daily process approach. *Behaviour Research and Therapy, 49*, 352–360. doi:10.1016/j.brat.2011.03.004

Kennedy, S. H., & Rizvi, S. (2009). Sexual dysfunction, depression, and the impact of antidepressants. *Journal of Clinical Psychopharmacology, 29*, 157–164. doi:10.1097/JCP.0b013e31819c76e9

Khan, S. I., Hudson-Rodd, N., Saggers, S., Bhuiyan, M. I., & Bhuiya, A. (2004). Safer sex or pleasurable sex? Rethinking condom use in the AIDS era. *Sexual Health, 1*, 217–225. doi:10.1071/SH04009

Kim, A., Galanter, M., Castaneda, R., Lifshutz, H., & Franco, H. (1992). Crack cocaine use and sexual behavior among psychiatric inpatients. *American Journal of Drug and Alcohol Abuse, 18*, 235–246. doi:10.3109/00952999209026064

Kingree, J. B., & Phan, D. (2002). Marijuana use and unprotected sexual intercourse among adolescent detainees: An event analysis. *Criminal Justice and Behavior, 29*, 705–717. doi:10.1177/009385402237923

Koelman, C. A., Coumans, A. B. C., Nijman, H. W., Doxiadis, I. I. N., Dekker, G. A., & Claas, F. H. J. (2000). Correlation between oral sex and a low incidence of preeclampsia: A role for soluble HLA in seminal fluid? *Journal of Reproductive Immunology, 46*, 155–166. doi:10.1016/S0165-0378(99)00062-5

Kruse, M. I., & Fromme, K. (2005). Influence of physical attractiveness and alcohol on men's perceptions of potential sexual partners and sexual behavior intentions. *Experimental and Clinical Psychopharmacology, 13*, 146–156.

Kuffel, S. W., & Heiman, J. R. (2006). Effects of depressive symptoms and experimentally adopted schemas on sexual arousal and affect in sexually healthy women. *Archives of Sexual Behavior, 35*, 160–174. doi:10.1007/s10508-005-9015-1

Langevin, R., Ben-Aron, M. H., Coulthard, R., Hucker, S. J., Purins, J. E., Russon, A. E., . . . Webster, C. D. (1985). The effect of alcohol on penile erection. In R. Langevin (Ed.), *Erotic preference, gender identity, and sexual aggression in men: New research studies* (pp. 102–111). Hillsdale, NJ: Erlbaum.

Langfeldt, T., & Porter, M. (1986). *Sexuality and family planning: Report of a consultation and research findings*. Copenhagen, Denmark: World Health Organization, Regional Office for Europe.

La Pera, G., Carderi, A., Marianantoni, Z., Peris, F., Lentini, M., & Taggi, F. (2008). Sexual dysfunction prior to first drug use among former drug addicts and its possible causal meaning on drug addiction: Preliminary results. *Journal of Sexual Medicine, 5*, 164–172.

La Pera, G., Giannotti, C. F., Carderi, A., Marianantoni, Z., Peris, F., Lentini, M., . . . Macchia, T. (2003). Prevalence of sexual disorders in those young males who later become drug abusers. *Journal of Sex and Marital Therapy, 29*, 149–156. doi:10.1080/713847172

Larson, J. S. (1996). The World Health Organization's definition of health: Social vs. spiritual health. *Social Indicators Research, 38*, 181–192. doi:10.1007/BF00300458

Laurent, S. M., & Simons, A. D. (2009). Sexual dysfunction in depression and anxiety: Conceptualizing sexual dysfunction as part of an internalizing dimension. *Clinical Psychology Review, 29*, 573–585. doi:10.1016/j.cpr.2009.06.007

Lee, S. J., & Levounis, P. (2008). Gamma hydroxybutyrate: An ethnographic study of recreational use and abuse. *Journal of Psychoactive Drugs, 40*, 245–253. doi:10.1080/02791072.2008.10400639

Leigh, B. C. (2002). Alcohol and condom use: A meta-analysis of event-level studies. *Sexually Transmitted Diseases 29*, 476–482.

Leigh, B. C., & Morrison, D. M. (1991). Alcohol consumption and sexual risk-taking in adolescents. *Alcohol Health and Research World, 15*, 64–72.

Leigh, B. C., Vanslyke, J. G., Hoppe, M. J., Rainey, D. T., Morrison, D. M., & Gillmore, M. R. (2008). Drinking and condom use: Results from an event-based daily diary. *AIDS and Behavior, 12*, 104–112. doi:10.1007/s10461-007-9216-9

Leitzmann, M. F., Platz, E. A., Stampfer, M. J., Willett, W. C., & Giovannucci, E. (2004). Ejaculation frequency and subsequent risk of prostate cancer. *JAMA, 291*, 1578–1586. doi:10.1001/jama.291.13.1578

Leutar, Z., & Mihokovic, M. (2007). Level of knowledge about sexuality of people with mental disabilities. *Sexuality and Disability, 25*, 93–109. doi:10.1007/s11195-007-9046-8

Lin, L. P., Yen, C., Kuo, F., Wu, J., & Lin, J. (2009). Sexual assault of people with disabilities: Results of a 2002–2007 national report in Taiwan. *Research in Developmental Disabilities, 30*, 969–975. doi:10.1016/j.ridd.2009.02.001

Líndal, E., & Stefánsson, J. G. (1993). The lifetime prevalence of psychosexual dysfunction among 55- to 57-year-olds in Iceland. *Social Psychiatry and Psychiatric Epidemiology, 28*, 91–95. doi:10.1007/BF00802098

Lindau, S. T., & Gavrilova, N. (2010). Sex, health, and years of sexually active life gained due to good health: Evidence from two US population based cross sectional surveys of ageing. *British Medical Journal, 340*(7746).

Lindman, R. E., Koskelainen, B. M., & Eriksson, C. J. (1999). Drinking, menstrual cycle, and female sexuality: A diary study. *Alcoholism: Clinical and Experimental Research, 23*, 169–173.

MacDonald, T. K., MacDonald, G., Zanna, M. P., & Fong, G. (2000). Alcohol, sexual arousal, and intentions to use condoms in young men: Applying alcohol myopia theory to risky sexual behavior. *Health Psychology, 19*, 290–298. doi:10.1037/0278-6133.19.3.290

Maisto, S. A., Carey, M. P., Carey, K. B., Gordon, C. M., & Schum, J. L. (2004). Effects of alcohol and expectancies on HIV-related risk perception and behavioral skills in heterosexual women. *Experimental and Clinical Psychopharmacology, 12*, 288–297. doi:10.1037/1064-1297.12.4.288

Malatesta, V. J., Pollack, R. H., Crotty, T. D., & Peacock, L. J. (1982). Acute alcohol intoxication and female orgasmic response. *Journal of Sex Research, 18*, 1–17. doi:10.1080/00224498209551130

Malatesta, V. J., Pollack, R. H., Wilbanks, W. A., & Adams, H. E. (1979). Alcohol effects on the orgasmic–ejaculatory response in human males. *Journal of Sex Research, 15*, 101–107. doi:10.1080/00224497909551027

Manolis, A., & Doumas, M. (2008). Sexual dysfunction: The "prima ballerina" of hypertension-related quality-of-life complications. *Journal of Hypertension, 26*, 2074–2084. doi:10.1097/HJH.0b013e32830dd0c6

Mao, L., Newman, E., Kidd, M. R., Saltman, D. C., Rogers, G. D., & Kippax, S. C. (2009). Self-reported sexual difficulties and their association with depression and other factors among gay men attending high

HIV-caseload general practices in Australia. *Journal of Sexual Medicine, 6*, 1378–1385. doi:10.1111/j.1743-6109.2008.01160.x

Marlatt, G. A., & Rohsenow, D. J. (1980). Cognitive processes in alcohol use: Expectancy and the balanced placebo design. In N. K. Mello (Ed.), *Advances in substance abuse* (pp. 159–199). Greenwich, CT: JAI Press.

Masters, N. T., George, W. H., Davis, K. C., Norris, J., Heiman, J. R., Jacques-Tiura, A. J., . . . Stappenbeck, C. A. (in press). Women's unprotected sex intentions: roles of sexual victimization, intoxication, and partner perception. *Journal of Sex Research*.

Masters, W. H., & Johnson, V. E. (1970). *Human sexual inadequacy*. Toronto, Ontario, Canada: Bantam Books.

Mazza, M., Harnic, D., Catalano, V., Di Nicola, M., Bruschi, A., Bria, P., . . . Mazza, S. (2011). Sexual behavior in women with bipolar disorder. *Journal of Affective Disorders, 131*, 364–367. doi:10.1016/j.jad.2010.11.010

McArthur, J. C., Brew, B. J., & Nath, A. (2005). Neurological complications of HIV infection. *Lancet Neurology, 4*, 543–555. doi:10.1016/S1474-4422(05)70165-4

McCabe, M. P., & Cobain, M. J. (1998). The impact of individual and relationship factors on sexual dysfunction among males and females. *Sexual and Marital Therapy, 13*, 131–143. doi:10.1080/02674659808406554

McNall, M., & Remafedi, G. (1999). Relationship of amphetamine and other substance use to unprotected intercourse among young men who have sex with men. *Archives of Pediatrics and Adolescent Medicine, 153*, 1130–1135. Retrieved from http://archpedi.ama-assn.org.offcampus.lib.washington.edu/cgi/reprint/153/11/1130

Meaddough, E. L., Olive, D. L., Gallup, P., Perlin, M., & Kliman, H. J. (2002). Sexual activity, orgasm and tampon use are associated with a decreased risk for endometriosis. *Gynecologic and Obstetric Investigation, 53*, 163–169. doi:10.1159/000058368

Meade, C. S., Fitzmaurice, G. M., Sanchez, A. K., Griffin, M. L., McDonald, L. J., & Weiss, R. D. (2011). The relationship of manic episodes and drug abuse to sexual risk behavior in patients with co-occurring bipolar and substance use disorders: A 15-month prospective analysis. *AIDS and Behavior, 15*, 1829–1833. doi:10.1007/s10461-010-9814-9

Meisler, A. W., & Carey, M. P. (1991). Depressed affect and male sexual arousal. *Archives of Sexual Behavior, 20*, 541–554. doi:10.1007/BF01550953

Mercan, S., Karamustafalioglu, O., Ayaydin, E. B., Akpinar, A., Goksan, B., Gonenli, S., & Guven, T. (2006). Sexual dysfunction in female patients with panic disorder alone or with accompanying depression. *International Journal of Psychiatry in Clinical Practice, 10*, 235–240. doi:10.1080/13651500600649994

Michael, A., & O'Keane, V. (2000). Sexual dysfunction in depression. *Human Psychopharmacology: Clinical and Experimental, 15*, 337–345. doi:10.1002/1099-1077(200007)15:5<337::AID-HUP207>3.0.CO;2-H

Middleton, L. S., Kuffel, S. W., & Heiman, J. R. (2008). Effects of experimentally adopted sexual schemas on vaginal response and subjective sexual arousal: A comparison between women with sexual arousal disorder and sexually healthy women. *Archives of Sexual Behavior, 37*, 950–961. doi:10.1007/s10508-007-9310-0

Mitchell, W. B., DiBartolo, P. M., Brown, T. A., & Barlow, D. H. (1998). Effects of positive and negative mood on sexual arousal in sexually functional males. *Archives of Sexual Behavior, 27*, 197–207. doi:10.1023/A:1018686631428

Monahan, J. L., Murphy, S. T., & Miller, L. C. (1999). When women imbibe: Alcohol and the illusory control of HIV risk. *Psychology of Women Quarterly, 23*, 643–651.

Mondaini, N., Cai, T., Gontero, P., Gavazzi, A., Lombardi, G., Boddi, V., & Bartoletti, R. (2009). Regular moderate intake of red wine is linked to a better women's sexual health. *Journal of Sexual Medicine, 6*, 2772–2777. doi:10.1111/j.1743-6109.2009.01393.x

Montejo, A., Majadas, S., Rizvi, S. J., & Kennedy, S. H. (2011). The effects of agomelatine on sexual function in depressed patients and healthy volunteers. *Human Psychopharmacology: Clinical and Experimental, 26*, 537–542. doi:10.1002/hup.1243

Moreno-Pérez, O., Escoín, C., Serna-Candel, C., Póco, A., Alfayate, R., Merino, E., . . . Portilla, J. (2010). Risk factors for sexual and erectile dysfunction in HIV-infected men: The role of protease inhibitors. *AIDS, 24*, 255–264. doi:10.1097/QAD.0b013e328334444b

Morlet, A., Watters, G. R., Dunn, J., Keogh, E. J., Creed, K. E., Tulloch, A. G. S., . . . Earle, C. M. (1990). Effects of acute alcohol on penile tumescence in normal young men and dogs. *Urology, 35*, 399–404. doi:10.1016/0090-4295(90)80080-7

Munoz, V., & Stravynski, A. (2010). Social phobia and sexual problems: A comparison of social phobic, sexually dysfunctional and normal individuals. *British Journal of Clinical Psychology, 49*, 53–66. doi:10.1348/014466509X436697

Myers, D. G. (2000). The funds, friends, and faith of happy people. *American Psychologist, 55*, 56–67. doi:10.1037/0003-066X.55.1.56

National Center for Health Statistics. (2007). *Health, United States, 2007*. Retrieved from http://www.cdc.gov/nchs/data/hus/hus07.pdf

National Institute on Drug Abuse. (2009). *NIDA InfoFacts: Prescription and over-the-counter medications*. Retrieved from https://www.drugabuse.gov/sites/default/files/painmed09.pdf

National Institute on Drug Abuse. (2010). *NIDA InfoFacts: Heroin*. Retrieved from https://www.drugabuse.gov/sites/default/files/heroin10.pdf

National Institute on Drug Abuse. (2011a). *Media guide: How to find what you need to know about drug abuse and addiction*. Retrieved from https://www.drugabuse.gov/sites/default/files/mediaguide_web.pdf

National Institute on Drug Abuse. (2011b). *Stimulants*. Retrieved from http://teens.drugabuse.gov/facts/facts_stim1.php

Newton, D. C., & McCabe, M. P. (2008a). Effects of sexually transmitted infection status, relationship status, and disclosure status on sexual self-concept. *Journal of Sex Research, 45*, 187–192.

Newton, D. C., & McCabe, M. P. (2008b). Sexually transmitted infections: Impact on individuals and their relationships. *Journal of Health Psychology, 13*, 864–869. doi:10.1177/1359105308095058

Nobre, P. J., & Pinto-Gouveia, J. (2006). Emotions during sexual activity: Differences between sexually functional and dysfunctional men and women. *Archives of Sexual Behavior, 35*, 491–499. doi:10.1007/s10508-006-9047-1

Nobre, P. J., & Pinto-Gouveia, J. (2008a). Cognitions, emotions, and sexual response: Analysis of the relationship among automatic thoughts, emotional responses, and sexual arousal. *Archives of Sexual Behavior, 37*, 652–661. doi:10.1007/s10508-007-9258-0

Nobre, P. J., & Pinto-Gouveia, J. (2008b). Cognitive and emotional predictors of female sexual dysfunctions: Preliminary findings. *Journal of Sex and Marital Therapy, 34*, 325–342. doi:10.1080/00926230802096358

Norris, J., Masters, N. T., & Zawacki, T. (2004). Cognitive mediation of women's sexual decision making: The influence of alcohol, contextual factors, and background variables. *Annual Review of Sex Research, 15*, 258–296.

Norris, J., Stoner, S. A., Hessler, D. A., Zawacki, T., Davis, K. C., George, W. H., . . . Abdallah, D. A. (2009). Influences of sexual sensation seeking, alcohol consumption, and sexual arousal on women's behavioral intentions related to having unprotected sex. *Psychology of Addictive Behaviors, 23*, 14–22. doi:10.1037/a0013998

Norris, J., Stoner, S. A., Hessler, D. A., Zawacki, T., George, W. H., Morrison, D. M., & Davis, K. C. (2009). Cognitive mediation of alcohol's effects on women's in-the-moment sexual decision making. *Health Psychology, 28*, 20–28. doi:10.1037/a0012649

Norton, G. R., & Jehu, D. (1984). The role of anxiety in sexual dysfunctions: A review. *Archives of Sexual Behavior, 13*, 165–183. doi:10.1007/BF01542150

Nosek, M. A., Foley, C. C., Hughes, R. B., & Howland, C. A. (2001). Vulnerabilities for abuse among women with disabilities. *Sexuality and Disability, 19*, 177–189. doi:10.1023/A:1013152530758

Nunnink, S. E., Goldwaser, G., Afari, N., Nievergelt, C. M., & Baker, D. G. (2010). The role of emotional numbing in sexual functioning among veterans of the Iraq and Afghanistan wars. *Military Medicine, 175*, 424–428.

Nusbaum, M. R., Hamilton, C., & Lenahan, P. (2003). Chronic illness and sexual functioning. *American Family Physician, 67*, 347–354.

O'Farrell, T. J., Choquette, K. A., Cutter, H. S. G., & Birchler, G. R. (1997). Sexual satisfaction and dysfunction among alcoholic, maritally conflicted, and nonconflicted couples. *Journal of Studies on Alcohol, 58*, 91–99.

Onder, G., Penninx, B., Guralnik, J. M., Jones, H., Fried, L. P., Pahor, M., & Williamson, J. D. (2003). Sexual satisfaction and risk of disability in older women. *Journal of Clinical Psychiatry, 64*, 1177–1182. doi:10.4088/JCP.v64n1006

Pae, C-U., Marks, D. M., Masand, P. S., Peindl, K., Hooper-Wood, C., Han, C., . . . Patkar, A. A. (2009). Methylphenidate extended release (OROS MPH) for the treatment of antidepressant-related sexual dysfunction in patients with treatment-resistant depression: Results from a 4-week, double-blind, placebo-controlled trial. *Clinical Neuropharmacology, 32*(2), 85–88.

Palha, A. P., & Esteves, M. (2002). A study of the sexuality of opiate addicts. *Journal of Sex and Marital Therapy, 28*, 427–437. doi:10.1080/00926230290001547

Pantalone, D. W., Bimbi, D. S., & Parsons, J. T. (2008). Motivations for the recreational use of erectile enhancing medications in urban gay and bisexual men. *Sexually Transmitted Infections, 84*, 458–462. doi:10.1136/sti.2008.031476

Parrott, A. C., Milani, R. M., Parmar, R., & Turner, J. J. D. (2001). Recreational ecstasy/MDMA and other drug users from the UK and Italy: *Psychiatric symptoms and psychobiological problems. Psychopharmacology, 159*, 77–82. doi:10.1007/s002130100897

Partnership for Solutions. (2004). *Chronic conditions: Making the case for ongoing care*. Retrieved from http://www.partnershipforsolutions.org/DMS/files/chronicbook2004.pdf

Perez, K., Gadgil, M., & Dizon, D. S. (2009). Sexual ramifications of medical illness. *Clinical Obstetrics and Gynecology, 52*, 691–701. doi:10.1097/GRF.0b013e3181bf4b4c

Perlis, R. H., Fava, M., Nierenberg, A. A., Pollack, M. H., Falk, W. E., Kienke, A. S., & Rosenbaum, J. F. (2002). Strategies for treatment of SSRI-associated sexual dysfunction: A survey of an academic psychopharmacology practice. *Harvard Review of Psychiatry, 10*(2), 109–114.

Peterson, Z. D., & Janssen, E. (2007). Ambivalent affect and sexual response: The impact of co-occurring positive and negative emotions on subjective and physiological sexual responses to erotic stimuli. *Archives of Sexual Behavior, 36*, 793–807. doi:10.1007/s10508-006-9145-0

Philpott, A., Knerr, W., & Boydell, V. (2006). Pleasure and prevention: When good sex is safer sex. *Reproductive Health Matters, 14*, 23–31. doi:10.1016/S0968-8080(06)28254-5

Ponizovsky, A. M. (2008). Clinical and psychosocial factors associated with quality of life in alcohol-dependent men with erectile dysfunction. *Journal of Sexual Medicine, 5*, 2347–2358. doi:10.1111/j.1743-6109.2008.00882.x

Pownall, J. D., Jahoda, A., Hastings, R., & Kerr, L. (2011). Sexual understanding and development of young people with intellectual disabilities: Mothers' perspectives of within-family context. *American Journal on Intellectual and Developmental Disabilities, 116*, 205–219. doi:10.1352/1944-7558-116.3.205

Prause, N., Staley, C., & Finn, P. (2011). Effects of acute ethanol consumption on sexual arousal and sexual risk taking. *Archives of Sexual Behavior, 40*, 373–384. doi:10.1007/s10508-010-9718-9

Prestage, G., Jin, F., Kippax, S., Zablotska, I., Imrie, J., & Grulich, A. (2009). Use of illicit drugs and erectile dysfunction medications and subsequent HIV infection among gay men in Sydney, Australia. *Journal of Sexual Medicine, 6*, 2311–2320. doi:10.1111/j.1743-6109.2009.01323.x

Purdie, M. P., Norris, J., Davis, K. C., Zawacki, T., Morrison, D. M., George, W. H., & Kiekel, P. A. (2011). The effects of acute alcohol intoxication, partner risk level, and general intention to have unprotected sex on women's sexual decision making with a new partner. *Experimental and Clinical Psychopharmacology, 19*, 378–388. doi:10.1037/a0024792

Raj, A., Saitz, R., Cheng, D. M., Winter, M., & Samet, J. H. (2007). Associations between alcohol, heroin, and cocaine use and high risk sexual behaviors among detoxification patients. *American Journal of Drug and Alcohol Abuse, 33*, 169–178. doi:10.1080/00952990601091176

Rawson, R. A., Washton, A., Domier, C. P., & Reiber, C. (2002). Drugs and sexual effects: Role of drug type and gender. *Journal of Substance Abuse Treatment, 22*, 103–108. doi:10.1016/S0740-5472(01)00215-X

Rehm, J., Shield, K. D., Joharchi, N., & Shuper, P. A. (2012). Alcohol consumption and the intention to engage in unprotected sex: Systematic review and meta-analysis of experimental studies. *Addiction, 107*, 51–59. doi:10.1111/j.1360-0443.2011.03621.x

Rubin, H. B., & Henson, D. E. (1976). Effects of alcohol on male sexual responding. *Psychopharmacology, 47*, 123–134.

Sadeghi-Nejad, H., Wasserman, M., Weidner, W., Richardson, D., & Goldmeier, D. (2010). Sexually transmitted diseases and sexual function. *Journal of Sexual Medicine, 7*, 389–413. doi:10.1111/j.1743-6109.2009.01622.x

Sadovsky, R., Basson, R., Krychman, M., Morales, A. M., Schover, L., Wang, R., & Incrocci, L. (2010). Cancer and sexual problems. *Journal of Sexual Medicine, 7*, 349–373. doi:10.1111/j.1743-6109.2009.01620.x

Sánchez, J., Comerford, M., Chitwood, D. D., Fernandez, M. I., & McCoy, C. B. (2002). High-risk sexual behaviours among heroin sniffers who have no history of injection drug use: Implications for HIV risk reduction. *AIDS Care, 14*, 391–398. doi:10.1080/09540120220123793

Sanjuan, P. M., Langenbucher, J. W., & Labouvie, E. (2009). The role of sexual assault and sexual dysfunction in alcohol/other drug use disorders. *Alcoholism Treatment Quarterly, 27*, 150–163. doi:10.1080/07347320902785541

Satcher, D. (2001). *The Surgeon General's call to action to promote sexual health and responsible sexual behavior.* Washington, DC: U.S. Department of Health and Human Services.

Schacht, R. L., George, W. H., Davis, K. C., Heiman, J. R., Norris, J., Stoner, S. A., & Kajumulo, K. F. (2010). Sexual abuse history, alcohol intoxication, and women's sexual risk behavior. *Archives of Sexual Behavior, 39*, 898–906. doi:10.1007/s10508-009-9544-0

Schacht, R. L., George, W. H., Heiman, J. R., Davis, K. C., Norris, J., Stoner, S. A., & Kajumulo, K. F. (2007). Effects of alcohol intoxication and instructional set on women's sexual arousal vary based on sexual abuse history. *Archives of Sexual Behavior, 36*, 655–665. doi:10.1007/s10508-006-9147-y

Schilder, A. J., Lampinen, T. M., Miller, M. L., & Hogg, R. S. (2005). Crystal methamphetamine and ecstasy differ in relation to unsafe sex among young gay men. *Canadian Journal of Public Health, 96*, 340–343. Retrieved from http://journal.cpha.ca/index.php/cjph/article/view/667/667.

Schnatz, P. F., Whitehurst, S. K., & O'Sullivan, D. M. (2010). Sexual dysfunction, depression, and anxiety among patients of an inner-city menopause clinic. *Journal of Women's Health, 19*, 1843–1849. doi:10.1089/jwh.2009.1800

Schrooten, W., Colebunders, R., Youle, M., Molenberghs, G., Dedes, N., Koitz, G., . . . Dreezen, C. (2001). Sexual dysfunction associated with protease inhibitor containing highly active antiretroviral treatment. *AIDS, 15*, 1019–1023. doi:10.1097/00002030-200105250-00010

Schweitzer, I., Maguire, K., & Ng, C. (2009). Sexual side-effects of contemporary antidepressants [Review]. *Australian and New Zealand Journal of Psychiatry, 43*, 795–808. doi:10.1080/00048670903107575

Scott, J. L., & Kayser, K. (2009). A review of couple-based interventions for enhancing women's sexual adjustment and body image after cancer. *Cancer Journal, 15*, 48–56. doi:10.1097/PPO.0b013e31819585df

Semple, S. J., Strathdee, S. A., Zians, J., & Patterson, T. L. (2009). Sexual risk behavior associated with co-administration of methamphetamine and other drugs in a sample of HIV-positive men who have sex with men. *American Journal on Addictions, 18*, 65–72. doi:10.1080/10550490802544466

Servais, L. (2006). Sexual Health Care in Persons with Intellectual Disabilities. *Mental Retardation and Developmental Disabilities Research Reviews, 12*, 48–56. doi:10.1002/mrdd.20093

Seto, M. C. (1992). A review of anxiety and sexual arousal in human sexual dysfunction. *Annals of Sex Research, 5*, 33–43. doi:10.1177/107906329200500102

Shacham, E., & Cottler, L. B. (2010). Sexual behaviors among club drug users: Prevalence and reliability. *Archives of Sexual Behavior, 39*, 1331–1341. doi:10.1007/s10508-009-9539-x

Shindel, A. W., Eisenberg, M. L., Breyer, B. N., Sharlip, I. D., & Smith, J. F. (2011). Sexual function and depressive symptoms among female North American medical students. *Journal of Sexual Medicine, 8*, 391–399. doi:10.1111/j.1743-6109.2010.02085.x

Shrier, L. A., Schillinger, J. A., Aneja, P., Rice, P. A., Batteiger, B. E., Braslins, P. G., . . . Fortenberry, J. D. (2009). Depressive symptoms and sexual risk behavior in young, chlamydia-infected, heterosexual dyads. *Journal of Adolescent Health, 45*, 63–69. doi:10.1016/j.jadohealth.2008.11.016

Siebelink, E. M., de Jong, M. T., Taal, E., & Roelvink, L. (2006). Sexuality and people with intellectual disabilities: Assessment of knowledge, attitudes, experiences, and needs. *Mental Retardation, 44*, 283–294. doi:10.1352/0047-6765(2006)44[283:SAPWID]2.0.CO;2

Sikkema, K. J., Watt, M. H., Drabkin, A. S., Meade, C. S., Hansen, N. B., & Pence, B. W. (2010). Mental health treatment to reduce HIV transmission risk behavior: A positive prevention model. *AIDS and Behavior, 14*, 252–262. doi:10.1007/s10461-009-9650-y

Smith, A. M. A., Ferris, J. A., Simpson, J. M., Shelley, J., Pitts, M. K., & Richters, J. (2010). Cannabis use and sexual health. *Journal of Sexual Medicine, 7*, 787–793. doi:10.1111/j.1743-6109.2009.01453.x

Smith, G. D., Frankel, S., & Yarnell, J. (1997). Sex and death: Are they related? Findings from the Caerphilly Cohort Study. *British Medical Journal, 315*, 1641–1644. doi:10.1136/bmj.315.7123.1641

Smith, J. F., Breyer, B. N., Eisenberg, M. L., Sharlip, I. D., & Shindel, A. W. (2010). Sexual function and depressive symptoms among male North American medical students. *Journal of Sexual Medicine, 7*, 3909–3917. doi:10.1111/j.1743-6109.2010.02033.x

Sobczak, J. A. (2009a). Alcohol use and sexual function in women: A literature review. *Journal of Addictions Nursing, 20*, 71–85. doi:10.1080/10884600902850095

Sobczak, J. A. (2009b). Struggling to reconnect: Women's perspectives on alcohol dependence, violence, and sexual function. *Journal of the American Psychiatric Nurses Association, 14*, 421–428. doi:10.1177/1078390308325577

Sprecher, S., & Cate, R. M. (2004). Sexual satisfaction and sexual expression as predictors of relationship satisfaction and stability. In J. Harvey, A. Wenzel, & S. Sprecher (Eds.), *Handbook of sexuality in close relationships* (pp. 235–256). Mahwah, NJ: Erlbaum.

Steele, C. M., & Josephs, R. A. (1990). Alcohol myopia: Its prized and dangerous effects. *American Psychologist, 45*(8), 921–933. doi:10.1037/0003-066X.45.8.921

Stefánsson, J. G., Líndal, E., Björnsson, J. K., & Güdmundsdóttir, Á. (1994). Period prevalence rates of specific mental disorders in an Icelandic cohort. *Social Psychiatry and Psychiatric Epidemiology, 29*, 119–125.

Stein, L. A. R., Lebeau, R., Clair, M., Martin, R., Bryant, M., Storti, S., & Monti, P. (2011). A web-based study of gamma hydroxybutyrate (GHB): Patterns, experiences, and functions of use. *American Journal on Addictions, 20*, 30–39. doi:10.1111/j.1521-0391.2010.00099.x

Steinke, E. E. (2005). Intimacy needs and chronic illness. *Journal of Gerontological Nursing, 31*, 40–50.

Stewart, J. G., & Harkness, K. L. (2012). Symptom specificity in the acute treatment of Major Depressive Disorder: A re-analysis of the treatment of depression collaborative research program. *Journal of Affective Disorders, 137*, 87–97. doi:10.1016/j.jad.2011.12.015

Stinson, J., Christian, L., & Dotson, L. (2002). Overcoming barriers to the sexual expression of women with developmental disabilities. *Research and Practice for Persons with Severe Disabilities, 27*, 18–26. doi:10.2511/rpsd.27.1.18

Stoner, S. A., Norris, J., George, W. H., Morrison, D. M., Zawacki, T., Davis, K. C., & Hessler, D. M. (2008). Women's condom use assertiveness and sexual risk-taking: Effects of alcohol intoxication and adult victimization. *Addictive Behaviors*, 33, 1167–1176. doi:10.1016/j.addbeh.2008.04.017

Substance Abuse and Mental Health Services Administration. (2011). *Results from the 2010 National Survey on Drug Use and Health: Detailed tables (NSDUH Series H-41, HHS Publication No. (SMA) 11–4658)*. Retrieved from http://oas.samhsa.gov/NSDUH/2k10NSDUH/tabs/Cover.pdf

Sutherland, M. A., Fantasia, H. C., & McClain, N. (in press). Abuse experiences, substance use, and reproductive health in women seeking care at an emergency department. *Journal of Emergency Nursing: JEN*. doi:10.1016/j.jen.2011.09.011

Taylor, M. J. (2006). Strategies for managing antidepressant-induced sexual Dysfunction: A review. *Current Psychiatry Reports, 8*, 431–436. doi:10.1007/s11920-006-0047-6

ter Kuile, M. M., Both, S., & van Uden, J. (2010). The effects of experimentally-induced sad and happy mood on sexual arousal in sexually healthy women. *Journal of Sexual Medicine, 7*, 1177–1184. doi:10.1111/j.1743-6109.2009.01632.x

Valencia, L. S., & Cromer, B. A. (2000). Sexual activity and other high-risk behaviors in adolescents with chronic illness: A review. *Journal of Pediatric and Adolescent Gynecology, 13*, 53–64. doi:10.1016/S1083-3188(00)00004-8

van den Hout, M., & Barlow, D. H. (2000). Attention, arousal and expectancies in anxiety and sexual disorders. *Journal of Affective Disorders, 61*, 241–256. doi:10.1016/S0165-0327(00)00341-4

Van Minnen, A., & Kampman, M. (2000). The interaction between anxiety and sexual functioning: A controlled study of sexual functioning in women with anxiety disorders. *Sexual and Relationship Therapy, 15*, 47–57. doi:10.1080/14681990050001556

Verschuren, J. E. A., Enzlin, P., Dijkstra, P. U., Geertzen, J. H. B., & Dekker, R. (2010). Chronic disease and sexuality: A generic conceptual framework. *Journal of Sex Research, 47*, 153–170. doi:10.1080/00224491003658227

Volkow, N. D., Wang, G., Fowler, J. S., Telang, F., Jayne, M., & Wong, C. (2007). Stimulant-induced enhanced sexual desire as a potential contributing factor in HIV transmission. *The American Journal of Psychiatry, 164*, 157–160. doi:10.1176/appi.ajp.l64.1.157

Wang, D., Noda, Y., Tsunekawa, H., Zhou, Y., Miyazaki, M., Senzaki, K., & Nabeshima, T. (2007). Behavioural and neurochemical features of olfactory bulbectomized rats resembling depression with comorbid anxiety. *Behavioural Brain Research, 178*, 262–273. doi:10.1016/j.bbr.2007.01.003

Weinhardt, L. S., & Carey, M. P. (2000). Does alcohol lead to sexual risk behavior? Findings from event-level research. *Annual Review of Sex Research, 11*, 125–157.

Werneke, U., Northey, S., & Bhugra, D. (2006). Antidepressants and sexual dysfunction. *Acta Psychiatrica Scandinavica, 114*, 384–397. doi:10.1111/j.1600-0447.2006.00890.x

Wiegel, M., Scepkowski, L. A., & Barlow, D. H. (2007). Cognitive-affective processes in sexual arousal and sexual dysfunction. In E. Janssen (Ed.), *The psychophysiology of sex* (pp. 143–165). Bloomington: Indiana University Press.

Wilsnack, S. C., Klassen, A. D., Schur, B. E., & Wilsnack, R. W. (1991). Predicting onset and chronicity of women's problem drinking: A five-year longitudinal analysis. *American Journal of Public Health, 81*, 305–318. doi:10.2105/AJPH.81.3.305

Wilsnack, S. C., Plaud, J. J., Wilsnack, R. W., & Klassen, A. D. (1997). Sexuality, gender, and alcohol use. In R. W. Wilsnack & S. C. Wilsnack (Eds.), *Gender and alcohol: Individual and social perspectives* (pp. 250–288). Piscataway, NJ: Rutgers Center of Alcohol Studies.

Wilson, G. T., & Lawson, D. M. (1976). Effects of alcohol on sexual arousal in women. *Journal of Abnormal Psychology, 85*, 489–497. doi:10.1037/0021-843X.85.5.489

Wilson, G. T., & Lawson, D. M. (1978). Expectancies, alcohol, and sexual arousal in women. *Journal of Abnormal Psychology, 87*, 358–367. doi:10.1037/0021-843X.87.8.358

Wilson, G. T., Lawson, D. M., & Abrams, D. B. (1978). Effects of alcohol on sexual arousal in male alcoholics. *Journal of Abnormal Psychology, 87*, 609–616.

Wilson, G. T., Niaura, R. S., & Adler, J. L. (1985). Alcohol, selective attention and sexual arousal in men. *Journal of Studies on Alcohol, 46*, 107–115.

Wilson, T. E., Jean-Louis, G., Schwartz, R., Golub, E. T., Cohen, M. H., Maki, P., . . . Lindau, S. (2010). HIV infection and women's sexual functioning. *Journal of Acquired Immune Deficiency Syndromes, 54*, 360–367.

Wolchik, S. A., Beggs, V. E., Wincze, J. P., Sakheim, D. K., Barlow, D. H., & Mavissakalian, M. (1980). The effect of emotional arousal on subsequent sexual arousal in men. *Journal of Abnormal Psychology, 89*, 595–598. doi:10.1037/0021-843X.89.4.595

Woods, N. F., Mitchell, E. S., & Julio, K. S. (2010). Sexual desire during the menopausal transition and early postmenopause: Observations from the Seattle Midlife Women's Health Study. *Journal of Women's Health, 19*, 209–218. doi:10.1089/jwh.2009.1388

World Association for Sexual Health. (2008). *Sexual Health for the Millennium. A Declaration and Technical Document*. Minneapolis, MH: World Association for Sexual Health. Retrieved from http://www.world-sexology.org/sites/default/files/Millennium%20Declaration%20(English).pdf

World Health Organization. (1946). *Official records of the World Health Organization*. Geneva, Switzerland: Author.

World Health Organization. (1975). *Education and treatment in human sexuality: The training of health professionals* (Technical Report Series No. 572). Geneva, Switzerland: Author.

World Health Organization (2010). *Developing sexual health programmes: A framework for action*. Retrieved from http://whqlibdoc.who.int/hq/2010/WHO_RHR_HRP_10.22_eng.pdf

Wormith, J. S., Bradford, J. M., Pawlak, A., Borzecki, M., & Zohar, A. (1988). The assessment of deviant sexual arousal as a function of intelligence, instructional set and alcohol ingestion. *Canadian Journal of Psychiatry, 33*, 800–808.

Yeh, H. C., Lorenz, F. O., Wickrama, K. A., Conger, R. D., & Elder, G. H. (2006). Relationships among sexual satisfaction, marital quality, and marital instability in midlife. *Journal of Family Psychology, 20*, 339–343. doi:10.1037/0893-3200.20.2.339

Zawacki, T. (2011). Effects of alcohol on women's risky sexual decision making during social interactions in the laboratory. *Psychology of Women Quarterly, 35*, 107–118. doi:10.1177/0361684310384106

Zawacki, T., Norris, J., Hessler, D. M., Morrison, D. M., Stoner, S. A., George, W. H., . . . Abdallah, D. A. (2009). Effects of relationship motivation, partner familiarity, and alcohol on women's risky sexual decision making. *Personality and Social Psychology Bulletin, 35*, 723–736. doi:10.1177/0146167209333043

Zemishlany, Z., Aizenberg, D., & Weizman, A. (2001). Subjective effects of MDMA ("Ecstasy") on human sexual function. *European Psychiatry, 16*(2), 127–130. doi:10.1016/S0924-9338(01)00550-8.

CHAPTER 22

SEXUALITY AND HIV/AIDS PREVENTION

José A. Bauermeister, Katherine S. Elkington, and David Huebner

The HIV/AIDS epidemic has had long-term and ongoing influences on how sexuality-related behavioral research and interventions are conceptualized, implemented, and evaluated. The pressing need to intervene in the HIV/AIDS epidemic promoted discussions of sexuality in public and scientific forums, highlighted the need to proactively communicate about sex in our communities, and facilitated the development of HIV/AIDS prevention approaches that considered the context and meaning of sexual behavior (Aggleton, 2004; Boyce et al., 2007; R. Parker et al., 2004). Propelled by the continued demands of the epidemic, sexuality research continues to influence the field of HIV-related research in the way that we conceive of HIV risk, prevention, treatment, and care.

This chapter provides a synthesis of the HIV/AIDS prevention approaches that have focused on sexual behavior over the past 30 years, and notes the reciprocal influences of the fields of sexuality and HIV research. The chapter begins with a brief overview of the HIV/AIDS epidemic. It then presents a review of HIV/AIDS prevention approaches focused on individual, interpersonal, ecologic, and biomedical strategies. Finally, it concludes with a call for integrated, multilevel HIV/AIDS research and intervention approaches.[1]

STATE OF THE EPIDEMIC

On June 5, 1981, the Centers for Disease Control and Prevention (CDC) published a report on five young gay men in Los Angeles with a rare form of pneumonia usually seen among severely immunosuppressed individuals (CDC, 1981b). The report suggested presciently that it was possible that this unusual epidemic could somehow be related to sexual behavior or some other aspect of the "homosexual lifestyle." A month later, the CDC reported a similarly unusual outbreak of Kaposi's sarcoma among 26 gay men in both New York and Los Angeles as well as an additional 10 cases of pneumocystis pneumonia, some in the same men (CDC, 1981a). Although it is now clear that the disease that would come to be known as acquired immune deficiency syndrome (AIDS) had been circulating in isolated places around the world for decades, these reports marked the first public recognition of what was soon to become an international epidemic.

In the three decades since those original reports, approximately 30 million people have died from AIDS around the world, and another 33.3 million are living with HIV (UNAIDS, 2010). Estimates suggest that 2.6 million people are newly infected each year, and that 1.8 million people die annually from AIDS-related causes. Although no part of the world is unaffected by HIV/AIDS, the most dramatic impact has been felt in Sub-Saharan Africa, where approximately 69% of all new infections in the world occur (see Volume 2, Chapter 9, this handbook). In this region, heterosexuals account for the large majority of new infections, although virtually

[1]Consistent with the scope of our chapter, we do not include in our review behavioral prevention strategies that focus on injection drug use nor on secondary prevention or treatment adherence approaches targeting HIV-positive individuals (a recent synthesis of these and other HIV/AIDS related topics is available in a recent publication by Hall, Hall, & Cockerell, 2011).

http://dx.doi.org/10.1037/14193-022
APA Handbook of Sexuality and Psychology: Vol. 1. Person-Based Approaches, D. L. Tolman and L. M. Diamond (Editors-in-Chief)

every subset of the population is affected. In contrast, other regions of the world have more specific epidemics. For instance, in Asia, the populations most affected include sex workers and their clients, injection drug users (IDUs), and men who have sex with men (MSM). In Eastern Europe, international heroin trade routes through the region have led to an explosion of injection drug use, and a corresponding HIV epidemic that is concentrated in IDUs but that more recently is spreading among sex workers and their clients.

In the United States, sexual activity is the most common route of HIV transmission. MSM continue to account for the largest proportion of new infections each year (61%), followed by heterosexuals (27%), and IDUs (9%). Within each of these groups, people of color, in particular African Americans, are represented disproportionately. Although African Americans represent only 14% of the U.S. population, they accounted for 44% of new infections in 2009 (CDC, 2011a). Given the critical role sexual behavior plays in the spread of HIV around the world, we now turn our attention to different HIV/AIDS prevention approaches employed over the past 30 years of the epidemic.

Sexuality Research and Its Applications to the HIV/AIDS Epidemic

The proliferation of HIV to virtually every part of the world, together with its affinity for populations who are historically marginalized, necessitated that researchers find ways to study and understand diverse sexual practices across a host of cultural contexts (see Volume 2, Chapter 6, this handbook). The early stages of the HIV/AIDS epidemic highlighted our limited understanding of sexuality at that time, one that relied on primarily biomedical or psychiatric conceptualizations of sexuality largely characterized by an absence of the social context (R. Parker, 2009b; R. Parker et al., 2004; see Chapter 5, this volume). When information about sexual behavior was needed to understand and address sexual transmission of HIV/AIDS, the limited body of knowledge regarding sexuality and sexual practices became apparent, particularly in marginalized groups most affected by HIV/AIDS early in the epidemic—MSM, IDUs, immigrants, and sex workers (Gagnon, 1988). Undoubtedly, sexuality as a field would be vital to provide a context and theoretical framework by which to understand human sexual behavior. From an applied public health perspective, however, the field of sexuality was somewhat fragmented and marginalized, with limited infrastructure in place to support scholarly research in this area (Gagnon, 1988; R. Parker, 2009b). The urgency created by the epidemic, specifically the need to understand disease transmission, identify the epidemiology of the riskiest behaviors, and develop prevention programming, all resulted in a large increase of resources in both social and behavioral research for examining sexuality and sexual risk behavior among diverse population groups (R. Parker, 2009b). Thus, as the epidemic advanced, the field of sexuality evolved and expanded, being both influenced by and influencing HIV/AIDS research. As a result, HIV/AIDS research became populated by sexuality researchers as well as by psychologists and other health-oriented social scientists.

"DISEASE" AND INDIVIDUAL-LEVEL MODELS

The initial model or understanding that emerged as a result of this rapid increase in research on sexual behavior was a disease model of HIV/AIDS, concerned mostly with sexual risk behaviors and transmission (Aggleton, 2004; Boyce et al., 2007; Michaels & Giami, 1999; R. Parker, 2009a, 2009b). Within this disease model, HIV transmission was conceptualized as being the result of three interrelated factors: the agent, the vector, and the host. Consequently, sexual behaviors (e.g., condomless sexual intercourse, multiple partners of unknown or serodiscordant status) and injection drug use (e.g., sharing needles) were thought of merely as transmission routes (i.e., vectors) through which an HIV-infected individual (i.e., the host) could transmit the virus (i.e., the agent). Consequently, public health efforts sought to curtail transmission by encouraging individuals to adopt behavioral strategies that would decrease transmission.

Considerable emphasis was placed on "counting" sexual behaviors and practices (e.g., number of sexual partners, number of protected and unprotected sexual occasions, type of sexual partner) and identifying sex-related attitudes, information, or knowledge to develop informed prevention and care programs. Most of this research, however, was carried out in large-scale surveys in primarily Western or resource-rich settings. Although these sexual behavior studies collected little if any information on orgasm, masturbation, procreation, and desire, the considerable emphasis placed on diverse sexual practices such as same-sex or bisexual behaviors was an important addition to the literature. In so doing, it underscored that our knowledge of heterosexual normative behaviors would be inadequate and insufficient to respond to the populations most affected early in the epidemic (R. Parker, 2009b). This epidemiological understanding of sexual risk was the foundation for developing and evaluating HIV prevention interventions designed to change behavior that previously had been largely unexplored, particularly in more marginalized populations (Gagnon, 1988; R. Parker, 2009b; R. Parker et al., 2004; see Volume 2, Chapter 8, this handbook).

This epidemiological framework or disease model facilitated our early understanding of how the virus was transmitted. It conceptualized transmission as an individual-level problem requiring individual-level approaches. A fundamental corollary of this public health perspective was that *individual responsibility* was key to stopping the epidemic. For example, the National Institute of Mental Health (NIMH) created a task force to improve HIV prevention efforts and concluded that HIV is "first and foremost a consequence of behavior. *It is not who you are but what you do* that determine(s) whether or not you expose yourself to HIV, the virus that causes AIDS" (Fishbein et al., 1992, p. 5). This perspective was motivated further by well-meaning public health officials who sought to destigmatize the disease and the affected communities by decoupling identity from risk behaviors. Although this effort undoubtedly helped reduce stigma in already marginalized communities (e.g., gay men), it nevertheless contributed to an approach that examined sexual behavior apart from any social, relational, or cultural context.

Congruent with this philosophy, and having had success in explaining other health behaviors, value-expectancy theories such as the health belief model (Becker, 1974), the theory of reasoned action and planned behavior (Ajzen, 1991; Fishbein & Ajzen, 1975), and social cognitive theory (Bandura, 1986) were used to explain sexual behavior and informed HIV preventive interventions. At their core, these value-expectancy theories shared the assumption that if individuals, who possess autonomy to make behavioral choices, were provided with accurate information combined with attitudes, motivation, and skills to engage in safe sex behaviors, they would make careful and reasoned choices about sexual risk (D. Albarracín et al., 2005; Fishbein & Yzer, 2003). Researchers and public health practitioners, however, differed on what were the most important constructs to consider when targeting factors that influenced an individual's intention to engage in risk reduction behaviors. Using the health belief model, for example, it was posited that the likelihood of a behavior occurring (e.g., using condoms) was dependent on whether individuals had a high perceived threat toward HIV/AIDS; that is, risk reduction behaviors would occur only if individuals believed that they were susceptible to HIV infection (i.e., perceived susceptibility) and that the consequences of becoming HIV-infected were severe (i.e., perceived severity). Therefore, interventions based on this model targeted increasing perceived susceptibility to and severity of HIV. Interventions guided by the theory of reasoned action addressed behavior-specific attitudes and norms (e.g., beliefs and feelings about condom use), rather than the threat of disease, as predictors of someone's willingness (i.e., behavioral intention) to adopt and maintain risk-reducing behaviors (e.g., consistent condom use). Conversely, interventions based on social cognitive theory emphasized increasing an individual's self-efficacy (e.g., confidence to enact a behavior) to increase the likelihood of engaging in safer sex practices. Thus, as researchers tested the efficacy of these different HIV prevention interventions, each targeting different constructs in an attempt to reduce sexual risk behavior in various populations (Janz et al., 1996), salient constructs from each theory were identified and integrated into new HIV-specific intervention models, such as the AIDS risk reduction model (Catania, Kegeles, & Coates, 1990) or the information-motivation-behavioral skills model (Fisher & Fisher, 2002).

At present, very few interventions rely solely on a single theoretical model. Rather than focusing on the testing of these theories as originally developed, scholars and practitioners alike have sought to integrate theoretical concepts effective from each theory into new comprehensive frameworks, such as the integrated behavioral model (Fishbein & Cappella, 2006), to maximize the prediction of behavioral change and inform the adequate development of HIV prevention interventions. Several recent reviews and meta-analyses have found that individual-level interventions have proven efficacious in achieving reductions in risky sexual behavior (e.g., unprotected sex). For example, a meta-analysis of 14 behavioral HIV and sexually transmitted infection (STI) prevention interventions conducted between 1988 and 1996 for heterosexual adults found significant effects in reducing sex-related risks. The interventions also had significant effects in reducing STI infections (Neumann et al., 2002). Similarly, a review of 18 HIV/STI prevention interventions for drug-using adults published between 1985 and 1998 also found that interventions were successful in reducing overall risk, including targeting HIV-related knowledge, beliefs, and attitudes toward safer sex, sexual behavior, and risk reduction skills (Prendergast, Urada, & Podus, 2001). Finally, a recent review of 67 adolescent HIV/STI prevention programs published between 1985 and 2008 demonstrated efficacy overall in reducing new STIs, increasing condom use, reducing or delaying penetrative sex, and increasing skills to negotiate safer sex (Johnson, Scott-Sheldon, Huedo-Medina, & Carey, 2011).

Other individual-level HIV/AIDS prevention approaches have sought to reduce risk-related behaviors that may hinder safer sex practices, in particular, alcohol and substance use (Stevens et al., 2006; Thurstone, Riggs, Klein, & Mikulich-Gilbertson, 2007). Several meta-analyses and studies have documented the negative association between sexual risk behaviors and alcohol and drug use across numerous populations (e.g., MSM, IDU, sex workers, minority youth), although the strength of these associations varies depending on the specific type of substance use, how substance use is conceptualized (e.g., alcohol consumption frequency, alcohol use before or concurrent with sex, or problem drinking), and how use is measured across studies (Baliunas, Rehm, Irving, & Shuper, 2010; Collins et al., 2005; Fisher, Bang, & Kapiga, 2007; Leigh, 2002; D. Parker, Harford, & Rosenstock 1994; Shuper, Joharchi, Irving, & Rehm, 2009; Vosburgh, Mansergh, Sullivan, & Purcell, 2012). Nonetheless, this robust body of literature on the association between substance use and sexual risk highlighted for researchers and interventionists the importance of targeting substance use in addition to sexual risk in an effort to achieve sustained reductions in HIV risk behaviors (Collins et al., 2005).

Reviews of individual-level interventions designed for specific high-risk groups, such as adolescents, minorities, or HIV-positive adults, however, have found mixed results. Although the review by Johnson et al. (2011) suggested interventions for adolescents are effective, prior reviews found that effects of these adolescent interventions diminished over time with gains returning to baseline or near-baseline levels (DiClemente, Salazar, & Crosby, 2007; Pedlow & Carey, 2003). Furthermore, interventions for very high-risk youth populations, such as youth involved in the juvenile justice system, show modest ability to reduce sexual risk with more than 50% of interventions failing to have any effect compared with control conditions (Tolou-Shams, Stewart, Fasciano, & Brown, 2010). Similarly, a review of 277 studies worldwide, published before 2006, found that interventions groups with higher proportions of Latinos (more than 50%) were less likely to increase condom use and acquired less knowledge than groups with lower proportion of Latinos (less than 50%; J. Albarracín, Albarracín, & Durantini, 2008). In a review of 33 intervention studies in the United States, Semaan et al. (2002) found that the proportion of drug users who reduced their risk behavior was 12% greater in the intervention conditions as compared with control groups, highlighting the importance of developing sexual risk reductions for drug users. Finally, a review of 15 studies examining risk reduction in HIV-infected participants found that interventions successfully increased condom use compared with control interventions, but they were more likely to be successful at increasing condom use if the sample included fewer MSM (Johnson, Carey, Chaudoir, & Reid, 2006). Taken together, these findings are troubling given that interventions have been less effective in reducing risk in the populations that are disproportionately affected by HIV/AIDS.

In light of these literature reviews and meta-analyses, evidence suggests that individual-level interventions may not adequately address HIV risk prevention for certain high-risk groups. Undoubtedly, the use of these individual-level models will continue to evolve as a critical piece of the arsenal to reduce and eliminate HIV; however, for high-risk groups, researchers have argued that interventions could be improved by targeting aspects of the individual's larger social or environmental context (D. Albarracín, Rothman, DiClemente, & Rio, 2010; D. Albarracín, Tannenbaum, Glasman, & Rothman, 2010; Johnson et al., 2010; Latkin, Weeks, Glasman, Galletly, & Albarracín, 2010). One direction that shows promise is the combination of these individual-level models with theoretical frameworks focused on social-relational, community, and structural perspectives.

Ecological Approaches

The approach to understanding sex strictly in the context of an individual at risk for disease has been criticized because of its tendency to create a quantified, rational explanation of sexual behavior and for its lack of attention to the differences in sexual behavior across different populations and settings (Aggleton, 2004; Boyce et al., 2007). Many, including those in the field of sexuality, have argued that quantifying specific behaviors alone was insufficient to understand the experience of an individual's sexuality and sexual behavior, which is informed by a complex interplay of individual, intrapersonal, and cultural and contextual factors (Aggleton, 2004; Boyce et al., 2007). Given the emphasis on keeping people alive via rational changes in risk behavior, some have argued that HIV behavior research and related risk reduction programming had abandoned the understanding of sex and sexuality, and how it fit into social, cultural, and psychological life (Aggleton, 2004; Gagnon, 1988). For example, referring to the 1992 NIMH Task Force report, Díaz and Ayala (2001) noted that the individual-level perspective had "failed to note that 'who you are'—not in terms of individual identity, but in terms of social location within a context of social oppressive factors—determines to a great extent what you can and cannot do" (p. 4). Acknowledging that individuals do not live in a systemic vacuum, Díaz and Ayala (2001) highlighted how community factors are associated with successful HIV prevention initiatives:

> We must first acknowledge that HIV risk is not simply an intra-individual factor or the property of certain individuals. In other words, HIV is not transmitted simply because there are risky individuals who practice risky behaviors on account of their individual personal deficits in morality, cognition or behavioral skills. Rather, our findings demand a conceptualization of "health risk" as a characteristic of socially produced contexts. These are social contexts of risk where individuals lose their power to enact their protective intentions, or where unsafe practices are perhaps the only viable and adaptive survival strategy. While individuals' values, cognitions, emotions and skills do become an integral part of the social contexts in which they participate, risk is the product of such social and contextual participation, rather than simply a personal trait that individuals bring along and enact across all situations and circumstances. (p. 24)

Thus, as HIV research embraced a more nuanced view of sexual behavior informed by a more comprehensive view of sexuality, the field moved beyond intraindividual models, and research and intervention approaches focused on interpersonal (e.g., dyadic, familial, and peer) and ecological contexts (e.g., community) were integrated into ongoing efforts and strategies (see Volume 2, Chapters 6, 8, and 9, this handbook). We present a synthesis of these different domains below.

Interpersonal and Social-Relational Models

With an increased awareness of the importance of the larger context in individual sexual behavior came a gradual shift in the emphasis of HIV behavioral research. The field began to attend more directly to approaches previously taken by the broader sexuality literature. Specifically, the field acknowledged the importance of the interpersonal or relational context as a key component to understanding HIV/AIDS risk (J. Kelly & Kalichman, 1995). Foci of such research included the examination of how the romantic or sexual relationship context influenced the enactment of sexual scripts within couples (e.g., power imbalance, meaning of condom use, sexual experience within close or romantic versus casual relationships), or how key social processes across social–relational contexts, including family (e.g., parental communication and monitoring) and peer processes (e.g., peer norms), influenced sexual behavior (see Chapter 10, this volume). We briefly synthesize work carried out in these settings below.

Couples

The dominant theories of behavior change underpinning many of the individual-level interventions previously described tend to focus primarily on the role of cognitive or behavioral processes that operate at the level of the individual, such as self-efficacy, personal beliefs, motivations, or intentions to perform specific behaviors. A larger body of literature, however, began to identify the influence of partner and relationship factors on sexual behavior, such as gender roles, intimacy, communication, negotiation, relationship dependencies, and balance of sexual power (Amaro, 1995; Diamond, 2003; Gebhardt, Kuyper, & Greunsven, 2003; Gómez & VanOss Marín, 1996; Hoff et al., 1997; J. Kelly & Kalichman, 1995; Tolman & Diamond, 2001; see Chapters 1 and 2, this volume). For example, within the dyadic research carried out, sexual relationship power became a focus to understand the gender inequality in men and women's vulnerability for HIV/AIDS. Sexual relationship power refers to the relative ability of one partner to act independently, to dominate decision making, to engage in behavior against a partner's wishes, or to control a partner's actions (Pulerwitz, Amaro, De Jong, Gortmaker, & Rudd, 2002). Unequal power relations in sexual relationships can have a detrimental influence on an individual's sexual health (Bauermeister, Zimmerman, Caldwell, Xue, & Gee, 2010; Bowleg, Belgrave, & Reisen, 2000; Gómez & VanOss Marín, 1996; R. Parker, 2001; Salazar et al., 2004). In their adaptation of the theory of gender and power to HIV prevention, Wingood and DiClemente (2002) proposed that HIV/STI risks are greatest for females because they may be overexposed to social, physical, and economic risks that promote unequal gender power imbalances, limit safer sex decision making, and increase their vulnerability to HIV/AIDS, STIs, and unintended pregnancy.

Drawing on this larger body of work, several researchers developed HIV/STI prevention interventions that address ongoing dynamic social processes within couples that contribute to sexual risk behaviors. The first evidence to suggest that couples-based interventions were efficacious in reducing risk comes from voluntary counseling and HIV testing (VCT) studies conducted mainly overseas (Allen et al., 1992; Deschamps, Pape, Haffner, Hyppolite, & Johnson, 1991; Padian, O'Brien, Chang, Glass, & Francis, 1993). For example, although not designed as a couples study, Allen et al. (1992) conducted a study of VCT among 1,458 Rwandan women and found that at the 2-year follow-up, HIV-negative women whose partners had participated were 50% less likely to seroconvert than were those whose partners had not participated. In one of the first studies to evaluate a couples-based VCT prevention program in the United States, Padian et al. (1993) examined behavioral change among 144 HIV serodiscordant heterosexual couples. About half (49%) of the couples reported consistent condom use before the intervention, whereas 88% reported consistent condom use at first follow-up.

Building on these early successes, interventionists began to theorize that couples-based intervention programs may be more successful in reducing sexual risk and HIV transmission in serodiscordant couples than traditional individual-level approaches (NIMH Multisite HIV Prevention Trial for African American Couples Group, 2008). Couples-based programs reduce sexual risk by increasing commitment to the relationship and to protecting the other partner from HIV/STIs, reducing gendered power imbalances that influence condom use, and improving communication and condom negotiation skills (Basen-Engquist, 1992; J. Kelly, 1995; Mintz, 1994; O'Leary & Wingood, 2000; Tanner & Pollack,

1988). This frequently is achieved by targeting the intimate relationship as the *focus* of change and defining the couple as the *agent* of change (El-Bassel et al., 2003, 2005). Relationship-based couples HIV/STI prevention interventions have been successful in decreasing unprotected sex and increasing the use of condoms in heterosexual couples (El-Bassel et al., 2003, 2005), reducing the risk of HIV transmission in serodiscordant couples (Davis & Friel, 2001; Deschamps et al., 1991; El-Bassel et al., 2010), and increasing condom use and decreasing unsafe injection acts at the 3-month follow-up in IDUs (Gilbert, El-Bassel, Terlikbayeva, & Rozental, 2010). Compared with individual-based interventions, however, fewer couples-based interventions have been developed and empirically tested. Despite the success of couples-based interventions, authors of a recent meta-analytic review of randomized controlled trials published between 2000 and 2007 (Burton, Darbes, & Operario, 2010) concluded that given the heterogeneity of samples, intervention approaches, and control groups, further research on the key components of successful behavior change in couples interventions is warranted.

Family, Peers, and Social Networks

In addition to appreciating the inherently dyadic nature of a sexual encounter, researchers also began to explore other interpersonal or social settings that may shape sexual behaviors, such as the family or peer groups. This was particularly true among youth who emerged as a group at increased risk for HIV infection later in the epidemic (CDC, 2000; see Chapter 15, this volume). Because adolescents exist in multiple interconnected systems that affect their behavior either directly and indirectly (Bronfenbrenner, 1979b) and given the limited success of youth-only intervention programs, some researchers have argued that to achieve sustained sexual risk reduction in youth, interventions must not only target individual-level determinants of risk but also address the larger context (DiClemente et al., 2007; DiClemente & Wingood, 2000; Elkington, Bauermeister, & Zimmerman, 2011; Malow, Rosenberg, Donenberg, & Devieux, 2006; Tolou-Shams et al., 2010). The family, one of the most proximal influences on youth, is widely recognized to play an important role in the emotional and behavioral development of children and adolescents, and it is seen as a key agent of change in adolescent sexual risk behavior (Repetti, Taylor, & Seeman, 2002). In particular, affective characteristics such as family involvement, cohesion, and parental support are integral to a youth's development of healthy romantic or intimate relationships and practice of safer sexual behavior (Donenberg, Paikoff, & Pequegnat, 2006). Close family relationships and involvement and parental support have been associated with more condom use, less exposure to risky situations, and later onset of sexual activity in youth (Donenberg, Bryant, Emerson, Wilson, & Pasch, 2003; Perrino, Gonzalez-Soldevilla, Pantin, & Szapocznik, 2000; Repetti et al., 2002; Teitelman, 2004). Conversely, youth who grow up in families characterized by overt family conflict and parental substance use or abuse and who have neglectful or unsupportive family relationships are more likely to engage in risky behaviors, including substance abuse and risky sexual activity (Donenberg et al., 2003; Repetti et al., 2002).

Guided by ecological models of behavior change, family-based HIV prevention programs successfully have reduced HIV risk behavior by adding components to standard individual-level interventions that improve processes such as parent-child communication, quality of relationships, and parental monitoring and involvement (DiIorio et al., 2006; Forehand et al., 2007; McKay et al., 2004; Prado et al., 2007; Repetti et al., 2002). A recent review of 21 U.S. family-based interventions published between 1990 and 2010, however, found inconsistent effects of family or parent-based HIV/STI prevention interventions on youth sexual risk behavior, with several interventions showing success in reducing adolescent sexual risk behavior outcomes. Several of these studies were effective in improving targeted intervention mediators, such as parent–child communication; family functioning; and parent or child norms, attitudes, and HIV-related knowledge. Increases in these outcomes, however, did not always translate into decreases in adolescent sexual risk (Downing, Jones, Bates, Sumnall and Bellis 2011). Again, the authors concluded that given the heterogeneity of samples, control groups, intervention approaches, and targeted outcomes, continued research on the successful mechanisms of change in family-based interventions remains crucial.

In addition to family dynamics, peer relationships are another important social influence on sexual behavior. HIV/AIDS interventions for adolescents have focused particular attention on peer beliefs and norms. In a recent review of the literature, Buhi and Goodson (2007) identified peer norms regarding acceptability of sexual behavior and the number of peers who are perceived to be sexually active as two peer-related indicators that were associated with sexual onset and sexual risk behaviors among adolescents. Peers within adolescents' social networks may reinforce positive or negative attitudes and behaviors regarding safer sex practices (D. Albarracín, Kumkale, & Johnson, 2004; Lewis, DeVellis, & Sleath, 2002) and may be mobilized to promote condom use and shift group norms among peers (Fang, Stanton, Li, Feigelman, & Baldwin, 1998). For example, youth engaged in risky sexual activity or substance use are more likely to be involved with a peer group who engages in that risky behavior and to associate with peer groups who possess favorable attitudes toward sex or drug use (Bachanas et al., 2002; Bauermeister, Elkington, Brackis-Cott, Dolezal, & Mellins, 2009; Elkington, Bauermeister, Brackis-Cott, Dolezal, & Mellins, 2009). On the other hand, peers who are supportive and engage in prosocial behaviors and whose norms support condom use and other safe sex behaviors are associated with protective behaviors (e.g., reduced substance use, increased condom use) in youth (Buhi & Goodson, 2007; Romer et al., 1994; Stanton et al., 2002).

Despite the importance of the peer context in either promoting or off-setting risk, comparatively few HIV/STI interventions include adolescent friend groups or target youth–friend dyads. Those that do have shown mixed results with some evidence to suggest reduced risk behavior (Dolcini, Harper, Boyer, & Pollack, 2010; Dolcini et al., 2008; Fang et al., 1998; Medley, Kennedy, O'Reilly, & Sweat, 2009), whereas others have shown minimal if any effects (Morrison et al., 2007), or diminishing effects over time, particularly in comparison with other intervention modalities such as school-based interventions (Fisher, Fisher, Bryan, & Misovich, 2002; Stanton, Kim, Galbraith, & Parrott, 1996). Furthermore, some peer-based interventions have had problematic impacts on outcomes (Dishion, McCord, & Poulin, 1999; Luna & Rotheram-Borus, 1999), with unintended negative effects labeled as "risk training" or "deviancy training." For example, outcomes associated with sexual risk such as delinquency and substance use have been affected negatively by peer-based intervention approaches, leading to worse HIV-related outcomes in adulthood (Dishion, McCord, & Poulin, 1999). Researchers hypothesize that high-risk youth are more susceptible to frequent interactions with negative or deviant peers compared with their low-risk counterparts. Such interactions with negative or deviant peers in treatment settings (e.g., intervention groups) in adolescence, under some circumstances, inadvertently may reinforce risky behaviors (for further discussion, see Dishion et al., 1999). Similarly, peer-led interventions also have shown inconsistent results with respect to achieving reductions in risky sexual behavior (C. Kim & Free, 2008; Maticka-Tyndale & Barnett, 2010), suggesting that further research on the involvement of peers and friendship groups in interventions also is warranted. Despite the limited success of peer-led or peer-based interventions for youth, the majority of individual or family-based interventions developed for youth do target peer norms, include building behavioral skills for navigating peer pressure.

In contrast, peer-led or peer-based interventions for adults have met with greater success. These social network interventions are predicated on the idea that social situational factors likely have a stronger influence or effect on an individual's behavior than individual-level factors (Johnson et al., 2010). In addition, given the decay or lessening of intervention effects seen in individual-level interventions over relatively brief periods of time (e.g., more than 1 year), targeting social influences experienced in an individual's social network is posited to lead to longer or more sustained sexual risk behavior change (Wang, Brown, & Shen, 2011). As part of social network interventions, researchers identify an "index" network member who is the initial recruit. This individual either recruits known peers to participate in an intervention (referred to as network members) or, after completing an intervention him- or herself, identifies network members to whom she or he will relay intervention material via a process of diffusion of information.

In a recent review of 11 social network interventions implemented worldwide for a variety of populations, including IDUs, young MSM, youth, substance abusers, or female sex workers, Wang et al. (2011) found that all interventions were successful at either improving condom use or biological outcomes, with several studies reporting sustained behavior change at 12 months and beyond. The majority of reduction in unprotected sex was seen with casual rather than main partners. Despite successes, social network interventions can be complex and difficult to implement, requiring an important understanding of the social networks involved in each intervention. Furthermore, intervention success relies heavily on the motivation of the index participants to not only identify or involve network members in the intervention but also to disseminate this information (Wang et al., 2011).

Taken together, findings from interpersonal approaches and interventions have highlighted the importance of considering the reduction of sexual risk behaviors as a process situated in relational exchanges. In the context of examining these relationships, however, researchers have acknowledged that these exchanges are situated within, and may vary on the basis of, the psychosocial characteristics of the communities where individuals live. This acknowledgment has underscored the importance of developing HIV/AIDS prevention interventions that consider how social contexts may influence the expression of sexuality. The following section illustrates how community-level characteristics may shape the expression of sexual behavior and create unequal vulnerability to HIV/AIDS infection across communities.

COMMUNITY-LEVEL APPROACHES

One of the enduring characteristics of HIV/AIDS, throughout the history of the epidemic, has been its disproportionate impact on populations who are socially marginalized or economically disadvantaged (see Volume 2, Chapter 7, this handbook). In the face of an unwavering global epidemic, the field of sexuality had been spurred to examine larger ecological contexts to further our understanding of sexual behavior (Michael, Gagnon, Laumann, & Kolata, 1994). Drawing from this body of work, the field of HIV research moved beyond intraindividual models to those that appreciated the dyadic, familial, and cultural contexts for sexual behavior and also was forced to acknowledge the reality that the HIV/AIDS epidemic was fueled by even larger ecological contexts. That is, factors such as a community's degree of social organization, access to power and resources, and sociopolitical circumstances all had the potential to influence sexual behaviors (R. Parker, 2001). Moreover, they were linked to the very dynamics of infectious disease transmission as well as organizational efforts to intervene and disrupt those dynamics. Several ecological theorists have attempted to comprehensively describe how the multitude of relationships, systems, and forces outside of an individual shape that individual's behaviors (Barker, 1968; Bronfenbrenner, 1979a; Moos, 1974; see Volume 2, Chapter 9, this volume). This section of the chapter describes the somewhat-heterogeneous group of theories and HIV prevention methodologies that focus on understanding the factors that influence sexual behavior beyond the levels of the dyad, family, and peers described in previous sections. Thus, the emphasis in this section is on describing those components of the ecology of HIV-related sexual behavior that exist *at the level of the community and beyond.* For our purposes, we define *community* as a group of individuals who share characteristics or interests, such as culture, geography, or social position within society that distinguishes them from the larger population. This shared social identity serves to create collective psychological characteristics and patterns of social interaction and common experiences within formal organizations (Minkler & Wallerstein, 2002). The discussion is organized into three sections: psychological characteristics of communities (e.g., norms, empowerment), physical characteristics of communities (e.g., housing availability), and socioeconomic characteristics of communities (e.g., income, availability of employment). Although it is clear that these three areas are inextricably tied, and certainly overlap with one another, we have adopted this organization to simplify an extraordinarily large literature.

Psychological Characteristics of Communities

HIV/AIDS spotlighted a number of ways in which the psychological characteristics of communities could sustain or inhibit sexual behaviors that placed individuals at risk for disease. Community mobilization efforts focused on increasing communities' empowerment through grassroots HIV-prevention programming and developing preventative social norms (R. Parker, 2001; R. Parker, Easton, & Klein, 2000; see Volume 2, Chapters 7 and 8, this handbook). Long before HIV/AIDS emerged as a public health threat, theorists from a variety of disciplines had written about how a community's psychological characteristics, such as its norms or sense of empowerment, were important determinants of community health (Rappaport, 1977). Although these ideas were not incorporated explicitly into the earliest generation of HIV prevention interventions, the field gradually began to recognize the constructs at work in the way those early interventions unfolded. For example, early in the epidemic, gay men, a historically disenfranchised population with limited social influence, recognized that the federal government was not acting quickly enough to address the epidemic threatening their community. "Stop AIDS," a grassroots organization originating in San Francisco, began a house-party campaign in which gay men would invite other friends to their homes and educate one another about how to avoid HIV transmission (Puckett, Bart, Bye, & Amory, 1985). Although the emphasis was on providing information to individuals so that they would have the knowledge necessary to change their individual sexual behaviors, two additional processes were unfolding. First, this process of harnessing and developing indigenous resources and skills is central to the philosophy of community empowerment that previously had been described by scholars from a variety of disciplines (Ramirez-Valles, 2002; Wallerstein & Bernstein, 1988; Zimmerman, 2000), one that appeared to maximize the effects of the individual-level education that was occurring by demonstrating to men the power they had to collectively improve their community's health. Second, because friends in a social atmosphere provided the education, a redefinition of acceptable community norms for sexual behavior gradually emerged. That is, men not only obtained the information and skills that they needed to protect themselves but also learned that many of their friends were doing the same thing, thereby reinforcing their own individual motivation to change their behaviors. As messages about safer sex diffused throughout the community through these prevention efforts, observers of the phenomenon recognized this as an example of "diffusion of innovations" (Bertrand, 2004; Rogers, 1995), a theoretical framework that describes how, why, and at what pace new ideas or technologies spread through a community. Empowerment and diffusion of innovations subsequently became foundational pieces of many community-level interventions for HIV prevention.

Using the empowerment approach, scholars have argued that optimal behavior change will be more likely to occur and be sustained when individuals become conscious of the social barriers hindering their health, gain mastery of these social processes by transforming the conditions that create inequities, and work collectively to create a shared view of the future through active citizenship and community participation. For example, Zimmerman, Ramirez-Valles, Suarez, de la Rosa, and Castro (1997) tested an empowerment-based intervention among Mexican gay men and found that men in the empowerment condition reported increases in HIV/AIDS knowledge and consistent condom use at a 12-month follow-up, as compared with men who did not receive the intervention. Carballo-Diéguez et al. (2005), on the other hand, found no support for an empowerment intervention with Latino gay men in New York City. Although there was a decrease in risk behaviors across both the intervention and control condition, the researchers argued that empowerment-based interventions may be adequate only in contexts in which participants feel like they do not have control over their lives, as opposed to just being categorized as a marginalized group or community. Together, these findings underscore the importance of aligning the population's needs and assets when considering whether to design and implement empowerment-based intervention.

Other interventions focused on the principle of diffusion of innovations. Community popular opinion leader interventions (CPOL) focused on disseminating HIV/AIDS prevention messages through influential members in the community. In the original application of the CPOL model, staff at gay bars nominated popular, influential gay men in the community to be trained as HIV educators. The men then committed to having specified numbers of conversations with their peers about HIV and ways to reduce their sexual risks. The hope was that by having popular men in their social network advocate for condom use, the behavioral acceptability of unprotected sex within the community would shift. Initial trials of the model with gay men showed success in the United States (J. Kelly et al., 1997). It has since been attempted with less success in international settings (NIMH Multisite HIV Prevention Trial Group, 1998). The variability in its success has been attributed to differences across intervention settings, cultural norms and processes, and salience of group-based norming to sexual behavior (Schneider & Laumann, 2011).

Finally, some combined both principles of diffusion and empowerment. For example, the Mpowerment project was one of the first community-level HIV prevention interventions targeted toward young gay and bisexual men (Kegeles, 1996). The intervention created a structure necessary to empower a "core group" of 10–15 young men to plan activities in their community that would set in motion an ever-widening diffusion process through which men encourage and communicate with each other about HIV prevention. Two large-scale trials of the intervention demonstrated its efficacy in curbing sexual risk behaviors among young gay and bisexual men (Kegeles, Hays, Pollack, & Coates, 1999). Similarly, Morisky et al. (2010) successfully applied these theories to HIV prevention in a community-based intervention focused on reducing the sexual risk behaviors of female bar workers (FBW), some of whom engage in commercial sex work, in the Philippines. Rather than focusing exclusively on FBW as intervention participants (e.g., teaching how to adequately use a condom), Morisky et al. also trained bar managers to promote procondom use policies in the bar (e.g., enforcement of 100% condom use) as well as to encourage regular STI testing. Findings from their quasi-experimental study found increases in HIV/STI testing and consistent condom use among participants receiving the intervention condition. Together, these studies underscore the importance of using empowerment processes and social norming as strategies to encourage health-promotive sexual behaviors.

In addition to empowerment and diffusion of innovation, some scholars have begun to examine how individuals who feel a bond or connection with their community may relate to HIV-related behaviors and norms. Past research has found that after controlling for demographic variables and usual source of care, individuals with a higher sense of community and neighborhood participation were more likely to decrease negative behaviors (Kawachi, 2000; Sampson, Raudenbush, & Earls, 1997), and report better general health and fewer depressive symptoms (E. Parker et al., 2001). Frye et al. (2010), for example, used archival data from a probability sample of young MSM (YMSM) living in NYC during 1999–2000 and found that consistent condom use during anal intercourse was higher among YMSM living in neighborhoods with a greater "gay-presence" (percent of households headed by same-sex partners) than counterparts from neighborhoods with less gay presence. These findings suggest that interventions geared toward creating and strengthening bonds at the community-level may provide opportunities to curtail HIV risk correlates (e.g., psychological distress) and promote safer sex norms. Future work is necessary to replicate these findings and apply them to interventions.

Physical Characteristics of Communities

The physical characteristics of communities also have the potential to influence HIV transmission and shape sexual behavior. Physical characteristics of the built environment may structure the frequency and access to social settings whereby individuals interact with each other in their communities. Physical characteristics may include geographic distance between members of a community and access to housing. Researchers have noted, for example, that individuals often select sexual partners in geographic proximity. As a result, individuals may be at greater risk of HIV exposure if they live in areas with greater HIV concentration (Rothenberg, Muth, Malone, Potterat, & Woodhouse,

2005). Similarly, researchers have noted that the lack of housing increases the likelihood of engaging in transactional sex or sexual victimization, with high rates noted among homeless youth and adults (Aidala, Cross, Stall, Harre, & Sumartojo, 2005). Efforts to reduce sexual risk by targeting housing stability have met with mixed success. In a recent randomized trial, Wolitski et al. (2010) found that residentially unstable HIV-positive individuals who received assistance to secure housing in three sites (Baltimore, Chicago, or Los Angeles) reported improved psychological well-being (e.g., depression symptoms and perceived stress) and decreased medical care costs over an 18-month period. The intervention also noted marginal trends ($p < .10$) regarding decreased number of sexual partners, likelihood of engaging in transactional sex, and likelihood of having unprotected sex with a serodiscordant or HIV-unknown partner.

The quality of the physical characteristics of the built environment (e.g., vacant or deteriorated property) also may encourage the expression of HIV risk behaviors. Several theoretical approaches, including social disorganization theory (Sampson & Groves, 1989) and broken windows theory (Kelling & Coles, 1996), for example, have been used to document how individuals living in more disorganized neighborhoods may be more likely to manifest higher rates of problem behaviors than counterparts living in more organized neighborhoods. These perspectives have posited that individuals living in chronically disinvested areas may lack sufficient access to quality health and human services, or adopt risk behaviors (e.g., transactional sex, substance use) to cope with deleterious social conditions (Gupta, Parkhurst, Ogden, Aggleton, & Mahal, 2008; Phelan, Link, & Tehranifar, 2010 Rhodes, Singer, Bourgois, Friedman, & Strathdee, 2005; Wallace, 1990). In one study, Cohen et al. (2000) developed a "broken window" index, composed of assessments of housing quality, graffiti, trash, and public school deterioration, and they explored the association between this index and the number of gonorrhea cases across neighborhoods. Even after controlling for socioeconomic markers, such as unemployment, income, and low education, the broken window index continued to predict gonorrhea rates, suggesting that the physical conditions of local neighborhoods might somehow be related to the sexual risk behaviors of local community members. Although these quasi-experimental studies support the relationship between physical characteristics and sexual risk, HIV/AIDS interventions focused on revitalizing physical neighborhoods remain to be tested.

Research on bathhouses represents another example of how sexuality and HIV research have conceptualized physical space as a contributor to risk. Sexuality research, in the context of addressing HIV risk, identified that physical characteristics also facilitate sociocultural interactions and the development of shared meanings and experiences, often referred to as "sexual spaces," which in turn shape sexual behavior (B. Kelly & Muñoz-Laboy, 2005). Early in the epidemic, a debate erupted over the existence of bathhouses (private clubs where men could meet for casual sex). Central to the debate were questions of whether the mere presence of such facilities in the community encouraged sexual risk behavior. Whereas some argued that sexual behaviors were individual acts, carried out independently of whether bathhouses existed, health department officials insisted that the presence of these facilities encouraged risky sexual behavior that otherwise might not occur if sex were restricted to other locations. Bathhouse managers responded with voluntary regulations of their own, such as increasing the amount of lighting in the clubs, or closing large rooms previously designated for group sexual activities, thus tacitly acknowledging that certain aspects of the built environment might contribute to risk behaviors. Ultimately, the bathhouses were closed by legal action, although the scientific question of whether their existence or design contributed to sexual risk behavior had yet to be clearly determined and later would suggest that the construction of their space was unrelated to risk (Woods et al., 2003). Despite the lack of conclusive evidence at the time, however, the act of closing the bathhouses and their subsequent reopening without doors on the rooms (in an effort to reduce certain behaviors by modifying the environment), remains one of the classic examples of an environmental intervention designed to change sexual behavior.

Since that time, other interventions have taken advantage of bathhouses as a setting in which to deliver prevention services, such as counseling and testing for HIV (Daskalakis et al., 2009; Huebner et al., 2006, 2010), to men who may be at relatively higher risk for infection. Although these interventions generally are conceptualized using individual-level principles of behavior change, some have found that their physical location within a setting in which sexual behavior occurs might increase their efficacy either by increasing the salience of prevention messages for the individual, or by shifting the way in which a sexual space is experienced by its clientele as a whole (Godin et al., 2008; Ko et al., 2009). Taken together, these built environment findings underscore the importance of considering how the physical characteristics of communities may create disproportionate vulnerability to HIV/AIDS exposure among certain population groups (e.g., homeless youth) as well as promote sexual behaviors within specific physical spaces (e.g., parks, bath houses). Interventions focused on altering the physical characteristics of a community as a strategy to redefine sexual exchanges in a community may be a promising strategy to reduce HIV/AIDS risk.

Socioeconomic Characteristics of Communities

Connections between sexuality and economics have been clear to observers of human behavior long before HIV/AIDS came into the public awareness. Indeed, the fact that sex work has been dubbed "the oldest profession" is evidence of the fact that throughout recorded history, and across cultures, people have recognized that sex has value as a resource (see Volume 2, Chapter 2, this handbook). Thus, the idea that economics might somehow affect individuals' sexual behaviors certainly did not first emerge in the context of HIV research. As with other influences on sexuality, however, the HIV/AIDS epidemic provided new incentives to understand the specific nature of the relationship between socioeconomic status and sexual health, and it spawned a body of empirical work that exponentially advanced our understanding of these dynamics (see Volume 2, Chapter 10, this handbook).

In the context of HIV/AIDS research, the impact of socioeconomic characteristics on HIV-related sexual behaviors has been studied both at the level of the individual (e.g., does my own personal income affect my sexual behavior?) and the community (e.g., does my neighborhood's income affect my sexual behavior?). At the individual level, socioeconomic status may influence individuals' ability to access HIV/AIDS preventative services and sexual health education as well as increase their immunologic susceptibility by having higher morbidity as a result of limited access to broader medical prevention and care (Obermeyer & Osborn, 2007). In addition, individuals of lower socioeconomic status may have less access to social privileges attained through schooling and socially upward work opportunities (Gillespie, Kadiyala, & Greener, 2007; Hargreaves et al., 2008). As a result, individuals may feel sexually disempowered to negotiate consistent condom use if their sexual partners assist with financial earnings, or they may engage in commercial sex work to produce earnings (Gupta et al., 2008).

In the context of these findings, interventions (e.g., microfinance initiatives) have been proposed to reduce economic disadvantage and reduce HIV risk (Dworkin & Blankenship, 2009). Given that women are more likely to be excluded from educational and employment opportunities (Higgins, Hoffman, & Dworkin, 2010), most HIV-related microfinance initiatives have focused on economically disadvantaged women. In so doing, microfinancing or microcredit programs for women have been implemented successfully to increase the economic status of women and empower their household influence and decision making (Dworkin & Blankenship, 2009; J. Kim et al., 2007; Pronyk, Hargreaves, & Morduch, 2007). Given that economic independence and decision-making status or power are strong predictors of condom use (Blankenship, Friedman, Dworkin, & Mantell, 2006), such movement toward household equality, both as they relate to economic empowerment and shared household decision making, is thought to translate to increased negotiating power within the sexual relationship and to encourage condom negotiation and use with partners. Domestically, Sherman, German, Cheng, Marks, and Bailey-Kloche (2006) provided drug-using sex workers with HIV/AIDS education as well as training in creating, marketing, and selling jewelry (Project JEWEL). Using a pre–post design, participants reported reductions in transactional sex for money and drugs and a reduction in the median number of clients at follow-up. Furthermore, the researchers noted a negative association between income earned from jewelry sales and the number of sexual partners reported at the 3-month follow-up. Internationally, the IMAGE (Intervention for Microfinance and Gender Equity) Program has provided additional support for microfinance interventions. IMAGE provided women in South Africa with modules on HIV/AIDS education, violence prevention, and gender equity. Using a randomized controlled trial, IMAGE participants reported decreases in likelihood of engaging in unprotected sex with a nonspousal partner as well as increased use of VCT and communication about HIV/AIDS (Pronyk et al., 2006; Pronyk et al., 2008). In addition, domestic violence decreased by half at the end of year one among IMAGE participants (Pronyk et al., 2006). Given that the use of economic interventions to prevent and reduce HIV risk, both in the United States and internationally, has occurred only relatively recently in the context of the epidemic, their long-term sustainability and program effects require further exploration and evaluation. Nevertheless, the integration of economic initiatives and HIV/AIDS education are promising, and they highlight the intersections between gender inequality, individual economic disadvantage, and HIV risk.

At the community level, researchers have examined the relationship between concentrated economic disadvantage within a specified geographic locale (sometimes referred to as "economic disadvantage") and HIV prevalence. Researchers have noted that economic disadvantage might influence the composition of sexual networks in a manner that facilitates risk for HIV and other STIs (Baumer & South, 2001; Browning, Burrington, Leventhal, & Brooks-Gunn, 2008; Dembo, Belenko, Childs, Wareham, & Schmeidler, 2009) and shape localized norms regarding sexuality (Bauermeister, Zimmerman, & Caldwell, 2011; Browning et al., 2008; Cubbin, Santelli, Brindis, & Braveman, 2005). For example, Burgard and Lee-Rife (2009) found greater neighborhood disadvantage was associated with earlier sexual onset and inconsistent condom use among adolescents and young adults in South Africa. Similarly, in a study of Chicago neighborhoods, Browning et al. (2008) found that youth living in neighborhoods with greater concentrated poverty were more likely to be sexually active than youth living in less concentrated poverty areas. Moreover, neighborhood disadvantage might increase perceptions of stress and contribute to the use of maladaptive coping mechanisms known to facilitate HIV risk (e.g., psychological distress and substance use; Galea et al., 2007; Haney, 2007; Latkin, Forman, Knowlton, & Sherman, 2003; Winstanley et al., 2008). These findings suggest that initiatives focused on improving the economic well-being of communities may be an innovative HIV/AIDS prevention strategy; however, structural interventions of this large scale (e.g., poverty alleviation programs) remain to be tested empirically.

Taken together, these ecological approaches have underscored the intersection between sexual risk and the larger social structures in which sexual behaviors are expressed and given meaning. In the context of HIV/AIDS prevention, these findings illustrate how "sexual risk" is contextualized by the community characteristics (e.g., psychological, physical, economic) where individuals live, including how HIV prevention information and norms are disseminated and enacted across communities. Furthermore, these data underscore the importance of considering and addressing how structural barriers hinder individuals' ability to engage in safer sex practices. The development, buy-in, and implementation of programs to address community-level characteristics linked to HIV/AIDS risk are vital. Acknowledging that these social changes may not be feasible across all contexts, HIV/AIDS researchers also have sought to develop biomedical approaches that reduce individuals' vulnerability to HIV/AIDS infection, particularly in settings in which consistent condom use is not viable. We discuss these biomedical alternatives in the following section.

BIOMEDICAL APPROACHES

Despite the success of HIV prevention intervention programs that target individual as well as ecological factors, the state of the epidemic suggests that behavioral approaches to eliminating HIV alone may not be sufficient. Epidemiologic simulations of HIV transmission have suggested that reducing the "community viral load" (i.e., aggregate number of HIV-positive individuals in a community whose viral loads pose risks for transmission) may be one of the most effective prevention approaches to curtail HIV incidence at the population level (Das et al., 2010). Thus, to supplement sociobehavioral approaches, researchers also are pursuing biomedical strategies to avert new transmissions by mitigating the body's biological vulnerability to the virus through circumcision, inoculation, or medication. In so doing, the intent behind these biomedical approaches is to provide alternative prevention methods to condom use (e.g., vaccine) and reduce the dependence on adherence to behavioral approaches (e.g., consistent condom use) as the sole method to reduce HIV exposure and transmission. The sections that follow summarizes recent successes of several biomedical approaches and highlight the ways in which behavioral research on sexuality continues to inform these strategies.

Circumcision

Ecologic studies of HIV incidence and circumcision have suggested a negative association between circumcision and HIV. There are several reasons why circumcision may be a protective factor. Circumcision may reduce tears in the foreskin that may occur during sex and facilitate exposure to the virus, may remove foreskin cells that are particularly susceptible to HIV infection, and may increase the toughness of the skin surrounding the head of the penis; however, studies examining causal relationships have been less conclusive. Several randomized trials conducted in Africa found that male circumcision has a strong protective effect against HIV infection among men in opposite sex relationships (Millett et al., 2007). In a meta-analysis of studies, Weiss, Quigley, and Hayes (2000) found an approximate 50% reduction in risk in circumcised men from 21 studies; Auvert et al. (2005) found a 60% reduction in risk for circumcised men in a randomized controlled trial. In these studies, the protective effects of male circumcision chiefly concerned HIV transmission from females to their uninfected male partners. Weiss, Hankins, and Dickson (2009) conducted a meta-analysis on male circumcision and male-to-female HIV transmission and found inconclusive evidence of a direct protective effect of circumcision for women, yet findings suggested that male circumcision may decrease male-to-female HIV transmission indirectly by decreasing HIV rates among men.

Examining circumcision's impact on male-to-male transmission also suggests inconclusive evidence of a protective effect from circumcision. Although some studies have suggested a protective effect of circumcision (Buchbinder et al., 2005; Kreiss & Hopkins, 1993), other studies have failed to find a protective effect on male-to-male transmission (Millett et al., 2007). Sullivan et al. (2007) suggested rectal rather than penile acquisition of HIV may nullify protective factors of circumcision in male-to-male transmission routes. These findings underscore the need to understand the biological differences in sexual intercourse.

Although accumulating evidence explores when and how circumcision could decrease HIV infection, male circumcision may be a promising biomedical approach for HIV prevention because of low rates of circumcision among some populations. Some advocates and scholars, however, have cautioned that this biomedical approach ignores the body and how its alteration may affect sexual, religious, and cultural heritage (see Volume 2, Chapters 6 and 13, this handbook). Sorrells et al. (2007), for example, noted that circumcision may be associated with less penile sensitivity. Similarly, Vincent (2008) has cautioned that large-scale circumcision initiatives should be considered through a cultural lens before their implementation. In many cultures, male circumcision has symbolic meaning, such as the transition from childhood into adulthood, virility, identification with a specific religious denomination, and acceptance of the man into the community. Furthermore, it remains unclear whether the use of circumcision status as a marker of HIV vulnerability will shift social norms and result in a higher number of new cases in the long term by conferring a false sense of security for engaging in unsafe sex practices, a concept known as behavioral disinhibition (Kalichman, 2010). Consequently, sexuality research will be vital to determine the acceptability of circumcision initiatives as they are implemented globally.

Microbicides

In the absence of a vaccine, an HIV prevention option other than condoms is needed urgently (Coggins et al., 2000; van de Wijgert & Coggins, 2002; Weber, Desai, & Darbyshire, 2005). Microbicides are products currently under development that could be presented as a gel, film, foam, or enema and administered before intercourse to prevent, or at least decrease, the risk of HIV transmission. Vaginal or rectal microbicides could help prevent HIV and other STIs by offering the receptive sexual partner an opportunity to decrease their risk of infection in situations in which they may lack the agency to engage in safer sex, be unable to decline sex with a partner, or seek a safer option for serodiscordant couples (Potts, 1994; van de Wijgert & Shattock, 2007). As these microbicides are developed, multiple biologic mechanisms are being considered. These mechanisms include limiting the virus from reaching vulnerable cells by placing a biochemical barrier, enhancing the body's natural defense mechanisms (e.g., acidic pH levels), or hindering the virus' replication once it enters the body.

Microbicide development for both vaginal and anal intercourse is still in its infancy. Recently, however, researchers found a 39% decrease in HIV infection and 51% reduction in herpes simplex among women who had used a microbicide containing tenofovir during sex and who also had received behavioral counseling (Abdool Karim et al., 2010). Data also suggested a dose-response effect, with greater efficacy among women who consistently used the microbicide (54% reduction among women who used the gel during 80% or more of their sexual acts vs. 28% reduction among those who intermittently used the gel). In light of these findings, enthusiasm for microbicides is strong. Additional female controlled methods are also in development (e.g., microbicide-releasing diaphragm or vaginal ring). The diaphragm would offer a means of contraception and HIV prevention controlled by the woman, and a vaginal ring would offer long-term protection for women; however, both are dependent on a proven effective microbicide (Major et al., 2010).

As biomedical researchers continue to seek out a chemical compound that may serve as a microbicide, sexuality and behavioral scientists are examining the potential acceptability and adherence of these products were they to become available. Specifically, sexuality researchers have advocated for a deeper understanding of the sexual practices that precede or follow sexual intercourse. For example, it is believed that for a microbicide to be efficacious, it should thoroughly cover the mucosa, whether vaginal or rectal, that may be susceptible to exposure of HIV. Therefore, certain sexual hygiene practices of some cultures (e.g., douching) could limit the effectiveness of these products by disrupting the lining of the vaginal and rectal mucosa. Evolving research on vaginal douching suggests that it is a behavior that is initiated during adolescence (Oh, Merchant, & Brown, 2002), may be more common among certain ethnic groups (Annang, Grimley, & Hook, 2006), and could be particularly resistant to change (Ness et al., 2003). Similar findings have been voiced among MSM (Carballo-Diéguez et al., 2008). Consequently, for microbicides to be successful beyond clinical trials, we need to better understand douching and other behaviors that cooccur with sexual intercourse, which might undermine the effectiveness of these chemicals.

Innoculation

Several biomedical strategies under development seek to reduce or completely prevent HIV infection. Undoubtedly, the development of a safe and efficacious vaccine has been one of the most important priorities in the field of HIV/AIDS prevention as it would circumvent behavioral obstacles that may occur when considering or adopting condom use consistently. Although condom use would be required to avoid other STIs and unintended pregnancies, a vaccine could create an adaptive immune response upon administration that could generate an effective response to HIV (Chhatbar, Mishra, Kumar, & Singh, 2011; Johnston & Fauci, 2008). Although some progress has been made in developing and testing safe and immunogenic inoculations, clinical trials with vaccine candidates have failed to demonstrate efficacy against HIV transmission (Buchbinder et al., 2008). Nevertheless, forthcoming evidence suggests progress is being made. An efficacy trial in Thailand (Vaccinia + gp160) demonstrated 31% efficacy against HIV-1 acquisition in predominately heterosexual men and women (Rerks-Ngarm et al., 2009); however, this finding, although significant, was only a modest reduction in the rate in HIV-1 infection. As efficacy trials suggest greater immunogenic inoculation, it will be vital for sexuality and behavioral researchers to examine individual and community vaccine acceptability and to propose strategies that encourage their adoption (e.g., social marketing campaigns) or remove barriers (e.g., medical mistrust) to their use.

Another biomedical intervention has used highly active antiretroviral therapy (HAART) as a preventive inoculation measure (Golub, Kowalczyk, Weinberger, & Parsons, 2010; Liu et al., 2008; Romanelli, 2010). By using HAART, individuals at high risk for exposure to HIV (e.g., commercial sex workers, serodiscordant couples) will be protected from infection through daily HAART use. Preexposure prophylaxis (PrEP) involves the use of antiretroviral medications (e.g., tenofovir and emtricitabine) before potential exposure, whereas postexposure prophylaxis (PEP) seeks to reduce HIV transmission postexposure. Several trials currently are under way to test the efficacy of daily or intermittent PrEP and PEP use. In one multinational trial (iPrEx), the efficacy of daily oral tenofovir and emtricitabine use was tested among 3,000 MSM in six countries (Grant et al., 2010). There were 44% fewer HIV infections among participants receiving the oral HAART combination alongside comprehensive HIV prevention package. Similarly, the HTN 052 trial found that HIV infection risk decreased in serodiscordant couples if HIV-positive men and women had begun their HAART regimen while their immune system was relatively healthy (e.g., CD4 >250 cells/mm^3). The efficacy of the aforementioned trials was more protective among individuals who had greater adherence to the product. Nevertheless, the long-term success of both approaches will require that individuals have access to comprehensive HIV prevention packages (e.g., counseling on safe sex practices, free condoms, treatment for STIs, regular HIV testing, and frequent evaluation and treatment for any complications related to HIV). The availability of these services remains unequal in the population, raising concerns about how structural factors may influence individuals' acceptability, access, and adherence to these treatments.

The use of PrEP/PEP as an inoculation strategy has been documented among individuals who could become infected as a result of occupational exposure (CDC, 2011b, 2011c). Currently, researchers are considering whether PEP may be an acceptable strategy to reduce HIV/AIDS infections occurring through nonoccupational exposures, particularly when balanced against HAART toxicity and adverse drug reactions in the body, or potential increases in virus resistance. Other concerns exist as to whether these biomedical interventions may increase risk behavior via behavioral disinhibition or risk compensation (Buchbinder & Liu, 2011; Golub et al., 2010; Hogben & Liddon, 2008). Golub et al. (2010) noted that PrEP may offer alternative prevention strategies among men who find condom use difficult in high-arousal situations, yet they cautioned that the availability of PrEP could reduce baseline condom use (e.g., more than 35% of those who would use PrEP also indicated they would be less likely to use condoms while using PrEP). Brooks et al. (2012) noted similar results; however, men interviewed as part of their study also noted that the availability of medical prophylaxis would reduce anxiety when having sex with an HIV-positive partner, particularly if they were in a serodiscordant relationship. Undoubtedly, the novelty of these biobehavioral strategies will require researchers to examine how prophylaxis use will influence sexual behavior as well as whether individuals will use these products, particularly if they reduce the physical or emotional pleasure of the sexual encounter or have taxing side-effects.

MOVING FORWARD TOWARD AN INTEGRATED APPROACH

In light of the renewed interest in biomedical approaches, scholars have underscored the importance of remaining aware of the role of sexuality in the marketing, roll-out, and delivery of these products. Furthermore, these biomedical strategies will be difficult to scale-up at a global scale because of limited economic and structural resources across and within countries (see Volume 2, Chapter 9, this handbook). In recognition of these challenges, researchers and advocates have advocated for an integrated approach in the delivery of HIV/AIDS prevention services.

Public health systems, including the World Health Organization and the CDC, have called for the development of HIV/AIDS prevention strategies that combine best practices across the multiple approaches summarized above. Recently, the White House presented the National HIV/AIDS Strategy (NHAS) as a framework to guide these HIV/AIDS prevention efforts. Using a three-pronged strategy, the NHAS seeks to (a) decrease new infections by proposing behavioral strategies that reduce the number of HIV transmissions and increase HIV-status awareness among HIV-positive individuals, (b) increase the proportion HIV-positive individuals who have comprehensive clinical care and have stable housing, and (c) reduce HIV disparities among socially marginalized populations (e.g., gay and bisexual men, racial or ethnic minorities) by improving access to prevention and care services. For such an integrated approach to succeed, it will be vital that HIV/AIDS prevention strategies reach and affect large numbers of people more efficiently, establish procedures that maximize the diffusion of interventions, increase program sustainability by building institutional capacity, and incorporate the needs of specific communities into their tailored services (Bauermeister, Tross, & Ehrhardt, 2009).

The systematic delivery of integrated prevention services, however, may encourage a "desexualization" of the epidemic (Boyce et al., 2007; R. Parker, 2009a; see Chapter 15, this volume). Devoid of an awareness of the social and relational meanings of sexuality, integrated prevention strategies may not resonate with their intended audiences, have limited acceptability and adoption, and ultimately may fail (Fenton, 2010). Consequently, it will be vital that social scientists conducting sexuality research underscore the psychosocial meanings embedded within sexual behavior and provide a lens to document the reasons why HIV/AIDS risk occurs across multiple levels (e.g., individual, relational, community) as well as how to create tailored, feasible, and efficacious programs across social contexts.

CONCLUSION

Reflecting back on the 30 years of the HIV/AIDS epidemic, we must not lose sight of the mounting progress that has been achieved. The epidemic forced issues surrounding sex and sexuality (e.g., gender power imbalances, homophobia) to become visible and, when necessary, to be challenged and contested. Through this visibility, we have been able to propose and test behavior change programs, some with more success than others and to learn new prevention and treatment strategies that reduce HIV/AIDS prevalence and incidence in our communities. In tandem, findings from HIV/AIDS research have provided opportunities to examine and rethink how we conceptualize sexuality and sexual behavior.

These successes, although noteworthy, have been insufficient in eradicating the epidemic globally. First, beyond developing and testing HIV/AIDS prevention interventions for different populations and risk outcomes, we still need to disseminate interventions proven to be efficacious and cost-effective to large numbers of people. Second, given increasing budget cuts and competing demands within health systems, research and policies that inform how to best sustain these interventions both within communities and across the globe are needed direly, particularly as we consider the integration of biomedical and behavioral strategies (e.g., PrEP). Finally, many of these interventions have been found to have short-lived effect sizes. From a sexuality standpoint, this is not surprising as people's expressions of sexual behavior constantly are changing depending on where they are in their life course, their partner characteristics, and the sociocultural contexts in which they interact. Consequently, rather than promoting a single approach, we encourage sexuality and HIV prevention researchers to consider how to integrate HIV programs across levels (e.g., individual, interpersonal, community, biomedical) as a strategy to strengthen the effect size longevity of HIV prevention interventions.

As the field of HIV/AIDS behavioral research has evolved over the past 30 years, it has changed from a field largely focused on understanding and intervening upon individual risk behaviors to incorporate foci of sexual meaning and of the larger context and settings that shape sexual behaviors. The influence of sexuality research has contributed greatly to this paradigm shift, as prevention programming incorporates aspects of risk reduction through targeted individual-based interventions as well as attempts to reduce vulnerability within the larger context, creating interventions that promote social, economic, or cultural change (Aggleton, 2004; Blankenship et al., 2006). Undoubtedly, sexuality researchers must remain central to the development, implementation, and evaluation of HIV/AIDS prevention programs across all intervention approaches.

References

Abdool Karim, Q., Abdool Karim, S. S., Frohlich, J. A., Grobler, A. C., Baxter, C., Mansoor, L. E., . . . Omar, Z. (2010). Effectiveness and safety of tenofovir gel, an antiretroviral microbicide, for the prevention of HIV infection in women. *Science*, *329*, 1168–1174. doi:10.1126/science.1193748

Aggleton, P. (2004). Sexuality, HIV prevention, vulnerability and risk. *Journal of Psychology and Human Sexuality*, *16*, 1–11. doi:10.1300/J056v16n01_01

Aidala, A., Cross, J. E., Stall, R., Harre, D., & Sumartojo, E. (2005). Housing status and HIV risk behaviors: Implications for prevention and policy. *AIDS and Behavior*, *9*, 251–265. doi:10.1007/s10461-005-9000-7

Ajzen, I. (1991). The theory of planned behavior. *Organizational Behavior and Human Decision Processes*, *50*, 179–211. doi:10.1016/0749-5978(91)90020-T

Albarracín, D., Gillette, J. C., Earl, A. N., Glasman, L. R., Durantini, M. R., & Ho, M. H. (2005). A test of major assumptions about behavior change: A comprehensive look at the effects of passive and active HIV-prevention interventions since the beginning of the epidemic. *Psychological Bulletin*, *131*, 856–897. doi:10.1037/0033-2909.131.6.856

Albarracín, D., Kumkale, G. T., & Johnson, B. T. (2004). Influences of social power and normative support on condom use decisions: A research synthesis. *AIDS Care*, *16*, 700–723. doi:10.1080/0954012041233 1269558

Albarracín, D., Rothman, A. J., Di Clemente, R., & Rio, C. (2010). Wanted: A theoretical roadmap to research and practice across individual, interpersonal, and structural levels of analysis. *AIDS and Behavior*, *14*(Suppl. 2), 185–188. doi:10.1007/s10461-010-9805-x

Albarracín, D., Tannenbaum, M. B., Glasman, L. R., & Rothman, A. J. (2010). Modeling structural, dyadic, and individual factors: The inclusion and exclusion model of HIV related behavior. *AIDS and Behavior*, *14*(Suppl. 2), 239–249. doi:10.1007/s10461-010-9801-1

Albarracín, J., Albarracín, D., & Durantini, M. (2008). Effects of HIV-prevention interventions for samples with higher and lower percents of Latinos and Latin Americans: A meta-analysis of change in condom use and knowledge. *AIDS and Behavior*, *12*, 521–543. doi:10.1007/s10461-007-9209-8

Allen, S., Serufilira, A., Bogaerts, J., Van de Perre, P., Nsengumuremyi, F., Lindan, C., . . . Hulley, S. (1992). Confidential HIV testing and condom promotion in Africa: Impact on HIV and gonorrhea rates. *JAMA*, *268*, 3338–3343. doi:10.1001/jama.1992.03490230068030

Amaro, H. (1995). Love, sex, and power: Considering women's realities in HIV prevention. *American Psychologist*, *50*, 437–447. doi:10.1037/0003-066X.50.6.437

Annang, L., Grimley, D. M., & Hook, E. W. (2006). Vaginal douche practices among black women at risk: Exploring douching prevalence, reasons for douching, and sexually transmitted disease infection. *Sexually Transmitted Diseases*, *33*, 215–219. doi:10.1097/01.olq.0000205046.11916.c5

Auvert, B., Taljaard, D., Lagarde, E., Sobngwi-Tambekou, J., Sitta, R., & Puren, A. (2005). Randomized, controlled intervention trial of male circumcision for reduction of HIV infection risk: The ANRS 1625 trial. *PLoS Medicine*, *2*(11), e298.

Bachanas, P. J., Morris, M. K., Lewis-Gess, J. K., Sarett-Cuasay, E. J., Sirl, K., Ries, J. K., & Sawyer, M. K. (2002). Predictors of risky sexual behavior in African American adolescent girls: Implications for prevention interventions. *Journal of Pediatric Psychology*, *27*, 519–530. doi:10.1093/jpepsy/27.6.519

Baliunas, D., Rehm, J., Irving, H., & Shuper, P. (2010). Alcohol consumption and risk of incident HIV infection: A meta-analysis. *International Journal of Public Health*, *55*, 159–166. doi:10.1007/s00038-009-0095-x

Bandura, A. (1986). *Social foundations of thought and action: A social cognitive theory*. New York, NY: Prentice Hall.

Barker, R. G. (1968). *Ecological psychology: Concepts and methods for studying the environment and human behavior*. Stanford, CA: Stanford University Press.

Basen-Engquist, K. (1992). Psychosocial predictors of "safer sex" behaviors in young adults. *AIDS Education and Prevention*, *4*(2), 120–134.

Bauermeister, J. A., Elkington, K. S., Brackis-Cott, E., Dolezal, C., & Mellins, C. A. (2009). Sexual behavior and perceived peer norms: Comparing perinatally infected and affected youth. *Journal of Youth and Adolescence*, *38*, 1110–1122. doi:10.1007/s10964-008-9315-6

Bauermeister, J. A., Tross, S., & Ehrhardt, A. A. (2009). A review of HIV/AIDS system-level interventions. *AIDS and Behavior*, *13*, 430–448. doi:10.1007/s10461-008-9379-z

Bauermeister, J. A., Zimmerman, M., Caldwell, C., Xue, Y., & Gee, G. (2010). What predicts sex partner age differences among African American youth? A longitudinal study from adolescence to young adulthood. *Journal of Sex Research*, *47*, 330–344. doi:10.1080/00224490903015850

Bauermeister, J. A., Zimmerman, M. A., & Caldwell, C. H. (2011). Neighborhood disadvantage and changes in condom use among African American adolescents. *Journal of Urban Health*, *88*, 66–83. doi:10.1007/s11524-010-9506-9

Baumer, E. P., & South, S. J. (2001). Community effects on youth sexual activity. *Journal of Marriage and Family*, *63*, 540–554. doi:10.1111/j.1741-3737.2001.00540.x

Becker, M. H. (1974). *The health belief model and personal health behavior.* Thorofare, NJ: Charles B. Slack.

Bertrand, J. T. (2004). Diffusion of innovations and HIV/AIDS. *Journal of Health Communication*, *9*(Suppl. 1), 113–121. doi:10.1080/10810730490271575

Blankenship, K. M., Friedman, S. R., Dworkin, S., & Mantell, J. E. (2006). Structural interventions: Concepts, challenges and opportunities for research. *Journal of Urban Health*, *83*, 59–72. doi:10.1007/s11524-005-9007-4

Bowleg, L., Belgrave, F. Z., & Reisen, C. A. (2000). Gender roles, power strategies, and precautionary sexual self-efficacy: Implications for Black and Latina women's HIV/AIDS protective behaviors. *Sex Roles*, *42*, 613–635. doi:10.1023/A:1007099422902

Boyce, P., Huang Soo Lee, M., Jenkins, C., Mohamed, S., Overs, C., Paiva, V., . . . Aggleton, P. (2007). Putting sexuality (back) into HIV/AIDS: Issues, theory and practice. *Global Public Health*, *2*, 1–34. doi:10.1080/17441690600899362

Bronfenbrenner, U. (1979a). *The ecology of human development.* Cambridge, MA: Harvard University Press.

Bronfenbrenner, U. (1979b). *The ecology of human development: Experiments by nature and design.* Cambridge, MA: Harvard University Press.

Brooks, R. A., Landovitz, R. J., Kaplan, R. L., Lieber, E., Lee, S. J., & Barkley, T. W. (2012). Sexual risk behaviors and acceptability of HIV pre-exposure prophylaxis among HIV-negative gay and bisexual men in serodiscordant relationships: A mixed methods study. *AIDS Patient Care and STDs*, *25*, 87–94. doi:10.1089/apc.2011.0283

Browning, C. R., Burrington, L. A., Leventhal, T., & Brooks-Gunn, J. (2008). Neighborhood structural inequality, collective efficacy, and sexual risk behavior among urban youth. *Journal of Health and Social Behavior*, *49*, 269–285. doi:10.1177/002214650804900303

Buchbinder, S. P., & Liu, A. (2011). Pre-exposure prophylaxis and the promise of combination prevention approaches. *AIDS and Behavior*, *15*(Suppl. 1), S72–S79. doi:10.1007/s10461-011-9894-1

Buchbinder, S. P., Mehrotra, D. V., Duerr, A., Fitzgerald, D. W., Mogg, R., Li, D., . . . Robertson, M. N. (2008). Efficacy assessment of a cell-mediated immunity HIV-1 vaccine (the Step Study): A double-blind, randomised, placebo-controlled, test-of-concept trial. *Lancet*, *372*, 1881–1893. doi:10.1016/S0140-6736(08)61591-3

Buchbinder, S. P., Vittinghoff, E., Heagerty, P., Celum, C., Seage, G., Judson, F. N., . . . Koblin, B. (2005). Sexual risk, nitrite inhalant use, and lack of circumcision associated with HIV seroconversion in men who have sex with men in the United States. *Journal of Acquired Immune Deficiency Syndromes*, *39*, 82–89. doi:10.1097/01.qai.0000134740.41585.f4

Buhi, E. R., & Goodson, P. (2007). Predictors of adolescent sexual behavior and intention: A theory-guided systematic review. *Journal of Adolescent Health*, *40*, 4–21. doi:10.1016/j.jadohealth.2006.09.027

Burgard, S. A., & Lee-Rife, S. M. (2009). Community characteristics, sexual initiation, and condom use among young black South Africans. *Journal of Health and Social Behavior*, *50*, 293–309. doi:10.1177/002214650905000304

Burton, J., Darbes, L. A., & Operario, D. (2010). Couples-focused behavioral interventions to prevention of HIV: Systematic review of the state of evidence. *AIDS and Behavior*, *14*, 1–10. doi:10.1007/s10461-008-9471-4

Carballo-Diéguez, A., Bauermeister, J. A., Ventuneac, A., Dolezal, C., Balan, I., & Remien, R. H. (2008). The use of rectal douches among HIV-uninfected and infected men who have unprotected receptive anal intercourse: Implications for rectal microbicides. *AIDS and Behavior*, *12*, 860–866. doi:10.1007/s10461-007-9301-0

Carballo-Diéguez, A., Dolezal, C., Leu, C. S., Nieves, L., Diacuteaz, F., Decena, C., & Balan, I. (2005). A randomized controlled trial to test an HIV-prevention intervention for Latino gay and bisexual men: Lessons learned. *AIDS Care*, *17*, 314–328. doi:10.1080/09540120512331314303

Catania, J. A., Kegeles, S., & Coates, T. (1990). Towards an understanding of risk behavior: An AIDS risk reduction model (ARRM). *Health Education Quarterly*, *17*, 53–72. doi:10.1177/109019819001700107

Centers for Disease Control and Prevention. (1981a). Kaposi's sarcoma and pneumocystis pneumonia among homosexual men: New York City and California. *Morbidity and Mortality Weekly Report*, *30*, 305–308.

Centers for Disease Control and Prevention. (1981b). Pneumocystis pneumonia: Los Angeles. *Morbidity and Mortality Weekly Report*, *30*(21), 1–3.

Centers for Disease Control and Prevention. (2000). *Young people at risk: HIV/STI among America's youth.* Retrieved from http://www.cdc.hiv/pubs/facts/youth.pdf

Centers for Disease Control and Prevention. (2011a). *HIV in the United States: Fact sheet.* Retrieved from http://www.cdc.gov/hiv/resources/factsheets/us.htm

Centers for Disease Control and Prevention. (2011b). Interim guidance: Preexposure prophylaxis for the prevention of HIV infection in men who have sex with men. *Morbidity and Mortality Weekly Report*, *60*(3), 65–68.

Centers for Disease Control and Prevention. (2011c). *Pre-exposure prophylaxis (PrEP) for HIV prevention: Promoting safe and effective use in the United States.* Retrieved from http://www.cdc.gov/hiv/prep/pdf/PrEPfactsheet.pdf

Chhatbar, C., Mishra, R., Kumar, A., & Singh, S. K. (2011). HIV vaccine: Hopes and hurdles. *Drug Discovery Today*, *16*, 948–956. doi:10.1016/j.drudis.2011.08.013

Coggins, C., Blanchard, K., Alvarez, F., Brache, V., Weisberg, E., Kilmarx, P. H., . . . Ellertson, C. (2000). Preliminary safety and acceptability of a carrageenan gel for possible use as a vaginal microbicide. *Sexually Transmitted Infections*, *76*, 480–483. doi:10.1136/sti.76.6.480

Cohen, D., Spear, S., Scribner, R., Kissinger, P., Mason, K., & Wildgen, J. (2000). "Broken windows" and the risk of gonorrhea. *American Journal of Public Health*, *90*, 230–236. doi:10.2105/AJPH.90.2.230

Collins, R. L., Ellickson, P. L., Orlando, M., & Klein, D. J. (2005). Isolating the nexus of substance use, violence and sexual risk for HIV infection among young adults in the United States. *AIDS and Behavior*, *9*, 73–87. doi:10.1007/s10461-005-1683-2

Cubbin, C., Santelli, J., Brindis, C. D., & Braveman, P. (2005). Neighborhood context and sexual behaviors among adolescents: Findings from the national longitudinal study of adolescent health. *Perspectives on Sexual and Reproductive Health*, *37*, 125–134. doi:10.1363/3712505

Das, M., Chu, P. L., Santos, G.-M., Scheer, S., Vittinghoff, E., McFarland, W., & Colfax, G. N. (2010). Decreases in community viral load are accompanied by reductions in new HIV infections in San Francisco. *PLoS ONE*, *5*(6), e11068.

Daskalakis, D., Silvera, R., Bernstein, K., Stein, D., Hagerty, R., Hutt, R., . . . Marmor, M. (2009). Implementation of HIV testing at 2 New York City bathhouses: From pilot to clinical service. *Clinical Infectious Diseases, 48*, 1609–1616.

Davis, E. C., & Friel, L. V. (2001). Adolescent sexuality: Disentangling the effects of family structure and family context. *Journal of Marriage and Family*, *63*, 669–681. doi:10.1111/j.1741-3737.2001.00669.x

Dembo, R., Belenko, S., Childs, K., Wareham, J., & Schmeidler, J. (2009). Individual and community risk factors and sexually transmitted diseases among arrested youths: A two level analysis. *Journal of Behavioral Medicine*, *32*, 303–316. doi:10.1007/s10865-009-9205-8

Deschamps, M. M., Pape, J. W., Haffner, A., Hyppolite, R., & Johnson, W. D. (1991). *Heterosexual activity in at risk couples for HIV infection.* Presentation offered in the VII International Conference on AIDS, Florence, Italy.

Diamond, L. M. (2003). Love matters: Romantic relationships among sexual-minority adolescents. In P. Florsheim (Ed.), *Adolescent romantic relations and sexual behavior: Theory, research, and practical implications* (pp. 85–107). Mahwah, NJ: Erlbaum.

Díaz, R., & Ayala, G. (2001). *Social discrimination and health: The case of Latino gay men and HIV risk.* New York, NY: Policy Institute of the National Gay and Lesbian Task Force.

DiClemente, R. J., Salazar, L. F., & Crosby, R. A. (2007). A review of STD/HIV preventive interventions for adolescents: Sustaining effects using an ecological approach. *Journal of Pediatric Psychology*, *32*, 888–906. doi:10.1093/jpepsy/jsm056

DiClemente, R. J., & Wingood, G. M. (2000). Expanding the scope of HIV prevention for adolescents: Beyond individual-level interventions. *Journal of Adolescent Health, 26*, 377–378. doi:10.1016/S1054-139X(00)00126-9

DiIorio, C., Resnicow, K., McCarty, F., De, A. K., Dudley, W. N., Wang, D. T., & Denzmore, P. (2006). Keepin' it R. E. A. L.! Results of a mother–adolescent HIV prevention program. *Nursing Research, 55*, 43–51. doi:10.1097/00006199-200601000-00006

Dishion, T. J., McCord, J., & Poulin, F. (1999). When interventions harm: Peer groups and problem behavior. *American Psychologist*, *54*, 755–764. doi:10.1037/0003-066X.54.9.755

Dolcini, M. M., Harper, G. W., Boyer, C. B., & Pollack, L. M. (2010). Project ÒRÉ: A friendship-based intervention to prevent HIV/STI in urban African American adolescent females. *Health Education and Behavior*, *37*, 115–132. doi:10.1177/1090198109333280

Dolcini, M. M., Harper, G. W., Boyer, C. B., Watson, S. E., Anderson, M., Pollack, L. M., & Chang, J. Y. (2008). Preliminary findings on a brief friendship-based HIV/STI intervention for urban African American Youth: Project Ore. *Journal of Adolescent Health, 42*, 629–633. doi:10.1016/j.jadohealth.2007.11.003

Donenberg, G. R., Bryant, F. B., Emerson, E., Wilson, H. W., & Pasch, K. E. (2003). Tracing the roots of early sexual debut among adolescents in psychiatric care. *Journal of the American Academy of Child and Adolescent Psychiatry*, *42*, 594–608. doi:10.1097/01.CHI.0000046833.09750.91

Donenberg, G. R., Paikoff, R., & Pequegnat, W. (2006). Introduction to the special section on families, youth, and HIV: Family-based intervention studies. [Research Support, N. I. H., Extramural]. *Journal of Pediatric Psychology*, *31*, 869–873. doi:10.1093/jpepsy/jsj102

Downing, J., Jones, L., Bates, G., Sumnall, H., & Bellis, M. A. (2011). A systematic review of parent and family-based intervention effectiveness on sexual outcomes in young People. *Health Education Research*, *26*, 808–833. doi:10.1093/her/cyr019

Dworkin, S. L., & Blankenship, K. (2009). Microfinance and HIV/AIDS prevention: Assessing its promise and limitations. *AIDS and Behavior, 13*, 462–469. doi:10.1007/s10461-009-9532-3

El-Bassel, N., Gilbert, L., Witte, S., Wu, E., Hunt, T., & Remien, R. H. (2010). Couple-based HIV prevention in the United States: Advantages, gaps, and future directions. *Journal of Acquired Immune Deficiency Syndromes, 55*, S98–S101. doi:110.1097/QAI.1090b1013e3181fbf1407

El-Bassel, N., Witte, S. S., Gilbert, L., Wu, E., Chang, M., Hill, J., & Steinglass, P. (2003). The efficacy of a relationship-based HIV/STD prevention program for heterosexual couples. *American Journal of Public Health*, *93*, 963. doi:10.2105/AJPH.93.6.963

El-Bassel, N., Witte, S. S., Gilbert, L., Wu, E., Chang, M., Hill, J., & Steinglass, P. (2005). Long-term effects of an HIV/STI sexual risk reduction intervention for heterosexual couples. *AIDS and Behavior*, *9*, 1–13. doi:10.1007/s10461-005-1677-0

Elkington, K. S., Bauermeister, J. A., Brackis-Cott, E., Dolezal, C., & Mellins, C. A. (2009). Substance use and sexual risk behaviors in perinatally Human Immunodeficiency Virus-exposed youth: Roles of caregivers, peers and HIV status. *Journal of Adolescent Health*, *45*, 133–141. doi:10.1016/j.jadohealth.2009.01.004

Elkington, K. S., Bauermeister, J. A., & Zimmerman, M. A. (2011). Do parents and peers matter? A prospective socio-ecological examination of substance use and condom use among African American youth. *Journal of Adolescence*, *34*, 1035–1047. doi:10.1016/j.adolescence.2010.11.004

Fang, X., Stanton, B., Li, X., Feigelman, S., & Baldwin, R. (1998). Similarities in sexual activity and condom use among friends within groups before and after a risk-reduction intervention. *Youth and Society*, *29*, 431–450. doi:10.1177/0044118X98029004002

Fenton, K. A. (2010). Time for change: Rethinking and reframing sexual health in the United States. *Journal of Sexual Medicine, 7*, 250–252. doi:10.1111/j.1743-6109.2010.02057.x

Fishbein, M., & Ajzen, I. (1975). *Belief, attitude, intention, and behavior: An introduction to theory and research.* Reading, MA: Addison-Wesley.

Fishbein, M., Bandura, A., Triandis, H. C., Kanfer, F. H., Becker, M. H., & Middlestadt, S. E. (1992). *Factors influencing behavior and behavior change: Final report, Theorists' Workshop.* Bethesda, MD: National Institute on Mental Health.

Fishbein, M., & Cappella, J. N. (2006). The role of theory in developing effective health communications. *Journal of Communication, 56*, S1–S17. doi:10.1111/j.1460-2466.2006.00280.x

Fishbein, M., & Yzer, M. C. (2003). Using theory to design effective health behavior interventions. *Communication Theory*, *13*, 164–183. doi:10.1111/j.1468-2885.2003.tb00287.x

Fisher, J. C., Bang, H., & Kapiga, S. (2007). The association between HIV infection and alcohol use: A systematic review and meta-analysis of African studies. *Sexually Transmitted Diseases*, *34*, 856–863. doi:10.1097/OLQ.0b013e318067b4fd

Fisher, J. D., Fisher, A. F., Bryan, A. D., & Misovich, S. J. (2002). Information-motivation-behavioral skills model–based HIV risk behavior change intervention for inner-city high school youth. *Health Psychology*, *21*, 177–186. doi:10.1037/0278-6133.21.2.177

Fisher, J. D., & Fisher, W. A. (2002). The information-motivation-behavioral skills model. In R. J. DiClemente, R. A. Crosby, & M. C. Kegler (Eds.), *Emerging theories in health promotion practice and research: Strategies for improving public health* (pp. 40–70). San Francisco, CA: Jossey-Bass.

Forehand, R., Armistead, L., Long, N., Wyckoff, S. C., Kotchick, B. A., Whitaker, D., . . . Miller, K. S. (2007). Efficacy of a parent-based sexual-risk prevention program for African American preadolescents: A randomized controlled trial. *Archives of Pediatrics and Adolescent Medicine*, *161*, 1123–1129. doi:10.1001/archpedi.161.12.1123

Frye, V., Koblin, B., Chin, J., Beard, J., Blaney, S., Halkitis, P., . . . Galea, S. (2010). Neighborhood-level correlates of consistent condom use among men who have sex with men: A multi-level analysis. *AIDS and Behavior*, *14*, 974–985. doi:10.1007/s10461-008-9438-5

Gagnon, J. H. (1988). Sex research and sexual conduct in the era of AIDS. *Journal of Acquired Immune Deficiency Syndromes, 1*, 593–601.

Galea, S., Ahern, J., Nandi, A., Tracy, M., Beard, J., & Vlahov, D. (2007). Urban neighborhood poverty and the incidence of depression in a population-based cohort study. *Annals of Epidemiology*, *17*, 171–179. doi:10.1016/j.annepidem.2006.07.008

Gebhardt, W. A., Kuyper, L., & Greunsven, G. (2003). Need for intimacy in relationships and motives for sex as determinants of adolescent condom use. *Journal of Adolescent Health*, *33*, 154–164. doi:10.1016/S1054-139X(03)00137-X

Gilbert, L., El-Bassel, N., Terlikbayeva, A., & Rozental, Y. (2010). Couple-based HIV prevention for injecting drug users in Kazakhstan: A pilot intervention study. *Journal of Prevention and Intervention in the Community*, *38*, 162–176. doi:10.1080/10852351003640914

Gillespie, S., Kadiyala, S., & Greener, R. (2007). Is poverty or wealth driving HIV transmission? *AIDS*, *21*, S5–S16. doi:10.1097/01.aids.0000300531.74730.72

Godin, G., Naccache, H., Cote, F., Leclerc, R., Frechette, M., & Alary, M. (2008). Promotion of safe sex: Evaluation of a community-level intervention programme in gay bars, saunas and sex shops. *Health Education Research*, *23*, 287–297. doi:10.1093/her/cym033

Golub, S. A., Kowalczyk, W., Weinberger, C., & Parsons, J. T. (2010). Preexposure prophylaxis and predicted condom use among high-risk men who have sex with men. *Journal of Acquired Immune Deficiency Syndromes*, *54*, 548–555. doi:10.1097/QAI.0b013e3181e19a54

Gómez, C., & VanOss Marín, B. (1996). Gender, culture, and power: Barriers to HIV-prevention strategies for women. *Journal of Sex Research*, *33*, 355–362. doi:10.1080/00224499609551853

Grant, R. M., Lama, J. R., Anderson, P. L., McMahan, V., Liu, A. Y., Vargas, L., . . . Glidden, D. V. (2010). Preexposure chemoprophylaxis for HIV prevention in men who have sex with men. *New England Journal of Medicine*, *363*, 2587–2599. doi:10.1056/NEJMoa1011205

Gupta, G. R., Parkhurst, J. O., Ogden, J. A., Aggleton, P., & Mahal, A. (2008). Structural approaches to HIV prevention. *Lancet*, *372*, 764–775. doi:10.1016/S0140-6736(08)60887-9

Hall, J. C., Hall, B. J., & Cockerell, C. J. (2011). *HIV/AIDS in the post-HAART era: Manifestations, treatment and epidemiology*. Shelton, CT: People's Medical Publishing House.

Haney, T. J. (2007). "Broken windows" and self-esteem: Subjective understandings of neighborhood poverty and disorder. *Social Science Research*, *36*, 968–994. doi:10.1016/j.ssresearch.2006.07.003

Hargreaves, J. R., Bonell, C. P., Boler, T., Boccia, D., Birdthistle, I., Fletcher, A., . . . Glynn, J. (2008). Systematic review exploring time trends in the association between educational attainment and risk of HIV infection in sub-Saharan Africa. *AIDS*, *22*, 403–414. doi:10.1097/QAD.0b013e3282f2aac3

Higgins, J. A., Hoffman, S., & Dworkin, S. L. (2010). Rethinking gender, heterosexual men, and women's vulnerability to HIV/AIDS. *American Journal of Public Health*, *100*, 435–445. doi:10.2105/AJPH.2009.159723

Hoff, C. C., Stall, R., Paul, J., Acree, M., Daigle, D., Phillips, K., . . . Coates, T. J. (1997). Differences in sexual behavior among HIV discordant and concordant gay men in primary relationships. *Journal of Acquired Immune Deficiency Syndromes and Human Retrovirology, 14*, 72–78. doi:10.1097/00042560-199701010-00012

Hogben, M., & Liddon, N. (2008). Disinhibition and risk compensation: Scope, definitions, and perspective. *Sexually Transmitted Diseases*, *35*, 1009–1010.

Huebner, D. M., Binson, D., Dilworth, S. E., Neilands, T., Grinstead, O., & Woods, W. J. (2010). Rapid vs. standard HIV testing in a bathhouse setting: What is gained and lost? *AIDS and Behavior, 14*, 688–696. doi:10.1007/s10461-008-9442-9

Huebner, D. M., Binson, D., Woods, W. J., Dilworth, S. E., Neilands, T., & Grinstead, O. (2006). Bathhouse-based voluntary counseling and testing is feasible and shows preliminary evidence of effectiveness. *Journal of Acquired Immune Deficiency Syndromes*, *43*, 239–246. doi:10.1097/01.qai.0000242464.50947.16

Janz, N. K., Zimmerman, M. A., Wren, P. A., Israel, B. A., Freudenberg, N., & Carter, R. J. (1996). Evaluation of 37 AIDS prevention projects: Successful approaches and barriers to program effectiveness. *Health Education Quarterly*, *23*, 80–97. doi:10.1177/109019819602300106

Johnson, B. T., Carey, M. P., Chaudoir, S. R., & Reid, A. E. (2006). Sexual risk reduction for persons living with HIV: Research synthesis of randomized controlled trials, 1993–2004. *Journal of Acquired Immune Deficiency Syndromes*, *41*, 642–650. doi:10.1097/01.qai.0000194495.15309.47

Johnson, B. T., Redding, C. A., DiClemente, R. J., Dodge, B., Mustanski, B. S., Sheeran, P., et al. (2010). Toward a network-individual-resource framework for HIV prevention. *AIDS and Behavior*, *14*(Suppl. 2), 204–221. doi:10.1007/s10461-010-9803-z

Johnson, B. T., Scott-Sheldon, L. A. J., Huedo-Medina, T., & Carey, M. (2011). Interventions to reduce sexual risk for human immunodeficiency virus in adolescents: A meta-analysis of trials, 1985–2008. *Archives of Pediatrics and Adolescent Medicine*, *165*, 77–84. doi:10.1001/archpediatrics.2010.251

Johnston, M. I., & Fauci, A. (2008). An HIV vaccine: Challenges and prospects. *New England Journal of Medicine, 359*, 888–890. doi:10.1056/NEJMp0806162

Kalichman, S. C. (2010). Neonatal circumcision for HIV prevention: Cost, culture, and behavioral considerations. *PLoS Medicine*, *7*(1), e1000219.

Kawachi, I. (2000). Social cohesion and health. In A. R. Tarlov & R. F. St. Peter (Eds.), *The society and population health reader: A state and community perspective* (pp. 57–74). New York, NY: New Press.

Kegeles, S. M. (1996). The Mpowerment Project: A community-level HIV prevention intervention for young gay men. *American Journal of Public Health, 86*, 1129–1136. doi:10.2105/AJPH.86.8_Pt_1.1129

Kegeles, S. M., Hays, R. B., Pollack, L. M., & Coates, T. J. (1999). Mobilizing young gay and bisexual men for HIV prevention: A two-community study. *AIDS, 13*, 1753–1762. doi:10.1097/00002030-199909100-00020

Kelling, G. L., & Coles, C. M. (1996). *Fixing broken windows: Restoring order and reducing crime in our communities.* New York, NY: Touchstone.

Kelly, B. C., & Muñoz-Laboy, M. A. (2005). Sexual place, spatial change, and the social reorganization of sexual culture. *Journal of Sex Research, 42*, 359–366. doi:10.1080/00224490509552292

Kelly, J. A. (1995). Advances in HIV/AIDS education and prevention. *Family Relations, 44*, 345–352. doi:10.2307/584989

Kelly, J. A., & Kalichman, S. C. (1995). Increased attention to human sexuality can improve HIV-AIDS prevention efforts: Key research issues and directions. *Journal of Consulting and Clinical Psychology, 63*, 907–918. doi:10.1037/0022-006X.63.6.907

Kelly, J. A., Murphy, D. A., Sikkema, K. J., McAuliffe, R. L., Roffman, R. A., Solomon, L. J., . . . Kalichman, S. C. (1997). Randomised, controlled, community-level HIV-prevention intervention for sexual-risk behaviour among homosexual men in US cities. *Lancet, 350*, 1500–1505. doi:10.1016/S0140-6736(97)07439-4

Kim, C. R., & Free, C. (2008). Recent evaluations of the peer-led approach in adolescent sexual health education: A systematic review. *Perspectives on Sexual and Reproductive Health, 40*, 144–151. doi:10.1363/4014408

Kim, J. C., Watts, C. H., Hargreaves, J. R., Ndhlovu, L. X., Phetla, G., Morison, L. A., . . . Pronyk, P. M. (2007). Understanding the impact of a microfinance-based intervention on women's empowerment and the reduction of intimate partner violence in South Africa. *American Journal of Public Health, 97*, 1794–1802. doi:10.2105/AJPH.2006.095521

Ko, N.-Y., Lee, H.-C., Hung, C.-C., Chang, J.-L., Lee, N.-Y., Chang, C.-M., . . . Ko, W.-C. (2009). Effects of structural intervention on increasing condom availability and reducing risky behaviours in gay bathhouse attendees. *AIDS Care, 21*, 1499–1507. doi:10.1080/09540120902923022

Kreiss, J. K., & Hopkins, S. G. (1993). The association between circumcision status and Human Immunodeficiency Virus infection among homosexual men. *Journal of Infectious Diseases, 168*, 1404–1408. doi:10.1093/infdis/168.6.1404

Latkin, C., Weeks, M. R., Glasman, L., Galletly, C., & Albarracín, D. (2010). A dynamic social systems model for considering structural factors in HIV prevention and detection. *AIDS and Behavior, 14*(Suppl. 2), 222–238. doi:10.1007/s10461-010-9804-y

Latkin, C. A., Forman, V., Knowlton, A., & Sherman, S. (2003). Norms, social networks, and HIV-related risk behaviors among urban disadvantaged drug users. *Social Science and Medicine, 56*, 465–476. doi:10.1016/S0277-9536(02)00047-3

Leigh, B. C. (2002). Alcohol and condom use: A meta-analysis of event-level studies. *Sexually Transmitted Diseases, 29*, 476–482. doi:10.1097/00007435-200208000-00008

Lewis, M. A., DeVellis, B. M., & Sleath, B. (2002). Social influence and interpersonal communication in health behavior. In K. Glanz, B. K. Rimer, & F. M. Lewis (Eds.), *Health behavior and health education: Theory, research, and practice* (pp. 240–264). San Francisco, CA: Jossey-Bass.

Liu, A. Y., Kittredge, P. V., Vittinghoff, E., Raymond, H. F., Ahrens, K., Matheson, T., . . . Buchbinder, S. (2008). Limited knowledge and use of HIV post- and pre-exposure prophylaxis among gay and bisexual men. *Journal of Acquired Immune Deficiency Syndromes, 47*, 241–247. doi:10.1097/QAI.0b013e31815e4041

Luna, G. C., & Rotheram-Borus, M. J. (1999). Youth living with HIV as peer leaders. *American Journal of Community Psychology, 27*, 1–23. doi:10.1023/A:1022861610985

Major, I., Lowry, D., Malcolm, K., Woolfson, D., Cohen, J., LaBarre, P., . . . Friend, D. (2010). *Development of a microbicide-releasing diaphragm as an HIV prevention strategy.* 32nd Annual International Conference of the IEEE EMBS, Buenos Aires, Argentina.

Malow, R. M., Rosenberg, R., Donenberg, G. R., & Devieux, J. G. (2006). Interventions and patterns of risk in adolescent HIV/AIDS prevention. *American Journal of Infectious Diseases, 2*, 80–89. doi:10.3844/ajidsp.2006.80.89

Maticka-Tyndale, E., & Barnett, J. P. (2010). Peer-led interventions to reduce HIV risk of youth: A review. *Evaluation and Program Planning, 33*, 98–112. doi:10.1016/j.evalprogplan.2009.07.001

McKay, M. M., Chasse, K. T., Paikoff, R., McKinney, L. D., Baptiste, D., Coleman, D., . . . Bell, C. C. (2004). Family-level impact of the CHAMP Family Program: A community collaborative effort to support urban families and reduce youth HIV risk exposure. *Family Process, 43*, 79–93. doi:10.1111/j.1545-5300.2004.04301007.x

Medley, A., Kennedy, C., O'Reilly, K., & Sweat, M. (2009). Effectiveness of peer education interventions for HIV prevention in developing countries: A systematic review and meta-analysis. *AIDS*

Education and Prevention, 21, 181–206. doi:10.1521/aeap.2009.21.3.181

Michael, R. T., Gagnon, J. H., Laumann, E., & Kolata, G. (1994). *Sex in America: A definitive survey*. Boston, MA: Little, Brown.

Michaels, S., & Giami, A. (1999). Sexual acts and sexual relationships: Asking about sex in surveys. *Public Opinion Quarterly, 63*, 401–420. doi:10.1086/297727

Millett, G. A., Ding, H., Lauby, J., Flores, S., Stueve, A., Bingham, T., . . . Marks, G. (2007). Circumcision status and HIV infection among black and Latino men who have sex with men in 3 US cities. *Journal of Acquired Immune Deficiency Syndromes, 46*, 643–650. doi:10.1097/QAI.0b013e31815b834d

Minkler, M., & Wallerstein, N. (2002). Improving health through community organization and community building: A health education perspective. In M. Minkler (Ed.), *Community organizing and community building for health* (pp. 30–52). New Brunswick, NJ: Rutgers University Press.

Mintz, E. (1994). "Narrow vs. broad targeting of HIV/AIDS education": Response. *American Journal of Public Health, 84*, 498–499. doi:10.2105/AJPH.84.3.498-a

Moos, R. H. (1974). *Evaluating treatment environments: A social ecological approach*. New York, NY: Wiley.

Morisky, D. E., Malow, R. M., Tiglao, T. V., Lyu, S.-Y., Vissman, A. T., & Rhodes, S. D. (2010). Reducing sexual risk among Filipina female bar workers: Effects of a CBPR-developed structural and network intervention. *AIDS Education and Prevention, 22*, 371–385. doi:10.1521/aeap.2010.22.4.371

Morrison, D. M., Casey, E. A., Beadnell, B. A., Hoppe, M. J., Gillmore, M. R., Wilsdon, A., . . . Wells, E. A. (2007). Effects of friendship closeness in an adolescent group HIV prevention intervention. *Prevention Science, 8*, 274–284. doi:10.1007/s11121-007-0075-4

Ness, R. B., Hillier, S. L., Richter, H. E., Soper, D. E., Stamm, C., Bass, D. C., . . . Aral, S. (2003). Why women douche and why they may or may not stop. *Sexually Transmitted Diseases, 30*, 71–74. doi:10.1097/00007435-200301000-00014

Neumann, M. S., Johnson, W. D., Semaan, S., Flores, S. A., Peersman, G., Hedges, L. V., & Sogolow, E. (2002). Review and meta-analysis of HIV prevention intervention research for heterosexual adult populations in the United States. *Journal of Acquired Immune Deficiency Syndromes, 30*, S106–S117.

NIMH Multisite HIV Prevention Trial for African American Couples Group. (2008). Eban HIV/STD risk reduction intervention: Conceptual basis and procedures. *Journal of Acquired Immune Deficiency Syndromes, 49*, S15–S27. doi:10.1097/QAI.0b013e318184255d

NIMH Multisite HIV Prevention Trial Group. (1998). The NIMH multisite HIV prevention trial: Reducing HIV sexual risk behavior. *Science, 280*, 1889–1894. doi:10.1126/science.280.5371.1889

Obermeyer, C. M., & Osborn, M. (2007). The Utilization of Testing and Counseling for HIV: A Review of the Social and Behavioral Evidence. *American Journal of Public Health, 97*, 1762–1774. doi:10.2105/AJPH.2006.096263

Oh, M. K., Merchant, J., & Brown, P. (2002). Douching behavior in high-risk adolescents. What do they use, when and why do they douche? *Journal of Pediatric and Adolescent Gynecology, 15*, 83–88. doi:10.1016/S1083-3188(01)00148-6

O'Leary, A., & Wingood, G. M. (2000). Interventions for sexually active heterosexual women. In J. L. Peterson & R. J. DiClemente (Eds.), *Handbook of HIV prevention* (pp. 179–200). New York, NY: Plenum. doi:10.1007/978-1-4615-4137-0_9

Padian, N. S., O'Brien, T. R., Chang, Y. C., Glass, S., & Francis, D. (1993). Prevention of heterosexual transmission of human immunodeficiency virus through couple counseling. *Journal of Acquired Immune Deficiency Syndromes, 6*, 1043–1048.

Parker, D. A., Harford, T. C., & Rosenstock, I. M. (1994). Alcohol, other drugs, and sexual risk-taking among young adults. *Journal of Substance Abuse, 6*, 87–93. doi:10.1016/S0899-3289(94)90117-1

Parker, E. A., Lichtenstein, R. L., Schulz, A. J., Israel, B. A., Schork, M. A., Steinman, K. J., & James, S. A. (2001). Disentangling measures of individual perceptions of community social dynamics: Results of a community survey. *Health Education and Behavior, 28*, 462–486. doi:10.1177/109019810102800407

Parker, R. (2001). Sexuality, culture, and power in HIV/AIDS research. *Annual Review of Anthropology, 30*, 163–179. doi:10.1146/annurev.anthro.30.1.163

Parker, R. (2009a). Sexuality, culture and society: Shifting paradigms in sexuality research. *Culture, Health, and Sexuality, 11*, 251–266. doi:10.1080/13691050701606941

Parker, R. (2009b). Unintended consequences: Evaluating the impact of HIV and AIDS on sexuality research and policy debates. *Cadernos de Saude Publica, 25*(Suppl. 2), S251–S258. doi:10.1590/S0102-311X2009001400007

Parker, R., Di Mauro, D., Filiano, B., Garcia, J., Munoz-Laboy, M., & Sember, R. (2004). Global transformations and intimate relations in the 21st century: Social science research on sexuality and the emergence of sexual health and sexual rights frameworks. *Annual Review of Sex Research, 15*, 362–398.

Parker, R., Easton, D., & Klein, C. (2000). Structural barriers and facilitators in HIV prevention: A review of international research. *AIDS, 14*(Suppl. 1), S22–S32. doi:10.1097/00002030-200006001-00004

Pedlow, C. T., & Carey, M. P. (2003). HIV sexual risk-reduction interventions for youth: A review and methodological critique of randomized controlled trials. *Behavior Modification, 27*, 135–190. doi:10.1177/0145445503251562

Perrino, T., Gonzalez-Soldevilla, A., Pantin, H., & Szapocznik, J. (2000). The role of families in adolescent HIV prevention: A review. *Clinical Child and Family Psychology Review, 3*, 81–96. doi:10.1023/A:1009571518900

Phelan, J. C., Link, B. G., & Tehranifar, P. (2010). Social conditions as fundamental causes of health inequalities: Theory, evidence, and policy implications. *Journal of Health and Social Behavior, 51*(Suppl. 1), S28–S40. doi:10.1177/0022146510383498

Potts, M. (1994). The urgent need for a vaginal microbicide in the prevention of HIV transmission. *American Journal of Public Health, 84*, 890. doi:10.2105/AJPH.84.6.890

Prado, G., Pantin, H., Briones, E., Schwartz, S. J., Feaster, D., Huang, S., . . . Szapocznik, J. (2007). A randomized controlled trial of a parent-centered intervention in preventing substance use and HIV risk behaviors in Hispanic adolescents. *Journal of Consulting and Clinical Psychology, 75*, 914–926. doi:10.1037/0022-006X.75.6.914

Prendergast, M. L., Urada, D., & Podus, D. (2001). Meta-analysis of HIV risk-reduction interventions within drug abuse treatment programs. *Journal of Consulting and Clinical Psychology, 69*, 389–405. doi:10.1037/0022-006X.69.3.389

Pronyk, P. M., Hargreaves, J. R., Kim, J. C., Morison, L. A., Phetla, G., Watts, C., . . . Porter, J. D. H. (2006). Effect of a structural intervention for the prevention of intimate-partner violence and HIV in rural South Africa: A cluster randomized trial. *Lancet, 368*, 1973–1983. doi:10.1016/S0140-6736(06)69744-4

Pronyk, P. M., Hargreaves, J. R., & Morduch, J. (2007). Microfinance programs and better health: Prospects for sub-Saharan Africa. *JAMA, 298*, 1925–1927. doi:10.1001/jama.298.16.1925

Pronyk, P. M., Kim, J. C., Abramsky, T., Godfrey, P., Hargreaves, J. R., Morison, L. A., . . . Porter, J. D. H. (2008). A combined microfinance and training intervention can reduce HIV risk behaviour in young female participants. *AIDS, 22*, 1659–1665. doi:10.1097/QAD.0b013e328307a040

Puckett, S. B., Bart, M., Bye, L., & Amory, J. (1985). Self-reported behavioural changes among gay and bisexual men: San Francisco. *Morbidity and Mortality Weekly Report, 34*, 613–615.

Pulerwitz, J., Amaro, H., De Jong, W., Gortmaker, S. L., & Rudd, R. (2002). Relationship power, condom use and HIV risk among women in the USA. *AIDS Care, 14*, 789–800. doi:10.1080/0954012021000031868

Ramirez-Valles, J. (2002). The protective effects of community involvement for HIV risk behavior: A conceptual framework. *Health Education Research, 17*, 389–403. doi:10.1093/her/17.4.389

Rappaport, J. (1977). *Community psychology: Values, research and action*. New York, NY: Holt, Rinehart & Winston.

Repetti, R. L., Taylor, S. E., & Seeman, T. E. (2002). Risky families: Family social environments and the mental and physical health of offspring. *Psychological Bulletin, 128*, 330–366. doi:10.1037/0033-2909.128.2.330

Rerks-Ngarm, S., Pitisuttithum, P., Nitayaphan, S., Kaewkungwal, J., Chiu, J., Paris, R., . . . Kim, J. H. (2009). Vaccination with ALVAC and AIDSVAX to prevent HIV-1 infection in Thailand. *New England Journal of Medicine, 361*, 2209–2220. doi:10.1056/NEJMoa0908492

Rhodes, T., Singer, M., Bourgois, P., Friedman, S. R., & Strathdee, S. (2005). The social structural production of HIV risk among injecting drug users. *Social Science and Medicine, 61*, 1026–1044. doi:10.1016/j.socscimed.2004.12.024

Rogers, E. M. (1995). *Diffusion of innovations* (4th ed.). New York, NY: Free Press.

Romanelli, F. (2010). Systemic preexposure prophylaxis for Human Immunodeficiency Virus infection. *Pharmacotherapy, 30*, 1021–1030. doi:10.1592/phco.30.10.1021

Romer, D., Black, M., Izabel, R., Feigelman, S., Kaljee, L., Galbraith, J., . . . Stanton, B. (1994). Social influences on the sexual behavior of youth at risk for HIV exposure. *American Journal of Public Health, 84*, 977–985. doi:10.2105/AJPH.84.6.977

Rothenberg, R., Muth, S. Q., Malone, S., Potterat, J. J., & Woodhouse, D. (2005). Social and geographic distance in HIV risk. *Sexually Transmitted Diseases, 32*, 506–512. doi:10.1097/01.olq.0000161191.12026.ca

Salazar, L. F., DiClemente, R. J., Wingood, G. M., Crosby, R. A., Harrington, K., Davies, S., . . . Oh, M. K. (2004). Self-concept and adolescents' refusal of unprotected sex: A test of mediating mechanisms among African American girls. *Prevention Science, 5*, 137–149. doi:10.1023/B:PREV.0000037638.20810.01

Sampson, R. J., & Groves, W. B. (1989). Community structure and crime: Testing social-disorganization theory. *American Journal of Sociology, 94*, 774–802. doi:10.1086/229068

Sampson, R. J., Raudenbush, S. W., & Earls, F. (1997). Neighborhoods and violent crime: A multilevel study of collective efficacy. *Science, 277*, 918–924. doi:10.1126/science.277.5328.918

Schneider, J. A., & Laumann, E. (2011). Alternative explanations for negative findings in the community popular opinion leader multisite trial and recommendations for improvements of health interventions through social network analysis. *Journal of Acquired Immune Deficiency Syndromes*, *56*, e119–e120. doi:10.1097/QAI.0b013e318207a34c

Semaan, S., Des Jarlais, D., Sogolow, E., Johnson, W., Hedges, L., Ramirez, G., . . . Needle, R. (2002). A meta-analysis of the effect of HIV prevention interventions on the sex behaviors of drug users in the United States. *Journal of Acquired Immune Deficiency Syndromes*, *30*, S73–S93.

Sherman, S. G., German, D., Cheng, Y., Marks, M., & Bailey-Kloche, M. (2006). The evaluation of the JEWEL project: An innovative economic enhancement and HIV prevention intervention study targeting drug using women involved in prostitution. *AIDS Care*, *18*, 1–11. doi:10.1080/09540120500101625

Shuper, P. A., Joharchi, N., Irving, H., & Rehm, J. (2009). Alcohol as a correlate of unprotected sexual behavior among people living with HIV/AIDS: Review and meta-analysis. *AIDS and Behavior*, *13*, 1021–1036. doi:10.1007/s10461-009-9589-z

Sorrells, M. L., Snyder, J. L., Reiss, M. D., Eden, C., Milos, M. F., Wilcox, N., & van Howe, R. S. (2007). Fine-touch pressure thresholds in the adult penis. *BJU International*, *99*, 864–869. doi:10.1111/j.1464-410X.2006.06685.x

Stanton, B., Kim, N., Galbraith, J. S., & Parrott, M. (1996). Design issues addressed in published evaluations of adolescent HIV-risk reduction interventions: A review. *Journal of Adolescent Health*, *18*, 387–396. doi:10.1016/1054-139X(95)00169-S

Stanton, B., Xiaoming, L., Pack, R., Cottrell, L., Harris, C., & Burns, J. M. (2002). Longitudinal influence of perceptions of peer and parental factors on African American adolescent risk involvement. *Journal of Urban Health*, *79*, 536–548. doi:10.1093/jurban/79.4.536

Stevens, S., Leybas-Amedia, V., Bourdeau, B., McMichael, L., & Nyitray, A. (2006). Blending prevention models: An effective substance use and HIV prevention program for minority youth. *Child and Adolescent Social Work Journal*, *23*, 4–23. doi:10.1007/s10560-005-0027-4

Sullivan, P. S., Kilmarx, P. H., Peterman, T. A., Taylor, A. W., Nakashima, A. K., Kamb, M. L., . . . Mastro, T. D. (2007). Male circumcision for prevention of HIV transmission: What the new data mean for HIV prevention in the United States. *PLoS Medicine*, *4*(7), e223.

Tanner, W. M., & Pollack, R. H. (1988). The effect of condom use and erotic instructions on attitudes toward condoms. *Journal of Sex Research*, *25*, 537–541. doi:10.1080/00224498809551481

Teitelman, A. M. (2004). Adolescent girls' perspectives of family interactions related to menarche and sexual health. *Qualitative Health Research*, *14*, 1292–1308. doi:10.1177/1049732304268794

Thurstone, C., Riggs, P. D., Klein, C., & Mikulich-Gilbertson, S. K. (2007). A one-session Human Immunodeficiency Virus risk-reduction intervention in adolescents with psychiatric and substance use disorders. *Journal of the American Academy of Child and Adolescent Psychiatry*, *46*, 1179–1186. doi:10.1097/chi.0b013e31809fe774

Tolman, D. L., & Diamond, L. M. (2001). Desegregating sexuality research: Cultural and biological perspectives on gender and desire. *Annual Review of Sex Research*, *12*, 33–74.

Tolou-Shams, M., Stewart, A., Fasciano, J., & Brown, L. K. (2010). A review of HIV prevention interventions for juvenile offenders. *Journal of Pediatric Psychology*, *35*, 250–261. doi:10.1093/jpepsy/jsp069

UNAIDS. (2010). *UNAIDS report on the global HIV/AIDS epidemic* Retrieved from http://www.unaids.org/en/aboutunaids/unitednationsdeclarationsandgoals/2011highlevelmeetingonaids

van de Wijgert, J., & Coggins, C. (2002). Microbicides to prevent heterosexual transmission of HIV: Ten years down the road. *BETA: A Bulletin of Experimental Treatments for AIDS*, *15*(2), 23–28.

van de Wijgert, J. H. H. M., & Shattock, R. J. (2007). Vaginal microbicides: Moving ahead after an unexpected setback. *AIDS*, *21*, 2369–2376. doi:10.1097/QAD.0b013e3282ef83fd

Vincent, L. (2008). "Boys will be boys": Traditional Xhosa male circumcision, HIV, and sexual socialization in contemporary South Africa. *Culture, Health, and Sexuality*, *10*, 431–446. doi:10.1080/13691050701861447

Vosburgh, H. W., Mansergh, G., Sullivan, P. S., & Purcell, D. W. (2012). A review of the literature on event-level substance use and sexual risk behavior among men who have sex with men. *AIDS and Behavior*, *16*, 1394–1410. doi:10.1007/s10461-011-0131-8

Wallace, R. (1990). Urban desertification, public health and public order: "planned shrinkage," violent death, substance abuse, and AIDS in the Bronx. *Social Science and Medicine*, *31*, 801–813. doi:10.1016/0277-9536(90)90175-R

Wallerstein, N., & Bernstein, E. (1988). Empowerment education: Freire's ideas adapted to health education. *Health Education Quarterly*, *15*, 379–394. doi:10.1177/109019818801500402

Wang, K., Brown, K., & Shen, S.-Y. (2011). Social network–based interventions to promote condom use: A systematic review. *AIDS and Behavior*, *15*, 1298–1308.

Weber, J., Desai, K., & Darbyshire, J. (2005). The development of vaginal microbicides for the prevention of HIV transmission. *PLoS Medicine*, *2*(5), e142. doi:10.1371/journal.pmed.0020142

Weiss, H. A., Hankins, C. A., & Dickson, K. (2009). Male circumcision and risk of HIV infection in women: A systematic review and meta-analysis. *Lancet*

Infectious Diseases, 9, 669–677. doi:10.1016/S1473-3099(09)70235-X

Weiss, H. A., Quigley, M. A., & Hayes, R. J. (2000). Male circumcision and risk of HIV infection in sub-Saharan Africa: A systematic review and meta-analysis. *AIDS, 14*, 2361–2370. doi:10.1097/00002030-200010200-00018

Wingood, G. M., & DiClemente, R. (2002). The theory of gender and power: A social structural theory for guiding public health interventions. In R. J. DiClemente, R. A. Crosby, & M. C. Kegler (Eds.), *Emerging theories in health promotion practice and research: Strategies for improving public health* (pp. 313–346). San Francisco, CA: Jossey-Bass.

Winstanley, E. L., Steinwachs, D. M., Ensminger, M. E., Latkin, C. A., Stitzer, M. L., & Olsen, Y. (2008). The association of self-reported neighborhood disorganization and social capital with adolescent alcohol and drug use, dependence, and access to treatment. *Drug and Alcohol Dependence, 92*, 173–182. doi:10.1016/j.drugalcdep.2007.07.012

Wolitski, R. J., Kidder, D. P., Pals, S. L., Royal, S., Aidala, A., Stall, R., . . . Courtenay-Quirk, C. (2010). Randomized trial of the effects of housing assistance on the health and risk behaviors of homeless and unstably housed people living with HIV. *AIDS and Behavior, 14*, 493–503. doi:10.1007/s10461-009-9643-x

Woods, W. J., Binson, D., Pollack, L., Wohlfeiler, D., Stall, R., & Catania, J. (2003). Public policy regulations and public space in gay bathhouses. *Journal of Acquired Immune Deficiency Syndromes, 32*, 417–423. doi:10.1097/00126334-200304010-00011

Zimmerman, M. A. (2000). Empowerment theory: Psychological, organizational, and community levels of analysis. In J. Rappaport & E. Seidman (Eds.), *Handbook of community psychology* (pp. 43–63). New York, NY: Kluwer Academic/Plenum. doi:10.1007/978-1-4615-4193-6_2

Zimmerman, M. A., Ramirez-Valles, J., Suarez, E., de la Rosa, G., & Castro, M. A. (1997). An HIV/AIDS prevention project for Mexican homosexual men: An empowerment approach. *Health Education and Behavior, 24*, 177–190. doi:10.1177/109019819702400206

CHAPTER 23

SEXUALITY AND REPRODUCTIVE HEALTH

Ronna Popkin and John Santelli

More than 65 years ago, the World Health Organization (WHO) took an affirmative approach to defining health, claiming in the preamble to its constitution that health is "a state of complete physical, mental, and social well-being and not merely the absence of disease or infirmity" (WHO, 1946, p. 1). Thus, definitions of sexual and reproductive health, like all areas of health, stem from these baseline principles that suggest that health in multiple arenas of life ought to be defined not just by the negative conditions that they lack, but also by the positive states that they encompass. Public health surveillance, research, and programs related to reproductive and sexual health, however, frequently have been focused on eliminating dysfunctions or diseases, such as sexually transmitted diseases (STDs), unwanted pregnancies, and sexual violence, rather than promoting reproductive choice, pleasure, and personal agency (see Chapters 11 and 21, this volume). Furthermore, although in recent years sexual and reproductive health increasingly have been researched and explored together, this is a relatively recent historical trend, emerging largely since the mid-1990s.

This chapter reviews the various conceptions of public health, reproductive health, sexuality, and sexual health and explains their interrelationships. It then briefly outlines the strengths and limitations of the typical public health focus on preventing disease and disability, explaining how public health goals and surveillance shape reproductive and sexual health priorities, research, programs, policies, and practices. Finally, it highlights new initiatives that reflect the increasing integration of the fields of sexual and reproductive health and issues suggestions for future directions in surveillance, research, and programming that will build off of these innovative approaches.

PUBLIC HEALTH DEFINITIONS AND FRAMEWORKS ON SEXUAL AND REPRODUCTIVE HEALTH

As medicine incorporates a scientific and technical approach to making health better, public health often has focused on using technical, medical, and scientific knowledge to improve health and prevent death and disability. Both social epidemiology and social medicine, which emphasize the social conditions that influence health and disease, preceded and have served as counterbalances to this technical approach by the two professions. Conventionally, the public health approach to reproductive health issues, such as family planning, pregnancy, and childbirth, has been motivated by concrete health outcomes like maternal and infant mortality, and these efforts often have been concurrent with efforts to expand women's rights (see Volume 2, Chapters 9 and 10, this handbook). For example, Margaret Sanger, the creator of the modern family planning movement, embraced both the mantle of medicine and the importance of political action to expand women's rights to control their own fertility (Chesler, 1992). Although some have denounced her work given her political alliances with eugenicists, she understood both the public health aims (e.g., preventing maternal mortality and morbidity)

http://dx.doi.org/10.1037/14193-023
APA Handbook of Sexuality and Psychology: Vol. 1. Person-Based Approaches, D. L. Tolman and L. M. Diamond (Editors-in-Chief)

and the broader vision of women's empowerment (Gordon, 2002). Reducing maternal and infant morbidity and mortality are worthy and necessary goals; however, focusing on these areas has meant that issues that more commonly fall under the rubric of sexuality, such as pleasure, agency, and choice, typically have not been the focus of public health efforts. Furthermore, only recently have more modern conceptions of public health developed that are based on a framework of rights, the elimination of health disparities, and positive visions of health.

In the mid-twentieth century, public health work related to reproduction, both in the United States and abroad, became linked with population control initiatives, which were critiqued heavily by feminist and women's health activists in the 1970s and 1980s as coercive infringements on women's reproductive rights and freedoms (Bandarage, 1997; Correa & Petchesky, 1994; Dixon-Mueller, 1993a). After the 1994 International Conference on Population and Development (ICPD) in Cairo and the 1995 Fourth World Conference on Women in Beijing, the dominant public health perspective on reproduction became women's rights and empowerment and reproductive choice, shifting from a narrower focus on controlling population levels and promoting family planning and maternal and child health. After Cairo, access to education and family planning were redefined as supporting women's empowerment; empowerment was important on its own terms, but it also typically led to smaller family sizes. The Report of the ICPD provided a clear definition of reproductive health (see Exhibit 23.1) that was noteworthy in several regards. It not only emphasized reproductive freedoms and choices but also mentioned sexual health and the right to a "satisfying and safe sex life" (United Nations, 1995). Before that point, most policy makers and researchers had viewed and treated sexual health as part of the field of human sexuality, not public health. Thus, the "reproductive health" paradigm that emerged in the mid-1990s was a progressive reframing that linked reproductive health, sexual health, and human rights (Correa & Petchesky, 1994).

Despite this broader framework that emerged in the 1990s, most public health research, surveillance, and programs related to sexual and reproductive health in the United States continue to emphasize issues related to reproduction rather than sexuality. This emphasis partly is due to cultural and religious barriers to addressing human sexuality. The United States, especially when compared with its peer nations in Western Europe, is a sexually conservative nation. For example, at the national level, condoms are rarely advertised on primetime network television (Brodesser-Akner, 2007; Wilke, 2001),

Exhibit 23.1
Definitions of Health

Health: "A state of complete physical, mental, and social well-being and not merely the absence of disease or infirmity" (WHO, 1946, p. 1).

Reproductive health: "Reproductive health is a state of complete physical, mental and social well-being and not merely the absence of disease or infirmity, in all matters relating to the reproductive system, and to its functions and processes. Reproductive health therefore implies that people are able to have a satisfying and safe sex life and that they have the capability to reproduce and the freedom to decide if, when and how often to do so. Implicitly in this last condition are the right of men and women to be informed and to have access to safe, effective, affordable and acceptable methods of family planning of their choice, as well as other methods of their choice for regulations of fertility which are not against the law and the right of access to appropriate health-care services that will enable women to go safely through pregnancy and childbirth and provide couples with the best chance of having a healthy infant. In line with the above definition of reproductive health, reproductive health care is defined as the constellation of methods, techniques and services that contribute to reproductive health and well-being by preventing and solving reproductive health problems. It also includes sexual health, the purpose of which is the enhancement of life and personal relations, and not merely counseling and care related to reproduction and sexually transmitted diseases" (United Nations, 1995, p. 40).

Sexual health: "Sexual health is a state of physical, emotional, mental, and social well-being in relation to sexuality; it is not merely the absence of disease, dysfunction, or infirmity. Sexual health needs a positive and respectful approach to sexuality and sexual relationships, and the possibility of having pleasurable and safe sexual experiences that are free of coercion, discrimination, and violence. For sexual health to be attained and maintained, the sexual rights of all individuals must be respected, protected, and satisfied" (WHO, 2006, p. 5).

and conservative members of congress have made consistent, repeated attempts to defund family planning programs because they believe that facilitating access to contraception threatens public morality (Miles, 2011; Sonfield & Gold, 2005). At the state level, there are minority, but vocal, oppositions to providing comprehensive sexuality education in schools, which includes instruction on contraceptive efficacy and use and topics such as homosexuality, gender identity, and masturbation (Fields, 2008; Irvine, 2002; Luker, 2006; Santelli et al., 2006; see also Volume 2, Chapters 10 and 11, this handbook). In addition, state legislatures frequently attempt to restrict the use of state funds for family planning services and curtail access to abortion (Guttmacher Institute, 2011). Finally, at the family level, as sociologist Schalet (2011) has asserted on the basis of her research comparing the United States and the Netherlands, United States parents tend to dramatize teen sex, whereas Dutch parents tend to normalize it. This conservative sexual culture both limits the pool of funders willing to provide support for sexuality research and programs and makes it difficult for social and governmental institutions to approve research.

When public health work has focused on sexuality, it has tended to rely on narrow definitions and to emphasize technical and scientific approaches to the risks of pregnancy and disease rather than the positive aspects of sexuality, such as pleasure (Dixon-Mueller, 1993b; Higgins & Hirsch, 2007, 2008). In fact, public health recently has focused on "sexual risk-taking," underscoring United States cultural and religious discomfort with sexuality. As a result of this emphasis on reproduction, in 2002, the WHO organized a technical consultation on sexual health to examine sexual health issues on their own rather than subsuming them within studies of reproductive health (WHO, 2006). Building on previous efforts to define the concept in 1975 and 1987, the WHO developed a working definition of sexual health that included both positive and negative aspects and acknowledged the physical, mental, and social dimensions of sexual health (Edwards & Coleman, 2004; Sandfort & Ehrhardt, 2004; see also Exhibit 23.1). The two definitions of reproductive health and sexual health are useful because they reflect how they are distinct yet related concepts and fields. Thus, much like gender and science studies scholar Jordan-Young (2010) has argued that sex, gender, and sexuality are a "three-ply yarn" in which the strands largely function together but can be analytically pulled apart, sexual and reproductive health can be conceived of as a "two-ply yarn"—both intimately related yet also distinct.

GOALS AND SURVEILLANCE

Public health goals and objectives, which often are quantitatively defined and measured, are important in identifying health disparities and determining priority areas for the funding of research and programs. The Millennium Development Goals (MDGs) and *Healthy People 2020* are examples of sets of comprehensive public health-related goals. The MDGs are a set of measurable objectives for reducing poverty and better meeting the needs of the impoverished across the globe by 2015. They were produced in 2000 at the Millennium Development Summit and have been agreed upon by all nations and the leading global development institutions. The eight MDGs are not all explicitly focused on health, but four of them are—end poverty and hunger, child health, maternal health, and combat HIV/AIDS—and the latter two include targets specifically related to sexual and reproductive health (United Nations, 2010).

Healthy People 2020 is a comprehensive national agenda for health promotion and disease prevention. Each one of the Healthy People initiatives includes goals and measurable, science-based objectives centered on improving the nation's health over a 10-year period. *Healthy People 2020* is the fourth Healthy People initiative. The first, *Promoting Health/Preventing Disease: Objectives for the Nation*, was developed in 1980 as a response to the 1979 publication *Healthy People: The Surgeon General's Report on Health Promotion and Disease Prevention. Healthy People 2000: National Health Promotion and Disease Prevention Objectives* was released in 1990 and was followed in 2000 by *Healthy People 2010: Objectives for Improving Health*. The objectives and targets specified in *Healthy People*, which are developed through a collaborative process involving input from experts in multiple federal agencies and feedback from public comments, provide the federal government, state, and local governments, public health agencies, nongovernmental organizations (NGOs), and other groups focused on improving health with tools and guidelines for monitoring and measuring the health of United States populations. *Healthy People 2020* includes 42 topic areas, five of which are related specifically to sexual and reproductive health: family planning; HIV; lesbian, gay, bisexual, and transgender health; maternal and child health; and STDs (Department of Health and Human Services, 2012).

Many of the specific objectives outlined in these topic areas or goals are focused on eliminating or reducing negative health outcomes, and the few positive ones are related mostly to reproduction, not sexuality. For example, in *Healthy People 2020*, the objectives include reducing unintended pregnancies, rates of teen pregnancy, and STD rates and increasing the proportion of abstinent teens, rates of contraceptive use, access to reproductive health services, and the proportion of adolescents receiving reproductive health education (Department of Health and Human Services, 2012). Similarly, in the MDGs, the targets include increasing access to reproductive health services and reducing the spread of HIV/AIDS (United Nations, 2010). Neither of these sets of goals contains positive objectives related solely to sexuality, such as increasing rates of sexual pleasure or satisfaction. Furthermore, as of 2012, the lesbian, gay, bisexual, and transgender topic area, which was new in *Healthy People 2020*, contained no specific objectives; they were noted as "under development" (Department of Health and Human Services, 2012). Presumably it was difficult to reach consensus on such goals, for which deep cultural divisions on acceptance of sexual diversity exist (see Volume 2, Chapters 6 and 7, this handbook).

All of the objectives in *Healthy People 2020* and the targets in the MDGs are tied to specific public health indicators, which are metrics that will be used to evaluate whether those objectives and targets have been met. These indicators typically are collected via public health surveillance systems, which provide ongoing collection and analysis of health data (Thacker & Berkelman, 1988). In the United States, the major public health surveillance systems monitoring aspects of sexual and reproductive health include the National Survey of Family Growth (NSFG), the National Vital Statistics System (NVSS), the Youth Risk Behavior Surveillance System (YRBSS), and the Behavioral Risk Factor Surveillance System (BRFSS; see Exhibit 23.2). Although states are not required to report abortion data to the Centers for Disease Control and Prevention (CDC), the CDC issues an annual Abortion Surveillance Report that includes data from the states that collect and voluntarily provide such information (CDC, 2011c). Additional abortion data are also available from the Guttmacher Institute's periodic survey of abortion providers, which, because of the variations in state-level abortion monitoring and reporting, often are combined with the CDC data to generate comprehensive information about abortions in the United States (Jones & Kooistra, 2011). For non-United States data, other countries maintain their own public health surveillance and vital statistics systems, and, in addition, the Demographic and Health Surveys (DHS) collect sexual and reproductive health data in developing nations (Measure DHS, 2012).

Each of these surveys and surveillance systems collects a range of information on sexual and reproductive health. The NSFG, which is the most extensive national survey on sexual and reproductive health, collects data on pregnancy, birth, abortion, and adoption histories; marital and relationship histories; contraceptive histories; family planning and medical services; pregnancy and birth desires, intentions, and outcomes; infertility and reproductive health services; sexual behavior, orientation, and assault; and attitudes toward sex, contraception, marriage, gender, and parenthood (CDC, 2012b). The YRBSS asks teens questions about age of sexual initiation, condom and birth control use, numbers of sexual partners, use of alcohol and drugs before or during intercourse, depressive feelings, and experiences of violence, including bullying and attempted suicide (CDC, 2011h). Some BRFSS modules include questions on birth control use, pregnancy intentions, sexual violence, number of sexual partners, and sexual behaviors (CDC, 2012a). None of these surveys or surveillance systems, however, measure factors like relationship quality, sexual

Exhibit 23.2
United States Public Health Surveys and Surveillance Systems on Sexual and Reproductive Health Issues

National Survey of Family Growth (NSFG): The NSFG is a National Center for Health Statistics (NCHS) survey of men and women ages 15–44 that gathers data on a range of sexual and reproductive health topics, including sexual behaviors, experiences, and orientation; marriage, families, and relationships; fertility and infertility; contraceptive use; pregnancy desires, intentions, and outcomes; and attitudes toward sex, contraception, marriage, gender, and parenthood. The first NSFG was conducted in 1973, and it was then conducted in five additional periodic cycles: 1976, 1982, 1988, 1995, and 2002. In 2006, the NSFG switched to continuous data collection with periodic releases of the data, which are currently available through 2010 (Centers for Disease Control and Prevention, 2012b).

National Vital Statistics System (NVSS): In the United States, the legal authority and responsibility for the registration of key vital events—births, deaths, marriages, and divorces—resides with the 50 states, five territories, and two cities (Washington, DC, and New York City). The NVSS is the NCHS system that develops standard forms and model procedures to guide vital event registration in these various legal jurisdictions and then collaborates with them to collect, integrate, and disseminate the data (CDC, 2012c).

Youth Risk Behavior Surveillance System (YRBSS): The YRBSS, which was developed in 1990 and is managed by the CDC Division of Adolescent and School Health, monitors the prevalence of obesity and asthma and six categories of health risk behaviors among adolescents and young adults: tobacco use; physical inactivity; dietary behaviors; alcohol and other drug use; sexual risk behaviors; and behaviors or experiences that contribute to unintentional injuries and violence, including depression, bullying, and attempted suicide. It consists of biannual, representative national, state, territory, tribal, and local school-based surveys of 9th through 12th graders (CDC, 2011h).

Behavioral Risk Factor Surveillance System (BRFSS): The BRFSS is a system of state health surveys conducted by state health departments that gather data on adult health risk behaviors, preventative health practices, and health care access. The CDC established BRFSS in 1984, and currently all 50 states, three United States territories, and the District of Columbia participate. The core survey does not contain questions related to sexual and reproductive health, but optional modules include human papilloma virus (HPV), family planning, women's health, sexual violence, and sexual behavior (CDC, 2012a).

Abortion Surveillance Report (ASR): The ASR is an annual report issued by the CDC's Division of Reproductive Health that compiles and analyzes state data on the incidence and characteristics of women obtaining legal abortions. Unlike vital statistics records, states are not required to collect or report abortion surveillance data. Currently 47 states (all but California, Maryland, and New Hampshire), New York City, and the District of Columbia voluntarily provide information to the CDC; however, the scope and granularity of the data vary by location (CDC, 2011a, 2011c).

Abortion Provider Survey (APS): The APS is a periodic survey of United States abortion providers that monitors abortion availability and service information, including the number, type, and geographic distribution of abortions and providers. The Guttmacher Institute, a global leader in sexual and reproductive health research, policy, and education, developed the APS in 1973 and has conducted 14 surveys, most recently in 2009 (Jones & Kooistra, 2011).

pleasure or satisfaction, positive motivations to engage in sexual activity, the quality of sexual experiences, or the relationships between mental health and sexual health (see Chapters 10, 12, and 21, this volume). Instead, like the goals that these data are used to measure, they gather information on sexual and reproductive health risk and protective factors, which are social factors that protect against sexual risk-taking. Hence, public health goals and surveillance are mutually constitutive—the goals shape what is measured, but what is measured also shapes future goals and priorities. Even further, public health goals and surveillance both drive and circumscribe public health research—the goals identify priority areas for assessment, while the surveillance systems provide key data for analyses. This feedback loop between goals, surveillance, and research is another reason that more public health research has been conducted on reproductive health rather than sexuality.

RESEARCH

Challenges to conducting quality research on sexuality include selection bias and methodological limitations. Because of the conservative sexual culture in the United States, many people are uncomfortable discussing sexuality with others. Hence, selection bias is likely in studies on sexuality because individuals who are willing to participate in sexuality research have been shown to be different than those who are not in ways that are related to the behaviors and outcomes of interest (Dunne et al., 1997; Trivedi & Sabini, 1998; Wiederman, 1999).

In addition, there are strengths and limitations to different methodological approaches to studying sexuality. Quantitative surveys are good at identifying the *who* and *what* of sexuality—they indicate the prevalence of, and key disparities in, sexual attitudes and behaviors (see Chapter 4, this volume). The format and structure of surveys also typically provide greater degrees of anonymity or privacy than other research techniques, which might encourage greater honesty and disclosure on sensitive topics like sexuality (Davidson & Layder, 1994; Metzger et al., 2000; Turner, Miller, & Rogers, 1997). Because structured surveys require researchers to delineate the range of possible answers in advance, however, they often fail to capture the complexity and richness of people's attitudes, feelings, and experiences related to sexuality. Qualitative studies, in which participants are observed in action or are interviewed at length about their feelings and experiences, address these gaps; they are useful for studying the *why* and *how* of sexuality (see Chapter 6, this volume). However, qualitative research is limited in its generalizability; is extremely time intensive; and, to have good internal validity, requires well-trained interviewers who are skilled at building trust and rapport with participants (Creswell, 2007; Kvale & Brinkman, 2009; Warren & Karner, 2010).

Finally, in sexuality research with adolescents, investigators can face difficulties in obtaining parental permission or institutional review board (IRB) approval. Federal regulations classify children as vulnerable populations and require that both permission from a parent or guardian and assent from the child be obtained in all research involving children (National Commission for the Protection of Human Subjects of Biomedical and Behavioral Research, 1977). Researchers, however, can seek a waiver from the IRB when obtaining parental permission is not reasonable, which includes studies conducted in health care settings on services for which adolescents can legally consent (such as sexual and reproductive health care) and "minimal risk" research involving mature minors (Santelli, 1997). Federal regulations define a research activity as minimal risk when the probability of harm or discomfort is not greater than what one would encounter in normal daily life or in routine physical and psychological tests (Office of Human Research Protections, 2009). According to both the WHO and the Society for Adolescent Medicine, interview research with adolescents, even on sensitive topics like sexuality, should classify as minimal risk because previous studies have not shown that the potential discomfort generated from discussing sensitive subjects is more harmful than what participants would encounter in daily life or routine exams (Ringheim, 1995; Society for Adolescent Medicine, 1995). Yet some IRBs may be unfamiliar with these recommendations and, as a result, researchers who wish to study adolescent sexuality may face barriers in getting their projects approved (see Chapter 15, this volume).

Because of these barriers, there is considerably more research on reproductive health than sexual health; however, despite these challenges, funders are supporting—and organizations and investigators are conducting—rigorous, well-designed sexuality and sexual health research. The Robert Wood Johnson Foundation is one example of a funder that provides grants and fellowships to health scholars, many of whom study sexual and reproductive health issues. Another example is the Ford Foundation, which currently lists "Sexual and Reproductive Health and Rights" as one of its priority issue areas (Ford Foundation, 2012). Private foundations like these, along with grants from offices and institutes within the National Institutes of Health, such as the National Institute for Child Health and Human Development, support sexuality and sexual health research at leading academic institutions and organizations throughout the country. One example of such an organization is the Kinsey Institute, a nonprofit organization affiliated with Indiana University that has been conducting quality research on sexuality for more than 60 years. Investigators working with the Kinsey Institute hail from a range of disciplinary backgrounds—anthropology, psychology, sociology, neuroscience, and gender studies—and research a variety of sexuality and sexual health topics, including cross-cultural comparisons of sexual health in marriages; sexual decision making, arousal, and response; barriers to condom use; and women's desire and sexual well-being (Kinsey Institute, 2012; see Foreword, this volume). Indiana University is also home to the Center for Sexual Health Promotion (CSHP), a collaborative research, education, and training center for scholars working in the field of sexual health. The CSHP recently conducted the largest nationally representative study of sexual behavior and health in the United States, the National Survey of Sexual Heath and Behavior (Herbenick et al., 2010; Indiana University, 2012a, 2012b).

Furthermore, in recent years, there has been a shift toward integrating sexual and reproductive health education, research, and advocacy, and therefore most organizations that are conducting research on sexuality also study reproduction. In fact, even the Kinsey Institute includes research on reproduction in its mission (Kinsey Institute, 2012). One example of an organization that conducts domestic and international research on both sexual and reproductive health is the Guttmacher Institute. Although perhaps better known for its work on reproductive health, researchers at the Guttmacher Institute also explore such topics as sexuality education, sexual behavior, and beliefs and attitudes about sexuality, particularly among adolescents. Reflecting their efforts in both areas, the Guttmacher Institute's two peer-reviewed journals, *Family Planning Perspectives* and *International Family Planning Perspectives*, were renamed *Perspectives on Sexual and Reproductive Health* and *International Perspectives on Sexual and Reproductive Health* in 2001 and 2008, respectively.

PROGRAMS AND SERVICE

A variety of public health programs that promote sexual and reproductive health have been demonstrated to be effective in reducing disparities and improving health (CDC, 2011d; Kirby, 2007; Sills, 2007). The major United States domestic programs include family planning programs, infant and children's health programs, STD and HIV/AIDS prevention and control programs, comprehensive sexuality education programs, and school-based health clinics (see Chapter 22, this volume; Volume 2, Chapters 9 and 10, this handbook). Funding for sexual and reproductive health programs comes from a range of sources, including private foundations and federal, state, and local governments; the majority of these programs are implemented at the community level through community-based organizations, schools, and local health centers.

Examples of successful sexual and reproductive health programs include Title X, the federal family planning program that currently provides funding to more than 4,500 community-based clinics across the country to assist them in delivering vital sexual and reproductive health services to low-income and uninsured individuals. These services include contraceptive counseling and care; STD and HIV education, counseling, and testing; breast and cervical cancer screenings; gynecological exams; and pregnancy testing and counseling (Office of Population Affairs [OPA], 2012). In addition, the CDC, through its Division of Adolescent and School Health, provides funds to state and local governmental agencies to assist school districts in developing and implementing educational programs designed to reduce HIV infection, STD transmission, and unintended pregnancy (CDC, 2011e). In a new national effort, the Office of Adolescent Health in the Department of Health and Human Services issues grants to state and local institutions to support the implementation of evidence-based teen pregnancy prevention programs (Mathematica Policy Research & Child Trends, 2010; Office of Adolescent Health, 2012). The CDC's Division of STD Prevention (DSTDP) offers resources and guidance to clinicians and state and local health workers on counseling, screening, and treating adolescents and young adults for STDs. In addition, DSTDP engages in innovative partnerships, like the Get Yourself Tested campaign, a collaborative effort implemented in conjunction with MTV, the Kaiser Family Foundation, and Planned Parenthood Federation of America, that encourages young people to know their HIV and STD status and communicate with partners about sexual health (CDC, 2012d; National Center for HIV/AIDS, Viral Hepatitis, STD, and TB Prevention, 2010). These are just a select few of the numerous public health programs designed to improve sexual and reproductive health in the United States.

There are, however, several specific areas in which sexual and reproductive health research, programs, and services could use strengthening and improvement. For example, few public health programs are focused on infertility. The DSTDP and OPA collaborate to support the Infertility Prevention Program, which provides funds to local health clinics to offer chlamydia and gonorrhea screening and treatment services to low-income women; undiagnosed and untreated bacterial STDs are a leading cause of women's infertility (CDC, 2011f; Sloane, 2002). Although these prevention efforts are helpful, there is little public health support or guidance for individuals once they face fertility challenges, as many fertility treatments and care are not covered by private insurance or Medicaid (CDC, 2010a; Macaluso et al., 2010; Peterson, 2005). In addition, there is minimal monitoring and research on the health effects of assisted reproductive technologies (ARTs) used to treat infertility (Almeling, 2011; CDC, 2010b; Chavkin, 2010; Macaluso et al., 2010). Building on previous data collection efforts from the 1990s, the CDC's Division of Reproductive Health launched the National ART Surveillance System in 2006, which monitors the success rates for procedures at fertility clinics across the United States. Data on the immediate and long-term health risks of these procedures for donors, recipients, and children are not systematically tracked, however, which makes these topics difficult to research (CDC, 2011b).

In addition, because public health efforts have been more focused on reproduction, the sexual and reproductive health issues and needs of individuals who do not gestate and birth babies, such as older adults and younger men, have been largely underresearched, underfunded, and underserved. Several researchers have documented the paucity or inadequacy of public health surveillance, research, and services devoted to young men's sexual and reproductive health (Lindberg, Sonfield, & Gemmill, 2008; Marcell, Wibbelsman, & Seigel, 2011; Sonenstein, 2000; Sonfield, 2002). Anthropologist Gutmann (2009) has identified a number of social and cultural misconceptions that may help explain why men's needs have not been prioritized. They include beliefs that reproduction and reproductive health concern only women, that men are not interested in taking responsibility for birth control, and that men's sexuality is natural and given. To address these gaps, researchers have recommended more clearly defining and measuring men's sexual and reproductive health needs, engaging in more research and advocacy on men's sexual and reproductive health issues, improving the quality of young men's sexuality education, and better training health care providers to offer sexual and reproductive health services to young men (Lindberg et al., 2008; Marcell et al., 2011; Sonfield, 2002). One example of a model program attempting to better meet young men's sexual and reproductive health needs is the Young Men's Clinic (YMC), which is a collaborative effort between the Center for Community Health and Education at Columbia University's Mailman School of Public Health and New York Presbyterian Hospital. The YMC provides a range of health services to young men, including HIV and STD testing and health education, and it recently offered an intervention that resulted in increased knowledge about and frequency of safer sexual behaviors (Armstrong, Kalmuss, Franks, Hecker, & Bell, 2010; New York Presbyterian & Columbia University, 2012). Additional public health programs like the YMC are needed to improve young men's sexual and reproductive health.

Older adults are another population whose sexual health needs historically have been overlooked by public health researchers and practitioners. Most older adults remain regularly sexually active (see Chapter 17, this volume), many through their 80s, but they are significantly less likely to use condoms than teens and young adults (Calvet, 2003; Jena, Goldman, Kamdar, Lakdawalla, & Lu, 2010; Laumann, Glasser, Neves, & Moreira, 2009; Schick et al., 2010). Older adults are also less likely to be asked about sexuality and sexual health by their health care providers or to approach their providers with questions about these aspects of health (Laumann et al., 2009; Lindau et al., 2007; Politi, Clark, Armstrong, McGarry, & Sciamanna, 2009). These combined factors may increase older adults' risks of exposure to HIV and other STDs. Although older adults account for a low proportion of overall STD incidence, studies have indicated that STD rates among this population have been rising in the past decade (CDC, 2011g; von Simson & Kulasegaram, 2012). These rising rates are associated with increased health and longevity among the elderly, divorce and widowhood, more liberal social mores about sexual behavior, and the increased use of erectile dysfunction drugs (American Association of Retired Persons, 1999; Bancroft, 2007; Jena et al., 2010; Lindau et al., 2007). Thus, improved public health surveillance, research, and services tailored to the sexual health of adults are needed.

NEW INITIATIVES AND RECOMMENDATIONS

Although historically most public health programs have focused more heavily on reproductive health issues, in the past decade, there have been several efforts to specifically target sexual health and promote the integration of sexual and reproductive health. For example, in 2001, Surgeon General David Satcher issued *The Surgeon General's Call to Action to Promote Sexual Health and Responsible Sexual Behavior* (*Call to Action*), which was the first formal government acknowledgment of the importance of sexual health to enhancing population health in the United States (CDC, 2010b; Satcher, 2001). The primary goal of the *Call to Action* was to initiate a thoughtful, national dialogue on sexual health and responsible sexual behavior to develop an evidence-based national strategy to improve sexual health that included efforts in three main areas: increasing public awareness of sexual health issues, providing interventions to promote and enhance sexual health, and investing and engaging in research on sexual health (Satcher, 2001).

Since its release, several organizations have heeded the *Call to Action* (Satcher, 2001) and have attempted to move forward with developing comprehensive sexual health strategies and frameworks (Center of Excellence for Sexual Health, 2006; CDC, 2010b; Fathalla, Sindling, Rosenfield, & Fathalla, 2006). For example, in 2006, Satcher, while serving as interim president for the Morehouse School of Medicine, founded the first Center of Excellence for Sexual Health (CESH) with support from the Ford Foundation (Morehouse School of Medicine, 2012). Through the CESH, he initiated the National Consensus Process (NCP) on Sexual Health and Responsible Sexual Behavior, a series of eight meetings with leaders from 25 major sexual health stake-holding organizations that spanned the political and ideological spectrum. The goals of the NCP were to openly communicate in order to discover areas of understanding and disagreement, develop a common vision of sexual health and responsible sexual behavior, and identify both shared and individual projects to promote sexual health that participating organizations could implement (Center of Excellence for Sexual Health, 2006). Unfortunately, social conservatives involved in the consensus process often have been unwilling to endorse many ideas to promote sexual health; dialogue has faltered over such issues as sexual diversity and sexual activity outside of marriage.

Similarly, in 2010, the CDC developed a "green paper" titled *A Public Health Approach for Advancing Sexual Health in the United States* and held a 2-day consultation with more than 65 leading sexual health experts to clarify the rationale and vision for a national public health framework that promotes sexual health and healthy sexual behaviors across the life span. Participants at the consultation discussed six draft objectives for priority action: (a) increasing healthy and responsible sexual attitudes and behaviors, (b) increasing awareness and the ability to make responsible and healthy sexual choices, (c) promoting healthy sexual functioning and relationships, (d) optimizing and educating about reproductive health, (e) increasing access to effective sexual health services, and (f) decreasing adverse health outcomes. Participants also analyzed ways to implement these goals through six strategies: providing national leadership; promoting effective policy actions; promoting communication, awareness, and education; expanding surveillance, monitoring, evaluation, and research; enhancing strategic partnerships; and strengthening service infrastructure. Some areas of general agreement among the consultants were the need to more clearly define and affirmatively frame sexual health; to identify clear measures of sexual health, including positive indicators; to engage media in sexual health promotion efforts; and to include diverse social and political perspectives (CDC, 2010b).

Many researchers have echoed and added to the recommendations developed at the NCP and the CDC's consultation. For example, pointing to outcomes in the United Kingdom, where a national sexual health strategy implemented in 2001 helped to expand the quality and reach of sexual health services, researchers from Johns Hopkins recently issued a call for the development of a national strategic agenda to improve sexual health in the United States (Swartzendruber & Zenilman, 2010). They suggested using the National HIV/AIDS Strategy as a template to develop a broader sexual health strategy that includes integrating currently fragmented sexual health services into primary care; providing medically accurate, comprehensive health education; and ensuring funding and coverage for contraception and other sexual health services (Fenton, 2010; Swartzendruber & Zenilman, 2010). Building on Dixon-Mueller's (1993b) call to explore how structures and ideologies of gender and power organize sexual and reproductive experiences and behaviors, sexuality researchers Higgins and Hirsch (2007) outlined several specific recommendations for better integrating sexuality and pleasure into health research and services (see Chapter 2, this volume; Volume 2, Chapter 9, this handbook). These included engaging in systematic research on how pleasure, sexual functioning, and enjoyment shape the use of contraceptive and safer sex measures; using "pleasure profiling" in contraceptive counseling; offering sexuality training to all health care providers, not just reproductive health professionals; and promoting, through education programs and the media, the use of behaviors and techniques that eroticize safer sex practices (Higgins & Hirsch, 2007).

CONCLUSIONS

In sum, public health goals and objectives, which are linked to surveillance systems and measurable outcomes, shape priority areas for the funding of sexual and reproductive health research and programs. As a result, most attempts at improving reproductive and sexual health in the United States have focused on eliminating or reducing negative outcomes, like maternal morbidity and mortality, rather than on increasing positive outcomes, such as sexual satisfaction and pleasure. In addition, there is considerably more research on reproductive health than sexual health because of the challenges investigators face when attempting to conduct quality research on sexuality. These include the potential for selection bias when researching a highly sensitive topic, the various limitations of different methodological approaches for studying sexuality, the conservative sexual culture in the U.S., and additional ethical considerations when studying high risk or vulnerable populations. Furthermore, the heightened focus on reproduction in the field of public health has led the needs of individuals who do not gestate and birth children, such as younger men and older adults, to often be overlooked. Yet despite these challenges and barriers, several organizations are funding and conducting research and programs designed to investigate and improve sexual health in the United States. In fact, several new initiatives are specifically focused on targeting the needs of underserved populations and more effectively integrating research and practice on sexual and reproductive health.

Each of the recommendations issued by other researchers that were summarized in the previous section would help to remove some of the barriers to integrating sexuality and reproductive health that we have identified in this chapter. For example, media campaigns and comprehensive education programs that foster open, honest dialogue about sexual health might help to shift the conservative sexual culture in the United States. More thoroughly researching the role of pleasure in contraceptive practices and decision-making would aid in the development of interventions and practices designed to increase the use of safer sex measures.

Psychologists can make especially useful contributions to a research agenda focusing on sexual health and well being by explicating how the social, interpersonal, and intra psychic dynamics of sexuality are both distinct from and inexorably linked to reproduction. Research that explores how these dynamics change over the life-span will enhance the success of programmatic innovations. Psychologists can illuminate the psychological dimensions of sexual and reproductive health by identifying how religious beliefs, temperament, gender roles, and histories of sexual abuse, violence, and pleasure shape people's decisions and their use of health services. An interdisciplinary approach is needed—one that includes collaboration among psychologists, public health researchers, and other social scientists.

But in addition to these important suggestions, we also would advocate for the targeted development of more comprehensive sexual health services for neglected populations, including men, LGBT individuals, and older adults. Even further, since public health research and funding is largely driven by measurable goals, we believe that the first step to implementing these changes is to identify and add measures of sexual pleasure and satisfaction to existing public health surveillance systems; sexuality-related items could easily be added to the NSFG, YRBS, and BRFSS questionnaires. Kevin Fenton, the director of the CDC's National Center for HIV/AIDS, Viral Hepatitis, and TB Prevention, recently stated:

> Public health can only assert its role in this evolving domain with a strong commitment to the systematic measurement and tracking of the nation's sexual attitudes and behaviors; a more critical approach to selecting, implementing, and bringing to scale the most effective evidence-based interventions; and fostering a sustained commitment to maintaining supportive policy environments for success. (Fenton, 2010, pp. 250–251)

We agree with Fenton's call for the U.S. to "seize this moment" to remake its public health model for managing sexual and reproductive health and believe that clear goal setting, systematic surveillance, and the collection of robust data are the cornerstones of this transformation.

References

Almeling, R. (2011). *Sex cells: The medical market for eggs and sperm.* Berkeley, CA: University of California Press.

American Association of Retired Persons. (1999). *AARP/Modern Maturity Sexuality Study.* Atlanta, GA: Author.

Armstrong, B. J., Kalmuss, D., Franks, M., Hecker, G., & Bell, D. (2010). Creating teachable moments: A clinic-based intervention to improve young men's sexual health. *American Journal of Men's Health, 4*, 135–144. doi:10.1177/1557988309331796

Bancroft, J. H. J. (2007). Sex and aging. *New England Journal of Medicine, 357*, 820–822. doi:10.1056/NEJMe078137

Bandarage, A. (1997). *Women, population and global crisis: A political-economic analysis.* London, NJ: Zed Books.

Brodesser-Akner, C. (2007). Sex on TV is OK as long as it's not safe. *Advertising Age, 78*(37), 1, 66.

Calvet, H. M. (2003). Sexually transmitted diseases other than human immunodeficiency virus infection in older adults. *Clinical Infectious Diseases, 36*, 609–614. doi:10.1086/367892

Center of Excellence for Sexual Health. (2006). *The national consensus process on sexual health and responsible sexual behavior.* Atlanta, GA: Morehouse School of Medicine.

Centers for Disease Control and Prevention. (2010a). *Outline for a national action plan for the prevention, detection and management of infertility.* Atlanta, GA: Author.

Centers for Disease Control and Prevention. (2010b). *A public health approach for advancing sexual health in the United States: Rationale and options for implementation,* Meeting report of an external consultation. Atlanta, GA: Author.

Centers for Disease Control and Prevention. (2011a). Abortion surveillance–United States, 2008. *Morbidity and Mortality Weekly Report, 60*(15), 1–42.

Centers for Disease Control and Prevention. (2011b). *Assisted reproductive technology surveillance system.* Retrieved from http://www.cdc.gov/ReproductiveHealth/DRH/activities/ART.htm

Centers for Disease Control and Prevention. (2011c, November 23). *CDC's abortion surveillance system FAQs.* Retrieved from http://www.cdc.gov/reproductivehealth/Data_Stats/Abortion.htm

Centers for Disease Control and Prevention. (2011d, August 12). *Compendium of evidence-based HIV behavioral interventions.* Retrieved from http://www.cdc.gov/hiv/topics/research/prs/compendium-evidence-based-interventions.htm

Centers for Disease Control and Prevention. (2011e, March 1). *Funded national, state, local, territorial, and tribal programs.* Retrieved from http://www.cdc.gov/healthyyouth/partners/index.htm

Centers for Disease Control and Prevention. (2011f, August 23). *Infertility prevention project.* Retrieved from http://www.cdc.gov/std/infertility/ipp.htm

Centers for Disease Control and Prevention. (2011g). *Sexually transmitted disease surveillance 2010.* Atlanta, GA: U.S. Department of Health and Human Services.

Centers for Disease Control and Prevention. (2011h, March 1). *YRBSS in brief.* Retrieved from http://www.cdc.gov/healthyyouth/yrbs/brief.htm

Centers for Disease Control and Prevention. (2012a, February 24). *BRFSS.* Retrieved from http://www.cdc.gov/brfss/index.htm

Centers for Disease Control and Prevention. (2012b, February 23). *National Survey of Family Growth.* Retrieved from http://www.cdc.gov/nchs/nsfg.htm

Centers for Disease Control and Prevention. (2012c, March 13). *National Vital Statistics System*. Retrieved from http://www.cdc.gov/nchs/nvss.htm

Centers for Disease Control and Prevention. (2012d, March 29). *STD awareness: Reaching young people*. Retrieved from http://www.cdc.gov/std/sam/default.htm

Chavkin, W. (2010). The globalization of motherhood. In W. Chavkin & J. Maher (Eds.), *The globalization of motherhood: Deconstructions and reconstructions of biology and care* (pp. 3–15). London, England: Routledge.

Chesler, E. (1992). *Woman of valor: Margaret Sanger and the birth control movement in America*. New York, NY: Simon & Schuster.

Correa, S., & Petchesky, R. (1994). Reproductive and sexual rights: A feminist perspective. In R. Parker & P. Aggleton (Eds.), *Culture, society, and sexuality: A reader* (2nd ed., pp. 298–315). New York, NY: Routledge.

Creswell, J. W. (2007). *Qualitative inquiry and research design: Choosing among the five approaches* (2nd ed.). Thousand Oaks, CA: Sage.

Davidson, J. O. C., & Layder, D. (1994). *Methods: Sex and madness*. New York, NY: Routledge. doi:10.4324/9780203423455

Department of Health and Human Services. (2012, February 22). *HealthyPeople.gov*. Retrieved from http://www.healthypeople.gov/2020/default.aspx

Dixon-Mueller, R. (1993a). *Population policy and women's rights: Transforming reproductive choice*. Westport, CT: Praeger.

Dixon-Mueller, R. (1993b). The sexuality connection in reproductive health. *Studies in Family Planning, 24*, 269–282. doi:10.2307/2939221

Dunne, M. P., Martin, N. G., Bailey, J. M., Heath, A. C., Bucholz, K. K., Madden, P. A. F., & Statham, D. J. (1997). Participation bias in a sexuality survey: Psychological and behavioural characteristics of responders and nonresponders. *International Journal of Epidemiology, 26*, 844–854. doi:10.1093/ije/26.4.844

Edwards, W. M., & Coleman, E. (2004). Defining sexual health: A descriptive overview. *Archives of Sexual Behavior, 33*, 189–195. doi:10.1023/B:ASEB.0000026619.95734.d5

Fathalla, M. F., Sindling, S. W., Rosenfield, A., & Fathalla, M. M. F. (2006). Sexual and reproductive health for all: A call to action. *Lancet, 368*, 2095–2100. doi:10.1016/S0140-6736(06)69483-X

Fenton, K. A. (2010). Time for change: Rethinking and reframing sexual health in the United States. *Journal of Sexual Medicine, 7*, 250–252. doi:10.1111/j.1743-6109.2010.02057.x

Fields, J. (2008). *Risky lessons: Sex education and social inequality*. New Brunswick, NJ: Rutgers University Press.

Ford Foundation. (2012). *Issues*. Retrieved from http://www.fordfoundation.org/issues

Gordon, L. (2002). *The moral property of women: A history of birth control politics in America*. Urbana: University of Illinois Press.

Gutmann, M. C. (2009). The missing gamete? Ten common mistakes or lies about men's sexual destiny. In M. C. Inhorn, T. Tjornhoj-Thomsen, H. Goldberg, & M. C. Mosegaard (Eds.), *Reconceiving the second sex: Men, masculinity, and reproduction* (pp. 21–44). Brooklyn, NY: Berghahn Books.

Guttmacher Institute. (2011). *Laws affecting reproductive health and rights: 2011 State policy review*. New York, NY: Guttmacher Institute.

Herbenick, D., Reece, M., Schick, V., Sanders, S. A., Dodge, B., & Fortenberry, J. D. (2010). Sexual behavior in the United States: Results from a national probability sample of men and women ages 14–94. *Journal of Sexual Medicine, 7*(Suppl. 5), 255–265 doi:10.1111/j.1743-6109.2010.02012.x

Higgins, J. A., & Hirsch, J. S. (2007). The pleasure deficit: Revisiting the "sexuality connection" in reproductive health. *Perspectives on Sexual and Reproductive Health, 39*, 240–247. doi:10.1363/3924007

Higgins, J. A., & Hirsch, J. S. (2008). Pleasure, power, and inequality: Incorporating sexuality into research on contraceptive use. *American Journal of Public Health, 98*, 1803–1813. doi:10.2105/AJPH.2007.115790

Indiana University. (2012a). *Center for Sexual Health Promotion*. Retrieved from http://www.sexualhealth.indiana.edu/index.html

Indiana University. (2012b). *National Survey of Sexual Health and Behavior*. Retrieved from http://www.nationalsexstudy.indiana.edu

Irvine, J. M. (2002). *Talk about sex: The battles over sex education in the United States*. Berkeley: University of California Press.

Jena, A. B., Goldman, D. P., Kamdar, A., Lakdawalla, D. N., & Lu, Y. (2010). Sexually transmitted diseases among users of erectile dysfunction drugs: Analysis of claims data. *Annals of Internal Medicine, 153*, 1–7.

Jones, R. K., & Kooistra, K. (2011). Abortion incidence and access to services in the United States, 2008. *Perspectives on Sexual and Reproductive Health, 43*, 41–50. doi:10.1363/4304111

Jordan-Young, R. M. (2010). *Brainstorm: The flaws in the science of sex differences*. Cambridge, MA: Harvard University Press.

Kinsey Institute. (2012). *Research program*. Retrieved from http://www.kinseyinstitute.org/research/index.html

Kirby, D. (2007). *Emerging answers 2007: Research findings on programs to reduce teen pregnancy and sexually transmitted diseases.* Washington, DC: National Campaign to Prevent Teen and Unplanned Pregnancy.

Kvale, S., & Brinkman, S. (2009). *InterViews: Learning the craft of qualitative research interviewing* (2nd ed.). Los Angeles, CA: Sage.

Laumann, E. O., Glasser, D. B., Neves, R. C., & Moreira, E. D., Jr. (2009). A population-based survey of sexual activity, sexual problems and associated help-seeking behavior patterns in mature adults in the United States of America. *International Journal of Impotence Research, 21*, 171–178. doi:10.1038/ijir.2009.7

Lindau, S. T., Schumm, L. P., Laumann, E. O., Levinson, W., O'Muircheartaigh, C. A., & Waite, L. J. (2007). A study of sexuality and health among older adults in the United States. *New England Journal of Medicine, 357*, 762–774. doi:10.1056/NEJMoa067423

Lindberg, L. D., Sonfield, A., & Gemmill, A. (2008). Reassessing adolescent male sexual and reproductive health in the United States: Research and recommendations. *American Journal of Men's Health*, 2, 40–56. doi:10.1177/1557988307309460

Luker, K. (2006). *When sex goes to school: Warring views on sex—and sex education—since the sixties.* New York, NY: W. W. Norton.

Macaluso, M., Wright-Schnapp, T. J., Chandra, A., Johnson, R., Satterwhite, C. L., Pulver, A., . . . Pollack, L. A. (2010). A public health focus on infertility prevention, detection, and management. *Fertility and Sterility, 93*, 16 e11-10. doi:10.1016/j.fertnstert.2008.09.046

Marcell, A. V., Wibbelsman, C., & Seigel, W. M. (2011). Male adolescent sexual and reproductive health care. *Pediatrics, 128*, e 1658–1676 doi:10.1542/peds.2011-2384

Mathematica Policy Research & Child Trends. (2010). Identifying programs that impact teen pregnancy, sexually transmitted infections, and associated sexual risk behaviors. Washington, DC: Mathematica Policy Research.

Measure DHS. (2012). *Measure DHS: Demographic and Health Surveys.* Retrieved from http://www.measuredhs.com

Metzger, D. S., Koblin, B., Turner, C., Navaline, H., Valenti, F., Holte, S., . . . Seage, G. R., III. (2000). Randomized controlled trial of audio computer-assisted self-interviewing: Utility and acceptability in longitudinal studies. *American Journal of Epidemiology, 152*, 99–106. doi:10.1093/aje/152.2.99

Miles, A. (2011). *A guide to GOP proposals on family planning funds.* Kaiser Health News. Washington, DC: Henry J. Kaiser Family Foundation.

Morehouse School of Medicine. (2012). *Center of Excellence for Sexual Health.* Retrieved from http://www.msm.edu/research/research_centersandinstitutes/SHLI/aboutUs/CESH.aspx

National Center for HIV/AIDS, Viral Hepatitis, STD, and TB Prevention. (2010, April 10). *MTV asks audience: Do you GYT? MTV, Kaiser Family Foundation, CDC, Planned Parenthood and others urge young people to GYT: Get yourself talking and tested.* Retrieved from http://www.cdc.gov/nchhstp/newsroom/SAMGYTPressRelease.html

National Commission for the Protection of Human Subjects of Biomedical and Behavioral Research. (1977). *Report and recommendations: Research involving children.* Washington, DC: Department of Health, Education, and Welfare.

New York Presbyterian & Columbia University. (2012). *Young men's clinic.* Retrieved from http://www.youngmensclinic.org/index.php

Office of Adolescent Health. (2012). *Teen pregnancy prevention programs.* Retrieved from http://www.hhs.gov/ash/oah/oah-initiatives/tpp

Office of Human Research Protections. (2009). *Human subjects research: Definitions.* Retrieved from http://www.hhs.gov/ohrp/humansubjects/guidance/45cfr46.html#46.102

Office of Population Affairs. (2012). *Title X family planning.* Retrieved from http://www.hhs.gov/opa/title-x-family-planning

Peterson, M. M. (2005). Assisted reproductive technologies and equity of access issues. *Journal of Medical Ethics, 31*, 280–285. doi:10.1136/jme.2003.007542

Politi, M. C., Clark, M. A., Armstrong, G., McGarry, K. A., & Sciamanna, C. N. (2009). Patient-provider communication about sexual health among unmarried middle-aged and older women. *Journal of General Internal Medicine, 24*, 511–516. doi:10.1007/s11606-009-0930-z

Ringheim, K. (1995). Ethical issues in social science research with special reference to sexual behaviour research. *Social Science and Medicine, 40*, 1691–1697. doi:10.1016/0277-9536(94)00279-3

Sandfort, T. G. M., & Ehrhardt, A. A. (2004). Sexual health: A useful public health paradigm or a moral imperative? *Archives of Sexual Behavior, 33*, 181–187. doi:10.1023/B:ASEB.0000026618.16408.e0

Santelli, J. (1997). Human subjects protection and parental permission in adolescent health research. *Journal of Adolescent Health, 21*, 384–387. doi:10.1016/S1054-139X(97)00199-7

Santelli, J., Ott, M. A., Lyon, M., Rogers, J., Summers, D., & Schleifer, R. (2006). Abstinence and abstinence-only education: A review of U.S. policies and programs. *Journal of Adolescent Health, 38*, 72–81. doi:10.1016/j.jadohealth.2005.10.006

Satcher, D. (2001). *The Surgeon General's call to action to promote sexual health and responsible sexual behavior*. Washington, DC: Office of the Surgeon General, Department of Health and Human Services.

Schalet, A. (2011). *Not under my roof: Parents, teens, and the culture of sex*. Chicago, IL: University of Chicago Press.

Schick, V., Herbenick, D., Reece, M., Sanders, S. A., Dodge, B., Middlestadt, S. E., & Fortenberry, J. D. (2010). Sexual behaviors, condom use, and sexual health of Americans over 50: Implications for sexual health promotion for older adults. *Journal of Sexual Medicine, 7*(Suppl. 5), 315–329 doi:10.1111/j.1743-6109.2010.02013.x

Sills, S. (2007). *Cost-effectiveness of Medicaid family planning demonstrations*. Washington, DC: National Academy for State Health Policy.

Sloane, E. (2002). *Biology of women* (4th ed.). Albany, NY: Delmar.

Society for Adolescent Medicine. (1995). Guidelines for adolescent health research. *Journal of Adolescent Health, 17*, 264–269. doi:10.1016/1054-139X(95)00180-8

Sonenstein, F. L. (2000). *Young men's sexual and reproductive health: Toward a national strategy*. Washington, DC: Urban Institute.

Sonfield, A. (2002). Looking at men's sexual and reproductive health needs. *Guttmacher Report on Public Policy, 2*, 7–10.

Sonfield, A., & Gold, R. B. (2005). *Conservatives' agenda threatens public funding for family planning*. The Guttmacher Report on Public Policy. New York, NY: Guttmacher Institute.

Swartzendruber, A., & Zenilman, J. (2010). A national strategy to improve sexual health. *JAMA, 304*, 1005–1006. doi:10.1001/jama.2010.1252

Thacker, S. B., & Berkelman, R. L. (1988). Public Health surveillance in the United States. *Epidemiologic Reviews, 10*, 164–190.

Trivedi, N., & Sabini, J. (1998). Volunteer bias, sexuality, and personality. *Archives of Sexual Behavior, 27*, 181–195. doi:10.1023/A:1018634614590

Turner, C. F., Miller, H. G., & Rogers, S. M. (1997). Survey measurement of sexual behavior: Problems and progress. In J. Bancroft (Ed.), *Researching sexual behavior: Methodological issues* (pp. 37–60). Bloomington: Indiana University Press.

United Nations. (1995). *Report of the International Conference on Population and Development, Cairo, 5–13 September 1994*. New York, NY: Author.

United Nations. (2010). *Millennium Development Goals: We can end poverty by 2015*. Retrieved from http://www.un.org/millenniumgoals

von Simson, R., & Kulasegaram, R. (2012). Sexual health and the older adult: Trends show that doctors must be more vigilant. *Student British Medical Journal, 20*, e688. doi:10.1136/sbmj.e688

Warren, C. A. B., & Karner, T. X. (2010). *Discovering qualitative methods: Field research, interviews, and analysis* (2nd ed.). New York, NY: Oxford University Press.

Wiederman, M. W. (1999). Volunteer bias in sexuality research using college student participants. *Journal of Sex Research, 36*, 59–66. doi:10.1080/00224499909551968

Wilke, M. (2001). *Changing standards: Condom advertising on American television*. Washington, DC: Henry J. Kaiser Family Foundation.

World Health Organization. (1946). *Constitution of the World Health Organization*. New York, NY: Author.

World Health Organization. (2006). *Defining sexual health: Report of a technical consultation on sexual health, 28–31 January 2002, Geneva*. Geneva, Switzerland: Author.

CHAPTER 24

TRANSGENDER IDENTITY DEVELOPMENT

Walter O. Bockting

Transgender people have become an increasingly visible part of society. Throughout history and across cultures, the existence of transgender people has been documented (Feinberg, 1996; Bullough & Bullough, 1993). Examples of transgender people in other cultures include two-spirit people among Native American tribes (Roscoe, 1991; Williams, 1986); the *hijras* in India (Nanda, 1999); *travestis* in Brazil, Mexico, and Costa Rica (Kulick, 1998; Prieur, 1998; Schifter, 1999); the *acault* in Myanmar (Coleman, Colgan, & Gooren, 1992), and the Muang Thai in Thailand (Taywaditep, Coleman, & Dumronggittigule, 1997). Examples of transgender people in history include female transvestism in early modern Europe (Dekker & van de Pol, 1989) and Chevalier d'Eon in 18th-century France (Kates, 1995). Many of the descriptions of the identities of these transgender people challenge binary conceptualizations of gender, that is, in addition to men and women, it appears that there always have been people who are differently gendered, their identities described as both man and woman (Williams, 1986), neither man nor woman (Nanda, 1999), third gender (Roscoe, 1991), or—more recently—transgender (Bockting, 1999, 2008) or genderqueer (Harrison, Grant, & Herman, 2011–2012).

This chapter reviews what we currently know about the identity development and health of contemporary transgender and transsexual people on the basis of scientific research and clinical experience. After defining several common terms, existing theories about transgender identity development and etiology are reviewed. Subsequently, salient health issues in childhood, adolescence, adulthood, and later life are discussed. The chapter concludes with a review of clinical practice, advocacy, and directions for future research.

TERMINOLOGY

Transgender-related terminology continues to evolve. New terms emerge, old terms are redefined, and some terms gradually fade into history. In addition, the definition and meaning of terms can vary across geographic regions, even within the United States. Although a lack of agreement on terms may pose a challenge to research, it also is reflective of advances in our understanding of gender diversity as well as perhaps indicative of the ambiguity and fluidity inherent in many manifestations of transgender identity and expression. Nevertheless, it is worthwhile to have an understanding of some of the basic terms and their time- and culture-bound definitions.

At least four components of sexual identity can be distinguished (Shively & DeCecco, 1977): (a) natal sex, (b) gender identity, (c) social sex role, and (d) sexual orientation. Sex is assigned at birth (natal sex) as either male or female on the basis of the appearance of the external genitalia. In case the external genitalia are ambiguous in their appearance, other aspects of sex are assessed (e.g., internal genitalia,

The original research reported in this chapter was supported by grants from the National Institutes of Health (1R01DA015269 and 9R01HD057595, Walter Bockting, Principal Investigator).

http://dx.doi.org/10.1037/14193-024
APA Handbook of Sexuality and Psychology: Vol. 1. Person-Based Approaches, D. L. Tolman and L. M. Diamond (Editors-in-Chief)

chromosomal sex, hormonal sex) to assign a sex that is most likely to be consistent with the second component, gender identity. Gender identity is one's basic conviction of being a boy/man or girl/woman, or, for some, an alternative gender (e.g., transgender, genderqueer; see Table 24.1; see also Bockting, 2008).

The third component of sexual identity is social sex role (or gender role or expression), which refers to characteristics in appearance, personality, and behavior considered masculine or feminine in a given culture. A person can be masculine or feminine in varying degrees. The fourth component is sexual orientation, referring to sexual attraction, fantasies, behavior, and emotional attachment (e.g., love) toward men or women or transgender persons (see Chapter 19, this volume). Transgender people may be attracted to men, women, both, or other transgender persons (see Table 24.2; see also Iantaffi & Bockting, 2011), and sexual orientation is best defined on the basis of their gender identity.

TABLE 24.1

Transgender Identity Self-Descriptions of a National, Online Sample of the U.S. Transgender Population (N = 1,229)

Assigned male at birth (n = 697)	**Assigned female at birth (n = 532)**
Female	Male
	Man-to-male
	Displaced male
	XX man
Woman with a correctible birth defect	God just made a slight error; boy whose syringe gives him the testosterone his balls cannot
Woman with a transsexual history; formerly transsexual; survivor of transsexuality	
	Gay man of trans experience; post-op man of transsexual experience
	Born with a female body but on the male end of the gender spectrum, but more than just male
Female with the genitalia of a male	
Pre-op transsexual; post-op male to female transsexual	Post op FTM transsexual
Closet transsexual	
Transgender	Transgender
MTF trans	FTM trans
M2f person	Boy-type person
Two spirit; bigender; equal part male/female	Two-spirit, bigender, girl-boy
Androgynous; androgyne	Androgynous; androgyne; ambiguous
75% female, no plans on surgery or hormones	
M2F dyke tomboy/butch queen	TGStonebutch; FTM fag
Intergendered	In-between and beyond
Third gender	Third gendered
Pangender	Pan-, poly-, or omnigendered; multigendered
Dynamically gendered/gender fluid	Fluid
	Neither male nor female; genderless; female-bodied, but not necessarily female in gender and possibly not male either; gender neutral, but female-bodied, f-to-n; (nonbiological) intersexed or female-to-none of the above
Genderqueer	Genderqueer

Note. From all of the entries submitted by the total sample of 1,229 participants, qualitative data analysis extracted these representative quotes as illustrative of the diversity of self-descriptions found among the sample, and classified these by sex assigned at birth. Many but not all of the descriptions were matched by the same or a very similar description across these two groups. In cases in which there was not a matching counterpart, the field in the table was left blank. FTM = female to male; MTF = male to female; M2f = male to female.

TABLE 24.2

Sexual Orientation of a National, Online Sample of the U.S. Transgender Population (N = 1,229)

Sex	Male assigned at birth (n = 697)	Female assigned at birth (n = 532)
Sexual attraction		
Toward men	188 (27%)	53 (10%)
Toward both	254 (37%)	182 (35%)
Toward women	252 (36%)	290 (55%)
Sexual fantasy		
About men	241 (35%)	77 (15%)
About both	283 (41%)	227 (43%)
About women	169 (24%)	222 (42%)
Sexual behavior		
With men	141 (20%)	46 (9%)
With both	162 (23%)	169 (32%)
With women	342 (49%)	286 (54%)
No partners	50 (7%)	26 (5%)
With transgender partners	97 (14%)	115 (22%)

For example, a person assigned male at birth, who identifies as a woman and is attracted to other women, most likely would describe her sexual orientation as lesbian (rather than heterosexual).

Transgender is an adjective used to refer to a diverse group of individuals whose gender identity varies significantly from their sex assigned at birth, and who cross or transcend culturally defined categories of gender (Bockting, 1999; Coleman et al., 2011). *Transsexual* is an adjective used to refer to a subgroup of the larger transgender population who desire or have undergone hormone therapy or surgery to feminize or masculinize their body, and who tend to identify with and live full-time in the role of the other sex. *Trans* is an adjective that is inclusive of, and short for, individuals who identify as transgender or transsexual. *Bigender* refers to identifying as both man and woman. *Genderqueer* is a term popular among the younger generations to describe their gender identity as different from the norm. Male-to-female, trans woman, or transfeminine spectrum refers to being assigned male at birth but identifying (to varying degrees) as female. Female-to-male, trans man, or transmasculine spectrum refers to being assigned female at birth but identifying (to varying degrees) as male. Conversely and more recently, the term *cisgender* has come into usage to refer to "individuals who have a match between the gender they were assigned at birth, their bodies, and their personal identity" (Schilt & Westbrook, 2009, p. 461). In addition to these terms, individuals might use a variety of other terms to describe their gender identity (Table 24.1).

THEORY

Theory in transgender identity development covers two main areas: typologies and stage models. In addition, theory has informed research on the etiology of a transgender or transsexual identity, which is reviewed separately here.

Typologies

A number of similar typologies have been proposed (Table 24.3). Benjamin's (1966) scale distinguished between nonsurgical, moderate intensity true, and high intensity true transsexualism; and pseudo, fetishistic, and true transvestism. The distinction between transsexualism and transvestism was also reflected in the third revision of the *Diagnostic Statistical Manual of Mental Disorders* (*DSM–III;* American Psychiatric Association, 1980). This distinction has not always been clear-cut because of a commonly observed trajectory of development for some individuals from transvestism to transsexualism. Person and Ovesey (1974a, 1974b) referred to this trajectory as secondary transsexualism, along with a less commonly observed development from

TABLE 24.3

Typologies of Male-to-Female Transsexualism and Transvestism

Author	Typology					
Benjamin (1966)	Pseudotransvestite	Fetishistic transvestite	True transvestite	Nonsurgical transsexual	True transsexual, moderate intensity	True transsexual, high intensity
Person & Ovesey (1974a, 1974b)	Not applicable		Secondary transsexualism		Primary transsexualism	
Buhrich & McConaghy (1977, 1979)	Nuclear transvestite		Marginal transvestite		Fetishistic transsexual	Not applicable
Blanchard (1985, 1989)	Not applicable		Nonhomosexual transsexualism		Homosexual transsexualism	

homosexuality to transsexualism. Primary transsexualism distinguished itself from these two forms of secondary transsexualism by an early (in childhood) versus late (in adolescence) onset of cross-gender identification and expression. Docter and colleagues (Docter, 1988; Docter & Prince, 1997) found empirical support for the development of transsexualism out of a history of transvestism, confirming Buhrich and McConaghy's (1977, 1979) typology of marginal versus nuclear transvestites. Finally, Blanchard (1985, 1989) distinguished between homosexual and nonhomosexual male-to-female transsexualism (using sex not gender identity as the anchor for sexual orientation), describing the latter as developing from *autogynephilia*, defined as sexual arousal to the image or thought of oneself as a woman. Chivers and Bailey (2000) extended this typology to female-to-male transsexualism. The various typologies largely overlap and describe similar phenomena, but differ in what the key distinguishing criterion is: age of onset of cross-gender identification versus sexual orientation (Lawrence, 2010).

An alternative way to understand the two commonly observed developmental pathways is to consider the impact of social stigma attached to gender role nonconformity on transgender identity development (Bockting & Coleman, 2007). As described above, gender identity and gender role or expression are two related, yet distinct, components of sexual identity. A child with cross-gender feelings who is also nonconforming in gender role has little choice but to come out and develop resilience in the face of stigma at an early age. During development, the child's authentic self is being mirrored (Fraser, 2009). In contrast, a child with cross-gender feelings who is conforming in gender role is able to conceal these cross-gender feelings from others. A normative, heterosexual sexual orientation only reinforces the ability to conform and fit in. Such concealment, however, can lead to dissociation of identity or "identity split"—two selves develop: one mirrored in relationship with others and the world, the other in (sexual) fantasy and through cross-dressing in secret. This schism may not be broken until much later in life, opening up a path to integration. The alternative theory of transgender coming out brings together transvestism and transsexualism, primary and secondary transsexualism, and nuclear and marginal transvestites into a theory of transgender identity development shaped by the context of social stigma attached to gender nonconformity.

Stage Models

Transgender identity development has been described as a series of developmental stages, informed by qualitative research findings (Devor, 2004; Gagné, Tewksbury, & McGaughey, 1997; Lewins, 1995) or clinical experience (Lev, 2004). Bockting and Coleman (2007) adapted Coleman's (1982) model of developmental stages of the coming-out process for gay and lesbian individuals to describe the transgender coming-out process and illustrated it with clinical vignettes. Each stage is characterized by specific developmental tasks. In the first stage, pre–coming out, the individual struggles with feeling different. In the second stage, coming out, the individual acknowledges this to self and to others. In the third stage, exploration, the individual explores community resources and connections, experiments with gender expression, and finds a gender role that is comfortable, turning shame into pride. In the fourth stage, intimacy, the individual risks fears of rejection and abandonment, establishing intimacy and first relationships in the preferred gender role. Sexual orientation may be redefined. In the fifth stage, identity integration, grief over lost time, missed opportunities, or not being able to truly change sex are resolved, contributing to a deeper level of acceptance of one's transgender or transsexual identity. If important before, *passing* becomes less and less of a focus, making room for tolerance of ambiguity. Being transgender becomes one among several signifiers of personal identity.

These stages are simply a model, individuals do not necessarily progress in linear fashion from stage to stage, and each individual's developmental path is unique (see Chapter 19, this volume). This model, however, does reflect the context of stigma in which transgender and transsexual individuals explore and define their identity; the importance of the peer group (transgender community) as an alternative reference group and source of support to develop resilience; and, if applicable, the continuation of identity development beyond the gender transition phase.

Etiology

The etiology of a transgender or transsexual identity remains largely unknown (Cohen-Kettenis & Pfäfflin, 2003). It is most likely the result of a complex interaction between biological and environmental factors (Money & Ehrhardt, 1972). Research on the influence of family of origin dynamics has found some support for separation anxiety among gender-nonconforming boys and psychopathology among mothers (Marantz & Coates, 1991; Zucker, Bradley & Lowry Sullivan, 1996; Zucker et al., 2003), but this could not be fully replicated (Wallien, Swaab, & Cohen-Kettenis 2007). Prenatal hormonal influences have been shown to affect gender role behavior but not gender identity (Hines, 2006; Meyer-Bahlburg et al., 2004). Genetic factors appear to play a role (Coolidge et al., 2002; Coolidge, Thede, & Young, 2002; van Beijsterveldt, Hidziak, & Boom 2006). One study found a higher concordance of transsexuality among monozygotic as compared with dizygotic twins of the same sex (Heylens et al., 2012). Current research focuses primarily on the sexual differentiation of the brain. The central bed nucleus of the stria terminalis in the hypothalamus of postmortum brains of transsexual women (natal males) was found to be smaller and contained fewer neurons than the brains of nontranssexual men, and was found to be more similar to that of nontranssexual women (Kruijver et al., 2000; Zhou, Hofman, Gooren, & Swaab, 1995). The reverse was found for the brain of a transsexual man. More recent functional magnetic resonance imaging research also found that transsexuals have brain structure and function similar to that of nontranssexual individuals with the same gender identity (for an overview, see Kreukels, 2011), although not all of these findings could be replicated.

DEVELOPMENT AND CHALLENGES ACROSS THE LIFE COURSE

Transgender identity development is a lifelong process with specific challenges and corresponding needs for affirmation and support. The sections that follow discuss the challenges that may occur in childhood, adolescence, adulthood, and later life and illustrate these with clinical vignettes.

Childhood

Particularly in childhood, it is important to distinguish between gender identity and gender expression or role. Gender identity refers to the basic sense of being a boy or girl, whereas gender expression or role refers to characteristics in appearance, personality, and behavior. According to their parents, 4.8% of boys and 10.6% of girls are gender role nonconforming, whereas 1% of boys and 3.5% of girls expressed the wish to be of the other sex, the latter being a possible indication of a cross-gender identity and associated gender dysphoria (i.e., discomfort with the sex or gender role assigned at birth; Zucker, Bradley, & Sanikhani, 1997). Gender identity and gender expression or role often are confounded (Bockting & Ehrbar, 2005). Only in a minority of children is gender role nonconformity accompanied by early cross-gender identification. Moreover, many adult transgender or transsexual individuals do not report a history of childhood gender role nonconformity (Cole, Eyler, & Samons, 2000; Landén, Wålinder, & Lundström, 1998; Lawrence, 2010). In no more than about one in four children does gender dysphoria persist from childhood to adolescence or adulthood (Steensma, Biemond, de Boer, & Cohen-Kettenis, 2011; Wallien & Cohen-Kettenis, 2008). The majority of boys with gender dysphoria (who may have expressed the wish to be of the other sex in childhood) later on identified as gay (63–100%), not transgender; for girls, 32–50% later identified as lesbian, not transgender.

Children may experience stigma associated with gender role nonconformity. Stigma can take the form of teasing, ridicule, and bullying, particularly from peers. Compared with controls, gender-nonconforming children have more difficulties with peer relationships (Zucker et al., 1997), which were found to be associated with behavior problems (Cohen-Kettenis, Owen, Kaijer, Bradlay, & Zucker 2003). Stigma also may take the form of a clear message of what is expected in terms of gender identity and expression and pressure to conform to these expectations. Parents, teachers, and other caregivers can help by creating an environment in which the child can safely explore and express gender identity and role. Particularly at this stage of development, ambiguity in gender identity and role should be tolerated. Premature labeling of gender identity should be avoided. Early social transition (i.e., change of gender role, such as registering a birth-assigned boy in school as a girl) should be approached with caution to avoid foreclosing this stage of (trans)gender identity development. Early social transition may be necessary for some; however, the stress associated with possible reversal of this decision has been shown to be substantial (Steensma et al., 2011). When gender dysphoria has been persistent and worsens with the onset of puberty, puberty-delaying hormones (gonadotropin-releasing hormone or GnRH analogues) can alleviate dysphoria and give hope for development of the body in a direction more congruent with gender identity.

Vignette: John

John was brought in by his mother to see a health provider at a gender identity clinic at the age of 6 years to obtain an evaluation for a legal name change. The mother explained that John was assigned female at birth, named Karin, but had consistently been highly gender nonconforming. Karin reportedly felt like a boy since age 2–3 years. She began to identify with male names and characters at the age of 2 1/2 years. At age 4 years, the name John was chosen, and his parents began to use this name and male pronouns to refer to him. By now, everyone was using the name John and referring to him as male. When meeting with John, it was indeed hard to think of him in any other way than as a boy. John denied ever thinking that he would like to live as a girl. John played co-ed soccer. In preschool, he was "Karin" on the team and now he was "John." John stated he does not like girlish things ("princess stuff"), liking boyish things instead ("Star Wars"). The mother explained that, initially, John did not express any dysphoria about his body or private parts, yet more recently, he reportedly had cried over the fact that his body was female. Last semester, John went to school in the male gender role. His parents had informed the school and teachers that John was transgender. John's situation was unusual as most children with a cross-gender identification do not make such an early gender role transition.

Adolescence

The prevalence of nonconformity in gender identity or role among adolescence is unknown (Zucker & Lawrence, 2009). Persistence of gender dysphoria from adolescence to adulthood is considerably higher than persistence from childhood to adolescence. For example, two studies showed that one half to two thirds of adolescents with gender dysphoria went on to have sex reassignment surgery (Cohen-Kettenis & van Goozen, 1997; Smith, van Goozen, & Cohen-Kettenis 2001).

Adolescence is a time of exploration and experimentation for everyone, gender-nonconforming adolescents included, and in that sense, the questions and concerns of gender-nonconforming adolescents can be normalized. For transgender youth, however, adolescence can be an extra challenging time as they may experience a level of discomfort with their sexual and gender development that is of a different magnitude than that of their peers. Although some adolescents who are gender nonconforming in identity or role are comfortable with their gender identity and expression, others experience a level of clinical distress (i.e., gender dysphoria) and may seek consultation. Distress can be related to the incongruence between sex assigned at birth and gender identity or role, primary or secondary sex characteristics (and their further development during puberty), or both. For some, this distress may necessitate changes in gender role, puberty suppression, or feminizing or masculinizing hormone therapy.

As in childhood, adolescents may be stigmatized by peers, family, teachers, and others because of their gender nonconformity (Grossman & D'Augelli, 2006; Grossman, D'Augelli, & Salter, 2006). Stigma may take the form of rejection, bullying, and discrimination, and it may contribute to shame and isolation, suicidal ideation and attempts, school dropout, homelessness, substance abuse, and entrance into prostitution (Garofalo, Deleon, Osmer, Doll, & Harper, 2006; Leichtentritt & Arad, 2004; Sausa, 2005; Wyss, 2004). One study showed that about half of parents reacted negatively to transgender youth's gender nonconformity (Grossman, D'Augelli, Howell, & Hubbard, 2005) and most were told by their parents to stop acting like a sissy or tomboy (Grossman, D'Augelli, Salter, & Hubbard, 2005). Verbal and physical abuse by parents and transgender-related negativity (e.g., feeling bad about being transgender, not being able to accept being transgender) were associated with transgender youths attempted suicide (Grossman & D'Augelli, 2007).

Also at this age, parents, teachers, and other caregivers as well as peers can help by affirming the adolescent's gender identity and expression and by providing protection and support. Lesbian, gay, bisexual, transgender (LGBT)–straight alliance groups in schools can provide much needed support, although participation from transgender youth in these groups may be limited because of the hesitancy of transgender youth to come forward and by being outnumbered by LGB youth. School psychologists can play an important role in supporting gender-nonconforming adolescents in their identity development and expression. Schools can facilitate the adjustment of transgender youth by training teachers and staff to avoid gender-segregated activities and to provide gender-neutral bathrooms; incorporate examples of gender diversity in the curriculum; accommodate preferred names and pronouns; and institute a zero-tolerance policy for bullying (Sausa, 2005).

Vignette: Alex

Alex was 14 years old when presenting at the gender identity clinic with gender dysphoria, social isolation, a history of self-harm (cutting), and recent suicidal ideation. Alex was female bodied. She recently wrote a letter to her parents coming out as genderqueer and preferring male pronouns. In this letter, Alex explained how challenging puberty had been for him and how self-conscious and distressed he was by his feminine shape, and he requested hormone therapy and chest surgery. All of this had come as a surprise to Alex's parents, as they had not observed a consistent pattern of gender role nonconformity; to the contrary, Alex had gone through a period of time of what appeared to be indulgence in femininity. Alex explained that this period was his last attempt at trying to make it as a girl.

Vignette: Lynette

Lynette was 17 years old when she came with her parents to the gender identity clinic. Lynette who was assigned male at birth had been living for about a year in the female gender role. While growing up, she was not interested in "boy's stuff." She was visibly gender role nonconforming and was severely teased and ridiculed for that in school, which eventually led to leaving school for a learning center. She stated that "not being able to be completely myself" had been her biggest challenge. Lynette endorsed several symptoms of depression, including feeling empty, lonely, sad, tired, and at times moody. She shared that she has had multiple boyfriends, many of whom she did not really know but with whom she had sex. The attention she received from young men had been an important source of affirmation of her femininity and attractiveness. Lynette requested feminizing hormone therapy followed by genital reconstructive surgery.

Adulthood

The prevalence of transgenderism in adulthood is estimated at 1:200 (Conron, Scott, Stowell, & Landers, 2012). The prevalence of transsexualism is estimated at 1:11,900 for male to female transsexualism (male assigned at birth, female gender identity and pursuing physical feminization) and 1:30,400 for female to male transsexualism (female assigned at birth, male gender identity and pursuing physical masculinization). Adults may come out at any age and, if applicable, make changes in gender role or undergo medical interventions to feminize or masculinize their body. Research among those who have changed their gender role permanently, have taken hormones, and have had surgery has shown that very few (less than 1%) at some point return to the original gender role (Kuiper & Cohen-Kettenis, 1998; Pfäfflin, 1992). The vast majority (80%) is satisfied and reports improved quality of life (Murad et al., 2010).

Transgender and transsexual adults can identify in various ways in terms of their gender identity (Table 24.1), may pursue various changes in gender role and expression, and potentially have access to a range of medical interventions to feminize or masculinize the body. These options range from GnRH analogues, anti androgens, estrogens, testosterone, chest or breast surgery, gonadectomy, hysterectomy, genital reconstructive surgery, facial feminization or masculinization surgery, hip removal, and body contouring. There is no one way of being transgender; rather, there is great diversity in gender identity and gender expression. Some very strongly identify as a member of the other sex and will pursue every way possible to achieve physical congruence. Others identify beyond the gender binary and may or may not feminize or masculinize their body in various ways.

Transgender and transsexual adults are diverse in other respects as well, including sexual orientation, race or ethnicity, and socioeconomic status. All of these factors can play a role in the coming-out process. Building on the two developmental pathways outlined previously, two main categories of transgender or transsexual women (i.e., with or without a history of childhood gender role nonconformity) and one main category of transgender or transsexual men (most of whom were gender role nonconforming in childhood) can be distinguished.

Most transgender and transsexual women (assigned male at birth but identifying as women) who have been outwardly gender role nonconforming from an early age will develop resilience over time (Nuttbrock et al., 2010). As adults, they can draw on extensive experience living with a stigmatized identity and typically have learned to negotiate accommodation of their gender-variant identity. Their sexual orientation is most often heterosexual (attracted to men).

Most transgender and transsexual women (assigned male at birth but identifying as women) who were outwardly gender role conforming, typically have tried their best to conform in every way to what they thought was expected of them, often quite successfully. They likely married and have children. They have expressed their female gender identity for many years in private, then part time more publicly, and not until later in life may pursue permanent changes in gender role. At that time, they typically go through a second adolescence, during which they begin to develop resilience. In addition to addressing their gender identity and expression, the responsibility of family, particularly spouse and children, weighs heavily. After coming out, they explore their sexual orientation, which is most often lesbian or bisexual (attracted to women, or to women and men).

Transgender and transsexual men (assigned female at birth but identifying as men) typically come out early in life and are less likely to conform to what is expected of them on the basis of normative gender expectations. They may be heterosexual, gay, or bisexual. Some transgender and transsexual men attracted to women are vulnerable to affirmation of their masculinity by taking care of women in need, sometimes to their own detriment. Developmentally, these relationships can be seen as "first" relationships that often do not last, but rather they begin a process of developing intimacy and relationship skills in the male gender role.

Among transgender and transsexual adults, stigma, discrimination, and violence are well documented (Bockting, Miner, Swinburne Romine, Hamilton, & Coleman, 2013; Lombardi, Wilchins, Priesing, & Malouf, 2002; Xavier, Bobbin, Singer, & Budd, 2005), with rates of verbal harassment ranging from 56% to 70%, physical violence ranging from 19% to 24%, and employment discrimination ranging from 37% to 38%. Gender-related stigma and discrimination has been associated with psychological distress among transgender and transsexual adults, and peer support (from other transgender and transsexual people) was identified as a protective factor (Bockting et al., 2013; Nuttbrock et al., 2010). Compared with lesbian or bisexual, gay, and heterosexual controls, transgender women and men have higher rates of depression and suicidal ideation and lower levels of social support (Bockting, Huang, Ding, Robinson, & Rosser, 2005; Mathy, 2002, 2003). Rates of depression among transgender Americans range from 37% to 55% among transgender men to 49% to 62% among transgender women (Bockting et al., 2013; Clements-Nolle, Marx, Guzman, & Katz, 2001). Especially for the younger generation, however, depression declined during later stages of life, presumably as a result of the development of resilience (Nuttbrock et al., 2010). A meta-analysis of transgender health studies indicated that 44% of transgender individuals surveyed indicated a desire for mental health counseling to address transgender-specific issues (Herbst et al., 2008).

Vignette: Ray

Ray was 31 years old when he was referred to the gender identity clinic by a crisis center. Ray had been suicidal. Assigned female at birth, Ray had lived for several years in the male role by now, had taken masculinizing hormones, and had completed chest surgery. He explained that he had continued to struggle with his mental health and with "genital ambiguity." Ray had done everything he could to pass as a man, including facial surgery to create a more masculine appearance. Other than the clitoris enlarged as a result of the hormones, he disliked his genital area and felt "not finished." When asking about family and social support, Ray stated that he had little to no contact with his family of origin and that none of his current friends knew about his transsexuality. He had turned to alcohol, marijuana, and prescription drug use to cope with his isolation and shame. Now in recovery, he became very active in Alcoholics Anonymous and joined a therapy group specifically for transgender men. In this group, Ray became more comfortable with his transgender identity and, taking calculated risks, disclosed his "secret" to his inner circle of friends and support system. He also accepted psychiatric care to alleviate symptoms of depression. Thankful for the newly found stability in his life, he began to research options for genital reconstructive surgery.

Later Life

"Coming out" as transgender does not end with finding comfort with gender identity and expression, but rather it is a lifelong process (Bockting & Coleman, 2007). Even transsexual individuals with a strong cross-gender identity who set out to completely change their sex and succeed in many ways in doing so, eventually are likely to discover the added value of their experience and incorporate it into an identity that transcends the gender dichotomy of male versus female, man versus woman, masculine versus feminine. In addition, many transgender and transsexual individuals of the older generation may have postponed their coming out because of having come of age in a time when gender variance was considerably more stigmatized than it is in the 21st century. Indeed, 70% of transgender seniors (age 65 years and older) in the National Transgender Discrimination Survey reported having delayed their gender transition to avoid discrimination in employment (Grant et al., 2011).

Besides anecdotal clinical experience, little is known about the identity development and health of the aging transgender or transsexual person. Descriptive small studies of transgender individuals age 50 years and older indicated that 36% had some form of disability and that experiences of emotional or psychological abuse (65%), health care discrimination (42%), and self-neglect (27%) were common; some participants were extremely afraid of elder abuse (Cook-Daniels & Munson, 2010). In long-term care facilities, more than 10% reported refusal by staff to call a transgender resident by the preferred name or pronoun (National Senior Citizens Law Center, 2011). This may lead transgender individuals to avoid medical care until their condition worsens and help is sought at an emergency department (Grant et al., 2011).

Research on the mental health of transgender elders indicates high levels of depression and suicidal ideation. Seventy-one percent of transgender older adults reported having considered suicide at least once in their lifetime, which was significantly higher than 35–40% among LGB older adults (Fredriksen-Goldsen et al., 2011). One study showed that for the younger generation of transgender women, depression declined significantly from adolescence into early middle age, whereas for the older generation, levels of depression remained relatively constant throughout their lives and into later middle age (Nuttbrock et al., 2010). Moreover, transgender older adults were found to have lower levels of social support than nontransgender older adults (Fredriksen-Goldsen et al., 2011).

Vignette: Alicia

Alicia was 50 years old when she presented at the gender identity clinic with a request for feminizing hormone therapy. Alicia was married to a woman named Sue; they had been together for a total of 12 years. Alicia told Sue before getting married of her desire to cross-dress, something Sue had accepted. Alicia struggled for many years with fear of losing the marriage if Sue were to find out that she considered a permanent transition to living in the female gender role. Alicia had cross-dressed since early adolescence. Initially, cross-dressing was sexually arousing for her, which diminished over time. Gradually, Alicia had explored her female identity further and, prompted by reaching the age of 50, felt it was time to pursue her desire to live full time in the female gender role and pursue feminizing hormone therapy. Alicia came out to her friends, faith community, parents, and siblings. Alicia had two children from a previous marriage. The oldest was a young adult son, who, after an initial adjustment period, accepted Alicia's transgender identity. The youngest was still a teenager with whom Alicia had little contact as she lived with the mother, from whom Alicia was estranged since the divorce. Sue got involved in a support group for spouses of transgender individuals and ended up being very supportive of Alicia's transition. Alicia's biggest concern now was to come out on the job.

Findings from a national online survey of the U.S. transgender population provide information on stigma, mental health, and such protective factors as family support, peer support, and pride in identity (Bockting et al., 2013). Table 24.4 presents selected findings organized by stage of life. The data are from a convenience sample as no sampling frame to draw a representative sample was available (Institute of Medicine [IOM], 2011); the geographic distribution of participants approximated that of the U.S. Census, but overall, participants were younger, more White, and more educated yet with less household income (Rosser, Oakes, Bockting, & Miner, 2007). Youth and elders were less likely than adults to have transitioned to living in another gender role (Table 24.4). Compared with both youth and adults, fewer elders reported verbal and physical abuse, employment discrimination, and barriers to accessing health care. A substantial proportion of all three groups, however, reported clinical levels of depression (assessed with the Brief Symptoms Inventory; Derogatis, 2000). Elders reported significantly lower levels of felt stigma and shame, and higher levels of pride in being transgender. Family support was the lowest among elders (which could be of particular concern when in need of care), yet perhaps this lack of family support is offset by the higher levels of peer support. Interestingly, youth and adults up to age 50 years did not differ significantly on any of the stigma, mental health, or social support measures. Although these results confirm the high levels of stigma found in

TABLE 24.4

Stigma, Mental Health, and Social Support for Youth, Adults, and Elders Among a National, Online Sample of the U.S. Transgender Population ($N = 1{,}229$)

	Youth (18–24; *n* = 429)	Adults (25–49; *n* = 651)	Elders (50–70; *n* = 148)
	n (%)	*n* (%)	*n* (%)
Identity and relationship status			
Gender			
Transgender woman	133 (31%)[a]	422 (65%)[a]	142 (96%)[a]
Transgender man	296 (69%)[a]	229 (35%)[a]	6 (4%)[a]
Currently taking hormones	119 (28%)[a]	351 (54%)	69 (47%)
Transitioned to living full time in another gender role	100 (23%)	253 (39%)[a]	36 (24%)
In a primary relationship	232 (54%)	383 (59%)	52 (35%)
Enacted stigma/discrimination			
Gender-related verbal abuse/harassment	299 (76%)	442 (72%)	69 (51%)[a]
Gender-related physical abuse	93 (24%)	166 (27%)	17 (13%)[a]
Gender-related sexual abuse	53 (13%)	106 (17%)	14 (10%)
Gender-related employment discrimination	171 (44%)	247 (40%)	20 (15%)[a]
Gender-related barriers accessing health care	95 (24%)	171 (28%)	18 (13%)[a]
Mental health			
Depressed	174 (41%)	255 (39%)	53 (36%)
	M (SD)	*M* (SD)	*M* (SD)
Felt stigma and shame[b]			
Felt stigma	4.58 (.70)	4.63 (.90)	4.32 (.94)[a]
Shame about being transgender	2.44 (1.44)	2.36 (1.47)	1.76 (1.31)[a]
Pride and social support[a]			
Pride in being transgender	4.38 (1.27)	4.30 (1.38)	4.86 (1.25)[a]
Family support	3.94 (1.79)	4.05 (1.94)	3.37 (1.76)[a]
Peer support	4.31 (1.32)	4.30 (1.37)	4.53 (1.24)[a]

[a]Indicates significantly different from the other two groups. [b]Scores are on 7-point Likert scales with higher scores indicating more stigma, shame, pride, and support.

other studies of the transgender population, despite these challenges, the majority is not depressed and levels of pride outweigh the levels of shame.

PRACTICE

Psychologists may encounter transgender people across different practice environments and settings (see Volume 2, Chapter 4, this handbook). Little training traditionally has been available, thus many transgender people have had less than satisfying experiences with psychologists (e.g., Cook-Daniels & Munson, 2010; Grossman & D'Augelli, 2006; Grant et al., 2011; Nemoto, Operario, & Keatley, 2005; Rachlin, Green, & Lombard, 2008; Sperber, Landers, & Lawrence, 2005). More recently, however, visibility of transgender people has increased, awareness of their needs has improved, and resources are becoming available to enhance psychologists' cultural competency in this area (American Psychological Association, Task Force on Gender Identity and Gender Variance, 2009; Burnes et al., 2010; Harper et al., 2013; Singh & Burnes, 2009) and, for those who are interested, develop clinical competence in transgender-specific care (Bockting & Goldberg, 2006).

To create a welcoming environment and effectively interact with transgender and transsexual individuals, it is key to respect and accommodate the gender diversity found among this population. This involves referring to the individual with the preferred name and pronoun and use forms and data entry systems that allow for differentiation between sex assigned at birth and gender identity. Staff at all levels, from scheduling, front desk, service provider, and billing personnel, should participate in training and continuing education to serve transgender and transsexual clients sensitively. Such training increasingly is provided by professionals in human resources and LGBT diversity and capacity building programs, either locally or nationally (e.g., Center of Excellence for Transgender Health, University of California, San Francisco; National LGBT Education Center, Fenway Health, Boston). In addition, providers should be aware of the evidence base, including health disparities, affecting transgender and transsexual clients in their particular area of practice. When clients are in need of specialized services, particularly when it comes to exploring gender identity and expression that may involve medical interventions, consultation and referral with providers competent in transgender-specific health care is essential.

Clinical competence criteria for mental health professionals assisting individuals with transition-related health care include specific training in the assessment and treatment of gender dysphoria, relevant continuing education, and supervision from an experienced provider—in addition to the basic competencies for clinical work with children, adolescents, or adults (Coleman et al., 2011). The Standards of Care of the World Professional Association for Transgender Health provide guidelines for the roles of mental health professionals in promoting transgender health (Coleman et al., 2011). This may include assessment, supportive psychotherapy, family and relationship counseling, treatment of mental health concerns, facilitating peer support, and evaluation and referral for medical interventions to feminize or masculinize the body (see also Bockting, Knudson, & Goldberg, 2006).

Approaches to working with gender-nonconforming children and their families vary. One approach attempts to lessen the child's gender dysphoria and nonconformity and reduce the likelihood of its persistence into adolescence and adulthood (Zucker, 2008), an approach that has been controversial as it may reinforce shame (Ehrensaft, 2012). A second approach aims to assist the environment (family, school, community) in fully accepting the gender-variant identity of the child (e.g., Menvielle, 2012). This approach runs the risk of neglecting individual problems the child might be experiencing and may involve an early gender role transition that might be challenging to reverse if cross-gender feelings do not persist (Steensma et al., 2011). A third approach monitors the child's gender identity development and resolves or prevents gender-related and non-gender-related adjustment problems, with involvement of both the child and the environment (family, school; de Vries & Cohen-Kettenis, 2012). This approach evaluates the child's gender dysphoria in the context of overall development, including psychosocial and cognitive adjustment, academic achievement, and family functioning, and incorporates identified concerns in the overall treatment plan. This may involve support as well as limits for gender-variant expression, considered by parents to guard against negative reactions and the associated harm. Parents are encouraged to allow for space and time for the child's exploration of gender identity and expression and to tolerate uncertainty about the eventual outcome (see also Roen, 2011).

For transgender and transsexual individuals of any age, gender dysphoria may be alleviated by exploring gender identity and finding a gender expression that is comfortable (Coleman et al., 2011). For some, this means integrating transgender feelings into a gender identity and role that corresponds to the sex they were assigned at birth. For others, this may include changes in gender role and expression, either part or full time. Medical interventions to feminize or masculinize may be part of reducing dysphoria and actualizing one's (trans)gender identity, whether this involves hormone therapy, surgery, or both.

For transgender youth, starting at Tanner Stage II of development (shortly after the onset of puberty), GnRH analogues can be used to suppress and delay puberty (de Vries, Cohen-Kettenis, & Delmarre-van der Waal, 2006; Hembree et al., 2009). This reversible intervention allows for additional time to explore gender identity and expression, alleviates the distress associated with puberty that some youth experience (when the body develops in a way that is incongruent with their perceived gender identity), and prevents the development of sex characteristics that are not reversible. For example, in female-bodied youth, it would prevent the development of breasts that otherwise might have to be removed later, resulting in significant scarring. In male-bodied youth, it would prevent such irreversible changes as a lowering of the voice and the growth of facial hair. Research has indicated that delaying puberty for up to several years appears to be safe. If gender dysphoria persists, cross-sex hormones subsequently may be initiated to facilitate pubertal development that is congruent with the youth's gender identification. If gender dysphoria and cross-gender identification do not persist, the puberty-delaying hormones can be discontinued, and puberty congruent with the youth's sex assigned at birth would resume. Follow-up of youth who received puberty-delaying hormones followed by cross-sex hormones showed a decrease in behavioral and emotional problems, a decrease in depression, and improvement in general functioning (de Vries, Steensma, Doreleijers, & Cohen-Kettenis, 2011), and they had better mental health than transsexual adults who did not receive early intervention during adolescence (de Vries, Kreukels et al., 2011).

For adolescents and adults, treatment with cross-sex hormones is available (Coleman et al., 2011; Hembree et al., 2009). Feminizing hormone therapy usually consists of antiandrogen agents and estrogen. Effects include breast development, a reduction in body hair but not in facial hair, redistribution of body fat, and decrease in sexual desire and fertility. Masculinizing hormone therapy consists of androgens. Effects include body and facial hair growth, male pattern baldness, redistribution of body fat, deepening of the voice, cessation of menses, clitoral growth, increased sexual desire, and decreased fertility.

For adults, chest or breast surgery, genital reconstructive surgery, and facial feminization or masculinization surgery are available (Bockting & Allen, 2012; Coleman et al., 2011). If 18 months or more of feminizing hormone therapy has not resulted in sufficient breast growth, augmentation is available. For transsexual men, the breasts can be removed and a male-appearing chest can be created. Genital reconstructive surgery for transsexual women includes orchiectomy (removal of testes), vaginoplasty, and creation of a clitoris. Most common is the penile inversion technique, where the outer skin of the penis becomes the inner lining of the vagina. The glans of the penis is reduced to form a clitoris. The testicles are removed and scrotum tissue is issued to create the labia. Genital reconstructive surgery for transsexual men includes hysterectomy, oophorectomy (removal of ovaries), metoidioplasty, or phalloplasty. Metoidioplasty involves release of the clitoris bringing it forward, extension of the urethra so one can stand to void, and creation of a scrotum from the labia with testicle implants inserted. It is a simpler procedure than phalloplasty and does not require an extensive skin graft. For phalloplasty, a skin graft is needed and often is taken from the forearm. For the phallus to become erect, a penile implant is required. Facial surgery is available to feminize or masculinize the appearance of the face, and neck. This may include surgery of the nose, brow bone, cheeks, jaw, chin, and Adam's apple.

Advocacy

Although much progress has been made in terms of the visibility and rights of transgender and transsexual people (see Volume 2, Chapters 3 and 10, this handbook), society often remains ill equipped to accommodate gender-variant identities and expressions. Multiple barriers exist in access to health care and other services, ranging from a lack of cultural and clinical competence on the part of providers (e.g., Grossman & D'Augelli, 2006; Lurie, 2005; Sperber et al., 2005) and exclusionary policies of medically necessary transgender-specific health care procedures, particularly surgery (e.g., Gehi & Arkles, 2007), to the negative effects of stigma (e.g., socioeconomic marginalization, lack of trust in the health care system, and internalized transphobia—i.e., discomfort with one's own transgenderism as a result of internalizing society's normative gender expectations) on the part of transgender and transsexual individuals and their families (Bockting, Robinson, Benner, & Scheltema, 2004; Cook-Daniels & Munson, 2010; Grant et al., 2011; Xavier et al., 2005). Thus, much work is yet to be done in the realm of advocacy and public policy to promote transgender health.

Psychologists and other health professionals have the opportunity to educate and advocate within their communities and the profession as well as provide expertise and scientific evidence to inform policy development. Examples of education and advocacy include educating families and schools about gender variance (e.g., Brill & Pepper, 2008); facilitating gender role transitions in the workplace (e.g., Taranowski, 2008); assisting with gender marker changes on identity documents (e.g., Thaler, Bermudez, & Sommer, 2009); training students, residents, fellows, and established professionals in gender diversity and transgender care (e.g., Bockting & Goldberg, 2006); arguing for coverage of medically necessary care (e.g., World Professional Association for Transgender Health, 2008); and supporting the inclusion of gender identity and expression in anti-discrimination and human rights policies and legislation (American Psychological Association, Task Force on Gender Identity and Gender Variance, 2009).

Opportunities for Research

Research in the area of transgender identity development and health remains limited. There are many opportunities for research (Lombardi, 2011). IOM (2011) identified transgender-specific health needs as one of five priority areas in the development of a comprehensive research agenda to advance knowledge and understanding of LGBT health. To date, such research is based on small, nonprobability samples; clinical trials are few and far between and rarely include a control group (Byne et al., 2012). Examples of future research include demographic and epidemiological studies; rigorous evaluation of the Standards of Care's eligibility criteria for hormone therapy and surgery; outcome research of transition or coming-out processes that do not conform to binary conceptualizations of sex and gender (e.g., transitions with hormones but no genital surgery or chest surgery but no hormones; see also Roen, 2011); clinical trials of hormone therapy; studies of transgender identity development and resilience across the life course; and research on dating and relationships, sexuality, parenting, family, and community.

CONCLUSION

Throughout history and across cultures, examples of transgender people have been documented (e.g., Feinberg, 1996). In the 20th century, gender-variant expressions and identities were medicalized, initially to advocate for the freedom of transgender individuals who were arrested for their gender-nonconforming expression (Hirschfeld, 1910/1991) and later in response to the plea of transsexual individuals to feminize their bodies through hormones and surgery as they "changed sex" and attempted to pass as members of the other sex (e.g., Benjamin, 1966; Hastings, 1969, 1974). In the 1990s, however, a generation of transgender and transsexual individuals "came out" and formed community to combat the stigma attached to their gender nonconformity and established coalitions with lesbian, gay, and bisexual communities in the pursuit of equality in civil and human rights (e.g., Bockting, 1997; Bockting, Rosser, & Coleman, 1999; Stone, 1991). In the 21st century, we are rediscovering the diversity in gender identity and expression. Typologies and theory of transgender identity development are being reconsidered on the basis of an increased understanding of lived experiences and new scientific knowledge. Most of the research to date has been qualitative and exploratory, and, when quantitative, has been based on clinical and convenience samples (IOM, 2011). More rigorous research is needed urgently to inform the emerging field of clinical practice in transgender health and to inform public policies to better accommodate and ensure the rights of transgender and transsexual people. Each stage of the life course has unique developmental features. Although there has been a surge in research of transgender and gender-nonconforming adolescents, adding to the knowledge about adults, little is known about the development into midlife and beyond and the needs of transgender elders. Psychologists can play a valuable role in furthering this research and provide evidence-based care, advocacy, and other services to this special population.

References

American Psychiatric Association. (1980). *Diagnostic and statistical manual of mental disorders* (3rd ed.). Washington, DC: Author.

American Psychological Association, Task Force on Gender Identity and Gender Variance. (2009). *Report of the task force on gender identity and gender variance.* Washington, DC: Author.

Benjamin, H. (1966). *The transsexual phenomenon.* New York, NY: Julian Press.

Blanchard, R. (1985). Typology of male-to-female transsexualism. *Archives of Sexual Behavior, 14*, 247–261. doi:10.1007/BF01542107

Blanchard, R. (1989). The classification and labeling of nonhomosexual gender dysphorias. *Archives of Sexual Behavior, 18*, 315–334. doi:10.1007/BF01541951

Bockting, W. O. (1997). Transgender coming out: Implications for the clinical management of gender dysphoria. In B. Bullough, V. Bullough, & J. Elias (Eds.), *Gender blending* (pp. 48–52). Amherst, NY: Prometheus Books.

Bockting, W. O. (1999). From construction to context: Gender through the eyes of the transgendered. *SIECUS Report*, *28*, 3–7.

Bockting, W. O. (2008). Psychotherapy and the real-life experience: From gender dichotomy to gender diversity. *Sexologies*, *17*, 211–224. doi:10.1016/j.sexol.2008.08.001

Bockting, W. O., & Allen, M. P. (2012). Gender dysphoria, transgenderism, and transsexuality. In T. Cash (Ed.), *Encyclopedia of body image and human appearance* (pp. 445–452). Kidlington, England: Elsevier. doi:10.1016/B978-0-12-384925-0.00071-7

Bockting, W. O., & Coleman, E. (2007). Developmental stages of the transgender coming out process: Toward an integrated identity. In R. Ettner, S. Monstrey, & E. Eyler (Eds.), *Principles of transgender medicine and surgery* (pp. 185–208). New York, NY: Haworth Press.

Bockting, W. O., & Ehrbar, R. (2005). Commentary: Gender variance, dissonance, or identity disorder. *Journal of Psychology and Human Sexuality*, *17*(3–4), 125–134.

Bockting, W. O., & Goldberg, J. M. (Eds.). (2006). *Guidelines for transgender care.* Binghamton, NY: Haworth Medical Press.

Bockting, W. O., Huang, C. Y., Ding, H., Robinson, B., & Rosser, B. R. S. (2005). Are transgender persons at higher risk for HIV than other sexual minorities? A comparison of HIV prevalence and risks. *International Journal of Transgenderism*, *8*, 123–131. doi:10.1300/J485v08n02_11

Bockting, W. O., Knudson, G., & Goldberg, J. M. (2006). Counseling and mental health care for transgender adults and loved ones. *International Journal of Transgenderism*, *9*, 35–82. doi:10.1300/J485v09n03_03

Bockting, W. O., Miner, M. H., Swinburne Romine, R. E., Hamilton, A., & Coleman, E. (2013). Stigma, mental health, and resilience in an online sample of the U.S. transgender population. *American Journal of Public Health, 103*, 943–951. doi:10.2105/AJPH.2013.301241

Bockting, W. O., Robinson, B. E., Benner, A., & Scheltema, K. (2004). Patient satisfaction with transgender health services. *Journal of Sex and Marital Therapy*, *30*, 277–294. doi:10.1080/00926230490422467

Bockting, W. O., Rosser, B. R. S., & Coleman, E. (1999). Transgender HIV prevention: Community involvement and empowerment. *International Journal of Transgenderism*, *3*(1–2).

Brill, S., & Pepper, R. (2008). *The transgender child: A handbook for families and professionals.* San Francisco, CA: Cleis Press.

Buhrich, N., & McConaghy, N. (1977). The clinical syndromes of femmiphilic transvestism. *Archives of Sexual Behavior, 6*, 397–412. doi:10.1007/BF01541183

Buhrich, N., & McConaghy, N. (1979). Three clinically discrete categories of fetishistic transvestism. *Archives of Sexual Behavior, 8*, 151–157. doi:10.1007/BF01541235

Bullough, V. L., & Bullough, B. (1993). *Cross dressing, sex, and gender*. Philadelphia: University of Pennsylvania Press.

Burnes, T. R., Singh, A. A., Harper, A. J., Harper, B., Maxon-Kann, W., Pickering, D. L., . . . Hosea, J. (2010). American Counseling Association Competencies for Counseling with Transgender Clients. *Journal of LGBT Issues in Counseling, 4*(3–4), 135–159.

Byne, W., Bradley, S. J., Coleman, E., Eyler, A. D., Green, R., Menvielle, E. J., . . . Tompkins, D. A. (2012). Report of the American Psychiatric Association Task Force on treatment of gender identity disorder. *Archives of Sexual Behavior, 41*, 759–796. doi:10.1007/s10508-012-9975-x

Chivers, M. L., & Bailey, J. M. (2000). Sexual orientation of female-to-male transsexuals: A comparison of homosexual and nonhomosexual types. *Archives of Sexual Behavior, 29*, 259–278. doi:10.1023/A:1001915530479

Clements-Nolle, K., Marx, R., Guzman, R., & Katz, M. (2001). HIV prevalence, risk behaviors, health care use, and mental health status of transgender persons: Implications for public health intervention. *American Journal of Public Health, 91*, 915–921. doi:10.2105/AJPH.91.6.915

Cohen-Kettenis, P. T., & Pfäfflin, F. (2003). *Transgenderism and intersexuality in childhood and adolescence: Making choices*. Thousand Oaks, CA: Sage.

Cohen-Kettenis, P. T., Owen, A., Kaijser, V. G., Bradley, S. J., & Zucker, K. J. (2003). Demographic characteristics, social competence, and behavior problems in children with gender identity disorder: A cross-national, cross-clinic comparative analysis. *Journal of Abnormal Child Psychology, 31*, 41–53. doi:10.1023/A:1021769215342

Cohen-Kettenis, P. T., & van Goozen, S. H. M. (1997). Sex reassignment of adolescent transsexuals: A follow-up study. *Journal of the American Academy of Child and Adolescent Psychiatry, 36*, 263–271. doi:10.1097/00004583-199702000-00017

Cole, S., Eyler, D., & Samons, S. (2000). Issues of transgender. In L. Szuchman & F. Muscarella (Eds.), *Psychological perspectives on human sexuality* (pp. 149–168). New York, NY: Wiley.

Coleman, E. (1982). Developmental stages of the coming out process. *Journal of Homosexuality, 7*(2–3), 31–43. doi:10.1300/J082v07n02_06

Coleman, E., Bockting, W., Botzer, M., Cohen-Kettenis, P., DeCuypere, G., Feldman, J., . . . Zucker, K. (2011). Standards of care for the health of transsexual, transgender, and gender nonconforming people, 7th version. *International Journal of Transgenderism, 13*, 165–232. doi:10.1080/15532739.2011.700873

Coleman, E., Colgan, P., & Gooren, L. (1992). Male crossgender behavior in Myanmar (Burma): A description of the acault. *Archives of Sexual Behavior, 21*, 313–321. doi:10.1007/BF01542999

Conron, K. J., Scott, G., Stowell, G. S., & Landers, S. J. (2012). Transgender health in Massachusetts: Results from a household probability sample of adults. *American Journal of Public Health, 102*, 118–122. doi:10.2105/AJPH.2011.300315

Cook-Daniels, L., & Munson, M. (2010). Sexual violence, elder abuse, and sexuality of transgender adults, age 50+: Results of three surveys. *Journal of GLBT Family Studies, 6*, 142–177. doi:10.1080/15504281003705238

Coolidge, F. L., Thede, L. L., & Young, S. E. (2002). The heritability of gender identity disorder in a child and adolescent twin sample. *Behavior Genetics, 32*, 251–257. doi:10.1023/A:1019724712983

Dekker, R. M., & van de Pol, L. C. (1989). *The tradition of female transvestism in early modern Europe*. New York, NY: St. Martin's Press.

Derogatis, L. R. (2000). *Brief Symptom Inventory (BSI 18)*. Minneapolis, MN: National Computer Systems, Pearson.

Devor, A. H. (2004). Witnessing and mirroring: A fourteen stage model of transsexual identity formation. *Journal of Gay and Lesbian Psychotherapy, 8*, 41–67.

de Vries, A., Cohen-Kettenis, P. T., & Delmarre-van der Waal, H. (2006). Clinical management of gender dysphoria in adolescents. *International Journal of Transgenderism, 9*, 83–94. doi:10.1300/J485v09n03_04

de Vries, A. L., & Cohen-Kettenis, P. T. (2012). Clinical management of gender dysphoria in children and adolescents: The Dutch approach. *Journal of Homosexuality, 59*, 301–320. doi:10.1080/00918369.2012.653300

de Vries, A. L., Kreukels, B. P., Steensma, T. D., Doreleijers, T. A., & Cohen-Kettenis, P. T. (2011). Comparing adult and adolescent transsexuals: An MMPI–2 and MMPI–A study. *Psychiatry Research, 186*, 414–418. doi:10.1016/j.psychres.2010.07.033

de Vries, A. L., Steensma, T. D., Doreleijers, T. A., & Cohen-Kettenis, P. T. (2011). Puberty suppression in adolescents with Gender Identity Disorder: A prospective follow-up study. *Journal of Sexual Medicine, 8*, 2276–2283. doi:10.1111/j.1743-6109.2010.01943.x

Docter, R. F. (1988). *Transvestites and transsexuals: Toward a theory of cross-gender behavior*. New York, NY: Plenum Press. doi:10.1007/978-1-4613-0997-0

Docter, R. F., & Prince, V. (1997). Transvestism: A survey of 1032 cross-dressers. *Archives of Sexual Behavior, 26*, 589–605. doi:10.1023/A:1024572209266

Ehrensaft, D. (2012). From gender identity disorder to gender identity creativity: True gender self child therapy. *Journal of Homosexuality, 59*, 337–356. doi: 10.1080/00918369.2012.653303

Feinberg, L. (1996). *Transgender warriors*. Boston, MA: Beacon Press.

Fraser, L. (2009). Depth psychotherapy with transgender people. *Sexual and Relationship Therapy, 24*, 126–142. doi:10.1080/14681990903003878

Fredriksen-Goldsen, K. O., Kim, H. J., Emlet, C. A., Muraco, A., Erosheva, E. A., Hoy-Ellis, C. P., . . . Petry, H. (2011). *The aging and health report: Disparities and resilience among lesbian, gay, bisexual, and transgender older adults*. Seattle, WA: Institute for Multigenerational Health.

Gagné, P., Tewksbury, R., & McGaughey, D. (1997). Coming out and crossing over. *Gender and Society, 11*, 478–508. doi:10.1177/089124397011004006

Garofalo, R., Deleon, J., Osmer, E., Doll, M., & Harper, G. W. (2006). Overlooked, misunderstood, and at risk: Exploring the lives and HIV risk of ethnic minority male-to-female transgender youth. *Journal of Adolescent Health, 38*, 230–236. doi:10.1016/j.jadohealth.2005.03.023

Gehi, P. S., & Arkles, G. (2007). Unraveling injustice: Race and class impact of Medicaid exclusions of transition-related health care for transgender people. *Sexuality Research and Social Policy, 4*, 7–35. doi:10.1525/srsp.2007.4.4.7

Grant, J. M., Mottet, L. A., Tanis, J., Harrison, J., Herman, J. L., & Kiesling, M. (2011). *Injustice at every turn: A report of the national transgender discrimination survey*. Washington, DC: National Center for Transgender Equality and National Gay and Lesbian Task Force.

Grossman, A. H., & D'Augelli, A. R. (2006). Transgender youth: Invisible and vulnerable. *Journal of Homosexuality, 51*, 111–128. doi:10.1300/J082v51n01_06

Grossman, A. H., & D'Augelli, A. R. (2007). Transgender youth and life-threatening behaviors. *Suicide and Life-Threatening Behavior, 37*, 527–537. doi:10.1521/suli.2007.37.5.527

Grossman, A. H., D'Augelli, A. R., Howell, T. J., & Hubbard, S. (2005). Parents' reactions to transgender youth's gender nonconforming expression and identity. *Journal of Gay and Lesbian Social Services, 18*, 3–16. doi:10.1300/J041v18n01_02

Grossman, A. H., D'Augelli, A. R., & Salter, N. P. (2006). Male-to-female transgender youth: Gender expression milestones, gender atypicality, victimization, and parents' responses. *Journal of GLBT Family Studies, 2*, 71–92. doi:10.1300/J461v02n01_04

Grossman, A. H., D'Augelli, A. R., Salter, N. P., & Hubbard, S. M. (2005). Comparing gender expression, gender nonconformity, and parents' responses of female-to-male and male-to-female transgender youth: Implications for counseling. *Journal of LGBT Issues in Counseling, 1*, 41–59. doi:10.1300/J462v01n01_04

Harper, A., Finnerty, P., Martinez, M., Brace, A., Crethar, H. C., Loos, B., . . . Hammer, T. R. (2013). Association for Lesbian, Gay, Bisexual, and Transgender Issues in Counseling competencies for counseling with lesbian, gay, bisexual, queer, questioning, intersex, and ally individuals. *Journal of LGBT Issues in Counseling, 7*, 2–43. doi:10.1080/15538605.2013.755444

Harrison, J., Grant, J., & Herman, J. L. (2011–2012). *A gender not listed here: Genderqueers, gender rebels, and otherwise in the national transgender discrimination survey*. Los Angeles: Williams Institute, University of California, Los Angeles.

Hastings, D. W. (1969). Inauguration of a research project on transsexualism in a university medical center. In R. Green & J. Money (Eds.), *Transsexualism and sex reassignment* (pp. 243–251). Baltimore, MD: The Johns Hopkins Press.

Hastings, D. W. (1974). Postsurgical adjustment of male transsexual patients. *Clinics in Plastic Surgery, 1*, 335–344.

Hembree, W. C., Cohen-Kettenis, P., Delmarre-van der Waal, H. A., Gooren, L. J., Meyer, W. J., III, Spack, N. P., . . . Montori, V. M. (2009). Endocrine treatment of transsexual persons: An Endocrine Society clinical practice guideline. *Journal of Clinical Endocrinology and Metabolism, 94*, 3132–3154. doi:10.1210/jc.2009-0345

Herbst, J. H., Jacobs, E. D., Finlayson, T. J., McKleroy, V. S., Neumann, M. S., & Crepaz, N. (2008). Estimating HIV prevalence and risk behaviors of transgender persons in the United States: A systematic review. *AIDS and Behavior, 12*, 1–17. doi:10.1007/s10461-007-9299-3

Heylens, G., De Cuypere, G., Zucker, K. J., Schelfaut, C., Elaut, E., Vanden Bossche, H., . . . T'Sjoen, G. (2012). Gender identity disorder in twins: A review of the case report literature. *Journal of Sexual Medicine, 9*, 751–757. doi:10.1111/j.1743-6109.2011.02567.x

Hines, M. (2006). Prenatal testosterone and gender-related behaviour. *European Journal of Endocrinology, 155*, S115–S121. doi:10.1530/eje.1.02236

Hirschfeld, M. (1991). *Transvestites: The erotic drive to crossdress* (M. Lombardi-Nash, Trans.). Buffalo, NY: Prometheus Books. (Original work published 1910)

Iantaffi, A., & Bockting, W. O. (2011). Views from both sides of the bridge? Gender, sexual legitimacy, and transgender people's experiences of relationships. *Culture, Health, and Sexuality, 13*, 355–370. doi:10.1080/13691058.2010.537770

Institute of Medicine. (2011). *The health of lesbian, gay, bisexual, and transgender people: Building a foundation for better understanding*. Washington, DC: National Academies Press.

Kates, G. (1995). *Monsieur d'Eon is a woman: A tale of political intrigue and sexual masquerade*. New York, NY: Basic Books.

Kreukels, B. (2011). Beeldvormend onderzoek naar de effecten van geslachtshormonen op de hersenen: Onderzoek bij transseksuelen. *Neuropraxis, 15*, 151–158. doi:10.1007/s12474-011-0029-2

Kruijver, F. P. M., Zhou, J.-N., Pool, C. W., Hofman, M. A., Gooren, L. J. G., & Swaab, D. F. (2000). Male-to-female transsexuals have female neuron numbers in a limbic nucleus. *Journal of Clinical Endocrinology and Metabolism, 85*, 2034–2041. doi:10.1210/jc.85.5.2034

Kuiper, A. J., & Cohen-Kettenis, P. T. (1998). Gender role reversal among postoperative transsexuals. *International Journal of Transgenderism*, 2(3).

Kulick, D. (1998). *Travesti: Sex, gender, and culture among Brazilian transgendered prostitutes*. Chicago, IL: University of Chicago Press.

Landén, M., Wålinder, J., & Lundström, B. (1998). Clinical characteristics of a total cohort of female and male applicants for sex reassignment: A descriptive study. *Acta Psychiatrica Scandinavica, 97*, 189–194. doi:10.1111/j.1600-0447.1998.tb09986.x

Lawrence, A. A. (2010). Sexual orientation versus age of onset as bases for typologies (subtypes) for gender identity disorder in adolescents and adults. *Archives of Sexual Behavior, 39*, 514–545. doi:10.1007/s10508-009-9594-3

Leichtentritt, R. D., & Arad, B. D. (2004). Adolescent and young adult male-to-female transsexuals: Pathways to prostitution. *British Journal of Social Work, 34*, 349–374. doi:10.1093/bjsw/bch042

Lev, A. I. (2004). *Transgender emergence: Therapeutic guidelines for working with gender-variant people and their families*. Binghamton, NY: The Haworth Press.

Lewins, F. (1995). *Transexualism in society: A sociology of male-to-female transsexuals*. South Melbourne, Australia: Macmillan Education Australia.

Lombardi, E. (2011). Transgender health: A review and guidance for future research—Proceedings from the Summer Institute at the Center for Research on Health and Sexual Orientation, University of Pittsburgh. *International Journal of Transgenderism, 12*, 211–229. doi:10.1080/15532739.2010.544232

Lombardi, E. L., Wilchins, R. A., Priesing, D., & Malouf, D. (2002). Gender violence: Transgender experiences with violence and discrimination. *Journal of Homosexuality*, *42*, 89–101. doi:10.1300/J082v42n01_05

Lurie, S. (2005). Identifying training needs of health-care providers related to treatment and care of transgendered patients: A qualitative needs assessment conducted in New England. *International Journal of Transgenderism*, *8*, 93–112. doi:10.1300/J485v08n02_09

Marantz, S., & Coates, S. (1991). Mothers of boys with gender identity disorder: A comparison of matched controls. *Journal of the American Academy of Child and Adolescent Psychiatry, 30*, 310–315. doi:10.1097/00004583-199103000-00022

Mathy, R. M. (2002). A nonclinical comparison of transgender identity and sexual orientation—A framework for multicultural competence. *Journal of Psychology and Human Sexuality*, *13*, 31–54. doi:10.1300/J056v13n01_02

Mathy, R. M. (2003). Transgender identity and suicidality in a nonclinical sample—Sexual orientation, psychiatric history, and compulsive behaviors. *Journal of Psychology and Human Sexuality*, *14*, 47–65. doi:10.1300/J056v14n04_03

Menvielle, E. (2012). A comprehensive program for children with gender variant behaviors and Gender Identity Disorders. *Journal of Homosexuality*, *59*, 357–368. doi:10.1080/00918369.2012.653305

Meyer-Bahlburg, H. F. L., Dolezal, C., Baker, S. W., Carlson, A. D., Obeid, J. S., & New, M. I. (2004). Prenatal androgenization affects gender-related behavior but not gender identity in 5–12-year-old girls with congenital adrenal hyperplasia. *Archives of Sexual Behavior*, *33*, 97–104. doi:10.1023/B:ASEB.0000014324.25718.51

Money, J., & Ehrhardt, A. A. (1972). *Man and woman, boy and girl: The differentiation and dimorphism of gender identity from conception to maturity*. Baltimore, MD: Johns Hopkins University Press.

Murad, M. H., Elamin, M. B., Garcia, M. Z., Mullan, R. J., Murad, A., Erwin, P. J., & Montori, V. M. (2010). Hormonal therapy and sex reassignment: A systematic review and meta-analysis of quality of life and psychosocial outcomes. *Clinical Endocrinology, 72*, 214–231.

Nanda, S. (1999). *Neither man nor woman: The Hijras of India*. Belmont, CA: Wadsworth.

National Senior Citizens Law Center. (2011). *LGBT older adults in long-term care facilities: Stories from the field*. Washington, DC: National Senior Citizens Law Center, National Gay and Lesbian Task Force, Services and Advocacy for GLBT Elders (SAGE), Lambda Legal, National Center for Lesbian Rights & National Center for Transgender Equality.

Nemoto, T., Operario, D., & Keatley, J. (2005). Health and social services for male-to-female transgender persons of color in San Francisco. *International Journal of Transgenderism*, *8*, 5–19. doi:10.1300/J485v08n02_02

Nuttbrock, L., Hwahng, S., Bockting, W., Rosenblum, A., Mason, M., Macri, M., & Becker, J. (2010). Psychiatric impact of gender-related abuse across the life course of male-to-female transgender persons. *Journal of Sex Research*, *47*, 12–23. doi:10.1080/00224490903062258

Person, E., & Ovesey, L. (1974a). The transsexual syndrome in males: I. Primary transsexualism. *American Journal of Psychotherapy*, *28*, 4–20.

Person, E., & Ovesey, L. (1974b). The transsexual syndrome in males: II. Secondary transsexualism. *American Journal of Psychotherapy*, *28*, 174–193.

Pfäfflin, F. (1992). Regrets after sex reassignment surgery. *Journal of Psychology and Human Sexuality*, *5*, 69–85. doi:10.1300/J056v05n04_05

Prieur, A. (1998). *Mema's house, Mexico City*. Chicago, IL: University of Chicago Press.

Rachlin, K., Green, J., & Lombardi, E. (2008). Utilization of health care among female-to-male transgender individuals in the United States. *Journal of Homosexuality*, *54*, 243–258. doi:10.1080/00918360801982124

Roen, K. (2011). The discursive and clinical production of trans youth: Gender variant youth who seek puberty suppression. *Psychology and Sexuality*, *2*, 58–68. doi:10.1080/19419899.2011.536316

Roscoe, W. (1991). *The Zuni man-woman*. Albuquerque: University of New Mexico Press.

Rosser, B. R. S., Oakes, J. M., Bockting, W. O., & Miner, M. (2007). Capturing the social demographics of hidden sexual minorities: An Internet study of the transgender population in the United States. *Sexuality Research and Social Policy*, *4*, 50–64. doi:10.1525/srsp.2007.4.2.50

Sausa, L. A. (2005). Translating research into practice: Trans youth recommendations for improving school systems. *Journal of Gay and Lesbian Issues in Education*, *3*, 15–28. doi:10.1300/J367v03n01_04

Schifter, J. (1999). *From toads to queens: Transvestism in a Latin American setting*. Binghamton, NY: Harrington Park Press.

Schilt, K., & Westbrook, L. (2009). Doing gender, doing heteronormativity: "Gender normals," transgender people, and the social maintenance of heterosexuality. *Gender and Society, 23*, 440–464. doi:10.1177/0891243209340034

Shively, M. G., & DeCecco, J. P. (1977). Components of sexual identity. *Journal of Homosexuality*, *3*, 41–48. doi:10.1300/J082v03n01_04

Singh, A. A., & Burnes, T. R. (2009). Creating developmentally appropriate, safe counseling environments for transgender youth: The critical role of school counselors. *Journal of LGBT Issues in Counseling*, *3*(3–4), 215–234. doi:10.1080/15538600903379457

Smith, Y. L., van Goozen, S. H., & Cohen-Kettenis, P. T. (2001). Adolescents with gender identity disorder who were accepted or rejected for sex reassignment surgery: A prospective follow-up. *Journal of the American Academy of Child and Adolescent Psychiatry, 40*, 472–481. doi:10.1097/00004583-200104000-00017

Sperber, J., Landers, S., & Lawrence, S. (2005). Access to health care for transgenderered persons: Results of a needs assessment in Boston. *International Journal of Transgenderism*, *8*, 75–91. doi:10.1300/J485v08n02_08

Steensma, T. D., Biemond, R., de Boer, F., & Cohen-Kettenis, P. T. (2011). Desisting and persisting gender dysphoria after childhood: A qualitative follow-up study. *Clinical Child Psychology and Psychiatry*, *16*, 499–516. doi:10.1177/1359104510378303

Stone, S. (1991). The empire strikes back: A posttranssexual manifesto. In J. Epstein & K. Straub (Eds.), *Body guards: The cultural politics of gender ambiguity* (pp. 280–304). New York, NY: Routledge.

Taranowski, C. J. (2008). Transsexual employees in the workplace. *Journal of Workplace Behavioral Health*, *23*, 467–477. doi:10.1080/15555240802540186

Taywaditep, K. J., Coleman, E., & Dumronggittigule, P. (1997). Thailand (Muang Thai). In R. Francouer (Ed.), *International encyclopedia of sexuality* (pp. 1192–1265). New York, NY: Continuum.

Thaler, C., Bermudez, F., & Sommer, S. (2009). Legal advocacy on behalf of transgender and gender nonconforming youth. In G. P. Mallon (Ed.), *Social work practice with transgender and gender variant youth* (pp. 139–162). New York, NY: Routledge.

van Beijsterveldt, C. E. M., Hidziak, J. J., & Boomsma, D. I. (2006). Genetic and environmental influences on cross-gender behavior and relation to behavior problems: A study of Dutch twins at ages 7 and 10 years. *Archives of Sexual Behavior, 35*, 647–658. doi:10.1007/s10508-006-9072-0

Wallien, M. S., & Cohen-Kettenis, P. T. (2008). Psychosexual outcome of gender-dysphoric children. *Journal of the American Academy of Child and Adolescent Psychiatry, 47*, 1413–1423. doi:10.1097/CHI.0b013e31818956b9

Wallien, M. S. C., Swaab, H., & Cohen-Kettenis, P. T. (2007). Psychiatric comorbidity among children with gender identity disorder. *Journal of the American Academy of Child and Adolescent Psychiatry*, *46*, 1307–1314. doi:10.1097/chi.0b013e3181373848

Williams, W. L. (1986). *The spirit and the flesh: Sexual diversity in American Indian culture.* Boston, MA: Beacon Press.

World Professional Association for Transgender Health, Inc. (2008). WPATH clarification on medical necessity of treatment, sex reassignment, and insurance coverage in the U.S.A. Retrieved from http://www.wpath.org/documents/Med%20Nec%20on%202008%20Letterhead.pdf

Wyss, S. E. (2004). "This was my hell": The violence experienced by gender non-conforming youth in U.S. high schools. *International Journal of Qualitative Studies in Education, 17*, 709–730. doi:10.1080/0951839042000253676

Xavier, J. M., Bobbin, M., Singer, B., & Budd, E. (2005). A needs assessment of transgendered people of color living in Washington, DC. *International Journal of Transgenderism, 8*, 31–47. doi:10.1300/J485v08n02_04

Zhou, J.-N., Hofman, M. A., Gooren, L. J., & Swaab, D. F. (1995). A sex difference in the human brain and its relation to transsexuality. *Nature, 378*, 68–70. doi:10.1038/378068a0

Zucker, K. J. (2008). Children with gender identity disorder: Is there a best practice? *Neuropsychiatrie de l'Enfance et de l'Adolescence, 56*, 358–364. doi:10.1016/j.neurenf.2008.06.003

Zucker, K. J., Bradley, S. J., Ben-Dat, D. N., Ho, C., Johnson, L., & Owen, A. (2003). Psychopathology in the parents of boys with gender identity disorder. *Journal of the American Academy of Child and Adolescent Psychiatry, 42*, 2–4. doi:10.1097/00004583-200301000-00003

Zucker, K. J., Bradley, S. J., & Lowry Sullivan, C. B. (1996). Traits of separation anxiety in boys with gender identity disorder. *Journal of the American Academy of Child and Adolescent Psychiatry, 35*, 791–798. doi:10.1097/00004583-199606000-00019

Zucker, K. J., Bradley, S. J., & Sanikhani, M. (1997). Sex differences in referral rates of children with gender identity disorder: Some hypotheses. *Journal of Abnormal Child Psychology, 25*, 217–227. doi:10.1023/A:1025748032640

Zucker, K. J., & Lawrence, A. A. (2009). Epidemiology of gender identity disorder: Recommendations for the standards of care of the World Professional Association for Transgender Health. *International Journal of Transgenderism, 11*, 8–18. doi:10.1080/15532730902799946

CHAPTER 25

SEXUALITY AND EMBODIMENT

Deborah L. Tolman, Christin P. Bowman, and Breanne Fahs

Our bodies are the permeable boundary between our individual sense of self and the society in which we live. From the most banal bodily acts of life—how we dress, the magazines we read, with whom we sleep—to the big questions of social organization regarding marriage, family, sexual morality, and sexual health, the body is always involved in some way. The body is at once our own, something we share with others, and also something that is important to and shaped by the social world. Almost everything about sex is also about the body; sexuality is an intrinsic part of an embodied self. Although there is certainly much research that focuses on particular biological functions of sexual bodily parts and physiological processes associated with, and in some cases considered to comprise, sexuality, this line of research is predicated on the body as fundamentally and exclusively organic and, for the most part, hardwired (see Chapters 7 and 23, this volume). We begin the introduction to this chapter by articulating social concepts of "the body" and their relationship to understandings of and research about sexuality.

Until very recently, the body has been considered a natural object and therefore the domain of the natural sciences. Conceptualizations of the body as a production that incorporates the physical and the social rather than as a biological—given theories of embodiment—have constituted a burgeoning field of inquiry, particularly within the disciplines of sociology, literature, cultural studies, feminist studies, education, and psychology. In an era in which forms of sexual interactions, identities, and representations have proliferated so profoundly, where evidence and vestiges of sex saturate landscapes from the visual to the virtual, the question of where and how bodies enter to constitute sexual feelings, thoughts, and actions is currently a primary one (Attwood, 2007; Coy & Garner, 2012). Embodiment theories have enabled us to reformulate research inquiries that are anchored in and about bodily experiences of the sexual and of sexuality. Grounded in a set of fundamentally social theories, embodiment theories and studies depart from much of sexuality research in that they are also inherently political, that is, they locate and provide insight into how bodies and sexuality, as experienced and made sense of, are not simply natural but exist, are apprehended, and are understood within social structures of power. These structures imbue bodies and bodily processes with meanings and significance, both inside and out. Embodiment epistemologically locates the sexual body, and the sexual person who "lives in" *any* body, in phenomenology, or the ways in which people apprehend and experience their sexual bodies.

It is ironic to recognize that the notion of how actual bodies—material, sexual bodies themselves—are experienced or come into being or consciousness has been overlooked frequently in current academic research on sex and sexuality. The long-established approach to studying the sexual body, exemplified in the work of Masters and Johnson's (1966) study of the (human) body's sexual response cycle, has been understood exclusively in terms of the body as a

The authors acknowledge the contributions of Gary Dowsett and Duane Duncan to the initial formulations of the chapter, and Jennifer Chmielewski for assistance with references and manuscript preparation.

http://dx.doi.org/10.1037/14193-025
APA Handbook of Sexuality and Psychology: Vol. 1. Person-Based Approaches, D. L. Tolman and L. M. Diamond (Editors-in-Chief)

biological mechanism, with biological substrates, and determined by the body's biology, a closed-system paradigm in which context did not matter. The study of biological substrates of many sexual bodily processes has blossomed and provided critical understanding of human sexuality (Lloyd, 2006; see Chapter 7, this volume), whereas other claims have been challenged by researchers whose premise is a social understanding of sexual bodily processes, that is, the ongoing debates over female sexual dysfunction (FSD; Shifren, Brigitta, Russo, Segretti, & Johannes, 2008; Tiefer, 2006; see Chapters 8 and 11 this volume) and gender identity (Stryker, 2006). As the beginnings of postmodernism seeped into sexuality research, the social construction of sexuality provided an alternative way to map and understand sexuality, including sexual desire, sexual identities, and sexual relationships (Plante, 2006; Tiefer, 2004), and it emerged as a prominent paradigm. New ways of thinking about and conducting research on sex and sexuality flourished, challenging the idea that sexuality was a natural or innate expression of each individual's true self, and drawing attention to the ways in which sexuality as a field of ideas or discourses constituted truths about subjectivities or lived experience or understanding of various aspects of selves (i.e., Gamson, 2000; Seidman, 1996; see Chapter 3, this volume). These two lines of theory came to clash as polar opposites through the 1990s (DeLamater & Hyde, 1998), as the "essentialism–social constructionism" debates, yielding antithetical understandings of what sexuality was and how it emerged over individual lifetimes and across historical time and human societies. In the eyes of biological determinism (often referred to as *essentialism*), sexuality is an essence, an objective and unchanging set of biological processes. In the eyes of social construction, sexuality is not a fixed essence or inherently determined by biology but is constituted through social meanings and understandings about what sexuality is, how it is expressed, and what it means (Tiefer, 2004). The emergence of embodiment theories has provided one alternative to the impasse that these debates generated (Tolman & Diamond, 2001; see Chapter 1, this volume). The very questions that an embodiment lens poses constitute a useful reframing of the mind–body binary that has fractured sexuality research: How do we connect the body as a material, biological entity to the body as a social entity or entities? How do we make sense of the sexual body in the context of, or as an "effect" (an outcome) of, social life? How do we understand the individual in relation to the social world via the body?

As Plummer (2002, 2012) and Dowsett (1996, 2000) have each argued, the actual desiring, heaving, sexual body is hardly anywhere to be found in sexuality research (see also Schilling, 2003). Ironically, the vast majority of sexuality research does not have much sex in it; what people actually do, think, and feel when expressing sexual feelings or use their bodies in sexual ways, is very rare. Sexuality research is for the most part more sanitized than the messiness of actual sex. As scholarship on embodiment has developed, it in fact has been more theoretical than empirical and more textual than involving actual bodies. The plethora of theoretical scholarship on embodiment, however, has begun to make possible a growing body of sexuality research grounded in or about embodiment that mobilizes and connects theoretical formulations of embodiment to empirical investigation of sexuality as embodied experiences and phenomena. This chapter presents the major embodiment theories and, in particular, how embodiment in relation to sexuality is theorized in psychology. We then present a critical review of a wide range of empirical research on sexuality that has utilized these theoretical frameworks to explore the body, embodiment, sex, and sexuality, including gendered sexual bodies, the sexual body and its parts, the sexual body in action, the sexual body across the life span, sexual-minority sexual bodies, and the "disobedient" sexual body. Finally, we consider briefly some implications of this relatively new knowledge for clinical practice and interventions as well as for the future of embodiment and sexuality and how the accomplishments and shortcomings of what has been done might be leveraged to expand this new arena of research.

WHAT IS EMBODIMENT?

Embodiment refers to the experience of living in, perceiving, and experiencing the world from the very specific location of our bodies. The concept of embodiment within psychology and other social sciences actually refers to two distinct processes or phenomena: *being embodied* and *embodying the social*. These conceptualizations of embodiment are by no means incompatible or mutually exclusive; we can rely on both simultaneously, and thereby paint a much fuller picture of embodiment as it relates to sexuality (see, e.g., Crossley, 1996; Rubin, 1984).

Being embodied refers to an experiential awareness of the feelings and sensations within one's body, which reflects our corporeality (Grosz, 1994) or the reality that we "live in skin" (J. Ward, 2002). This awareness can be characterized as *lived embodiment*, because it refers to the body as we live in it and feel it (e.g., see Merleau-Ponty, 1962; Young, 1990). Merleau-Ponty (1962) described the lived body as a "body-subject," meaning that the body itself, not cognition, is capable of genuine experience. That is, the body is not just a passive sensory-data receptor that then relies on our consciousness and cognition to give it meaning, but the body experiences the world directly because the body is forever entangled with the world. He referred to this "body which is better informed than we are" as having a "latent knowledge" (Merleau-Ponty, 1962, p. 238). Similarly, Young (1984) suggested that it is possible to "locate consciousness and subjectivity in the body itself" (p. 161). That is, our bodies themselves experience sensations and awareness, rather than simply collecting external stimuli and information in service to a cognitive, meaning-making psyche.

G. Lindemann (1996) deftly wove social influences into an understanding of the material, physical body, by theorizing distinctions between *objectified*, *experiencing*, and *experienced* bodies. The *objectified* body is the visible, material body that moves through physical and social space. The *experiencing* body is the sensory (or *lived* or *phenomenological*) body, experiencing the environment through the five senses; this lived body has also been described as being in a specific sociocultural context or a *body in situation* (Young, 1990, p. 16; see also Moi, 2001). The *experienced* body is our cognitive sense of our own bodies, for instance, our understanding of our own pleasure or pain. The *experiencing* body, then, is the kinesthetic, affective, emotional, and desiring body. For Lindemann, the *experiencing* and *experienced* bodies come together to make up the *living body*. In applying Lindemann's account to a social psychological analysis of sexuality, we can understand the objectified body as the one onto which all societal presumptions (e.g., requirements of masculinity and femininity) are projected. Sexual desires as well as sexual pleasures, therefore, can be understood as experienced within the body itself. This is not to say that bodily sensations are somehow independent from the realm of the social. Indeed, bodily sensations are constantly modified, interpreted, and informed by the social contexts in which these bodies exist. A countervailing conception of embodiment is the notion of intersubjectivity (or derivatization), that is, that the body is experienced in relationship to or with another person. In this context, sexual objectification is not a form of alienation but a form of personification, such that the sexual bodies of two people in a sexual encounter can be sexual subjects and sexual objects, with a mutuality of desire and being desired simultaneously (Cahill, 2011).

Conversely, embodiment can refer to the ways our social and historical environments enter into and become entangled with our bodies. This social constructionist viewpoint emphasizes the mechanisms by which our bodies come to behave in certain normative fashions; in short, by living day to day in a society that makes certain demands on our bodies and psyches, we come to internalize these norms or discourses and embody them (e.g., see Bartky, 1990; Foucault, 1978). These norms and discourses form and inform our bodily feelings, behaviors, and comportment, and they constitute the phenomenology of embodiment (Bartky, 1990; Bordo, 1993, 2000; Young, 1990). Some theorists have referred to this concept as *social inscription*, as the body can be understood as a surface onto or into which social norms are written by others or by the self. The key psychological theories of embodiment are the psychodynamic processes of internalization and dissociation, understood as providing mechanisms of inscription that are not conscious. These processes are conceived as relational, that is, the production or experience of the self in relation to specific others or in relation to proximate or distal social contexts (Henriques, Hollway, Urwin, Venn, & Walkerdine, 1998; Ussher, 1989; Young, 1990).

Embodiment also can constitute conscious ways that we might form or "perform" our bodies as part of the production of identities (Butler, 1994). These related conceptualizations of embodiment, then, can be characterized as *inscribed embodiment*.

It is within these multiple understandings of embodiment that we review theoretical frameworks that are used heavily by sexuality researchers and psychologists primarily working in gender and sexuality. Although there has been a useful proliferation of embodiment theories (i.e., "visible identities," Alcoff, 2005; "bodily imaginaries," Gatens, 1996; "cyborg bodies," Haraway, 1991), the work of Foucault and Butler are the foundational theories in which these developments are anchored, and our review reflects this emphasis. We also have highlighted the emerging developments in feminist and queer theory that have come to play an important role in research on embodiment and sexuality.

Foucault and Butler: Production of Embodied Subjects

One of Foucault's anchor projects was the history of sexuality (1978) as it connected to the archaeology of power (1975). Whereas we tend to think of sexuality as a distinct thing that individuals "have," Foucault's insights suggest an alternative: that sexuality is in fact a condition of the time and place in which we live and reflects the dynamic relationship between sexual bodies, sexual practice, institutional power, and knowledge. Foucault's (1966, 1975) work thus has been of enormous value in thinking about how bodies and sexuality are socially constructed. He demonstrated how hegemonic (that is, dominant) discourses emerged and continued to both enable and constrain how bodies might be experienced and lived, explicating the development of regulations specifically related to the management of bodies, including fertility, reproductive health, and sexuality (Foucault, 1969, 1975). All of these regulations emerged as key areas of personal life that the state had an interest in regulating. Each of these concerns produced authoritative discourses related to personal conduct, against which individuals came to evaluate and categorize themselves and others in acts of self-surveillance and self-discipline. Foucault (1975) demonstrated how institutional or state power induced compliance not by force but through more insidious coercive means: via authoritative discourses that regulate social conduct through the bodies and subjectivities of individuals. As such, Foucault's work opened up a distinctly social approach to understanding the body and its place in social relations, all while problematizing or debunking the notion that the body is predetermined, ahistorical, or existing materially outside of culture.

Foucault proposed that a set of ideas or discourses produce and sanction particular practices, experiences, and identities as normal (or pathological) and acceptable (or abjected, wrong, and thus "appropriately" marginal). These discourses produce regulation, control, and "surveillance" that exist, in essence, simultaneously nowhere and everywhere, difficult to pinpoint but reliably effective in shaping and regulating. By discourse, Foucault meant not only a way of speaking but also an integrated way of being and knowing that includes the body, the mind, and relationships. Hegemonic or dominant discourses exert intangible but forceful pressure to comply with a set of interlocking norms or ideologies, communicated through language and produced, reproduced, and sanctioned through practices and institutions that both reflect and enact these discourses (Foucault, 1969). Rather than operating through the direct imposition of power and force, discourse regulates conduct, thoughts, and feelings through reliance on socially agreed-on authorities sanctioned by the state, such as medicine and the law. In Foucault's view, power is not a thing but a relation; power is not simply repressive but productive. Foucault's approach to discourse as social practice provides a way to analyze how bodies and sexualities reflect and enact the power relations of the societies in which they can be seen to exist.

This understanding of social organization and the development and lived experiences of individuals within it is predicated on the dissolution of the fixed subject, who presumably enters into social relations as a whole and biologically determined agent. From Foucault's perspective, there is no such fixed subject who precedes his or her meaningful recognition in discourse; instead, subjectivity must be constituted by the subject in the course of social relations. He or she "takes up" subject positions in discourse or can be understood to perform subject positions or to be composed of (potentially changing, multiple, and contradictory) subjectivities. These generally are not conscious acts. The insidiousness and effectiveness of the operation of discourses, especially those that are hegemonic, is that they are not visible as such; it is the very self that abides by, reproduces, and reinforces the state's regulations and interests. Most important, Foucault demonstrated the "situated nature of subjectivity" (Braidotti, 1994, p. 238), that is, that subjectivity is always constituted in and by specific historical and social contexts.

Foucault understood that subjects cannot have access to the body except through discourses about the body that constrain how we might think about and understand it. Rather than requiring the repression of sexual instincts, the proliferation of discourses on the management and regulation of sexuality led individuals to view themselves as having an innate sexuality, as an extension of their character or true nature. Foucault's primary example is the invention of homosexuality as a category of identification for men and women who participate in same-sex sexual behavior. Before the 1880s, there was no such thing as a homosexual person, nor before the 1930s was there such a term as *heterosexual*.

Although one of the key critiques of Foucault centers on his silence about gender, many feminist scholars have used, extended, and elaborated Foucault's work in important ways, particularly at the intersection of gender and sexuality. The most significant contribution is Butler's (1990) work, which echoed Foucault's challenge to biological determinism and provided an alternative understanding of gender as a set of embodied social practices. Butler (1990) argued that rather than being predestined, gender and gendered bodies are constituted through the repeated stylization of highly regulated acts and practices that, when applied to and through the body over time, give the appearance of being natural. She explained the way in which the sexed body is in fact a product of binary gender discourses, which she denoted as a "process of materialization which stabilizes over time to produce the effect of boundary, fixity, and surface we call matter" (Butler, 1993, p. 9). Thus, gender is not something that people have but something people do, a notion Butler termed "performativity." This endless doing or practice is regulated by conformity through an alignment of sex, gender, and sexuality that she termed "the heterosexual matrix" (Butler, 1990, p. 151). The heterosexual matrix demands and organizes individual and social behavior such that compliant productions of femininity by women, masculinity by men, and heterosexuality by everyone, constitute "normal" or what Butler (1993) described as "intelligible"—recognizable or understandable—embodiment (see also Rich, 1980; Rubin, 1984).

Feminist scholars have infused Foucault's understanding of bodies as produced through regulatory and authoritative discourses with Butler's notion of performativity to argue for the fundamental role of *heterosexuality* as an institutionalized, regulatory discourse that functions to produce experiences and meanings of gendered bodies (Bordo, 2000). Although Butler's work has proven foundational to contemporary embodiment studies, critics have highlighted that Butler's articulation of the performativity of embodied practices sometimes leaves aside the physicality of the body—that is, the ways in which illness, aging, or pregnancy inform identity and experience (Turner, 1995; Longhurst, 2001)—and also fails to consider actual differences between bodies (Schilling, 2003). For instance, Green (2008) has theorized that sexual desire should be conceptualized at both the micro and macro levels, ideally analyzing the somatization of social relations (embodiment), in addition to identifying structural predictors of sexual desire.

Feminist Theories of Embodiment

Given the history of the male–female binary which has constituted women as "more biological, more corporeal, and more natural than men" (Grosz, 1994, p. 14), feminists have developed alternative theoretical frameworks that recognize women's corporeality without eliding into a naturalized, reductionistic, essentialized mind–body dualism that attributes minds to men and bodies to women (see Chapter 2, this volume). Feminists also have powerfully critiqued the historical association of the body with a range of "lesser" individuals and statuses, including colonized people, people of color, people with disabilities, and those living in poverty, grounding these critiques in the concept of intersectionality (Crenshaw, 1991), whereby every corporeal body is situated within, constructed, and experienced through interlocking and inseparable standpoints constituted by specific structural realities and meanings. Embodiment provides a way to understand social differences emanating from race, class, and able-bodiedness as embedded in the flesh, situated in bodies constructed through culturally and historically specific discourses (Spelman, 1990). Postcolonial and transnational scholars have drawn attention to the ways in which racial discourses intersect with sexuality discourses to constitute some bodies as closer to nature (and thus more sexually dangerous and out of control) than others (i.e., Howe & Rigi, 2009; Magubane, 2001; Minh-Ha, 1989)

Shildrick and Price (1999) observed that embodiment theory enables feminist scholars to recognize and account for the materiality or physicality of female bodies (and other marginalized bodies), while at the same time interrogating our living-in-bodies in a social world that informs, forms, and organizes how bodies are known and recognized. That is, embodiment theory rejects the mind–body dualism on which notions of hard-wired sexual difference have been predicated while respecting the materiality and situatedness of women's bodies as they intersect with other structural contexts (see also de Beauvoir, 1949/2009; Irigaray, 1984). Grosz (2008) has deepened feminist embodiment theory by stressing "the virtualities, the potentialities, within biological existence that enable cultural, social, and historical forces to work with and transform that existence" (p. 24). An alternative imaginary is a "Mobius strip," whereby mind and body are inextricably entangled (Braidotti, 1994; Fausto-Sterling, 2000; Grosz, 2008) within the specifics of historical and social moments and institutions. Feminist theoretical perspectives on embodiment provide insight into and understanding of how patriarchy reproduces itself and regenerates oppression in and through bodies. This work has focused explicitly on gender and sexuality as core "vectors" for the perpetuation of institutionalized heterosexuality (Bartky, 1990; Bordo, 1993; Butler, 1993).

Thus, feminist theorists have articulated the specific ways that bodies are under pressure to become socially inscribed as female–male or feminine–masculine (Bartky, 1990; Bordo, 1993; Young, 1990). For instance, by regimes of dieting, makeup, exercise, dress, and cosmetic surgery, women, and increasingly men, try to sculpt their bodies into shapes that reflect the dominant societal norms. Bartky (1990) explicated how women produce feminine embodiment, for instance, by taking norms of femininity into their bodies (i.e., sitting with our legs crossed, taking up as little space as possible); Young (1990) demonstrated how "throwing like a girl" is an effect of endemic yet subtle bodily training and consequential production of a body through femininity discourses about what female bodies can and cannot do. Young (1990) outlined how women learn to experience menstruation as disgusting and necessary to hide, and how women learn to apprehend their breasts as objects of (male) desire and public consumption that require constant management, compelling women to experience their breasts as alien and separate from their own sense of integrated feeling and experience. Such disciplinary practices attach not only to the production of appropriately gendered bodies but also to other aspects of bodily identity subjected to social normalization, such as race. For instance, hair straightening, blue-tinted contact lenses, and surgical reconstruction of noses and lips exemplify practices that extend the hegemonic discourse of feminine beauty to "unruly" black bodies.

Queer Theories of Embodiment

Queer theorists have highlighted the force of institutionalized heterosexuality as heteronormativity, whereby embodying and participating as "properly" gendered heterosexual men and women is equated with normality (Sedgwick, 1990). Importantly, queer theories deconstruct the heterosexual–homosexual binary and help illuminate the ways in which non-normative bodies and sexualities help to constitute and consolidate heterosexual bodies and sexual practices as natural, normal, and prior to culture; non-normative bodies and sexualities also can instigate transformation of the social norms that contain and maintain "proper" sexuality and acceptable embodiments (Berlant & Warner, 2000; Butler, 1994). These processes are produced and induced by making sexual acts and human intimacies that are not circumscribed within heteronormativity invisible or seen only as maligned or criminalized. Queer theories fuel and explain embodied practices that defy heteronormativity and thus make sexuality and bodies that are not contained by its norms into visible, knowable, and increasingly recognizable ways of being, such as dressing in drag, participating in gay pride parades, and engaging in "flaunting" (Berlant & Warner, 2000). These practices and lived experiences were described as "epistemologies of the closet" by Sedgwick (1990), meaning that knowledge about (and from) such lives, desires, and experiences was shut out or shut up rather than pathological or wrong. Queer theory and research focuses on decentering and destabilizing socially given or normative standards and identities of sexuality and gender—what has been called "upending categories"—to reveal that normalized embodiment is compelled and how it can be resisted (Halberstam, 1998). Queer theory emphasizes both the possibility and necessity of resistance to normative discourses—in particular through alternative, often previously unnamed, marginalized or demonized embodied practices. In fact, such resistance is necessary for the regulatory system of heteronormativity itself to be made visible and has the effect of showing how it can be vulnerable to change. By revealing how heteronormativity attempts to regulate and contain bodies and sexualities that do not comply, queer theory demonstrates its regulatory function through and on bodies (Butler, 1993; Moraga & Anzaldúa, 1981).

One way that this theoretical perspective is utilized is by unpacking the lived embodied experiences of those who do not or refuse to embody gendered and heterosexual bodily norms, such as fat women (Shaw, 2006), feminine men (Connell, 1995), masculine women (Halberstam, 1998), and transgender people (Feinberg, 1997) Recent research on embodiment embeds queer theory within conventional research techniques to examine messy and unstable multilayered subjectivities (Epstein, 1994). Both feminist and queer theorists have been challenged for "overtextualizing" the body, that is, for focusing so much on the meanings that bodies have taken up through discourses that the corporeality or materiality of the body has been given short shrift (Braidotti, 1994; Grosz, 2008). As Connell (1995) noted, "bodies, in their own right as bodies, do matter" (p. 51).

Scholarship on sexuality and embodiment comes from an array of disciplines. These embodiment theories have been useful to social science researchers' investigation of people's lived experience and understanding of where sexuality and embodiment meet at the individual, interpersonal, and cultural levels. Psychologists have contributed to this growing body of research and have drawn on and often developed and complicated psychological theories to articulate research questions about sexuality and bodies that are distinctly relevant to the discipline. Psychoanalytic concepts have been especially important mechanisms underlying theorized processes of embodiment. The next section reviews several key psychological theories that are important.

PSYCHOLOGICAL THEORIES AND THE SEXUAL BODY

William James (1890) understood the self, the "I," as fundamentally embodied: "the world experienced (otherwise called 'the field of consciousness') comes at all times with our body as its center. . . [e]verything circles around it, and is felt from its point of view" (cited in Young, 1990, pp. 89–90). It could be argued that being embodied—that is, living, experiencing, sensing in and through one's body, and being (in simple terms) connected with one's body and through one's body to oneself and to others in relational contexts—is an implicit default state of what might be considered psychologically healthy. Empirical psychology has been from the mid-1950s until quite recently oriented toward inquiry into what is broken, wrong, dysfunctional, or unhealthy (Gable & Haidt, 2005), especially in relation to sexuality (Diamond, 2006; Rutherford, 2012). Thus, psychological theories relating to embodiment most often have described processes and states of *disembodiment*, with an eye toward how to prevent, cure, or ameliorate disembodiment.

Disembodiment is understood in psychology as an effect of dissociation. In the literature on sexual abuse, for instance, disembodiment has been recognized as the outcome of the psyche's response to trauma, the dissociation from knowledge (sensory, cognitive) that constitutes an ongoing state of disconnection from the felt body experience as well as from particular memories (Freud, 1900; Herman, 1992; Young, 1990). Embodiment also has been understood as a key element of identity or a sense of self, what is known or experienced "as me" (Young, 1990).

Sexual subjectivity has been articulated in psychology as one's sense, awareness, or knowledge of one's perspectives, feelings, beliefs, and desires as a sexual being situated in the body; it has been articulated as including sexual body–esteem, entitlement to self-pleasure and pleasure from a partner, sexual self-efficacy, sexual agency, and reflection about sexual behavior (Fine, 1988; Hirschman, Impett, & Schooler, 2006; Horne & Zimmer-Gembeck, 2005; Phillips, 2000; Tolman, 1994, 2002). Identity theories position sexual subjectivity as an ongoing process of constructing and experiencing a coherent sexual self through available discourses (e.g., Hammack & Cohler, 2009; Ussher, 1989). The theory of self-objectification provides an explanation for individuals' conscious and less conscious monitoring and shaping of their bodies to comply with conventions of "attractive" and "normal" sexual bodies. This process relies on positing (for women and gay men) the internalization of a "male (desiring) gaze," such that a person turns her or his own body into an object, observed not only by others but also by the self. Rather than existing as a feeling subject, an individual moves a specific dimension of the social world from the interpersonal to the intraindividual to organize one's perception of one's body and bodily experience (Fredrickson & Roberts, 1997; McKinley & Hyde, 1996). This theory was developed to understand women's relationships with their bodies under the conditions of patriarchy in which their bodies are the focus, in practices and in discourses, of male desire and originally was demonstrated as a part of women's and not men's psychological repertoire (Fredrickson, Roberts, Noll, Quinn, & Twenge, 1998), although its applicability to men and ethnically diverse populations is being evaluated (e.g., Hebl, King, & Lin, 2004; Roberts & Gettman, 2004). Piran (e.g., Piran & Ross, 2005; Piran & Teall, 2012) has developed and tested the developmental theory of embodiment, which incorporates both positive or connected risk and "disrupted" embodiment and is composed of five factors: embodiment, body journey, physical freedom versus physical corseting, mental freedom versus mental corseting, and social power versus social disempowerment.

Another psychological concept that is salient to embodiment is agency or choice. A critical and often-contested dimension of embodiment is the place of agency and choice in how it is conceptualized. That is, to what extent might conscious processes be involved in what people do or feel or want in, with, or for their bodies, and in what ways is embodiment predicated on unconscious processes? Some feminist theorists have discussed agency and choice as key sites of contestation around the body and sexuality (Gill, 2008). Another area in which the rhetoric of "choice" appears is in disagreements about Foucault, particularly critiques that his theory lacked the capacity for an agentic, resistant subject who could articulate and enact counterhegemonic discourses—discourses that explicitly challenge or refute what dominant practices or norms determine to be acceptable, normal, or valued (Alcoff, 1988; for a critique of this perspective, see also Lacombe, 1996). If bodily experience is constructed by hegemonic discourses, then are individuals doomed to enact and abide by its regulatory power? The psychological concept of agency is a capacity to recognize and enact choices, that is, "the ability of human beings to create viable lives even when they are constrained by social forces" (Eitzen, Baca Zinn, & Gold, 1999, p. 469). The self-determination theory model of internalization provides a framework linking the intrapsychic, social, and subjective dimensions of agency and choice:

> Individuals may feel autonomous while meeting social expectations as a result of internalization, a process by which

> individuals over time increasingly come to identify with social expectations, so that subjectively they experience these constraints in a highly agentic way, that is, in a way that involves a subjective sense of autonomy or choice. (Miller, Das, & Chakravarthy, 2011, p. 46)

Agency can range from conscious resistance to oppressive forces or cultural constraints to survival strategies that are neither transformative nor meant to be. Agency has been conceptualized as "strategies" of action, ranging from unconscious capitulation that does not intend resistance to the much more deliberate and organized resistances people engage in because they have the agency to do so. Furthermore, agency can be exercised as accommodation to, or resistance toward, norms and structures that manage, control, and discipline the body (Dillaway, 2011; Komter, 1989). Currently there is much debate about the place of agency and choice in relation to embodiment (Gill, 2008; Peterson, 2010), with some scholarship tackling it as a central question related to sexuality and embodiment (Albanesi, 2009). One of the key questions in this debate is how people's understanding of their decision making may be impeded by what appears to be a set of viable choices that in fact is impoverished (Tolman, 2012).

Gendered Sexual Bodies

In the field of sexuality, femininity traditionally is understood as a collection of heteronormative scripts, norms, or ideologies that require women to suppress their needs and desires (Greene & Faulkner, 2005; J. Holland, Ramazanoglu, Sharpe, & Thomson, 2004), to play "gatekeeper" roles for male desire (Byers, 1995; Gagnon, 1990), and to remain ignorant about sex in general (Gagnon, 1990; J. Holland et al., 2004). At the same time, femininity also requires attending to one's sexual body, as many scholars have pointed to the increasing pressure on women to "perfect" their genital appearances via labiaplasty and other cosmetic procedures meant to render women's genitalia more "feminine" by making them more "virginal" or "childlike" (Braun, 2005; Braun & Kitzinger, 2001; Sanger, 2009; Tiefer, 2008). Furthermore, femininity requires constant self-surveillance and self-objectification, as women internalize an observer's perspective and endeavor to live up to impossible standards of sexual desirability (Fredrickson & Roberts, 1997; J. Holland et al., 2004). Many feminists, therefore, have argued that traditional femininity ideologies play an alienating role in the lives of women, estranging them from their bodies and their sexualities (Bartky, 1990; J. Holland et al., 2004, Tolman, 2002). Indeed, women who endorse traditional femininity ideologies report experiencing less sexual agency and less comfort with their bodies during sex (Curtin, Ward, Merriweather, & Carruthers, 2011). It follows, then, that when women are thinking about their bodies during sex (high levels of body consciousness), they have less sexual self-esteem (Wiederman, 2000), experience less sexual pleasure (Sanchez & Kiefer, 2007), have more difficulty achieving orgasm (Sanchez & Kiefer, 2007), and have greater sexual anxiety (Wiederman, 2000) and emotional disengagement during sex (Yamamiya, Cash, & Thompson, 2006). This distancing of women's psyches from their bodies during sexual encounters may make it difficult for women to negotiate safe and pleasurable sexual experiences (Curtin et al., 2011).

Just as femininity plays a key role in regulating the behaviors and attitudes of women within compulsory heterosexuality (Rich, 1980), traditional masculine ideals prescribe what sexual activities and desires are acceptable for men (Byers, 1995; J. Holland, Ramazanoglu, Sharpe, & Thomson, 2003; J. Holland et al., 2004). Some scholars have even argued that "heterosexuality is not, as it appears to be, masculinity-and-femininity in opposition: it *is* masculinity" (J. Holland et al., 2004, p. 10). That is, both women and men alike are held to the standards of what J. Holland et al. (2004) have described as an internalized "male-in-the-head," or a hegemonic, heterosexual masculine observer that resides within the minds of all people, submitting us to the surveillance of a "male gaze" (J. Holland et al., 2004; Storr, 2000). Within sexuality, traditional ideals of masculinity both include and demand urgent and insatiable heterosexual male sexual desire (Falomir-Pichastor, Manuel, & Mugny, 2009; Forrest, 2000) as well as an innate knowledge of sexuality that requires no additional learning (Kehily, 2001). Masculinity often constructs male bodies as dominant (Kehily, 2001; Simpson, 2007) and penetrative (whereas female or feminine bodies are receptive; Forrest, 2000). Men's first experiences with (hetero)sexual intercourse may make them feel like they are really "being a man," and some men recall very embodied experiences of sexual pleasure in which "something mysterious happens all over your body" (Simpson, 2007, p. 177). Hegemonic masculinity intersects with race and other social identities as, for example, Black men may be presumed to have better sexual performance (Nyanzi, Rosenberg-Jallow, Bah & Nyanzi, 2005), thus positioning these men as hypermasculine and, as such, more ruled by sexual impulses and thus animalistic and in greater need of social control.

The Sexual Body and Its Parts

Researchers often conceptualize bodies by focusing on the particular social and cultural messages directed at particular *parts* of the body, particularly breasts, genitals, and other easily sexualized body parts. Consequently, a sizeable body of research has emerged that examines the particular anxieties and challenges associated with different body parts and with conceptualizations of the exposed body. In general, research on sexualized body parts suggests that compliance with social norms is expected for numerous regions of the body, whereas deviance from social norms elicits rejection and social disapproval.

Studies examining nudity often have questioned the relationship between individuals and their social contexts, particularly in the public regulation and personal assessment of the nude female body. Eck (2003) found that both men and women had readily accessible cultural scripts about the naked female body (e.g., overt sexualization and acceptance), whereas the naked male body elicited more diverse and less scripted responses (e.g., feelings of guilt, rejecting the body). This may influence women's subjective feelings about their nude bodies, as Weinberg and Williams (2010a) found that women's positive feelings about nudity were more strongly associated with sexual behavior and pleasure compared with men and were strongly mitigated through positive relationships with their partners. This suggests that compared with men, women's feelings about nudity reference cultural scripts that imagine female nudity as only and inherently sexual. Cover (2003) noted that recent slippages have occurred between sites once considered "nonsexual" and sites imbued with the "sexual," particularly communal showers, places where children bathe, and public nude beaches, indicating that our cultural panics surrounding nudity have extended into sites previously considered nonsexual.

In more specific analyses of sexualized body parts, women's breasts have received much attention as a site of embodiment and a locus for cultural anxieties about small versus large breasts. Millsted and Frith (2003) found that women's breasts are invested with social, cultural, and political meanings that shape women's understandings of their embodied selves, particularly as they associate self-worth with the size of their breasts. After interviewing eight large-breasted women, they concluded that these women experience a mix of feeling feminine and attractive while also recognizing their breasts as appropriated and consumed by others. Echoing these findings, Young (2005) asserted that breasts represent sites of conflict that reveal the depth of patriarchy, as women's quests toward cosmetic surgery (breast enlargement and postmastectomy procedures) link femininity with the size and shape of women's breasts.

Just as breasts have signified the essence of femininity for women, the penis has signified ultimate masculinity for men. In the comparable way that small breasts often create anxiety for women, small penises have elicited subjective feelings of distress for men. The anxiety is caused, in part, by ambiguity about what constitutes "small" in a context in which size is imbued with a fundamental gender "performance." Del Rosso's (2011) online ethnography found that men who self-identified as having small penises felt more anxiety in face-to-face encounters with partners than in online encounters, perhaps suggesting that online sexual exchanges can mediate the negative impact of feeling that one has a small penis. Furthermore, as Nugteren et al., (2010) found in their study of men seeking treatment for small penises, the majority of men found relief with psychotherapy, although a small percentage required surgery to alleviate the stressors caused by perceived small penis size. Looking more broadly at social and cultural trends, both pornography and the rise of the Viagra culture have influenced men's experiences of "phallic embodiment," setting larger (and harder) standards for "typical" masculinity beyond average bodies (Loe, 2007; Maddison, 2009; see Volume 2, Chapter 1, this handbook).

Although both men and women face pressures to groom body hair in socially scripted ways—often with women as completely hairless and men as hairy (or, at most, increasingly "manscaped" (Boroughs, Cafri, & Thompson, 2005)—research on body hair has found that women who deviate from social scripts face more severe social punishments and rejection than do men (Fahs, 2011a). With approximately 99% of women reporting that they had removed body hair at some point in their lives (Toerien, Wilkinson, & Choi, 2005), women who do not shave their body hair face internal feelings of disgust and external appraisals of their bodies as "manly" and unattractive, suggesting that heterosexist and sexist scripts both inform assessments of body hair (Fahs, 2011a). Furthermore, women of color who choose to have body hair face more severe social penalties than White women, particularly from family members concerned with "respectability" (Fahs & Delgado, 2011). Aside from body hair (i.e., underarm, leg, facial), women have experienced increasing pressures to remove all or most of their pubic hair (Tricklebank, Braun, & Clarke, in press), with younger and partnered women reporting more frequent pubic hair removal than older and nonpartnered women (Herbenick, Schick, Reece, Sanders, & Fortenberry, 2010).

Researchers also recently identified a new line of work examining women's genital self-image, particularly how women feel about their vulvas and pubic hair. Roberts and Waters (2004) posited that because media messages convey women's fundamental unacceptability in their natural state, women internalize ideas that they need sanitizing, deodorizing, exfoliating, and denuding (see also Bartky, 1990). These self-objectifying feelings can translate into women's disgust toward their vaginas, menstrual cycles, and bodily functions. More precisely, researchers have developed the Female Genital Self-Image scale, finding that more positive genital self-image correlated with greater likelihood of seeking gynecological exams, particularly for women who regularly practiced vaginal penetrative intercourse (DeMaria, Hollub, & Herbenick, 2011). Associations between positive female genital self-image and women's sexual health and functioning also have been identified (Herbenick & Reece, 2010; see Chapter 11, this volume), as women with more positive feelings toward their genitals reported more frequent vibrator use, masturbation, genital self-examinations, and gynecological visits (Herbenick et al., 2011).

Perhaps because social scripts about the body remain relatively rigid, particularly for women, expectations that women will modify, alter, and conform their bodies to existing cultural standards have led to a slew of plastic surgeries promoted to women. In addition to pressures women face to enlarge their breasts, new surgeries target women's genitals, particularly their labia and vaginas. Braun and Tiefer (2010) outlined how trends toward "disease mongering" have created new ways for women's self-consciousness to translate into surgical procedures, including labiaplasties (e.g., removing "excess" labial tissue in a manner that produces a more child-like vulva), vaginal "rejuvenation," and vaginal tightening. Despite the medical community finding no medically indicated reason for such surgeries, a new market of genital surgeries has arisen in the past decade (Braun, 2005). In qualitative research on women who underwent a labiaplasty, Bramwell, Morland, and Garden (2007) found that women's expectations for how a labiaplasty would improve their sex lives did not translate into reality.

Many feminists caution that plastic surgeries can instigate urgent and endless renovations of the self (M. Jones, 2008), with debates emerging about the efficacy and agency of women who undergo elective plastic surgery. Pitts (1999) has argued that when mental health discourses dominate discussions about body modification, alternative accounts of female embodiment become obscured by discussions of the "normal" and "pathological" body. Schover et al. (1995) studied women who had cancer and underwent partial mastectomies and mammoplasties and found that fewer than 20% of women reported poor psychosocial adjustment, poor body image, or poor sexual functioning, although women who had elected chemotherapy treatments reported poorer sexual functioning and body image (see Chapter 21, this volume). Adding to these debates, Gagné and McGaughey (2002) noted that women who underwent elective mammoplasty (i.e., not postcancer reconstruction) felt greater power and control over their bodies even while embodying hegemonic ideals of feminine beauty. They argued that cosmetic surgery can empower individual women while also reinforcing ideals and norms that oppress women as a group.

The Sexual Body in Action

Commonly heard phrases like "sexual performance" and "sexual satisfaction" have roots in pathologizing sexuality and sexual bodies (Irvine, 1990) as well as in empirical work on these same topics, as scholars have examined the sexual body in action. Evaluating the meaning of sexual desire, sexual satisfaction, orgasm, sexual performances, and technologies exerted on (or embraced by) the sexual body have all constituted emerging areas of research in recent years.

Sexual desire constitutes one of the most complex and difficult topics to assess, explore, theorize, and make claims about. As issues of safety, consent, pleasure, commitment, taboo, and cultural scripts about the "erotic" (broadly defined) fuse, research on sexual desire provides a window into the complexity of psychological research on embodiment. As a more concrete examination of desire, research has directed much recent attention to the desires and practices of young women. Sieg (2007) noted that although young women's sexualities more recently often are portrayed as liberating and empowered, young women's qualitative accounts of their experiences reveal discrepancies between their relational desires and relational realities in that they compromised their own needs and desires within their heterosexual relationships. Similarly, Backstrom, Armstrong, and Puentes (2012) interviewed 43 college women about their experiences with cunnilingus and found that women in relationships could expect and ask for cunnilingus, whereas women merely "hooking up" often could not unless they asserted these desires clearly. Furthermore, women in relationships alternatively found both pleasure and difficulty with cunnilingus, particularly related to their partner's feelings about it and the social scripts they had internalized about receiving oral sex (Bay-Cheng & Fava, 2011; see also Burns, Futch, & Tolman, 2011)

Similar controversies surrounding the meaning of sexual satisfaction and orgasm have also appeared in recent literatures on embodiment. Deciding how to measure sexual satisfaction, along with considerations about how satisfaction may interact with social identities and social justice concerns, has been taken up in McClelland's (2010) call for better understandings of social and sexual stigmas as antecedents to sexual satisfaction ratings. Fahs and Swank (2011) found sexual satisfaction and sexual activity as often misaligned. In particular, younger women, women of color, less educated women, and lower socioeconomic status women describe having low sexual satisfaction and high sexual activity. Social identity variables also appeared as significant in a recent study by Seal, Smith, Coley, Perry, and Gamez (2008), who found that age differentials between partners and the presence of a Black male partner predicted more traditional interpersonal scripts about sexuality.

Research on orgasm also has revealed much about the way men and women internalize scripts about sexual normality and "acceptable" desires. Fahs (2011b) found that women faked orgasm for a number of reasons, primarily to please their (male) partners, to end the encounter (often because of fatigue), and to seem sexually normal. Jackson and Scott (2007) theorized the gendered dimensions of women faking orgasm and noted that the production of fake orgasms signifies the quintessential problems of conceptualizing embodiment too broadly: namely, broad sociological views on embodiment neglect the more concrete modes in which material gendered bodies behave in everyday life. Theoretical accounts of orgasm have given new and fruitful direction to the study of the sexual body in action. Performance artist Frueh (2003) explored orgasm as an artistic expression, whereas Jagose (2010) asserted that the fake orgasm reveals the counterfeit nature of heterosexual sex by showing the pleasures inherent in a queer deconstruction of heterosexual penetrative intercourse.

Along these lines, embodiment researchers have examined, theoretically and empirically, the notion of *performances* of the sexual body. Although the concept of "sexual performance" has a long history in sexuality research and therapy (i.e., Kaplan, 1974), the performance of the sexual body in action refers to productions and enactments of certain forms of embodiment rather than achievement by specific body parts. The ways people consume sexuality and perform sexuality has cast a wide net, capturing research not only on body norms but also sexual desire, practices, and feelings. As Weber (1998) argued, sexual performances can expand widely (e.g., the nation state) or remain incredibly detailed and small (e.g., the individual orgasm). In particular, embodiment researchers have captured the ways women manage others' anxieties about their bodies by performing their own bodies within certain socially prescribed limits. Fahs (2011a) argued that much of contemporary women's sexuality reflects the simultaneously liberating and disempowering aspects of sexual performance, particularly when women fake orgasms, pretend bisexuality at parties in front of men, discuss female Viagra, and minimize sexual coercion and violence as "okay" or "not really rape." Women learn to manage their identities and "do gender" (West & Zimmerman, 1987) in particular ways that conform to, and rebel against, cultural and social expectations. Berkowitz (2006) found that women and men manage their self-presentation and negotiate gender performances even in adult novelty stores, where people both enact and resist hegemonic masculinity, femininity, and compulsory heterosexuality.

Ultimately, questions have arisen about the benefits and problems of adhering to traditional performances of gender and sexuality, particularly for the embodied self. In a review of the empirical literature, Sanchez, Fetterolf, and Rudman (2012) found that traditional gender role adherence had negative consequences for women's sexuality and led to more sexual problems and less sexual satisfaction. When women internalized traditional connections between sexuality and male power, and when men enacted such connections, both men and women experienced less rewarding and authentic sexual expressions (see Chapter 2, this volume). To address other performances of male sexuality, Jewkes and Morrell (2010) found that enacting black African manhood that emphasized toughness, strength, and prodigious sexual success was associated with more sexual risk-taking, as men resisted condoms and HIV treatment, whereas women who espoused this perspective were more tolerant of infidelity and violence. In a more subversive example, Shapiro's (2007) study of drag kings found that intentional transgressive performances of gender encouraged interrogation, play, and adoption of new social roles, as gender performances formed the basis for "oppositional communities" of differently embodied selves.

Sexual performances are beholden to their particular social and political contexts, particularly as women adopt new ways to attract the sexually endorsing male gaze. An increasing number of studies have interrogated the phenomenon of women engaging in same-sex eroticism for the viewing benefit of men (Diamond, 2005). Just as Fahs (2009) theorized this "performative bisexuality" as a potentially new manifestation of compulsory heterosexuality, Hamilton (2007) also found that college women affiliated with the Greek party scene catered to male sexual desire by performing interest in same-sex eroticism and by rejecting lesbians because of their assumed disinterest in garnering men's sexual attention. Yost and McCarthy (2012) found that 33% of college women had engaged in same-sex kissing at college parties, while 69% of college men and women had observed this behavior. High levels of alcohol consumption, pressure to engage in same-sex kissing, heterosexist attitudes, and the belief that college is a time for experimentation predicted greater likelihood of women engaging in public same-sex eroticism at college parties (see Chapter 20, this volume).

As a more literal example of the performing sexual body, sexualized dancing also has appeared in the contemporary literatures on women's embodiment. Regehr (2012) has theorized the increasing popularity of recreational burlesque dancing as enhancing women's feelings of empowerment and self-efficacy even while connecting to a history of women offering their bodies for men's visual consumption (e.g., pornography and strip clubs). In an interview study of young women contestants on a burlesque reality television show in which they spent 6 weeks learning techniques to perform, Regehr found that some of the women shifted from an exclusive focus on looking at their bodies to beginning to feel more sexy or sexy once again through engagement in a sexualized practice that was new to them. She found that by the final performance, these women were more focused on their own embodied experiences, with an imagined viewership that was present but also receded as their own practice had developed. Looking at sexualized dancing at college parties, Ronen (2010) described this dancing in less liberating terms, finding that men initiated sexual "grinding" more often than women and thus reproduced systematic gender inequalities by limiting women's access to agency and pleasure because of men's control of, and intrusion into, women's space. In this dancing, women had to privilege men's pleasures over their own while confirming men's higher status. Similar arguments could be made for the appropriation of stripping into "strip aerobics," as it packages "women's empowerment" within the guise of something that reveals the "everyday" aspects of sexual exploitation (Whitehead & Kurz, 2009).

Performances of sexuality also can extend into the realm of reproductive technology, as ideas about gender and power infuse medical understandings of the body and its processes. Embodiment scholars have found clear connections among gender, embodiment, and reproductive control. Carpenter and Casper (2009) examined public debates about the human papillomavirus (HPV) vaccine, known to prevent many cervical cancers, and found that attempts to mandate HPV vaccination have activated intense concerns about adolescent girls' "promiscuity," whereas discourses surrounding the promotion of male circumcision to prevent HIV have not triggered similar anxieties around boys' sexuality. Such technologies also can become a mechanism to reproduce meanings of gender and sexuality as they interact with age and race. Along these lines, Lowe (2005) found that although women can access contraceptive technologies and assert bodily autonomy by controlling their reproduction, this conflicts with dynamics present in heterosexual couplings that demand attention to, and concern with, men's preferences and needs, sometimes at women's expense. Angulo-Olaiz (2009) found that Latina women struggled with prioritizing sexual health because of gendered perceptions of love and motherhood, associations between commitment and sexual risk-taking, and unequal access to economic opportunities. In discussions of sexual safety and condom use, women as the carriers of disease have appeared frequently, particularly in discussions of the HPV vaccine (Carpenter & Casper, 2009). Analyzing research findings on safer heterosexual practices, Vitellone (2002) found that heterosexual masculine self-identity, rather than avoidance of disease or risk, plays a key role in the creation of discourse surrounding condoms.

Technologies of sexual embodiment can be understood as medical or technological efforts to create particular kinds of desires, appearances, or sexual norms as enacted onto the embodied female self. As a quintessential example, the rise of Viagra (Loe, 2006) and experimentation with female Viagra and sexual performance drugs (e.g., flibanerin, sildenafil; Fahs, 2011a) exemplify the medicalization of sexual performance. Feminists, particularly Tiefer (2004), have devoted significant critical attention to the widespread advertisement and dispersion of Viagra, noting that it prescribes not only medicalized erections but also incites desire for "overperformance," while ignoring the sociocultural bases of sexual desire and performance. Demonstrating the necessity of seeing Viagra as socially situated, Castro-Vásquez (2006) posited that the introduction of Viagra in Japan coincided with anxieties about pollution, men's unwillingness to perform their "appropriate" gender roles, decreased adherence to marriage norms, and declining birth rates. A similar study of New Zealand men conducted by Grace, Potts, Gavey, and Vares (2006) found that Viagra connects with men seeing their partner's pleasure as a measure of success and their own sexuality as based in performance. Conversely, Loe (2004) found that women in the United States did not view Viagra as universally positive, as some aging women were becoming less interested in sex at the same time as their longtime partners were now having pharmaceutically induced erections.

Lifestyle drugs that refashion the body according to socially acceptable or socially demanded criteria carry with them the need for caution and concern by those who advocate social views of sexuality. Marshall (2006) cautioned that Viagra represents not only the medicalization of sexuality but also the expansion of consumer culture and the manufactured notion of the "sexual expert" who decides what "normal" sexual functioning looks like, thus normalizing and defining dysfunction according to pharmaceutical priorities. Mamo and Fishman (2001) argued that Viagra, much like antidepressants, performs ideological work and reinforces traditional notions of hegemonic masculinity (e.g., erection as "manly"). Marshall (2006) noted that Viagra has created new standards for male virility by distorting the naturally occurring declines in virility that coincide with age. Nuancing this claim, Wentzell (2011) studied Mexican men from different generations and noted that younger men expressed more interest in Viagra than older men, although these younger men wanted to use it to sustain positive marital sexual attachments rather than in the service of *machismo*. Still, opportunities for resistance to these medically reinforced social scripts abound, as some have found ways to subvert the intended uses of Viagra in meaningful ways. Holt (2009) found that medical understandings of Viagra as a drug guaranteed to produce erectile performance compared with gay men's recreational use of Viagra produces questions about the public health and social understandings of safe sex and "good" sex within different subcultures of men. Potts (2004) theorized that although Viagra has created new definitions of "normal" sexuality, its inconsistent ability to induce consistent erections and the failure of female Viagra underscore the necessity for experimentation, creativity, and transformation in the erotic realm.

As a note on the future of the performing sexual body, the development of, and failure to gain U.S. Food and Drug Administration (FDA) approval for, female sexual desire disorder drugs have illuminated additional gendered debates about the medicalization of sexuality. More than a decade has passed since the FDA approved Viagra for men in 1998, and a successful female counterpart has yet to be produced (Hartley, 2006; Tiefer, 2006), suggesting that sexual dysfunction among men and women may differ more than had been previously assumed (McHugh, 2006; Tiefer, 2006; see also Chapters 7 and 8, this volume). The New View campaign, a group of feminist researchers, activists, and therapists who work on female sexuality, has articulated a critical stance toward the medicalization of women's sexual problems (Cacchioni, 2007; Tiefer, 2001, 2010). The campaign has fought against the increasingly automatic and first response to women's concerns with their sexual bodies to be medicalizing women's desires, orgasms, or physiological functioning. The campaign claims that such medicalization of women's bodies obfuscates and suppresses more complex understandings of women's sexual functioning. Hartley (2006) reported that for drug companies to effectively create a market for FSD drugs, they had to problematize or "disease" the vicissitudes of women's sexuality while also promoting off-label uses of men's Viagra to women. Consequently, drug companies have promoted FSD as increasingly widespread and have worked to infuse mainstream media with ideas about the "failing" female sexual body (Hartley & Tiefer, 2003). Recognizing that what constitutes "normal" sexual functioning for women is complex and ambiguous at best (see Chapter 8, this volume), an embodied analysis of the social underpinnings of the market for drugs demonstrates how discourses about sexual bodies can be leveraged into bodily experience, individual and social practices, and social policy.

THE SEXUAL BODY ACROSS THE LIFE SPAN

As sexuality develops across the life span, so does the sexual body itself. Corporeal changes in physiology and hormones are infused with social meanings. Social meanings and corporeality shift inextricably over the course of a life. Embodiment itself is both continuous, as embodied processes are always already infused in the development of sexuality, and dynamic in form and experience.

Childhood

Studies of childhood sexuality are generally few and far between (Sandfort & Rademakers, 2000; see Chapter 14, this volume), and they tend to focus almost exclusively on sexual abuse (Bancroft, 2003; Ryan, 2000). Other weaknesses of this literature include an overreliance on retrospective accounts (Graham, 2003) and an overemphasis on charting and tabulating the specific behaviors in which children engage (Friedrich, 2003). Although some studies have begun to focus on children's sexual identities and sexual cultures, and in particular have explored how heteronormativity organizes these aspects of sexuality as early as the childhood years (Renold, 2005), inquiry into embodied dimensions of childhood sexuality remains scarce. Because the notion of childhood sexuality poses a profound threat to hegemonic notions of childhood as a time of innocence, children are denied knowledge about sexuality and any form of sexual citizenship (Angelides, 2004; Renold, 2005; Robinson, 2012). The prohibition on knowledge of childhood sexuality extends to children's apprehension of their own bodily feelings (Lamb, 2001; Sandfort & Rademakers, 2000). We know little about whether children's embodied feelings, experiences of arousal, and genital sensations can even be considered sexual (Ryan, 2000), and what expected development of these bodily sensations and experiences entails (Lamb & Coakley, 1993). Western societies generally relegate children's sexual feelings to a liminal developmental state called "emerging sexuality" (Renold, 2005, p. 37), which prepares the child for adult sexuality but is itself inherently incomplete. There is disagreement about whether children's sexual play is actually sexual or just another form of play (Renold, 2005; Robinson, 2012) or evidence of sexual abuse (Hyde, 2003). We also do not understand the degree to which children's developing cognitive capacities shape their capacity for making meaning of pleasurable feelings in the body as *sexual* (Robinson, 2012). In the few studies that have incorporated questions about children's bodily experiences of sexuality, it remains difficult to resolve these questions. Some studies have traced how girls transition from child to adolescent in middle school, by repositioning these subjectivities through embodied activities, such as from "innocent play" to the "heterosexualization of boy-girl friendships" (Renold, 2006, p. 495), in which girls begin to experience and engage with boys as potential boyfriends rather than playmates (see also Hauge, 2009).

In one study of young children's body awareness and physical intimacy (Rademakers, Laan, & Straver, 2003), researchers interviewed 31 children 8 to 9 years old and their parents, about romping, cuddling, and being in love. Most children enjoyed cuddling because of the bodily sensations or feeling of safety they felt, and many more of the children than their parents said that children need cuddling; more than half said they had been in love, said it was positive, "nice," "fun," and a "tickling sensation" (Rademakers et al., 2003, p. 124). When shown a naked same-sexed body, all children were able to identify what were "pleasant" parts for them, with fewer indicating "exciting"; even fewer indicated that genitals, bottom, or anus were either "exciting" or "pleasant" parts of their own bodies. No gender differences were identified. Although there is evidence that both boys and girls masturbate in childhood (Strachan & Staples, 2012), there is little inquiry into what these experiences feel like for them, in either prospective or retrospective reports. Herdt and McClintock (2000) have argued for a "magical age of 10," when awareness of sexual feelings and attractions as distinctly sexual—and the emergence of unequivocally sexual subjectivity—is associated with an interplay between adrenarche (maturational increase in adrenal androgen production) and changing cultural meanings and roles. In their formulation, these braided developments mark the prepubertal shift from childhood to adolescent sexuality. Although their theory is anchored in an overview of cross-cultural studies, no systematic or empirical work has confirmed this model, specifically the critical role that they posit for adrenal androgens in this transition.

Adolescence

The body offers and has been imbued with meanings associated with the emergence of adult sexuality over the course of adolescence. One key and increasingly troubled bodily focus has been the loss of virginity, typically defined, and instantly problematized, as the first experience of sexual intercourse. Even the term "loss" has been challenged as positioning this experience as both passive and commodified. The emergence of "secondary virginity" is an exquisite case in point, a reclamation discourse arising out of the abstinence-only movement whereby both girls and boys who have had sexual intercourse could proclaim the status of virginity contingent on their desire and commitment to not having sex overriding their bodily history (Loewenson, Ireland, & Resnick, 2004).

Most of the literature on embodied adolescent sexuality has focused on girls' experiences, primarily because this literature rests on cultural assumptions that adolescent boys' sexual experiences are predicated on bodily (and unbridled) sexual desire and the complementary assumption of girls either not having or not acting on their own sexual feelings (Fine, 1988; J. Holland & Thomson, 2010; Tolman, 2006). These discursive studies are organized by questions of how young people "take up" subject positions, identified by how they describe their experiences, that is, what discourses they use to make sense of their sexual and relational experiences. Other studies within this conceptual context address how young people experience, make meaning of, and negotiate their sexual desires and other dimensions of sexual experiences. This research situates girls' and boys' embodied practices within the theoretical framework of heteronormativity, investigating how constructions of femininity and masculinity underpin and shape their individual bodily experiences (e.g., Epstein, Calzo, Smiler, & Ward, 2009; Impett, Henson, Breines, Schooler, & Tolman, 2011). Another set of questions is how adolescents constitute, are constituted by, and also resist heteronormativity in and via their bodies in their (primarily heterosexual) relationships (Hauge, 2009; Maxwell & Aggleton, 2010; Renold & Ringrose, 2011).

In particular, this line of research has investigated how feminine heterosexual practices embody the power relations through which masculinity and femininity are constructed (Burns et al., 2011; J. Holland, Ramazanoglu, Sharpe, & Thomson, 1994; J. Holland et al. 2004; Martin, 1996; Pascoe, 2007; Tolman, 2002). J. Holland et al. (1994) found that for most of the 150 diverse young women in their narrative study, who for the most part provided disembodied accounts of sexual experience, they heard "points of tension where physical bodies interrupt idealized relationships" (p. 23). The disembodiment required and produced by enacting practices of proper femininity, regimes of dress and diet, and subsequent alienation from their material or sensate bodies yielded pressure on girls to be passive objects of others' sexual desire (J. Holland & Ramazanoglu, 1994).

They found that girls' concern about their reputations and having to contend with both the specter and experience of sexual coercion and violence (see also Burns et al., 2011; Tolman, 1994, 2002) produced at best struggles with their sexual feelings and responses. For some, "normal sex" did not include a girl's sexual pleasure but did require faking orgasm; one girl expressed her surprise at having a real orgasm, when she had understood faking as part of "normal sex." These authors' notion of "the male in the head," those heteronormative demands of a set of sexual practices predicated on patriarchal surveillance and organization of sexuality around male sexual needs, dominated the accounts they heard. J. Holland et al. (2004) did hear of girls' resistance to embodied femininity in the realm of sexual practices in this research. More often, "experiential empowerment," that is, enacted within and through the body, was overridden by "intellectual empowerment," in which girls' belief in their ability to choose sexual agency was difficult to play out. Enactments of "good" and "bad" girl performances, through sexualized clothing to explicit sexual agency, have been found to fluctuate between stark and ambiguous, with girls balancing the benefits and costs of these mutually reinforcing embodiments and also maintaining ambiguity about meanings (Gleeson & Frith, 2004; Hauge, 2009). Interviews with young men have revealed the tensions between the variability in their actual bodily sexual feelings and the flat yet powerful message of being "up for it" all the time (J. Holland & Thomson, 2010). These researchers noted the difficulty of discerning embodied sexual experience through talk, given the limited language for, and social condemnation and even titillation of, talking explicitly about sex and sexual activity. In a recent reflection on the continuity and changes in young people's sexual experiences, J. Holland and Thomson (2010) found that although the cultural milieu is far more sexualized than it was a decade ago, with pornography being part of the mainstream, sexual diversity being visible, and information about condoms and contraception being more available, for young people, negotiating heterosexuality remains "fragile and uncertain" (p. 348).

The array of discourses about the bodies and sexualities of girls, and to some extent, boys, of diverse ethnicities and socioeconomic statuses has been explicated in this area of research (French, 2012). Tolman (2002; Tolman & Szalacha, 1999) found continuities and distinctions in the desire narratives of girls in urban and suburban contexts in which (urban) Black and Latina girls' negotiation of assumed hypersexuality was evident in their struggles to embody their sexuality and (suburban) White girls navigated assumptions of an absence of sexual feelings in their own bodies. Curtis (2009) described "the geography of girls' sexual pleasure" (p. 151) in her study of girls' sexuality on Nevis using surveys, focus groups, and individual interviews with girls ages 12–17 years old. Focusing on the context of a changing social landscape in which new discourses and images of female sexual pleasure infuse traditional beliefs about sex and women's sexuality, she found that girls described experiences of intense physical sexual pleasure in an array of sexual contexts—the first willingly bestowed kiss, the negotiation of sexual progression with overeager boyfriends, and the endurance of the pain of first intercourse. Although sexual pleasure wove through these girls' narratives, sexual coercion often anchored their stories (see also, Fine & McClelland, 2006; Tolman, 1994; Vance, 1984). That is, embodied sexual pleasure for these young women was clear and present even as they engaged in experiences that they resisted or did not want.

Another line of research has investigated sexual subjectivity, the sense and experience of the self as sexual, which is predicated in part on experience anchored in the body and has been considered in relation to sexual health. Curtin et al. (2011) observed that concerns about body image or discomfort with one's body can make it difficult to experience one's own body and sexual pleasure in sexual activity. They found a relationship between diverse young women objectifying their own bodies and both body comfort and body self-consciousness around sexual partners. Impett and Tolman (2006) found that young women with a stronger sense of self as sexual were more likely to experience sexual satisfaction. Ringrose (2013) suggested that narratives told by early adolescent girls in individual interviews and mixed-ethnicity focus groups reflect combinations of simultaneous resistance to and desire for sexual subjectivities predicated on being the object of a male sexual gaze, undergirded by the possible presence of their own desires. Maxwell and Aggleton (2012) examined how young women described and understood their own bodies in their sexual and relational encounters with boys. The majority of young women in the study described sexually feeling bodies, including "sparks" and "sexual tensions" in their narratives (Maxwell & Aggleton, 2012, p. 314). Acting in relation to their physical responses for and to another person, participants narrated confidence and a sense of their bodies as powerful. Maxwell and Aggleton suggested that these narratives reflect these girls' bodies as providing a space for becoming more knowledgeable and comfortable with their sexuality and grounding their choices about how they wanted to be sexual. They concluded that these narratives illuminate four agentic practices within and beyond sexual interactions anchored in these girls' bodily sexual experiences: assertive, refusing, proactive, and interrogative strategies.

Although there is now a fast-growing literature on the development of gay, lesbian, and bisexual identity construction (Diamond, 2005; Thompson & Morgan, 2008; see Chapters 19 and 20, this volume), including uses of the body to construct and convey resistance to heteronormative expectations to produce these identities, actual sexual experiences of sexual-minority young (or older) people have received insufficient attention by researchers. Diamond's developmental study of 89 sexual-minority women over a 10-year period identified "fluidity" in women's sexuality, such that their attractions and behaviors changed over time, suggesting shifting embodied sexual feelings. She concluded that many women's desires may not be fixed on a particularly gendered object. In comparison, the research on young sexual-minority men's emerging sexual desire indicates more stability in desire for other men (e.g., Ainsworth & Baumeister, 2012).

Boislard & Zimmer-Gembeck (2011) found that young women with a history of same-sex sexual experience and a monogamous steady partner reported a greater sense of entitlement to self-pleasure and more self-efficacy in their sexual pleasure.

Adulthood

Most of this chapter is about embodiment and sexuality among adults, but several specific dimensions can be noted from a life span perspective. Expectations that sexual practices become associated with bodily sexual satisfaction, especially for women, consolidate for adults. Some research has demonstrated associations for women between their feelings about their bodies and their experiences of their sexual desire or arousal, that is, their feelings in their bodies, whereas some research has demonstrated positive perceptions of one's body and increases in levels in sexual desire, especially in midlife and as women age (Woertman & Brink, 2012). In her clinical and theoretical work, Young (1990) elaborated explicitly how dissociation induced by sexual trauma can produce disembodiment among women, particularly dissociation or disconnection from sexual feelings. Sanchez and Kiefer (2007) found that body shame led to sexual self-consciousness during intercourse, which in turn predicted lower sexual arousability and less sexual satisfaction. These studies did not investigate differences by race, ethnicity, or sexual orientation. Questions of embodiment are raised rather than explained by these findings. In general, whereas bodily sexual feelings associated with sexual orientation has been an area of study (see the section The Sexual Body in Action earlier in this chapter), explicit experiences of the actual (i.e., "the heaving, sweating") body engaged in sexual expression have been studied even less among heterosexuals. Although "controlling images" (Collins, 1990) of Black and Latina women's sexuality have been explicated (e.g., Miller-Young, 2010, M. Ward & Wyatt, 1994; Zavella, 2008), the impact of those stereotypes on experiences of embodied sex itself among people of color is largely unexplored. Shildrick (2005) has delineated the anxiety that bodily disconformity and limited bodily control characterizing disabled people and their sexuality incites in able-bodied individuals about their own sexuality (see the section Body-Related Disobedience later in this chapter). McClelland (2011) has problematized our knowledge of sexual satisfaction among marginalized populations not only because of inadequate sampling but because assumptions of sexual entitlement (to bodily pleasure in particular) infuse the very items of scales used to measure bodily satisfaction.

Dimensions and parts of the sexual body that are taken up in reproduction also have been studied (see Chapter 23, this volume). Roberts and Waters (2004) observed that mandates of femininity demanding that women keep their bodies sanitized and deodorized mean that menstruation must be "kept under wraps" (p. 5). Roberts (2004) found that the more women self-objectified, that is, viewed themselves as sexual objects, the more likely they were to associate their menstruating bodies with disgust, shame, and embarrassment. Although the phenomenon of women's pregnant bodies becoming newly sexualized in the media has been elaborated (Oliver, 2010), experiences of their own bodies as sexual (e.g., having sexual desires or feelings) during pregnancy have not been studied. In a study of White breastfeeding mothers, Reich (2011) found women having to negotiate even potential exposure of their breasts in public as a violation of norms of femininity and sexuality, in which case the embodiment of their breasts as providing sustenance to their babies ironically violated the sanctioned embodiment of their breasts as providing sexual excitement as objects of desire. In a phenomenological study of menopausal hot flashes, Dillaway (2011) found, among primarily heterosexual, Black and White women from a range of socioeconomic backgrounds, that the physical sensation, while mostly intense, was less distressing than the visibility and sense of loss of bodily control. In addition, these women also felt they had violated cultural norms of proper female comportment, what Dillaway called "nontransformative acts of agency" (2011, p. 205), managing the evidence of this bodily change in their individual bodies but not purposefully refusing to comply with restrictive cultural norms. Middle-class White women also reported that having their bodies become menopausal was a positive experience, liberating them from concerns about contraception and ushering in greater sexual enjoyment (Dillaway, 2005; Loe, 2004).

In a single study of the association between being nude and experiencing sexual pleasure among 184 heterosexual men and women, Weinberg and Williams (2010a) found that comfort with one's nude body was associated with a sexually expansive point of view but with sexual pleasure only for women. They also found that women's feeling objectified interfered with their sexual intimacy and pleasure. They explained these feelings in part as an effect of structured gender inequality and acknowledged the study's race and age limitations. Although there is research on gay men's sexual embodiment (see the section Sexual-Minority Men's Sexual Embodiment later in this chapter), there is surprisingly little study of heterosexual men's embodiment of sexuality (Marshall & Katz, 2002), outside of medicalized sexual function (see the section Body-Related Disobedience later in this chapter). In their study, Weinberg and Williams (2010a) found that although some men felt self-conscious about penis size, their experiences of their bodies as sexual were not affected. In one study of men's experience of masturbation for in vitro fertilization semen collection, Inhorn (2007) found this process especially anxiety provoking for Muslim men, for whom masturbation is an act of impurity (see also Moore, 2007). Sperm itself is a new disembodied commodity that is ironically very much of the body of individual (sexual) men but is now accessible outside of sexual relationships through sperm banking, producing a panicked disembodiment of fatherhood among some and freedom of choice about a variety of reproductive technologies (and embodiments) among others (Moore, 2007).

Sexuality among aging adults has become an emergent area of study, as social norms have changed to represent greater acceptance of sexuality in late life, and as consumer markets have endeavored to create and sustain a new target population for sexuality-related products and services (Katz & Marshall, 2003; see Chapter 17, this volume). Apart from research related to sexual dysfunction, some research on older women's sexual embodiment finds a mix of resistance to stereotypes of declining sexual interest as well as growing discomfort with the evident sexuality of older people. For instance, some older women report active resistance to stereotypes and cultural mandates about the inevitability of low sexual interest in late life and the increasing asexuality of the aging body. In fact, Loe (2004) found that some aging heterosexual women continue to pursue pleasure, for example reporting regular vibrator use, and also reporting frustration because of a lack of male sexual partners and men's loss of sexual function. These studies contradict the notion that older women are more interested in cuddling and emotional intimacy than sexual pleasure. Quite to the contrary, one woman noted that "cuddling gets you hot and bothered and you need a man down there" (Loe, 2004, p. 308). Even as new representations of aging bodies as "sexy oldies" are emerging, older and more repressive notions persist. One study found that older women (ages 45–89) in a focus group study reacted with disgust to open discussions and representations of sexuality in later life, finding these images "unwatchable" (Vares, 2009, p. 520). Dickerson and Rousseau (2009) describe aging Black women's sexuality as obsolescent, their bodies rendered invisible in the sexual landscape. There is an absence of research on aging lesbian, gay, and bisexual people's experiences with their sexual bodies.

SEXUAL-MINORITY SEXUAL BODIES

The sexual bodies of sexual-minority people constitute compelling material challenges to compulsory heterosexuality. By demanding and enacting sexuality, sexual expression, and gender expression that elude and defy the terms of heterosexuality, sexual-minority sexual bodies demonstrate and demand recognition of the variability of sexuality. Regardless of debates about the etiology of sexual-minority sexualities, embodiments outside of heterosexuality raise fundamental questions about its legitimacy and justification (see Chapter 18, this volume).

Sexual-Minority Men's Sexual Embodiment

Traditional notions of power in sexual relationships draw on ideals of masculinity and femininity within heterosexual couplings. Conventional understandings of sexuality, when applied to sexual-minority men, would suggest that more masculine men should occupy the "top" or penetrative position during anal sex, whereas less masculine men or feminine men occupy the "bottom" or receptive position (Hoppe, 2011; Kippax & Smith, 2001). Thus, "tops" may be presumed to hold more power than "bottoms," and this position is assumed to be one of domination (Kippax & Smith, 2001). Although many sexual-minority men have fear or anxiety about being anally penetrated (Middelthon, 2002), it also can be considered masculine and powerful to "take it like a man" as the "bottom" (Dowsett, Williams, Ventuneac, & Carballo-Dieguez, 2008; Middelthon, 2002; Ridge, 2004), and these "bottoms" expressed feelings of embodied pleasure that they attributed to the very act of pleasing their partners and giving up their power (Hoppe, 2011).

Power is also visible in the sexualized body images of sexual-minority men (Kong, 2002; Pyle & Klein, 2011). Traditionally, the gay male community has valued and rewarded male bodies that are young, White, thin, muscular, and hairless (Duncan, 2010; Kong, 2002; Poon & Ho, 2008; Pyle & Klein, 2011). Despite the fact that these narrow prescriptions may facilitate body image dissatisfaction among sexual-minority men (Duncan, 2010), in recent years, sexual-minority men whose bodies do not conform to this ideal, or who are attracted to men whose bodies do not fit this ideal, have created alternative spaces for sexual expression (Pyle & Klein, 2011; Shiu-Ki, 2004). In this way, "chubs," "bears," and "chasers"—as well as non-White, hairy, or other male bodies that do not conform—challenge the existing power dynamics within the gay male community (Pyle & Klein, 2011).

In attempting to limit the spread of HIV and practice safe sex, sexual-minority men, regardless of serostatus, must monitor their embodied feelings of sexual desire and pleasure. Sexual-minority men frequently articulate that they are not solely interested in sexual pleasure but also crave intimacy, love, and romance (Slavin, 2009). As condom use is seen as detracting from intimacy (Dowsett et al., 2008; Villaamil & Jociles, 2011), spontaneity (Davis, 2002), and pleasure (Davis, 2002; Dowsett, 2003; Villaamil & Jociles, 2011), sexual-minority men sometimes find it difficult to negotiate a balance between intense sexual desire, arousal, or pleasure and safe sex practices. The Internet and social networking websites increasingly have been employed by men seeking other men with whom to engage in sexual activities (Dowsett et al., 2008; see Volume 2, Chapter 3, this handbook). Men using this technology often enact inscribed embodiment in their performances of masculinity and "macho talk" in their interactions with other users and, indeed, following Butler (1990), *do* gay (Dowsett et al., 2008; White, 2010).

Sexual-Minority Women's Sexual Embodiment

Unlike the empirical research on sexual-minority men, sexuality research focused on sexual-minority women is decidedly less sexually embodied. That is, although the research on sexual-minority men focuses on actual bodies in sexual acts (e.g., "tops" vs. "bottoms," power dynamics during sex, negotiating desire and condom use during sex), and how these acts are interpreted by the actors, research on sexual-minority women's embodied sex lives remains sparse. The following research focuses mainly on how sexual-minority women relate to their social worlds rather than to one another. This is a shortcoming in the literature on sexual minorities' sexual embodiment and likely reflects the widespread bias in research on same-sex sexuality toward male sexuality.

In a fashion complementary to sexual-minority men, sexual-minority women are socialized in a culture that values traditional notions of heterosexual performance and especially normative femininity among women (Rooke, 2007). Within the lesbian community, however, a variety of socially inscribed gender performances have come into acceptance, including "butch" (more "masculine" gender presentations) and "femme" (more "feminine" gender presentations; J. Walker, Golub, Bimbi, & Parson, 2012). Sexual-minority women are sometimes complicit in gender policing: "gaydar," or the ability for sexual-minority women to identify one another, often relies on bodily performances of female masculinity, which excludes sexual-minority women with feminine or conventionally heterosexual gender presentations (Levitt & Horne, 2008; L. Walker, 2001). Gender presentations often are assumed to translate to sexual behaviors among sexual-minority women, in that "butch" women are presumed to be more sexually aggressive, and "femme" women are presumed to be more receptive. These stereotypes are not supported by the research, however, which instead suggests that sexual behaviors among sexual-minority women are fluid across labels or gender-specific identities and socially inscribed embodiments of gender (J. Walker et al., 2012).

Sexual-minority women historically have been denied legitimacy through discourses that render invisible the possibilities of eroticism between women (Farquhar, 2000; Rooke, 2007). For example, defining female–female sex has been challenging, with sexual activity between women often conceived as mutual genital stimulation (Rothblum, 1994). This definition overlooks many other important erotic behaviors pursued between women (Rothblum, 1994) ranging from kissing (Ussher & Mooney-Somers, 2000) to bondage and exhibitionism (Tomassilli, Golub, Bimbi, & Parsons, 2009).

The concepts of choice and agency play out in the lives of sexual-minority women in unique ways. Some scholars have argued that female–female relationships exemplify female sexual agency in sexual-minority women's ability to choose a wider range of supportive and intimate partners and network structures than those who fit neatly into heterosexual norms (Weeks, Heaphy, & Donovan, 2001) and that sexual-minority women are more able to attend to their own sexual desires rather than to the desires of someone else (Hammers, 2008). Still, others demonstrate how such agency is moderated by social class (McDermott, 2009), race (Tomassilli et al., 2009), and other social factors (Blackwood, 2005; Hammers, 2008; Pasko, 2010). Nevertheless, women with a history of same-sex sexual experience tend to have higher sexual entitlement and sexual self-efficacy overall (Boislard & Zimmer-Gembeck, 2011).

Although we have used the phrase "sexual-minority" instead of lesbian to include the full range of individuals with same-sex attractions and behavior, regardless of identification, it bears noting that the vast majority of research on sexual minorities has focused on openly identified lesbians and openly identified gay men. The literature on sexual embodiment among bisexually identified individuals is nearly nonexistent. One possible explanation for this dearth is that "sexual embodiment" is a concept that refers to bodies in sexual relationships and that for bisexually identified men and women, unless they are having sex with men and women *simultaneously*, each individual sexual relationship they may have likely would be with *either* a man or a woman. These embodied sexual experiences, then, might fall into the literatures on either gay and lesbian sexual embodiment or heterosexual embodiment. Still, some empirical work specifically has explored bisexuals' experiences, especially those of women. Diamond's (2008) work on sexual fluidity demonstrates that mixed patterns of attraction (i.e., to both men and women) are more common than exclusive same-sex attractions and that even lesbian-identified women tended to report bisexual experiences and behaviors as time went on. Some of the women Diamond (2008) studied described themselves as "attracted to 'the person, not the gender'" (p. 172), suggesting that current notions of sexual orientation might be too focused on gender as an organizing construct. In a narrative study of four in-depth cases of women with bisexual patterns of attraction, Hammack, Thompson, and Pilecki (2009) illuminated how shifting embodied feelings of desire for both men and women can infuse young women's negotiation of rigid sexual identity categories with unique complexity and can render the body a source of confusion and questioning rather than clarification.

The Sexual Body in Society and the Media

One of the key debates in which embodiment and sexuality are embroiled is how the increasing widespread commodification and objectification of sexual bodies, in particular through sexualization and in pornography, informs people's experiences and negotiations of their sexuality (Garner, 2012). As the divide between pornography and mainstream depictions of sexuality evaporates (McNair, 1996), current arguments center less on questions about morality and more on questions about the possible implications of pornography for people's own changing experiences of their sexuality (Corsianos, 2007; Garlick, 2011; see Volume 2, Chapter 1, this handbook) and on sexual aesthetics (Attwood, 2007). An intensified focus on looks and physical appearance is displacing attention to embodied feelings (Frost, 2005; Tolman, 2002, 2012). In the global context in which Western media and sexual representations now circulate, this shift is extending beyond the West and affecting people transnationally (De Casanova, 2004; Howe & Rigi, 2009; see Volume 2, Chapter 9, this handbook). In 2007, the American Psychological Association's (APA) Task Force on the Sexualization of Girls released its report on the state of knowledge about this growing phenomenon. The report defined sexualization as (a) a person's value comes only from his or her sexual appeal or behavior, to the exclusion of other characteristics; (b) a person is held to a standard that equates physical attractiveness (narrowly defined) with being sexy; (c) a person is sexually objectified—that is, made into a thing for others' sexual use rather than seen as a person with the capacity for independent action and decision-making; and (d) sexuality is inappropriately imposed upon a person (APA, Task Force on the Sexualization of Girls, 2007, p. 1). The report yielded a notable increase in research on sexualization and its impact and ignited public debate and discussion, within and beyond the academy (e.g., Bragg, Buckingham, Russell, & Willett, 2011; Egan & Hawkes, 2008). The explosion of online pornography has meant that it has become accessible and pertinent to how people think, learn and imagine possibilities for their own sexual experience (Owens, Behun, Manning, & Reed, 2012; Short, Black, Smith, Wetterneck, & Wells, 2012).

One line of inquiry in psychology is how sexualization reflects or affects current modes of sexual being, behavior, or experience, and if so, whether those manifestations are positive or problematic, particularly for women. Given that women who feel more positively about their bodies have been found to express more comfort with their own sexual feelings (Ackard, Kearney-Cooke, & Peterson, 2000; Trapnell, Meston, & Gorzalka, 1997; Wiederman, 2000), the power of sexualization to diminish or negatively affect women's feelings about their bodies raises important questions about women's sexual embodiment. For instance, narrow sociocultural ideas of women's sexual attractiveness predict women's sexual intentions about and their acceptance of different types of sexual behavior, hindering their subjective experience of their own sexuality (Nowatzki & Morry, 2009). Sanchez and Kiefer (2007) found that body shame in women was linked more strongly to greater sexual problems than in men, including lower sexual arousability, less ability to reach orgasm, and having less pleasure from physical intimacy. These changes were mediated by sexual self-consciousness, regardless of relationship status or age. Focusing attention during sexual encounters on how one looks rather than on how one feels can lead to diminished sexual pleasure (Wiederman, 2000, 2001). A woman who has been socialized to dissociate from her own sexual arousal and desire may find it difficult to be aware of her desires, to assert her desires, or to feel entitled to satisfaction in sexual situations (Brotto, Heiman, & Tolman, 2009; see Chapter 8, this volume).

The process of self-sexualization, apprehending and experiencing the self as a sexual object for the desire of others or for commodification by the self, has received growing empirical attention (Roberts & Zurbriggen, 2012). For instance, self-sexualization has been associated with African American girls' increased focus on looks and beauty (Gordon, 2008). Complicated questions about what constitutes self-sexualization have been raised as well, illuminating the liminality of experiences of empowerment that attach to bodily expression associated with sexuality. For instance, pole dancing is a wildly popular physical fitness activity that underscores and relies on how looking youthfully sexy and performing a very particular bodily trope trumps feeling sexy or even sexual (Donaghue, Whitehead, & Kurz, 2011). Ironically, pole dancing takes advantage of the disconnection from their bodies that many women have in the wake of their own sexual socialization and the societal context of the sexualization of girls (Tolman, 2012). Yet research also has demonstrated the complexity of how pole dancing as exercise makes ambiguous its association with sexual display, and thus it may entail for women a reworking of a practice for sexual titillation with feelings of power in one's body and, possibly because of this ambiguity, feeling powerful or sexy without the physical presence of a male audience, perhaps through the context of a space safe from an actual sexualizing gaze (S. Holland & Attwood, 2009). The question, however, of whether experience of embodied feelings of power in this particular context may carry over beyond a given moment and space into women's sexual lives remains contested and unexplored (Tolman, 2012).

Another realm of psychological research on sexualization is phenomenological, seeking to understand how an increasingly sexualized mainstream landscape shapes embodied experiences of sexuality. Analysis of public discourses and representations, by which increasingly sexualizing and pornographic sentiments are communicated and circulated, are critical to understanding how lived experience may be constructed (Bartky, 1990; Hardy, 2009). This research primarily is composed of content and discursive analyses of sexualized images, especially their meanings for different constituencies, although much of the research has centered on girls' and women's bodies (Brookes & Kelly, 2009; Fabrianesi, Jones, & Reid, 2008; Hernandez, 2009; Merskin, 2004; Sanger, 2009), For instance, Goodin, Denberg, Murnen, and Smolak (2011) evaluated the presence of sexualizing clothing for girls on the websites of 15 popular stores and found that 30% of images had sexualizing qualities ("garments worn to enhance, exaggerate, call attention to, or accentuate the curves or angles of any part of the body . . . to arouse interest of physical intimacy from others," p. 5), with the highest being for "tween" markets. Joshi, Peter, and Valkenberg (2011) evaluated representations of sexual wanting (expressing sexual urges and sexual desires or expressing their own sexual wishes) in an analysis of U.S. and Dutch teen magazines, finding that in the U.S. coverage, boys' sexual wanting received more attention than girls' sexual wanting, whereas in the Dutch coverage sexual wanting was depicted equally often for boys and girls (see Volume 2, Chapter 12, this handbook).

Some research has focused on whether and how girls in particular are attempting or preferring a particular kind of "sexy" body (Coy, 2009a; Ringrose, 2010). For instance, in one study, young girls presented with girls wearing sexualized clothing versus nonsexualized clothing indicated that they greatly preferred the former, both for their ideal self and for being popular (Starr & Ferguson, 2012). Gill (2009) suggested that White, heterosexual young women have shifted from sexual objectification to "sexual subjectification"; that is, rather than being shown as passive objects of desire, these young women (and only these young women) are portrayed as being active "subjects" of their own sexuality. Rather than being "liberating," however, such portraits may constitute a new set of limiting mandates about how young women should express or appear to express their sexuality that is anchored in the "midriff-bearing," actively desiring young woman, requiring a toned but not too strong body that looks youthful but should not be too physically capable (Fahs, 2009). Yet Attwood (2011), in a study of women's digital representations of their sexuality in interactive new media, identifies new sexual femininities that defy simple binaries of passive object and active subject, with women producing themselves as sexual actors as "camgirls" or depicting sexually defiant women in "altporn." The question of whether or how these women's own bodily sexual feelings inform or result from these subversive acts of representation is an important next step in understanding the interplay between representations of others' sexual bodies and how people experience their own sexual bodies.

The participation of boys and men in these productions may incite their sexual feelings, despite the duality of their dedicated purpose of creating marketable images and not identifying as men who objectify women (Garner, 2012). Representations of sexiness in middle age are becoming extensive, promising both a challenge to narrow conventions of female attractiveness and a new repressive regime for women as they age (Tally, 2006; Vares, 2009). Representations of "lesbian" sexual performance are more pervasive, but there is no research on how such representations are experienced by sexual-minority women. These performances of same-sex desire may constitute "heteroflexibility," wherein women's same-sex kissing or touching as a public endeavor produces an embodiment of male sexual fantasy to consolidate a heterosexual identity (Diamond, 2005; Fahs, 2009). There is no evidence to date that these experiences reflect or incorporate embodied sexual desire, feelings, or responses, although the emergence of "bi-curiosity" as an intelligible identity may reflect or enable exploration or experience of actual erotic pleasure and enjoyment rather than being just a function of pressure alone.

One particular debate in which embodiment has emerged is the relationship between sexualization and sexual empowerment. On one side of the debate is the contention that sexualized images may reflect and provide cultural space for a more assertive and entitled or empowered sexuality, trumping traditional conceptions of appropriately feminine sexuality (Lamb, 2010; Peterson, 2010). Others argue that sexualization may reinstantiate and invigorate gender inequalities in sexual interactions and that a sense of sexual empowerment that does not embody one's own sexual feelings may be problematic (Fahs, 2009; Gavey, 2012; Tolman, 2012). Egan and Hawkes (2008) suggested that an unintended consequence of the current debate is that sexualization is framed as deterministic and restrictive regarding young women's sexuality, although others have argued for young women's subversion and resistance to an objectified sexuality under these conditions (e.g., Attwood, 2007). Teasing apart the complex, contradictory, and commercial dimensions of the "new sexual empowerment" means raising challenges about what is missing from it—women's embodied sexual pleasure as an anchor to sexual subjectivity and real choices that flesh out rather than laminate female sexual agency. Evans, Riley, and Shankar (2010) suggested the concept of new "technologies of sexiness" (p. 119), whereby women could utilize the contradictory yet proliferating discourses about women's sexuality to construct subversive sexual subjectivities, eluding the disembodiment attached to sexualization (see also Coy, 2009b).

A long history of research on the impact of pornography on sexuality has yielded inconsistent evidence (Segal, 1992). However, the explosion of the availability and possibility for new forms of engagement with porn through the Internet, a specific and increasingly salient context, has yielded more specific research on pornography's interplay with embodied sexuality. Rather than simply investigating whether viewing porn has negative effects on sexual behavior, sexual arousal, or sexual self-appraisal, more recent research on pornography focuses on the ways in which people produce, consume, and integrate it into their daily lives (van Doorn, 2011; Wilson-Kovacs, 2009). The emergence of the Internet as a site for constructing and experiencing male and female bodies by real women and men both reproduces gendered sexual bodily norms and emerges as a forum for resistance to them (Alexias, Kountria, & Tsekeris, 2011). More racial diversity is accompanied by less variation in the shapes of women's bodies in porn—now thinner, larger chested, with surgically or digitally altered labia—with ramifications for real women's dissatisfaction with or concern about their material bodies (Tibbals, 2010). In one study of women's self-published porn sites, DeVoss (2002) found that women are "inserting their embodied subjectivities into public space" (p. 75), thus challenging notions of female sexual submission and production for male pleasure.

Cyberspace is one of the new frontiers of the intersections among sexuality, media, and embodiment; the concept of the cyborg subject, wherein bodies and technology meet and comingle, ushers in new conceptions of the body and challenges the very terms of what constitutes a material body (Haraway, 1991). Cybersexuality (i.e., sexual behavior, desires, and bodies transmitted online and imbued with sensations and attitudes that mimic so-called real bodies and sexualities) has appeared more forcefully in recent years. In one sense, cybersex has been implicated in, enacted in, and constructed through mediations of sexual media (van Doorn, 2011; Waskul, 2002). van Doorn (2011) explored how virtual performances of gender, sexuality, and embodiment become materialized in digital space and may inform actual signification of gender norms, sexual identities, and even what is understood as sexual practice, particularly for engagement with heteronormativity. Eklund (2011) explored how the online game World of Warcraft imbues players with gender and sexuality scripts and makes way for numerous queer performances, even while seemingly promoting heterosexual exchanges between players. Looking at social networking sites, Ringrose (2011) argued that because mainstream online spaces demand and assume heterosexuality, they create new and intensified gendered and sexualized identities among young people. The ambiguous boundary and interplay between behavior in cyberspace and offline has inspired empirical questions about online sexual embodiments and actual bodies. Analyzing harassment on social networking sites, Ybarra and Mitchell (2008) found that although social networking sites do create contexts for unwanted sexual solicitation, problems of disembodying and harassing youth and teens extend far beyond the reach of cyberspace. In a study of relationship and marriage possibilities between men in the United States and women in other countries, Constable (2007) raised the question of how cultural and structural differences present challenges to expectations generated online through sexual images and talk and offline realities.

Although there is a depth of textual analysis of cybersex (e.g., Campbell, 2004; R. Jones, 2008; Wolmark, 1999), the material sexual body has received far less scholarly attention, in part because digital bodies raise questions about what an intelligible body is. There is some research on how cyberspace provides a new venue for individual exploration and construction of what constitutes embodied erotic experience that challenges the everyday conception of what is named *erotic*. For instance, in a study of online gay chat communities for gay self-identified bears and muscle worshippers that constitute a sexual space, Campbell (2004) demarcated the centrality of the physical body in social relations through these online interactions. As Waskul (2002) noted, cybersex involving videos becomes an embodied experience that creates both a viewed object and an experienced subject, yet he did not address the experiencing sexual subject. Attwood (2002) suggested that new media technologies may render a kind of "autosexuality" (p. 101), in which sex with other people (i.e., their bodies) is replaced by fundamentally disembodied sex that brings less danger, less mess, and less inconvenience. Yet she is one of the few scholars to recognize the engagement of the material body in cybersex; in her assessment of the sexualization of culture, she provided an explicit anecdotal description of a woman's bodily sexual response at the abrupt end of an online sex chat, offline physical frustration at coming close to orgasm. The "heaving body" does not appear to be a topic of research but rather an illustration of how cyberspace and media complicate what constitutes sex and how questions about sexual identities have dominated research on cybersex, which have yet to engage material bodies. Alapack, Blichfeldt, and Elden (2005) observed that as virtual sex "wins the war between desire and technology," neglect of "live embodiment" proliferates (p. 52). In an ethnography of trading "sexpics" on an online site, Slater (1998) found that rather than a realm of deconstruction and ideal possibilities, participants exerted tremendous energy attempting to refix bodies and identities in search of material forms of authenticity. Even as disembodiment motives for online chatting have been associated with loneliness, depression, and diminished social support, when used as a technology for social connection, online engagement can lead to offline connectivity (Kang, 2007), suggesting a potential line of inquiry for cybersex and its multiple embodiments.

THE DISOBEDIENT SEXUAL BODY

Bodies that do not reflect or refuse to conform to either explicit or unwritten hegemonies of normality or acceptability are often declared "not sexual." Notions of which bodies are eligible to be sexual are entangled with the material diversities of bodies that defy such criteria. There are many people who are assumed not to be sexual or disallowed status as sexual people predicated on what we are calling "disobedient" embodiments in such hierarchies of normality who refute and resist this exclusion. We review three types of such disobedience: body related, sexuality related, and gender related.

Body-Related Disobedience

When a person's physical body becomes ill, he or she must negotiate many changes in his or her sexual activities. Cancer patients, for example, often feel that the body that they had once mastered now enslaves them (Waskul & van der Riet, 2002) or feels "invaded" by an alien (Mairs, 1997). Similarly, people who have limited or no bladder or bowel control have an acute awareness of the proximity of their excretory organs to their anatomical sites of sexual pleasure (Koch, Kralik, & Eastwood, 2002; Manderson, 2005). For these people, as well as for women who experience chronic vulvar pain, good communication with one's sexual partner and partner receptivity to different "sexual scripts" is crucial to maintaining a satisfying sex life (Koch et al., 2002; Labuski, 2011).

Women who have been treated for breast cancer experience many changes in their sexualities, often related specifically to their bodies (Emilee, Ussher, & Perz, 2010). Because of the intense nature of the treatment regimen for breast cancer, women experience a range of changes in sexual functioning, including disruptions in arousal, lubrication, orgasm, sexual desire, and sexual pleasure (Emilee et al., 2010). Women who have undergone mastectomies may presume (often wrongly) that their sexual partners will be repulsed by their changed bodies (Sheppard & Ely, 2008). Similarly, in the case of testicular or prostate cancer among men, many men feel that the loss of a testicle or the inability to maintain an erection signifies a loss in masculinity, and they worry that their sexual function will be forever compromised (Gurevich, Bishop, Bower, Malka, & Nyhof-Young, 2004; Kelly, 2004). Even in cases in which men experience impotence as a result of cancer treatment, some men discover new avenues to sexual satisfaction, including redefining intimacy and exploring non-penile-penetrative erotic behaviors (Oliffe, 2005). Regardless of the specific bodily ailment, the psychological impact men and women experience as a result of their illnesses depends greatly on the social and relational contexts in which these individuals engage in sexual behaviors (Emilee et al., 2010).

People with physical disabilities often are desexualized actively in Western culture (Erickson, 2010; Guldin, 2000; Kim, 2011; Shildrick, 2007). Women with disabilities have reported as much sexual desire (Nosek et al., 2001; Vansteenwegen et al., 2003) and sexual motivation (Vansteenwegen et al., 2003) as nondisabled women, but they report significantly lower sexual satisfaction overall (Nosek et al., 2001; Vansteenwegen et al., 2003). Disabled people often internalize cultural ideals of what a "sexy body" should look like (Guldin, 2000) or what "real sex" should be (Tepper, 2000), and in feeling that they do not measure up to these ideas, they may experience feelings of inadequacy or emotional pain (Guldin, 2000; Tepper, 2000). These people's sexualities are not overdetermined by such societal ideals, however, and many disabled people view themselves as sexy (Erickson, 2010; Guldin, 2000), find alternatives to the traditional methods of achieving sexual pleasure (Tepper, 2000), or may even happily embrace an asexual identity (Kim, 2011). For example, some people redefine for themselves what an orgasm should be or feel like and explore nongenital or non-ejaculatory orgasms that may be centralized in other areas of the body, such as the lips or mouth (Guldin, 2000). Disabled men may choose to focus not on their difficulty maintaining an erection but instead on their prowess in giving partners oral sex or pleasurable manual stimulation, thus improving their feelings of self-worth (Guldin, 2000).

Overweight or fat people in our culture often are judged to be physically unattractive and are assumed, therefore, to find sexuality problematic (Bess, 1997). These stereotypes are more stringently applied to women than men, as our society is more accepting of large or fat men and even equates male largeness with strength and power (Bess, 1997). Fat men and women report fewer sexual partners than people with healthy weights (Bajos, Wellings, Laborde, & Moreau, 2010), which may be a result of a self-conscious fear of rejection and internalization of social stigmas about obesity (Bess, 1997). Fat men in particular are more likely to report sexual dysfunction (Bajos et al., 2010) and report less sexual desire and fewer erotic fantasies than men with more average weights (Jagstaidt, Golay, & Pasini, 1997). Many people who have undergone bariatric surgery feel they are more sexually attractive after surgery (Camps, Zervos, Goode, & Rosemurgy, 1996), and some also enjoy sex more (Camps et al., 1996; Kinzl et al., 2001). Sexual satisfaction, however, is not contingent on body weight; the outdated theory that fat individuals eat to avoid sex is not supported by the literature (Bess, 1997). Although fatness is not always associated with or a result of a less healthy lifestyle or eating habits, the fat body often is understood as diseased, pathological, sexually unattractive, and asexual (Braziel & LeBesco, 2001; Murray, 2004; Rothblum, Solovay, & Wann, 2009). As Murray noted, "[a fat woman is] expected to deny [her] own sexual desires and identity because [her] body stands as an 'embolism' (Sedgwick, 1993, p. 217) . . . between [her] sexuality and [her] society" (p. 239) and that fat women are denied sexual subjectivity and desirability outside of being fetishized objects.

Pitman (1999) observed that for fat lesbians, internalizing both homophobia and fat hatred can yield complex dissatisfaction with their sexual bodies as well as their bodies more generally.

Sexuality-Related Disobedience

Reported sexual dysfunction among men and women has become widespread, largely because Western culture has convinced people that sexuality is "natural" and therefore no learning should be necessary to produce high levels of pleasure and satisfaction (Tiefer, 2006). This conceptualization of sexuality as automatic and unlearned predisposes people to feel that if they are experiencing any disturbances or dissatisfaction in desire, performance, or pleasure, this must be a simple medical problem with a simple medical solution (Tiefer, 2006). The biomedical model of sexual dysfunction sets the stage for pharmaceutical production and leverage of a specific dysfunction discourse that frames sexual dissatisfaction as exclusively biological in nature and curable with "magic bullet" approaches (Cacchioni, 2007; McHugh, 2006; Moynihan, 2003; Tiefer, 2006). This increasingly popular discourse of sexual difficulty is especially problematic for women, as FSD and hypoactive sexual desire disorder (HSDD) have remained hard to define (Moynihan, 2003; Tiefer, 2006; see Chapter 8, this volume). Because FSD and HSDD have been based on the assumption that females experience biologically parallel sexual problems to those of men (Hartley, 2006; McHugh, 2006), some have argued that these diagnoses are an example of starting with a non-evidence-based presupposed "condition" and then trying to produce confirmatory evidence through research—often without success (Mayor, 2004; McHugh, 2006).

Similar challenges surrounding the debates about sexual dysfunction also influence academic understandings of asexuality (generally defined as a lack of sexual attraction; Carrigan, 2011): Is sexual desire, arousal, or behavior most important? Is sexual desire the same as sexual attraction? Can any of this be understood without exploring the social and psychological contexts within which it takes place (Carrigan, 2011; Scherrer, 2008)? An absence of sexual feelings of any kind generally has been assumed to signal sexual or psychological problems, predicated on the notion of the feeling sexual body as normal. The fifth edition of the Diagnostic and Statistical Manual of Mental Disorders (DSM-5), however, introduces an absence of distress about lack of sexual desire as contraindicating a diagnosis of HSDD. There has been a recent explosion of websites dedicated to the asexual community, providing much needed space for discussion online. Within the academy, however, very scholars have taken up asexuality as an area of investigation, with a few exceptions in the past 5 to 10 years. Asexuality traditionally has been pathologized as, for example, sexual aversion disorder or HSDD, rather than studied as an acceptable self-chosen identity (Prause & Graham, 2007; Scherrer, 2008), although this increasingly is changing in the literature (Boaert, 2004). Individuals who self-identify as asexual may have diverse reasons for doing so and may understand their asexuality in a variety of ways, ranging from regarding sex apathetically to feeling complete disgust at the prospect of sex (Carrigan, 2011). Many asexuals make an explicit distinction between the ideas of romance and sexuality, feeling that emotional attraction, companionship, and romance are desirable within relationships but that sex is not (Brotto, Knudson, Inskip, Rhodes, & Erskine, 2010; Scherrer, 2008). Developmentally, asexuals may express that they always have felt that they were somehow different from their peers who feel sexual attraction, and that this feeling of difference led them to believe something was wrong with them, until they discovered the concept (and sometimes the community) of asexuality (Brotto et al., 2010; Carrigan, 2011; Scherrer, 2008). Masturbation has proven to be a site of variability among asexuals, as some people feel no desire for sex with others or with themselves, whereas other people find masturbation occasionally satisfying and consistent with their asexual identities (Prause & Graham, 2007; Scherrer, 2008). Additionally, some individuals, who do not identify as asexual, nevertheless find fulfillment in romantic relationships that lack a sexual component, and this pattern, in particular among women (e.g., Boston marriages) has been documented for centuries (Rothblum & Brehony, 1993; Smith-Rosenberg, 1975).

Sexual dysfunction and asexuality are not the only sites in which individuals challenge normative frameworks for healthy sexuality. People who engage in exhibitionist or sadomasochistic sexual practices, for example, also resist social and medical norms. According to the DSM-IV, exhibitionism is still considered a mental disorder that involves exposing one's genitals to a stranger (American Psychiatric Association, 1994), and the vast majority of the literature pertaining to exhibitionism has focused on men (Hugh-Jones et al., 2005). The pathologization of exhibitionist behavior has been supported by theories regarding faulty brain chemistry as well as psychodynamic processes, such as castration anxiety (Hugh-Jones et al., 2005). Recent work on exhibitionism, however, has focused more on the performative nature of exhibitionism and has shown that much exhibitionism is evident online and on websites where people can post naked or erotic pictures of themselves for others to view for their own personal enjoyment (Hugh-Jones et al., 2005). Female exhibitionists who post on these websites report feeling powerful and socially supported (Hugh-Jones et al., 2005), demonstrating that women who exhibit may use the practice as a means to sexual empowerment. There is no research on embodied sexuality in sex club contexts, where performing and consuming exhibitionism is condoned.

Sadomasochism in particular and BDSM practices in general (including bondage and discipline, dominance and submission, and sadism and masochism) have been similarly pathologized historically (American Psychiatric Association, 1994). On-the-ground and online communities of sadomasochists actively reject the idea that their style of kinky sex is harmful, and instead they focus on mutually consenting partners and communication as most important (Langdridge & Butt, 2004; Weiss & Weiss, 2011). Sadomasochistic practices rely heavily on extreme performances of power, domination, and submission socially inscribed on the body, and this performativity may mirror traditional understandings of masculinity and femininity (D. Lindemann, 2011). Furthermore, as some scholars have pointed out, lived embodied links between pleasure and pain are not uncommon (Deckha, 2011). Sexual performances of sadomasochism may not exist solely on the fringes of society. As sadomasochistic practices have become increasingly trendy, the topic has become more prevalent in mainstream magazines, mainstream booksellers, and mainstream advertisements (Hanna, 2001). Yet Weiss (2006) found in a study employing surveys, focus groups, and interviews that current practices of accepting sadomasochism through normalization or understanding it through pathologization both reinforce privileges of normative sexuality (see Chapter 9, this volume).

Gender-Related Disobedience

Many people experience their bodies and their genders in ways that do not conform to traditional understandings of male–female or masculine–feminine. Transgender individuals (those whose gender presentation does not conform to conventional notions of masculinity or femininity and may run counter to their own biological assignment as male or female), including but not exclusively transsexuals (those who feel that their psychological sex does not match the sex they were assigned at birth, and who desire bodily modifications to bring these into alignment), may or may not actually use these terms to understand their genders. Some gender-nonconforming individuals prefer such gender identifications as "butch" or "femme" (Valentine, 2007) or simply may identify themselves as their preferred gender without reference to any "trans" identities (Wilson, 2002). Transgender individuals experience their sexualities in unique ways, especially because the medical expectation of any transition is that an individual will become a heterosexual man or woman (Pardo, 2011; see Chapter 24, this volume). Many transgender people challenge compulsory heterosexuality (Rich, 1980) at the point of both lived and inscribed embodiment, in that they understand their sexual attractions as distinct from the bodies assigned a gender at birth, and therefore they "subvert the cultural assumption that sex between male- and female-bodied individuals equals heterosexuality" (Rich, 1980, p. 109; Hines, 2007; Schleifer, 2006). For example, many female-to-male transsexuals change their sexual orientation after transitioning or find themselves attracted to both men and women (Dozier, 2005; Schleifer, 2006). Cisgender people (those whose preferred gender matches the gender they were assigned at birth) who are sexually attracted to transgender people may construct unique sexual desires on the basis of their own sexual orientations (Weinberg & Williams, 2010b). For example, in a study of cisgender men who were sexually interested in transwomen (in this study defined as male-to-female transsexuals who retain their penises), those who identified as heterosexual tended to ignore the transwoman's penis, whereas bisexually oriented men incorporated the transwoman's penis into the sexual experience (Weinberg & Williams, 2010b).

People who are born with atypical or ambiguous genitalia (referred to as "intersex," although less frequently currently than in the past) also must navigate gender norms and expectations in their expressions of their sexualities. Often, intersex infants, who are born with ambiguous genitalia that do not fit into the presumed binary framework of sex, are understood by doctors to require "corrective" or "reparative" surgery to "fix" the atypical sexual bodies (Kessler, 2002; Roen, 2008). It is most common for an infant born with an atypically small penis or an atypically large clitoris to be surgically altered to fit into one or the other side of the sex binary, and these corrective procedures often entail numerous follow-up surgeries over the course of development (Minto, Liao, Woodhouse, Ransley, & Creighton, 2003). Ironically, since the incidence of ambiguous genitalia in the population has been estimated to be as high as 2% (Blackless et al., 2000), it seems that the occurrence of intersexuality is relatively common (Roen, 2008). There is debate about these surgeries, with some critiquing this practice as "correcting" ambiguous bodies to match "intelligible" bodies that fit into an essentialized gender binary (Kessler, 2002; Roen, 2008) and others noting that such surgeries frequently are required for physical or psychological reasons (Creighton & Liao, 2004; Holmes, 2002; Woodhouse, 2004). Infants who undergo surgical procedures may have compromised sexual functioning as adults (Minto et al., 2003). For example, people who had undergone feminizing surgery as infants and were then living as adult females had more difficulty achieving orgasm than individuals who had not had surgery (Creighton & Liao, 2004; Minto et al., 2003). Results such as these have prompted medical professionals to take much greater care in surgical decisions, often delaying genital surgeries until a person is old enough to contribute meaningfully to the discussion and explicitly consent to any surgical procedures (Woodhouse, 2004). Additionally, many of these individuals now reject the label "intersex," because of its negative associations with terms like "hermaphrodite," or because they may feel that "intersex" was something "done to" them and therefore not a part of their chosen identity (Grabham, 2007; Koyama, n.d.).

Interventions for Embodiment

A number of researchers have proposed various interventions to assist and support people who are experiencing challenges or difficulties with sexuality as social inscription on the body or as living experience of the body. Sensate approaches to sex therapy, in which the therapist guides the client, either as an individual or as a couple, to refocus and, in essence, reconnect with their physical sexual feelings and responses, can be understood as a form of embodiment intervention and continues to be a central approach to sexual distress (see Chapter 8, this volume). An embodiment lens may underscore that a purely mechanistic approach is impoverished or may not be appropriate depending on the complaint. Therapeutic work connecting embodiment and psychotherapy has been particularly successful in treating disorders like anorexia and bulimia, posttraumatic stress disorder, and childhood sexual abuse. Lester (1997) argued that to successfully treat anorexia, therapists should deconstruct notions of "inside" and "outside" to allow the patient to experience a connection with their own bodies. Similarly, Langmuir, Kirsh, and Classen (2012) suggested that sensorimotor psychotherapy—in which patients use their bodies actively to improve body awareness and to decrease dissociation—can successfully treat trauma disorders. Adding a more psychoanalytic twist, Baker-Pitts (2007) argued that female therapists can use their patients' projections about both the therapists' and patients' bodies to grapple more intensely with defense mechanisms of dependency and broader projections made onto the female body.

Research also has worked to establish the embodied bases of existing psychotherapy processes. Dekeyser, Elliott, and Leijssen's (2009) work on empathy argued for empathy as a cooperative, dialogical process vividly grounded in the body. More expansively, Phelan (2009) analyzed the benefits and contraindications of therapists and patients touching before, during, or after psychotherapy sessions, finding a wide range of outcomes depending on the reasons for touch, the patient's perceptions of touch, cultural and religious considerations, and rationale for touch. Ultimately, issues of embodiment in psychotherapy—for the therapists and their patients—can serve as meaningful interventions when working with clients with a range of complaints and disorders.

CONCLUSION AND FUTURE DIRECTIONS

This chapter demonstrated how a lens of embodiment offers a unique and important understanding of sexuality. Leveraging and building from embodiment theories, researchers have generated a new and substantive body of research predicated on the *physicality* of sexuality that is foundationally social rather than biologically deterministic. Reviewing the prominent theories that guide thought and research on embodiment, we have provided both broad strokes about and intimate looks into knowledge about sexual bodies that are situated in time, space, action, and society. In particular, the chapter focused attention on intersections of embodied sexuality and psychology. This relatively new line of research both includes psychology and has much to offer the discipline. The chapter has argued that developing these lines of inquiry within psychology will constitute a significant contribution to the understanding of sexuality. It concludes with suggestions for future directions.

Recent work from neuroscience supports embodiment theory as a useful framework for social science research, suggesting that the body in and beyond sexuality research is seen as more plastic, with "hard wiring" incorporating the environmental contexts in which it develops, exists, performs, and malfunctions (Cromby, 2004; see Chapter 7, this volume). This work not only challenges the debate between "nature" and "nurture" but also offers further evidence that the interactionist perspective embedded in embodiment theory enables it as a functional conceptual framework (Tolman & Diamond, 2001; see Chapter 1, this volume). For instance, evidence from men recovering a sexual life following treatment for prostate cancer suggests that all of us may generate new capacities for sexual feeling and expression following the loss of other capacities or valued practices (Litwin, Melmed, & Nakazon, 2001). The constraints on our ability to do so are likely to be as much social as they are physical and psychological. Diamond (2005) has suggested applying dynamical systems theory (DST) to our understanding of women's same-sex sexuality development. She argued that DST, in explaining how interactions among internal and external features of experience produce abrupt transitions, new patterns, and sensitivity to fluctuations, accounts for the changing patterns she identified in this population. It is possible that DST may provide a way to understand embodiment of sexuality among other groups and practices, providing a roadmap to the interplay between our physicality and our relational, environmental, and cultural contexts characterized by shifting discursive, sociopolitical, and historic dimensions. These examples demonstrate the ways in which thinking of the mind and body as separate, or of bodies as independent from society, limits our potential for understanding sexuality. Embodiment theories provide tools for observing, posing, and investigating daring and difficult questions about sexuality that can contribute to resisting oppressive binaries that so many bodies and psyches labor under, struggle, subvert, or resist.

Looking forward, we imagine many new threads of research on embodiment and sexuality. In particular, future research can interrogate the limitations of the "rhetoric of choice" and agency with regard to sexual decision making, particularly as debates intensify about which kinds of embodiment, and which embodied expressions, signify "liberation" and "empowerment" and which signify the internalization of oppression (and negative stereotypes). More nuanced work that theorizes the body into contemporary cultural narratives, such as strip clubs, commodification of sex, and the untethering of sex from morally determined and condoned contexts, and that leverages these theories in posing and answering the innovative research questions that will emerge represents the potent future of research on embodiment. We foresee that embodiment research likely will venture more and more into thinking about and theorizing nonconforming bodies, particularly disability studies, fat studies, and queer studies. How these nonconforming bodies yield intersectional understandings of gender, power, and sexuality will form the cutting edge of embodiment research. The material and bodily dimensions of subjects engaged in practices is a rich arena that will both inform and be informed by research grounded in embodiment perspectives.

Ultimately, as so many of these studies testify, research on embodiment and sexuality places the corporeal body at the center of fields that have largely ignored the body as a "knowing subject". Transcending, sidestepping, or solving the biological determinism versus social construction debate, embodiment theory, and research afford an exciting new strategy to move forward, in a complex way, how we understand the very real complexities of sexuality.

References

Ackard, D. M., Kearney-Cooke, A., & Peterson, C. B. (2000). Effect of body image and self-image on women's sexual behaviors. *International Journal of Eating Disorders,28*, 422–429. doi:10.1002/1098-108X(200012)28:4<422::AID-EAT10>3.0.CO;2-1

Ainsworth, S. E., & Baumeister, R. F. (2012). Changes in sexuality: How sexuality changes across time, across relationships, and across sociocultural contexts. *Clinical Neuropsychiatry,9*, 32–38.

Alapack, R., Blichfeldt, M., & Elden, A. (2005). Flirting on the Internet and the hickey: A hermeneutic. *Cyberpsychology and Behavior, 8*, 52–61. doi:10.1089/cpb.2005.8.52

Albanesi, H. P. (2009). *Gender and sexual agency: How young people make choices about sex.*Lanham, MD: Lexington Books.

Alcoff, L. (1988). Cultural feminism vs. post-structuralism: The identity crisis in feminist theory. *Signs: Journal of Women in Culture and Society,13*, 405–436. doi:10.1086/494426

Alcoff, L. (2005). *Visible identities: Race, gender, and the self.*Oxford, England: Oxford University Press.

Alexias, G., Kountria, A., & Tsekeris, C. (2011). Sex and the web: The embodiment of female sexuality in online pornography. *Facta Universitatus: Series Philosophy, Sociology, and Psychology,10*, 217–231.

American Psychiatric Association. (1994). *Diagnostic and statistical manual of mental disorders* (4th ed.). Washington, DC: Author.

American Psychological Association, Task Force on the Sexualization of Girls. (2007). *Report of the APA Task Force on the Sexualization of Girls*. Retrieved from http://www.apa.org/pi/women/programs/girls/report-full.pdf

Angelides, S. (2004). Feminism, child sexual abuse, and the erasure of child sexuality. *GLQ: A Journal of Lesbian and Gay Studies,10*, 141–177. doi:10.1215/10642684-10-2-141

Angulo-Olaiz, F. (2009). The role of pap smears in negotiating risk: Latinas' perceptions of trust and love in sexual relationships with men. *NWSA Journal,21*, 166–190. doi:10.1353/nwsa.0.0095

Attwood, F. (2002). Reading porn: The paradigm shift in pornography research. *Sexualities,5*, 91–105. doi:10.1177/1363460702005001005

Attwood, F. (2007). No money shot? Commerce, pornography, and new sex taste cultures. *Sexualities,10*, 441–456. doi:10.1177/1363460707080982

Attwood, F. (2011). The paradigm shift: Pornography research, sexualization, and extreme images. *Social Compass, 5*, 13–22. doi:10.1111/j.1751-9020.2010.00356.x

Backstrom, L., Armstrong, E. A., & Puentes, J. (2012). Women's negotiations of cunnilingus in college hookups and relationships. *Journal of Sex Research, 49*, 1–12. doi:10.1080/00224499.2011.585523

Bajos, N., Wellings, K., Laborde, C., & Moreau, C. (2010). Sexuality and obesity, a gender perspective: Results from French national random probability survey of sexual behaviours. *British Medical Journal*.doi:10.1136/bmj.c2573

Baker-Pitts, C. (2007). Two bodies in the room: An intersubjective view of female objectification. *Psychoanalysis, Culture, and Society,12*, 124–141. doi:10.1057/palgrave.pcs.2100117

Bancroft, J. (Ed.). (2003). *Sexual development in childhood.*Bloomington: Indiana University Press.

Bartky, S. L. (1990). *Femininity and domination: Studies in the phenomenology of oppression.*New York, NY: Routledge.

Bay-Cheng, L. Y., & Fava, N. M. (2011). Young women's experiences and perceptions of cunnilingus during adolescence. *Journal of Sex Research,48*, 531–542. doi:10.1080/00224499.2010.535221

Berkowitz, D. (2006). Consuming eroticism: Gender performances and presentations in pornographic establishments. *Journal of Contemporary Ethnography,35*, 583–606. doi:10.1177/0891241605285402

Berlant, L., & Warner, M. (2000). Sex in public. In L. Berlant (Ed.), *Intimacy* (pp. 311–330). Chicago, IL: University of Chicago Press.

Bess, B. E. (1997). Human sexuality and obesity. *International Journal of Mental Health,26*, 61–67.

Blackless, M., Charuvastra, A., Derryck, A., Fausto-Sterling, A., Lauzanne, K., & Lee, E. (2000). How sexually dimorphic are we? Review and synthesis. *American Journal of Human Biology,12*, 151–166. doi:10.1002/(SICI)1520-6300(200003/04)12:2<151::AID-AJHB1>3.0.CO;2-F

Blackwood, E. (2005). Transnational sexualities in one place: Indonesian readings. *Gender and Society,19*, 221–242. doi:10.1177/0891243204272862

Boaert, A. F. (2004). Asexuality: Prevalence and associated factors in a national probability sample. *Journal of Sex Research,41*, 279–287. doi:10.1080/00224490409552235

Boislard, P. M., & Zimmer-Gembeck, M. J. (2011). Sexual subjectivity, relationship status and quality, and same-sex sexual experience among emerging adult females. *Journal of Educational and Developmental Psychology,1*, 54–64. doi:10.5539/jedp.v1n1p54

Bordo, S. (1993). *Unbearable weight: Feminism, western culture, and the body.*Berkeley: University of California Press.

Bordo, S. (2000). *The male body: A new look at men in public and private.*New York, NY: Farrar, Straus and Giroux.

Boroughs, M., Cafri, G., & Thompson, J. K. (2005). Male body depilation: Prevalence and associated features of body hair removal. *Sex Roles,52*, 637–644. doi:10.1007/s11199-005-3731-9

Bragg, S., Buckingham, D., Russell, R., & Willett, R. (2011). Too much too soon? Children, "sexualization" and consumer culture. *Sex Education,11*, 279–292. doi:10.1080/14681811.2011.590085

Braidotti, R. (1994). *Nomadic subjects: Embodiment and sexual difference in contemporary feminist theory.*New York, NY: Columbia University Press.

Bramwell, R., Morland, C., & Garden, A. S. (2007). Expectations and experience of labial reduction: A qualitative study. *BJOG: An International Journal of Obstetrics and Gynecology,114*, 1493–1499. doi:10.1111/j.1471-0528.2007.01509.x

Braun, V. (2005). In search of (better) sexual pleasure: Female genital "cosmetic" surgery. *Sexualities,8*, 407–424. doi:10.1177/1363460705056625

Braun, V., & Kitzinger, C. (2001). The perfectible vagina: Size matters. *Culture, Health and Sexuality,3*, 263–277. doi:10.1080/13691050152484704

Braun, V., & Tiefer, L. (2010). The "designer vagina" and the pathologisation of female genital diversity: Interventions for change. *Radical Psychology,8*, 1393–1407. doi:10.1089/jwh.2009.1728

Braziel, J. E., & LeBesco, K. (2001). *Bodies out of bounds: Fatness and transgression.* Berkeley: University of California Press.

Brookes, F., & Kelly, P. (2009). Dolly girls: Tweenies as artifacts of consumption. *Journal of Youth Studies,12*, 599–613. doi:10.1080/13676260902960745

Brotto, L. A., Heiman, J. R., & Tolman, D. L. (2009). Narratives of desire in mid-age women with and without arousal difficulties. *Journal of Sex Research,46*, 387–398. doi:10.1080/00224490902792624

Brotto, L. A., Knudson, G., Inskip, J., Rhodes, K., & Erskine, Y. (2010). Asexuality: A mixed-methods approach. *Archives of Sexual Behavior,39*, 599–618. doi:10.1007/s10508-008-9434-x

Burns, A., Futch, V. A., & Tolman, D. L. (2011). "It's like doing homework": Academic achievement discourse in adolescent girls' fellatio narratives. *Sexuality Research and Social Policy,8*, 239–251. doi:10.1007/s13178-011-0062-1

Butler, J. (1990). *Gender trouble: Feminism and the subversion of identity.*New York, NY: Routledge.

Butler, J. (1993). *Bodies that matter: On the discursive limits of sex.*New York, NY: Routledge.

Butler, J. (1994). Contingent foundations: Feminism and the question of "postmodernism". In S. Seidman (Ed.), *The postmodern turn: New perspectives on social theory* (pp. 153–170). Cambridge, MA: Cambridge University Press. doi:10.1017/CBO9780511570940.011

Byers, E. S. (1995). How well does the traditional sexual script explain sexual coercion? Review of a program of research. *Journal of Psychology and Human Sexuality,8*, 7–25. doi:10.1300/J056v08n01_02

Cacchioni, T. (2007). Heterosexuality and "the labour of love": A contribution to recent debates on female sexual dysfunction. *Sexualities,10*, 299–320. doi:10.1177/1363460707078320

Cahill, A. J. (2011). *Overcoming objectification: A carnal ethics.*New York, NY: Routledge.

Campbell, J. (2004). *Getting it on online: Cyberspace, gay male sexuality, and embodied identity.*Binghamton, NY: Harrington Park Press/Haworth Press.

Camps, M. A., Zervos, E., Goode, S., & Rosemurgy, A. S. (1996). Impact of bariatric surgery on body image perception and sexuality in morbidly obese patients and their partners. *Obesity Surgery,6*, 356–360. doi:10.1381/096089296765556700

Carpenter, L. M., & Casper, M. J. (2009). A tale of two technologies: HPV vaccination, male circumcision, and sexual health. *Gender and Society,23*, 790–816. doi:10.1177/0891243209352490

Carrigan, M. (2011). There's more to life than sex? Difference and commonality within the asexual community. *Sexualities,14*, 462–478. doi:10.1177/1363460711406462

Castro-Vásquez, G. (2006). The politics of Viagra: Gender, dysfunction, and reproduction in Japan. *Body and Society,12*, 109–129. doi:10.1177/1357034X06064328

Collins, P. H. (1990). *Black feminist thought: Vol. 2. Knowledge, consciousness, and the politics of empowerment*. Boston, MA: Unwin Hyman.

Connell, R. W. (1995). *Masculinities*. Cambridge, England: Polity Press.

Constable, N. (2007). Love at first site? Visual images and virtual encounters with bodies. In M. B. Padilla, J. S. Hirsch, M. Muñoz-Laboy, R. Sember, & R. G. Parker (Eds.), *Love and globalization: Transformations of intimacy in the contemporary world* (pp. 252–269). Nashville, TN: Vanderbilt University Press.

Corsianos, M. (2007). Mainstream pornography and "women": Questioning sexual agency. *Critical Sociology, 33*, 863–885. doi:10.1163/156916307X230359

Cover, R. (2003). The naked subject: Nudity, context, and sexualization in contemporary culture. *Body and Society,9*, 53–72. doi:10.1177/1357034X030093004

Coy, M. (2009a). Milkshakes, lady lumps, and growing up to want boobies: How the sexualisation of popular culture limits girls' horizons. *Child Abuse Review,18*, 372–383. doi:10.1002/car.1094

Coy, M. (2009b). This body which is not mine: The notion of the habit body, prostitution and (dis)embodiment. *Feminist Theory,10*, 61–75. doi:10.1177/1464700108100392

Coy, M., & Garner, M. (2012). Definitions, discourses and dilemmas: Policy and academic engagement with the sexualisation of popular culture. *Gender and Education,24*, 285–301. doi:10.1080/09540253.2012.667793

Creighton, S., & Liao, L. M. (2004). Changing attitudes to sex assignment in intersex. *BJU International,93*, 659–664. doi:10.1111/j.1464-410X.2003.04694.x

Crenshaw, C. (1991). Mapping the margins: Intersectionality, identity politics, and violence against women of color. *Stanford Law Review,43*, 1241–1299. doi:10.2307/1229039

Cromby, J. (2004). Between construction and neuroscience: The societal co-constitution of embodied subjectivity. *Theory and Psychology,14*, 797–821. doi:10.1177/0959354304048107

Crossley, N. (1996). Body-subject/body-power: Agency, inscription and control in Foucault and Merleau-Ponty. *Body and Society,2*, 99–116. doi:10.1177/1357034X96002002006

Curtin, N., Ward, L., Merriwether, A., & Caruthers, A. (2011). Femininity ideology and sexual health in young women: A focus on sexual knowledge, embodiment, and agency. *International Journal of Sexual Health,23*, 48–62. doi:10.1080/19317611.2010.524694

Curtis, D. (2009). *Pleasure and perils: Girls' sexuality in a Caribbean consumer culture.* New Brunswick, NJ: Rutgers University Press.

Davis, M. (2002). HIV prevention rationalities and serostasis in the risk narratives of gay men. *Sexualities,5*, 281–299. doi:10.1177/1363460702005003002

de Beauvoir, S. (2009). *The second sex*(C. Borde & S. Malovany-Chevallier, Trans.). New York, NY: Knopf. (Original work published 1949)

De Casanova, E. M. (2004). "No ugly women": Concepts of race and beauty among adolescent women in Ecuador. *Gender and Society,18*, 287–308. doi:10.1177/0891243204263351

Deckha, M. (2011). Pain as culture: A postcolonial feminist approach to S/M and women's agency. *Sexualities,14*, 129–150. doi:10.1177/1363460711399032

Dekeyser, M., Elliott, R., & Leijssen, M. (2009). Empathy in psychotherapy: Dialogue and embodied understanding. In J. Decety & W. Ickes (Eds.), *The social neuroscience of empathy* (pp. 113–124). Cambridge: Massachusetts Institute of Technology Press.

DeLamater, J. D., & Hyde, J. S. (1998). Essentialism vs. social constructionism in the study of human sexuality. *Journal of Sex Research,35*, 10–18. doi:10.1080/00224499809551913

Del Rosso, J. (2011). The penis as public art: Embodiment and the performance of masculinity in public settings. *Sexualities,14*, 704–724. doi:10.1177/1363460711420461

DeMaria, A. L., Hollub, A. V., & Herbenick, D. (2011). Using genital self-image, body image, and sexual behaviors to predict gynecological exam behaviors of college women. *Journal of Sexual Medicine,8*, 2484–2492. doi:10.1111/j.1743-6109.2011.02379.x

DeVoss, D. (2002). Women's porn sites—Spaces of fissure and eruption or "I'm a little bit of everything."*Sexuality and Culture,6*, 75–94. doi:10.1007/BF02912229

Diamond, L. (2005). "I'm straight, but I kissed a girl": The trouble with American media representations of female–female sexuality. *Feminism and Psychology,15*, 104–110. doi:10.1177/0959353505049712

Diamond, L. (2006). What we got wrong about sexual identity development: Unexpected findings from a longitudinal study of young women. In A. Omoto & H. Kurtzman (Eds.), *Recent research on sexual orientation* (pp. 73–94). Washington, DC: American Psychological Association.

Diamond, L. (2008). *Sexual fluidity: Understanding women's love and desire.* Cambridge, MA: Harvard University Press.

Dickerson, B., & Rousseau, N. (2009). Ageism through omission: The obsolescence of Black women's sexuality. *Journal of African American Studies, 13*, 307–324. doi:10.1007/s12111-008-9084-z

Dillaway, H. E. (2005). Menopause is the "good old": Women's thoughts about reproductive aging. *Gender and Society, 19*, 398–417. doi:10.1177/0891243204271350

Dillaway, H. E. (2011). Menopausal and misbehaving: When women "flash" in front of others. In C. Bobel & S. Kwan (Eds.), *Embodied resistance: Challenging the norms, breaking the rules* (pp. 197–208). Nashville, TN: Nashville University Press.

Donaghue, N., Whitehead, K., & Kurz, T. (2011). Spinning the pole: A discursive analysis of the websites of recreational pole dancing studios. *Feminism and Psychology, 21*, 443–457. doi:10.1177/0959353511424367

Dowsett, G. (1996). *Practicing desire: Homosexual sex in an age of AIDS.* Palo Alto, CA: Stanford University Press.

Dowsett, G. W. (2000). Bodyplay: Corporeality in a discursive silence. In R. Parker, R. M. Barbarosa, & P. Aggleton (Eds.), *Framing the sexual subject: The politics of gender, sexuality, and power* (pp. 29–45). Berkeley: University of California Press.

Dowsett, G. W. (2003). Some considerations on sexuality and gender in the context of AIDS. *Reproductive Health Matters, 11*, 21–29. doi:10.1016/S0968-8080(03)02290-0

Dowsett, G. W., Williams, H., Ventuneac, A., & Carballo-Dieguez, A. (2008). "Taking it like a man": Masculinity and barebacking online. *Sexualities, 11*, 121–141. doi:10.1177/1363460707085467

Dozier, R. (2005). Beards, breasts, and bodies: Doing sex in a gendered world. *Gender and Society, 19*, 297–316. doi:10.1177/0891243204272153

Duncan, D. (2010). Embodying the gay self: Body image, reflexivity and embodied identity. *Health Sociology Review, 19*, 437–450. doi:10.5172/hesr.2010.19.4.437

Eck, B. A. (2003). Men are much harder: Gendered viewing of nude images. *Gender and Society, 17*, 691–710. doi:10.1177/0891243203255604

Egan, R. D., & Hawkes, G. L. (2008). Endangered girls and incendiary objects: Unpacking the discourse on sexualization. *Sexuality and Culture, 12*, 291–311. doi:10.1007/s12119-008-9036-8

Eitzen, D. S., Baca Zinn, M., & Gold, S. J. (1999). Integrating professional socialization and training for sociology graduate students. *American Sociologist, 30*(4), 56–63. doi:10.1007/s12108-999-1023-5

Eklund, L. (2011). Doing gender in cyberspace: The performance of gender by female World of Warcraft players. *Convergence: The International Journal of Research into New Media Technologies, 17*, 323–342. doi:10.1177/1354856511406472

Emilee, G., Ussher, J. M., & Perz, J. (2010). Sexuality after breast cancer: A review. *Maturitas, 66*, 397–407. doi:10.1016/j.maturitas.2010.03.027

Epstein, M., Calzo, J. P., Smiler, A. P., & Ward, L. M. (2009). "Anything from making out to having sex": Men's negotiations of hooking up and friends with benefits scripts. *Journal of Sex Research, 46*, 414–424. doi:10.1080/00224490902775801

Epstein, S. (1994). Integration of the cognitive and the psychodynamic unconscious. *American Psychologist, 49*, 709–724. doi:10.1037/0003-066X.49.8.709

Erickson, L. (2010). Out of line: The sexy femmegimp politics of *flaunting* it! In M. Stombler, D. M. Baunach, E. O. Burgess, D. J. Donnelly, W. O. Simonds, & E. J. Windsor (Eds.), *Sex matters: The sexuality and society reader* (3rd ed., pp. 135–140). Boston, MA: Allyn & Bacon.

Evans, A., Riley, S., & Shankar, A. (2010). Technologies of sexiness: Theorizing women's engagement in the sexualization of culture. *Feminism and Psychology, 20*, 114–131. doi:10.1177/0959353509351854

Fabrianesi, B., Jones, S. C., & Reid, A. (2008). Are pre-adolescent girls' magazines providing age-appropriate role models? *Health Education, 108*, 437–449. doi:10.1108/09654280810910854

Fahs, B. (2009). Compulsory bisexuality? The challenges of modern sexual fluidity. *Journal of Bisexuality, 9*, 431–449. doi:10.1080/15299710903316661

Fahs, B. (2011a). Dreaded "otherness": Heteronormative patrolling in women's body hair rebellions. *Gender and Society, 25*, 451–472. doi:10.1177/0891243211414877

Fahs, B. (2011b). *Performing sex: The making and unmaking of women's erotic lives.* Albany, NY: SUNY Press.

Fahs, B., & Delgado, D. (2011). The specter of excess: Race, class, and gender in women's body hair narratives. In C. Bobel & S. Kwan (Eds.), *Embodied resistance: Challenging the norms, breaking the rules* (pp. 13–25). Nashville, TN: Vanderbilt University Press.

Fahs, B., & Swank, E. (2011). Social identities as predictors of women's sexual satisfaction and sexual activity. *Archives of Sexual Behavior, 40*, 903–914. doi:10.1007/s10508-010-9681-5

Falomir-Pichastor, J. M., Manuel, J., & Mugny, G. (2009). "I'm not gay . . . I'm a real man!": Heterosexual men's gender self-esteem and sexual prejudice. *Personality and Social Psychology Bulletin, 35*, 1233–1243. doi:10.1177/0146167209338072

Farquhar, C. (2000). "Lesbian" in a post-lesbian world? Policing identity, sex, and image. *Sexualities,3*, 219–236. doi:10.1177/136346000003002007

Fausto-Sterling, A. (2000). *Sexing the body: Gender politics and the construction of sexuality.*New York, NY: Basic Books.

Feinberg, L. (1997). *Transgender warriors: Making history from Joan of Arc to Dennis Rodman.*Boston, MA: Beacon Press.

Fine, M. (1988). Sexuality, schooling, and adolescent females: The missing discourse of desire. *Harvard Educational Review,58*, 29–53.

Fine, M., & McClelland, S. I. (2006). Sexuality education and desire: Still missing after all these years. *Harvard Educational Review,76*, 297–338.

Forrest, S. (2000). "Big and tough": Boys learning about sexuality and manhood. *Sexual and Relationship Therapy,15*, 247–261. doi:10.1080/14681990050109845

Foucault, M. (1966). *The order of things.*New York, NY: Vintage.

Foucault, M. (1969). *The archaelogy of knowledge.*New York, NY: Harper & Row.

Foucault, M. (1975). *Discipline and punish.*New York, NY: Pantheon.

Foucault, M.(1978). *The history of sexuality* (Vol. 1). New York, NY: Random House.

Fredrickson, B. L., & Roberts, T.(1997). Objectification theory: Toward understanding women's lived experiences and mental health risks. *Psychology of Women Quarterly,21*, 173–206. doi:10.1111/j.1471-6402.1997.tb00108.x

Fredrickson, B. L., Roberts, T. A., Noll, S. M., Quinn, D. M., & Twenge, J. M. (1998). That swimsuit becomes you: Sex differences in self-objectification, restrained eating, and math performance. *Journal of Personality and Social Psychology,75*, 269–284. doi:10.1037/0022-3514.75.1.269

French, B. H. (2012). More than Jezebels and freaks: Exploring how black girls navigate sexual coercion and sexual scripts. *Journal of African American Studies,17*, 35–50. doi:10.1007/s12111-012-9218-1

Freud, S.(1900). *The interpretation of dreams* (Vol. 4). London, England: Hogarth Press.

Friedrich, W. (2003). Studies of sexuality of nonabused children. In J. Bancroft (Ed.), *Sexual development in childhood* (pp. 107–120). Bloomington: Indiana University Press.

Frost, L. (2005). Theorizing the young woman in the body. *Body and Society,11*, 63–85. doi:10.1177/1357034X05049851

Frueh, J. (2003). The aesthetics of orgasm. *Sexualities,6*, 459–478. doi:10.1177/136346070363012

Gable, S. L., & Haidt, J. (2005). What (and why) is positive psychology? *Review of General Psychology,9*, 103–110. doi:10.1037/1089-2680.9.2.103

Gagné, P., & McGaughey, D. (2002). Designing women: Cultural hegemony and the exercise of power among women who have undergone elective mammoplasty. *Gender and Society,16*, 814–838. doi:10.1177/089124302237890

Gagnon, J. H. (1990). The explicit and implicit use of the scripting perspective in sex research. *Annual Review of Sex Research,1*, 1–43.

Gamson, W. A. (2000). Sexualities, queer theory, and qualitative research. In N. K. Denzin & Y. Lincoln (Eds.), *Handbook of qualitative research* (Vol. 2, pp. 347–365). Thousand Oaks, CA: Sage.

Garlick, S. (2011). A new sexual revolution? Critical theory, pornography, and the Internet. *Canadian Review of Sociology,48*, 221–239. doi:10.1111/j.1755-618X.2011.01264.x

Garner, M. (2012). The missing link: The sexualisation of culture and men. *Gender and Education,24*, 325–331. doi:10.1080/09540253.2012.670392

Gatens, M. (1996). *Imaginary bodies: Ethics, power, and corporeality.*London, England: Routledge.

Gavey, N. (2012). Beyond "empowerment"? Sexuality in a sexist world. *Sex Roles,66*, 718–724. doi:10.1007/s11199-011-0069-3

Gill, R. (2008). Empowerment/sexism: Figuring female sexual agency in contemporary advertising. *Feminism and Psychology,18*, 35–60. doi:10.1177/0959353507084950

Gill, R. (2009). Beyond the "sexualization of culture" thesis: An intersectional analysis of "sixpacks," "midriffs," and "hot lesbians" in advertising. *Sexualities,12*, 137–160. doi:10.1177/1363460708100916

Gleeson, K., & Frith, H. (2004). Pretty in pink: Young women presenting mature sexual identities. In A. Harris (Ed.), *All about the girl: Culture, power, and identity* (pp. 103–114). New York, NY: Routledge.

Goodin, S. M., Denberg, A., Murnen, S. K., & Smolak, L. (2011). "Putting on" sexiness: A content analysis of the presence of sexualizing characteristics in girls' clothing. *Sex Roles,65*, 1–12. doi:10.1007/s11199-011-9966-8

Gordon, M. K. (2008). Media contributions to African American girls' focus on beauty and appearance: Exploring the consequences of sexual objectification. *Psychology of Women Quarterly,32*, 245–256. doi:10.1111/j.1471-6402.2008.00433.x

Grabham, E. (2007). Citizen bodies, intersex citizenship. *Sexualities*, *10*, 29–48. doi:10.1177/1363460707072951

Grace, V., Potts, A., Gavey, N., & Vares, T. (2006). The discursive condition of Viagra. *Sexualities,9*, 295–314. doi:10.1177/1363460706065050

Graham, C. (2003). Methodological issues involved in adult recall of childhood sexual experiences. In J. Bancroft (Ed.), *Sexual development in childhood* (pp. 67–76). Bloomington: Indiana University Press.

Green, A. I. (2008). Erotic habitus: Toward a sociology of desire. *Theory and Society,37*, 597–626. doi:10.1007/s11186-007-9059-4

Greene, K., & Faulkner, S. L. (2005). Gender, belief in the sexual double standard, and sexual talk in heterosexual dating relationships. *Sex Roles,53*, 239–251. doi:10.1007/s11199-005-5682-6

Grosz, E. (1994). *Volatile bodies: Towards a corporeal feminism.*Bloomington: Indiana University Press.

Grosz, E. (2008). Darwin and feminism: Preliminary investigations for a possible alliance. In S. Alaimo (Ed.), *Material feminisms* (pp. 23–51). Bloomington: Indiana University Press.

Guldin, A. (2000). Self-claiming sexuality: Mobility impaired people and American culture. *Sexuality and Disability,18*, 233–238. doi:10.1023/A:1005690009575

Gurevich, M., Bishop, S., Bower, J., Malka, M., & Nyhof-Young, J. (2004). (Dis)embodying gender and sexuality in testicular cancer. *Social Science and Medicine,58*, 1597–1607. doi:10.1016/S0277-9536(03)00371-X

Halberstam, J. (1998). *Female masculinity.*Durham, NC: Duke University Press.

Hamilton, L. (2007). Trading on heterosexuality: College women's gender strategies and homophobia. *Gender and Society,21*, 145–172. doi:10.1177/0891243206297604

Hammack, P. L., & Cohler, B. J. (2009). *The story of sexual identity: Narrative perspectives on the gay and lesbian life course.*Oxford, England: Oxford University Press.

Hammack, P. L., Thompson, E. M., & Pilecki, A. (2009). Configurations of identity among sexual minority youth: Context, desire, and narrative. *Journal of Youth and Adolescence,38*, 867–883. doi:10.1007/s10964-008-9342-3

Hammers, C. J. (2008). Making space for an agentic sexuality? The examination of a lesbian/queer bathhouse. *Sexualities,11*, 547–572. doi:10.1177/1363460708094267

Hanna, C. (2001). Sex is not a sport: Consent and violence in criminal law. *Boston College Law Review Boston College Law School,42*, 239–290.

Haraway, D. (1991). *Simians, cyborgs and women: The reinvention of nature.*New York, NY: Routledge.

Hardy, S. (2009). The new pornographies: Representation or reality? In F. Attwood (Ed.), *Mainsteaming sex: The sexualization of western culture* (pp. 3–18). London, England: IB Tauris.

Hartley, H. (2006). The "pinking" of Viagra culture: Drug industry efforts to create and repackage sex drugs for women. *Sexualities,9*, 363–378. doi:10.1177/1363460706065058

Hartley, H., & Tiefer, L. (2003). Taking a biological turn: The push for a "female Viagra" and the medicalization of women's sexual problems. *Women's Studies Quarterly,31*, 42–54.

Hauge, M. (2009). Bodily practices and discourses of hetero-femininity: Girls' constitution of subjectivities in their social transition between childhood and adolescence. *Gender and Education,21*, 293–307. doi:10.1080/09540250802667625

Hebl, M. R., King, E. B., & Lin, J. (2004). The swimsuit becomes us all: Ethnicity, gender, and vulnerability to self-objectification. *Personality and Social Psychology Bulletin*, *30*, 1322–1331. doi:10.1177/0146167204264052

Henriques, J., Hollway, W., Urwin, C., Venn, C., & Walkerdine, V. (1998). *Changing the subject: Psychology, social regulation and subjectivity.* New York, NY: Routledge.

Herbenick, D., & Reece, M. (2010). Original research—Outcomes assessment: Development and validation of the female genital self-image scale. *Journal of Sexual Medicine,7*, 1822–1830. doi:10.1111/j.1743-6109.2010.01728.x

Herbenick, D., Schick, V., Reece, M., Sanders, S., Dodge, B., & Fortenberry, D. (2011). The female genital self-image scale (FGSIS): Results from a nationally representative probability sample of women in the United States. *Journal of Sexual Medicine,8*, 158–166. doi:10.1111/j.1743-6109.2010.02071.x

Herbenick, D., Schick, V., Reece, M., Sanders, S., & Fortenberry, D. (2010). Pubic hair removal among women in the United States: Prevalence, methods, and characteristics. *Journal of Sexual Medicine,7*, 3322–3330. doi:10.1111/j.1743-6109.2010.01935.x

Herdt, G., & McClintock, M. (2000). The magical age of 10. *Archives of Sexual Behavior,29*, 587–606. doi:10.1023/A:1002006521067

Herman, J. L. (1992). *Trauma and recovery: The aftermath of violence.* New York, NY: Basic Books.

Hernandez, J. (2009). "Miss, you look like a bratz doll": On chonga girls and sexual–aesthetic excess. *National Women's Studies Association Journal,21*, 63–90. doi:10.1353/nwsa.0.0102

Hines, S. (2007). *Transforming gender: Transgender practices of identity, intimacy and care.*Bristol, England: Policy Press.

Hirschman, C., Impett, E. A., & Schooler, D. (2006). Dis/embodied voices: What late-adolescent girls can teach us about objectification and sexuality. *Sexuality Research and Social Policy*, *3*(4), 8–20. doi:10.1525/srsp.2006.3.4.8

Holland, J., & Ramazanoglu, C. (1994). Coming to conclusions: Power and interpretation in researching young women's sexuality. In M. Maynard & J. Purvis (Eds.), *Researching women's lives from a feminist perspective* (pp. 125–148). London, England: Taylor & Francis.

Holland, J., Ramazanoglu, C., Sharpe, S., & Thomson, R. (1994). Power and desire: The embodiment of female sexuality. *Feminist Review*, *46*, 21–38. doi:10.1057/fr.1994.2

Holland, J., Ramazanoglu, C., Sharpe, S., & Thomson, R. (2003). When bodies come together: Power, control and desire. In J. Weeks, J. Holland, & M. Waites (Eds.), *Sexualities and society: A reader* (pp. 84–94). Oxford, England: Polity Press.

Holland, J., Ramazanoglu, C., Sharpe, S., & Thomson, R. (2004). *The male in the head: Young people, heterosexuality, and power* (2nd ed.). London, England: Tufnell Press.

Holland, J., & Thomson, R. (2010). Revisiting youthful sexuality: Continuities and changes over two decades. *Sexual and Relationship Therapy*,*25*, 342–350. doi:10.1080/14681991003767370

Holland, S., & Attwood, F. (2009). Keeping fit in six-inch heels: The mainstreaming of pole dancing. In F. Attwood (Ed.), *Mainsteaming sex: The sexualization of Western culture* (pp. 129–146). London, England: IB Tauris.

Holmes, M. (2002). Rethinking the meaning and management of intersexuality. *Sexualities*,*5*, 159–180. doi:10.1177/1363460702005002002

Holt, M. (2009). "Just take Viagra": Erectile insurance, prophylactic uncertainty, and deficit correction in gay men's accounts of sexuopharmaceutical use. *Sexualities*,*12*, 746–764. doi:10.1177/1363460709346112

Hoppe, T. (2011). Circuits of power, circuits of pleasure: Sexual scripting in gay men's bottom narratives. *Sexualities*,*14*, 193–217. doi:10.1177/1363460711399033

Horne, S., & Zimmer-Gembeck, M. J. (2005). Female sexual subjectivity and well-being: Comparing late adolescents with different sexual experiences. *Sexuality Research and Social Policy*,*2*, 25–40. doi:10.1525/srsp.2005.2.3.25

Howe, C., & Rigi, J. (2009). Transnationalizing desire: Sexualizing culture and commodifying sexualities. *Ethnos: Journal of Anthropology*,*74*, 297–306. doi:10.1080/00141840903053071

Hugh-Jones, S., Gough, B., & Littlewood, A. (2005). Sexual exhibitionism as "sexuality and individuality": A critique of psycho-medical discourse from the perspectives of women who exhibit. *Sexualities*,*8*, 259–281. doi:10.1177/1363460705049576

Hyde, J. (2003). The use of meta-analysis in understanding the effects of child sexual abuse. In J. Bancroft (Ed.), *Sexual development in childhood* (pp. 82–91). Bloomington: Indiana University Press.

Impett, E. A., Henson, J. M., Breines, J. G., Schooler, D., & Tolman, D. L. (2011). Embodiment feels better: Girls body objectification and well being across adolescence. *Psychology of Women Quarterly*,*35*, 46–58. doi:10.1177/0361684310391641

Impett, E. A., & Tolman, D. L. (2006). Late adolescent girls' sexual experiences and sexual satisfaction. *Journal of Adolescent Research*,*21*, 628–646. doi:10.1177/0743558406293964

Inhorn, M. C. (2007). Masturbation, semen collection and men's IVF experiences: Anxieties in the Muslim world. *Body and Society*,*13*, 37–53. doi:10.1177/1357034X07082251

Irigaray, L. (1984). *An ethics of sexual difference*(C. Burke & G. C. Gill, Trans.). London, England: Althone.

Irvine, J. M. (1990). From difference to sameness: Gender ideology in sexual science. *Journal of Sex Research*,*27*, 7–24. doi:10.1080/00224499009551539

Jackson, S., & Scott, S. (2007). Faking like a woman? Towards an interpretive theorization of sexual pleasure. *Body and Society*,*13*, 95–116. doi:10.1177/1357034X07077777

Jagose, A. (2010). Counterfeit pleasures: Fake orgasm and queer agency. *Textual Practice*,*24*, 517–539. doi:10.1080/09502361003690849

Jagstaidt, V., Golay, A., & Pasini, W. (1997). Relationships between sexuality and obesity in male patients. *New Trends in Experimental and Clinical Psychiatry*,*13*, 105–110.

James, W. (1890). *The principles of psychology* (Vol. 1). New York, NY: Henry Holt & Co. doi:10.1037/11059-000

Jewkes, R., & Morrell, R. (2010). Gender and sexuality: Emerging perspectives from the heterosexual epidemic in South Africa and implications for HIV risk and prevention. *Journal of the International AIDS Society*,*13*, 1–11. doi:10.1186/1758-2652-13-6

Jones, M. (2008). Makeover culture's dark side: Breasts, death, and Lolo Ferrari. *Body and Society*,*14*, 89–104. doi:10.1177/1357034X07087532

Jones, R. (2008). The role of text in televideo cybersex. *Text and Talk*, 453–473. doi:10.1515/TEXT.2008.022

Joshi, S. P., Peter, J., & Valkenberg, P. M. (2011). Scripts of sexual desire and danger in U.S. and Dutch teen girl magazines: A cross-national content analysis. *Sex Roles*,*64*, 463–474. doi:10.1007/s11199-011-9941-4

Kang, S. (2007). Disembodiment in online social interaction: Impact of online chat on social support and psychosocial well-being. *Cyberpsychology and Behavior, 10*, 475–477. doi:10.1089/cpb.2006.9929

Kaplan, H. S. (1974). *The new sex therapy.*New York, NY: Brunner/Mazel.

Katz, S., & Marshall, B. (2003). New sex for old: Lifestyle, consumerism, and the ethics of aging well. *Journal of Aging Studies,17*, 3–16. doi:10.1016/S0890-4065(02)00086-5

Kehily, M. (2001). Bodies in school: Young men, embodiment, and heterosexual masculinities. *Men and Masculinities,4*, 173–185. doi:10.1177/1097184X01004002005

Kelly, D. (2004). Male sexuality in theory and practice. *Nursing Clinics of North America,39*, 341–356. doi:10.1016/j.cnur.2004.02.016

Kessler, S. (2002). Defining and producing genitals. *Gender: A Sociological Reader.*London, England: Routledge.

Kim, E. (2011). Asexuality in disability narratives. *Sexualities,14*, 479–493. doi:10.1177/1363460711406463

Kinzl, J. F., Trefalt, E., Fiala, M., Hotter, A., Biebl, W., & Aigner, F. (2001). Partnership, sexuality, and sexual disorders in morbidly obese women: Consequences of weight loss after gastric banding. *Obesity Surgery,11*, 455–458. doi:10.1381/096089201321209323

Kippax, S., & Smith, G. (2001). Anal intercourse and power in sex between men. *Sexualities,4*, 413–434. doi:10.1177/136346001004004002

Koch, T., Kralik, D., & Eastwood, S. (2002). Constructions of sexuality for women living with multiple sclerosis. *Journal of Advanced Nursing,39*, 137–145. doi:10.1046/j.1365-2648.2002.02253.x

Komter, A. (1989). Hidden power in marriage. *Gender and Society,3*, 187–216. doi:10.1177/089124389003002003

Kong, T. S. K. (2002). The seduction of the golden boy: The body politics of Hong Kong gay men. *Body and Society,8*, 29–48. doi:10.1177/1357034X02008001002

Koyama, E.(n.d.). Being accountable to the invisible community: A challenge for intersex activists and allies. *Intersex Initiative.*Retrieved from http://www.intersexinitiative.org/articles/invisible-community.html

Labuski, C. (2011). "It's hard to say": Moving beyond the mystery of female genital pain. In S. Kwan & C. Boble (Eds.), *Embodied resistance: Challenging the norms, breaking the rules* (pp. 143–155). Nashville, TN: Vanderbilt University Press.

Lacombe, D. (1996). Reforming Foucault: A critique of the social control thesis. *British Journal of Sociology*, 47, pp. 332–352. doi:10.2307/591730

Lamb, S. (2001). *The secret lives of girls: What good girls really do—sex play, aggression, and their guilt.*New York, NY: The Free Press.

Lamb, S. (2010). Feminist ideals for a healthy female adolescent sexuality: A critique. *Sex Roles,62*, 294–306. doi:10.1007/s11199-009-9698-1

Lamb, S., & Coakley, M. (1993). 'Normal' childhood sexual play and games: Differentiating play from abuse. *Child Abuse and Neglect,17*, 515–526. doi:10.1016/0145-2134(93)90026-2

Langdridge, D., & Butt, T. (2004). A hermeneutic phenomenological investigation of the construction of sadomasochistic identities. *Sexualities,7*, 31–53. doi:10.1177/1363460704040137

Langmuir, J. I., Kirsh, S. G., & Classen, C. C. (2012). A pilot study of body-oriented group psychotherapy: Adapting sensorimotor psychotherapy for the group treatment of trauma. *Psychological Trauma: Theory, Research, Practice, and Policy,4*, 214–220. doi:10.1037/a0025588

Lester, R. J. (1997). The (dis)embodied self in anorexia nervosa. *Social Science and Medicine,44*, 479–489. doi:10.1016/S0277-9536(96)00166-9

Levitt, H. M., & Horne, S. G. (2008). Review of the book *Challenging lesbian norms: Intersex, transgender, intersectional and queer perspectives* by A. P. Aragon (ed.). *Sex Roles,59*, 296–297. doi:10.1007/s11199-008-9401-y

Lindemann, D. (2011). "Is that any way to treat a lady?": The dominatrix's dungeon. In C. Boble & S. Kwan (Eds.), *Embodied resistance: Challenging the norms, breaking the rules* (pp. 26–36). Nashville, TN: Nashville University Press.

Lindemann, G. (1996). The body of gender difference (J. Wolfgang, Trans.). *European Journal of Women's Studies,3*, 341–361. doi:10.1177/135050689600300402

Litwin, M. S., Melmed, G. Y., & Nakazon, T. (2001). Life after radical prostectomy: A longitudinal study. *Journal of Urology,166*, 587–592. doi:10.1016/S0022-5347(05)65989-7

Lloyd, E. A. (2006). *The case of the female orgasm: Bias in the science of evolution.*Cambridge, MA: Harvard University Press.

Loe, M. (2004). Sex and the senior woman: Pleasure and danger in the Viagra era. *Sexualities,7*, 303–326. doi:10.1177/1363460704044803

Loe, M. (2006). The Viagra blues: Embracing or resisting the Viagra body. In D. Rosenfeld & C. Faircloth (Eds.), *Medicalized masculinities* (pp. 21–44). Philadelphia, PA: Temple University Press.

Loe, M. (2007). *The rise of Viagra: How the little blue pill changed sex in America.* New York: New York University Press.

Loewenson, P. R., Ireland, M., & Resnick, M. D. (2004). Primary and secondary sexual abstinence in high school students. *Journal of Adolescent Health,34*, 209–215. doi:10.1016/j.jadohealth.2003.05.002

Longhurst, R. (2001). Breaking corporeal boundaries: Pregnant bodies in public spaces. In R. Holliday & J. Hassard (Eds.), *Contested bodies* (pp. 81–94). London, England: Routledge.

Lowe, P. (2005). Contraception and heterosex: An intimate relationship. *Sexualities,8*, 75–92. doi:10.1177/1363460705049575

Maddison, S. (2009). "The second sexual revolution": Big pharma, porn, and the biopolitical penis. *Topia: The Canadian Journal of Cultural Studies,22*, 35–53.

Magubane, Z. (2001). Which bodies matter? Feminism, poststructuralism, race, and the curious theoretical odyssey of the "hottentot venus."*Gender and Society,15*, 816–834. doi:10.1177/089124301015006003

Mairs, N. (1997). Carnal acts. In K. Conboy, N. Medina, & S. Stanbury (Eds.), *Writing on the body: Female embodiment and feminist theory* (pp. 296–305). New York, NY: Columbia University Press.

Mamo, L., & Fishman, J. R. (2001). Potency in all the right places: Viagra as a technology of the gendered body. *Body and Society,7*, 13–35. doi:10.1177/1357034X01007004002

Manderson, L. (2005). Boundary breaches: The body, sex, and sexuality after stoma surgery. *Social Science and Medicine,61*, 405–415. doi:10.1016/j.socscimed.2004.11.051

Marshall, B. L. (2006). The new virility: Viagra, male aging, and sexual function. *Sexualities,9*, 345–362. doi:10.1177/1363460706065057

Marshall, B. L., & Katz, S. (2002). Forever functional: Sexual fitness and the ageing male body. *Body and Society,8*, 43–70. doi:10.1177/1357034X02008004003

Martin, B. (1996). *Femininity played straight: The significance of being lesbian.*New York, NY: Routledge.

Masters, W. H., & Johnson, V. E. (1966). *Human sexual response.*Boston, MA: Little, Brown.

Maxwell, C., & Aggleton, P. (2010). Agency in action—Young women and their sexual relationships in a private school. *Gender and Education,22*, 327–343. doi:10.1080/09540250903341120

Maxwell, C., & Aggleton, P. (2012). Bodies and agentic practice in young women's sexual and intimate relationships. *Sociology,46*, 306–321. doi:10.1177/0038038511419192

Mayor, S. (2004). Pfizer will not apply for a license for sildenafil for women. *Social Science and Medicine,328*, 542. doi:10.1136/bmj.328.7439.542

McClelland, S. (2010). Intimate justice: A critical analysis of sexual satisfaction. *Social and Personality Psychology Compass,4*, 663–680. doi:10.1111/j.1751-9004.2010.00293.x

McClelland, S. (2011). Who is the "self" in self-reports of sexual satisfaction: Research and policy implications. *Sexuality Research and Social Policy,8*, 304–320. doi:10.1007/s13178-011-0067-9

McDermott, E. (2009). Review of the book *Working-class lesbian life: Classed outsiders* by Yvette Taylor. *American Journal of Sociology,115*, 273–275. doi:10.1086/605741

McHugh, M. C. (2006). What do women want? A new view of women's sexual problems. *Sex Roles,54*, 361–369. doi:10.1007/s11199-006-9006-2

McKinley, N. M., & Hyde, J. S. (1996). The Objectified Body Consciousness Scale development and validation. *Psychology of Women Quarterly,20*, 181–215. doi:10.1111/j.1471-6402.1996.tb00467.x

McNair, B. (1996). *Mediated sex: Pornography and postmodern culture.*London, England: Arnold.

Merleau-Ponty, M. (1962). *Phenomenology of perception.* London, England: Routledge.

Merskin, D. (2004). Reviving Lolita? A media literacy examination of sexual portrayals of girls in fashion advertising. *American Behavioral Scientist,48*, 119–129. doi:10.1177/0002764204267257

Middelthon, A. (2002). Being anally penetrated: Erotic inhibitions, improvisations and transformations. *Sexualities,5*, 181–200. doi:10.1177/1363460702005002003

Miller, J. G., Das, R., & Chakravarthy, S. (2011). Culture and the role of choice in agency. *Journal of Personality and Social Psychology,101*, 46–61. doi:10.1037/a0023330

Miller-Young, M. (2010). Putting hypersexuality to work: Black women and elicit eroticism in pornography. *Sexualities,13*, 219–235. doi:10.1177/1363460709359229

Millsted, R., & Frith, H. (2003). Being large-breasted: Women negotiating embodiment. *Women's Studies International Forum,26*, 455–465. doi:10.1016/S0277-5395(03)00105-5

Minh-Ha, T. T. (1989). *Woman, native, other: Writing postcoloniality and feminism.*Bloomington: Indiana University Press.

Minto, C. L., Liao, L. M., Woodhouse, C. R. J., Ransley, P. G., & Creighton, S. M. (2003). The effect of clitoral surgery on sexual outcome in individuals who have intersex conditions with ambiguous genitalia: A cross-sectional study. *Lancet,361*, 1252–1257. doi:10.1016/S0140-6736(03)12980-7

Moi, T. (2001). *What is a woman? And other essays.*Oxford, England: Oxford University Press.

Moore, L. J. (2007). *Sperm counts: Overcome by a man's most precious fluid.*New York: New York University Press.

Moraga, C., & Anzaldúa, G. (1981). *This bridge called my back: Writings by radical women of color*. Watertown, MA: Persephone Press.

Moynihan, R. (2003). The making of a disease: Female sexual dysfunction. *British Medical Journal,326*, 45–47. doi:10.1136/bmj.326.7379.45

Murray, S. (2004). Locating aesthetics: Sexing the fat woman. *Social Semiotics,14*, 237–247. doi:10.1080/10350330408629678

Nosek, M. A., Howland, C., Rintala, D. H., Young, M. E., & Chanpong, G. F. (2001). National study of women with physical disabilities: Final report. *Sexuality and Disability,19*, 5–40. doi:10.1023/A:1010716820677

Nowatzki, J., & Morry, M. M. (2009). Women's intentions regarding, and acceptance of, self-sexualizing behavior. *Psychology of Women Quarterly,33*, 95–107. doi:10.1111/j.1471-6402.2008.01477.x

Nugteren, H. M., Balkema, G. T., Pascal, A. L., Schultz, W. C. M., Nijman, J. M., & Van Driel, M. F. (2010). 18-year experience in the management of men with a complaint of a small penis. *Journal of Sex and Marital Therapy,36*, 109–117. doi:10.1080/00926230903554438

Nyanzi, S., Rosenberg-Jallow, O., Bah, O., & Nyanzi, S. (2005). Bumsters, big black organs and old white gold: Embodied racial myths in sexual relationships of Gambian beach boys. *Culture, Health and Sexuality,7*, 557–569. doi:10.1080/13691050500245687

Oliffe, J. (2005). Constructions of masculinity following prostatectomy-induced impotence. *Social Science and Medicine,60*, 2249–2259. doi:10.1016/j.socscimed.2004.10.016

Oliver, K. (2010). Motherhood, sexuality, and pregnant embodiment: Twenty-five years of gestation. *Hypatia, 25*, 760–777. doi:10.1111/j.1527-2001.2010.01134.x

Owens, E., Behun, R., Manning, J., & Reed, R. (2012). The impact of Internet pornography on adolescents: A review of the research. *Sexual Addiction and Compulsivity,19*, 99–122. doi:10.1080/10720162.2012.660431

Pardo, S. T. (2011). Queering transgender: Towards a sociology of transgender. *Journal of Sex Research,48*, 409–410. doi:10.1080/00224499.2010.487769

Pascoe, C. J. (2007). "What if a guy hits on you?" Intersections of gender, sexuality, and age in fieldwork with adolescents. In A. L. Best (Ed.), *Representing youth: Methodological issues in critical youth studies* (pp. 226–247). New York: New York University Press.

Pasko, L. (2010). Setting the record "straight": Girls, sexuality, and the juvenile correctional system. *Social Justice,37*, 7–26.

Peterson, Z. D. (2010). What is sexual empowerment? A multidimensional and process-oriented approach to adolescent girls' sexual empowerment. *Sex Roles,62*, 307–313. doi:10.1007/s11199-009-9725-2

Phelan, J. E. (2009). Exploring the use of touch in the psychotherapeutic setting: A phenomenological review. *Psychotherapy: Theory, Research, Practice, Training,46*, 97–111. doi:10.1037/a0014751

Phillips, L. M. (2000). *Flirting with danger: Young women's reflections on sexuality and domination*. New York: New York University Press.

Piran, N., & Ross, E. (2005). The transition from girlhood to womanhood. In J. Worell & C. Goodhart (Eds.), *Handbook of girls' and women's psychological health* (pp. 178–195). London, England: Oxford Press.

Piran, N., & Teall, T. (2012). The developmental theory of embodiment. In G. McVey, M. P. Levine, N. Piran, & H. B. Ferguson (Eds.), *Preventing eating-related and weight-related disorders: Collaborative Research, Advocacy, and Policy Change* (pp. 171–199). Waterloo, ON: Wilfred Laurier Press.

Pitman, G. E. (1999). Body image, compulsory heterosexuality, and internalized homophobia. *Journal of Lesbian Studies,3*, 129–139. doi:10.1300/J155v03n04_17

Pitts, V. (1999). Body modification, self-mutilation, and agency in media accounts of a subculture. *Body and Society,5*, 291–303. doi:10.1177/1357034X99005002016

Plante, R. F. (2006). *Sexualities in context: A social perspective.*Boulder, CO: Westview.

Plummer, K. (2002). *Telling sexual stories: Power, change, and social worlds*. New York, NY: Routledge.

Plummer, K. (2012). Critical sexuality studies. In G. Ritzel (Ed.), *The Wiley-Blackwell companion to sociology* (pp. 243–268). New York, NY: Blackwell. doi:10.1002/9781444347388.ch14

Poon, M. K., & Ho, P. T. (2008). Negotiating social stigma among gay Asian men. *Sexualities,11*, 245–268. doi:10.1177/1363460707085472

Potts, A. (2004). Deleuze on Viagra (or, what can a 'Viagra-body' do?). *Body and Society,10*, 17–36. doi:10.1177/1357034X04041759

Prause, N., & Graham, C. A. (2007). Asexuality: Classification and characterization. *Archives of Sexual Behavior,36*, 341–356. doi:10.1007/s10508-006-9142-3

Pyle, N., & Klein, N. L. (2011). Fat, hairy, sexy: Contesting standards of beauty and sexuality in the gay community. In C. Boble & S. Kwan (Eds.), *Embodied resistance: Challenging the norms, breaking the rules* (pp. 78–87). Nashville, TN: Nashville University Press.

Rademakers, J., Laan, M. J. C., & Straver, C. J. (2003). Body awareness and physical intimacy: An exploratory study. In J. Bancroft (Ed.), *Sexual development in childhood* (pp. 121–125). Bloomington, Indiana: Indiana University Press.

Regehr, K. (2012). The rise of recreational burlesque: Bumping and grinding towards empowerment. *Sexuality and Culture,16*, 134–157. doi:10.1007/s12119-011-9113-2

Reich, J. (2011). Public Mothers and private practices: Breastfeeding as transgression. In C. Bobel & S. Kwan (Eds.), *Embodied resistance: Challenging the norms, breaking the rules* (pp. 130–142). Nashville, TN: Vanderbilt University Press.

Renold, E. (2005). *Girls, boys, and junior sexualities.*New York, NY: Routledge.

Renold, E. (2006). "They won't let us play . . . unless you're going out with one of them": Girls, boys and Butler's "heterosexual matrix" in the primary years. *British Journal of Sociology of Education,27*, 489–509. doi:10.1080/01425690600803111

Renold, E., & Ringrose, J. (2011). Schizoid subjectivities? Re-theorizing teen girls' sexual cultures in an era of "sexualization."*Journal of Sociology*, *47*, 389–409. doi:10.1177/1440783311420792

Rich, A. (1980). Compulsory heterosexuality and lesbian existence. *Signs: Journal of Women in Culture and Society,5*, 631–660. doi:10.1086/493756

Ridge, D. T. (2004). "It was an incredible thrill": The social meanings and dynamics of younger gay men's experiences of barebacking in Melbourne. *Sexualities,7*, 259–279. doi:10.1177/1363460704040138

Ringrose, J. (2010). Sluts, whores, fat slags and playboy bunnies: Teen girls' negotiations of "sexy" on social networking sites and at school. In C. Jackson, C. Paechter, & E. Renold (Eds.), *Girls and education: Continuing concerns, new agendas* (pp. 170–182). New York, NY: Open University Press.

Ringrose, J. (2011). Are you sexy, flirty, or a slut? Exploring "sexualization" and how teen girls perform/negotiate digital sexual identity on social networking sites. In R. Gill & C. Scharff (Eds.), *New femininities: Postfeminism, neoliberalism, and subjectivity* (pp. 99–116). New York, NY: Palgrave-MacMillan.

Ringrose, J. (2013). *Postfeminist education? Girls and the sexual politics of schooling.*London, England: Routledge.

Roberts, T. (2004). Female trouble: The menstrual self-evaluation scale and women's self-objectification. *Psychology of Women Quarterly,28*, 22–26. doi:10.1111/j.1471-6402.2004.00119.x

Roberts, T., & Gettman, J. Y. (2004). Mere exposure: Gender differences in the negative effects of priming a state of self-objectification. *Sex Roles,51*, 17–27. doi:10.1023/B:SERS.0000032306.20462.22

Roberts, T. A., & Waters, P. L. (2004). Self-objectification and that "not so fresh feeling": Feminist therapeutic interventions for healthy female embodiment. *Women and Therapy,27*, 5–21. doi:10.1300/J015v27n03_02

Roberts, T. A., & Zurbriggen, E. L. (2012). *The sexualization of girls and girlhood: Causes, consequences, and resistance.* New York, NY: Oxford University Press.

Robinson, K. H. (2012). "Difficult citizenship": The precarious relationships between childhood, sexuality, and access to knowledge. *Sexualities,15*, 257–276. doi:10.1177/1363460712436469

Roen, K. (2008). But we have to do something: "Surgical correction" of atypical genitalia. *Body and Society,14*, 47–66. doi:10.1177/1357034X07087530

Ronen, S. (2010). Grinding on the dance floor: Gendered scripts and sexualized dancing at parties. *Gender and Society,24*, 355–377. doi:10.1177/0891243210369894

Rooke, A. (2007). Navigating embodied lesbian cultural space: Toward a lesbian habitus. *Space and Culture,10*, 231–252. doi:10.1177/1206331206298790

Rothblum, E. D. (1994). Transforming lesbian sexuality. *Psychology of Women Quarterly,18*, 627–641. doi:10.1111/j.1471-6402.1994.tb01051.x

Rothblum, E. D., & Brehony, K. A. (1993). *Boston marriages: Romantic but asexual relationships among contemporary lesbians.*Amherst: University of Massachusetts Press.

Rothblum, E. D., Solovay, S., & Wann, M. (2009). *The fat studies reader.*New York: New York University Press.

Rubin, G. S. (1984). Thinking sex: Notes for a radical theory of the politics of sexuality. In H. Abelove, M. A. Barale, & D. M. Halperin (Eds.), *The lesbian and gay studies reader* (pp. 143–178). New York, NY: Routledge.

Rutherford, A. (2012). Problems of sex and the problem with nature: A commentary on "beyond Kinsey."*History of Psychology,15*, 228–232. doi:10.1037/a0027668

Ryan, G. (2000). Childhood sexuality: A decade of study. Part 1: Research and curriculum development. *Child Abuse and Neglect,24*, 33–48. doi:10.1016/S0145-2134(99)00118-0

Sanchez, D. T., Fetterolf, J. C., & Rudman, L. A. (2012). Eroticising inequality in the United States: The consequences and determinants of traditional gender role adherence in intimate relationships. *Journal of Sex Research,49*, 168–183. doi:10.1080/00224499.2011.653699

Sanchez, D. T., & Kiefer, A. K. (2007). Body concerns in and out of the bedroom: Implications for sexual pleasure and problems. *Archives of Sexual Behavior,36*, 808–820. doi:10.1007/s10508-007-9205-0

Sandfort, T. G. M., & Rademakers, J. (Eds.). (2000). *Childhood sexuality: Normal sexual behavior and development.*Binghamton, NY: Haworth Press.

Sanger, N. (2009). New women, old messages? Constructions of femininities, race and hypersexualized bodies in selected South African magazines, 2003–2006. *Social Dynamics,35*, 137–148. doi:10.1080/02533950802667301

Scherrer, K. S. (2008). Coming to an asexual identity: Negotiating identity, negotiating desire. *Sexualities,11*, 621–641. doi:10.1177/1363460708094269

Schilling, C. (2003). *The body and social theory.*London, England: Sage.

Schleifer, D. (2006). Make me feel mighty real: Gay female-to-male transgenderists negotiating sex, gender, and sexuality. *Sexualities,9*, 57–75. doi:10.1177/1363460706058397

Schover, L. R., Yetman, R. J., Tuason, L. J., Meisler, E., Esselstyn, C. B., Hermann, R. E., . . .Dowden, R. V. (1995). Partial mastectomy and breast reconstruction: A comparison of their effects on psychosocial adjustment, body image, and sexuality. *Cancer, 75*, 54–64. doi:10.1002/1097-0142(19950101)75:1<54::AID-CNCR2820750111>3.0.CO;2-I

Seal, D. W., Smith, M., Coley, B., Perry, J., & Gamez, M. (2008). Urban heterosexual couples' sexual scripts for three shared sexual experiences. *Sex Roles,58*, 626–638. doi:10.1007/s11199-007-9369-z

Sedgwick, E. K. (1990). *Epistemology of the closet.* Berkeley: University of California Press.

Sedgwick, E. K. (1993). *Tendencies.*Durham, NC: Duke University Press. doi:10.4324/9780203202210

Segal, L. (1992). Introduction. In L. Segal & M. McIntosh (Eds.), *Sex exposed: Sexuality and the pornography debate* (pp. 1–11). London, England: Virago.

Seidman, S. (Ed.). (1996). *Queer theory/sociology.*Oxford, England: Blackwell.

Shapiro, E. (2007). Drag kinging and the transformation of gender identities. *Gender and Society,21*, 250–271. doi:10.1177/0891243206294509

Shaw, A. E. (2006). *The embodiment of disobedience: Fat black women's unruly political bodies.* Lanham, MD: Lexington Books.

Sheppard, L. A., & Ely, S. (2008). Breast cancer and sexuality. *Breast Journal,14*, 176–181. doi:10.1111/j.1524-4741.2007.00550.x

Shifren, J. L., Brigitta, M., Russo, P., Segretti, A., & Johannes, C. B. (2008). Sexual problems and distress in United States women: Prevalence and correlates. *Obstetrics and Gynecology, 112*, 970–978. doi:10.1097/AOG.0b013e3181898cdb

Shildrick, M. (2005). Unreformed bodies: Normative anxiety and the denial of pleasure. *Women's Studies,34*, 327–344. doi:10.1080/00497870590964219

Shildrick, M. (2007). Dangerous discourses: Anxiety, desire, and disability. *Studies in Gender and Sexuality,8*, 221–244. doi:10.1080/15240650701226490

Shildrick, M., & Price, J. (1999). Breaking the boundaries of the broken body. In J. Price & M. Shildrick (Eds.), *Feminist theory and the body: A reader* (pp. 432–444). New York, NY: Routledge.

Shiu-Ki, T. K. (2004). Queer at your own risk: Marginality, community and Hong Kong gay male bodies. *Sexualities,7*, 5–30. doi:10.1177/1363460704040136

Short, M. B., Black, L., Smith, A. H., Wetterneck, C. T., & Wells, D. E. (2012). A review of Internet pornography use research: Methodology and content from the past 10 years. *Cyberpsychology, Behavior, and Social Networking,15*, 13–23. doi:10.1089/cyber.2010.0477

Sieg, E. (2007). "What you want, or what you get?" Young women talking about the gap between desired and lived heterosexual relationships in the 21st century. *Women's Studies International Forum,30*, 175–186. doi:10.1016/j.wsif.2007.01.007

Simpson, A. (2007). Learning sex and gender in Zambia: Masculinities and HIV AIDS risk. *Sexualities,10*, 173–188. doi:10.1177/1363460707075799

Slater, D. (1998). Trading sexpics on IRC: Embodiment and authenticity on the Internet. *Body and Society, 4*, 91–117. doi:10.1177/1357034X98004004005

Slavin, S. (2009). "Instinctively, I'm not just a sexual beast": The complexity of intimacy among Australian gay men. *Sexualities, 12*, 79–96. doi:10.1177/1363460708099114

Smith-Rosenberg, C. (1975). The female world of love and ritual: Relations between women in 19th-century America. *Signs: Journal of Women in Culture and Society, 1*, 1–29. doi:10.1086/493203

Spelman, E. V. (1990). *Inessential woman.* Boston, MA: Beacon Press.

Starr, C., & Ferguson, G. (2012). Sexy dolls, sexy grade-schoolers: Media and maternal influences on young girls' self-sexualization. *Sex Roles, 67*, 463–476. doi:10.1007/s11199-012-0183-x

Storr, M. (2000). Review of the book *The male in the head: Young people, heterosexuality, and power* by J. Holland, C. Ramazanoglu, S. Sharpe, and R. Thomson. *Feminist Review, 66*, 151–153.

Strachan, E., & Staples, B. (2012). Masturbation. *Pediatrics,33*, 190–191. doi:10.1542/pir.33-4-190

Stryker, S. (2006). (De)subjugated knowledges: An introduction to transgender studies. In S. Stryker & S. Whittle (Eds.), *The transgender studies reader* (pp. 1–17). New York, NY: Routledge.

Tally, M. (2006). "She doesn't let age define her": Sexuality and motherhood in recent "middle-aged chick flicks." *Sexuality and Culture,10*, 33–55. doi:10.1007/s12119-006-1014-4

Tepper, M. S. (2000). Sexuality and disability: The missing discourse of pleasure. *Sexuality and Disability,18*, 283–290. doi:10.1023/A:1005698311392

Thompson, E. M., & Morgan, E. M. (2008). "Mostly straight" young women: Variations in sexual behavior and identity development. *Developmental Psychology,44*, 15–21. doi:10.1037/0012-1649.44.1.15

Tibbals, C. A. (2010). From the devil in Ms Jones to DMJ6: Power, inequality, and consistency in the content of U.S. adult films. *Sexualities,13*, 625–644. doi:10.1177/1363460710376493

Tiefer, L. (2001). A new view of women's sexual problems: Why new? Why now? *Journal of Sex Research,38*, 89–96. doi:10.1080/00224490109552075

Tiefer, L. (2004). *Sex is not a natural act and other essays.*Boulder, CO: Westview Press.

Tiefer, L. (2006). Female sexual dysfunction: A case study of disease mongering and activist resistance. *PLoS Medicine,3*, 10436–10440. doi:10.1371/journal.pmed.0030178

Tiefer, L. (2008). Female genital cosmetic surgery: Freakish or inevitable? Analysis from medical marketing, bioethics, and feminist theory. *Feminism and Psychology,18*, 466–479. doi:10.1177/0959353508095529

Tiefer, L. (2010). Activism on the medicalization of sex and female genital cosmetic surgery by the New View campaign in the United States. *Reproductive Health Matters,18*, 56–63. doi:10.1016/S0968-8080(10)35493-0

Toerien, M., Wilkinson, S., & Choi, P. Y. L. (2005). Body hair removal: The "mundane" production of normative femininity. *Sex Roles,52*, 399–406. doi:10.1007/s11199-005-2682-5

Tolman, D. (1994). Doing desire: Adolescent girls' struggles for/with sexuality. *Gender and Society,8*, 324–342. doi:10.1177/089124394008003003

Tolman, D. (2002). *Dilemma of desire: Teenage girls and sexuality.*Cambridge, MA: Harvard University Press.

Tolman, D. (2006). In a different position: Conceptualizing female adolescent sexuality development within compulsory heterosexuality. *New Directions for Child and Adolescent Development,2006*, 71–89. doi:10.1002/cd.163

Tolman, D. (2012). It's bad for everyone: Impact of sexualization on boys, men, and women. In E. Zurbriggen & T. Roberts (Eds.), *Hot girls? Sexualization of girls* (pp. 84–106). New York, NY: Oxford University Press.

Tolman, D., & Diamond, L. (2001). Desegregating sexuality research: Synthesizing cultural and biological perspectives on gender and desire. *Annual Review of Sexuality Research,12*, 33–74.

Tolman, D., & Szalacha, L. A. (1999). Dimensions of desire: Bridging qualitative and quantitative methods in a study of female adolescent sexuality. *Psychology of Women Quarterly,23*, 7–39. doi:10.1111/j.1471-6402.1999.tb00338.x

Tomassilli, J. C., Golub, S. A., Bimbi, D. S., & Parsons, J. T. (2009). Behind closed doors: An exploration of kinky sexual behaviors in urban lesbian and bisexual women. *Journal of Sex Research,46*, 438–445. doi:10.1080/00224490902754202

Trapnell, P. D., Meston, C. M., & Gorzalka, B. B. (1997). Spectatoring and the relationship between body image and sexual experience: Self-focus or self-valence? *Journal of Sex Research,34*, 267–278. doi:10.1080/00224499709551893

Tricklebank, G., Braun, V., & Clarke, V. (in press). "It shouldn't stick out from your bikini at the beach": Gender, pubic hair, and pubic hair removal. *Psychology of Women Quarterly.*

Turner, B. S. (1995). Aging and identity: Some reflections on the somatization of the self. In M. Featherstone & A. Wernick (Eds.), *Images of aging* (pp. 245–260). London, England: Routledge.

Ussher, J. M. (1989). *The psychology of the female body.* London, England: Routledge.

Ussher, J. M., & Mooney-Somers, J. (2000). Negotiating desire and sexual subjectivity: Narratives of young lesbian avengers. *Sexualities,3*, 183–200. doi:10.1177/136346000003002005

Valentine, D. (2007). *Imagining transgender: An ethnography of a category.*Durham, NC: Duke University Press Books.

Vance, C. S. (1984). *Pleasure and Danger: Toward a politics of sexuality.*Boston, MA: Routledge & Kegan Paul.

van Doorn, N. (2011). Digital spaces, material traces: How matter comes to matter in online performances of gender, sexuality and embodiment. *Media Culture and Society,33*, 531–547. doi:10.1177/0163443711398692

Vansteenwegen, A., Jans, I., & Revel, A. T. (2003). Sexual experience of women with a physical disability: A comparative study. *Sexuality and Disability,21*, 283–290. doi:10.1023/B:SEDI.0000010070.46481.17

Vares, T. (2009). Reading the "sexy oldie": Gender, age(ing) and embodiment. *Sexualities,12*, 503–524. doi:10.1177/1363460709105716

Villaamil, F., & Jociles, M. I. (2011). Risk and community: The impact of HIV among gays in Madrid: The case of sex clubs. *Sexualities,14*, 580–596. doi:10.1177/1363460711415334

Vitellone, N. (2002). Condoms and the making of sexual differences in AIDS heterosexual culture. *Body and Society,8*, 71–94. doi:10.1177/1357034X02008003004

Walker, J. J., Golub, S. A., Bimbi, D. S., & Parson, J. T. (2012). Butch bottom—femme top? An exploration of lesbian stereotypes. *Journal of Lesbian Studies,16*, 90–107. doi:10.1080/10894160.2011.557646

Walker, L. (2001). *Looking like what you are: Sexual style, race, and lesbian identity*.New York: New York University Press.

Ward, J. (2002). *The skin we're in: Teaching our teens to be emotionally strong, socially smart, and spiritually connected*.New York, NY: Free Press.

Ward, M., & Wyatt, G. E. (1994). The effects of childhood sexual messages on African American and White women's adolescent sexual behavior. *Psychology of Women Quarterly,18*, 183–201. doi:10.1111/j.1471-6402.1994.tb00450.x

Waskul, D. D. (2002). The naked self: Being a body in televideo cybersex. *Symbolic Interaction,25*, 199–227. doi:10.1525/si.2002.25.2.199

Waskul, D. D., & van der Riet, P. (2002). The abject embodiment of cancer patients: Dignity, selfhood, and the grotesque body. *Symbolic Interaction,25*, 487–513. doi:10.1525/si.2002.25.4.487

Weber, C. (1998). Performative states. *Millennium—Journal of International Studies,17*, 77–95. doi:10.1177/03058298980270011101

Weeks, J., Heaphy, B., & Donovan, C. (2001). *Same sex intimacies: Families of choice and other life experiments*.London, England: Routledge. doi:10.4324/9780203167168

Weinberg, M. S., & Williams, C. J. (2010a). Bare bodies: Nudity, gender, and the looking glass body. *Sociological Forum,25*, 47–67. doi:10.1111/j.1573-7861.2009.01156.x

Weinberg, M. S., & Williams, C. J. (2010b). Men sexually interested in transwomen (MSTW): Gendered embodiment and the construction of sexual desire. *Journal of Sex Research*, *47*, 374–383. doi:10.1080/00224490903050568

Weiss, M., & Weiss, M. D. (2011). *Techniques of pleasure: BDSM and the circuits of sexuality*.Durham, NC: Duke University Press.

Weiss, M. D. (2006). Mainstreaming kink. *Journal of Homosexuality,50*, 103–132. doi:10.1300/J082v50n02_06

Wentzell, E. (2011). Generational differences in Mexican men's ideas of age-appropriate sex and Viagra use. *Men and Masculinities,14*, 392–407. doi:10.1177/1097184X10394780

West, C., & Zimmerman, D. H. (1987). Doing gender. *Gender and Society,1*, 125–151. doi:10.1177/0891243287001002002

White, M. (2010). Listing eBay masculinity: Erotic exchanges and regulation in "gay" and "gay interest" underwear and swimwear auctions. *Journal of Gender Studies,19*, 43–58. doi:10.1080/09589230903525437

Whitehead, K., & Kurz, T. (2009). Investigation of the reinvention of pole dancing as a recreational activity. *Feminism and Psychology,19*, 224–244. doi:10.1177/0959353509102218

Wiederman, M. W. (2000). Women's body image self-consciousness during physical intimacy with a partner. *Journal of Sex Research,37*, 60–68. doi:10.1080/00224490009552021

Wiederman, M. W. (2001). "Don't look now": The role of self-focus in sexual dysfunction. *Family Journal,9*, 210–214. doi:10.1177/1066480701092020

Wilson, M. (2002). I am the prince of pain, for I am a princess in the brain: Liminal transgender identities, narratives and the elimination of ambiguities. *Sexualities,5*, 425–448. doi:10.1177/1363460702005004003

Wilson-Kovacs, D. (2009). Some texts do it better: Women, sexually explicit texts and the everyday. In F. Attwood (Ed.), *Mainstreaming sex: The sexualization of women and culture* (pp. 147–163). London, England: IB Tauris.

Woertman, L., & Brink, F. (2012). Body image and female sexual functioning and behavior: A review. *Journal of Sex Research,49*, 184–211. doi:10.1080/00224499.2012.658586

Wolmark, J. (1999). *Cybersexualities: A reader on feminist theory, cyborgs and cyberspace*.Edinburgh, Scotland: Edinburgh University Press.

Woodhouse, C. R. J. (2004). Intersex surgery in the adult. *British Journal of Urology International,93*, 57–65. doi:10.1111/j.1464-410X.2004.04712.x

Yamamiya, Y., Cash, T. F., & Thompson, J. K. (2006). Sexual experiences among college women: The differential effects of general versus contextual body images on sexuality. *Sex Roles,55*, 421–427. doi:10.1007/s11199-006-9096-x

Ybarra, M. L., & Mitchell, K. J. (2008). How risky are social networking sites? A comparison of places online where youth sexual solicitation and harassment occurs. *Pediatrics,121*, e350–e357. doi:10.1542/peds.2007-0693

Yost, M. R., & McCarthy, L. (2012). Girls gone wild? Heterosexual women's same-sex encounters at college parties. *Psychology of Women Quarterly,36*, 7–24. doi:10.1177/0361684311414818

Young, I. M. (1990). *Throwing like a girl and other essays in feminist philosophy and social theory*. Bloomington: Indiana University Press.

Young, I. M. (2005). Breasted experience: The look and the feeling. In I. M. Young (Ed.), *On female body experience: "Throwing like a girl" and other essays* (pp. 75–96). New York, NY: Oxford University Press. doi:10.1093/0195161920.003.0006

Zavella, P. (2008). Playing with fire?: The gendered construction of Chicana/Mexicana sexuality. In M. C. Gutmann, F. V. Matos Rodriguez, L. Stephen, & P. Zavella (Eds.), *Perspectives on Las Americas: A reader in culture, history, and representations* (pp. 229–244). Malden, MA: Blackwell.